Professional XML 2nd Edition

Mark Birbeck
Jason Diamond
Jon Duckett
Oli Gauti Gudmundsson
Pete Kobak
Evan Lenz
Steve Livingstone
Daniel Marcus
Stephen Mohr
Nikola Ozu
Jonathon Pinnock
Keith Visco
Andrew Watt
Kevin Williams
Zoran Zaev

Wrox Press Ltd. ®

Professional XML 2nd Edition

Published by Wrox Press Ltd,
Arden House, 1102 Warwick Road, Acocks Green,
Birmingham, B27 6BH, UK
Printed in Canada
ISBN 1861005059

Trademark Acknowledgements

Credits

Authors
Mark Birbeck
Jason Diamond
Jon Duckett
Oli Gauti Gudmundsson
Pete Kobak
Evan Lenz
Steve Livingstone
Daniel Marcus
Stephen Mohr
Nikola Ozu
Jonathon Pinnock
Keith Visco
Andrew Watt
Kevin Williams
Zoran Zaev

Technical Architect
Timothy Briggs

Technical Editors
Phil Jackson
Simon Mackie
Chris Mills
Andrew Polshaw

Category Managers
Dave Galloway
Sonia Mulineux

Project Administrator
Beckie Stones

Author Agent
Marsha Collins

Proof Reader
Agnes Wiggers

Production Manager
Simon Hardware

Technical Reviewers
Daniel Ayers
Martin Beaulieu
Arnaud Blandin
Maxime Bombadier
Joseph Bustos
David Carlisle
Pierre-Antoine Champin
Robert Chang
Michael Corning
Chris Crane
Steve Danielson
Phil Powers DeGeorge
Chris Dix
Sébastien Gignoux
Tony Hong
Paul Houle
Craig McQueen
Thomas B. Passin
Dave Pawson
Gary L Peskin
Eric Rajkovic
Gareth Reakes
Matthew Reynolds
David Schultz
Marc H. Simkin
Darshan Singh
Paul Warren
Karli Watson

Production Co-ordinator
Pip Wonson

Indexers
Andrew Criddle
Bill Johncocks

Diagrams
Shabnam Hussain

Cover
Chris Morris

About the Authors

Mark Birbeck

Mark Birbeck is Technical Director of Parliamentary Communications Ltd. where he has been responsible for the design and building of their political portal, ePolitix.com. He is also managing director of XML consultancy x-port.net Ltd., responsible for the publishing system behind spiked-online.com. Although involved in XML for a number of years, his special interests lay in meta data, and in particular the use of RDF. He particularly welcomes Wrox's initiative in trying to move these topics from out of the shadows and into the mainstream.

Mark would particularly like to thank his long-suffering partner Jan for putting up with the constant smell of midnight oil being burned. He offers the consolation that at least he will already be up when their first child Louis demands attention during the small hours.

Jon Duckett

Jon has been using and writing about XML since 1998, when he co-authored and edited Wrox's first XML publication. Having spent the past 3 years working for Wrox in the Birmingham UK offices, Jon is currently working from Sydney, so that he can get a different view out of the window while he is working and supping on a nice cup of tea...

Oli Gauti Gundmundsson

Oli is working for SALT, acting as one of two Chief System Architects of the SALT Systems, and Development Director in New York. He is currently working on incorporating XML and XSL into SALT's web authoring and content management systems. He has acted as an instructor in the Computer Science course (Java) at the University of Iceland, and Java is one of his greatest strengths (and pleasures!). As a hobby he is trying to finish his BS degree in Computer Engineering.

His nationality is Icelandic, but he is currently situated in New York with his girlfriend Edda. He can be reached at `oli.gauti@salt.is`.

Pete Kobak

Pete Kobak built and programmed his first computer from a kit in 1978, which featured 256 bytes of RAM and a single LED output. After a fling as an electrical engineer for IBM, Pete gradually moved into software development to support mainframe manufacturing. He earned geek programmer status in the late '80s when he helped to improve Burroughs' Fortran compiler by introducing vectorization of DO loops. Justified by his desire to continue to pay his mortgage, Pete left Burroughs in 1991 to put lives in jeopardy by developing medical laboratory software in OS/2. In 1997, Pete somehow convinced The Vanguard Group to hire him to do Solaris web development, even though he could barely spell "Unix". He has helped to add new features to their web site since then, specializing in secure web communication.

Pete's current interest is in web application security, trying to find the right techniques to enforce the strong security needed by a serious financial institution while meeting their need to rapidly extend business relationships. Pete is thankful to be able to introduce interesting web technologies in the service of helping millions of people to reach for their financial dreams. He can be contacted at `kobak@ieee.org`.

I'd like to dedicate my humble contribution to my wife Geraldine, and to my children Mary, John, and Patricia. They have sacrificed my time and attention for me to be able to complete this project. This chapter is a family effort.

Evan Lenz

Evan Lenz currently works as a software engineer for XYZFind Corp. in Seattle, WA. His primary area of expertise is in XSLT, and he enjoys exploring new ways to utilize this technology for various projects. His work at XYZFind includes everything from XSLT and Java development to writing user's manuals, to designing the XML query language used in XYZFind's XML database software. Wielding a professional music degree and a philosophy major, he hopes to someday bring his varying interests together into one grand, masterful scheme.

Thanks to my precious wife, Lisa, and my baby son, Samuel, for putting up with Daddy's long nights. And praise to my Lord and Savior, Jesus Christ, without whom none of this would be possible or meaningful.

Steve Livingstone

Steve Livingstone is an IT Architect with IBM Global Services in Winnipeg, Canada. He has contributed to numerous Wrox books and magazine articles, on subjects ranging from XML to e-Commerce. Steven's current interests include e-Commerce, ebXML, .NET, and Enterprise Application Architectures.

Steve would like to thank everyone at Wrox, especially for their understanding as he emigrated from Scotland to Canada (and that could be another book itself ;-) Most importantly he wants to thank Loretito for putting up with him whilst writing – gracias mi tesoro.

Congratulations Celtic on winning the Treble :)

Daniel Marcus

Dr. Marcus has twenty years of experience in software architecture and design. He is co-founder, President, and Chief Operating Officer at Speechwise Technologies, an applications software company at the intersection of speech, wireless, and Internet technologies. Prior to starting Speechwise, he was Director of e-Business Consulting at Xpedior, leading the strategy, architecture, and deployment of e-business applications for Global 2000 and dot-com clients. Dr. Marcus has been a Visiting Scholar at Princeton's Institute for Advanced Study, a research scientist at the Lawrence Livermore National Laboratory, and is the author of over twenty papers in computational science. He is a Sun-Certified Java Technology Architect and holds a Ph.D. in Mechanical Engineering from the University of California, Berkeley.

Stephen Mohr

Stephen Mohr is a software systems architect with Omicron Consulting, Philadelphia, USA. He has more than ten years' experience working with a variety of platforms and component technologies. His research interests include distributed computing and artificial intelligence. Stephen holds BS and MS degrees in computer science from Rensselaer Polytechnic Institute.

For my wife, Denise, and my sons James and Matthew.

Nikola Ozu

Nikola Ozu is an independent systems architect who lives in Wyoming at the end of a few miles of dirt road – out where the virtual community is closer than town, but only flows at 24kb/s, and still does not deliver pizza.

His current project involves bringing semantic databases, text searching, and multimedia components together with XML – on the road to Xanadu. Other recent work has included the usual web design consulting, some XML vocabularies, and an XML-based production and full-text indexing system for a publisher of medical reference books and databases.

In the early 90s, Nik designed and developed a hypertext database called *Health Reference Center,* followed by advanced versions of *InfoTrac.* Both of these were bibliographic and full-text databases, delivered as monthly multi-disc CD-ROM subscriptions. Given the large text databases involved, some involvement with SGML was unavoidable. His previous work has ranged from library systems on mainframes to embedded micro systems (telecom equipment, industrial robots, toys, arcade games, and videogame cartridges). In the early 70s, he was thrilled to learn programming using patch boards, punch cards, paper tape, and printouts (and Teletypes, too).

When not surfing the 'net, he surfs crowds, the Tetons, and the Pacific; climbs wherever there is rock; and tries to get more than a day's walk from the nearest road now and then. He enjoys these even more when accompanied by his teenage son, who's old enough now to appreciate the joy of mosh pits and sk8ing the Mission District after midnight.

To Noah: May we always think of the next (23 - 1) generations instead of just our own 20.

My thanks to the editors and illustrators at Wrox and my friend Deanna Bauder for their help with this project. Also, thanks and apologies to my family and friends who endured my disappearances into the WriterZone for days on end.

Jonathan Pinnock

Jonathan Pinnock started programming in Pal III assembler on his school's PDP 8/e, with a massive 4K of memory, back in the days before Moore's Law reached the statute books. These days he spends most of his time developing and extending the increasingly successful PlatformOne product set that his company, JPA, markets to the financial services community. He seems to spend the rest of his time writing for Wrox, although he occasionally surfaces to say hello to his long-suffering wife and two children. JPA's home page is www.jpassoc.co.uk.

Keith Visco

Keith Visco currently works for Intalio, Inc., the leader in Business Process Management, as a manager and project leader for XML based technologies. Keith is the project leader for the open source data-binding framework, Castor. He has been actively working on open source projects since 1998, including the Mozilla project where he is the original author of Mozilla's XSLT processor (donated by his previous employer, The MITRE Corporation) and is the current XSLT module owner.

In all aspects of his life, Keith is most inspired after drinking a large Dunkin' Donuts Hazelnut Coffee. Keith relieves what little stress his life does encounter by playing guitar or keyboards (he apologizes to his neighbors). He is also a firm believer that life cannot exist without three basic elements: music, coffee, and Red Sox baseball.

I would like to acknowledge Intalio, Inc. and The Exolob Group for giving me the opportunity to work on many industry-leading technologies. I would like to thank my team at Intalio, specifically Arnaud Blandin and Sebastien Gignoux, for their hard work as well as their invaluable feedback on this chapter. I would also like to thank my family for their unconditional support and incessant input into all phases of my life. A special thanks to Cindy Iturbe, whose encouragement means so much to me and for teaching me that with a little patience and hard work all things are possible, no matter how distant things may seem.

Andrew Watt

Andrew Watt is an independent consultant who enjoys few things more than exploring the technologies others have yet to sample. Since he wrote his first programs in 6502 Assembler and BBC Basic in the mid 1980s, he has sampled Pascal, Prolog, and C++, among others. More recently he has focused on the power of web-relevant technologies, including Lotus Domino, Java and HTML. His current interest is in the various applications of the Extensible Markup Meta Language, XMML, sometimes imprecisely and misleadingly called XML. The present glimpse he has of the future of SVG, XSL-FO, XSLT, CSS, XLink, XPointer, etc. when they actually work properly together is an exciting, if daunting, prospect. He has just begun to dabble with XQuery. Such serial dabbling, so he is told, is called "life-long learning".

In his spare time he sometimes ponders the impact of Web technologies on real people. What will be the impact of a Semantic Web? How will those other than the knowledge-privileged fare?

To the God of Heaven who gives human beings the capacity to see, think and feel. To my father who taught me much about life.

My heartfelt thanks go to Gail, who first suggested getting into writing, and now suffers the consequences on a fairly regular basis, and to Mark and Rachel, who just suffer the consequences.

Kevin Williams

Kevin's first experience with computers was at the age of 10 (in 1980) when he took a BASIC class at a local community college on their PDP-9, and by the time he was 12, he stayed up for four days straight hand-assembling 6502 code on his Atari 400. His professional career has been focused on Windows development – first client-server, then onto Internet work. He's done a little bit of everything, from VB to Powerbuilder to Delphi to C/C++ to MASM to ISAPI, CGI, ASP, HTML, XML, and any other acronym you might care to name; but these days, he's focusing on XML work. Kevin is a Senior System Architect for Equient, an information management company located in Northern Virginia. He may be reached for comment at `kevin@realworldxml.com`.

Zoran Zaev

Zoran is a Sr. Web Solutions Architect with Hitachi Innovative Solutions, Corp. in the Washington DC area. He has worked in technology since the time when 1 MHz CPUs and 48Kb was considered a 'significant power', in the now distant 1980s. In mid 1990s, Zoran became involved in web applications development. Since then, he has worked helping large and small clients alike leverage the power of web applications. His more recent emphasis has been web applications and web services with XML, SOAP, and other related technologies. When he's not programming, you'll find him traveling, exploring new learning opportunities.

I would like to thank my wife, Angela, for her support and encouragement, as well as sharing some of her solid writing knowledge. And, you can never go wrong thanking your parents, so 'fala' to my mom, Jelica and dad, Vanco. On the professional side, I would like to thank Ellen Manetti for her strong project management example, and Pete Johnson, founder of Virtualogic, Inc., for his vision inspiring influence. Finally, thanks to Beckie and Marsha from Wrox for their always-timely assistance and to Jan from "Images by Jan".

Zoran can be reached at `zoran.zaev@hitachisolutions.net`

Table of Contents

Introduction

Extensible Markup Language (XML) has emerged as nothing less than a phenomenon in computing. It is a concept elegant in its simplicity driving dramatic changes in the way Internet applications are written. This book is a revision to the first edition to keep pace with this fast-changing technology as many technologies have been superseded, and new ones have emerged.

What Does This Book Cover?

This book explains and demonstrates both the essential techniques for designing and using XML documents, and many of the related technologies that are important today. Almost everything in this book will be based around a specification provided by the World Wide Web Consortium (W3C). These specifications are at various levels of completion and some of the technologies are nascent, but we expect them to become very popular when their specifications are finalized because they are useful or essential. The wider XML community is increasingly jumping in and offering new XML-related ideas outside the control of the W3C, although the W3C is still central and important to the development of XML.

The focus of this book is on learning how to use XML as an enabling technology in real-world applications. It presents good design techniques, and shows how to interface XML-enabled applications with web applications. Whether your requirements are oriented toward data exchange or presentation, this book will cover all the relevant techniques in the XML community.

Most chapters contain a practical example (unless the technology is so new that there were no working implementations at the time of writing). As XML is a platform-neutral technology, the examples cover a variety of languages, parsers, and servers. All the techniques are relevant across all the platforms, so you can get valuable insight from the examples even if they are not implemented using your favorite platform.

Who Is This Book for?

This book is for the experienced developer, who already has some basic knowledge of XML, to learn how to build effective applications using this exciting but simple technology. Web site developers can learn techniques, using XSLT stylesheets and other technologies, to take their sites to the next level of sophistication. Other developers can learn where and how XML fits into their existing systems and how they can use it to solve their application integration problems.

XML applications can be distributed and are usually web-oriented. This book focuses on this kind of application and so we would expect the reader to have some awareness of multi-tier architecture – preferably from a web perspective. Although we will retread over XML, in case some of the XML fundamentals have been missed in your experience, we will cover the full specification thoroughly and fairly quickly.

A variety of programming languages will be used in this book, and we do not expect you to be proficient in them all. The techniques taught in this book can be transferred to other programming languages. As XML is a cross-platform language, Java will be a language used in this book, especially because it has a wealth of tools to manipulate XML. Other languages covered include JavaScript, VBScript, VB, C#, and Perl. We expect the reader to be proficient in a programming language, but it does not matter which one.

How Is this Book Structured?

Although many authors have contributed towards this book, we have tied the chapters together under unifying themes. As you will read below, the book has effectively been split into six sections.

A small number of the chapters, for example Chapter 23, rely heavily on a previous chapter, but this will be made clear. Most of the chapters will be relatively self-contained.

Learning Threads

XML is evolving into a large, wide-ranging field of related markup technologies. This growth is powering XML applications. With growth comes divergence. Different readers will come to this book with different expectations. XML is different things to different people.

Foundation

Chapter 1 introduces the XML world in general, discussing the technologies that are relevant today and may be relevant tomorrow, but with very little code. Chapters 2 (Basic XML Syntax) and 3 (Advanced XML Syntax) cover the fundamentals of XML 1.0. Chapter 2 gives you the basic syntax of an XML document, while Chapter 3 covers slightly more advanced issues like namespaces. These chapters form the irreducible minimum you need to understand XML and, depending on your experience, you may want to skip these introductory chapters. Chapter 4 teaches you about the Infoset, a standard way of describing XML, which provides an abstract representation for XML data.

In Chapter 5, we cover document validation using DTDs. Although, as you learn in the subsequent two chapters, other schema-based validation languages exist that supersede DTDs, they are not quite dead as many more XML parsers validate with DTDs than any other schema language, and DTDs are relatively simple. Following this, in Chapter 6, we cover XML Schema and show how to validate your XML documents using this new XML-based validation language specified by the W3C. Chapter 7 covers other schema-based validation languages, including James Clark's TREX proposal, and the Schematron.

In Chapter 8, we explain the XPath specification – a method of referring to specific fragments of XML that is relevant to and used by other XML technologies. These include XSLT, described in Chapter 9. Here we teach you how to transform your XML documents into anything else, based on certain stylesheet declarations. In Chapter 10, we show various linking technologies, such as XLink and XPointer and describe the XML Fragment Interchange specification.

These ten chapters are enough for you to learn about all of the immediately useful XML technologies – for those who just use XML. You may already have a lot of experience of XML and so some of these chapters will be re-treading over well-walked ground, but everybody should be able to learn something new, especially because XML Schema acquired Proposed Recommendation status, the penultimate stage of the W3C specifications, just two months before this book was printed. Although a wealth of XML techniques lie ahead, you will have a firm foundation upon which to build.

So the Foundation thread includes:

- **Chapter 1**: Introducing XML
- **Chapter 2**: Basic XML Syntax
- **Chapter 3**: Advanced XML Syntax
- **Chapter 4**: The XML Information Set
- **Chapter 5**: Validating XML: Schemas
- **Chapter 6**: Introducing XML Schema
- **Chapter 7**: XML Schema Alternatives
- **Chapter 8**: Navigating XML – XPath
- **Chapter 9**: Transforming XML
- **Chapter 10**: Fragments, XLink, and XPointer

XML Programming

XML is both machine and human readable and, not surprisingly, some standard APIs have been created to manipulate XML data. These APIs are implemented in JavaScript, Java, Visual Basic, C++, Perl, and many other languages. These provide a standard way of manipulating, and developing for, XML documents.

In Chapter 11, we consider the first API, which emerged from the HTML world, the DOM. This has been released as a specification from the W3C, and Level 2 of this specification has recently been released. XML data can be thought of as hierarchical and object-oriented, and the DOM provides methods and properties for retrieving and manipulating XML nodes. Chapter 12 discusses the SAX, a lightweight alternative to the DOM. When manipulating the DOM, the entire document has to be read into memory; with the SAX, however, it only retrieves as much data as is necessary to retrieve or manipulate a specific node.

Chapter 13 is the last chapter in this section, and it covers declarative programming with XML. Most programmers use procedural languages, but XML and the XML specifications don't care about how a particular language or application performs a job, just that it does it according the declarations made. This chapter explains how to use schemas to design your applications.

The Programming thread therefore includes:

- **Chapter 11**: The Document Object Model
- **Chapter 12**: SAX 2
- **Chapter 13**: Schema Based Programming

XML As Data

There are four chapters in this section, all targeted specifically at the storage, retrieval, and manipulation of data – as it relates to XML. Chapter 14, Data Modeling, explains how to plan your project 'properly', and so model your XML on your data and build better applications because of it. Chapter 15 extends this concept by covering the binding of the data to XML (and vice versa). Querying XML covers a nascent technology known as XML Query. It aims to provide the power of SQL in an XML format. This short chapter teaches you how to use the technology as it stands at the time of writing.

The final chapter covered is a case study, which describes how to relate your databases to your XML data and so integrate your XML and RDBMS in the best way possible.

This means that the Data thread contains:

- **Chapter 14**: Data Modeling
- **Chapter 15**: Data Binding
- **Chapter 16**: Querying XML
- **Chapter 17**: Case Study: XML and Databases

Presentation of XML

Chapter 18 covers an XML technology called SVG – Scalable Vector Graphics. This XML technology, when coupled with an appropriate viewer (for example, Adobe SVG Viewer), allows quite detailed graphics files to be displayed and manipulated. In Chapter 19, we describe VoiceXML, an XML technology to allow voice recognition and processing on the Web. XML data can be converted to VoiceXML and, using the appropriate technology, can be spoken and interacted with over a telephone.

Chapter 20 covers the final technology in this section, XSL-FO. This is an emerging technology that allows the layout of pages to be specified exactly, much in the same way as PDF does now. The main difference is, this is XML too and so can be manipulated using the same XML tools you may be used to. Also, XSL-FO can be converted to PDF if necessary for users without XSL-FO viewers.

In the Presentation thread, therefore, we cover:

- **Chapter 18**: Presenting XML Graphically
- **Chapter 19**: VoiceXML
- **Chapter 20**: XSL Formatting Objects: XSL-FO

XML As Metadata

In this thread, we discuss how XML can be used to represent metadata – that is, the meaning or semantics of data, rather than the data itself. In Chapter 21, we cover the setting up of an index of XML data. This chapter uses a Java indexing application, but the techniques are applicable to any indexing tool. Chapter 22 is where we really get to the meat of the topic, where we talk about RDF – a language to describe metadata. We cover the elements and syntax of this technology. In Chapter 23, we go over some practical examples of RDF technology, before describing RDDL – a method of bundling resources at the URL of a namespace, so that a RDDL-enabled application can learn what the technology of which the namespace is referring to, actually is and access schema and standard transforms.

In the Metadata thread, we cover:

- **Chapter 21**: Case Study: Generating a Site Index
- **Chapter 22**: RDF
- **Chapter 23**: RDF Code Samples and RDDL

XML Used for B2B

The final section of this book describes what is quite possibly the most important use of XML – B2B and Web Services. In the past, the communication protocols for B2B (for example, EDI) have been proprietary, and expensive – both in terms of cost, and processor power. Using XML vocabularies, an open and programmable model can be used for B2B transactions.

In Chapter 24, we describe **S**imple **O**bject **A**ccess **P**rotocol. SOAP was a mostly Microsoft initiative (although the W3C are developing the XML Protocol specification, which should be very similar to SOAP), which allows two applications to specify services using XML. We cover the intricacies of this protocol, so that you can use it to web-enable any service you would care to mention.

Chapter 25 covers Microsoft's BizTalk Server. This server can control all B2B transactions, using the open BizTalk framework. BizTalk is just one method of using SOAP to conduct business transactions, but it is Microsoft's and is very popular. In Chapter 26, we have a case study discussing e-Business integration using XML. There are a number of business standards for commerce, and this chapter explains how you can integrate all of the standards, without having to write code for every possible B2B transaction between competing standards.

We end in Chapter 27, with a discussion of the Web Services Description Language, which allows us to formalize other XML vocabularies by defining services that a SOAP, or other client, can connect to. WSDL describes each service and what it does. In addition, in this chapter, we cover UDDI (Universal Description, Discovery, and Integration), which is a way of automating the discovery and transactions with various services. In many cases, it should not be necessary for human interaction to find a service, and using public registration services, UDDI makes this possible. Both of these technologies are nascent, but their importance will grow as more and more businesses make use of them.

In summary, in the B2B thread, we describe in each chapter the following:

- **Chapter 24**: SOAP
- **Chapter 25**: B2B with Microsoft BizTalk Server
- **Chapter 26**: E-Business Integration
- **Chapter 27**: B2B Futures: WSDL and UDDI

What You Need to Use This Book

The book assumes that you have some knowledge of HTML, some procedural object-oriented programming languages (for example Java, VB, C++), and some minimal XML knowledge. For some of the examples in this book, a Java Runtime Environment (http://java.sun.com/j2se/1.3/) will need to be installed on your system, and some other chapters, require applications such as MS SQL Server, MS Index Server, and BizTalk.

The complete source for larger portions of code from the book is available for download from: http://www.wrox.com/. More details are given in the section of this Introduction called, "Support, Errata, and P2P".

Conventions

To help you get the most from the text and keep track of what's happening, we've used a number of conventions throughout the book.

For instance:

> **These boxes hold important, not-to-be forgotten information, which is directly relevant to the surrounding text.**

While this style is used for asides to the current discussion.

As for styles in the text:

When we introduce them, we **highlight** important words

We show keyboard strokes like this: *Ctrl-A*

We show filenames, and code within the text like so: `doGet()`

Text on user interfaces is shown as: File | Save

URLs are shown in a similar font, as so: http://www.w3c.org/

We present code in two different ways. Code that is important, and testable is shown as so:

```
In our code examples, the code foreground style shows new, important,
    pertinent code
```

Code that is an aside, shows examples of what *not* to do, or has been seen before is shown as so:

```
Code background shows code that's less important in the present context,
    or has been seen before.
```

In addition, when something is to be typed at a command line interface (for example a DOS prompt), then we use the following style to show what is typed, and what is output:

```
> java com.ibm.wsdl.Main -in Arithmetic.WSDL
>> Transforming WSDL to NASSL ..
>> Generating Schema to Java bindings ..
>> Generating serializers / deserializers ..
Interface 'wsdlns:ArithmeticSoapPort' not found.
```

Support, Errata, and P2P

The printing and selling of this book was just the start of our contact with you. If there are any problems, whatsoever with the code or the explanation in this book, we welcome input from you. A mail to support@wrox.com, should elicit a response within two to three days (depending on how busy the support team are).

In addition to this, we also publish any errata online, so that if you have a problem, you can check on the Wrox web site first to see if we have updated the text at all. First, pay a visit to www.wrox.com, then, click on the Books | By Title(Z-A), or Books | By ISBN link on the left-hand side of the page. See below:

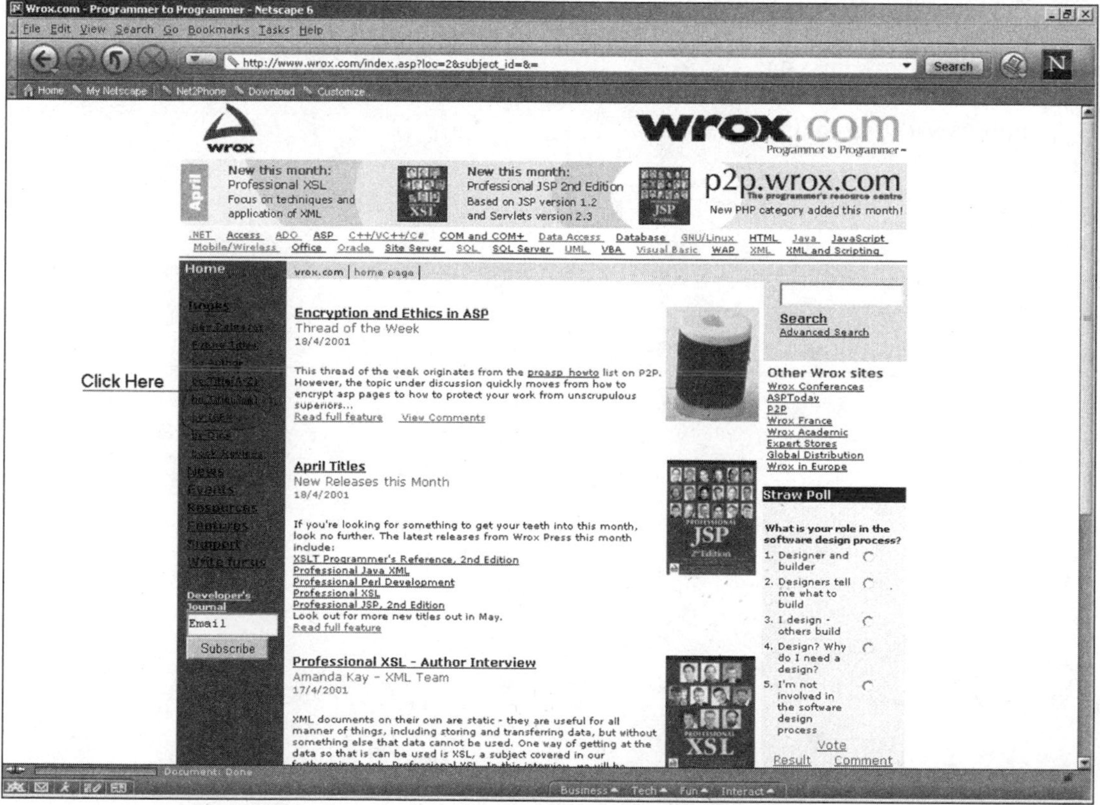

Navigate to this book (this ISBN is 1861005059, if you choose to navigate this way) and then click on it. As well as giving some information about the book, it also provides options to download the code, view errata, and ask for support. Just click on the relevant link. All errata that we discover will be added to the site and so information on changes to the code that has to be made for newer versions of software may also be included here – as well as corrections to any printing or code errors.

All of the code for this book can be downloaded from our site. It is included in a zip file, and all of the code samples in this book can be found within, referenced by chapter number.

In addition, at p2p.wrox.com, we have our free "Programmer to Programmer" discussion lists. There are a few relevant to this book, and any questions you post will be answered by either someone at Wrox, or someone else in the developer community. Navigate to http://p2p.wrox.com/xml, and subscribe to a discussion list from there. All lists are moderated and so no fluff or spam should be received in your Inbox.

Tell Us What You Think

We've worked hard to make this book as useful to you as possible, so we'd like to know what you think. We're always keen to know what it is you want and need to know.

We appreciate feedback on our efforts and take both criticism and praise on board in our future editorial efforts. If you've anything to say, let us know on:

```
feedback@wrox.com
```

Or via the feedback links on:

http://www.wrox.com

1

Introducing XML

In this chapter, we'll look at the origins of XML, the core technologies and specifications that are related to XML, and an overview of some current, and future applications of XML. The later sections of this introduction should also serve as something of a road map to the rest of the book.

Origins and Goals of XML

"XML", as we all know, is an acronym for Extensible Markup Language – but what is a markup language? What is the history of markup languages, what are the goals of XML, and how does it improve upon earlier markup?

Markup Languages

Ever since the invention of the printing press, writers have made notes on manuscripts to instruct the printers on matters such as typesetting and other production issues. These notes were called "markup". A collection of such notes that conform to a defined syntax and grammar can certainly be called a "language". Proofreaders use a hand-written symbolic markup language to communicate corrections to editors and printers. Even the modern use of punctuation is actually a form of markup that remains with the text to advise the reader how to interpret that text.

These early markup languages use a distinct appearance to differentiate markup from the text to which it refers. For example, proofreaders' marks consist of a combination of cursive handwriting and special symbols to distinguish markup from the typeset text. Punctuation consists of special symbols that cannot be confused with the alphabet and numbers that represent the textual content. These symbols are so necessary to understanding printed English that they were included in the ASCII character set, and so have become the foundation of modern programming language syntax.

The ASCII character set standard was the early basis for widespread data exchange between various hardware and software systems. Whatever the internal representation of characters; conversion to ASCII allowed these disparate systems to communicate with each other. In addition to text, ASCII also defined a set of symbols, the **C0 control characters** (using the hexadecimal values 00 to 1F), which were intended to be used to mark-up the structure of data transmissions.

Only a few of these symbols found widespread acceptance, and their use was often inconsistent. The most common example is the character(s) used to delimit the end of a line of text in a document. Teletype machines used the physical motion-based character pair CR-LF (carriage-return, line-feed). This was later used by both MS-DOS and MS-Windows; UNIX uses a single LF character; and the MacOS uses a single CR character. Due to conflicting and non-standard uses of `C0` control characters, document interchange between different systems still often requires a translation step, since even a simple text file cannot be shared without conversion.

Various forms of **delimiters** have been used to define the boundaries of containers for content, special symbol glyphs, presentation style of the text, or other special features of a document. For example, the C and C++ programming languages use the braces {} to delimit units of data or code. A typesetting language, intended for manual human editing, might use strings that are more readable, like "`.begin`" and "`.end`".

> **Markup is a method of conveying meta data (information about another dataset).**

XML is a relatively new markup language, but it is a subset of, and is based upon, a mature markup language called **Standard Generalized Markup Language (SGML)**. The WWW's **Hypertext Markup Language (HTML)** is also based upon SGML; indeed, it is an application of SGML. There is a new version of HTML 4 that is called **Extensible Hypertext Markup Language (XHTML)**, which is similarly an application of XML. All of these markup languages are for meta data, but SGML and XML may be further considered meta-languages, since they can be used to create other meta data languages. Just as HTML was expressed in SGML, XHTML and others will use XML.

> **SGML-based markup languages all use literal strings of characters, called** tags **to delimit the major components of the meta data, called** elements.

Tags represent object delimiters and other such markup, as opposed to its content (no matter whether it's simple text or text that is program code). Of course, there has often been conflict between different sets of tags and their interpretation. Without common delimiter vocabularies, or even common internal data formats, it has been very difficult to convert data from one format to another, or otherwise share data between applications and organizations.

For example, the following two markup excerpts (`Chapter_01_01.html` & `Chapter_01_01.xml`) show familiar HTML and similar XML elements with their delimiting tags:

```
<HTML>
<HEAD>
   <TITLE>Product Catalog (Toysco-only)</TITLE>
</HEAD>
<BODY>
   <H1>Product Catalog (Internal-use only!)</H1>
   <HR>
```

```
    <H2>Product Descriptions</H2>
    <HR WIDTH=33% ALIGN=LEFT>
    <H3>Mega Wonder Widget</H3>
    <P>The <EM>Mega Wonder Widget</EM> is a popular toy with a 20 oz. capacity. It
costs only $12.95 to make, whilst selling for $33.99 (plus $3.95 S&H).<BR>
    <H3>Giga Wonder Widget</H3>
    <P>The <EM>Giga Wonder Widget</EM>is even more popular, because of its
larger 55 oz. capacity. It has a similar profit margin (costs $19.95,
sells for $49.99).
...
    <HR>
    <P><I>Updated:</I> 2001-04-01 <I>by Webmaster Will</I>
</BODY>
</HTML>
```

This rather simplistic document uses the few structural tags that exist in HTML, such as `<TITLE>`, `<H1>`, `<H2>`, and `<H3>` for headers, and `<P>` for paragraphs. This structure is limited to a very basic *presentation* model of a document as a printed page. Other tags, such as `<HR>` and `<EM>`, are purely about the appearance of the data. Indeed, most HTML tags are now used to describe the presentation of data, interactive logic for user input and control, and external multimedia objects. These tags give us no idea what structured data (names, prices, etc.) might appear within the text, or where it might be in that text.

On the other hand, XML allows us to create a *structural* model of the data within the text. Presentation cues *can* be embedded as with HTML tags, but the best XML practice is to separate the data structure from presentation. An external **style sheet** can be used with XML to describe the data's presentation model. So, we might convert – and extend – the above HTML example into the following XML data file (`Chapter_01_01.xml`):

```
<?xml version="1.0" ?>
<!DOCTYPE ProductCatalog
[
   <!ELEMENT ProductCatalog  (HEAD?, BODY?) >
   <!ELEMENT HEAD  (TITLE, Updated, Author+, Security*) >
   <!ELEMENT BODY  (H1, H2, (H3, Products)+ ) >
   <!ELEMENT Products  (Product+) >
   <!ELEMENT Product  (#PCDATA|Prodname|Capacity|Cost|Price|Shipfee)* >

   <!ELEMENT H1     (#PCDATA) >
   <!ELEMENT H2     (#PCDATA) >
   <!ELEMENT H3     (#PCDATA) >
   <!ELEMENT TITLE (#PCDATA) >

   <!ELEMENT Updated  (#PCDATA) >
   <!ELEMENT Author   (#PCDATA) >
   <!ELEMENT Security (#PCDATA) >

   <!ELEMENT Prodname (#PCDATA) >
   <!ELEMENT Capacity (#PCDATA) >
   <!ELEMENT Cost     (#PCDATA) >
   <!ELEMENT Price    (#PCDATA) >
   <!ELEMENT Shipfee  (#PCDATA) >

   <!ENTITY MWW "Mega Wonder Widget" >
   <!ENTITY GWW "Giga Wonder Widget" >
```

```
]>
<ProductCatalog>
   <HEAD>
      <TITLE>Product Catalog</TITLE>
      <Updated>2001-04-01</Updated>
      <Author>Webmaster Will</Author>
      <Security>Toysco-only (TRADE SECRET)</Security>
   </HEAD>
   <BODY>
      <H1>Product Catalog</H1>
      <H2>Product Descriptions</H2>
      <Products>
         <H3>&MWW;</H3>
         <Product>
            The <Prodname>&MWW;</Prodname> is a popular toy with a
            <Capacity unit="oz.">20</Capacity> capacity. It costs only
            <Cost currency="USD">12.95</Cost> to make, whilst selling for
            <Price currency="USD">33.99</Price> (plus
            <Shipfee currency="USD">3.95</Shipfee> S&amp;H).<BR/>
         </Product>
         <H3>&GWW;</H3>
         <Product>
            The <Prodname>&GWW;</Prodname> is popular, because of its
            larger <Capacity unit="oz.">55</Capacity> capacity. It has a
            similar profit margin (costs <Cost currency="USD">19.95</Cost>,
            sells for <Price currency="USD">33.99</Price>).<BR/>
         </Product>
         ...
      </Products>
   </BODY>
</ProductCatalog>
```

The XML document looks very similar to the HTML version, with comparable text content, and some equivalent tags (as XHTML). XML goes far beyond HTML by allowing the use of custom tags (like `<Prodname>` or `<Weight>`) that preserve some structured data that is embedded within the text of the description. We can't do this in HTML, since its set of tags is more or less fixed, changing slowly as browser vendors embrace new features and markup. In contrast, anyone can add tags to their own XML data. The use of tags to describe data structure allows easy conversion of XML to an arbitrary DBMS format, or alternative presentations of the XML data such as in tabular form or via a voice synthesizer connected to a telephone.

We have also assumed that we will use a stylesheet to format the XML data for presentation. Therefore, we are able to omit certain labels from our text (such as the $ sign in prices, and the "oz." after the capacity value). We will then rely upon the formatting process to insert them in the output, as appropriate. In a similar fashion, we have put the document update information in the header (where it can be argued that it logically belongs). When we transform the data for output, this data can be displayed as a footer with various string literals interspersed. In this way, it can appear to be identical to the HTML version.

It should be obvious from the examples that HTML and XML are very similar in both overall structure and syntax. Let's look at their common ancestor, before we move on to the goals of XML.

SGML and Document Markup Languages

SGML is an acronym for **Standard Generalized Markup Language**, an older and more much complex markup language than XML. It has been codified as an international standard by the **ISO** (**International Organization for Standardization**) as ISO 8879 and **WebSGML**.

> *The **ISO** doesn't put very much of its standards information online, but they do maintain a website at* http://www.iso.ch, *and offer the paper version of **ISO 8879** for sale at* http://www.iso.ch/cate/d16387.html. *General **SGML** information and links can be found at* http://www.w3.org/MarkUp/SGML *and* http://xml.coverpages.org. ***WebSGML** (ISO 8879:1986 TC2. Information technology – Document Description and Processing Languages) is described online at* http://www.sgmlsource.com/8879rev/n0029.htm.

SGML has been widely used by the U.S. government and its contractors, large manufacturing companies, and publishers of technical information. Publishers often construct paper documents, such as books, reports, and reference manuals from SGML. Often, these SGML documents are then transformed into a presentation format such as PostScript, and sent to the typesetter and printer for output to paper. Technical specifications for manufacturing can also be exchanged via SGML documents. However, SGML's complexities and the high cost of its implementation have meant that most businesses and individuals have not been able to afford to embrace this powerful technology.

SGML History

In 1969, a person walked on the Moon for the first time. In the same year, Ed Mosher, Ray Lorie, and Charles F. Goldfarb of IBM Research invented the first modern markup language, **Generalized Markup Language** (**GML**). GML was a self-referential language for marking the structure of an arbitrary set of data, and was intended to be a meta-language – a language that could be used to describe other languages, their grammars and vocabularies. GML later became SGML. In 1986, SGML was adopted as an international data storage and exchange standard by the ISO. When Tim Berners-Lee developed HTML in the early 1990s, he made a point of maintaining HTML as an application of SGML.

With the major impact of the World Wide Web (WWW) upon commerce and communications, it could be argued that the quiet invention of GML was a more significant event in the history of technology than the high adventure of that first trip to another celestial body. GML led to SGML, the parent of both HTML and XML. The complexity of SGML and lack of content tagging in HTML led to the need for a new markup language for the WWW and beyond – XML.

Goals of XML

In 1996, the principal design organization for technologies related to the WWW, the **World Wide Web Consortium** (**W3C**) began the process of designing an extensible markup language that would combine the flexibility of SGML and the widespread acceptance of HTML. That language is XML.

> *The W3C home page is at* http://www.w3.org, *and its XML pages begin with an overview at* http://www.w3.org/XML. *Most technical documents can be found at* http://www.w3.org/TR.

XML version 1.0 was defined in a February 1998 W3C Recommendation, which, like an Internet Request for Comments (**RFC**), is an informal "standard". Various minor errors in documentation and some changes in underlying standards led to the publication of a Second Edition in October 2000, which corrects and updates the documentation, but doesn't change XML itself.

*The current XML 1.0 Recommendation (which we'll abbreviate as **XML 1.0 REC**) can be found at* http://www.w3.org/TR/REC-xml.

The W3C developed ten design goals for XML, to quote from the Recommendation:

The design goals for XML are:

1. XML shall be straightforwardly usable over the Internet.
2. XML shall support a wide variety of applications.
3. XML shall be compatible with SGML.
4. It shall be easy to write programs that process XML documents.
5. The number of optional features in XML is to be kept to the absolute minimum, ideally zero.
6. XML documents should be human-legible and reasonably clear.
7. The XML design should be prepared quickly.
8. The design of XML shall be formal and concise.
9. XML documents shall be easy to create.
10. Terseness in XML markup is of minimal importance.

Like all specifications intended to be standards, XML has been defined in a formal and concise manner, using a formal notation, **Extended Backus-Naur Form (EBNF)** that satisfies design goal 8. The other design goals have been met by several characteristics of XML 1.0 and its "normative" (pre-requisite) references to existing Internet standards. We can categorize these as:

- Extensibility and separation of semantics and presentation (an implicit goal)
- Simplicity (design goals 4, 5, 6, 7, and 10)
- Internationalization (1, 2, 6, and 9)
- Usable over the Internet (1 and 2)
- Interoperability with SGML (3)

We'll look at a few of these in slightly greater depth, and then show some additional resources for XML information, vocabularies, and software tools.

Extensibility

SGML is a highly extensible and open-ended markup language, and so is XML. A significant aspect of this was illustrated in the example in the *Markup Languages* section, where we were able to add our own tags to a document and thus include some structured data within the text. XML provides a basic syntax but does not define the actual tags; the tag set can be extended by anyone for their own purposes.

Separation of Semantics and Presentation

HTML is a markup language that describes data *and* its presentation. Despite the advent of external **Cascading Style Sheets** (CSS) to format HTML data, most web pages still use numerous presentation tags embedded within the data.

> **XML is all about the description of data, with nothing said about its presentation. HTML combines some rudimentary descriptive markup, plus a great deal of markup that describes the presentation of the data.**

The XML specification not only describes the XML data format and grammar, it also specifies a two-tier client architecture for handling XML data. The first tier is the XML Processor (also known as the **XML parser**, which is the term we'll use in this book). The parser ensures that the presumed XML data is **well-formed** (has the correct structure and syntax), and may be used to check the validity of the user's data structure. The parser must comply with the XML specification, and pass the content and structure of the XML data to a second tier application (the XML Application) in a prescribed manner.

The XML parser can use a separate document, generically called a schema, to describe and validate that instance of XML data. One type of schema, called a **Document Type Definition** (**DTD**), is specified in the XML 1.0 REC. There are other forms of schemas in use and under development. We will look at several of these, including the W3C's **XML Schema** and **XML-Data Reduced (XDR)**, currently used by Microsoft as their schema language – although they will be using XML Schema in the future, just not at this time of writing.

> **The initial layer of XML processing is the XML parser, which can optionally use a DTD or schema to describe and validate the XML data.**

As we mentioned earlier, the presentation of XML data is also defined in a separate document, the style sheet, which uses the **Extensible Stylesheet Language** (**XSL**). XSL is to XML, as CSS is to HTML.

XML can be transformed for presentation or just simple data conversion using an **XSL Transformations (XSLT)** tool, such as MSXML, Saxon, or XT. These tools can be used on server-side XML data, transforming it to a combination of HTML and CSS, for display in existing web browsers. An XSL processor can also be implemented on the client side (such as MSXML in the IE5 browser), so that XML data is sent directly to the client, without requiring server-side transformation.

> **The application layer of XML processing, such as a browser or editor, can use an XSL style sheet to describe the presentation of the XML data.**

One stylesheet can ensure a uniform presentation style for multiple XML documents. Contrariwise, a single XML document might be presented in a variety of ways, using multiple style sheets. The application layer can choose to present the XML data as synthetic speech over a telephone or radio using **VoiceXML**, or reformat it to fit a PDA display screen (using WML, for example).

For that matter, there is no requirement that XML be presented as text, or displayed at all. XML data can also be used as the basis of a messaging system, either computer-mediated person-to-person messages like e-mail, or computer-to-computer messages such as Remote Procedure Calls (RPCs). We will look at some of these, like **XML-RPC** and **SOAP**, later in this chapter.

> **XML data can be used for computer-to-computer messages, as well as for human-readable documents.**

This non-document use of XML is one of the most exciting applications of XML and its supporting tools and specifications. Just as XML might be used to present web pages that are more sophisticated to users and tagged data to search engines, XML may also serve in the underlying technical infrastructure. E-commerce applications may use XML to describe business rules and XML (as SOAP or XML-RPC) for distributed processing calls and messages. Financial transactions may be encoded in signed XML packets, and so on, right on down to the configuration and administration of the very computers that implement the world-wide e-commerce system.

Internationalization (I18N)

Although the WWW is already an international phenomenon, XML was designed for much better support of non-European languages and internationalization (also known as "**i18n**" or "I18N". This is yet another shorthand notation, obviously from the minds of programmers, that is derived from the first and last letters, and the count of 18 letters between. XML is based upon several ISO standards, including the Universal Character Set (UCS), defined in the **ISO/IEC 10646 character set** standard (which is currently congruent with the somewhat better-known **Unicode** standard).

*The current **Unicode 3.0** specification can be found at:* http://www.unicode.org ***ISO/IEC 10646*** *documentation can be ordered at* http://www.iso.ch.

Like most aspects of XML, names have been extended beyond the old-fashioned Anglo-centric ASCII-only limitation to allow the use of most any of the world's languages.

> **XML text *and* names may use any of the world's different alphabets, scripts, and writing systems as defined in the ISO/IEC 10646 and Unicode 3.0 standards.**

The value of this design goal extends far beyond merely presenting text in different human languages. The XML meta data can also be described in the local vernacular, and style. XML is the basis of a truly international Internet, accessible to people all over the world, in their native language.

XML Works with the Internet

XML is based upon a simple text format. Even though this means Unicode text, not just simple ASCII text, it may be converted to the UTF-8, or ASCII encoding for reliable transmission over the oldest of Internet connections and hardware (Teletype, anyone?). This also eliminates some considerable issues related to the interpretation of binary data formats on different computer hardware and operating systems.

XML also uses existing Internet protocols, software, and specifications wherever possible, for easier data processing and transmission. These range from basic syntax, like **Uniform Resource Identifiers** (**URI**s), to directories of code numbers, like ISO Country Codes. We will look at the more important of these Internet specifications in some detail, in Chapter 3.

There is even a version of HTML represented in an XML-compatible form, called (rather verbosely): "**XHTML 1.0**: The Extensible Hypertext Markup Language – A Reformulation of HTML 4.0, in XML 1.0". This provides a migration path from millions of existing HTML pages to pure XML representation. Once XHTML support in browsers is widespread, further development of HTML and Dynamic HTML (DHTML) can leverage all the benefits of expression in XML syntax and common XML tools.

XML is a text format that is easily transmitted over the Internet and other communications links. XML works with basic WWW protocols, including HTTP or HTTPS.

Like HTML, XML is often transmitted using the WWW's Hypertext Transfer Protocol (HTTP). This means that XML can be handled easily by existing web server software, and pass through corporate network firewalls.

XHTML 1.0 is described at http://www.w3.org/MarkUp. *The current **HTTP** specification can be found at* http://www.w3.org/Protocols.

Although XML is not a direct replacement for HTML, future versions of HTML will be expressed in XML syntax as XHTML. XML enables enhanced web architecture by moving more of the burden of presentation from the server to the client's browser or other application. XML provides a syntax that can be used for almost any data, its descriptive meta data, and even the message protocols used to move the XML data between server and clients.

XML will enable an enhanced WWW architecture. XML can also be used as a universal data exchange and long-term storage format, with or without the Internet.

Improved searching is another benefit – instead of attempting to find a price buried within a lump of text, enclosed in HTML `<P>` tags, the price information can be found easily and reliably using explicitly tagged XML data. This same tagging will provide for vastly improved data exchange between a web site and its users, between co-operating websites, and/or between software applications. XML will enable a much more powerful Web, and it will also empower most other computing applications.

XML is Simplified SGML

A major design goal for XML was ease-of-use, so the XML design team was able to use SGML as an already working starting point, and focus upon simplifying SGML. Due to its many optional features, SGML was so complex that is was difficult to write generic parsers, whereas XML parsers are much simpler to write. XML is also intended to be easy to read and write by developers using simple and commonly available tools.

XML is constrained by design to be interoperable with SGML.

This design constraint allowed early adopters of XML to use SGML tools. However, it also means that there are some quirky constraints on XML data, declarations, and syntax necessary to maintain SGML compatibility. This is the downside of XML being a subset of SGML. At some point in the future, there may be a break between XML and SGML, but for some years to come, SGML-based XML 1.0 syntax is likely to be the norm.

Resources

The formal XML specifications, including grammars in EBNF notation, are readily available on the Web from the W3C. There is also an excellent annotated version of the XML 1.0 Recommendation by Tim Bray (one of the co-editors of the XML specification). These web pages are tremendous resources that also provide extensive links to various other topics related to XML.

*The current **XML 1.0 REC** is at* http://www.w3.org/TR/REC-xml. *This is the Second Edition, and so there is a very useful color-coded version showing changes from the 1998 edition at* http://www.w3.org/TR/2000/REC-xml-20001006-review.html.

The first edition is at http://www.w3.org/TR/1998/REC-xml-19980210, *with Bray's annotated version available at* http://www.xml.com/axml/axml.html.

There is an XML 1.0 FAQ (Frequently Asked Questions) web site, maintained by Peter Flynn, *et al.* on behalf of the W3C's XML Special Interest Group.

*The **XML 1.0 FAQ** can be found at* http://www.ucc.ie/xml.

There are some other non-commercial resources that are very useful XML information sources, and serve as depositories for communally developed XML vocabularies, namespaces, DTDs, and schemas. There are also numerous e-mail lists devoted to various XML-related issues.

The **Organization for the Advancement of Structured Information Standards** (**OASIS**) is a non-profit, international consortium that is devoted to accelerating the adoption of product-independent vocabularies based upon public standards, including SGML, HTML, and XML. This organization is working with the United Nations to specify a modular electronic business framework based on XML (ebXML), and with various other organizations to produce other XML vocabularies.

OASIS hosts **The XML Industry Portal** for news and information of XML at XML.org, and **The XML Cover Pages**, one of the best web sites for researching all aspects of XML, including current tools and vocabularies.

OASIS has also become the host for **XML-DEV**, the XML developers mailing list. This list is primarily for the developers of XML parsers and other tools, so the technical level is quite high and focused upon some of the more esoteric issues of XML syntax, grammar, schemas, and specifications. Any questions concerning XML may be posted to this list, but browse the archives *first* for pertinent threads (and a sense of the list's scope) before posting any questions – this is *not* the list for simple XML questions.

***OASIS** is at* http://www.oasis-open.org. ***The XML Industry Portal** is at* http://www.xml.org, ***The XML Cover Pages** are at* http://www.oasis-open.org/cover/, *and the **XML-DEV** home page and archives are at* http://www.xml.org/xml-dev/index.shtml.

The **XML-L** and **dev-xml** e-mail lists are much better choices than XML-DEV for basic questions, and for developers of XML applications. Questions about XSL should be posted to the **xsl-list** e-mail list, rather than posting to any of the more generic XML lists. In addition, cross-posting between these lists is strongly discouraged.

*The **XML-L** home page is at* http://listserv.heanet.ie/xml-l.html, ***dev-xml** is available at* http://groups.yahoo.com/group/dev-xml, *and **xsl-list** is at* http://www.biglist.com/lists/xsl-list/. *All of these sites provide subscription information and list archives.*

There is also a USENET newsgroup for XML at comp.text.xml.

The Various Stages of W3C Specifications

Before we delve deeper into XML and all of the specifications of its related technologies, it would be a good idea to explain what each level of the specifications actually means. More detail can be found at the W3C at: http://www.w3.org/Consortium/Process-20010208/tr.html than is given here, but we give a quick overview to help understand how near completion the various standards are.

Once the W3C wants to publish a standard, it moves through five stages before reaching its final form. They are detailed below, from the first appearance at Working Draft, until it reaches the final Recommendation status.

Every specification enters the W3C through a **Note**; it is then considered by a **working group** who will want to move it through the various stages so it can become a Recommendation. There are various processes that have to be performed and conditions to be satisfied before it can be moved up. A specification can be returned to an earlier stage at any time before it becomes a Recommendation, so its position in the different stages is no guarantee that it is any nearer completion.

Working Draft

At this stage, there is no guarantee as to the quality of the specification; it just means that a working group is working with the specification, redrafting it in association with external parties.

Last Call Working Draft

After a number of conditions have been met, the specification is put through to Last Call Working Draft. It generally remains at this stage for three weeks only. It can last longer if the "...technical report is complex or has significant external dependencies" and the length of this review period has to be specified at the start of this stage. During this stage, the working group must address all comments on the specification from all parties, including external agencies. If the Director is satisfied that all objections have been noted and all comments addressed, it may move up to Candidate or Proposed Recommendation status. Once it moves up from this stage, the technical report or specification will change very little, unless it is rejected further up the process and sent back to Working Draft status.

Candidate Recommendation

At this stage, the comments made during the Last Call have to have been addressed, and the Working Group have to attempt to implement all features of the technical report. The technical report can be updated during this stage for clarity, and the period lasts as long as it takes to implement all the details.

Proposed Recommendation

For the specification to have reached this level, a working implementation of the technical report has to exist. All issues raised during the previous implementation period have to be addressed, possibly by amending the technical report. During this stage, the working group should address all "...informed and relevant issues..." raised by the public or other Working Groups. The specification must remain at this stage for at least four weeks before moving on. It can either move up to Recommendation status or move back down to Candidate Recommendation, or Working Draft, status.

Recommendation

This is the final stage of the process. The Director must be satisfied that there is significant support for the technical report before progressing to this stage. The W3C should make every effort to maintain the Recommendation, updating any errata and assisting in the creation of test bed software.

We will now move on to summarize the rest of XML, starting with the XML core.

The XML Core

The core of XML and its key components and extensions are:

- XML 1.0 syntax, including Document Type Definitions (DTDs)
- **Namespaces** in XML
- XML Schema (or one of its alternatives or supplemental validation tools: XDR, SOX, RELAX, TREX, and The Schematron)

These basic specifications describe the syntax of XML 1.0 and provide a standard validation grammar (DTDs). The extensions support multiple and shared vocabularies (Namespaces), and more rigorous and powerful validation (XML Schema *et al.*). In conjunction with the XML parser (which is also defined in the XML 1.0 REC), these comprise the first tier of XML processing.

Technology without application is useless, so several important (second tier) applications of XML are also becoming part of XML-based systems. These related specifications provide some of the key features that are commonly required in XML applications.

- Describing XML data structure: The XML Information Set (**XML Infoset**) and XML Path Language (**XPath**).
- Navigating & Linking: XML Linking (**XLink**), XML Pointer Language (**XPointer**), XML Inclusions (**XInclude**), XML Fragment Interchange (**XFI**), and XML Query Language (**XQuery**).
- Transforming & Presenting: XSLT and **XSL-FO** (XSL Formatting Objects).

We will look at the core syntax first, and then we'll look at the practical applications of these technologies and some widely shared XML vocabularies.

XML 1.0 Syntax

As we've seen before, the basic syntax of XML is described in a W3C recommendation called Extensible Markup Language (XML) 1.0 (Second Edition). This recent revision (2000-10-06) is strictly a documentation update, including some clarifications and minor code changes. There are no fundamental changes to XML as described in the original XML 1.0 recommendation (1998-02-10).

Several facets of basic XML should be understood to fully appreciate and effectively use XML for markup.

Self-Describing Data

The tags that delimit the different components of an XML document can also be interpreted to provide some semantic information about the document content. The use of descriptive element tag and attribute names in a shared XML vocabulary allows software to extract structured data from XML documents. For instance, if we consider an excerpt from the example XML text earlier in this chapter, we can see how a product name, price or other data can easily be extracted from the text, by searching for the appropriate tag:

```
<?xml version="1.0" ?>
<!DOCTYPE  ProductCatalog
[
 <!-- DTD declarations omitted -->
]>
<ProductCatalog>
   <HEAD>
      <!-- contents of <HEAD> omitted -->
   </HEAD>
   <BODY>
      <H1>Product Catalog</H1>
      <H2>Product Descriptions</H2>
      <Products>
         <H3>&MWW;</H3>
         <Product>
            The <Prodname>&MWW;</Prodname> is a popular toy with a
            <Capacity unit="oz.">20</Capacity> capacity. It costs only
            <Cost currency="USD">12.95</Cost> to make, whilst selling for
            <Price currency="USD">33.99</Price> (plus
            <Shipfee currency="USD">3.95</Shipfee> S&amp;H).<BR/>
         </Product>
         <!-- Second <H3> and <Product> omitted -->
         ...
      </Products>
   </BODY>
</ProductCatalog>
```

A stylesheet might be used to present some of this data in a Products table:

Name	Cost (US$)	Price (US$)	Capacity (Oz.)	Description
...				...
Mega Wonder Widget	12.95	33.99	20	The Mega Wonder Widget is a popular toy with a 20 oz. capacity. It costs...
Giga Wonder Widget	19.95	49.99	55	The Giga Wonder Widget is...
...				...

More significantly, a search engine or a user shopping agent (a "shopbot") can build a dynamic custom product list by extracting pertinent data from XML web pages and other XML data sources.

Use of Existing Standards

XML is built on top of existing Internet and other international standards. We've already mentioned the ISO and Unicode in conjunction with the definition of legal XML characters. Several other ISO standards are part of XML, including code numbers for countries and languages of the world. Numerous **Internet Engineering Task Force** (**IETF**) specifications, in the form of RFCs, also serve to define certain components of XML, such as URI/URL/URN references, and country or language codes.

*The **IETF** has a home page at* http://www.ietf.org.

Extensions to basic XML 1.0, such as XML Schemas, also use existing technical standards. For example, XML data types can be defined in terms of IEEE floating-point numbers or ISO date-time codes. The WWW is woven of myriad standards ranging from character encoding to resource references to protocols, and XML is a new thread in this web.

Well-Formed XML

All data objects (documents) that conform to the basic XML 1.0 syntax specification are known as **well-formed** XML data. Such documents can be used without a DTD or schema to describe their structure, and are known as **DTD-less** XML documents. These documents cannot rely upon external declarations, and attribute values will receive no special processing or default values.

A well-formed XML document contains one or more elements (delimited by start- and end-tags) that nest properly within each other. There is one element, the document element, which contains any and all other elements within the document. All elements form a simple hierarchical tree, and so the only direct element-to-element relationship is that of parent-child. Sibling relationships can often be inferred using data structures internal to the XML application, but these are neither direct, nor reliable (due to the possibility of elements being inserted between the common parent and one or more of its children). Document content can include other markup and/or character data.

> **Well-formed XML data conforms to the XML syntax specification, and includes no references to external resources (unless a DTD is provided). It is comprised of elements that form a hierarchical tree, with a single** root node **(the document element).**

The XML text example earlier in this chapter is also an example of well-formed XML data.

The existence of well-formed documents allows use of XML data without the burden of constructing and referencing an external description of that data. The term "well-formed" has a similar meaning in formal mathematical logic – an assertion is well-formed if it meets grammatical rules, without any concern as to whether the assertion is "true" or not.

Valid XML

Any XML data object is considered a **valid** XML document if it is well-formed, meets certain further validity constraints, *and* matches a grammar describing the document's content (the DTD). Like SGML, XML can provide such a description of document structure and its grammar in the form of a Document Type Definition (DTD). See Chapter 5 for more details about these.

> **Valid XML data is well-formed, and it conforms to additional validity constraints of the XML syntax specification and those defined in a DTD or schema.**

Validation using a DTD ensures that element parent-child relationships are respected, that attributes have valid values, that all referenced entities have been properly defined, and that numerous other specific validity constraints are obeyed.

> ***SGML Note****: The SGML equivalent of a well-formed document is known as* ***tag-valid****. The SGML equivalent of a valid document is* ***type-valid****.*

Given its SGML origins, XML will continue to be used for complex documents and websites. However, much current interest in XML is as a basis for electronic commerce. This application of XML requires more complex and robust methods of organizing XML vocabularies, and a way to maintain strong data typing when moving data to and from modern object and RDBMS systems. Since the restrictions imposed upon DTDs make them inadequate for this task, the W3C is in the process of defining a more robust validation method using XML Schema. When an XML application uses these extensions, validation of the XML data using a DTD becomes unnecessary. It is likely that there will be something of a divide in the use of XML: the "traditional" XML documents will be validated using DTDs, and "non-document" applications of XML like SOAP and ebXML will be based upon XML Schema validation.

Parsers

In addition to specifying the syntax of XML, the W3C described some of the behavior (but not the specific implementation) of the lower tier of XML's client architecture (the XML parser). There are two types of parsers:

- **Non-validating** – the parser merely ensures that a data object is well-formed XML
- **Validating** – the parser uses a DTD (or other type of schema) to ensure the validity of a well-formed data object's form and content

Some parsers work as both types, with configuration switches that determine whether or not the document will be validated. We will discuss parsers in Chapters 2 and 5, "*Basic XML Syntax*" and "*Validating XML: DTDs*".

The behavior of XML parsers has been defined with the intent of easing the burden upon an application's handling of XML data. For example, the character sequences used to delimit the end of text records are often OS-specific. However, an XML application needn't be concerned with this, because the XML parser will normalize all standard text line delimiters to a single line-feed (hexadecimal 0A) character. Text macro strings, (known as general entity strings), are expanded by the parser for the use of the application.

Any XML parser that encounters a construct within the XML data that is not well-formed, must report this error to the application as a "fatal" error. Fatal errors need not cause the parser to terminate – it may continue processing in an attempt to find other errors, but it may not continue to pass character data and/or XML structures to the application in a normal fashion. Similarly, a validating parser must report any validity errors encountered when processing the XML data.

This approach to error-handling is the result of XML's design goal of compactness, and the intention that XML be used for much more than just document display. This rather brutal requirement for error handling was designed to keep XML parsers simple, by avoiding the proliferation of non-well-formed XML documents. Hopefully this will avoid the problems associated with HTML, where parsers have to do their best to handle the large quantities of badly written HTML that are available on the Web. Let's continue looking at some of the other technologies that use and extend XML.

Description and Validation

For many applications, simple well-formed XML data is not enough – we must ensure that the data is also valid, using either XML 1.0 DTDs, or an extension such as XML Schema.

DTDs

As we mentioned in the "*Valid XML*" section, and we will describe in Chapter 5, DTDs are an integral part of the XML 1.0 Recommendation, although they do not use XML syntax. Any validating parser will be able to validate XML data using a DTD. The DTD can also supply definitions for XML entities, which are a form of text macros that are expanded by the parser. We will discuss the various declarations that can be used in DTDs to define and validate XML data.

Our earlier XML data example uses the following simplistic data model:

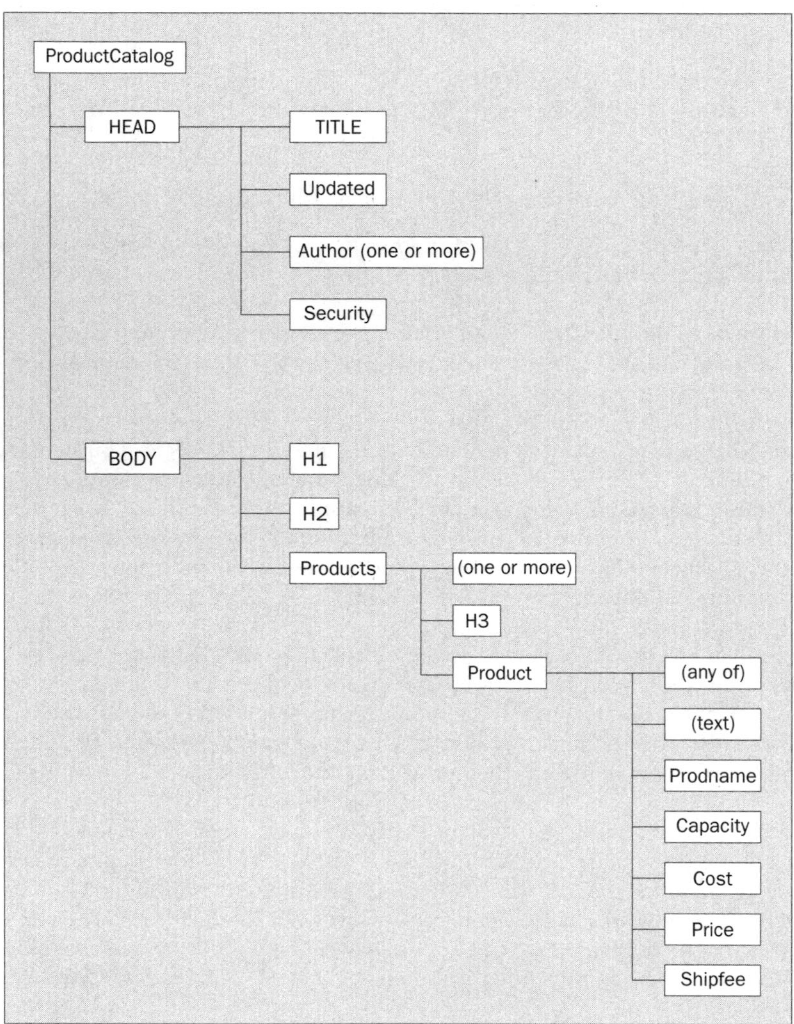

A partial set of the DTD declarations for an excerpt from this example might look something like this:

```
<!DOCTYPE  ProductCatalog
[
   <!ELEMENT ProductCatalog  (HEAD?, BODY?) >

   <!ELEMENT HEAD (TITLE, Updated, Author+, Security*) >
```

```
    <!ELEMENT BODY (H1, H2, (H3, Products)+ ) >

    <!ELEMENT Products (Product+) >
    <!ELEMENT Product (#PCDATA|Prodname|Capacity|Cost|Price|Shipfee)* >
]>
```

The above example describes the some of the structure of our example `<ProductCatalog>` elements (using `<!ELEMENT>` declarations). Don't worry about the syntax (or missing declarations) in the above example; we will deal with these in detail in the Chapter 5.

We can convert many existing SGML DTDs to XML DTDs. Though there are certain features of SGML that are not supported in XML, there are workarounds for most of these differences.

Schemas

We've touched on some limitations to DTDs as a validation schema. The W3C has created another form of schema called: XML Schema. Unlike DTDs, this new form uses XML 1.0 syntax and can therefore be edited and processed with generic XML tools. A fragment of an XML Schema that is almost equivalent to the above DTD excerpt would be:

```
<?xml version="1.0" ?>
<xsd:schema xmlns:xsd="http://www.w3.org/2001/XMLSchema" >

   <xsd:element name="ProductCatalog" >
      <xsd:complexType content="eltOnly" >
         <xsd:sequence>
            <xsd:element name="HEAD" type="eltOnly" />
            <xsd:element name="BODY" type="eltOnly" />
         </xsd:sequence>
      </xsd:element>
      <!-- <!ELEMENT  ProductCatalog  (HEAD?, BODY?) > -->

      <!-- declarations for "HEAD", etc. are omitted for brevity -->

   <xsd:element name="Products" >
      <xsd:complexType content="eltOnly" >
         <xsd:sequence>
            <xsd:element ref="H3" />
            <xsd:element ref="Product" maxOccurs="unbounded" />
         </xsd:sequence>
   </xsd:element>
   <!-- <!ELEMENT  Products  (Product+) > -->

   <xsd:element name="Product" >
      <xsd:complexType content="mixed" >
         <xsd:choice>
            <xsd:element name="Prodname" type="text" />
            <xsd:element name="Capacity" type="decimal" minOccurs="0"
               maxOccurs="1" />
            <xsd:element name="Cost" type="decimal" />
            <xsd:element name="Price" type="decimal" maxOccurs="5" />
            <!-- allows 1 to 5 <Price> elements for different currencies -->
            <xsd:element name="Shipfee" type="decimal" minOccurs="0"
               maxOccurs="1" />
```

```
            </xsd:choice>
        </xsd:complexType>
    </xsd:element>
    <!-- <!ELEMENT Product (#PCDATA|Prodname|Capacity|Cost|Price|Shipfee)* >
    -->

</xsd:schema>
```

The above example redefines the structure of our example `<ProductCatalog>` elements using XML Schema syntax instead of a DTD. The expression of an XML Schema in XML syntax is more verbose than its equivalent in DTD syntax. In this verbosity however, we gain a great deal more control over the description of our data, such as the use of common data types (such as `type="decimal"`) and more precise specification of an element's structure, such as the number of occurrences of child elements (allow 1 to 5 `<Price>` elements, instead of the DTD's unlimited one or more). A "mixed" content element may also be more precisely specified in XML Schema than in a DTD. The XML comment below each section of the above schema shows the corresponding DTD declaration. We will discuss these declarations in detail in Chapter 6.

We can easily convert the element structural descriptions, content models, and attribute descriptions in DTDs to XML Schemas, using a variety of editors and conversion tools. If we use special character or other entity references, we will still need to define these entities in a DTD. Validation with an XML Schema takes place *after* the parser has expanded any entity references (using a DTD). Schemas are designed to work with XML Namespaces (see the next section) and other related XML specifications such as the XML Infoset and XPath, which we will discuss shortly.

Schema Alternatives

Although XML Schema is an "official" development effort of the W3C, there are some alternatives that either pre-date XML Schema, or extend it with special schema formats and tools.

Two early proposals for an enhanced XML schema format were **XML-Data** and its offshoot **XDR** (XML-Data Reduced), and the Schema for Object-oriented XML **(SOX)**. XDR is currently implemented in Internet Explorer (IE5) and Microsoft's XML parser (MSXML). XDR is also the basis for the BizTalk Framework, while SOX is used as the basis for CommerceOne's e-business initiative.

There are some other proposals that are intended to provide a simpler and easier-to-implement form of a schema for the validation of XML data, such as the Regular Expression Language for XML **(RELAX)** and Tree Regular Expressions for XML **(TREX)**. Like DTDs and XML Schema, these are grammar-based validation tools. A different approach, using rules-based tree patterns instead of a grammar, is used in **The Schematron**. The Schematron relies upon conventional XPath patterns and XSLT processing (more about these shortly), and it can be used in conjunction with XML Schema to extend the validation of XML data.

We will discuss these different schema approaches in detail in Chapter 7.

Data Modeling in XML

One key to the success of an XML application is an effective XML vocabulary. This is the specification of elements, their attributes, and the structure of the XML data that will be used by the application. An effective vocabulary is critical to the success of an XML application, just as a good schema is to the success of a traditional database application. An effective data model also enables the exchange of the XML data between a variety of different platforms and applications.

Creating a good XML vocabulary is an exercise in data modeling. It describes components of the data as objects with certain characteristics and relations to each other. There are no hard and fast rules, nor rote algorithms for data modeling. There are, however, some best practices, techniques, and tools that can be applied to modeling XML data – many of them derived from such practices with relational data and DBMSs.

We will devote an entire chapter (Chapter 14) to data modeling in an XML context, including the conversion of object models and RDBMS schemas to XML Schemas. This chapter can be seen as like a lot of good software design or programming practices. You don't need this material before you start writing code or markup, but the applications and vocabularies that you design will benefit greatly from having studied this material.

Namespaces in XML

If we want to share a definition of an XML vocabulary with others, the possibility exists of name collisions between different users of the shared vocabulary. Just about any XML data could contain an element named `<name>` or `<title>`, so there must be some means to distinguish otherwise identical names that belong to different vocabularies. XML Namespaces provides a means to this end, and allows us to create XML data that merges multiple vocabularies within a single document type.

XML Namespaces provides a compound name syntax that extends the definition of XML 1.0 names to ensure that unique names can be generated for shared vocabularies.

This extension uses already legal XML names, and so remains backward compatible with simple XML 1.0 data and non-namespace aware applications. Namespaces will be discussed in Chapter 3, as they are a critical component of other XML technologies such as XML Schema and the XML Infoset.

Now that we've considered the core of XML, its basic syntax and its description and validation, we will look at some other related specifications that use and extend various different aspects of XML.

The XML Information Set

The XML Information Set (**XML Infoset**) is a specification for use with other specifications. It has been created to standardize the *terms* used to describe various components of XML data as an object model, rather than just as a sequence of simple tagged text. This allows other specifications to precisely define their relationship to, and possible effect upon, certain parts of an XML document. Every well-formed *and* Namespace-aware XML document can have an associated Infoset. This Infoset can then be used when describing a precise *specification* for the transformation or linking of the data (rather than their actual implementations). We will reuse the terms defined in the XML Infoset in many related XML standards, such as **XLink**, **XPath**, **XPointer**, and XSLT (see the next section). The XML Infoset is described in more detail in Chapter 4.

Navigating & Linking XML

One of the defining characteristics of HTML is linking, with links between different web pages being the very essence of the WWW. Links can also be used within a document to provide a navigable Table of Contents, Index, and cross-references. RDBMS tables also use links in the form of foreign keys that reference other tables. When it comes down to it, almost any computing application will require some method of connecting different bodies of data together.

Query systems are another common technology that is being adapted to work with XML. There needs to be a standard way to pass some selection criteria to an XML parser and receive fragments of the XML data that correspond to that query criteria. Quite apart from these database-like aspects of XML querying, these query methods are also central to XML transformations (XSLT), a key way to modify XML data for presentation and other purposes, as we will see in the next section.

We can navigate XML data and provide both internal and external linking using **XML Base**, the XML Path Language (XPath), the XML Pointer Language (XPointer) and the XML Linking Language (XLink). Multiple XML data sources can be combined into a single XML document using **XML Inclusions (XInclude)**, and fragments of XML documents may be exchanged using **XML Fragment Interchange (XFI)**, a work-in-progress. Queries against XML data can use XPath expressions or perhaps the new **XQuery** language.

XPath

The XML Path Language (XPath) is a querying language that is used to address specific parts of an XML data object as nodes within a tree. In support of this, XPath can also handle strings, numbers, and Boolean variables. XPath expressions use a compact non-XML syntax, which allows for easier use within URIs and XML attribute values.

This language handles XML data as paths within an abstract hierarchical tree structure of nodes, and a current **context node**, rather than using the superficial syntax of tags and attributes. The addressing capability of XPath also implies the ability to match patterns in the XML data, thus providing a simple method of querying that data.

> *The Recommendation for* ***XPath*** *(1999-11-16) is at* http://www.w3.org/TR/xpath.

XPath, which will be discussed in Chapter 8, is currently used by XSLT and XPointer, and it provides a simpler and complementary tool to XQuery.

XPointer

The XML Pointer Language (XPointer) is based upon XPath expressions, and is therefore yet another non-XML syntax language that is used in association with XML. XPointer is also used to address specific internal structures of XML data objects. XPointer extends XPath by:

- Providing addressing of arbitrary points and ranges as relative positions within the XML data
- String matching within the XML data
- The possibility that it can be used as the fragment identifier in a URI reference

The locations found with an XPointer can be used as link targets, or in any other way that might be useful to an XML application – however, no resource retrieval or link traversal is implied.

> *The Last Call Working Draft for* ***XPointer*** *(2001-01-08) is at http://www.w3.org/TR/WD-xptr. There may still be changes to this specification before it becomes a Recommendation.*

XLink

The XML Linking Language (XLink) defines some special elements that can be used within XML data to *create links* between resources – which may be other XML data, related meta data, or even non-XML data (such as images). These elements use XML syntax and URIs to provide various kinds of links, including the simple unidirectional links that are similar to hyperlinks (HREFs) in HTML. A powerful addition is the ability of XLink to *describe links* to a different XML document, without modifying the content of that document.

XLink not only specifies linking data structures, it also defines a simple link behavior model, which may be extended by higher-level applications layers.

> *The Proposed Recommendation for **XLink** (2000-12-20) is at* http://www.w3.org/TR/xlink.

XInclude

Most programming languages provide some kind of inclusion mechanism (such as the C/C++ `#include` statement) that facilitates modular storage of parts of a program. XInclude provides a processing model and syntax for general-purpose inclusion of XML data. This is accomplished by merging multiple XML Infosets into one composite XML Infoset. Note that XInclude operates upon post-parsing Infosets, rather than the underlying XML data in raw form.

The XInclude merging process is controlled using elements and attributes in the XML 1.0 syntax, with the additional use of XML Namespaces to ensure unique names for this special markup. XInclude is a low-level process that is intended to transform an XML Infoset and pass it to a higher-level application.

> *The Working Draft for **XInclude** (2000-10-26) is at* http://www.w3.org/TR/xinclude/.

XInclude is complementary to external entities. DTD, and external entity processing occurs while parsing XML data, but XInclude uses a completely different approach, based upon the data's Infoset.

XFI (XML Fragment Interchange)

XML 1.0 already supports the creation of logical documents composed of multiple external entities. XFI is a way to describe and transmit fragments of XML data for viewing or editing, without needing to send the entire data object, and without using explicitly defined external entities. A key feature of XFI is the maintenance of the fragment's context within its original data source. This allows the fragment to be parsed correctly (as if it were still in its original context).

> *The Candidate Recommendation for **XFI** (2001-02-12) is located at* http://www.w3.org/TR/xml-fragment.html.

XFI will be discussed in Chapter 10.

XQuery

XQuery is a proposal for a new query language that is expressed in a non-XML syntax. It is used to make queries against XML data, using the proposed XPath 2.0 expressions, plus many expressions that are similar to SQL query expressions (including FLWR expressions, which use `FOR`, `LET`, `WHERE`, and `RETURN` clauses, hence the name).

> *The Working Draft for **XQuery** (2001-02-15) can be found at* http://www.w3.org/TR/xquery/, *and the **XML Query** working group home page is* http://www.w3.org/XML/Query.

XQuery will be discussed in the Chapter 16.

Some of these navigational languages, like XPath, are also the basis for transforming XML data.

Transforming XML

A very powerful XML technique is transformation, which is implemented as a declarative programming language, and stored in a stylesheet. These stylesheets specify the conversion of XML data from one forms, into another form, using a set of rules that are applied to the data in the first form. XML data can be transformed into HTML using Cascading Style Sheets, level 2 (CSS2), or into a different form of XML (or almost any text-based format) using the Extensible Stylesheet Language (XSL).

*The **XSL** home page at the W3C is* http://www.w3.org/Style/XSL/.

A common use of XSL is to transform some server-side XML data into HTML for display in a web browser.

Cascading Style Sheets (CSS)

Level 1 (CSS1) of this well-known style sheet format is already supported by most web browsers, with CSS2 support emerging. It can be used to display either HTML (CSS1 or CSS2), or XML (CSS2). CSS can be used to specify most details concerned with the presentation of data, including typeface, size, style, color, margins, spacing, etc. The details of this technology are beyond the scope of this book.

A good CSS reference is Wrox's Professional Stylesheets for HTML and XML, ISBN 1-861001-65-7.

CSS is designed for the presentation of data as web pages, with some multimedia extensions (much like HTML). Printing support is weak, and browser support for CSS2 is still sparse. Both CSS1 and CSS2 predate the original XML 1.0 REC, so an extensible style sheet language is a useful addition to extensible markup.

XSL Transformations (XSLT)

One subset of XSL is called **XSLT** (XSL for Transformations). It is a declarative language, which means that we don't have to specify *how* to handle the XML data (as with procedural code), we merely need to state some rules that describe *what* we want to do with the data. The XSLT processor will then use these templates to determine how to achieve the desired transformation goals.

XSLT is generally used to organize XML data for use with XSL presentation styling, and is flexible enough to perform most conversion, data extraction, and sorting tasks without resorting to any procedural code in the application. Scripting code can be embedded within an XSL style sheet to further enhance the processing of dynamic data.

*The Recommendation for **XSLT** (1999-11-16) is at* http://www.w3.org/TR/xslt.

XSLT will be discussed in Chapter 9. A fuller and much more detailed explanation can be found in *Pro XSL, Wrox Press, ISBN-1-861003-57-9.*

XSL Formatting Objects (XSL-FO)

An XML vocabulary, called **XSL-FO** (XSL Formatting Objects), is oriented toward the precise display and print presentations of XML data. XSL-FO describes detailed formatting specifications, much like CSS, but with a more sophisticated layout model. Styling can be based upon the *content* of the XML data, rather than just the *structure*, as with CSS. Where CSS is able to style all `<Price>` elements, XSL-FO can do this and have special styling for a range of values for individual `<Price>` elements.

XSL-FO also supports truly internationalized text with right-to-left and top-to-bottom text, and additional features like margin notes and footnotes.

We will discuss XSL-FO in more detail in Chapter 20, but it can be thought of as having the same amount of power as PostScript or PDF has for laying out information. As (X)HTML doesn't exactly specify how content should look on all viewers, a language like this would be necessary for many publishing operations.

These two XSL subsets can be used together – for example, XSLT might be used to transform some XML data from a verbose data exchange format into a smaller excerpt, and then it could be formatted for print publishing using XSL-FO.

Practical XML

Now that we've had an overview of some of the core XML technologies, let's discuss some practical applications of XML: vocabularies and APIs.

XML Vocabularies

The most significant feature of XML is its extensibility. In comparison, HTML began as a simple markup language for scientific papers (with a fixed tag set), but it quickly evolved as browser developers added new features and tags to their software. Many of these additions to HTML were to provide for the delivery of multimedia features and flashy commercial web pages. Unfortunately, these tags were the semi-proprietary creations of individual companies, and often caused problems for other browsers. Some additions have become a formal part of HTML, but many remain proprietary. Unfortunately, little has been added to HTML in the way of improved data modeling, semantic markup, or structured information exchange protocols.

On the other hand, XML has always been intended to allow the easy and rapid construction of custom tag-sets specific to corporations, scientific disciplines, and other such domains. While every corporation (or even individual!) could choose to define their own XML vocabulary, one of the strengths of XML is the sharing of such vocabularies, all of which use the same basic syntax, parsers, and other tools. Shared XML vocabularies provide more easily searchable documents and databases, and a way to exchange information between many different organizations and computer applications.

An XML "vocabulary" is a description of XML data that is used as the medium for information exchange, often within a specific domain such as business, chemistry, math, law, or music.

There is a universe of potential XML vocabularies to exchange scientific and business information, model data objects, design databases, provide "boilerplate" legal documents, and perhaps even to control the Internet, and switches of the international telephone network. We'll take a brief look at samples of XML vocabularies for a variety of domains.

Scientific vocabularies

The first real use of XML was Peter Murray-Rust's JUMBO browser for the **Chemical Markup Language (CML)**, originally developed in early 1997 based on a preliminary draft of XML. CML has been referred to as "HTML with Molecules", but CML also provides for the conversion of various proprietary file formats without semantic loss, and the creation of structured documents suitable for professional publication.

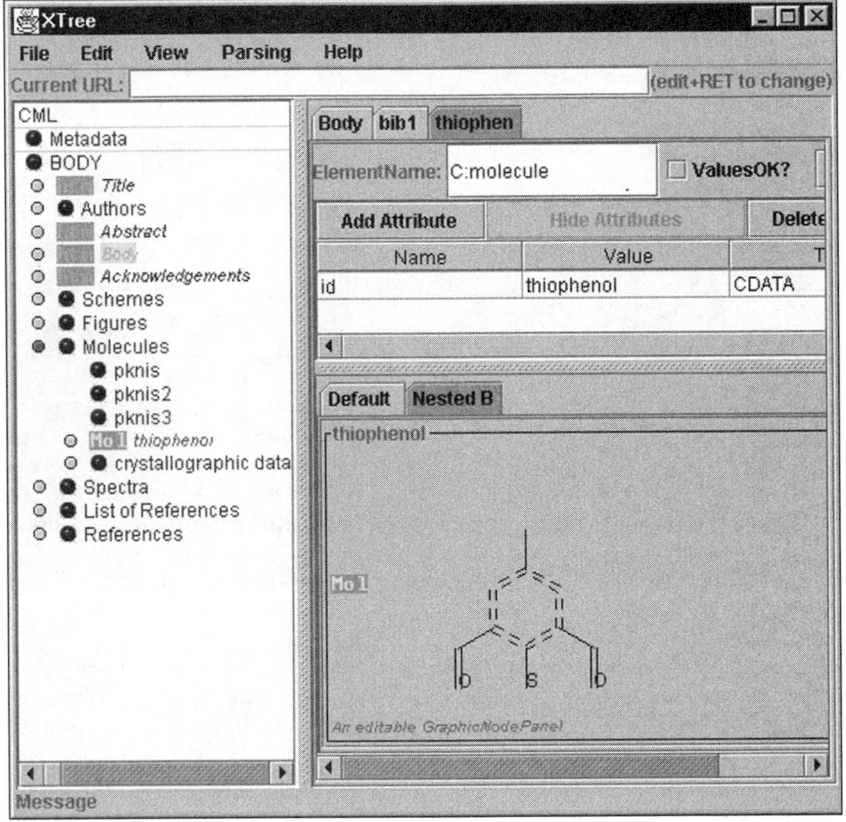

The fundamental language of science is mathematics, and there is an XML vocabulary named **MathML** that provides a way of exchanging mathematical expressions. MathML will replace the display of equations as mere pictures and/or ugly ASCII approximations, and provides an interchange format for symbolic algebra, geometry, statistics, and other math software tools.

Other scientific vocabularies include NASA's Instrument Markup Language (**IML**) for the control of lab instruments, and its first implementation, Astronomical Instrument Markup Language (**AIML**). These markup languages are classic uses of XML vocabularies for structured technical documents, and the precise dissemination of scientific and technical information. This use of XML has great promise for very powerful educational tools, as well.

*The definitive website for **CML** is* http://www.xml-cml.org. *Visit* http://www.w3.org/Math *for the **MathML** home page and specifications. **IML** is at* http://pioneer.gsfc.nasa.gov/public/iml/ *and **AIML** is at* http://pioneer.gsfc.nasa.gov/public/aiml/.

Business vocabularies

The most popular application of computing is commerce. The financial lifeblood of the world flows through computer networks using a variety of data formats. Most of these data formats are proprietary, indeed common public knowledge of international monetary wire-transfer protocols is probably undesirable! However, much fiscal and business information does need to be exchanged between companies, and this information benefits greatly from common information standards.

This is such a significant application of XML that we will devote many chapters at the end of the book to the use of XML business vocabularies, as well as the various standards and frameworks that strive to connect businesses. We'll look at some specific vocabularies in the "Foundation of eBusiness" section later in this chapter.

Legal vocabularies

Digital representation of paper forms remains a problem for the business, legal, and medical communities. One possible solution is PureEdge and Tim Bray's Extensible Forms Description Language (**XFDL**). This XML vocabulary supports; precision layout, computations, input validation, digital signatures, legally binding transaction records, and audit trails.

> *XFDL is described at* http://www.pureedge.com/resources/xfdl.htm.

Legally binding XML documents will also be able to rely upon the W3C's Canonical XML and XML Signature specifications.

> *Both Canonical XML and XML Signature are described at http://www.w3.org/Signature/.*

Canonical XML provides a single common representation of XML data that can be used for data comparison and secure packaging. XML Signature provides a way to digitally sign these packages.

Medical vocabularies

Medical information can be covered by the gamut of XML's technologies. Medical reference materials and related scientific papers using XML markup can be easily translated for presentation in various forms, and are also more readily found, and retrieved using structured searches that are more focused and powerful than simple Boolean free-text searches. Clinical, financial, and administrative information must be exchanged between numerous independent computer systems, at numerous different organizations, ranging from hospitals, to pharmacies, to insurance companies, and/or government agencies.

In 1987, an ANSI X12 initiative produced the **Health Level 7** (**HL7**) standard, which is used in the majority of large US hospitals today; it is also used in Australia, Western Europe, Israel and Japan. Although this standard is not currently implemented using XML, progress is being made toward an XML version.

> *The HL7 organization's home page is at* http://www.hl7.org.

Computer vocabularies

The Internet and the WWW both require ways to describe the exchange of information from disparate sources and of various formats.

Scalable Vector Graphics (**SVG**) is an XML vocabulary for describing two-dimensional graphics, including: vector graphic shapes, images and text. These graphical objects can be grouped, styled, and transformed; they can also be used with XML Namespaces (as we discuss in Chapter 18). The **Synchronized Multimedia Integration Language** (**SMIL**) is a very early XML vocabulary (it became a Recommendation within a few months of XML 1.0). SMIL is used to describe time-based multimedia presentations, including temporal management, display formatting, and hyperlinks to multimedia objects.

> *The overview page for* ***SVG*** *is at* http://www.w3.org/Graphics/SVG/Overview.htm8. *The* ***SMIL 1.0*** *Recommendation is at* http://www.w3.org/TR/REC-smil/.

The **Resource Descriptor Framework** (**RDF**) uses an XML interchange format for describing the structure of web sites and other resources, using sitemaps, content ratings (such as PICS), and stream channel definitions, superseding the older Channel Definition Format (**CDF**). We will discuss this vital XML vocabulary, RDF, in a chapter of its own (and a little in its own section here in this chapter).

> *The home page for the W3C's* ***RDF*** *activity is at* http://www.w3.org/RDF/.

Structured Graph Format (SGF) is another XML format for describing the structure of web sites, based upon the formal mathematics of structure graphs.

> ***SGF*** *is described at* http://www.isl.hiroshima-u.ac.jp/projects/SGF/index.html.

Netscape's Mozilla project is using an XML-based User interface Language (**XUL**), as a cross-platform way of describing user interfaces. XUL can contain element types for UI controls, HTML 4 markup for content data, and JavaScript for user event handling.

> ***XUL*** *is described at* http://www.mozilla.org/xpfe/languageSpec.html.

IBM's Bean Markup Language (**BML**) is an XML-based component configuration markup language that is customized for the JavaBean component model. BML can be used to describe the creation of new JavaBeans, access and/or configure existing JavaBeans, bind events from one JavaBean to another, and call arbitrary methods in other JavaBeans.

> ***BML*** *is available at the alphaWorks web site:* http://www.alphaworks.ibm.com/formula/xml, *click on* Java *and then the* Bean Markup Language *link in the navigation box on the left.*

Modern database design uses a rigorous design process that is based upon data modeling, often using the Unified Modeling Language (UML). The Object Management Group (OMG) is the developer of the Common Object Request Broker Architecture (CORBA) specification. The OMG, large systems companies (such as IBM, Sun, HP, and Unisys), and database software companies (such as Oracle, Rational, and Sybase) have promoted the merger of XML, UML, and MOF (Meta-Object Facility) in the form of the **XML Meta data Interchange (XMI)** specification. Whilst this isn't strictly an XML vocabulary (since it's a superset of XML), XMI is a good example of the power of XML for non-document purposes.

> ***UML*** *resources are available from the OMG at* http://www.omg.org/uml/ *and from Rational Software at* http://www.rational.com/uml/index.jsp. *The* ***XMI*** *specification is available at:* http://www.omg.org/technology/documents/formal/xml_metadata_interchange.htm.

Telephony Vocabularies

One of the most conservative technology domains is the switched public telephone network. For years, this network has used a rather complex protocol, Signaling System 7 (SS7). Recently, several XML-based alternatives have been proposed, including the Call Policy Markup Language (**CPML**). This is a by-product of a trend toward more open standards in the traditionally proprietary telecom industry. Voice-over-IP is another indication of the coming convergence between the voice and packet-switched networks, with key support from Lucent Technologies (formerly Bell Labs), Nortel Networks, and Cisco Systems.

CPML is described at http://www.oasis-open.org/cover/cpml.html.

Most of these XML vocabularies were defined collaboratively by groups of companies and organizations, with their primary purpose being the convenient exchange of data, using XML.

So how do we use these vocabularies in programs or within the context of the WWW?

Programming with XML

Two major programming models can be used to access XML data: the DOM and the SAX.

Document Object Model (DOM)

Since well-formed XML data is a hierarchical tree of elements and other document entities each node can be modeled and accessed using familiar tree traversal routines. The entire tree is usually constructed in memory, so virtual memory is a necessity for large documents, but random access performance is greatly improved.

The standard tree object model that is used for access to XML data is the **Document Object Model** (**DOM**). This neutral interface allows dynamic access and modification of structured data, such as XML, from different languages and platforms. The DOM is implemented in standard Java, C++, Visual Basic, and script libraries.

The DOM, its various levels and its origins are discussed at http://www.w3.org/DOM/.

We will discuss programming with the DOM in Chapter 11.

SAX

The other approach is for a parser to read the XML data sequentially and signal events for each individual node, which can then be used by an application to process the data. This event-driven approach is similar to the event-handling model of modern graphical user interfaces (GUIs), and can handle immense XML documents without requiring massive amounts of memory to store a tree model.

SAX (**Simple API for XML**) is a standard interface for event-driven XML parsers that was developed by members of the XML-DEV e-mail list. The current version, released 2000-05-02, is SAX 2.0 – it supersedes the original SAX 1.0 version, which is still widely supported.

SAX is described at http://www.megginson.com/SAX/index.html.

We will discuss programming with SAX in Chapter 12.

Presentation of XML

We've stressed the importance of structural markup of XML data, and its separation from presentation issues and markup. Indeed, much XML data may never be seen by human eyes – XML messaging will move terabytes of text that is for the computer's eyes only. Yet, whatever the percentage, a large amount of XML data *will* be seen by people, at least by developers, and therefore will need to be styled for presentation. We will also look at an alternate presentation method in Chapter 20.

XML in Browsers

Web browsers will continue to be among the most common human-Internet interactions, for the near future. Browsers can present HTML pages using a default style, but no such crutch exists for XML. Any XML data to be displayed in a browser will require transformation of some sort. We've already mentioned the concept of style sheets ("Transforming XML"), where a CSS2 or XSL style sheet can be used to style XML data for presentation. Most browsers support CSS, with a few now offering real XSLT support.

Server-side XML, Client-side HTML

Most browsers do not yet support XML directly, so it is common to use XSLT or another transformation tool on the server to convert the XML data to semi-styled HTML data, which is sent on to the client and then styled for presentation there. By storing the server data in XML, we gain all the content markup advantages of XML, but still have the option to send simpler HTML documents to clients.

> *The hierarchical tree model of XML data that is shown in IE5 by default is actually being styled using a built-in style sheet.*

From HTML To XHTML

HTML that is converted to XHTML must follow these rules and restrictions:

- Data must be well-formed: with opening and closing tags, and no overlapping elements. For example, the following is legal:

```
This <i>is</i> <b>legal</b>
```

  However, this is not legal:

```
This <i> is <b>il</i>legal<b>
```

- All element and attribute names must use lowercase letters (`<p>` instead of `<P>`, etc.)
- End tags are required for non-empty elements (must use `<p>...text...</p>`, instead of `<p/>...text...`)
- Attribute values must always be enclosed in quotes (must use `<hr width="33%"/>` instead of `<hr width=33%>`)
- No attribute minimalization is allowed (must use `<p align="left">` instead of the minimized form, like `<P LEFT>`)
- Empty elements must be explicitly terminated with either an end-tag or an empty-element tag (for example, the familiar `<BR>` tag must be replaced with `<br></br>` or `<br/>`)
- Scripting language code must be contained within `<script>` elements – the common practice of hiding script code in comments does not work in XHTML or XML

- Leading and trailing white space characters will be stripped from attribute values, and runs of multiple such characters will be replaced with a single space character.

The W3C's Dave Raggett has developed a utility program, called **HTML Tidy**, which fixes ill-formed HTML files and validates element and attribute names. It can do most, if not all, of the conversion from HTML to XHTML.

> *A version of HTML Tidy for almost any operating system can be downloaded from* http://www.w3.org/People/Raggett/tidy/.

Multiple Presentations from a Single Document

The XML data can even be custom-formatted for each individual client, and transformations to support older browsers are easily done. Alternative interfaces, such as speech-based telephone access to the data, can also be supported from the same basic XML dataset. Instead of creating web pages full of browser-specific quirks and conditional expressions, the data can be transformed into an optimal form for each different type of browser. Eventually, most web browsers are likely to support XML directly, therefore eliminating this conversion step and further improving application performance.

Non-text Data in XML Documents

Much of the massive growth in the popularity of the WWW is due to its inclusion of graphics and other visual and audio (multimedia) features. People can watch movies, listen to the radio, browse photo galleries, or just look at animated ads, in addition to reading text articles and viewing databases.

Even though XML is a textual format and cannot *contain* embedded binary data (such as images), XML data can contain *references* to data of any sort. This is no different from HTML web pages, which display images as if they were embedded within the text, even though the image is an external resource that is included by reference. Of course, the HTML text only has references to the images (using `<img...>` tags), it is the browser that retrieves, formats, and displays images from separate resources. Unlike HTML, there are no pre-defined elements in XML, so those `<img...>` tags could be used in XML data, but we'd have to write explicit instructions in our style sheet to actually display the associated images.

An exciting application of XML is the creation of **aural browsers**, such as IBM's VoiceXML and HP's SpeechML browsers. With XML and these tools, we are no longer limited to a two-dimensional presentation of text and graphics on computer screens. The entire XML data stream might be converted to speech for either broadcast or local listening. We might present some data as text, and provide audio cues and feedback to the user as s/he views our web page. This is also a decoupling of the WWW from a user's computer – that user can just as easily access the XML data through a cell phone or receive structured information in a radio broadcast. Improvements in speech recognition software mean that soon, WWW research could be conducted as a dynamic conversation with an English (or French or Hindi or Klingon!) speaking search engine (perhaps named HAL, Holly, or just Computer).

We will discuss some of these issues in Chapter 19.

XML for Servers and Databases

XML is the future of database technology. While proprietary storage formats may endure for the sake of performance, many data exchanges between applications and systems will use XML.

There are numerous different Relational and Object-Oriented Database Management Systems (RDBMSs and OODBMSs), each with its own internal storage format. The exchange of data between two of these systems usually requires some kind of conversion or transformation. To exchange data between N possible formats would require N^2 conversion filters. If we use XML to provide an intermediate data exchange format, we would only need to create 2N conversion filters (one for each direction from the RDBMS to XML, and vice versa). This use of XML goes beyond the Internet to any traditional computer that can exchange data, by almost any means.

All of the major commercial RDBMS products (DB2, Oracle, SQL Server, and Informix) have become XML-enabled databases. This means that conversion tools are provided, and some XML handling may be integrated into the regular database.

> *IBM's* ***DB2 XML Extender*** *can be found at:* http://www-4.ibm.com/software/data/db2/extenders/xmlext/. *Both* ***Oracle 8i*** *and* ***9i*** *support XML, with the page at* http://technet.oracle.com/tech/xml *being the best entry point for Oracle's copious XML tools. A good overview of Microsoft's SQL Server 2000 is at* *http://msdn.microsoft.com/library/periodic/period00/sql2000.htm. It uses XML as an internal data exchange format. Informix supports XML with its Object Translator and Web DataBlade tools, at* http://www.informix.com/idn-secure/webtools/ot/ *and* http://www.informix.com/datablades/dbmodule/informix1.htm, *respectively.*

The structure of much XML data makes it an excellent companion to OODBMS databases. Object structure and relationships can be preserved when sending extracted data to other databases or human clients.

Perhaps the best way to store XML data is in a native XML database, such as the open source **dbXML** or Software AG's **Tamino**. Another related possibility is the XML:DB Initiative, which is an industry collaboration to develop XML database specifications and open source reference implementations.

> *The dbXML project is at* http://www.dbxml.org/. *Tamino is described at* http://www.softwareag.com/tamino/. *The XML:DB Initiative for XML Databases is at* http://www.xmldb.org/.

Both OO and RDBMS transactions can benefit from the use of XML as the transport format. As we see in the next section, even Remote Procedure Calls (RPCs) can be transported in XML.

> *An excellent, and reasonably current, list of XML databases is maintained by Ronald Bourret at* http://www.rpbourret.com/xml/XMLDatabaseProds.htm.

We discussed some of the presentational advantages of having XML data on a web server in the last section. In addition to multiple presentational formats, multiple types of clients can effectively also query the XML data. These can range from the typical user-driven browser, to a data-structure-aware web crawler (spider). The use of XML instead of unstructured HTML text means that shopping agents and other automated search agents will get far better results when looking for specific data such as price or availability.

Modern information appliances aren't just limited to computers; handheld PDAs, smart cell phones, and bi-directional pagers all exchange messages, keep name and address information, and perform various forms of human and network-oriented communications. In the past, synchronizing data between these devices and a home computer required proprietary docking cradles and synchronization software.

The use of an XML vocabulary called **SyncML** will enable data synchronization between any devices that can handle XML and TCP/IP. Once again, XML provides a simple and commonly supported syntax that unites disparate systems and software.

> *SyncML is a cross-industry initiative sponsored by IBM, Lotus, Starfish, and several cell phone and PDA manufacturers. It is at* http://www.syncml.org/.

We will discuss these issues in Chapters 14 and 15, and look at a specific application in Chapter 17.

Extensible Communications Protocols

XML may have been originally designed to be an extensible *markup* language, but it has become the basis for almost any extensible data format. Communications protocols have traditionally been rigidly defined and difficult to modify. For example, object brokers such as CORBA and DCOM perform similar tasks but in an incompatible fashion – they cannot call each other's objects without an intermediary. In the past, these interfaces were written for each pair of object brokers, or any other pair of incompatible protocols. With XML, we can use one common intermediate format (like XML-RPC or SOAP), which will greatly streamline the development of protocol converters. Eventually, many protocols will use XML as their native syntax, with all the associated benefits of extensibility, internationalization, and easy transport over the Internet.

> **The combination of the WWW and HTTP is becoming a universal data bus, using XML as its fundamental syntax.**

We will look at the use of XML as the data format for various communications protocols in the last four chapters of this book.

XML-RPC

Distributed computing is based upon objects, with one system being able to call on objects on other systems, using a Remote Procedure Call (RPC). Similar, but incompatible RPC standards include the multi-platform CORBA and Microsoft-specific DCOM. Encoding RPCs in XML and transmitting them over HTTP provides a new avenue for RPCs and distributed computing.

XML-RPC is an XML vocabulary that describes RPCs, and has been widely implemented on many different operating systems. The platform independence means that a browser on a Macintosh might pass an RPC to some CORBA-based UNIX systems for one task, and another RPC to a Microsoft NT system with DCOM. Instead of needing protocol drivers for each different type of object broker and RPC format, the Macintosh client need only handle RPCs in the XML-RPC format. It is now also possible to write the drivers for XML-RPC, and use a stylesheet to convert to SOAP if necessary.

> *The home page for **XML-RPC** is* http://www.xml-rpc.org/.

While XML-RPC remains a good choice for developers interested in a simple and lightweight RPC system, most new work in this area is focused on SOAP – a more complex and capable way to handle RPCs and other messaging using XML data.

SOAP

SOAP (the **Simple Object Access Protocol**) is similar to XML-RPC – they share some of the same developers. SOAP can handle RPCs like XML-RPC, but also provides access to an object's methods and properties, and is the basis for an object messaging system using XML. SOAP is a general wire protocol that provides access not just to objects, but also services and servers, in a platform-independent manner. SOAP messages are represented in XML and can be transported using HTTP or SMTP (though implementations of the latter are uncommon).

> *SOAP is described in a W3C NOTE at* http://www.w3.org/TR/SOAP/. *For more information, we can start by looking at* http://www.soapware.org/, http://www.soaprpc.com/, *or* http://www.perfectxml.com/soap.asp.
>
> *Don't bother with the obvious website names: "soap.com" is a janitorial supply company and "soap.org" is the Society for Obstetric Anesthesia and Perinatology!*

There are quite a few new XML technologies based on SOAP messaging, such as Microsoft's .NET and HailStorm initiatives. As we'll see in the "eBusiness" section, several protocols such as automated service discovery also rely heavily upon SOAP.

XML Protocol

XML-RPC was developed by an independent group of companies, and SOAP was adopted and pushed by Microsoft, but only the latter has become as much as a W3C Note. The W3C has an XML Protocol Working Group that is writing the requirements for a generic **XML Protocol** (**XMLP**). This process is being informed by SOAP 1.1 and its implementations.

> *The W3C's home page for XML Protocol is at* http://www.w3.org/2000/xp/, *and the Working Draft of XMLP requirements is at* http://www.w3.org/TR/xmlp-reqs/.

It is unclear whether the W3C, which more or less sat on the sidelines while XML-RPC and SOAP were being developed, will be able to produce an XMLP specification that is compelling enough to replace SOAP in the real world.

The Foundation of eBusiness

The WWW has grown in large part due to its commercial potential. The buying and selling of goods and services over the Web is a new kind of electronic commerce, better known as **e-commerce** or **eBusiness**. XML is poised to be the data language of choice for all sorts of messages, transactions, and other commercial data exchanges.

Business-to-Business (B2B)

Much of this commerce is between different businesses, and is called **business-to-business** (**B2B**) commerce to differentiate it from business-to-consumer (B2C) transactions.

Electronic Data Interchange (EDI)

Businesses transactions usually involve the exchange of legally binding documents on paper. These documents can also be exchanged electronically, using **Electronic Data Interchange** (**EDI**) standards. EDI in North America is based upon the ANSI X12 standards (also known as "ASC X12"). In the US, the (not-for-profit) Data Interchange Standards Association (**DISA**) oversees the development of these standards.

DISA 's home page is at http://www.disa.org *and the X12 standards group is at* http://www.x12.org.

For many years, Electronic Data Interchange (EDI) has been used for business-to-business transactions and data exchange. EDI uses complicated proprietary data formats and networks, which have made it too expensive for anyone but large companies with high volumes of transactions. Most major EDI formats are now being redesigned to use XML due to all the associated advantages that XML provides in the form of tools and transport mechanisms.

Many groups have used X12 as the basis for newer SGML or XML-based specifications.

The ebXML Framework

CommerceOne and SAP have developed the XML-based **Common Business Library** (**xCBL**), with support from Microsoft, Sun, and Compaq, and in collaboration with OASIS and others. This framework is derived from the earlier CBL and cXML efforts, and is being merged into the more internationally viable **ebXML Framework**.

Like many North American standards, X12 is not commonly used elsewhere in the world. Most of the world uses the United Nations / Electronic Data Interchange for Administration, Commerce and Transport (**UN/EDIFACT**) standard. The maintenance, development, and promotion of UN/EDIFACT are the responsibility of the UN/EDIFACT Working Group (EWG), an empowered group under The Center for Facilitation of Administration, Commerce and Trade (**UN/CEFACT**). The international ebXML framework development effort is being conducted by ebXML.org, which is a joint effort by UN/CEFACT and OASIS.

xCBL is described at http://www.xcbl.org. *UN/CEFACT 's home page is at* http://www.unece.org/cefact/, *and the ebXML home page is at* http://www.ebxml.org.

The BizTalk Framework

Microsoft has also created the **BizTalk Framework** initiative, which has support from companies like SAP, CommerceOne, Boeing and BP/Amoco. This repository of XML schemas and message descriptions is intended "to enable electronic commerce and application integration".

BizTalk 's home page is at http://www.biztalk.org/.

Since Microsoft is promoting BizTalk, it has used some Microsoft-specific XML technologies like XDR schemas (instead of XML Schema). This may ultimately hamper the widespread adoption of BizTalk, though Microsoft is determined to base BizTalk schema design upon the W3C standard XML Schema as these standards are adopted by other organizations.

The BizTalk Framework truly does embrace the extensible and open spirit of XML. BizTalk is designed with the assumption that messages will be passed between loosely coupled systems – there is no need for a common OS, DBMS, transport protocol, or object model – applications just need to be able to pass XML messages.

Other Business Initiatives

A few years ago, Microsoft, Intuit, and CheckFree, joined to develop an open SGML specification for the online transfer of financial data called Open Financial Exchange (OFX). However, OFX was never fully developed, and when XML was introduced in 1998, migration to XML became the goal of OFX. A newer financial markup language, called Interactive Financial Exchange (**IFX**), is being developed by a group within the DISA, based upon the earlier OFX work.

IFX is described at http://www.ifxforum.org/ *and* http://www.oasis-open.org/cover/ifx.html.

Another industry initiative, with widespread support among high-tech companies, is the **RosettaNet** organization. The initial focus of RosettaNet is supply-chain management for the Information Technology, Electronic Components, and Semiconductor Manufacturing industries, but with a foundation for more general business applications.

The ***RosettaNet*** *home page is at* http://www.rosettanet.org.

Automated Service Negotiations

Much inter-business communication involves the bid-contract-supply cycle for goods and services. Prospective business partners first need to find each other, determine if they have a complementary business need, and then negotiate the terms of a contract for a service or delivery of goods. Many of these exchanges are mediated by brokers, such as distributors or supply cartels. The Internet has created new business models that provide direct connections between businesses without the need for so many intermediaries.

At the traditional business level, we have the **Universal Description, Discovery, and Integration** (**UDDI**) specification that provides an international, Internet-based business directory, much like a telephone company's yellow pages. At a more technical level, there are several protocols for the discovery of and negotiation for network services. The most prominent of these is probably the **Web Services Description Language** (**WSDL**). WSDL is based upon SOAP, and has the support of Microsoft, IBM, and other large companies.

For more information about ***UDDI****, see* http://www.uddi.org/. ***WSDL*** *is described at* http://www.w3.org/TR/wsdl *and* http://msdn.microsoft.com/xml/general/wsdl.asp.

It will come as no surprise that all of these specifications rely upon XML as the data transport format.

We will look at various flavors of B2B systems based on XML in the last three chapters of this book.

Semantics and Meta Data

In this section, we discuss how XML describe data in a semantic way. That is, describing and representing the actual *meaning* or *content* of data, as well as the data itself.

The Semantic Web

The Semantic Web is the W3C's vision of the WWW described and linked so that it can be used by computers, as well as by people. Shared vocabularies and open protocols will allow applications to share data and work together, via messages in XML and using meta data descriptions of resources. We've already mentioned some XML vocabularies designed to facilitate automated network resource discovery. These are some of the building blocks for the Semantic Web.

The W3C's ***Semantic Web*** *home page is at* http://www.w3.org/2001/sw/.

For the sake of human viewers and search engines alike, many web sites use HTML's `<meta>` tag to include information *about* a web page, within that page. This resource meta data may also be maintained separately from the resource that is being described. Informal web logs and directories often include this sort of information, along with a link to the resource in question. Since this is a generic sort of description, the W3C has created a foundation for the automated exchange of meta data, called the Resource Descriptor Framework (RDF).

RDF

RDF is an XML vocabulary that provides a generic structure for resource meta data. This takes the form of RDF statements that include a **subject** (the resource being described), a **predicate** (a property associated with resource), and its **object** (the value of the property). For example, this book could be the subject of an RDF statement with a predicate called `publisher` and the object equal to "`Wrox Press Inc.`"

> ***RDF** syntax and its data model are defined at* http://www.w3.org/TR/REC-rdf-syntax/.

RDF is intended to be the basis for a new generation of web crawlers, distributed authoring systems (such as WebDAV), and digital library collections. Specific descriptive elements will vary depending upon the type of resource being described. One of the most commonly used element sets comes from the **Dublin Core Metadata Initiative** (**DCMI**).

Dublin Core

The Dublin Core bibliographic meta data vocabulary comes primarily from the library science community. It includes fifteen elements for common meta data descriptive terms, and some common attributes to further qualify the meaning of the meta data.

> *The home page of the **Dublin Core Metadata Initiative** is at* http://dublincore.org/.

An expanded form of our earlier RDF example could be expressed as an XML document using RDF and Dublin Core like so:

```
<?xml version="1.0"?>
<rdf:RDF
   xmlns:rdf="http://www.w3.org/1999/02/22-rdf-syntax-ns#"
   xmlns:dc="http://purl.org/dc/elements/1.1/" >
   <rdf:Description about="urn:ISBN:1-861003-11-0" >
      <dc:Title>Professional XML</dc:Title>
      <dc:Publisher>Wrox Press Inc.</dc:Publisher>
      <dc:Date>2000-01</dc:Date>
      <dc:Language>en-US</dc:Language>
      <dc:Subject>Internet</dc:Subject>
      <dc:Subject>Internet programming</dc:Subject>
      <dc:Subject>XML</dc:Subject>
      <dc:Description>
         This book is a comprehensive XML reference, with numerous examples,
         and several case studies.
      </dc:Description>
   </rdf:Description>
</rdf:RDF>
```

The tags that have names beginning with `rdf:` are defined in the RDF Recommendation, and those tag names beginning with `dc:` are defined in the Dublin Core vocabulary. Although this description is certainly human readable, it also provides a structured description of the meta data that can be used by search engines to find books (or other resources) about a particular subject, in a specific language, or from a particular publisher.

This also illustrates the slippery definition of meta data. XML is considered a "meta data" language but not all data in XML is meta data. RDF statements are just another form of XML data, though they should always be interpreted as meta data.

We will look at RDF in Chapter 22 and 23.

Summary

Although we haven't discussed anything in any detail here, we have touched on a great number of different technologies, most of which are covered in this book. The reader should now have a good overview of the XML technologies, and will be better informed when exploring these technologies further.

To sum up, detailed below are some of the technologies that we have mentioned so far, which are covered elsewhere in this book:

- XML syntax and its core technologies
- Namespaces in XML – a method to uniquely identify tags
- The XML Infoset – an abstract representation of XML data
- Validation of XML – using DTDs, XML Schema, The Schematron, RELAX, and TREX
- XPath – a method of navigating XML data
- XLink, XPointer, XFI – XML linking technologies
- XSLT – a method of transforming XML data into another format (XML or otherwise)
- DOM and SAX – APIs for manipulating XMT
- Advantages of representing and querying XML data, with standard and XML-aware DBMSs
- XSL-FO, SVG, and VoiceXML – different methods of presenting data using XML
- RDF – an XML vocabulary for meta data
- SOAP, BizTalk, and UDDI – methods of performing eBusiness

Some other technologies that were beyond the scope of this book were mentioned, with pointers for information should these technologies prove useful to the reader. These included:

- SGML – XML's predecessor, in that XML is also a subset of SGML
- MathML, CML – mathematical and chemical markup languages
- XInclude and XBase
- XFDL, HL7, BML – a legal vocabulary, a (non-XML) medical standard, and the Bean Markup Language (a way of communicating with JavaBeans in XML), respectively
- XML-RPC – an XML-based remote procedure call vocabulary
- XMLP – XML Protocol; the W3C's attempt at creating a communication protocol

In the next chapter, we get down to the meat of the material and formally describe what it means to be a well-formed XML document.

References

This chapter contained many references to many numerous technologies. Most of them are repeated on the following page for easy reference.

W3C Specifications

XML 1.0 Recommendation	http://www.w3.org/TR/REC-xml
XHTML 1.0 Recommendation	http://www.w3.org/TR/xhtml1/
HTTP Specification	http://www.w3.org/Protocols
SGML Specification and Links	http://www.w3.org/MarkUp/SGML
XPath Recommendation	http://www.w3.org/TR/xpath
XPointer Working Draft	http://www.w3.org/TR/xptr
XLink Proposed Recommendation	http://www.w3.org/TR/xlink
XML Fragment Interchange Candidate Recommendation	http://www.w3.org/TR/xml-fragment.html
XQuery Working Draft	http://www.w3.org/TR/xquery/
XSLT Recommendation	http://www.w3.org/TR/xslt
MathML Specifications, Recommendation	http://www.w3.org/Math
XML Signature	http://www.w3.org/Signature/
Canonical XML, Recommendation	http://www.w3.org/TR/2001/REC-xml-c14n-20010315
SMIL 1.0 Recommendation	http://www.w3.org/TR/REC-smil/
XML Protocol Working Draft	http://www.w3.org/TR/xmlp-reqs/
UDDI Note	http://www.w3.org/TR/wsdl
RDF syntax and data model	http://www.w3.org/TR/REC-rdf-syntax/

Other Web References

OASIS – Organization for the Advancement of Structured Information Standards:	http://www.oasis-open.org
XML Industry Portal:	http://www.xml.org
Annotated XML 1.0 Recommendation:	http://www.xml.com/axml/axml.html
XML 1.0 FAQ:	http://www.ucc.ie/xml
The Internet Engineering Task Force:	http://www.ietf.org
The XSL home page:	http://www.w3.org/Style/XSL/
SVG Overview:	http://www.w3.org/Graphics/SVG/Overview.htm8
RDF Homepage:	http://www.w3.org/RDF/
XUL Homepage:	http://www.mozilla.org/xpfe/languageSpec.html

Table continued on following page

UML Resources:	http://www.omg.org/uml/ http://www.rational.com/uml/index.jsp
The DOM:	http://www.w3.org/DOM/
SAX:	http://www.megginson.com/SAX/index.html
The Unicode Specification:	http://www.unicode.org
The HTML Tidy utility:	http://www.w3.org/People/Raggett/tidy/
List of XML databases:	http://www.rpbourret.com/xml/XMLDatabaseProds.htm
The SyncML Initiative:	http://www.syncml.org/
XML-RPC home page:	http://www.xml-rpc.org/
SOAP Information:	http://www.perfectxml.com/soap.asp
XML Protocol home page:	http://www.w3.org/2000/xp/
ebXML home page:	http://www.ebxml.org
BizTalk Framework:	http://www.biztalk.org/
UDDI Information:	http://www.uddi.org/
The Semantic Web:	http://www.w3.org/2001/sw/
The Dublin Core Metadata Initiative:	http://dublincore.org/

Distribution Lists

XML DEV	http://www.xml.org/xml-dev/index.shtml
XML-L home page	http://listserv.heanet.ie/xml-l.html
Dev-XML home page	http://groups.yahoo.com/group/dev-xml
XSL-List	http://www.biglist.com/lists/xsl-list/
XML USENET Newsgroup	news:comp.text.xml

2

Basic XML Syntax

In this chapter we will take a detailed look at the basics of XML syntax, as defined by the W3C's Recommendation of 6th October 2000: **Extensible Markup Language (XML) 1.0 (Second Edition)**. This is still about the same XML 1.0 – this new edition merely includes errata from the original 1998 Recommendation, as well as some clarifying revisions to the documentation.

By the end of the chapter we will:

- Be reminded how to author basic XML documents.
- Begin developing an invoice application using XML to describe/model the data required by a simple business invoice.

The main source for XML and its related technologies is the W3C's web site: http://www.w3.org/XML. *The XML Recommendation (which we'll abbreviate as **XML 1.0 REC**) is at* http://www.w3.org/TR/REC-xml. *An excellent annotated version of the First Edition is at* http://www.xml.com/axml/axml.html.

Markup Syntax

XML markup describes and provides structure to the content of an XML document or data packet. We will generally use the phrase **XML data** to refer to this content. This markup is comprised of tags that delimit different sections of the content, provide references to special symbols and text macros, convey special instructions to the application software, and provide comments to the document's editors.

You are probably familiar with the markup tags of HTML:

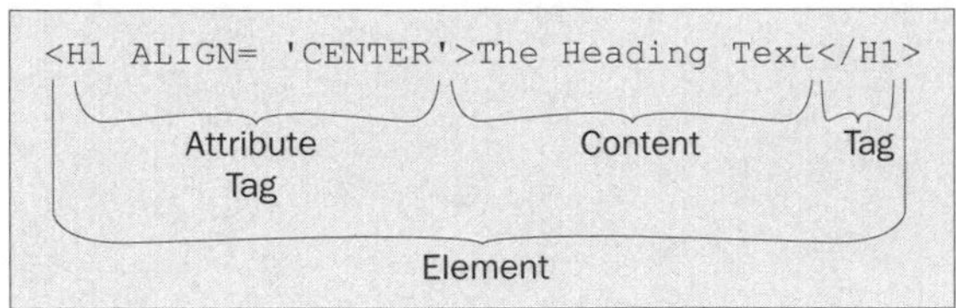

The tag markup syntax of XML is very similar to HTML (both are based upon SGML), with angle brackets used to delimit tags. All tags begin with a less-than sign (<) and end with a greater-than sign (>).

> **Unlike HTML, XML is case-sensitive, including element tags and attribute values, that is:**
> **`<Invoice> ≠ <INVOICE> ≠ <invoice> ≠ <INvoice>`**

XML's design goals of internationalization (often referred to as **I18N**) and simplified processing are the main reasons for case sensitivity. Most non-English languages don't divide the alphabet into separate cases, and many letters (even within the Roman alphabet) may not have an upper or lower case equivalent. For example, en français, the upper-case equivalent of ç is not necessarily Ç (it may be C). The Greek letter Sigma has one upper case form, but two lower case forms; Arabic uses multiple forms of the same letter, and so on. Case folding has numerous pitfalls, particularly with non-ASCII encodings, and XML's designers chose to avoid these problems.

Let's look at how XML provides for international characters.

Characters

Because XML is intended for worldwide use, characters are not limited to the 7-bit ASCII character set. XML uses most of the characters that are defined in the 16-bit **Unicode** character set (currently congruent with ISO/IEC 10646). There are two Unicode formats that are used as the basis of XML characters: **UTF-8** and **UTF-16**. XML allows the use of almost any character encoding that can be mapped to Unicode (such as EBCDIC, Big5, etc.). There are numerous other character encodings that can be used with *some* XML tools, but UTF-8 and UTF-16 support is required of all XML processors.

> *The current Unicode specification can be found at:* http://www.unicode.org, *and ISO/IEC 10646 documentation can be ordered at* http://www.iso.ch. *The UTF acronym can mean "Unicode Transformation Format" (according to Unicode), or "UCS Transformation Format" (in IEC or IETF documents) – essentially they mean the same thing, since Unicode and ISO/IEC 10646 are nearly identical.*

UTF-8 is commonly used in North America and Europe, since the first 128 character values map directly to 7-bit US-ASCII (conversely any 7-bit ASCII string is valid UTF-8). UTF-8 is a multi-byte encoding, with character values represented in one to six bytes. This encoding is less popular in Asia, since most Asian characters and ideographs require the longest encoded forms.

> UTF-8 is described at: http://www.ietf.org/rfc/rfc2279.txt.

The UTF-16 encoding uses 16-bit values for characters, with the full range of 65,536 possible 16-bit values being split into two parts. There are 63,486 values available to represent single 16-bit character values. The other 2,048 values are reserved to provide paired 16-bit code values for an additional 1,048,544 character values. These are called **surrogate pairs**, but so far none of these values are being used.

UTF-16 is described at: http://www.ietf.org/rfc/rfc2781.txt.

These are relatively new standards, and so much of the world's text isn't yet stored in Unicode. However, it was designed to be a superset of most existing character encodings, and so the conversion of legacy data to Unicode is straightforward. For example, converting ASCII to the UTF-16 form of Unicode merely requires stuffing a zero into the high-order byte of the 16-bit character, and simply preserving the low-order byte as is. Of course, this means that twice the storage space is required, compared to the same text in ASCII. As noted above, 7-bit ASCII doesn't even need conversion to be treated as the UTF-8 encoding.

Another bit of computer character history involves ligatures (for example: combined `fi` or `ff` characters inherited from various typesetting systems) and half-width katakana (from early attempts to handle Japanese text). Although these relics are included in the Unicode standard and are legal XML characters, their use must be discouraged. For instance, ligatures aren't really characters, but rather a form of print styling that is best handled during the presentation of text (for example: XSLT can easily transform "`fi`" or "`ff`" pairs into the Unicode ligatures, if desired).

Unicode for XML

Legal XML characters include three ASCII control characters (from the "C0" section), all normal ASCII display characters, and almost all other Unicode character values. The following table shows legal XML character values:

Character values (hexadecimal)	Description
09	ASCII control – Horizontal tab (HT)
0A	ASCII control – Line-feed (LF)
0D	ASCII control – Carriage-return (CR)
20 • 7F	ASCII characters (Basic Latin)
80 • D7FF	Other Latin and non-Latin characters and ideographs, symbols, etc.
E000 • FFFD	Private Use Area, additional CJK (Chinese-Japanese-Korean), ligatures and other presentation forms, and Unicode Specials
10000 • 10FFFF	Unicode Surrogate equivalents and High Private Use Area

Unicode has provided blocks of characters called the **Private Use Areas** for application-specific characters. Of course, any exchange of XML data using these private characters requires separate agreements as to the interpretation of these characters. Therefore, this portion of Unicode should never be used for XML data that is to be widely exchanged.

There are some Unicode (and other) character values that are *not* legal for XML:

Character values (hexadecimal)	Description
00 • 08	ASCII C0 control characters
0B • 0C	ASCII C0 control characters
0E • 1F	ASCII C0 control characters
D800 • DB7F	Unicode High Surrogates
DB80 • DBFF	Unicode High Private Use Surrogates
DC00 • DFFF	Unicode Low Surrogates
FFFE	Byte-order Mark (BOM)
FFFF	(Not a character)
110000 • FFFFFFFF	(Values beyond Unicode 3.0)

The key thing to remember is that XML has broken the chains of US-ASCII character representations, and thus most of the world can use XML in their native language. This is significant for XML names, as we will see in the next section.

Special Markup Characters

Five characters have special meaning in XML mark-up:

- < – Less-than sign (left angle bracket)
- > – Greater-than sign (right angle bracket)
- & – Ampersand
- ' – Apostrophe (single quotation mark)
- " – Quotation mark (double quotation mark)

Since these characters are used to delimit markup and strings, they may not generally appear within regular text data. Therefore, all of these characters have alternate representations in the form of **entity references**. We will discuss these in greater detail later, but for now it is sufficient to know to replace each of these characters with their corresponding entity reference:

- Use < for <
- Use > for >
- Use & for &
- Use ' for '
- Use " for "

There are some specific circumstances where these need not (or should not) be used, but we will get to those in the "Character and Entity References" section, later in this chapter.

Simple Names

Most XML structures are named. All XML names must begin with a letter or one of two punctuation characters. All subsequent characters are known as **name characters** as shown in this table of those characters that are allowed in XML names:

Initial Name character (`Name1`)	Other Name characters (`NmToken`)
`any Unicode letter character`	`any Unicode letter character`
	`any Unicode number character`
`_ (underscore)`	`_ (underscore)`
`: (colon)`	`: (colon)`
	`- (hyphen)`
	`. (period, full-stop)`

In actual practice, the colon character should not be used, except as a namespace delimiter (see Chapter 3 – "Advanced XML Syntax" for more about this). It is important to remember that letters are not limited to ASCII characters, so that users of XML can use almost any language for their markup.

> *The XML 1.0 REC defines a related concept called a* ***name token*** *(abbreviated as* ***NmToken*** *or* ***NMTOKEN****). This is any mixture of name characters with the restriction upon the initial character. This concept isn't used in basic XML syntax, but it will be important when we discuss valid XML in Chapter 5 ("Validating XML: DTDs"), and later chapters.*

The one other restriction upon names is that they may not begin with the strings `xml`, `XML`, or any other string that would match any variation of those three characters, in that sequence (for example, `xMl`, `Xml`). Names beginning with these characters are reserved for W3C use only.

The following are legal names:

- Invoice
- INVOICE
- Wrox:Invoice
- ΔΓΦ
- CERN_Conseil_Européen_pour_la_Recherche_Nucléaire
- 日本語

The first two names are *not* equivalent – XML names are case-sensitive (unlike HTML). The third is an example of a name that uses the namespace delimiter character (`:`). This is perfectly acceptable for plain XML data that doesn't make use of XML `Namespaces`. However, if an XML `Namespace` has been declared, use of this character is restricted based upon that supplementary XML specification (see the "Advanced XML Syntax" Chapter 3 for more information on this). The last three examples are reminders that Greek, French, and Japanese (and in fact just about any other language) are just as acceptable as English for XML names.

The following are *not* legal names:

- AmountIn$
- AT&T
- E=mc²
- -Book
- 42book
- XmlData
- XML_on_NeXt_machines

The first three examples use characters that are never legal in a name (`$`, `&`, and the superscript `2`). The fourth and fifth examples use characters that are not legal as the first character of a name, even though they are legal name characters (`-` and `4`). The last two examples violate the "no `XML` at the beginning of a name" restriction (unless, of course, they had been defined by the W3C). The last four examples could be made legal if the first character was changed to, say, an underscore (for example: `_-book`, `_XmlData`).

There are a few other aspects of XML syntax that we will discuss later in this chapter: **String Literals**, **Whitespace**, and **End-of-Line Characters**. For now, let's look at how to create XML tags using the basic syntax we've just discussed.

Elements

Elements are the basic building blocks of XML markup, and may be thought of as containers. They may have associated **attributes** and/or contain other elements, **character data, character references**, **entity references**, **comments**, **processing instructions (PIs)**, and/or **CDATA sections**. Don't worry about all these new terms – we'll explain them in detail later in this chapter. In fact, most XML data (except for comments, PIs, and whitespace) *must* be contained within elements.

> **An element is XML's basic container for content – it may contain character data, other elements, and/or other markup (comments, PIs, entity references, etc.). Since they represent discrete objects, elements can be thought of as the "nouns" of XML.**

Elements are delimited with a **start-tag** and an **end-tag**. If an element has no content, it is known as an **empty element**, and may be represented with either a start-tag/end-tag pair or using an abbreviation: the **empty-element tag**. Unlike the looser syntax of HTML and SGML, *the end-tag cannot be omitted*, except when using an empty-element tag.

All three types of tags are shown in this example:

```
<html>                              <!-- start-tag -->
  <img src="logo.png" />        <!-- empty-element tag -->
</html>                             <!-- end-tag -->
```

Each of these tags consists of the **element type name** (this must be a valid XML name) enclosed within a pair of angle brackets (< >). Let's look at XML tags in more detail.

Tags

The opening delimiter of an element is called the **start-tag**. Start-tags are comprised of an **element type name**, and perhaps some attributes (which we'll look at later in this chapter), enclosed within a pair of angle brackets.

We can think of start-tags as "opening" a container – which is then "closed" with an **end-tag**. End-tags are comprised of a forward slash (/) followed by an element type name, enclosed within the usual angle brackets. The name in an end-tag must match the element name in a corresponding start-tag.

Everything between the start-tag and the end-tag of an element is contained within that element.

The following are legal pairs of start- and end-tags:

- `<Invoice> ... </Invoice>`
- `<INVOICE> ... </INVOICE>`
- `<INVOICE > ... </INVOICE >`
- `<Wrox:Invoice> ... </Wrox:Invoice>`
- `<ΔΓΦ> ... </ΔΓΦ>`
- `<CERN_Conseil_Européen_pour_la_Recherche_Nucléaire> ...`
  `</CERN_Conseil_Européen_pour_la_Recherche_Nucléaire>`
- `<日本語>...</日本語>`

In the third example, the space trailing the name is legal – moreover it will be ignored, so the second and third examples are equivalent. The first two examples are, of course, *not* equivalent tags; also remember that element type names may use any legal name characters, not just ASCII letters. The following are *not* legal start-tags:

```
< INVOICE >
<AmountIn$>
<AΓΔ and/or ΦBK>
```

Whitespacebetween the opening < and the element type name is *not* permitted. In the latter two cases, illegal name characters are present (the $ in the first example, the / and spaces in the second).

Note that the slash character in an end-tag may only appear immediately following the opening angle bracket, and there may only be one such slash in the tag. The following are *not* legal end-tags:

- `< /INVOICE >`
- `</AΓΔ/ΦBK>`

There is another form of start-tag that is not used to delimit a container – it is used for elements with no content.

Empty-Element Tags

Empty elements are those that have no content, though there may be associated attributes. Let's say that we wanted to explicitly indicate certain points within our XML data (see the next section). We could just add a start- and end-tag pair without any text between, for example:

```
<point></point>
```

Of course, we just want to indicate a point, not provide a container. It would be nice to save some space with an abbreviation, and also to indicate that there can never be any content in our `<point>` element. So, XML specifies that an empty element may also be represented in an abbreviated form that is a hybrid of the start- and end-tags. This has the advantages of both brevity and giving an explicit indication that the element shouldn't have any content.

Empty-element tags are comprised of an element type name *followed* by a forward slash (/), and enclosed within angle brackets, for example:

```
<point/>
<point />
```

These two examples are considered identical (whitespace trailing the element name in a tag is ignored). There may not be any whitespace between the / and the >, nor, as before, between the opening < and the tag name.

*HTML note: The common use of unclosed tags (
, <P>, <IMG>, etc.) is an artifact of HTML's origins in SGML – they are not the same as empty-element tags (though they could be converted to those), and they are not allowed in XML.*

Another common use of an empty-element tag includes one or more attributes. This is similarly based upon the idea of a point within the XML data. For example, we might use the following empty element to insert an image within text data:

```
<img src='logo.png' alt='Logo image' />
```

Now that we've discussed the three kinds of XML tags, let's look at a simple example using these tags.

Tags: A Simple Example

Any simple ASCII text file is a singular container (the file), holding a sequence of smaller containers (the text lines), which in turn contain characters. The file is also implicitly contained by its physical existence within a parent file system. All text files have explicit "end-line" delimiters, and some file systems also use an explicit "end-of-file" delimiter. For example, MS-DOS uses a pair of characters, the carriage-return (hexadecimal `0D`, commonly known as "CR") and line-feed (hex `0A` or "LF"), to delimit the end of a text line. The *Ctrl-Z* (hex `1A`) character is used as an explicit end-of-file.

For example, here is a simple ASCII file (note: for the sake of illustration, we'll use **#$** to illustrate the CR-LF pair and **&** for the *EOF*):

```
A Simple Example#$
 by Yours Truly#$
```

```
This is the 3rd line of a simple 5-line text file.#$
..the middle line.. #$
And lastly, a final line of text.#$
&
```

When the same text is represented in XML, the implicit structure of the data can now be made explicit:

```
<textfile>
   <line>A Simple Example</line>
   <line> by Yours Truly</line>
   <line>This is the 3rd line of a simple 5-line text file.</line>
   <line>..the middle line..</line>
   <line>And lastly, a final line of text.</line>
   <EOF/>
</textfile>
```

Note that the indentation in the above example is only used to emphasize the hierarchical structure of these elements, and has no other significance.

In this example, we've explicitly marked the beginning and end of the entire file content (the `<textfile>` element), the beginning and end of each line of text therein (the `<line>` elements), and included an empty-element representation for the *Ctrl-Z* end-of-file marker (the `<EOF/>` element). This is an explicitly described and verifiable structure, comprised of seven individual elements (one of which contains the rest) that are represented by three different element types (`<textfile>`, `<line>`, and `<EOF/>`).

Now that we know the basics of XML name syntax, elements, and the tags that delimit elements, let's step back and look at the overall structure of XML data.

The Structure of XML Data

All XML data must conform to both syntax requirements and a simple container structure. Such data is known as **well formed** (see relevant section later in this chapter for more details). All well-formed XML documents can be comprised of one to three parts:

- An optional **prolog**, which may contain important information about the rest of the data.
- The **body**, which consists of one or more elements in the form a hierarchical tree.
- An optional "miscellaneous" **epilog** that follows the element tree.

These parts, and the unfamiliar syntax in the following illustration, will be described in greater detail later in this chapter.

Prolog

```
<?xml version="1.0"?>
<!-- Comments and/or PIs allowed here -->
<!DOCTYPE textfile SYSTEM "http://www.mySite.com/MyDTDs/Textfile.dtd">
<!-- Comments and/or PIs allowed here -->
```

Body

```
<textfile>
   <line>A Simple Example</line>
   <line> by Yours Truly</line>
   <line>This is the 3rd line of a simple 5-line text file.</line>
   <line>..the middle line..</line>
   <line>And lastly, a final line of text.</line>
   <EOF/>
</textfile>
```

Epilog

```
<!-- ..some more comments and/or PIs... -->
```

In this example, the prolog, document element (`<textfile>`), and the epilog are all part of the document root. `<EOF/>` is an example of an empty-element tag.

Since XML data may be well formed without including either a prolog or epilog, we'll look into the details of those later, after we've described in detail the most important part – the body, with its element tree.

Hierarchical Tree Structure

Well-formed XML data is defined as being in the form of a simple hierarchical tree, with one, and only one, root node, called the **document entity** or the **document root**. This node may contain a prolog and/or epilog, and it will always contain a body. The body is comprised of a sub-tree of elements.

The first levels of the maximum document tree for any XML data is:

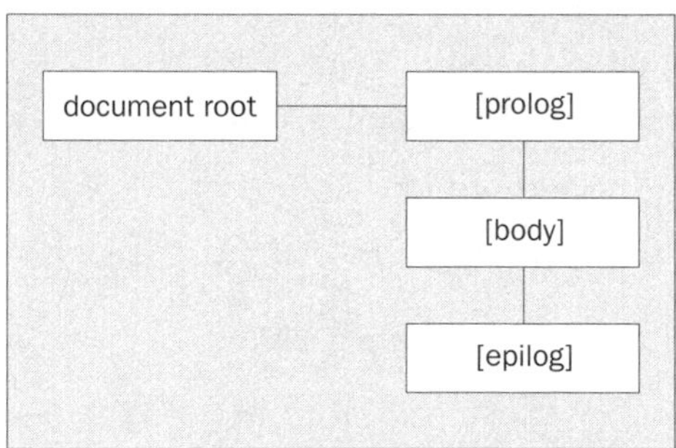

The minimum document tree is:

[document root] [body]

The body sub-tree always has a single root node called the **document element** (sometimes referred to as the **root element**) – if not, the data is *not* well-formed XML!

> **Any well-formed XML document must be a simple hierarchical tree with a single root node, called the "document root". This document tree contains a secondary tree of elements, with its own singular root node, called the "document element".**

The document root of each XML document is also the main point of attachment for the document's description using a DTD or Schema (see Chapters 5 and 6 for more about these). A **Processing Instruction** (**PI** – more about these later) is often used to attach a stylesheet as well (see Chapter 9).

Since well-formed XML data has a tree structure, it can be modeled and manipulated as a tree. A standard model for this approach is the W3C **Document Object Model** (**DOM**), which will be discussed in Chapter 11.

Now let's look at the body of the XML document in greater depth.

The Document Element

This element is the parent of all other elements in the tree, and thus it may not be contained in any other element. Because the document root and the document element are *not* the same thing, it is better not to refer to the document element as the "root element" (even though it is the root of the element sub-tree).

Child Elements

All other elements in an XML document are descendants ("children") of the document element. In the earlier "textfile" example, the `<textfile>` element is the document element, and the `<line>` and `<EOF>` elements are its children. Its element tree is:

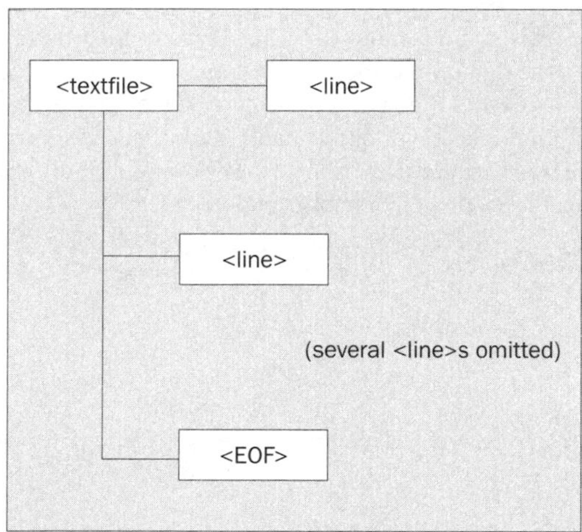

The element tree and its parent-child relationships are an important feature of XML. Tree manipulation code has been developed and refined over many years, and this also greatly simplifies the use of stylesheets to both format and transform XML data for different presentations.

Element Nesting

XML imposes a key constraint upon elements – they must be properly nested. An analogy to physical objects helps illustrate what is meant by "properly nested". In fact, we might even claim that XML elements are things ("nouns") that must follow the same rules as any material thing.

Consider how this book might have been transported to you. After printing, this book and 23 others like it were packed into a box. Two boxes were packed into a larger carton, and cartons were loaded onto a truck and delivered to a bookstore.

This could be represented by the following XML elements (many books and cartons have been omitted for brevity):

```
<truck>
  <carton>
    <box>
      <book>...</book>
      <book>...</book>
      <book>...</book>
      ...
      <book>...</book>
    </box>
    <box>
      <book>...</book>
      ...
      <book>...</book>
    </box>
  </carton>
  <carton>
   ...
  </carton>
   ...
</truck>
```

A physical box can contain complete books, but can't have part of the book inside the box and part outside (for the sake of this example, let's ignore that moment in time when we're placing the book into the box; and sub-atomic particle behavior, as well!) Likewise, a book can only be in one box, not partly in one and partly in another (again, I plead: let's not tear the books in half). And the boxes must be contained within cartons, which are in turn always contained within the truck (please, no open doors and bumps in the road). XML elements must also follow this basic law of physical containment.

The element tree that is implied by this example is:

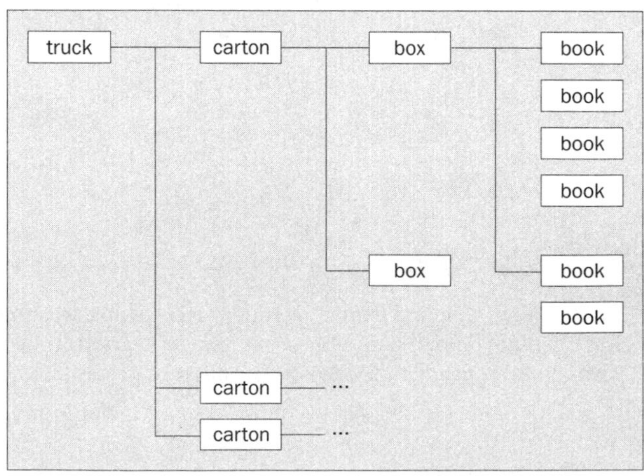

Improper Nesting

HTML and many word processing formats are not nearly so rigorous as XML when it comes to element nesting. The following is an all-too-common example of overlapping HTML tags that is *illegal* in XML:

```
<B>..some bold text, with <I>bold-italic</B> followed by plain italic text..</I>
```

Most HTML browsers have no trouble displaying this, but different browsers often do so in different ways:

```
..some bold text, with bold-italic followed by plain italic text..
```

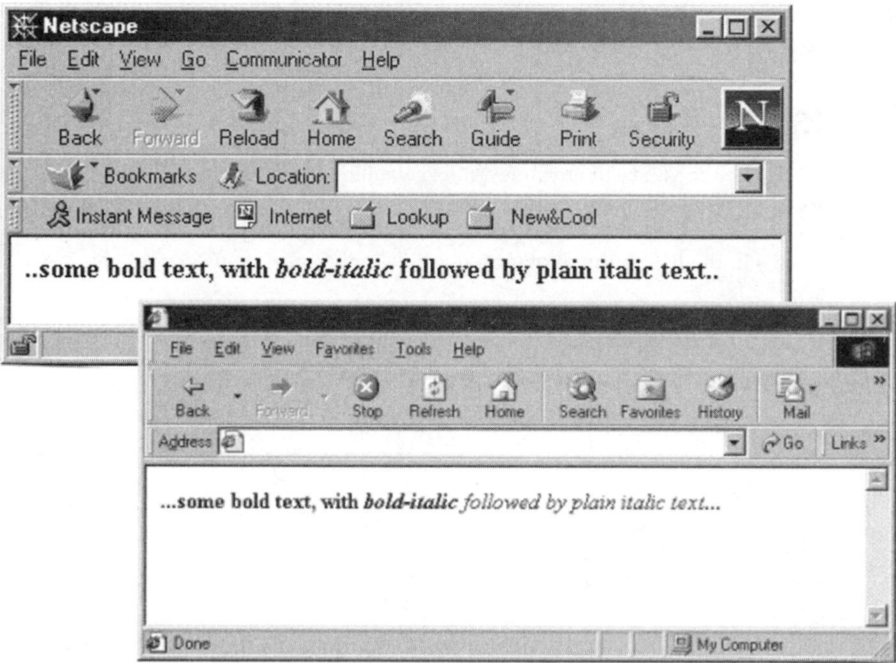

This situation might be fine for trivial text formatting, but when the tags are intended to describe real content, such as a name and address, this kind of overlap is ambiguous, or worse. Imagine trying to interpret the following (**illegal**) XML construct:

```
<name>Joe Lee<address>Park Lane</name>Anytown</address>
```

The "tree" that would be implied by this example is:

```
name --- {name ∩ address} --- address
```

Since tags are not properly nested, a simple hierarchical tree of elements cannot be constructed. The middle element type above hasn't been defined and doesn't really exist; it's just a synthetic placeholder to indicate the intersection of the two properly defined element types. While set theory and non-hierarchical trees would certainly allow us to use this sort of structure, its actual programming implementation would be a nightmare.

Since there's no way to differentiate between presentable and ambiguous overlaps, and the manipulation of the tree that is created by these overlaps would be so complex, XML simply prohibits any overlapping tags. The first time an improperly nested tag is encountered, the XML Parser must report a "not well-formed" error, and will usually quit processing the document and report a "fatal" error (see the "*XML Parsers*" section later in this chapter for more about fatal errors).

HTML browsers will usually render even seriously broken tags, and SGML tools often attempt to continue processing a document, even after encountering errors. By design, XML does not allow this behavior.

Now that we've looked at both the structure of XML data and the basic syntax of elements, let's expand our understanding of elements by looking at an alternate way to include information within the element start-tag (**attributes**) and another type of element content (**character data**). But first, we'll look at the syntax of string literals in XML since they are used for attribute values.

String Literals

String literals are used for the values of attributes, internal entities, and external identifiers. All string literals in XML are enclosed by delimiter pairs, using either an apostrophe (`'`) or a quotation mark (`"`). The one restriction upon these literals is that the character used for the delimiters may not appear within the literal – if an apostrophe appears in the literal, the quotation mark delimiter must be used, and vice versa.

If both delimiter characters are needed within the literal, the one being used for the delimiters must be escaped, using an appropriate entity reference (`'` for the `'` or `"` for the `"`). There is more about these later in this chapter, in the "Character and Entity References" section.

The following are legal string literals:

```
"string"
'string'
"..Jack's cow said &quot;moo&quot;"
'..Jack&apos;s cow said "moo"'
```

The delimiter character in the latter two examples has been properly escaped using the `"` and `'` entity references.

The following are *illegal* string literals:

```
"string'
'..Jack's cow said "moo"'
```

In the first example, the closing delimiter does not match the opening delimiter. The second example uses both possible delimiter characters within the string, but doesn't use the appropriate entity reference to escape the character that has been used to delimit the literal.

Attributes

If elements are the "nouns" of XML, then attributes are its "adjectives".

Often there is some information about an element that we wish to attach *to* it, as opposed to including it as a string *inside* the element, or one of its children. This can be done using **attributes**, each of which is comprised of a name-value pair. Both start-tags and empty-element tags may include attributes within the tag. Attribute values must always be string literals, so the attribute value can use either of the two delimiters:

```
<tagname attribute_name="attribute_value">
<tagname attribute_name='attribute_value'>
```

Attribute values may contain text characters, entity references, and/or character references (the latter two are explained later in this chapter). However, neither of the protected markup characters (< and &) may be used as simple characters – they must always be escaped using the `<` or `&` entity references (see the "*Entity References*" section above for more information on these).

HTML note*: HTML permits the use of attribute names without values, and values that don't have delimiters, such as* `<IMG WIDTH=300...>` *or* `<P ALIGN=LEFT>`*, but this is not allowed in XML.*

Another restriction upon XML attributes is that only one instance of an attribute name is allowed within a given tag. For example, the following (legal) HTML tag would *not* be legal in XML:

```
<img src="image1.jpg" src="altimage.jpg" />
```

This restriction greatly simplifies the XML parser's handling of attributes. It also helps to discourage the notion that attributes are part of the XML data content – they're intended to modify the associated elements, much as an adjective modifies a noun.

Going back to our earlier "truck-full-of-books" example, we might attach a number to each carton of our book shipment using attributes:

```
<carton number="0-666-42-1">
  ...
</carton>
<carton number='0-666-42-2'>
  ...
</carton>
```

In this example, the attribute name is `number` and the values are `0-666-42-1` and `0-666-42-2`. Note that both legal string literal delimiter characters (`"` and `'`) are illustrated in this example.

In our even earlier "textfile" example, the `<EOF/>` empty-element tag could perhaps include the hex value of the original text file end-of-file character:

```
<EOF char="1A"/>
```

In this example, the attribute name is `char` and its value is `1A` (MS-DOS's infamous *Ctrl-Z*).

There is another way to look at the choice between element and attribute that makes sense for structured text data (a "document"). If the data should appear within the normal view of the document, it should be contained in an element. If the data describes something *about* the element or is for behind-the-scenes processing (like a link target such as the one contained within the `href` attribute below), it should be in an attribute. An HTML hyperlink anchor element (`<a>`) in a snippet of text illustrates this distinction:

```
More at the <a href="http://www.wrox.com/">Wrox Press</a> website.
```

Although we've referred to elements and attributes as nouns and adjectives, this is not an enforceable (or even a universal!) distinction.

Elements vs. Attributes

The decision to use an element versus an attribute is not a simple one. Much discussion and argument has occurred about this topic on both the XML-L and XML-DEV lists. Some argue that attributes should never be used – that they add unnecessary processing complexity, and that anything that can be represented as an attribute would be better contained within a child element. Others extol the advantage of being able to validate attribute values and assign default values using a DTD. Experiments have shown that, despite superficial appearances, use of generic data compression (such as **gzip**, **zlib**, or **LZW**) has shown that neither form has an inherent advantage for data storage or transmission.

Two of the editors of the XML 1.0 REC and some other SGML/XML experts have written on this topic. Most of the following are deep links to Robin Cover's excellent SGML/XML web pages:

- "XML Syntax Recommendation for Serializing Graphs of Data" by Andrew Layman – http://www.w3.org/TandS/QL/QL98/pp/microsoft-serializing.html
- "Elements or attributes?" by Eliot Kimber – http://www.oasis-open.org/cover/attrKimber9711.html
- "Elements vs. Attributes" by Michael Sperberg-McQueen – http://www.oasis-open.org/cover/attrSperberg92.html
- "SGML/XML: Using Elements and Attributes" by Robin Cover – http://www.oasis-open.org/cover/elementsAndAttrs.html
- "When is an attribute an attribute?" by Tim Bray – http://www.oasis-open.org/cover/brayAttr980409.html
- "When to use attributes as opposed to elements" by G. Ken Holman – http://www.oasis-open.org/cover/holmanElementsAttrs.html

Character Data

Character data is plain text that contains no element tags or other markup, except perhaps, character and entity references. Remember too, that because XML is intended for worldwide use, text means Unicode, not just ASCII (see the "Characters" section earlier in this chapter).

The ampersand (&) and less-than (<) characters are used as XML's opening delimiters, and thus may never appear in their literal form (except in CDATA sections, which are discussed later). If these characters are needed within character data, they *must* be escaped using the entity references; `<` or `&`. It is not necessary to escape the other markup characters (like >), but they *may* be escaped (using `>` in this case), if only for the sake of consistency within the character data.

These escape sequences are part of the set of five such strings defined by the XML specification, and implemented in all compliant XML parsers.

Whitespace

Whitespace is an important linguistic concept for both human and computer languages. Only four characters are treated as whitespace in XML data:

Character values (hexadecimal)	Description
`09`	Horizontal tab (HT)
`0A`	Line-feed (LF)
`0D`	Carriage-return (CR)
`20`	ASCII space character

There is no expansion of tab characters, so each tab is simply treated as a single space character (though it could be used to trigger special handling in the application). Similarly, any special formatting that might be implied by an end-of-line is left to the XML application and/or stylesheet. However, there is a quirk in the interpretation of the carriage-return character, as we will see in the next section.

Unicode defines a variety of different kinds of non-ASCII spaces, but none of these are considered whitespace within the context of XML markup.

The XML specification requires that the XML parser pass all characters, including all whitespace characters, to the application. If a validating parser is used, it is required to inform the application when whitespace characters appear within element content (and thus, by implication, those whitespace characters that are part of an element's character data). It is always up to the application to handle whitespace.

> **XML's rule for handling whitespace is very simple: all whitespace characters (except for the CR character) within the content are preserved by the parser and passed unmodified to the application, while whitespace within element tags and attribute values *may* be removed. This is unlike the rampant removal of whitespace carried out in HTML browsers.**

Indenting tags and other markup is a common practice in both SGML and HTML documents. Even within the document's content, HTML browsers often remove all but a single whitespace character between words and other identifiable units of text. This feature has some advantages for the author: it makes the markup easier to read and emphasizes the structure of the document. However, different browsers have different rules for whitespace removal, and many HTML authors use the `<pre>` tag, the ` ` (non-breaking space) entity and/or the table tags to force more deterministic spacing of text. Elimination of this ambiguity in HTML and the complexity of SGML's whitespace rules were XML design goals.

An HTML browser usually ignores whitespace between markup. On the other hand, SGML has a bunch of complex rules for deciding whether or not to preserve whitespace caused by markup – whatever that means (these rules have never been very clear nor concise).

We mentioned some funniness concerning the carriage-return character, so let's look at the gory details of special end-of-line character handling.

End-of-line Handling

Since XML is considered a "text" (rather than binary) format, XML data is often stored in discrete computer files that are divided into "lines" of text. Two of the four XML white space characters are the standard ASCII end-of-line control characters. There are three common combinations of these two characters that are used to indicate end-of-line: CR-LF (MS-Windows, MS-DOS, CPM), LF only (Unix, GNU/Linux), and CR only (MacOS).

An XML parser will convert all three common ASCII end-of-line strings to a single LF (line-feed) character.

In an effort to simplify coding of XML applications, an XML parser is required to normalize all end-of-line strings to use the Unix style. Naturally, this pleased Unix programmers, and befuddled many MS-Windows programmers (MacOS users have already been conditioned to handle multiple end-of-line strings). Tim Bray (one of the editors of the XML 1.0 REC) has stated that there were some second thoughts about this "feature", given the MS-Windows market-share. But the fact remains that XML forces the use of Unix-style end-of-line characters.

OS/390 note: *The EBCDIC newline character (*`NEL` *or #x0085) is* not *correctly handled as an end-of-line character. This oversight in the original XML 1.0 specification is an open issue, with a NOTE at* *http://www.w3.org/TR/newline*.

Before we plunge into entity references and other special purpose syntax, let's have a quick summary of the syntax we've discussed so far.

Summary of Element and Attribute Syntax

The simple XML tag forms:

Example	Description
`<tagname>`	Element start-tag.
`</tagname>`	Element end-tag.
`<tagname attr="value">`	Element start-tag with attribute.
`<tagname/>`	Empty-element tag.
`<tagname attr1="value1" attr2='value2'/>`	Empty-element tag with two attributes, and using both string delimiters.

Now let's look at the markup syntax of character and entity references.

Character and Entity References

Like SGML and HTML before it, XML provides two simple methods of representing characters that don't exist within the basic US-ASCII character set:

- Character references.
- Entity references.

Let's look at the simpler of these first.

Character References

Character references are used to represent a displayable character that cannot be conveniently input into a document (such as Chinese characters in a European-language word processor), or as a substitute for a literal form that would violate the syntax rules of XML (such as the ampersand character).

A character reference is comprised of a decimal or hexadecimal number, preceded by an `&#` or `&#x` string literal (respectively) and followed by a semi-colon (`;`) character:

- `&#NNNNN;`
- `&#xXXXX;`

The `NNNNN` and `XXXX` strings may be one to five decimal, or one to four hexadecimal digits respectively, that correspond to any Unicode character value that is allowed by XML. Although decimal numbers are more commonly used in HTML, the hex form is preferred for XML, since Unicode character encoding is defined using hex numbers.

For example:

```
<test>&#169; is the same as &#xA9; and &#174; is the same as &#xAE;</test>
```

This would be displayed (in an HTML browser) as shown in the screenshot below:

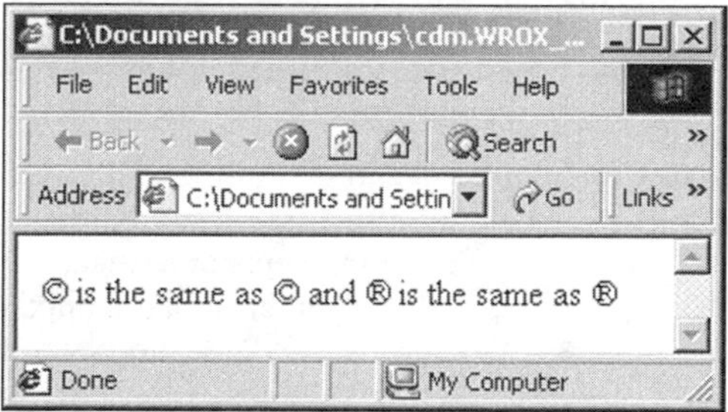

Two of the three non-English names we showed earlier in the chapter, are shown below:

- ΔΓΦ
- CERN_Conseil_Européen_pour_la_Recherche_Nucléaire

These could also be represented using plain ASCII characters, plus some character references:

```
&#x0394;&#x0393;&#x03A6;
CERN_Conseil_Europ&#xE9;en_pour_la_Recherche_Nucl&#xE9;aire
```

Character references suffice for representing single characters or symbols using their numeric Unicode value. It would be nicer to be able to represent characters with a name, or embed named strings of characters – for this we can use **entity references**.

Entity References

Entity references allow the insertion of any string literal into element content or attribute values, as well as providing mnemonic alternatives to character references.

An entity reference is a legal XML name string, preceded by an ampersand (`&`) and followed by a semi-colon (`;`) character, for example:

```
&name;
```

In this case, `name` refers to an entity that is defined elsewhere. We'll tackle entity definition in Chapter 5, so let's just stipulate that the entity has been defined as something (*what* doesn't really matter for now).

We've already seen that there are five entity references built in to XML, and used as escape sequences for the XML markup delimiter characters:

Entity Reference	Usage
`&`	Always used to escape the (`&`) character literal (except within a CDATA section – more about these later in this chapter).
`<`	Always used to escape the (`<`) character (except within a CDATA section).
`>`	May be used to escape the (`>`) character – must be used in a CDATA section if preceded by (`]]`).
`'`	May need to be used to escape the (`'`) character in string literals.
`"`	May need to be used to escape the (`"`) character in string literals.

Except for these five entities' entity references, all entities must be defined prior to their use in a document (just like traditional programming macro definition and use). Entities are defined in the document's **Document Type Definition** (**DTD**) – see the Prolog section later in this chapter, and Chapter 5, "Validating XML: DTDs", for more details. If an XML parser encounters an undefined entity references, the parser is obligated to report a fatal error – see the "Well-formed XML" section later in this chapter.

Numerous named character and symbol entities have been defined as part of HTML (and can be made available to XML). The following examples have a mixture of XML built in and standard HTML entity references:

```
&copy; AT&amp;T
```

This would be displayed (in an HTML browser) as shown below:

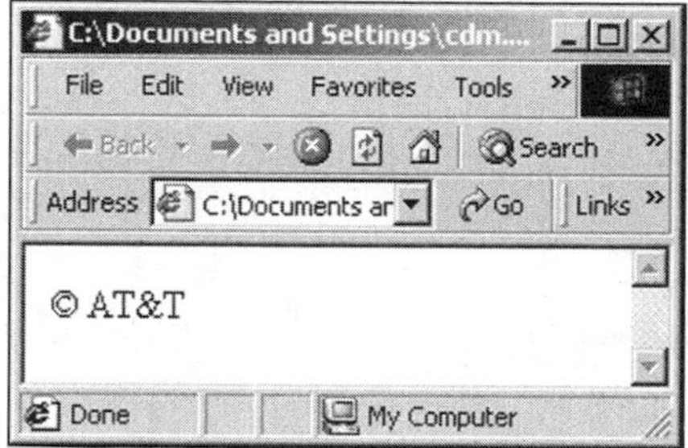

In addition:

```
&quot;Jack's Tracks&quot; &reg; by DJ Chris
```

This would be displayed as:

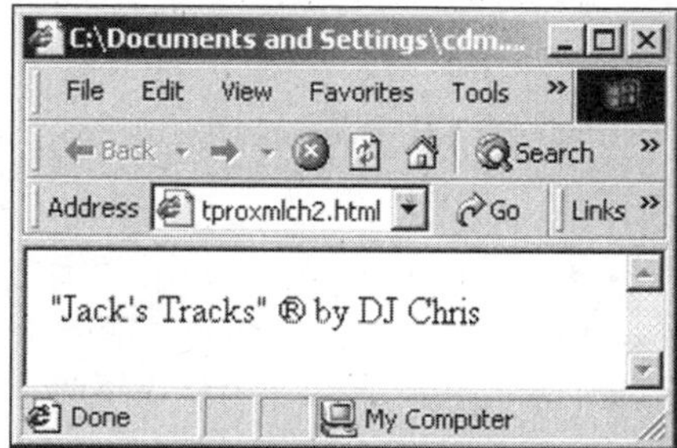

Entity references may also be used as general text macros ("boilerplate"). For example, the following text includes several entity references:

```
&Warn; - &Disclaimer; &lt; &copy; 2001 &USCG; &amp; &USN; &gt;
```

This might be displayed as:

WARNING! – Not to be used for navigation! <© 2001 U.S. Coast Guard & U.S. Navy >

Of course, we're assuming for the moment that the non-built in entities have already been defined as follows (*how* they're defined is unimportant for now):

Entity Reference	Text Equivalent
`&Warn;`	`WARNING!`
`&Disclaimer;`	`Not to be used for navigation!`
`©`	©
` `	
`®`	®
`&USCG;`	`U.S. Coast Guard`
`&USN;`	`U.S. Navy`

When the replacement text for an entity is declared to include another entity reference, that reference is expanded in turn, and so on, until all such nested references are resolved. However, a nested "`name`" must not contain a recursive reference to itself, either directly or indirectly. We will address the details of entity expansion in the "Advanced XML Syntax" and "Validating XML: DTDs" chapters (3 and 5, respectively).

Let's move on to the remaining special-purpose markup syntax.

Special-Purpose Markup

We've already discussed just about every aspect of XML syntax that is necessary to create well-formed XML data (elements, attributes, and character/entity references). There are three additional syntactic constructs that deviate from the familiar syntax of tags (`<tagname>`) or entity references (`&ref;`). These are:

- Comments
- Processing Instructions (PIs)
- CDATA sections

We'll look at their details in the above sequence.

Comments

It is often useful to insert notes, or **comments**, into a document. These comments might provide a revision log, historical notes, or any other sort of meta-data that would be meaningful to the creator and editors of a document (serving to enhance its human readability), but aren't truly part of the document's content. Comments may appear anywhere in a document outside of other markup (that is, you can't put a comment in the middle of a start- or end-tag).

The basic syntax of an XML comment is:

```
<!--...comment text...-->
```

The "`...comment text...`" portion can be any character string that doesn't include the "`--`" string literal (this restriction is for SGML compatibility). Furthermore, this portion cannot end with a hyphen (`-`) since this could cause misinterpretation of the closing delimiter.

> **Comments are not part of a document's character data! Within a comment section, markup is not interpreted, and entity references are not expanded.**

The XML 1.0 REC allows, *but does not require*, an XML processor to provide a method for the application to retrieve the text of comments. Therefore, an XML application may never rely on using comments to transmit special instructions (an all-to-common HTML trick).

Let's see some examples of legal XML comments:

```
<tag> ..some content.. </tag>  <!-- this is a legal comment -->
<!--======= Beginning of some more comments ========-->
<!--
   this is a comment containing unexpanded <tag> and &entity_reference;'s
    - that is also continued on another line..
-->
<!--======= End of comments ========-->
```

The following are illegal comments:

```
<tag> ..some content.. </tag <!-- (no comments within tags) --> >
<!-- Comments cannot <!-- be nested --> like this -->
<!-- Comments cannot end with an extra hyphen, like this --->
```

Comments cannot be used within element tags, and comments may never be nested.

The following comment is technically legal XML, but it isn't legal SGML, so its use is discouraged for the sake of compatibility.

```
<!-- (an incompatible comment -- because of the double hyphen within) -->
```

Until the creation of the `<script>` element, many HTML browsers extracted script code from HTML comments. This does not work in XML, since comments need *not* be passed to the application. XML has provided a substitute for both `<script>` elements and code in comments, as we will see in the next section.

Processing Instructions (PIs)

XML, like SGML, is a descriptive markup language, and so it does not presume to try to explain how to actually process an element or its contents. This is a powerful advantage in that it provides presentation flexibility, and OS- and application-independence. However, there are times when it is desirable to pass processing hints (or perhaps some script code) to the application along with the document. The Processing Instruction (PI) is the mechanism that XML provides for this purpose.

PIs use a variation of XML element tag syntax:

```
<?target ...instruction... ?>
```

The PI `target` is required, and must be a valid XML name that is used to identify the application (or other object) to which the PI is directed. The `...instruction...` portion of the PI is merely a string literal that may include any valid character string, except the `?>` string literal (the PI's ending delimiter). There is no further definition of PI syntax in the XML 1.0 REC.

An example of a nearly ubiquitous PI that is used to associate a stylesheet with an XML document:

```
<?xml-stylesheet href="mystyle.css" type="text/css" ?>
```

Note that this PI uses a target name that begins with the string "`xml`" – this would be illegal for any non-W3C-defined PI, since its use is reserved for W3C specifications. See "Transforming XML", Chapter 9, for more about the use of this PI.

> *This PI was not included in the XML 1.0 REC, but instead rated its very own W3C recommendation: "Associating Style Sheets with XML documents Version 1.0" (29 June 1999) which is available at* http://www.w3.org/TR/xml-stylesheet/.

There has been something of a debate in the XML developer community as to whether or not PIs are truly useful, or are instead a bit of special syntax that will hinder the acceptance of XML (because of lack of support for PIs in existing browsers, or by allowing incompatible markup to be generated due to the lack of standardized target names). Another argument against PIs is that many of the hints that might be conveyed using a PI are better kept in external stylesheets.

On the other hand, there are several possible advantages of PIs: a hook for scripts or server-side includes (without resorting to the abuse of HTML's `<!-- ... -->` comment syntax); a mechanism for extending schemas that cannot otherwise be modified; a method of extending documents without altering DTD validation; or another way to pass document presentation information (such as line- or page-breaks) embedded in the document without affecting that document's element content or structure.

> *Although XML does not specify any format for a PI (other than the target name), the* `xml-stylesheet` *PI uses the same name-value syntax as XML start-tag attributes. This is a good approach to PI syntax, and should probably be used for consistency and ease of processing.*

Let's now turn our attention to the last of the special-purpose markup syntax.

CDATA Sections

CDATA sections are a method of including text that contains characters that would otherwise be interpreted as markup. This feature is primarily useful to authors who wish to include examples of XML markup in their documents (like the examples in this book). This is probably the only good reason to include CDATA sections in a document, since almost all advantages of XML are lost when using these sections.

CDATA sections are *not* a good way to include binary data within an XML file. Such data could never include most of the ASCII C0 and C1 control character values (hex `00 • 2F`), nor the three-byte hex sequence `5D`, `5D`, `3E`, or "`]]>`" (which would be misinterpreted as the end of the CDATA section). The binary data could be encoded with base64, or some other technique that can assure that the encoded data never contains illegal or greater-than (>) characters. However, if this method is used, the base64-encoded binary data could just as easily be included in any element's content, and thus a CDATA section would be unnecessary.

CDATA sections:

- May contain most markup characters (which will *not* be interpreted as such, so character and entity references are not expanded).
- May occur anywhere that character data may occur.
- Cannot be nested.
- Cannot be empty (just delimiters with no data).

The only markup string that's recognized within a CDATA section is its end delimiter "`]]>`", so less-than characters (`<`) and ampersands (`&`) may occur in their literal form; they need not be escaped.

The basic syntax of a CDATA section is:

```
<![CDATA[...]]>
```

The "`...`" portion can be any character string that doesn't include the "`]]>`" string literal.

We might want to include our boilerplate entity references example (from a while back) in an XML document, without letting the XML parser expand the entities. We could simply copy the example to a CDATA section:

```
<![CDATA[&Warn; - &Disclaimer; &lt;&copy; 2001 &USCG; &amp; &USN; &gt; ]]>
```

Otherwise, if we wanted to include the example in regular element content (character data), we would need to replace all the ampersand characters with the `&` entity reference, so that they will not be misinterpreted:

```
<example>&amp;Warn; - &amp;Disclaimer; &amp;lt;&amp;copy; 2001 &amp;USCG;
&amp;amp; &amp;USN; &amp;gt;
</example>
```

The former approach is obviously easier to read and write, and has the additional advantage of permitting the direct cutting-and-pasting of XML examples from elsewhere. The latter method is rather unreadable – we have to mentally parse all the `&` entity references back into the `&` characters that delimit the other various entity references (for example: `&` becomes `&` and so on).

Document Structure

Now that we've discussed the various aspects of XML syntax, let's put it all together and take a detailed look at the structure of well-formed XML data. As we've seen before, well-formed XML data is comprised of three major parts: an optional prolog, the body (including the hierarchical element tree), and an optional epilog.

Prolog

The prolog is the appetizer – used to signal the beginning of XML data. It describes the data's character encoding, and provides some other configuration hints to the XML parser and application.

The prolog should consist of an **XML Declaration**, followed by zero or more comments, PIs, and/or whitespace characters, then an optional **Document Type Declaration**, and perhaps some more comments, PIs, and/or whitespace characters.

Since all parts of the prolog are optional, this implies that the prolog may be omitted and the data will still be well formed.

XML Declaration

All XML documents *should* begin with an XML Declaration. This declaration is not required in most XML documents, but it serves to explicitly identify the data as XML, and does permit some optimizations when processing the document. If the XML data uses an encoding other than UTF-8 or UTF-16, then an XML Declaration with the correct encoding *must* be used.

If this declaration is included, then the string literal "`<?xml `" must be the very first six characters of the document – no preceding whitespace or embedded comments are allowed.

While this declaration looks exactly like a processing instruction, strictly speaking it is *not* a PI (it is a unique declaration defined by the XML 1.0 REC). Nevertheless, the XML Declaration uses PI-like delimiters and an attribute-like parameter syntax that is similar to the one used in element tags (either `"` or `'` may be used to delimit the value strings). For example:

```
<?xml version="1.0" encoding='utf-8' standalone="yes"?>
```

Three parameters have been defined by the XML 1.0 specification:

- `version` – This is *required*, and its value currently must be "`1.0`" (no other versions have been defined). This parameter enables support for possible future versions of XML.
- `encoding` – This is optional, and its value must be a legal character encoding name, such as "`UTF-8`", "`UTF-16`", or "`ISO-8859-1`" (Latin-1). If this parameter is not included, UTF-8 or UTF-16 encoding is assumed, depending upon the format of the initial "`<?xml `" string. See the "IANA" and "Character Encoding Autodetection" sections in the next chapter for more details.
- `standalone` – This is optional, and its value must be either "`yes`" or "`no`". A "`yes`" means that all required entity declarations are contained within the document, and "`no`" means that an external DTD is required (more about this in Chapter 5, "Validating XML: DTDs").

Even though the above name-value pairs look a lot like XML attributes, there are a couple of key differences. Unlike XML attributes (which can be in any order), these must be in the order shown above. On the other hand, but again unlike most XML attributes, the `encoding` values are *not* case-sensitive. This apparent inconsistency is due to XML's dependence upon existing ISO and IANA (Internet Assigned Numbers Authority) standards for character encoding names.

Early drafts of XML did not specify case sensitivity for names, and many early implementers, including Microsoft, used an upper case version of this declaration "`<?XML...?>`". However, the final W3C recommendation specified case sensitivity, and defined the "`xml`" name as lower case. Thus some so-called XML documents are no longer legal XML 1.0 data.

Although HTTP provides a method for a server to tell the client (like a browser) what encoding is being used, sometimes there is no server (as when viewing files on a local file system). Using the `encoding` parameter is also more reliable than trying to rely upon auto-detection of the character encoding (this technique can often get close, but can't distinguish UTF-8 from ISO-8859-1, or reliably detect the UTF-7 encoding).

For the examples in the rest of this chapter, we'll use the basic version of the XML Declaration:

```
<?xml version='1.0' encoding='utf-8'?>
```

If the XML declaration is used, `version` is required (`'1.0'` is the only currently valid version). If any encoding other than UTF-8 or UTF-16 is used, then an explicit `encoding` is required.

Still, "best practice" is to always include an XML declaration with both `version` and `encoding` explicitly declared.

Document Type Declaration

This should *not* be confused with the DTD (Remember: Document Type *Definition*)! Rather, the **Document Type Declaration** can refer to an external DTD and/or contain part of the DTD. Simple well-formed documents do not necessarily require this declaration (as long as they do not contain any entity references other than the five built in XML entity references). Since these will not be used in any of the examples in this chapter, we will defer the detailed discussion of this declaration to the "Advanced XML Syntax" and "Validating XML: DTDs" chapters (3 and 5, respectively).

Body

This is, of course, the main course of the XML data, which we've discussed at length in terms of its components: elements, attributes, character data, etc. It is worth reiterating that the body may contain comments, PIs, and/or whitespace characters interleaved with elements and character data. The elements must comprise a hierarchical tree, with a single root node.

Epilog

The XML epilog is the dessert with potentially unpleasant consequences! It may include comments, PIs, and/or whitespace. Comments and whitespace don't cause any significant problems. However, it is unclear whether PIs in the epilog should be applied to the elements in the preceding XML data, or a subsequent XML document (if any).

This may well be a solution in search of a problem, or it may just be a problem in and of itself. XML does not define any end-of-document indicator, and many applications will use the document element end-tag for this purpose. In this case, the epilog is never read, let alone processed.

This is a "real design error" as considered by Tim Bray (one of the XML 1.0 REC editors). It is probably inadvisable to use it without a very compelling reason – and the prior knowledge that it will likely not be interoperable with other XML applications.

Well-Formed XML

As we've already mentioned, all documents (or data) that conform to the basic rules of the XML 1.0 REC are known as well formed. This data can be used without a DTD or schema to describe their structure, and is also known as **standalone** (or **DTD-less**) XML data. Such data cannot rely upon any external declarations, and attribute values will receive no special processing or default values.

All well-formed XML data contains one or more elements (delimited by start- and end-tags) that nest properly within each other. There is one element, which contains any and all other elements within the document – the document element. All these elements form a simple hierarchical tree, and so the only direct element-to-element relationship is that of parent-child. Sibling relationships can often be inferred using data structures internal to the XML application, but these are neither direct, nor reliable (due to the possibility of elements being inserted between the common parent and one or more of its children). Document content can include markup and/or character data.

To summarize, data is **well-formed** XML if:

- The end-tag matches the corresponding start tag, and there is:

    no overlapping in element definitions.

    no instances of multiple attributes with the same name for one element.

- Syntax conforms to the XML specification, including:

    Start-tags all have matching end-tags (or are empty-element tags).

    Element tags do not overlap.

    Attributes have unique names.

    Markup characters are properly escaped.

- Elements form a hierarchical tree, with a single root node.
- There are no references to external entities (unless a DTD is provided).

Any XML parser that encounters a construct within the XML data that is not well formed must report this error to the application as a fatal error. Fatal errors need not cause the parser to terminate – it may continue processing in an attempt to find other errors, but it may not continue to pass character data and/or XML structures to the application in a normal fashion.

This approach to error handling is the result of XML's design goal of compactness, and the intention that XML be used for much more than just document display. Hopefully, this rather brutal error handling will prevent the creation of bloated software like Internet Explorer and Navigator (which have all sorts of special code to figure-out how to handle ambiguous HTML). Besides, it's just not that hard to make well-formed XML data.

Tools for both HTML and SGML, are much more forgiving than XML tools. An HTML browser can usually render most of a seriously broken web page, a fact that contributed to the rapid acceptance of HTML. Yet, the actual rendering varies from browser to browser. Similarly, SGML tools usually try to continue processing a document even after encountering errors.

The existence of well-formed documents allows use of XML data without the burden of constructing and referencing an external description of that data. The term "well-formed" has a similar meaning in formal mathematical logic – an assertion is well-formed if it meets grammatical rules, without any concern as to whether the assertion is "true" or not.

Valid XML (A Brief Look)

Any XML data object is considered **valid XML** if it is well formed, *and* it meets certain further validity constraints and matches a grammar describing the document's content. Like SGML, XML can provide such a description of document structure in the form of an **XML Schema** or a DTD. See Chapter 5 for details about DTD validation, and Chapter 6 for validation with XML Schema.

Validation using a DTD ensures that element parent-child relationships are respected, that attributes have valid values, that all referenced entities have been properly defined, and that numerous other validity constraints are obeyed.

> *The SGML equivalent of a well-formed document is known as* ***tag-valid****. The SGML equivalent of a valid document is* ***type-valid****.*

Given its SGML origins, XML will continue to be used for complex documents and websites. However, much of the current interest in XML is as a basis for electronic commerce. This application of XML requires more complex and robust methods of organizing XML vocabularies, and a way to maintain strong data typing when moving data to and from modern relational and object-oriented DBMSs.

Since the restrictions imposed upon DTDs have proven them inadequate for this task, the W3C has provided two extensions to the basic specification: **Namespaces** (see Chapter 3, "Advanced XML Syntax") and **XML Schemas** (see Chapter 6, "Introducing XML Schemas"). Namespaces and DTDs simply don't work well together. XML Schemas work well with Namespaces, and are generally a more powerful alternative to DTDs for validation.

XML Parsers

In addition to specifying the syntax of XML, the W3C described some of the behavior of the lower tier of XML's client architecture (the **XML processor** or **parser**).

Parser Levels

Two levels of parser ("processor") behavior are defined in the XML 1.0 REC:

- **Non-validating** – ensures that the data is well-formed XML, but need not resolve any external resources
- **Validating** – ensures both well-formedness and validity using a DTD, and must resolve external resources

Some parsers can work either way, with configuration switches that determine whether or not the data will be validated. See Chapter 5 for more about validating parsers.

Some of the behavior of XML parsers has been defined with the intent of easing the burden upon an application's handling of XML data. For example, as previously described, the character sequences used to delimit the end of text records are often OS-specific. However an XML application needn't be concerned with this, because the XML parser will normalize all standard text record delimiters to a single line-feed (LF or hex 0A) character. Whitespace handling is another area where parsers are constrained – unlike HTML or SGML, all whitespace must be passed from the document to the application.

Parser Implementations

There are two different implementation approaches to processing the XML data:

- **Event-driven parser** – Processes XML data sequentially, handling components one at a time
- **Tree-based parser** – Constructs a tree representation of the entire document and provides access to individual nodes in the tree (can be constructed on top of an event-driven parser)

Much quasi-religious argument has occurred about this dichotomy, but each approach has its merits. Like so many other real-world problems, XML processing may have vastly different requirements, and thus different approaches may be best for different situations.

Event-driven Parsers

The event-driven model should be quite familiar to programmers of modern GUI interfaces and operating systems. In this case, the XML parser executes a call-back to the application for each component of the XML data: element (with attributes), character data, processing instructions, notation, or comments. It's up to the application to handle the XML data as it is provided via the call-backs – the XML parser does not maintain the element tree structure, or any of the data after it has been parsed. The event-driven method requires very modest system resources, even for extremely large documents; and because of its simple, low-level access to the structure of the XML data, provides great flexibility in handling the data within the XML application.

All major event-driven parsers support a standard API, called **SAX** (**Simple API for XML**), with two versions available: SAX1 and SAX2. This API was created by Members of the XML-DEV mailing list, led by David Megginson (author of Open Text's **Ælfred** parser). It has current implementations in Java, Perl, and Python, and will be discussed in depth in Chapter 12.

> *See also* http://www.megginson.com/SAX/index.html *for more information about SAX. The* ***Ælfred*** *parser is now available from Open Text at* http://www.opentext.com/microstar/.

Tree-based Parsers

One of the most widely used structures in software engineering is the simple hierarchical tree. All well-formed XML data is defined to be such a tree, and thus common and mature algorithms may be used to traverse the nodes of an XML document, search for content, and/or edit the document tree. These tree algorithms have the advantage of years of academic and commercial development.

XML parsers that use this approach generally conform to the W3C's Document Object Model (DOM). The DOM is a platform- and language-neutral interface that allows manipulation of tree-structured documents. On the other hand, the DOM tree must be built in memory, before the document can be manipulated – high-performance virtual memory support is imperative for larger documents! Once the tree is built, an application may access the DOM via a related API. See Chapter 11 for more details and programming examples.

> *See the W3C Technical Reports and Publications site at* http://www.w3.org/DOM/DOMTR/ *for more about the various DOM levels and specifications.*

Some Specific Parsers

The following is a sample of the numerous XML parsers available. In several cases, we've also shown more general XML resources that are associated with parser vendors.

IBM and Apache Software Foundation

IBM has developed numerous tools for processing XML data, including the XML Parser for Java (**XML4J**) and the XML Parser for C++ (**XML4C**). These are both validating XML parsers that provide both tree-structured (see next part of this section), and event-based access to the XML data. IBM donated early versions of these parsers to the Apache Software Foundation for the **Xerces-J** and **Xerces-C** projects. Things have come full-circle, and now IBM's current parsers are based upon the Apache projects' parsers. A significant feature of Xerces-J is its support of the 24th October 2000 draft of XML Schema (XML4J supports the 7th April 2000 draft).

- **IBM's XML4C** – http://alphaworks.ibm.com/tech/xml4c
- **IBM's XML4J** – http://alphaworks.ibm.com/tech/xml4j

- **Xerces-C** – http://xml.apache.org/xerces-c/index.html
- **Xerces-J** – http://xml.apache.org/xerces-j/index.html
- **XML tools from Apache** – http://xml.apache.org/
- **XML tools from alphaWorks** – http://www.alphaworks.ibm.com/tech/ (click on "XML")

Microsoft (MSXML, IE5)

Microsoft developed an early XML parser called **MSXML**, which was supplied as an add-on for IE4. Later, XML support was included as part of Internet Explorer 5 (IE5), using a different parser. In addition, the .NET Framework uses XML extensively as its data format, which may greatly hasten the adoption of XML. At the same time, it should be made clear that many aspects of XML have not yet made their way to final recommendation status. Microsoft has been working ahead of these standards and there may be differences between Microsoft's implementation and the formal W3C standards (particularly XML Schemas).

- **Internet Explorer** – http://www.microsoft.com/windows/ie/
- **MSXML 3.0** – http://msdn.microsoft.com/xml/general/xmlparser.asp
- **XML tools** – http://msdn.microsoft.com/xml/general/xmltools.asp

Mozilla (AOL-Netscape)

Prior to its purchase by AOL, Netscape has promised full XML 1.0 and XSL support in its next generation browser. It is still being built by the Mozilla.org open source project. The current version at time of editorial is Mozilla 0.8, and a look at the release notes shows that this is still very much cutting-edge software.

- **Mozilla releases** – http://www.mozilla.org/releases/

Oracle (XML Parser for Java)

Oracle has also developed numerous tools for processing XML data, including their own **XML Parser for Java (v1 and v2), XML Parser for C, XML Parser for C++, XML Parser for PL/SQL and related tools.** All of these parsers support both SAX and the DOM.

- **Oracle XML Parser for Java** – http://technet.oracle.com/tech/xml/parser_java2/
- **Oracle XML tools** – http://technet.oracle.com/tech/xml

Expat and XP

One of the earliest and most elegant examples of an event-driven parser is James Clark's **expat**, written in portable ANSI-C. Clark was the Technical Lead for the XML 1.0 REC, wrote some of the best SGML tools, and has written another XML parser in Java called **XP**. The expat parser is now being maintained as a SourceForge project, led by Clark Cooper. It is also available with C++ (**expatpp**), Perl (**XML::Parser**), Python (**Pyexpat**), and even Common Lisp (**xml.expat**) wrappers.

- **expat** (current, v1.95.1) – http://expat.sourceforge.net/
- **expat** (original, v1.2) – http://www.jclark.com/xml/expat.html
- **Pyexpat** (part of PyXML) – http://www.python.org/sigs/xml-sig/status.html
- **XML::Parser** – http://search.cpan.org/doc/COOPERCL/XML-Parser.2.30/Parser.pm

- **xml.expat** – ftp://lambda-codex.sourceforge.net/pub/lambda-codex/expat-1.0-beta.tgz
- **XP** – http://www.jclark.com/xml/xp/index.html

Parser Link Websites

Since there are so many XML tools now available, it is also worth looking at the following web sites for links to the latest parsers and other tools:

- **Free XML Tools** – http://www.garshol.priv.no/download/xmltools/cat_ix.html#SC_XML
- **OASIS** – http://www.oasis-open.org/cover/xml.html#xmlSoftware
- **PerfectXML** – http://www.perfectxml.com/toolsoft.asp?SoftCat=6
- **Sun** – http://java.sun.com/xml/
- **Web Developer's Virtual Library (WDVL)** – http://wdvl.com/Software/XML/parsers.html

Summary of XML Syntax

Before we put all of this together in our Invoice examples, let's quickly review the syntax we've learned so far.

The simple XML tag forms:

Example	Description
`<tagname>`	Element start-tag.
`</tagname>`	Element end-tag.
`<tagname attr="value">`	Element start-tag with attribute.
`<tagname/>`	Empty-element tag.
`<tagname attr1="value1" attr2='value2'/>`	Empty-element tag with two attributes, and using both string delimiters.

XML entity references:

Example	Description
`ʚ`	Character reference, using a decimal value (`666` in this example).
`Ω`	Character reference, using a hexadecimal value (`03A9` here).
`&entity_ref;`	Reference to a defined entity (such as a text macro or boilerplate string).

Special XML instructions and declarations:

Example	Description
`<!-- some text -->`	A comment.
`<?target string?>`	Processing Instruction (PI).
`<![CDATA[ text ]]>`	An unparsed Character Data (CDATA) section.

Examples: Simple Invoices

Throughout this book we will return to the **ToysCo** invoice application as a way to provide an ongoing illustration of various features of XML. Since we've only discussed basic XML syntax, the following examples are of necessity rather simple minded.

A paper invoice is a sales and shipping document that helps convey products from a vendor to a customer. It includes the customer's name and address, products ordered, payment information, etc. We will use a very simple data model. Initially, we will only use a few main objects (each in the form of an element):

- <Toysco> – the document element (just a place-holding container).
- A single <Customer> – the recipient of the invoice.
- A few <Invoice> and <InvoiceOrder> elements – the pivotal objects of this application.

Every invoice needs customer information. Instead of copying this information into every one of the customer's invoices, we will refer to a single <Customer> element via an identifier (customerID). Similarly, each invoice will refer to one or more <Product> elements via productID.

A <Customer> element includes name, address, phone numbers, and so forth. A <Product> element includes a name, description, price, and similar product information. An <Invoice> element refers to a <Customer>, and contains one or more <InvoiceOrder> elements, one for each <Product> ordered.

This <Toysco> example is located in Chapter_02_01.xml and is shown below:

```
<?xml version="1.0" encoding="utf-8" ?>
<Toysco>

   <Customer customerID="CU02">
      <Name>
         <FirstName>Buffy</FirstName>
         <LastName>Summers</LastName>
      </Name>
      <BillingAddress>
         <Street>1630 Matilda Drive</Street>
         <City>Sunnyvale</City>
         <State>CA</State>
         <Zip>94086</Zip>
         <Country>USA</Country>
      </BillingAddress>
```

```
      <ContactDetails>
         <Email>buffy@buffster.com</Email>
         <Phone phonetype="HOME">408/555-5555</Phone>
         <Phone phonetype="WORK">650/555-5555</Phone>
      </ContactDetails>
   </Customer>

   <Product productID="BL4123"
      name="Blood Ball"
      description="Pretend blood squirts out when bitten on" >
      <Price>40.00</Price>
      <Units>3</Units>
      <Stock>75</Stock>

   </Product>

   <Product productID="CV4533"
      name="Scrabble"
      description="The world&apos;s favorite word board game" >
      <Price>24.99</Price>
      <Units>1</Units>
      <Stock>31</Stock>
   </Product>

   <Product productID="SC4323"
      name="Chess"
      description="Beautiful ornate pieces and a dull cardboard chess board" >
      <Price>9.99</Price>
      <Units>1</Units>
      <Stock>45</Stock>
   </Product>

   <Invoice invoiceID="TC2787" customerID="CU02"
      date="2001-01-16"
      terms="Immediate"
      paid="true" >
      <InvoiceOrder productID="CV4533" units="1" />
      <InvoiceOrder productID="BL4123" units="10" />
   </Invoice>

</Toysco>
```

We have used a mixture of elements and attributes for different types of information. We put the customer data into a bunch of child elements because this is the sort of data that is likely to be transformed in a variety of ways, and elements offer some conveniences for this purpose. For instance, one part of the `<Customer>` element is used for mailing labels, bits of the customer's name might be used in "personalized" letters, and the entire element might find its way onto an invoice.

Numeric data, like an order or a price, is contained in elements. These can also then have attributes that describe the contained data, like a currency attribute for a price. This will allow us to validate the content more easily, using a controlled vocabulary for attributes like currency or units of measurement. In doing this, we've tried to distinguish between the real "nouns" (say, `<Price>` or `<Customer>` or `<Product>`) and descriptive "adjectives" (`currency`, `name`, etc.).

At the moment, the linkage between the `<Invoice>` and `<Customer>` elements is merely implied by the existence of a unique customer identifier attribute (`<Invoice ... customerID="CU02" >`). The `<InvoiceOrder>` empty elements and `<Product>` elements are connected in the same way with the `productID` attribute. Later, we'll show how to use some more advanced features of XML to validate and traverse this implied linkage – for now, just consider it a provocative placeholder. We used an empty element with attributes for `<InvoiceOrder>` because it is used strictly as a simple data point, which points to a container object (the `<Product>`), rather than being a container itself.

In the next chapter ("Advanced XML Syntax"), we will look at how XML Namespaces will allow us to make a distinction between a name attribute that describes an `<Item>` and the like-named attribute that refers to a person or company (`<Customer>` or `<Vendor>`).

Later, in Chapter 5 ("Validating XML: DTDs"), we will use a DTD to limit the various attributes to a limited set of values, and to ensure that our elements have the proper children and relationships to each other. Still later, we will do the same with XML Schema and some alternatives that provide even more extensive and rigorous validation. These will allow us to constrain the content of elements and attributes to specific data types (such as Boolean or integer), or specific ranges of values (such as an integer in the range 1 to 100, inclusive).

Summary

In this chapter, we've shown the basic syntax that is required for all XML data. We can create simple well-formed documents without any other knowledge or tools, but this wouldn't begin to take advantage of much of the power of XML.

For example, nothing in this basic syntax provides for the "HT" in HTML – hypertext. Improved linking syntax is a very important aspect of some of the XML extensions (such as XLink and XPath) that are discussed later in this book (see the "Navigating XML", "Linking/Hyperlinking XML", and "Querying XML" chapters (8, 10 and 16, respectively)).

The sharing of data is greatly enhanced by the use of Namespaces (see the next chapter, "Advanced XML Syntax"). These may be standard namespaces such as the XHTML namespace, or a specific agreement between organizations exchanging XML data.

In its simplest form, XML is a powerful medium of data exchange. When extended with DTDs or schemas, namespaces, linking, and stylesheets, XML is the basis for a new era of a much more powerful Internet. Coupled with Java or another portable language, XML will lead to many more widespread and portable computing applications.

3

More XML Syntax

In the last chapter, we looked at the basics of XML syntax. In this chapter, we'll look at some of the more subtle details of those basic structures (such as special attributes and entity expansion) and some other XML-based syntax specifications that extend the core of XML. We'll also look at the various specifications that serve as the basis for some of the implementation details of XML (such as Unicode).

We will discuss two XML-based syntax specifications from the W3C that are fundamental to advanced use of XML:

- *Namespaces in XML*, known as **XML Namespaces**.
- *XML Base*.

Although the popular view of the Internet seems to begin and end with the World Wide Web, the fact remains that the Internet is a much larger and older piece of technology than just XML, HTML, or HTTP. Although it was largely the US government and academia that built the early Internet, later development was largely the result of a semi-formal online technical process called the **Internet Engineering Task Force (IETF)**.

When the WWW made the transition from an academic project at CERN to mass consumption, an alternative development process was spawned in the form of the W3C. Although there is often active collaboration between the W3C and IETF, both organizations also continue to develop technical specifications from their own perspectives. Of course, there is considerable cross-fertilization and collaboration, so some IETF standards have been incorporated into and referenced from some W3C specifications.

Since internationalization is one of the key design requirements of XML, the use of the ISO/IEC 10646 (Unicode) characters was imperative. These character set standards will be discussed, and we will briefly look at the contributions from four other Internet and international standards organizations:

- International Organization for Standardization (**ISO**)
- Unicode, Inc.
- IETF
- Internet Assigned Numbers Authority (**IANA**)

Lastly, we will show how the use of XML Namespaces and XML Base can enhance our Invoice example documents with reusable and more maintainable components.

First, let's look at some of the advanced syntax and processing aspects of XML.

Advanced Processing Considerations

In the previous chapter, we glossed over some of the more esoteric details of XML syntax, and here we continue our look. These details include seldom-used features (the "Special Attributes" section) and parser details that can have an impact upon authors or users of XML documents (see the "Attribute Values Normalization" section, also below).

Special Attributes

The XML 1.0 REC has defined a pair of attributes with special meaning:

- `xml:lang`
- `xml:space`

These attributes can be used to pass content and formatting signals to an XML application (such as a browser), by the XML document author or generating software. Both make use of the XML Namespace syntax, that is, a namespace prefix ("`xml`"), followed by a colon ("`:`"), and then the attribute name ("`space`" or "`lang`"). Even if Namespaces are not used, these are valid names (the prohibition against names beginning with "xml" doesn't apply since these are part of XML). We'll learn more about Namespaces later in this chapter.

xml:lang Attribute

This attribute exists because of the XML design goal of internationalization. The use of Unicode provides a standard method of *encoding* the characters used by a given human language – Unicode is mostly silent about the *rendering* of the text (though there are some special display characters and the "BIDI" algorithm used to render bi-directional Semitic text; as well as cues for composite Asian characters). There are several other language-specific considerations: sorting order of characters and symbols; how to delimit words for full-text indexing; spell checking; hyphenation; and gender-specific pronouns or phrases.

> **The `xml:lang` attribute specifies the human language used in the associated XML data, just as the encoding parameter of the XML Declaration specifies the character encoding used to represent that language.**

The `xml:lang` attribute values are constrained to use one of the following basic formats:

- A two-letter ISO 639 language code.
- A two-letter ISO 639 language code followed by a three-letter ISO 3166 country code.
- A two-letter ISO 639 language code followed by one or more sub-tags, which usually describe a dialect, a regional variation, or different written forms of a language.
- A registered IANA language tag ("`I-`" or "`i-`", followed by a one to eight character IANA language name).
- An unregistered ("user") IANA language tag ("`X-`" or "`x-`", followed by a string that does *not* correspond to a registered ISO language code or IANA language tag).

The following examples include two or three each of the different forms of the ISO language code:

```
fr
en
en-US
en-GB
en-cockney
no-bokmaal
no-nynorsk
az-arabic
az-cyrillic
```

French (`fr`) and English (`en`) are the common or standard versions of the language, with sub-tags for specific national versions of English (`GB` and `US`) or a regional dialect (`en-cockney`). There are two commonly used versions of Norwegian, and Azerbaijani can be written in either Arabic or Cyrillic script.

IANA language tags can be registered or ungregistered, beginning with an "`I-`" or an "`X-`" respectively:

```
I-navajo
i-klingon
X-Inverse-My
```

Registered tags, such as those for the language of the Diné or the invented language Klingon, are often temporary (many such tags are replaced with standard ISO 639 codes). Unregistered tags are intended for private use, and as such, will never become part of the IANA or ISO language lists.

The value of the `xml:lang` attribute is not just applied to the element including the attribute; it also applies to all child elements and attributes of that element. This isn't at all consistent with XML's general treatment of attributes, but this deviation is formally specified.

There is a strong tradition in the Internet community to use lower-case letters for language codes, and upper-case letters for country codes. Even though these attribute values are *not case-sensitive* (unlike most XML names), it would be best to adhere to this custom (remember the XML design goal of the easy use of existing Internet protocols).

The following XML snippet illustrates a few possibilities:

```
<example>
   <song xml:lang="de">
      <title>Sagt mir wo die Blumen sind</title>
```

```
        <lyrics>...</lyrics>
        <question>
           Welche Farbe Blumen magst Du am liebsten?
        </question>
        <question xml:lang="en-GB">
           What is your favourite colour of flower?
        </question>
        <question xml:lang="en-US">
           What is your favorite color of flower?
        </question>
        <question xml:lang="X-Inverse-My">
           What flower is your color?
        </question>
     </song>
  </example>
```

Since the `xml:lang` attribute applies to its own element and its children, the content of the `<lyrics>` element and the first `<question>` element are presumed to be in Deutsch (German). Those children with their own `xml:lang` attributes override the initial designation. In this example, an application (or stylesheet) could use the `xml:lang` attribute to decide what `<question>` to present, based upon some user language configuration setting.

There is no obligation on the application to pay any attention to the `xml:lang` attribute. However, this attribute can be very useful when styling XML data, and it is likely that the `xml:lang` attribute will become an essential feature of most internationalized XML documents.

xml:space Attribute

This attribute exists to allow the XML document author (or generating software) to tell an application that it should preserve all whitespace, instead of relying on the application's implicit behavior. Content such as programming source code or poetry often imparts significance to whitespace, which therefore should not be cavalierly discarded. Another example of this behavior is the HTML `<pre>` element, used to preserve text formatting.

As with the `xml:lang` attribute, the value of the `xml:space` attribute is applied to its associated element and all of its children – not just to the element with this attribute. For example, we might use this attribute to describe some source code contained within an XML element:

```
<code xml:space='preserve' >
   for (i = 0; i &lt; imax; i++)
   {
      do_something ();
   }
</code>
```

The `xml:space` attribute has two valid values:

- `preserve` – An application should preserve all whitespace within specified elements.
- `default` – Merely affirms that the applications' default processing is acceptable.

A non-validating parser can't enforce this restriction, so the use of this attribute then becomes application-specific. Unfortunately, there is no obligation for the application to do anything in response to this signal – there is no formal XML requirement that this attribute be honored, so it is unclear whether it will really be of much value. The argument can also be made that this sort of processing hint is more the domain of stylesheets (see also Chapter 9, "Transforming XML").

Since we've just looked at a few of XMLs special attributes, now is probably a good time to look at the processing of attribute *values* in greater detail.

Attribute Value Normalization

Every XML parser is responsible for normalizing attribute values *before* validating or passing to the application (we'll discuss validation starting from Chapter 5, "XML Validation: DTDs"). Non-validating parsers do *not* necessarily provide the same normalized attribute value to the application as validating parsers, as the two types differ in their handling of whitespace.

> **Attribute value normalization is more than a detail of parser implementation. Since validating and non-validating parsers may legitimately handle this process differently, the XML application must not rely upon significant whitespace in attribute values.**

For the sake of illustration, assume that there have been several entities declared with the following replacement text (we'll discuss the actual syntax of these DTD declarations in Chapter 5):

Entity Name	Replacement Text (in quotes)
`copy`	`'©'`
`nbsp`	`' '`
`ent1`	`'&ent1x;'`
`ent1x`	`'{   text   }'`

We will begin with the following un-normalized attribute value, where the three plain space characters have been underlined, and the other whitespace characters are represented by symbols. A § character represents a horizontal tab (`#x0009`), ¶ is used for a carriage-return (`#x000D`), and ¬ is a line-feed (`#x000A`) character:

```
attvalue = "__e.g._§&copy;§&ent1;_¶¬"
```

First, all whitespace is normalized as described in the last chapter: all CRLF pairs (`#x000D#x000A`), and individual CR or LF characters are replaced with a single LF (`#x000A`) character:

```
attvalue = "__e.g._§&copy;§&ent1;_¬"
```

Then comes the recursive step, where all remaining characters are normalized following these rules:

- A character reference (in the form `�` or `�`) is converted to the actual character.
- An entity reference causes a recursion of this entire step using the entity replacement text.
- All horizontal tab HT (`#x0009`), LF (`#x000A`) characters are replaced with a single space character.
- All other characters are simply copied, as is.

Replacing the HT and LF characters with spaces, we get:

```
attvalue = "__e.g.__&copy;_&ent1;__"
```

The first entity reference (`©`) is expanded, becomes the character reference "`©`" and then the actual "©" character:

```
attvalue = "__e.g.__©_&ent1;__"
```

The next entity reference (`&ent1;`) is also expanded, this time through another entity reference to *its* replacement text:

```
attvalue = "__e.g.__©_{__text__}__"
```

If the attribute value has been declared as simple CDATA, one more normalization step is applied – both leading and trailing whitespace is stripped, and multiple whitespace characters are replaced with a single space character:

```
attvalue = "e.g._©_{_text_}"
```

Non-validating parsers *should* always assume that all attribute values are CDATA and strip whitespace, but this is *not* a required behavior.

Notice the differences between the last two lines of this example – an application might receive the normalized attribute value in either of these two forms, depending on the type of attribute and/or parser. This difference can cause problems when exchanging XML data, unless all parties use validating parsers or attach no significance to whitespace in attribute values.

Let's turn our attention to the standards that underlie XML.

Use of Existing Standards

Although there may sometimes be overlap, or even competition, between it, and other technical specifications organizations, the W3C has wisely taken advantage of existing international standards and de facto Internet standards whenever possible.

> *Strictly speaking, "Standards" (big "S") come from national standards bodies and the ISO. The de facto IETF standards (little "s") that define the Internet are called "Requests for Comments" (RFCs), and those of the W3C are called "Recommendations" (or "RECs" for short). So, when the word "standard" is used in this book, we mean it in the generic sense, rather than the legalistic sense.*

We'll take a brief look at some important reference terminology pertaining to the W3C's documents, and then we'll outline the various IANA, IETF, ISO/IEC, and Unicode standards that are used for XML.

XML 1.0 References

There are two kinds of references to other specifications in the W3C's documents:

- "**Normative**" – The specification or code list in the reference is a critical part of the W3C document (such as the use of Unicode in XML).

- "**Other**" or "**Non-normative**" – The more typical sort of reference, which is useful in understanding the basis of the W3C document (such as academic papers about regular languages), or something which is a useful addition to the W3C document but isn't considered an integral part (such as URIs, URLs, or URNs).

The first sort of reference is obviously critical to both understanding a given W3C specification, and processing data that conforms to it. We will look at several such references from the XML 1.0 REC in detail later in this chapter. Many other XML-related specifications also depend upon these standards, so these sections will be useful background for various chapters within this book.

Normative References

There are six standards (two big "S" and four little "s") relating to XML 1.0 (the last four are essentially different versions of the XML character set). For further information, see the "References" section at the end of the chapter:

- **ISO/IEC 10646** – *ISO/IEC 10646-1993 (E).*
- **ISO/IEC 10646-1** – *ISO/IEC 10646-1:2000 (E).*
- **Unicode 2.0** – *The Unicode Standard, Version 2.0.*
- **Unicode 3.0** – *The Unicode Standard, Version 3.0.*
- **IETF Language Tags** – *RFC 1766.*
- **IANA Character Set Names** – *Official Names for Character Sets.*

Note that two of these (ISO/IEC 10646-1 and Unicode 3.0) were among the additions to the Second Edition of XML 1.0, updating the earlier references. In fact, there are now provisions within the XML 1.0 REC to allow such ongoing updates to these and some of the other normative references, without needing to change the text of the actual XML specification. On the other hand, two normative references from the original REC were demoted to the "Other References" section in the Second Edition (namely ISO 639 and ISO 3166, see the next section). The text that was related to these in the XML 1.0 REC was also removed.

Other (Non-normative) References

These standards either affected the design of XML, or are used in XML for specific values within attributes. We will look at them in individual sections, organized by their associated standards organization – ISO/IEC, Unicode, the IETF, and the IANA. See the "References" section at the end of this chapter for more details:

- **ISO/IEC**
  - **SGML** – ISO 8879:1986 (E)
  - **Web SGML** – ISO 8879:1986 TC2
  - **HyTime** – ISO/IEC 10744-1992 (E)
  - **ISO 639 Language Codes** – ISO 639:1988 (E)
  - **ISO 3166 Country Codes** – ISO 3166-1:1997 (E)
- **Others**
  - **UTF-8** – *RFC 2279*
  - **UTF-16** – *RFC 2781*

- **URI** - *RFC 2396*
- **URL** - *RFC 1738*
- **Relative URLs** - RFC *1808*
- **IPv6 Addresses in URLs** - IETF *RFC 2732*
- **URN** - *RFC 2141*
- **MIME types for XML** - *RFC 2376*
- **IANA Language Tags** - IANA *Registry of Language Tags*

We'll now take a more detailed look at these related non-W3C standards.

ISO

The **International Organization for Standardization** (**ISO**) is a consortium of various national standards bodies and international organizations, such as the United Nations. The ISO's scope is any technical standard, *except* those for electrical and electronic engineering, which are the responsibility of the International Engineering Consortium (IEC).

> *The general websites for these organizations are:* http://www.iso.ch *(ISO) and* http://www.iec.org *(IEC).*

We'll look at the one normative XML reference (the ISO/IEC 10646 character set), and briefly visit several other related references to ISO standards.

ISO/IEC 10646 - Universal Character Set (UCS)

Unicode is probably better known than ISO/IEC 10641, due to its origins as an American business consortium's de facto "standard". Strictly speaking, Unicode tracks the "real" international standard: ISO/IEC 10646. However, the ISO's reluctance to publish these international standards on the international WWW has inhibited access by many programmers, who can get almost any information they might need regarding Unicode or RFCs, free and online. Also, Microsoft's Windows NT provided Unicode support, *not* support for the ISO/IEC standard – Java is also based upon Unicode, rather than 10646.

> *ISO/IEC 10646* – ISO/IEC 10646-1993 (E). Information technology – Universal Multiple-Octet Coded Character Set (UCS) – Part 1: Architectures and Basic Multilingual Plane *[1993]. This standard has been replaced by: ISO/IEC 10646-1* – ISO/IEC 10646-1:2000 (E). Information technology – Universal Multiple-Octet Coded Character Set (UCS) -- Part 1: Architectures and Basic Multilingual Plane *[2000]* – http://www.iso.ch/cate/d29819.html *(order the official standard on paper).*

> *For a comparison of the ISO 10646 standards and Unicode, see* http://www.usenix.org/publications/login/standards/38.labonte.html.

Not all ISO standards have another "standard" counterpart, such as Unicode. Language and country codes remain the domain of the ISO, although these are maintained by organizations like the United Nations and the U.S. Library of Congress – both of which are willing to publish these code-lists on the WWW for free and widespread use.

ISO 639 Language Codes

We will discuss the syntax of these tags in the *Language Tags (RFC 3066 & 1766)* sections. It is the actual code lists that are maintained by the ISO (or more precisely the US Library of Congress, in this case).

> ***ISO 639 Language Codes*** – ISO 639:1988 (E). Code for the representation of names of languages *[1988] – Online code lists for both 639-1 and 639-2 are available from the Library of Congress at* http://lcweb.loc.gov/standards/iso639-2/termcodes.html*, and an overview of the standard is at* http://lcweb.loc.gov/standards/iso639-2/langhome.html. *If you must have the "official" standard on paper, it can be ordered at* http://www.iso.ch/cate/d4766.html.

Although XML 1.0 originally specified the older two-character language codes (ISO 639-1), there is a transition underway to the newer three-character codes (as defined in ISO 639-2). In fact, the Second Edition of the XML 1.0 REC mentions the pending change, and implies that XML will specify the newer codes in the future.

All new XML data should use the three-character language codes whenever possible.

ISO 3166 Country Codes

As you might expect, ISO 3166 Country Codes are used to label the countries of the world, using abbreviated terms from a controlled vocabulary. The two-character codes are maintained by the **Deutsches Institut für Normung** (**DIN**), and the three-character codes are maintained (and widely used) by the **United Nations**.

> ***ISO 3166 Country Codes*** – ISO 3166-1:1997 (E). Codes for the representation of names of countries and their subdivisions – Part 1: Country codes. *[2000] – Online code lists are at* http://www.din.de/gremien/nas/nabd/iso3166ma/codlstp1/en_listp1.html *(the 2-character "Internet" codes) or* http://www.un.org/Depts/unsd/methods/m49alpha.htm *(the new 3-character codes). Use* http://www.iso.ch/cate/d24591.html *to order the official standard on paper.*

As with ISO 639, there is an ongoing transition from two- to three-character codes. The former are still widely used for Internet domain addresses (such as: bbc.co.uk, and www.iso.ch), and thus will continue to be used for some time.

The three-character codes are widely used in computer *and* real world applications – broadcasts of the Olympics or the World Cup identify national teams using these codes, and the oval national-origin plates on motor vehicles are another example. Except for specific Internet-related or legacy applications, the newer three-character language codes should be used whenever possible.

Other Markup Standards

SGML (ISO 8879) and Web SGML (For Compatibility Issues)

XML (including DTDs) is a subset of SGML. Therefore, any well-formed XML data can be processed with SGML tools. DTDs are inherited from SGML, though XML DTDs are more limited than their ancestors.

Web SGML is a formal Annex to ISO 8879. It corrects some errors and resolves some issues that were raised by the use of SGML on the WWW (though it does extend to all applications of SGML).

SGML – ISO 8879:1986 (E). Information processing – Text and Office Systems – Standard Generalized Markup Language (SGML). *[1986-10-15]* – http://www.iso.ch/cate/d16387.html *(paper version). A good introduction to SGML is available at* http://etext.virginia.edu/bin/tei-tocs?div=DIV1&id=SG.

Web SGML – ISO 8879:1986 TC2. Information Technology – Document Description and Processing Languages. *[1998]* – http://www.sgmlsource.com/8879rev/n0029.htm.

Much like XML with its related specifications, SGML has been extended by other standards, such as **DSSSL** (**Document Style Semantics and Specification Language**) and HyTime.

HyTime (ISO/IEC 10744)

HyTime is the Hypermedia/Time-based Structuring Language, an ISO/IEC standard that is now in its second edition. It is an application of SGML, for information markup as required by hypertext and multimedia applications (including synchronization of multimedia resources such as video, audio, and images).

HyTime – ISO/IEC 10744:1997 Information Technology – Hypermedia/Time-based Structuring Language (HyTime) *[1992, 1996] – the all too rare online version at* http://www.ornl.gov/sgml/wg8/docs/n1920/html/n1920.html *– to order the paper version, go to* http://www.iso.ch/cate/d29303.html.

Although XML does *not* rely upon HyTime, the concepts developed for this SGML application do apply to the design of XML vocabularies and data models.

Now that we've briefly discussed the XML-related ISO standards, let's look at the most fundamental normative reference in XML, the Unicode character set.

Unicode

The grand goal of the Unicode consortium is to provide a "universal character set" that includes all of the world's languages, alphabets and scripts. Unicode 1.0 was published in 1991, followed by version 2.0, which formed the basis for the original XML 1.0 Recommendation. The current version is 3.0.1 (published in August 2000), and is the basis for XML 1.0 Second Edition.

Unicode 3.0 – The Unicode Standard, Version 3.0 *[2000-02-11]* – http://www.unicode.org/unicode/standard/standard.html*, with an associated online edition:* http://www.unicode.org/unicode/uni2book/u2.html*, and the book: ISBN 0-201-61633-5. The latest revision (documentation changes only – no new characters) notes are at* http://www.unicode.org/unicode/standard/versions/Unicode3.0.1.html.

Unicode 2.0 – The Unicode Standard, Version 2.0 *[1996-09] – Replaced by Unicode 3.0, but still available in book form: ISBN 0-201-48345-9.*

As of February 2001, most of the world's languages have Unicode representation(s) for their writing systems. There are about a dozen current languages, and several dozen archaic or historic languages (including Mayan, Linear B, and Old Persian Cuneiform) that are currently unsupported. Sadly for *Star Trek* enthusiasts, the addition of Klingon characters to Unicode remains "under investigation".

As with other normative references in the XML 1.0 REC, the text of the REC provides that changes to Unicode will be reflected in XML 1.0 – any XML processor must accept any characters within the specified ranges. See the "*Unicode for XML*" section in the previous chapter for details.

Character Encodings

Unicode was originally designed as a simple set of 16-bit scalar values, since this would include most of the special symbols or characters needed for any modern language. However, the needs of scholars and historians, coupled with the dynamic nature of ideographic languages, demanded more space. Unicode has added the **surrogate pairs** (never called surrogate characters) to accommodate future expansion. These pairs of 16-bit values are used to represent an additional 1,048,576 characters.

> **Unicode identifies characters using numeric values that correspond to those of the ISO/IEC 10646 Universal Character Set (UCS).**

Both Java and Microsoft's Windows NT use 16-bit Unicode characters for their default character sets.

There are several acceptable ways of storing these numbers. The XML design goal of widespread network use demands that various encoding methods be allowed. By specification, all XML parsers must at least support the UTF-8, and UTF-16 encodings. Although these encodings have been defined by the IETF in RFC 2279 (UTF-8) and RFC 2781 (UTF-16), the Unicode documentation of these remains the definitive version.

UTF-8

The UTF-8 encoding is widely used in various Internet standards and protocols and a great deal of XML data, because it allows 7-bit US-ASCII characters to appear without any modification. However, UTF-8 requires 2 to 4 bytes (each within the range of 80_{16} to FD_{16}) to encode all the other Unicode characters.

See Chapter 3; Section 3.8 (Transformations) *of the Online Unicode Standard* http://www.unicode.org/unicode/uni2book/ch03.pdf *for more details.*

This encoding is wonderful for predominately ASCII text, but is not that nice for the rest of the world. Given this inefficiency of UTF-8 for non-ASCII data, it isn't a very good choice for truly international use. However, it does avoid issues of internal numeric representations that can plague the 16- and 32-bit encodings.

UTF-16

The UTF-16 encoding is the simplest, storing 16-bit characters in one of the two traditional ways (little-endian or big-endian). Any character value from `0` to `FFFF` is represented directly as 16-bit integers. Those in the range from `10000` to `10FFFF` are represented by surrogate pairs. Characters with values greater than `10FFFF` cannot be encoded in UTF-16.

UCS-4

The main concerns about UTF-8 and UTF-16 comes from East Asia, where four bytes may already be required to represent a single character (as in UTF-8 or surrogate pairs). In those circumstances, the UCS-4 encoding has the advantage of programming simplicity, and thus this is a very popular encoding in Asia. However, for most European languages the use of this encoding doubles (or quadruples!) the storage space required by each individual character, so it remains much less popular in Europe and the Americas.

Byte-order Marks

The first two bytes of any XML data encoded in UTF-16 are required to be the Unicode character U+`FEFF`, called the **ZERO WIDTH NO-BREAK SPACE** character. When used in this context, the character is also known as the **Byte-order Mark** (**BOM**). It is used to differentiate between the little- and big-endian versions of UTF-16. The BOM is the signal that one of the two UTF-16 encodings is being used (since the values $\texttt{FE}_{16}$ and $\texttt{FF}_{16}$ may never appear in UTF-8 data).

To preserve this signal, Unicode specifically does not assign any character with the value U+FFFE. It is also important to note that the U+FEFF character may also be used anywhere else within the XML data. If so, it must be interpreted as the ZERO WIDTH NO-BREAK SPACE character, and not a BOM.

Character Encoding Auto-Detection

The XML Declaration and its `encoding` attribute must always use US-ASCII characters; so that it's possible for an XML parser to reliably auto-detect an XML document's encoding, or at least get close enough to read the declaration for the explicit encoding information. This can mitigate the effects of erroneous or unreliable encoding information at the operating system or transport-protocol level.

> **Best Practice: Always use an XML Declaration with the version number and an explicit character encoding declaration.**

Any XML data that does not use UTF-8 or UTF-16 *must* begin with an XML Declaration that includes the `encoding` attribute. The first five characters of this declaration must always be "`<?xml`" (followed by one or more whitespace characters). Therefore, some Unicode encodings can be detected from signature values in the first two or four bytes of the data stream.

In the absence of one of these patterns or an explicit XML Declaration, XML data is assumed to be UTF-8. This may cause serious problems if the data is actually another encoding, or even fragmented or corrupted. This constitutes yet another argument for always using an XML Declaration, even though it isn't strictly required.

Now let's look at the largest source of XML-related standards and specifications, the IETF.

IETF

The IETF is the ad hoc organization that evolved to develop almost all aspects of the Internet. The mechanism for this distributed development is the publishing of Requests for Comments (RFCs) by the Internet Society.

> *Almost any of these RFCs may be viewed on the WWW using a URL of the form:* 'http://www.ietf.org/rfc/rfcNNNN.txt ", *where* 'NNNN " *is the 4-digit RFC number (using leading zeros if necessary). The list of all RFCs is available at* http://www.ietf.org/rfc.html.

One of the RFCs in this section (RFC 3066, Language Tags) is a normative reference for the XML 1.0 REC, while the rest are informational or non-integral components of XML.

Language Tags (RFCs 3066 & 1766)

Both of these RFCs describe the *syntax* of tags that are used to describe textual data as representing a specific human language (computer "languages" are explicitly excluded, sorry HAL). Lists of the actual tag strings are maintained by the ISO (see the *ISO* section), and the IANA (see "IANA" section).

> ***IETF Language Tags*** – RFC 3066: Tags for the Identification of Languages *[2001-01]* – http://www.ietf.org/rfc/rfc3066.txt. *This replaces the RFC of the same name that is cited in XML 1.0,* RFC 1766 *[1995-03]* – http://www.ietf.org/rfc/rfc1766.txt.

A language tag is comprised of one or more parts. All tags include at least one alphabetic string of 1 to 8 ASCII characters ("A" to "Z", or "a" to "z"). There may optionally be one or more additional subtags that are also 1 to 8 ASCII characters, and which may also include the ASCII numeric digits ("0" to "9"). If multiple subtags are used, they must be separated by the ASCII hyphen ("-"). No whitespace or other characters are permitted in these tags, and they are *not* case-sensitive.

See the earlier "xml:lang" attribute section for examples of valid IEO 639 language tags in the RFC 3066 format.

We'll touch on the IETF's descriptions of the UTF-8 and UTF-16 encodings, and then move on to the ISO standards that are a significant part of XML.

UTF-8 and UTF-16

When the RFC for UTF-8 was published in 1998, it was intended to become an Internet standard. Yet the RFC for UTF-16, published in 2000, is explicitly *not* intended to be a standard. It is labeled "Informational" only, and it defers to the Unicode and ISO/IEC 10646 standards for the formal definition of the UTF-16 encoding.

> *UTF-8* – RFC 2279: UTF-8, a transformation format of ISO 10646 *[1998-01]* – http://www.ietf.org/rfc/rfc2279.txt
>
> *UTF-16* – RFC 2781: UTF-16, an encoding of ISO 10646 *[2000-02]* – http://www.ietf.org/rfc/rfc2781.txt

It seems safe to view the earlier document in the same light as the later one, so we will leave the discussion of these encodings to the *ISO* and *Unicode* sections.

MIME Types for XML

A great deal of XML data is transmitted by means other than HTTP, such as File Transfer Protocol (FTP) or an Internet mail protocol (like SMTP). When mail protocols are used for such transfers, the data is typically contained in a MIME (Multipurpose Internet Mail Extensions) envelope. These envelopes require a label for the type of data within, in order to be able to preserve message integrity during the various intermediate-processing steps (MIME user agents).

> ***MIME types for XML*** – RFC 3023: XML Media Types *[2001-01]* – http://www.ietf.org/rfc/rfc3023.txt. *This replaces* RFC 2376 *[1998-07]* – http://www.ietf.org/rfc/rfc2376.txt

There are five new MIME types for XML documents and data:

- `text/xml`
- `application/xml`
- `text/xml-external-parsed-entity`
- `application/xml-external-parsed-entity`
- `application/xml-dtd`

In theory, the first two types are for well-formed XML data, with `text/xml` generally used for XML documents readable by a casual human user, while `application/xml` is for system-oriented XML data, such as XML-RPC or SOAP messages. In practice, most XML data should use `application/xml`, as we will see in a moment.

The next two types should be used for XML external parsed entities, with the same distinction between the `text/` and `application/` types. The `application/xml-dtd` type should only be used for external DTD subsets or external parameter entities (these DTD components will all be discussed in detail in Chapter 5, "Validating XML: DTDs"). Since DTDs are not well-formed XML data, the first four MIME types must never be used for this type.

All these MIME types allow an optional, but strongly recommended, "`charset`" parameter to describe the character encoding used in the MIME message. For example, a common XML media type is:

```
application/xml; charset=utf-8
```

`UTF-8` is the best choice for maximum interoperability since it may be sent over 8-bit clean transport without base64 encoding. Encoding is not required for binary clean transports (like HTTP). Of course, anything but `US-ASCII` must be encoded in base64 or quoted-printable on 7-bit transports.

> **The `application/xml` type should be used for most XML data, particularly that transferred via MIME.**

The most important distinction between the `text/xml` and `application/xml` types concerns their handling by MIME user agents. Agents that do not explicitly support `text/xml` will treat it as `text/plain`. This may cause a serious loss of data integrity for any XML data that isn't US-ASCII, if the character encoding isn't explicitly specified as recommended.

URIs, URLs, and URNs

Several RFCs, written over a period of five years have defined and refined the specification for **Uniform Resource Identifiers (URIs)**.

URI – RFC 2396: Uniform Resource Identifiers (URI): Generic Syntax *[1998-08]* – http://www.ietf.org/rfc/rfc2396.txt – *this updates URLs as defined in RFCs 1738 and 1808, is amended by RFC 2732, and refers to RFC 2141*

URL – RFC 1738: Uniform Resource Locators (URL) *[1994-12]* – http://www.ietf.org/rfc/rfc1738.txt

Relative URLs – RFC 1808: Relative Uniform Resource Locators *[1995-06]* – http://www.ietf.org/rfc/rfc1808.txt

IPv6 Addresses in URLs – RFC 2732: Format for Literal IPv6 Addresses in URLs *[1999-12]* – http://www.ietf.org/rfc/rfc2732.txt.

URN – RFC 2141: URN Syntax *[1997-05]* – http://www.ietf.org/rfc/rfc2141.txt

There are two subsets of URIs, one concrete, and the other abstract:

- **Uniform Resource Locator (URL)** – a concrete network resource locator
- **Universal Resource Name (URN)** – an abstract name

URLs are familiar to almost everyone who has ever used a web browser, but we will look at some of the interesting implications of the more generalized URIs and URNs.

Character Escape Mechanism

Since the physical syntax of these identifiers is limited to US-ASCII characters, we can encode other characters that may be useful within these strings. Any 7- or 8-bit binary value can be encoded in a three-character string, beginning with the percent character (`%`), and followed by a 2-digit hexadecimal number (xx), corresponding to the value to be escaped:

```
%xx
```

The arbitrary string "`a|b\50%`" would be encoded like this:

```
a%7Cb%5C50%25
```

While there are different restrictions upon which characters are permissible for a given URI/URN/URL string or substring, all three use this same character escape mechanism.

URIs

URIs are defined in RFC 2396. Since they are more generic than URLs, this RFC supersedes RFCs 1738 (URL) and 1808 (Relative URLs).

> **A URI may identify an abstract resource, a physical resource, or both.**

These are all represented as character strings. Since these specifications were designed for maximum interoperability, they all use US-ASCII characters, so when we mention letters or numbers in this section, we mean plain ASCII rather than XML's more extensive Unicode character set.

Different types of resource identifiers can be handled despite different access mechanisms; new types of identifiers may be added without disturbing existing schemes, and identifiers may be reused in different contexts.

A URI can be transcribed from one medium to another – it can appear on a computer display, a cocktail napkin, or be spoken over the radio. The use of US-ASCII characters increases the probability that the URI can easily be typed on any keyboard. When possible, meaningful components are used to make the URI easier for a person to remember, such as the use of the "at" sign (`@`) in e-mail addresses.

URI Syntax

All upper- and lower-case letters, numeric digits, and the following punctuation marks are valid URI characters:

```
-_.!~*'()
```

The following characters *may* be allowed within an URI, but are *reserved* for special purposes (some of which will be discussed in this section):

```
;/?:@&=+$,
```

The following characters are excluded from URIs:

```
<>"{}|\^[]`
```

The first three characters (<>") cannot be used within URIs, since they are often used as delimiters around the URI in both text and protocol headers. The remaining characters are excluded because they may be used as delimiters, or may be modified during transport.

Two characters have special meanings within a URI:

```
#%
```

The # character is used as the URI fragment identifier (see below), and the % character is used for escaped characters (see the previous section).

URIs are comprised of two major parts:

```
scheme-name:scheme-specific-part
```

The `scheme-name` is a string that begins with a letter, followed by any combination of letters, numeric digits, plus (+), period (.), and/or hyphen (-) characters. These names are *not* case-sensitive. A single colon (:) is used as a separator between the two parts of the URI. The `scheme-specific-part` is also a string, the syntax of which depends upon the specific named scheme.

Some well-known URI schemes are:

- `file` – System-specific file names (such as `file:///c:\windows\fonts\arial.fon`).
- `ftp` – File Transfer Protocol (like `ftp://ftp.is.co.za/rfc/rfc2141.txt`).
- `http` – Hypertext Transfer Protocol (the typical web address: `http://www.wrox.com/Books/Books.asp?section=1`).
- `mailto` – An e-mail address (an address like `mailto:errata@wrox.com`, *not* a "send an e-mail to..." action).
- `news` – A USENET newsgroup (such as `news:comp.text.sgml`).
- `telnet` – Interactive remote system access (for example, `telnet://melvyl.ucop.edu/`).
- `urn` – A Universal Resource Name (URN), such as the one used to identify Microsoft's XDR schema: `urn:schemas-microsoft-com:xml-data`.

A URI may have a `path` component in the scheme-specific portion. If so, it has a hierarchical nature, and its levels are separated using the slash (/) character. Although some file systems use this same character for their own hierarchies, this should not be taken to imply any specific mapping between URIs and file systems.

The following is a complete URI that illustrates all these components, and will even take us to a list of useful XML books from Wrox Press:

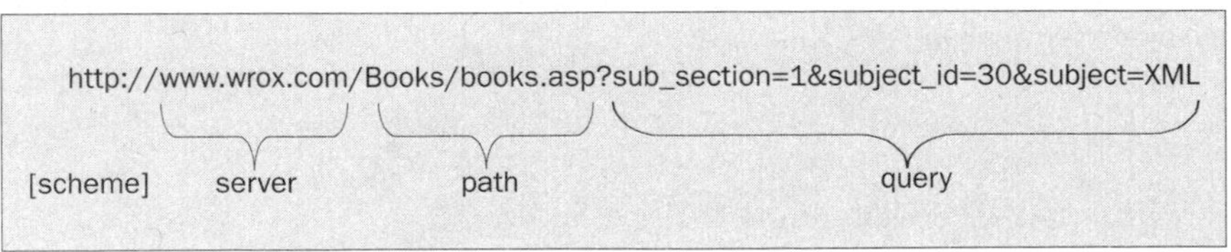

URI References

The term "**URI reference**" denotes the common usage of a URI in an XML document, written on paper, or keyed into a browser. It may be absolute or relative, and may include additional information attached after a fragment identifier. An absolute reference is a reference to a resource without regard to the context of the identifier. Conversely, a relative URI refers to a resource by the difference, within a hierarchical namespace, between the current context and an absolute identifier.

> **The actual URI that results from a URI reference includes only the absolute URI – a relative reference must first be resolved to its absolute form, and any information after the fragment identifier must be removed.**

Absolute URIs are distinguishable from relative URIs because the former will have a scheme name, whereas relative URIs inherit their scheme from the base URI. A relative URI can inherit the server and portions of the path components of its base URI.

A relative URI is meaningless unless there exists an absolute "base URI". A base URI can be established in one of four ways, in order of precedence:

- Base URI is embedded within content (for example, using the `xml:base` attribute that we will discuss in the *XML Base* section)
- Use base URI of encapsulating entity (file / document / message)
- Use URI that was used to retrieve the encapsulating entity
- An application-dependent base URI

For example, using the familiar HTML hyperlink syntax:

```
<head><base href='http://www.wrox.com' /></head>
<body>
   <a href='http://www.wrox.com/index.asp'>An absolute reference</a>
   <a href='#index'>
      A reference within the current page (fragment indentifier)
   </a>
   <a href='images/logo.png'>
      A relative reference within a tree of resources, using above 'base'
   </a>
   <a href='here:now/eat.html'>An invalid relative reference</a>
   <a name='index' />
</body>
```

The first hyperlink is to a specific and absolute location (a different web page). The second is a fragment identifier that refers to a location named "`index`" within the current page. The third relies upon a location for the image called `logo.png` that is relative to the specified `<base>` address. The fourth is an invalid relative reference because of the colon – this URI would be interpreted as using the mythic "`here:`" scheme with a path of "`now/eat.html`".

Let's now look briefly at the two subsets of URIs: URLs and URNs.

URLs

URLs describe a concrete network "location" and are used to access resources on that network.

URL syntax is nearly identical to that of URIs, although since URLs are an older standard, they are slightly more permissive concerning certain characters. URL references can be either absolute or relative, and most of the schemes mentioned in the URI section imply the use of URLs (the obvious exception being the "`urn:`" scheme). For the sake of present and future interoperability, it is best to limit URLs to the URI syntax as described in the preceding section.

Numeric literal IP addresses (IPv4 and IPv6) may be used in URLs, instead of the more familiar domain names. IPv4 addresses in a URL require no special delimiters, for example:

```
http://138.80.11.31:80/index.html
```

To avoid problems with delimiter characters, IPv6 addresses are simply enclosed within a pair of square brackets:

```
http://[FEDC:BA98:7654:3210:FEDC:BA98:7654:3210]/index.html
```

Although URLs are probably the most familiar form of URIs, the abstract form has the potential to become even more ubiquitous, since it can be useful even without a computer.

URNs

URNs are persistent, globally unique, location-independent, resource *names* as defined in RFC 2141. They are intended to provide an easy mapping from more generic namespaces into URN-space.

It is critical to remember that these resources do *not* need to exist on the Internet, or on any other computer for that matter: a URN can refer to a box of biscuits or a printed book. Universal Product Codes (UPCs) or International Standard Book Numbers (ISBNs), could also be described using URNs.

The basic syntax of a URN is:

```
urn:NID:NSS
```

In the above example, `NID` is the **Namespace Identifier** (**NID**), `NSS` is the **Namespace Specific String** (**NSS**), and the leading string literal ("`urn`") is *not* case-sensitive. The NID and NSS must be separated by a colon (`:`) and no embedded whitespace is allowed. Like the more generic URIs, URN syntax also provides an encoding scheme that works with most existing protocols and equipment.

The NID is also *not* case-sensitive, and its value will be used to determine the syntax of the NSS. The NID is a string of 1 to 32 characters, which begins with a letter or number, and is continued with these and/or hyphens (-). An NID may *not* be the string "`urn`", so as to avoid confusion with the URN prefix string.

The NSS may vary depending upon the NID, but the canonical form is a string of one or more characters, with certain restrictions as to the valid characters. All letters (upper- and lower-case), numeric digits, and the following punctuation marks are valid URN characters:

```
()+,-.:=@;$_!*'
```

It is permissible to create an NSS that uses other characters than those shown above, but these strings *must* be translated into the canonical form before being used with Internet protocols or other applications. This translation requires the non-URN characters to first be encoded into UTF-8, and then the resulting bytes are encoded again using the "%xx" character escape mechanism.

These are the key IETF syntax specifications that are used with XML 1.0, so let's now look at some Internet code lists that are also used in XML.

IANA

The IANA serves as the registry for numerous Internet codes, names, and numbers. The XML 1.0 REC uses two of the registered lists, those for character set names and language identifiers.

Character Set Names

As we saw in the previous chapter, the second attribute of the XML Declaration (encoding) is used to signal the character set encoding of the subsequent data. The value of this attribute must conform to a controlled vocabulary of character set names, as registered by the IANA.

> ***IANA Character Set Names*** – Official Names for Character Sets *[2000-10-30]* – ftp://ftp.isi.edu/in-notes/iana/assignments/character-sets.

For example, the following declaration would be used to indicate that the subsequent XML data is encoded in the Taiwan version of Chinese:

```
<?xml version="1.0" encoding="Big5"?>
```

These **encoding names** may be up to 40 characters long, and must themselves be expressed using the printable characters of US-ASCII (0x20 to 0x7E). These names are *not* case-sensitive, that is, the name "UTF-8" is equivalent to "Utf-8" or "utf-8".

Remember that an XML parser is only required to support the UTF-16 and UTF-8 encodings, so if we need to handle any of the others we must select our tools accordingly. Some tools, like Oracle's offerings, support numerous encodings, while others only handle the required pair. Thus, most XML data is likely to be converted to the UTF-16 or UTF-8 encodings, especially if universal XML tool support is desirable.

Any data in regular 7-bit US-ASCII can be used unmodified, since it is a proper subset of UTF-8.

Language Tags

IANA language tags provide a set of values for the special xml:lang attribute (which we'll also discuss later in this chapter), or any other attributes that are intended to convey the name of a human language.

> **IANA Language Tags** – Registry of Language Tags *[2001-01-25]* – http://www.isi.edu/in-notes/iana/assignments/languages *(index of registrations).*

This IANA registry conforms to the syntax rules of RFCs 3066 and 1766 (Language Tags), and supplements the larger list of ISO 639 language codes (see those sections for more details). Once a language tag is accepted by the ISO, it is removed from the IANA list – which often functions as the receiving station for new codes.

There is also a provision for language tags that will likely not become part of the ISO 639 list, but rather remain listed only by the IANA. These tags always begin with "`i-`" or "`I-`", followed by the descriptive name or abbreviation. At the present time, there are only 12 such tags listed, with the following three representing the range of the list from minority languages (Luxembourgish and the Diné of the Southwestern USA) to an invented, but actually spoken, language (Klingon):

```
i-lux
I-navajo
i-klingon
```

This IANA list will probably remain a short one, as these tags often migrate to the ISO 639 list. See the "*Special Attributes*" section earlier in this chapter for examples of the use of these tags in the `xml:lang` attribute.

Now that we've discussed the details of XML 1.0 syntax and its prerequisite standards, it's time to start looking at some optional syntax extensions, starting with some additional rules pertaining to the names of elements and attributes.

Namespaces in XML

Our Invoice example at the end of the previous chapter uses several different sorts of data: name and address for the `<Customer>` elements; inventory control for `<Product>`s and `<Invoice>`s; and even Internet components, such as website names and e-mail addresses. These vocabularies might have been developed separately, and yet we want to use them together in one Invoice application.

We could attempt to negotiate non-overlapping names between the different vocabulary developers, modifying attribute names as needed. Or, we could just prefix the element context to each attribute name (such as `vendorname` or `Vendor.name`), but this clearly becomes cumbersome rather quickly. Neither of these approaches would work very well when it comes to element names, which might have similar meanings, but have different structures or include different content.

This naming problem becomes even more noticeable when we try to share XML vocabularies and documents that have been written by others, or embed excerpts of XML data from others into our own. A name like `Name` could be used in almost every vocabulary, with diverse meanings covering all the possible definitions of the word (the name of a customer, the name of a product that the customer is buying, the name of the shipping company that is to deliver said product to the customer).

The W3C has provided a way to resolve naming conflicts with a Recommendation that was published shortly after the original XML 1.0 Recommendation.

> Namespaces in XML *[Recommendation 1999-01-14]* – http://www.w3.org/TR/REC-xml-names.

This relatively simple and straightforward specification relies upon only three other specifications, yet there has been much confusion about some of the implications of XML Namespaces. Hopefully, we will be able to clear up some of the misconceptions about this important extension to basic XML in the following section.

What is an XML Namespace?

An XML Namespace is a concept: a named collection of names. Period! It is *not* a DTD reference, nor a pointer to an XML schema. A namespace does not even need to exist as a physical or network resource.

> **An XML Namespace is simply a group of names, usually with a related purpose or context, where the *group* has a globally unique name (the "namespace name"). This is often ensured by using a domain name (from Internet DNS) as the first part of the namespace name.**

Unfortunately, numerous myths have arisen about XML Namespaces. Some myths are due to the differences between XML Namespaces and the more widely-understood namespaces in the context of programming languages, others have resulted from misreading the W3C specification, and yet others reflect unsatisfied desires about shared DTDs and other deficiencies of XML 1.0 syntax and processing. Even the statements at the beginning of this section could be misleading if the reader insists on assuming that a "group of names" implies a tangible list.

It is important to understand that XML Namespaces are *not*:

- Resources that exist anywhere (other than conceptually).
- A part of XML 1.0 syntax.
- Directly related to DTDs or XML Schemas.
- A redefinition of XML data validity.
- Something with any semantic meaning.
- An object, an interface, or something with a specific internal structure.

Given these statements of what an XML Namespace is *not*, let us look at what they are, and how they work within the context of existing XML 1.0 syntax and Internet standards.

How Are XML Names Made Unique?

The *Namespaces in XML* REC provides a method of creating globally unique names (and we mean this literally, as in the WWW), as long as the namespace is made universally known, and people stick to using it (although this can never be totally guaranteed). We could simply apply a contextual prefix to name every name we wanted to use (say `Invoice.Customer.Name`), but this would just move the problem of differentiating names in shared vocabularies to a different level – we would still need a "name prefix authority" to ensure non-overlapping name prefixes. The W3C wisely decided to avoid a whole new name infrastructure by specifying that prefixes for XML names could be based upon the Internet's existing Domain Name System (DNS), using URIs.

Take the following XML data snippet from the example at the end of the previous chapter:

```
<Customer>
   <Name>
      <FirstName> ... </FirstName>
      <LastName> ... </LastName>
   </Name>
</Customer>
...
<Product productID='SC4323' hire='false' >
   <Name>Chess set</Name>
      ...
</Product>
```

Here, the <Name> element is used in two different contexts, once as the name of a person or company (the customer), and again as the name of a thing (the product). These two uses also have completely different structures – one is a container for some child elements and the other is a simple character data element.

We could just change one of the conflicting element type names, for example:

```
<Product productID='SC4323' hire='false' >
   <ProductName>Chess set</ProductName>
   ...
</Product>
```

This would be fine if we were working in isolation, but sooner or later we will want to use some other XML data in conjunction with our own, and this situation would likely recur. In that case, we might not be able to change any names in either the external data or our own.

Given that we would like to be able to use these overlapping names, we would need to be able to differentiate between them. We could use a domain name in URI syntax as a part of our names, but this would violate XML name restrictions. There are many characters that are legal in URIs that cannot be used in XML names, which means that the use of raw URIs is not possible without changing XML 1.0 syntax rules.

Maybe we could use some characters (say the curly brackets) that aren't permitted in either URIs or XML names as special name separators, like so:

```
<Product productID='SC4323' hire='false' >
  <{http://www.wrox.com/Invoice}Name>Chess set
  </{http://www.wrox.com/Invoice}Name>
  ...
</Product>
```

This is, in fact, a common way of representing examples of XML Namespace-prefixed names in technical articles. But this would once again break the rules for XML names, and we really don't want to modify the XML 1.0 REC to accommodate namespaces.

Namespace Name and Prefix

The solution the W3C devised is to create an *alias* for the URI that would be restricted to legal XML name characters, and restrict the use of the colon (":") character in XML names to be the namespace delimiter. Remember that URIs can be in the form of a concrete URL or an abstract URN.

> *The XML 1.0 REC does* allow *the use of colons in XML names, but includes the caution that the pending* Namespaces in XML *specification had reserved this character for its own use.*

This URI is called the **namespace name**, which is intended to be unique and persistent. We will associate each with an XML-legal name (say "Per" and "Inv"), known as the **namespace prefix**. We can then use the prefixes as needed in our XML data:

```
<Toysco xmlns:Per='urn:ProXML2e:www.wrox.com/Persons'
        xmlns:Inv='urn:ProXML2e:www.wrox.com/Invoices' >

   <Customer customerID='CU02' >
      <Per:Name>
         <Per:FirstName> ... </Per:FirstName>
         <Per:LastName> ... </Per:LastName>
```

```
        </Per:Name>
    </Customer>
    ...
    <Product productID='SC4323' hire='false' >
        <Inv:Name>Chess set</Inv:Name>
          ...
    </Product>
        ...
</Toysco>
```

The prefixes are associated with URIs in the two attributes of the `<Toysco>` element that begin with "`xmlns:`":

- **`Per`** is the prefix for the urn:ProXML2e:www.wrox.com/Persons namespace name.
- **`Inv`** is the prefix for urn:ProXML2e:www.wrox.com/Invoices.

We will discuss the specifics of these declarations in the next section. The use of the URN form for the two URIs in this example is intentionally provocative, a reminder that namespaces are about *names*, not specific addresses or resources.

URNs would seem to be ideal for XML Namespaces, since they even include a defined "Namespace Identifier" field (the bit between the two colons). Unfortunately, since there is no central URN name authority to register these identifiers (like DNS for URLs), there is no way to guarantee that a URN is unique.

The use of concrete URIs (that is, URLs) for namespace names is another cause for confusion about XML Namespaces. We have become so used to retrieving web pages using the URL form of URIs that we forget that, strictly speaking, they are just names and it is actually HTTP that provides for the retrieval of web pages. The widespread misuse of URIs like mailto:you@foo.com to automatically launch e-mail clients also contributes to this confusion between names and protocols or resources.

Qualified Names

The W3C refers these prefixed names as **qualified names** (usually abbreviated as **QName**). A QName consists of two parts: the namespace prefix, (`per` or `inv`) as shown in the example above; and the **local part**, which is the simple element name that we've been using all along (`Name`).

A qualified name will not match an unqualified name that uses the same local part. For example, `<Per:Name>` would not be the same as `<Name>`. Therefore, if a qualified name is used in a start-tag (such as `<Per:Name>`), it must also be used in the closing end-tag (`</Per:Name>`).

> **XML Namespaces are for the use of the XML parser, and as such, the prefix is only a placeholder that is *not* available to the application. If qualified names are to be used outside that context, the namespace *name* must be used to construct a unique name.**

The use of namespaces and qualified names makes the construction of XSLT and XPath expressions, for stylesheets and such, much more complicated (as we will see in Chapter 9, "Transforming XML"). Structured editing of XML data and manipulation of element types using the DOM are also both greatly complicated by the use of namespaces (more about this later).

Let's look at the association of a namespace name with a prefix in more detail.

Declaring Namespaces

Although we have conceptually associated a pair of namespace prefixes with a couple of URNs in our example above, how does this really work?

Namespaces in XML provides a mechanism to associate namespace URIs and prefixes, known as a **namespace declaration**, using yet another special attribute called "xmlns". We declared two namespaces in our ongoing example as follows:

```
<Toysco xmlns:Per='urn:ProXML2e:www.wrox.com/Persons'
        xmlns:Inv='urn:ProXML2e:www.wrox.com/Invoices' >
 ...
</Toysco>
```

Note that the use of the leading "xml" string in an attribute name *is* legal here – it is reserved for just such use (officially assigned by the W3C). This restriction also ensures that no one can use "xmlns" as their own namespace prefix.

This example also illustrates some key aspects of namespace declarations:

- There may be multiple namespace declarations in a single element – "xmlns:Per" is not the same attribute name as "xmlns:Item", so XML 1.0 attribute name rules are not violated.
- These declarations are backwards compatible with XML 1.0 parsers that are not aware of XML Namespaces. These attributes are ignored, but the two different prefixes ensure that each element still has a unique name.

You may have noticed that we have not used namespace prefixes for any of the other element names in our earlier examples. Strictly speaking, these elements do not belong to any namespace. This is fine if we're using the data in a single application, but leaves the potential name collision problem if we are sharing our data with others.

We *could* apply the Inv prefix to all the other elements and some attributes:

```
<Inv:Toysco xmlns:Per='urn:ProXML2e:www.wrox.com/Persons'
        xmlns:Inv='urn:ProXML2e:www.wrox.com/Invoices' >

  <Inv:Customer customerID='CU02' >
    <Per:Name>
      <Per:FirstName> ... </Per:FirstName>
      <Per:LastName> ... </Per:LastName>
    </Per:Name>
  </Inv:Customer>
   ...
  <Inv:Product Inv:productID='SC4323' Inv:hire='false' >
    <Inv:Name>Chess set</Inv:Name>
     ...
  </Inv:Product>
   ...
</Inv:Toysco>
```

This example illustrates some other aspects of namespaces:

- A namespace declaration applies to the element in which it is declared – the `Inv` prefix can be applied to the `<Toysco>` element, as well as its children.
- Unqualified attribute names (like "`customerID`") do not explicitly belong to any namespace.
- Qualified attribute names (like "`productID`") belong to the associated namespace.

It's easy to see that requiring the use of a namespace prefix on every single element and attribute name becomes rather tedious, particularly when most of the names in a document belong to the same namespace. There is a solution to this inconvenience, as we will see in the next section.

Default Namespaces

A namespace declaration need not include a namespace prefix. In this case, all element (but *not* attribute) names would be assumed to belong to this single unnamed namespace, known as the **default namespace**. Since there is only one namespace, it is not necessary to use a namespace prefix with every element name within the `<Toysco>` element, only those that belong to other namespaces.

In our ongoing example, we can keep using the "`Inv`" namespace, but we can also make it the default namespace with an additional declaration that omits the colon and namespace prefix from the `xmlns` attribute:

```
<Toysco xmlns:Per='urn:ProXML2e:www.wrox.com/Persons'
        xmlns='urn:ProXML2e:www.wrox.com/Invoices'
        xmlns:Inv='urn:ProXML2e:www.wrox.com/Invoices' >
  ...
</Toysco>
```

This eliminates the need to use prefixed names for all of the elements within the `<Toysco>` data; they now belong to the declared default namespace. However, attributes are not explicitly part of any default namespace. We will look at this in more detail in the "Namespaces and Attributes" section below.

> **A default namespace must be declared, and it then applies to any subsequent element name without an explicit prefix.**

Of course, there may only be one default namespace in any given context, but that does not preclude the use of multiple default namespaces in a single document.

In these examples, we have stated that we could declare each namespace once at the document element, and it would apply to the entire document. This is true enough, but let's look at the scope of XML Namespaces in more detail. This will open the door to multiple default namespaces and limited use of namespaces.

Scope

The value of the `xmlns` (or `xmlns:`*`prefix`*) attribute is explicitly considered to apply to both the element where it is specified *and* to all of its child elements, unless overridden by another namespace declaration using the same namespace prefix.

A very common practice with XML Namespaces uses this rule of inheritance and declares all the namespaces that are to apply to the XML data in the document element. The scope of such namespace declarations is thus the entire element tree of that document. In our ongoing Invoice example, we did indeed declare the two namespaces in the document element.

There are advantages to collecting all the namespace declarations at the beginning of the XML data: both easier maintenance (for the author) and processing (for the parser). This is not unlike keeping all `#include` directives at the beginning of a C/C++ program.

Multiple Default Namespaces

If our XML data includes distinct sections of data that belong to different namespaces, we might want to use multiple default namespaces. This can be accomplished by overriding the original default namespace declaration. For example, say that we want to include XHTML descriptions within each invoice `<Product>` element, yet keep using the existing `Inv` default namespace. All our example code would remain unchanged, except for the `<Inv:Description>` element and its children:

```
<Toysco xmlns:Per='urn:ProXML2e:www.wrox.com/Persons'
        xmlns='urn:ProXML2e:www.wrox.com/Invoices'
        xmlns:Inv='urn:ProXML2e:www.wrox.com/Invoices' >

   <Customer customerID='CU02' >
      <Per:Name>
         <Per:FirstName> ... </Per:FirstName>
         <Per:LastName> ... </Per:LastName>
      </Per:Name>
   </Customer>
      ...
   <Product productID='SC4323' hire='false' >
      <Inv:Name>Chess set</Inv:Name>
      <Inv:Description xmlns='http://www.w3.org/1999/xhtml' >
         <html>
            <head><title>Toysco Product Description</title></head>
            <body>
            <h1>Toysco Chess set</h1>
               <p>
                  Beautiful ornate pieces, and an elegant inlaid board
               </p>
            </body>
         </html>
      </Inv:Description>
      <Units>1</Units>
       ...
   </Product>
      ...
</Toysco>
```

All the familiar HTML elements would be associated with the XHTML namespace, so we could use similar element names elsewhere in this example without any name conflicts.

Since namespace scope is always limited to the element containing the namespace declaration and its children, the default namespace would revert to the `Inv` namespace once the `<Inv:Description>` element is closed. Thus, the `<Units>` element is part of the `Inv` default namespace and doesn't require a prefix. However, the `<Description>` element now requires an explicit prefix to remain in the `Inv` namespace, instead of being considered part of the newly declared XHTML default namespace.

Similarly, we can disable the default namespace completely by using an empty attribute value in the default namespace declaration:

```
<Inv:Description xmlns="" >
   ...
</Inv:Description>
```

This change means that any unqualified element names within (and including) `<Description>` would then not belong to any default namespace. The element names outside of this scope would continue to belong to the previously declared default namespace (if any).

As we've noted several times, there are some differences between element and attribute names as they relate to XML Namespaces.

Namespaces & Attributes

There are several rules pertaining to the use of namespaces with attributes:

- No start-tag may contain two attributes with the same name, whether the attribute name is qualified or not (this is an extension of the XML 1.0 rule).
- No start-tag may contain two qualified attribute names with the same local part and different prefixes that resolve to the same namespace name (see the examples below).
- Attribute names may contain only zero or one colon (":") characters. If included, the colon will be interpreted to separate the namespace prefix from the local part of a qualified name.
- Some attribute values may be declared to be of a type that must be a legal XML name (see Chapter 5, "Validating XML: DTDs", for more about attribute types). Attributes of one of these types (`ID`, `IDREF`, `IDREFS`, `ENTITY`, `ENTITIES`, or `NOTATION`) may not use any colons within their values. However, unless a validating parser is used, this rule cannot be enforced.
- Default namespace declarations have no effect upon any attribute names.
- An unqualified attribute name does not *explicitly* belong to any namespace!

There is much confusion about this last item, since attributes *are* associated with their element's start-tags in XML processing (the DOM, XSLT, etc.). Furthermore, the non-normative Appendix A of *Namespaces in XML* describes "Namespace Partitions" and includes unqualified attribute names in the "Per-Element-Type" partition. This has often been misread as associating an attribute with its element's namespace.

In this otherwise well-formed example, two of the following attribute names are *not* legal:

```
<Document
   xmlns:n1='urn:example:some-names'
   xmlns:n2='urn:example:some-names' >

      <BadAttrs_XML_1.0 att='1' att='2' />
      <BadAttrs_Namespaces n1:att='1' n2:att='2' />
      <OkAttrs_Namespaces att='1' n2:att='2' />

</Document>
```

The first child element violates the XML 1.0 rule that attribute names must be unique. The second is not valid because both the "n1" and "n2" prefixes refer to the same URI. Yet the third is acceptable because "att" is an unqualified name and does not belong to any namespace, while "n2:att" is a qualified name belonging to the "urn:example:some-names" namespace. This example is also a reminder that a namespace name may be either kind of URI: a URL or a URN.

Summary: Namespaces

As we've seen, XML Namespaces are a powerful extension to basic XML 1.0 syntax. Namespaces allow the use of shared vocabularies without the worry of name collisions. As we have seen, they support intermixing of XML and XHTML data, provide a foundation for the use of advanced XML-related validation technologies (see chapter 6, "Introducing XML Schemas"), and the description of XML metadata (see chapter 22, "RDF").

XML Namespaces do *not* provide a locator for any tangible resources (such as schemas), do *not* have an implied structure or meaning, and do *not* affect the validation specified in XML 1.0 – they are simply a *conceptual* collection of unique names.

Unfortunately, XML Namespaces also do not work well with DTDs. Since DTDs do not understand qualified names, we would have to include the namespace prefix and colon within every declaration in the DTD. This could cause problems when mixing data from other namespaces, and most of the advantages of namespaces would be lost.

XML Namespaces are based upon URI references, and such references may be relative; we would like a way to specify a "base URI" for this purpose. The XML method of defining base URIs is known as XML Base (though ironically, we cannot use XML Base with XML Namespaces).

XML Base

One of the design considerations for XML has been interoperability with SGML, and to a limited extent, with certain key features of HTML. One of the HTML features that demands support in XML is linking (the very essence of the "HT" in "HTML"). XML's linking uses the XML Linking Language (XLink), which will be discussed in chapter 10, "Linking/Hyperlinking XML".

One of the basic concepts of HTML linking is the use of a "base URI" to allow relative links to external images, style sheets, etc. This is implemented in HTML using the <base> element. The XML Base specification uses the xml:base attribute to accomplish a similar result in XML. Although this new attribute was developed primarily to support XLink, it was done so in a modular fashion so that xml:base can be used in other specifications, such as the XML Infoset.

The XML Base specification has reached the status of Proposed Recommendation (one step before becoming a Candidate Recommendation).

> XML Base *[2000-12-20]* – http://www.w3.org/TR/xmlbase/.

XML Base relies upon both the XML 1.0 and Namespaces specifications.

Syntax

The basic syntax of the xml:base attribute is:

```
<element xml:base="base_URI"> ... </element>
```

As with XML namespace declarations and the two special attributes (xml:lang and xml:space), the value of xml:base is applied to all children of the element that includes the xml:base attribute. Once again, this is unlike the scope of most attributes in XML. Thus, including the xml:base attribute in the document element means that all elements within the document can use the value of this attribute. As with the other special attributes, any xml:base attribute may be overridden by a subsequent xml:base attribute, but only within that subsequent attribute's element and its children.

The following example shows how xml:base attributes may be nested to modify the base URI for different elements and their children:

```
<?xml version='1.0' encoding='utf-8' ?>
<Catalog xml:base='http://www.wrox.com/'>
   <Head>
      <Title>Some Books on Parade</Title>
      <Logo xml:base='/logos/'>
         <Image source='Wrox.png'>Wrox Press Ltd's logo</Image>
      </Logo>
      <Homepage>main.html</Homepage>
   </Head>
   <Body xml:base='/covers/'>
      <Book>
         <Title>Beginning XML</Title>
         <Cover><Image source='BegXML.png' />
      </Book>
      <Book>
         <Title>Professional XML</Title>
         <Cover><Image source='ProXML.png' />
      </Book>
   </Body>
</Catalog>
```

In the above example, we could use an XML Base-aware browser to link to a homepage and display PNG images from two different (hypothetical!) directories at the Wrox website, after resolving the relative URIs:

- The <Logo> image would be located at "http://www.wrox.com/logos/Wrox.png".
- The <Homepage> would be linked to at "http://www.wrox.com/main.html".
- The <Cover> images would be located at "http://www.wrox.com/covers/BegXML.png" and "http://www.wrox.com/covers/ProXML.png".

The scope of the first xml:base attribute (the one within <Catalog>) is the entire document. The second xml:base attribute only applies to the <Logo> element and its child <Image>. Once we move on to the <Homepage> element, we revert to the initial base URI. Then, the third xml:base covers the <Body> element and all its children.

Note that these are illustrative examples only – there is nothing in basic XML syntax to imbue meaning to any of these elements. We've just constructed some relative URIs, while respecting the rules of XML Base. For more concrete examples, see the XLink material in Chapter 10, "Linking/Hyperlinking".

Effect On Other XML Specifications

At the present time, only three XML-related specifications rely upon XML Base as one of their normative references: XLink, XML Infoset, and Canonical XML.

Other XML specifications have little or no connection with XML Base:

- XML 1.0 only uses URIs in Document Type Declarations which are outside the document element, and thus outside of the scope of an `xml:base` attribute.
- XML Namespaces use URIs, but they should *not* be resolved with respect to an `xml:base` attribute.
- XML Schema data types include a `uriReference` primitive datatype that should probably use XML Base, though this has not yet been done.
- XPath has no use for relative URI references, and thus no use for XML Base.
- XSLT uses base URIs in a way that is incompatible with XML Base.

Now that we've covered XML Namespaces and XML Base, let's revise our ongoing example to use these XML 1.0 extensions.

Example: An Invoice with Namespaces

We will use the "Toysco" example from the last chapter as a starting point. We'll add some XML Namespace declarations (like those we used as examples in that section of this chapter). We will also add a base URI and some `xml:lang` attributes.

> ***IE5 Note**: IE5 (v5.5) not only supports XML Namespaces, it requires them! The MSXML parser is no longer a conformant XML 1.0 parser, since it does not allow the use of names containing a colon unless there is an associated namespace declaration.*

The full version of this example is in `Chapter_03_01.xml`. For the sake of brevity, we will omit most of the element instances in this example:

```
<?xml version='1.0' encoding='utf-8'?>
<Toysco xml:base='http://www.wrox.com/ProXML2e/'
        xmlns:Addr='urn:ProXML2e:www.wrox.com/Addresses'
        xmlns:Inv='urn:ProXML2e:www.wrox.com/Invoices'
        xmlns:Per='urn:ProXML2e:www.wrox.com/Persons'
        xmlns='urn:ProXML2e:www.wrox.com/Invoices' >

  <Customer customerID='CU02'>
    <Per:Name>
      <Per:FirstName>Buffy</Per:FirstName>
      <Per:LastName>Summers</Per:LastName>
    </Per:Name>
    <Addr:BillingAddress>
      <Addr:Street>1630 Matilda Drive</Addr:Street>
      <Addr:City>Sunnyvale</Addr:City>
      <Addr:State>CA</Addr:State>
      <Addr:Zip>94086</Addr:Zip>
```

```
      <Addr:Country>USA</Addr:Country>
    </Addr:BillingAddress>
    <ContactDetails>
      <Email>buffy@buffster.com</Email>
      <Phone phonetype='HOME'>408/555-5555</Phone>
      <Phone phonetype='WORK'>650/555-5555</Phone>
    </ContactDetails>
  </Customer>

   ...

  <Product productID='CV4533' hire='false' picture='prod.CV4533.png' >
    <Inv:Name>Scrabble</Inv:Name>
    <Inv:Description xmlns='http://www.w3.org/1999/xhtml' xml:lang='en' >
      <html>
        <head><title>Toysco Product Description</title></head>
        <body>
          <h1>Toysco Chess set</h1>
          <p>The world&apos;s favorite word board game</p>
        </body>
      </html>
    </Inv:Description>
    <Price currency='USD'>24.99</Price>
    <Units>1</Units>
    <Stock>31</Stock>
  </Product>

  <Product productID='SC4323' hire='false' picture='prod.SC4323.png' >
    <Inv:Name>Chess set</Inv:Name>
    <Inv:Description xmlns='http://www.w3.org/1999/xhtml' xml:lang='en' >
      <html>
        <head><title>Toysco Product Description</title></head>
        <body>
          <h1>Toysco Chess set</h1>
          <p>Beautiful ornate pieces, and an elegant inlaid board</p>
        </body>
      </html>
    </Inv:Description>
    <Units>1</Units>
    <Price>9.99</Price>
    <Stock>45</Stock>
  </Product>

   ...

  <Invoice invoiceID='TC2787'
    customerID='CU02'
    date='2001-01-16'
    terms='Immediate'
    paid='true' >
    <InvoiceOrder productID='CV4533' units='1' />
    <InvoiceOrder productID='BL4123' units='10' />
  </Invoice>

</Toysco>
```

We added an `xml:base` attribute to the `<Toyco>` element to establish a base URI for the entire document. To illustrate the effect of this, we also added a new `picture` attribute to the `<Product>` element, which has a PNG image name that is relative to the base URI. An application handling this particular value might take advantage of this to locate the actual image file on Wrox's website.

We declared three namespaces in the document element start-tag, so they will apply to all elements within this entire document. We use the `Per` and `Inv` prefixes to ensure that the different `Name` elements will be handled differently. The `Addr` prefix is used for any data pertaining to a physical address.

The namespace that is named `urn:ProXML2e:www.wrox.com/Invoices` is also declared as the default namespace (except when it's overridden within the `<Inv:Description>` element), so all element names that don't have an explicit namespace prefix will be considered part of this namespace.

The other namespace is declared in instances of the `<Inv:Description>` elements to illustrate a limited-scope default namespace. This overrides the original default namespace, but only within the scope of these `<Inv:Description>` elements.

Summary

In this chapter, we've discussed some of the more obscure aspects of XML 1.0 syntax. We have now covered all of XML 1.0 as it relates to simple well-formed data. The only aspects of this specification that we haven't discussed are those related to Document Type Definitions (DTDs) – the subject of Chapter 5.

We looked at an extension of XML 1.0 syntax – XML Namespaces – that further constrains the syntax of element and attribute names.

We also looked at the XML Base attribute, which will be used in our discussions in the next chapter of the XML Information Set, and other XML-related specifications (in several later chapters).

Well-formed documents may be adequate for some applications, but this implies that any interpretation or validation of the data must be hard-coded in the XML application that handles the data. A more portable approach is to provide a second document that is used to validate the first (and any others of its general type). This validation document may be in the form of a DTD, or an XML Schema (see Chapters 5 and 6 respectively for details of these two forms of validation).

References

What follows below is an expanded version of the list of Normative and Non-normative references that we first met in the "Use of Existing Standards" section, to provide you with a quick reference to them, and further information.

Normative References

In this list, the names in **bold** are the common (but unofficial) terms for the standard, followed by its official name/title. The standards can all be found in full in the "*Normative References*" section at http://www.w3.org/TR/REC-xml:

- **ISO/IEC 10646** – *ISO/IEC 10646-1993 (E). Information technology -- Universal Multiple-Octet Coded Character Set (UCS) -- Part 1: Architectures and Basic Multilingual Plane.* Replaced by ISO/IEC 10646-1.

- **ISO/IEC 10646-1** – *ISO/IEC 10646-1:2000 (E). Information technology -- Universal Multiple-Octet Coded Character Set (UCS) -- Part 1: Architectures and Basic Multilingual Plane.* There is a pending update, which will be called ISO/IEC 10646-2.
- **Unicode 2.0** – *The Unicode Standard, Version 2.0.*
- **Unicode 3.0** – *The Unicode Standard, Version 3.0.*
- **IETF Language Tags** – *RFC 1766: Tags for the Identification of Languages.* Replaced by *RFC 3066: Tags for the Identification of Languages.*
- **IANA Character Set Names** – *Official Names for Character Sets.*

Non-normative References

These can be found in the "*Other References*" section at http://www.w3.org/TR/REC-xml:

ISO/IEC

- **SGML** – *ISO 8879:1986 (E). Information processing – Text and Office Systems – Standard Generalized Markup Language (SGML)*
- **Web SGML** – *ISO 8879:1986 TC2. Information technology – Document Description and Processing Languages*
- **HyTime** – *ISO/IEC 10744-1992 (E). Information technology – Hypermedia/Time-based Structuring Language (HyTime)*
- **ISO 639 Language Codes** – *ISO 639:1988 (E). Codes for the representation of names of languages*
- **ISO 3166 Country Codes** – *ISO 3166-1:1997 (E). Codes for the representation of names of countries and their subdivisions – Part 1: Country codes*

Others

- **UTF-8** – *RFC 2279: UTF-8, a transformation format of ISO 10646*
- **UTF-16** – *RFC 2781: UTF-16, an encoding of ISO 10646*
- **URI** – *RFC 2396: Uniform Resource Identifiers (URI): Generic Syntax*
- **URL** – *RFC 1738: Uniform Resource Locators (URL)*
- **Relative URLs** – *RFC 1808: Relative Uniform Resource Locators*
- **IPv6 Addresses in URLs** – IETF *RFC 2732: Format for Literal IPv6 Addresses in URLs*
- **URN** – *RFC 2141: URN Syntax*
- **MIME types for XML** – *RFC 2376: XML Media Types*; replaced by *RFC 3023: XML Media Types*
- **IANA Language Tags** – IANA *Registry of Language Tags*

4

The XML Information Set

As more XML-based technologies have been developed, there has been a divergence in some of the terms used to describe various components of XML data and processing. Slight deviations in dialect have created some confusion when describing aspects of XML, confusion that could develop into subtly different processing models and incompatible data and/or applications.

For example, the **document element**, as described by XML 1.0 is often called the **document root** or root element, yet these are not all the same thing. XPath refers to location paths and context nodes (see Chapter 8), while the DOM might refer to a `NamedNodeMap` or a `NodeList` (see Chapter 11). These aren't equivalent objects with different names, but these terms all relate to the hierarchical tree of XML data in a slightly different way. As new specifications are created, there is a tendency to also create new terms that fit within the new point of view.

The W3C has begun an effort to check the proliferation of terms that refer to the same or similar aspects of XML, called the **XML Information Set** (also known as the **XML Infoset**).

> **The XML Infoset is a set of consistent definitions for components of a well-formed XML document that need to be referred to in other XML-related specifications.**

The XML Infoset specification still has Working Draft status, which means more time before it can next progress to Proposed Recommendation status.

XML Information Set [2001-02-01] – http://www.w3.org/TR/xml-infoset/.

As with most XML-related specifications, XML Infoset relies upon some other specifications and standards, including the Second Edition of XML 1.0, Namespaces in XML and XML Base. We covered the details of these in Chapters 2 and 3.

What is the Information Set?

XML data has an Information Set if the data is well-formed *and* it conforms to the "Namespaces in XML" extension to the XML 1.0 syntax. The data does *not* need to be valid to have an Information Set. This set is comprised of a number of information items, which are abstract representations of certain parts of the XML data, each with an associated set of properties. These three terms are similar to the more generic terms *tree*, *node*, and *properties*. However, these new terms are used instead to avoid confusion with any other data models, in particular XPath and the DOM. Information items do *not* map directly to the nodes of either of these two XML-related specifications.

> **An Information Set only exists for well-formed XML data that also complies with the naming rules as extended by "Namespaces in XML". Validation is *not* required.**

Entity References

The information set is intended to describe XML data with its entity references already expanded, that is, the information items correspond to the replacement text of an entity reference, not the reference itself. Yet, there are several circumstances when entity expansion may not occur in well-formed XML data: an entity may be undeclared, an external entity may be irretrievable, or a non-validating parser may choose not to expand, or even read, external entity references.

Base URIs

Any information item that uses the base URI property must comply with the XML Base specification (see Chapter 3). The base URI that is used for the Infoset is the final URI after all redirection (if any) has been resolved.

Information Items

Seventeen types of information items have been defined:

- The Document
- Namespace
- Element
- Attribute
- Character
- Comment
- Processing Instruction
- CDATA Start Marker
- CDATA End Marker
- Internal Entity

- External Entity
- Unparsed Entity
- Unexpanded Entity Reference
- Entity Start Marker
- Entity End Marker
- Document Type Declaration
- Notation

This is *not* an exhaustive list of all conceivable information items – there presently doesn't appear to be one; it is merely the collection of those deemed useful for use in other specifications.

The Document Information Item

There is one and only one document information item in the information set. It corresponds to the entire XML document, and all other information items are accessed from its properties, either directly or indirectly.

The document information item has the following properties:

Property	Description
Children	A list of all top-level information items, in document order. This list contains exactly one element information item (for the document element), one PI information item for each PI outside the document element (in either the prolog or the epilog), one comment information item for each comment outside the document element. If a Document Type Declaration is present, there will be exactly one document type declaration information item. PIs and comments within the internal subset of a DTD (if any) are *not* included here.
Document entity	An entity information item that corresponds to the document entity.
Document element	An element information item that corresponds to the document element.
Notations	An *un*ordered set of notation information items, one for each notation declaration in a DTD.
Entities	An *un*ordered set of all internal, external, and unparsed entity information items, one for each general entity that has been declared in a DTD. This set will always include five information items for the five predefined markup protection entities (`lt`, `gt`, `amp`, `apos`, and `quot`).
Base URI	The base URI of the document entity, if known. If not, this property's value is Null.

Table continued on following page

Property	Description
Standalone	One of three values: `yes`, `no`, or null, depending on the value of the Standalone Document Declaration (or null if the SDD is absent).
Version	A string copied from the XML Declaration, or null if there is no XML Declaration.
(All declarations processed)	Strictly speaking, a signal, rather than a part of the Infoset. The signal is `true` if the parser has read the complete DTD; otherwise, it is `false` (as will be the case with many non-validating parsers). If `true`, a null value for a DTD-related declaration means that no such declaration was present. If the signal is `false`, such null values may instead reflect a declaration that was never read.

Namespace Information Items

There is one namespace information item for each namespace declaration in the XML data.

A namespace information item has the following properties:

Property	Description
Prefix	A string representing the namespace prefix defined in the associated namespace declaration, that is, the second part of an attribute name that begins with "`xmlns:`". If the declaration is for a default namespace (the attribute name is simply `xmlns`) then this property is an empty string.
Namespace name	The name of the declared namespace, that is, the URI that is the attribute value.

Element Information Items

There is an element information item for each element in the XML data. As with the well-formed XML data, there is one element information item for the document element, and all other element information items are children of that root information item.

An element information item has the following properties:

Property	Description
Namespace name	A string representing the name of the namespace, if the element belongs to a namespace. Otherwise, this property is null.
Local name	The local part of the element-type name.
Prefix	The namespace prefix of the element-type name, if any. If the element does not belong to a namespace, this property is an empty string.

Property	Description
Children	A list of all child information items, in document order, containing element, PI, unexpanded entity reference, character, and/or comment information items for each such item contained within this element. If its content includes an entity references, the list will include pairs of entity start and end markers. If there are any `CDATA` sections within the element, the list will include pairs of `CDATA` start and end markers. If the element is empty, so too is this list.
Attributes	An *un*ordered set of attribute information items, one for each of the element's attributes, whether specified or declared as defaults in a DTD, and *excluding* Namespace declarations (if any). If there are no attributes, this list is empty.
Namespace attributes	An *un*ordered set of attribute information items, one for each namespace declaration within this element's start-tag (or as provided by a default in a DTD). If no such declarations are present, this set is empty.
In-scope namespaces	An *un*ordered set of namespace information items, with one for each namespace that is in effect for this element. This set is never empty; it will always contain at least one namespace information item with the `xml` prefix.
Base URI	The base URI of the element, which may be inherited from the document entity, or may be null if no such URI is known.
Parent	The element information item, which is the parent of this element. If this element is the document element, its parent is the document information item.

Attribute Information Items

There is an attribute information item for each attribute, whether explicitly specified or defaulted, of each element in the XML data. These information items do include namespace declarations, but they are segregated from other attribute information items in the properties for the element information item.

An attribute information item has the following properties:

Property	Description
Namespace name	A string representing the name of the namespace, if the attribute belongs to a namespace. Otherwise, this property is null.
Local name	The local part of the attribute name.
Prefix	The namespace prefix of the attribute's element-type name, if any. If the element-type does not belong to a namespace, this property is an empty string.
Normalized value	The normalized attribute value.

Table continued on following page

Property	Description
Specified	A flag that is yes if the attribute was specified in the start-tag, or no, if the attribute was included as a DTD default.
Attribute type	The type of the attribute as specified in the DTD. The value may be one of the following: ID, IDREF, IDREFS, ENTITY, ENTITIES, NMTOKEN, NMTOKENS, NOTATION, CDATA, or ENUMERATION. If no declaration has been read for this attribute, this property is null.
Owner element	The element information item that contains this information item.

Character Information Items

There is one character information item for *each character* in the document's character data or within a CDATA section. This excludes any characters that were discarded due to end-of-line handling (see the section in Chapter 2).

A character information item has the following properties:

Property	Description
Character code	The hexadecimal value of the ISO 10646 (Unicode) character code, in the range #x0000 to #x10FFFF.
Element content whitespace	A flag that is yes if the character is whitespace appearing within element content, or no if it isn't such whitespace. If no DTD declaration was read for the containing element, this property is null.
Parent	The element information item that contains this information item.

Comment Information Items

There is one comment information item for each XML comment in the XML data.

A comment information item has the following properties:

Property	Description
Content	A string that contains the characters between comment delimiters ("<!--" and "-->").
Parent	The document, element, or document type declaration information item, which contains this information item.

Processing Instruction (PI) Information Items

There is one processing instruction (PI) information item for each PI in the XML data.

A PI information item has the following properties:

Property	Description
Target	A string that contains the target part of the PI (this must be a legal XML name).
Content	A string that contains the characters after the PI target (and excluding intervening whitespace) and before the closing delimiter ("?>"). If there is no content, this property is an empty string.
Base URI	The base URI of the PI, if known. If not, this property's value is null.
Parent	The document, element, or document type declaration information item, which contains this information item.

CDATA Start and End Marker Information Items

A CDATA start marker information item appears for each CDATA start delimiter ("<![CDATA[\") in the XML data. Likewise, a CDATA end marker information item appears for each CDATA end delimiter ("]]>").

These information items both have the following property:

Property	Description
Parent	The element information item that contains this information item.

Internal Entity Information Items

There is an internal entity information item for each internal general entity declared in the DTD. There are always at least five of these for the five predefined character entities.

An internal entity information item has the following properties:

Property	Description
Name	The name of the entity.
Content	The replacement text of the entity.

External Entity Information Items

There is an external entity information item for each external general entity declared in the DTD. There is always at least one external entity information item for the document entity.

An external entity information item has the following properties:

Property	Description
Name	The name of the entity. If this information item is for the document entity, this property is null.
System identifier	A string that contains the entity's system identifier.
Public identifier	A string that contains the entity's public identifier.
Base URI	The base URI of the entity. If the entity was not read, this property is null. If this information item is for the document entity, this property *may* be null.
Charset	The name of the entity's character encoding, derived from either the optional encoding declaration at the beginning of the entity, or from a MIME header. If the entity was not read, this property is null.

The system identifier, public identifier, and base URI properties may *be null if this information item is for the document entity. Otherwise, these properties may* not *be null if the entity was read.*

Unparsed Entity Information Items

There is an unparsed entity information item for each unparsed general entity declared in the DTD.

An unparsed general entity information item has the following properties:

Property	Description
Name	The name of the entity.
System identifier	A string that contains the entity's system identifier.
Public identifier	A string that contains the entity's public identifier. If none is declared, this property is null.
Notation	The notation information item associated with this entity.

Unexpanded Entity Reference Information Items

There is one unexpanded entity reference information item for each unexpanded external general entity reference. These placeholders may only be present when using a non-validating parser that does not read and expand external general entities.

An unexpanded entity reference information item has the following properties:

Property	Description
Name	The name of the entity being referenced.
Entity	The internal or external entity information item corresponding to this reference, if any. This property is null if no declaration was read for this entity.
Parent	The element information item, which contains this information item.

Entity Start and End Marker Information Items

An entity start marker information item appears at that point in an element's content just prior to the beginning of a general entity's replacement text (which is being included due to an entity reference), and an entity end marker information item appears after the end of the replacement text. These are *not* used with parameter entity references in the DTD.

These information items both have the following properties:

Property	Description
Entity	The entity information item referred to by the entity reference.
Parent	The element information item that contains this information item.

Document Type Declaration Information Item

If the XML data contains a document type declaration, there will be exactly one information item for the document type declaration in the Infoset. Any entities or notations that are declared within the DTD will appear as properties of the document information item, not this information item.

The information item for the document type declaration has the following properties:

Property	Description
System identifier	A string that contains the system identifier of the external DTD subset.
Public identifier	A string that contains the public identifier of the external DTD subset.
Children	A list containing the comment and PI information items representing the comments and PIs appearing in the DTD, in the original document order. All items from the internal DTD subset appear before those in the external subset.
Parent	This is always the document information item.

The system identifier and/or public identifier properties are null if the identifier is not present in the document type declaration.

Notation Information Items

There is one notation information item for each notation declared in the DTD.

A notation information item has the following properties:

Property	Description
Name	The name of the notation.
System identifier	A string that contains the system identifier of the notation.
Public identifier	A string that contains the public identifier of the notation.

The system identifier and/or public identifier properties are null if the identifier is not present in the notation declaration.

Summary

Since the XML Infoset is an abstract construct, there are many ways to implement this specification. Although we have described the Infoset in the context of a hierarchical tree for simplicity, it need not be presented in this fashion. Alternate representations could include (but aren't limited to) an event-based interface (like SAX) or a query-based interface. The fundamental requirement of this specification is that the various information items and their properties are made available to XML applications in some way or another.

Remember, though, that the XML Infoset is intended to provide information primarily to other specifications. Therefore, it is the specifications, not their implementations, which need to conform to the Infoset. To achieve conformance, the specification must:

- List all information items and properties needed for the specification
- Specify how unnecessary information items and properties are handled
- Note any aspects of XML data that are needed, but not specified in the Infoset
- Note any deviation from definitions in the Infoset (such deviations are strongly discouraged!)

Since the XML Infoset specification, as currently published, is *not* intended to be a comprehensive list of all *possible* information items, future changes can be anticipated. The current version includes XML 1.0, DTDs, and Namespaces; later versions will need to take into account XML Schemas (this may require a major expansion of the Infoset!), and other such extensions to basic XML 1.0 syntax.

In the next chapter, we will discuss DTDs, and the explanation should be made clearer because of an understanding of the Infoset.

5

Validating XML: DTDs

In the previous chapters, we discussed the basic rules of the XML syntax, how to construct properly nested, well-formed XML data, and the use of namespaces as a method of identifying individual XML vocabularies. Simple well-formed XML data *can* be exchanged, processed, and displayed using only this minimal set of syntax rules, but we will often want to ensure that this data conforms to some specific structure and ses of values.

In this chapter, we'll look at valid XML, and validation using **Document Type Definitions (DTDs)**. DTDs are a set of rules that define how XML data should be structured. Being able to define such rules will become more important as we exchange, process, and display XML in a wider environment, such as in business-to-business (B2B) or e-commerce systems. Using DTDs will allow us not only to determine that XML data follows some advanced syntax rules of XML 1.0, but also that the data follows our own rules regarding its content and structure.

We will discuss:

- Why we might need DTDs, and the benefits of using them
- How to write DTDs
- How to use and reuse DTDs

For illustrating the various DTD declarations and concepts, we'll create a Toysco DTD, using the same XML data as we used in the earlier syntax chapters. In later chapters, we'll use some different methods – XML Schemas and XDR Schemas – to describe this same vocabulary.

Why Validate XML?

Well-formed XML data is guaranteed to use proper XML syntax, and a properly nested (hierarchical) tree structure. This may be sufficient for relatively static internal applications, particularly if the XML data is computer-generated and/or computer-consumed. In this case, it's the responsibility of the applications using the data to perform any structural or content verification, error handling, and interpretation of the data. The XML structural information, and the logic to do this, is usually hard-coded separately within the sending and receiving applications, from a common specification. Therefore, any change to the XML data structure must be made in three places: the specification, and the sending and receiving applications.

This *can* be a high-performance approach to handling XML data in certain limited circumstances. For example, an internal corporate application might use well-formed XML as a data transfer mechanism between two different Relational Database Management Systems. The sending RDBMS would be assumed to generate good data. At the other end, the receiving RDBMS is likely to already have an input data verification feature, so any data validation could occur *after* the XML-to-DBMS translation step. There would be no need to re-validate the data while it was within the XML domain – in this limited case, well-formed XML would be sufficient for the data transfer.

However, when there's no formal description of XML data, it can be difficult to describe or modify the structure of that data, since its structure and content constraints are buried within the application code. Without the use of a formal description of our XML data, we're only using a fraction of the power of XML.

Data Needs Description and Validation

In addition to ensuring that XML data is well formed, many, if not most, XML applications will also need to ensure that the data is **valid XML**. To do this, we need to:

- Describe and validate the data structure, preferably in a rigorous and formal manner
- Communicate this data structure to others – both applications and people
- Constrain element content
- Constrain attribute types and values, and perhaps provide default values

These functions *could* be handled by specific code within a pair of cooperating applications and their accompanying documentation. However, in cases where the XML data is more widely shared, say between multiple applications or users, maintaining these functions in each application becomes an exponential nightmare. This is a problem common to most XML applications, so ideally we'd like to take a more standardized approach.

Separating the XML data description from individual applications allows all cooperating applications to share a single description of the data, known as the **XML vocabulary**. A group of XML documents that share a common XML vocabulary is known as a **document type**, and each individual document that conforms to a document type is a **document instance**.

> *This is similar to the basic principle of object-oriented ("OO") programming: objects are grouped and described as an object* ***class*** *(comparable to a document type); each individual object conforming to that class description is known as an* ***instance*** *of that object (comparable to the document instance).*

First, let's briefly describe what a DTD is, and how it is used to validate XML data.

Valid XML

As we've already seen, we can use an XML parser to ensure that an XML document is well formed. Many parsers, known as **validating parsers**, can also provide a more rigorous verification option to check that the content of the XML document is valid. This means that the parser itself can verify that the document conforms to the rules of a specific XML vocabulary. This validation is accomplished by comparing the content of the document with an associated template in the form of a DTD.

> **Valid XML data is well-formed data that also complies with syntax, structural, and other rules as defined in a Document Type Definition (DTD). XML Schemas can also be used for this purpose, as we will see in the next chapter.**

Although it's possible for an XML application to handle validation, there are some real advantages to using a validating parser and a DTD to handle this task. Multiple documents and applications can share DTDs. Having a central description of the XML data and a standardized validation method lets us move both data description and validation code out of numerous individual applications. The data description code becomes the DTD, and the validation code is already present in the validating XML parser. This greatly simplifies our application code, and therefore improves both performance and reliability.

Valid XML is also preferable to simple well-formed XML for most document-oriented data. Human authors can be guided (and restricted) by the structural and syntax constraints imposed by the DTD and validating parser. This prevents authors from creating documents that don't conform to exchange standards (the DTD), and can provide default values and structures to simplify the authoring process. The use of valid XML also simplifies writing programs to handle the data, since most of the validation chores are handled by the validating parser and DTD.

The Document Type Definition (DTD)

Document Type Definitions (DTDs) for XML are derived from the more complex DTDs that were used with SGML (XML's parent markup language). DTDs use a formal grammar to describe the structure and syntax of an XML document, including the permissible values for much of that document's content. These rules, called validity constraints, ensure that any XML data conforms to its associated DTD.

XML DTDs are described in sections 3 and 4 of the XML 1.0 Recommendation, available at http://www.w3.org/TR/REC-xml.

Since DTDs are part of the XML 1.0 specification, there is already widespread support for this method of data description and validation in XML parsers and other tools.

> **A DTD is a set of declarations which can be incorporated within XML data, or exist as a separate document. The DTD defines the rules that describe the structure and permissible content of the XML data. Only one DTD may be associated with a given XML document or data object.**

Although DTDs are *not* represented using well-formed XML, DTD declarations are superficially similar in syntax to XML: angle brackets delimit the declarations, and a special form of entity references may be used within DTDs. Comments within DTDs use the syntax identical to that of XML comments.

For example, the following excerpt of a DTD shows some comments and the three major declarations used in DTDs: <!ENTITY>, <!ELEMENT>, and <!ATTLIST> (which describe entities, elements, and attributes respectively):

```
<!-- 'toysco.dtd' (excerpt #1) -->

<!ENTITY  WROX  'Wrox Press Ltd.' >

<!ENTITY % IDREF_Req   'IDREF #REQUIRED' >
<!ENTITY % IDREF_Opt   'IDREF #IMPLIED' >

<!ELEMENT FirstName   (#PCDATA) >
<!ELEMENT MiddleName  (#PCDATA) >
<!ELEMENT LastName    (#PCDATA) >

<!ELEMENT Name   (FirstName, MiddleName*, LastName) >

<!ELEMENT Invoice  EMPTY>
<!ATTLIST Invoice
   invoiceID      ID     #REQUIRED
   customerID     IDREF  #REQUIRED
   date           CDATA  #REQUIRED
   terms          CDATA  #REQUIRED
   paid (true | false) #REQUIRED
   hire (true | false) "false"
   notes          CDATA  #IMPLIED >

<!ELEMENT InvoiceOrder EMPTY >
<!ATTLIST InvoiceOrder
   invoiceID IDREF_Req
   productID IDREF_Req
   units CDATA #REQUIRED
   notes CDATA #IMPLIED >

<!-- End of 'toysco.dtd' (excerpt #1) -->
```

We will look at the specifics of these declarations a little later in this chapter.

Features of DTDs

The most significant aspect of DTD validation is the definition of the structure of the hierarchical tree of elements. A validating parser and a DTD can ensure that all necessary elements and attributes are present in a document, and that there are no unauthorized elements or attributes. This ensures that the data has a valid structure *before* it is handed over to the application.

A DTD can be used in conjunction with a validating parser to validate existing XML data or enforce validity during the creation of XML documents by a human author, by:

- Checking that required elements are present
- Prompting the author for their inclusion when using a DTD-aware XML editor
- Checking that no disallowed elements are included, and preventing the author from using them
- Enforcing element content and tree structure (using <!ELEMENT> declarations)
- Enforcing element attributes and their permissible values (with <!ATTLIST> declarations)

DTDs can also provide information and shortcuts that may be used in instances of the XML data:

- Default values for attribute values that are omitted from the XML data (also with `<!ATTLIST>` declarations)
- Replaceable content (internal and external entities, and the `<!ENTITY>` declaration)
- Standardized content (using ISO and other character entity sets)

DTDs also have some additional features for the author of the DTD:

- Replaceable content for the DTD (parameter entities)
- Describing non-XML data (the `<!NOTATION>` declaration)
- Conditional sections (using the `INCLUDE` and `IGNORE` directives)

These features will be discussed in detail throughout this chapter.

Sharing DTDs

Shared DTDs are the basis for many XML vocabularies. Using a shared data description greatly simplifies the creation and maintenance of an XML vocabulary; any application code can be simpler, and therefore more reliable and easier to maintain. With a shared DTD, there is only one place that we'd make modifications to the vocabulary's data description.

Furthermore, the rules of the XML vocabulary description (in the DTD), and how those rules are applied (by the validating parser), are well defined in the XML 1.0 REC. This alone can go a long way towards a more reliable data exchange, particularly between diverse business partners. It is no longer necessary for each partner to create its own custom tools – both partners can use the same standard XML tools and technologies to handle their shared data vocabulary.

Many common XML vocabularies are represented by DTDs. Quite often these are simplified versions of DTDs that were previously implemented using SGML.

> *For example, there is a common bibliographic metadata standard known as the* ***Dublin Core standard****. It describes the various items used to describe books, such as title, author, ISBN, and the like. It is available at* http://www.dublincore.org.

Standardized XML vocabularies for common things, such as bibliographic information, allows developers to reuse existing DTDs, saving the cost of developing custom DTDs. Custom DTDs isolate their users and applications from others that might otherwise be able to share commonly formatted documents and data. Shared DTDs are one foundation of XML data interchange and reuse.

Alternatives to DTDs

There are some proposed alternatives to DTDs, including **XML Schema**, **XML-Data**, and its simpler relative, **XML-Data Reduced** (also called **XDR**). At the time this chapter is being written, XML Schemas are well on their way to becoming a formal W3C Recommendation. The XDR subset of XML-Data is currently integrated into Microsoft's Internet Explorer 5, and the MSXML parser (including the retrofit version for IE4), and has been used as the basis for the BizTalk e-commerce initiative. We will look at these alternatives in the next two chapters.

Current versions of the proposed XML Schema specifications are:

- **Part 0: Primer** at http://www.w3.org/TR/xmlschema-0,
- **Part 1: Structures** at http://www.w3.org/TR/xmlschema-1, and
- **Part 2: Datatypes** at http://www.w3.org/TR/xmlschema-2.

A description of XML-Data can be found at http://www.w3.org/TR/1998/NOTE-XML-data. XDR is a Microsoft-specific schema language, which is described at http://msdn.microsoft.com/xml/reference/schema/start.asp.

These alternatives to DTDs will be discussed in Chapters 6 and 7: "Introducing XML Schemas" and "Schema Alternatives" respectively.

For now, let's look at the basic structure of a DTD and the declarations therein.

DTD Structure

Although only one DTD can be associated with a given XML document, that DTD may be divided into two parts: the **internal subset** and the **external subset**. These two subsets are named relative to the XML document instance:

- The internal subset is that portion of the DTD included within the XML data
- The external subset is the set of declarations that are located in a separate document

The external subset is often referred to as "*the* DTD", since it is often contained in a file with a `.dtd` extension. Despite this common usage, an external DTD need not be a separate file – it could be stored as a record contained in a database – and the internal subset is part of the same DTD.

There is no requirement that a DTD use either subset – although without any DTD we can't validate the XML data (we can at least ensure that it's well formed, however). A DTD might be contained entirely within the XML data (an internal subset), with no external subset, or a document may simply refer to an external subset and contain no DTD declarations of its own. In many cases, the DTD will use a combination of both of these subsets (both internal and external subsets are used).

> **DTD declarations in the internal subset have priority over those in the external subset – when similar declarations exist in both subsets, the one from the internal subset will be used (the one in the external subset will be ignored).**

For example, the external subset description of an element might allow several child elements, while the internal subset version specifies an empty element. Any XML data containing this DTD combination had better use an empty element, or it would be considered invalid.

Since it is impossible to experiment with DTDs without knowing how to associate a DTD with a document, let's first discuss how to link a DTD to an XML document or data object.

Associating a DTD with XML Data

In a confusing clash of names, DTDs are linked to XML data objects using markup called the **Document Type Declaration** – which is *never* abbreviated to DTD. This declaration is commonly referred to as the DOCTYPE declaration, to differentiate it from a DTD (Document Type *Definition*).

> **"DTD" refers only to the *definition* of a document type – *not* the DOCTYPE declaration that associates a DTD with the XML document instance.**

Validating parsers use this declaration to retrieve the DTD (if it exists) and validate the document according to the DTD's rules. If the DTD is not found, the parser will send an error message, and be unable to validate the document.

> **An XML document can be associated with only one DTD, using a single DOCTYPE declaration (though this one DTD may be divided into internal and external subsets).**

The limit of one DTD per document can be an unfortunate restriction. For example, our `Toysco` vocabulary contains information about businesses, individuals, and products. The former might best be described using a standard industry vocabulary that describes a generic business. Individuals also have common name and address information that might also be described in a standard DTD. Product descriptions might be unique to our vendor, and therefore contained in a DTD of their own. It would be useful if we could include references to these three DTDs in each of our `Toysco` documents.

Unfortunately, this is not very easy to do with XML DTDs. There *are* some workarounds to the limitation that we'll discuss later in the "Parameter Entities" section of this chapter, but first, let's take a closer look at the syntax of the DOCTYPE declaration.

The Document Type (DOCTYPE) Declaration

This declaration may appear only once in an XML document. It must follow the document's XML declaration, if any, and precede any elements or character data content. Only comments and PIs can be inserted between the `<?xml...?>` declaration and the DOCTYPE declaration. Although this declaration is optional for simple well-formed XML documents, any document that needs to be validated using a DTD must have a DOCTYPE declaration.

There are two forms of the DOCTYPE declaration (`SYSTEM` and `PUBLIC` sources):

```
<!DOCTYPE doc_element SYSTEM location [ internal_subset ] >
```

...and...

```
<!DOCTYPE doc_element PUBLIC identifier location [ internal_subset ] >
```

The common aspects of these are:

- The usual XML tag delimiters (< and >)

- The exclamation mark (`!`) that signifies a DTD declaration
- The `DOCTYPE` keyword
- The name of the document element (*`doc_element`*)
- Optionally, some additional DTD declarations comprising the internal subset, contained within the pair of square brackets (`[` and `]`)

We will discuss the two specific aspects (*`identifier`* and *`location`*) of the two different forms in their respective sections below.

The Document Element Name

The first variable parameter of any DOCTYPE declaration is the name of the document element. This name is required, for example:

```
<?xml version='1.0'?>
<!DOCTYPE Toysco SYSTEM "http://www.wrox.com/DTDs/Toysco.dtd" >

<Toysco>
   ...
</Toysco>
```

Since all XML documents must be well formed, there can only be one `<Toysco>` element in the document with which to connect the DTD.

> **DTDs are associated with the entire element tree via the document element.**

If the DOCTYPE declaration and the document element don't match, a validating parser will report this as an error and will stop further processing of the document. When we want to associate an external DTD subset with a document, we need to declare at least one source for that DTD (`SYSTEM` or `PUBLIC`).

Let's look at the details of both forms of the DOCTYPE declaration.

Using SYSTEM Locations

The `SYSTEM` keyword is used to explicitly specify the location of the DTD. According to the XML 1.0 REC, a `SYSTEM` location will be dereferenced, so it uses the URL form of a URI reference. In our previous example we used this type of DTD reference:

```
<!DOCTYPE Toysco SYSTEM "http://www.wrox.com/DTDs/Toysco.dtd" >
```

In this case, the parser will attempt to retrieve the DTD from the specified URL at Wrox's website. If the DTD isn't found, an error will be reported and the parser won't be able to validate the document.

URIs, URL, and URNs are discussed in Chapter 3.

Of course, a document residing on the same file system as the DTD could also access the DTD directly, without using an external address:

```
<!DOCTYPE Toysco SYSTEM "file:///DTDs/Toysco.dtd" >
```

Although general-purpose URLs may use the hash mark/number sign (#) character as a **URL fragment identifier**, we shouldn't use these in the location of a DTD. XML parsers might report such URLs as errors, so they won't be able to locate or process the DTD.

The following is an *illegal* DTD location, since it uses a URL fragment:

```
<!DOCTYPE  Toysco  SYSTEM "http://www.wrox.com/DTDs/Toysco.dtd#Part1" >
```

In all of these examples, the declarations needed to validate a document would be found in the external subset DTD (in the file named `Toysco.dtd`). This approach is most useful when the DTD and all of its related document instances will be accessible on the Internet, for use by anyone authorized to access that URL.

Using PUBLIC Identifiers

The use of `PUBLIC` identifiers should probably be limited to internal systems and SGML legacy applications. Any organization that uses these must also share catalogs that map them to real resource locations. This primary location is used in some application-specific way that is beyond the scope of XML.

For example, the `Toysco` DTD might be a corporate standard, in which case we might refer to it using the following declaration:

```
<!DOCTYPE Toysco PUBLIC "BigBusinessConsortium/DTDs/Toysco" >
```

In this example, the XML application would have more flexibility in locating the DTD – a local copy of the DTD might be used, a shared DTD might be available via a private network, or the declarations could even be stored in a non-XML database server. This means that finding the DTD at a `PUBLIC` location and handling its possible absence is left to the application (which sets up the parser environment).

This works fine if we have a mechanism to resolve this identifier into a discrete resource. Usually, we should also specify a secondary `SYSTEM`-style location. This provides a fallback location if the `PUBLIC` location cannot be used. Ironically, any XML data for public exchange must always include a `SYSTEM` location, since there aren't any real standards for handling these identifiers (and URI redirection can provide most of the advantages of a `PUBLIC` identifier, anyway). This preferred form still uses the `PUBLIC` keyword and identifier, but adds a location (a URL reference):

```
<!DOCTYPE Toysco PUBLIC "BigBusinessConsortium/Toysco"
    "http://www.wrox.com/DTDs/Toysco.dtd" >
```

If the application cannot locate the DTD using the primary (`PUBLIC`) location, the secondary (`SYSTEM`) location is used. Note that the `SYSTEM` keyword is *implied* in this example – it is never included in the same declaration as a `PUBLIC` keyword. Any of these forms of the DOCTYPE declaration can be used to associate a DTD with XML data.

Most of the examples in this book will use the simpler `SYSTEM` location. We should find this to be a better option for our own experiments with DTDs as well, since we are likely to keep our XML data and the associated DTD on a local file system.

Internal Subset Declarations

One or more DTD declarations may be included in the internal subset, which is contained within the DOCTYPE declaration. These declarations are delimited by square brackets (`[...]`), and must appear after all the other parameters of the DOCTYPE declaration:

```
<?xml version="1.0"?>
<!DOCTYPE Toysco PUBLIC "BigBusinessConsortium/Toysco"
   "http://www.wrox.com/DTDs/Toysco.dtd"
[
   DTD declaration #1
   DTD declaration #2
   ...
   DTD declaration #N
]>

<!-- The external subset is referenced by the PUBLIC keyword -->
<!-- The internal subset is included between the "[ ]" above -->

<Toysco>
   ...
</Toysco>
```

It's a common markup style to put the `[ ]` delimiters, and each DTD declaration, on separate lines to visually separate these declarations from the other parts of the DOCTYPE declaration.

We will use both internal and external subset DTDs in the various examples in the rest of this chapter. The former are most useful for simple examples with just a few DTD declarations. The latter are necessary to show some of the advanced features of DTDs, and will be used for our ongoing `Toysco` example, at the end of the chapter.

Internal and External DTD Subsets

Most DTDs use the external subset, since this allows sharing the DTD with multiple documents and separates the XML data and its description. However, as we will see shortly, there are some circumstances when the internal subset is not only useful, but also necessary.

When To Use the External Subset

We should generally use the external subset for DTD declarations that will be shared by multiple documents. Using only the internal subset would require copies of the DTD declarations in all document instances – an obvious maintenance nightmare, which also eliminates the advantages of shared DTDs.

It's obviously much easier to update shared declarations if they're kept in a single separate document. Keeping a separate DTD also provides a description of all XML data that refers to that DTD. Often, a DTD is shared by multiple organizations, with a working group to maintain the DTD and publish copies of it to each of the participants. Such a DTD could also be maintained and stored in some form of central repository (though copies of the DTD might still be cached in multiple locations for performance reasons). Shared DTDs are a very powerful aspect of XML.

Using the Internal Subset To Override

The priority of the DTD's internal subset can be either a blessing or a curse.

On one hand, the use of internal subset declarations to override an external DTD can be the only way to use an existing DTD that doesn't match our needs exactly. As long as we don't use any unintentionally conflicting declarations, the external subset can provide the bulk of the description and validation information. Our additional declarations would be added in the internal subset, perhaps to add some new elements and/or attributes. We may also choose to override some existing declarations (remember that the internal subset always takes priority).

The internal subset can also be useful during the development of the DTD. For instance, during the creation of our examples in this book, we might want to try different specifications for some element. We can accomplish this by copying the appropriate declarations from the external subset to the internal subset, and then modifying those internal declarations to try the new constraints. Once we are satisfied with the change, we can then move the new declaration to its permanent home in the external subset.

Of course, this priority can also be seen as a drawback – someone with whom we share XML data and DTDs might choose to override some of our constraints in the original DTD, and this might cause problems if that XML data were then sent back without the newly modified internal subset.

There is another downside – we cannot completely rely on an external subset of the DTD for validation, since a document could override it using internal subset declarations, and so change the validation criteria.

Now that we've discussed the basic structure of DTDs and the method of associating them with XML data, let's look at the basic DTD declarations that define elements, their attributes, and the hierarchical tree of elements.

Basic DTD Declarations

DTD declarations are delimited with the usual XML tag delimiters (< and >). Like the DOCTYPE declaration, all DTD declarations are indicated by the use of the exclamation mark (`!`) followed by a keyword, and its specific parameters:

```
<!keyword parameter1 parameter2 ... parameterN>
```

Although we've only used single spaces between the parameters in the above example, any amount of whitespace is permitted – as with most XML declarations and content, whitespace is *not* significant, and tabs or spaces may be used to align text for greater clarity. However, this general rule doesn't apply to the initial keyword strings of a declaration, which must appear exactly as shown above.

For example, the following element type declaration is *illegal*, due to the spaces around the `!` character (all the other extra whitespace *is* legal):

```
< ! keyword   parameter1
   parameter2
   ...
   parameterN
>
```

Assuming the two illegal spaces are removed, this example shows an otherwise valid and very useful format for DTD declarations. Multi-line declarations are commonly used to clarify element structure, sequence, and other constraints.

There are four basic keywords used in DTD declarations:

Keyword	Description
`ELEMENT`	Declares an XML element type name and its permissible sub-elements ("children").

Table continued on following page

Keyword	Description
ATTLIST	Declares XML element attribute names, plus permissible and/or default attribute values.
ENTITY	Declares special character references, text macros (much like a C/C++ `#define` statement), and other repetitive content from external sources (like a C/C++ `#include`).
NOTATION	Declares external non-XML content (for example, binary image data) and the external application that handles that content.

The first two keywords are essential for describing any XML content or data model (elements and their attributes). The latter two provide useful shortcuts for creating documents with reusable content, plus methods for handling non-XML data.

First, let's look at those two DTD declarations that are required to describe most XML documents.

Element Type (ELEMENT) Declarations

Elements are the fundamental building blocks of XML data. Any useful document will include several element types, some nested within others (perhaps many levels deep). Many documents will also use element attributes, but we'll discuss those in the next section.

Elements are described using the **element type declaration**. This declaration can have one of two different forms, depending on the value of the *content_category* parameter (which is implied in the latter form):

```
<!ELEMENT name content_category >
<!ELEMENT name (content_model) >
```

The *name* parameter is the **element type name** that is being described – it must be a legal XML name.

Remember that (as we saw in Chapters 2 and 3) XML names must only comprise of letters, digits, and four punctuation marks (". ", "_", ": ", "- "). Letters and digits are any valid Unicode characters, not just ASCII. These are known as **NameChar** *characters. Additional restrictions apply to the first character of an XML name (the* `Name1` *character). Also remember that colons (:) should* not *be used in XML names, except as the XML Namespace delimiter character.*

The **content_category** and **content_model** parameters describe what kind of content (if any) may appear within elements of the given name.

Element Content Categories

There are five categories of element content:

- Any – any well-formed XML data
- None (or Empty) – may *not* contain any text or child elements – only element attributes are permitted
- Text only – contains any text (character data), but no child elements

- Element only – contains only child elements, and no text outside of those children
- Mixed – may contain a mixture of child elements and/or text data

All of these categories allow the use of attributes within the element start-tag.

> *These attributes are defined using an Attribute (`ATTLIST`) Declaration, which will be covered later in this chapter.*

We'll look at the two simplest of these categories first – all (any) or nothing (empty). They both use the simple (first) form of the element type declaration:

```
<!ELEMENT name content_category >
```

The rest of these content categories require the use of the content model (second) form of the declaration.

The Any Category

As the name implies, elements defined in this category may contain any well-formed XML. This could include character data, other elements, comments, PIs, CDATA sections – anything goes, as long as it's well-formed XML.

The following element type declaration is an example of this category:

```
<!ELEMENT AnythingGoesInHere ANY >
```

An element in this category could be empty, or have almost any kind of content:

```
<AnythingGoesInHere/>
<AnythingGoesInHere>
   <AnElementWithText>..some character data...</AnElementWithText>
   <AnElementWithChildren>
      <AnotherElement/>
      <!-- comments can go almost anywhere... -->
   </AnElementWithChildren>
   <?somePI with_its_target ?>
</AnythingGoesInHere>
```

In the above example, we could shuffle the order of the elements, omit or add some elements, insert character data almost anywhere, and otherwise change the content of `<AnythingGoesInHere>`, without causing any validity error(s).

This sort of element should be used very sparingly, as we lose almost all validity checking if we only use this most permissive category. One common use of this category is for an element that contains some arbitrary XML data.

The Empty Category

At the other end of the element spectrum are elements that can't *contain* anything, though they may still have attributes. These empty elements are defined using the `EMPTY` keyword. Examples of empty elements include (X)HTML's familiar line-break and image reference tags:

```
<br />
<img src="logo.png" />
```

Empty elements can also be used for configuration files that use name-value pairs (element attributes), organized in named sections (the element type name):

```
<ParserConfig validate="yes" externalEntity="no" keepComments="no" />
<BrowserConfig showtags="yes" showcomments="no" showPIs="no" />
```

The above examples all use the abbreviated empty element form. While this form is commonly used, it is also acceptable to use explicit start- and end-tags, as long as nothing appears between those tags.

So, the previously shown `<br />` empty element could also be represented as:

```
<br></br>
```

Both `<br>` element examples above are equivalent, so both forms would be considered valid empty elements. However, using the longer form in documents is not recommended since it might imply that it was possible to insert content into what is supposed to be an empty element. The abbreviated form implies that no such content is allowed, and it's more compact.

> *Some browsers and other applications (such as older versions of MSXML) will change the abbreviated form into its longer start-tag plus end-tag form upon display, but it's still an empty element (and will be validated as such).*

The element type declarations describing the above empty elements are:

```
<!ELEMENT br EMPTY>
<!ELEMENT img EMPTY>
<!ELEMENT ParserConfig EMPTY>
<!ELEMENT BrowserConfig EMPTY>
```

The last three of the above element type declarations would be supplemented with `!ATTLIST` declarations to describe their various attributes and values, but we'll ignore them until a later section.

Other Categories

The other content categories (element, mixed, and PCDATA) are used to restrict an element's content to data of a certain type. These all use the second form in our basic syntax example, and therefore require the use of a content model:

```
<!ELEMENT name (content_model)cardinality >
```

The entire context model within the parentheses may also have an optional **cardinality operator** within the element declaration (which describe how many occurrences of a child element are valid, and which we'll discuss a few sections from now).

So let's look at the syntax and grammar of content models and these other three content categories.

Content Models

The content model in an element declaration is used to describe the structure and content of a given element type. As we saw above, this content may be:

- Text only – contains any text (character data), but no child elements
- Element only – contains only child elements, and no text outside of those children
- Mixed – may contain a mixture of child elements and/or text data

No content model is needed (or allowed) for the ANY or EMPTY categories.

The basic syntax of a content model is a list of child element type names and/or the `#PCDATA` keyword contained within a pair of parentheses. Additional pairs of parentheses may be used to nest various sub-expressions, but they must always be matched pairs.

These examples show content models for the three categories:

```
<!ELEMENT name (#PCDATA) >
<!ELEMENT name ((child1, child2) | (child3, child4)) >
<!ELEMENT name (#PCDATA | child1 | child2)* >
```

Two kinds of element lists may appear within content models:

- **Sequence lists** – child elements must appear in the order specified, using a comma to separate element names in the list – as in the second example above, within the inner parentheses.
- **Choice lists** – only one of several mutually exclusive child elements may appear, separated by the vertical bar character (|) – as in both the second and third examples.

Content models may use combinations of these sequence and choice lists, to limit the child elements. We can also exert additional control upon the child element structure using the cardinality operators to specify the number of occurrences of a given child element.

Combinations of these two types of lists and cardinality operators provide very powerful and complex content models. These combinations can be nested using additional pairs of parentheses.

Text-only (PCDATA) Content

The following document excerpt shows an element with text only (character data) content:

```
<foo>
   Character data can also include entity references (such as &amp; or &lt;)
</foo>
```

Elements in the `PCDATA` content category only allow textual data and entity references, and the `#PCDATA` keyword is the only parameter allowed in such a content model. The above example would be described using the following declaration:

```
<!ELEMENT foo (#PCDATA) >
```

Note that the whitespace between the closing parenthesis and angle bracket is a stylistic choice that is used for clarity only – whitespace is permitted here, but not required.

Element-only Content

As the name suggests, elements that are defined as having **element content** may only contain other (child) elements, but no text content outside of child elements. An example document fragment that would conform to this category might be:

```
<foo>
   <a_child_element>Some elemental content..</a_child_element>
   <another_child>
      ...some other child's content..
   </another_child>
   <a_third_child>...yet another child's content...</a_third_child>
</foo>
```

You have probably noticed that no text (other than some insignificant whitespace) appears outside of any element tags in the above example. This is the essence of element content – the only data that may appear within a `<foo>` element are the three child elements named `<a_child_element>`, `<another_child >`, and `<a_third_child>`.

This `<foo>` element in the example above, would be declared as having only element content like so:

```
<!ELEMENT foo (a_child_element, another_child, a_third_child) >
```

The example above uses a comma-separated list of child element names – a sequence list. We specify that `<foo>` may only have three child elements, and they must always appear in the same order as they appear in the content model.

Element content is both the most versatile and yet potentially most restrictive content model. It allows the most control over the presence and/or absence of child elements, their sequence of appearance, and the possibility of alternative children. The only drawback to this content model is that all text (character data) must be contained within one of the child elements.

We'll look at sequence lists, choice lists and cardinality operators in greater detail, right after we take a quick look at the last kind of content model – mixed content.

Mixed Content

In a mixed content model, content is constrained to character data and/or a simple list of valid child element types. Child elements in mixed content can appear (or not) in any order, any number of times.

The following example shows a document excerpt with mixed content:

```
<foo>
   Mixed content element types can include other elements, as well as
   character data, and/or entity references.
   <a_child_element>More text..</a_child_element>
   <another_child>Its text.</another_child>
   And even some additional character data in the &lt;name&gt; element.
   <a_child_element>Can't constrain number of occurrences!</a_child_element>
</foo>
```

In this example, the content of the `<foo>` element includes four child elements and the text outside of these children as well. Mixed content is always specified using a choice list, but in this content model, the choices are *not* mutually exclusive.

Since both character data and elements are allowed, the element must be declared as having mixed content by using the #PCDATA keyword as the first item in the content model:

```
<!ELEMENT foo (#PCDATA | a_child_element | another_child)* >
```

The list of valid child elements does not imply that there's any required sequence of those elements. Therefore, the previous declaration is equivalent to this one:

```
<!ELEMENT foo (#PCDATA | another_child | a_child_element)* >
```

In both of these example declarations, we've included the required and constant cardinality operator (the *) after the closing parenthesis. This is needed because the mixed content model doesn't constrain the number of occurrences of child elements. We'll discuss these shortly, but it is sufficient to know that this cardinality operator implies that all content specified within the parentheses is optional and allows zero or multiple instances. This allows any combination of these elements and character data within <foo>.

Whenever the #PCDATA keyword is used, it must always be the first item in the content model (followed by the child element type names, if any). Therefore, the following is *illegal*, since a child element type name appears before the #PCDATA keyword:

```
<!ELEMENT foo (a_child_element | #PCDATA | another_child)>
```

A very common example of XML's mixed content model is the body of an HTML web page. The entire web page may well be contained within <html>, <head>, and <body> elements. However, the rest of the body is clearly mixed content, since it is usually a mixture of text, entity references, empty elements (such as <br/ > and <img/ >), and regular non-empty elements (such as <b>...</b>).

For example:

```
<html>
<body>
   This is some text that is part of the &lt;body&gt; element's content. It
   may also contain other child elements that tell the browser to
   <em>emphasize</em> the text, or make the text <b>bold</b> or
   <i>italic</i>.<br/>
   Empty elements may appear anywhere within the mixed content, usually to
   indicate the end of a line or paragraph.<p/>
   Other empty elements provide links to external data, such as images:
   <img src="someImage.jpg"/><br/>
</body>
</html>
```

In the above example, the value of mixed content becomes apparent: we'd be very hard-pressed to construct a content model that handled all the variations of text and child element sequences. There is really no reason that we would even want to try to limit the sequence of child elements – it is enough to list the element types that *may* appear within the <body> element; no other constraints are needed.

The above example uses XHTML 1.0 syntax, which is version 4.01 of HTML expressed in well-formed XML syntax. Therefore we have added the slashes that indicate XML empty elements, such as
 and <img /> *instead of the commonly used*
 and <img>. *Although HTML is* not *case sensitive, XHTML (like XML)* is *case sensitive – by specification, all XHTML element and attribute names must use only lower case.*

This is an important markup language option for those who are interested in using HTML within an XML environment. It also provides a compatible version of HTML that can be embedded within XML documents for display in existing HTML browsers.

There are times when it is desirable to be more restrictive about the content of an element. This does require the use of element content and is implemented using choice and/or sequence lists, and cardinality operators.

Using Sequence and Choice Lists

These lists comprise the child element type names within a pair of parentheses, separated by one of the two list operator characters we have already mentioned ("," and "|"). Each child element type name in a list may have a cardinality operator appended, and/or the list as a whole may also include a cardinality operator (as we'll see in the very next section). Parentheses can be used to group lists. This simple grammar allows the construction of some powerful expressions to describe an element's children.

Let's look at an example. A simple, five-element sequence list for a person's name could be declared as:

```
<!ELEMENT PersonName (Title, FirstName, MiddleName, LastName, Suffix) >

<!ELEMENT Title      (#PCDATA) >
<!ELEMENT FirstName  (#PCDATA) >
<!ELEMENT MiddleName (#PCDATA) >
<!ELEMENT LastName   (#PCDATA) >
<!ELEMENT Suffix     (#PCDATA) >
```

By declaring `<PersonName>` to have element content, we are restricting this element to the five specific child elements in the specified order, and no other data. The children in this example can only contain character data, so they're declared to use the `PCDATA` content model.

A document instance that conforms to this declaration might be:

```
<PersonName>
   <Title>Mr</Title>
   <FirstName>John</FirstName>
   <MiddleName>Q</MiddleName>
   <LastName>Public</LastName>
   <Suffix>Jr</Suffix>
</PersonName>
```

In common practice, neither the `<Title>` nor `<Suffix>` element is a free-form text element; there are a limited number of commonly used titles and suffixes (though we won't clutter our examples with an attempt to include all of them, like "Miss", "Right Rev.", "II", "VIII", etc.)

We could use choice lists of specific empty elements to replace these two text-containing elements:

```
<!ELEMENT PersonName
   (
   (Mr | Ms | Dr | Rev), FirstName, MiddleName, LastName, (Jr | Sr | III)
   )
>
```

```
<!ELEMENT Mr  EMPTY >
<!ELEMENT Ms  EMPTY >
<!ELEMENT Dr  EMPTY >
```

```
<!ELEMENT Rev EMPTY >

<!ELEMENT FirstName  (#PCDATA) >
<!ELEMENT MiddleName (#PCDATA) >
<!ELEMENT LastName   (#PCDATA) >

<!ELEMENT Jr  EMPTY >
<!ELEMENT Sr  EMPTY >
<!ELEMENT III EMPTY >
```

In this example, a person's name still comprises five child elements in a specific sequence. However, two of the child elements are derived from a list of mutually exclusive choices. Instead of `<Title>` or `<Suffix>` elements that contain text, specific empty elements are used. Whichever child element is chosen from a choice list, that element still must appear in the same place in the child element sequence, as specified in the sequence list.

The conforming document instance would now become:

```
<PersonName>
   <Mr />
   <FirstName>John</FirstName>
   <MiddleName>Q</MiddleName>
   <LastName>Public</LastName>
   <Jr />
</PersonName>
```

There is an unaddressed problem with all of the examples we've shown so far – we've had no way of indicating *optional* elements, or that an element may occur more than once, or otherwise constraining the number of *occurrences* of child elements (cardinality). Let us look at how we can dictate these constraints.

Cardinality

As we've mentioned a few times already, any content model may have a cardinality operator appended, and any child element within a content model will have an indication of how many times it may occur.

> **Cardinality operators define how many child elements may appear in a content model.**

There are four cardinality operators:

Cardinality Operator	Description
None	The absence of a cardinality operator character indicates that one, and only one, instance of the child element is allowed (and it is *required*)
?	Zero or one instance – optional singular element
*	Zero or more instances – optional element(s)
+	One or more instances – required element(s)

In all the content model examples that we've seen so far, the absence of any explicit cardinality operators means that each child element must occur only once. This is a problem for our personal name example – not everyone has a middle name, and most people don't have any suffix attached to their name.

Let's revise that example to use some cardinality operators:

```
<!ELEMENT PersonName
   (
      (Mr | Ms | Dr | Rev)?, FirstName, MiddleName*,
         LastName, (Jr | Sr | III)?
   )
>
```

The absence of cardinality operators for `<FirstName>` and `<LastName>` means that there must always be exactly one of each of these child elements in every `<PersonName>`. This also applies to the empty elements in the choice lists – if anything is chosen from the list, it must be singular. Both choice lists are declared as singular, but optional (the "`?`" operator). The `<MiddleName>` element type is declared optional, but with multiple occurrences permitted (the `*` operator), to allow for common Latino names, for example. Therefore, we have declared that `<FirstName>` and `<LastName>` are the only required children of the `<PersonName>` element type: all other children are optional.

The above content model pretty much handles almost any kind of name, with one exception – many people use only a single name. This may be cultural, as in Brazil or Indonesia; or affected, as in Balthus or Ice-T. So, let's make one more revision to allow this other form of a personal name, and illustrate an even more complex nested declaration:

```
<!ELEMENT PersonName
   (
      SingleName |
      ((Mr | Ms | Dr | Rev)?, FirstName, MiddleName*, LastName,
         (Jr | Sr | III)? )
   )
>
```

You'll notice that we've kept the existing content model for the "typical" `<PersonName>`, but we've now wrapped this in another pair of parentheses and included it in a new choice list. With these additions, `<PersonName>` may contain either a single child (`<SingleName>`), or two to five children that conform to the sequence and choice lists from the previous example.

> *Remember that "**internationalization**" (commonly abbreviated as "**I18N**" or "**i18n**", as in "I" + 18 other letters + "N") is one of the design goals of XML. In an international marketplace, it is very important to leave any Anglo-centric (or any* other*-centric) bias out of one's XML designs. The old "last name first, only 20 characters for a name, and only one middle initial" data design restriction is an example of the kind of practice that's no longer acceptable.*

Here are some conforming instances of our revised `<PersonName>` element:

```
<PersonName>
   <Mr/>
   <FirstName>John</FirstName>
   <MiddleName>Q</MiddleName>
   <MiddleName>P</MiddleName>
```

```
    <LastName>User</LastName>
    <Jr/>
</PersonName>
```

```
<PersonName>
    <FirstName>Jane</FirstName>
    <LastName>Doe</LastName>
</PersonName>
```

```
<PersonName>
    <SingleName>Madonna</SingleName>
</PersonName>
```

In each of the above examples, the data conforms to the required content and sequence of child elements and would be accepted by a validating parser. Of course, any of the examples here (above or below) would always be accepted by a non-validating parser, since all are well-formed XML.

Some non-conforming ("not valid") examples include:

```
<PersonName>
    <LastName>Smith</LastName>
    <FirstName>Bob</FirstName>
</PersonName>
```

The required elements are present, but in the wrong order. Or:

```
<PersonName>
    <Miss/>
    <FirstName>Jane</FirstName>
    <LastName>Doe</LastName>
</PersonName>
```

Here, the element structure is correct, but an invalid title (not present in the choice list) is used. Finally:

```
<PersonName>
    <SingleName>Madonna</SingleName>
    <SingleName>Ciccone</SingleName>
</PersonName>
```

In this case, the `<SingleName>` element isn't singular.

Now that we've described the elemental nouns of XML data, let's look at the adjectives: attributes and their related DTD declaration.

Attribute (ATTLIST) Declarations

Attributes can be used to describe the metadata or properties of their associated element. Attributes are also an alternative way to markup document data.

For example, either of the following document excerpts could be used to describe a person's name. The first is derived from the simple example that we used earlier in this chapter:

```
<PersonName>
   <Mr/>
   <FirstName>John</FirstName>
   <MiddleName>Q</MiddleName>
   <MiddleName>P</MiddleName>
   <LastName>User</LastName>
   <Jr/>
</PersonName>
```

However, the same data could just as easily be represented using element attributes, instead of child elements:

```
<PersonName title="Mr" first="John" middle="Q P" last="User"
   suffix="Jr" />
```

This attributes-only representation of the same data uses an empty element since all the data is now in those attributes.

> *In keeping with the "element = noun" and "attribute = adjective" metaphor, we are using a stylistic convention for element and attribute names. Element names use the proper noun form (Capitalized Names) and attribute names are shown entirely in lower case. This is a common style for both XML and SGML markup (at least in English and other cased languages), and has some obvious benefits to the reader of the markup.*

Element attributes are described using the **attribute-list declaration**, also called the **ATTLIST declaration**. This declaration has the usual DTD declaration format, using the `ATTLIST` keyword plus zero or more attribute definitions:

```
<!ATTLIST elementName
   attrName1 attrType1 attrDefault1 defaultValue1
   attrName2 attrType2 attrDefault2 defaultValue2
   ...
   attrNameN attrTypeN attrDefaultN defaultValueN >
```

Both the *`elementName`* and the *`attrNameN`* parameters are required, and they must be legal XML names. The former is the name of the associated element type, the latter the name of the individual attribute. Each attribute requires a separate definition, and these are usually shown on separate lines for greater readability.

The **attribute default** (*`attrDefaultN`*) parameter dictates XML parser behavior. It tells the parser whether or not the attribute's presence is required (using the `#REQUIRED` keyword), and how to handle its absence if it is an optional attribute (the `#IMPLIED` keyword). The parser can use the DTD's optional *`defaultValueN`* parameter to provide an attribute value to the application, even when the attribute is not present in the document.

In the second example excerpt at the beginning of this section, we have a `<PersonName>` element that uses five attributes. We could describe this attributes-only version of `<PersonName>` in the following fashion:

```
<!ELEMENT PersonName EMPTY >
<!ATTLIST PersonName
   title  CDATA #IMPLIED
   first  CDATA #REQUIRED
   middle CDATA #IMPLIED
   last   CDATA #REQUIRED
   suffix CDATA #IMPLIED >
```

Because we've replaced all the child elements of `<PersonName>` with attributes, the content model has also been changed to disallow any content (it's now an EMPTY element). The five attributes are all normal character data (CDATA), two of them are required to always be present (`#REQUIRED`), and the other three are optional (`#IMPLIED`). Even though we have listed these attributes in an order similar to the earlier element-only example, this order cannot be enforced – by specification, the order of attributes cannot be defined or constrained, and an XML parser is free to pass these attributes to the application in any order.

The next few sections will describe the ATTLIST declaration in detail. First, let's look at the various parameters of this declaration, beginning with the last two parameters: the **attribute default declaration**.

Attribute Defaults

Every ATTLIST declaration contains an attribute default declaration to dictate whether or not an attribute's presence is required, and if it is not required, how a validating parser should handle its absence from a document.

There are four different attribute defaults:

Attribute Default	Description
`#REQUIRED`	Attribute *must* appear in every instance of the element.
`#IMPLIED`	Attribute is optional.
`#FIXED` (plus default value)	Attribute is optional. If it does appear, it *must* match the default value. If the attribute doesn't appear, the parser *may* supply the default value.
Default value (only, no keyword)	Attribute is optional. If it does appear, it may be any value conforming to its attribute type. If the attribute doesn't appear, the parser *may* supply the default value.

You may have noticed the phrase "the parser may *supply" in the table above. This is a reminder that a non-validating parser is* not *required to supply default values for attributes.* Validating *parsers* are *required to provide defaults from a DTD (and usually do so even if the validation option is turned off).*

#REQUIRED

Let's look at an example of a simple `ATTLIST` declaration with the `#REQUIRED` keyword (we can ignore the `CDATA` attribute type for now – it simply means the attribute value is character data):

```
<!ATTLIST AnElement its_attr CDATA #REQUIRED >
```

When `<AnElement>` is declared in this fashion, the `its_attr` attribute must appear in every instance of this element type, or the data is not valid (though it's still well formed). Since the value is required, no default value may be specified.

The following example is *not* valid therefore:

```
<AnElement> ... </AnElement>
```

It doesn't have the required `is_attr` attribute.

#IMPLIED

A similar declaration with the #IMPLIED keyword:

```
<!ATTLIST AnElement its_attr CDATA #IMPLIED >
```

In this case, the its_attr attribute is optional, so it may or may not appear in instances of <AnElement>. Even though the attribute might be absent, no default value may be specified for an #IMPLIED attribute.

#FIXED

Attributes may be optional, yet still be constrained to a single specific value. We use the #FIXED attribute default to restrict that value, while allowing the parser to supply the value if the attribute is absent.

For example, a document might have a version number that, like the XML specification, is currently limited to a single valid value:

```
<Doc version="1.00"> ... </Doc>
```

This would be declared in the DTD using the #FIXED keyword with a default value (we'll assume that the element allows character data content):

```
<!ELEMENT Doc   (#PCDATA) >
<!ATTLIST Doc version CDATA #FIXED "1.00" >
```

If a <Doc> element appeared with a version attribute value other than "1.00", a validating parser would report an error. Some non-validating and all validating parsers would supply the default value, if the attribute were absent from an instance of <Doc>.

This form of the ATTLIST declaration is relatively uncommon. If the attribute value is truly fixed and yet is required, it might just as well be hard-coded into the application, unless our application is intended to work with several versions of <Doc>, using a different DTD for each. Since we can't rely on a non-validating parser to provide default attribute values, any #FIXED attribute value must appear in the XML data if its value is significant to the application.

Default Values

If we wanted to be more liberal with our document versions, we could let the parser supply this default value, without *requiring* it to be present in every instance of the element type. However, this does mean we lose the capacity to restrict the attribute to a single value. For example:

```
<!ELEMENT Doc (#PCDATA) >
<!ATTLIST Doc version CDATA "1.00" >
```

This declaration is similar to an #IMPLIED declaration – in both cases the attribute value is *optional*. The absence of the #IMPLIED keyword lets the parser know that a default value can be supplied by the DTD.

For example, our document could contain elements with or without the version attribute, with any character data attribute value being valid:

```
<Doc version="6.66"> ... </Doc>
<Doc version="1.00"> ... </Doc>
<Doc> ... </Doc>
```

A validating parser would present the third instance of the <Doc> element to the application as if the element had an explicit `version="1.00"` attribute. The latter two examples would be functionally equivalent as far as the application was concerned. However, since we've lost the ability to force a single attribute value, the first instance would also be valid.

> *Some XML parsers (such as those in the SAX and the DOM) will inform the application whether the attribute value was actually in the data or was supplied as a default value from the DTD. This is not required by the XML 1.0 Recommendation, but can be useful information for some applications.*

If we wanted to require the version attribute to be constrained to a single value, yet not require the attribute to be present in every instance of the element, we could use an enumerated attribute type (see the next section for more about these) with the `#IMPLIED` keyword instead:

```
<!ELEMENT Doc (#PCDATA) >
<!ATTLIST Doc version (1.00) #IMPLIED >
```

Let's look at one last parameter of the `ATTLIST` declaration: the attribute type.

Attribute Types

There are ten different types of attributes defined in the XML 1.0 Recommendation:

Attribute Type	Attribute Value Description
`CDATA`	Character data (simple text string)
Enumerated values (attribute choice list)	One of a series that is explicitly defined in the DTD
`ID`	A unique identifier for each instance of this element type; it must be a valid XML name
`IDREF`	A reference to an element with an `ID` type attribute
`IDREFS`	A list of `IDREF` values separated by whitespace character(s)
`NMTOKEN`	A **name token**, that is a text string that conforms to the XML name rules, except that the first character of the name may be any valid `NameChar` (see below)
`NMTOKENS`	A list of `NMTOKEN` values separated by whitespace character(s)
`ENTITY`	The name of a pre-defined **entity**
`ENTITIES`	A list of ENTITY names separated by whitespace character(s)
`NOTATION`	A **notation type** that is explicitly declared elsewhere in the DTD (see the NOTATION declaration section)

The *values* (as well as the names) of all `ID`, `IDREF`, and `IDREFS` attribute types must conform to XML name rules. The *values* of all enumerated, `NMTOKEN`, and `NMTOKENS` attribute types must exclusively comprise of `NameChar` characters (we discussed these and `Name1` characters at the beginning of this section).

Let's look at the details of these attribute types.

CDATA (Character Data) Attribute Type

Most attribute values are nothing more than plain text. These attributes are declared using the CDATA type, which is similar to #PCDATA for elements. For example:

```
<!ATTLIST AnElement its_attr CDATA #REQUIRED >
```

This example states that an element type (named <AnElement>) has a *required* single attribute (named its_attr) that has a text string for its value.

An example document excerpt that conforms to the above declaration might be:

```
<AnElement its_attr="some text string"> ... </AnElement>
```

As long as the attribute value is nothing but text, it will be considered valid by a validating parser. Since XML uses Unicode, such values are not constrained to be only plain ASCII text. Another valid instance of this element type might use Greek text:

```
<AnElement its_attr="ΔΓΦ"> ... </AnElement>
```

However, no *external* entity references are allowed in CDATA attribute values, so the following version of the same Greek text using the equivalent ISO external entity references, would be *illegal*:

```
<AnElement its_attr="&Delta;&Gamma;&Phi;"> ... </AnElement>
```

This restriction does not apply to internally-defined entities (such as the five built-in entities: <, >, &, ', and ") or character references (such as or *), so we *could* use the Unicode character numbers to represent our Greek attribute value:

```
<AnElement its_attr="&#913;&#915;&#916;"> ... </AnElement>
```

These different types of entity types and references will be described later in this chapter.

Another related restriction upon all attribute values involves the beginning element tag delimiter, the left angle bracket, or less-than sign (<). No well-formed XML document is allowed to use this character within an attribute value: it must always be escaped using the < entity reference. For example, an attribute value that needs to represent the mathematical expression "A < B < C" must use text modified to appear like this:

```
<AnElement its_attr="A &lt; B &lt; C"> ... </AnElement>
```

The greater-than sign (right angle bracket, >) doesn't have to use an entity reference, but it is good practice to escape it like the other special markup characters.

Let's now look at the other commonly used attribute type.

Enumerated Values Attribute Type

We'll often want to use one of a set of specific text strings for an attribute value.

In the simple <PersonName> element that we defined earlier in this chapter, we confined the honorific title and name suffix to a limited set of valid element types using choice lists in the element content model. A similar mechanism exists for attribute values, using a nearly identical syntax. Valid choices are one or more name tokens in a list separated by vertical bar (|) characters, with the list enclosed in parentheses.

> **All enumerated values must be legal XML name tokens (comprised exclusively of `NameChar` characters).**

So let's redefine the simple <PersonName> element, using two new attributes, instead of the two child element choice lists (the other child elements remain defined as before):

```
<!ELEMENT PersonName (FirstName, MiddleName, LastName) >
<!ATTLIST PersonName
   title  (Mr | Ms | Dr | Rev) #IMPLIED
   suffix (Jr | Sr | III)      #IMPLIED >
```

Both attributes are NameChar text strings, but each must have a value that exactly matches one of the values shown in the above declaration.

A document excerpt that conforms to this new definition of <PersonName> might be:

```
<PersonName title="Mr" suffix="Jr">
   <FirstName>John</FirstName>
   <MiddleName>Q</MiddleName>
   <LastName>Public</LastName>
</PersonName>
```

Remember that XML is case-sensitive, so "Mr" is *not* equivalent to "MR" If we're creating a DTD for documents that will be manually entered, we might want to allow for all the various case-insensitive permutations of such strings (though this quickly becomes ridiculous in practice). A better practice is to establish a convention for attribute values – always use upper case, or always use lower-case, and then use the DTD and a validating XML editor to enforce this rule.

ID Attribute Type (Element Identifier)

Attributes using the ID type provide a unique identifying name for a given instance of an element. The *value* of an ID attribute must conform to the rules for XML names, and this value must be unique within a given document. This also means that all-numeric IDs, such as the U.S. Social Security Number (SSN), or a database record number, cannot be used as an ID attribute value in XML (unless we prefix the number with a legal Name1 character).

Each element type may use only one ID attribute, and thus every instance of that element can be referred to using a single unique identifier. One more rule: any attribute of this type must be declared as #IMPLIED (optional) or #REQUIRED – it would make no sense to use a #FIXED (constant) or default value for what is supposed to be a unique identifier for each element.

> *The "one ID per element" restriction is another rule inherited from SGML. The ID attribute type is intended to be the unique name for an instance of an element – not the equivalent of a database record key (which often allows for the use of both primary and secondary keys).*

Let's create a new <Person> element type that has a required ID attribute, and a content model that includes a few familiar children:

```
<!ELEMENT Person (PersonName, CorpName?, Email*, Address?, Biography?) >
<!ATTLIST Person perID ID #REQUIRED >
```

We always want this element to always have an ID, so perID is declared to be #REQUIRED.

All of our example attributes of the ID *type have the string* "ID" *in the attribute name. This is a common and suggested style of markup (and another SGML practice). At the same time, using any variation of* "id" *or* "ID" *for any* non-ID *attributes is strongly discouraged.*

This new element type's content model includes one (and only one each) of our previously defined <PersonName> and <Address> element types. We've also added three simple PCDATA child elements for the person's corporate affiliation and biography (zero or one of each of these), and e-mail address (zero or more).

A document excerpt that conforms to this definition of <Person> might be:

```
<Person perID='JHN_Q_PBLC'>
   <PersonName honorific='Mr.' suffix='Jr.'>
      <FirstName>John</FirstName>
      <MiddleName>Q</MiddleName>
      <LastName>Public</LastName>
   </PersonName>
   <CorpName>Acme XML Writers</CorpName>
   <Email>jqpublic@notmail.com</Email>
   <Biography>John, Jr. is a swell fellow, son of John, Sr.</Biography>
</Person>
```

Remember that an ID attribute is not only case-sensitive (like all XML names and content), it must also be a valid XML name that is unique within a given document instance. In this example, no other element in the same document could have an ID of "JHN_Q_PBLC", though the string "jhn_q_pblc" would be acceptable.

> **The *value* of an ID attribute must be a legal XML name, unique within a document, and use the #IMPLIED or #REQUIRED default value. There may only be one ID attribute for each element type.**

The following is an example of an *invalid* ID attribute, because the *value* is not a legal XML name (it begins with a numeric digit and also contains two illegal punctuation characters):

```
<Person perID="2Pac(RIP)" ... >
```

This attribute type can be very useful when using XML as an exchange format for data from an RDBMS.

You might be tempted to use a database record number (maybe a numeric primary key) as the value of an ID *attribute. However, don't forget that an* ID *attribute's value must be a legal XML name (which cannot begin with a numeric digit), so you must precede this with a letter or some other legal XML* Name1 *character in this situation, such as an underscore.*

For example, an invoice that was stored in an RDMBS would probably have a unique number, and the customer might be referred to using their Tax ID Number. We have prefixed an underscore (_) or a text string ("TIN-") to ensure that our numeric database IDs are legal XML names:

```
<Invoice invID="_1234-56">
   <Customer custID="TIN-123-45-6789"> ... </Customer>
</Invoice>
```

An ID attribute can also be used as a link target, in conjunction with IDREF or IDREFS attributes elsewhere in the XML data.

IDREF / IDREFS Attribute Types (Relationships Between Elements)

We can use an IDREF attribute (the **link source**) to establish a link from an element to a different element with an ID attribute. Although the target must always be unique, we can have many different link sources (elements with IDREF attributes) that refer to a single ID attribute.

> **The *value* of an IDREF attribute must be a legal XML name, and must match the *value* of an ID attribute within the same document. Multiple IDREF links to the same ID are permitted.**

For example, a <Book> element might link to an author in this way:

```
<Book author="JHN_Q_PBLC">
```

This link attribute would be declared in the DTD as follows:

```
<!ATTLIST Book author IDREF #REQUIRED >
```

Of course, many books have multiple authors (a one-to-many relationship). We might try to use multiple instances of the IDREF attribute to represent these links, but since a well-formed element may only have one attribute of a given name, the following example is *illegal* syntax:

```
<Book author="JHN_Q_PBLC" author="JN_D">
```

Fortunately, XML does have a way to handle multiple IDREF attributes in a single element: the IDREFS type.

> **An IDREFS attribute is a white space-delimited list of individual IDREF attributes, each of which must conform to all the rules of the IDREF type of attribute.**

Now, to allow multiple authors for <Book>, using IDREFS links, we will re-declare this attribute:

```
<!ATTLIST Book author IDREFS #REQUIRED>
```

We can then use a space-delimited list of the IDREF values within a single author attribute value:

```
<Book author="JHN_Q_PBLC JN_D TW_PC">
```

The XML parser will present the application with a single value for the author attribute, and it will be up to that application to separate each individual IDREF value from the list. In this case, we'd end up with three such values: "JHN_Q_PBLC", "JN_D", and "TW_PC".

These attribute types allow us to express both one-to-one and one-to-many relationships between elements.

NMTOKEN / NMTOKENS Attribute Types (Name Tokens)

Sometimes, it's desirable to restrict the syntax of an attribute value, but still allow the use of unspecified values. The CDATA attribute type allows any string of characters without any restrictions. At the other end of the spectrum, we have enumerated values – only those strings specified in the DTD are permitted. There is a middle ground in the form of the NMTOKEN and NMTOKENS attribute types.

These types restrict the attribute values to use only XML NameChar characters. Unlike ID values, any of these characters may be used at the beginning of the string – there is no Name1 character restriction. Unlike enumerated values, the value of an NMTOKEN is not limited to a finite set of specific values.

As with the IDREFS type, there is a plural form (NMTOKENS), which allows a whitespace-delimited list of multiple NMTOKEN values.

> *These attribute types are another part of XML that was inherited from SGML, and are mostly useful for interoperability with SGML tools and DTDs. Another possible use would be the direct use of numeric keys as attribute values, though the parser would not be able to enforce unique values within a document (as with the ID and IDREF attribute types).*

We could change the declarations of <PersonName>'s title and suffix attributes to use the NMTOKEN and NMTOKENS types, instead of limiting these to a set of enumerated values:

```
<!ATTLIST PersonName
   title  NMTOKENS #IMPLIED
   suffix NMTOKEN  #IMPLIED >
```

An example use of this in a document might be:

```
<PersonName title="Rev. Dr." suffix="Jr."> ... </PersonName>
```

There are two advantages to this approach:

- We aren't constrained to pre-specified short lists of valid honorific titles and suffixes.
- We can now use multiple titles ("Rev. Dr.") without having to specify every possible combination.

Of course, this flexibility can also be a disadvantage – without the constraints of enumerated values, an author could use "Dr. Rev.", "Mr. Ms.", "foobar", or some other nonsensical title or suffix.

There is another major drawback to these attribute types. Since their legal values aren't specified in the DTD, a validating parser can only enforce the simple NameChar syntax rule – all further validation must now be handled by the application. As with IDREFS, an NMTOKENS list must also be processed by the application – the parser will simply pass the entire list as a single attribute value.

The only real difference between a CDATA and NMTOKEN attribute is that the latter prevents the inclusion of whitespace and some punctuation characters. While the NMTOKEN and NMTOKENS attribute types may be useful in certain limited circumstances, in most cases a CDATA or enumerated value attribute will work as well, or better.

ENTITY / ENTITIES Attribute Types (Replaceable Content)

These two related attribute types are used to allow a reference to an unparsed external entity to appear within a document. Like the IDREF / IDREFS pair, these two provide a singular and plural form of the same basic attribute type. The attribute value must always be a legal XML name, and the plural form uses a whitespace-delimited list of names. For example, we might want to add product pictures to our <Product> elements:

```
<Product productID='SP4544' hire='true' imgtype='png' imgsrc='tn_SP4544'>
   <Name>Spell Book</Name>
   ...
</Product>
```

The imgtype attribute is a NOTATION type, and imgsrc is an ENTITY attribute type.

NOTATION Attribute Type (Non-XML Data)

This special form of an enumerated attribute value can be used by a validating parser to associate the value of the attribute with a <!NOTATION> declaration elsewhere in the DTD.

> **The *value* of a NOTATION attribute must be a legal XML name, and must match a <!NOTATION> declaration in the same DTD. There may only be one NOTATION attribute for each element type, and this attribute type may not be used with EMPTY elements (these three limitations are all validity constraints).**

For example, a pseudo-HTML <IMG> element type that permits three different types of images could be defined as:

```
<!NOTATION gif  SYSTEM 'http://www.wrox.com/Programs/GIF_Viewer' >
<!NOTATION jpg  SYSTEM 'http://www.wrox.com/Programs/JPG_Viewer' >
<!NOTATION png  SYSTEM 'http://www.wrox.com/Programs/PNG_Viewer' >

<!ELEMENT img (#PCDATA) >
<!ATTLIST img
   src  CDATA #REQUIRED
   type NOTATION (png | jpg | gif)  #IMPLIED >
```

The src attribute value can be any text string. On the other hand, the type attribute may only use one of the three enumerated values, and there must be a matching <!NOTATION> declaration for each such value (more details in the next section).

Use of NOTATION and ENTITY Attribute Types

We might modify the definition of the <Product> in our Invoice DTD to allow an associated image of the product. Of course, the image will probably be in some binary image file format, so we need to provide both an external unparsed entity (for the image file), a notation for the associated image format (the image viewer), and a reference to the image entity.

This element would be defined like so:

```
<!ATTLIST Product
   productID ID #REQUIRED
   hire      (true | false)  "false"
   imgtype   NOTATION (png | jpg | gif) #IMPLIED
   imgsrc    ENTITY #IMPLIED >
```

If we want to use the imgtype and imgsrc attributes in a valid XML document, we will also need three associated NOTATION declarations for the png, jpg, and gif attribute types. So let's look at the various forms of the NOTATION declaration.

Notations – Non-XML Data

XML is based upon text data, but not all data is textual. We need some way to include *references* to external data, such as images, spreadsheet files, and other binary data formats. Thus, we describe the non-XML data in the DTD and include a reference to an external application that will handle the data (since an XML parser can't do this for us). The XML application will then have this information available either for its own use, or to pass on to a helper application.

A **notation** is used by the XML application as a hint about handling an unparsed entity (see the next section for more details about these) or some other non-XML data.

Notations can be used to identify (by name):

- The format of unparsed entities
- The format of element attributes of the ENTITY and ENTITIES types
- The application associated with a processing instruction (PI)

The basic syntax of the NOTATION declaration is:

```
<!NOTATION name SYSTEM "location" >
<!NOTATION name PUBLIC "identifier" "location" >
```

The *name* is the identifier for a particular notation type. Any <!ENTITY> declaration, NOTATION attribute, or PI that pertains to this notation type, will also use this exact *name* as the means of associating an external resource with its handler.

> **All notation *names* that are used in a document must be declared with a <!NOTATION>**

The *identifier* and *location* parameters are the same as those for any external reference in XML, such as those in the Document Type Declaration: *identifier* is a unique name for application-specific use, and *location* is a URL, which in this case locates a non-XML resource (such as an image file).

The handlers for the three image types we used in the last section might be declared like this:

```
<!NOTATION png SYSTEM 'http://www.wrox.com/Programs/PNG_Viewer.exe' >
<!NOTATION jpg SYSTEM 'http://www.wrox.com/Programs/JPG_Viewer.exe' >
<!NOTATION gif SYSTEM 'http://www.wrox.com/Programs/GIF_Viewer.exe' >
```

When the XML parser encounters our <Product> example, it will extract the imgtype value (which is png) and look for a matching name amongst the notation declarations. If the name is matched, the URI from the above declaration will be passed on to the application for further processing.

The XML parser need only provide the names of the unparsed entity and its associated notation declaration to the application. Any further processing is strictly within the application's domain. An XML document can include unparsed entities and notations without necessarily having any means to process them – no error is reported for unknown notation types, nor those for which no handler is available.

These declarations can have a very similar effect to the HTML <img> element. Images are typically included in web pages with a statement like:

```
<img src="picture.png">
```

This tells a browser to go find an image named picture.png, and display it within the page. It is up to the browser to determine what kind of image format is being used, often based upon the filename extension (which is .png in this case, for the Portable Network Graphics format) or an embedded MIME type (which would be image/png). This means that a browser that does not understand the PNG format cannot display the image.

Since XML parsers and applications don't have any such built-in behavior associated with tags like <img>, we must explicitly notify the application of the kind of image format(s) we're using and how to handle this non-XML data. To do this, we need to use the combination of XML's ENTITY and NOTATION attribute types and the NOTATION declaration.

Of course, many browsers have these image viewer capabilities already built-in, so we may not need the helper application for any of these examples. However, it is still necessary to include these NOTATION declarations (using dummy PUBLIC identifiers) to satisfy a validating XML parser:

```
<!NOTATION png PUBLIC '//Wrox/PNG_Viewer' >
<!NOTATION jpg PUBLIC '//Wrox/JPG_Viewer' >
<!NOTATION gif PUBLIC '//Wrox/GIF_Viewer' >
```

We've mentioned entities several times in this chapter, so let's look at how we define and declare the various kinds of entities.

Entities

Replaceable content is a key maintenance and timesaving concept. Instead of using the same text repeatedly in multiple documents, we can put this boilerplate text in a separate file, and then include it by reference in our XML data. We can also use symbolic names for special characters, by including references to pre-defined character entity sets. Many of these are standardized by international organizations such as the ISO, while others have been created for specific industries or purposes. All XML documents are comprised of units of storage called **entities**. The **document entity** serves as the entry point for an XML parser, and contains the entire document – including the document element and its tree of children, and any other declarations that precede or follow the document element. The internal and external subsets of the DTD are also entities, albeit unnamed ones. Other types of entities are always identified and referred to by name. These are the key to replaceable content in both DTDs and documents, so we will look at several different forms of entities in this chapter.

The two main categories of entities are:

- **General entities** – used within XML data
- **Parameter entities** – only used in DTDs

Not only do these two types use different syntax, they also occupy different symbol namespaces. It's therefore possible (though probably inadvisable) to have a general entity and a parameter entity use the same name without any conflict.

There are two other ways to classify entities. They may be:

- **Parsed entities** – can include any well-formed content, known as the **replacement text**, which may include other markup
- **Unparsed entities** – non-XML data (can even be non-text data)

There are two forms of parsed entities:

- **Internal** – the actual replacement text is included in the declaration
- **External** – the replacement text (or non-XML data) is located in an external file or other resource

Parameter entities are always parsed entities, and so can be either internal or external.

Parsed Entities

The replacement text of a parsed entity can be considered part of the document in which it is referenced, as if it had simply been included everywhere it was referenced. Parsed entities are always referenced by name using an **entity reference**, which may be either a general or a parameter reference (for data or DTD).

```
<!ENTITY TheName "The replacement text" >
...
<foo>&TheName;</foo>
```

The above document fragment first shows the definition of a simple text entity using an **entity declaration**, and then its inclusion in the XML data by means of an entity reference.

Unparsed Entities

An unparsed entity is something that may or may not be text, and if it is, need not be XML text. These general entities are always named, and can only be used as the value of an attribute having the `ENTITY` or `ENTITIES` type. All unparsed entities must have an associated notation (as described in the previous section), which is also identified by name. For example:

```
...
<!NOTATION png SYSTEM 'http://www.wrox.com/Programs/PNG_Viewer.exe' >
<!ENTITY  TheImageRef  SYSTEM 'image.png'  NDATA png >
<!ELEMENT foo EMPTY >
<!ATTLIST foo img ENTITY #IMPLIED >
...
<foo img="TheImageRef"/>
```

The above document fragment shows the definition of a notation (the first line), the definition of an unparsed entity referring to that notation (the second line), and then an empty element that refers to the unparsed entity (as an attribute value).

Let's now look again at the entity references that cause an entity's replacement text to be inserted into a document.

Entity References

All parsed entities are included in a document or DTD by means of an entity reference, which we discussed in the "Character and Entity References" section of Chapter 2.

Parsed general entity references use the ampersand (`&`) and semi-colon (`;`) as the beginning and end delimiters, respectively:

```
&name;
```

Parameter entity references use similar syntax, but with the percent sign (`%`) as the beginning delimiter:

```
%name;
```

Unparsed general entity references can only be used as an attribute value, so they require no special reference syntax. In fact, entity references are not allowed to contain the name of an unparsed entity.

In both cases, the entity name must conform to the general rules for XML names, just like element type or attribute names. This *name* must also match the name of an entity declaration; otherwise, the document containing the entity reference won't be well formed.

In general, the defining declaration should precede any references to the entity. A parameter entity declaration must precede any references to that declaration. Any general entity that's used as the default value of an attribute must also be defined before such use.

We've already seen how we can use the five built-in general entities to avoid conflicts with special markup characters, particularly the ampersand (&) and less-than sign (<). It's not necessary to explicitly define any of these in a DTD for use with well-formed documents. However, for any would-be valid documents with a DTD, they should be defined for the sake of interoperability with existing SGML-based tools.

The strings on the left are all legal XML *general* entity references (with XML comments on the right):

```
&amp;              <!-- built-in general entity - ampersand -->
&lt;               <!-- built-in general entity - less-than sign -->
&copy;             <!-- symbolic entity for copyright (©) character -->
&ProductDisclaimer; <!-- some boiler-plate legal text -->
```

These two are legal *parameter* entity references:

```
%ISO_Latin1;      <!-- include an ISO entity set in the DTD -->
%ToyscoElements; <!-- the <!ELEMENT..>s for Toysco DTD -->
```

Later in this chapter, we'll look at how these are interpreted by an XML parser, how the referenced entity was originally declared, and how the replacement text might appear in an XML application.

First, we'll revisit character references.

Character References

XML, like SGML before it, has a reference mechanism for any non-ASCII characters that don't have a direct input method (say, on an ASCII keyboard). Any XML-legal character in Unicode (or ISO/IEC 10646) may be the target of a **character reference**, using syntax similar to parsed general entities. These characters are referred to by the assigned Unicode integer value of the character.

Contrary to common belief (perhaps reinforced by Microsoft's Unicode support in Windows NT), these values are not limited to 16-bit integers – there are several ISO/IEC 10646 encodings that use 32-bit numbers (UCS-4, UTF-32) or variable-length multi-byte formats (UTF-16, UTF-8, UTF-7).

Like general entity references, character references are delimited with an ampersand and semi-colon. The numeric value is further delimited with a preceding hash mark/number sign (#) – this is how an XML parser can easily differentiate a character reference from a general entity reference. Two forms of numbers may be used in these references – decimal and hexadecimal. These are distinguished by using a lower-case x to precede all hex numbers.

For example, here are two Unicode character references, the first using a decimal value, the second a hex value:

```
&#2014;  <!-- decimal value - refers to the em-dash character -->
&#x0199; <!-- hex value - refers to capital C with cedilla (Ç) -->
```

There's no requirement that either one or the other of these formats be used. For most XML applications, hex is preferred since that's how the Unicode standards documents present character values. These are usually shown in the form "U+*nnnn*", where *nnnn* is a 4-digit hex number, with leading zeros.

Note to C/C++ programmers: there are no octal numbers in XML or ISO/IEC 10646, so these leading zeros will never cause a number to be interpreted as an octal value.

This method of including special characters doesn't require a DTD or any other definition of the character value – as long as its numeric value is that of a legal XML character, the parser will pass it on to the application for display or other handling. Refer back to Chapter 3 for more details about Unicode.

Remembering over 16,000 character values for the world's letters, numbers, and symbols is both unfeasible and somewhat ludicrous. Symbolic names have been created for the most common Unicode characters, using general entities, as we'll see in the next and later sections.

General Entities

As we've already mentioned, general entities may be either parsed or unparsed; they can include any well-formed content (the replacement text), and they are always referenced by name. A by-product of this well-formedness is that all XML structures remain properly nested – no XML component (for example tags, elements, PIs) can begin in one entity and end in another.

Any of the following would cause fatal XML parser errors:

- Any reference to an unparsed entity
- Any character or general-entity reference in the DTD, except within an entity or attribute value
- Any reference to an external entity from within an attribute value

We've seen how to refer to entities, so let's look at how they're defined..

Parsed Entities

A parsed general entity is defined in the DTD, in either the internal or external subset.

> **A parsed entity's replacement text must always be well-formed XML.**

As we already mentioned, parsed entities may be either internal or external.

Internal Parsed Entities

The basic format of an **internal parsed entity** declaration is:

```
<!ENTITY name "replacement_text" >
```

The *name* must conform to the general rules for XML names, while the *replacement_text* may be any well-formed XML content (as long as it doesn't include any entity references to the same entity that is being defined).

For example, we can re-declare a simplified version of our `<Invoice>` element to contain standard notice and include a `name` attribute (we'll omit the others we've already used for clarity). Both of these can use a pair of internal parsed entities to provide some appropriate text:

```
<?xml version="1.0" ?>

<!DOCTYPE Invoice
[
   <!ENTITY  copy  "&#x00A9;" >
   <!ENTITY  Vendor  "Toysco Inc. Ltd." >
   <!ENTITY  Disclaimer  "No warranty! &copy; 2001 &Vendor;" >

   <!ELEMENT  Invoice  (Notice?) >
   <!ATTLIST  Invoice  name  CDATA  #REQUIRED >

   <!ELEMENT  Notice  (#PCDATA) >
]>

<Invoice name='&Vendor;' />
   <Notice>&Disclaimer;</Notice>
</Invoice>
```

This file (`ProXML2e.Entity-internal-parsed.xml`) would be displayed in IE5 like so (with the two entity references expanded):

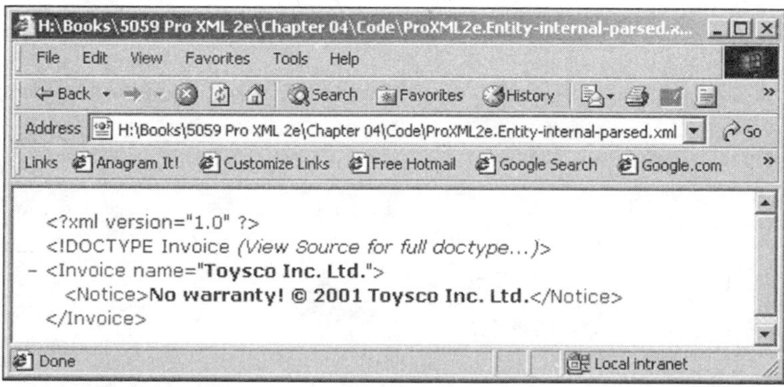

There are two important limitations to the use of parsed entities:

- No entity can refer to itself by its own name, directly or indirectly (in other words, no recursive references are allowed)
- The ending delimiter character of an attribute value (" or ') cannot be contained in an entity

For example, the following simple circular references are *not* well-formed:

```
<!ENTITY BadSelfRef "This is a &BadSelfRef; to one's own self" >
<!ENTITY BadRefToA "This is a &BadRefToB; because B refers back to A" >
<!ENTITY BadRefToB "This is a &BadRefToA; because A refers back to B" >
```

The first of the above declarations is the prohibited direct self-recursion; the rest illustrate an indirect, but still illegal, self-reference.

Although the parser treats entity reference delimiters as such when they appear within the replacement text (as in our previous example), the quotation marks are treated as nothing more than normal data characters. Therefore, the following would *not* be well-formed:

```
<!ENTITY  ValueWithApos  "The End'" >
...
<an_element an_attribute='Some text, then &ValueWithApos; / >
```

An XML parser fully expands the `&ValueWithApos;` entity reference (to "`The End'`"), and *then* starts looking for the attribute value's closing apostrophe *after* the closing semi-colon of the entity reference. Therefore, this attribute value is *not* well-formed.

Not all parsed entities need their replacement text to be included in an `<!ENTITY>` declaration within the DTD. It's also possible to refer to parsed entities that are external to the XML document.

External Parsed Entities

The same example replacement text that we used in the last section could instead be included using an **external parsed entity**. Instead of putting the disclaimer message directly in the DTD, we could instead store the message text in an external text file. Like the `<!DOCTYPE>` declaration and any other external reference, we can use either a `PUBLIC` location, a `SYSTEM` location, or both, to refer to this external resource.

We will simply move the text within the quotation marks in the Disclaimer entity declaration to an external file (named "`ProXML2e.Disclaimer.txt`"):

```
No warranty! &copy; 2001 &Vendor;
```

We then change the Disclaimer entity declaration to (the rest of example remains unchanged):

```
<?xml version='1.0' ?>

<!DOCTYPE Invoice
[
   <!ENTITY  copy  "&#x00A9;" >
   <!ENTITY  Vendor  "Toysco Inc. Ltd." >
   <!ENTITY  Disclaimer  SYSTEM 'ProXML2e.Disclaimer.txt' >
```

```
   <!ELEMENT  Invoice  (Notice?) >
   <!ATTLIST  Invoice  name  CDATA  #REQUIRED >

   <!ELEMENT  Notice  (#PCDATA) >
]>

<Invoice name='&Vendor;' />
   <Notice>&Disclaimer;</Notice>
</Invoice>
```

If the changed document (`ProXML2e.Entity-external-parsed.xml`) is displayed in IE5 and if both the document and the external entity text file are in the same folder, it will appear to be identical to the previous example.

When the XML parser encounters the external entity reference (`&Disclaimer;`), it will refer back to the earlier `<!ENTITY Disclaimer ...>` declaration, read the named file (at the `SYSTEM` location), process the declaration therein, and then pass *its* replacement text to the application, just as if the entity were declared in the document itself (as before).

This method has the advantage of completely segregating the definitions of the boilerplate text from the DTD – any vendor could use the exact same DTD, with the custom text for the vendor's name and legalese coming from an external entity.

The downside of this approach is most significant in an Internet environment. The multiple reads and data transfers implied by a document that comprises multiple entities, can greatly degrade performance when every piece is another HTTP transfer. This is less of a problem for an internal network application, where it can be a powerful method of sharing and reusing DTDs for multiple documents and applications.

In fact, the XML version of the text of this whole book could be included in a "master" XML document with the use of external parsed entities:

```
<?xml version="1.0"?>

<!DOCTYPE ProXML2eBook
[
  <!ENTITY copy  "&#x00A9;" >          <!-- This is used in 'TextFront' -->
  <!ENTITY Wrox  "Wrox Press Ltd." >  <!-- Ditto -->

  <!ENTITY textFront     SYSTEM "ProXML2e.BookFront.txt" >
  <!ENTITY textChapter1 SYSTEM "ProXML2e.BookChapter1.txt" >
  <!ENTITY textChapter2 SYSTEM "ProXML2e.BookChapter2.txt" >
  <!ENTITY textChapter3 SYSTEM "ProXML2e.BookChapter3.txt" >
  <!ENTITY textChapter4 SYSTEM "ProXML2e.BookChapter4.txt" >
]>

<ProXML2eBook>
  <front_matter>&textFront;</front_matter>
  <chapter>&textChapter1;</chapter>
  <chapter>&textChapter2;</chapter>
  <chapter>&textChapter3;</chapter>
  <chapter>&textChapter4;</chapter>
    ...
</ProXML2eBook>
```

This method is commonly used to construct a number of documents that share the same basic structure – the DTD and most of the master XML document can remain unchanged, but the contents can vary depending upon the content of the external entities.

External Parsed Entity – Text Declaration

Any *external* parsed entity can begin with a **text declaration**. This is a truncated version of the XML declaration, which may include the `version` and/or `encoding` attributes (but unlike the XML declaration, the `version` attribute may be omitted). This declaration must be a string literal – entity references aren't allowed within it. If this declaration is included, it may only appear at the very beginning of the entity (and nowhere else).

The following are both legal text declarations (assume that each is at the beginning of its own external entity). The first declares that the entity uses a mythic version of XML, encoded as Big5 (Taiwan Chinese) characters:

```
<?xml version="1.x" encoding="Big5" ?>
<foo>Some text in the Big5 encoding...</foo>
```

And this one just declares that the entity contains text in a common Japanese encoding:

```
<?xml encoding="Shift_JIS" ?>
<foo>...</foo>
```

The scope of these declarations is just the external entity itself – there's no effect on other document content. In the first example above, the contents of `<foo>` would be Big5 text, but the rest of the document (which refers to this external entity) could be in ASCII or UTF-8, or some other encoding.

This mechanism allows us to construct XML documents from data with different character encodings, or even from multiple versions of XML.

> **Any external parsed entity that is not stored in UTF-16 or UTF-8 (the default encoding), *must* always include a text declaration with the `encoding` attribute set to the appropriate value. It is a fatal error if the parser cannot handle a particular encoding in the external entity.**

It is an error for an external entity to declare an incorrect encoding value. If there is no `encoding` attribute and no Byte-Order-Mark (BOM) at the beginning of the entity, the data *must* be encoded in UTF-8. This implies that plain 7-bit ASCII documents don't need to use the text declaration, since ASCII is a subset of UTF-8 and all ASCII characters would be properly recognized.

Unparsed Entities

By definition, unparsed entities are always external entities. As such, the entity declaration for these entities will always reference an external location (`PUBLIC` or `SYSTEM`), and must always supplement the location with the `NDATA` keyword and the associated notation type name. There are no constraints on the contents of unparsed entities – they need not even be text, much less XML text.

The basic format of an **external unparsed entity** declaration is either of the following:

```
<!ENTITY name SYSTEM "location" NDATA notation_type >
<!ENTITY name PUBLIC "location1" "location2" NDATA notation_type >
```

The NDATA keyword is how the XML parser differentiates parsed and unparsed external entities. The parser's only obligation for processing these declarations is to provide the name, location, and notation_type values to the application for its own use.

Every name must match a name in a <!NOTATION> declaration for the document to be considered valid.

> **An unparsed external entity is a *reference to an external resource* (for example, an image file). The entity's associated notation is a *reference to the handler or application* that will process the external resource (for example, an image viewer).**

The following is an example of an unparsed entity being used to refer to a PNG image file:

```
<!ENTITY WroxLogo SYSTEM "http://www.wrox.com/Images/Logo.png" NDATA png >
```

Whenever a reference is made to WroxLogo within an attribute value, the location of the image file and the notation for the png type will be associated with this entity and passed on to the application for further handling.

Now that we've looked at the various forms of general entities that may be used in XML documents, let's look at a similar mechanism for DTDs.

Parameter Entities

As we've noted before, parameter entities are used exclusively in DTDs and must always be parsed entities. This also means that the replacement text must be well-formed in the context of DTD syntax. These entities are a very powerful way to reuse groups of DTD declarations, include entity sets for non-ASCII characters, and/or include entire DTDs within the external subset of a DTD.

The basic format of a **parameter entity** declaration is:

```
<!ENTITY % name "replacement_text" >
```

This declaration is nearly identical to a general parsed internal entity declaration – the only difference is the percent sign (%) that must appear between the "<!ENTITY " string literal and the name parameter. In addition, the parameter entity reference syntax is also slightly different from that of general entity references.

As before, the *name* must conform to the general rules for XML names, while replacement_text may be any well-formed XML content that would be legal within a DTD. As with external parsed entity declarations, the replacement text may be stored in an external resource that's located using the usual external reference form (a URI that may be a PUBLIC and/or SYSTEM identifier). The constraint against using recursive references also applies to this type of entity declaration.

Parameter entities are convenient shorthand for repetitive DTD declarations, or portions thereof. For example, we could save some typing by defining a few parameter entities like this:

```
<!ENTITY % CDATA_Req "CDATA #REQUIRED" >
<!ENTITY % CDATA_Opt "CDATA #IMPLIED" >
<!ENTITY % IDREF_Req "IDREF #REQUIRED" >
<!ENTITY % IDREF_Opt "IDREF #IMPLIED" >
```

Then, when we later declare an element's attributes that used some of these types, we could use parameter entity references, instead of explicitly typing the latter portions of each attribute description:

```
<!ATTLIST  InvoiceOrder
            invoiceID   %IDREF_Req
            productID   %IDREF_Req
            units       %CDATA_Req
            notes       %CDATA_Opt >
```

These parameter entity references would be expanded, and the appropriate replacement text would be inserted within each line of the attribute declaration. The end result would be identical to a version that used the strings directly. Although this example just provides some shorthand, we can implement rudimentary data types and other standardized DTD content with this technique.

This potentially powerful use of parameter entities has two major drawbacks. First, when these are used everywhere in a DTD, it quickly becomes impossible to read the DTD without much flipping of pages (or the use of many windows in an IDE). Unless the parameter entity names are quite descriptive, we've greatly reduced the readability of the DTD, in an effort to save some typing and/or reuse some previously defined declarations. Extensive use of such parameter entities in SGML is one of the many reasons that SGML documents, DTDs, and tools are so complex and expensive to maintain.

The other drawback depends upon how we provide the parameter entity declarations. If we were using entities from many different sources, such as many different files over a network, our document processing performance would be greatly reduced. This is because each time an external entity is used, the parser will need to fetch the entity declaration and expand it at the point of reference (caching can help, but won't eliminate all of the additional network traffic).

A reasonable rule of thumb would be to severely restrict the use of any such parameter entities in XML data that will be used in a dynamic network environment. The use of this feature of XML is best reserved for documents that are more traditional.

The parameter entity mechanism is a powerful way to reuse DTD declarations. It is especially useful for including entity sets that have been standardized by the ISO and other organizations, as we'll see in the next section.

ISO and Other Standard Entity Sets

Both character and general entities have been used for many years in SGML. As a result, numerous standard sets of entity definitions were created, and it's been very easy to convert these SGML resources to XML. SGML's status as an international standard (ISO 8879) means that many of these components are also international standards.

Standard Character Entity Reference Sets

There are two widely used sets of character entity references that provide names for the Unicode (ISO/IEC 10646) Latin-1, Greek, and many mathematical and other symbol characters:

- HTML 3.2 characters – *HTML 3.2 Reference Specification* [1997-01-14] – http://www.w3.org/TR/REC-html32#latin1.
- HTML 4 characters – *Character entity references in HTML 4* [§24 of *HTML 4.01 Specification*, 1999-12-24] – http://www.w3.org/TR/html40/sgml/entities.html#iso-88591.

Some examples of these symbols and their declarations, which have been converted from SGML to well-formed XML, are shown in the following table:

Symbol	Character Number	Entity Declaration
À	U+00C0	<!ENTITY Agrave "À">
Á	U+00C1	<!ENTITY Aacute "Á">
Â	U+00C2	<!ENTITY Acirc "Â">
Ã	U+00C3	<!ENTITY Atilde "Ã">
Ä	U+00C4	<!ENTITY Auml "Ä">
Å	U+00C5	<!ENTITY Aring "Å">
Æ	U+00C6	<!ENTITY AElig "Æ">

The complete DTDs for these character entity definitions have been collected in two files that accompany this book:

- `ProXML2e.Latin1.dtd` – Latin-1 characters (similar to ISO 8859-1)
- `ProXML2e.Greek.dtd` – Modern Greek characters

The typical method of including these character entity definitions in our DTD uses parameter entities. The following example shows a simple DTD that does nothing but include the two entity sets:

```
<!-- 'ProXML2e.EntitySets.dtd' -->

<!ENTITY % CharsLatin1 SYSTEM "ProXML2e.Latin1.dtd" >
<!ENTITY % CharsGreek  SYSTEM "ProXML2e.Greek.dtd" >

%CharsLatin1;
%CharsGreek;

<!-- End of 'ProXML2e.EntitySets.dtd' -->
```

This DTD entity can be included in your XML data with the following `DOCTYPE` declaration:

```
<!DOCTYPE doc_element SYSTEM "ProXML2e.EntitySets.dtd" >
```

Of course, if you are using your own DTD to validate your data, you will need to include the contents of this DTD within your DTD, as yet another parameter entity. We've also created a simple XML test file (`ProXML2e.EntitySets.xml`) to show these character entity references in action.

These test files demonstrate an IE5 limitation: none of the three special Greek symbols are displayed correctly (at least in IE5 5.0 or 5.5). Of course, the current production Netscape browsers (6) are not only incapable of displaying these special characters; they can't handle XML data at all.

Let us now turn our attention from replaceable content in DTDs and XML data, to conditional content in DTDs.

Conditional Sections

When programming, we may have used compiler directives to create **conditional sections** of code. In other words, code that may or may not be included and used based upon some run-time condition or compiler flag. Many standard code libraries (particularly those used with Microsoft Windows) are a maze of these conditional sections, which can depend on the CPU, the target operating system (OS), the locale (for internationalization), and a whole bunch of other variables.

DTDs have a similar feature, albeit one with much more limited capabilities. Often when one is developing a new DTD, or adding a new section to an existing DTD, it is useful to be able to include different declarations in the DTD, depending upon different situations. For example, we may want to test the additions to an existing DTD, without having to create a completely separate DTD.

DTD conditional sections are almost useless without the use of parameter entities. With parameter entities, we can construct quite elaborate multi-purpose DTDs, which use entities defined in the internal subset to modify the conditional section directives in the external subset. We can then use this to allow documents to select their own "level" of validation, or even allow radically different element structures, depending on a few carefully designed declaration structures.

> *Although the use of the internal subset of a DTD is discouraged for production DTDs and/or when DTDs are shared, the internal subset can be very useful during the development of a DTD.*

There are two declarations that are used to create conditional sections in a DTD. They use syntax that is very similar to the `CDATA` declarations we've already discussed.

The basic syntax of these declarations is:

```
<![keyword
[
   ...the conditional DTD declarations go here...
]]>
```

The two valid *keywords* are: `INCLUDE` and `IGNORE`. As the names suggest, any declarations within an `INCLUDE` section are to be used for validation, and declarations within an `IGNORE` section are read, but not processed, by the parser. Neither of these declarations can be used within the internal subset of the DTD – they may only be present in the external subset.

Unlike most programming languages, there is no "`if...else`" grammar to control the inclusion or exclusion of conditional sections in a DTD. So, at first glance the `INCLUDE` and `IGNORE` declarations seem useless. For example, there is no functional difference between the following two examples:

```
<!ELEMENT Toysco (Product, Customer*, Invoice*) >
```

```
<![INCLUDE
[
 <!ELEMENT Toysco (Product, Customer*, Invoice*) >
]]>
```

The element declaration for `<Toysco>` will always be included in the DTD in both these cases. Similarly, there's no significant difference between simply omitting a declaration, and enclosing the same declaration within an `IGNORE` section (except perhaps as a means of documenting the deletion of a formerly useful declaration from the current DTD).

Of course, there is a way to make these declarations quite useful – we just use a parameter entity reference in place of the *keyword* in our basic syntax example above. This little trick allows us to change our conditional section to be either an INCLUDE or IGNORE section, as we'll see in the following example (ProXML2e.Conditional.dtd):

```
<!-- ProXML2e.Conditional.dtd -->

<!ENTITY % useSuppliers   "IGNORE">
<!ENTITY % useNoSuppliers "INCLUDE">

<![%useSuppliers;
[
 <!ELEMENT  Toysco  (Product, Supplier*, Customer*, Invoice*) >

 <!ELEMENT  Supplier  (#PCDATA) >
]]>
<![%useNoSuppliers;
[
 <!ELEMENT  Toysco  (Product, Customer*, Invoice*) >
]]>

<!ELEMENT  Product    (#PCDATA)>
<!ELEMENT  Customer   (#PCDATA)>
<!ELEMENT  Invoice    (#PCDATA)>
```

The above two parameter entities (useSuppliers and useNoSuppliers) must be defined in this DTD, since a parameter entity must always be defined before it is used. For the sake of this illustration, we've simplified the definition of the children of <Toysco> to be trivial text elements.

We've set these two default values in such a way that the production version (no <Supplier> elements) won't need to include any additional declarations. We will need to redefine both useSuppliers and useNoSuppliers in the internal subset of all development version documents that need to use the <Supplier> element and its children. Here is the related XML file, ProXML2e.Conditional.xml:

```
<?xml version="1.0" encoding="UTF-8" standalone="no"?>

<!-- ProXML2e.Conditional.xml -->

<!DOCTYPE  Toysco  SYSTEM "ProXML2e.Conditional.dtd"
[
   <!ENTITY % useSuppliers   "INCLUDE">
   <!ENTITY % useNoSuppliers "IGNORE">
]>

<Toysco>
   <Product>...</Product>
   <Supplier>...</Supplier>
   <Customer>...</Customer>
   <Invoice>...</Invoice>
</Toysco>
```

The internal subset of the DTD has priority, so it's read and processed before the external subset. All declarations in the external subset that duplicate those in the internal subset are ignored. Therefore, when the two parameter entities are expanded within the external DTD, the resulting conditional declarations would be:

```
<![INCLUDE
[
 <!ELEMENT  Toysco  (Product, Supplier*, Customer*, Invoice*) >
]]>
<![IGNORE
[
 <!ELEMENT  Toysco  (Product, Customer*, Invoice*) >
]]>
```

Documents that don't need to include any <Supplier> elements would simply never use the two parameter entity redefinitions in the internal subset. A validating parser would report an error if the document without these redefinitions included any of the now-prohibited <Supplier> elements.

Once we've completed the development process, it's a simple matter to remove the conditional section declarations from the shared DTD. It would *not* be necessary to delete the two parameter entity declarations from any of the documents they've already been defined in – these declarations would just be ignored. All subsequent documents could just omit them, as they'd no longer be needed.

Nesting Conditional Sections

Conditional sections may be nested within each other, with the outermost directive controlling the rest. This situation might occur during DTD development, but otherwise nested conditionals only make sense if we're using the parameter entity trick we just discussed.

The following example illustrates some nested conditional sections, all of which will be ignored:

```
<![IGNORE
[
   <!-- Any declaration in this section will be bypassed. -->
   <![INCLUDE
   [
      <!-- Despite the INCLUDE, anything herein will also be ignored, -->
      <!--  due to the presence of the outermost IGNORE directive. -->
      <![IGNORE
      [
         <!-- This section is always ignored. -->
      ]]>
   ]]>
]]>
```

While we can use the combination of parameter entities and conditional sections to create very complex DTDs from multiple sources, it's probably easier to use external parsed entities in most cases where you need variable content.

Now that we've discussed the various aspects of DTD structure and declarations, let's look at a related declaration that appears in most XML data.

The Standalone Document Declaration

As we discussed in Chapter 2, the XML declaration looks just like an XML processing instruction (though technically it is *not* a PI) with three specific attributes: the required version; and optional encoding and standalone attributes.

The third of these pertains to the use of DTDs, and how the XML processor or parser will interpret the DOCTYPE declaration. There are only two legal values for this attribute:

- `yes` – the document is self-contained, and no other data is required
- `no` – the document uses markup contained in an external DTD

This XML declaration has appeared in several recent examples:

```
<?xml version="1.0" encoding="UTF-8" standalone="yes" ?>
```

In this example, we declare that the document conforms to XML 1.0 syntax, it uses the UTF-8 character encoding, and that *no* external entities are required.

When the `standalone` attribute is changed to `no`, we are telling the XML parser that the DTD contains references to external resources that may be needed to validate the document instance, and/or resolve external entities.

It's important to remember that this attribute is primarily a hint to the XML parser, not an absolute command. A non-validating parser is allowed to ignore external entity references completely, though it must report an error if the document has `standalone="yes"` in the declaration and an undeclared external entity is encountered.

Let's now make a brief survey of the tools that can be used to validate XML using DTDs: validating XML parsers and an online validator.

Validating XML Parsers

We've already discussed XML Parsers (also known as XML Processors) in Chapter 2. Now let's look at a special kind of parser, the validating parser. All XML parsers must be able to process well-formed XML and report any problems encountered with the basic syntax and structure of a document. However, as we've discussed in this chapter, there are often times when we want to ensure that an XML document is not just well formed, but valid, as well. To accomplish this, we need to use a validating parser in conjunction with a DTD.

Some Current Validation Tools

There are numerous XML parsers and tools available, with more being released almost daily. Therefore, we will only include some interesting academic projects and a few of the offerings from major software vendors in this section.

> *Useful listings of XML tools include: Robin Cover's SGML/XML pages [2001-03-03] at* http://www.oasis-open.org/cover/xml.html#xmlSoftware*; the Perfect XML website [2001-03-05] at* http://www.perfectxml.com/toolsoft.asp?SoftCat=6*; and Lars Marius Garshol's Free XML Tools listing [2001-03-06] at* http://www.garshol.priv.no/download/xmltools/cat_ix.html.

Academic Projects (RXP, fxp, and STG Validator)

Three offerings from the academic community are of interest to those who want to validate XML documents using DTDs. The first (**RXP**, written in C, by Richard Tobin at the University of Edinburgh, Scotland) is one of the earliest XML 1.0 validating parsers to have been developed. The second (**fxp**, written in the functional programming language SML) is another validating parser, developed by Andreas Neumann, *et al.* at the University of Trier in Germany. As can be seen from the revision dates below, both of these parsers benefit from ongoing development at their respective universities.

The third (STG Validator) is not a parser *per se* – it is an online XML document validation service, provided by Brown University in the USA. Anyone with a browser can go to the STG website and have their document validated, and receive an HTML report describing any validation errors or warnings.

> *RXP [2001-03-06] is available at* http://www.cogsci.ed.ac.uk/~richard/rxp.html*, and fxp [2000-10-30] is available at* http://www.informatik.uni-trier.de/~aberlea/Fxp/*. The STG Validator is at* http://www.stg.brown.edu/service/xmlvalid.

Apache (Xerces-C and Xerces-J) and IBM (IBM4C and IBM4J)

The Apache Software Foundation is well known for its widely used open source web server software. It is not surprising therefore, that Apache has also embarked upon a pair of open source XML parser projects, working in both C++ (Xerces-C) and Java (Xerces-J).

IBM was an early developer of XML tools. In an interesting strategic move, IBM chose to donate its parser software to the Apache Foundation. There is now a complete circle, since current IBM parsers (IBM4C v3.3.1 and IBM4J v3.0.1) are now based upon the Xerces parsers, which were based on the earlier IBM efforts.

All of these parsers are validating, with support for Namespaces, DOM, and SAX. A key aspect of the two Java parsers is their partial support for XML Schema: the 24 October 2000 draft in Xerces-J and the 7 April 2000 draft in XML4J at time of writing. Now that XML Schema is nearing the end of the design process, all of these parsers will soon have current schema support.

> *Xerces-C [2000] and Xerces-J [2000] are both available from the Apache Software Foundation at* http://xml.apache.org/xerces-c/index.html *and* http://xml.apache.org/xerces-j/index.html*, respectively. IBM4C [2000-11-17] and IBM4J [2001-01-18] are available from IBM at* http://alphaworks.ibm.com/tech/xml4c *and* http://alphaworks.ibm.com/tech/xml4j.

Microsoft (MSXML, IE5)

Although Microsoft was one of the earliest supporters of XML, they chose to follow their own path for several related technologies (such as using XDR instead of XML Schemas, and a non-conforming version of XSL in older versions). As a result of this approach, the other parsers shown here may be a better choice for those readers who are most interested in conformance to the W3C Recommendations and pending standards such as XML Schema.

Still, these are arguably the most widely used XML parsers, and at the time of writing, IE5 remains the only commercial WWW browser that supports XML – the W3C's Amaya browser is a non-commercial browser that serves as a testbed for new technologies, including XML, XSLT, etc. The MSXML 3.0 parser is available as a standalone program, as well as being used to retrofit IE4 with XML capabilities.

> *IE 5.5 (SP1) is available at* http://www.microsoft.com/windows/ie/ *and MSXML 3.0 is at* http://msdn.microsoft.com/xml/general/xmlparser.asp.

Oracle (XML Parser for Java v2)

Oracle Corp. has also been a particularly aggressive developer of XML parsers and other tools, in Java, C++, and other languages (there is even an XML Parser for PL/SQL, the Oracle DBMS language). Since the release of Oracle 8i, XML capabilities have been built into Oracle's ubiquitous RDBMS. The XML Parser for Java v2 is a validating parser that supports Namespaces, the DOM, and SAX. It has support for numerous Asian character encodings, in addition to the typical European encodings.

XML Parser for Java v2 is available at http://technet.oracle.com/tech/xml/parser_java2/ *and the PL/SQL version is at* http://technet.oracle.com/tech/xml/parser_plsql/.

Sun (JAXP and Java Project X TR2)

It is no surprise that Sun Microsystems chose to develop their XML tools in Java. They have released version 1.1 of the Java API for XML Processing (JAXP), which provides support for SAX2, DOM Level 2, and includes XSLT support, as well.

The Java Project X TR2 (Technology Release 2) parser is a validating parser that supports Namespaces, the DOM, and SAX. It requires JDK 1.1.6 or later (preferably JDK 1.2), and Java 2 may be used. Although this parser is available to Java Developer Connection (JDC) subscribers only, membership is free and can be easily set up on the first visit to the Project X website.

See http://java.sun.com/xml *for information about JAXP and other Sun XML projects. The Java Project X TR2 parser is available at* http://developer.java.sun.com/developer/products/xml.

Now that we've discussed the various aspects of XML data validation using DTDs and validating parsers, let's look at some limitations of DTDs that caused the development of alternative schema languages.

Limitations of DTDs

Like XML itself, XML DTDs are a subset of SGML. Although DTDs are one of the most complex aspects of SGML, they are essential to describing documents and their markup. Many existing SGML tools could be used immediately with XML, thus easing the usual adoption pains of a new technology. However, it's important to remember that SGML was always intended for complex documents (such as aircraft technical manuals, government regulations, etc.), and not usually for more general data exchange.

The abstract of the XML 1.0 Recommendation explicitly states: "XML is a subset of SGML.... ...to enable... SGML... on the Web... XML has been designed for ... interoperability with both SGML and HTML".

While XML (and early HTML) shared a similar origin, these markup languages have been used for more than technical documents. HTML began as a way to represent hypertext, but quickly became a way to present multimedia and, with the addition of JavaScript, also became the programming environment for the WWW's client-side. XML is now touted as the foundation of new e-commerce applications, a replacement for HTML (via XHTML), and a generic data exchange format for connecting disparate RDBMS and other corporate databases. XML is even being used within embedded systems, such as cellular phones and other wireless devices.

Since XML came from the SGML community, the stated design goals and even the choice of terms (for example "document") reflect a focus on technical documentation and monolithic document/DTD units. However, XML has rapidly become much more than a document markup language and the limitations of DTDs for more generic data description have become all too apparent. This rapid adoption of XML owes a lot to IBM and Microsoft's tools for XML, and the latter's early implementation of XML in MSXML and IE5, plus their use of XML as the basis for the BizTalk Framework and .NET initiatives. These tools have been the basis for considerable experimentation and even production use on the server-side of WWW and Internet applications. E-commerce initiatives, such as BizTalk, have spurred widespread interest in XML as a messaging format, with no connection to the document-centric model of yore.

Some limitations of DTDs include:

- Non-XML syntax
- DTDs are not extensible (unlike XML itself!)
- Only one DTD may be associated with each document
- DTDs do not properly support XML Namespaces
- Very weak data typing
- No OO-type object inheritance
- Data can ignore the external DTD by using the internal subset
- No DOM support
- Relatively few, older, more expensive, tools

Let's look at these limitations in a little more detail.

Non-XML Syntax

Despite the use of angle brackets to delimit declarations, DTDs do not use well-formed XML syntax. Every validating parser must include two different parsers: one for XML and one for the DTD. These parsers keep the DTD information hidden from the application and user, even though it would often be useful to view or manipulate this data.

DTDs are Not Extensible

When a DTD is used to describe the rules of an XML vocabulary, all those rules must be present in that single DTD. An external entity mechanism allows inclusion of declarations from multiple sources. However, this document-centric approach is limited and rather complex, and it can greatly reduce processing performance (particularly in the network environment for which XML is intended).

Only One DTD Per Document

The restriction of one DTD per document may be evaded using external parameter entities, but otherwise it's impossible to validate a document against multiple descriptions. For example, in an ideal world our `Toysco` vocabulary would draw from a generic name and address DTD, a product description DTD, and perhaps some e-commerce DTD. The parameter entity evasion would work, but it would be very difficult to read, and isn't feasible without a great deal of work and cooperation between the creators of the different DTDs.

Limited Support of Namespaces

Two of the advantages of XML Namespaces are the ability to:

- Prevent conflicting element type names
- Resolve different name strings that are intended to mean the same thing

If namespaces are used, every element type from each namespace must be included in the DTD – which somewhat defeats the purpose of using multiple namespaces from various independent sources.

Weak Data Typing

DTDs really work with only one data type – the text string. While it is true that some constraints may be applied to some strings (for example `ID`, `NMTOKEN`, and related attribute types), these are very weak and limited checks. There is no provision for numeric data types, or much less for more complex (but very common) structures like dates, times, encoded numbers or strings, or URI references.

No Inheritance

Modern OO systems are based on the idea that it's very often more reliable and efficient to describe new objects in terms of existing ones. Given that element types are analogous to object classes, it would be very powerful to be able to describe one element type in terms of another – but DTDs cannot do this.

Document Can Override an External DTD

Isn't it ironic that an external DTD may be completely ignored or overridden by the internal DTD subset within a document instance (given the lack of DTD support for inheritance)? Since the internal subset has precedence over the external subset, there is no assurance that the rules of a DTD will be followed by the documents with which it is associated!

This becomes a significant problem when XML data is used for e-commerce, and other critical applications where data validation is important. The internal DTD subset could actually become something of a "Trojan Horse", used to subvert the intentions of the DTD's designer and misrepresent data in the XML document.

No DOM Support

The DOM is a commonly used way to manipulate XML data, but it doesn't provide access to the rules of the document model in the DTD. Given the investment in applications based on the DOM, it would be a great advantage to be able use this to view/modify not just an XML document, but its meta data also.

Limited Tools

The rapid adoption of XML was due, in some part, to its design goal of interoperability with SGML and HTML. Early users and developers of XML documents and vocabularies could use existing SGML tools, and with the advent of MSXML, a standard HTML browser (IE5). However, most SGML tools are both complex and expensive, and have always been targeted for a rather esoteric and specialized market. Recent HTML browsers have provided some support for XML, but very little support for DTDs.

If DTDs were written in XML, we could use any of the multitudes of available XML tools to view the DTD, extract content models, or even provide dynamic selection of validation information.

Getting Around Some of the Limitations

Despite the opinions of many XML pundits, some experts argue that "DTDs Aren't Completely Dead Yet!" (This was the title of an interesting and controversial thread on XML-DEV earlier this year.) XML Schema may represent the future of XML validation, but at the time of this writing, it is still at Proposed Recommendation status. Although there is still little support available in existing XML tools, several vendors should be able to adapt their existing schema support to the final version of XML Schema in a very short period.

Parameter Entities Mitigate "Only One DTD Per Document"

It is true that we can only include one DTD reference (DOCTYPE declaration) in a given XML document. However, we can use carefully nested external parameter entities to separate various components of our DTD into logical modules (as we saw in the ***Parameter Entities*** section). The DTD referenced in our XML data is simply a shell that includes whichever components we need for that particular data.

The major drawback to this approach is the inability to use Namespaces – all modules must be designed to share a single namespace, which is a difficult proposition for in-house DTDs, much less publicly shared DTDs! Nevertheless, significant applications have been built using this method (such as very complex technical documentation systems using the SGML standards).

SGML and XML 1.0 Tools Already Handle "Non-XML Syntax"

DTDs are part of XML 1.0, and so all conformant validating XML parsers already use DTDs as their schema language. Many XML editors also provide DTD editing using modern IDEs. If your application does not require the rich datatypes or other features of XML Schemas, DTDs may suffice for your purposes.

Now let's put everything we've discussed in this chapter together, and build a DTD to validate our ongoing `Toysco` example.

The <Toysco> Example

At the end of Chapter 2, we had a simple `<Toysco>` document that included a `<Customer>` element, some `<Product>` elements, and a few `<Invoice>` elements. We will add one line to this earlier example, the DOCTYPE declaration necessary to associate a DTD with the data:

```
<?xml version="1.0" encoding="utf-8" ?>
<!DOCTYPE  Toysco  SYSTEM  "toysco.dtd" >

<!-- "toysco.xml" -->

<Toysco>
<!-- Customers -->
   <Customer customerID="CU02">
      <Name>
         <FirstName>Buffy</FirstName>
         <LastName>Summers</LastName>
      </Name>
      <BillingAddress>
         <Street>1630 Matilda Drive</Street>
         <City>Sunnyvale</City>
         <State>CA</State>
         <Zip>94086</Zip>
```

```
        <Country>USA</Country>
      </BillingAddress>
      <ContactDetails>
        <Email>buffy@buffster.com</Email>
        <Phone phonetype="HOME">408/555-5555</Phone>
        <Phone phonetype="WORK">650/555-5555</Phone>
      </ContactDetails>
    </Customer>

  <!-- Other <Customer> elements deleted for illustrative brevity -->

  <!-- Products -->
    <Product productID="CV4533" hire="false" >
      <ProductName>Scrabble</ProductName>
      <Description>The world&apos;s favorite word board game</Description>
      <Price currency="USD">24.99</Price>
      <Units>1</Units>
      <Stock>31</Stock>
    </Product>

    <Product productID="SC4323" hire="false" >
      <ProductName>Chess set</ProductName>
      <Description>
        Beautiful ornate pieces and a dull cardboard chess board
      </Description>
      <Units>1</Units>
      <Price>9.99</Price>
      <Stock>45</Stock>
    </Product>

    <!-- Other <Product> elements deleted for illustrative brevity -->

  <!-- Invoices -->
    <Invoice invoiceID="TC4543"
      customerID="CU03"
      date="2001-04-01"
      terms="Immediate"
      paid="true" >
      <InvoiceOrder productID="SP4544" units="1" />
      <InvoiceOrder productID="ST4545" units="10" />
    </Invoice>

    <Invoice invoiceID="TC2787"
      customerID="CU02"
      date="2001-01-16"
      terms="Immediate"
      paid="true" >
      <InvoiceOrder productID="CV4533" units="1" />
      <InvoiceOrder productID="BL4123" units="10" />
    </Invoice>

    <!-- Other <Invoice> elements deleted for illustrative brevity -->
  </Toysco>
```

The complete version of this file is called `Chapter_04_Toysco.xml`.

A Simple Invoice DTD

We will assume a very simple data model: each <Toysco> can have one or more <Product> elements, and zero or more <Customer>, <Invoice>, and <InvoiceOrder> elements – and no other (mixed) content.

We will use a pair of parameter entities to centralize our enumerated attribute values, both as an illustration of this feature and a good practice to simplify maintenance of these values.

The beginning of this DTD would be:

```
<!-- 'Toysco.dtd' -->

<!-- Parameter entity for 'currency' and 'phonetype' attributes -->

<!ENTITY % attdef_currency  "currency (CDN | DM | UKP | USD | YEN)" >
<!ENTITY % attdef_phonetype  "phonetype (HOME | WORK | FAX | CELL)" >

<!-- <Toysco> -->

<!ELEMENT Toysco (Customer*, Product+, Invoice*, InvoiceOrder*) >
```

Since the currency attribute in any element will use the enumerated list of values above, only one of the five values shown would be considered valid.

The <Customer> element has four children and a single required ID attribute. Three are required and must be singular: <Name>, <BillingAddress>, and <ContactDetails>. The fourth is an optional singular <MailingAddress> element:

```
<!-- <Customer> + its children -->

<!ELEMENT Customer (Name, BillingAddress, MailingAddress?, ContactDetails)>
<!ATTLIST Customer
   customerID ID #REQUIRED >

<!ELEMENT Name (FirstName, MiddleName*, LastName) >

<!ELEMENT FirstName  (#PCDATA) >
<!ELEMENT MiddleName (#PCDATA) >
<!ELEMENT LastName   (#PCDATA) >

<!ELEMENT BillingAddress (Street+, City, State, Zip, Country) >
<!ELEMENT MailingAddress (Street+, City, State, Zip, Country) >

<!ELEMENT Street  (#PCDATA) >
<!ELEMENT City    (#PCDATA) >
<!ELEMENT State   (#PCDATA) >
<!ELEMENT Zip     (#PCDATA) >
<!ELEMENT Country (#PCDATA) >

<!ELEMENT Email   (#PCDATA) >

<!ELEMENT ContactDetails (Email*, Phone+) >

<!ELEMENT Phone (#PCDATA) >
<!ATTLIST Phone %attdef_phonetype; #IMPLIED >
```

The last ATTLIST declaration (for the Phone element) shows the use of a parameter entity to declare the name and values of the phonetype attribute.

The <Product> element has several children, mostly simple text-only elements. All of these children are required and must be singular. Once again, the parent element has a required ID attribute, plus an additional enumerated value (Boolean) attribute:

```
<!-- <Product> -->

<!ELEMENT Product (ProductName, Description, Price, Units, Stock) >
<!ATTLIST Product
   productID ID #REQUIRED
   hire (true | false) "false" >

<!ELEMENT ProductName (#PCDATA) >
<!ELEMENT Description (#PCDATA) >

<!ELEMENT Price (#PCDATA) >
<!ATTLIST Price %attdef_currency; #REQUIRED >

<!ELEMENT Units (#PCDATA) >
<!ELEMENT Stock (#PCDATA) >
```

Like the Phone element in the previous section of this example, the Price element uses a parameter entity for part of its attribute declaration.

The <Invoice> element is the key to all the others. It is an empty element that uses five required and two optional attributes. These include the usual ID attribute to identify the invoice, an IDREF attribute that provides a link to the customer, invoice date, and the like:

```
<!-- <Invoice> -->

<!ELEMENT Invoice EMPTY>
<!ATTLIST Invoice
   invoiceID  ID     #REQUIRED
   customerID IDREF #REQUIRED
   date       CDATA #REQUIRED
   terms      CDATA #REQUIRED
   paid (true | false)  #REQUIRED
   hire (true | false)  "false"
   notes      CDATA #IMPLIED >
```

The last kind of element is the <InvoiceOrder>. It connects the billing aspects of the invoice system (such as <Invoice> and <Customer>) with the <Invoice> inventory part, via its IDREF attributes:

```
<!-- <InvoiceOrder> -->

<!ELEMENT  InvoiceOrder EMPTY >
<!ATTLIST  InvoiceOrder
   invoiceID IDREF #REQUIRED
   productID IDREF #REQUIRED
   units     CDATA #REQUIRED
   notes     CDATA #IMPLIED >

<!-- End of 'toysco.dtd' -->
```

We now have a DTD that can be used to validate our example <Toysco> document (and to provide entity replacement text and attribute default values). This DTD is named Chapter_05.dtd, and can be used to validate the Chapter_05_Toysco.xml example data.

Summary

In this chapter, we've seen how to use DTDs to define and constrain the structure and content of XML data. We've seen:

- The difference between well-formed and valid XML data
- That DTDs comprise an internal and an external subset
- How to associate a DTD with a document
- How to describe elements and their content
- How to describe attributes
- How to define the various kinds of entities (replaceable content) for both XML data and DTDs
- How to handle non-XML data
- How to use conditional sections in DTDs
- The limitations of DTDs

Although we've concentrated on what can be done with DTDs, there are limitations, which imply that an alternative method of validating XML data is needed for some applications. Given XML's origins in SGML, many generic text documents can be handled adequately with DTDs. However, many new uses of XML demand more rigorous data typing and other features that will be provided by XML Schema, as we will see in the next chapter.

6

Introducing XML Schema

The W3C XML Schema specification is aimed at offering an alternative way to constrain documents other than DTDs. It is a powerful and flexible language, which permits authors to create either tighter or looser restrictions over documents than DTDs, while still allowing them to be validated. It introduces data typing, which makes for richer documents that can be processed more easily. Furthermore, its syntax is written in XML, which means you do not have to learn a different syntax (such as EBNF) and there are a number of tools that are already at your disposal for working with such schemas. In this chapter, we will be looking at the syntax and construction of XML Schema, and examples of how to write our own.

Most XML documents are largely composed of elements and attributes that mark up the text into segments that are labeled so that they can be easily processed. Schemas describe the structure of documents and constrain what they can contain. In the time it has taken for the W3C XML Schema specification to come this far, there have been many competing or complementary specifications for defining data structures. We will look at some of the alternatives to XML Schemas in Chapter 7, "Schema Alternatives", but in this chapter we will be focusing on the W3C's XML Schema specification, and when we talk about an XML Schema that is what we mean.

> **When we refer to XML Schemas (big 'S') in this chapter, we specifically mean schemas written according to the W3C XML Schema specification. When we refer to schemas (small 's'), we mean schemas in general (remember that a DTD is a 'type of schema').**

By the end of this chapter the reader should have learned about the following:

- The syntax of, and how to write, XML Schemas
- The advantages of XML Schemas over DTDs
- Some example schemas

However, first of all we will look at the importance of schemas in general:

Why Schemas Are Important

Schemas not only describe the permissible content of a document, they can:

- Create an abstract description of the structure of documents an application will be dealing with. This means that we can create an application around the schema, rather than having to write an application that is tied to a proprietary vendor implementation. We can then just work with a subset or extension of this schema if it is more appropriate. Building on a common schema is far less risky than building on a proprietary structure.
- Describe how a document will be exchanged, which acts as an enforceable (validatable) contract between senders and receivers, as seen in initiatives such as the BizTalk framework.
- Save each application from the need to check whether this contract is enforced (they do still have the option to, and can pass this on to a validating component).
- Be shared between communities, allowing different companies to share the same data or model.
- Make it easier for different applications to create, manage, and process the same files.

In this chapter, we will be focusing on the syntax of how to design XML Schemas, with a number of design considerations that relate to the new features that schemas offer. There is also some complementary material in Chapter 14, "Data Modeling", which will say more about design issues and structures of your models.

Before we start looking at the syntax in detail, we would benefit from looking at some of the aims of XML Schema, how the specifications are divided up, and how documents are validated with XML Schema

Background To W3C XML Schemas

When the W3C put together a working group to devise the XML Schema specification, the group had several aims. A full list of what they intended to achieve can be found in the requirements document at http://www.w3.org/TR/NOTE-xml-schema-req. Their aims included:

- The creation of a mechanism for constraining document structure that would be analogous to DTDs.
- Allowing markup constructs and constraints to be specified in XML-based syntax.
- The provision of a richer set of data-types than DTDs (including byte, date, integer, and SQL and Java primitive data-types). This would have to be adequate to import and export data from a relational, object-oriented or OLAP database (helpful in mapping database data to an XML document and describing relationships in the XML document form).
- Allowing users to derive their own data-types.
- Integration with namespaces.
- To allow inheritance of element, attribute, and data-type definitions.
- Distinguish lexical data representation from an underlying information set, as the processing model works on the Infoset.

Along the way, there have been many revisions, and some high-profile discussions of the resulting W3C XML Schema language. The resulting specification addressing these concerns has been divided into three parts:

- **XML Schemas Part 0: Primer**. The first part is a primer, which explains what W3C XML Schemas are, how they differ from DTDs, and how someone writes such a schema according to the new syntax. This is easy to read, and offers a very different approach from any previous W3C specifications; it is a good start for getting to grips with XML Schemas and what they are capable of. Some would go as far as saying that it was a necessary addition, due to the complexity of the specification itself. As such it is classed as **Non-normative**; it is not the standard or specification of the W3C XML Schema language, rather an introduction to it.
- **XML Schemas Part 1: Structures**. The next part describes how we can constrain the structure and contents of XML documents using the new XML syntax, and defines rules governing schema validation of documents. It is analogous to the specification of DTDs in the XML 1.0 specification, explaining how we declare the **information items** that can appear in the instance documents. It covers the declaration of elements, attributes, notations, etc. This section is **Normative**; it is the official documentation as opposed to the primer, which is an introduction.
- **XML Schemas Part 2: Data-types**. The third part defines a set of simple data-types, which can be associated with XML element content and attribute values. When we declare an element's content to be of a particular data-type, we are saying that it should, for example, be a string, date, number, integer, or byte etc. It describes the set of data-types that are built into the schemas specification, which all conforming processors are required to implement by default. It also explains how we can add further restrictions to these built-in data-types to derive our own data-types. This allows XML software to do a better job of managing dates, numbers, and other special forms of information. This section, like the Structures specification, is **Normative**.

Advantages of W3C XML Schemas

As we will really see when we start looking at how to write XML Schemas, they have several advantages over their DTD counterparts. Let's take a brief look at some of these to see why the W3C Schema technology is so valuable.

Support for Data-types

This is one of XML Schemas greatest strengths. As XML is being used increasingly in applications, the ability to know whether the content of an element or attribute is a string, integer, Boolean, float, or whatever, is a great asset. With XML 1.0 the only data-types that were available were:

Data-type	Description
`string`	Representing a string type
`entity`	Representing the XML `ENTITY` type
`entities`	Representing the XML `ENTITIES` type
`enumeration`	Representing the enumerated type (of attributes)
`id`	Representing the XML `ID` type
`idref`	Representing the XML `IDREF` type

Table continued on following page

Data-type	Description
idrefs	Representing the XML IDREFS type
nmtoken	Representing the XML NMTOKEN type
nmtokens	Representing the XML NMTOKENS type
notation	Representing an NMTOKEN type

This meant that if you wanted to represent a data-type such as an integer or a date, you would either write this into the application logic or make your elements carry attributes to indicate the data-type of their element content. For example:

```
<!ELEMENT MyElement (#PCDATA)>
<!ATTLIST MyElement datatype CDATA  #IMPLIED >
```

When represented in the instance document, it would look something like this:

```
<MyElement datatype="integer">12882774</MyElement>
```

This means that applications have to:

- Validate the document before passing it to the application
- Read the correct data-type from the attribute
- Convert the element content from a string into an integer before it can process it

Using XML Schema's ability to specify the data-type of element content and attribute values in the schema, applications will be able to use a validation component that not only ensures that the document is valid, but also ensures that the information matches the specified data-type. A W3C XML Schema conformant processor would therefore save us from writing application code to validate that the data that we receive into our applications is within an allowable range and of the correct type.

It would also be possible (if the schema processor was written in the same language as the application) to remove the stage where the string has to be converted into the correct data-type, allowing programs to perform calculations on the data directly.

The benefits stretch further, when we consider that you can limit the size of your XML documents by specifying a data-type for element content and attribute values. This works in the same way as constraining the type of data held within fields of a relational database using database schemas. In fact, as we shall see, there are a number of features of the W3C XML Schema specification that make working with existing data stored in a relational database much easier.

As we will see later in the chapter, we can create what are known as complex types, built up from simple data-types and other complex types, which create reusable blocks of code that offer the conceptual and maintenance benefits of the OO inheritance of data-types *and* structures. This is because, once we have defined a type, we can reuse it or build upon it.

The ability of XML Schemas to enforce types helps bridge the divide between using XML to mark up documents and data. When it comes to defining documents such as invoices, we can specify them with dates, quantities and currencies, both abstractly and completely, so that different processing applications can make use of them, and so that data and documents become integrated without losing information from either.

As a result, we will also be able to make use of the XML Schema to create search engines that search XML document instances more specifically. For example, we could search for dates or ranges of dates, or a type that we have created.

Use XML Syntax

When you look at your first XML Schema, probably the most striking difference between it and DTDs is that XML Schemas are actually written in XML. The W3C XML Schema specification describes an XML vocabulary that can be used to constrain XML documents. This means that all the tools you would use to create and manipulate XML documents, are also available to work with XML Schemas – standard XML parsers, the DOM, SAX, XSLT, XML-aware browsers. It also means that it will be possible to construct schemas or transform them on the fly using standard XML technologies such as the DOM, or XSLT.

When first learning XML, many people found the notation used to write DTDs difficult to understand. The syntax was defined in **Extended Backus Naur Form** (**EBNF**). Like many things, DTDs are not too difficult when we get the hang of using them, but often they are a lot more complex than the data they describe. Because XML Schemas use XML to describe a document, it means that users do not have to learn another syntax and its associated rules before creating the schema.

Stronger Support for Content Models

DTDs content models are weak, only allowing us to constrain the document to a simple sequence or choice list. They cannot be used to validate any mixed content models (elements that can contain character data as well as other markup), they can only contain zero, one, or many occurrences of an element (rather than a fixed number or range), and there are no named element or attribute groups (which allow us to reuse content models). XML Schemas, on the other hand, allow for more detailed and flexible content models. They can be used to validate mixed content; they can be used to specify exact numbers of occurrences, and can be used to name groups of elements. These are all valuable additions whether you are working with representing text or other forms of data.

There are also much more powerful mechanisms for:

- Creating reusable constructs: the ability to group together attributes and elements so that they can be used in other content models, to inherit from them, and to alter their meaning in different contexts (far better than the use of parameter entities for this purpose)
- Controlling order and nesting in the content model
- Specifying patterns using regular expressions to check that the sequence of characters in an element's content or attribute's value matches the pattern

Applications such as e-commerce, data exchange, and RPC (remote procedure calls) all benefit from the more advanced features of schemas, including the ability to create complex content models, and the stronger description and validation of mixed content.

Extensible

When we think about the full name of XML, it is somewhat ironic that the description language that was released with the specification is not extensible too; which is another drawback of DTDs. The W3C XML Schema specification, however, changes all this with features such as:

- The ability to reuse parts of schemas in other schemas
- The ability to define complex structures that can be reused in different schemas
- The ability to derive our own, new data-types from existing ones
- The ability to reference multiple schemas from a document instance

Overall, this means that we will be able to share standard vocabularies with greater ease, and be able to tailor existing schemas to our own needs rather than everyone creating their own.

If we think about the use of XML for data interchange, and think about some of the examples where XML documents are generated on the fly from several data sources, we can see why the ability to support content models from different schemas is important. As we share more data between companies or departments, sending the same data between different programs, the ability to support multiple schemas will be very useful. Imagine we were writing an application that required sets of data both from our supplier and from our accounts department, and that we were getting data from these two sources into our one application. With XML Schemas, we could write a schema that the processing application could use to validate the documents content that had come from different sources, based upon sharing the two vocabularies.

Self Documenting

Using the `annotation` elements defined in the XML Schema specification, we can describe the intended purpose of an element, attribute, or section of the schema – as with all programming, use of comments is simply good practice that leads to more maintainable code. Indeed if you intend others to share the schema, or you intend to make it public, good use of the annotations will help make sure that those who want to use your schema use it in the way that you intended.

Furthermore, by simply attaching a style sheet to a properly annotated schema, it is possible to display the descriptions in the `annotation` elements alongside the constructs and constraints, effectively creating your own documentation.

Choosing a Parser

In order to work with the examples in this chapter, we will need to choose a schema-compliant parser. At the time of writing, there was a limited range of parsing tools to work with XML Schemas. At the time of writing, two parsers that offer limited compliance are:

- **Xerces-j** from the Apache XML Project, which is based on technology from IBMs XML4C and XML4J parsers – http://xml.apache.org.
- Oracle's **XML Parser for Java v2** can be found online at http://technet.oracle.com/tech/xml/. It is integrated into the Oracle 8i DBMS, and therefore provides XML support on the multitude of systems that can run this popular DBMS.

A proliferation of other parsers will no doubt become available when the specification becomes a firm Recommendation.

Working with XML Schemas

Before we start looking at the syntax of XML Schemas, it is worth noting that XML Schemas work on an abstract data model as defined in the Infoset (see Chapter 4), not an instance document. This is similar to the way the W3C DOM API works: first, the document is parsed, and then validation occurs (after any entity expansion and attribute value defaulting or normalization have taken place) on the resulting information set. This ensures that the document that has been parsed is well formed, and that it conforms to the rules of the Namespace specification.

One of the tasks of the specification is to explain what a W3C XML Schema-aware processor must be able to do in order to conform to it. To do this, it talks in terms of operations that occur on the **abstract model**, because it cannot talk in terms of an implementation of a processor that is XML Schema-compliant.

Schema Components is a generic term for the blocks that make up the abstract data model of the schema. In all, there are twelve components, split into three groups:

- **Primary components**: simple type and complex type definitions, and element and attribute declarations
- **Secondary components**: attribute groups, identity constraints, model group definitions and notation declarations
- **Helper components**: these are different from the first two, because they cannot be named or independently accessed

This actually provides us with a natural path for learning about schemas, and indeed for writing our own data model. (Data modeling is covered in detail in Chapter 14). We will look at the use of these types in detail below, including examples of the use of each.

For a start then, we will concentrate on the primary components.

Primary Components

As we have just said, there are four primary components:

- **Element declarations**
- **Simple type definitions** can only hold values, not child elements or attributes
- **Complex type definitions** are allowed to have sub-elements, and to carry attributes
- **Attribute declarations**

*Note the terminology: we **declare** attributes and elements, but we **define** types.*

Declaring Elements

The main building blocks of all XML documents are elements and attributes. Because XML is intended to be a self-describing format, it is hardly surprising that XML Schemas use elements called `element` and `attribute` to declare an element and attribute respectively.

In its simplest form, you declare an element like so:

```
<xsd:element name="dateReceived" />
```

The name of the element is the value of an attribute unsurprisingly called, `name`. The namespace prefix `xsd:` indicates that the `element` construct has come from the W3C XML Schema namespace – this will be declared in the root element when we come to write our first full schema, but it is good to get in practice and start using them now. As we said, one of the important features of XML Schemas is that they add data typing. If we do not specify a type on the element, the default is that the element content will be a string. In order to specify that the content of an element should be a date, we add a `type` attribute to our element declaration, like so:

```
<xsd:element name="dateReceived" type="xsd:date" />
```

This should take the format `YYYY-MM-DD`, so we could expect something like this: `<dateReceived>2001-12-25</dateReceived>`. We have used the `xsd:` namespace prefix in the value of the `type` attribute, because (as we shall see) the date type is part of the XML Schema namespace.

The declaration of an element is an association of its name with a type.

While this statement may seem a little strange, having seen that we can specify data-types for element content with the addition of the `type` attribute on the element declaration, you can understand it better. In fact, as we will come to see, when we come to creating content models for elements we are still associating a name with a type.

If we want to specify the legal number of times an element can occur, we have two optional attributes that help us: `minOccurs` and `maxOccurs`, whose value can be any non-negative integer.

```
<xsd:element name="dateReceived" type="xsd:date"
        minOccurs="0" maxOccurs="1" />
```

This makes the `dateReceived` element optional, because it can occur a minimum of zero times, but it can only occur once if it is included (denoted by the maximum of 1).

Both attributes have a default value of `1`, meaning that if they are omitted, there may only be one occurrence of the element and it is required (just like the absence of a cardinality operator in a DTD). The following table shows the equivalents of DTD cardinality operators for values of `minOccurs` and `maxOccurs` Schema attributes:

Cardinality Operator	minOccurs Value	maxOccurs Value	Number of times the element can appear
[none]	1	1	One and only one
?	0	1	Zero or one
*	0	unbounded	Zero or more
+	1	unbounded	One or more

A couple of points worth noting here are that:

- The maxOccurs attribute can also take the special value of unbounded, which means that the element must occur at least as many times as the value of minOccurs, but that there is no upper limit on how many times it occurs over and above the minimum.
- If minOccurs is present and maxOccurs is omitted, the value of maxOccurs is assumed to be equal to the value of minOccurs.

For example, imagine we were working an invoice, and were declaring the Line-Item element; we would want to ensure that this occurred at least once:

```
<xsd:element name="LineItem" type="xsd:string"
  minOccurs="1" maxOccurs="unbounded" />
```

Here we are saying that the LineItem element must occur at least once, but can occur more than once without a limit to the number of line items that can appear in the order.

For us to continue, it is important to understand that the W3C XML Schema specification makes a clear distinction between **simple types** and **complex types**. Simple types refer to atoms of data (whether element content or attribute values) that cannot be divided in terms of XML Schema and we use **data-types** to define the data-type of information in a simple type. For example, the value of the dateReceived element was a date in the format YYYY-MM-DD, and this cannot be split up into constituent parts of year, month and date by the schema (that would have to be done by a processing application or the element content would have to be split into the constituent parts). An element whose content includes child elements is not a simple type, because the information can be split up into sections contained in each of the child elements only the value of an element with no children is a simple type.

Complex types can contain other elements and attributes. In fact, in order for an element to carry even one attribute or to have a single child element we would have to define a complex type. It is by using complex types that we define content models for elements.

Let's have a look at each of these, after which we will come back to look at how we declare attributes.

Simple Types

We have already established that simple types are the atoms of information considered distinct to XML Schema and that they cannot be split up, for example:

```
<myElement>Here is some simple type content.</myElement>
```

This string is a unique atom of information. In the same way, each of the attribute values on the following element are separate simple types:

```
<myElement attribute1="simpleType" attribute2="simpleType" />
```

Here the string simpleType is the simple type.

We are now able to specify the data-type of simple types because of the added functionality that XML Schemas allow.

The data-types specification defines two varieties of data-types: built-in types and user-derived types.

- **Built-in types** are available to all XML Schema authors, and should be implemented by a conforming processor. There are two varieties of built-in type:
  - **Primitive types**, which are types in their own right, they are not defined in terms of other data-types.
  - **Derived types**, which are built from definitions of other data-types, are created by restricting existing data-types, and the type that they are derived from is known as their **base type**.
- **User-derived types** are derived by the author of the Schema, and are particular to that Schema (Although we can import these definitions into other definitions).

Built-in Types

Here are the built-in primitive types that are available to Schema authors:

Primitive type	Description	Example
`string`	Represents any legal character strings in XML that match the Char production in XML 1.0 Second Edition.	`Bob Watkins` Note, if you need to use a character such as an angled bracket or an ampersand, these should be escaped using the escape characters or numeric character references defined in XML 1.0 Second Edition, such as: ❑ < or < for < (an opening angled bracket) ❑ > or > for > (a closing angled bracket) ❑ & or for & (an ampersand) ❑ &apos or ' for ' (an apostrophe) ❑ " or " for " (a quotation mark).
`boolean`	Represents binary logic, `true` or `false`	`true`, `false`, `1`, `0`
`number`	Represents arbitrary precision decimal numbers, and must be capable of handling a number to 18 decimal places at least.	`-1.75`, `0`, `23.67`, `2234.5` The representation of one hundred can be `100` or `1.0E2`.

Primitive type	Description	Example
`float`	Standard concept of real numbers corresponding to a single precision 32 bit floating point type	`-INF, -1E4, 4.5E-2, 37, INF, NaN` NaN means **Not a Number**
`double`	Standard concept of real numbers corresponding to a single precision 64 bit floating point type	`-INF, -1E4, 4.5E-2, 37, INF, NaN`
`decimal`	Represents arbitrary precision decimal numbers	
`duration`	Represents a duration of time in the format `P`*n*`Y`*n*`M`*n*`DT`*n*`H`*n*`M`*n*`S`. Where: ❑ `P` is a designator that must always be present ❑ *n*`Y` represents number of years ❑ *n*`M` represents number of months ❑ *n*`D` represents number of days ❑ `T` is the date/time separator ❑ *n*`H` is number of hours ❑ *n*`M` is number of minutes ❑ *n*`S` is number of seconds	`P1Y0M1DT20:25:30` 1 year and a day, 20 hours, 25 minutes and 30 seconds.
`dateTime`	A specific instance in time in the format: `CCYY-MM-DDThh:mm:ss` where: ❑ `CC` represents the century ❑ `YY` represents the year ❑ `MM` represents the month ❑ `DD` represents the day `T` is the date/time separator ❑ `hh` represents hours ❑ `mm` represents minutes ❑ `ss` represents seconds The year `0000` is prohibited.	`2001-04-16T15:23:15` Represents the 16th of April 2001, at 3:23 and 15 seconds in the afternoon.

Table continued on following page

Primitive type	Description	Example
time	Represents an instance of time that occurs every day in the format HH:MM:SS	14:12:30 Represents 12 minutes and thirty seconds past two in the afternoon.
date	Represents a calendar date from the Gregorian calendar (the whole day) in the format CCYY-MM-DD	2001-04-16 Represents the 16th of April 2001.
gYearMonth	Represents a month in a year in the Gregorian calendar, in the format CCYY-MM	1999-02 Represents February 1999
gYear	Represents a year in the Gregorian calendar in the format CCYY.	1986 Represents 1986
gMonthDay	Represents a day of the month in the Gregorian calendar in the format -MM-DD.	-16-04 Represents the 16th of April, ideal for birthdays, holidays, and recurring events.
gDay	Represents a day in the Gregorian calendar in the format -DD.	-16 Represents the sixteenth day of a month. Ideal for monthly occurrences, such as payday.
gMonth	Represents a month in the Gregorian calendar in the format -MM.	-12 Represents December
hexBinary	Represents arbitrary hex-encoded binary data	111110110111
base64Binary	Represents Base64-encoded arbitrary binary data	111110110111
AnyURI	Represents a URI. The value can be absolute or relative, and may have an optional fragment identifier, so it can be a URI reference	http://www.example.com
QName	Represents an XML namespace QName (or qualified name)	xsd:element
Notation	Represents the NOTATION type from XML 1.0 Second Edition. It should not appear directly in a schema; it should only be used for deriving other data-types by specifying a value for enumeration which can be used in a schema	

To create a new data-type, you further restrict an existing built-in or user-derived data-type, which is known as the **base type** of your definition. These new types are therefore a subset of the existing type. The XML Schema specification authors devised some built-in derived types, which are again available to all XML Schema authors, because they thought they were so important to using XML that they would only end up being recreated anyway. Here are the derived data-types that are built into XML schemas:

Derived type	Description	Base type	Example
`normalizedString`	Represents whitespace normalized strings. Whitespace normalized strings do not contain carriage return, line feed or tab (#x9) characters	`string`	`This is a normalized string`
`token`	Represents tokenized strings, which do not contain line feed or tab characters, leading or trailing spaces, and internal sequences of more than two spaces	`normalizedString`	`One Two Three Four`
`language`	Language identifiers, as defined in RFC 1766, and valid values for `xml:lang` as defined in XML 1.0	`token`	`en-GB`, `en-US`, `fr`
`IDREFS`	`IDREFS` attribute type from XML 1.0		
`ENTITIES`	`ENTITY` attribute type from XML 1.0		
`NMTOKEN`	XML 1.0 `NMTOKEN`	`token`	`small, medium, large`
`NMTOKENS`	XML 1.0 `NMTOKENS`		`small medium large`
`name`	Represents XML Names	`token`	
`NCName`	Represents XML "non-colonized" Names – a QName without the prefix and colon	`name`	`Address`
`ID`	Represents the ID attribute type from XML 1.0 second edition.	`NCName`	
`IDREF`	Represents the IDREF attribute type from XML 1.0 Second edition	`NCName`	

Table continued on following page

Derived type	Description	Base type	Example
ENTITY	Represents the ENTITY attribute type from XML 1.0 Second edition.	NCName	
integer	Standard mathematical concept of integer numbers	number	-4, 0, 2, 7
nonPositive Integer	Standard mathematical concept of a non-positive integer (includes 0)	integer	-4, -1, 0
negativeInteger	Standard mathematical concept of negative integers (does not include 0)	integer	-4, -1
long	An integer between - 9223372036854775898 and 922372036854775807	long	-23568323, 52883773203 895
int	An integer between -2147483648 and 2147483647	interger	-24781982, 24781924
short	An integer between - 32768 and 32767	int which is derived from long	-31353, -43, 345, 31347
byte	An integer between -128 and 127	short	-127, -42, 0, 54, 125
nonNegative Integer	A positive integer including zero	integer	0, 1, 42
unsignedLong	A nonNegativeInteger between 0 and 18446744073709551615	nonNegativeInteger	0, 356, 23875382938 3
unsignedInt	A nonNegativeInteger between 0 and 4294967295	unsignedLong	46, 4255774, 2342823723
unsignedShort	A nonNegativeInteger between 0 and 65535	unsignedInt	78, 64328
unsignedByte	A nonNegativeInteger between 0 and 255	unsignedShort	0, 46, 247
positiveInteger	An integer of 1 or higher	nonNegativeInteger	1, 24, 345343

We will look at creating our own simple data-types later in the chapter, in the section entitled "Creating Our Own Data-Types".

In all, XML Schema defines three varieties of simple type:

- Atomic data-types
- List data-types
- Union data-types

We will now go on to look at these three types in more detail.

Atomic Data-types

As we saw earlier, an **atomic data-type** is one that has a value that cannot be divided, at least not within the context of XML Schema. Therefore, if we had an atomic type representation of the string "`A B C`" it would be interpreted as a single string of three letters and two whitespace characters, rather than three separate units separated by whitespace. While a derived type can be an atomic type, the derived type must be a restriction on a primitive built-in XML Schema data-type. This means we can only use the constraining facets that apply to that primitive built-in type.

> **Note that atomic is not analogous to primitive.**

Numbers and strings are atomic types since their values cannot be described using any smaller pieces. The former is obvious, but can't a string be defined in terms of a smaller component, such as characters? While it is true in the abstract sense, XML Schema has no concept of a character as a data-type – and thus the string is an atomic primitive type, (of `string`):

```
<atom>This string is fine as we can slice textual data - there are no character
atoms in XML Schema.</atom>
```

The second example is an atomic derived type. It is a `date`, which could be derived from the `string` primitive type, though in XML Schema they are derived indirectly from three other types:

```
<atom2>1927-01-16</atom2>
```

The third example is also an atomic derived type; an `integer` is derived from the `float` primitive type.

```
<atom3>469557</atom3>
```

List Types

As well as atomic types, XML Schema also provides a **list type**. To understand list types you have to remember that XML Schema considers **atomic types** to be indivisible. For example, a string such as "`This is my element content`" would be considered indivisible. Furthermore, if you were representing clothes sizes, you could create an element whose content is of type `NMTOKEN` whose value is `XL`. The content of the element (whose type is `NMTOKEN`) is indivisible or atomic, so the letters `X` and `L` have no meaning of their own. However, if you had an element whose type is `NMTOKENS` and whose value is "`S M L XL`", these would be treated as separate white space delimited values – a sequence of four atoms.

You can create your own list types by deriving them from existing atomic types, but you cannot create your own list types by deriving from existing list or complex types. If we wanted to derive a list type from a simple type `oneToTen`, as seen here:

```
<listFromOneToTenType>1 4 7 9</listFromOneToTenType>
```

we could create it like this:

```
<xsd:simpleType name = "listFromOneToTenType">
   <xsd:list itemType = "oneToTen" />
</xsd:simpleType>
```

There are three built-in list types in XML Schemas: `NMTOKENS`, `IDREFS` and `ENTITIES`.

One thing to be aware of is that deriving from strings can be difficult, because you cannot use strings that contain whitespace, for example if you had a list of internet search engine sites, such as "`AltaVista Ask Jeeves Google Yahoo`" it would be treated as five items because there is whitespace between `Ask` and `Jeeves`, although it is intended to be one item.

Union Types

Union types enable element content or attribute values to be of a type provided from a union of different atomic and list types. If you imagine that we sold clothes in sizes `S`, `M`, `L`, or `XL` and in numeric sizes from `1` to `10`, we could create a union type so that allowable content would be either one of the abbreviated letterforms or a number between 1 and 10.

```
<xsd:simpleType  name = "sizesUnion">
<xsd:union  memberTypes = "clothesSizes oneToTen" />
</xsd:simpleType>
```

We just provide the types to participate in the union as a white space separated list.

Now let's move on to look at complex types.

Complex Types

We need to be able to define complex types in order to create element content models and allow elements to carry attributes.

Here we can see the power of being able to create content models that we can inherit from and reuse. We will create a type called `Address` to indicate the child elements that we would expect to see in a content model representing an address.

```
<xsd:complexType name = "Address">
   <xsd:sequence>
      <xsd:element name="Street1" />
      <xsd:element name="Street2" />
      <xsd:element name="City" />
      <xsd:element name="State" />
      <xsd:element name="Zip" />
   </xsd:sequence>
</xsd:complexType>
```

Here we have the `complexType` element, which holds the definition of our complex type. It has an attribute called `name` whose value holds the name of the complex type we are creating. This is followed by a `sequence` element to indicate that the child elements should appear in the order in which they are declared. The element declarations themselves, representing the content model, are then nested inside.

Having declared this complex type, we can now use it with any elements that should contain address details. For example, imagine that we had a document, which contains customer, employee, and supplier addresses. We would be able to reuse this same content model in elements for each, like so:

```
<xsd:element name="mailingAddress" type="Address" />
<xsd:element name="billingAddress" type="Address" />
```

Each of these elements would now contain the same child elements, like so:

```
<MailingAddress>
   <Street1></Street1>
   <Street2></Street2>
   <City></City>
   <State></State>
   <Zip></Zip>
</MailingAddress>
```

It is best to create a **named complex type** when we are going to reuse the content model. However, if we are just declaring a content model to be used in a single element, we can declare an **anonymous type**, like so:

```
<xsd:element name = "Name">
   <xsd:complexType>
      <xsd:sequence>
         <xsd:element name = "FirstName" />
         <xsd:element name = "MiddleInitial"
                      minOccurs = "0" maxOccurs = "unbounded" />
         <xsd:element name = "LastName" />
      </xsd:sequence>
</xsd:complexType>
```

Here we have declared an element called `Name`, and then used the `complexType` element without the addition of a `name` attribute (making it anonymous). Inside the sequence element, we again have element declarations that are the child elements of `Name`. In this case, we have added the optional `minOccurs` and `maxOccurs` attributes to the `MiddleInitial` element to indicate that it can appear repeatedly, or not at all. The other elements will be required to appear but can only appear once.

This also helps keep the design tidy because we are not creating references to types that are defined elsewhere in the schema. Let's put these two together now and create a schema for contact details (this can be found in the download available from `wrox.com` as `06_01.xsd`).

```
<?xml version = "1.0" ?>

<xsd:schema xmlns:xsd = "http://www.w3.org/2001/XMLSchema">

<xsd:element name = "ContactDetails">
   <xsd:complexType>
      <xsd:sequence>
         <xsd:element ref = "Contact"
          minOccurs = "1" maxOccurs = "unbounded" />
      </xsd:sequence>
   </xsd:complexType>
</xsd:element>

<xsd:element name = "Contact">
   <xsd:complexType>
```

```
        <xsd:sequence>
           <xsd:element name = "Name">
              <xsd:complexType>
                 <xsd:sequence>
                    <xsd:element name = "FirstName" />
                    <xsd:element name = "MiddleInitial"
                     minOccurs = "0" maxOccurs = "unbounded" />
                    <xsd:element name = "LastName" />
                 </xsd:sequence>
           </xsd:complexType>

        <xsd:element ref = "billingAddress" type = "Address" />
        <xsd:element ref = "mailingAddress" type = "Address" />

        <xsd:sequence>
     </xsd:complexType>
  </xsd:element>

  <xsd:complexType name = "Address">
     <xsd:sequence>
        <xsd:element name="Street1" />
        <xsd:element name="Street2" />
        <xsd:element name="City" />
        <xsd:element name="State" />
        <xsd:element name="Zip" />
     </xsd:sequence>
  </xsd:complexType>

  </xsd:schema>
```

W3C XML Schemas are normally saved with the extension .xsd

As this is an XML document, we have included the XML declaration. Next, you can see that we have introduced the `schema` root element. This contains the namespace for the W3C XML Schema, and associates the prefix `xsd:` with markup from that schema.

```
<?xml version = "1.0" ?>

<xsd:schema xmlns:xsd = "http://www.w3.org/2001/XMLSchema">
```

We then declare an element called `ContactDetails` to be the root element. Inside this can be one or more `Contact` elements used to hold the details of the individual. Note here that we are using an attribute called `ref` on the element declaration for the `Contact` element. This is because we have defined it elsewhere in the schema document. We are passing a reference to this element declaration.

```
<xsd:element name = "ContactDetails">
   <xsd:complexType>
      <xsd:sequence>
         <xsd:element ref = "Contact"
                      minOccurs = "1" maxOccurs = "unbounded" />
      </xsd:sequence>
   </xsd:complexType>
</xsd:element>
```

Next, we declare the `Contact` element and define its content model using an anonymous type definition. This includes the element declaration for `Name` (and its anonymous type definition), and the declaration of two new elements `billingAddress` and `mailingAddress`, which are both of type `Address` and therefore contain the child elements defined in the `Address` type.

```
<xsd:element name = "Contact">
   <xsd:complexType>
      <xsd:sequence>
         <xsd:element name = "Name">
         ...
         </xsd:element>

      <xsd:element name = "mailingAddress" type = "Address"
                   minOccurs = "0" maxOccurs = "1" />
      <xsd:element name = "billingAddress" type = "Address"
                   minOccurs = "0" maxOccurs = "1" />

      </xsd:sequence>
   </xsd:complexType>
</xsd:element>
```

After this, we define the `Address` type as we saw earlier and close the `schema` element.

Extending ComplexTypes

This address type may be ideal for most uses, but if one department needed an extra attribute, it would be possible to extend this definition to add another element just for their use. This illustrates the power of type reuse. Let's say that the finance department needs to know how long a customer has lived at an address for credit checking purposes. We can extend the `addressType` to include two attributes called `residentFrom` and `residentTo`. To do this, we use the `extension` element, inside a `complexContent` element to indicate that the base type that we are extending is a `complexType` already:

```
<xsd:element name="CreditAddressReference">
   <xsd:complexType>
      <xsd:complexContent>
         <xsd:extension base="addressType">
            <xsd:attribute name="residentFrom" type="xsd:date" />
            <xsd:attribute name="residentTo" type="xsd:date" />
         </xsd:extension>
      </xsd:complexContent>
   </xsd:complexType>
</xsd:element>
```

Declaring Attributes

We have already seen how to declare elements, and define simple types and complex types. Now we should look at how to declare attributes and add them to elements. The declaration of an attribute is rather similar to the declaration of an element; we use an element called `attribute` to declare the attribute, which carries an attribute called `name` whose value is the name of the attribute we are declaring:

```
<attribute name = "paid" />
```

We can also add a data-type for the value of the attribute using the `type` attribute:

```
<attribute name = "paid" type = "boolean" />
```

Obviously, there is no requirement for `minOccurs` and `maxOccurs`, as an attribute can only occur once on an element. Nevertheless, there are some other additional ways of controlling whether the attribute is required to appear, or merely optional. If it must appear, we can add another one to the declaration called `use` whose value should be set to `required`.

```
<attribute name = "paid" use = "required" />
```

The default is that it is optional, although we can say this using the `use` attribute again, this time with a value of `optional`.

```
<attribute name = "paid" use = "optional" />
```

You can even say that an attribute may not appear on an element by using the value of `prohibited` on the `use` attribute:

```
<attribute name = "paid" use="prohibited" />
```

We can also supply fixed or default content for attributes using attributes of the same name:

```
<attribute name = "paid" use = "required" fixed = "True" />
```

to indicate that the attribute's value should always be `True`, or

```
<attribute name = "paid" use = "optional" default = "True" />
```

to indicate that if no value has been given for the `paid` attribute, or if it has been missed off, that the parser should add the value `True` for the attribute. If you are going to specify a default value, the attribute's presence *must* be optional.

So far, this type of declaration would have to be a direct child of the schema element, and it could then be used by reference in other declarations. So, let's see how we attach an attribute to an element. We can declare the element inside the complex type (whether the complex type is anonymous or named):

```
<xsd:element name = "invoice">
   <xsd:complexType>
      <attribute name = "paid" use = "optional" default = "True" />
   </xsd:complexType>
</xsd:element>
```

Remember we have to define the attribute as part of a complex type because simple types can only hold atomic values, and not carry attributes or have child elements.

Or if we had declared the attribute as a child of the `schema` element, we could use it with the `ref` attribute on the attribute declaration like so:

```
<xsd:element name = "invoice">
   <xsd:complexType>
```

```
        <attribute ref = "paid" />
    </xsd:complexType>
</xsd:element>
```

We might have done this if we needed to use the `paid` attribute on a number of different elements.

Content Models

Having seen how to declare elements and attributes, we should look at other content specifications that will be familiar to DTD authors:

- Any
- Empty
- Element-only
- Mixed

The two simplest content models are **empty** elements and **any**.

Any

The any content model is the default content model when you declare an element in XML Schema, which means that element can contain any text, whitespace, and child elements. It is completely unconstrained and equivalent to the `ANY` keyword in DTDs, but in XML Schema it is known as the `anyType`. If we were to declare this, it would take the form:

```
<xsd:element name = "myElement" type = "xsd:anyType" />
```

But as it is the default, this would be equivalent:

```
<xsd:element name = "myElement" />
```

This really illustrates the idea that, when we are writing schemas, we have to constrain the allowable content for document instances. It should also become apparent that this is why we have to define types for all kinds of element content.

We add constraints in the form of a **content specification** – while the `anyType` type does count as a content specification, the others are **empty**, **element**, **mixed**, and **text-only** content.

Empty

Empty elements can carry attributes, but prevent any content appearing as text or child elements. They are ideal for placeholders. In order to define an empty element in XML Schema we first have to define a complex type, and then we have to restrict it from the `anyType` so that it can only carry attributes.

```
<xsd:element name = "product">
    <xsd:complexType>
        <xsd:complexContent>
            <xsd:restriction base = "xsd:anyType">
                <xsd:attribute name = "productID"
                               use = "required" type = "xsd:id" />
```

```
            <xsd:attribute name = "name" use = "required"
                           type="xsd:string" />
          </xsd:restriction>
        </xsd:complexContent>
      </xsd:complexType>
    </xds:element>
```

Here we have declared the element, added a `complexType` element to define the complex type, and then introduced a new element called `complexContent`, to indicate that we either wish to extend or restrict the content model of this complex type. In our case, we want to restrict the `anyType` type, so we add a `restriction` element. The `restriction` element has an attribute called `base`, whose value is the base type that we want to restrict, which in this case is the `anyType` type. Then we just add the attributes, so that we indicate that this is all the element can contain.

Element

We have already seen how we create element content by defining a complex type, and we have seen how to define both named complex types and anonymous complex types. The elements can have element content, could be empty elements, and they can carry attributes (depending on the restrictions we have placed upon the complex type). We will come again to look at element content when we look at model groups shortly.

Mixed

For information that is more complicated, we might choose a mixed model, where an element can contain a mix of text content, child elements and attributes. The mixed content model is particularly useful for adding emphasis to text and for dealing with representations of documents that you may wish to view and process. This helps break down the traditional divide between documents and data – as we will see in the example (which allows us to create and process what might be considered more like a traditional paper document) .

DTDs did not offer powerful methods of constraining mixed content models; it was not possible to use them to constrain the order and number of child elements appearing in an instance document. XML Schema, as we have already seen, does offer these features.

If we look at the following example:

```
<AutomaticResponse>

  <Header>
    Thank you for question regarding The Wrox Online Store. Your query has
    been received and will be answered in a queue by one of our support
    staff.
  </Header>

  <QueryDetails>
    For reference, your Customer ID is<CustomerID>116725</CustomerID>
    regarding order <OrderID>2001-01-16-1455</OrderID>
  </QueryDetails>

</AutomaticResponse>
```

As you can see, this document is an automatic acknowledgement generated in response to a customer query. Mixed in with the text, we have customer details and order details.

So, let's define a complex type representing the mixed content in the AutomaticResponse element. To indicate that we want a mixed content model, we simply add the mixed attribute to our complexType element, with a value of true.

```
<xsd:element name = "AutomaticResponse">
   <xsd:complexType mixed = "true">
      <xsd:sequence>
         <xsd:element name = "Header" />
         <xsd:element name = "QueryDetails">
            <xsd:complexType>
               <xsd:sequence>
                  <xsd:element name = "CustomerID" type = "xsd:number" />
                  <xsd:element name = "OrderID" type = "xsd:number" />
               </xsd:sequence>
            <xsd:complexType>
         </xsd:element>
      </xsd:sequence>
   </xsd:complexType>
</xsd:element>
```

Here we have defined the complex type to have mixed content, which means there can be character data between any of the child elements. Then we have declared that there should be a Header element and a QueryDetails element in that order. We have missed off the minOccurs and maxOccurs attributes on the element declarations, so they are expected to appear once and once only. We then define another anonymous complex type in the QueryDetails element, to indicate that it should contain elements called CustomerID and OrderID and that the content of these elements should be a number. Again, there should be one, but only one instance of each of these in the QueryDetails element.

So, we have been able to control the order, the presence of, and the data-types of the elements within the mixed model, which is far more powerful than the capabilities of DTDs for dealing with mixed content.

When we come to build up a content model, we see the idea of restricting the allowable content of a document. We are restricting the default anyType type for element content, either by restricting the anyType type, which we saw in the example for an empty element, or by defining a new complex type and specifying this as the type for the element. Having covered the primary components, let's move on to look at the secondary components of XML Schema. Here we will see another important schema component for building content models – namely model groups.

Secondary Components

The secondary components of XML Schemas are model group definitions, attribute groups, notation declarations and identity constraints. In particular, groups facilitate reuse and inheritance. We will soon see how they can extend the way we use complex types and create complex types.

Model Group Definitions

XML Schema allows us to create a **group** of element definitions and gives us the option of naming them (using a name attribute), so that we can use these groups to build up content models of complex types – in this sense they are rather like the use of parameter entities in XML 1.0. A model group can consist of element declarations, wildcards, and other model groups.

To create a named model group we use the group element. This must be declared as a top-level schema component, which means it must be a child of the schema element.

Once a set of elements has been grouped together with a name, we can also indicate that there can only be a choice of one element from the group, or that all of them should appear, using elements called `choice` and `all` respectively. Let's look at `choice` first. We create a group called `MealOptions`, which contains a fish, meat and vegetarian option, and specify it in an element called `FlightDinner`, which will associate a passenger's name with their choice of food:

```
<xsd:element name = "FlightDinner">
   <xsd:sequence>
      <xsd:element ref = "Name" />
      <xsd:group ref = "MealOptions" />
   </xsd:sequence>
</xsd:element>

<xsd:group name = "MealOptions" >
   <xsd:choice>
      <element name = "Fish" type = "Meal" />
      <element name = "Meat" type = "Meal" />
      <element name = "Vegetarian" type = "Meal" />
   </xsd:choice>
<xsd:group>
```

Here we have named the group `MealOptions`, this group allows a choice of the elements `Fish`, `Meat` or `Vegetarian`. Each of these elements is of type `Meal`, which could then contain a list of the courses for that meal. The `MealOptions` group is used by reference in an element called `FlightDinner`, which consists of the passenger's name and their choice of meal option (be it fish, meat or vegetarian).

The `all` group may only appear at the top level of any content model, and its children must be individual, unique elements – we cannot use groups within the `all` group and the elements can only appear once within that group. This means that the value of `minOccurs` must be `1` and `maxOccurs` must be `1` (although this is the default, so we have left it out). For example:

```
<xsd:group name = "CreditCardDetails">
   <xsd:all>
      <xsd:element name = "CardType" />
      <xsd:element name = "CardHoldersName" />
      <xsd:element name = "CardNumber" />
      <xsd:element name = "CardExpiryDate" />
   </xsd:all>
</xsd:group>
```

If you declare an element inside an `all` group, it can only be used within that group. It may not appear anywhere else in the document, even if we are referencing an element that is declared outside the group definition.

There is another element we can use within a group, which we have met already: the `sequence` element. This would be used within a named group just like the `choice` element. As you might have noticed, however, we have been using it without it being a child of the `group` element. In fact, we can use `choice`, `all` and `sequence` on their own, to create what is known as an **unnamed group**.

Unnamed groups do not have to be top-level schema components – they can be used inside `complexType` elements and element declarations to create content models. We can just use either the `choice` or `all` elements within a complex type just as we have been doing with `sequence` to indicate an unnamed group, like so:

```
<xsd:complexType name = "Address">
   <xsd:all>
      <xsd:element name="Street1" />
      <xsd:element name="Street2" />
      <xsd:element name="City" />
      <xsd:element name="State" />
      <xsd:element name="Zip" />
   </xsd:all>
<xsd:complexType>
```

If we use `all`, remember that it still has to be at the top level of the content model. If we wanted `all` to appear for child elements nested further inside a content model, we would have to either use a named group, or rely on the occurrence indicators.

You can also use the `minOccurs` and `maxOccurs` attributes on the `group`, `choice`, `sequence` and `all` elements. By combining and nesting the groups, and setting `minOccurs` and `maxOccurs`, we have a flexible way of recreating content models that were expressed in DTDs.

> *Strictly speaking, while a named model group is a secondary component of the schema specification, an unnamed model group is a helper component, although the same rules apply to both, you cannot use a name to reference an unnamed group.*

Attribute Groups

In the same way that we can group together elements, we can create a group of attributes. Attribute groups let us define a set of attributes that would be used on a set of elements. For example, if we had an element that had several attributes as children, we can group together the attributes associated with the element and include a reference to them in the element declaration. This can make the schema easier to read, and also allow us to reuse the group of attributes on other elements, should another element use the same group of attributes (again like parameter entities in XML 1.0). Indeed, if the attribute group is reused in several elements, should one of the attributes change, we would only need to change the one instance of the attribute group for the change to be reflected in all elements that use that group.

For example, let's take the `product` element and add an attribute group for all the attributes it carries:

```
<xsd:element name = "product">
   <xsd:complexType>
      <xsd:attributeGroup ref = "productDetails" />
   </xsd:complexType>
</xsd:element>

<xsd:attributeGroup name = "productDetails" >
   <xsd:attribute name = "productID" use = "required"
                  type = "xsd:ID"/>
   <xsd:attribute name = "name" use = "required" type = "xsd:string"/>
   <xsd:attribute name = "description" use = "required"
                  type = "xsd:string"/>
   <xsd:attribute name = "unit" type = "xsd:positiveInteger"/>
   <xsd:attribute name = "price" use = "required"
                  type = "xsd:decimal"/>
   <xsd:attribute name = "stock" type = "xsd:integer"/>
   <xsd:attribute name = "hire" type = "xsd:string"/>
</xsd:attributeGroup>
```

Attribute groups can nest other attribute groups inside of them, and rather like attribute declarations, they should appear at the end of a complex type.

Notation Declarations

Notation declarations associate a name with an identifier for an application used to view that sort of notation, for example an image with a program that displays that type of image. The notation declaration does not participate in validation itself, but we can restrict the simple type for the element's content to be appropriate for the notation the element contains (for example, you can make sure that an element containing a binary representation of a JPEG is hex-binary encoded). So, in an instance document we could represent the appearance of a JPEG (in hex-binary encoded form) like so:

```
<xsd:image format="jpeg">111110110111...</xsd:image>
```

The content of this element would be a binary definition of the JPEG. In the schema, we would restrict the content of the `image` element to a hex-binary simple type. What we have here is an element called `image` and an attribute called `format`, so that we can use the `image` element to represent images in different formats: JPEGs, GIFs, bitmaps, etc.

In the schema, we will have to declare the notation, the associated application we use to view the image, and an element called `image`. We also need to declare an attribute enumerated to associate the format of the image with the appropriate notation declaration. This is what the schema looks like:

```
<xsd:notation name="jpeg" public="image/jpeg" system="viewer.exe" />

<xsd:element name="image">
   <xsd:complexType>
      <xsd:complexContent>
         <xsd:extension base="xsd:hexBinary">
         <xsd:attribute name="format">
            <xsd:simpleType>
               <restriction base="xsd:NOTATION">
                  <xsd:enumeration value="jpeg"/>
                  <xsd:enumeration value="bmp"/>
                  <xsd:enumeration value="png"/>
                  <xsd:enumeration value="gif"/>
              </xsd:restriction>
            </xsd:simpleType>
         </xsd:extension>
      </xsd:complexContent>
   </xsd:complexType>
</xsd:element>
```

The `public` attribute of the notation element takes a public identifier as used in SGML, which is taken from the ISO 8879 specification, while the `system` attribute takes a URI reference.

Identity Constraints

XML Schema introduces `ID`, `IDREF`, and `IDREFS` as simple types that we can use with attributes, just as we would in XML 1.0. In addition, it introduces two elements that are a lot more powerful, namely `key` and `keyref`. These can be used to specify a relationship between any attribute, element, its value/content, or even from a combination of element and attribute content. It also allows you to specify the scope within which the constraints apply (whereas an XML 1.0 ID applies to the whole document).

Furthermore, using another element called `unique`, we can specify that the value of an attribute or content of an element should be unique within a document instance. As you might imagine, these are particularly useful for those working with relational databases. Let's have a look at these new powerful concepts.

Unique Values

There are times when you need to ensure that there are unique values for elements and attributes, for example if you are using a value as a unique identifier, such as a customer `ID`. Furthermore, if you are using an element or attribute to represent a primary key, you want to ensure that this is unique within that table, but not necessarily unique to the document. The `unique` element allows you to specify which values should be unique and the scope within which the restriction applies (and it would be the job of a validating processor to ensure that the values were unique as intended).

In order to ensure the uniqueness of values both across the document and within a range of elements or attributes, a clever use of XPath statements is employed. For example, if we want to make sure that the `productID` attribute of the `Product` element is unique, we can use the following syntax:

```
<xsd:unique name="uniqueProdID">
   <xsd:selector xpath="tc:Product/" />
   <xsd:field xpath="tc:@ProductID" />
</xsd:unique>
```

This would be declared at the same level as the type (in this case the complex type definition of `Product`). The `tc:` namespace prefix refers to the schema that we are creating here (as opposed to schema declarations laid out in the schema specification using the `xsd:` namespace prefix), which would have to be declared in the root `schema` element. There are three key steps going on here:

- First, we specify the `unique` element, and give it a name. While you could use the same value for the `name` attribute as the name of the element or attribute you are trying to constrain, it is clearer if you use a different name. So, while the attribute we are constraining is called `ProductID`, we have given the `unique` element a different value as its name – `uniqueProdID`. No two values for `<unique's>` `name` attribute can be the same in a schema.
- Then we use an XPath expression to select the range of elements that we want to make sure contain some unique value, this is done with the `<selector>` element, whose `xpath` attribute holds the XPath expression that retrieves the range of elements, in this case all `Product` elements.
- In our case we want to make sure that the value of the `Product` element's `productID` attribute is unique (after all we would not want two products to have the same ID). We have already specified that this constraint only applies to the `Product` elements, therefore we have to specify the child node that we want to be unique within this context. To do this we use the `field` element, which also carries an `xpath` attribute. This time, the value of the `xpath` attribute is an XPath expression indicating the node within the range (which we have already specified) is to be unique. In this case, the `productID` attribute of the given range.

This will ensure that all values of the `productID` attribute on `Product` are unique. If we had another element called `Order`, which also used the `productID` attribute, this would not ensure that values of the `productID` attribute on the `Order` element were unique also.

If we wanted to make the uniqueness constraint apply to more than one value in the document, we could just add more field paths, like so:

```
<unique name="uniqueIDs">
   <selector xpath="tc:Customers/" />
   <field xpath="tc:tradeCustomer/@CustID" />
   <field xpath="tc:publicCustomer/@CustID" />
</unique>
```

Here we are making sure that when a new customer is added, whether they are a trade or public customer, that they are given a unique customer ID.

Key and KeyRef

The use of ID, IDREF, and IDREFS as a method of describing relationships in XML 1.0 is common, but traversal of these relationships is resources intensive. In addition, there are limits to their value because an ID has to be unique to the whole document, and could only be used with attribute values.

ID, IDREF, and IDREFS are still provided in XML Schema as built-in simple types, however this also introduces the more powerful and flexible key and keyref constructs which can be used with element content as well as attribute values. Rather than repeating values in XML documents, we can use the key element to make sure that an item of information only needs to appear once, and that other items are related to it (mimicking the functionality of link tables in relational databases). Furthermore, we can limit the scope of keys and their references, so that it is possible to create a key that is only unique to a certain level of the markup (allowing a key to be unique for a chosen table, if the table is represented as an element).

For example, if we have several invoices for the same customer, we do not need to store their personal details several times; rather we can use a <key> element for the customers and associate this with a <keyref> for their invoices. Here <key> acts like the primary key, while <keyref> acts as a foreign key. Let's have a look at an example:

```
<key name="customerID">
   <selector xpath="tc:SalesData/" />
   <field xpath="tc:Customer/@CustID" />
</key>

<keyref name="item" refer="customerID">
   <selector xpath="tc:SalesData/" />
   <field xpath="tc:Invoice/@invoiceID" />
</keyref>
```

As you will notice, the syntax is similar to that of the unique element, where we use selector and field elements as children of the key and keyref elements to describe where we want the key relationship to be placed, and in what range it must be unique. The refer attribute on the keyref element is the name of the key we want to refer back to. The constraints are independent from the types of attributes and elements, so you can still indicate that an invoice ID is an integer or a string if you require (whereas if you were using a simple type of ID, that would specify the data-type of the attribute value). As with the unique element, key and keyref elements should be declared in the schema at the same level as the complex type.

Furthermore, because this is actually a constraining mechanism, a valid document instance cannot contain an Invoice element unless it contains an invoiceID attribute whose value corresponds to an existing CustID attribute on a given Customer element.

Default or Fixed Element Content

If we want to specify a default or fixed value on element content, we can use attributes of the same name: `default` and `fixed`. They take the value we want to set.

If we specify a default value for an element, and that element is empty in the instance document, the default value will be inserted when an XML Schema-compliant parser parses the document. By default, the default type will be a string. Therefore, in the following example we have a fragment of an XML instance document, which is used to profile a member's subscription to a site:

```
<mailOut>
   <subscribe></subscribe>
</mailOut>
```

If we had specified a default value, like so:

```
<element name="subscribe" default="yes" />
```

once parsed, the `subscribe` element's information set item would contain the value `yes` as a string.

If we specify that an element's content will be fixed, the element content must either be empty (in which case it behaves like `default`), or the element content must match the value of the `fixed` attribute, otherwise the document would not be valid.

Specifying Null Values in Document Instances

Specifying that an element should still appear in an instance document, even if it has no content, becomes especially useful when working with XML that is coming from a database. If we wanted to represent an element as having a null value when sending information to or from a database, you can use the `nillable` attribute in the element declaration (which takes a Boolean, whose default is `False`), to indicate that an empty element is required if there is no element content. For example, in the schema we could add the `nillable` attribute to an element like so:

```
<element name="ackReceived" nillable="true" />
```

In the instance document, we then represent that the `ackReceived` element has a null value using the `nill` attribute (this is defined in the XML Schema namespace for instances at http://www.w3.org/2000/10/XMLSchema-instance, and must therefore use the `xsi` namespace prefix):

```
<ackReceived xsi:nill="true"></ackReceived>
```

This means that the Schema for namespace instances must be declared in any instance documents that contain nillable elements.

Annotations

There are two types of `<annotation>` element in XML Schema, both of which appear as children of the `annotation` element:

- `documentation` – which serves a function similar to a comment used to describe the relevant part of the schema to another human user

- appInfo – whose intended use is similar to a processing instruction in XML 1.0, because it passes information to a processing application

As with all aspects of programming, good use of comments helps ensure that others know what was intended when the code was written, and helps those who wrote it when they come back to look at it again. This is particularly important with XML Schemas that are intended for industrial or public use. Furthermore, it is always very helpful to summarize and highlight differences between subsequent versions of schemas and their predecessors. Another useful addition to the documentation element is the presence of an `xml:lang` attribute.

```
<xsd:annotation>
   <xsd:documentation xml:lang="en">
This price element should always carry an attribute called currency, whose value
is taken from the enumerated type.
   </xsd:documentation>
</xsd:annotation>
```

The `appInfo` element is particularly interesting if parsers implement a way of raising these events to an application. This is because XML Processing Instructions often required you to use a custom parser to work with them. With the addition of the `appInfo` element, we will be able to pass information directly to the application when information is inserted. It would also be possible to put further processing code in the `appInfo` element.

```
<xsd:annotation>
   <xsd:appInfo>
      order.process(orderID, customerID);
   </xsd:appInfo>
</xsd:annotation>
```

Employee Schema

Let's have a look at how we can create an employee schema, which will create types and groups that are reusable. Here is some XML that we will represent in the `employee.xsd` file:

```
<Employee lastUpdated="2001-04-10">
   <Name firstName="Matt" middleInitial="J" lastName="Thomas" />
   <Contact>
      <Address>
         <Street>121 East Street</Street>
         <City>HeresVille</City>
         <State>Washington</State>
         <Zip>WA 12765</Zip>
      </Address>
      <HomePhone>012235567</HomePhone>
      <Email1>matt@thomas.org</Email1>
   </Contact>
</Employee>
```

Here is that schema:

```
<xsd:schema xmlns:xsd="http://www.w3.org/2000/10/XMLSchema">
<xsd:element name="Employee" type="personType" />
```

```
<xsd:complexType name="personType">
   <xsd:sequence>
      <xsd:element name="Name" type="nameType" />
            <xsd:choice>
               <xsd:group   ref="Contact" />
               <xsd:element name="AddressOnly" type="addressType" />
            </xsd:choice>
         <xsd:element   name="notes" minOccurs="0" maxOccurs="1" />
      </xsd:sequence>
   <xsd:attribute name="lastUpdated" type="xsd:date" />
</xsd:complexType>

<xsd:complexType name="nameType">
   <xsd:attribute name= "firstName" />
   <xsd:attribute name= "middleInitial" />
   <xsd:attribute name= "lastName" />
</xsd:complexType>

<xsd:complexType name="addressType">
   <xsd:sequence>
      <xsd:element name="Street" />
      <xsd:element name="City" />
      <xsd:element name="State" />
      <xsd:element name="Zip" />
   </xsd:sequence>
</xsd:complexType>

<xsd:group name="Contact">
   <xsd:sequence>
      <xsd:element name="Address" type="addressType" />
      <xsd:group ref="PhoneFaxEmail" />
   </xsd:sequence>
</xsd:group>

<xsd:group name="PhoneFaxEmail">
   <xsd:any>
      <xsd:element name="HomePhone" type="phoneType" />
      <xsd:element name="WorkPhone" type="phoneType" />
      <xsd:element name="CellPhone" type="phoneType" />
      <xsd:element name="Fax" type="phoneType" />
      <xsd:element name="Email1" type="emailType" />
      <xsd:element name="Email2" type="emailType" />
   </xsd:any>
</xsd:group>
<xsd:schema>
```

In this example, we start by declaring the `<employee>` element, which is of `personType`. We defined a complex type for details regarding all kinds of people, so that it can be reused for employees, customers, contacts, etc.

The `personType` uses a `nameType` for defining data about names, again to facilitate reuse, holding details in attribute values. There is also an option for notes to appear in the `nameType` in case we want to store anything with the employee details. After the `Name` element, there is then a choice between a group of elements that hold all contact details (both address and phone, fax and email details, or just an address that is held in an `addressType`, which is used by the `Contact` group in any case.

The `Contact` group is made up of an `Address` element that is of the `addressType` and a group called `PhoneFaxEmail`, which holds phone numbers, fax number and email addresses.

Creating your Own Data-Types

Having looked earlier in the chapter at the built-in simple types, in this section we will look at creating our own simple types, known as **user-derived simple types**. We create our own simple types by constraining either the built-in types or other user-derived types using **facets**. So, when we create a user-defined type it is actually a subset of an existing type. We can see how this works in the following diagram, which shows the built-in types that are already available to schema authors and how they have been derived:

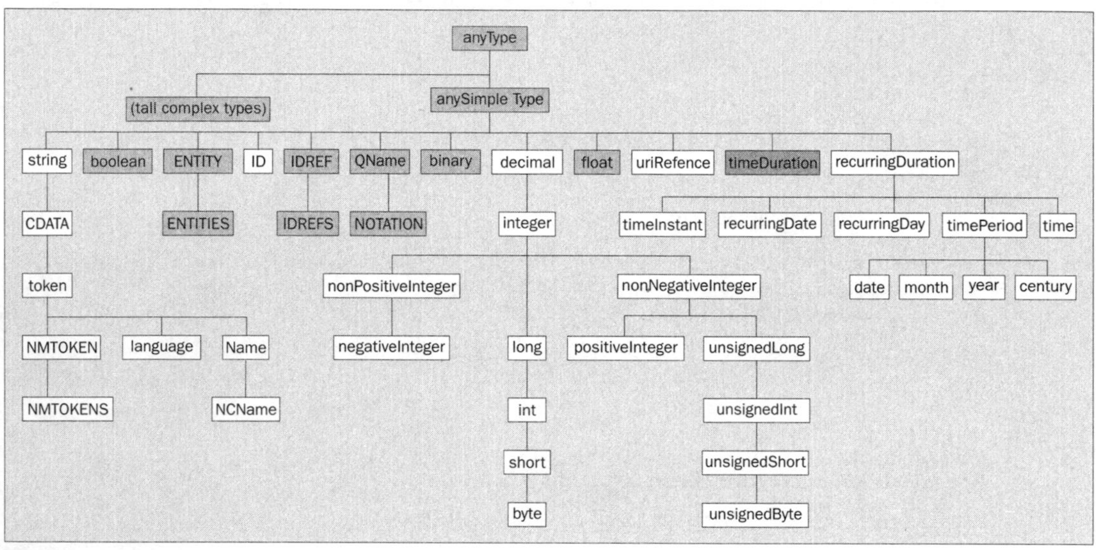

This tree shows how simple types are derived from the `anyType` type, which allows any form of string. We can derive our own user-derived types from any of these built-in types. The type we add restrictions to, when creating our own types, is known as the **base type**. For example, the simple type `year` is derived from the `timePeriod` type, which is itself derived from the `recurringDuration` type. As we go down the tree, the types become increasingly specialized.

In XML 1.0 we were limited to the string data-type and the XML 1.0 types of `entity`, `entities`, `enumeration`, `ID`, `idref`, `idrefs`, `nmtoken`, `nmtokens`, and `notation`. The ability to further constrain element content or an attribute value using data-types is one of the strongest advantages to XML Schemas over DTDs. Because XML 1.0 limited us to the XML 1.0 types and the basic string data-type, a lot of programmers wrote their own validation logic, to ensure that element content and attribute values were legal, before passing them into the application. A lot of this effort can now be avoided by using an XML Schema compliant parser. Not only do we have a set of built-in types to call at our fingertips, we can also create tighter constraints to represent data-types that specify permitted ranges of values (such as allowable order quantities) that sequences and patterns (such as telephone numbers or zip/postal codes) may take.

The constraints also explain how the strings in the XML document instance should be represented after being processed. Before a value is processed, it is known as an initial value and, after processing, it is known as normalized value. Normalization is the process of stripping the whitespace from the sequence of characters that make the string. This is done in accordance with what is known as a facet, which we shall meet soon, called `whiteSpace`.

When deriving new simple types from primitive built-in data-types the base type used will be `anySimpleType`*, the simplest version of the* `ur-type` *definition, which is itself restricted from the* `ur-type` *definition. The* `ur-type` *definition is actually a third definition type in XML Schema, which lies at the top of the schema's type hierarchy; it is like a super-class, to borrow from object oriented terminology. It is the root definition of the schemas type definition, and is named* `anyType`*. It can act as both a simple and a complex type.*

Aspects of Data-types

All XML Schema data-types are composed of three parts:

- A **value space** – the set of distinct values where each of the values is denoted by one or more literals in the data-type's lexical space
- A **lexical space** – the set of lexical representations, in other words a set of valid literal strings representing values
- A set of **facets** – properties of the value space, its individual values, and/or lexical items

> **A Simple Type Definition is a set of constraints on the value space *and* the lexical space of a data-type.**

To illustrate the difference between lexical and value spaces, we'll look at a fragment of a document:

```
<Order>
   <Item>Widgets</Item>
   <Quantity>465000</Quantity>
</Order>
```

In the `<Item>` element, the value and lexical spaces are the same thing – the lexical representation of a string is also its value.

The `<Quantity>` element, however, is represented in XML as a string, but we really want this to represent the mathematical concept of "`four hundred and sixty five thousand`". Any comparison of `<Quantity>` elements (such as multiplying them by the price to get a total) would mean using their numeric values (their value spaces), not their lexical string representations. There are various forms we could use to represent the same value, although they are lexically different: four hundred and sixty five thousand, 465000, 465000.00, 4650.00E2. If, however, we were to say that the element content had to be an `integer` type, we would only be able to use 465000.

Let's take a closer look at these concepts.

Value Spaces

Each schema data-type has a range of possible values. These value spaces are **implicit** in the definition of a primitive data-type. For example, the built-in `float` data-type has a value space that ranges from negative to positive infinity. The `string` data-type is composed of values that correspond to any of the legal XML characters.

Derived types inherit their value space from their base type, and may constrain that value space to an explicit subset of the base type's value space.

A derived data-type such as `integer` would allow any positive or negative whole number value, but wouldn't allow decimal fractions. Another integer type could be derived from `integer`, but this type might limit the range of acceptable values to only positive numbers, or to only 3-digit numbers. Value spaces may also have a set of explicitly enumerated values, or be derived from the members of a list of types.

Value spaces always have certain facets (or abstract properties), such as **equality**, **order**, **bounds**, **cardinality**, and the age-old **numeric/non-numeric** dichotomy, which will be familiar if you have studied math and logic. These are intrinsic to the data-type and cannot be used to further constrain a type within XML Schemas.

Lexical Spaces

A lexical space is the set of string literals that *represent* the values of a data-type. These literals are always composed of "text" characters, which may be any of the XML-legal subset of the Unicode character set. For example:

```
<a_string>
The name of the sorority was ΑΓΔ, and their motto was "plus ça change, plus c'est
la même chose"
</a_string>
```

By definition, string literals only have one lexical representation. On the other hand, numeric values may have several equivalent and equally valid lexical representations. For example, the string literals "`100`", "`1.0E2`", and "10^2" obviously have different lexical values, but they have identical numeric values in the floating-point number value space.

Derivation and Facets

You define a new simple type by deriving it from an existing type (be it built-in or derived). Every data-type has a set of facets that characterize the properties of the data-type, for example the length of a string. By restricting some of the many facets, a new data-type can be derived. This is done by restricting an existing type's range of values, so it is hardly surprising that we do so using an element called `restriction`. The `restriction` element is used to indicate the existing or **base** type, and to identify the facets that constrain the range of values. There are two types of facets in XML Schemas: these are fundamental facets and constraining facets.

- **Fundamental facets** – abstract properties that define the semantic characteristics of a value space. These are standard number and logic concepts: equality, order, bounds, cardinality and numeric/non-numeric; but they are intrinsic to the data-type and cannot be used as a restriction mechanism in XML Schema.
- **Constraining facets** – optional limits on the permissible values of a data-type's value space.

Fundamental Facets

XML Schema defines twelve fundamental facets for simple types.

Simple Type Facet	Scope of Use
`length`	Constrains the length of a simple type in terms of the number of units of length that it can have. The units of length will be characters, octets, or list items the simple type is allowed to contain
`minLength`	Constrains the minimum number of units of length that a simple type can have for its value
`maxLength`	Constrains the maximum number of units of length that a simple type can have for its value
`pattern`	Constrains the literals comprising the value of a facet to a pattern defined by a regular expression
`enumeration`	Constrains the value of a facet to a specific value
`maxInclusive`	Constrains the value of a facet to a specific inclusive upper bound
`maxExclusive`	Constrains the value of a facet to a specific exclusive upper bound
`minInclusive`	Constrains the value of a facet to a specific inclusive lower bound
`minExclusive`	Constrains the value of a facet to a specific exclusive lower bound
`whiteSpace`	Constrains the value of a facet according to the rules for whitespace normalization as defined in the XML 1.0 specification
`totalDigits`	Constrains the value space to values with a specific maximum number of decimal digits
`fractionDigits`	Constrains the value space to values with a specific maximum number of decimal digits in the fractional part

It should be obvious from the list above that not all facets apply to all base types – after all, we are not going to apply a period facet to anything other than something representing a time period. Therefore, we are limited to the facets that are relevant to the base-type we are deriving from.

Let's look at the details of these constraining facets.

length, minLength, maxLength

These three facets all deal with the number of units of length of a data-type, the value of which must always be a non-negative integer. The nature of the units will vary, depending on the base data-type:

- For those derived from the string type, length is the number of characters (Unicode code points).
- Types that are derived from the binary type measure length as the number of octets (8-bit bytes) of the binary data.
- List types define length as the number of items in the list.

For example, if we wanted to constrain some data-type (such as a North American area code for phone numbers) to always be a 3-digit number, we could use the `length` facet with a value of `three`.

```
<xsd:simpleType name="AreaCode">
   <xsd:restriction base="int">
      <xsd:length value="3" />
   </xsd:restriction>
</xsd:simpleType>
```

Note that the restrictions are held within a `restriction` element, and the base type we are deriving from is defined by the `base` attribute.

You cannot use this along with `minLength` or `maxLength`. Also, `maxLength` cannot be greater than the value space of the parent element, so a type derived from a `byte` cannot have a `maxLength` of `4` or higher.

pattern

This facet is a constraint on the data-type's *lexical* space, which indirectly constrains the value space. A `pattern` is a regular expression (**regexp**) that a data-type's lexical representation must match for that latter literal to be considered valid. The regexp language used in XML Schema is similar to the one defined for the Perl programming language.

Let's have a look at a pattern dealing with telephone area codes, which requires the first digit to be a zero:

```
<xsd:simpleType name="AreaCode">
   <xsd:restriction base="string">
      <xsd:minLength value="3" />
      <xsd:maxLength value="3" />
      <xsd:pattern value="[1][0-9][0-9]" />
   </xsd:restriction>
</xsd:simpleType>
```

For more about the use of regular expressions, see:

http://www.perl.com/pub/doc/manual/html/pod/perlre.html

or

Appendix E of "**XML Schema Part 2: Data-types**" at http://www.w3.org/TR/xmlschema-2/#regexs

enumeration

This facet is very much like a DTD's specification of an element type choice list or the enumerated values of an attribute. Enumeration limits a value space to a specific set of values – if the value isn't specified in the schema, it isn't valid.

This facet is particularly useful for all simple types except `Boolean`. It limits a `simpleType` to a set of distinct values (such as allowable departments or regions).

```
<xsd:simpleType name="DepartmentType">
   <xsd:restriction base="xsd:string">
      <xsd:enumeration value="Accounts" />
      <xsd:enumeration value="Sales" />
      <xsd:enumeration value="Warehouse" />
      <xsd:enumeration value="Web" />
```

```
        <xsd:enumeration value="Marketing" />
        <xsd:enumeration value="Customer support" />
    </xsd:restriction>
</xsd:simpleType>
```

Using this facet does *not* impose an additional or different order relation on the value space due to the order of the enumerated values – any ordered property of the derived data-type remains the same as that of its base type.

whiteSpace

This facet is a constraint on whether whitespace is allowed in a value space. It takes the values `preserve`, `replace` or `collapse`.

minExclusive, maxExclusive, minInclusive, maxInclusive

All of these facets can only apply to a data-type that has an order relation:

- The two "min" facets define the minimum (lower bound) of a value space
- The two "max" facets define its maximum (upper bound)
- An exclusive bound means that the bounding value is *not* included in the value space (meaning that for all values `V` in the value space, `minExclusive` < `V` < `maxExclusive`)
- An inclusive bound is one that *is* included within the value space (`minInclusive` ≤ `V` ≤ `maxInclusive`)

These two types of bounds are not coupled – a lower bound might be *ex*clusive, while the upper bound is *in*clusive. Obviously, you must choose between the two types of bound for each end of the spectrum – it's never possible for a bound to be both *in*clusive and *ex*clusive!

totalDigits, fractionDigits

`totalDigits` constrains the value space to a maximum number of decimal places, while `fractionDigits` constrains the maximum number of decimal digits in the fractional part.

The value for either of these should be a `nonNegativeInteger`. `totalDigits` cannot have a greater value than the parent; for example, you could not have a value of four if the type you were constraining was a byte. `fractionDigits` cannot be greater than `totalDigits`.

Here is a table that shows which constraining facets can be applied to which simple data-types:

Simple Types	Facets					
	length	minLength	maxLength	pattern	enumeration	whiteSpace
string	x	x	x	x	x	x
normalizedString	x	x	x	x	x	x
token	x	x	x	x	x	x
byte				x	x	x
unsignedByte				x	x	x
base64Binary	x	x	x	x	x	x
hexBinary	x	x	x	x	x	x
integer				x	x	x
positiveInteger				x	x	x
negativeInteger				x	x	x
nonNegativeInteger				x	x	x
nonPositiveInteger				x	x	x
int				x	x	x
unsignedInt				x	x	x
long				x	x	x
unsignedLong				x	x	x
short				x	x	x
unsignedShort				x	x	x
decimal				x	x	x
float				x	x	x
double				x	x	x
boolean				x		x
time				x	x	x
dateTime				x	x	x
duration				x	x	x
date				x	x	x
gMonth				x	x	x
gYear				x	x	x
gYearMonth				x	x	x
gDay				x	x	x
gMonthDay				x	x	x
Name	x	x	x	x	x	x
QName	x	x	x	x	x	x
NCName	x	x	x	x	x	x
anyURI	x	x	x	x	x	x

Simple Types	Facets					
	length	minLength	maxLength	pattern	enumeration	whiteSpace
language	x	x	x	x	x	x
ID	x	x	x	x	x	x
IDREFS	x	x	x		x	x
ENTITY	x	x	x	x	x	x
ENTITIES	x	x	x		x	x
NOTATION	x	x	x	x	x	x
NMTOKEN	x	x	x	x	x	x
NMTOKENS	x	x	x		x	x

In the second table, not all facets are listed because they only apply to elements that are ordered:

Simple Types	Facets					
	maxInclusive	maxExclusive	minInclusive	minExclusive	totalDigits	fractionDigits
byte	x	x	x	x	x	x
unsignedByte	x	x	x	x	x	x
integer	x	x	x	x	x	x
positiveInteger	x	x	x	x	x	x
negativeInteger	x	x	x	x	x	x
nonNegativeInteger	x	x	x	x	x	x
nonPositiveInteger	x	x	x	x	x	x
int	x	x	x	x	x	x
unsignedInt	x	x	x	x	x	x
long	x	x	x	x	x	x
unsignedLong	x	x	x	x	x	x
short	x	x	x	x	x	x
unsignedShort	x	x	x	x	x	x

Table continued on following page

Simple Types	Facets					
	maxInclusive	maxExclusive	minInclusive	minExclusive	totalDigits	fractionDigits
decimal	x	x	x	x	x	x
float	x	x	x	x		
double	x	x	x	x		
time	x	x	x	x		
dateTime	x	x	x	x		
duration	x	x	x	x		
date	x	x	x	x		
gMonth	x	x	x	x		
gYear	x	x	x	x		
gYearMonth	x	x	x	x		
gDay	x	x	x	x		
gMonthDay	x	x	x	x		

Limitations

There are some limitations that we should be aware of. In XML Schemas, there is no provision for:

- Overriding facets in the instance document
- Creating quantity/unit pairs in a simple type (although it is possible in complex types)
- Declaring n-dimensional arrays of tokens, where n > 1
- Specifying inheritance effects
- Declaring complex constraints where the value of some other information item in the instance (for example, an attribute) has an effect on the current data-type.

The ToysCo Example

Let's revisit the toysco schema that we have been using throughout the book. We will be making a few changes, because we can constrain the allowable contents far better with XML Schema than we could with a DTD and will also be able to add relationships that will save space in resulting document instances.

A conforming document that will represent the daily sales from Toysco will have a root element called `<toysco>`. This element contains three child elements:

- `customer` – which holds customer details
- `product` – which holds details about each product sold that day
- `invoice` – which contains details about the invoices for items sold

Let's look at some of the points you should take special note of regarding the move to XML Schema.

Rather than repeating the customer's details in each invoice (after all a customer may have placed more than one order in a day), we make the `customerID` attribute a `key` element, which relates to the `customerKeyRef attribute` in the `<invoice>` element, to show the advantages of the `key` and `keyref` mechanisms in XML Schema. We also make sure that the `customerID` values are unique within the document using the `unique` mechanism.

Because the billing address may be different from the delivery address – and indeed there may be more than one delivery address – we create a complex type that can be reused in the billing and delivery address elements, so that they contain the same content model.

We have specified simple types for some of the element content and attribute values so that they are restricted to the specified data-type. Furthermore, we create two new `simpleTypes`, one to restrict the length of fields that are strings, the other to enumerate payment methods.

Here is the schema in full (`toysco.xsd`):

```
<?xml version = "1.0" encoding = "UTF-8"?>
<!-- Conforms to w3c http://www.w3.org/2001/XMLSchema -->
<xsd:schema xmlns:xsd = "http://www.w3.org/2001/XMLSchema"
            targetNamepsace = "http://www.toysco.com/schemas/dailyReport"
            xmlns:tc = "http://www.toysco.com/schemas/dailyReport" >

   <xsd:annotation>
      <xsd:documentation>
         The toysco element is the root element of a document instance
         containing the daily summary info of sales from toysco. It contains
         three child elements: customer, product, and invoice. There is a
         relationship between customer details and orders to save repeating
         customer details should they place more than one order.
      </xsd:documentation>
   </xsd:annotation>

   <xsd:element name = "toysco">

      <xsd:complexType>
         <xsd:sequence>
            <xsd:element ref = "customer"
                         minOccurs = "1" maxOccurs = "unbounded"/>
            <xsd:element ref = "product"
                         minOccurs = "1" maxOccurs = "unbounded"/>
            <xsd:element ref = "invoice"
                        minOccurs = "1" maxOccurs = "unbounded"/>
         </xsd:sequence>
      </xsd:complexType>
```

```
</xsd:element>

<xsd:annotation>
   <xsd:documentation>
      The customer element contains four child elements: name (required),
      deliveryAddress, billingAddress(required), and
      contactDetails(required).
   </xsd:documentation>
</xsd:annotation>

<xsd:element name = "customer">
   <xsd:complexType>
      <xsd:sequence>
         <xsd:element name = "name">
            <xsd:complexType>
               <xsd:sequence>
                  <xsd:attribute name = "firstName" use = "required"
                                 type = "limitedString"/>
                  <xsd:attribute name = "lastName" use = "required"
                                 type = "limitedString"/>
               </xsd:sequence>
            </xsd:complexType>
         </xsd:element>

         <xsd:element name = "deliveryAddress" type="addressType"
                      minOccurs = "1" maxOccurs = "unbounded" >
            <xsd:complexType>
               <xsd:attribute name = "addressID" type = "xsd:ID" />
            </xsd:complexType>
         </xsd:element>

         <xsd:element name = "billingAddress" type="addressType" />

         <xsd:element name = "contactDetails">
            <xsd:complexType>
               <xsd:sequence>
                  <xsd:element name = "email" type = "limitedString" />
                  <xsd:element name = "homePhone" type = "xsd:integer" />
                  <xsd:element name = "workPhone" type = "xsd:integer" />
                  <xsd:element name = "cellPhone" type = "xsd:integer" />
                  <xsd:element name = "fax" type = "xsd:integer" />
               </xsd:sequence>
            </xsd:complexType>
         </xsd:element>
      </xsd:sequence>
      <xsd:attribute name = "customerID" use = "required" type = "xsd:ID"/>

            <xsd:unique name = "uniqueCustomerKey">
               <xsd:selector xpath = "tc:customer" />
               <xsd:field xpath = "@customerID" />
            </xsd:unique>

            <xsd:key name = "customerKey">
               <xsd:selector xpath = "tc:customer" />
               <xsd:field xpath = "@customerID" />
            </xsd:key>
```

```
    </xsd:complexType>
  </xsd:element>

  <xsd:complexType name = "addressType">
    <xsd:sequence>
      <xsd:element name = "Street" type = "limitedString"/>
      <xsd:element name = "City" type = "limitedString"/>
      <xsd:element name = "State" type = "limitedString"/>
      <xsd:element name = "Zip" type = "limitedString"/>
    </xsd:sequence>
  </xsd:complexType>

  <xsd:annotation>
    <xsd:documentation>
      The product element is a single element with seven attributes that
      hold the details of the each product sold that month.
    </xsd:documentation>
  </xsd:annotation>

  <xsd:element name = "product">
    <xsd:complexType>
      <xsd:attribute name = "productID" use = "required" type = "xsd:ID"/>
      <xsd:attribute name = "name" use = "required" type = "xsd:string"/>
      <xsd:attribute name = "description" use = "required"
                     type = "xsd:string"/>
      <xsd:attribute name = "unit" type = "xsd:positiveInteger"/>
      <xsd:attribute name = "price" use = "required" type = "xsd:decimal"/>
    </xsd:complexType>
  </xsd:element>

  <xsd:annotation>
    <xsd:documentation>
      The invoice element holds details of each individual invoice that
      is made for the day. It holds a repeatable lineItem element and
      eight attributes.
    </xsd:documentation>
  </xsd:annotation>

  <xsd:element name = "invoice">
    <xsd:complexType>
      <xsd:sequence>
        <xsd:element name = "lineItem"
                     minOccurs = "1" maxOccurs = "unbounded">
          <xsd:complexType>
            <xsd:attribute name = "productIDref" use = "required"
                           type = "xsd:IDREF"/>
            <xsd:attribute name = "units" use = "required"
                           type = "xsd:byte"/>
            <xsd:attribute name = "price" use = "required"
                           type = "xsd:decimal"/>
          </xsd:complexType>
        </xsd:element>
      </xsd:sequence>
      <xsd:attribute name = "invoiceID" use = "required" type = "xsd:ID"/>
      <xsd:attribute name = "customerRef" use = "required" />
      <xsd:attribute name = "date" use = "required" type = "xsd:date"/>
```

```
        <xsd:attribute name = "notes" type = "xsd:string"/>
        <xsd:attribute name = "paymentTerms" type = "paymentOptions" />
        <xsd:attribute name = "paid" use = "required" type = "xsd:boolean"/>
        <xsd:attribute name = "deliverTo" use = "required"
                       type = "xsd:IDREF"/>
      </xsd:complexType>

      <xsd:keyref name = "customerRef" ref = "customerKey">
        <xsd:selector xpath = "tc:invoice" />
        <xsd:field xpath = "@customerRef" />
      </xsd:keyref>

    </xsd:element>

    <xsd:simpleType name = "limitedString">
      <xsd:restriction base = "string">
        <xsd:maxLength value = "100" />
      </xsd:restriction>
    </xsd:simpleType>

    <xsd:simpleType name = "paymentOptions">
      <xsd:restriction base = "string">
        <xsd:enumeration value = "cashOnDelivery" />
        <xsd:enumeration value = "30dayCredit" />
        <xsd:enumeration value = "90dayCredit" />
      </xsd:restriction>
    </xsd:simpleType>

  </xsd:schema>
```

Now let's look at the schema step by step. We start with the XML declaration, followed by the root <schema> element, which declares three namespaces: the XML Schema namespace, the target namespace (which is the namespace for the schema we are defining), and we also specify this explicitly so that we can qualify our own data-types. We could have made either of these the default namespace (in particular we could have done this with the XML Schema namespace so that we did not have to keep using the xsd: namespace prefix on schema elements and attributes), but all namespace prefixes have been used.

```
  <?xml version = "1.0" encoding = "UTF-8"?>
  <xsd:schema xmlns:xsd = "http://www.w3.org/2001/XMLSchema"
              targetNamepsace = "http://www.toysco.com/schemas/dailyReport"
              xmlns:tc = "http://www.toysco.com/schemas/dailyReport" >
```

Next, we have the first use of a <documentation> element, which helps users of the schema understand what the syntax does. This nests inside the <annotation> element, as it is one of the two types of annotation available in XML Schema (the other being <appInfo>, which acts like a processing instruction).

```
    <xsd:annotation>
      <xsd:documentation>
        The toysco element is the root element of a document instance
        containing the daily summary info of sales from toysco. It contains
        three child elements: customer, product, and invoice. There is a
        relationship between customer details and orders to save repeating
        customer details should they place more than one order.
      </xsd:documentation>
    </xsd:annotation>
```

Now we come to the root element for conforming document instances. The root element is called `<toysco,>` and would have one or more `customer`, `product` and `invoice` elements as children. The elements are declared by reference, as their full declarations are offered beneath in global element declarations. The number of times they can appear is indicated using the occurrence indicators `minOccurs` and `maxOccurs`, their values indicate that they can appear a minimum of once, and there is no limit on the maximum number of times it can appear. The child elements are part of an anonymous complex type, and an anonymous `sequence` group.

```
<xsd:element name = "toysco">
   <xsd:complexType>
      <xsd:sequence>
         <xsd:element ref = "customer"
                      minOccurs = "1" maxOccurs = "unbounded"/>
         <xsd:element ref - "product"
                      minOccurs = "1" maxOccurs = "unbounded"/>
         <xsd:element ref = "invoice"
                      minOccurs = "1" maxOccurs = "unbounded"/>
      </xsd:sequence>
   </xsd:complexType>
</xsd:element>

<xsd:annotation>
   <xsd:documentation>
      The customer element contains four child elements: name (required),
      deliveryAddress, billingAddress(required), and
      contactDetails(required).
   </xsd:documentation>
</xsd:annotation>
```

The next element is the `<customer>` element. This contains two elements whose content models are defined inline anonymously (namely `name` and `contactDetails`), and two whose content models are defined by reference to the `address` complex type (namely `billingAddress` and `deliveryAddress`). This way, if we want to change the way we store addresses, we only have to change it once – we facilitate reuse – and keep a clean design.

The children of the <name> element are the first to make use of a new simple type that we will come to at the end of the schema. The simple type (called `limitedString`) limits the length of a string to 100 characters.

```
<xsd:element name = "customer">
   <xsd:complexType>
      <xsd:sequence>
         <xsd:element name = "name">
            <xsd:complexType>
               <xsd:sequence>
                  <xsd:attribute name = "firstName" use = "required"
                                 type = "limitedString"/>
                  <xsd:attribute name = "lastName" use = "required"
                                 type = "limitedString"/>
               </xsd:sequence>
            </xsd:complexType>
         </xsd:element>
```

Note that the `deliveryAddress` element has an attribute called `addressID`, whose simple type is the XML 1.0 `ID` type. This allows us to reference the `addressID` for the delivery address when we come to the `<invoice>` element.

```
          <xsd:element name = "deliveryAddress" type="addressType"
                       minOccurs = "1" maxOccurs = "unbounded" >
            <xsd:complexType>
              <xsd:attribute name = "addressID" type = "xsd:ID" />
            </xsd:complexType>
          </xsd:element>

          <xsd:element name = "billingAddress" type="addressType" />

          <xsd:element name = "contactDetails">
            <xsd:complexType>
              <xsd:sequence>
                <xsd:element name = "email" type = "limitedString" />
                <xsd:element name = "homePhone" type = "xsd:integer" />
                <xsd:element name = "workPhone" type = "xsd:integer" />
                <xsd:element name = "cellPhone" type = "xsd:integer" />
                <xsd:element name = "fax" type = "xsd:integer" />
              </xsd:sequence>
            </xsd:complexType>
          </xsd:element>
        </xsd:sequence>
        <xsd:attribute name = "customerID" use = "required" />
```

The `customer` element carries an attribute called `customerID` whose use is required. This attribute is the unique identifier for the customer, which is used in the `<invoice>` element to save us having to include customer details for each invoice. We use the new facilities in XML Schema to make this attribute a `key`, and therefore make sure that its value is `unique`. These have to be declared at the same level as the element in question.

```
            <xsd:unique name = "uniqueCustomerKey">
              <xsd:selector xpath = "tc:customer" />
              <xsd:field xpath = "@customerID" />
            </xsd:unique>

            <xsd:key name = "customerKey">
              <xsd:selector xpath = "tc:customer" />
              <xsd:field xpath = "@customerID" />
            </xsd:key>

      </xsd:complexType>
    </xsd:element>
```

Having completed the child elements of `customer`, we now define the `addressType` unnamed model group, which serves as a reusable content model for address elements. Each of these elements uses the `limitedString` data-type, which we derive from `string`, to limit the length of the string to 100 characters. When we declare an element to use this type (as we did with `billingAddress` and `deliveryAddress`), they will have to include one occurrence of each of these child elements, in the given order.

```
<xsd:complexType name = "addressType">
   <xsd:sequence>
      <xsd:element name = "Street" type = "limitedString"/>
      <xsd:element name = "City" type = "limitedString"/>
      <xsd:element name = "State" type = "limitedString"/>
      <xsd:element name = "Zip" type = "limitedString"/>
   </xsd:sequence>
</xsd:complexType>
```

Next, we declare the `product` element. This contains an attribute called `productID`, which is used with the `invoice` element. To save us from repeating all of the details about a product every time someone buys one (as several customers are likely to order the same products), we use the traditional XML 1.0 `ID` mechanism to create a relationship. This element also makes use of some more of the built-in types in its attribute values.

```
<xsd:annotation>
   <xsd:documentation>
      The product element is a single element with seven attributes that
      hold the details of each product sold that month.
   </xsd:documentation>
</xsd:annotation>

<xsd:element name = "product">
   <xsd:complexType>
      <xsd:attribute name = "productID" use = "required" type = "xsd:ID"/>
      <xsd:attribute name = "name" use = "required" type = "xsd:string"/>
      <xsd:attribute name = "description" use = "required"
                     type = "xsd:string"/>
      <xsd:attribute name = "unit" type = "xsd:positiveInteger"/>
      <xsd:attribute name = "price" use = "required" type = "xsd:decimal"/>
   </xsd:complexType>
</xsd:element>
```

Next, we come to the `invoice` element. This declaration contains declarations for `lineItem` child elements to indicate the products purchased (which themselves carry attributes), and attributes that indicate details about the invoice. The attributes range from whether the customer has paid, and how they intend to, to the XML `IDREF` attributes that link back to delivery address details and the `keyref`'d attribute which relates to the customer's ID.

```
<xsd:annotation>
   <xsd:documentation>The invoice element holds details of each individual
         invoice that is made for the day.
         It holds repeatable lineItem elements and seven attributes.
   </xsd:documentation>
</xsd:annotation>

<xsd:element name = "invoice">
   <xsd:complexType>
      <xsd:sequence>
         <xsd:element name = "lineItem"
                      minOccurs = "1" maxOccurs = "unbounded">
            <xsd:complexType>
               <xsd:attribute name = "productIDref" use = "required"
                              type = "xsd:IDREF"/>
               <xsd:attribute name = "units" use = "required"
                              type = "xsd:byte"/>
               <xsd:attribute name = "price" use = "required"
                              type = "xsd:decimal"/>
```

```
            </xsd:complexType>
         </xsd:element>
      </xsd:sequence>
      <xsd:attribute name = "invoiceID" use = "required" type = "xsd:ID"/>
      <xsd:attribute name = "customerRef" use = "required" />
      <xsd:attribute name = "date" use = "required" type = "xsd:date"/>
      <xsd:attribute name = "notes" type = "xsd:string"/>
      <xsd:attribute name = "paymentTerms" type = "paymentOptions" />
      <xsd:attribute name = "paid" use = "required" type = "xsd:boolean"/>
      <xsd:attribute name = "deliverTo" use = "required"
                     type = "xsd:IDREF"/>
   </xsd:complexType>
```

Here is where we create a reference to the key that uniquely identifies the customer. As with the `key` declaration, it is on the same level as the declaration of the item it is being used for. It is the `customerRef` attribute on the `<invoice>` element that becomes the `<keyref>`.

```
   <xsd:keyref name = "customerRef" ref = "customerKey">
      <xsd:selector xpath = "tc:invoice" />
      <xsd:field xpath = "@customerRef" />
   </xsd:keyref>

</xsd:element>
```

As we mentioned earlier, we have created our own simple type in this schema to limit the length of some of the strings to 100 characters (such as the individual element content representing each line of the address and the attribute values of the first and last names). We do this simply by restricting the `maxLength` facet of the string data-type to indicate a maximum length of `100` characters.

```
<xsd:simpleType name = "limitedString">
   <xsd:restriction base = "string">
      <xsd:maxLength value = "100" />
   </xsd:restriction>
</xsd:simpleType>
```

Finally, we should note how the `paymentOptions` attribute is enumerated. The enumerated data-type is created to ensure that one of the allowed payment options is given as a value for `paymentType` attribute on the `invoice` element, so the customer can either pay cash on delivery, or put it on their account with either 30 or 90 days to pay for the items.

```
   <xsd:simpleType name = "paymentOptions">
      <xsd:restriction base = "string">
         <xsd:enumeration value = "cashOnDelivery" />
         <xsd:enumeration value = "30dayCredit" />
         <xsd:enumeration value = "90dayCredit" />
      </xsd:restriction>
   </xsd:simpleType>

</xsd:schema>
```

There we have it – the XML Schema version of the toysco schema. As you can see, we have been able to add more restrictions to the document than we would with a DTD. We have created our own data-types (one to specify allowable payment options, the other to limit the length of a string), which has a normalizing effect on the data. We have also used two types of relationship: the standard XML 1.0 `ID` and `IDREF` relationships, and the new XML Schema `key` and `keyref` relationships. The XML Schema relationship allows us to only ensure that the values provided as keys are unique to the customer element, not the whole document, and we have enforced this value to be unique using the `unique` mechanism provided in XML Schema. In addition, we created complex types and model groups to show how we can reuse element content models, particularly in the case of the address.

Summary

In this chapter, we have had a look at the syntax and rules for creating XML Schemas. While they are at Proposed Recommendation stage at the time of writing, it is unlikely that they will change much before the official Recommendation.

We have seen that there are strong advantages to using XML Schemas over DTDs, namely that they provide us with much more control over the content of a document instance. In particular, they allow us to define our own types and support a rich enough set of data-types that we are able to work with processing applications and databases with a lot more flexibility. The ability to process XML Schemas with the wealth of XML tools currently available is also a distinct benefit.

We have seen that there are several ways to constrain our document content, some of which mirror the capabilities of DTDs; others of which extend it, allowing us to validate and describe both structures that are both looser, and structures that offer a lot more control.

XML Schemas are a powerful addition to the toolkit of any XML developer. The advantages they provide will mean that anyone involved in XML will have to be at least aware of them.

7

Schema Alternatives

In this chapter we will take a look at some of the current alternatives (and supplements) to the W3C's XML Schema, currently a *Proposed* Recommendation (as of 2001-04-15).

Since XML 1.0 and DTDs were introduced in 1998, there has been an effort to develop alternatives to DTDs for XML data validation and description. Various companies and organizations made numerous proposals, resulting in the development of XML Schema by a W3C working group. We will look briefly at several of the more significant of these alternative schema proposals. While this may seem to be of only historical interest, several of these proposals are the basis for XML Schema and/or were implemented in major XML tools (and therefore some shared XML data may depend upon these alternative schemas).

One of these early schema proposals, called **XDR** (XML-Data Reduced), was developed and submitted to the W3C by several companies, including Microsoft. It was just another early proposal, but Microsoft then chose to implement XDR as the schema language for IE5 and the MSXML parser, instead of waiting for a final version of XML Schema. XDR is also the schema used in the .NET and BizTalk Frameworks. It is incompatible with XML Schema, but Microsoft has promised to upgrade their software and revise specifications based upon XDR, once the final XML Schema Recommendation is published.

Two major contributors to XML and related technologies have developed a pair of interesting alternatives to XML Schema, known as **RELAX** (Regular Language for XML) and **TREX** (Tree Regular Expressions for XML). Both of these are based upon grammars, as are DTDs and XML Schema. However, both are less complex than the *XML Schema Part 1: Structures* specification, and so represent a middle ground between DTDs and XML Schema. Since RELAX and TREX processors are currently available, they allow experiments with schema-based validation that aren't yet possible with XML Schema. They may also continue to be useful in circumstances where DTDs are inadequate, but full XML Schema support is too costly in terms of resources (such as when using XML in embedded systems such as cellphones or PDAs).

Another member of the XML Schema Working Group has developed a very different approach to XML data validation, called **The Schematron** (which is usually referred to as just "**Schematron**"). It takes a very different approach to validation, using patterns in the XML data's tree structure instead of using a formal grammar. Schematron uses XPath and XSLT expressions to describe constraints upon part(s) of the XML data (element and/or attribute *types* or even specific *instances* of elements and/or attributes). These constraints aren't limited to the parent-child relationships of hierarchy-based grammars, and may also use calculations and other validity tests that aren't possible with XML Schema or any of the other alternatives. Since Schematron was designed to work *with* XML Schema validation, rather than act as a replacement, it is likely to continue to be very useful even after the latter reaches final Recommendation status and has widespread support in XML tools.

We will re-work our Invoice example from Chapter 6 in XDR, and we'll also look at some examples of simple validation tests for the same data using RELAX, TREX, and Schematron. However, let's first look at some of those earlier schema proposals.

Early Schema Proposals

The limitations of DTDs led to many proposals for an "XML schema language". We will look at six of these proposals:

- **DDML** (Document Definition Markup Language)
- **DT4DTD** (Datatypes for DTDs)
- **SOX** (Schema for Object-Oriented XML)
- **XML-Data**
- **XML Data-Reduced (XDR), a subset of XML-Data**
- **DCD** (Document Content Description)

The first four of these are cited in the XML Schema specifications – they can be seen as the basis for the structure and syntax of the current XML Schema proposal. SOX is significant because it remains the basis for CommerceOne's e-business initiative. The DCD proposal is included because of its association with the development of XDR.

> *An excellent academic* Comparative Analysis of Six XML Schema Languages: DTD 1.0, XML Schema (April 2000 draft), XDR 1.0, SOX 2.0, DSD 1.0, and Schematron 1.4 *is at* http://www.cobase.cs.ucla.edu/tech-docs/dongwon/sigmod-record-00.html.

Arguably the most significant of these is XDR, because of its implementation in Microsoft's MSXML parser and IE5 browser, and its use as the basis for the .NET and BizTalk initiatives.

DDML

The DDML (Document Definition Markup Language) specification became a W3C NOTE on 19 January 1999, and was previously known as **XSchema**.

> ***DDML** is described at* http://www.w3.org/TR/NOTE-ddml*. Four developers working on the XML-DEV mailing list wrote it: Ronald Bourret (Darmstadt University of Technology), John Cowan, Ingo Macherius (GMD – the German National Research Center for Information Technology), and Simon St. Laurent.*

DDML was designed to be a simple base for preliminary XML schema implementations, encoding the logical content of DTDs in schemas using XML syntax. It does not include data types or provisions for schema reuse (both of these are now present in XML Schema).

DT4DTD

The DT4DTD (Datatypes for DTDs) specification became a W3C NOTE on 13 January 2000.

DT4DTD is described at http://www.w3.org/TR/dt4dtd, *and free open source code for both SAX and the DOM implementations is available at* http://www.extensibility.com/dt4dtd. *The specification was written by Lee Buck (Extensibility), Charles F. Goldfarb (co-inventor of SGML), and Paul Prescod (ISOGEN International).*

DT4DTD is intended to support legacy systems that must continue to use DTDs instead of XML Schema, but would benefit from stronger data-typing than is provided in XML 1.0 DTDs. These data types are intended to be compatible with both XML Schema and XML-Data (and XDR) data types, with an extensible architecture that provides for custom data types. The consistent use of these compatible data types will simplify the migration from DTDs to validation using XML Schema.

Because DT4DTD is intended to work with XML 1.0 DTDs, XML Namespaces are *not* supported and DTD syntax is used for the new data types instead of XML syntax. Two special attributes are used (`e-dtype` and `a-dtype`) for element and attribute data typing. `NOTATION` declarations are used to associate the names of data types with their definition elsewhere, like so:

```
<!NOTATION  string  SYSTEM "urn:schemas-microsoft-com:datatypes/string" >
<!NOTATION  number  SYSTEM "urn:schemas-microsoft-com:datatypes/number" >
```

These data types could be those in XDR or XML Schema, or even user-defined types. An example DTD excerpt declares both element and attribute data types:

```
<!ELEMENT  Invoice  EMPTY>
<!ATTLIST  Invoice
            invoiceID   ID     #REQUIRED
            customerID  IDREF  #REQUIRED
            date        CDATA  #REQUIRED
            terms       CDATA  #REQUIRED
            paid  (true | false)  #REQUIRED
            hire  (true | false)  "false"
            notes       CDATA  #IMPLIED

            a-dtype  CDATA  #FIXED
               "invoiceID id
               customerID idref
               date dateTime" >

<!ELEMENT  Price   (#PCDATA) >
<!ATTLIST  Price
            currency  (CDN | DM | UKP | USD | YEN)  #REQUIRED
            e-dtype  CDATA  #FIXED "number" >
```

As long as basic XML 1.0 DTDs continue to be used to validate XML data, extensions such as DT4DTD data types will also continue to be viable. This approach to data types has been used in Financial Products Markup Language (FPML) from JPMorgan and PriceWaterhouseCoopers, and some early versions of the Common Business Library (CBL) from CommerceOne. This specification provides a major benefit of XML Schema (data types), without the massive overhead and complexity of a full XML Schema implementation.

SOX

The SOX (Schema for Object-oriented XML) specification first became a W3C NOTE on 30 September 1998. A W3C member company, CommerceOne Inc. submitted it. A new revision (**SOX 2.0**) was accepted as a W3C NOTE on 30 July 1999, again at the request of CommerceOne.

SOX 2.0 is described at http://www.w3.org/TR/NOTE-SOX/. *Eight XML developers (from various organizations) wrote it.*

The design of SOX took note of the contemporary XML-Data and DCD proposals, the international standard **EXPRESS** language (ISO-10303-11), and was also heavily influenced by the Java language. It uses XML syntax for its schemas, supports XML Namespaces, extensible data types, element type inheritance, and embedded documentation.

The main reason that SOX remains of interest is its use in the CommerceOne ebXML Framework. Like the use of XDR in the BizTalk Framework, SOX will likely be replaced by XML Schema, but it is being used today in various ebXML implementations.

XML-Data

The XML-Data specification became a W3C Note on 5 January 1998, one of the earliest schema language proposals. It was one of the most comprehensive proposals, and is the basis for XDR, as well as a major influence upon the design of XML Schema.

XML-Data is described at http://www.w3.org/TR/1998/NOTE-XML-data-0105/. *Eight XML developers (from Microsoft, DataChannel, Inso, ArborText, and the University of Edinburgh) wrote it.*

XML-Data was written to describe classes of objects as schemas, such as those used to validate the structure of XML data or relational databases. XML-Data schemas use XML syntax, numerous data types were provided, and it was designed to work with XML Namespaces (though the XML-Data proposal actually predates the Namespaces in XML Recommendation).

XML-Data Reduced (XDR)

The **XML-Data Reduced (XDR)** specification became a W3C Note on 5 January 1998, another of the earlier schema language proposals. It is a non-standard schema that is used in Microsoft's MSXML parser, their IE5 browser, and as the basis for the BizTalk Framework.

XDR is a subset of XML-Data (hence its name), with functionality comparable to DCD. Like XML-Data, XDR is written in XML, supports data types, and is namespace-aware.

Microsoft's current "XML Schema" overview (although it actually covers XDR) is available at http://msdn.microsoft.com/xml/XMLGuide/schema-overview.asp *and the reference guide is at* http://msdn.microsoft.com/xml/reference/schema/datatypes.asp. *The original (somewhat different) version of XDR is described at* http://www.ltg.ed.ac.uk/~ht/XMLData-Reduced.htm. *The specification was written by Charles Frankston (Microsoft), and Henry S. Thompson (University of Edinburgh).*

The acronym "XDR" is unofficial, but it is commonly used – however, it shouldn't be confused with the IETF's RFC 1832, "XDR: External Data Representation Standard" (August 1995).

The future of XDR is somewhat murky. On one hand, Microsoft has promised to replace XDR with XML Schema, once the latter "standards are adopted". Microsoft has been in this position before – early XML and XSL support in MSXML were based on pre-Recommendation specifications. Once the W3C published these Recommendations, Microsoft did update their software. There are already conversion tools to produce XML Schema from XDR schemas (see the end of this section for more about these).

DCD

The DCD specification became a W3C NOTE on 31 July 1998, yet another of the early schema language proposals.

DCD is described at http://www.w3.org/TR/NOTE-dcd. *It was written by Tim Bray (Textuality, and a co-editor of XML 1.0), Charles Frankston (see also XDR), and Ashok Malhotra (IBM).*

DCD was based upon a subset of XML-Data, and was designed to be consistent with the Resource Description Framework (for more information on RDF, see Chapter 22), which was then also a specification under development – DCD is an RDF vocabulary. DCD schemas are a superset of DTDs that use RDF syntax and provide basic data types. Like XML-Data, DCD was designed to work with XML Namespaces, and other W3C specifications. It doesn't provide sub-classing or inheritance, though these were suggested as future enhancements to DCD.

Now that we've had an overview of some of the XML schema proposals that were early alternatives to DTDs, let's take a look at a widely-deployed alternative to XML Schema, Microsoft's XDR. We will then look at some other current proposals that can supplement or replace XML Schema.

Structure of an XDR Schema

An XDR schema consists of a preamble, followed by the schema's actual description and validation declarations in a fragment of well-formed XML data. These declarations deal with elements, attributes, entities, notations, comments, and data types. We will look at each type of these in turn, discussing how XDR differs from XML Schema.

Preamble

There are a few differences between an XDR preamble and its XML Schema equivalent:

- XDR uses `<Schema>` where XML Schema uses `<schema>`
- Microsoft uses URNs to refer to its schemas, while the W3C uses URLs.
- XDR requires its schemas to be named, using the `name` attribute

The preamble of the XML Schema for the Invoice example had the following declarations and document element:

```
<?xml version="1.0" encoding="UTF-8" ?>
<!-- Conforms to w3c http://www.w3.org/2000/10/XMLSchema -->
<xsd:schema xmlns:xsd="http://www.w3.org/2000/10/XMLSchema" >
  ...
</xsd:schema>
```

The XDR version of our Invoice schema would instead use the following:

```
<?xml version="1.0" encoding="UTF-8" ?>
<!-- Conforms to Microsoft's XDR Schema -->
<xdr:Schema
   name="Invoice_VersionInXDR"
   xmlns:xdr="urn:schemas-microsoft-com:xml-data"
   xmlns:dt="urn:schemas-microsoft-com:datatypes"
   version="1.42.57" >
   ...
</xdr:Schema>
```

The namespace ("xmlns:") declarations have changed to refer to the XDR schema and data types, using URNs rather than URLs. We use the xdr: namespace prefix to distinguish XDR schemas from XML Schema (which generally use an xsd: prefix).

Let's look at the differences between XML Schema and XDR declarations for elements and attributes.

Elements and Attributes

As with the schema preamble, XDR uses slightly different syntax for describing elements, their content models, and their attributes.

The elements used in XDR (we'll also call them "declarations" since they are used to declare the structure and content of XML data, just like declarations in a DTD) are:

XDR Element Name	XML Schema Equivalent	Description
<Schema>	<schema>	The top-level element of an XDR schema, which is used to name and version the schema, and declare XDR namespaces.
<ElementType>	<element name="...">	Declares an element type (within a <Schema>)
<group>	<attributeGroup> or <group>	Contains a group of child elements or attributes
<element>	<element ref="...">	Declares a child element within a content model
<AttributeType>	<simpleType> or <complexType>	Declares an attribute type
<attribute>	<attribute>	Declares an attribute within an <ElementType>

XDR Element Name	XML Schema Equivalent	Description
<datatype>	<simpleType> or <complexType>	Declares an <ElementType> or <AttributeType> to be of the specified data type.
<description>	<annotation>	Documents an <ElementType> or <AttributeType>

There are also some structural differences, which will be illustrated in the following examples of the XML Schema and XDR versions of another part of our Invoice schema.

For an ongoing example in these sections, we'll start with an excerpt of our previous Invoice XML Schema that describes the <MailingAddress> element and its children:

```
<xsd:element name="Street"  type="xsd:string" />
<xsd:element name="City"    type="xsd:string" />
<xsd:element name="State"   type="xsd:string" />
<xsd:element name="Zip"     type="xsd:string" />
<xsd:element name="Country" type="xsd:string" />

<xsd:element name="MailingAddress" >
   <xsd:complexType>
      <xsd:sequence>
         <xsd:element ref="Street" />
         <xsd:element ref="City" />
         <xsd:element ref="State" />
         <xsd:element ref="Zip" />
         <xsd:element ref="Country" />
      </xsd:sequence>
   </xsd:complexType>
</xsd:element>
```

And its comparable XDR schema form:

```
<xdr:ElementType name="Street"  content="textOnly" model="closed" />
<xdr:ElementType name="City"    content="textOnly" model="closed" />
<xdr:ElementType name="State"   content="textOnly" model="closed" />
<xdr:ElementType name="Zip"     content="textOnly" model="closed" />
<xdr:ElementType name="Country" content="textOnly" model="closed" />

<xdr:ElementType name="MailingAddress"
                  model="open" content="eltOnly" order="seq">
   <xdr:element type="Street" />
   <xdr:element type="City" />
   <xdr:element type="State" />
   <xdr:element type="Zip" />
   <xdr:element type="Country" />
</xdr:ElementType>
```

These same schema excerpts would be expressed in a DTD as:

```
<!ELEMENT  Street    (#PCDATA) >
<!ELEMENT  City      (#PCDATA) >
<!ELEMENT  State     (#PCDATA) >
<!ELEMENT  Zip       (#PCDATA) >
<!ELEMENT  Country   (#PCDATA) >
<!ELEMENT  MailingAddress  (Street, City, State, Zip, Country) >
```

The following excerpt of XML data would be considered valid by any of these schemas:

```
<MailingAddress>
   <Street>123 Park Avenue</Street>
   <City>Skokie</City>
   <State>IL</State>
   <Zip>60606</Zip>
   <Country>USA</Country>
</MailingAddress>
```

We used XDR's <xdr:ElementType> and <xdr:element> declarations (elements) instead of the <xsd:element>, <xsd:sequence>, and <xsd:ComplexType> elements in XML Schema. These elements also fit together in slightly different ways, as we'll see in the next few sections.

Declaring Elements: <ElementType>

XDR uses <ElementType> to declare an element type, and <element> to declare an "instance" of an element within a content model. The basic syntax of an <ElementType> is:

```
<ElementType
   name="id"
   dt:type="valid_data_type"
   model="{ open | closed }"
   content="{ empty | textOnly | eltOnly | mixed }"
   order="{ one | seq | many }" >
```

The first of these attributes is required:

- name is the name of the element type being declared, which must be a legal and unique XML name, so its value must be a valid ID (like the DTD attribute type of the same name, and not an IDREF, as described in Microsoft's reference!) – this name will be the target of a reference from an <element> element
- dt:type must have a value that is the name of a valid XDR data type – see the XDR "Data Types" section later in this chapter

We will discuss the remaining three of these optional attributes in context in the next section (***Content Models***). The attribute values in curly braces ({...}) are a set of mutually exclusive enumerated values shown here using the typical DTD choice operator character (|). The braces and spaces (and |) should *not* be included in the actual declaration.

Content Models

A significant difference between XDR and XML Schema is XDR's use of a default **open content model**. This means that XDR allows undeclared elements and/or attributes to be present in the XML data, which would still be considered valid. DTDs and XML Schema both require all content to be explicitly declared (except that of the completely permissive any content model).

From this example on, we'll just stipulate that the XDR schema namespace was declared as the default namespace, so we can omit the `xdr:` *prefix from the rest of our XDR schema examples for the sake of brevity and clarity.*

In our earlier XDR schema example, we declared an element named `<MailingAddress>`, with an *open* element-only content model (`model="open" content="eltOnly"`) of a four-element sequence of singular child elements (`order="seq"`). We'll glance at the beginning of this declaration once again:

```
<ElementType name="MailingAddress"
                        model="open" content="eltOnly" order="seq" >
   ...
   <element type="Country" />
</ElementType>
```

Since the default value of the `model` attribute is `open`, we could have omitted that attribute in the above example, but we'll leave the explicit declaration as a reminder that XDR content models can be open or closed.

When converting from a DTD to an XDR schema, be sure to explicitly declare all elements with `model="closed"` to ensure comparable validation (all DTD content models are closed).

For example, with the open content model, we could add an extra `<Note>` element to an instance of our `<MailingAddress>` element, without causing a validation error:

```
<MailingAddress>
   <Street>123 Park Avenue</Street>
   <City>Skokie</City>
   <State>IL</State>
   <Zip>60606</Zip>
   <Country>USA</Country>
   <Note>That's &quot;IL&quot; for Illinois</Note>
</MailingAddress>
```

Open content is *not* the same as any content, and does not imply that an explicitly declared content model can be broken. The following XML data would *not* be considered valid open content, since we inserted a new element (`<Note>`) within the explicitly declared sequence of elements:

```
<MailingAddress>
   <Street>123 Park Avenue</Street>
   <City>Skokie</City>
   <State>IL</State>
   <Note>That's &quot;IL&quot; for Illinois</Note>
   <Zip>60606</Zip>
   <Country>USA</Country>
</MailingAddress>
```

Because we have specified that a `<MailingAddress>` element is comprised of a sequence of five child elements, we may not break the declared sequence with a `<Note>` element.

When these added elements or attributes are in the same namespace as the declared element's content model, they must also be defined with an appropriate `<ElementType>` or `<AttributeType>`. If they are from a different namespace, no definition is necessary (and naturally no validation can be performed on the unspecified content). Thus, in this example, we *would* need to have an `<ElementType>` declaration for the `<Note>` element, or an error would be reported.

Content Types

XDR provides four content types that are comparable to those in DTDs as the permissible values for the `content` attribute (the default value is `"mixed"`):

- `empty` – the element cannot contain anything (equivalent to `EMPTY` in a DTD)
- `textOnly` – character data content only (equivalent to `#PCDATA` in a DTD) – this is only true when `model="closed"` – when the `model` attribute value is `open`, then there is no difference between this and the `mixed` content type with an open content model
- `eltOnly` – the element can only contain other (specified) elements
- `mixed` – the element can contain mixed element and character data content, with specific elements (this is really only useful for closed content models)

In our example, we chose an element-only content type:

```
<xdr:ElementType ... content="eltOnly" ... >
```

With this content type, the sequence (or choice) list of child elements can also be constrained.

Order Constraints

XDR provides three content types to specify the pattern of child elements that are similar to the different kinds of content models in DTDs. These types are the permissible values for the `order` attribute:

- `one` – One element from those listed within the `<ElementType>` declaration corresponds to the OR content model in a DTD (that is, a choice list, which uses the `"|"` operator)
- `seq` – Child elements must appear in the same order as listed within the `<ElementType>` declaration (this is the default for `eltOnly` content) – analogous to a sequence list in a DTD (which uses the `","` operator)
- `many` – Child elements may appear (or not) in any order – this corresponds to a DTD choice list with an unlimited cardinality constraint, such as `<!ELEMENT foo (child1 | child2)* >`

The default value for the `order` attribute is `many`, except if `content="eltOnly"` (element content only) then the default is `order="seq"`.

In our example, we chose a sequenced list of child elements:

```
<xdr:ElementType ... order="seq" >
```

The actual list of child elements is declared with a series of `<element>` declarations, as we will see two sections from now. Lists of single elements would be rather limited, so we also need a way to specify the cardinality of the children; in other words, the range of occurrences for each child within the list.

Cardinality Constraints

XDR provides two attributes that are functionally equivalent to the cardinality operators in a DTD: minOccurs and maxOccurs. These attributes can be used in either the <element> or <group> declaration (we will discuss <group> a little later).

The minOccurs attribute is optional, and its value is the minimum number of times that the group may appear. It may be one of two values:

- 0 – The element/group is optional
- 1 – The element/group must occur at least once

The maxOccurs attribute is also optional, and its value is the maximum number of times that the group may appear. It may also be one of two values:

- 1 – The element/group can occur only once, at most
- * – Unlimited occurrences (equivalent to unbounded in XML Schema)

Unlike XML Schema, which allows these attributes to have any positive integer value, XDR is limited to the same constraints as DTDs. The following combinations of these two attribute's values correspond to the cardinality operators in a DTD:

minOccurs	maxOccurs	Cardinality Operator in DTD
unspecified	unspecified	None – One and only one occurrence is allowed
0	1	? – Zero or one
0	*	* – Zero or more
1	1	None – One and only one occurrence allowed
1	*	+ – One or more

The default value for both the minOccurs and maxOccurs attributes is 1 (as implied by the first row in the above table).

Let's now look at more details of how to declare the individual child elements that may be contained within another element.

Declaring Child Elements: <element>

The sequence of child elements is implied by the presence of a series of <element> declarations, one for each child element. The basic syntax of an <element> is:

```
<element
   type="element-type"
   minOccurs="{ 0 | 1 }"
   maxOccurs="{ 1 | * }" >
```

The value of the type attribute must correspond to a name attribute value in an ElementType declaration elsewhere in the schema. The minOccurs and maxOccurs attributes were just described in the previous section.

In our example, the sequence of child elements is implied by the sequence of the five <element> declarations, one for each possible child. Since we've just discussed cardinality constraints, we'll change a few of these declarations from the earlier example to illustrate a slightly more complex content model:

```
<ElementType name="MailingAddress"
             model="open" content="eltOnly" order="seq" >
   <element type="Street" maxOccurs="*" />
   <element type="City" />
   <element type="State" />
   <element type="Zip" minOccurs="0" />
   <element type="Country" />
</ElementType>
```

Remember that the minOccurs and maxOccurs attributes are optional, and their absence leaves them with default values of 1.

We changed the <Street> element to allow multiple occurrences, but still require at least one such element within each <MailingAddress>. We also changed the cardinality of the <Zip> element to make it optional – not all countries use postal codes. As with the other element declarations, we could have omitted the minOccurs and maxOccurs attributes anywhere their value is equal to the default value ("1"). We've left them here for the sake of illustration.

Grouping Child Elements: <group>

XDR schemas provide a way to group the child elements of an <ElementType> content model in separate sequence and/or choice lists, just like the parentheses in a DTD. Each group is contained within a <group> declaration that can use order and cardinality constraints to produce the various possible content models of a DTD.

The basic syntax of a <group> is:

```
<group
   order="{ one | seq | many }"
   maxOccurs="{ 1 | * }"
   minOccurs="{ 0 | 1 }" >
```

The attributes are optional:

- order has the same meaning (and seq default value) as the like-named attribute in <ElementType> – see the earlier section
- minOccurs and maxOccurs use the values described in the previous section (their default value for both these attributes is 1)

The attribute values in curly braces ({...}) are a set of mutually exclusive enumerated values shown here using the typical DTD choice operator character (|). The braces and spaces (and |) should *not* be included in the actual declaration.

For example, a DTD might allow one of two different groups of child elements:

```
<!ELEMENT  Point ((x1,y1) | (x2,y2)) >
```

This would be represented in XDR using two <group> elements:

```
<ElementType name="Point" model="closed" content="eltOnly" order="one" >
   <group>
      <element type="x1" />
      <element type="y1" />
   </group>
   <group>
      <element type="x2" />
      <element type="y2" />
   </group>
</ElementType>
```

For the sake of brevity, we can just assume that the four child element types have already been declared in their own <ElementType> declarations.

Data Types: <datatype>

The <ElementType> and <AttributeType> declarations may each have one (and only one) data type declaration, using the <datatype> element. This element should be empty and must have a single attribute:

```
<datatype dt:type="valid_data_type" />
```

The value of the dt:type attribute (*valid_data_type*) must be one of the names of valid XDR data types – see the "XDR Data Types" section later in this chapter.

For example, we could redeclare the <Zip> element to allow only integer values, using this element:

```
<ElementType name="Zip" content="textOnly" model="closed" >
   <datatype dt:type="int" />
</ElementType>
```

The <datatype> element is simply an alternative to the use of the dt:type attribute within the <ElementType> declaration:

```
<ElementType name="Zip" content="textOnly" model="closed" dt:type="int" />
```

Either of these forms can also be used in the same way with <AttributeType> declarations. Speaking of the latter, let's look at how we can declare attributes in XDR.

Declaring Attributes

XDR uses the <AttributeType> declaration to declare a type of attribute, and the <attribute> declaration to declare an *instance* of an attribute with an <ElementType>.

In our ongoing ToysCo example, we have a <Price> element that uses a single attribute for the type of currency. It was declared in the DTD as:

```
<!ELEMENT  Price  (#PCDATA) >
<!ATTLIST  Price  currency  (CDN | DM | UKP | USD | YEN)  #REQUIRED >
```

The same constraints can be expressed in XDR as follows:

```
<AttributeType name="currency" dt:type="enumeration"
   dt:values="CDN DM UKP USD YEN" />

<ElementType name="Price" content="textOnly" model="closed" >
   <datatype dt:type="fixed.14.4" />
   <attribute type="currency" required="yes" default="USD" />
</ElementType>
```

The parallels in these two completely different kinds of schema declarations are fairly clear, and you can see that we've taken advantage of XDR's data types to further constrain the price to be a number. We put the required and default attributes in the <attribute> declaration (instead of in the <AttributeType>) since we might want to reuse this attribute type for other purposes, with a different default currency or as an optional attribute.

Now let's look at these two XDR elements in greater detail.

Attribute Types: <AttributeType>

The basic syntax of an <AttributeType> declaration is:

```
<AttributeType
   name="idref"
   dt:type="valid_data_type"
   dt:values="enumerated_values"
   required="{ yes | no }"
   default="default_value" >
```

The first of these attributes is required – the rest are optional:

- name is the name of the attribute type being declared, which must be a legal and unique XML name (its value must be a valid ID attribute) – this name will be the target of a reference from an <attribute> element
- dt:type must be the name of a valid XDR data type – see the "XDR Data Types" section later in this chapter
- dt:values is only used if dt:type="enumerated", in which case its value must be a space-delimited list of nmtoken values; just like enumerated values in a DTD
- required may be either yes or no, and specifies whether or not the attribute must be present within every instance of the element type
- the default value (if any) must be valid for the declared data type (it *must* appear in the dt:values list if the attribute is an enumerated type)

The current IE5 implementation of dt:type allows the following values: string, enumeration, id, idref, idrefs, nmtoken, nmtokens, entity, entities, or notation. These are almost all identical to attribute types in DTDs (string is equivalent to CDATA), and will be described in detail in the "XDR Data Types" section.

The {} braces and spaces (and |) in the description above should *not* be included in the actual declaration

Attribute Instances: <attribute>

The basic syntax of an <attribute> declaration is:

```
<attribute
   type="attribute_type"
   required="{ yes | no }"
   default="default_value" >
```

The first of these attributes is required, the second is sometimes required, and the third is always optional:

- type is a reference to the *value* of the name attribute of an <AttributeType> declaration within this schema or another (indicated with an associated namespace prefix)
- required may be either yes or no, and overrides the attribute of the same name in the corresponding <AttributeType> declaration – if there isn't such a corresponding attribute, then it is required here
- default overrides, and has the same value restrictions as, the like-named attribute in the associated <AttributeType>

The order of attributes cannot be constrained, nor can an element have more than one attribute of the same name (these are restrictions of the XML 1.0 syntax).

Comments and Application Information

Since an XDR schema uses XML syntax, regular XML comments may be used as desired. However, remember that an XML parser need *not* pass such comments to the XML application.

Instead of using an XML comment or Processing Instruction, we can use a <description> element within any other element to pass information to the XML application. This is similar to a conflation of the <documentation> and <appinfo> elements in XML Schema.

For example, we could embed some (fictional) script code for the application to do additional validation tests that are beyond the scope of the XDR schema:

```
<ElementType name="MailingAddress" model="open" content="eltOnly" >
   ...
   <element type="Zip" minOccurs="0" maxOccurs="1" />
   <description>Use 'US_Zip' for non-international apps</description>
   <element type="Country" />
   <description>'Country' intable('ISO 3166')? </description>
</ElementType>
```

Of course, like PIs, it is up to the application to parse or otherwise process the contents of a <description> element – the parser will merely pass it on.

Scope

Element type declarations (<ElementType>) are always global in scope.

Attribute type declarations (<AttributeType>) are different, because they can have a local scope within an element type declaration. This allows the same attribute name to be used for a different purpose in different elements.

Attribute type declarations can also be global in scope, simply by putting them outside of any element type declaration. Attributes declared in this fashion can be useful – multiple elements can share common attributes that need only be declared once.

Data Types

The XML 1.0 DTD provides some simple attribute data types, all of which are string types, mostly constrained to be some form of XML name (an `NCName` or `NmToken`). XDR extends this capability to provide a variety of common numeric and specialized string types, which may also be applied to elements as well as to attributes.

> **Unlike the real XML Schema, data types in XDR are *not* extensible.**

Many of these XDR data types also correspond to specific data types in the XML Document Object Model (DOM). These new data types allow more precise validation of XML data, can imply a valid lexical format, and enable additional processing in the XML application.

Data Types From XML 1.0 DTD Attribute Types

XDR supports the following data types that correspond to the like-named DTD attribute types, with only minor variations (as noted in parentheses):

- `string` – character data (`CDATA` in a DTD)
- `enumeration` – a list of `NmTokens`, see `nmtoken` below (an implied type in a DTD)
- `id` – a unique identifier for an instance of an element, it must be a valid XML name
- `idref` – a reference to an element with an ID type attribute, must be a valid XML name
- `idrefs` – a list of whitespace-separated `idref` values
- `nmtoken` – a name token (or `NmToken`), a valid XML name without the first character restrictions
- `nmtokens` – a list of whitespace-separated `nmtoken` values
- `entity` – the name of a pre-defined entity
- `entities` – a list of whitespace-separated `entity` names
- `notation` – a declaration of non-XML data, it must correspond to a `<!NOTATION..>` declaration in a DTD

We've already seen the `string` and `enumeration` types used in earlier examples in this chapter. Another element from the Toysco example is the `<Invoice>` element, which in DTD form looks like this:

```
<!ELEMENT  Invoice  EMPTY>
<!ATTLIST  Invoice
            invoiceID   ID      #REQUIRED
            customerID  IDREF   #REQUIRED
            date        CDATA   #REQUIRED
            terms       CDATA   #REQUIRED
            paid   (true | false)  #REQUIRED
            hire   (true | false)  "false"
            notes       CDATA   #IMPLIED >
```

And in XDR equivalent, we'd use four different DTD-compatible data types:

```
<AttributeType name="invoiceID" dt:type="id" required="yes" />
<AttributeType name="customerID" dt:type="idref" required="yes" />

<AttributeType name="date" dt:type="string" required="yes" />
<AttributeType name="terms" dt:type="string" required="yes" />

<AttributeType name="paid"
   dt:type="enumeration" dt:values="true false" required="yes" />

<AttributeType name="hire"
   dt:type="enumeration" dt:values="true false" default="false" />

<AttributeType name="notes" dt:type="string" required="no" />

<ElementType name="Invoice" content="empty" model="closed" >
   <attribute type="invoiceID" />
   <attribute type="customerID" />
   <attribute type="date" />
   <attribute type="terms" />
   <attribute type="paid" />
   <attribute type="hire" />
   <attribute type="notes" />
</ElementType>
```

Beware of Microsoft's "XML Schema Developer's Guide" when it comes to some of these so-called "primitive" data types – their documentation sometimes uses `IDREF` in a way that is different to its definition in XML 1.0 DTDs! Fortunately, this does seem to be an error in the documentation rather than in the XDR implementation.

Additional XDR-specific Data Types

In addition to the basic data types that are used in DTDs (and implicitly defined in XML 1.0), the current IE5 implementation of XDR also supports the following data types:

- `bin.base64` – value is MIME-style Base64 encoded binary data
- `bin.hex` – hexadecimal digits (`0` to `9`, `A` to `F` or `a` to `f`) representing binary data
- `boolean` – can only be a `0` or `1`, with `0` meaning false and `1` meaning true
- `char` – a single-character string
- `date` – a calendar date in abbreviated ISO 8601 format, without time, such as "`2001-01-16`"
- `dateTime` – a calendar date in abbreviated ISO 8601 format, with an optional time, but no time zone – for example, "`2001-03-20T06:31:57`"
- `dateTime.tz` – a calendar date in abbreviated ISO 8601 format, with an optional time and time zone – for example, "`2001-03-20T06:31:57-07:00`"
- `time` – a time in abbreviated ISO 8601 format, with no time zone – for example, "`06:31:57`"
- `time.tz` – a time in abbreviated ISO 8601 format, with an optional time zone – for example, "`06:31:57-07:00`"

- number – can be either an int or a float with unlimited digits, though the value range is limited to that of a float or an r8
- fixed.14.4 – same as a number, but with no more than 14 digits to the left of the decimal point, a maximum of 4 digits to the right, and no exponents
- float – a real number of unlimited digits, using US English style punctuation – values can be in the range from 2.2250738585072014E-308 to 1.7976931348623157E+308
- r4 – a four byte signed real number with 7 digit precision (as described in the Microsoft documentation) – values range from 1.17549435E-38F to 3.40282347E+38F
- r8 – an eight byte signed real number with 15 digit precision – value range is the same as float
- int – an integer number with an optional sign (+ or -), but with neither fractions nor exponents
- i1 – a one byte signed integer – values can range from -128 to +127
- i2 – a two byte signed integer – values can range from -32768 to +32767
- i4 – a four byte signed integer – values can range from -2,147,483,648 to +2,147,483,647
- i8 – an eight byte signed integer – values can range from -9,223,372,036,854,775,808 to 9,223,372,036,854,775,807
- ui1 – a one byte unsigned integer – values can range from 0 to +256
- ui2 – a two byte unsigned integer – values can range from 0 to +65,535
- ui4 – a four byte unsigned integer – values can range from 0 to +4,294,967,295
- ui8 – an eight byte unsigned integer – values can range from 0 to +18,446,744,073,709,551,615
- uri – a Universal Resource Identifier (URI), which can be a URL or URN – for example: "urn:schemas-micorsoft-com:Office2000" or "http://www.w3.org/xml/Namespaces/"
- uuid – A unique sixteen byte binary value, with each byte represented by a pair of hexadecimal digits (optional embedded hyphens are ignored) – for example: "ABCD4257-1A2B-113F-BC00-A9B8C7D6E5F4"

We can take advantage of one of XDR's extended data types to more precisely define the date attribute type in our above example:

```
<AttributeType name="date" dt:type="date" required="yes" />
```

If it were possible to change our XML data, we could also change the paid and hire attribute types to use the XDR boolean data type:

```
<AttributeType name="paid" dt:type="boolean" required="yes" />
<AttributeType name="hire" dt:type="boolean" default="0" />
```

Then, instead of using true and false values for this attribute, we'd use 0 and 1. None of these changes would affect the <attribute> elements or the <ElementType> declaration.

Many of these data types are also available in XML Schema (though perhaps with slightly different names). There is a table comparing these XDR types with their XML Schema equivalents in the next section.

XDR and XML Schema

Some of the basic differences between XDR and XML Schema are:

- XML Schema allows the creation of user-defined data types, while XDR can only use its built-in data types
- XML Schema data types can be used for both attributes and elements, but these must be declared separately in XDR
- XML Schema has extensive object-oriented features to build modular schemas from multiple smaller schemas which are lacking in XDR
- XML Schema element names can be reused and redefined in different contexts, while XDR can only have one type of element per element name
- XML Schema can describe attributes or child elements inline within the parent element's description, but XDR requires a separate description (in the form of `<AttributeType>` and `<ElementType>`)
- XML Schema describes its content models using elements, such as `<choice>` and `<sequence>`, while XDR uses a combination of elements and attributes (such as `<group>` and `order="seq"`)
- On the other hand, XDR has a more permissive model for attributes (when `model="open"`, XDR allows attributes from other namespaces that haven't been defined in the schema)

Schema Declarations

Most declarations in XDR have a counterpart in XML Schema, though often with a different name and sometimes even a completely different structure (the use of attributes as opposed to the use of elements).

Some comparable declarations in XDR and XML Schema:

XDR	XML Schema
`<ElementType>`	`<element name="...">`
`<ElementType order="one" ...>`	`<choice>`
`<ElementType order="seq" ...>`	`<sequence>`
`<element>`	`<element ref="...">`
`<group>`	`<group>`
`<AttributeType>`	`<attribute>`
`<attribute>`	`<attribute>`
`<description>`	`<appinfo>`

The XML Schema <element> is a combination of the XDR <element> and <ElementType>, and the <attribute> element is similar in this respect. Content models are described in different fashions as well. There are also numerous XML Schema elements and attributes that have no counterparts in XDR, and a few aspects of XDR that aren't part of XML Schema.

Schema Data Types

With the recent publication of the XML Schema Proposed Recommendation, numerous XML Schema data types have changed names, many to names similar to those used in XDR. Comparable data types in XDR and XML Schema (ignoring the common DTD types) are:

XDR	XML Schema
`bin.base64`	`base64Binary`
`bin.hex`	`hexBinary`
`boolean`	`boolean`
`char`	**No built-in equivalent**
`date`	`date`
`dateTime`	`dateTime (actually same as XDR's dateTime.tz)`
`dateTime.tz`	`dateTime`
`fixed.14.4`	**No built-in equivalent**
`float`	`float`
`i1`	`byte`
`i2`	`short`
`i4`	`int`
`i8`	`long`
`int`	`integer`
`number`	`decimal`
`r4`	`float`
`r8`	`double`
`time`	`time` (actually the same as XDR's `time.tz`)
`time.tz`	`time`
`ui1`	`unsignedByte`
`ui2`	`unsignedShort`
`ui4`	`unsignedInt`
`ui8`	`unsignedLong`
`uri`	`anyUri`
`uuid`	**No built-in equivalent**

The XDR and XML Schema date and time formats have slightly different data types with conflicting names, though all of them are based on the same ISO 8601 formats. The `char` and `fixed.14.4` types can be converted to derived types in XML Schema, with the appropriate lexical and value constraints. If XDR's `uuid` type is needed in XML Schema, a regular expression pattern-constrained string type will have to suffice (`hexBinary` doesn't allow hyphens).

We've discussed XDR in the context of its differences from XML Schema. The two could continue to co-exist, but this would be like another "browser war", and this kind of obstacle to interoperability is one of the things XML is supposed to avoid. If we assume that XML Schema is the future and that XDR will eventually become obsolete, how will we make the transition from one to the other?

Converting XDR to XML Schema

A simple schema can be manually converted from one form to another. However, multiple or complex schemas require some form of automated conversion. Evidence of Microsoft's commitment to eventually replace XDR with XML Schema is the availability of their XDR to XML Schema conversion process, which uses an XSLT style sheet.

This conversion stylesheet produces a schema conforming to the *2000-10-25 draft* of XML Schema, which has been superseded by the Proposed Recommendation of 2001-03-16.

> *The **XDR-XSD Converter** from Microsoft is currently available at http://msdn.microsoft.com/downloads/default.asp?URL=/code/sample.asp?url=/msdn-files/027/001/539/msdncompositedoc.xml. Someday maybe Microsoft will pay attention to Dr. Jakob Nielsen and Tim Berners-Lee, and use simple, persistent, and reasonable URLs! See the former's* "URL as UI" *at http://www.useit.com/alertbox/990321.html and the latter's* "Cool URIs don't change" *at http://www.w3.org/Provider/Style/URI for more on this issue.*

There are two key design differences between XDR and XML Schema that cannot be converted automatically:

- The open content model of XDR is forgiving of unspecified attributes
- XDR allows separate validation of attributes in the target namespace and other namespaces

Since XDR was the schema used for the BizTalk Framework, numerous XDR schemas have been developed and deployed. Those that depend on these features may slow the overall conversion process from XDR to XML Schema, but since most new schema designs now use XML Schema, this will be a diminishing problem.

Example – An XDR Schema for Invoices

Throughout this chapter, we've looked at various bits and pieces of our `Invoice` example in XDR and its XML Schema version. Now let's look at a large portion of both schemas – the `<Customer>` element and its children – section by section.

Most conversions between these two types of schemas are likely to be *from* XDR to XML Schema. However, for the sake of illustration, and to build upon the previous chapter, we will look at these examples in the opposite order, with the more familiar XML Schema first.

First, we'll revisit the XML Schema preamble:

```
<?xml version="1.0" encoding="UTF-8" ?>
<!-- "toysco.xsd" -->
<!-- Conforms to 2001-03-16 XML Schema PR (Proposed Recommendation) -->
<xsd:schema xmlns:xsd="http://www.w3.org/2001/XMLSchema"
   xmlns:inv="http://www.wrox.com/examples/ProXML2"
   targetNamespace="http://www.wrox.com/examples/ProXML2" >
```

Its equivalent in XDR:

```
<?xml version="1.0" encoding="UTF-8" ?>
<!-- "toysco.xdr" -->
<xdr:Schema
   xmlns:xdr="urn:schemas-microsoft-com:xml-data"
   xmlns:dt="urn:schemas-microsoft-com:datatypes"
   xmlns:inv="http://www.wrox.com/examples/ProXML2" >
```

These are almost the same, with the principal difference being the use of URNs (instead of URIs) in the XDR namespace declarations. Also, XDR does not specify a target namespace like XML Schema.

The separate XDR declarations for structures (the one with the `xdr:` prefix) and datatypes (`dt:` prefix) used to be a feature of XML Schema as well, but they have now been combined into a single namespace (`http://www.w3.org/2001/XMLSchema`).

Now, let's look at a simple element declaration in XML Schema:

```
<xsd:element name="Name" >
   <xsd:complexType>
      <xsd:element name="FirstName" type="xsd:string" />
      <xsd:element name="MiddleName" type="xsd:string"
         minOccurs="0" maxOccurs="unbounded" />
      <xsd:element name="LastName" type="xsd:string" />
   </xsd:complexType>
</xsd:element>
```

We are describing a `<Name>` element with three children that must appear in the sequence shown. The first and last children are required and they must be singular; the middle element is optional and can have more than one instance (or none at all). Unlike some of our earlier examples, we've chosen to declare the child elements directly within the parent, rather than as separate complex types. This emphasizes a difference between XML Schema and XDR (which *must* use the separate type declarations).

In XDR, this same element is described as so:

```
<xdr:ElementType name="FirstName" dt:type="dt:string" />
<xdr:ElementType name="MiddleName" dt:type="dt:string" />
<xdr:ElementType name="LastName" dt:type="dt:string" />

<xdr:ElementType name="Name" content="eltOnly" order="seq" >
   <xdr:element type="FirstName" />
   <xdr:element type="MiddleName" minOccurs="0" maxOccurs="*" />
   <xdr:element type="LastName" />
</xdr:ElementType>
```

The differences here are superficial:

- XDR declares element types and instances with different elements (<ElementType> and <element>), while XML Schema merges the two together (and uses <complexType> to describe the types)
- XDR uses a separate namespace for data types
- XDR uses the content and order attributes, instead of separate elements like XML Schema
- XDR uses maxOccurs="*" instead of maxOccurs="unbounded"

Let's look at another rather simple element description. First, in XML Schema:

```
<xsd:complexType name="Address" >
   <xsd:sequence>
      <xsd:element name="Street" type="xsd:string" />
      <xsd:element name="City" type="xsd:string" />
      <xsd:element name="State" type="xsd:string" />
      <xsd:element name="Zip" type="xsd:string" />
      <xsd:element name="Country" type="xsd:string" />
   </xsd:sequence>
</xsd:complexType>
```

There are no declarations needed for the <MailingAddress> and <BillingAddress> elements since they will simply be declared later within the definition of the <Customer> element (see below). This serves to simplify these examples, as well as remind of differences between XML Schema and XDR.

The equivalent elements in XDR:

```
<xdr:ElementType  name="Street" dt:type="dt:string" />
<xdr:ElementType  name="City" dt:type="dt:string" />
<xdr:ElementType  name="State" dt:type="dt:string" />
<xdr:ElementType  name="Zip" dt:type="dt:string" />
<xdr:ElementType  name="Country" dt:type="dt:string" />

<xdr:ElementType name="MailingAddress" content="eltOnly" order="seq" >
   <xdr:element type="Street" />
   <xdr:element type="City" />
   <xdr:element type="State" />
   <xdr:element type="Zip" />
   <xdr:element type="Country" />
</xdr:ElementType>

<xdr:ElementType name="BillingAddress" content="eltOnly" order="seq" >
   <!-- Declarations omitted - identical to "MailingAddress" above -->
</xdr:ElementType>
```

Since XDR doesn't have XML Schema's object-oriented type structures, we need to declare the element *types* for the <MailingAddress> and <BillingAddress> elements here, so we can refer to them when we define the <Customer> element.

The definition of the phonetype attribute of the <Phone> element is a little more verbose in XML Schema:

```
<xsd:simpleType name="PhoneType" >   <!-- for "phonetype" attribute -->
   <xsd:restriction base="xsd:string" >
      <xsd:enumeration value="HOME" />
      <xsd:enumeration value="WORK" />
      <xsd:enumeration value="CELL" />
      <xsd:enumeration value="FAX" />
   </xsd:restriction>
</xsd:simpleType>
```

...than in XDR:

```
<xdr:AttributeType name="phonetype"
   dt:type="dt:enumeration" dt:values="HOME WORK CELL FAX" />
```

However, there are two ways that XML Schema enumerated types are more powerful than in XDR. First, the XML Schema version declares a general data type (`PhoneType`), which may be used for elements and/or attributes, while XDR can only declare an attribute type. The XDR `dt:enumeration` data type is also limited to `NMTOKEN` values (strings constrained to legal XML name characters, with no embedded whitespace), rather than the more general strings of this type in XML Schema.

The `<Customer>` element and its other children are straightforward – in XML Schema:

```
<xsd:element name="Email" type="xsd:string" />

<xsd:element name="Phone" type="xsd:integer" >
   <xsd:complexType>
      <xsd:attribute name="phonetype" type="PhoneType" />
   </xsd:complexType>
</xsd:element>

<xsd:element name="ContactDetails">
   <xsd:complexType>
      <xsd:sequence>
         <xsd:element ref="Email" minOccurs="0" maxOccurs="2" />
         <xsd:element ref="Phone" minOccurs="0" maxOccurs="4" />
      </xsd:sequence>
   </xsd:complexType>
</xsd:element>
```

...and the very similar declarations as converted to XDR:

```
<xdr:ElementType name="Email" dt:type="dt:string" />

<xdr:ElementType name="Phone" dt:type="dt:integer" content="textOnly" >
   <xdr:attribute type="phonetype" />
</xdr:ElementType>

<xdr:ElementType name="ContactDetails" content="eltOnly" order="seq" >
   <xdr:element type="Email" minOccurs="0" maxOccurs="*" />
   <xdr:element type="Phone" minOccurs="0" maxOccurs="*" />
</xdr:ElementType>
```

This excerpt shows another subtle advantage of XML Schema over XDR, greater control of the number of occurrences of an element. While the former can dictate 0-2 <Email> elements, followed by 0-4 <Phone> elements, XDR is limited to the same granularity as DTDs. The minOccurs attribute value can only be zero or one, whilst maxOccurs can be zero, one, or many.

Lastly, we will bring together all the children into a <Customer> element in our final XML Schema excerpt:

```
   <xsd:element name="Customer" >
      <xsd:complexType>
         <xsd:sequence>
           <xsd:element ref="Name" />
           <xsd:element name="MailingAddress" type="Address" minOccurs="0"/>
           <xsd:element name="BillingAddress" type="Address" />
           <xsd:element ref="ContactDetails" />
         </xsd:sequence>
         <xsd:attribute name="customerID" type="xsd:ID" use="required" />
      </xsd:complexType>
   </xsd:element>
   <!-- Remaining declarations omitted for brevity -->
</xsd:schema>
```

We haven't forgotten the <MailingAddress> and <BillingAddress> elements – they are both defined and used as part of the <Customer> content model right here.

The XDR version's <MailingAddress> and <BillingAddress> element types were declared at the beginning of this example, and are simply referenced in the content model here. This end of the XDR schema also has an additional attribute type declaration:

```
   <xdr:AttributeType name="customerID" dt:type="dt:ID" />

   <xdr:ElementType name="Customer" content="eltOnly" order="seq" >
      <xdr:element type="Name" />
      <xdr:element type="MailingAddress" minOccurs="0" />
      <xdr:element type="BillingAddress" />
      <xdr:element type="ContactDetails" />
      <xdr:attribute type="customerID" />
   </xdr:ElementType>
   <!-- Remaining declarations omitted for brevity -->
</xdr:Schema>
```

With XDR, the customerID attribute must first be declared as a type (in the <AttributeType> declaration) and then can be used by reference as an attribute for one or more elements. In a similar fashion, we had already declared the <MailingAddress> and <BillingAddress> elements in earlier <ElementType> declarations. XML Schema *allows* element types to be declared separately like XDR, but does not *require* them to be declared like XDR. Other than this difference, most of the conversion is simple name changing, with a few different structural approaches, such as content models in attributes as opposed to content models being represented as elements. Neither form is as compact as similar constraints in a DTD, but both XDR and XML Schema have several advantages over DTDs, as we saw in the last chapter.

The above examples show the very similar syntax of XDR and XML Schema. XDR has a few built-in data types (such as `uuid` or `fixed.14.4`) that aren't in XML Schema, but these *can* be similarly defined as derived types in the latter. Since XML Schema has extensible data types, it allows many more complex types than XDR's small fixed set.

At times, either one can be more verbose than the other when expressing certain content models or such. However, the power *and* complexity are not reciprocal – XML Schema really does have an edge when it comes to data type extensibility, the ability to create complex data types for either elements or attributes, redeclaration of elements with the same name, object-oriented inclusion mechanisms, and a variety of other features.

XDR Summary

Although XDR is widely deployed in BizTalk Framework schemas and custom IE5-based applications, there will certainly be a transition to XML Schema. At such time, XDR will be relegated to historical interest, like its contemporaries DDML and DCD. The implementation of XDR in IE5 informed the development of the XML Schema specifications, gave many developers early experience with non-DTD schemas for XML, and helped hasten the adoption of XML for non-traditional uses.

Let's now look at some of those other alternatives to XML Schema.

Alternative Validation Tools

There are four interesting proposals for schema languages that may be seen as replacing or supplementing XML Schema for the description and validation of XML data:

- **DSD** (Document Structure Description)
- **RELAX** (Regular Language for XML)
- **TREX** (Tree Regular Expressions for XML)
- **Schematron**

DSD is another current proposal that addresses some concerns about the complexity of XML Schema and its ability to scale-up gracefully for extremely large documents and databases. DSD is a potential alternative to XML Schema, but its development has been outside the W3C process, so this may not be a viable alternative. As such, we'll just give a brief overview of DSD, and then move on to the latter three significant schema alternatives.

RELAX and TREX are intended to be less complex alternatives to "XML Schema Part 1: Structures" that may be useful as a validation method that is more powerful than a DTD but less complex than XML Schema. These first three schema proposals are based on formal grammars, much like XML and XML Schema.

Schematron is an interesting schema alternative that instead uses patterns in the tree structure of XML and an XSLT processor to apply constraints, rather than a syntax-based grammar with an XML parser.

All of these proposals might be seen as providing lighter-weight alternatives to an implementation using XML Schemas. None of them (except perhaps DSD) are intended to replace XML Schema since it has many capabilities that are not present in these other proposals.

All of these specifications remain outside of the scope of the W3C, though the authors are respected members of the XML developer communities.

DSD

Though the DSD specification is being developed outside of the scope of the W3C, it *is* designed to work with HTML and CSS. It is being developed by AT&T Labs Research (New Jersey, USA) and BRICS (Basic Research in Computer Science at the University of Aarhus in Denmark), with the most recent update in October 2000.

> ***DSD** is described at* http://www.brics.dk/DSD/ *with a more detailed description at* http://www.brics.dk/DSD/dsd.html. *It was written by Nils Klarlund (AT&T), Anders Møller, and Michael I. Schwartzbach (the latter two at BRICS).*

Like XML Schema, a DSD schema is self-describing and is expressed in XML syntax. DSD is intended to work much like a CSS or XSL style sheet, providing a declarative and readable specification of XML data that can be processed with XSLT. Presently, DSD does *not* work with XML Namespaces.

DSD claims to be both simple and more expressive than XML Schema, with features that are not available in XML Schema, such as context dependencies (see also Schematron) and schema evolution (the modification of existing schemas). For the sake of simplicity (and given the focus on using DSD in an HTML/CSS context), DSD does *not* adopt the object-oriented programming notions of XML Schema like final, abstract, and equivalence.

A key design feature of DSD is the guarantee of processing time that is in linear proportion to the size of the XML data – in contrast to XML Schema's potentially devastating open-ended processing time scaling.

DSD's use of CSS style declarative syntax and context-free grammars is a different approach than XML Schema. Given the scaleable performance and special features of DSD, it may remain a viable alternative to XML Schema for certain applications involving large datasets. It is also possible that aspects of DSD will be folded into XML Schema, though the key feature of linear time scaling may be unattainable with the current XML Schema design.

We will discuss the other three proposals in their own sections. First, we'll take a look at RELAX.

RELAX

"Just relax" is good advice for developers who are concerned that XML Schema is unnecessarily complex for their XML applications. RELAX, the Regular Language for XML, is a way to describe and validate XML data using **RELAX grammars**.

RELAX is intended to be a bridge from DTDs to XML Schemas, and may persist as an approach to validation. While the design of XML Schema has a very broad scope, that of RELAX is more modest. RELAX grammars can easily be converted to XML Schema since they share data types. RELAX structural validation is similar to that of a DTD, so they can easily be made into RELAX grammars.

> **RELAX offers the structural validation of DTDs (with some extensions), plus the rich data types of XML Schema and support for XML namespaces.**

The RELAX specification is a Japanese Information Standard Technical Report (JIS TR X 0029:2000) that has also been submitted to the ISO for consideration as an international standard.

> ***RELAX** is described at http://www.xml.gr.jp/relax/. It was created by Murata Makoto of IBM, a member of the W3C XML and XML Core Working Groups, contributor to the XML Schema specification, and the co-author of the XML Media Types RFC (#3023).*
>
> *The Fast Track ISO Draft is: ISO/IEC DTR 22250-1, "Document Description and Processing Languages – Regular Language Description for XML (RELAX)" – Part 1: RELAX Core, 2000 October. As usual with ISO documents, this is* not *readily available online.*

The key features of RELAX are that they:

- Use standard XML syntax
- Are based on regular expressions, hedge automata theory (see below), and grammars
- Work with XML Namespaces
- Work with data types from "XML Schema Part 2: Datatypes" (RELAX doesn't define its own data types, but does provide two extensions to the standard data types, as we shall see in a few sections)
- Can have dynamic content models, based upon an element's context (its parent element) or one of its attribute values

Regular expressions are familiar to most programmers, but **hedge automata theory** is a little more esoteric. A **hedge** can be informally defined as a sequence of trees. In XML, this is a series of elements, perhaps with interspersed character data. Therefore, any well-formed XML data is a hedge. Hedges can be generated using **regular hedge grammars** (**RHG**), which can be used as a formal representation of an XML schema. The creator of RELAX has been using hedge grammars to describe and transform structured document schemas since 1993, first with SGML, and now for XML.

> *An excellent summary of regular expressions in the context of XML is in Appendix D of the* "XML Schema Part 0: Primer" *at http://www.w3.org/TR/xmlschema-0/. Murata-san's paper, "Hedge automata: a formal model for XML schemata" is available at http://www.xml.gr.jp/relax/hedge_nice.html. More links on this are at http://www.oasis-open.org/cover/hedgeAutomata.html.*

This theory is good background material that can greatly enhance one's understanding of tree theory and structured data such as XML. But let's look at more practical matters, like our ongoing `<MailingAddress>` example:

```
<MailingAddress>
   <Street>AMK Building</Street>
   <Street>123 Park Avenue</Street>
   <City>Skokie</City>
   <State>IL</State>
   <Zip>60606</Zip>
   <Country>USA</Country>
</MailingAddress>
```

A simple RELAX grammar that describes and validates this structure would be:

```
<module
   moduleVersion='1.2'
   relaxCoreVersion='1.0'
   targetNamespace='http://www.wrox.com/examples/ProXML2'
   xmlns='http://www.xml.gr.jp/xmlns/relaxCore'>

   <interface>
      <export label='MailingAddress' />
   </interface>

   <elementRule role='Street' type='string' />
   <elementRule role='City' type='string' />
   <elementRule role='State' type='string' />
   <elementRule role='Zip' type='string' />
   <elementRule role='Country' type='string' />

   <tag name='Street' />
   <tag name='City' />
   <tag name='State' />
   <tag name='Zip' />
   <tag name='Country' />

   <elementRule role='MailingAddress' >
      <sequence>
         <ref label='Street' occurs='*' />
         <ref label='City' />
         <ref label='State' />
         <ref label='Zip' />
         <ref label='Country' />
      </sequence>
   </elementRule>

   <tag name='MailingAddress' />

</module>
```

This kind of schema is starting to look familiar, with a default namespace, a hook to the document element (the <interface> and <export> elements), and the rules describing the element, its content model, and its children (the <elementRule> element and *its* children).

We will take a look at the structure of RELAX, and then some of the specific elements that comprise a RELAX grammar. Finally we'll look at some implementations of RELAX and validation of our ongoing <Customer> example using RELAX.

RELAX Structure

As the above example suggests, a RELAX grammar consists of a <module> element that has the typical "header" (the <interface> element and its children) and "body" structure (<tag> and <elementRule> elements, and their children). Provisions have been made for reusable content in the grammar (<hedgeRule> and <attPool> elements), structured comments like those in XML Schema (<annotation>, etc.) and even a presentation element (<div>).

RELAX is available in two basic configurations:

- **RELAX Core** – a single namespace version that can work as a direct replacement for a DTD ("classic" conformance level) or provide additional validation features ("fully relaxed" level)
- **RELAX Namespace** – as the name implies, this version works with multiple XML namespaces

Most of our discussion in this section will deal with RELAX Core since it is the closest to DTDs and is the most portable version of RELAX. Of course, almost everything we discuss applies to the namespace version, as well.

> *There is an excellent tutorial by Murata-san, called* "How to RELAX", *available in English at* http://www.xml.gr.jp/relax/html4/howToRELAX_full_en.html *and in Japanese at* http://www.xml.gr.jp/relax/html4/howToRELAX_full_ja.html.

This tutorial is probably the best place to learn the details of RELAX elements, but we'll provide a summary of these elements here, along with some simple examples of their use.

RELAX Elements

Since RELAX is based upon XML syntax, it uses regular elements and attributes for its declarations.

Top-level Elements: <module>, <interface>, and <export>

These three elements comprise the "header" portion of a RELAX grammar.

<module>

The `<module>` element is always the top-level element of a RELAX grammar. Its basic syntax is:

```
<module
   moduleVersion="schema version#"
   relaxCoreVersion="1.0"
   targetNamespace=""
   xmlns="http://www.xml.gr.jp/xmlns/relaxCore" >
```

All of the following attributes are optional:

- `moduleVersion` is the version number for this grammar
- `relaxCoreVersion` is the version number for RELAX, currently at "`1.0`"
- `targetNamespace` is the namespace of the XML data that is described/validated by this module
- `xmlns` is the namespace declaration for the RELAX Core, which we will designate as the default namespace in this and other examples (so that we can use unprefixed names for the RELAX elements for the sake of clarity)

Like the `<schema>` element in XML Schema or the `<Schema>` element in XDR, the `<module>` element is the entry point to a RELAX grammar which identifies it and declares any necessary namespaces. It is also the container for all other elements in the grammar. The `<module>` element must contain an `<interface>` element followed by one or more `<elementRule>` elements.

<interface>

All RELAX <module> elements must begin with a single <interface> element. It is simply a container element for one or more <export> elements.

<export>

The <export> element is used to specify an element in the XML data that is the document element. This allows a single RELAX grammar to describe a variety of XML data that might use different document elements.

The <export> element is an empty element with a single required attribute:

```
<export label="name_of_document_element" />
```

Our ongoing example has two different elements for addresses, which can both be handled by a common RELAX grammar:

```
<interface>
   <export label='MailingAddress' />
   <export label='BillingAddress' />
</interface>
```

Although our Invoice example uses these elements within others, this example is for illustrative purposes only, so we'll pretend that these two are the document elements of different types of similar address data. It might actually be used in this form if these elements were promoted to be the document element, as would be the case if they were XML data islands.

The "body" of a RELAX grammar can include element and attribute declarations, reusable rules, and documentation elements. There is no container element for the body – it just follows the required <interface> element. Let's look at how to describe elements first.

Element Type Declarations

The <!ELEMENT...> declaration in a DTD is replaced in RELAX with a combination of <elementRule> and <tag> elements. These allow more flexible and reusable declaration of element content models and attributes.

<elementRule>

The <elementRule> element is used to specify the type of an element and its content model. In RELAX, a content model has been generalized as a hedge model, which is similar enough to be considered the same thing for our current discussion.

The <elementRule> element is a container element with up to three attributes:

```
<elementRule role="element_type" type="data_type" label="context" >
   <!-- describe content model or value constraints here -->
</elementRule>
```

None of these attributes are required, though role is used in most circumstances:

- role is the element type name being described
- type is one of RELAX's valid data types that constrains the element's content (see the "Data Types" section later in the chapter)
- label is used when we have multiple rules for a single element type, which are chosen based upon some context or dynamic value (see the later "Data-dependent Content Models" section)

Like XML Schema, RELAX allows an element to be constrained to be a specific data type, and may also provide further constraints upon the value of the element. For example, we can require a <Zip> element to be a number, and limit its values as well:

```
<elementRule role="Zip" type="integer" >
   <minInclusive value="01000" />
   <maxInclusive value="99999" />
</elementRule>
```

Within each <elementRule> element are one or more additional elements that describe and constrain the target element's content model in the usual ways. These children include: <empty>, <sequence>, <choice>, <ref>, <mixed>, and <none>.

<empty>

The <empty> element is used to declare an element to be empty. For example:

```
<elementRule role="Product" >
   <empty/>
</elementRule>
```

There are no attributes for this element, and as befits its purpose, it may not contain any other elements.

<sequence>

The <sequence> element is the equivalent of a sequence list in a DTD content model, which are those lists that use the comma (,) as the separator character. It is a container element that has an optional attribute:

```
<sequence occurs="cardinality" >
   <!-- child elements are listed here -->
</sequence>
```

The occurs attribute value (if any) must be one of the usual XML cardinality operators:

- * – zero or more occurrences
- + – one or more
- ? – zero or one

Also as usual, the absence of this attribute is interpreted to mean that "one and only one" occurrence is permitted. This attribute can be used in much the same way as a cardinality operator in a DTD, and thus is an option for most of the following RELAX elements, as well.

<choice>

The `<choice>` element is the equivalent of a choice list in a DTD, which are lists that use the vertical bar character (|) as the separator. Its form is the same as that of the `<sequence>` element:

```
<choice occurs="cardinality" >
   <!-- child elements are listed here -->
</choice>
```

The `occurs` attribute is optional and uses one of the usual three XML cardinality values as specified above.

<ref>

The `<ref>` element is an empty element that is used to specify the occurrence(s) of a child element. Its basic syntax is:

```
<ref label="element_type_name" occurs="cardinality" />
```

The first attribute is required, while the second is optional:

- `label` is the name of an element type in the XML data
- `occurs` uses one of the usual three values

Our `<MailingAddress>` element is a simple container for a sequence of several child elements. As we saw earlier, it would be described in RELAX as follows:

```
<elementRule role="MailingAddress" >
   <sequence>
      <ref label="Street" occurs="*" />
      <ref label="City" />
      <ref label="State" />
      <ref label="Zip" />
      <ref label="Country" />
   </sequence>
</elementRule>
```

This RELAX rule is identical to our earlier DTD and XDR schema specifications.

Character Data (#PCDATA) Content

The easiest way to declare an element with text content in RELAX uses its data type capability. The optional `type` attribute of an `<elementRule>` is set to the `string` data type. For example:

```
<elementRule role="Street" type="string" />
```

The other method is more complex, and has little to recommend its use.

<mixed>

The `<mixed>` element is a container element that is used to declare the target element to have mixed content. RELAX allows much more complex mixed content models than those in DTDs. Remember that a DTD cannot constrain the sequence or occurrences of child elements in a mixed content model.

Our ongoing example could be converted to a mixed content model, while still specifying the sequence of the child elements:

```
<elementRule role="MailingAddress" >
   <mixed>
      <sequence>
         <ref label="Street" occurs="*" />
         <ref label="City" />
         <ref label="State" />
         <ref label="Zip" />
         <ref label="Country" />
      </sequence>
   </mixed>
</elementRule>
```

This simply changes our earlier example to allow *any* characters between the child elements.

Assume that the three children below are all simple text (#PCDATA) elements as part of a more complicated example of mixed content in RELAX:

```
<elementRule role="Name" >
   <mixed>
      <sequence>
         <ref label="FirstName" />
         <ref label="MiddleName" occurs="*" />
         <ref label="LastName" />
      </sequence>
   </mixed>
</elementRule>
```

For example, this XML data conforms to the above model:

```
<Name>
   The late Mr. <FirstName>Walter</FirstName> &quot;Sweetness&quot;
   <LastName>Payton</LastName>
</Name>
```

But this example does *not*, since the child element sequence is invalid:

```
<Name>
  <LastName>Public</LastName>, <FirstName>John</FirstName>
  <MiddleName>Q</MiddleName>.
</Name>
```

This is a significant advantage over DTDs when using mixed content models.

<none>

The <none> element is unique to RELAX – it is used to declare an element is not permitted to have any content. Although this seems identical to an <empty> element, it has a slightly different meaning in a hedge model (see the <hedgeRule> element and its children).

Element Type Names: <tag>

The `<tag>` element is another empty element that is used to specify the actual tag of an element type. The combination of this and the `<elementRule>` element are equivalent to an `<!ELEMENT...>` declaration in a DTD.

> **In RELAX, every element type name must be described in a `<tag>` element.**

This declaration must be made for every element type. Its basic syntax is:

```
<tag name="element_type_name" />
```

The `name` attribute is required since it is the whole basis of this element. It is a legal XML name that will be the target of a reference in an `<elementRule>` elsewhere in the grammar.

The `<tag>` element must be an empty element if there are no attributes associated with the element type being named. Otherwise, the attributes are defined within the `<tag>` element, as we will see in the next section.

The elements we have used in several earlier examples would have their tags described as follows:

```
<tag name="MailingAddress" />
<tag name="Name" />
```

These use the empty element form since neither is defining an element type with attributes. We will see the container form of the `<tag>` element in the very next section.

Attribute List Declarations

Earlier in this chapter, we declared an empty `<Product>` element from our ongoing invoice example. Now we will define its tag and the attributes associated with that element type:

```
<tag name="Product" >
   <!-- attributes are declared here -->
</tag>
```

Each attribute of our `<Product>` element will be defined with its own declaration contained within the RELAX `<tag>` element .

<attribute>

The `<attribute>` element is an element that is used to specify the name, type, and value constraints (if any) of an element's attribute. It is equivalent to an `<!ATTLIST...>` declaration in a DTD, and it usually appears as an empty element.

This declaration must be made for every element type. Its basic syntax is:

```
<attribute name="attribute_name" required="{ true | false }"
   type="data_type" />
```

The first attribute is required, whereas the latter two are optional:

- name is the name of the attribute (a legal XML name)
- required may be either "true" (which is the same as #REQUIRED in a DTD) or "false" (the default value, which means the attribute is optional)
- type may be any valid RELAX data type – its default value is "string"

For example, our <Product> element could be defined as so:

```
<tag name="Product" >
   <attribute name="name" required="true" type="ID" />
   <attribute name="description" required="true" type="string" />
   <attribute name="unit" required="true" type="string" />
   <attribute name="price" required="true" type="string" />
   <attribute name="stock" required="true" type="string" />
   <attribute name="hire" required="false" type="boolean" />
</tag>
```

We could have omitted the type="string" and required="false" attributes, since they just repeat the default values, but we have left them here as an illustration (and as some explicit documentation of our intentions for this element).

<enumeration>

RELAX does support the DTD's enumerated values attribute type, using an <enumeration> element for each possible value. For example, we could explicitly declare the hire attribute of the <Product> element to allow one of two values:

```
<tag name="Product" >
   ...
   <attribute name="hire" required="false" type="string" >
      <enumeration value="true" />
      <enumeration value="false" />
   </attribute>
</tag>
```

In this case, a non-empty <attribute> element must be used.

<attPool>

Often, XML data will have sets of recurring attributes that are shared by numerous element types. For example, numerous elements might use the first two attributes in our <Product> element (name and description). RELAX provides the <attPool> element, which is roughly equivalent to the use of a DTD parameter entity in an <!ATTLIST...> declaration.

For example, we can take the first two attributes from our previous example to make a common pair for elements that are described and named:

```
<attPool role="Generic.ElementIds" >
   <attribute name="name" required="true" type="ID" />
   <attribute name="description" required="true" type="string" />
```

In this case, our example <Product> element could then be redefined as:

```
<tag name="Product" >
   <ref role="Generic.ElementIds" />
   <attribute name="unit" required="true" type="string" />
   <attribute name="price" required="true" type="string" />
   <attribute name="stock" required="true" type="string" />
   <attribute name="hire" required="false" type="boolean" />
</tag>
```

More than one <ref> element may be used within a <tag> element, but they must precede any <attribute> elements. It is also permissible for <attPool> elements to directly contain other <attPool> elements, but there may be no recursive references, either direct or indirect. An <attPool> element need *not* precede its use by reference.

Just as we can reuse attribute lists (or parts thereof) with an <attPool> element, we can also reuse common content models in a RELAX grammar.

Reusable Rules: <hedgeRule> and <hedgeRef>

Like XML Schema, RELAX can establish sets of rules that may be reused in various contexts. The <hedgeRule> element is like a macro definition or a parameter entity definition in a DTD – it:

- may only be used to describe element content models
- may *not* include mixed content (the <mixed> element) or data types
- can reference another <hedgeRule> element (using a <hedgeRef> element)
- may not refer to itself, directly or indirectly (no recursive references)
- need not precede its use in a RELAX grammar

A <hedgeRule> element has a single required attribute named label, which is a legal XML name that will be used to refer to the rule elsewhere in the grammar. For example, we can recast our earlier definition of the <MailingAddress> element as a generic address, and then use this common rule to define two different types of address elements:

```
<elementRule role="MailingAddress" >
   <hedgeRef label="Invoice.Address" />
</elementRule>

<elementRule role="BillingAddress" >
   <hedgeRef label="Invoice.Address" />
</elementRule>

<hedgeRule label="Invoice.Address" >
   <sequence>
      <ref label="Street" occurs="*" />
      <ref label="City" />
      <ref label="State" />
      <ref label="Zip" />
      <ref label="Country" />
   </sequence>
</hedgeRule>
```

Both <elementRule> elements would be interpreted to contain the equivalent of everything between, and including, the <sequence> elements in the <hedgeRule> element. Although we would probably want to define our hedge rules at the beginning of a grammar, it is *not* necessary to have them before their use, as this example illustrates.

We can also have a content model that extends a hedge rule, such as

```
<hedgeRule label="Invoice.Name" >
   <sequence>
      <ref label="FirstName" />
      <ref label="MiddleName" occurs="*" />
      <ref label="LastName" />
   </sequence>
</hedgeRule>

<elementRule role="NameAndTitle" >
   <sequence>
      <ref label="Honorific" occurs="?" />
      <hedgeRef label="Invoice.Name" />
      <ref label="Suffix" occurs="*" />
   </sequence>
</elementRule>
```

Here too, the <sequence> element and its children in the <hedgeRule> element would be included within this <elementRule> as if they were literally present (no nesting of sequence list implied).

This allows an optional honorific like "Mrs." or "Dr." to precede the children of <Name> that are defined in the <hedgeRule>, and zero or more <Suffix> elements that might be titles (such as "M.D." or "Esq.") or parts of the name (like "Jr." or "III"). For example:

```
<Name>
  <Honorific>The Rev. Dr.</Honorific>
  <FirstName>Martin</FirstName>
  <MiddleName>Luther</MiddleName>
  <LastName>King</LastName>
  <Suffix>Jr.</Suffix>
  <Suffix>Div.D.</Suffix>
  <Suffix>Nobel Laureate</Suffix>
</Name>
```

The last group of elements used in RELAX grammars that we will discuss are those used for documentation and presentation purposes.

Documentation and Presentation

RELAX provides three elements for documentation and application information that are similar to the like-named elements in XML Schema, plus a presentation grouping element from HTML:

- <annotation>
- <documentation>
- <appinfo>
- <div>

XML comments can also be used, but XML parsers are not obligated to pass these onwards to an application. The RELAX elements should be used for any important comments about the grammar and/or its target, so they will be included in the data output from the parser, and can be styled and shown like the rest of the grammar.

<annotation>

Like a similar structure in XML Schema, the `<annotation>` element is the container element for the `<documentation>` and `<appinfo>` elements. It may appear in almost any other RELAX element, but only once, and its appearance is usually constrained to be the first child element.

<documentation>

The `<documentation>` element is intended to contain a natural language description of the associated aspect of the RELAX grammar. It can have text-only content, such as:

```
<annotation>
  <documentation xml:lang="en">
      This rule ensures valid ZIP codes.
   </documentation>
</annotation>
```

The optional `xml:lang` attribute identifies the language used for the text content.

An alternate form of this element uses a `uri` attribute in an empty element to provide the documentation in an external resource. For example, we might document our `Invoice` grammar in a web page:

```
<annotation>
   <documentation uri="http://www.wrox.com/ProXML2/Invoice.in.RELAX.html" />
</annotation>
```

If this type of `<documentation>` element is used, it must be in the form of an empty element (in other words, it must have no additional text content).

<appinfo>

The `<appinfo>` element is intended to convey hints or script code to an application program, just like the XML Schema element of the same name, or an XML Processing Instruction (PI). This element may also use either an inline or URI reference form, like the `<documentation>` element above.

<div>

The `<div>` element is similar to the HTML element of the same name. It is used to contain logical groups of the `<module>` element's children. These groups might be divided based upon distinct parts of the target data, or based upon the type of validation being described. In either case, this element has no effect upon standard validation; it is merely a way to group rules together for styling or application-specific processing.

Reusable Modules

Like most programming languages, RELAX provides some declarations that can be used to split a grammar into smaller modules. These are merged into a grammar using the `<include>` element. For example, we could split our `Invoice` grammar into several separate modules, and then bring them all together in one master module:

```
<module
   moduleVersion="1.2"
   relaxCoreVersion="1.0"
   targetNamespace="http://www.wrox.com/examples/ProXML2"
   xmlns="http://www.xml.gr.jp/xmlns/relaxCore">

   <interface>
      <export label="Invoice" />
   </interface>

   <include moduleLocation="Invoice.NameAddress.rlx" />
   <include moduleLocation="Invoice.Customer.rlx" />
   <include moduleLocation="Invoice.Product.rlx" />
   <include moduleLocation="Invoice.Invoice.rlx" />
</module>
```

Each of these included modules will in effect be copied into this <module>. Each included module must conform to RELAX syntax rules, and so will have both <module> and <interface> elements. The former will be ignored, but must match the values in the main module. Any <interface> elements in the included modules will be ignored, since the main module will specify the document element.

Data-dependent Content Models

RELAX can make different content models for a single element type, depending upon an element's parent or the value of one of the element's attributes. This is a very flexible and powerful extension to simple DTD validation.

> *A discussion of dynamic content models in RELAX is in the* How to RELAX *tutorial at* *http://www.xml.gr.jp/relax/html4/howToRELAX_full_en.html#id_37_*.

To make an element's content model dependent upon its parent, we can define multiple <elementRule> models with the same `role` attribute, but different `label` attributes. The appropriate content model is then referenced by a `label` in the parent <elementRule> element.

Making an element's content model dependent upon the value of one of its associated attributes works in the same way, except that the content model is referenced from a <tag> element via the `role` attribute.

Another major advantage of RELAX is its ability to constrain element content to be of a certain specific data type.

Data Types

RELAX uses the same data types as XML Schema. These include eight of the types used in XML 1.0 DTDs:

- ID
- IDREF
- IDREFS
- NMTOKEN
- NMTOKENS

- ENITITY
- ENITITIES
- NOTATION

Also included are all the new data types that are defined in XML Schema Part 2, and two types that are unique to RELAX:

- none
- emptyString

Like XML Schema, RELAX can constrain the values of a given instance of a data type, as we saw in our earlier <Zip> element example. Unlike DTDs, which have a limited ability to constrain only attribute values, RELAX rules may apply to element content or attributes.

> *A more complete reference for RELAX data types is within the* How-to RELAX *tutorial at* http://www.xml.gr.jp/relax/html4/howToRELAX_full_en.html#id_29_. *The XML Schema Datatypes are defined at* http://www.w3.org/TR/xmlschema-2.

Unlike XML Schema, RELAX cannot have user-defined data types, only those in the pre-defined set. This is one of the limitations of RELAX that ensures that it is much simpler to implement than XML Schema.

Now that we have discussed the components of RELAX, let's make a brief survey of some implementations.

Implementations

First of all, no special API is needed since RELAX works in cooperation with existing XML processors (parsers). Yet, there *is* a Java API for invoking RELAX verifiers (something like SAX for XML 1.0 parsers).

A RELAX grammar is applied to XML data using a **RELAX processor**. Its inputs are the grammar and an instance of the XML data, and it produces a validation report. One such processor converts the grammar to an XSL style sheet so that a regular XSLT processor can be used to do the validation.

Links to Tools

There are quite a few free programs to handle RELAX, most of which are written in Java (though there are a few in C++, VisualBASIC, and XSLT).

> *The key resource for developers interested in RELAX is the public* ***RELDEVE mailing list*** *at* http://groups.yahoo.com/group/reldeve, *and its collections of files including verifiers in C++ and Java, the DTD for RELAX, sample RELAX grammars, and more documentation at* http://groups.yahoo.com/group/reldeve/files.

A pair of Java programs that convert DTDs to RELAX grammars and vice versa can be found at:

- **DTD2RELAX** at http://www.horobi.com/Projects/RELAX/Archive/DTD2RELAX.html
- **RELAX2DTD** at http://www.geocities.co.jp/SiliconValley-Bay/4639/relax2dtd.htm

There are several RELAX verifiers:

- **RELAX Verifier for XSLT** at http://www.geocities.co.jp/SiliconValley-Bay/4639/intro.htm
- **RELAX Verifier for Java** by K. Kawaguchi *et al.* is available at http://www.swiftinc.co.jp/en/frame/products/RELAX/ and also at http://groups.yahoo.com/group/reldeve/files/Verifier%20for%20Java/
- **VBRELAX** (an ActiveX server component in VisualBASIC) is at http://www.geocities.co.jp/SiliconValley-Bay/4639/vbrelaxen.htm
- Other verifiers in C++ and Java at the RELDEVE e-group (see above)
- A Java program that uses RELAX Namespace and a "divide-and-validate" approach is at http://www.xml.gr.jp/relax/divideAndValidate.html

There is even an interactive web-based viewer for RELAX grammars:

- **viewRELAX** at http://www.geocities.co.jp/SiliconValley-Bay/4639/viewRELAX/viewRELAX2.html

There is a free trial version of some commercial software that supports RELAX Core:

- TIBCO Extensibility's **XML Authority** (now part of their Turbo XML v2.1 package) can be downloaded from http://www.extensibility.com

RELAX Summary

An advantage of RELAX is its simplicity relative to XML Schema. RELAX can do the same validation as a DTD, plus extended features similar to those of XML Schema. A key feature is the use of data types from "XML Schema Part 2: Datatypes". A DTD is still needed for default values or notations, which RELAX does not provide. RELAX allows dynamic content models, based upon a parent or other ancestor element, or the value of an attribute. Attributes and elements may be mutually exclusive or grouped together, perhaps with local scoping.

Applications willing to forgo the use of default values or notations can use a non-validating parser and a RELAX processor together as a low overhead solution to XML parsing and validation. This may hold an advantage over XML Schema for embedded systems that have limited resources, such as PDAs or cell phones.

A draft of RELAX has been accepted by the JIS and ISO, so it may well become an international standard for validating XML data. On the other hand, some standards languish on the shelf with few real-world implementations. RELAX satisfies many XML validation needs without using the more advanced features of XML Schema, and so RELAX may continue to be a viable alternative to XML Schema for some time to come.

The second of our alternatives to XML Schema, TREX, has some similarities with RELAX as we will soon see.

TREX

TREX is an acronym for "Tree Regular Expressions for XML". It might equally be thought of as tree regular expressions *in* XML, since the syntax of the proposed TREX validation (or schema) language is compliant with XML 1.0 syntax. TREX was created by James Clark, who also created the first TREX processor (described later), and arose out of a perceived need for an "easy-to-learn XML schema language". A significant body of potential users believe that W3C XML Schema is too complex. An advantage of TREX for such users is that with TREX you can "start simple" and work up.

TREX is, at the time of writing, one of the newest of the alternatives to W3C XML Schema, having been announced as a proposal by its creator, James Clark, on 8th January 2001 on the XML-Dev mailing list. If you are interested in XML history, the original announcement is located at http://lists.xml.org/archives/xml-dev/200101/msg00306.html.

James Clark is well regarded in the XML world. He was the technical lead for the XML 1.0 Recommendation at the W3C and was also the editor of the XSLT 1.0 and XPath 1.0 Recommendations. Thus TREX has attracted a lot of interest from sections of the XML community.

> *At the time of writing it is barely three months since the TREX proposal was made. In the interim it has been submitted to OASIS (the Organization for the Advancement of Structured Information Standards) with a view to creating a specification for validating XML documents using TREX. It is possible that significant changes may be made during the consideration of TREX at OASIS. Therefore, be aware that almost any detail of the specification or implementation of TREX described here is subject to change.*

At the moment, the primary source of information about the TREX proposal James Clark's web site at http://www.thaiopensource.com/trex/.

As originally proposed, TREX does not claim to be a full schema language. Its primary purpose is to permit validation of XML documents using a schema that is written in XML syntax. TREX defines a tree structure and content of specific classes of XML documents, but it does not aim to assist in further processing of XML documents, nor does it change the Infoset; the post-schema validation Infoset is the same as the pre-schema validation Infoset. For more information on how XML Schemas use the Infoset, see the section "Working with XML Schemas" in Chapter 6.

Advantages of TREX

The claimed features or advantages of TREX are that it

- Is simple
- Is easy to learn
- Uses XML syntax
- Does not change the Infoset of an XML document
- Supports XML namespaces
- Treats attributes uniformly with elements so far as possible
- Has unrestricted support for unordered content, using 'interleaving'
- Has unrestricted support for mixed content

- Permits the use of a wildcard for the name of an element, which could be useful with respect to literal result elements in XSLT
- Has a solid theoretical basis in regular expressions
- Can partner with a separate datatyping language (such as W3C XML Schema Datatypes, http://www.w3.org/TR/xmlschema-2/)

TREX Elements

A TREX schema document is an XML 1.0 compliant document. Therefore it has an optional XML declaration as its first element.

Simple Element Type Declarations

The document element of a simple TREX schema is typically an `<element>` element, with a `name` attribute that defines the element name of the document element of the target XML document. An alternative syntax is to use a `<grammar>` element as the document element (see the later section, "TREX Named Patterns").

For example, if we wished to create a TREX schema for a class of XML documents which had a `<book>` element as the document element then we would have a simple **TREX pattern** (TREX's term for a schema) like this:

```
<?xml version="1.0"?>

<element name="book">
  <!-- Other elements and attributes would be defined here. -->
</element>
```

Cardinality

TREX has several elements that describe the permitted frequency with which an element may occur in the class of XML documents to which the TREX schema relates. If, for example, our `<book>` element were allowed to have one or more `<Chapter>` children, then the **TREX pattern** would use the TREX `<oneOrMore>` element and look like this:

```
<?xml version="1.0"?>

<element name="book">
  <oneOrMore>
    <element name="Chapter">
      <!-- The allowable content of a Chapter
      element would be defined here. -->
    </element>
  </oneOrMore>
  <!-- Other elements would be defined here. -->
</element>
```

If we wished to allow an optional preface and to allow the presence of several appendices but also to allow for no appendices, our TREX pattern would need to use the TREX `<optional>` and `<zeroOrMore>` elements and look like this:

```
<?xml version='1.0'?>

<element name="book">
  <optional>
    <element name="Preface">
      <!-- The permitted content of a Preface would be defined here. -->
    </element>
  </optional>
  <oneOrMore>
    <element name="Chapter">
      <!-- The allowable content of a Chapter element would be defined here.
      -->
    </element>
  </oneOrMore>
  <zeroOrMore>
   <element name="Appendix">
     <!-- The permitted content of appendices would be defined here. -->
   </element>
  </zeroOrMore>
</element>
```

Thus cardinality in TREX is provided using the <optional>, <zeroOrMore> and <oneOrMore> elements, which is similar to the functionality found in DTDs. One of the issues under consideration by OASIS is whether other options should be added, such as functionality equivalent to the flexible usage of the minOccurs and maxOccurs attributes provided in W3C XML Schema.

TREX allows choices to be made between various elements. Let's suppose you had a class of XML documents that recorded the version of a document in <Draft> or <Final> elements but you didn't want the document to have both. In TREX you could express this dichotomy using the <choice> element:

```
<?xml version="1.0"?>

<element name="Version">
  <choice>
    <element name="Draft">
      <!-- the definition of a Draft element would go here. -->
    </element>
    <element name="Final">
      <!-- the definition of a Final element would go here. -->
    </element>
  </choice>
</element>
```

The TREX <choice> element defines that one and only one of its child elements is allowed in an instance of the class of XML documents.

TREX also allows a choice to be made between single elements and a group of elements. For example, to return to the simple example for customers that you saw at the beginning of the chapter, let's suppose we had an international range of customers. In Western societies a first name/last name pattern is normal but in some societies a single name is used for a person. To express in TREX the choice of a single <SingleName> element and the group made up of <FirstName> and <LastName> elements we use the TREX <group> element like this:

```
<?xml version="1.0"?>

<element name="Customers">
  <choice>
    <element name="SingleName">
      <anyString/>
    </element>
    <group>
      <element name="FirstName">
        <anyString/>
      </element>
      <element name="LastName">
        <anyString/>
      </element>
    </group>
  </choice>
</element>
```

Again the choice is between the child elements of the `<choice>` element. On this occasion the choice is between an `<element>` element and a `<group>` element.

Note too the `<anyString/>` element nested within each of the `<element>` elements above. The `<anyString/>` element indicates that the element in question may contain any string. This provides similar functionality to a DTD. Thus:

```
<element name="SingleName">
      <anyString/>
    </element>
```

is equivalent to:

```
<!ELEMENT SingleName (#PCDATA)>
```

in a DTD.

Attribute List Declarations

TREX deals with the declaration of attributes very much as the declaration of elements is treated.

Let's suppose that we wish our `<Chapter>` elements to have a required `title` attribute but an optional `version` attribute. Then we would use the TREX `<attribute>` element, without any indication of cardinality, to define that the `title` attribute for the `<Chapter>` element is required. Clearly, when writing a book we would not wish the title of a chapter to be arbitrarily constrained and so we use the `<anyString/>` element to indicate that the value of the `title` attribute may be any string. To allow an optional version attribute we follow the technique used for elements and simply nest the definition of the `version` attribute in `<optional>` tags.

```
<?xml version='1.0'?>

<element name="book">
  <optional>
    <element name="Preface">
```

```
      <!-- The permitted content of a Preface would be defined here. -->
    </element>
  </optional>
  <oneOrMore>
    <element name="Chapter">
    <attribute name="title">
      <anyString/>
    </attribute>
    <optional>
      <attribute name="version">
        <anyString/>
      </attribute>
    </optional>
      <!-- Other allowable content of a Chapter element would be defined here.
      -->
    </element>
  </oneOrMore>
  <zeroOrMore>
   <element name="Appendix">
     <!-- The permitted content of appendices would be defined here. -->
   </element>
  </zeroOrMore>
</element>
```

Given that the norm for attributes of an XML element is that there cannot be more than one attribute with the same name on an element, then use of the <oneOrMore> or <zeroOrMore> TREX elements is inappropriate here.

Up to this point when dealing with strings we have used the TREX <anyString/> element to indicate that any string content is allowed. Let's suppose that we want to constrain the content of the version attribute, when present, to be either "draft" or "final". Then we change:

```
<attribute name="version">
  <anyString/>
</attribute>
```

in the above example to:

```
<attribute name="version">
  <choice>
    <string>draft</string>
    <string>final</string>
  </choice>
</attribute>
```

You may also similarly constrain the permitted values of an element.

Putting It Together

Before we move on to look at more complex TREX patterns let's put all this together. Let's suppose you want to create a TREX pattern for the <Employee> information you saw previously. Here, for convenience, is the XML.

```
<Employee lastUpdated="2001-04-10">
   <Name firstName="Matt" middleInitial="J" lastName="Thomas" />
   <Contact>
      <Address>
         <Street>121 East Street</Street>
         <City>HeresVille</City>
         <State>Washington</State>
         <Zip>WA 12765</Zip>
      </Address>
      <HomePhone>012235567</HomePhone>
      <Email1>matt@thomas.org</Email1>
   </Contact>
</Employee>
```

The corresponding TREX pattern (schema), assuming that each element is required and occurs only once, would look like this. Note the addition of the namespace URI for the TREX namespace.

```
<?xml version='1.0'?>

<element name="Employee" xmlns="http://www.thaiopensource.com/trex">
 <attribute name="lastUpdated">
   <anyString/>
 </attribute>
 <element name="Name">
  <attribute name="firstName">
   <anyString/>
  </attribute>
  <attribute name="middleInitial">
   <anyString/>
  </attribute>
  <attribute name="lastName">
   <anyString/>
  </attribute>
 </element> <!-- End element "Name" -->
 <element name="Contact">
  <element name="Address">
   <element name="Street">
    <anyString/>
   </element>
   <element name="City">
    <anyString/>
   </element>
   <element name="State">
    <anyString/>
   </element>
   <element name="Zip">
    <anyString/>
   </element>
  </element> <!-- End element "Address" -->
  <element name="HomePhone">
   <anyString/>
  </element>
  <element name="Email1">
   <anyString/>
  </element>
 </element> <!-- End element "Contact" -->
</element> <!-- End element "Employee" -->
```

The TREX schema indicates that the corresponding class of XML documents have an <Employee> element as root element which must contain one <Contact> child element. The <Employee> element has a lastUpdated attribute. The first element child of <Employee> is a <Name> element that has three attributes, firstName, middleInitial, and lastName. The content of each of those attributes may be any string as defined by the <anyString/> element in the TREX pattern. The second child of the <Employee> element is a <Contact> element that has an <Address> child element (which itself has four child elements), plus a <HomePhone> element and an <Email1> element.

You may have noticed that the content of each attribute in the TREX pattern is an <anyString/> element. TREX is intended to be used with a schema language that defines datatypes, such as Part 2 of the W3C XML Schema. TREX is thus, at least for some purposes, a potential replacement for Part 1 (Structures) of W3C XML Schema.

The approach we have seen so far is the one I described earlier as "start simple", and those techniques do allow us to define the content of simple XML documents. For more substantial XML documents there are advantages in a more structured approach.

Interleaving

TREX provides an <interleave> element which allows the use of XML elements in any order (attributes of an XML element may occur in any order). Normally in XML the ordering of elements is significant, so to allow them in some arbitrary order requires to be explicitly stated.

Let's suppose in some document we wanted to allow the three elements (excuse the pun) <earth>, <wind> and <fire> to occur in any order then we could use a TREX pattern like this:

```
<element name="document">
 <interleave>
  <element name="earth">
   <anyString/>
  </element>
  <element name="wind">
   <anyString/>
  </element>
  <element name="fire">
   <anyString/>
  </element>
 </interleave>
</element>
```

The <interleave> element indicates that there is flexibility in the *ordering* of elements. Each of the elements in the above example must occur once and exactly once, but there is freedom regarding the ordering of the elements. Be careful not to confuse that flexibility in ordering with the flexibility in cardinality of elements provided by <zeroOrMore> or <oneOrMore> elements.

Let's move on and look at how we might apply TREX interleaving to a possible pattern for XSLT, assuming we were using a simple TREX pattern rather than the named patterns technique.

The Extensible Stylesheet Language Transformations, XSLT, has a number of elements which must be immediate children of the <xsl:stylesheet> element but whose ordering within the document is flexible. The XSLT 1.0 specification allows 12 top-level elements, with the <xsl:import> element preceding the other top-level elements, which may occur in any order. In the following example, I will only show three of those. I have omitted namespaces (all elements have the namespace URI of http://www.w3.org/1999/Transform) and the allowed element content here for simplicity.

```
<?xml version='1.0'?>
<element name='stylesheet'>
 <zeroOrMore>
   <element name='import'>
    <!-- Allowed content goes here. -->
   </element>
 </zeroOrMore>
 <interleave>
  <zeroOrMore>
   <element name='include'>
    <!-- Allowed content goes here. -->
   </element>
  </zeroOrMore>

  <oneOrMore>
   <element name='template'>
    <!-- Allowed content goes here. -->
   </element>
  </oneOrMore>
<!-- Patterns defining any of the other nine top-level elements could go here. -->
 </interleave>
</element>
```

The <xsl:template>, <xsl:import>, <xsl:include> (and the other XSLT 'top level' elements) must all be immediate children of the <xsl:stylesheet> element. However, the <xsl:import> element must precede all the others, which can occur in any order. The TREX <interleave> element expresses that situation.

> *Given the complexity of the XSLT specification, it may be more convenient when expressing patterns for the full XSLT specification to use the alternate approach described in the "Named Patterns" section below.*

It is not only possible to interleave elements as in the previous example, but we can also use the <interleave> element to mix strings and elements as here, where we have something akin to the TREX pattern for a very simplified HTML <p> element:

```
<element name="p">
 <interleave>
  <anyString/>
  <element name="b">
   <anyString/>
  </element>
 </interleave>
</element>
```

As written, our greatly simplified <p> element could have strings of characters interleaved with <b> elements (bold, if you wish) which themselves could have strings of characters as children.

TREX also provides an alternate syntax using the <mixed> element to express the same thing.

```
<element name="p">
 <mixed>
  <element name="b">
```

```
      <anyString/>
    </element>
  </mixed>
</element>
```

Again, this would correspond to a pattern for a greatly simplified HTML <p> element, which allowed either <b> element children (which could themselves contain any string) or strings of characters in any order.

TREX Named Patterns

In TREX patterns for XML documents whose structure is anything but simple the succession of <element> elements can become visually confusing. Therefore TREX provides an alternate syntax, **named patterns**. A named pattern consists of a single TREX pattern which is constructed by incorporating, by reference, named TREX <define> elements within the same TREX document.

In constructing a named pattern we make use of the natural structure of the TREX pattern, by locating suitably sized blocks of elements. If we look again at the TREX pattern for Employee we can see that all other elements are nested within the <element> that refers to the <Employee> element in the instance documents. Within the <element> representing the <Employee> element we can see that there are <element> elements that represent <Name> and <Contact> elements.

```
<?xml version='1.0'?>

<element name="Employee" xmlns="http://www.thaiopensource.com/trex">
 <element name="Name">
  <attribute name="firstName">
   <anyString/>
  </attribute>
  <attribute name="middleInitial">
   <anyString/>
  </attribute>
  <attribute name="lastName">
   <anyString/>
  </attribute>
 </element> <!-- End element "Name" -->
 <element name="Contact">
  <element name="Address">
   <element name="Street">
    <anyString/>
   </element>
   <element name="City">
    <anyString/>
   </element>
   <element name="State">
    <anyString/>
   </element>
   <element name="Zip">
    <anyString/>
   </element>
  </element> <!-- End element "Address" -->
  <element name="HomePhone">
   <anyString/>
```

```
    </element>
    <element name="Email1">
     <anyString/>
    </element>
  </element> <!-- End element "Contact" -->
</element> <!-- End element "Employee" -->
```

Named patterns allow us to break the succession of <element> elements down into components, which are more easily read and understood. Since the <Name> and <Contact> elements have nested within them a suitably self-contained structure, they seem suitable for creating named patterns.

In a TREX named pattern we have a <grammar> element as document element, rather than a TREX <element> element. The first child of a <grammar> element is a <start> element which, using a referencing <ref> element, tells the TREX processor which of the definitions contained in <define> elements it should process first.

For example, a TREX named pattern for the Employee document would look like this:

```
<?xml version='1.0'?>
<grammar>
```

The document element of a TREX named pattern is a <grammar> element.

```
  <start>
    <ref name="EmployeeDefn"/>
  </start>
```

The TREX <start> element contains a <ref> element whose name attribute references a TREX named pattern within the same document where the definition for "EmployeeDefn" begins. Note that the value of the name attribute of the <ref> element need not be the same as the element name that it contains, although it need not be different. In this example, I have used "EmployeeDefn" as the value of the name attribute and used the same value for the name attribute on the referenced <define> element. Clearly, the value of the name attributes of the <ref> and <define> elements must match exactly.

```
  <define name="EmployeeDefn">
    <element name="Employee">
     <attribute name="lastUpdated">
      <anyString/>
     </attribute>
     <ref name="Name"/>
     <ref name="Contact"/>
    </element>
  </define>
```

The definition for the <Employee> element is contained in the TREX <define> element. The structure nested within the TREX <element> element may be <element> elements, <attribute> elements or further <ref> elements which reference other <define> elements which make up the TREX named pattern. In our example we see that there is a required lastUpdated attribute and that two further definitions (for the <Name> and <Contact> elements) are referenced. The definitions for the <Name> and <Contact> elements follow.

```
<define name="Name">
<element name="Name">
  <attribute name="firstName">
    <anyString/>
  </attribute>
  <attribute name="middleInitial">
    <anyString/>
  </attribute>
  <attribute name="lastName">
    <anyString/>
  </attribute>
</element>
</define>
```

The definition for the <Name> element indicates that it contains three attributes with names of firstName, middleInitial, and lastName. Each of those attributes may contain any string. Since there is no indication of cardinality, we know that the attributes are required.

```
<define name="Contact">
<element name="Contact">
  <ref name="Address"/>
  <element name="HomePhone">
   <anyString/>
  </element>
  <element name="Email1">
   <anyString/>
  </element>
</element>
</define>
```

The definition for the <Contact> element includes a reference to the Address pattern, which is defined later, plus two elements called <HomePhone> and <Email1> which are fully defined within the present <define> element. We then need to look at the definition for the "Address".

```
<define name="Address">
 <element name="Address">
  <element name="Street">
   <anyString/>
  </element>
  <element name="City">
   <anyString/>
  </element>
  <element name="State">
   <anyString/>
  </element>
  <element name="Zip">
   <anyString/>
  </element>
  <element name="Country">
   <anyString/>
  </element>
 </element>
</define>
```

The definition for the "Address" indicates that it contains an <Address> element nested within which are <Street>, <City>, <State>, and <Zip> elements, each of which may contain any string as content.

```
</grammar>
```

The named pattern finishes with the end tag for the <grammar> element.

In the examples towards the end of this section we will look at a TREX named pattern that defines the W3C XLink specification.

Modularization of TREX

If an XML structure is likely to be contained in several TREX patterns, it makes a lot of sense to modularize the pattern that describes that structure, not least since maintenance or updating becomes easier to manage if there is only one place where changes need to be made. TREX allows one TREX pattern to reference another TREX pattern in an external file.

To see a simple example of how that is done let's look again at the early part of the named pattern for an employee:

```
<?xml version='1.0'?>
<grammar>

  <start>
    <ref name="employee"/>
  </start>

  <define name="employee">
    <element name="Employee">
     <attribute name="lastUpdated">
      <anyString/>
     </attribute>
     <ref name="Name"/>
     <ref name="Contact"/>
    </element>
  </define>
```

As written, the <ref> to "Contact" references another TREX <define> element in the same file. However, if we wanted to modularize the structure for contact details, and placed that pattern in the separate file contact.trex, we could replace the <ref> element with a TREX <include> element:

```
<define name="employee">
    <element name="Employee">
     <attribute name="lastUpdated">
      <anyString/>
     </attribute>
     <ref name="Name"/>
     <include href="contact.trex"/>
    </element>
</define>
```

The <include> element is also allowed as a child of a <grammar> element. For example, if we wanted to include a (fictional) previous TREX pattern, called oldEmployee.trex we could modify the beginning of the Employee.trex file as follows:

```
<?xml version='1.0'?>
<grammar>

<include href="oldEmployee.trex"/>

  <start>
    <ref name="employee"/>
  </start>

  <define name="employee">
    <element name="Employee">
     <attribute name="lastUpdated">
      <anyString/>
     </attribute>
     <ref name="Name"/>
     <ref name="Contact"/>
    </element>
  </define>
```

Normally duplication of a definition in a TREX pattern would be an error. However, when a TREX grammar is included we can combine the grammars. TREX provides a combine attribute, which allows us to replace the included definition with another or to group the definitions. The permitted values of the combine attribute are replace, group, choice, and interleave.

Namespaces

You may use namespaces with TREX, as you saw when we used the <grammar> element as the document element of the Employee schema.

```
<?xml version='1.0'?>
<element name="Employee" xmlns="http://www.thaiopensource.com/trex">
```

It is also possible to use namespaces when declaring elements in a TREX pattern. Let's suppose we wanted to declare a <x:book> element whose namespace URI was http://www.xmml.com/trex/:

```
<?xml version="1.0"?>
<element name="book" ns="http://www.xmml.com/trex/">
 <!-- The allowed content of the <x:element> element would go here. -->
</element>
```

This would match:

```
<x:book xmlns:x="http://www.xmml.com/trex/">
```

but TREX would also allow:

```
<book xmlns="http://www.xmml.com/trex/">
```

or any other syntactically correct namespace declaration which used the relevant namespace URI.

TREX also allows the ns attribute to be an empty string. Thus the pattern:

```
<element name="book" ns="">
```

would match:

```
<book xmlns="">
```

For elements, TREX follows the Namespaces in XML Recommendation in allowing the use of the default namespace to be applied to all contained elements that are not associated with another namespace URI.

Thus:

```
<element name="book" ns="http://www.xmml.com/trex/">
 <element name="Preface">
   <anyString/>
 </element>
 <element name="Chapter">
  <anyString/>
 </element>
</element>
```

is equivalent to:

```
<element name="book" ns="http://www.xmml.com/trex/">
 <element name="Preface" ns="http://www.xmml.com/trex/">
   <anyString/>
 </element>
 <element name="Chapter" ns="http://www.xmml.com/trex/">
  <anyString/>
 </element>
</element>
```

While the use of namespaces for elements is straightforward, when it comes to attributes some care needs to be taken. Remember that the default namespace declaration is not applied to attributes in the Namespaces in XML Recommendation (http://www.w3.org/TR/REC-xml-names). To ensure that the default namespace declaration is applied to an attribute we make use of the TREX **global** attribute within the <attribute> element and set its value to true, as in the following example:

```
<element name="book" ns="http://www.xmml.com/trex/">
 <element name="Preface" ns="http://www.xmml.com/trex/">
   <anyString/>
 </element>
 <element name="Chapter" ns="http://www.xmml.com/trex/">
  <attribute name="title" global="true">
   <anyString/>
  </attribute>
  <anyString/>
 </element>
</element>
```

Data Types

The initial release of the Java implementation of TREX did not support datatyping, but the first version of the TREX proposal alluded simply to the possible use of Part 2 of the W3C XML Schema specification (datatyping), or other datatyping vocabulary, in conjunction with TREX. In February 2001 James Clark issued an update to the TREX implementation in Java, which made use of the then current version (Candidate Recommendation) of W3C XML Schema. That version of the TREX processor allows us to use W3C XML Schema datatypes within TREX patterns.

Thus, if we wanted to constrain an element to have only integers as content we could use a TREX pattern like this:

```
<element name="AnInteger" xmlns:xsd="http://www.w3.org/2001/XMLSchema">
  <data type="xsd:integer">
</element>
```

Support of data types in TREX is, at the time of writing, as follows:

Fully Supported	Partially Supported	Not Supported
boolean	ENTITIES	binary
byte	ENTITY	century
CDATA	ID	date
decimal	IDREF	month
double	IDREFS	recurringDate
float	language	recurringDay
int	NOTATION	recurringDuration
integer	timeDuration	time
long	timeInstant	timePeriod
Name	uriReference	year
NCName		
negativeInteger		
NMTOKEN		
NMTOKENS		
nonNegativeInteger		
nonPositiveInteger		
positiveInteger		
QName		
short		
string		
token		

Table continued on following page

Fully Supported	Partially Supported	Not Supported
unsignedByte		
unsignedInt		
unsignedLong		
unsignedShort		

It is clear that support for date/time data types is the area where significant further work is required.

Anonymous Data Types

The derivation of new data types by restriction, enumeration or union is supported. An element bearing the attribute `trex:role="datatype"` must be a `restriction`, `list`, `union` or `simpleType` element.

For example, if we wanted to define an element for a child and ensure that only those aged under 18 were included we could do this using a TREX pattern something like this:

```
<element name="child" xmlns="http://www.thaiopensource.com/trex">
 <element name="age"
  xmlns:xsd="http://www.w3.org/2001/XMLSchema"
  xmlns:trex="http://www.thaiopensource.com/trex">
  <xsd:restriction base="xsd:nonNegativeInteger" trex:role="datatype">
    <xsd:maxInclusive value="17"/>
  </xsd:restriction>
 </element>
</element>
```

Support for **facets** is as follows:

Fully Supported	Not Supported
enumeration	duration
length	encoding
maxExclusive	period
maxInclusive	
maxLength	
minExclusive	
minInclusive	
minLength	
pattern (but requires the use of an external regular expressions package)	
precision	
scale	
whiteSpace	

Further information on datatype support in the Java implementation of TREX can be found at http://www.thaiopensource.com/trex/jdatatypes.html. It is likely that the gaps in support will be progressively addressed.

TREX Processors

There are already two implementations of TREX available. Languages that currently have TREX processors are Java and Python. Other implementations may be available by the time you read this.

Jtrex

Jtrex is the first TREX processor and has been implemented in Java by James Clark. It is available for download, either as a JAR file or as a Windows executable from http://www.thaiopensource.com/trex/jtrex.html.

If you download the Windows executable and install it in a suitable directory, say `c:\trex`, then from the command line you can issue a command:

```
> trex file.trex file.xml
```

If the file `file.xml` does not correspond to the constraints defined in the TREX pattern contained in `file.trex` then error messages should result, detailing where the error occurred in the document. If the `.xml` file correctly corresponds to the `.trex` schema then a message indicating the elapsed time is output.

PyTrex

PyTrex is an open-source implementation of a TREX processor in Python, created by James Tauber. At the time of writing it is at version 0.7.1.

Further information is to be found at http://pytrex.sourceforge.net/.

TREX Schemas

If TREX is to be a generally useful schema language for XML documents then it ought to be capable of describing widely available document types, including W3C specifications. Already TREX schemas for some W3C specifications have been produced.

Among those available are:

- A TREX schema for TREX itself, which may be downloaded from http://www.thaiopensource.com/trex/trex.trex.
- A TREX schema for Extensible Stylesheet Language Transformations, XLST, version 1.0. Available for download from http://www.thaiopensource.com/trex/xslt.trex.
- A TREX schema for RELAX core available from http://www.thaiopensource.com/trex/relaxCore.trex.
- A range of TREX schemas for the various flavors of XHTML 1.0, for XHTML Basic and for the Modularization of XHTML Candidate Recommendation. A description of the approach taken is located at http://www.thaiopensource.com/trex/xhtml/. Note that a number of the TREX schemas don't exactly follow the DTD's presented in the W3C Candidate Recommendation. A full list of the available TREX schemas is located at http://thaiopensource.com/trex/xhtml/modules/.

- Several versions of TREX schemas for DocBook are located on the OASIS Web site. At the time of writing there was no official TREX schema for DocBook. You can access the various TREX schemas for DocBook from http://www.oasis-open.org/docbook/trex/index.html.
- A TREX schema is currently available for XLink (currently at Proposed Recommendation at W3C, http://www.w3.org/TR/xlink). In an example that follows later, we will walk through the TREX schema for XLink to help understand how a "real life" TREX schema works.

Stylesheet To Convert from RELAX

An XSLT stylesheet is available for download which will convert from RELAX (see the earlier section of this chapter) to TREX. The URL for download is http://www.thaiopensource.com/trex/from-relax.xsl.

Examples

In this section let's take a look at a couple of examples of TREX patterns. First we will build step by step a TREX pattern to correspond to the ToysCo invoice document. Second, we will examine how TREX has been used to create a pattern for the XLink specification, currently at Proposed Recommendation at W3C.

Example - TREX Pattern for Invoices

Let's build up our TREX pattern for the ToysCo invoice. The root element is a <Toysco> element and nested within that we have zero or more <Customer> elements, one or more <Product> elements, zero or more <Invoice> elements and zero or more <InvoiceOrder> elements.

Let's use the named pattern syntax. We can capture the basic structure within a <Toysco> element like this:

```
<?xml version='1.0'?>
<grammar>

  <start>
    <ref name="toysco"/>
  </start>

  <define name="toysco">
    <element name="Toysco">
    <zeroOrMore>
      <ref name="Customer"/>
    </zeroOrMore>
    <oneOrMore>
     <ref name="Product"/>
    </oneOrMore>
    <zeroOrMore>
     <ref name="Invoice"/>
    </zeroOrMore>
    </element>
  </define>
<!-- Other TREX definitions will go here. -->

</grammar>
```

Essentially we can treat the definitions of the <Customer>, <Product>, and <Invoice> elements as modules to be contained within TREX <define> elements in the same document.

The pattern for the <Customer> element would look like this:

```
<define name="Customer">
<element name="Customer">
```

The definition for Customer starts with the <Customer> element.

```
<attribute name="customerID">
 <anyString/>
</attribute>
```

The <Customer> element has a customerID attribute, which can contain any string.

```
<element name="Name">
 <element name="FirstName">
   <anyString/>
 </element>
 <zeroOrMore>
 <element name="MiddleName">
  <anyString/>
 </element>
 </zeroOrMore>
 <element name="LastName">
   <anyString/>
 </element>
</element>
```

Nested within the <Customer> element is the <Name> element, which has a <FirstName> element as child, zero or more middle names and a <LastName> element. Each of those elements may contain any string.

```
  <optional>
    <element name="MailingAddress">
     <oneOrMore>
      <element name="Street">
       <anyString/>
      </element>
     </oneOrMore>
     <element name="City">
       <anyString/>
     </element>
     <element name="State">
       <anyString/>
     </element>
     <element name="Zip">
       <anyString/>
     </element>
     <optional>
       <element name="Country">
         <anyString/>
       </element>
     </optional>
    </element>
  </optional>
```

The mailing address is optional and therefore is nested within TREX <optional> elements. The <MailingAddress> element has one or more <Street> elements, followed by a <City> element, a <State> element,<Zip> element, and an optional <Country> element. Each of those elements may contain any string.

```
<element name="BillingAddress">
  <oneOrMore>
  <element name="Street">
    <anyString/>
  </element>
  </oneOrMore>
  <element name="City">
   <anyString/>
  </element>
  <element name="State">
    <anyString/>
  </element>
  <element name="Zip">
    <anyString/>
  </element>
  <optional>
    <element name="Country">
      <anyString/>
    </element>
  </optional>
 </element>
```

The structure of the <BillingAddress> element is the same as that of the <MailingAddress> element, described above.

```
<element name="ContactDetails">
 <zeroOrMore>
   <element name="Email">
     <anyString/>
   </element>
 </zeroOrMore>
 <zeroOrMore>
   <element name="Phone">
     <attribute name="phonetype">
       <choice>
         <string>HOME</string>
         <string>WORK</string>
         <string>FAX</string>
         <string>CELL</string>
       </choice>
     </attribute>
   </element>
 </zeroOrMore>
</element> <!-- End element ContactDetails -->
```

The <ContactDetails> element contains zero or more <Email> elements nested within a TREX <zeroOrMore> element. In addition it contains zero or more <Phone> elements, which are nested within a TREX <zeroOrMore> element. The phonetype attribute of the <Phone> element allows a choice of four string values, which we see nested within a TREX <choice> element.

```
</element> <!-- End element Customer -->
</define>
```

The definition for the <Customer> element ends with the end tag for the TREX <element> named "Customer" and the end tag for the corresponding TREX <define> tag.

The definition module for the <Product> element is quite a bit simpler:

```
  <define name="Product">
   <element name="Product">
   <attribute name="productID">
    <anyString/>
   </attribute>
   <attribute name="hire">
     <choice>
       <string>true</string>
       <string>false</string>
     </choice>
   </attribute>
   <element name="ProductName">
    <anyString/>
   </element>
   <element name="Description">
    <anyString/>
   </element>
   <element name="Price">
     <attribute name="currency">
     <anyString />
     </attribute>
   </element>
   <element name="Units">
    <anyString/>
   </element>
   <element name="Stock">
    <anyString/>
   </element>
   </element>
  </define>
</define> <!-- End of definition for Product. -->
```

Note that the hire attribute uses the TREX <choice> element to constrain the value of the attribute to either "true" or "false" (note that this is case-sensitive).

```
  <define name="Invoice">
   <element name="Invoice">
    <attribute name="invoiceID">
      <anyString/>
    </attribute>
    <attribute name="customerID">
      <anyString/>
    </attribute>
    <attribute name="date">
      <anyString/>
    </attribute>
```

```
      <attribute name="terms">
        <anyString/>
      </attribute>
      <attribute name="paid">
       <choice>
         <string>true</string>
         <string>false</string>
       </choice>
      </attribute>
      <optional>
        <attribute name="hire">
         <choice>
           <string>true</string>
           <string>false</string>
         </choice>
        </attribute>
      </optional>
      <optional>
        <attribute name="notes">
          <anyString/>
        </attribute>
      </optional>
      <zeroOrMore>
       <ref name="InvoiceOrder"/>
      </zeroOrMore>
    </element>
  </define> <!-- End of definition for Invoice -->
```

The definition for the <Invoice> element is very similar to that for the <Product> element. There are multiple attributes, most of which are required and can take any string value. The paid and hire attributes can take only values of "true" and "false" therefore the TREX <choice> element is used to constrain the allowed strings. The last element nested inside <Invoice> is <InvoiceOrder>:

```
  <define name="InvoiceOrder">
   <element name="InvoiceOrder">
    <attribute name="invoiceID">
      <anyString/>
    </attribute>
    <attribute name="productID">
      <anyString/>
    </attribute>
    <attribute name="units">
      <anyString/>
    </attribute>
    <attribute name="notes">
      <anyString/>
    </attribute>
   </element>
  </define> <!-- End of definition for InvoiceOrder -->
```

Example - TREX pattern for XLink

If you are not already familiar with XLink take a look at Chapter 10 where the basics of XLink are explained. In addition you may find it helpful to review the tables of relationships between XLink linking elements laid out in chapters 4.1 and 4.2 of the XLink specification (http://www.w3.org/TR/xlink/).

I will show you the TREX schema for XLink which James Clark has posted and interpolate within the sections of the TREX schema fairly extensive comments which will, hopefully, help you to appreciate how the TREX schema for XLink works.

The TREX schema looks like this. The comments within the code are those provided by James Clark.

```
<?xml version="1.0"?>
<!-- $Id: xlink.trex,v 1.2 2001/01/26 11:22:06 jjc Exp $ -->
<!-- This disallows things that don't have an XLink-defined meaning. -->
```

A TREX schema is an XML document therefore it has an (optional) XML declaration. The XLink specification permits certain linking structures whose meaning is stated in the XLink specification to be undefined. The TREX schema shown here does not allow those XLink structures with undefined meaning, which seems to be a sensible pragmatic choice. The TREX schema uses the named pattern syntax.

```
<grammar xmlns="http://www.thaiopensource.com/trex"
  xmlns:xlink="http://www.w3.org/1999/xlink">
```

On the root TREX element, `<grammar>`, the namespace for TREX is declared as the default and the XLink namespace is also declared.

```
<start name="any">
  <choice>
    <ref name="simple"/>
    <ref name="extended"/>
    <ref name="other"/>
    <anyString/>
  </choice>
</start>
```

The `<start>` element indicates where a TREX processor will begin to work through the `<define>` elements in the schema. In this example James Clark has used a shorthand syntax, which includes the name of a definition as the value of the name attribute of the `<start>` element. That is shorthand for:

```
<start>
 <ref name="any">
</start>

<define name="any">
 <choice>
    <ref name="simple"/>
    <ref name="extended"/>
    <ref name="other"/>
    <anyString/>
  </choice>
</define>
```

The above section (in either of the alternate syntaxes) indicates that the name of the element that contains the XLink links can be `any`, that is, an XLink linking attribute can be added to any XML element within the XML document being referenced. Within the TREX `<choice>` element we see that any of three values of XLink type attributes are supported in this context – `simple`, `extended` and `other`. This allows us to use the two basic XLink types of `simple` and `extended`.

```
<define name="simple">
  <element>
    <anyName/>
    <attribute name="xlink:type">
      <string>simple</string>
    </attribute>
    <optional>
      <attribute name="xlink:href"/>
    </optional>
    <optional>
      <attribute name="xlink:role"/>
    </optional>
    <optional>
      <attribute name="xlink:arcrole"/>
    </optional>
    <optional>
      <attribute name="xlink:title"/>
    </optional>
    <ref name="behave.atts"/>
    <ref name="other.atts"/>
    <zeroOrMore>
      <ref name="any"/>
    </zeroOrMore>
  </element>
</define>
```

The above section provides a definition for the allowable structure of a `simple` XLink link. Note that there is no `name` attribute on the `<element>` element, since XLink global attributes are not limited to only one named element but may be applied to any XML element. The empty element `<anyName/>` indicates that XLink attributes, which are global attributes, may be attached to any XML element. The `xlink:type` attribute may only have the value of "`simple`", which makes sense for the definition of a simple XLink link. The XLink `xlink:href` attribute is declared to be optional, reflecting the fact that XLink links are allowable, according to the XLink specification, even when not fully defined. Further, in addition to the `type` and `href` attributes there may additionally optionally be `xlink:role`, `xlink:arcrole`, and `xlink:title` attributes on an XLink simple link. The presence of multiple `<optional>` elements indicates that each of these attributes is optional. There is also a reference to the XLink "behavior attributes", which are described more fully later in this TREX schema.

Then we move on the definition of extended links:

```
<define name="extended">
  <element>
    <anyName/>
    <attribute name="xlink:type">
      <string>extended</string>
    </attribute>
    <optional>
      <attribute name="xlink:role"/>
    </optional>
    <optional>
      <attribute name="xlink:title"/>
    </optional>
    <ref name="other.atts"/>
```

```
      <zeroOrMore>
        <choice>
          <ref name="any"/>
          <ref name="title"/>
          <ref name="resource"/>
          <ref name="locator"/>
          <ref name="arc"/>
        </choice>
      </zeroOrMore>
    </element>
  </define>
```

The above section of the TREX file defines an XLink extended link. The `<anyName/>` element reminds us that the XLink global attributes can be associated with any XML element. As with the simple link seen earlier, an XLink extended link has an `xlink:type` attribute of fixed value, in this case "`extended`", contained within a TREX `<string>` element. An extended XLink has optional `xlink:role` and `xlink:title` attributes. In addition, the `<choice>` element indicates that there may also be `title`, `locator`, `resource` or `arc` attributes which are defined elsewhere in the TREX schema.

The XLink `locator` was referenced above and is now defined:

```
  <define name="locator">
    <element>
      <anyName/>
      <attribute name="xlink:type">
        <string>locator</string>
      </attribute>
      <attribute name="xlink:href"/>
      <optional>
        <attribute name="xlink:role"/>
      </optional>
      <optional>
        <attribute name="xlink:title"/>
      </optional>
      <optional>
        <attribute name="xlink:label"/>
      </optional>
      <ref name="other.atts"/>
      <zeroOrMore>
        <choice>
          <ref name="any"/>
          <ref name="title"/>
        </choice>
      </zeroOrMore>
    </element>
  </define>
```

The above section defines an XLink `locator` attribute. The `<anyName/>` element indicates that, as with other XLink global attributes, the `locator` attribute may be applied to any XML element. The `xlink:type` attribute may only have one value in this case which is "`locator`". The `xlink:href` attribute is required in association with a `locator` type attribute, but `xlink:role`, `xlink:label` and `xlink:title` attributes are indicated as optional.

```
<define name="arc">
  <element>
    <anyName/>
    <attribute name="xlink:type">
      <string>arc</string>
    </attribute>
    <optional>
      <attribute name="xlink:arcrole"/>
    </optional>
    <optional>
      <attribute name="xlink:title"/>
    </optional>
    <ref name="behave.atts"/>
    <optional>
      <attribute name="xlink:from"/>
    </optional>
    <optional>
      <attribute name="xlink:to"/>
    </optional>
    <ref name="other.atts"/>
    <zeroOrMore>
      <choice>
        <ref name="any"/>
        <ref name="title"/>
      </choice>
    </zeroOrMore>
  </element>
</define>
```

The above section defines an `arc` type Xlink, therefore the value of the `xlink:type` attribute may only take the value of "`arc`". It may optionally be associated with `xlink:arcrole`, `xlink:title`, `xlink:from` and `xlink:to` attributes. The `xlink:title` attribute provides a human-readable description of the arc, and the `xlink:from` and `xlink:to` attributes define the starting resource and ending resource of the arc.

```
<define name="resource">
  <element>
    <anyName/>
    <attribute name="xlink:type">
      <string>resource</string>
    </attribute>
    <optional>
      <attribute name="xlink:role"/>
    </optional>
    <optional>
      <attribute name="xlink:title"/>
    </optional>
    <attribute name="xlink:label"/>
    <ref name="other.atts"/>
    <zeroOrMore>
      <ref name="any"/>
    </zeroOrMore>
  </element>
</define>
```

The above section defines a `resource` type of XLink. The `xlink:type` attribute may only have the value of "`resource`". It may optionally be combined with `xlink:role`, `xlink:title` and `xlink:label` attributes.

```
<define name="title">
  <element>
    <anyName/>
    <attribute name="xlink:type">
      <string>title</string>
    </attribute>
    <ref name="other.atts"/>
    <zeroOrMore>
      <ref name="any"/>
    </zeroOrMore>
  </element>
</define>
```

The above definition relates to the `title` type of XLink, therefore the `xlink:type` attribute may only have a string value of "`title`".

```
<define name="other">
  <element>
    <anyName/>
    <ref name="other.atts"/>
    <zeroOrMore>
      <ref name="any"/>
    </zeroOrMore>
  </element>
</define>

<define name="behave.atts">
  <optional>
    <attribute name="xlink:show">
      <choice>
     <string>new</string>
     <string>replace</string>
     <string>embed</string>
     <string>other</string>
     <string>none</string>
      </choice>
    </attribute>
  </optional>
  <optional>
    <attribute name="xlink:actuate">
      <choice>
     <string>onLoad</string>
     <string>onRequest</string>
     <string>other</string>
     <string>none</string>
      </choice>
    </attribute>
  </optional>
</define>
```

XLink has what are called "behavior attributes" which are defined in the above section. The xlink:show attribute has a choice of values: "new", "replace", "embed", "other", or "none". If the value is "new" then this means that the link results in a new window being opened to display the linked resource. If it has the value "replace" then the linked resource is displayed in the same window (similar to the default behavior of HTML/XHTML links).

The XLink xlink:actuate attribute may take the values of "onLoad", "onRequest", "other" or "none" as indicated in the above section of the TREX schema. When the xlink:actuate attribute has the value "onRequest" that would correspond closely to the behavior of the HTML/XHTML <a> element with which you may be familiar. If the xlink:actuate attribute had the value of "onLoad" it could be combined with the xlink:show attribute value of "new" to display a pop up window, displaying possibly useful or important information.

```
<define name="other.atts">
  <zeroOrMore>
    <attribute>
      <not>
     <nsName ns="http://www.w3.org/1999/xlink"/>
      </not>
    </attribute>
  </zeroOrMore>
</define>
```

The above section sates that the element on which the XLink global attributes exist may also have attributes that are not from the XLink namespace URI.

```
</grammar>
```

An appropriate end tag closes the document element of the TREX document.

TREX at OASIS

TREX has been submitted to OASIS for further development as a specification for validating XML documents.

> *OASIS operates by a mechanism of Technical Committees. The home page for the TREX technical committee is at* http://www.oasis-open.org/committees/trex/index.shtml. *A little like W3C, much of the discussion at OASIS takes place out of the public gaze. However, membership of OASIS is open to interested individuals for the relatively modest sum of $250 per year (personal membership of the W3C is $5000 per year).*

In addition to facilitating individual membership OASIS also provides access to the archives of the otherwise private discussions on its mailing lists. The TREX mailing list home page is located at http://lists.oasis-open.org/archives/trex/. If you are seriously interested in TREX this will be the place to check stay on the cutting edge.

As we went to press, the Technical Committee had just issued the minutes of their first meeting. One of the decisions was that the charter for the committee should be to create a single schema language based on both RELAX and TREX, so keep checking the web sites to keep up to date with the latest information.

The target date for the delivery of the first TREX specification from the Technical Committee is 1st July 2001.

TREX Summary

TREX is a schema language expressed in XML that, in its simpler forms, is very easy to use. It also has considerable power to express the structure of 'real-world' XML documents such as the W3C XHTML Modularization and XLink specifications. Further development of TREX is likely to take place at a rapid rate; be sure to check at the URLs given for the fully up to date situation.

The third of our alternatives to XML Schema, Schematron, is very different from almost every other schema proposal. So let's look at it in more detail.

Schematron

Schematron is a truly innovative supplement to XML schemas. Unlike most kinds of schemas, Schematron is not grammar-based, but rather is based on finding patterns in trees. Also, Schematron limits itself to validation of XML data – it doesn't replace entity expansion in DTDs, nor provide the extensive data types of XML Schema.

The key features of Schematron are that it:

- uses standard XSL syntax
- is based on finding patterns in trees (using XPath paths and expressions)
- uses XPath and XSLT to describe and transform patterns
- works with XML Namespaces
- works with XML Schema (Schematron expressions can even be embedded within an XML Schema `<appinfo>` element)
- requires no special software, other than an XSLT processor (such as Saxon, XT or Xalan)

Schematron schemas are like most other schema proposals that we've seen, in that they use XML syntax. Schematron goes a step further and makes extensive use of XPath expressions (actually an extended form, XSLT patterns) within its schemas.

> **Schematron is based upon tree patterns, instead of using a descriptive grammar.**

Grammars can be a very good method of describing structured data. But, because of XML's rigid syntax and tree structure, grammars are not strictly necessary to validate XML data. The structure of any well-formed XML data is a hierarchical tree, so validation can just as easily be described as a pattern within the tree.

On the other hand, grammars cannot express constraints between different branches of the tree, only in terms of parent-child relationships. An element can choose its children, but often children need to choose their parents. In our ongoing examples, an address without its customer parent is worthless. This just isn't possible using a DTD. However, it is simple in Schematron. In other circumstances, it may also be desirable to validate the contents of one element based upon an attribute in a completely different part of the tree. An example of this might be the use of different format `<Address>` element structures, based upon some global setting for the country. This is something that is straightforward in Schematron, but is not so easy using a grammar-based schema approach.

> ***Schematron** is available at http://www.ascc.net/xml/resource/schematron/. It was developed by Rick Jelliffe, a member of the XML Schema Working Group, while he was at the Academia Sinica Computing Centre (ASCC) in Taiwan. Its current version is 1.5 (as of March 2001). This is the definitive website, with the various Schematron "compiler" style sheets, some validation applications for common XML vocabularies, news, and reference materials.*
>
> *After doing initial development work in cooperation with other XML developers, notably Oliver Becker, Jelliffe has placed further development of Schematron (starting from version 1.5) in the hands of the open source community at http://sourceforge.net/projects/schematron.*
>
> *An excellent tutorial for Schematron is at http://www.zvon.org/xxl/SchematronTutorial/General/contents.html.*

There is another easily overlooked, but fundamental, limitation to the use of grammars in an international context such as XML. Jelliffe has raised an interesting issue concerning cultural perceptions of grammars when ideographic languages are involved – there is a tendency to go more directly from syntax to semantics, without bothering with a formal grammar. As XML becomes more and more popular in Asia, this cultural difference may become better known. It is probably no coincidence that Schematron was developed in Taiwan. Coincidently, the RELAX and TREX proposals are also from Asia (Japan and Thailand respectively).

Jelliffe and his collaborators set several design goals for Schematron:

- Easy implementation on top of XSL and XPath
- Complement validation with XML 1.0 DTDs – be able to handle content models and other patterns that cannot be validated using DTDs (or in many cases, using XML Schemas)
- Validation based on the absence of patterns – those patterns that do *not* appear in the data may also be significant for validation
- Handle language variants (such as HTML 4.0 Basic, Traditional, etc.) that may be used at different phases in workflow or document life cycle.
- Avoid abstraction like type hierarchies (elements, attributes) and content models – instead, provide a direct pattern model (XPath paths and expressions)
- Easy GUI implementation for a schema tree navigator

Let's look at the structure of Schematron, its use of XSLT and XPath, and the small set of elements that enable its implementation.

Schematron Structure

The crux of Schematron is a set of assertions about the XML data. These assertions may be positive or negative and are grouped together to form rules, which are in turn grouped in patterns. These patterns serve as the container and reference point for the various different validation rules within – a pattern is a collection of the rules that provide the actual validation tests.

In DTD validation, there is a direct relation to element and attribute types within the XML data – separate rules for specific instances of these are not possible, nor can the validation rules be applied to non-hierarchical groups or patterns within the data. Furthermore, the constraints that can be applied in a DTD are rather simple, with the testable number of occurrences, for example, being limited to zero, one, or many – greater precision is possible, but only for small numbers and even these are quite cumbersome.

Use of XSLT and XPath

Schematron rules can be much more complex, and are not constrained to simple nodes within the tree structure. Schematron uses XSLT patterns to locate the target of its validation rules. These patterns can match single types of elements or attributes, just like a DTD, or they can match subsets of an element type (such as, "all <name> elements within a <person>, but nowhere else"), or even individual instances of elements (say, "all <name> elements containing a <lastName> matching Smith or Jones"). This is a very powerful ability that transcends the limits of location and validation in a DTD.

XSLT patterns are an extended form of XPath expressions that can use grouping parentheses and OR lists. These lists are compound expressions separated by the typical XML choice character (|).

> **Schematron rules can be applied to any of the elements and/or attributes within the XML data that match a specific XSLT pattern.**

XPath is a pattern language used to identify discrete parts of XML data. As it is a meta-language for a meta-language, it does not use XML syntax. The primary use of XPath is in the form of XPath expressions, which can be evaluated as an object, which may be a Boolean, a number, a string, or a collection of nodes from the XML data tree. Such expressions are evaluated relative to a **context node** within the XML data. An important kind of XPath expression is the **location path**, which is a pattern that selects a group of nodes *relative* to the context node.

Let's consider this variation on our ongoing <MailingAddress> example of XML data:

```
<MailingAddress>
   <Street>AMK Building</Street>
   <Street>123 Park Avenue</Street>
   <City>Skokie</City>
   <State>IL</State>
   <Zip>60606</Zip>
   <Country>USA</Country>
</MailingAddress>
```

We could establish the <MailingAddress> element type as the context node using the expression:

```
/self::MailingAddress <!--"MailingAddress" is the document element here-->
```

Although our example only has one such element, it is important to realize that the above expression would match *all* instances of a <MailingAddress> element that appeared within our data. Of course, we can always be more specific, as we will see momentarily. Assuming this context, some example location paths include:

```
child::State          <!-- select the 'State' child element -->
child::*              <!-- select all child elements -->
ancestor::customer    <!-- select a 'customer' ancestor element -->
descendent::name      <!-- select a 'name' element that is a child (or
                           grandchild, etc.) of the current context node -->

child::Street[position()=last()]
<!-- select the last 'Street' child element -->
```

```
self::MailingAddress[child::State='IL']
<!-- select all "MailingAddress" elements in Illinois -->
```

XPath expressions can become extremely complex, allowing us to select a single customer or address with peculiar criteria (such as "the 100th customer from the 60606 ZIP code who orders a Jumbo Widget"). Or, we could select all customers from Illinois, or only those with multi-line addresses, or simply all elements in the XML data. The above examples show the basic syntax of some XPath expressions. There is also an abbreviated syntax that is terser, and therefore more useful for most schemas.

See Chapter 8, "Navigating XML" for further details of XPath expressions. XPath 1.0 is described in the W3C Recommendation at http://www.w3.org/TR/xpath. *XSLT 1.0 is also a Recommendation at* http://www.w3.org/TR/xslt.

These expressions are the key to Schematron. With them, we can make positive assertions about our data, such as "all `<MailingAddress>` elements must contain one and only one `<City>` element". Of course, this can be accomplished with a DTD or XML Schema as well, but there are many simple and more complex assertions that can only be validated using Schematron.

The structure of an address is expressed in the now-familiar DTD:

```
<!ELEMENT  Street    (#PCDATA) >
<!ELEMENT  City      (#PCDATA) >
<!ELEMENT  State     (#PCDATA) >
<!ELEMENT  Zip       (#PCDATA) >
<!ELEMENT  Country   (#PCDATA) >
<!ELEMENT  MailingAddress  (Street, City, State, Zip, Country) >
```

The following excerpt of a Schematron schema would express the same constraints as the DTD, plus some additional constraints:

```
<schema>
   <title>Validate &lt;MailingAddress&gt;</title>
   <!-- comments, of course -->

   <pattern name="MailingAddress type" >
      <rule context="Street | City | State | Zip | Country" >
      <!-- group the children together -->
         <assert test="parent::*/Street"
         ><name/> element must contain a 'Street' element.</assert>
         <assert test="parent::*/City"
         ><name/> element must contain a 'City' element.</assert>
         <assert test="parent::*/State"
         ><name/> element must contain a 'State' element.</assert>
         <assert test="parent::*/Zip"
         ><name/> element must contain a 'Zip' element.</assert>
         <assert test="parent::*/Country"
         ><name/> element must contain a 'Country' element.</assert>
      </rule>
      <rule context="/Street | /City | /State | /Zip | /Country" >
         <report test="self::*"
```

```
        >Element can't be top-level.</report>
      </rule>
    </pattern>

    <pattern name="Elements" >
      <rule context="Street">
        <report test="child::*"
        ><name/> element should not have child elements</report >
        <assert test="parent::MailingAddress"
        ><name/> element can only appear in a 'MailingAddress'</assert>
      </rule>
      <!-- ... -->
      <rule context="Zip">
        <report test="child::*"
        ><name/> element should not have child elements</report>
        <assert test="parent::MailingAddress"
        ><name/> element can only appear in a 'MailingAddress'</assert>
        <assert test="floor(.) = number(.)"
        ><name/> element must be an integer</assert>
      </rule>
      <!-- and so on... -->
    </pattern>
</schema>
```

The somewhat unusual use of the closing tag delimiter (>) allows us to indent the contents of these elements without inserting unwanted white space.

We could extend the above example, and assert the format of our `<Zip>` element, based upon the *value of the contents* of an associated `<Country>` element. For example, a `<MailingAddress>` in the USA would only allow a simple five-digit number ("nnnnn") or the ZIP+ format ("nnnnn-nnnn") with a hyphen as the valid separator. Canadian and British addresses would only permit the appropriate alphanumeric patterns with a space as the separator ("xnx nxn" and "xxnn nxx", respectively).

Now that we've had an overview and example of Schematron's pattern-based approach, let's look at the specifics of the elements that are used to produce Schematron schemas.

Schematron Elements

One of Schematron's design goals was simplicity, and the ability to use standard GUI tree navigation tools to view a schema. This is ensured by a simple, four levels deep, tree structure with just seven main elements:

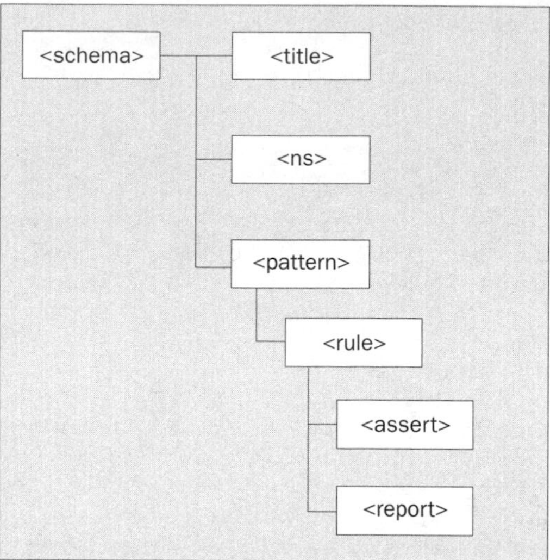

There are several other Schematron elements that are used to improve output styling of Schematron reports, provide multiple versions of the schema for workflow or document versioning, or show diagnostic information. These are all refinements, so we will look at these seven first, since we need only these to create a schema to validate our XML data.

Top-level Element: <schema>

The `<schema>` element is always the top-level element of a Schematron schema, but it need not be the document element of the XML data containing the schema. Remember that Schematron schemas can be embedded in other documents, such as within an `<appinfo>` element in an XML Schema. The basic syntax of a `<schema>` is:

```
<schema
    id="identifier" fpi="identifier" schemaVersion="version#"
    icon="imageURI" xml:lang="langcode"
    defaultPhase="idref"
    version="Schematron version#" xsi:schemaLocation="uri"
    xmlns="default_ns_declaration"
    xmlns:prefix="ns_declaration" >
```

All of the following attributes are optional. The first six describe the individual Schematron schema:

- `id` can be used to provide a unique identifier for the schema (using an DTD `ID` type attribute). As such, its value is constrained to be a legal XML name and must be unique within a given schema
- `fpi` is an SGML Formal Public Identifier that is useful when using SGML tools or catalogs
- `schemaVersion` is the version number for this schema
- `icon` is a URI reference to a small image that could be used to visually identify the schema
- `xml:lang` is the special XML language attribute which uses a RFC 1766 language code to specify the human language used in the schema – see Chapter 3, "Advanced XML Syntax" for more about these
- `defaultPhase` is an `IDREF` reference to the `<phase>` element (see below) that is to be used for the initial validation – intended to support document versioning and workflow variations

The next two describe which Schematron is used:

- `version` is the version number for *Schematron*, which is currently "1.5"
- `xsi:schemaLocation` is used to identify the XML Schema for Schematron – useful when validating a new meta-stylesheet

The last set is used to declare one or more XML Namespaces (those attributes beginning with `xmlns`).

There may also be one or more XML Namespace declarations for elements used within the schema. These would typically include a namespace for the Schematron elements, and perhaps a reference to the XML Schema instance namespace. For example:

```
<sch:schema
   xmlns:sch="http://www.ascc.net/xml/schematron"
   xmlns:xsi="http://www.w3.org/2000/10/XMLSchema-instance" >
```

If a namespace prefix is used for the Schematron namespace, `sch:` is the preferred prefix. For the sake of clarity, we will make Schematron the default namespace in all of the examples in this section, that is:

```
<schema xmlns="http://www.ascc.net/xml/schematron" >
```

The `<schema>` element contains all other Schematron elements, directly or indirectly. Its immediate children include the preamble (`<title>` and `<ns>`), one or more `<pattern>` elements, optional grouping (`<phase>`), an optional `<diagnostics>` element, and may also contain descriptive text paragraphs (`<p>`).

Preamble: <title> and <ns>

The preamble is optional, but it should be included for the sake of documentation and diagnostic reporting.

Schema Title: <title>

The `<title>` element is simply used to document and identify the Schematron schema. It contains some plain character data. It has no attributes, and can optionally include `<dir>` element(s) for internationalization. For example:

```
<title>Schematron 1.5 schema to validate Toysco customers</title>
```

Namespaces: <ns>

The `<ns>` element is used to describe any namespaces used in the schema, and make this metadata explicitly available for diagnostic or application-specific purposes. The basic syntax of the `<ns>` element is:

```
<ns prefix="ns_prefix" uri="ns_uri" />
```

This is always an empty element and the `uri` attribute is required. The `prefix` attribute is optional to allow for the declaration of a default namespace (which does have an associated prefix).

For example, consider a typical XML namespace declaration:

```
... xmlns:sch="http://www.ascc.net/xml/schematron" ...
```

This would be restated in an <ns> element:

```
<ns prefix="sch" uri="http://www.ascc.net/xml/schematron" />
```

There should be one <ns> element for each namespace being validated.

The Container: <pattern>

The <pattern> element is the container for all schema rules related to given context. All of these rules are applied to the context, one by one. Once a rule matches a specified pattern, its assertion is applied and processing moves on to the next pattern.

The <pattern> element is the child of the top-level <schema> element, either directly or indirectly (as an IDREF from a <phase> element).

> **A <pattern> contains <rule>, which can contain <assert> and/or <report>. Rules are applied in context, and only the first matching rule is used in a pattern.**

The basic syntax of <pattern> is:

```
<pattern name="pattern_name" id="identifier" see="docURI" icon="imageURI" >
```

The first attribute (name) is required, while the rest are optional:

- name is required to provide a name (NMTOKEN) for this pattern
- id can be used to provide a unique identifier for this pattern, so that it can be reused by reference
- see is a URI reference to an external human-readable document that describes this pattern
- icon is a URI reference to a small image to signify the pattern

The see attribute could be used in a hypertext system to provide help and documentation for both the schema and the results of the validation process. The icon could be used with both the help system and to visually identify the pattern.

An example of a <pattern> is:

```
<pattern
   name="Invoice Name &amp; Address"
   id="INV_NAMEADDR_P1"
   see="http://www.wrox.com/schemas/InvoiceNameAddr.xhtml"
   icon="http://www.wrox.com/schemas/InvoiceNameAddr_P1.png" >
   <rule> ... </rule>
   <rule> ... </rule>
   ...
</pattern>
```

Each pattern is comprised of one or more rules.

The Crux: <rule>, <assert>, and <report>

These three closely related elements are the key to validation using Schematron.

All `<rule>` elements are contained within `<pattern>` elements. All `<assert>` and/or `<report>` elements are, in turn, children of `<rule>`. A variety of other elements within these are used for things like HTML presentation will be described later, and ignored for the moment.

Group of Assertions: <rule>

A rule is a group of assertions. Rules operate on a context described by an XPath expression, the context being any and all elements in the XML data that match the expression.

The basic syntax of the `<rule>` element is:

```
<rule context="path" id="identifier" role="role_name"
   abstract="{ yes | no }" >
```

These attributes are all optional:

- `context` is the XSLT pattern that describes the context element that is the object of the `<rule>` and its assertions (`<assert>` and/or `<report>` children) – this is required if `abstract="false"` (the default value) or is prohibited if `abstract="true"`
- `id` can be used to provide a unique identifier for the rule (and it is absolutely necessary for an abstract rule to be useful)
- `role` is a name (NMTOKEN) that can be used to describe the nature of the rule
- `abstract` is an enumerated type that may have one of two values: `false` (the default) or `true` – if `true`, then this rule will be used as a template of assertions that can be included within other rules – and the `context` attribute *must* be omitted

The XSLT pattern in `context` is either a simple XPath path or group of XPath paths using the OR (|) operator and parentheses for sub-grouping. The `role` attribute is up to the user's discretion, perhaps using an external controlled vocabulary to identify standardized rules. Schematron 1.5 does not define any values for this attribute.

An example:

```
<rule context="/Customer/MailingAddress" id="INV_NAMEADDR_R1"
   role="USPS_OK" >
   <assert> ... </assert>
   <assert> ... </assert>
   ...
   <report> ... </report>
   ...
</rule>
```

The `<rule>` element contains one or more `<assert>`, `<report>`, `<key>`, and/or `<extends>` elements. The two kinds of assertions (`<assert>` and `<report>`) are tested against the context established by their `<rule>` parent. We will describe each of these in their respective sections.

Positive Assertion: <assert>

The `<assert>` element makes a positive assertion about the XML data in plain language – what *should* be found in the data. These are implemented with an attribute value that is an XSLT pattern. For example, we might say the following about a person's name: "It contains one first name and one last name."

Or in a snippet of a Schematron schema:

```
<assert test="(self::name and child::firstName) and count(firstName) = 1" >
   A 'name' element must contain one 'firstName' element.
</assert>
<assert test="(self::name and child::lastName) and count(lastName) = 1" >
   A 'name' element must contain one 'lastName' element.
</assert>
```

If our data conforms to these assertions (`test` evaluates as `false`), then it is considered valid in this context and no output will result.

If one of these was *not* true (the test expression evaluates to `false`), then the text within the associated `<assert>` element would be output, perhaps to be shown in a validation report.

> **The contents of an `<assert>` element are output if the XSLT pattern is *false*.**

The basic syntax of the `<assert>` element is:

```
<assert
   test="XPath_expression"
   id="identifier" role="role_name" icon="imageURI" xml:lang="langcode"
   subject="path" diagnostics="idrefs" >
   ...a positive assertion about the test...
</assert>
```

The `test` attribute is required – it is the XSLT pattern that describes the condition that we are testing. This pattern is either a simple XPath expression or group of XPath expressions using the OR (|) operator and parentheses for sub-grouping.

Our first `<assert>` example above used a simple three-part AND statement that would match a `<name>` element (`self::name`) with a single `<firstName>` child element (the `count` expression and `child::firstName`). The second example is almost identical, but checks for a single `<lastName>` child element.

The other attributes are optional:

- `id` can be used to provide a unique identifier for the assertion
- `role` is a name (NMTOKEN) that can be used to describe the nature of the rule
- `icon` is a URI reference to a small image that could be used for visual highlighting in the output of the validation process
- `xml:lang` specifies the language used in the assertion

- `subject` is an XPath expression that directly describes the subject of this assertion. It could be used to automatically generate a document, such as an RDF description, from the XML data.
- `diagnostics` is a whitespace-delimited list of identifier references (`IDREFs`), each of which is a link to a descriptive `<diagnostic>` element – these can also be used to provide additional information about the result of the assertion in the validation output

The following XML data excerpt would be considered valid by both the `<assert>` examples above:

```
<name>
   <firstName>Tim</firstName>
   <lastName>Berners-Lee</lastName>
</name>
```

The following excerpt would *not* be considered valid by the second `<assert>` example above:

```
<name>
   <firstName>Tim</firstName>
   <lastName>Berners</lastName>
   <lastName>Lee</lastName>
</name>
```

The presence of the second `<lastName>` element causes the third part of our XSLT pattern (the `test` attribute) to fail, and so the following text would be output to our validation report:

```
   A 'name' element must contain only one 'lastName' element.
```

Of course, these particular tests could have been done just as easily with a DTD. We'll look at the sort of extended validation that makes Schematron so valuable, after we've looked at the rest of its schema elements.

Negative Assertion: <report>

The `<report>` element is the inverse of the `<assert>` element. The only real difference is that the `<report>` element is making a negative assertion – what *has* been found – if the result is `false`, it passes the test and nothing is output. The attributes are the same, with the same meanings.

> **The contents of a `<report>` element are output if the XSLT pattern is *true*.**

A common use of `<report>` is to output a simple "OK" message for a complete element-by-element validation report. Another use would be to output confirmation messages that certain key elements are present.

For example, a comprehensive validation report might include the following `<report>` element:

```
<report test="((self::name and child::firstName) and count(firstName) = 1)
   and ((self::name and child::lastName) and count(lastName) = 1))" >
   OK - 'name' element has all its children.
</report>
```

This "active reporting" approach might use an additional XSLT transform to verify that all messages are "OK", resolving a whole series of validation tests into a simple "go" / "no go" result.

Rule Macros: <extends>

The <extends> element provides a simple macro mechanism for rules. This empty element always contains a `rule` attribute, which is an `IDREF` to another (abstract) rule. The abstract rule cannot have a context; so all of its assertions are applied to the context of this element's parent (a non-abstract <rule>).

Matching Character Data: <key>

The <key> element allows any simple character data in the XML data to be treated as a key.

The basic syntax of this empty element is:

```
<key path="XPath_expression" name="identifier" icon="imageURI" />
```

This empty element requires the first two attributes, and has an optional third:

- `path` is the required XSLT pattern that describes the path from the current context to the field in the XML data that is to be used as a key
- `name` is required to provide a name (`NmToken`) for this key
- `icon` is a URI reference to a small image that visually identifies the key

This is a very powerful, if obscure, feature of Schematron and XPath – we can find and validate graphs within our XML data beyond just simple hierarchical trees!

Assertion Context: <name>

The <name> element can be embedded within the message text of an <assert> or <report> element to describe the related context element that triggered the assertion. It can alternatively use an `xpath` attribute to include mention of elements that are not the context element.

Presentation: <p>, <dir>, <emph>, and <span>

Two of these four elements (<emph> and <span>) are essentially the same as those in HTML (<em> and <span>). The <p> element has some Schematron-specific attributes, but is easily transformed into an HTML <p> element. The <dir> element is different from the one of the same name in HTML.

Text Paragraph: <p>

The <p> element simply contains a paragraph of descriptive or diagnostic text, just like its use in HTML. It may appear in a <schema> or <pattern> element. The basic syntax of the <p> element is:

```
<p id="identifier" class="classname(s)" icon="imageURI"
   xml:lang="langcode" >
```

All of these attributes are optional:

- `id` can be used to provide a unique identifier for the paragraph
- `class` is a name (or whitespace-delimited list of names) that can be used to style the schema's HTML output with a CSS style sheet – it could also be used as a hook for some other external user agent or post-processor

- `icon` is a URI reference to a small image that could be used for visual highlighting of the text
- `xml:lang` specifies the language used in the paragraph

Within a paragraph, we may want to apply some additional organization or abstract text styling.

Text Styling: <emph>

The `<emph>` element simply states that the text within is to be emphasized when it is shown. It is equivalent to HTML's `<em>` element, and has no attributes.

Text Paragraph: <span>

The `<span>` element is similar to its counterpart in HTML, providing some inline structured text, often for localized styling, a quotation, or some other kind of embedded text that should be grouped or styled as a single entity. Of course, this is unnecessary in XML data, but this element (and `<div>`) are as close as HTML gets to generic structural tagging.

The basic syntax of the `<span>` element is:

```
<span class="classname(s)" >
```

As with the `<p>` element, the optional `class` attribute is intended to aid output styling. This element could be useful as a way to preserve some vestige of structure in an output message.

Text Direction: <dir>

The `<dir>` element simply states the reading direction of the text with the paragraph, using an empty element with a single attribute. It is an element version of the `dir` *attribute* from HTML or CSS, and shares the same values.

The basic syntax of the `<dir>` element is:

```
<dir value="{ ltr | rtl }" />
```

The `value` attribute *is* optional, though this element isn't very useful without the attribute. The `ltr` value specifies left-to-right text, and `rtl` specifies right-to-left text.

> *Do not confuse this `<dir>` element with the HTML* element *of the same name – which is used to create indented "directory" text.*

This element is essential for truly internationalized schemas.

Let's now return to some higher-level elements that enhance the production and presentation of Schematron schemas.

Conditional Sections: <phase> and <active>

The life cycle of a document often reflects various levels of validation. At first, very loose standards may be applied as the various parts of a document are being written, edited, and merged together. Numerous elements might be missing at this stage, so validation might be limited to basic syntax. Later, as the document comes together, structural validation becomes more important. Last of all, a very strict set of validation tests may be done to ensure that the document's structure is correct, its contents are appropriate, presentation hints are complete, and even that calculations embedded in the data have plausible results.

The <phase> and <active> elements provide a hook for an application to selectively process subsets of the validation patterns based upon specific phases of the XML document life cycle.

Schematron provides a simple hook to enable conditional processing. As we saw earlier, the <schema> element may contain a currentPhase attribute, which points (via an IDREF) to a particular <phase> element. Each phase of the document life cycle uses one such element to contain one or more empty <active pattern="..."/> elements. These point (via IDREFS) to all the <pattern> elements that should be active for the given phase of the document life cycle. Since all patterns will be used in normal XSLT processing, it is up to the application to provide a selection mechanism and the necessary XSLT processor parameters to do the appropriate set of validation patterns.

Diagnostics: <diagnostics>, <diagnostic>, and <value-of>

Many users of Schematron have extended the text of assertion messages to include a variety of diagnostic and advisory information. While this is a reasonable use, verbose text clouds the simplicity of having the text within an <assert> or <report> element simply restate the XSLT pattern as a natural language assertion. Schematron has therefore provided a simple mechanism for including diagnostic text that supplements the text elsewhere in the schema.

The Group: <diagnostics>

This element exists solely to group all <diagnostic> elements within a single parent, for convenient transformation and presentation. It is a child of the top-level <schema> element, and can only contain zero or more <diagnostic> elements, which contain the actual diagnostic text. This element has no attributes.

The Text: <diagnostic>

The <diagnostic> element is the container for the text that describes an assertion in more detail. Its basic syntax is:

```
<diagnostic id="identifier" icon="imageURI" xml:lang="langcode" >
   Some <emph>emphasized text</emph>, perhaps mentioning the name of the
   element that triggered the message: <value-of select="pattern" /> and so
   on...
</diagnostic>
```

The id attribute is required, and the other two are optional:

- id is required to provide a unique identifier for the diagnostic text
- icon is a URI reference to a small image
- xml:lang specifies the language used in the text

This element may contain three of the usual presentation elements (<emph>, <dir>, and <span>) plus <value-of> elements that are described presently.

Variable Data: <value-of>

The <value-of> element uses yet another XSLT pattern (as an attribute) that can be used to embed dynamic values within the diagnostic (or other) text. The pattern might be the name of an element or the value of some content that doesn't pass a validation test.

The basic syntax of this empty element is:

```
<value-of select="XSLT_pattern" />
```

The `select` attribute is the only one allowed and it is required. It is an XSLT pattern that describes the path from the current context node to the field in the XML data that is to be included with this text.

We now know the basic structure of Schematron, so let's look at its implementation using an XSLT processor.

Implementation of Schematron

The only software needed to implement Schematron is an XSLT processor. Validating XML data with Schematron is a two step process. Once we've written a Schematron schema, it must first be "compiled" using the XSLT processor and the Schematron "compiler stylesheet", which is also called a **meta-stylesheet**. Once compiled, our Schematron schema (now in the form of an XSL stylesheet) can then be used to validate our XML data. Unless the schema changes, it is not necessary to re-compile it every time we need to validate some data.

XSLT Processors with Schematron

The key tool for processing Schematron schemas is an XSLT processor, such as Saxon, XT, or Xalan. The XSLT processors in MSXML3 (MSXSL) and Oracle's XML Processor for Java also work well with Schematron schemas.

> ***Saxon*** *can be found at* http://users.iclway.co.uk/mhkay/saxon/index.html, *and was developed by Michael Kay.* ***xt*** *is another of James Clark's ubiquitous tools, at* http://www.jclark.com/xml/xt.html. ***Xalan*** *is available in both C and Java versions at* http://xml.apache.org/xalan-j/index.html *and* http://xml.apache.org/xalan-c/index.html. *Oracle's* ***XML Processor for Java*** *is at* http://technet.oracle.com/tech/xml/parser_java2/ *and* ***MSXML 3.0*** *is available at* http://msdn.microsoft.com/xml/general/xmlparser.asp.

Since Schematron relies upon existing XSLT processors, Jelliffe has tested a dozen or so implementations with some known style sheets. These tests have produced a warning about using XT with Schematron – do not use the `key()` feature, as it is not implemented in XT.

> ***The Screamatron Torture Test*** *examines how well Schematron 1.5 works with various XSLT processors, at* http://www.ascc.net/xml/schematron/1.5/conrep.html.

There are also implementations available in Perl and Python. Once we've chosen an XSLT processor, we need to select a meta-stylesheet to compile our schema.

Schematron Meta-Stylesheets

There are several flavors of Schematron meta-stylesheets that can be used to compile Schematron schemas. These are designed to work with specific tools or for different presentations, and are available at the Schematron website, by clicking on Download Schematron 1.5 Tools (the first four) or Download Schematron 1.3 Tools and Schemas (the rest).

- schematron-basic – concept demonstration – generates simple text
- schematron-message – generates messages for use with an editor such as emacs or XED

- schematron-conformance – tests Schematron 1.5 with XSLT processors
- schematron-report – generates HTML pages with error messages
- schematron-rdf – generates RDF statements for each pattern found in schema (context element located with an XPointer)
- schematron-pretty – a pretty-print formatter for schemas
- schematron-pretty (for IE5) – an XSL stylesheet for prettified schemas in IE5
- schematron-w3c – generates HTML pages with assertion messages and an extracted version of the XML data node causing the message; used in the online Web Content Accessibility Checking Service
- schematron-xml – generates XML data with suspected error location as an XPath in an attribute

One of these meta-stylesheets is used to compile our Schematron schema, which is then used to validate our data. The schematron-message meta-stylesheet is also useful for production purposes since it provides information to locate the portion of the XML data causing an error.

Several schemas have already been written for some common XML vocabularies.

Schematron Schemas

Schematron schemas have been developed to provide additional validation for some vocabularies that are based on DTDs. They are all available at the Schematron website. Some of the more generally useful and interesting schemas are for:

- XML Schema – validates the schema specifications (*not* XML data using an XML Schema)
- Web Accessibility Initiative (WAI) – this is a best-practice schema, rather than a usage or definitional schema
- News Interchange Transfer Format (NITF)
- Synchronized Multimedia Interchange Language (SMIL)
- RSS (Rich Site Summary) Validator – supplements RSS 0.91 DTD validation
- SOAP 1.1
- XLink

Schematron Summary

Schematron is not a good way to represent the complete structure of an XML tree – DTDs and XML Schema are better suited for this purpose. Some of Schematron's advantages come from the use of XPath expressions that can select all elements of a given type or a single instance of the element or range of instances. XPath comparisons and calculations allow validation constraints that are simply not possible with any other schema. Where an XML Schema can constrain an attribute value to be a numeric data type within a specific range of values, Schematron can make that range dynamic (perhaps as the result of a calculation) or specify multiple (discontinuous) ranges.

Schematron is designed to work in harmony with a DTD or XML Schema. A Schematron schema can be encapsulated in `<appinfo>` elements for individual validation tests that supplement element or attribute descriptions in an XML Schema.

There are several free open source XSLT processors, and XSLT support is being built into applications like web browsers, so it is relatively easy to implement Schematron – no special processor is needed. Schematron's use of standard XML specifications like XPath and XSLT, and its cooperative relationship to XML Schema, is an excellent example of how to extend XML.

Although initially the work of an individual, Schematron is now an open source project in the best tradition of worldwide Internet collaborative development. Schematron will likely endure as a supplement to XML Schema, for any application where it is desirable to provide more specific constraints upon the value of attributes or the content of elements.

Summary

In this chapter, we have looked at several alternatives (and supplements) to the W3C's XML Schema for validating XML documents. We concentrated on four of these technologies: XDR, RELAX, TREX, and Schematron. XDR is currently used by Microsoft in products like Internet Explorer and the BizTalk Framework, but is likely to be replaced by the W3c's XML Schema in the future. RELAX and TREX are suitable middleweight alternatives to "XML Schema Part 1: Structures". They are generally easier to use and can be implemented on platforms on which it would be difficult to implement the W3C's XML Schema, such as PDA's and cell phones. Schematron is not based on grammars like the other technologies that we looked at, but instead works by matching patterns in the XML tree structure, and is designed to complement, rather than replace, the W3C's XML Schema. Schematron, RELAX, and TREX are all new technologies that are likely to evolve rapidly in the future, so keep checking the web sites mentioned in the relevant sections.

8

Navigating XML – XPath

The XML 1.0 syntax provides a straightforward, standard way to exchange information between computer programs. The XML Path Language, **XPath**, plays an important part in such exchange of information between computers or computer applications because it allows selected or filtered information from within the source XML data or document to be exchanged or displayed.

In this chapter, we will introduce you to the theory and practice of using XPath. If you find the theory too dry on a first reading, feel free to skip ahead to the sections that include numerous example XPath expressions. You will need to master the theory, but the examples may help you to grasp the principles.

We will discuss XPath at times as if it were a standalone technology, but will also discuss XPath in the context of its current primary usage with Extensible Stylesheet Language Transformations, **XSLT**, as well as discussing its potential usage with other languages, including the XML Pointer Language (XPointer), the XML Schema Language, and the XML Query Language (XQuery).

XPath is a complex technology with many subtleties and a few potential pitfalls, although basic use can be straightforward. We will illustrate the use of XPath with examples towards the end of the chapter, hoping to bring to life what can potentially be a rather abstract technology.

Introduction to XPath

XPath is one of the most important, but probably one of the least understood, members of the XML family of technologies. In this chapter, we will introduce many of the basic aspects of XPath that should provide you with a foundation for using XPath, and particularly using it with XSLT, which is described more fully in Chapter 9.

In addition to its use with XSLT, XPath is being incorporated in several other XML-based technologies, which are reaching a stage of development where the scope for the practical use of XPath is widening (see the section on XPath 2.0 towards the end of the chapter). At the time of writing, none of those other technologies has been released as a W3C Recommendation; but during the lifetime of this book, you may well find that an understanding of XPath will be needed to make full use of many other XML-based technologies. However, it is with XSLT that XPath finds its widest use today and the examples in this chapter will focus on that.

Back in November 1999, when the XPath 1.0 Recommendation was released, XPath could be used with XSLT and nothing else. The potential use for XPath as a foundation for the XML Pointer Language, XPointer, was recognized in the XPath 1.0 Recommendation, but the XPointer technology was at a too early stage of development for the use of XPath in it to be anything other than an experimental, if clearly envisaged, proposition. By contrast, at the time of writing, XPointer is close to progressing to a Candidate Recommendation and some preliminary XPointer implementations are appearing. When, in some future XML-based application, we wish to navigate to a particular part of a local or a linked document, it will likely be some combination of XPath and XPointer that will make that navigation possible. In addition, the XML Schema Language is at the Proposed Recommendation stage of development and parts of XML Schema make significant use of XPath. Perhaps most important in the long term, will be the use of XPath in or with XQuery, the XML Query Language. At the time of writing XQuery had just been released in its first public Working Draft. XPath is an important technology, among several (including XSLT), on which XQuery is likely to be built. The potential uses of XPath in or with XML Schema and XQuery will be discussed when we look at what is being considered for development in XPath version 2.0, which is discussed at the end of this chapter. However, before we look at those exciting future prospects we will spend most of the chapter with our feet firmly on the ground looking at what XPath is now, how it works and what it can do for the XML developer. Except where otherwise stated, all unqualified references to XPath in this chapter will refer to XPath version 1.0, released by the W3C in November 1999, which you can find at http://www.w3.org/TR/ 1999/REC-xpath-19991116.

XPath and What It Does

XPath is designed to enable addressing of, or navigation to, chosen parts of an XML document. In support of that aim, XPath provides a number of functions for the manipulation of strings, numbers, Booleans, and nodesets.

In practice, the most important use of XPath at present is within XSLT, whether in transformation of XML to HTML or transformation of one form of XML to another (for example in business-to-business data interchange). The use of XPath in XSLT is extended by additional expressions and functions. Parts of XSLT operate using a subset of XPath that allows for testing whether or not an XPath **node** matches a **pattern**.

Before we begin to burrow into the dark recesses of XPath theory, let's take a brief look at how XPath may straightforwardly be used in practice with XSLT.

The XSLT that we will use is simple, but we will assume that you understand it, rather than take time to explain the XSLT here (XSLT will be covered in detail in Chapter 9, "Transforming XML".) We will highlight, within the text that follows, some XPath terms that will be explained in more detail in a later section. For the moment, the important thing is that the generality of the process is grasped, while seeing real (if simple) working XPath and XSLT code.

For example, let's suppose we have some source XML, either as a document or because of querying a data store, which we want to present on the Web as HTML in a simple table. Our source XML, `SalesReport.xml`, representing sales figures for a fictional company in Europe, North America, and Australasia might look something like this:

```
<?xml version="1.0" encoding="utf-8"?>
<?xml-stylesheet href="SalesToHTML.xsl" type="text/xsl" ?>
<!-- SalesReport.cml -->
<SalesReport>
   <Company>XMML.com</Company>
   <Period>2001-2002</Period>
   <Sales Region="EU">50,000</Sales>
   <Sales Region="NA">150,000</Sales>
   <Sales Region="AU">10,000</Sales>
</SalesReport>
```

To use this data to create an HTML web page we need to transform it using XSLT, which makes use of a number of XPath expressions to create the output page.

> *Please note that the XSLT examples in this chapter use XSLT compliant with XSLT version 1.0. If you are using an older version of Microsoft MSXML, such as the one supplied with Internet Explorer 5.5, you will need to upgrade to MSXML3 (released in October 2000) and install it in replace mode, because earlier versions of MSXML use an old version of XSLT that differs significantly from W3C XSLT 1.0.*

We can use the following simple XSLT stylesheet, `SalesToHTML.xsl`:

```
<?xml version='1.0'?>
<!-- SalesToHTML.xsl -->
<xsl:stylesheet version="1.0"
   xmlns:xsl="http://www.w3.org/1999/XSL/Transform">
   <xsl:output method="html" omit-xml-declaration="yes" />

   <xsl:template match="/">
      <html>
      <head>
         <title>
            Sales Report, <xsl:value-of select="/SalesReport/Company" />:
            <xsl:value-of select="/SalesReport/Period" />
         </title>
      </head>
      <body>
         <br />
         <h2>
            <xsl:value-of select="/SalesReport/Company"/>, Sales Report:
            <xsl:value-of select="/SalesReport/Period"/>
         </h2>
         <br />
         <table width="50%">
            <tr>
               <th>Region</th>
               <th>Sales ($ 000's)</th>
            </tr>
            <xsl:for-each select="/SalesReport/Sales">
```

```
            <tr>
               <td align="center"><xsl:value-of select="@Region"/></td>
               <td align="center"><xsl:value-of select="."/></td>
            </tr>
         </xsl:for-each>
      </table>
   </body>
   </html>
</xsl:template>

</xsl:stylesheet>
```

With this stylesheet, we can select parts of the source XML document to use, for example, in the `<title>` element and `<table>` element of the output HTML. Using this stylesheet to display the content of our source XML document in a simple HTML web page would look like this:

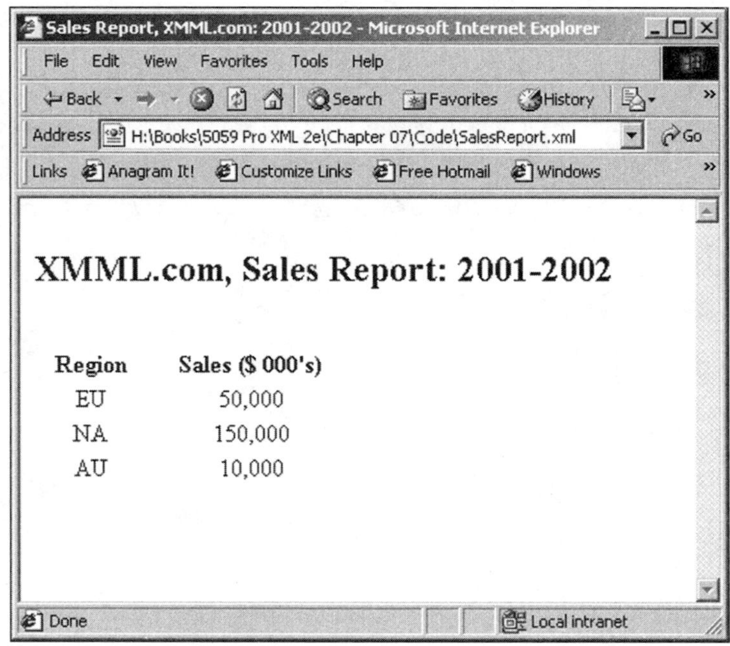

None of the data displayed on our web page was typed literally in the XSLT stylesheet. All of it was retrieved from within the source document by means of various XPath expressions or **location paths**. An XPath location path is a special type of XPath expression, widely used with XSLT, which returns a nodeset (XPath expressions can additionally return three other data types – string, Boolean, and number). For example, we used location paths to create the HTML `<title>` element within the `<head>` of the page using the following code:

```
<title>
   Sales Report, <xsl:value-of select="/SalesReport/Company" />:
   <xsl:value-of select="/SalesReport/Period" />
</title>
```

Some literal text is returned, such as "Sales Report", but the company name and the period to which the sales report refers are printed using XSLT `<xsl:value-of>` elements whose `select` attributes make use of XPath location paths to incorporate appropriate parts of the content from our source XML document within the HTML `<title>` element.

Each of the `select` attributes of the `<xsl:value-of>` elements in the above code snippet contains an XPath expression or location path that accesses the content of an element in the source XML document. For example, examine the XSLT element:

```
<xsl:value-of select="/SalesReport/Company"/>
```

This selected the content of the `<Company>` element, which was the child of the `<SalesReport>` element in our source XML document. The XPath expression `/SalesReport/Company` is the way in which the XSLT processor is informed about which part(s) of the source XML document is to be included in or displayed in that part of the HTML `<title>` element of our web page.

Similarly, the data cells of the simple HTML table are populated using the content of attributes and elements in our source XML document.

```
<xsl:for-each select="/SalesReport/Sales">
   <tr>
      <td align="center"><xsl:value-of select="@Region"/></td>
      <td align="center"><xsl:value-of select="."/></td>
   </tr>
</xsl:for-each>
```

The important tag is the following:

```
<xsl:for-each select="/SalesReport/Sales">
```

This selects the XPath node that represents the `<Sales>` elements that are children of the `<SalesReport>` element in our source XML document as the **context node**, which is the starting point for our expression. Therefore, each of the `<xsl:value-of>` elements nested within the `<xsl:for-each>` element are evaluated with the **element node** representing a `<Sales>` element as the context node.

The XPath location path, `@Region`, selects the **attribute node**, which represents the `Region` attribute of a `<Sales>` element. The successive values of the `Region` attribute are therefore output in the left column of the HTML table. The location path, `.`, is an abbreviated form of syntax for the context node which in this case is an element node representing the `<Sales>` element. Therefore, the content of each `<Sales>` element is inserted into the right column of the HTML table.

With the context nodeset as described above, and by making appropriate selections from the XML in the source document, we have, by using XPath location paths, created a simple, but informative, sales report suitable for display on the Web, using XPath location paths within XSLT. Of course, much more sophisticated or complex visual display is possible but that is not our purpose at present. The intent is to grasp a little of how XPath works with XSLT. Let's move on from that simple practical example to look in a little more detail at the theory of how XPath works.

How XPath Works

XPath is a complex specification with many subtleties, not all of which will be covered in this chapter due to space constraints. However, before we go deeper into the detail of XPath it is important that you understand the broad principles of how XPath works. Generally, the easiest way to explain it to someone not already familiar with XPath is to liken it to a set of street directions. That analogy is particularly relevant with respect to location paths, which are the most important type of XPath expression.

Let's assume we are in a city where the streets are laid out in a grid pattern in a North-South and East-West layout. If we are strangers in the city and we ask a knowledgeable and helpful citizen how to get to a desired destination, we are likely to be given a set of directions that, implicitly, take account of where we are starting. The directions might take the form "Go 2 blocks North, then turn left, go three blocks, and then it is the third building past the intersection."

XPath works in a broadly similar way. Of course, there are many differences. XPath, for example, is used to navigate a hierarchical structure (which we will look at in more detail shortly) rather than the rectilinear street pattern of many North American cities. However, XPath works similarly to street directions. It has a starting point, the context node, and we move in a particular direction, called an **axis** in XPath, and our arrival at our destination is determined by one or more steps, which in XPath are termed **location steps**.

The XPath expressions we saw in the code earlier are all a special type of XPath expression called a location path. As mentioned earlier, the important distinction of a location path is that it returns a nodeset rather than one of the other data types that XPath expressions can return. A location path is a series of one or more "street directions" telling an XSLT or other processor how to navigate around the XPath representation of the source XML document. A location path consists of one or more location steps.

A location step is broadly equivalent to a part of some street directions. Where street directions will typically have a direction, a location path has an axis. In XPath, there are 13 different axes, which will be discussed in more detail later in the chapter. For the moment, think of an axis as broadly equivalent to a compass direction.

The second part of a location step is a node test. The node test specifies the type of node selected and its expanded name, if it has one. As discussed in more detail in a little while, there are seven types of node in the XPath data model. Formally, the XPath specification designates that an expanded name is used in the node test. If the start tag of the root element of a document that is to be transformed included a namespace declaration as follows:

```
<ecxml:invoice xmlns:ecxml="http://www.ecxml.com/e-commerce/">
```

The expanded name of the node representing the `<ecxml:invoice>` element would be something like:

```
http://www.ecxml.com/e-commerce/:invoice
```

although there is no defined convention for displaying the expanded name, and some products use a circumflex (^) to separate the namespace URI and the local name.

Therefore, instead of using the namespace prefix, which is the more natural way for the human reader, the XPath (or XSLT) processor actually uses the namespace URI to which the namespace prefix is mapped within the expanded name.

If you need to refresh your memory about XML Namespaces, you may wish to look at theW3C's Namespaces in XML Recommendation of 14 January 1999, which is located at http://www.w3.org/TR/1999/REC-xml-names *or at the discussion of XML namespaces in Chapter 3.*

As you can see, an expanded name becomes unwieldy to handle within XPath expressions, at least for human beings. In most of the examples in this chapter, we will use source documents that do not involve namespace declarations. In the absence of a namespace declaration, the namespace URI is `null`; therefore the expanded name of such an element is the same as the element name. In other words, we can simply think of `invoice` as the expanded name, rather than as an expanded name such as `http://www.ecxml.com/e-commerce/:invoice`, which makes explanation or illustration of concepts in code much more manageable. However, be sure to remember that it is an expanded name that is being used in the XPath location paths or expressions, not simply the element's local name. If, as is likely in anything other than trivial XSLT transformations, we do have namespace declarations, then we will need to bear in mind considerations relating to the namespace URI and expanded name.

In addition to the axis and the node test, a location step may optionally have one or more **predicates**. XPath predicates help to refine or filter the nodeset selected by the axis and the node test.

Thus, a location step has three parts:

- An axis
- A node test, which specifies the node type and expanded name of the nodes selected by the location step
- Zero or more predicates, which use arbitrary XPath expressions to further refine the set of nodes selected by the location step

XPath has both an unabbreviated and abbreviated syntax. Both are described and discussed later in the chapter. The unabbreviated syntax for a location step is the axis name and node test separated by a double colon, followed by zero or more expressions (the predicates) each in square brackets.

For example, in `child::paragraph[position()=2]`, `child` is the name of the axis, the double colon is a separator between the axis and the node test, `paragraph` is the node test and `[position()=2]` is a predicate. The predicate makes use of the `position()` function, which is one of the functions contained in the XPath core function library described later in the chapter.

> **In XPath, the `position()` function returns the position of a node within a nodeset. Note that position 1 denotes the first position in a group of siblings. This is in contrast to, for example, the Java language, which uses index zero to represent the first element in an array. If you are used to programming in a language that uses a zero index, take particular care when using predicates like this, that you have chosen the element node intended.**

If we had a slightly longer location path:

```
child::chapter/child::paragraph[position()=2]
```

The first location step is `child::chapter`, which is separated by a forward slash from the following location step: `child::paragraph[position()=2]`. The first location step does not include a predicate, whereas the second location step does.

Just as when we were given our street directions they made sense only if we defined where we were starting from, so it is in XPath. Each XPath location path has a meaning that is determined by the context node, the starting point in the hierarchical tree that represents the source XML document. In the simple examples we have just looked at, the context would be determined by, for example, the XSLT template within which the XPath location path was contained.

The XPath Data Model

XPath operates on the abstract logical structure of an XML document rather than on its surface syntax. The representation of the abstract structure of the XML document is called a **data model**.

Earlier, we mentioned the XPath term node and now we will go on to explain what an XPath node is. First, we need to take a step back and think about the structure of a serialized XML document. When XML exists as a file, it is visible to a reader as a succession of elements each of which has a start tag and end tag, typically with other elements nested within it and/or within each other. XPath does not use that representation, but in its data model it models those XML elements within an XML document as a hierarchical structure of nodes.

The following diagram schematically represents the hierarchical structure within XPath representing the XML source document, `SalesReport.xml`, which we used in the example earlier in the chapter. Each ellipse represents an XPath node:

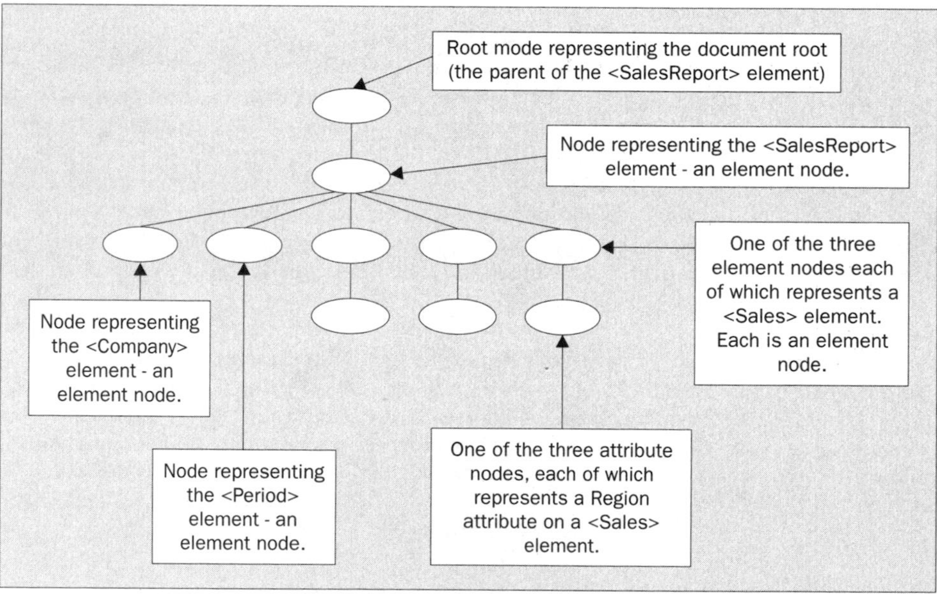

Each XML document has a **root node**, which is the parent of the node representing the **element root**. The element root is represented as an **element node**, which in the case of our sample document represents the `<SalesReport>` element.

In the diagram, the element node representing the `<SalesReport>` element has five other child element nodes respectively representing the `<Company>` element, the `<Period>` element, and each of the three `<Sales>` elements.

For instance, in a serialized XML 1.0 document we would see the `<Company>` element nested within the `<SalesReport>` element like this:

```
<SalesReport>
   <Company>XMML.com</Company>
   <!-- Other elements go here. -->
</SalesReport>
```

In XPath, we have an element node, representing the `<Company>` element as a child of the element node, which represents the `<SalesReport>` node.

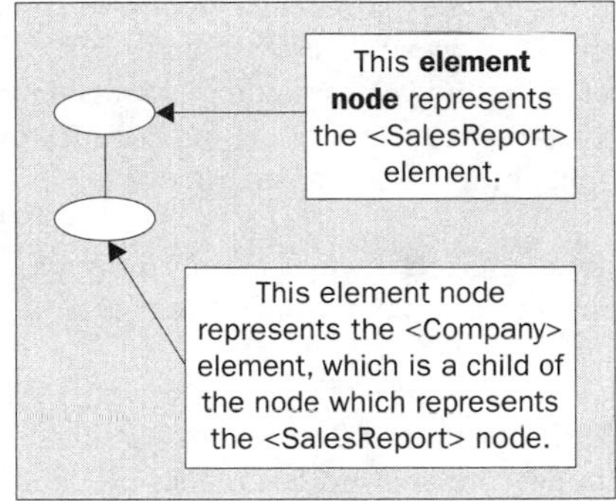
This **element node** represents the <SalesReport> element.
This element node represents the <Company> element, which is a child of the node which represents the <SalesReport> node.

In the first diagram, each of the three element nodes representing a `<Sales>` element is the parent of an attribute node representing the `Region` attribute of the `<Sales>` element. An element node is the parent of an attribute node, but, in XPath terminology, an attribute node is *not* the child of its parent element node. This, perhaps surprising, distinction is necessary so that the child axis, discussed later in the chapter, operates so as to select child *element* nodes but exclude attribute nodes (which are selected using a separate attribute axis).

Our document illustrates three of the seven node types in XPath. Here is the full list of node types:

- Root nodes – one and only one per document
- Element nodes – one element node represents the element root of a document
- Text nodes
- Attribute nodes
- Namespace nodes
- Processing instruction nodes
- Comment nodes

Be sure to avoid confusing the root node and its child, which is an element node that represents the element root.

Consider the following simple XML document:

```
<?xml version='1.0'?>
<?xml-stylesheet href="book.xsl" type="text/xsl" ?>
<!-- NodeTypes.xml -->

<book xmlns="http://www.xmml.com/">
   <title code="Navigating XML - XPath">
      XPath is cool - but not easy!
   </title>
</book>
```

Viewed conceptually in XPath, it contains all of the seven types of node in the XPath data model. The root node is present, although not visible in the document, and is the parent of the processing instruction node, the comment node and of the `<book>` element node. The `<title>` element node has a text node child, which has the string value "`XPath is cool - but not easy!`" and also has a child attribute node whose name is `code` and whose value is "`Navigating XML - XPath`". It also has a namespace node, whose value is inherited from the namespace node of its parent `<book>` element node. Note that, although it is enclosed in the `<? ?>` characters like processing instructions, the XML declaration at the top is not actually a processing instruction and therefore has no corresponding processing instruction node in the XPath data model. However the `<?xml-stylesheet?>` processing instruction would be represented by a processing instruction node in the XPath model of this XML document.

For each of the seven types of node, there is a way of determining a string value for a node of that type. For some types of node, the string value is part of the node. For other types of node, the string value is computed from the string value of descendant nodes.

The string value of a node is one illustration of the sometimes subtle differences of approach between DOM and XPath. For element nodes and root nodes, the string value of a node is not the same as the string returned by the DOM `nodeValue` method.

For further information on the Document Object Model, refer to Chapter 10.

XPath also includes a concept of **document order**. For elements from the same document, document order is the same as the order of the start tags in the original source. In terms of the XPath data model, a node is ordered after its preceding siblings, and these are ordered after their parent node. The ordering of attribute and namespace nodes, and of nodes from different source documents, is not fully defined.

Root nodes and element nodes have an ordered list of child nodes. Nodes never share children. Every node other than the root node has exactly one parent, which is either an element node or the root node. In other words, apart from the root node, only element nodes may be the parent of any other node. A root node or an element node is the parent of each of its child nodes. The descendants of a node are the children of the node, and the descendants of the children of the node. The following is a description of the different types of node:

Node	Description
Root	The root node is the root of the XPath tree. Each XPath tree may have exactly one root node. The string value of the root node is the concatenation of the string values of all text node descendants of the root node in document order. The root node does not have an expanded name.

Node	Description
Element	There is an element node for each element in the XML source document. An element node has an expanded name derived by expanding the **QName** (a qualified name; the element name including any prefix) in the element tag according to the W3C's Namespaces in XML Recommendation. The namespace URI of the element's expanded name will be `null` if the QName has no prefix and there is no applicable default namespace. The children of an element node are the element nodes, comment nodes, processing instruction nodes and text nodes for its content. Entity references to both internal and external entities are expanded. Character references are first resolved.
Attribute	Each element node has an associated set of attribute nodes, which may be empty. The element node is the parent of each of these attribute nodes. However, an attribute node is *not* a child of its parent element. In other words, when a location path begins with `child::` then no attribute nodes are selected. Note that this is a further difference from the DOM, which does not treat the element bearing an attribute as the parent of the attribute.
Namespace	Each element has an associated set of namespace nodes, one for each distinct namespace prefix that is in scope for the element (including the `xml` prefix, which is implicitly declared by the Namespaces in XML Recommendation) and one for the default namespace if one is in scope for the element. An element node is the parent of each of these namespace nodes. However, a namespace node is *not* a child of its parent element. This means that a location path that begins with `child::` does not return any namespace nodes. Elements never share namespace nodes. If one element node is not the same node as another element node, then none of the namespace nodes of the one element node will be the same node as the namespace nodes of another element node. In summary, this means that an element will have a namespace node: ❑ For every attribute on the element whose name starts with `xmlns:` ❑ For every attribute on an ancestor element whose name starts with `xmlns:`, unless the element itself or a nearer ancestor re-declares the prefix ❑ For an `xmlns` attribute, if the element or some ancestor has an `xmlns` attribute, and the value of the `xmlns` attribute for the nearest such element is non-empty
Processing Instruction	There is a processing instruction node for every processing instruction, except for any processing instruction that occurs within the Document Type Declaration. A processing instruction has an expanded name; the local part is the processing instruction's target and the namespace URI is `null`. The string value of a processing instruction node is the part of the processing instruction following the target (the application to which the PI applies) and any whitespace. It does not include the "?>" characters which terminate the processing instruction. As mentioned previously, the XML declaration is not a processing instruction and therefore there is no processing instruction node corresponding to the XML declaration.

Table continued on following page

Node	Description
Comment	There is a comment node for every comment in the source XML document, except for any comment that occurs within the Document Type Declaration. The string value of a comment is the content of the comment not including the opening `<!--` characters or the closing `-->` characters. A comment node does not have an expanded name.
Text	Character data in the source document is grouped into text nodes. As much character data as possible is grouped into each text node, thus a text node never has an immediately following or preceding sibling that is a text node. The string value of a text node is the character data. A text node always has at least one character of data. Each character within a CDATA section is treated as character data. Thus, `<![CDATA[<]]>` in the source document will be treated the same as `<`. Both will result in a single < character in a text node in the tree. Thus, a CDATA section is treated as if the `<![CDATA[` and `]]>` were removed and every occurrence of < and & were replaced by `<` and `&` respectively. A text node does not have an expanded name.
	Note that characters inside comments, processing instructions and attribute values do not produce text nodes. Line endings in external entities are normalized to `#xA` as specified in the XML 1.0 Recommendation.

We have introduced quite a few new terms in the last few paragraphs so before we move on and look at some more theory, let's look at how all this works with our example XML document.

Let's look again at the XSLT element in which part of the `<title>` element of our output document was selected:

```
<xsl:value-of select="/SalesReport/Company" />
```

The XPath location path (using the abbreviated syntax, as it happens) is `/SalesReport/Company`. It may help to see the unabbreviated syntax for the XPath expression that means the same, prior to working through in detail how such an XPath expression is processed.

```
/child::SalesReport/child::Company
```

The starting point for the location path, whatever the context node, is indicated by the first forward slash. The forward slash selects the root node of the document that contains the context node.

The axis is not actually expressed in the abbreviated syntax, indicating that the default axis (which is the child axis) is in use. The child axis selects only element nodes. Therefore, the presence of the child axis indicates, at this stage, that potentially all the element nodes in the document form part of the nodeset that might be returned.

The remainder of the location path is `child::SalesReport/child::Company` and (given that the child axis is operating and so we are looking for element nodes) this refines the resulting nodeset. The node test of the first location step `SalesReport` returns a nodeset, each node in which is then used as the context node for any following location step. The first location step is separated from the second, which is `Company`, by the forward slash separator. The nodeset resulting from the application of the first location step is processed, with each member successively being treated as context node, so that only element nodes which represent a `<Company>` element which is the child of a node representing a `<SalesReport>` element, which is itself the child of the root node, can be returned.

If there were a third location step, then the node set which would otherwise be returned from the second location step is used as the context node(s) when the third location step is evaluated.

In our XML document, we find that only one element node represents an element, whose name is `Company`, and which is a child of an element node, whose name is `SalesReport`, and which is itself a child of the root node. That element node representing a `<Company>` element has a text node containing the text "`XMML.com`" in our example.

In our example, there is no predicate. If our XPath location path had included a predicate like this: `/child::SalesReport/child::Company[position()=1]`, the returned nodeset would still have contained the node representing one `Company` element, since the only `Company` element in our document is in position 1.

However, if the XPath location path had included a different predicate like this: `/child::SalesReport/child::Company[position()=2]`, then an empty nodeset would have been returned since there is no node representing a `<Company>` element in position 2.

A similar XPath location path but with a different second location step: `/child::SalesReport/child::Sales[position()=2]`, would have selected the node representing the `<Sales>` element which has a `Region` attribute with value of "`NA`".

To reinforce understanding of how this works, let's step through this location path. The context node is first set to the root node, represented by the forward slash. The location path is `child::SalesReport/child::Sales`. The first location step selects all element nodes that represent a `<SalesReport>` element that is a child of the root node. That initial nodeset includes only one node. That node in the initial nodeset is used as the context node when the second of the two location steps is evaluated to provide another initial nodeset. The location path (before the predicate is applied) selects all nodes that represent `<Sales>` elements, which are also children of a node which represents a `<SalesReport>` element, which is itself a child of the root node. In our document there are three such element nodes representing three `<Sales>` elements and so satisfying the node test. So, at this stage, our possible returned nodeset contains three nodes.

However, the predicate `[position()=2]` further filters that nodeset. Only one of those three nodes satisfies the condition imposed by the predicate, which is the node in position 2. This node represents the `<Sales>` element whose `Region` attribute has the value "`NA`".

To summarize how XPath works:

- The **context node** defines the starting point for evaluation of the XPath location path, which may consist of one or more location steps
- The **axis** defines the direction that is taken through the hierarchical structure, given the context node. Initially the nodeset which would be returned is all nodes of the principal node type for the given axis and starting point
- The **node test** refines or filters the nodeset, excluding nodes from it which do not pass the node test
- The **predicate**(s), if present, further refines the nodeset which exists after application of the context node, axis and node test(s)
- After the first location step is processed, the nodeset produced from the location path is returned to the application, unless there are more location steps in the location path, in which case each node in that initial nodeset is used as the context node for the next location step

XPath Expressions and Location Paths

A location path is the most important type of XPath expression and is the focus of much of this chapter. A location path selects a nodeset relative to the context node in the XPath data model representation of a source XML document.

Location steps in a location path are separated by a forward slash. The following location path:

```
/child::chapters/child::appendices/child::appendix[attribute::name="A"]
```

consists of three location steps. The first two location steps have no predicate (remember that predicates are an optional part of a location step) whereas the third location step has a predicate `[attribute::name="A"]` that selects the node(s) representing an `<appendix>` element only if it also has a name attribute with the value of "`A`". Each of the element nodes representing an `<appendix>` element is, in succession, the context node and the predicate `[attribute::name="A"]` is evaluated in relation to those respective context nodes.

So far we have considered location paths that, when evaluated, yield a nodeset as a result. However, an XPath expression may be evaluated, as appropriate, to yield one of four types of object:

- Nodeset (an unordered collection of nodes without duplicates)
- Boolean (`true` or `false`)
- Number (a floating-point number)
- String (a sequence of Unicode characters)

A location path is a special form of XPath expression that returns only a nodeset.

Context in XPath

Up to this point, we have referred imprecisely to context in XPath without defining it explicitly, while focusing on the notion of the context node. However, context in XPath is actually made up of five parts of which the context node is only one. The five parts of XPath context are:

- A node (the context node)
- A pair of non-zero positive integers (the context position and the context size)
- A set of variable bindings
- A function library
- The set of namespace declarations in scope for the expression

The context node is of pivotal importance – all the other parts of the XPath context are defined in relationship to the context node.

The context position and context size are of particular relevance when one or more predicates exist within a location path. The context position is counted from 1 (not zero as in some languages). The context position is always less than or equal to the context size.

For an XPath expression, used as a predicate in a location step, the context position is the position of the context node in the nodeset selected prior to the predicate being evaluated. The context position determines the value returned by the `position()` function.

For example, in the XPath representation of the source XML document used early in the chapter, if the context node represented the `<Sales>` element with attribute value of `EU`, then the context position would be `1`. Since there are three `<Sales>` elements, the context size would be `3`.

The variable bindings consist of a mapping from variable names to variable values. The function library consists of a mapping from function names to functions. All XPath implementations must support a core function library, which is described later in the chapter.

For the examples of XPath in this chapter, the set of namespace declarations is an empty set, since no namespace declarations are present in the XML documents being represented in the XPath data model.However, where one or more namespace declarations exist within a source XML document then the namespace declarations represent a mapping from the prefixes to namespace URIs.

XPath Syntax

XPath syntax is not based on XML. The syntax that XML employs, if it were used in XPath, would not allow XPath expressions or location paths to be included in URIs, or in the attributes of XML elements. If, for example, the syntax of XPath were based on XML, we would find errors being generated if XPath elements were present within the attribute values of XML elements. Hence, a non-XML syntax is required to be used in XPath.

In some XPath expressions we may find predicates such as `[position() > 1]`. For example, in our sample document we might wish to choose the second and third `<Sales>` elements, so we would use this predicate as follows:

```
<xsl:value-of select="/SalesReport/Sales[position() > 1]" />
```

When literal strings occur within XPath location paths, they are delimited by pairs of single or double quotes. Similarly, the XML attributes, which may contain such location paths, are also delimited by single or double quotes. There are two solutions for avoiding the potential problems that may result. The first option is to use single quotes to delimit the XML attribute and double quotes to delimit the string within the XPath location path (or vice versa). It doesn't matter what we use single or double quotes for – the important thing is that we use a different type of quote for the XML attribute and for a string contained in a location path. The second option is to escape the quotation characters used to delimit the literal string contained in the location path. As a reminder, the escaped version of a double quotation mark is `"` and the escaped version of a single quotation mark is `'`. Except with built-in entities, you will have to define entities like these within the application using them.

XPath Axes

As mentioned earlier in the chapter, XPath has 13 axes:

- **Child** – The child axis contains the child or children of a context node. Note that attribute nodes and namespace nodes are not children of the element nodes to which they relate (although they have element node parents). Therefore, the child axis never returns any attribute or namespace nodes in the returned nodeset.

- **Parent** – The parent axis consists of the node that is the parent of the context node, if such a parent node exists. Of course, when the root node of the document is the context node it has no parent.
- **Descendant** – The descendant axis contains the descendants of the context node. Descendants of a node are its children and its children's children and so on, so while the child axis is part of the descendant axis, the reverse is not generally true; not all descendant nodes are child nodes. The descendant axis never contains attribute or namespace nodes.
- **Ancestor** – The ancestor axis consists of the ancestors of the context node. The ancestors of the context node consist of the parent of the context node and the parent's parent and so on. The ancestor axis will always include the root node, unless the context node is the root node. As mentioned previously, the root node has no parent node and therefore has no ancestor nodes.
- **Descendant-or-self** – The descendant-or-self axis includes the nodes on the descendant axis together with the context node itself.
- **Ancestor-or-self** – The ancestor-or-self axis includes the nodes on the ancestor axis together with the context node itself.
- **Following-sibling** – The following-sibling axis contains all the following siblings of the context node. If the context node is an attribute node or namespace node, the following-sibling axis is always empty. If an element node has multiple attributes, be careful to remember that for attribute nodes the following-sibling axis is empty. In our first example, if the context node were the node representing the `<Sales>` element with attribute of value `"EU"`, the nodeset returned from the following-sibling axis (if not otherwise further filtered) would contain two element nodes which represent the `<Sales>` elements whose attributes were of the value `"NA"` and `"AU"`.
- **Preceding-sibling** – The preceding-sibling axis contains all the preceding siblings of the context node. If the context node is an attribute node or namespace node then, as mentioned for the following-sibling axis, the preceding-sibling axis is empty. If the context node were the element node in position 3 from our first example, the preceding-sibling axis would (provided there was no other filtering of the nodeset) return a nodeset containing two element nodes whose attribute values would be `"EU"` and `"NA"`.
- **Following** – The following axis contains all nodes in the same document as the context node that are after the context node in document order, excluding any descendants and excluding attribute nodes and namespace nodes. Be careful not to confuse the following-sibling axis with the following axis.
- **Preceding** – The preceding axis contains all nodes in the same document as the context node that are before the context node in document order, excluding any ancestors and excluding attribute nodes and namespace nodes. Be careful to distinguish the preceding-sibling axis from the preceding axis.
- **Attribute** – The attribute axis contains the attributes of the context node. The attribute axis will be empty unless the context node is an element.
- **Namespace** – The namespace axis contains the namespace nodes of the context node. The namespace axis will be empty unless the context node is an element.
- **Self** – The self axis contains only the context node.

It may be helpful to realize that together the five axes: ancestor, descendant, self, following, and preceding do not overlap and together reference all nodes in a document, in the same way that North, South, here, East and West are sufficient (in theory!) to direct a person to any given street address.

An XPath axis is either a **forward** axis or a **reverse** axis. An axis that only ever contains the context node, or nodes that are after the context node in document order, is a forward axis. An axis that only ever contains the context node together with nodes that are before it in document order, or nodes that are before the context node in document order, is a reverse axis.

The forward axes are:

- Child
- Parent
- Descendant
- Descendant-or-self
- Following-sibling
- Following
- Attribute
- Namespace
- Self

The reverse axes are:

- Ancestor
- Ancestor-or-self
- Preceding-sibling
- Preceding

The XPath specification implies that the context node is both in a forward and reverse axis. In practice this inconsistency is of little importance since the context node itself, chosen in the self axis, is always a single node.

The importance of understanding whether an axis is a forward or reverse axis comes when evaluating the proximity position using the `position()` function, for example. The proximity position of a member of a nodeset with respect to an axis, is defined to be the position of the node in the nodeset ordered in document order if the axis is a forward axis, and ordered in reverse document order if the axis is a reverse axis.

XPath Functions

You may recall that we mentioned earlier that XPath included some basic facilities for manipulation of Booleans, numbers, and strings. Those facilities are contained in the core function library, which is provided by conforming processors.

A full discussion of XPath functions would require a very lengthy chapter, so here we provide an overview of the XPath functions rather than an exhaustive treatment of them. For a full description of the functions available in XPath, see the Wrox Press book "XSLT Programmer's Reference, 2nd Edition", by Michael Kay (ISBN 1-861005-06-7).

For a function in the core XPath function library the arguments of a function and the result returned by the function may be of four types:

- Nodeset
- Boolean
- Number
- String

XSLT and XPointer define additional functions that operate on the four basic types just listed. However, both XSLT and XPointer also operate on additional data types, which are defined in the XSLT and XPointer specifications. Other specifications, of which XQuery will likely be a prominent example, are free to add their own data types.

Nodeset Functions

We have already seen some of the XPath functions that operate on nodesets. The `position()` and `last()` functions are examples which we have seen in earlier examples.

- **count()** – The `count()` function takes a nodeset as its argument and returns the number of nodes present in the nodeset.
- **id()** – The `id()` function returns a nodeset which contains the node or nodes with a given `ID` attribute.
- **last()** – The `last()` function returns the value of the context size.
- **local-name()** – The `local-name()` function returns the local part of the name of a node.
- **name()** – The `name()` function returns a QName that represents the name of a node. Typically, this will be the name of the node in the source XML document, including a prefix if present.
- **namespace-uri()** – The `namespace-uri()` function returns a string representing the namespace URI in the expanded name of the node.
- **position()** – The `position()` function returns the value of the context position.

Boolean Functions

- **boolean()** – The `boolean()` function takes its argument and converts it to a Boolean value. Any argument may be converted to a Boolean value. When the argument is a number, then it is converted to the Boolean value `false` if it is zero, otherwise it evaluates to `true`. If the argument is a string, then the string is converted to the Boolean value `false` if it is of zero length, otherwise it is evaluated as `true`. If the argument is a nodeset, an empty nodeset is evaluated to `false`; a nodeset that is not empty is evaluated as `true`.

  Typically the `boolean()` function will be called automatically when needed. However, it can be called explicitly to force the conversion of its argument to Boolean.
- **false()** – The `false()` function returns the Boolean value `false`.
- **lang()** – The `lang()` function returns a Boolean value which tests whether the language of the context node, as defined by the `xml:lang` attribute, is in accordance with the language supplied as an argument.

- **not()** – The `not()` function returns the negation of its argument. If the argument is true, then the `not()` function returns `false`, and vice-versa.
- **true()** – The `true()` function returns the Boolean value `true`.

Number Functions

- **ceiling()** – The `ceiling()` function returns the smallest integer value which is equal to or greater than the argument of the function. In other words, a non-integer number is rounded up to the next integer value.
- **floor()** – The `floor()` function accepts a single numeric argument and returns the largest integer less than or equal to the argument of the function. In other words, a non-integer number is rounded down to the next lower integer value.
- **number()** – The `number()` function converts its argument to a number.
- **round()** – The `round()` function returns the integer closest to the numeric value of the argument.
- **sum()** – The `sum()` function adds a series of numbers supplied as a nodeset.

String Functions

- **concat()** – The `concat()` function takes two or more string arguments (or arguments which are converted to string) and concatenates the string arguments in sequence. The function call `concat('Hello', 'World!')` would yield the result string "Hello World!" (A single concatenated string, rather than two separate strings.)
- **contains()** – The `contains()` function tests whether one string value contains another string value as a sub string. For example, the function call `contains('concatenate', 'cat')` would return `True` since the string `"cat"` is present as a sub string within the string `"concatenate"`.
- **normalize-space()** – The `normalize-space()` function removes leading and trailing whitespace from a string, and also removes extraneous whitespace within a string by converting any sequences of whitespace within a string to a single-space character.
- **starts-with()** – The `starts-with()` function determines whether one string starts with another string.
- **string()** – The `string()` function converts its argument to a string.
- **string-length()** – The `string-length()` function returns the length of a string, or in other words, the number of characters in a string.
- **substring()** – The `substring()` function returns part of a string value, determined by numeric arguments describing the sub string selected. For example, the function `substring('Christmas', 1, 6)` would return the sub string `'Christ'`.
- **substring-after()** – The `substring-after()` function returns part of a string that occurs after the (first) occurrence of a specified sub string. For example, the function `substring-after('impair', 'im')` would return the string `"pair"`.
- **substring-before()** – The `substring-before()` function returns part of a string argument which occurs before the (first) occurrence of a specified sub string. For example, the function `substring-before('impartial', 'ial')` returns `"impart"`.

- **translate()** – The `translate()` function takes a string and two characters or sequences of characters as arguments and replaces characters within the string by replacing characters listed in the first sequence of characters by the equivalent characters in the second sequence of characters. For example, the `translate()` function could be used to convert a string to lowercase by using the following: `translate('XHTML', 'ABCDEFGHIJKLMNOPQRSTUVWXYZ', 'abcdefghijklmnopqrstuvwxyz')`.

Variations in XPath Syntax

XPath has two types of syntax in which XPath expressions can be expressed: **unabbreviated syntax** and **abbreviated syntax**. All XPath expressions can be expressed in unabbreviated syntax. Many common XPath expressions, or location paths, can be expressed in abbreviated syntax, but not all, so from time to time you may find that you have to use unabbreviated syntax. .

In addition to the distinction between unabbreviated syntax and abbreviated syntax, XPath also defines **relative location paths** and **absolute location paths**. Absolute location paths may be considered a special case of relative location paths – a special case where the context node refers to the root node of the XML document being represented in the XPath data model as the starting point of the location path.

With complex location paths, unabbreviated location paths can become quite lengthy. Since those same location paths may need to be included within the values of attributes of XSLT elements it makes a lot of sense, in terms of readability and debugging, to have a more concise syntax to express the more commonly used location paths or expressions, which is why there is an abbreviated syntax.

In the sections that follow, we will consider each of these forms of syntax in turn and give examples of each syntax form, thereby reinforcing some of the ideas introduced earlier in the chapter.

As well as discussing the meaning of the example location paths in an abstract way, we will also use the following example file to enable us to test our understanding of XPath location paths as we read. The example source XML is called `XPathLocPaths.xml`:

```
<?xml version='1.0'?>
<!-- An example XML representation of the book Professional XML, 2nd Ed. -->

<book>
   <title>Professional XML, 2nd Edition</title>

   <chapters>
      <chapter number="1" title="Introducing XML"></chapter>
      <chapter number="2" title="Basic XML Syntax">
         <section number="1">
            <paragraph number="1">
               First paragraph in Section 1 of Chapter 2.
            </paragraph>
            <paragraph number="2">
               Second paragraph in Section 1 of Chapter 2.
            </paragraph>
            <paragraph number="3">
               Third paragraph in Section 1 of Chapter 2.
            </paragraph>
            <paragraph number="4">
               Fourth paragraph in Section 1 of Chapter 2.
```

```
            </paragraph>
         </section>
         <section number="2">
            <paragraph number="1">
               First paragraph in Section 2 of Chapter 2.
            </paragraph>
            <paragraph number="2">
               Second paragraph in Section 2 of Chapter 2.
            </paragraph>
            <paragraph number="3">
               Third paragraph in Section 2 of Chapter 2.
            </paragraph>
            <paragraph number="4">
               Fourth paragraph in Section 2 of Chapter 2.
            </paragraph>
            <paragraph number="5">
               Fifth paragraph in Section 2 of Chapter 2.
            </paragraph>
         </section>
         <section number="3"></section>
      </chapter>
      <chapter number="3" title="Advanced XML Syntax"></chapter>
      <chapter number="4" title="InfoSet"></chapter>
      <chapter number="5" title="Validating XML - DTDs"></chapter>
      <chapter number="6" title="Introducing XML Schemas"></chapter>
      <!-- Many other chapters would in real life be listed here. -->
   </chapters>

   <appendices>
      <!-- The appendices listed here are for example purposes only. -->
      <appendix name="A">Appendix A</appendix>
      <appendix name="B">Appendix B</appendix>
      <appendix name="C">Appendix C</appendix>
      <appendix name="D">Appendix D</appendix>
      <appendix name="E">Appendix E</appendix>
      <appendix name="F">Appendix F</appendix>
   </appendices>
</book>
```

Unabbreviated Relative Location Paths

In this section, we will illustrate with a number of example XPath expressions, the unabbreviated syntax for relative location paths. For each we will give a general definition for the expression and then, using specific context nodes in the `XPathLocPaths.xml` example document, we will describe the nodeset that would result when the XPath expression is processed with such a context node.

The context for the relative location paths, when XPath is used with XSLT, will be determined by the structure of the XSLT stylesheet. In the examples that follow, we will simply state what the context node is, rather than using XSLT code to produce a particular context.

So, let's move on and start looking at the examples of XPath unabbreviated relative location paths.

child::paragraph

This expression selects the <paragraph> children of the context node. In our example file, if the context node were the <book> element node then an empty nodeset would be returned, because the <book> element has no child <paragraph> elements. If, however, the context node was the <section> element with the number attribute having the value of "1" in chapter 2 then a nodeset containing four element nodes representing <paragraph> elements would be returned. If the context node were the element node representing the <section> element with a number attribute of value "2" then the nodeset would contain five element nodes.

child::*

The expression child::* selects all element node children of the context node. The node test * selects all nodes of the principal node type for the axis. For the child axis the principal node type is the element node. If the context node has children other than element nodes, then those are not included within the nodeset. If the context node represented the <book> element, the nodeset would contain the element nodes which represent the <title>, <chapter>, and <appendix> elements. Remember, that only children, not descendants in general, are included in the nodeset.

child::text()

The above expression will select all text node children of the context node. In our example document, if the context node were the node representing the <book> element, an empty nodeset would be returned. If the context node was the node representing the <paragraph> number 1 in section number 2 of the chapter number 2, then a nodeset consisting of one text node with the string value "First paragraph in Section 2 of Chapter 2." would be returned.

child::node()

Now the expression will select *all* node children of the context node. Note that this differs from child::* which selects only element nodes within the nodeset, whereas child::node() will also include text nodes, comment nodes and processing instruction nodes, but not namespace or attribute nodes.

attribute::number

The attribute::number expression returns the number attribute node of the context node. Be careful to distinguish this type of location path (which selects an attribute node) from examples that you will see later, which select an element node based on attributes it may have. In our sample XML source document, if the context node were the node representing either a <paragraph>, <section>, or <chapter> element node then the node representing the number attribute would be returned in the nodeset. Otherwise, in our example source document, an empty nodeset would be returned since only <chapter>, <section> and <paragraph> elements have a number attribute.

attribute::*

Here, the expression returns all attribute nodes of the context node. The node test * selects all nodes of the **principal node type** for the axis. For the attribute axis the principal node type is the attribute node. If the context node were the node representing the <chapter> element for Chapter 1 then a nodeset would be returned which would contain two attribute nodes: those nodes representing the number and title attributes related to Chapter 1.

descendant::paragraph

This location path will select all <paragraph> elements that are descendants of the context node. In our sample document, if the context node were the node representing either the <book> element or the <chapters> element, we would retrieve a nodeset containing a total of nine nodes, one node for each of the <paragraph> elements in our document. If, however, our context node were the node representing the <section> element for Section 2 of Chapter 2, a nodeset containing five nodes representing <paragraph> elements would be returned. If the context node were the node representing the <appendix> element, an empty nodeset would be returned.

ancestor-or-self::chapter

The `ancestor-or-self::chapter` location path selects the element node(s) representing ancestors of the context node and if the context node is a `chapter` element, it will also be returned. In our example document, if the context node were the node representing the <chapters> element, this would equate to an empty node set (since the context node is neither a <chapter> element nor does it have any <chapter> element nodes as ancestors). If, however, our context node were a node representing a <section> element, then it would return a nodeset containing one element node, which would represent the <chapter> element within which the <section> element is contained.

descendant-or-self::section

Now our location path selects the node representing the <section> element descendants of the context node and, if the context node represents a <section> element, includes the context node as well. In our sample document, if the context node represented the <chapter> element for Chapter 2 a nodeset would be returned containing three nodes, representing the three <section> elements which are children of the <chapter> element for Chapter 2. If, however, the context node represented the <chapter> element for Chapter 3 it would return an empty nodeset, since our source document, as written, contains no <section> elements within Chapter 3. If the context node were the node representing the <chapters> element we would again have a returned nodeset containing three nodes including all nodes in the document representing <section> elements.

self::paragraph

The `self::paragraph` location path selects the context node if it represents a <paragraph> element if not, it will return an empty nodeset.

preceding-sibling::chapter

The `preceding-sibling::chapter` location path selects any preceding siblings of the context node which are also nodes representing `<chapter>` elements. In our sample document if the context node were an element node representing a `<section>` element, an empty set would be returned since the context node has no preceding sibling nodes that represent `<chapter>` elements. However, if the context node were the element node which represents the `<chapter>` element for Chapter 6, then the location path would return a nodeset containing five elements nodes, one each for Chapters 1 to 5.

preceding::chapter

The `preceding::chapter` location path selects any chapter elements which precede the context node in document order, but excluding the node's own ancestors. In our sample document if the context node were an element node representing a `<section>` element, a nodeset would be returned containing one element node representing the `<chapter>` element for Chapter 1. Let's take a moment to examine why. The context node has no preceding sibling nodes that represent `<chapter>` elements, but we are using the preceding axis (not the preceding-sibling axis). While the element node returned is not a sibling (and therefore not present in the preceding-sibling axis), it does precede in document order the element nodes representing `<section>` elements, which are all present in Chapter 2 and therefore, that one element node is present in the returned nodeset.

Using More Complex Paths

So far, the examples shown have been simple ones containing just a single location step. However as stated earlier, XPath location paths may include more than one location step. In the examples that follow we will illustrate some examples using multiple location steps, describing in abstract terms the meaning of those paths and by reference to our example source document, illustrating the nodesets which are produced.

child::chapter/descendant::paragraph

Here, the location path includes two location steps. It selects the nodes that represent the `<paragraph>` element descendants of the `<chapter>` element children of the context node. If the context node represented the `<chapters>` element in our sample document, it would return a nodeset containing nine element nodes representing the `<paragraph>` elements contained within Chapter 2. This is because the `<chapter>` element is a child of the `<chapters>` element and nine element nodes representing `<paragraph>` elements are descendants (but not children) of the node representing a `<chapter>` element.

Looking at location paths with multiple locations steps, we can read the location path left-to-right or right-to-left. Use whichever of the approaches you find most helpful to visualize which nodes are produced.

Taking the `child::chapter/descendant::paragraph` location path, we can therefore read it as "Look for all the `<chapter>` element nodes which are children of the context node, and for each of these, return any element nodes representing `<paragraph>` elements which are their descendants".

child::chapter/descendant::paragraph (cont'd)

If we adopt the right-to-left approach, the location path could be translated as, "Include all element nodes which represent <paragraph> elements and that are descendants of any element nodes which represent <chapter> elements, and which are children of the context node".

Note that these approaches do not necessarily represent the approach which an XPath or XSLT processor might use, they are offered simply as an aid for you to visualize which nodes will be included in the returned nodeset.

child::*/child::paragraph

Here again we have a multiple location step path. It selects all `paragraph` grandchildren of the context node. In our example document if the context node represented the <chapters> elements, it would return an empty nodeset, because the <chapters> element node has no children element nodes which themselves have nodes which represent <paragraph> element children. However, if the context node were the <chapter> element node for Chapter 2, it would return a nodeset containing nine `paragraph` nodes, namely the nodes representing the <paragraph> element children of the three <section> element node children of the context node. Of course, as the third <section> element node has no <paragraph> children, it doesn't add any elements to the result set.

Predicates

We mentioned earlier in the chapter that location paths consisted of an axis, a nodeset and an optional predicate. Up to now, I have shown you in examples of location paths that had an axis and nodeset but no predicate. So let's take a look at a few examples of unabbreviated relative location paths using predicates.

child::paragraph[position()=1]

The predicate is the code contained in square brackets, and allows us to select the node representing the first <paragraph> element child of the context node by use of the `position()` function. In our sample document, if the context node represented the first <section> element node in chapter 2, then the returned nodeset would contain just the <paragraph> element node with the text node child "`First Paragraph in Section 1 of Chapter 2.`"

child::paragraph[position()=last()]

This location path selects the node that represents the last <paragraph> element child of the context node. The predicate uses the function `position()` in combination with `last()` to return the position of the last <paragraph> element node child of the context node. In our example document, if the context node were the node representing the first <section> element in Chapter 2 then the node representing the fourth <paragraph> element would be returned, since it is last. However, if the context node were the node representing the second <section> element, then the node returned would be the node representing the fifth <paragraph> element, since in that section it is last.

child::paragraph[position()=last()-1]

The `child::paragraph[position()=last()-1]` location path is similar, but will return the last but one <paragraph> element child of the context node.

preceding::chapter[attribute::number]

The preceding::chapter[attribute::number] location path will return a nodeset containing element nodes that represent <chapter> elements that also possess a number attribute. If the context node were one of the element nodes representing a <section> element, a node set returning the element node that represents Chapter 1 would be returned since it precedes, in document order, the element node representing the <section> elements (all of which are in Chapter 2 in our example document) and it also possesses a number attribute.

child::*/child::*[attribute::name]

The child::*/child::*[attribute::name] location path returns a nodeset containing nodes which are grandchildren of the element node and which also possess a name attribute. If, in our example document, the context node were the node representing the <book> element the returned nodeset would contain six element nodes representing each of the six <appendix> nodes, since each is an element grandchild of the node representing the <book> element and also possesses a name attribute. The returned nodeset would not include the nodes representing the <chapter> elements since, although these are element grandchildren of the node representing the <book> element, they do not possess a name attribute.

Predicates Returning Multiple Nodes

The predicates you have seen so far in this section which use XPath functions have all chosen a single node for inclusion in the returned nodeset; for example, [position()=1]. However, XPath functions also allow the returned nodeset defined by an XPath function in a predicate to contain more than one node.

child::paragraph[position()>1]

Here a nodeset is implied which may contain more than one <paragraph> element node, depending on the number of matching <paragraph> element nodes. In essence, all but the first <paragraph> element node children of the context node are selected. Thus if there are more than two matching <paragraph> element nodes, the returned nodeset will have more than one contained node. Looking again at our sample document, with the context node as the first <section> element node in Chapter 2, then there are four child <paragraph> element nodes which match the child::paragraph axis and nodeset. The predicate [position()>1] excludes the <paragraph> element node at position 1, meaning that the remaining three <paragraph> element nodes make up the returned nodeset.

Similarly, in our sample document, if the context node were the node representing Section 2 of Chapter 2, then four nodes would be returned in the nodeset, which are all nodes representing <paragraph> children with the exception of the node in position 1.

In our example source document the position happens to be the same as the number attribute of the paragraphs selected. However, that is simply coincidental. For example, if our location path were child::appendix[position() > 1], assuming that the context node was the node representing the <appendices> element, the returned nodeset would contain five nodes – the nodes representing Appendices B, C, D, E and F.

following-sibling::chapter[position()=1]

Here our location path selects the next `<chapter>` sibling of the context node. Thus, in our example document, if the context node were representing the `<chapter>` element for Chapter 1, then the element node which is returned in the nodeset would be the `<chapter>` element node whose `number` attribute has the value of "2". Similarly, if Chapter 2 were the context node, the returned nodeset would contain one `<chapter>` element node whose number attribute would have the value of "3". Remember that it is document order, which determines the following-sibling, rather than any attribute that an element may have.

Again it is not the value of the `number` attribute that determines the node returned in the nodeset. For example, if our location path is `following-sibling::appendix[position()=1]`we would find, assuming our context node was the node representing Appendix C, that the node returned in the nodeset would be the node representing Appendix D, since that is the following sibling in document order in position 1 for the following-sibling axis.

preceding-sibling::chapter[position()=1]

The `preceding-sibling::chapter[position()=1]` returns the previous `<chapter>` element node sibling of the context node – it is the first sibling node encountered when travelling in reverse document order. Thus in our example document if the context node represented the `<chapter>` element whose number attribute had the value of "3", the returned nodeset would contain the element node representing the `<chapter>` element whose number attribute has the value of "2". Again, note that it is document order (in this example, reverse document order) that determines whether or not a node is in the nodeset. Remember, too, that the preceding-sibling axis is a reverse axis and that the sibling node returned is the first one encountered when moving in reverse document order.

Note that the `position()` function's meaning is relative to the axis involved it will have a different effect here to, say, its meaning when used with the following-sibling or child axes. When the preceding-sibling axis is applicable then `position()` returns element nodes met when going *backwards* through the sibling nodes. It may help to return to the notion of street directions and think of how the instruction "turn right" ends with heading East if we were originally on the North axis but if we were originally on a South axis, that same instruction of "turn right" would result in heading West.

child::chapters/child::chapter[position()=2]/child::section[position()=2]

This location path adds a third location step and contains two predicates. As you can see, such unabbreviated relative location paths can become fairly long. The location path selects the node representing the second `<section>` element child that is the child of the second `<chapter>` element node that is a child of the `<chapters>` element node. In our example document, if the context node represented the `<book>` element then the location path would return a nodeset containing the second `<section>` element of Chapter 2. If the context node were anything other than the node representing the `<book>` element then an empty nodeset would be returned, since no other nodes have great-grandchildren which represent `<section>` elements.

As well as selecting element nodes based on their position we can also select them based on the type or value of their attributes. First, let's look at selecting an element on the basis of the presence of a particular type of attribute.

child::chapter[attribute::number]

This location path will select all element nodes that represent `<chapter>` elements, which are children of the context node and which possess a `number` attribute. In our example document, if the context node represented the `<chapters>` element, then there are six element nodes, which represent `<chapter>` elements that are children of the context node. All six of those children happen to possess a `number` attribute; therefore, all six element nodes are included in the nodeset. If there were an element node representing a `<chapter>` element which was a child of the node representing the `<chapters>` element, but which did not possess a `number` attribute, then it would be excluded from the nodeset.

child::chapter[attribute::number][position()=3]

Here we see a combination of two predicates being used to make a more precise selection of element nodes than the preceding example, with the additional predicate `[position()=3]` refining the selection further. Our document has six nodes representing `<chapter>` elements which have a `number` attribute, but only one of those six nodes is in position 3. Therefore, when applied to our example document with the node representing the `<chapters>` node as context node, the returned nodeset is reduced from six `<chapter>` element nodes to just the element node representing the `<chapter>` element node in the third position in document order.

child::chapter[attribute::title="Introducing XML Schemas"]

This location path demonstrates the use of a predicate to choose elements based on the presence of an attribute of a particular *value* for the element. In our example document, if the context node were the node representing the `<chapters>` element, then there are six child nodes representing `<chapter>` elements. Each of those `<chapter>` elements has an attribute of type `title`, therefore all six `<chapter>` element nodes are included within the nodeset selected by the location step `child::chapter`, but only one of those has a `title` attribute with a value as specified in the predicate. Therefore, only one `<chapter>` element node is present after the predicate is applied. Remember, this location path selects an element node based on the value of one of its attributes; it does not select the attribute itself. The location path for selecting an attribute node was illustrated earlier in this section.

Predicate Order

We can combine predicates in different orders. Typically, that will mean selecting different nodes to be returned in the nodeset. For example, what if we reverse the order of the predicates used in the second to last example in the previous section

child::chapter[position()=3][attribute::number]

Here, the new location path selects the `<chapter>` element child of the context node which is in position 3 and, if that third `<chapter>` element has an attribute node of type "`number`", then the node will be included in the returned nodeset. However, if that third `<chapter>` element node had no `number` attribute, then an empty nodeset would be returned. In our example, if the context node were the element node representing the `<chapters>` element then the third element node representing a `<chapter>` element would be selected. Since it does have a `number` attribute, it can be included in the returned nodeset.

Let's look at another usage of relative locations paths that, quite possibly, will at first glance look similar to the previous example.

child::chapter[child::title="Introducing XML Schemas"]

What will this path give us in the returned nodeset? Let's suppose our context node is the node representing the `<chapters>` element. There are six `<chapter>` element nodes as children. When we come to evaluate the predicate we need to be careful not to walk into a trap. One of the `<chapter>` elements has a title attribute with the value "`Introducing XML Schemas`" but there is no `<title>` element node that is a child of that or any of the other of the `<chapter>` element nodes. Remember that, in this case, the predicate refers to an element node called `<title>` whose string value is equal to "`Introducing XML Schemas` ". So, an empty nodeset is returned.

If we did want to choose the element node representing Chapter 6, we would need to modify the predicate from `[child::title=" Introducing XML Schemas"]` to `[attribute::title="Introducing XML Schemas"]`.

child::*[self::appendix][position()=last()]

This location path uses the first predicate to select the last `<appendix>` child of the context node. In our example document, if the context node was the node representing the `<appendices>` element, we would find that the returned nodeset contained one node representing the `<appendix>` element for Appendix F.

Having looked at a representative selection of examples using unabbreviated relative location paths, we'd now like to move on to look at some examples that use unabbreviated absolute location paths.

Unabbreviated Absolute Location Paths

In this section, we will briefly explain and illustrate the usage of unabbreviated syntax for absolute location paths. Remember that, like relative location paths, absolute location paths have a context and one or more location steps. Absolute location paths can be viewed as a special case of relative location paths – a special case where the context node refers to a location path that consistently begins at the root node.

All absolute location paths start with the forward slash character to indicate that they are absolute location paths.

A forward slash by itself selects the root node of the document containing the context node. If qualified by a relative location path, the nodeset returned is that which the relative location path would imply were the root node of the document the context node. Let's look at some examples.

/child::*

This location path selects all element nodes that are children of the root node. In a well-formed XML document there can be only one child element node of the root node – the node representing the document element. In our sample document, the returned nodeset would therefore only contain the node representing the `<book>` element. The node representing the comment would not be included in the nodeset since it is not an XPath element node. If, however, the location path had read `/child::node()`, then the comment node would have been included in the returned nodeset.

/descendant::paragraph

This unabbreviated absolute location path selects all the <paragraph> elements in the same document as the context node. In other words, it selects all the <paragraph> element nodes. In our sample document the returned nodeset would contain nine nodes representing <paragraph> element nodes.

/descendant::section/child::paragraph

This location path selects all the nodes representing <paragraph> elements that have a <section> element node parent. In our sample document, there are three <section> element nodes, which together have nine <paragraph> element nodes. So the returned nodeset would contain those nine <paragraph> element nodes. In our example document, coincidentally, this example and the previous one return the same nodeset, but that occurs solely because all the element nodes which represent <paragraph> elements are children of element nodes which represent <section> elements. If we also had <paragraph> elements within, for example, appendices which were not children of nodes representing <section> elements, then the location path `/descendant::paragraph` would have included those, whereas the location path `/descendant::section/child::paragraph` would not.

/descendant::chapter[position()=3]

Here, the returned nodeset contains the third <chapter> element node in the document. In our sample document, this will be the third <chapter> element node in document order, which in this case has a number attribute which also happens to have the value "3". The node included in the returned nodeset is not determined by the value of the number attribute but by the position of the node.

Abbreviated Relative Location Paths

The XPath location paths that we saw in the example at the beginning of this chapter were abbreviated relative location paths. In practice, abbreviated location paths are a much more succinct method of expressing a location path compared to the unabbreviated syntax. Within XSLT elements and in other usages of XPath such succinct syntax improves readability. Sometimes abbreviated location paths may be so short that you have to think carefully to understand their intent.

One of the most commonly used axes in location paths is the child axis. In the abbreviated syntax, the `child` keyword and double colon separator can be omitted: in effect, the default axis is the child axis. This gives us very succinct location paths when using the child axis, as shown in the following examples.

paragraph

The location path `paragraph` selects those element nodes that are children of the context node and represent <paragraph> elements. The unabbreviated equivalent location path is `child::paragraph`. In general, any named child elements of the context node can be selected by using the element name on its own as the location path.

The star location path can be used also:

```
*
```

All element nodes that are children of the context node, are selected. The unabbreviated equivalent location path is `child::*`.

```
text()
```

The above location path selects all text node children of the context node. The unabbreviated equivalent location path is `child::text()`.

```
.
```

The "." location path selects the context node. The unabbreviated equivalent location path is `self::node()`.

```
..
```

The ".." location path selects the parent of the context node. The equivalent unabbreviated location path is `parent::node()`.

Just as the child axis can be abbreviated, so too can the attribute axis by use of the `@` symbol, as shown in a number of the following examples.

```
@number
```

The location path `@number` selects the `number` attribute of the context node. If the context node has a `number` attribute the returned nodeset has one node contained in it. If the context node does not have a `number` attribute, then the returned nodeset is empty. The unabbreviated equivalent location path is `attribute::number`.

```
@*
```

The location path `@*` selects all the attributes of the context node. The unabbreviated equivalent location path is `attribute::*`.

```
..@number
```

Here, we are selecting the `number` attribute of the parent element of the context node. The equivalent unabbreviated location path is `parent::node()/attribute::number`. Be careful not to confuse this location path with `..[@number]` which selects the parent element if and only if it possesses a `number` attribute. The equivalent unabbreviated location path for the latter is `parent::node()[attribute::number]`.

```
paragraph[1]
```

Remember that the child axis is the default axis and that the predicate must be interpreted in the light of the applicable axis. The predicate here `[1]` implies the default `position()` function to select the first `<paragraph>` child node of the context node. The unabbreviated equivalent location path is `child::paragraph[position()=1]`.

paragraph[last()]

Now we see a similar form to select the last `<paragraph>` child element node of the context node. The unabbreviated equivalent location path is:
`child::paragraph[position()=last()]`.

paragraph[@number="2"]

This location path selects all the `<paragraph>` element children of the context node having a number attribute with value "2". The equivalent unabbreviated location path is:
`child::paragraph[attribute::number="2"]`.

paragraph[@type="confidential"][3]

The location path now selects the third node representing a `<paragraph>` element child of the context node having a `type` attribute of value "`confidential`". The equivalent unabbreviated location path is:
`child::paragraph[attribute::type="confidential"][position()=3]`.

paragraph[4][@security="confidential"]

This time we are selecting the node representing the fourth `<paragraph>` child of the context node if it has a security attribute with value of "`confidential`". The equivalent unabbreviated location path is:
`child::paragraph[position()=4][attribute::security="confidential"]`.

***/paragraph**

This path selects all grandchildren element nodes of the context node that also represent `<paragraph>` elements. The unabbreviated equivalent location path is:
`child::*/child::paragraph`.

chapter[title="Introducing XML Schemas"]

The location path here selects the `<chapter>` children of the context node having one or more `<title>` element children with string value equal to "`Introducing XML Schemas`". The equivalent unabbreviated location path is:
`child::chapter[child::title="Introducing XML Schemas"]`.

chapter/section[1]/paragraph[3]

The location path here selects the third `<paragraph>` element node that is a child of the first `<section>` element node that is a child of the `<chapter>` node that is a child of the context node. The unabbreviated equivalent location path is:
`child::chapter/child::section[position()=1]/child::paragraph[position()=3]`.

.//paragraph

The double slash notation here indicates use of `descendant-or-self::` rather than `child::`. In other words, the `//` notation selects not the default node type for the axis but all node types. The above line thus selects all the `<paragraph>` element nodes that are descendants of the context node. The equivalent unabbreviated location path is: `self::node()/descendant-or-self::node()/child::paragraph`.

chapter//paragraph

This location path selects the nodes that represent the `<paragraph>` element descendants of the `<chapter>` element children of the context node. The equivalent unabbreviated location path is: `child::chapter/descendant::paragraph`.

chapter[@number and @title]

The predicate `[@number and @title]` only allows `<chapter>` children of the context node that have both a `number` attribute and a `title` attribute into the resultset. The equivalent unabbreviated location path is: `child::chapter[attribute::number and attribute::title]`.

Having looked at relative location paths that use the abbreviated XPath syntax, we're ready to move on to briefly look at some examples of absolute location paths that use the abbreviated syntax.

Abbreviated Absolute Location Paths

The abbreviated absolute location path syntax has similarities with both the unabbreviated absolute location path syntax (all location paths begin with a forward slash representing the root node) and with the abbreviated relative location paths (the remainder of the syntax is identical to that in the abbreviated relative location path syntax).

/

The unabbreviated absolute location path syntax for the root node, the forward slash character, cannot realistically be abbreviated further and is the same in the abbreviated syntax as in the unabbreviated absolute location path syntax.

//paragraph

The `//paragraph` location path selects all `<paragraph>` nodes which are descendants of the root node. Thus the location path selects all `<paragraph>` element nodes in the document. The unabbreviated equivalent location path is `/descendant-or-self::paragraph`. In practice this is equivalent to `/descendant::paragraph`, since the root node cannot be a `<paragraph>` element node.

/book/chapter[2]/section[1]/paragraph[3]

The above abbreviated absolute location path selects the third paragraph of the first section of the second chapter of the <book> element, the <book> element being a child of the root node. The unabbreviated equivalent location path is:
`/child::book/child::chapter[position()=2]/child::section[position()=1]`

`/child::paragraph[position()=3]`. As can be seen, the abbreviated syntax is substantially shorter than the unabbreviated for location paths such as this.

//chapter/section

Looking at this location path, we see it selects all <section> nodes that have <chapter> nodes as a parent element (and which are descendants of the root node). In other words, it selects all <section> elements in the same document as the context node that have a <chapter> element parent. The unabbreviated equivalent location path is:
`/descendant-or-self::chapter/child::section`.

This is also functionally equivalent to:
`/descendant::chapter/child::section`, since the root node cannot be an element node representing a <chapter> element.

//chapter[@number="2"]

Here, we are selecting all <chapter> descendants of the root node with a number attribute with value "2". The equivalent unabbreviated location path is:
`/descendant-or-self::chapter[attribute::number="2"]`, or practically
`/descendant::chapter[attribute::number='2']`. Those two unabbreviated location paths are functionally equivalent since the root node cannot be an element node (and therefore cannot be an element node representing a <chapter> element).

XPath as a foundation for XSLT

You saw in our simple transformation of XML to HTML at the beginning of the chapter that we can use XPath expressions within our XSLT stylesheets in order to reliably and predictably produce a suitable HTML document from our XML source.

The use of XPath location paths in the <xsl:value-of> element, which we saw in the example at the beginning of the chapter, is a particularly common use.

XSLT Patterns

The syntax of XPath expressions has a subset that contains XSLT **patterns**. A location path pattern uses only the child or attribute axis. It is used in four settings in an XSLT document:

- In the `match` attribute of the <xsl:template> element
- In the `match` attribute of the <xsl:key> element
- In the `count` attribute of the <xsl:number> element
- In the `from` attribute of the <xsl:number> element

For our purposes, the first setting is the most important. An XSLT transformation is achieved by associating a pattern with an XSLT template. A pattern is matched against an element or the document root in the source XML document.

For example, most XSLT stylesheets would include an association of the root node with a particular XSLT template like this:

```
<xsl:template match="/">
```

This would create a result tree, whose structure is dependent on the content of that XSLT template and any other XSLT templates applied or called from it.

Here are some example XSLT patterns which would match one or more than one element in the source document, XPathLocPaths.xml used earlier in the chapter:

- / – Matches the root node
- * – Matches any element
- chapters/chapter – Matches any <chapter> element which has a <chapters> parent
- text() – Matches any text node

We can see that XSLT patterns correspond to XPath abbreviated syntax, described earlier in the chapter.

A location path pattern is a location path whose steps use only the child and attribute axes. This makes sense since for an <xsl:template> we would wish to define the template either with respect to an element (on the child axis) or an attribute (on the attribute axis).

XPath as a Foundation for XPointer

The XML Pointer language, XPointer, is intended as a provider of fragment identifiers for XML documents. Expressed more formally, XPointer is the fragment identifier language for resources whose type is one of text/xml, application/xml, text/xml-external-parsed-entity, or application/xml-external-parsed-entity. XPointer is currently at the Working Draft stage. The Working Draft of January 2001, current at the time of writing, is described at http://www.w3.org/TR/2001/WD-xptr-20010108. Updates to the Working Draft will be located at http://www.w3.org/TR/xptr.

XPointer is based on XPath. Conformant XPointer processing depends on XPath processing. XPointer provides a means of examining the hierarchical representation of an XML document and the choice of internal parts of that representation by means of selecting, for example, element types, attribute values, and character content.

XPointer has a number of extensions to XPath which allow XPointer to:

- Address points and ranges as well as whole nodes
- Locate information by string matching
- Use addressing expressions in URI references as fragment identifiers (after suitable escaping)

XPointer includes the notion of a **point**, which corresponds to the notion of a position in the Document Object Model Level 2. In XPointer, the term point is used to avoid confusion with the notion of a position in XPath. XPointer also adds the concept of a **range**, which is the information contained between a pair of end points.

In addition, XPointer includes the notion of a **location**, which corresponds to a generalization of the XPath concept of a node, but with the addition of points and ranges. Note carefully that an XPointer location must be distinguished from an XPath location path or location step.

XPointer's **location-set** concept corresponds to a generalization of the XPath concept of a nodeset but with the addition of points and ranges.

Detailed consideration of XPointer syntax is beyond the scope of this chapter but it may be of interest to see the similarities in syntax between XPath and XPointer.

If we have an XML code snippet such as the following:

```
<list ID="MyList">
   <item>First list item</item>
   <item>Second list item</item>
   <item>Third list item</item>
</list>
```

If we want to refer to what XPointer terms a singleton location-set, consisting of the second of the items within the `<list>` element, we would use the following XPointer:

```
xpointer(id('MyList')/item[1]/range-to(following-sibling::item[2]))
```

The syntax of XPointer formally incorporates, by reference, the syntax of XPath. Thus to understand XPointer fully it is also necessary to have a full understanding of XPath. Any syntax error in an XPointer will cause a conformant XPointer processor to refuse to process the syntactically incorrect XPointer. Therefore, careful generation of XPointers will likely prove to be a necessity.

The XPointer specification refers to what it terms **iterative selections**. If we ponder the manner in which XPath location paths are processed by generating a nodeset, which is successively filtered by further node tests and/or predicates, we will have a good picture of what XPointer iterative selections are about.

The Future for XPath

As was indicated at the beginning of the chapter, the context for XPath has changed significantly since the time that the XPath 1.0 Recommendation was issued in November 1999. Back in November 1999 the only fully developed XML-based technology that had dependencies on XPath was XSLT. It was appreciated that XPath would also provide a foundation for XPointer, but XPointer was then at a very early stage of development.

XPath 2.0

At the time of writing the first public Working Draft of the Requirements for XPath 2.0 had just been released by W3C. The text of the Working Draft may be accessed at http://www.w3.org/TR/2001/WD-xpath20req-20010214.

The latest version of the Requirements document will always be located at http://www.w3.org/TR/xpath20req. If it still refers to the first Working Draft of 14 February 2001, then no further Working Drafts of the Requirements document have been issued. To look for full Working Drafts of XPath 2.0 that are developed in the light of the XPath 2.0 Requirements document, visit http://www.w3.org/TR/ and look under the heading of "Working Drafts".

While XPath 1.0 does many things well and succinctly, problems or limitations have been found, for example in the handling of strings. It is likely that XPath 2.0 will facilitate string replacement, string padding and case conversion. In addition, when the XPath Recommendation was issued, the XML Schema specification was in its infancy and the needs of XML Schema could, at least for a time, be put to one side.

It is intended that the Data Model of XPath 2.0 will be expressed in terms of the XML Infoset (described at http://www.w3.org/TR/xml-infoset/, and in Chapter 4 of this book). Furthermore, it is intended that XPath 2.0, XSLT 2.0, and XQuery 1.0 should share a common data model, if possible. Given that both XSLT (currently) and XQuery (in the future) will make extensive use of XPath expressions there is much sense in that aim of a common data model.

The draft document envisages that the expression language of XSLT 2.0 will be XPath 2.0 plus XSLT extensions, and that the expression language of XQuery 1.0 will be XPath 2.0 plus XQuery extensions. Presumably, although it is not mentioned in the draft, the expression language of XPointer will continue to be built on XPath with extensions. The XSLT 2.0 Requirements draft is located at http://www.w3.org/TR/xslt20req.

It is envisaged that XPath 2.0 will add semantics which allow "for any" and "for all" comparisons, which are not possible with XPath 1.0. In addition, XPath 2.0 is likely to add intersection and difference functions to those available for nodesets in XPath 1.0.

It is also anticipated that XPath 1.0 restrictions on what may be included in location steps after a forward slash separating location steps, will be loosened to bring XPath into closer alignment with XPointer. It is likely also that use of unions and functions after the forward slash will be supported in XPath 2.0.

Further possible or likely changes in XPath 2.0 are described in the sections on XML Schema, Regular Expressions, and XQuery, which follow.

XPath and XML Schema

The W3C XML Schema specification, which is presently at Proposed Recommendation stage aims, in XML syntax, to describe the structure and constrain the contents of XML documents. As we have already seen in earlier chapters, XML Schema has similar aims to the Document Type Definitions described in the XML 1.0 Recommendation, but incorporates usage of XML namespaces and also extends the capabilities provided by DTDs.

Full discussion of XML Schema is beyond the scope of this chapter; it was described more fully in Chapter 6. XML Schema is mentioned here primarily to draw attention to the anticipated use of XPath expressions within XML Schema, for example in **identity-constraint definitions**.

XPath is one of the W3C technologies upon which XML Schema depends. Indeed, the first stated goal of the XPath 2.0 Requirements document is to simplify the manipulation of XML Schema-typed content.

The XPath 1.0 data model supports nodeset, Boolean, String, and Number data types. In XPath 2.0, it is anticipated that the XPath data model will be extended to provide support for at least some XML Schema primitive data types.

XPath and Regular Expressions

Regular Expressions provide a powerful means of specifying string pattern matching. They play an important role in the XML Schema Proposed Recommendation in specifying pattern facets (facets constrain the content of an XML document). The XPath 2.0 Requirements draft indicates that XPath 2.0 must support regular expressions using the regular expression notation defined in XML Schema Part 2, Datatypes.

The addition of regular expressions functionality can be expected to add substantially to the power and flexibility of XPath expressions.

XPath and XQuery

XQuery is the term used for the W3C XML Query Language in the first public Working Draft of XQuery, which was issued just as this chapter was being written (February 2001). The important inter-relationships between XPath 2.0 and XQuery 1.0 are indicated by the fact that the XPath 2.0 Requirements document is a joint effort of the XSL Working Group and the XQuery Working Group of the W3C. The XQuery 1.0 Working Draft is located at http://www.w3.org/TR/2001/WD-xquery-20010215. Future updates to the Working Draft can be located via http://www.w3.org/TR/xquery.

As the volume of information stored as XML, or accessible as XML (for example, having been retrieved from a relational database management system) increases, it becomes very important for there to be a usable and efficient query language for such XML-based information.

XQuery has a total of eight forms of expression, of which one is a path expression founded on the XPath data model and (slightly modified) syntax. More specifically, the requirements enunciated for XPath 2.0, discussed above, and the XQuery 1.0 Working Draft, both indicate that a common data model and syntax (slightly extended in XQuery) is in view. Therefore, a full understanding of XPath will become a very important foundation for the use of the forthcoming XQuery 1.0 query language.

At the time of writing, given that the XQuery specification is only at first public Working Draft stage, it is clear that many changes in detailed syntax are possible. Yet it is equally clear that mastery of XQuery is an important XML-based skill, which itself will be partially dependent on knowledge of and skills in using XPath, specifically the abbreviated form of XPath syntax. More information about XQuery can be found in Chapter 16.

Summary

In this chapter, we have covered a lot of ground. We have looked at the current implementation of XPath, XPath 1.0. In particular we have looked at the XPath Data Model and how XPath expressions and location paths work. In addition, using a substantial number of examples, we examined both the unabbreviated and abbreviated forms of XPath syntax.

Hitherto, practical use of XPath has been with XSLT. Recent W3C documents promise a much more extensive and growing use of XPath in or with XPointer 1.0, XML Schema 1.0, and XQuery 1.0.

9

Transforming XML

The nice thing about XML is that it is standard. As we've seen, if you conform to the XML Recommendation, you can generate data documents that may be processed by anyone else who uses XML. The bad thing about XML is the 'X' – it's extensible. Although that is also a virtue, it means that sooner or later you will have to change the format of your data (this is, of course, also a potential problem in any data format subject to version changes, but XML will **always** be subject to it). The content – the specific values of your elements and attributes – is still meaningful, but someone else orients it differently. Even XML applications that take the data directly to the user have to change formats, say, when they want to present an XML document as an HTML page. Transformation is the process of taking an XML document and turning it into a document in another form. Although the two may not be precisely equivalent (you might, for example, suppress some information in the process, or present some data that is derived from the original set), the data that appears in both documents is basically the same.

Happily, the XML community anticipated this need. The key is an XML vocabulary termed the **Extensible Stylesheet Language** (**XSL**). XSL properly takes in two specialized technologies: **XSL-Formatting Objects** (XSL-FO, http://www.w3.org/TR/xsl), and **XSL-Transformation** (XSLT, http://www/w3/org/TR/xslt).

XSL-FO is a page formatting language intended primarily for the visual presentation of XML – it is covered in detail in Chapter 20. XSLT, which is the focus of this chapter, is a language for specifying transformations of XML documents. XSLT lets you apply some rules contained into a **stylesheet** document to XML documents to generate a second document. The process of applying the rules to the source document is called a **transformation**. Most programmers are accustomed to writing sometimes lengthy code to read a file and generate some output. The code must be changed when either the source vocabulary or the processing rules change. XSLT, by contrast, is **declarative**. You declare your intentions by writing rules. Each rule specifies some pattern in the source document. When the processor matches the pattern in the source document, it takes the actions listed in the rule to generate output or control the flow of the transformation.

Although you have control over the general course of the transformation, you do not have control over the step-by-step processing of the XSLT processor. While that might make some programmers uneasy, it is greatly liberating: you tell the processor what you want to happen and let it worry about the details. XSLT stylesheets are also portable: any processor that conforms to the XSLT Recommendation can make use of them. Now you can not only generate documents that may be used across platforms, but you can create transformations that are equally portable.

This chapter is an introduction to XSLT. We'll see what XSLT is, and from whence it came. You'll learn how to write XSLT stylesheets, and you'll learn the syntax and usage of the most common XSLT elements. An exhaustive treatment of XSLT is beyond the scope of this chapter, but you'll learn enough to get started and even write some fairly sophisticated stylesheets. We'll round out our coverage of XSLT with two examples. First, we'll take an XML document and use XSLT to convert it to an appropriate HTML page. With only a line or two of procedural code, we'll be able to craft a basic user interface from a data document. Next, we'll show you how XSLT can be used to solve the more general problem of transforming data from one XML vocabulary to another. This technique is at the heart of data conversion engines and B2B messaging software, such as Microsoft BizTalk Server, which will be examined in greater depth in Chapter 25, "B2B with Biztalk". You'll find it to be a useful utility tool as well. With it, you can write scripts that use XSLT to accomplish all sorts of data transformation and manipulation tasks.

If this introduction whets your appetite for XSLT, you may follow up with Professional XSL (Wrox Press, 2001, ISBN 1-861003-57-9) or the XSLT Programmer's Reference, Second Edition (Wrox Press, 2001, ISBN 1-86105-06-7). The XSLT Recommendation is found at http://www.w3.org/TR/xslt.html

Origins and Purpose of XSLT

Standards work at the World Wide Web Consortium (W3C) is organized within Activities and Domains. Thus, the W3C has a broad **User Interface Domain** (http://www.w3.org/UI/) to address all aspects of Web user interfaces and presentation. Within that Domain, the **Style Sheets Activity Statement** (http://www.w3.org/Style/Activity) shows how Working Groups are managed in matters pertaining to the development of both **Cascading Style Sheets** (CSS) and XSL. If you've created any moderately advanced HTML pages you've probably encountered CSS, either as an embedded `STYLE` tag or as a linked style sheet file with the extension `.css`. CSS is very easy to use once you learn the syntax. You pick a tag, or class of tags and specify the formatting styles for it. Whenever a browser encounters such tags, it automatically applies the styling you specified, overriding any default styling that may apply (such as the formatting applied to heading tags like H1, H2, etc.). CSS capabilities continue to be improved and provide Web authors with rich formatting capabilities in an easy to use form.

As of this writing (January 2001) CSS Level 2 is a W3C Recommendation (12 May 1998, http://www.w3.org/TR/REC-CSS2/), while CSS Level 3 has been broken into a number of modules to aid its development. Common browsers have varying levels of compliance with CSS Level 2. An introduction to CSS3 is available online at http://www.w3.org/TR/css3-roadmap/.

As useful as CSS is however, (Level 1 is well supported by the major browsers, Level 2 not so well as yet) it has its limits. Everything in the source document will appear, and the material will appear in the order in which it appears in the source document. You cannot reorder things, and you cannot conditionally perform styling without resorting to scripting. CSS is strictly a styling language. It helps you build HTML for presentation, but it offers nothing for structural transformations.

Recognizing these limits, the XSL Working Group was formed. XSL draws not only on CSS but also on a prior formatting language, an ISO standard named the **Document Style, Semantics and Specification Language** (**DSSSL**). The initial proposal for XSL was submitted to the W3C in August of 1997. While XSL has always had the two tracks – transformation and formatting objects – early progress was on transformations. Sean Russell introduced an independent XSL processor late in 1997, and Microsoft offered a widely available technical preview of an XSL processor in January 1998. XSLT achieved W3C Recommendation status on 16 November 1999.

Progress on XSL-FO has lagged somewhat. At the time of writing, it is in Candidate Recommendation status.

What is Transformation?

Let's be clear about the nature of transformations. They are not at all like procedural code, nor do they modify the source document. They are somewhat like the mathematical concept of transformations. They are a set of rules that produce an output from an input. They are not algorithmic in the sense of a traditional programming language. You will not see a step-by-step procedural flow. Instead, an XSLT stylesheet consists of a series of templates. Templates are the 'rules' we mentioned in the introductory remarks for this chapter. A template consists of an expression describing the form of some XML fragment and one or more elements specifying what output to generate when the form is matched in the source document. These expressions make use of another XML technology, **XPath**. This technology specifies syntax for describing paths through an XML document. Such paths locate desired nodes within the document. Consequently, the first part of a template, the expression, is an XPath expression that precisely locates the XML items on which you want to operate. This is done by locating them according to their structural form, and (optionally), some conditions regarding the values of these items. Without worrying about the specific syntax of XPath expressions, consider the following XML document (5059_09_1.xml):

```
<Person age="29">
   <Name>
      <First>John</First>
      <Last>Doe</Last>
   </Name>
</Person>
```

An XPath expression that retrieves the `<Last>` element would look like this. Note the path from the document element down to the element we wish to find:

```
/Person/Name/Last
```

The second part of a template, the body, describes the output that goes into the document resulting from the transformation. This description may be hard-coded text, but it usually includes some elements defined in XSLT that either generate output, or direct the processor to other templates for continued processing. These elements also make use of XPath. They may contain XPath expressions to locate some other element or attribute within the source document that contains a value needed in the output. Here is a template (implemented in full in the file `5059_09_1.xsl` from the code download) that goes with the XML document above and emits a string composed of the contents of the `<First>` element followed by some whitespace, which is in turn followed by the `<Last>`element:

```
<xsl:template match="Name">
  <xsl:value-of select="First"/>
  <xsl:text> </xsl:text>
  <xsl:value-of select="Last"/>
</xsl:template>
```

So, when you process 5059_09_1.xml with 5059_09_1.xsl, as described above, you get the following output:

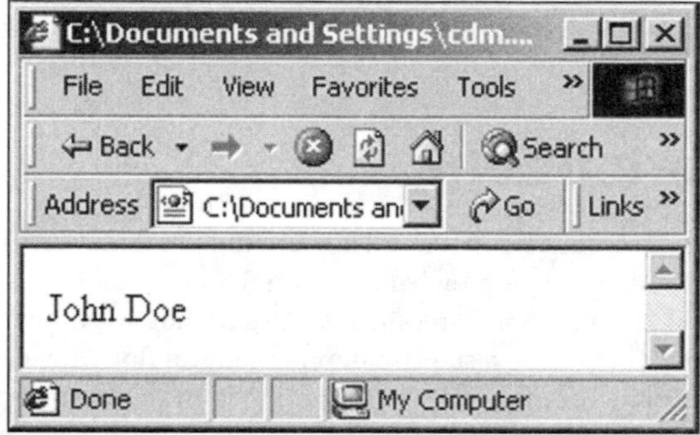

However, you can't do everything by just matching XML structures with XPath expressions. Although you can't control the execution of the XSLT processor in detail, you can direct it through the source document. To this end, XSLT includes some elements that are superficially similar to flow control statements in procedural languages. Each stylesheet contains a template that matches the root of the document, termed the root template. This gives the XSLT processor somewhere definite to begin. From there you provide instructions on how the processor should proceed. There are loops and conditional statements, as we shall see shortly. We say this superficially, however, because they do not work by directing the processor from line to line. Instead, they work by changing the **context** of processing. In a procedural language like JavaScript, the processor is executing a particular line of code. XSLT, as a declarative language, works its way through the structures in the source document, and the context is the node of the parse tree on which the processor is focusing.

The various elements of XSLT use XPath expressions to select a set of nodes, which for example, might all be elements named <Chapter>, or all <Book> elements, whose price attribute has a value greater than 50. When you iterate through such a set, the XSLT processor changes the context to each such element in turn. The context controls how expressions can be matched. If you do not provide any other processing instructions, you tell the processor to continue to apply the templates in the stylesheet, in which case the processor continues with the current context and checks the expression in each template in the order in which they appear until one matches.

That's the basic idea: a stylesheet consisting of templates that provide instructions on what to generate when certain patterns are found in the source XML. You control how the processor moves through the source document, not how it moves through an independent set of instructions. This is the key difference between procedural and declarative languages. A procedural language is totally focused on a body of code that hopefully, faithfully mirrors the data on which it operates. A declarative language doesn't have that luxury. XSLT doesn't have code in the algorithmic sense, so it must focus on the data. It moves from place to place in the data depending on what it finds, and what you tell it to do when it finds certain things.

Locating Data: XPath

Clearly, given the flexibility of XSLT, being able to precisely specify arbitrary items within an XML document is very important – you can't work on things you can't find. Since XSLT also lets you pick and choose what you want to work on, a means of filtering XML items according to their value must also be provided. For this, XSLT uses the XPath Recommendation (http://www.w3.org/TR/xpath).

When an XML document is parsed into a node tree, any given item – element, attribute, etc. – can be located by naming a path from the document root to the node in question. This is a location path in XPath. Location paths are analogous to the way we specify file paths in Windows or Unix. From a known starting point, you compile a string that is a delimited list of the names along the way. Anyone who starts at the known starting point and follows the named items along the way is sure to locate the item you wanted them to find.

XPath expressions were covered in detail in the last chapter. The following brief coverage is intended as a refresher focused on the needs of XSLT or as minimal coverage for those who skipped that chapter for any reason.

Location Paths

A location path is an XPath expression that selects a set of nodes – XML items in the parse tree – based on their location in the tree relative to the context node. An XSLT processor will start from the document element (root node in the tree), but the context changes throughout the course of processing. When you see a location path in a template, you must look at the template carefully to understand what the context is when the template is executed. We'll go into this in more detail when we get into the structure of stylesheets.

As we saw in Chapter 8, XPath uses some special characters as operators in its expressions. Location paths are built from these operators and the names of XML elements and attributes. Location paths are broken into **steps**. Think of a step as a choice to be made at each point in the node tree. To follow one path rather than another, you take a particular step, choosing to go one way rather than another. Location steps consist of **axes** to express a relationship between the context and the nodes to be selected, a **node test**, to actually specify what is to be selected at the final step, and, optionally, **predicates**, which filter the nodes selected by the node test, according to some criteria. An axis, then, is shorthand for a commonly used location step.

Axes

Axes are named, pre-defined paths that are frequently encountered in XSLT processing and XPath expressions. This is the complete list of XPath axes:

Axis Name	Meaning
`child`	All children of the context node
`descendant`	Recursive selection of children
`parent`	Immediate parent node of the context node, if any
`ancestor`	Recursive selection of parent nodes up to the document element (tree root node)
`following-sibling`	All nodes on the same level of the tree as, and which follow the context node

Table continued on following page

Axis Name	Meaning
`preceding-sibling`	All nodes on the same level as, and preceding the context node
`following`	All nodes following the context node in document order, excluding the descendant, attribute, and namespace axes
`preceding`	All nodes preceding the context node, in document order, excluding the ancestor, attribute, and namespace axes
`attribute`	All attributes of the context node
`namespace`	All namespace declarations on the context node
`self`	Context node
`descendant-or-self`	Union of the descendant and self axes
`ancestor-or-self`	Union of the ancestor and self axes

Node Tests

The final name in a location path selects the node(s) desired – this is known as the node test. For elements and attributes, we typically name the node desired. For other types of nodes, we need one of the following special node tests:

Node Test	Returns
`comment()`	`true` for comment nodes
`node()`	`true` for all nodes
`processing-instruction()`	`true` for processing instruction nodes
`text()`	`true` for text nodes

Abbreviated Form

It is useful to have a more compact representation of axes and node tests than the formal, named form shown above. To this end, XPath prescribes the **abbreviated form**, which uses special operators to represent some of the basic axes. Like file paths, abbreviated paths use the slash character (/) to delimit a parent-child relationship. Thus, to locate the `GrandChild` element in the following XML fragment:

```
<Node>
   <Child>
      <GrandChild>. . . </GrandChild>
   </Child>
   ...
</Node>
```

you need the following XPath expression:

```
/Node/Child/GrandChild
```

The initial slash denotes the root of the document, and each successive slash indicates that the name that follows it is a child of the name that precedes it. Sometimes, it is inconvenient to fully specify the location path, or you may not know the structure between the root and some desired child node. In that case, use the double slash (//) to denote recursive descent. In other words, it means to keep going to lower levels until you find the name following the double slash. Returning to the above example, then, we could replace the full path given with:

```
//GrandChild
```

or

```
/Node//GrandChild
```

In the preceding discussion, I was careful to say "name" rather than element name. XPath differentiates between elements and attributes by preceding an attribute name with the "at" character (@). If GrandChild were modified like this:

```
<GrandChild id="tmx1147" age="41">. . . </GrandChild>
```

We would reach the age attribute with the following path:

```
/Node/Child/GrandChild/@age
```

Here is the full list of special operators in the XPath abbreviated form:

Operator	Meaning
/	Child
//	Recursive descent child
.	Current context node
..	Parent of the context node
@	Attribute qualifier; used alone, it becomes a wildcard matching any attribute
:	Namespace separator
( )	Grouping for precedence
[ ]	Filter pattern or subscript operator for collections
+	Addition
-	Subtraction
div	Floating-point division
*	Multiplication
mod	Modulus arithmetic, that is: returns the remainder of a division

Predicates

Predicates are appended to the end of location paths to filter the node set returned by the axis and location steps. In this, they are like the `WHERE` clause in a SQL statement. Predicates take the following form:

```
[expression]
```

where expression is a location step, comparison, or some other logical expression. Here is a predicate that returns all `House` elements that have a `<Garage>` child element:

```
House[Garage]
```

`House` is the location step. The predicate is `[Garage]`. Now here is a predicate that contains a logical expression:

```
House[@roof="slate"]
```

Once again, we are looking at `<House>` elements, but in this case we use a predicate to select only those `<House>` elements whose `roof` attribute has the value `slate`.

Clearly, predicates will use logical operators. Here is the list of operators you can use for logical comparisons in predicates:

Expression	Meaning
`and`	Logical AND
`or`	Logical OR
`not()`	Logical negation, for example: `not(position()=1)`
`=`	Equal
`!=`	Not equal
`<`	Less than
`<=`	Less than or equal
`>`	Greater than
`>=`	Greater than or equal
`|`	Union

Functions

There are 37 functions defined in XPath and XSLT to return useful information about documents and the items within them. They are typically used within predicates to assist in filtering node sets. As we are merely summarizing XPath in this chapter, we cannot discuss all the functions here. You will see some of them used in our examples, where their meaning will be examined in context. Just to remind you of the scope of available functions, it is worth listing the functions by functional area. The functions are divided into five areas according to their purpose:

- Node set manipulation and information
- String manipulation
- Boolean tests
- Basic numeric utilities
- XSLT-specific functions

Node set manipulation	String Manipulation	Boolean Tests	Basic Numeric Utilities	XSLT-specific Functions
`count`	`concat`	`boolean`	`ceiling`	`current`
`document`	`contains`	`false`	`floor`	`element-available`
`id`	`normalize-space`	`lang`	`number`	`format-number`
`key`	`starts-with`	`not`	`round`	`function-available`
`last`	`string`	`true`	`sum`	`generate-id`
`local-name`	`string-length`			`node-set`
`name`	`substring`			`system-property`
`namespace-uri`	`substring-after`			`unparsed-entity-uri`
`position`	`substring-before`			
	`translate`			

Uses for XPath in Transformations

XSLT uses XPath expressions to:

- Match node sets in order to execute templates
- Evaluate node sets to control the execution of conditional XSLT elements
- Select node sets to change the current context and direct the flow of execution through the source document
- Select node sets to obtain an output value

This reflects the focus of XSLT on the data itself, the node tree representing the source XML document. You control the flow of execution by directing the XSLT processor through the source document, matching node sets to execute templates. Within those templates, you may make decisions, and these are based on values taken from the node tree. Selecting a new node set as the current context further directs the processor through the source document. Finally, at some point you must generate output. Much of that will be taken from the source tree's node values, so XSLT uses XPath to allow you to specify what values you need.

Transforming Data: XSLT

XPath is all well and good, and it has uses beyond XSLT, but we promised to show you how to transform XML, and we need something more for that. In this chapter, that something else is XSLT. XSLT is itself an XML vocabulary, so we need to discuss the elements and attributes of XSLT before we can show you any XSLT techniques for transformation.

XSLT Elements

XSLT is relatively compact, performing its tasks with thirty-seven elements and their attributes. Of course, XPath technology brings a great deal of power to XSLT, and it is used extensively in the elements we are going to discuss. As it turns out, the majority of transformations can be accomplished with a smaller subset of elements. We're going to take a casual approach to XSLT, showing you the elements you are most likely to need as you begin using XSLT.

> *This is intended to be an introduction to XSLT and its use for transforming XML documents in applications. In view of this, we will not be presenting every part of XSLT syntax and we will skip over useful but advanced topics. As we have said before, two excellent sources of in-depth information are XSLT Programmer's Reference (Wrox Press, 2000, ISBN 1-861003-12-9) and Professional XSL (Wrox Press, 2001, ISBN 1861003-57-9).*

The Full List

Although this chapter is not intended to be a comprehensive XSLT reference, we would be remiss in our duties if we did not show you the whole list of XSLT elements and allow you to gauge the extent of what is presented in this introductory coverage. The table that follows lists all the elements declared in XSLT. Elements covered in the following pages are shown in boldface. Note that only some of these elements may be used as immediate children of `xsl:stylesheet` or `xsl:transform` elements, while others occur only within the body of templates. We'll see the distinction as we go along.

xsl:apply-imports	**xsl:copy**	**xsl:import**	**xsl:output**	**xsl:template**
xsl:apply-templates	**xsl:copy-of**	**xsl:include**	**xsl:param**	**xsl:text**
xsl:attribute	xsl:decimal-format	xsl:key	xsl:preserve-space	**xsl:transform**
xsl:attribute-set	**xsl:element**	xsl:message	**xsl:processing-instruction**	**xsl:value-of**
xsl:call-template	xsl:fallback	xsl:namespace-alias	xsl:sort	**xsl:variable**
xsl:choose	**xsl:for-each**	xsl:number	xsl:strip-space	**xsl:when**
xsl:comment	**xsl:if**	**xsl:otherwise**	**xsl:stylesheet**	**xsl:with-param**

Commonly Used Elements

In keeping with our informal approach to XSLT, we'll divide the most commonly used elements into the following function categories:

- Building stylesheets
- Controlling transformation output
- Generating simple output
- Generating XML
- Iteration
- Conditional tests
- Programming constructs
- Modularity

Some elements will have subsections devoted to them, while others will be covered in passing as we need them. For any given element, we will cover all commonly used attributes, though we may occasionally bypass some attributes that are only used for advanced cases.

Building Stylesheets

We said that stylesheets are XML documents that contain one or more templates. That means that we need a root element that clearly indicates to an XSLT processor that it is dealing with a stylesheet that conforms to the XSLT Recommendation, as well as elements denoting templates. There must be a way to tell the processor where to start, as well as a way to tell it when to look for other templates to execute. Let's consider the XSLT elements that perform these functions.

<xsl:stylesheet> and <xsl:transform>

The very first element you will need is `<xsl:stylesheet>` or its synonym, `<xsl:transform>`. This is the top-most element in the document and serves to indicate that the document is an XSLT stylesheet. The element has two mandatory attributes: a namespace declaration for the XSLT namespace, and a `version` attribute. The current version is `1.0`. Here are two equivalent ways to start a stylesheet; XSLT treats `<xsl:transform>` as a synonym of `<xsl:stylesheet>`:

```
<xsl:stylesheet xmlns:xsl="http://www.w3.org/1999/XSL/Transform" version="1.0">
   ...
</xsl:stylesheet>
```

```
<xsl:transform xmlns:xsl="http://www.w3.org/1999/XSL/Transform" version="1.0">
   ...
</xsl:transform>
```

The namespace declaration used above is the one specified in the W3C Recommendation. Microsoft's technology preview implementation was based on a Working Draft, which specified the URI http://www.w3.org/TR/WD-xsl, so you may encounter stylesheets with that value. These are not XSLT-compliant stylesheets. The prefix declared in the namespace declaration is, of course, completely arbitrary, but it is customary to use `xsl`. Additionally, you will be highly unlikely to see the namespace made the default (without a prefix), as stylesheets need to use names from other vocabularies. The `<stylesheet>` and `<transform>` elements also provide for three optional attributes, but these are advanced usages beyond the scope of this introductory chapter.

<xsl:template>

Every stylesheet must contain templates to get some work done. Since stylesheets are declarative, not procedural, XSLT processors cannot assume that the first template is the appropriate place to begin. Consequently, there must be a convention that unambiguously tells the processor where to start processing. Every stylesheet must have a template that matches the root node of the document.

If you have more than one template matching the root node, you will get either an error or the result of applying the last matching template to appear in the document, depending on the XSLT implementation.

Templates are declared with the `<xsl:template>` element. This element has four optional attributes: `match`, `name`, `priority`, and `mode`. The `match` attribute is almost always necessary. In fact, we won't see a case when it isn't until we take up the elements dealing with programming in a later section of this chapter. The `match` attribute takes an XPath expression as its value. When the current context matches the node set defined by the expression, the template is executed. Remembering that the `/` character is shorthand for the root of the node tree, we can then write the required starting template for our stylesheet:

```
<xsl:stylesheet xmlns:xsl="http://www.w3.org/1999/XSL/Transform" version="1.0">
   <xsl:template match="/">
      ...
   </xsl:template>
      ...
</xsl:stylesheet>
```

The `name` attribute gives us a way to refer to a given template from elsewhere in the stylesheet, something that will be useful in the programming discussion coming up. The `priority` attribute takes a numeric value that allows a stylesheet author to tell the processor the order in which multiple templates should be executed when they all match the current context. The `mode` attribute takes a name as its value. When we get into programming techniques you will see how to define variables and assign them a name. When the name matches the value of `mode` and the current context matches the `match` attribute value, the template executes. If the context matches but the `mode` value does not, the template is skipped. This gives authors a bit of flexibility by allowing them to provide enhanced context information.

<xsl:apply-templates> and <xsl:output>

Now, how does the XSLT processor move from the root-matching template to other templates? We certainly need to be able to do this or the `<xsl:template>` element would be redundant and everything would be one long procedural mess in the body of the stylesheet. Instead, we want some sort of mechanisms analogous to function calls in a procedural language that will let us break up our XSLT instructions. This is where the `<xsl:apply-templates>` element comes in. Its only permitted child elements are `<xsl:with-param>`and `<xsl:sort>`, though it is commonly used as an empty element. If used with no attributes, it tells the processor to try to match the templates in the stylesheet against the current context node. If no matching templates are found, the XSLT processor will apply the default templates specified in the Recommendation. These defaults are specific to the type of node encountered, but the general effect is to continue processing recursively. You should not rely on default processing templates until you are expert in XSLT, however, as you are giving up control of processing to the processor. Upon finishing, it returns to the content immediately following the `<xsl:apply-templates>` element. Here is a stylesheet that performs an identity transformation, that is, it copies the source document without change. The second template, invoked in response to the `<xsl:apply-templates>` element in the first template, matches all nodes in the tree and simply copies them to the output document:

```
<xsl:stylesheet xmlns:xsl="http://www.w3.org/1999/XSL/Transform" version="1.0">
   <xsl:output method="xml" indent="yes"/>
```

```
    <xsl:template match="/">
       <xsl:apply-templates />
    </xsl:template>

    <xsl:template match = "node()">
       <xsl:copy-of select = "." />
    </xsl:template>

</xsl:stylesheet>
```

If we include the `select` attribute, however, we can pick a node set. The XSLT processor will then look at each of the templates in the stylesheet and see if any template matches the selected node set. If one does, it will be executed and control will return to the stylesheet following the `<xsl:apply-templates>` element. Note that this is not like a subroutine call in a procedural language. There might be more than one template match, in which case all will be executed.

Consider the following template:

```
    <xsl:template match="/">
       <Members><xsl:apply-templates select="/Team/Member"/></Members>
    </xsl:template>
```

Applied to our sample document, it will write out a `<Member>` element whose contents will be the output generated by the template matching the `<Member>` element in the source document.

Fine-Tuning Stylesheet Output

Before we get into the elements that go into templates, let's pause long enough to learn how to fine-tune the output resulting from a transformation. XSLT provides three elements for this purpose, `<xsl:output>`, `<xsl:preserve-space>`, and `<xsl:strip-space`. The first is the most commonly used, and we shall cover it here. The others control whitespace handling which is generally not useful in transformations of data. When transforming for presentation, you will use HTML's features to control the positioning of information on the screen.

The `<xsl:output>` element specifies certain broad information regarding the overall output of the XSLT processor. If used, it's as an immediate child of the `<xsl:stylesheet>` element. In practice, if one is used, it is invariably found directly after the opening `<xsl:stylesheet` tag>. The element is always empty. Here is a list of the element's attributes, all of which are optional:

Attribute	Usage and Meaning
`method`	Defines the output type using one of the following values: `xml`, `html`, `text`
`version`	Defines the version of the output
`encoding`	Specifies the character encoding of the output
`omit-xml-declaration`	Takes the values `yes` or `no`. If `yes`, causes the XML output to lack the XML declaration

Table continued on following page

Attribute	Usage and Meaning
standalone	Controls the value of the standalone attribute in the XML declaration of XML output. Takes the values yes or no.
doctype-public	Sets the URI for the public identifier in an XML DOCTYPE declaration
doctype-system	Sets the system identifier value in an XML DOCTYPE declaration
cdata-section-elements	A whitespace delimited list of element names whose textual content should be output as CDATA sections
indent	A suggestion to the processor regarding whether indentation (whitespace) should be used to indicate the hierarchical structure of the output document. Takes the values yes or no
media-type	Defines the output MIME type

The most commonly used attributes when using XSLT for applications are method and omit-xml-declaration, and perhaps, if the programmer is thorough, version. If method is given the value xml, then the output must be a well-formed XML fragment. Note that the output need not be a complete XML document, a fact that is useful when multiple transforms are combined programmatically. The only value for version in that case is 1.0. If html is specified, the output will default to 4.0 for version. You will see us use this value when we cover XSLT for visual presentation later in the chapter. Setting the value method to text is used when XSLT is employed to output data in flat file formats other than XML.

Generating Simple Output

Unless we put something inside a template, we'll have very little output. In fact, there are occasions when you will use empty template bodies to explicitly suppress certain elements. If we want to generate some output, though, the simplest thing to do is to take values from the source document and add them to the output.

xsl:value-of

If we merely want the value of some node expressed as a string, we can make use of the empty element <xsl:value-of>. This element, which may only be found within <xsl:template>, has a required select attribute. The value of this attribute is an XPath expression. The value of the nodes located by the expression will be copied to the output document in text form. If the expression returns a collection of nodes, only the value of the first node will be output. If a single node has children, however, the textual content of the entire sub-tree rooted by that node will be output. If the value in question is numeric, a string representation will be output. If it is a Boolean expression (such as when one of the XPath Boolean functions is used), it will be evaluated and the result will be output as either true or false. Consider the following XML:

```
<Team>
   <Leader id="a101">Bob Smith</Leader>
   <Member id="b234">Grace Hopper</Member>
   <Member id="c666">John von Neuman</Member>
</Team>
```

Now consider the following stylesheet:

```
<xsl:stylesheet xmlns:xsl="http://www.w3.org/1999/XSL/Transform"
   version="1.0">
<xsl:output method="text"/>
```

```
    <xsl:template match="/">
       Leader: <xsl:value-of select="/Team/Leader" /> (<xsl:value-of
          select="/Team/Leader/@id"/>)

       Member: <xsl:value-of select="/Team/Member" /> (<xsl:value-of
          select="Team/Member/@id"/>)
    </xsl:template>

</xsl:stylesheet>
```

The output of the transformation is:

```
Leader: Bob Smith (a101)
Member: Grace Hopper (b234)
```

Exactly how to invoke an XSLT transformation is a matter explicitly left out of the XSLT Recommendation. We'll explicitly cover one implementation later in the chapter, as well as mentioning tools for editing stylesheets and invoking transformations.

The `<xsl:output>` element was used to specify text as the output type through its `method` attribute. We haven't yet learned to create any XML output, so we need to resort to text if we want to avoid an error. Processing begins with the template whose `match` attribute specifies the root node through the XPath expression `/`. That's not a very big clue given that our stylesheet only has one template, but it is necessary to have this. Within the template, we see something interesting: the very first thing is literal text, specifically the string `"Leader:  "`. This is written directly to the output. Our new friend `<xsl:value-of>` comes into play as we use it to grab the textual value of the `Leader` node, followed by a literal character ("`(`"). The `<xsl:value-of>` element is then used to write the value of the `id` attribute to the output. After closing our parentheses with a literal "`)`", we follow the same pattern for the `<Member>` elements.

Making Copies

This is where we run afoul of the limitation on `<xsl:value-of>`. The expression `/Team/Member` returns a collection: nodes for the two `Member` elements that are children of `Team`. The `<xsl:value-of>` element operates on the first node in the collection, ignoring the rest. This is why the output only lists the first team member in the source document. We'll learn about the `<xsl:for-each>` element, which fixes the problem, in a little while. Our other team member will just have to be patient.

There are two other elements that are interesting right now, though their full value will only become apparent in later sections of this chapter. They are `<xsl:copy>` and `<xsl:copy-of>`. The `<xsl:copy>` element simply copies the current context node to the output. It does not copy any child nodes that the context node may have. This is more limiting than it might appear at first glance. The textual content of an element is itself a child text node of the element node. Using `<xsl:copy>` when the context is an element will copy the element node, but it will be empty, as `<xsl:copy>` will not bring along any attributes or child nodes. In consequence, the following template:

```
<xsl:template match="/Team">
   <xsl:copy/>
</xsl:template>
```

results in the following output:

```
<Team/>
```

Contrast that with the following stylesheet:

```
<xsl:stylesheet xmlns:xsl="http://www.w3.org/1999/XSL/Transform"
   version="1.0">
<xsl:output encoding="UTF-16" method="xml" indent="yes"/>

   <xsl:template match="/">
      <xsl:copy-of select="."/>
   </xsl:template>

</xsl:stylesheet>
```

When it is applied to our preceding example document, the output is (with some whitespace added for clarity):

```
<?xml version="1.0" encoding="UTF-16"?>
<Team>
   <Leader id="a101">Bob Smith</Leader>
   <Member id="b234">Grace Hopper</Member>
   <Member id="c666">John von Neuman</Member>
</Team>
```

Note that `<xsl:copy-of>` has a `select` attribute. Its value, an XPath expression, specifies the root node containing the nodes to be copied to the output.

If we want to get serious about transforming XML documents in applications however, we need to be able to create XML and HTML content other than text without simply copying it as is from the input. We need to be able to create new elements and attributes. Let's proceed to that task right now.

Generating XML Constructs Directly

XSLT includes five elements for creating each of the major constructs of XML. Each uses a combination of its attribute values and textual content to create a node of the appropriate type on the output tree. Here is the list:

Element Name	Attributes	Element Content Meaning
`xsl:attribute`	`name` – required; name of the attribute `namespace` – optional; URI identifying the attribute's namespace	Text denoting the attribute's value
`xsl:comment`	none	Text; comment body
`xsl:element`	`name` – required; name of the element `namespace` – optional; URI identifying the element's namespace `use-attribute-sets` – optional; whitespace delimited list of attribute set names	Element content; may be text for textual content, or literal child elements, or may contain instances of `xsl:element`, `xsl:attribute`, `xsl:comment`, `xsl:processing-instruction`, or `xsl:text` to create child nodes

Element Name	Attributes	Element Content Meaning
xsl:processing-instruction	name – required; PI target	Text; denotes the data portion of the PI
xsl:text	disable-output-escaping – optional; yes (if special XML characters should not be escaped on output but written as is), or no (default)	Textual content of the text node

While you can output XML structures as literal strings in an XSLT template, the use of these elements gives a transform author the flexibility of using other XSLT elements to obtain values from the source document or perform conditional tests before generating output. To create any one of the team members in the sample we've been using, you might use the following:

```
<xsl:element name="Staff">
   <xsl:attribute name="empID"><xsl:value-of select="@id"/></xsl:attribute>
   <xsl:value-of select="."/>
</xsl:element>
```

This results in the following output:

```
<Staff empID="b234">Grace Hopper</Staff>
```

Because <xsl:attribute> is contained within the <xsl:element> element, empID is created as an attribute of <Staff>. To pick up the textual content of the source <Member> element, we call <xsl:value-of> on the current context node, which at that point is the <Member> element. Here again though, we run into the same problem we had before. We need an XSLT element that lets us iterate through a collection of nodes.

Iteration

Anyone familiar with common procedural languages would suspect that the <xsl:for-each> element implements something like a loop. Indeed, <xsl:for-each> performs iteration, but it does not work by incrementing a variable like the for statement in C++ or Javascript. It operates on a collection of nodes designated by the value of its select attribute. The contents of the <xsl:for-each> element are executed once for each node in the collection. While the element is executed, the nodes in the collection become the current context node. Let's finish off our simple document example by creating a new document that lists the team leader and all team members but changes the structure very slightly by making the team members children of a new element. Here is the stylesheet:

```
<xsl:stylesheet xmlns:xsl="http://www.w3.org/1999/XSL/Transform" version="1.0">
<xsl:output encoding="UTF-16" method="xml" indent="yes"/>

   <xsl:template match="/">
      <xsl:element name="ProjectTeam">
         <xsl:apply-templates select="/Team/Leader"/>
      </xsl:element>
   </xsl:template>

   <xsl:template match="Leader">
      <xsl:element name="TeamLead">
         <xsl:attribute name="empID">
```

```
            <xsl:value-of select="@id"/>
         </xsl:attribute>
         <xsl:element name="TeamStaff">
            <xsl:for-each select="/Team/Member">
               <xsl:element name="Staff">
                  <xsl:attribute name="empID">
                     <xsl:value-of select="@id"/>
                  </xsl:attribute>
               <xsl:value-of select="."/>
               </xsl:element>
            </xsl:for-each>
         </xsl:element>
      </xsl:element>
   </xsl:template>
</xsl:stylesheet>
```

After matching the root, we transfer the context to the <Leader> element in the source document. We create a <TeamLead> element in the output and copy the leader's id information to it. While still within the <xsl:element> that creates <TeamLead>, we create a child element <TeamStaff>. Now we come to the iteration. The <xsl:for-each> element selects all the source <Member> elements. As each becomes the context node, we create a <Staff> element and copy the <Member> information to it. The output looks like this:

```
<?xml version="1.0" encoding="UTF-16"?>
<ProjectTeam>
   <TeamLead empID="a101">
      <TeamStaff>
         <Staff empID="b234">Grace Hopper</Staff>
         <Staff empID="c666">John von Neuman</Staff>
      </TeamStaff>
   </TeamLead>
</ProjectTeam>
```

The team leader loses his name in this transformation, but he gains ownership of the team members. While this might not be the most exciting stylesheet you will ever see, it should awaken you to the possibilities for data transformation using XSLT. The transformation is entirely data-driven. There is no procedural code. If an attribute or element does not appear in the source, it will be omitted from the output without resorting to conditional statements in procedural code. Later in the chapter, we'll tackle the problem of transforming a more complicated source document into a more sophisticated output document.

Conditional Tests

There will be times when you will wish to vary the output of the transformation based on some condition in the source document. It may be a matter of checking for the presence of some information, or you may want to change the output based on the value of some element or attribute. XSLT offers two forms of conditional execution that are similar to those found in procedural languages. If you combine these with the content creation elements and the <xsl:apply-templates> element, you can create dynamic output or change the flow of execution based on what the XSLT processor finds in the source document.

xsl:if

The first and simplest conditional element we will look at is the <xsl:if> element. It's a very basic sort of if statement – there is no else statement to go with it. The <xsl:if> element takes one attribute, test, which is an XPath expression. If it evaluates true, the body of the element is executed. Here's an example:

```
<xsl:if test="@id">. . . </xsl:if>
```

In this case, if the current context node has an `id` attribute, the body of `<xsl:if>` is executed. The following example shows how to branch, based on the value of some attribute:

```
<xsl:if test="Payment/@type = 'cc'"> ... </xsl:if>
```

Here, we are checking the `Payment` child element of the current context to see if the `type` attribute has the value `cc`.

Note that there is no "else" syntax. If you want alternative processing, you must use a combination of elements in the next section.

Evaluating Multiple Conditions

Now, if you wish to check more complicated cases for multiple values you will need to use a combination of `<xsl:choose>` and its child elements `<xsl:when>` and `<xsl:otherwise>`. This is analogous to the `switch` statement in C++, or the `Select Case` statement in Visual Basic. The `<xsl:choose>` element has no attributes. It exists solely to indicate the presence of a multi-part conditional check. Within it are one or more `<xsl:when>` elements. These are like `<xsl:if>` in that they have a `test` attribute, which controls whether the body of the element is executed. Note that unlike C++ case statements, you cannot fall through to the next `<xsl:when>`. Moreover, each `xsl:when` is evaluated in turn until one `<xsl:when>` element's `test` attribute evaluates `true`. When that happens, the body of the element is executed, after which control resumes after the `<xsl:choose>` element. Finally, the optional `<xsl:otherwise>` element allows you to provide a default body of instructions to execute if none of the `<xsl:when>` elements is applied. Here is a sample `<xsl:choose>` element. Note that the values of the `test` attribute do not have to be related, unlike the `case` statement in C++, for example:

```
<xsl:choose>
   <xsl:when test="@color='red'">
      <xsl:attribute name="paint-color">red</xsl:attribute>
   </xsl:when>
   <xsl:when test="/Department/Budget/@signature &gt; @cost">
      No signature required
   </xsl:when>
   <xsl:otherwise>
      <xsl:element name="comments">
         It's not red and it requires signature approval
      </xsl:element>
   </xsl:otherwise>
</xsl:choose>
```

This particular example may not make a lot of sense, but it is perfectly valid XSLT. Note also the need to use the `>` entity in the second `<xsl:when>` element's test attribute to avoid a stylesheet that is not well-formed.

Programming Constructs

XSLT offers several elements that are superficially similar to procedural programming statements. You may, for example, declare variables and parameters. You may call named templates in much the same way that you call subroutines in a procedural language. There are, however, some major distinctions, and understanding them is key to writing effective XSLT transformations.

Declaring Variables

You declare a variable with, not surprisingly, the `<xsl:variable>` element. It has a required `name` attribute and an optional `select` attribute. If it appears, the value of `select` is an XPath expression whose evaluated value becomes the value of the variable. For example:

```
<xsl:variable name="x" select="/Parent/Child"/>
<xsl:variable name="y" select="/Parent/Child/@age"/>
<xsl:variable name="z" select="number(2)">
```

The first variable, x, is an element node. We can use it in subsequent expressions just as if we repeated the XPath expression. The variable `y` has the value of the attribute `age`, while `z` has the numeric value `2` (`number()`) being one of the XPath functions we skipped over in an earlier section).

You refer to a variable following its declaration by prefacing it with the reserved character `$`. So, given the declaration of `x` above, we can rewrite the declaration of `y` as follows:

```
<xsl:variable name="y" select="$x/@age"/>
```

However we define `y`, we can use it like this:

```
<xsl:value-of select="$y"/>
```

We mentioned that the `select` attribute is optional. Since we have no use for parameters that lack value (as we shall see in just a moment), there is an alternative form. If `select` is missing and the `xsl:variable` is empty, its contents become the value of the variable. Thus, the following are equivalent to our prior declarations, with one exception:

```
<xsl:variable name="x">
   <xsl:value-of select="/Parent/Child"/>
</xsl:variable>
<xsl:variable name="y" />
   <xsl:value-of select="/Parent/Child/@age"/>
</xsl:variable>
<xsl:variable name="z">2</xsl:variable>
```

The last declaration generates a string variable with the value `2`. If we wanted a numeric value, as in the original declaration, we would have to use `<xsl:value-of>` as in the two preceding examples.

The scope of XSLT variables is similar to what you have encountered in procedural languages. Top-level declarations, that is; `<xsl:variable>` elements outside of `<xsl:template>` elements, have global scope and may be referenced anywhere within the stylesheet. Variables declared within a template go out of scope when processing leaves the template. A top-level declaration and a declaration with the same name in template scope do not conflict. The template-scope variable is said to **shadow** the top-level variable. It is available for use within the template, but the top-level variable value is not.

There is one extremely important distinction between XSLT variables and variables as implemented in procedural languages. Once set, an XSLT variable cannot have its value changed. There is no assignment operator. Any modifications you wish to make must either go into new variables (generally a bad idea, as it consumes resources) or directly into the output document in the desired form (usually the right thing to do).

Calling Templates

Back when we told you about `<xsl:template>`, we mentioned that the element had an optional `name` attribute. It is but a short step from declaring variables to declaring parameters, thereby turning templates into something that look a lot like subroutines in procedural languages. A named template uses the `<xsl:param>` element to declare parameters and, optionally, give them default values. These defaults are used in the event that the template is called without a value for the parameter. Unlike procedural languages, XSLT is relaxed when it comes to parameter lists. It is not an error to call a template without the required parameters, although processing may obviously be affected. Consider the following fragment of XML (`speakerlist.xml`):

```
<SpeakerList>
   <Person email="bill@bill.org">
      <First>William</First>
      <Last>Clinton</Last>
      <Biography>
         A fixture on the NYC and Hollywood social scenes,
         Mr. Clinton has extensive experience in fund raising,
         administration, and legal defense. Always an entertaining
         speaker...
      </Biography>
   </Person>

   <Person email="maggie@lords.org">
      <First>Margaret</First>
      <Last>Thatcher</Last>
      <Biography>
         Affectionately known as the 'Iron Lady', Baroness Thatcher
         owns an extensive collection of handbags...
      </Biography>
   </Person>
</SpeakerList>
```

We might generate all sorts of HTML that uses a well-formatted summary of personal information contained in a `<Person>` element such as the one above. It is useful to write a template that takes a `<Person>` element as a parameter, and then call that template whenever we need such formatting. Consider the following stylesheet:

```
<xsl:stylesheet xmlns:xsl="http://www.w3.org/1999/XSL/Transform"
   version="1.0">
<xsl:output method="html"/>
<xsl:template match="/">
   <xsl:element name="HTML">
      <xsl:element name="HEAD">
         <xsl:element name="TITLE">Speaker List</xsl:element>
      </xsl:element>
      <xsl:element name="BODY">
         <xsl:for-each select="/SpeakerList/Person">
            <xsl:call-template name="format-person">
               <xsl:with-param name="person" select="."/>
            </xsl:call-template>
         </xsl:for-each>
      </xsl:element>
   </xsl:element>
</xsl:template>

<xsl:template name="format-person">
   <xsl:param name="person"/>
   <xsl:element name="DIV">
      <xsl:attribute name="STYLE">
```

```
            background-color:teal; color:white; font-
            family:Verdana,arial,helvetica,sans-serif;font-size:12pt; padding:4px
         </xsl:attribute>
         <xsl:value-of select="$person/First"/><xsl:text> </xsl:text>
         <xsl:value-of select="$person/Last"/>
      </xsl:element>
      <xsl:element name="DIV">
         <xsl:attribute name="STYLE">
            font-size:10pt;color:gray
         </xsl:attribute>
            email: <xsl:value-of select="$person/@email"/>
      </xsl:element>
      <xsl:element name="DIV">
         <xsl:attribute name="STYLE">
            background-color:#EEEEEE; color:black; font-size:12pt
         </xsl:attribute>
         <xsl:value-of select="$person/Biography"/>
      </xsl:element>
      <xsl:element name="P"/>
   </xsl:template>

   </xsl:stylesheet>
```

The root-matching template generates the standard HTML shell, then iterates through all the `<Person>` elements in a list of speakers. In the body of the `<xsl:for-each>` element it calls the `format-person` template with the current context node, a `<Person>` element, as the value of the `person` parameter.

The `<xsl:template>` element for `format-person`, in turn, declares the named parameter `person`, then uses the parameter the same way we used variables in the last section, with the `$` character prefixed to the parameter name. This template puts our entire `<Person>` element formatting in one place without worrying about how `Person` elements are encountered in the source document.

Parameters are scoped in the same fashion as variables. You might wonder why you would declare parameters as children of a stylesheet. XSLT allows for processors to pass parameter values into the stylesheet when performing a transformation, but it is silent on the API for performing this feat. Each XSLT-compliant processor is free to implement this standard feature with a proprietary call.

The result of transforming `speakerlist.xml` with the above stylesheet is as follows:

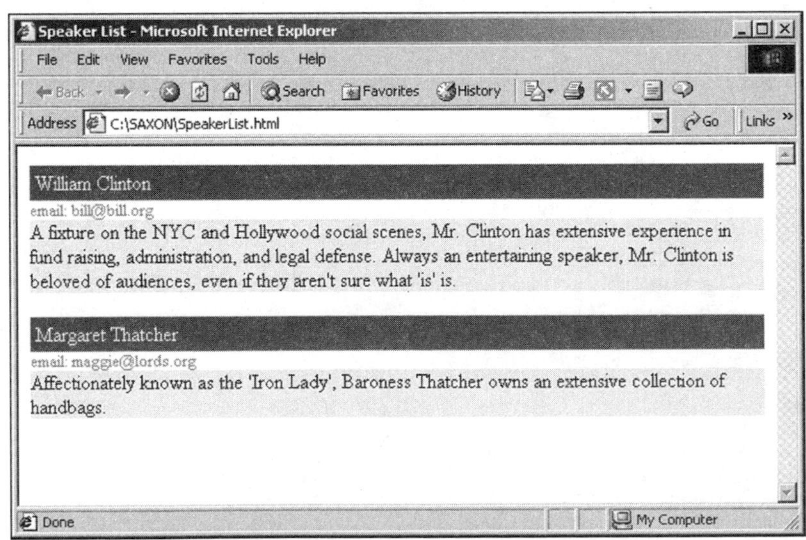

The above HTML example was created by applying the previous XSLT to the above XML, using Michael Kay's Saxon processor (see the "Transformations in Code" section for more details).

Modularity

It's also useful to be able to treat stylesheets as modular units, particularly if you develop an extended body of useful templates that handle a commonly encountered problem. To accommodate this, XSLT provides the `<xsl:include>` and `<xsl:import>` elements.

Both have the same syntax. They are empty elements that take a single, required attribute, `href`, whose value is a URI that identifies the stylesheet to bring into the calling stylesheet. Both are child elements of `<xsl:stylesheet>` or `<xsl:transform>`. Here are some samples:

```
<xsl:include href="http://www.my_org.net/xsl/v_important.xsl"/>
```

```
<xsl:import href="somewhatimportant.xsl"/>
```

When either element appears, the top-level elements – variable and parameter declarations as well as templates – are treated as if they were physically inserted into the importing or including stylesheet. The difference between the two is in how conflicting templates are handled. The `<xsl:include>` element gives included templates the same priority as templates from the including stylesheet. Any conflicts are resolved using the same rules that apply for conflicting templates native to the stylesheet. Content inserted with `<xsl:import>`, by contrast, have a lower priority than native templates. Thus, if an imported template matches the current context node and a native template matches as well, the native template will be executed in preference to the imported template.

If you wish to override this and have both templates apply, you may resort to `<xsl:apply-imports>` within the body of a template. Suppose two stylesheets have templates like this:

```
<xsl:template match="Person">   ...   </xsl:template>
```

If one stylesheet imports the other, the native template will be used in preference to the imported template that matches the `Person` element. The following stylesheet fragment, however, causes both to be applied:

```
<xsl:stylesheet version="1.0"
   xmlns:xsl="http://www.w3.org/1999/XSL/Transform">

   <xsl:import href="other_stylesheet.xsl"/>
      ...
   <xsl:template match="Person" />
      ...
   </xsl:template>
   <xsl:apply-imports/>
      ...
</xsl:stylesheet>
```

XSLT Programming Style

Despite the fact that XSLT includes elements that give authors of transformations a programming-like capability (for example, the `<xsl:for-each>` and `<xsl:if>` elements), working with XSLT requires a significant shift from procedural programming. Just getting around the lack of an assignment operator takes a shift in techniques. This can be beneficial. Not only do we learn new problem solving techniques, but also new techniques may teach us something we want to take back to the procedural world.

Whether we want to explore new techniques or not, we have to deal with them if we are going to be effective in writing non-trivial transformations. We'll briefly consider three areas with which you should become familiar if you want to use XSLT in your XML programming arsenal. These techniques are:

- Recursion
- Focusing on the data rather than the code
- Dealing with transformation tasks XSLT can't handle alone

Recursion

One of the most powerful techniques you will commonly use in XSLT transformations is recursion. This is, generally speaking, where a subroutine calls itself with some subset of the information originally passed to it. This continues until the data is broken down to a state where the routine can handle it without calling itself again. This is known as the exit condition. When writing a recursive routine, you must be sure you will always have an exit condition, unless your aim is to destroy your application in an amusing new way. Each time the subroutine is called, the local variables and calling parameters are pushed onto a stack. When the calls reach the bottom, the stack is unwound, using the simple solution to solve the next largest piece and so on until the original call to the routine is handled.

Recursion is widely used for two reasons: firstly, the lack of an assignment operator can be handled with recursion. Consider a traditional `for` loop. Instead of incrementing a variable and performing some unit of work until the variable reaches a limit, we arrange for the work to act as the counter. When the data is broken apart, the first unit of work is performed and the stack begins to unwind. Secondly, recursion can be a high performance technique when dealing with collections of nodes. Rather than create a new variable and execute an XPath selection that repeats some work performed earlier, we perform the selection once and pass it through a recursive algorithm.

Consider the following problem. We have some list of chapters in a book, and we want to represent them as a row of boxes on a browser page. In a procedural language, we'd have a variable that controlled the placement of each box on the page. As each chapter was processed, we'd increment the variable and proceed to the next one. Lacking an assignment operator, however, we can't do this with an `<xsl:for-each>` element or any other XSLT construct except recursion. Here's the code:

```
<xsl:template …
   <xsl:call-template name="list">
      <xsl:with-param name="x" select="8.0"/>
      <xsl:with-param name="y" select="0.5"/>
      <xsl:with-param name="nodelist" select="//Chapter[@category='core']"/>
   </xsl:call-template>
</xsl:template>

<xsl:template name="list">
   <xsl:param name="x"/>
   <xsl:param name="y"/>
   <xsl:param name="nodelist"/>
   <xsl:variable name="firstnode" select="$nodelist[1]"/>
   <xsl:variable name="rest-of-list" select="$nodelist[position()!=1]"/>
   <xsl:variable name="selID" select="//Book/@selected"/>
   <xsl:call-template name="output-box" >
      <xsl:with-param name="selected" select="boolean($selID =
                                 $firstnode/@id)"/>
      <xsl:with-param name="node" select="$firstnode"/>
```

```
            <xsl:with-param name="x" select="$x"/>
            <xsl:with-param name="y" select="$y"/>
        </xsl:call-template>

        <xsl:if test="$rest-of-list">
            <xsl:call-template name="list">
                <xsl:with-param name="x" select="number($x) + 4.5"/>
                <xsl:with-param name="y" select="$y"/>
                <xsl:with-param name="nodelist" select="$rest-of-list"/>
            </xsl:call-template>
        </xsl:if>
    </xsl:template>
```

Let's look at a template – for now, it does not matter which one – in the stylesheet that uses the `<xsl:call-template>` element. It sends the initial `x` and `y` coordinates for where the row of boxes is to begin, together with a list of nodes we want to output, to the named template, `list`. The `list` template splits the list into its first node and a list of remaining nodes. Using these variables, `firstnode` and `rest-of-list`, it does two things. First, it calls another template, `output-box` (not shown in the listing), which generates the HTML needed to render the box on the page. Next, if there are nodes remaining in the list, it calls itself. The value of `y` is unchanged (this is a single row), but the value passed as `x` is the current value of `x` plus a standard offset. We have not changed the value of `x` in this scope; the incremented value is passed as a parameter to a new instance of `list` on the call stack. When the last `Chapter` node is output, `rest-of-list` will be empty because there are no more elements to be selected by the expression `$nodelist[position()!=1]` and therefore, processing in `list` will cease.

Focus on Data, NOT Programming

One of the interesting side effects of XSLT's declarative nature is that a well-written stylesheet is forced to focus on the data in the source document and not programming. While XSLT contains familiar programming constructs like `xsl:for-each` and `xsl:if`, its lack of an assignment operator and the fact that so much processing is driven by the expression matching sequence rather than programmatic control means that your templates must reflect the structure of the data document. They cannot create data structures of their own to any great extent, but must instead draw from the data as it appears.

In a procedural language, the equivalent to the source document would be the public data structures of the application. A bad programmer (or a good programmer saddled with poorly conceived data structures) is free to create his own private structures, committing whatever sins he needs to implement an algorithm. If the values in these structures make their way back to the public structures, all is well – though not necessarily elegant. If the programmer forgets to make this change, the program ceases to be valid.

Now consider what happens in an XSLT stylesheet. You have a fixed structure to start: the source document. The form of the document is set in advance, and the particular document instance being processed must conform to it. If it does not, your templates will not match and little or nothing will be done. The other major structure with which you may work is the output document – this is wide open to you. Along the way, your opportunities for caching data in variables and interim structures are limited. You are encouraged to write templates that incrementally generate output as source data is encountered. In the words of Michael Corning, a speaker on schema-based programming, "the schema is the API". XSLT makes it hard for you to avoid the data – it is data driven and leaves little room for changing the data outside of writing to the output document. If you encounter a problem you can't solve within the limits of XSLT, you should first consider the structure of your stylesheet. Is it tracking the data or fighting it? If that isn't the problem, you should reflect on the structure of the source document. Does the vocabulary adequately represent what you are trying to accomplish?

Dealing with Tasks XSLT Can't Handle

Of course, no language is perfect. Declarative languages like XSLT have their limitations as well as their proper uses. Some tasks are better handled in procedural code.

We'll examine this issue in Chapter 13, "Declarative Programming", when we look at schema based programming in detail.

The XSLT Recommendation actually makes provisions for vendor-specific extensions. In essence, a vendor may use extension functions in XPath expressions, template bodies, or top-level elements by qualifying them within a specific namespace and providing an implementation in their XSLT processors. The use of namespaces prevents name collisions between XSLT and vendors, and between various vendors. It also flags extensions so that other processors can ignore the vendor-specific implementations.

To give you an idea of what is available, let's consider two implementations of extension functions. Several Java processor implementations permit extensions that refer to methods of a particular Java class. While all are similar, they have slight differences in syntax, so the extensions are not portable across processors even though all use the Java language. Either the namespace declaration or the specific extension usage provides a fully qualified Java class path to the class implementing the method to be used. For example:

```
<xsl:stylesheet version="1.0"
   xmlns:xsl="http://www.w3.org/1999/XSL/Transform"
   xmlns:date="http://www.oracle.com/XSL/Transform/java/java.util.Date" >
      ...
   <xsl:value-of select="date:toString(date:new())" />
      ...
```

The declaration of the `date` namespace tells Oracle's processor to use the class `java.util.Date`, and the `<xsl:value-of>` element uses the `toString` and `constructor` (`new()`) methods of that class to generate output.

The specific details of Java usage vary by vendor, so be sure to check your documentation carefully.

The Microsoft processor uses the `<msxsl:script>` element and its `implements-prefix` attribute to implement and denote, extension functions. For example:

```
<xsl:stylesheet xmlns:xsl="http://www.w3.org/1999/XSL/Transform"
   xmlns:msxsl="urn:schemas-microsoft-com:xslt"
   xmlns:guid="http://www.wrox.com/uuid" version="1.0">
      ...
   <xsxsl:script language="Javascript" implements-prefix="guid">
      function GenerateGuid( )
      {
         ...
      }
   </msxsl:script>
...
   <xsl:value-of select="guid:GenerateGuid()"/>
...
</xsl:stylesheet>
```

Microsoft's namespace permits the MSXML XSLT processor to locate script code within the body of the stylesheet. The `language` attribute tells the script runtime which interpreter to use, while the value of the `implements-prefix` attribute is the prefix of our extension functions. The XSLT processor uses this information to invoke the script runtime and look for a function within the `<msxsl:script>` element that implements the extension function. Elsewhere in the stylesheet, some template includes the `<xsl:value-of>` element shown. Since the `guid` prefix is encountered, the script function is located and executed to satisfy the `select` attribute. The value generated by the extension function is output as the result of the `<xsl:value-of>` element.

> *If you are familiar with the earlier Microsoft XSL technology preview, this usage, which is implemented in MSXML 3.0, replaces the proprietary* `<xsl: eval>` *element used in the preview implementation.*

Executing Transformations

We've made no mention so far about how to invoke an XSLT processor to apply XSLT transformations to XML documents. This is because the XSLT Recommendation provides no guidance other than to leave this issue to the vendors. That is, each vendor must provide one or more proprietary API calls to execute a transformation. The W3C is only concerned with the XSLT and XPath vocabularies and their semantics. As we move into the sample code portion of this chapter, it becomes an issue. The samples we will provide adhere to the XSLT Recommendation, so you are free to invoke them using the processor of your choice. Before we turn to them, though, we'll provide a bit of guidance in case you have never worked with an XSLT processor. There are two ways to go about applying a transformation: write your own code that calls the vendor-specific API functions, or use a third-party utility.

Transformations in Code

There isn't a lot to be said about writing XSLT-invoking code from a high level. Each vendor's implementation is unique, so we cannot simply list some core set of calls that will apply across processors. We've used Microsoft's processor extensively, so we will very briefly list the calls with which you should become familiar when working with that processor. If you are using some other processor, be sure to refer to the vendor's documentation.

> *You will also find extensive code samples using a variety of processors in XSLT Programmer's Reference (Wrox Press, 2001, ISBN 1-861005-06-7) and Professional XSL (Wrox Press, 2001, ISBN 1-861003-57-9).*

Microsoft's MSXML component provides XSLT transformations in two ways. It has added two methods to the Document Object Model, `transformNode` and `transformNodeToObject`. Both take a stylesheet object as an argument. When applied to a node in an XML document, `transformNode` returns the XML that results from the transformation specified in the supplied stylesheet. The `transformNodeToObject` method takes the same stylesheet argument, but returns the results of the transformation as an object. The object, which is also supplied as a parameter to the method, is a parser instance similar to the object on which the transformation was applied.

Beginning with version 3.0 of the parser component, Microsoft began supporting XSLT and addressed the issue of scalability. Users were increasingly performing transformations on Web servers, so a scalable method of performing transformations was urgently needed. The result is two new interfaces, `IXSLTemplate` and `IXSLProcessor`. The advantage to using these interfaces is that XSLT stylesheets are cached after having been parsed. The component's internal structures are retained, so each transformation is faster for not having to parse the stylesheet and prepare for transformation. The basic process of using these objects takes three steps. First, a stylesheet is loaded into a free-threaded instance of the parser component (created using the COM ProgID `Msxml2.FreeThreadedDOMDocument`).

Next, an instance of a template object is created using the ProgID `Msxml2.XSLTemplate` and that object's stylesheet property is set equal to the free-threaded parser component instance that holds the parsed stylesheet. Finally, the template object's `createProcessor` method is called to create an instance of the `IXSLProcessor` interface. That interface's transform method actually applies the transformation to a document. The following code fragment is a Javascript sample of this usage in an ASP page:

```
var xmlDoc = new ActiveXObject("MSXML2.FreeThreadedDOMDocument");
var xslSheet = new ActiveXObject("MSXML2.FreeThreadedDOMDocument");
var xslTemplate = new ActiveXObject("MSXML2.XSLTemplate");
xmlDoc.async = false;
xslSheet.async = false;
xslSheet.setProperty("SelectionLanguage", "XPath");

xmlDoc.load(Server.MapPath("source_doc.xml"));
xslSheet.load(Server.MapPath("transform.xsl"));
xslTemplate.stylesheet = xslSheet;
var xslProcessor = xslTemplate.createProcessor();

xslProcessor.input = xmlDoc;
xslProcessor.transform();
Response.Write(xslProcessor.output);
```

The advantages to using these interfaces and their slightly roundabout approach to transformations are scalability and the ability to pass parameters to the XSLT stylesheet. As noted, the template object may be cached, thereby avoiding the overhead of parsing the stylesheet and preparing internal structures. The processor object is more narrowly focused, having properties set for a particular source document and set of parameters. This is not suitable for caching, being instantiated instead at the time transformation is required. The second advantage, global parameter passing, was introduced in response to the finished XSLT Recommendation. The technical preview implemented an earlier draft of XSL, which did not incorporate the idea of parameters. In consequence, the older method of transformation, using the Document Object Model and the `transformNode` and `transformNodeToObject` methods, does not permit parameter passing. The XSLT processor component, however, has methods for setting parameters values prior to transformation.

A complete reference to programming the Microsoft XSLT processor is found on Microsoft's XML SDK site at http://msdn.microsoft.com/library/psdk/xmlsdk/xmls6g53.htm.

If we are merely dealing with transformations in isolation, however, we don't want to write scripts just so we can execute them. It would be nice to have a utility that provided this for us. While there are many XSLT processors available, we'd like to mention a couple of utilities in passing that can help you explore the stylesheets in the following sections.

Saxon

Saxon is a very useful open source XSL implementation, written by Michael Kay. It is available under the Mozilla Public License, allowing free use of it for any purpose. It can be invoked either from the command line, or as a Java class, and it allows you to run simple XSLTs, using syntax as shown below:

```
C:\> saxon SpeakerList.xml SpeakerList.xsl > SpeakerList.html
```

This is the command used to create an HTML file from the XML and XSL files we looked at earlier, where SAXON was first mentioned in the chapter, in the "Calling Templates" section. For it to work, the SAXON program has to be present in the same location as the source files; otherwise you'll need to include the full path to SAXON in the command when you invoke it.

For more information about SAXON, and to download the different versions, go to http://users.iclway.co.uk/mhkay/saxon/

We used "instant SAXON" in our example, a cut-down version, packaged as a windows executable for ease of use (no source code or examples – the **Full** version includes these).

VBXML's XSL Tester

This utility is called XSL Tester and is the product of VBXML.com, an association of XML authors and consultants. The source code for XSL Tester is available for download. This utility, which is a simple XSL editor, takes XML documents and stylesheets and applies the transformation, displaying the results in an output window, where they may be viewed as plain text or in a browser window. The utility was developed for the Microsoft XSL preview. When you create a new stylesheet, for example, the namespace on the stylesheet element is incorrect. This leaves you with two options. If you want to do things right, you may edit the source code to instantiate the correct version of the MSXML component and display the correct namespace on new stylesheets. If, however, you simply want to load and apply a transformation in a big hurry, you can run MSXML3 in replace mode. XSLT stylesheets, such as the samples, will execute correctly. When you write new stylesheets, however, you must remember to edit the namespace declaration.

XSL Tester is available at http://www.vbxml.com/xsltester. *The MSXML3 download is found at* http://msdn.microsoft.com/xml/general/xmlparser.asp. *If you wish to run it in replace mode (and understand what replace mode is), you must download the xmlinst utility at* http://msdn.microsoft.com/downloads/default.asp?URL=/code/sample.asp?url=/msdn-files/027/001/469/msdncompositedoc.xml. *Some recent versions of Microsoft products also install MSXML3 during installation.*

VBXML has other XSLT resources, including a beta version XSLT debugger. The site and the code on it change frequently, so it is worth checking on a regular basis.

XSLT for Presentation: XML To HTML Example

Let's look at an XML vocabulary that we will use for the two examples that follow. It is based on the exchange of data about books between booksellers, distributors, and publishers. The document is a partial catalog of books, and can be used in different ways by different parties. A publisher will want to list all the books they offer for sale, and distributors and booksellers might list selections across publishers that are organized by theme or imprint. This example will show us how to convert a `Catalog` document into an HTML page suitable for viewing in a browser. The example that follows will take exactly the same source document and two views that differ in format and content, each tailored to a different purpose. Both are created by XSLT transformations.

The Book Catalog Source Document

Each `Catalog` document includes a list of publishers, a list of subject matter threads, and a list of books. Each publisher has a list of authors who write for them, as well as a list of imprints. The threads are areas of interest – XML styling, for example, or database programming – for which someone might be searching for help. All the books in the document are listed together with no expectation of order or organization. There should be enough information to relate books to authors and publishers and threads to books. Here is a sample `Catalog` document (also found in the download as `BookCatalogSample.xml`):

```
<?xml version = "1.0"?>
<Catalog>
   <Publisher isbn = "186100">
      <CorporateName>Wrox Press Ltd</CorporateName>
      <Address headquarters = "yes">
         <Street>Arden House</Street>
         <Street>1102 Warwick Road, Acocks Green</Street>
         <City>Birmingham</City>
         <Country>UK</Country>
         <PostalCode>B27 6BH</PostalCode>
      </Address>
      <Address headquarters = "no">
         <Street>Suite 520</Street>
         <Street>29 S. Lasalle Street</Street>
         <City>Chicago</City>
         <PoliticalDivision>IL</PoliticalDivision>
         <Country>USA</Country>
         <PostalCode>60603</PostalCode>
      </Address>
      <Imprints>
         <Imprint shortImprintName = "XML">XML and Scripting</Imprint>
         <Imprint shortImprintName ="Linux">GNU/Linux</Imprint>
         <Imprint shortImprintName ="Java">Java</Imprint>
         <Imprint shortImprintName ="ASP">Active Server Pages</Imprint>
      </Imprints>
      <Author authorCiteID = "smohr">
         <FirstName>Stephen</FirstName>
         <LastName>Mohr</LastName>
         <Biographical>Stephen Mohr is a senior systems
            architect...
         </Biographical>
      </Author>
      <Author authorCiteID = "nozu">
         <FirstName>Nikola</FirstName>
         <LastName>Ozu</LastName>
         <Biographical>Nikola Ozu is a systems architect and
            consultant...
         </Biographical>
      </Author>
      <Author authorCiteID = "jond">
         <FirstName>Jon</FirstName>
         <LastName>Duckett</LastName>
         <Biographical>One of Wrox's in-house authors, Jon
            is...
         </Biographical>
      </Author>
      <Author authorCiteID = "mbirbeck">
         <FirstName>Mark</FirstName>
         <LastName>Birbeck</LastName>
         <Biographical>Mark Birbeck has been a professional programmer
            for...
         </Biographical>
      </Author>
      <Author authorCiteID = "mkay">
         <FirstName>Michael</FirstName>
         <LastName>Kay</LastName>
```

```
        <Biographical>Michael Kay, author of XSLT programmer's reference, has
           spent most of ...
        </Biographical>
     </Author>
     <Author authorCiteID = "scottwoo">
        <FirstName>Scott</FirstName>
        <LastName>Woodgate</LastName>
        <Biographical>Scott Woodgate, a Microsoft Certified Solution
           Developer, ...
        </Biographical>
     </Author>
  </Publisher>
  <Thread threadID = "coreXML">Core XML</Thread>
  <Thread threadID ="proXML">Advanced Topics in XML</Thread>
  <Thread threadID ="msXML">Microsoft XML Products</Thread>
  <Book ISBN = "1861005059" level = "pro" pubdate = "06-01-2001"
        pageCount = "800" authors = "smohr mbirbeck nozu jond"
        threads = "coreXML proXML" imprint = "XML">
     <Title>Professional XML, 2nd Edition</Title>
     <Abstract>An update to the wildly successful first edition, Pro XML
       covers the full ...
     </Abstract>
     <RecSubjCategories>
        <Category>Internet</Category>
        <Category>Internet Programming</Category>
        <Category>XML</Category>
     </RecSubjCategories>
     <Price currency = "USD">49.99</Price>
  </Book>
  <Book ISBN = "1861003129" level = "pro" pubdate = "07-2000" pageCount = "780"
        authors = "mkay" threads = "proXML" imprint = "XML">
     <Title>XSLT Programmer's Reference</Title>
     <Abstract>
        The definitive guide to XSLT and XSLT programming
     </Abstract>
     <RecSubjCategories>
        <Category>Internet</Category>
        <Category>XML</Category>
        <Category>XSL</Category>
     </RecSubjCategories>
     <Price currency = "USD">34.99</Price>
  </Book>
  <Book ISBN = "1861003293" level = "pro" pubdate = "12-2000" pageCount = "700"
        authors = "smohr scottwoo" threads = "proXML msXML" imprint = "XML">
     <Title>Professional BizTalk</Title>
     <Abstract>
        The first comprehensive guide to using and programming Microsoft
        BizTalk Server...
     </Abstract>
     <RecSubjCategories>
        <Category>XML</Category>
        <Category>E-Commerce</Category>
     </RecSubjCategories>
     <Price currency = "USD">49.99</Price>
  </Book>
</Catalog>
```

Note that the stem of the ISBN number uniquely identifies publishers. They have multiple physical locations listed, with one designated as the corporate headquarters. The imprints listed for them are the major themes or subject areas into which they group their books. Authors are identified by a unique `id` attribute, `authorCiteID`, whose value turns up in the `author's` attribute of the books themselves. That attribute is typed as `IDREFS`, which allows us to have multiple authors.

Each book has the full ISBN of the title, the book title, the cost of the books, a list of threads to which it belongs, and the author list. The threads attribute allows us to organize books according to some subject area, while `ISBN` allows us to find the book's publisher.

Now let's suppose we need a stylesheet that will take the `Catalog` document and render it as a list of books in HTML format. Our sample document looks like this after such a transformation:

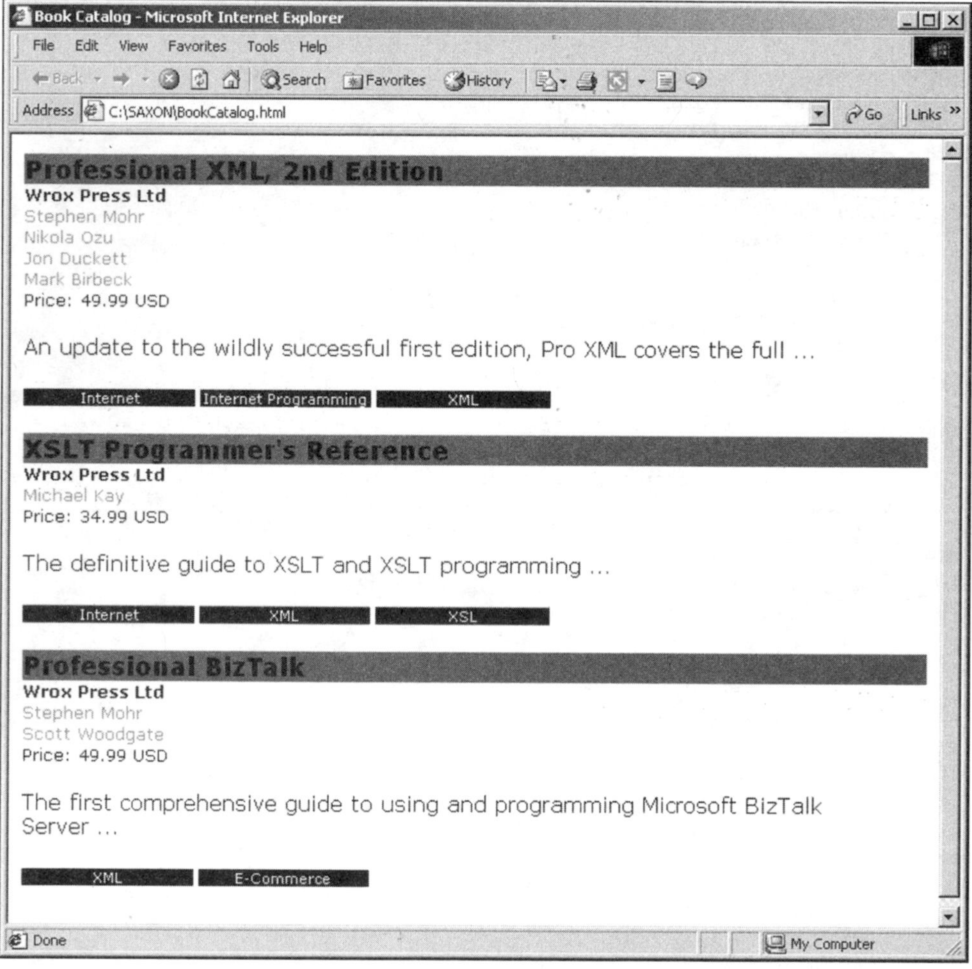

We begin our stylesheet (`catalog_ui.xsl` in the download) for this task with the standard `<xsl:stylesheet>` element and an `<xsl:output>` element that tells the processor we will be generating HTML output:

```
<xsl:stylesheet xmlns:xsl="http://www.w3.org/1999/XSL/Transform"
        version="1.0">
<xsl:output encoding="UTF-16" method="html" />
```

The template that matches the root is essential in that it determines the shell of the HTML page and organizes our processing:

```
<xsl:template match="/">
   <xsl:element name="HTML">
      <xsl:element name="HEAD">
         <xsl:element name="TITLE">Book Catalog</xsl:element>
      </xsl:element>
      <xsl:element name="BODY">
         <xsl:apply-templates select="/Catalog/Book"/>
      </xsl:element>
   </xsl:element>
</xsl:template>
```

The `<xsl:element>` elements create the standard shell of an HTML page as well as providing a title for it. Take a look at the element that creates the HTML `<BODY>` element, though. We want to direct the processor to the `<Book>` elements and skip over everything else unless and until we need it. To do this, we call on `<xsl:apply-templates>`, but we are specific in which template to apply. The result of applying this element with the value of the `select` attribute shown is to direct the processor to the template that matches `<Book>` elements. This template will be executed once for each `<Book>` element found in the source document. We obviously want to start our listing with the book's title. Following that, we have a number of attributes of the source `Book` element that must appear prior to any of the items in child elements. While we want to control the flow of execution as little as possible, we do have to take control for these early items. Let's look at this first part of the `Book`-matching template:

```
<xsl:template match="Book">
   <xsl:apply-templates select="Title"/>
   <xsl:variable name="isbn" select="@ISBN"/>
   <xsl:element name="DIV">
     <xsl:attribute name="style">
         font-family:Verdana;font-size:10pt;color:black;
         font-weight:bolder
      </xsl:attribute>
      <xsl:value-of select=
         "/Catalog/Publisher[contains($isbn,@isbn)]/CorporateName"/>
   </xsl:element>
   <xsl:variable name="by" select="@authors"/>
      <xsl:call-template name="fetch-authors">
      <xsl:with-param name="authors" select=
         "/Catalog/Publisher/Author[contains($by,@authorCiteID)]"/>
   </xsl:call-template>
   <xsl:element name="DIV">
      <xsl:attribute name="style">
         color:black;font-size:10pt;font-family:Verdana
      </xsl:attribute>
      <xsl:text>Price: </xsl:text>
      <xsl:value-of select="Price"/>
      <xsl:text> </xsl:text>
      <xsl:value-of select="Price/@currency"/>
```

```
    </xsl:element>
    <xsl:apply-templates select="*[name() != 'Title']"/>
    <xsl:element name="P"/>
</xsl:template>
```

The very first thing we are doing is invoking the `<Title>` matching template in much the same way we invoked the template we are examining. It creates a `<DIV>` with the appropriate styling:

```
<xsl:template match="Title">
    <xsl:element name="DIV">
        <xsl:attribute name="style">
            background:teal;color:black;font-family:Verdana;
            font-size:14pt;font-weight:bolder
        </xsl:attribute>
        <xsl:value-of select="."/>
    </xsl:element>
</xsl:template>
```

As soon as it completes and we return to the `Book`-matching template though, we want to list the publisher. Recall that the `<Publisher>` element has the stem of the ISBN for all their books as an attribute, and the current `Book` element has the complete ISBN of the book. The complete ISBN, of course, contains the stem denoting the related `Publisher` element. The XPath expression used in the `<xsl:value-of>` element -- `/Catalog/Publisher[contains($isbn,@isbn)]/CorporateName` locates the `<Publisher>` whose `isbn` attribute is contained in the `<Book>` element's `ISBN` attribute, denoted here by the variable `isbn`. We need this variable so we can refer to `<Book>` information while looking at information within the `<Publisher>` context.

Now we want to list the authors. We have their IDs in the `authors` attribute, but we need to assemble their full names from the related `<Author>` elements. We select the collection of `<Author>` elements that are related to the current `Book` element and pass that collection to the named template `fetch-authors`:

```
    <xsl:call-template name="fetch-authors">
        <xsl:with-param name="authors" select=
            "/Catalog/Publisher/Author[contains($by,@authorCiteID)]"/>
    </xsl:call-template>
```

Leaving the `Book`-matching template for a moment, let's look at `fetch-authors`:

```
<xsl:template name="fetch-authors">
    <xsl:param name="authors" select="anonymous"/>
    <xsl:variable name="first" select="$authors[1]"/>
    <xsl:variable name="rest" select="$authors[position()!=1]"/>
    <xsl:element name="DIV">
        <xsl:attribute name="style">
            font-family:Verdana;font-size:10pt;color:gray;
        </xsl:attribute>
        <xsl:value-of select="$first/FirstName"/>
        <xsl:text> </xsl:text>
        <xsl:value-of select="$first/LastName"/>
    </xsl:element>

    <xsl:if test="$rest">
     <xsl:call-template name="fetch-authors">
```

```
        <xsl:with-param name="authors" select="$rest"/>
      </xsl:call-template>
    </xsl:if>
  </xsl:template>
```

We want to create a string consisting of the <FirstName> and <LastName> element's textual values separated by a single space. This string is placed inside a <DIV> on which we'll set a style attribute containing color and font information.

There are two important things to observe about this template. The first is that we are using recursion to work through the list of authors. The variable first takes the first node in the list passed through the parameter authors. The variable rest takes any node whose position in the collection is not 1 – that is, all but the very first node in the collection. After processing first, we check to see if rest contains anything (this is in the <xsl:if> element). If it does, we again call fetch-authors, replacing the entire list of authors with the subset in rest. Eventually, we will call the template with the last node in the original collection, first will claim this value, rest will be empty, and the template will finish processing.

The other thing to observe is the use of <xsl:text>. Go ahead and try replacing it with a single space character. You will find that this literal whitespace is ignored and the first and last names of the authors are concatenated without a space. Whitespace is explicitly handled in XSLT. If you want some literal spaces, you need to formally tell the processor what you want.

Once fetch-authors finishes its processing, we return to the Book-matching template. At this point, we've output the book's title, the name of the publisher, and the list of authors. That leaves the price, the abstract of the book, and the list of recommended subject areas. <Price> is found at the end of the <Book> element, and we need the value of its currency attribute as well. We therefore need to keep control of the flow of execution, so that the XSLT elements to process this information are found within the Book-matching template. The instructions should be familiar to you by now. We create a <DIV> with appropriate styling, then we use <xsl:text> to emit the literal string Price:. Note the hard-coded space at the end of the string. Following that, we output the value of <Price>, following it with another hard-coded space. Finally, we emit the value of the currency attribute.

```
    <xsl:element name="DIV">
      <xsl:attribute name="style">
        color:black;font-size:10pt;font-family:Verdana
      </xsl:attribute>
      <xsl:text>Price: </xsl:text>
      <xsl:value-of select="Price"/>
      <xsl:text> </xsl:text>
      <xsl:value-of select="Price/@currency"/>
    </xsl:element>
```

The remaining items of information – the abstract and recommended subject lists – are found in the source document in the order in which we want to output them, so we can relinquish control at this point. This lets the XSLT processor optimize its processing, and it simplifies our Book-matching template. Recall, though, we are still in the context of the <Book> element, so we have to tell the processor to explicitly ignore the <Title> element or we will see this information repeated. We do this with <xsl:apply-templates>:

```
    <xsl:apply-templates select="*[name() != 'Title']"/>
    <xsl:element name="P"/>
  </xsl:template>
```

The value of the `select` attribute retrieves any node whose name is not <Title>, which is what we want. We are still not out of the Book-matching template, however. When all the other templates have completed, the processor will return to this template and create an HTML <P> element, thereby giving us a little space between books.

Once we relinquish control to the XSLT processor, it proceeds from its current context – the <Book> element – to child content. The first element it finds – remember, we've excluded <Title> explicitly – is <Abstract>. The template for this is straightforward. It creates a <DIV> element with the styling we desire and copies the content of <Abstract> into the output:

```
<xsl:template match="Abstract">
   <xsl:element name="P"/>
   <xsl:element name="DIV">
      <xsl:attribute name="style">
         font-family:Verdana;font-size:12pt</xsl:attribute>
      <xsl:value-of select="."/>
   </xsl:element>
</xsl:template>
```

Processing for <RecSubjCategories> is much the same. The only novelty here is that we want little black boxes such as are seen on the back covers of books. To get them, we create <SPAN> elements – these need to be on the same line and <DIV> is a block element – and give them fixed widths and colors:

```
<xsl:template match="RecSubjCategories">
   <xsl:element name="P"/>
   <xsl:for-each select="Category">
      <xsl:element name="SPAN">
         <xsl:attribute name="style">
            font-family:verdana;font-size:8pt;background:black;
            color:white;width:3.5cm;text-align:center
         </xsl:attribute>
         <xsl:value-of select="."/>
      </xsl:element>
      <xsl:text> </xsl:text>
   </xsl:for-each>
</xsl:template>
```

That would seem to be it. If we stopped there and ran the transformation, however, we'd see the textual content of the <Price> element repeated in the output. To turn that off, we add a final, empty template that matches all text nodes. The XSLT processor will still encounter <Price>, and finding no match will proceed to its child text node. Finding a match, it generates no output and goes on with the expression matching process:

```
<xsl:template match="text()"/>

</xsl:stylesheet>
```

Results

You've seen the visual results of the transformation we've just described. Here is the HTML output for a single book that results from applying the transformation using Microsoft's MSXML 3.0 processor. Some whitespace has been added for clarity:

```
<DIV style="background:teal;color:black;font-family:Verdana;
      font-size:14pt;font-weight:bolder">Professional XML, 2nd Edition
</DIV>
<DIV style="font-family:Verdana;font-size:10pt;color:black;
      font-weight:bolder">
   Wrox Press Ltd
</DIV>
<DIV style="font-family:Verdana;font-size:10pt;color:gray;">Stephen Mohr</DIV>
<DIV style="font-family:Verdana;font-size:10pt;color:gray;">Nikola Ozu</DIV>
<DIV style="font-family:Verdana;font-size:10pt;color:gray;">Jon Duckett</DIV>
<DIV style="font-family:Verdana;font-size:10pt;color:gray;">Mark Birbeck</DIV>
<DIV style="color:black;font-size:10pt;font-family:Verdana">
   Price: 49.99 USD
</DIV>
<P></P>
```

XSLT for Data Conversion: XML To XML Example

Let's suppose now that we aren't interested in generating a user interface for browser interaction, but instead are interested in generating data for further use elsewhere. Continuing with the book catalog example, let's explore the **Threads** concept. Threads are designed to organize books within the catalog according to some theme or thread of knowledge. Some training management application might determine the training themes of an organization and request reading lists that match those needs. It might take things a step further, generating a purchase request and ordering the books. To support this application, we need a transformation that accepts a thread ID as a parameter and generates a book list. The resultant reading list document might look like this:

```
<?xml version="1.0" encoding="UTF-16"?>
<ReadingList>
   <Topic totalCost="134.97USD">
      <TopicTitle>Advanced Topics in XML</TopicTitle>
      <Resource isbn="1861005059">Professional XML, 2nd Edition</Resource>
      <Resource isbn="1861003129">XSLT Programmer's Reference</Resource>
      <Resource isbn="1861003293">Professional BizTalk</Resource>
   </Topic>
</ReadingList>
```

The Transformation

To begin this transformation, we need to declare the parameter, which we shall call `desired-thread`:

```
<xsl:stylesheet xmlns:xsl="http://www.w3.org/1999/XSL/Transform"
      version="1.0">
<xsl:output encoding="UTF-16" method="xml" indent="yes"/>
<xsl:param name="desired-thread">proXML</xsl:param>
```

In addition to the usual `<xsl:stylesheet>` element, we've added an `<xsl:output>` element indicating that the result of the transformation is XML, not HTML. We've thrown in the `indent` attribute to help clean up the output for the benefit of programmers who might take a look at it. The important thing about this code fragment, however, is the `<xsl:param>` element. It appears as a top-level element, so it is global in scope. We've provided a default value of `proXML`. If the XSLT processor is not passed a value for `desired-thread`, it will use this default value.

The root-matching template generates the root of the output, <ReadingList>, and then directs the processor to the template for <Catalog>. These are one and the same, but it helps us organize our templates and gives us some flexibility should we bury <Catalog> within some other element later:

```
<xsl:template match="/">
   <xsl:element name="ReadingList">
      <xsl:apply-templates select="/Catalog"/>
   </xsl:element>
</xsl:template>
```

The Catalog-matching template performs a lot of work. It finds the <Thread> element in the source document that matches our desired-thread parameter. Having done so, it generates a <Topic> element. We want the total cost of all the books that belong to this thread so we have some idea what our reading list will cost to acquire. This total is not found anywhere in the source document, so we must calculate it from the individual book prices.

In a procedural language, you would locate the matching books and iterate through the collection incrementally adding the value of <Price> to some variable. This is unnecessary in XSLT. We rely on XPath to find the nodes we need, and do the arithmetic for us using the sum() function:

```
<xsl:template match="Catalog">
   <xsl:for-each select="Thread[@threadID=$desired-thread]">
      <xsl:element name="Topic">
         <xsl:attribute name="totalCost">
            <xsl:value-of select=
              "sum(/Catalog/Book[contains(@threads,$desired-thread)]/Price)"/>
```

If the vendor of our XSLT processor has done a good job of optimizing their code, this will be much more efficient than including procedural code in our stylesheet. Following the output of this calculated value, we output the currency attribute's value, generate a <TopicTitle> element, fill it with the textual value of the source document's <Thread> element (<xsl:for-each> changes the context from <Catalog> to <Thread>), then call the template for listing the books in the thread:

```
         <xsl:value-of select=
            "/Catalog/Book[contains(@threads, $desired-thread)]/Price/@currency"/>
         </xsl:attribute>
      <xsl:element name="TopicTitle">
         <xsl:value-of select="."/>
      </xsl:element>
      <xsl:call-template name="list-books">
         <xsl:with-param name="titles" select=
            "/Catalog/Book[contains(@threads,$desired-thread)]"/>
      </xsl:call-template>
      </xsl:element>
   </xsl:for-each>
</xsl:template>
```

The named template that handles the listing of books is similar to the author-listing template you saw in our HTML example. The list-books template uses recursion to process the collection of books, but it passes detailed processing for each book off to another template, expand-resource:

```
<xsl:template name="list-books">
   <xsl:param name="titles"/>
   <xsl:variable name="first" select="$titles[1]"/>
   <xsl:variable name="rest" select="$titles[position()!=1]"/>
```

```
    <xsl:call-template name="expand-resource">
       <xsl:with-param name="book" select="$first"/>
    </xsl:call-template>

    <xsl:if test="$rest">
       <xsl:call-template name="list-books">
          <xsl:with-param name="titles" select="$rest"/>
       </xsl:call-template>
    </xsl:if>
 </xsl:template>
```

The expand-resource template is very straightforward. It creates a <Resource> element, adorns it with an isbn attribute whose value is obtained from the ISBN attribute of the passed-in <Book> element, then outputs the value of the source <Title> element as the textual content of the output <Resource> element:

```
 <xsl:template name="expand-resource">
    <xsl:param name="book"/>

    <xsl:element name="Resource">
       <xsl:attribute name="isbn">
          <xsl:value-of select="$book/@ISBN"/>
       </xsl:attribute>
       <xsl:value-of select="$book/Title"/>
    </xsl:element>
 </xsl:template>
 </xsl:stylesheet>
```

Further Steps

This transformation limited itself to providing a reading list for a single thread whose ID was passed in as a parameter. The implicit schema, however, permits more than one Topic element per <ReadingList> element. We might modify the transformation so that the default value of the desired-thread parameter is all. Try doing this, adding an <xsl:choose> element wherever an XPath expression uses the desired-thread value. When desired-thread has the value all, the expression may be simplified so that it returns all books.

Summary

In the course of this chapter, you've been introduced to XSLT, a language that grew out of the styling community of the W3C to become a declarative language widely used to transform XML-encoded data. In fact, we saw that using XSLT to style HTML is merely a special case of the overall problem of transforming XML structures.

XSLT is a declarative language, and we spent considerable time discussing how this changes programming. Transformations require a somewhat different view of programming than programs written in procedural languages. Though XSLT includes elements that mimic certain procedural activities, well-written XSLT stylesheets follow the source data rather than an algorithm. A stylesheet is an exercise in saying what should happen, not when or how. In practice, the lines blur somewhat, but you should always remain open to the differences. If you do, you will occasionally encounter some elegant bit of transformation that reduces lengthy procedural code to a few well-written templates.

Following this introduction, we presented two practical examples. Both stemmed from the same set of data, a single document comprising a catalog of books and publishers. Originally conceived with Document Object Model manipulation in mind, this vocabulary was used in two different ways, once as a simple listing for human use, and once as a relational organization for use by applications. XSLT provides transforms, and many applications are just a matter of transforming data from one format to another.

In the course of this introduction to XSLT, you were exposed to the principal elements of XSLT. XSLT is critically dependent on XPath, so we presented an introduction to that XML technology as well. Both topics were, necessarily, an introduction. There are more elements in XSLT and functions in XPath than we have discussed. Certainly, you will come to appreciate the power of these technologies only after you have has some experience of writing transformations of your own. You will encounter dead ends and false starts, but the eventual resolution will move you to a new level of experience. Even if you decide that procedural code is more to your taste, your toolkit will be richer for experiencing XSLT. If you become proficient with XSLT, you will be well placed to participate in e-commerce projects. Many, if not most, of the latest generation of business-to-business software use XML for data transfer and XSLT for data transformation. We invite the more adventurous to join us in Chapter 13, "Declarative Programming", where we use XSLT to explore a new frontier in programming.

10

Fragments, XLink, and XPointer

While the XML 1.0 specification has been around and stable for a while now, there are other specifications currently under development by the W3C that will round out the functionality of XML. We've seen some of these in the last few chapters. For XML to reach its full potential, we need a standardized way to implement:

- Linking between XML documents
- Pointing at parts of an XML document
- Exchanging fragments of XML documents

As we begin to store more and more of our information in XML document repositories, we need to be able to navigate the information in a structured manner. We need a way of specifying relationships between parts of documents, and a way of accessing the portions (or *resources*) within the document that have relationships to other resources. These resources can be portions of the same document, portions of different documents, or even items that are not XML at all!

In this chapter we will look at four different key areas that address these needs:

- **XML Fragment Interchange** – the W3C specification for the transmission of partial XML documents. It provides a way to specify contextual information for a fragment of a document without transmitting the entire document.
- **XLink** – the W3C mechanism for linking to other resources from within an XML document. Roughly analogous to a hyperlink (but much more flexible), XLink also allows non-XML documents to be linked together.
- **XPath** – the W3C general language specification for addressing parts of an XML document. We've seen the details of this in Chapter 8, so in this chapter, we'll be focusing on how XPath works in conjunction with the other technologies we discuss.

- **XPointer** – the W3C mechanism for pointing to a particular location in, or portion of, an XML document. Note that XPointer relies on XPath – XPath is used to define the addressing mechanism, while XPointer provides a standard way to use that mechanism in references. XPointers may be used to point to XML documents from non-XML sources, such as HTML.

XML Fragment Interchange

As our XML document repositories grow, and our average document size increases as we store more information in each document, manipulating the documents becomes more and more unwieldy. It would be nice if we could just work with a small portion of the document instead of needing to transfer and load the full version of it every time. To address this need, the W3C has created a specification for **XML Fragment Interchange (XFI)** that defines some mechanisms for the creation and transfer of a portion of an XML document.

What Has Changed Since the First Edition of This Book?

Since the first edition of Professional XML was published, the XML Fragment Interchange specification has been promoted to Candidate Recommendation status (this version of the specification was released on February 12, 2001). The W3C specification for XML Fragment Interchange may be found at http://www.w3.org/TR/xml-fragment.

This specification has remained essentially unchanged since the first edition of Professional XML. Note that even though this specification has been around for quite some time essentially unchanged, there aren't really any fragment-aware processors out there yet – so this section is basically intended to familiarize you with the way fragments work and how they will be used once these processors become available.

I think that the reason there's been so little take-up of this technology is that there hasn't been much call for it – unlike XLink or even XPointer, there's no pressing practical application for fragments at the moment. This is likely to change as embedded computing moves into the XML space.

What Are Document Fragments?

A **document fragment** is defined by this specification to be any **well-balanced** subset of the original document. Well-balanced subsets of documents contain whole information items – but they do not necessarily need to be well formed in the sense that an XML document is well-formed. Specifically, well-balanced subsets must contain complete tags (no partial tags are allowed), and if a well-balanced subset contains a start tag, it must contain the corresponding end tag. However, a well-balanced subset may have text at the top level – indeed, a well-balanced subset may consist of only text – or it may have multiple elements at the top level. We'll see some examples of this later.

It is up to the application that serves the fragments to decide which pieces of information are useful to the receiver. The most common example would be to only transmit elements that are necessary for the receiver's function, but other types of fragments are possible. To help us understand what portion of a document may be a fragment, let's take a look at the diagram of a sample document structure:

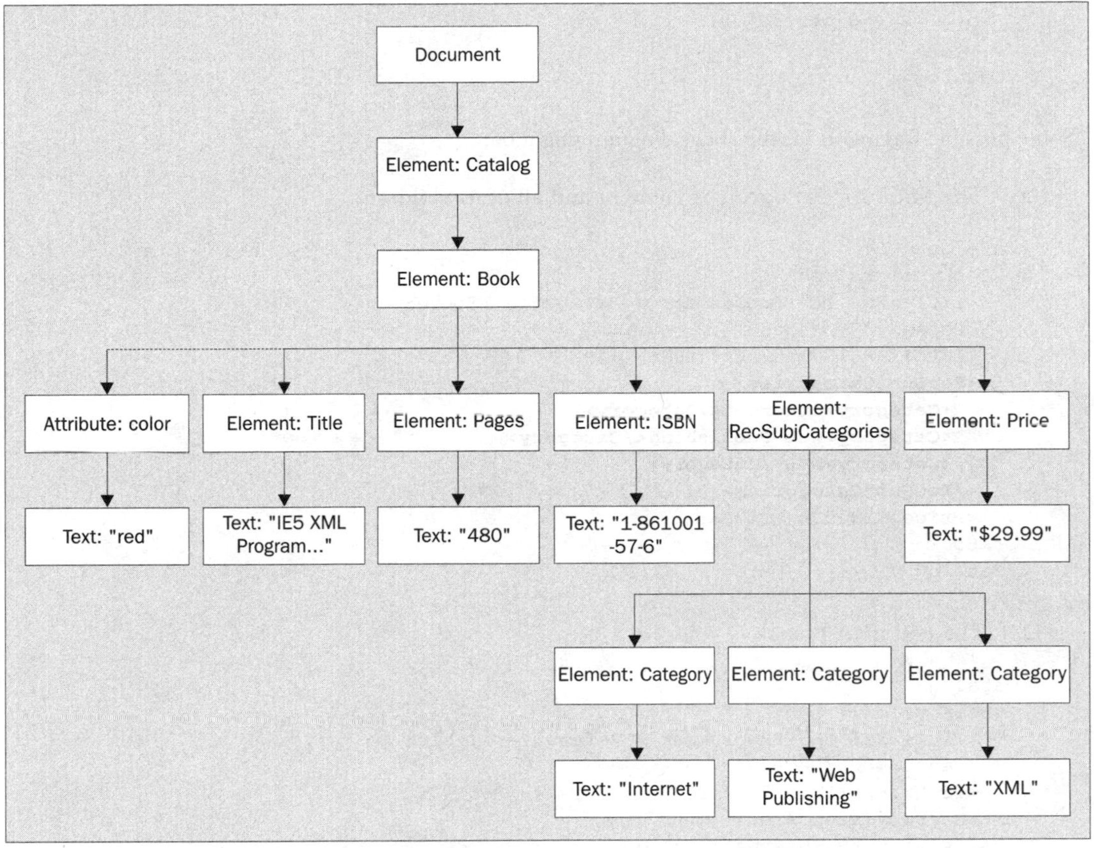

In the tree representation, any of the branches connected to the main tree by a solid line may be thought of as a possible fragment, because each branch is guaranteed to be contiguously defined within the original document. Attributes may not be defined as fragments, because they are embedded in tags and thus do not qualify as well balanced. In addition, adjacent siblings (and their children) may be defined together as a fragment, since they occur together in the original document. It may also help to think in terms of the original (serialized text) document: a valid fragment will appear as a contiguous block of text in the original document, while non-contiguous text may never be a valid fragment. Note, however, that we may have a contiguous block of text that is not a valid fragment – the above rules still apply.

The XML for the document in the diagram would be this:

```
<Catalog>
  <Book color="red">
    <Title>XML IE5 Programmer's Reference</Title>
    <Pages>480</Pages>
    <ISBN>1-861001-57-6</ISBN>
    <RecSubjCategories>
      <Category>Internet</Category>
      <Category>Web Publishing</Category>
      <Category>XML</Category>
    </RecSubjCategories>
```

```
    <Price>$29.99</Price>
  </Book>
</Catalog>
```

Some possible fragments for the above diagram might be:

- The RecSubjCategories element and all of its children

```
<Catalog>
  <Book color="red">
    <Title>XML IE5 Programmer's Reference</Title>
    <Pages>480</Pages>
    <ISBN>1-861001-57-6</ISBN>
    <RecSubjCategories>
      <Category>Internet</Category>
      <Category>Web Publishing</Category>
      <Category>XML</Category>
    </RecSubjCategories>
    <Price>$29.99</Price>
  </Book>
</Catalog>
```

- The text item "480"

```
<Catalog>
  <Book color="red">
    <Title>XML IE5 Programmer's Reference</Title>
    <Pages>480</Pages>
    <ISBN>1-861001-57-6</ISBN>
    <RecSubjCategories>
      <Category>Internet</Category>
      <Category>Web Publishing</Category>
      <Category>XML</Category>
    </RecSubjCategories>
    <Price>$29.99</Price>
  </Book>
</Catalog>
```

- The first two Category elements and their children

```
<Catalog>
  <Book color="red">
    <Title>XML IE5 Programmer's Reference</Title>
    <Pages>480</Pages>
    <ISBN>1-861001-57-6</ISBN>
    <RecSubjCategories>
      <Category>Internet</Category>
      <Category>Web Publishing</Category>
      <Category>XML</Category>
    </RecSubjCategories>
    <Price>$29.99</Price>
  </Book>
</Catalog>
```

However, the following would not be appropriate fragments:

- The first Category element and the third Category element (not contiguous)

```
<Catalog>
  <Book color="red">
    <Title>XML IE5 Programmer's Reference</Title>
    <Pages>480</Pages>
    <ISBN>1-861001-57-6</ISBN>
    <RecSubjCategories>
      <Category>Internet</Category>
      <Category>Web Publishing</Category>
      <Category>XML</Category>
    </RecSubjCategories>
    <Price>$29.99</Price>
  </Book>
</Catalog>
```

- The color attribute

```
<Catalog>
  <Book color="red">
    <Title>XML IE5 Programmer's Reference</Title>
    <Pages>480</Pages>
    <ISBN>1-861001-57-6</ISBN>
    <RecSubjCategories>
      <Category>Internet</Category>
      <Category>Web Publishing</Category>
      <Category>XML</Category>
    </RecSubjCategories>
    <Price>$29.99</Price>
  </Book>
</Catalog>
```

- The <Price> start tag, but not the </Price> end tag

```
<Catalog>
  <Book color="red">
    <Title>XML IE5 Programmer's Reference</Title>
    <Pages>480</Pages>
    <ISBN>1-861001-57-6</ISBN>
    <RecSubjCategories>
      <Category>Internet</Category>
      <Category>Web Publishing</Category>
      <Category>XML</Category>
    </RecSubjCategories>
    <Price>$29.99</Price>
  </Book>
</Catalog>
```

- The ISBN element without its Text child

```
<Catalog>
  <Book color="red">
    <Title>XML IE5 Programmer's Reference</Title>
```

```
      <Pages>480</Pages>
      <ISBN>1-861001-57-6</ISBN>
      <RecSubjCategories>
        <Category>Internet</Category>
        <Category>Web Publishing</Category>
        <Category>XML</Category>
      </RecSubjCategories>
      <Price>$29.99</Price>
    </Book>
  </Catalog>
```

Some Uses for Document Fragments

Now that we know what document fragments are, what can we do with them? Let's take a look at a few ways that fragments might be useful to us in application development. Using fragments can help us:

- Conserve resource consumption (processing time, memory requirements, network requirements, storage requirements, and so on).
- Isolate relevant subsets of information from a source document – as long as that information is contiguous. Non-contiguous information may not be sent in a single fragment, making fragments a less optimal choice than, say, XSLT, for the **redaction** (editing a subset of information that can be published) of certain pieces of information.
- Create a concurrent editing environment for large XML documents.

Conservation of Resources

The most obvious way fragments could be useful to us is to reduce the amount of information that is transferred across our networks and processed by our systems. For example, let's say that a user has requested information about a particular book from the Wrox catalog. Rather than transmitting the entire Wrox catalog (with all of the book details) to the receiver and forcing the receiver to fish out the information for the one book the user is interested in, the sender could simply send a fragment containing just the one book to the user. This will result in less bandwidth being consumed by the transmission, quicker parsing on the receiving end, and direct access to the desired information without having to traverse unnecessary information as well.

Collecting a Subset of Information

Say that Wrox included private information about royalties, distribution numbers, and so on in their XML catalog document. Unfortunately, unless that information is contiguous, XFI does not allow us to pass that information as a fragment, making XFI a poor solution to this problem. Let's take a look at an example:

```
<Catalog>
   <Book color="red">
      <Title>XML IE5 Programmer's Reference</Title>
      <Pages>480</Pages>
      <ISBN>1-861001-57-6</ISBN>
      <RecSubjCategories>
         <Category>Internet</Category>
         <Category>Web Publishing</Category>
         <Category>XML</Category>
```

```
      </RecSubjCategories>
      <Price>$49.99</Price>
      <Royalties>...</Royalties>
      <DistributedCopies>...<DistributedCopies>
   </Book>
</Catalog>
```

If someone asked for information about the XML IE5 Programmer's Reference book, a fragment could be created that only included the sibling elements for public information about the book, but did not include the private information:

```
      <Title>XML IE5Programmer's Reference</Title>
      <Pages>480</Pages>
      <ISBN>1-861001-57-6</ISBN>
      <RecSubjCategories>
         <Category>Internet</Category>
         <Category>Web Publishing</Category>
         <Category>XML</Category>
      </RecSubjCategories>
      <Price>$49.99</Price>
```

Unfortunately, fragments are not a good choice for redaction of information, since only contiguous nodes may be specified – if we wanted to send the entire catalog with private information removed, we wouldn't be able to use a fragment to do so. A much better choice for this type of manipulation would be XPath and XSLT. However, we should use fragments where possible because they allow us also to provide context information for the fragment (as we'll see later in the chapter).

Concurrent Editing and Version Control

Taking our example from above, let's presume that the catalog document goes a little deeper and actually contains the text of each book in question:

```
<Catalog>
   <Book color="red">
      <Title>XML IE5 Programmer's Reference</Title>
      <Pages>480</Pages>
      <ISBN>1-861001-57-6</ISBN>
      <RecSubjCategories>
         <Category>Internet</Category>
         <Category>Web Publishing</Category>
         <Category>XML</Category>
      </RecSubjCategories>
      <Price>$49.99</Price>
      <Chapter id="chap1">...</Chapter>
      <Chapter id="chap2">...</Chapter>
      <Chapter id="chap3">...</Chapter>
      <Chapter id="chap4">...</Chapter>
      ...
   </Book>
</Catalog>
```

Let's see how we could implement a crude form of concurrent editing and version control for the different chapters in this book.

We'll need some sort of database to track the current status of each chapter in a book:

Book	Chapter	Status
XML IE5 Programmer's Reference	1	Not checked out
XML IE5 Programmer's Reference	2	Checked out to "jond"
XML IE5 Programmer's Reference	3	Checked out to "kevinw"
XML IE5 Programmer's Reference	4	Not checked out

Of course, if we had control over the content, we could implement this as a status attribute on the `Chapter` elements as well.

We would then write an application to allow the various authors and editors to check out and check in each chapter. When a chapter is checked out to a particular author, only that fragment is sent to the author:

```
<Chapter id="chap3">...</Chapter>
```

This allows one author to work on a chapter at the same time as another author is editing a different chapter, without them overwriting each other's work. When the author is finished making changes to the chapter, he would send the modified fragment back to Wrox, who would then integrate it into the original document. It would be a simple matter at that point to update a version table in our database to indicate who had edited the document and when. There are commercial XML servers available that already implement this kind of functionality.

The Problem: Bare Document Fragments Aren't Always Enough

Having said that we can use XFI to retrieve a subsection of an XML document, there are times when a receiver needs more information than that included in the document fragment to do its job, they often require some kind of context. We'll examine some situations where bare document fragments don't provide enough information, and then we'll take a look at the W3C's solution to the problem.

What Do I Describe?

Often, in a well-designed XML document, elements are reused with different meanings depending on where they are located in the document structure. Take the following example:

```
<Bookstore>
   <Book>
      <Title>XML IE5 Programmer's Reference</Title>
      <Price>$49.99</Price>
   </Book>
   <Coffee>
      <CoffeeType>Double mocha latte</CoffeeType>
      <Price>$2.99</Price>
   </Coffee>
</Bookstore>
```

Now, let's say we received the following fragment of this document:

```
<Price>$2.99</Price>
```

What is this the price of: a programming book or a double mocha latte? Without any additional information, it's hard to tell. The sender could send the entire parent element:

```
<Coffee>
   <CoffeeType>Double mocha latte</CoffeeType>
   <Price>$2.99</Price>
</Coffee>
```

But now we've received information (`<CoffeeType>Double mocha latte</CoffeeType>`) that we didn't necessarily want or need. It would be nice if we could get some context information for our fragment without necessarily receiving all of the content of the context.

Using IDREF and IDREFS

Say that Wrox has implemented the version control management software described in the example earlier in the chapter. An author is writing Chapter 4 when she realizes she wants to include a reference back to something she had written in Chapter 1. She remembers that she had assigned an ID to that paragraph, but she doesn't remember what it was. Since she only has the Chapter 4 fragment to work with, she can't map to an `ID` in Chapter 1 using an `IDREF`. It would be nice if she could have some sort of information about the content in Chapter 1 – such as the section titles tagged with `IDREFS` – without needing to download an entire copy of the book.

Validating Processors

Imagine that we're using a DTD to specify the content in our catalog example:

```
<!DOCTYPE catalog SYSTEM "www.wrox.com/XML/Catalog.dtd">
<Catalog>
   <Book color="red">
      <Title>XML IE5 Programmer's Reference</Title>
      <Pages>480</Pages>
      <ISBN>1-861001-57-6</ISBN>
      <RecSubjCategories>
         <Category>Internet</Category>
         <Category>Web Publishing</Category>
         <Category>XML</Category>
      </RecSubjCategories>
      <Price>$49.99</Price>
      <Chapter id="chap1">...</Chapter>
      <Chapter id="chap2">...</Chapter>
      <Chapter id="chap3">...</Chapter>
      <Chapter id="chap4">...</Chapter>
      ...
   </Book>
</Catalog>
```

Again, an author wants to check one chapter out. If the author is using a validating processor to verify the structure of his chapter, he is going to have a problem using the original DTD to do so – the original DTD will be expecting a `Catalog` element, a `Book` element, and so on. An ideal version of the document would include placeholders to satisfy the DTD, but not include their content to minimize bandwidth consumption and processing time.

The Solution: Context Information

Fortunately, the W3C anticipated these problems when specifying XFI, and provided a mechanism for the transmission of **context information** along with the fragment to the receiver.

What Is Context Information?

Context information is information that is sent to a receiver to help describe the fragment's structural position within the original document. The XFI specification allows a lot of flexibility in exactly what information is provided for context to the user; this information should be delivered based on the receiver's needs. It might be as little as the fragment's ancestors up to the document element, or as much as all the various element tags in the original document – it's up to the XML server to decide what context information would be useful to the receiving processor.

While the specification does not explain exactly how the context information should be transported, it provides two suggestions. This first involves sending the requestor two files:

- The fragment context specification file, which contains all of the necessary information around the element, and a reference to the file that contains the fragment (using the `fragbody` element)
- The fragment itself in a separate file

While this requires two files to be generated, and that one of them be cached in some way (via a file persisted to disk or some other mechanism), it does mean that the receiving processor can provide information that would surround the fragment.

The other option is that it might be transferred in one single file using namespaces to separate the context information from the actual fragment content. To illustrate some examples of fragment interchange we will use the first of the two proposals (we will revisit the second shortly).

What Is Allowed To Be Part of Context Information?

The W3C specifies that the following information may be provided for the purposes of context for a fragment:

- The URI of the DTD used for the original document
- The URI of the internal subset for the document
- The URI of the original document this fragment was taken from
- A specification of the location of the fragment in the original document
- Ancestor information for the fragment body
- Sibling information for the fragment body
- Sibling information for any of the ancestors
- Descendant information for any of the ancestors or siblings
- Attribute information for any of the elements specified above

Note that this covers all of the nodes in our node tree except for those included in the fragment body we are sending. The author of the XML server can design the fragment generator (using the DOM, XSLT, or whatever other technology they choose) to include whatever portion of this information is relevant to the receiver for the purposes of interpreting the fragment (based on a prior negotiation between the sender and the receiver).

How are Fragments Represented?

The W3C has created the following namespace for fragment declarations:

```
http://www.w3.org/2001/02/xml-fragment
```

The `fcs` element (short for Fragment Context Specification) is the wrapper element for the specification of fragment contexts. All fragment contexts should be wrapped in an `fcs` element. It has the following four attributes:

- `extref` – the URI of the DTD for the original document
- `intref` – the URI of the 'externalized' internal subset
- `parentref` – the URI of the original document itself
- `sourcelocn` – the URI of the location of the fragment within the original document

Note that no encoding scheme is specified for this locator by the W3C at this time, although one might expect the W3C to use XPointer.

The children of the `fcs` element should be some portion of the document structure (possibly including attributes) for the original document. Again, the portion of the element tree represented is decided by the sending application, and should be dependent on the needs of the receiving application. At the position in the subtree where the fragment body should belong, a `fragbody` element should be included in its place. This element has one attribute, `fragbodyref`, which should be a URI reference to the actual fragment.

Let's look at an example. Say we have this catalog file (for the sake of this example, let's say it's located at http://www.wrox.com/Catalog/Catalog.XML):

```
<Catalog>
   <Book color="red">
      <Title>XML IE5 Programmer's Reference</Title>
      <Pages>480</Pages>
      <ISBN>1-861001-57-6</ISBN>
      <RecSubjCategories>
         <Category>Internet</Category>
         <Category>Web Publishing</Category>
         <Category>XML</Category>
      </RecSubjCategories>
      <Price>$29.99</Price>
      <Chapter id="chap1">...</Chapter>
      <Chapter id="chap2">...</Chapter>
      <Chapter id="chap3">...</Chapter>
      <Chapter id="chap4">...</Chapter>
      ...
   </Book>
</Catalog>
```

We want to transmit just the ISBN for the book to the receiver. We would create a fragment context specification that looks like this:

```
<f:fcs xmlns:f="http://www.w3.org/2001/02/xml-fragment"
       parentref="http://www.wrox.com/Catalog/Catalog.XML">
   <Catalog>
      <Book>
         <f:fragbody fragbodyref="http://www.wrox.com/Catalog/ISBN.XML"/>
      </Book>
   </Catalog>
</f:fcs>
```

Here you can see that the fragment context specification file contains the `Catalog` and `Book` elements to provide context for the fragment, and a reference to the second file, which actually contains the requested fragment. The fragment file itself, which is referenced in the `fragbody` element as http://www.wrox.com/Catalog/ISBN.XML, contains the following:

```
<ISBN>1-861001-57-6</ISBN>
```

Examples, Revisited

Let's take a look at our three examples again and see how we would use fragments and contexts to send the information to the receiver.

What Do I Describe?

Earlier, we were trying to figure out how to indicate that the price sent to the receiver was associated with coffee and not a book. If we transmitted the following fragment context specification,

```
<f:fcs xmlns:f="http://www.w3.org/2001/02/xml-fragment"
       parentref="http://www.wrox.com/Bookstore/Bookstore.XML">
   <Bookstore>
      <Coffee>
         <f:fragbody fragbodyref="http://www.wrox.com/Bookstore/Price.XML"/>
      </Coffee>
   </Bookstore>
</f:fcs>
```

the user would know that the following fragment (located at http://www.wrox.com/Bookstore/Price.XML) is a child of the `Coffee` element, and a grandchild of the `Bookstore` element:

```
   <Price>$2.99</Price>
```

It would then be obvious to the receiver what the `<Price>` element in the `Price.XML` file represented.

Using IDREF and IDREFS

OK, so how about the author that wanted to reference back to an `ID` for a paragraph in Chapter 1, if all she has to edit is Chapter 4? If we sent this fragment context specification:

```
<f:fcs xmlns:f="http://www.w3.org/2001/02/xml-fragment"
       parentref="http://www.wrox.com/FullText/FullText.XML">
<Catalog>
```

```
    <Book>
       <Chapter id="chap1">
          <para ID="IntroXML" />
          <para ID="IntroChap1" />
          <para ID="IntroChap2" />
          <para ID="IntroChap3" />
          <para ID="IntroChap4" />
          <para ID="IntroChap5" />
          <para ID="IntroChap6" />
       </Chapter>
       <Chapter id="chap2">
          <para ID="XMLKeywords">
            ...
          </para>
       </Chapter>
       <Chapter id="chap3">
          <para ID="XMLDTDs">
            ...
          </para>
       </Chapter>
       <f:fragbody fragbodyref="http://www.wrox.com/
                                FullText/XMLIE5Chapter4.xml"/>
    </Book>
 </Catalog>
 </f:fcs>
```

The author would have a reference to the context of their chapter, which is a fragment in the `XMLIE5Chapter4.xml` file.

```
<Chapter id="chap4">
   ...
</Chapter>
```

Now the author would have the `ID`s of the various positions in each chapter to refer back to in the fragment context specification file – and she could add an `IDREF` to, say, `IntroChap4` to point back to information given in the first chapter about Chapter 4. This provides the contextual information she needs to create her content without actually receiving all of the other content she needs to refer to.

Validating Processors

In order to keep a validating processor happy, we can include a copy of all required elements (that are allowed to be empty) with character data removed – optional elements may be discarded. The idea is to make the fragment as sparse as possible – just passing enough information that the document can be validated. So, for our example, we might transmit the following fragment context specification:

```
<f:fcs xmlns:f="http://www.w3.org/2001/02/xml-fragment"
       extref="http://www.wrox.com/XML/Catalog.dtd"
       parentref="http://www.wrox.com/FullText/FullText.XML">
<Catalog>
   <Book>
      <Title></Title>
      <Pages></Pages>
      <ISBN></ISBN>
```

```
        <RecSubjCategories>
        </RecSubjCategories>
        <Price></Price>
        <f:fragbody fragbodyref="http://www.wrox.com/
                                   FullText/IE5XMLChapter4.xml"/>
    </Book>
</Catalog>
</f:fcs>
```

This provides a fragment-aware processor with the required elements for the following fragment to be valid:

```
<Chapter id="chap4">
   ...
</Chapter>
```

Note that we dropped the `Category` elements (because we're assuming that `Category` is declared as optional in the DTD) and the additional `Chapter` elements (because `Chapter` is specified as having one or more occurrences in the DTD). On receiving these two files, the processor would parse the fragment body in place as if it were an external parsed entity, discard the context wrapper on the context piece, and be able to validate the document against the DTD.

How Fragments May Be Transmitted

Now that we've defined some fragments and fragment context specifications, how do we go about sending them to a receiver? The W3C doesn't constrain the transmission of fragments in the XFI specification, but it does offer a couple of different ways a fragment-aware receiving processor might accept transmissions.

The Separate File Mechanism

We've already seen the way fragments work with two separate files. One file contains the fragment itself and the other contains the fragment context specification file. To send this information to a receiver, the fragment context specification file is sent. The fragment-aware processor parses the fragment context specification file and goes to the location in the `fragbodyref` attribute to read the fragment body itself.

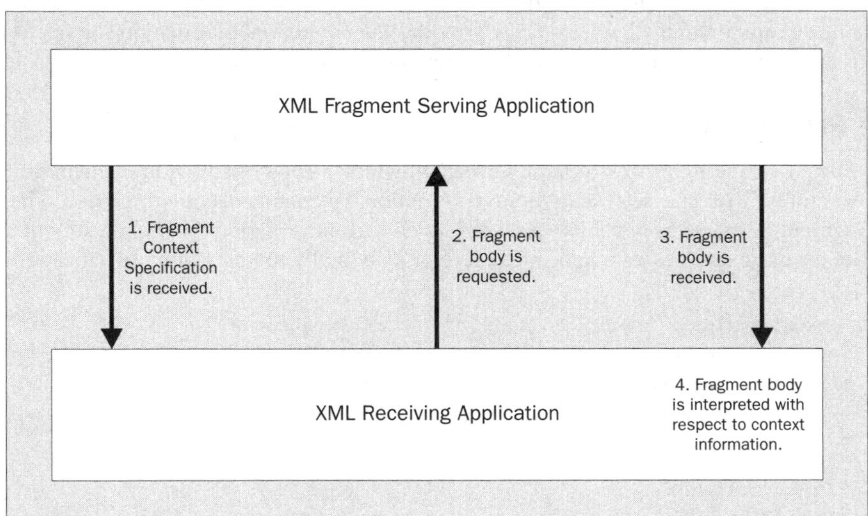

Unfortunately, this requires two files to be generated by the fragment serving application, and that one of them be cached in some way (via a file persisted to disk or some other mechanism). In addition, this requires an extra round trip across the network, which we'd like to avoid if possible.

The Proposed Package Mechanism

While the W3C declares that the transmission of fragments is outside the scope of the XFI specification, it does provide a **non-normative** (W3C code for suggested but not required) way that a fragment and a fragment body may be packaged together and sent as one file. Basically, a new namespace is defined that provides an element to contain a fragment body. Then, instead of two files with a fragment context specification like so,

```
<f:fcs xmlns:f="http://www.w3.org/2001/02/xml-fragment"
      parentref="http://www.wrox.com/Bookstore/Bookstore.XML">
   <Bookstore>
      <Coffee>
         <f:fragbody fragbodyref="http://www.wrox.com/Bookstore/Price.XML"/>
      </Coffee>
   </Bookstore>
</f:fcs>
```

and a fragment body such as this,

```
    <Price>$5.99</Price>
```

we would have just one file:

```
<p:package xmlns:p="http://www.w3.org/2001/02/xml-package"
           xmlns:f="http://www.w3.org/2001/02/xml-fragment">
   <f:fcs parentref="http://www.wrox.com/Bookstore/Bookstore.XML">
      <Bookstore>
         <Coffee>
            <f:fragbody/>
         </Coffee>
      </Bookstore>
   </f:fcs>
   <p:body>
      <Price>$5.99</Price>
   </p:body>
</p:package>
```

Note that we no longer specify a location for the fragment body – it is assumed to fall in the `p:body` element. The fragment-aware processor sees the `f:fragbody` element and understands that the content of the `p:body` element represents the fragment that occurs in this location with respect to the context information. In this scenario, only one trip to the server would be required:

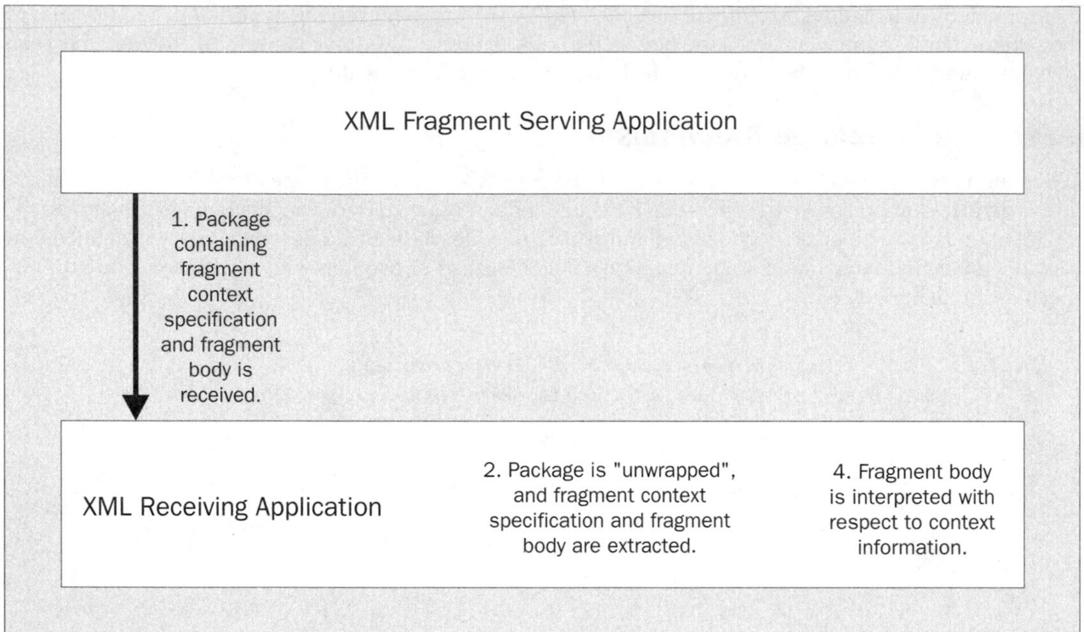

This technique allows us to reduce round trips to the server, and also reduces the complexity of the serving application itself.

Summary

The XML Fragment Interchange provides a way to describe a portion of an XML document to a receiver, along with enough context information to make the document usable by the receiver. We've taken a look at some ways fragments might be useful – allowing us to manage multiple authors for a document, for example, or decreasing the amount of unused information that is transmitted across our networks and processed by our XML processors. However, fragments returned by the XFI must correspond to contiguous elements in the source document, making sophisticated manipulation of the original content impossible.

While there aren't any widely-available fragment-aware processors yet, being comfortable with the concepts of fragment and context will get you ready for fragments when they do start hitting the streets. As the various XML technologies converge, XFI will likely be the method used to transfer partial documents, generated by queries or links, where context information is also required.

Linking

Next, let's take a look at how we can extend the functionality of XML by including links to external resources such as other XML documents, HTML documents, or images. As we will see, we may use links to define relationships between similar documents, to define a sequence in which documents should be navigated, or even to embed non-XML content in an XML document.

What Is Linking?

If you've used HTML, you are no doubt familiar with the concept of a **hyperlink**. You can specify an anchor that acts as a link to another document:

```
<A HREF="www.wrox.com/Catalog/Catalog.html">Book catalog</A>
```

This declaration tells us two things.

- First, it says that the text, `Book catalog`, is the start of a connection between two resources (because it's wrapped in an `<A>` tag that contains an `HREF` attribute)
- Second, it says that the URL, www.wrox.com/Catalog/Catalog.html, is the destination of that same connection

This is a simple example of a link – a connection between resources. XML linking is similar to HTML linking, but with greater functionality and flexibility (as we'll see a little later).

The Distinction Between Conceptual Linking and Rendering

Note that the above content is typically rendered by highlighting the start of the connection in some way (underlining it, changing its color, and so on), with a click of the mouse (or other navigation mechanism) causing navigation to the destination content. However, this behavior is not explicitly defined in the HTML specification – a content rendering engine is free to render it any way it sees fit. One has only to think about a browser for a visually impaired user to understand why.

Understanding the difference between linking and rendering is important if you are to understand the way XML linking works, since the XML linking specification only provides a conceptual model for linking.

The Problem with HTML Links

We mentioned earlier that HTML links are fairly inflexible. In particular, HTML anchor links have the following drawbacks:

HTML Links Are Embedded in the Source Document

This limitation prevents us from creating a link out of a document whose contents we cannot edit, for example, or a document that doesn't provide native markup capacity (such as an image file). If we could somehow take our links out of the documents they reference, we could also construct a store for our links (in a link database or file) that connects our content together but is managed from a central location. We'll revisit the subject of link databases later.

HTML Links Only Allow Navigation in One Direction

If we have a sequence of pages we want the user to be able to navigate between, we need to explicitly define hyperlinks between all of them. For example, we might have a document called `page1.htm` that contains the word Next hyperlinked to `page2.htm`. If we want to define a hyperlink (say for the word Previous) that allows us to navigate back to `page1.htm`, we need to explicitly define the link in the other direction here. It would be nice if we could state that the two pages are linked once, without worrying about the direction of the navigation.

HTML Links Only Connect Two Resources

We've all seen sites on the Internet where multiple pages of information are connected by lists of links, or by Previous and Next links:

```
<HTML>
<BODY>
<H3>Joe's Grill - Breakfast Menu</H3>

Breakfast:
  Two eggs, any style...............$1.95
  Bacon.............................$1.25
  Sausage...........................$1.25
  Pancakes..........................$3.00

<P><A HREF="http://www.joesgrill.com/beverages.htm">Beverages</A></P>
<P><A HREF="http://www.joesgrill.com/appetizers.htm">Appetizers</A></P>
<P><A HREF="http://www.joesgrill.com/sandwiches.htm">Sandwiches</A></P>
<P><A HREF="http://www.joesgrill.com/grill.htm">From the Grill</A></P>
<P><A HREF="http://www.joesgrill.com/dessert.htm">Desserts</A></P>
<P><A HREF="http://www.joesgrill.com/main.htm">Return to main menu</A></P>
</BODY>
</HTML>
```

Of course, all the other pages of the menu have a similar list of hyperlinks on them, making maintenance of the menu a nightmare. If Joe's Grill decides to add a pasta menu, for example, every page will need to have a link added to the pasta page. It would be great if we could specify that all the resources were linked in one place and let the browser take care of navigating between them.

HTML Links Do Not Specify the Behavior of the Rendering Engine

It would be nice to be able to specify some additional conceptual behavior for the engine rendering the content. Should the rendering engine automatically traverse the link, or should it wait for user interaction before doing so? Should the rendering engine create a new context (for a browser, a window) to render the linked content, or should it even be embedded in with the current content? With HTML links, only the target named window may be specified, and the browser will behave differently based on the browser's current state (if a window with the specified name is already open, for example, it will replace that content; otherwise, it will create a new window).

The W3C's specification for XML linking addresses all of these issues, as we will see.

The W3C Specification: XLink

The specification for XML linking is known as XLink. It currently has a status of proposed recommendation, which means it is likely to be promoted to a W3C recommendation with few if any changes. The latest version of this document may be found at http://www.w3.org/TR/xlink. (At the time of writing the latest version was from the 20th December 2000.)

Since the XLink specification is close to becoming a W3C recommendation, you should familiarize yourself with the various attributes that form the specification. Even though at this point there isn't a great deal of support for XLink in existing XML processors, you can still take advantage of its standardized linking mechanisms in your own XML documents if you like. In this section, we'll see how XLinks are declared and implemented; we'll also see an example of how XSLT may be used to transform XLinks into equivalent HTML navigation constructs.

Changes To the Specification Since the First Edition of the Book

There have been some significant changes to the XLink specification since the first edition of Professional XML was published. Specifically:

- The specification no longer provides XLink elements (`xlink:simple` and `xlink:extended`); instead, all XLinks must be asserted as attributes in the XML namespace attached to elements in the document's namespace
- The `xlink:arcrole` attribute has been added
- New enumerated values have been added to the `xlink:show` and `xlink:actuate` attributes
- Finally, the behavior formerly exhibited by the `xlink:role` attribute (defining types of locators for the purposes of arc declaration) has been split out into a separate attribute called `xlink:label`

XLink Declarations

The namespace declared by the W3C for XLink is:

```
http://www.w3.org/1999/xlink/
```

To assert a link from an XML document, this namespace must be defined for the subtree in which the link is asserted. Links are asserted by adding attributes of the XLink namespace to an element in the document.

An element that has XLink attributes associated with it looks like this:

```
<Authors xmlns:xlink="http://www.w3.org/1999/xlink"
         xlink:type="simple"
         xlink:href="authors.xml"
         xlink:role="author list"
         xlink:title="Author list"
         xlink:show="replace"
         xlink:actuate="onRequest"/>
```

Note that if you choose to add XLink attributes to one of your own elements and you're using a DTD, you'll need to define the attributes in an `<!ATTLIST>` for the linking element. Otherwise, your validating processor will complain that it doesn't recognize the `xlink:*` attributes! For the above example, you would need this element definition in your DTD:

```
<!ELEMENT Authors EMPTY>
<!ATTLIST Authors
   xmlns:xlink   CDATA #FIXED "http://www.w3.org/1999/xlink"
   xlink:type    (simple|extended|locator|arc|resource) "simple"
   xlink:href    CDATA #REQUIRED
   xlink:role    CDATA #IMPLIED
   xlink:title   CDATA #IMPLIED
   xlink:show    (new|replace|embed|other|none) "replace"
   xlink:actuate (onLoad|onRequest|other|none) "onRequest">
```

Link Types

The `xlink:type` attribute can take one of two values for a link assertion: `simple` and `extended`. (The other possible values for `xlink:type`, `locator`, `arc`, and `resource`, are used to define participants in a link and navigation rules for a link respectively – as we'll see later in the chapter.)

`Simple` links offer similar functionality to HTML hyperlinks, while `extended` links offer greater capabilities. As we'll see later, simple links are really just a subset of extended links – even though they use a different syntax.

Simple Links

Simple links are very similar to the HTML `<A HREF=...>` link you may already be familiar with. The following attributes are used when declaring a simple link:

xlink:type

For simple links, this attribute is always `simple`.

xlink:title

A human-readable string that describes the link. Again, the W3C does not specify how this is to be used in an XLink-aware renderer, but it could be used to provide some indication to the user that the element is a link.

xlink:href

The destination URI of the link. The exact form of this URI will depend on the processor's URI recognition capabilities; for example, if the processor is XPointer-aware, the URI may include XPointers.

xlink:role

A URI that describes the function of this link's content. While the W3C does not specify what the `role` may be used for, some implementations of XLink may use the role string to control rendering of the document.

xlink:arcrole

A URI that describes the function of the link itself. For example, a link between two pages of a menu might have an `arcrole` of `"NextPage"`. While the W3C does not specify what the `arcrole` may be used for, some implementations of XLink may use the `arcrole` URI to control rendering of the document.

xlink:show

This attribute defines how the target content is to be rendered for the user. It may take one of five values:

- `new` – the target content is to be rendered in a separate context (in a browser, this might be a new browser window).
- `replace` – the target content should replace the source content in its original context (in a browser, this would be normal hyperlink behavior).
- `embed` – the content will be embedded in the source document at the link position (in place of the link representation itself).

- `other` – the link does not specify the behavior when the link is traversed. If the `xlink:show` attribute has this value, the document will contain other clues about how the link is to be traversed, such as other (document type-specific) markup that describes the purpose of the link.
- `none` – the link does not specify the behavior when the link is traversed. In this case, the document will not contain other clues about how the link is to be traversed.

xlink:actuate

This attribute defines when the link should be triggered. It may take one of four values:

- `onRequest` – the user must take some action to trigger the link. This is analogous to the way HTML hyperlinks work, where a user must click the linked text to activate the link.
- `onLoad` – the link will automatically be activated when the source document is loaded. This is most useful when the `xlink:show` attribute is `embed`, but also has some applications when it is `new` (to automatically open an additional context window with the destination information when the source document is opened, for example).
- `other` – the link does not specify the behavior when the link is actuated. If the `xlink:actuate` attribute has this value, the document will contain other clues about how the link is to be actuated.
- `none` – the link does not specify the behavior when the link is actuated. In this case, the document will not contain other clues about how the link is to be actuated.

Simple Link Resources

Simple links are functionally equivalent to HTML hyperlinks – they link two locations in one direction, and the start of the link is always the declaration of the link itself:

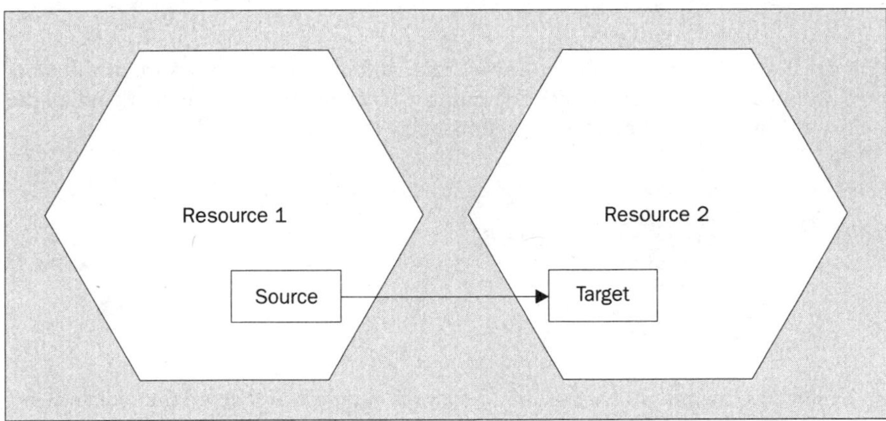

Note that even though we show the resources as being different, it's perfectly acceptable for both resources to be in the same document, or even be the same location within that document:

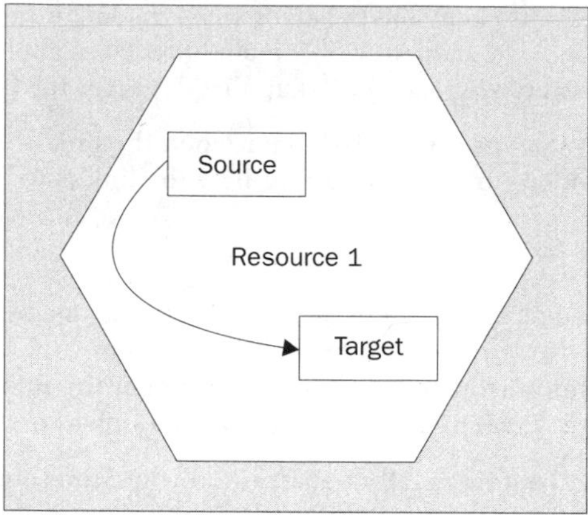

This will be an important point to remember later, when we're discussing extended links. XLink operates with resources or portions of resources (basically anything that can be addressed with a URI) – with the default location for a resource being the 'top', however that happens to be defined for the type of resource.

Simple Link Examples

Let's take a look at a couple of quick examples before we move on:

```
<Authors xmlns:xlink="http://www.w3.org/1999/xlink"
         xlink:type="simple"
         xlink:href="authors.xml"
         xlink:role="author list"
         xlink:title="Author list"
         xlink:show="new"
         xlink:actuate="onRequest"/>
```

This example creates a link with the title `Author list`, and makes the user aware that there is link information associated with it (perhaps by underlining it, as in an HTML document). When the user activates the link, the `authors.xml` document is opened in a new context.

```
<authors xmlns:xlink="http://www.w3.org/1999/xlink"
         xlink:type="simple"
         xlink:href="authors.xml"
         xlink:role="author list"
         xlink:title="Author list"
         xlink:show="embedded"
         xlink:actuate="onLoad"/>
```

This example indicates that the `authors.xml` document should be rendered immediately in place of the link reference when the source document is initially rendered (remembering that it is actually up to the user agent how it treats the link, so it may vary).

Note that there are some combinations of `show` and `actuate` that don't make a great deal of sense, such as `xlink:show="replace"` and `xlink:actuate="onLoad"`. This could potentially serve as a redirection from one document to another, but what will the renderer do if two such links are in the source document? As with all specific rendering behavior, the W3C specification makes no attempt to clarify what a renderer's behavior should be in circumstances like these, and only time will tell how specific implementations deal with the problem.

Extended Links

The other way links may be defined for XLink is as extended links. Extended links allow more than one resource to be linked together, and they may be specified out-of-line (that is, in a document other than the source document).

Here's a diagram to summarize the three ways that extended XLinks can describe a link between two resources:

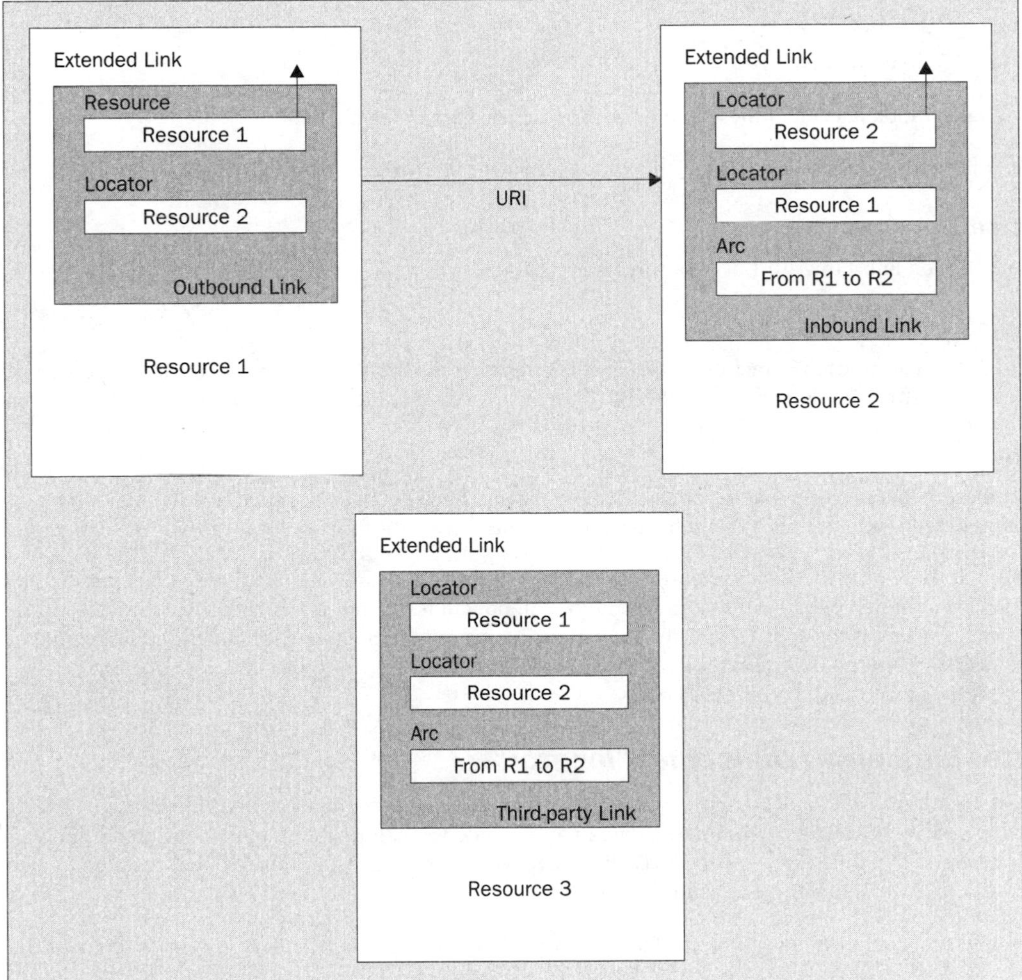

From the diagram we can see the following:

- There are three types of extended link – **inbound**, **outbound**, and **third-party**
- An extended link has **participants** (locators and resources) and **arcs**
- Resources are 'by-value' local resources while locators' use of URIs make them 'by-reference', whether in the same resource or a reference to another document

Defining Extended Links

XLink extended links are defined the same way simple links are – by adding attributes in the XLink namespace to existing XML documents. However, elements that have extended XLink attributes may also have sub-elements with XLink attributes identifying them as:

- Locator elements
- Resource elements
- Arc elements
- Title elements

We'll take a look at each of these and what they signify later in the chapter.

The following attributes are associated with an element that is an extended XLink element:

xlink:type

For extended links, this attribute is always `extended`.

xlink:role

A URI that describes the function of this link's content. While the W3C does not specify what the `role` may be used for, some implementations of XLink may use the role string to control rendering of the document.

xlink:title

A human-readable string that describes the link. Again, the W3C does not specify how this is to be used in an XLink-aware renderer, but it could be used to provide some indication to the user that the element is a link.

Note that there's no specification for the destination of the link – the `href` attribute is missing. Actually, the source isn't defined either – unlike simple links, extended links do not imply that their source is the document in which the link is located. To specify the various locations participating in an extended link and the connections between the links, we'll need to use the three sub-element types: `xlink:location`, `xlink:resource`, and `xlink:arc`.

Locator Elements (xlink:type="locator")

These elements should always appear as sub-elements of an element that is an XLink extended link. They are used to specify the locations that participate in an extended link. For example, if we wanted to implement a link between five different resources (say, five pages of a menu), we would have one locator child element for each of the five resources participating in the link.

Elements that are functioning as XLink locators always have the attribute `xlink:type` set to the value `locator`.

Locator elements have the following attributes associated with them:

- The `xlink:href` attribute defines the URI that locates a remote endpoint for the extended link being defined. This attribute is required for all locator elements. Note that if the processor can understand XPointer references, the URI may contain an XPointer reference to a subset of an XML document. Be aware when designing documents containing XLinks that, whatever functionality you use (such as XPointer references), all processors that will be consuming these documents must understand that functionality.

- The `xlink:role` attribute is optional, and specifies a URI reference for the endpoint.
- The `xlink:title` attribute is also optional, and specifies an alternate text description of the endpoint. Note that you can also specify title information in a sub-element with an `xlink:type` attribute of `title`, if you prefer.
- Finally, the `xlink:label` attribute is optional. This attribute contains a string that identifies the endpoint for the purpose of arc definition, as we'll see when we discuss arc elements later in the chapter.

If you're familiar with earlier drafts of the XLink specification, the function of `xlink:label` used to be fulfilled by the `xlink:role` attribute; this behavior has changed in the more recent versions of the specification.

Note that a locator does not explicitly indicate a link – it only specifies a location that is participating in the extended link. To define explicit connections between locators, we need to use the `xlink:arc` element.

Resource Elements (xlink:type="resource")

These elements appear as sub-elements of an extended link, and are used to define participants in the link that are within the scope of the extended link element itself (as opposed to `locator` elements, which are used to specify remote participants in the link). Elements that function as XLink resources always have the attribute `xlink:type` set to the value `resource`.

Resource elements have the following attributes associated with them:

- The `xlink:role` attribute is optional, and specifies a URI description for the endpoint.
- The `xlink:title` attribute is also optional, and specifies an alternate text description of the endpoint. Note that you can also specify title information in a sub-element with the `xlink:type` of `title`, if you prefer.
- Finally, the `xlink:label` attribute is optional. As with locator elements, this attribute contains a string that identifies the endpoint for the purpose of arc definition.

Arc Elements (xlink:type="arc")

Arc elements also appear as sub-elements of an extended link, and are used to define navigable connections (or 'arcs') between locators participating in an extended link. Elements that function as XLink arcs always have the attribute `xlink:type` set to the value `arc`.

Arc elements have the following attributes associated with them:

- The `xlink:arcrole` attribute is optional, and provides a URI description of the navigation defined by this arc element.
- The `xlink:title` attribute is also optional, and specifies an alternate text description of the endpoint. Note that you can also specify title information in a sub-element with the `xlink:type` of `title`, if you prefer.
- The `xlink:show` attribute is optional, and specifies the way in which the linked content is to be revealed (see our definition of `xlink:show` in the simple link section for more details).
- The `xlink:actuate` attribute is optional, and specifies when the linked content is to be revealed (see our definition of `xlink:actuate` in the simple link section for more details).

- The `xlink:from` attribute is optional, and defines the label for the resource(s) that will act as the starting resource(s) for this navigation. This label must match the `xlink:label` attribute on one or more locator or resource elements defined for this extended link. If the `xlink:from` attribute is not provided, this arc allows navigation from all locators and resources defined in the extended link.
- The `xlink:to` attribute is optional, and defines the label for the resource(s) that will act as the end point(s) for this navigation. This label must match the `xlink:label` attribute on one or more locator or resource elements defined for this extended link. If the `xlink:to` attribute is not provided, this arc allows navigation to all locators and resources defined in the extended link.

Note that if more than one locator or resource in an extended link have the same label, an arc element with a `xlink:from` or `xlink:to` attribute that matches that label will connect all locators with that label. For example, say we have the following document:

```
<family xmlns:xlink="http://www.w3.org/1999/xlink"
        xlink:type="extended"
        xlink:role="family"
        xlink:title="John Smith's family">
   <person
        xlink:type="locator"
        xlink:href="johnsmith.xml"
        xlink:label="parent"
        xlink:title="John Smith"/>
   <person
        xlink:type="locator"
        xlink:href="marysmith.xml"
        xlink:label="parent"
        xlink:title="Mary Smith"/>
   <person
        xlink:type="locator"
        xlink:href="billysmith.xml"
        xlink:label="child"
        xlink:title="Billy Smith"/>
   <person
        xlink:type="locator"
        xlink:href="kateysmith.xml"
        xlink:label="child"
        xlink:title="Katey Smith"/>
   <person
        xlink:type="locator"
        xlink:href="johnsmithjr.xml"
        xlink:label="child"
        xlink:title="John Smith Jr."/>
   <relationship
        xlink:type="arc"
        xlink:from="parent"
        xlink:to="child"
        xlink:title="See children"
        xlink:show="replace"
        xlink:actuate="onRequest"/>
</family>
```

The following connections are defined by the extended link:

```
John Smith to Billy Smith
John Smith to Katey Smith
John Smith to John Smith Jr.
Mary Smith to Billy Smith
Mary Smith to Katey Smith
Mary Smith to John Smith Jr.
```

Finally, if an arc definition results in an arc between a given start point and end point being defined more than once, only the first arc definition parsed for that start and end point will be used.

Title Elements (xlink:type="title")

Elements with the `xlink:type` attribute with the value `title` are used to associate semantic information with an extended link. Elements that function as XLink titles have one attribute, `xlink:type`, that always contains the string `title`.

For example, a link that associates the different pages of a menu might have a title element with the value `Menu`. Using title elements, rather than the `xlink:title` attribute, allows for richer description of the title – including XML structures, if it's meaningful to the document. Multiple titles may be specified (for example, if an XML document is being internationalized), using the `xml:lang` attribute to indicate which language this particular title is associated with. Title elements may also appear as sub-elements of `xlink:locator` and `xlink:arc` elements.

How titles are used is up to the specific processor implementation – so if multiple titles are provided, the processor decides how to use each one.

Before we continue, here's a table (from Section 4.1 of the XLink specification) that summarizes the allowed attributes for the different XLink types:

	simple	**extended**	**locator**	**arc**	**resource**	**title**
type	Required	Required	Required	Required	Required	Required
href	Optional		Required			
role	Optional	Optional	Optional		Optional	
arcrole	Optional			Optional		
title	Optional	Optional	Optional	Optional	Optional	
show	Optional			Optional		
actuate	Optional			Optional		
label			Optional		Optional	
from				Optional		
to				Optional		

Implicit versus Explicit Arcs

Note that some connection information may be determined by looking at the list of locations that participate in an extended link. Say we have the following extended link declaration:

```
<menu xmlns:xlink="http://www.w3.org/1999/xlink"
        xlink:type="extended"
        xlink:role="menuPages"
        xlink:title="Joe's menu">
   <menupage
        xlink:type="locator"
        xlink:href="menu1.xml"
        xlink:label="menuPage1"
        xlink:title="Beverages"/>
   <menupage
        xlink:type="locator"
        xlink:href="menu2.xml"
        xlink:label="menuPage2"
        xlink:title="Appetizers"/>
   <menupage
        xlink:type="locator"
        xlink:href="menu3.xml"
        xlink:label="menuPage3"
        xlink:title="Sandwiches"/>
   <menupage
        xlink:type="locator"
        xlink:href="menu4.xml"
        xlink:label="menuPage4"
        xlink:title="Desserts"/>
   <menuNavigation
        xlink:type="arc"
        xlink:from="menuPage1"
        xlink:to="menuPage2"
        xlink:title="Next menu page"
        xlink:show="replace"
        xlink:actuate="onRequest"/>
   <menuNavigation
        xlink:type="arc"
        xlink:from="menuPage2"
        xlink:to="menuPage3"
        xlink:title="Next menu page"
        xlink:show="replace"
        xlink:actuate="onRequest"/>
   <menuNavigation
        xlink:type="arc"
        xlink:from="menuPage3"
        xlink:to="menuPage4"
        xlink:title="Next menu page"
        xlink:show="replace"
        xlink:actuate="onRequest"/>
</menu>
```

The explicit links in this declaration are those defined by elements that have the `xlink:type` attribute of `arc`:

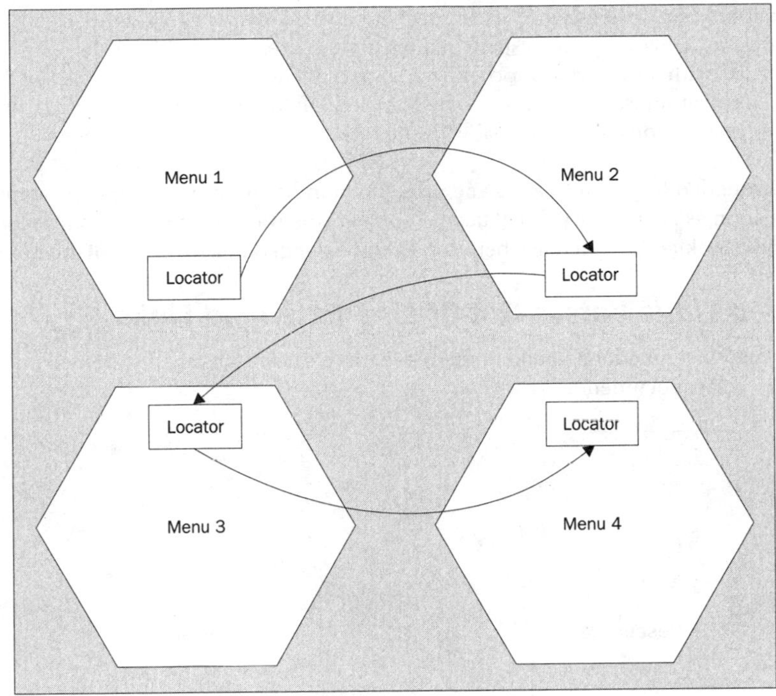

However, if we did not include any arc elements, XLink would assume that there was an implicit arc between each of the locators defined as part of the extended link definition:

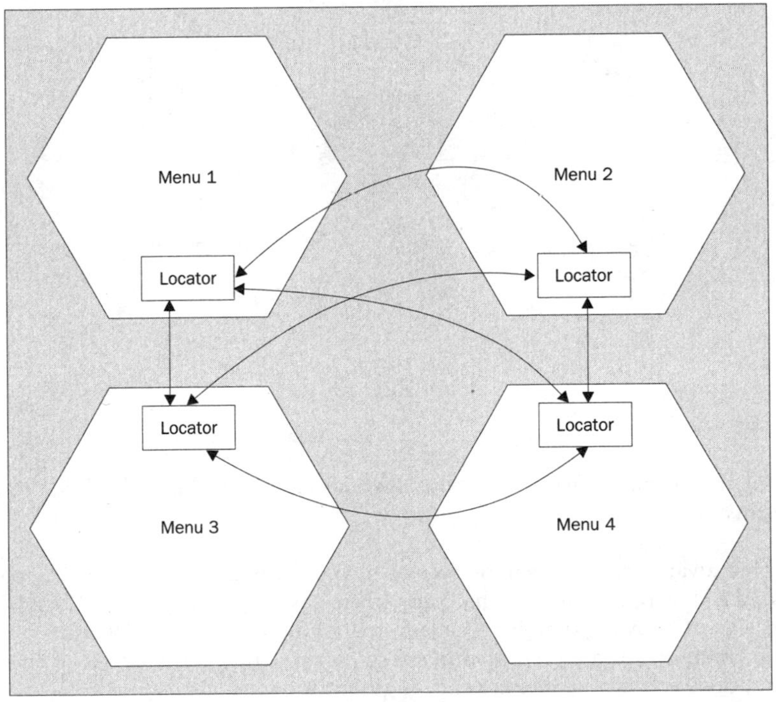

Note that implicit links are also assumed to be present between locators (or resources) and themselves – typically not a desired outcome – so it usually makes more sense to explicitly declare only the navigation you want using elements with an `xlink:type` of `arc`. The W3C doesn't specify whether an XLink-aware parser needs to handle implicit links, or if they are to be handled differently from explicit links. Again, it remains to be seen how implementations of XLink deal with the issue.

By defining an extended link with locators and arcs, any number of resources may be connected together in as complex a fashion as is necessary. We'll take a look at some ways extended links may be used a little later, but first let's take a look at the difference between **inline** extended links and **out-of-line** extended links.

Inline Extended Links Versus Out-Of-Line Extended Links

Extended links may be embedded in one of the resources participating in an extended link (if that resource happens to be an XML document).

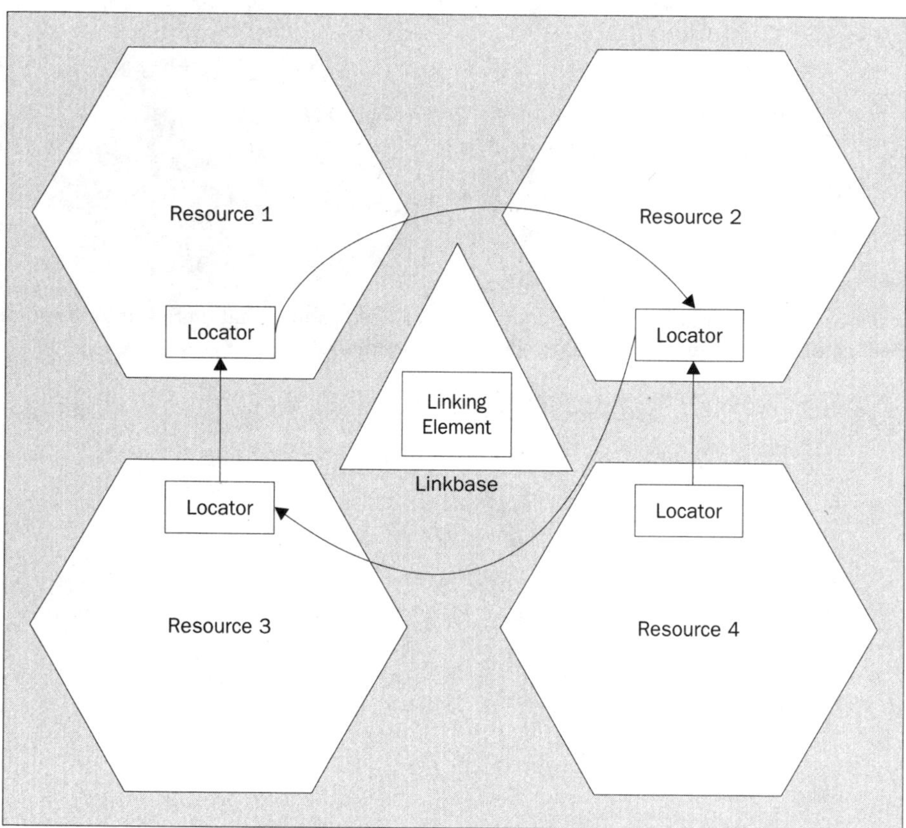

While embedding the extended link in one of the locations used in the link will work, this approach has a couple of problems:

- An XLink-aware processor will be able to navigate the links if the resource containing the extended link is read first, but what happens if, say, Resource 2 is read first? The processor has no way of knowing that there's a legitimate link to Resource 3 that may be navigated. The link information could be repeated in every resource that contains a locator in the extended link, but then you have a maintenance nightmare.

- The resource that contains the links must be an XML resource. What happens, for example, if we want to link four image resources together in the pattern shown above? Where can we put the link information?

Out-Of-Line Extended Links – Using Linkbases

A special type of arc element is used to indicate to an XLink-aware processor that out-of-line links exist for a particular document. The element's `arcrole` attribute must be set to:

```
http://www.w3.org/1999/xlink/properties/linkbase
```

Note that while this looks very much like a namespace, it actually represents the physical value that must be set in the `arcrole` attribute for the arc that asserts the linkbase. When an arc has its `arcrole` set to this value, the endpoint of the arc is loaded and all simple and extended links are extracted from it as if they were present in the original document. This may necessitate a redisplay of the original document to reflect links found in the linkbase. In order to automatically have the links in a linkbase available when a document is loaded, an arc must be defined as above with its `xlink:actuate` attribute set to `onLoad`, as in the following example:

```
<catalogLinks
        xmlns:xlink="http://www.w3.org/1999/xlink"
        xlink:type="extended">
    <linkStart
        xlink:type="resource"
        xlink:label="catalogLink" />
    <linkDatabase
        xlink:type="locator"
        xlink:label="catalogDocument"
        xlink:href="http://www.wrox.com/Catalog/linkdb.xml" />
    <linkArc
        xlink:type="arc"
        xlink:arcrole="http://www.w3.org/1999/xlink/properties/linkbase"
        xlink:from="catalogLink"
        xlink:to="catalogDocument"
        xlink:actuate="onLoad" />
</catalogLinks>
```

When an XLink-aware processor encounters an arc element with an `xlink:arcrole` of `http://www.w3.org/1999/xlink/properties/linkbase` (and the `xlink:actuate` attribute of the arc is set to `onLoad`), it reads the document(s) indicated in the locator or resources whose `xlink:label` matches the `xlink:to` attribute of the arc element. It then 'remembers' that information as if it were included in the original document. This makes it much easier to maintain linkages between items – in effect, solving the "Joe wants to add a pasta menu" problem we ran into earlier.

Here's our separate XML document containing out-of-line link information connecting our resources:

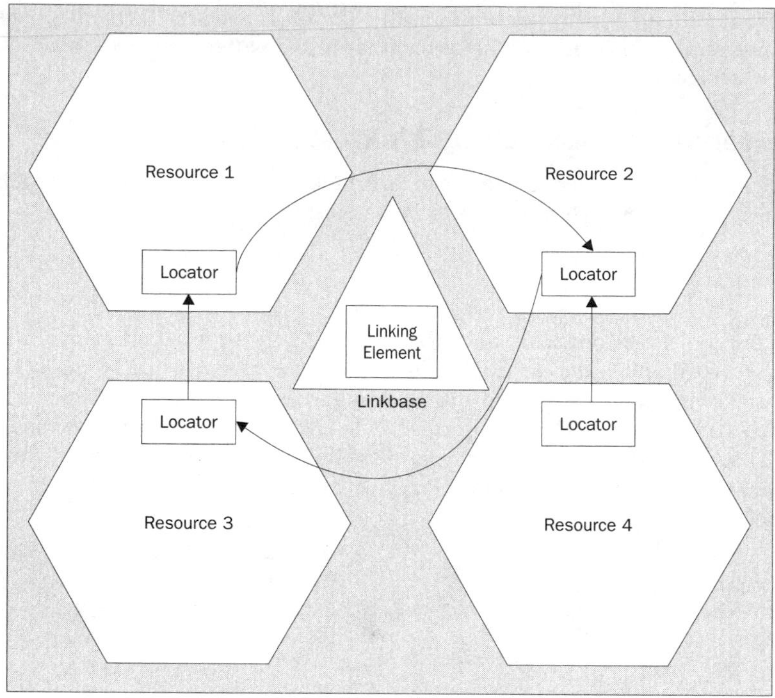

If we then add extended links containing linkbase arcs to the four linked documents, loading the links when the document is loaded by setting the `xlink:actuate` attribute on the arc to `onLoad`, information for the external link will then be available when any of the documents is the current document:

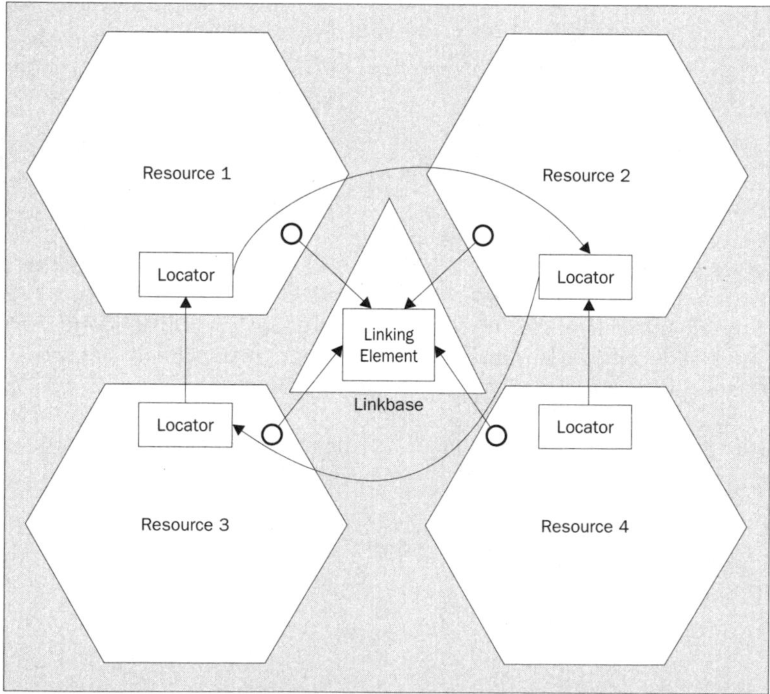

Some Examples of Extended XLinks

Let's take a look at the way extended links solve some of the problems we mentioned before with HTML links:

- HTML links must be embedded in the source document
- HTML links only allow navigation in one direction
- HTML links only connect two resources
- HTML links do not specify the behavior of the rendering engine

Link Databases

Using linkbases, we can maintain a list of links between documents. We might have the following linkbase document, `menulink.xml`:

```
<linkbase
       xmlns:xlink="http://www.w3.org/1999/xlink"
       xlink:type="extended"
       xlink:title="See other parts of menu">
  <endpoint
       xlink:type="locator"
       xlink:href="menu1.xml"
       xlink:label="menuPage1"
       xlink:title="Beverages"/>
  <endpoint
       xlink:type="locator"
       xlink:href="menu2.xml"
       xlink:label="menuPage2"
       xlink:title="Appetizers"/>
  <endpoint
       xlink:type="locator"
       xlink:href="menu3.xml"
       xlink:label="menuPage3"
       xlink:title="Sandwiches"/>
  <endpoint
       xlink:type="locator"
       xlink:href="menu4.xml"
       xlink:label="menuPage4"
       xlink:title="Desserts"/>
  <link
       xlink:type="arc"
       xlink:from="menuPage1"
       xlink:to="menuPage2"
       xlink:show="replace"
       xlink:actuate="onRequest"/>
  <link
       xlink:type="arc"
       xlink:from="menuPage2"
       xlink:to="menuPage3"
       xlink:show="replace"
       xlink:actuate="onRequest"/>
  <link
       xlink:type="arc"
       xlink:from="menuPage3"
       xlink:to="menuPage4"
       xlink:show="replace"
       xlink:actuate="onRequest"/>
</linkbase>
```

We can then have the following `menu1.xml` (the same general format applies to all the menu pages):

```
<menupage xmlns:xlink="http://www.w3.org/1999/xlink">
   <linkbase
            xlink:type="extended">
      <linkbaseStart
            xlink:type="resource"
            xlink:label="linkbaseStart"/>
      <linkbaseEnd
            xlink:type="locator"
            xlink:href="menulink.xml"
            xlink:label="linkbaseEnd"/>
      <loadLinkbase
            xlink:type="arc"
            xlink:arcrole="http://www.w3.org/1999/xlink/properties/linkbase"
            xlink:from="linkbaseStart"
            xlink:to="linkbaseEnd"
            xlink:actuate="onLoad"/>
   </linkbase>
   <menuitem>
      <name>Coffee</name>
      <price>$0.99</price>
   </menuitem>
   <menuitem>
      <name>Tea</name>
      <price>$1.09</price>
   </menuitem>
   <menuitem>
      <name>Soda</name>
      <price>$1.25</price>
   </menuitem>
</menupage>
```

When `menu1.xml` is opened, an XLink-aware processor will read the extended link information from the `menulink.xml` document and render the document in a way that will make it clear that this document links to `menu2.xml`. A browser might choose to render the information this way (of course, this is a mockup – no browser directly supports extended XLinks as of press time):

If Joe now wants to add a pasta menu, all we need to do is modify the link database document:

```
<linkbase
      xmlns:xlink="http://www.w3.org/1999/xlink"
      xlink:type="extended"
      xlink:title="See other parts of menu">
  <endpoint
      xlink:type="locator"
      xlink:href="menu1.xml"
      xlink:label="menuPage1"
      xlink:title="Beverages"/>
  <endpoint
      xlink:type="locator"
      xlink:href="menu2.xml"
      xlink:label="menuPage2"
      xlink:title="Appetizers"/>
  <endpoint
      xlink:type="locator"
      xlink:href="menu3.xml"
      xlink:label="menuPage3"
      xlink:title="Sandwiches"/>
  <endpoint
      xlink:type="locator"
      xlink:href="menu4.xml"
      xlink:label="menuPage4"
      xlink:title="Desserts"/>
  <endpoint
      xlink:type="locator"
      xlink:href="menu5.xml"
      xlink:label="menuPage5"
      xlink:title="Pasta"/>
  <link
      xlink:type="arc"
      xlink:from="menuPage1"
      xlink:to="menuPage2"
      xlink:show="replace"
      xlink:actuate="onRequest"/>
  <link
      xlink:type="arc"
      xlink:from="menuPage2"
      xlink:to="menuPage3"
      xlink:show="replace"
      xlink:actuate="onRequest"/>
  <link
      xlink:type="arc"
      xlink:from="menuPage3"
      xlink:to="menuPage4"
      xlink:show="replace"
      xlink:actuate="onRequest"/>
  <link
      xlink:type="arc"
      xlink:from="menuPage4"
      xlink:to="menuPage5"
      xlink:show="replace"
      xlink:actuate="onRequest"/>
</linkbase>
```

We then create the menu5.xml document for the pasta items, and that's it – we don't have to go back and modify any of the other menu pages! Our browser would reflect the change automatically.

If we wanted to change the order in which the menu pages were traversed, we could do so by modifying the link database document (instead of altering each participating document in the link, as we would need to with HTML). As you can see, the abstraction of link information away from content is a powerful way of controlling and maintaining links between documents, as well as allowing others who do not control your content to link to (and from!) it – as we'll see in the next section.

Note that if you want, you can always use XSLT to style XLink assertions into some sort of equivalent declarations for your target platform (such as HTML hyperlinks). How you do so (especially for extended links) is completely up to you, since XLink doesn't specify any particular behavior for the links. Let's see an example of this.

Transforming XLinks To HTML with XSLT

Say we have the following example XML document with an extended XLink declaration (menu.xml):

```
<menu xmlns:xlink="http://www.w3.org/1999/xlink" xlink:type="extended">
  <menuPage xlink:type="resource"
            xlink:label="menuPage"
            xlink:title="Appetizers">
    <menuItem>
      <itemName>French Fries</itemName>
      <itemPrice>$1.15</itemPrice>
    </menuItem>
    <menuItem>
      <itemName>Onion Rings</itemName>
      <itemPrice>$1.25</itemPrice>
    </menuItem>
    <menuItem>
      <itemName>Cheese Sticks</itemName>
      <itemPrice>$3.50</itemPrice>
    </menuItem>
  </menuPage>
  <menuPage xlink:type="resource"
            xlink:label="menuPage"
            xlink:title="Entrees">
    <menuItem>
      <itemName>Hamburger</itemName>
      <itemPrice>$1.80</itemPrice>
    </menuItem>
    <menuItem>
      <itemName>Hot Dog</itemName>
      <itemPrice>$1.40</itemPrice>
    </menuItem>
    <menuItem>
      <itemName>Veggie Burger</itemName>
      <itemPrice>$2.20</itemPrice>
    </menuItem>
  </menuPage>
  <menuPage xlink:type="resource"
            xlink:label="menuPage"
            xlink:title="Desserts">
    <menuItem>
```

```
      <itemName>Ice Cream</itemName>
      <itemPrice>$0.80</itemPrice>
    </menuItem>
    <menuItem>
      <itemName>Sundae</itemName>
      <itemPrice>$1.20</itemPrice>
    </menuItem>
    <menuItem>
      <itemName>Banana Split</itemName>
      <itemPrice>$2.20</itemPrice>
    </menuItem>
  </menuPage>
  <menuLink
     xlink:type="arc"
     xlink:from="menuPage"
     xlink:to="menuPage"
     xlink:show="embed"
     xlink:actuate="onLoad"/>
</menu>
```

We want to render this menu as HTML. Note that all the participants in the link are in-line – this would correspond to a large document that provides a way to move to specific portions of the document.

In our case, we've decided to render the links as HTML hyperlinks (although this isn't the only way you could do it – for example, you might put the links in a dropdown with a Go button and a little bit of JavaScript behind it). We can use the following stylesheet to do the transformation (`menu.xsl`):

```
<xsl:stylesheet version="1.0" exclude-result-prefixes="xlink"
  xmlns:xsl="http://www.w3.org/1999/XSL/Transform"
  xmlns:xlink="http://www.w3.org/1999/xlink" >
  <xsl:output method="html" />

  <xsl:template match="/">
    <html>
      <head>
        <title>Menu</title>
      </head>
      <body>
        <h1>Joe's Grill - Menu</h1>
        <xsl:apply-templates />
      </body>
    </html>
  </xsl:template>

  <xsl:template match="menuPage">
    <a name="{@xlink:title}" />
    <h2><xsl:value-of select="@xlink:title" /></h2>
    <table>
      <xsl:apply-templates />
    </table>
    <xsl:variable name="resourceLabel" select="@xlink:label" />

    <xsl:for-each
      select="../menuLink[@xlink:type='arc'][@xlink:from=$resourceLabel]">
```

```
      <xsl:variable name="destinationLabel" select="@xlink:to" />
      <xsl:for-each select="../menuPage[@xlink:label=$destinationLabel]">
        <br />
        <a href="#{@xlink:title}"><xsl:value-of select="@xlink:title" /></a>
      </xsl:for-each>
    </xsl:for-each>
  </xsl:template>

  <xsl:template match="menuItem">
    <tr>
      <td><xsl:value-of select="itemName" /></td>
      <td><xsl:value-of select="itemPrice" /></td>
    </tr>
  </xsl:template>
</xsl:stylesheet>
```

This stylesheet basically traverses the document looking for linkages and adds hyperlinks where appropriate. It produces the following page:

As you can see, you can write XSLT transforms to leverage XLink right now, without waiting for so-called 'native' XLink support in browsers and other processors.

Marking Up Read-Only Documents

Using out-of-line links is also a great way to annotate read-only documents from another source. Let's take a look at a brief example of how this might be done.

Say we have the following, read-only document, called quotelist.xml, which contains quotes, which we can then annotate to clarify:

```
<quotelist>
   <quote>
      Now is the time for all good men to come to the aid of their country.
   </quote>
</quotelist>
```

We want to add to this document in another document, comments.xml:

```
<comment>
   By men, the author obviously meant all people, not the male gender.
</comment>
```

We can specify a link document, commentlink.xml, which asserts a linkage between comments.xml and the read-only quotelist.xml:

```
<linkbase
        xmlns:xlink="http://www.w3.org/1999/xlink"
        xlink:type="extended"
        xlink:role="quoteComments"
        xlink:title="Comments">
   <endpoint
        xlink:type="locator"
        xlink:href="quotelist.xml"
        xlink:label="quotes"
        xlink:title="Famous quotes"/>
   <endpoint
        xlink:type="locator"
        xlink:href="comments.xml"
        xlink:label="comments"
        xlink:title="Commentary"/>
   <commentLink
        xlink:type="arc"
        xlink:from="quotes"
        xlink:to="comments"
        xlink:title="Show comments"
        xlink:show="new"
        xlink:actuate="onRequest"/>
</linkbase>
```

An XLink-aware processor would open the link document, read the extended link, and see that there is a link between the quotelist.xml document and the comments.xml document. It might then bring up the quotelist.xml content and render links from it to the comments.xml document:

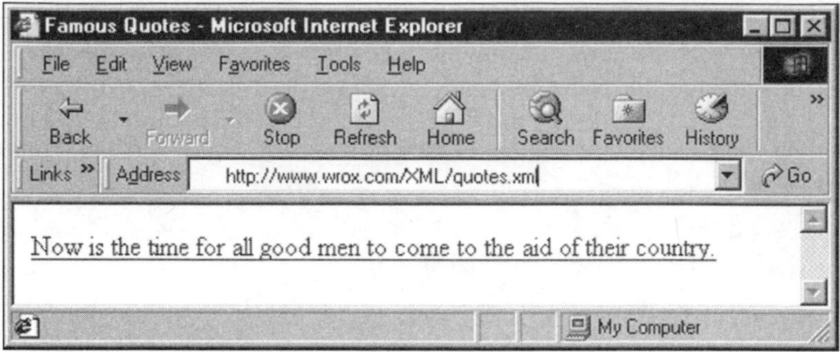

Clicking on the linked element would bring up the comment information:

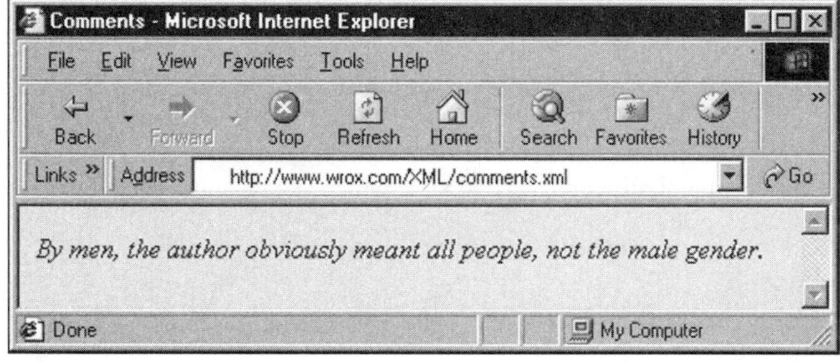

It would be even better if we could link to the precise location in the `quotelist.xml` document that corresponds to the word we are commenting on, `men` – but that's the job of **XPointer**, which we'll discuss next.

XLink Summary

XLink provides a flexible mechanism for defining links in XML documents that connect various resources together. These resources may even be resources that don't normally have the ability to contain links, like image files. XLink may be used to:

- Link one document to another, much as HTML hyperlinks work
- Link many different resources together
- Abstract link information away from content, allowing linkage information to be easily updated

However, XLink is not implemented in any serious fashion in the toolsets most commonly in use at this time – although some form of XLink will undoubtedly be available soon for use by XML developers, and it's a simple enough task to use XSLT to transform XLink declarations into HTML-style navigation. There are other ways XLink functionality can be leveraged as well – for example, transforming XLink information into RDF (see http://www.w3.org/TR/xlink2rdf for more details).

XPointer

We mentioned earlier that it would be nice if we could point not to an entire XML document, but to some portion of it – individual sub-trees, attributes, or even individual characters that are part of text content. The W3C has defined a mechanism that allows us to do just that.

HTML Pointers

Again, the concept of XML Pointers has an analogue in HTML: the `<A NAME=...>` markup. This markup indicates that the position marked by the `<A>` element may be linked to using the HTML pointer syntax. For example, if we have the following document, `content.htm`:

```
<HTML>
  <BODY>
    <A NAME="sentence1">This is the first sentence.<BR/></A>
    <A NAME="sentence2">This is the second sentence.<BR/></A>
    <A NAME="sentence3">This is the third sentence.<BR/></A>
  </BODY>
</HTML>
```

We can link to this document from another document, `index.htm`, using this syntax:

```
<HTML>
  <BODY>
    <A HREF="content.htm#sentence1">Go to the first sentence<BR/></A>
    <A HREF="content.htm#sentence2">Go to the second sentence<BR/></A>
    <A HREF="content.htm#sentence3">Go to the third sentence<BR/></A>
  </BODY>
</HTML>
```

HTML uses the # character (known as a **fragment specifier**) to indicate that the text following it refers to a named anchor point, or fragment identifier, in the targeted document. A browser will typically render the content by positioning the viewer at the marked position in the target document. As we'll see later in the chapter, XPointer references are declared in a similar way.

The Problem with HTML Pointers

Like HTML links, HTML pointers have shortcomings.

HTML Anchor Points Must Be Declared

In order to point to a specific location in an HTML document, that document must contain an `<A NAME=...>` anchor reference. HTML pointers may not point to a location in an HTML document that does not have this declaration, making it impossible to point into a read-only document that doesn't already have anchor points declared.

HTML Anchor Points Must Link To the Entire Target Document

There is no way to specify an HTML pointer that points to just a portion of a target document – all that may be specified is an anchor point in the full document. When HTML link targets are rendered, the entire document is rendered with the document positioned to the referenced anchor point. It would be nice if we could define a pointer that points to some portion of a target document, so the processor could only render that section instead of the full target.

The XML pointing mechanism addresses both of these issues, as we'll see later.

The XPointer Specification

The W3C specification for XML pointers is known as XPointer. It may be found at http://www.w3.org/TR/xptr. The most recent working draft of this specification was released in January 2001.

As of the time of writing, the XPointer specification is a working draft in last call status. This means it will be reviewed soon for promotion to candidate recommendation status, and the information found in it should be considered relatively stable.

Note that the XPointer specification essentially extends another specification, XPath. XPath is the W3C's common mechanism for addressing individual information items in an XML document, and is also a major component of XSLT. XPointer provides syntax for stating address information in a link to an XML document, as well as extending XPath with a few additional features. XPath is discussed in Chapter 8.

What's Changed Since the First Edition of the Book?

Well, even though it appears that not much has changed (the specification is once again in last call working draft status), it actually made it as far as candidate recommendation status before being downgraded again to working draft status. This was done because of the addition of syntax to assist in the resolution of namespace prefixes where the same prefix is associated with different URIs within the same document. We'll see how this namespace resolution is performed later in the chapter.

Specifying XPointers in a URI

XPointers are referenced in a similar way to HTML pointers. When working with an XPointer-aware processor, URIs may contain a reference to a position in an XML document by appending an XPointer fragment identifier to the URI of the document itself.

For example,

```
http://www.wrox.com/Catalog/catalog.xml#xpointer(book1)
```

would point to the element with the `ID` `book1` in the `catalog.xml` document. We'll talk about the way fragment identifiers may be specified next.

How May Fragment Identifiers Be Specified?

There are three ways of specifying fragment identifiers in XPointer:

- Bare names
- Child sequence
- Full XPointers

The full specification is quite complex and allows a great deal of flexibility in pointing into an XML document. It builds on the W3C XPath recommendation.

First, we'll talk about the first two ways fragment identifiers may be specified in XPointer.

Bare Name Fragment Identification

To provide a similar functionality to that we are used to in HTML pointers, a shorthand notation is provided for pointing to elements with specific IDs. For example, let's say we had the following document, catalog.xml:

```
<Catalog>
   <Book color="red" ID="book1">
      <Title>XML IE5 Programmer's Reference</Title>
      <Pages>480</Pages>
      <ISBN>1-861001-57-6</ISBN>
      <RecSubjCategories>
         <Category>Internet</Category>
         <Category>Web Publishing</Category>
         <Category>XML</Category>
      </RecSubjCategories>
      <Price>$29.99</Price>
   </Book>
</Catalog>
```

We may point to the Book element with the ID book1 using the following syntax:

```
#book1
```

If the fragment is simply an ID value, the pointer points to the element with that ID value. Note that for this shorthand to work, the document being pointed into must have a schema or DTD that specifies an attribute for the element with the type ID.

Child Sequence Fragment Identification

Child sequence fragment identifiers allow a document to be pointed into by walking through the child element tree. Some examples may be helpful. In our sample catalog document, catalog.xml,

```
<Catalog>
   <Book color="red" ID="book1">
      <Title>XML IE5 Programmer's Reference</Title>
      <Pages>480</Pages>
      <ISBN>1-861001-57-6</ISBN>
      <RecSubjCategories>
         <Category>Internet</Category>
         <Category>Web Publishing</Category>
         <Category>XML</Category>
      </RecSubjCategories>
      <Price>$29.99</Price>
   </Book>
</Catalog>
```

we may point to the second Category element with this URI fragment (the two examples are equivalent):

```
#/1/1/4/2
#xpointer(/1/1/4/2)
```

This syntax may be understood this way:

- Go to the first element in the document (the Catalog element)
- Then go to the first child element of that element (the book1 Book element)

- Then go to the fourth child element of that element (the `RecSubjCategories` element)
- Then go to the second child element of that element (the Web Publishing `Category` element)

These child sequence identifiers may also start from a named node, specified as in the bare name fragment identification method. The following URI is equivalent to the one above:

```
http://www.wrox.com/catalog/catalog.xml#xpointer(book1/4/2)
```

Namespace Resolution

It is possible for an XPointer expression to refer to a namespace that is not declared in the document containing the XPointer (for example, if the document containing the XPointer is not XML). In the previous drafts of XPointer, it was assumed that the prefix used for the namespace would be matched, and the appropriate element would be pointed to. However, it quickly came to light (necessitating a downgrade of the status of XPointer from a candidate recommendation to a working draft) that there was a problem with this namespace resolution scheme.

Consider the following document, `data.xml` (one hopes that documents like this wouldn't exist in the real world, but it is theoretically possible):

```
<?xml version="1.0" ?>
<root>
  <x:a xmlns:x="www.abc.com/xml" />
  <x:a xmlns:x="www.xyz.com/xml" />
</root>
```

Now consider this XPointer expression, found in a (hypothetical) XPointer-aware version of XHTML:

```
<a href="data.xml#xpointer(//x:a)">Which a element am I?</a>
```

The obvious problem is that the XPointer expression cannot determine which a element is intended to be the target of the XPointer – since there are two distinct a elements, in different namespaces, but with the same prefix.

The solution to the problem, added when XPointer was moved back to working draft status, is to add a way to declare a namespace prefix right in the XPointer expression itself:

```
<a href="data.xml#xmlns(x=http://www.abc.com/xml) xpointer(//x:a)">
  Now I know which a element I am!
</a>
```

If you have a complex namespace issue like this where there is the possibility of name clashes (based on unresolved namespace prefixes), you should declare the URI for the namespace of each prefix you are matching on to ensure that the XPointer-aware processor can find the appropriate target nodes in the target document. Note that in the new version of XPointer, the prefix used for the namespace is irrelevant – matching is performed on the URI declared for the prefix instead.

The Full XPointer Specification

With the full XPointer specification, the pointing mechanism being used in the URI must be identified by putting the pointing mechanism name and parentheses around the locator – for XPointers, this will always take the form `xpointer()`.

The full XPointer specification uses XPath for its location mechanism. XPath provides a universal way of specifying some portion of an XML document.

> *XPath is a specification that was worked on jointly by members of the XSL and XPointer Working Groups, as they realized that both required a way of selecting a part of an XML document. Both groups use and build upon the functionality offered by XPath. The specification for XPath has a status of Recommendation, meaning that it will not change from its current status in this version. It may be found at* http://www.w3.org/TR/xpath. *Here we will just look at some of the key points that you need to know to implement XPointers; for more detail on XPath, see Chapter 8.*

XPointer Extensions To XPath

XPointer extends XPath to allow for some additional functionality. It introduces the concepts of points and ranges as ways to declare portions of XML documents (in addition to the node construct in XPath), and provides some functions for manipulating these new position references.

Points

XPointer defines the concept of a **point** location, as distinct from a node. While a point location may be a node, it may also be a particular location within character content (for example, at the third character of the text value of the `Title` element). Points are useful in the definition of **ranges**, which we will look at next.

Ranges

XPointer also defines the concept of a **range** location, which is defined to be the XML structure and content between two points. Note that this might result in a section that is not well-formed, as only part of some elements may be enclosed in the range. The ability to specify ranges would allow, for example, a pointer to point to all the occurrences of a particular word in a target document (as the result of a search engine's output, for example). Ranges may be declared this way:

```
#xpointer(<locator>/range-to(<locator>))
```

So, a range that selects the range starting from the element with the `ID` `book1` and ending with the element with the `ID` `book3`, inclusive, including all of the content in document order that falls between them, would be specified as:

```
#xpointer(id("book1")/range-to(id("book3")))
```

Additional Functions

There are some additional functions defined in the XPointer specification to allow for the generation and manipulation of point and range locations. Let's take a look at the some of the most important ones.

The `string-range` function searches the text in the target document and returns a list of range locations for each discovered instance of a target string. For example, this locator would return all of the instances of the string `XML` in the `catalog.xml` document:

```
catalog.xml#xpointer(string-range(/, "XML"))
```

This function might be used, for example, in a search engine – each instance of the word would be a range in the XPointer, allowing an application to show contextual text around the instance and perhaps allowing the user to jump to that location in the document via an XLink.

The `here` function returns the element that contains the XPointer itself. This function allows XPointers to point to other locations relative to the XPointer's location in the pointing document itself. For example, the following XPointer would point to the parent of the XPointer element itself:

```
#xpointer(here()/..)
```

XPointer Errors

There are three errors that may be caused by an improper XPointer. Any parser that is XPointer-aware will need to handle these errors in some way (the XPointer specification leaves the exact mechanism up to the developer designing the XPointer-aware processor).

Syntax Error

A fragment identifier that does not correspond to the syntactical constraints of the XPointer specification results in a **syntax error**.

Resource Error

A fragment identifier that is syntactically correct, but is attached to an improper resource (such as an XPointer into an image file), causes a **resource error**.

Sub-Resource Error

A fragment identifier that is syntactically correct and is attached to a well-formed XML document but does not result in any valid locations causes a **sub-resource** error.

Summary

XPointers provide a mechanism for a URI to point to some portion of an XML document. While there are few serious implementations of XPointers at this time, the specification is currently in last call status, and implementations that use XPointers will be available very soon. For now, you can see how Amaya's XPointer support is used in combination with Annotea to annotate web resources, in Chapter 23.

Conclusions

In this chapter, we've taken a look at three technologies that will soon have an impact on the way we design and implement XML systems:

- XML Fragments may be used when part of a large document needs to be transferred to another system, and provides a way to also include contextual information where necessary to the receiving system.
- XLink provides a mechanism, analogous to HTML hyperlinks, that allows us to assert links between XML documents. We can define more complex, multiple-document linkages using XLink. We can also annotate read-only documents using XLink linkbases.
- XPointer provides a way, analogous to the HTML anchor mechanism, to specify a particular location or portion of an XML document as part of a URI. This allows non-XML documents, such as HTML documents, to reference XML documents with a good deal of control and granularity.

While none of these technologies has been formally blessed by the W3C as of this writing, they will all soon be part of the XML toolset – familiarizing yourself with these technologies now will prepare you to take advantage of these technologies as soon as they become available.

11

The Document Object Model

By now, you should be starting to get a handle on the structure of XML documents and the ways they can be used to describe hierarchical information. Next, we need to look at the ways you may access an XML document from your programs. One of those ways is via the **Document Object Model (DOM)**. In this chapter, we'll take a look at the Document Object Model and demonstrate its functionality with a couple of sample programs. We'll see:

- What the Document Object Model is and why we need it
- DOM Level 1 – how to parse, navigate, modify and create XML documents.
- Uses of DOM
- DOM Level 2
- The future of DOM with DOM Level 3

What Is the Document Object Model?

The term Document Object Model has been applied to web browsers for some time. Modern browsers allow programmatic access to their services through an object model – for scripting languages in the HTML page. Objects such as window, document, and history have long been considered part of the browser object model (BOM) – but due to the way in which Web development suddenly exploded and at least in part due to the rivalry between Microsoft and Netscape, these models have been notoriously different and difficult to code consistently for. In order to create a more standardized way of accessing and manipulating document structure over the web, the W3C produced specifications resulting in the current W3C DOM, which provides both an object model for HTML documents and a more generalized model for XML documents.

The W3C DOM is a **language-** and **platform-neutral** definition, that is, interfaces are defined for the different objects comprising the DOM, but no specifics of implementation are provided. The objects in the DOM allow the developer to read, search, modify, add to, and delete data from a document – they provide a definition of standard functionality for document navigation and manipulation of the content and structure of HTML and XML documents.

DOM implementations may be coded in any programming language for any platform. This allows, for example, legacy data stores to be accessed using the DOM by implementing the DOM interfaces as a thin wrapper around the legacy data accessor functions.

The most recent recommendations for the DOM (DOM level 2) are:

- Core DOM specification – http://www.w3.org/TR/DOM-Level-2-Core/
- Views specification – http://www.w3.org/TR/DOM-Level-2-Views/
- Events specification – http://www.w3.org/TR/DOM-Level-2-Events/
- Style specification – http://www.w3.org/TR/DOM-Level-2-Style/
- Traversal and Range specification – http://www.w3.org/TR/DOM-Level-2-Traversal-Range/

What Has Changed Since the First Edition of This Book?

Since the first edition of Professional XML, the DOM Level 2 has become a W3C recommendation. We'll take a look at the features of the DOM level 2, including traversal, ranges, and events, and how you can use them in your applications. We'll also take a look at what's coming in the DOM level 3, including (finally) a standard way to save and load your documents regardless of the specific implementation of the DOM.

XML Document Structure

Developers new to XML often assume that the main purpose of XML is to enable pieces of information in a file to be named so that others may easily understand them. As a result, documents prepared by novice XML developers often resemble "tag soup" – an unordered list of data elements with meaningful tag names, but containing about the same level of information as a flat file.

```
<INVOICE>
   <CUSTOMER>Homer J. Simpson</CUSTOMER>
   <ADDRESS>142 Evergreen Terrace</ADDRESS>
   <CITY>Springfield</CITY>
   <STATE>VA</STATE>
   <ZIP>00000</ZIP>
   <PRODUCT1>Plutonium</PRODUCT1>
   <UNITS1>10</UNITS1>
   <PRODUCT2>Donuts</PRODUCT2>
   <UNITS2>937</UNITS2>
   <PRODUCT3>Beer</PRODUCT3>
   <UNITS3>1028</UNITS3>
   <PRODUCT4>Peanuts</PRODUCT4>
   <UNITS4>1</UNITS4>
</INVOICE>
```

The ability of XML that many developers overlook is its ability to show relationships between elements – specifically, the ability to imply a parent-child relationship between two elements. One possible way (but not the only way) to express this information in a structured way would be this:

```
<INVOICE CUSTOMER="Homer J. Simpson"
         ADDRESS="142 Evergreen Terrace"
         CITY="Springfield"
         STATE="VA"
         ZIP="00000">
   <LINEITEM PRODUCT="Plutonium"
             UNITS="10"/>
   <LINEITEM PRODUCT="Donuts"
             UNITS="937"/>
   <LINEITEM PRODUCT="Beer"
             UNITS="1028"/>
   <LINEITEM PRODUCT="Peanuts"
             UNITS="1"/>
</INVOICE>
```

In this form of the document, it becomes immediately apparent that the invoice element has four children: the LINEITEM elements. It also makes it easier to search the document – if we're looking for all orders for plutonium, we can do so by looking for <LINEITEM> elements with a PRODUCT attribute value of "Plutonium" – instead of having to look at the <PRODUCT1> element, <PRODUCT2> element, and so on.

It's useful to think about our documents in terms of trees that show all the elements and their relationships to one another:

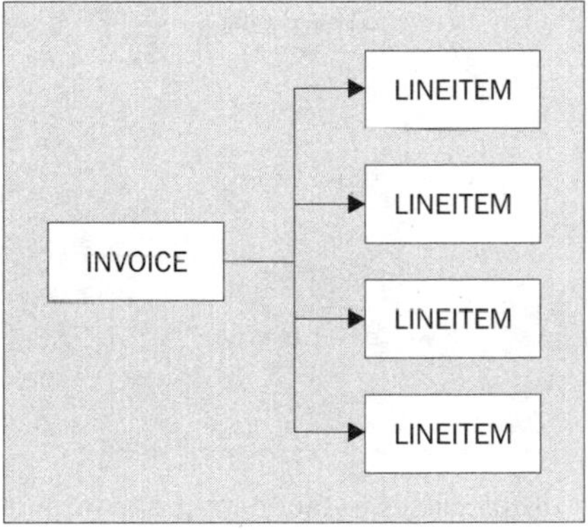

We can think of each item in this tree as a **node** – that is, an atomic piece of information that we can manipulate. When working with the DOM (as we will see), there are various types of nodes – element nodes, attribute nodes, text nodes, and so on. To add another line item to the invoice in the text file, we would have to read through the file until we got past the last line item element of the invoice, insert our new line item text, and then proceed with the rest of the document. As you can imagine, this technique becomes tricky quickly, especially if the node tree starts to become deep. However, if we could operate on the document in the node form with its tree structure, we'd be able to add the line item easily – we would simply create a new LINEITEM node and attach it as a child to the INVOICE node.

This is exactly how the DOM works.

When the DOM is used to manipulate an XML text file, the first thing it does is parse the file, breaking the file out into individual elements, attributes, comments, and so on. The DOM relies on the description of XML documents provided in the W3C's XML Information Set recommendation (covered in Chapter 4) to determine what portions of an XML document correspond to nodes. It then creates (in memory) a representation of the XML file as a node tree. The developer may then access the contents of the document through the node tree, and make modifications to it as necessary.

In fact, the DOM goes one step further and treats every item in the document as a node – elements, attributes, comments, processing instructions, and even the text that makes up an attribute. So, for our example above, the DOM representation would actually be:

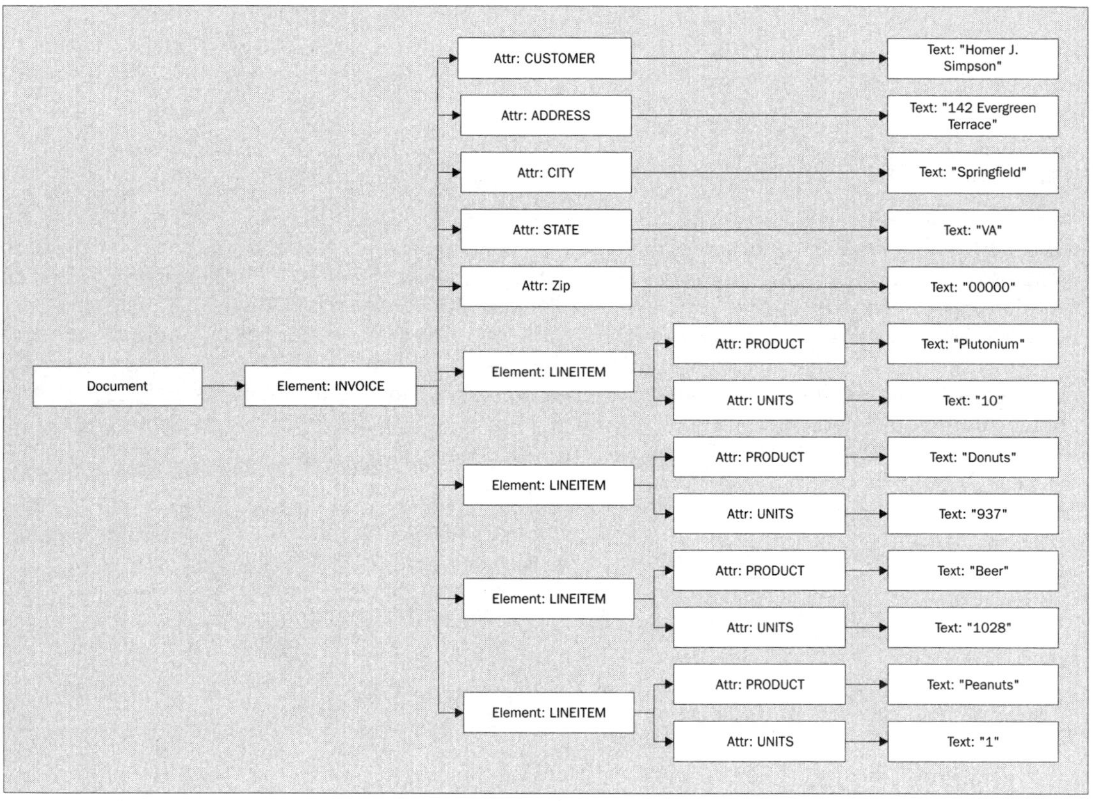

The DOM provides a robust set of interfaces to facilitate the manipulation of the DOM node tree.

Why Use the DOM?

Using the DOM to create and access XML documents provides several benefits:

- The DOM ensures proper grammar and well-formedness
- The DOM abstracts content away from grammar
- The DOM simplifies internal document manipulation
- The DOM closely mirrors typical hierarchical and relational database structures

Let's look at each of these in turn.

The DOM Ensures Proper Grammar and Well-Formedness

Because DOM parsers transform the text file into an abstract representation of a node tree, problems like unclosed tags and improperly nested tags can be completely avoided (as opposed to writing an XML document by manually serializing text, for example, and running the risk of forgetting to write an end tag). In addition, the DOM will prevent improper parent-child relationships in the document. For example, an `Attr` object will never be allowed to be the parent of another `Attr` object.

The DOM Abstracts Content Away From Grammar

The node tree created by the DOM is a logical and consistent representation of the content found in the XML file – it shows what information is present and how it is related without necessarily being bound to the XML grammar. The information exposed by the node tree may be used, for example, to update a relational database, or create an HTML page – and developers need not concern themselves with the specifics of the XML language.

The DOM Simplifies Internal Document Manipulation

A developer using the DOM to modify an XML file will have a much simpler task than one who is attempting to do so manually (by serializing the XML document to a stream directly). As we discussed in the previous example, adding an element to the middle of a document is a simple task with the DOM. In addition, global operations (such as deleting all elements with a particular tag name from a document) can be performed with a couple of commands, rather than the brute force method required to perform a scan of the file and remove the offending tags.

The DOM Closely Mirrors Typical HIerarchical and Relational Database Structures

The way in which the DOM represents the relationship between data elements is very similar to the way that this information is represented in modern object-oriented and relational databases. This makes it very easy to move information between a database and an XML file using the DOM.

Many databases represent hierarchical information using a **snowflake** structure, where the information in the database radiates out from a central "top-level" table much like the spokes on a wheel:

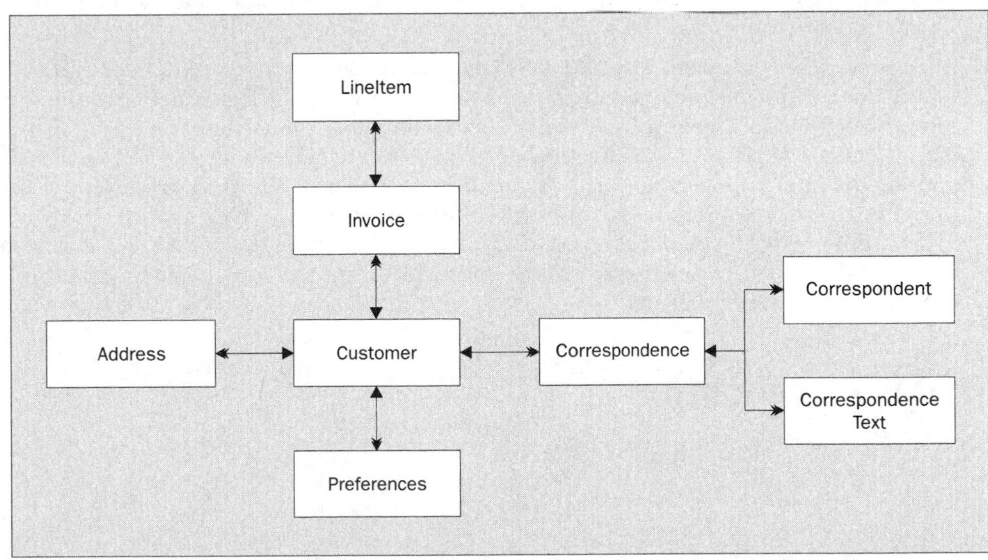

The XML equivalent of this structure might be:

```
<CUSTOMER>
   <INVOICE>
      <LINEITEM />
   </INVOICE>
   <ADDRESS />
   <PREFERENCES />
   <CORRESPONDENCE>
      <CORRESPONDENT />
      <CORRESPONDENCETEXT />
   </CORRESPONDENCE>
</CUSTOMER>
```

Using the DOM to build the tree structure of a document allows information to be easily transferred between systems.

Practical Considerations

Because the DOM loads an entire document into memory and parses it into a document tree, it tends to consume an inordinate amount of memory – depending on several factors such as the library being used and the details of its internal structure, a document can require up to four or five times its own size for a DOM representation! If you have a server that needs to work with several multi-megabyte documents at once, you can see how the DOM could rapidly become a bottleneck. The alternative would be to use some other processing mechanism to get at the information in your documents. Here are a couple of options:

- **Use SAX.** SAX, or the Simple API for XML, was designed specifically to avoid the memory problems encountered when using the DOM. Instead of loading the entire document into memory all at once, it streams the document through a parser and raises events based on the elements, attributes, and so on, that it encounters. If you need to extract a few pieces of information from a large XML document, SAX is usually the best way to accomplish it. However, if you need to extract the entire contents of an XML document, or your document has complex relationships (such as many `ID-IDREF` relationships), SAX will be a poorer choice – requiring multiple passes over the document or caching of the document information. You can learn more about SAX in Chapter 12.
- **Pre-process the document with XSLT.** If you need to access some well-defined subset of a large document, you could pre-process the document with XSLT and then load the resulting instance of the document with the DOM. This will reduce the memory footprint of your application dramatically, but also slow down processing (because it requires two passes to obtain the information from your document). Also, this method does not allow updating of the original document, so it can only be used to read the document. Note that pre-processing with XSLT only works if you're using an XSLT library that runs on top of SAX – if it runs on top of the DOM, the program will still load the entire document tree into memory! You can learn more about XSLT in Chapter 9.

The DOM Specification

As of press time, the W3C has prepared three documents on DOM – DOM Level 1, Level 2, and Level 3.

DOM Level 1

The W3C document for DOM Level 1 has a status of Recommendation. This means that the W3C has reviewed it, accepted member comment on it, revised it, and is now promoting it as a standard on the World Wide Web. The full text of the recommendation may be found at http://www.w3.org/TR/REC-DOM-Level-1/.

This document contains two main sections:

- **Document Object Model (Core) Level 1** contains the specification for interfaces that can access any structured document, with some specific extensions that allow access to XML documents. Every DOM library will provide at least the functionality found in the Document Object Model core.
- The second section of the document describes HTML-specific extensions to the DOM, and is outside the scope of this book. For information on the HTML DOM, please take a look at HTML Programmer's Reference, ISBN 1-861001-56-8 from Wrox Press.

The DOM specification describes how strings are to be manipulated by the DOM by defining the datatype `DOMString`. It is defined as a multiple-byte character set string, encoded using the UTF-16 encoding scheme (note that in accordance with recent revisions of Unicode, this may require up to four bytes for some characters). For specific implementations, the interfaces will usually be bound to system datatypes that are also UTF-16 encoded, such as Java's `String` type.

Let's take a look at the objects, methods, and properties that make up the DOM level 1 specification. Note that the behavior described is that for XML documents only; the DOM may behave differently when used to access HTML documents.

The following diagram shows the class hierarchy for the objects making up the DOM:

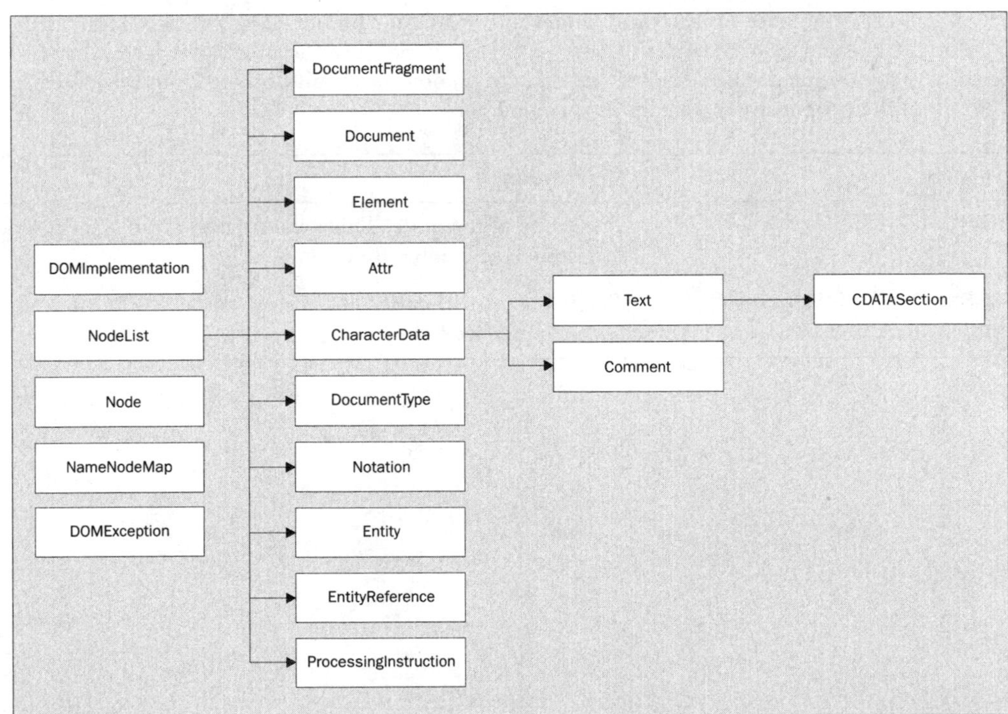

Moving from left to right on this diagram, interfaces to the right inherit from interfaces to the left.

In general, the DOM is accessed by traversing the various children, siblings, and parents of nodes in a tree. It does not (unfortunately) allow more complex addressing, such as that offered by XPath. In order to get to a particular piece of information in the tree, methods are available to search on that node's name or to manually walk down the tree to the node. Becoming familiar with the way the document tree may be traversed is crucial to getting the most out of your DOM code.

Next, let's take a look at each of these interfaces and how they fit into the DOM.

DOMImplementation

The `DOMImplementation` interface allows the code to interrogate the specific implementation of the DOM to find out about available support for various features. In the Level 1 DOM specification, the operational areas that may be tested are HTML and XML; however, as we'll see in our overview of Level 2, many more functional areas will be added to the DOM in future releases.

Method	Description
`boolean hasFeature( DOMString feature, DOMString version)`	Tests to see if the DOM implements a particular feature. In the Level 1 DOM specification, this feature may be the strings `"HTML"` or `"XML"`, and the version may be the string `"1.0"`. If the version is not specified, `true` is returned if any version of the feature is supported by the implementation. Returns `true` if the feature is implemented, or `false` otherwise.

Node

The `Node` object is the base object for all nodes in the DOM. The `Element`, `Attr`, `Text`, `CDATASection`, `EntityReference`, `Entity`, `ProcessingInstruction`, `Comment`, `Document`, `DocumentType`, `DocumentFragment`, and `Notation` objects are all derived from this object and support all of the properties and methods specified here.

Property	Description
`DOMString nodeName`	The name of the node. This varies based on the `nodeType` of this node (see below). Read-only.
`DOMString nodeValue`	The value for this node. This varies based on the `nodeType` of this node (see below).

Property	Description
unsigned short nodeType	The type of node. Read-only. The possible values are: ❑ ELEMENT_NODE = 1: This node is an Element. ❑ ATTRIBUTE_NODE = 2: This node is an Attr. ❑ TEXT_NODE = 3: This node is a Text object. ❑ CDATA_SECTION_NODE = 4: This node is a CDATASection. ❑ ENTITY_REFERENCE_NODE = 5: This node is an EntityReference. ❑ ENTITY_NODE = 6: This node is an Entity. ❑ PROCESSING_INSTRUCTION_NODE = 7: This node is a ProcessingInstruction. ❑ COMMENT_NODE = 8: This node is a Comment. ❑ DOCUMENT_NODE = 9: This node is a Document. ❑ DOCUMENT_TYPE_NODE = 10: This node is a DocumentType. ❑ DOCUMENT_FRAGMENT_NODE = 11: This node is a DocumentFragment. ❑ NOTATION_NODE = 12: This node is a Notation.
Node parentNode	The parent Node object of this node. Read-only. For Document, DocumentFragment, and Attr nodes, this is always NULL; also, if the node is currently disconnected with respect to the document, this property will also be NULL.
NodeList childNodes	A NodeList object containing a list of all the child nodes of this node. Read-only. Like all NodeLists, this property will change dynamically to reflect changes in other parts of the document.
Node firstChild	The first child Node object of this node. Read-only. If this node has no children, this property returns NULL.
Node lastChild	The last child Node object of this node. Read-only. If this node has no children, this property returns NULL.
Node previousSibling	The Node object immediately preceding this node in the document and sharing the same parent. Read-only. If this node is the first child of its parent or is the root node of the document, this property returns NULL.

Table continued on following page

Property	Description
`Node nextSibling`	The `Node` object immediately following this node in the document and sharing the same parent. Read-only. If this node is the last child of its parent or is the root node of the document, this property returns `NULL`.
`NamedNodeMap attributes`	If this node is an element, this property is a `NamedNodeMap` object containing all of the attributes of this node. Otherwise, this property returns `NULL`. Read-only.
`Document ownerDocument`	The `Document` object associated with this node. Read-only. If this node is a document, this property returns `NULL`.

Method	Description
`Node insertBefore( Node newChild, Node refChild)`	Inserts the node `newChild` before the existing child node `refChild`. ❑ If `refChild` is `NULL`, `newChild` will be added at the end of the list of children for this node. ❑ If the `newChild` node is a `DocumentFragment`, all of its children are inserted before `refChild` ❑ If `newChild` already exists, it is replaced by the new `newChild`. Returns the `newChild` node. May raise the following `DOMException` errors: ❑ `HIERARCHY_REQUEST_ERR` ❑ `WRONG_DOCUMENT_ERR` ❑ `NO_MODIFICATION_ALLOWED_ERR` ❑ `NOT_FOUND_ERR`
`Node replaceChild( Node newChild, Node oldChild)`	Replaces the `oldChild` node in the list of children with the `newChild` node. If `newChild` already exists, it is first removed. Returns the `oldChild` node. May raise the following `DOMException` errors: ❑ `HIERARCHY_REQUEST_ERR` ❑ `WRONG_DOCUMENT_ERR` ❑ `NO_MODIFICATION_ALLOWED_ERR` ❑ `NOT_FOUND_ERR`

Method	Description
`Node removeChild( Node oldChild)`	Removes the `oldChild` node from the list of children for this node. Returns the `oldChild` node. Note that the child node still exists even though it's not in the child list of any element – it may still be manipulated. May raise the following `DOMException` errors: ❑ `NO_MODIFICATION_ALLOWED_ERR` ❑ `NOT_FOUND_ERR`
`Node appendChild( Node newChild)`	Adds the `newChild` node to the end of the list of children for this node. If the `newChild` node is a `DocumentFragment`, all nodes in the fragment are appended to the list of children. Returns the `newChild` node. May raise the following `DOMException` errors: ❑ `HIERARCHY_REQUEST_ERR` ❑ `WRONG_DOCUMENT_ERR` ❑ `NO_MODIFICATION_ALLOWED_ERR`
`boolean hasChildNodes()`	Returns a `boolean` indicating whether this particular node contains any child nodes.
`Node cloneNode( boolean deep)`	Returns an exact copy of this node. If the `deep` parameter is `true`, all of the child nodes associated with this node are duplicated as well; otherwise, only the node itself is duplicated. Returns the new duplicate node. Note that the duplicate node has no parent.

The `nodeName` and `nodeValue` properties of the `Node` object take on different meanings based on the `nodeType`, as follows:

Node type	**`nodeName`** **represents**	**`nodeValue`** **represents**
`Element`	The element's tag name	Not used
`Attr`	The name of the attribute	The value of the attribute
`Text`	The literal "`#text`"	The content of the text node
`CDATASection`	The literal "`#cdata-section`"	The content of the CDATA section
`EntityReference`	The name of the referenced entity	Not used

Table continued on following page

Node type	nodeName represents	nodeValue represents
Entity	The name of the entity	Not used
ProcessingInstruction	The target	The remainder of the content (excluding the target name)
Comment	The literal "#comment"	The content of the comment
Document	The literal "#document"	Not used
DocumentType	The document type name	Not used
DocumentFragment	The literal "#document-fragment"	Not used
Notation	The notation name	Not used

Document

The Document object is the main object that can be instantiated in the DOM. None of the other objects make any sense outside the context of a Document object; therefore, the Document object contains factory methods to access the various other objects that make up the DOM.

The Document object is derived from the Node object.

Property	Description
DocumentType doctype	The DocumentType object that represents the Document Type Definition (DTD) for this document. Read-only. If there is no DTD associated with the document, this property will return NULL.
DOMImplementation implementation	The DOMImplementation object for this document. Read-only. This object may be interrogated to determine the capabilities of the DOM implementation being accessed.
Element documentElement	An Element object representing the root node in the DOM tree. Read-only. When using the DOM to walk the document tree of an XML document, this node should always be the starting point.

Method	Description
`Element createElement( DOMString tagName)`	Creates an `Element` object with the specified tag name. Note that this does not actually attach the new element to the node tree. Until a method like `appendChild()` is called on another node with this element as the parameter, this element will remain an orphan. The same applies to all other create methods on the `Document` object. Returns the created `Element` object. May raise the following `DOMException` errors: ❑ `INVALID_CHARACTER_ERR` ❑ `NOT_SUPPORTED_ERR`
`DocumentFragment createDocumentFragment()`	Creates and returns an empty `DocumentFragment` object.
`Text createTextNode( DOMString data)`	Creates and returns a `Text` object with the specified string as its text.
`Comment createComment( DOMString data)`	Creates and returns a `Comment` object with the specified string as its text.
`CDATASection createCDATASection( DOMString data)`	Creates and returns a `CDATASection` object with the specified string as its text.
`ProcessingInstruction createProcessingInstruction( DOMString target, DOMString data)`	Creates and returns a `ProcessingInstruction` object using the given name and data strings. May raise the following `DOMException` error: ❑ `INVALID_CHARACTER_ERR` ❑ `NOT_SUPPORTED_ERR`
`Attr createAttribute( DOMString name)`	Creates and returns an `Attr` object using the given name. May raise the following `DOMException` error: ❑ `INVALID_CHARACTER_ERR`
`EntityReference createEntityReference( DOMString name)`	Creates and returns an `EntityReference` object referencing the provided name. May raise the following `DOMException` errors: ❑ `INVALID_CHARACTER_ERR` ❑ `NOT_SUPPORTED_ERR`

Table continued on following page

Method	Description
`NodeList getElementsByTagName( DOMString tagname)`	Returns a `NodeList` object containing all the `Element` objects with a given tag name, in the order they would be encountered when traversing the node tree. An asterisk may be specified for `tagname` to create a `NodeList` containing all the `Element` objects in the document.

DocumentFragment

The `DocumentFragment` object is a 'lightweight' version of the `Document` object. It can be used to represent any arbitrary sub-tree of a document. A `DocumentFragment` object may be used to assemble a sub-tree of the main document tree, and then passed to a method such as `appendChild()` or `insertBefore()` to incorporate its child nodes into the main `Document` object.

As part of my work, I have written a rudimentary Word-XML converter using the MS Office 9 libraries. The code walks the Office 9 document tree and generates the analogous XML document. Since Word documents are broken up into paragraphs, and then sentences, I wrote a `renderParagraph()` *private method and a* `renderSentence()` *private method - each returning an XML fragment. To render the paragraph, I create a fragment and append to it each fragment returned by calling* `renderSentence()` *on the successive sentences in the paragraph. Document fragments are incredibly useful in this case.*

The `DocumentFragment` object is derived from the `Node` object.

The `DocumentFragment` object does not implement any additional methods or properties beyond those implemented by the `Node` object.

NodeList

The `NodeList` object is simply an ordered collection of `Node` objects. Typically, your program will need to manipulate `NodeLists` when they are returned by a call to the `getElementsByTagName()` method on the `Document` object.

Property	Description
`unsigned long length`	The number of `Node` objects in the `NodeList`. Read-only.

Method	Description
`Node item( unsigned long index)`	Returns the `index`ed item in the list of `Node` objects. The valid range for `index` is 0 to `length` - 1. If the `index` is out of range, this method returns `NULL`.

NamedNodeMap

The `NamedNodeMap` object is a collection of `Node` objects that may be accessed by name. The attributes associated with a particular element are expressed in the `attributes` property of that node as a `NamedNodeMap`.

Property	Description
`unsigned long length`	The number of `Node` objects in the `NamedNodeMap`. Read-only.

Method	Description
`Node getNamedItem( DOMString name)`	Returns a `Node` object from the `NamedNodeMap` specified by name. If the node with the specified name could not be found, this method returns `NULL`.
`Node setNamedItem( Node arg)`	Adds the specified `Node` object to the `NamedNodeMap`, using its `nodeName` to determine validity of the operation. Note that the same `Attr` node may not be added to more than one `Element`; the `Attr` node needs to be cloned before it may be added elsewhere. Returns the previous `Node` object in the `NamedNodeMap` with the same `nodeName` if one was present, or `NULL` otherwise. May raise the following `DOMException` errors: ❑ `WRONG_DOCUMENT_ERR` ❑ `NO_MODIFICATION_ALLOWED_ERR` ❑ `INUSE_ATTRIBUTE_ERR`
`Node removeNamedItem( DOMString name)`	Removes the `Node` object with the specified name from the `NamedNodeMap`. `Attr` nodes with defaults removed in this way are instead modified to take the default value. Returns the `Node` object removed from the `NamedNodeMap`, or `NULL` if no node matching the provided name was found. May raise the following `DOMException` error: ❑ `NOT_FOUND_ERR`
`Node item( unsigned long index)`	Returns the `index`ed item in the list of `Node` objects. The valid range for `index` is 0 to `length` - 1. If the `index` is out of range, this method returns `NULL`.

CharacterData

The `CharacterData` object is an object that defines some string manipulation methods that may be used to access raw text. In the DOM Level 1 specification, the `Text` and `Comment` objects inherit the `CharacterData` object's methods and properties.

The `CharacterData` object is derived from the `Node` object.

Property	Description
`DOMString data`	The character data for the node that is based on this object. Note that this property may be too large to be retrieved or updated at once; the various string manipulation methods provided for the `DOMString` object may then be used to read or update this property. May raise the following `DOMException` errors: ❑ `DOMSTRING_SIZE_ERR` ❑ `NO_MODIFICATION_ALLOWED_ERR`
`unsigned long length`	The length of the `data` property, in characters. Read-only.

Method	Description
`DOMString substringData( unsigned long offset, unsigned long count)`	Extracts a range of data from the `Node` object, starting from the `offset` position, and returning `count` characters. Returns the data extracted. May raise the following `DOMException` errors: ❑ `INDEX_SIZE_ERR` ❑ `DOMSTRING_SIZE_ERR`
`void appendData( DOMString arg)`	Appends the data to the end of the `Node` object's data. May raise the following `DOMException` error: ❑ `NO_MODIFICATION_ALLOWED_ERR`
`void insertData( unsigned long offset, DOMString arg)`	Inserts the data in the `arg` string into the `Node` object's data at the specified `offset`. May raise the following `DOMException` errors: ❑ `INDEX_SIZE_ERR` ❑ `NO_MODIFICATION_ALLOWED_ERR`
`void deleteData( unsigned long offset, unsigned long count)`	Deletes a range of data from the `Node` object, starting at the `offset` position, and deleting `count` characters. May raise the following `DOMException` errors: ❑ `INDEX_SIZE_ERR` ❑ `NO_MODIFICATION_ALLOWED_ERR`

Method	Description
`void replaceData( unsigned long offset, unsigned long count, DOMString arg)`	Replaces a range of data in the `Node` object starting at the `offset` position and going for `count` characters with the data in `arg`. Note that this function is simply shorthand for a `deleteData()` method call followed by an `insertData()` method call. May raise the following `DOMException` errors: ❑ `INDEX_SIZE_ERR` ❑ `NO_MODIFICATION_ALLOWED_ERR`

Attr

The `Attr` object contains information about an attribute associated with an element. Note that the DOM treats attributes differently from other nodes in the document tree – attributes are considered to be properties of an element, rather than separate nodes in their own right. Therefore, the properties `parentNode`, `previousSibling`, and `nextSibling` will always be `NULL` for attributes.

Because an `Attr` object may contain either text or unparsed entity references, an `Attr` will have one or more child nodes that are either `Text` nodes or `EntityReference` nodes.

The `Attr` object is derived from the `Node` object.

Property	Description
`DOMString name`	The name of this attribute. Read-only.
`boolean specified`	Indicates whether the value of this attribute was explicitly specified, or whether the DOM is supplying it based on a default in the `DocumentType` for this document. If the DOM is used to assign a value for the attribute, this flag will automatically be set to `true`. Read-only.
`DOMString value`	The value of the attribute. Entities are expanded to their text values. When setting this property, an `EntityReference` will be replaced with a `Text` node containing the new attribute value.

Element

The `Element` object contains information about an element in the document.

The `Element` object is derived from the `Node` object.

Property	Description
`DOMString tagName`	The tag name for the element. Read-only.

Method	Description
`DOMString getAttribute( DOMString name)`	Returns the value of an attribute associated with the element, or an empty string if the specified attribute was not found.
`void setAttribute( DOMString name, DOMString value)`	Sets the value of an attribute for the element. If the attribute does not already exist, it is created. Note that, like all the strings in the DOM, it contains raw (unescaped) text – the implementation will take care of escaping special characters when rendering the DOM tree to a file. May raise the following `DOMException` errors: ❑ `INVALID_CHARACTER_ERR` ❑ `NO_MODIFICATION_ALLOWED_ERR`
`void removeAttribute( DOMString name)`	Removes the `name` attribute from the element. Note that if the attribute has a default value defined in the `documentType` object associated with this document, calling `removeAttribute()` will simply reset the value of the attribute to the default. May raise the following `DOMException` error: ❑ `NO_MODIFICATION_ALLOWED_ERR`
`Attr getAttributeNode( DOMString name)`	Returns the `Attr` node for the attribute associated with this element named `name`, or `NULL` if the attribute does not exist.
`Attr setAttributeNode( Attr newAttr)`	Adds an `Attr` node to the element. If an `Attr` node with the same name already exists, the new one replaces it. Returns the old version of the `Attr` node, if it already existed, or `NULL` otherwise. May raise the following `DOMException` errors: ❑ `WRONG_DOCUMENT_ERR` ❑ `NO_MODIFICATION_ALLOWED_ERR` ❑ `INUSE_ATTRIBUTE_ERR`

Method	Description
`Attr removeAttributeNode( Attr oldAttr)`	Removes the specified `Attr` node from the element. Note that if the attribute has a default value defined in the `documentType` object associated with this document, calling `removeAttributeNode()` will simply reset the value of the attribute to the default. Returns the removed `Attr` node. May raise the following `DOMException` errors: ❑ NO_MODIFICATION_ALLOWED_ERR ❑ NOT_FOUND_ERR
`NodeList getElementsByTagName( DOMString name)`	Returns a `NodeList` object containing all the descendant subelements of this element with the given `name`. Passing an asterisk for the `name` will retrieve all descendant elements of this element.
`void normalize()`	Concatenates adjacent `Text` nodes in the sub-tree of this element into single `Text` nodes. This will ensure that the structure of the document can be reproduced if the document is written to file and reloaded. Here's an example: If an element called `MyElement` had only two children, both `Text` nodes, one with the data value `"123"` and one with the data value `"456"`, when written to a file it would be expressed as: `<MyElement>123456</MyElement>` The `normalize()` method concatenates the two `Text` nodes into one `Text` node with the value `"123456"`. If you eliminate markup, for example, take out ` ` elements from a web page, using `normalize()` makes sure your document has no adjacent text blocks, which are just confusing.

Text

The `Text` object represents the text data in an `Element` or `Attr` node. If there is mixed content (both markup and character data) in an element, the element's children will be a sequence of `Text` and `Element` nodes.

The `Text` object is derived from the `CharacterData` object.

Method	Description
`Text splitText( unsigned long offset)`	Splits a `Text` node in two, leaving both of them in the document tree as siblings, at the specified `offset`. Returns the new `Text` node created. May raise the following `DOMException` errors: ❑ `INDEX_SIZE_ERR` ❑ `NO_MODIFICATION_ALLOWED_ERR`

Comment

The `Comment` object contains the content of a comment. In XML, this is the text information found between the begin comment marker `<!--` and the end comment marker `-->`.

The `Comment` object is derived from the `CharacterData` object.

The `Comment` object does not implement any additional methods or properties.

CDATASection

The `CDATASection` object contains the content of an unparsed block of text. In XML, this is the text information found between the begin CDATA marker `<![CDATA[` and the end CDATA marker `]]>`.

The `CDATASection` object is derived from the `Text` object.

The `CDATASection` object does not implement any additional methods or properties.

DocumentType

The `DocumentType` object is intended to contain structural information about the document, gathered either from the DTD associated with the document or from some other structural source (an XML Schema, for example). However, since these document type specifications are still in flux, the DOM Level 1 specification requires only that a list of entities and notations declared in the DTD be maintained in this object. Future versions of the DOM will include much more detailed information in this object, allowing strong type checking and validation of content by the implementation of the DOM.

The `DocumentType` object is derived from the `Node` object.

Property	Description
`DOMString name`	The name of the supplied structural source (the name of the DTD or schema). For the DTD, this will be the name following the `DOCTYPE` keyword in the XML document's prolog. Read-only.
`NamedNodeMap entities`	A `NamedNodeMap` containing a list of the entities declared in the DTD. All nodes in this list will be `Entity` nodes. Read-only.

Property	Description
NamedNodeMap notations	A NamedNodeMap containing a list of the notations declared in the DTD. All nodes in this list will be Notation nodes. Read-only.

Notation

The Notation object contains information about notations declared in the DTD.

The Notation object is derived from the Node object.

Property	Description
DOMString publicId	The public identifier for the notation, or NULL if no public identifier was supplied. Read-only.
DOMString systemId	The system identifier for the notation, or NULL if no system identifier was supplied. Read-only.

Entity

The Entity object contains information about an entity defined in the document. Note that for some XML processors, all substitutions will be performed before the tree model is made available to the developer via the DOM; therefore, an EntityReference may instead have the child node list of the Entity object referenced. The Entity object will still exist and may still be referenced by adding EntityReference objects.

The Entity object is derived from the Node object.

Property	Description
DOMString publicId	The public identifier for the entity, or NULL if no public identifier was supplied. Read-only.
DOMString systemId	The system identifier for the entity, or NULL if no system identifier was supplied. Read-only.
DOMString notationName	The name of the notation used for the entity, or NULL if the entity is a parsed entity. Read-only.

EntityReference

The EntityReference object contains information about a reference to an entity in the document being parsed. Note that some XML processors will perform all substitutions before making the tree model available to the developer via the DOM.

The EntityReference object is derived from the Node object.

The EntityReference object does not implement any additional methods or properties.

ProcessingInstruction

The `ProcessingInstruction` object contains information about processing instructions embedded in the document – that is, instructions inside the special tag delimiters `<?` and `?>`. For example, a reference to an XML style sheet is represented as a processing instruction within the DOM tree model.

The `ProcessingInstruction` object is derived from the `Node` object.

Property	Description
`DOMString target`	The target of the processing instruction. Within the processing instruction, this will be the first token beyond the start tag (up to the first whitespace). Read-only.
`DOMString data`	The data to be used by the processing instruction. Defined as the remaining content between the target declaration and the end tag of the processing instruction. May raise the following `DOMException` error: ❑ `NO_MODIFICATION_ALLOWED_ERR`

DOMException

The `DOMException` object is the principal error-handling object for the DOM. In implementations that support the raising of errors, this object will be raised by a method that has a problem. For implementations that don't support the raising of errors, the error codes that the `DOMException` object provides may be returned as extended error information to the call that caused the exception.

The following exception codes may be reported by the `DOMException` object:

Exception Code	Condition
`INDEX_SIZE_ERR`	If the specified index or size value is negative, or greater than the largest allowed value
`DOMSTRING_SIZE_ERR`	If the specified range of text cannot be expressed as a `DOMString` (a multi-byte character set string)
`HIERARCHY_REQUEST_ERR`	If a node is improperly inserted somewhere it does not belong (for example, attempting to attach an `Attr` node to another `Attr` node)
`WRONG_DOCUMENT_ERR`	If a node is used in a different document from the one that created it
`INVALID_CHARACTER_ERR`	If an invalid character is specified as part of a name or other property
`NO_DATA_ALLOWED_ERR`	If data is specified for a node that does not allow data
`NO_MODIFICATION_ALLOWED_ERR`	If an attempt is made to modify a read-only object
`NOT_FOUND_ERR`	If an attempt is made to reference a node in a context where it does not exist

Exception Code	Condition
NOT_SUPPORTED_ERR	If the implementation does not support the type of object requested
INUSE_ATTRIBUTE_ERR	If an attempt is made to add an attribute that is already in use elsewhere

The DOM in the Real World

So far, we've been looking at the DOM from a purely theoretical perspective – discussing it in terms of the general recommendation from the W3C. Next, let's take a look at the way the DOM is implemented in the real world.

The DOM in Current Browsers

As this book goes to press, the version of Internet Explorer 5.5 on Windows 2000 comes with the MSXML 2.5 libraries. In addition, Internet Explorer 6.0 Beta 1 comes with MSXML 3.0. These libraries provide a full implementation of the DOM Level 1, although the DOM Level 2 is not available yet.

The Microsoft implementation of the DOM as COM components may be downloaded free of charge from http://msdn.microsoft.com/xml.

Netscape version 6 supports the DOM Level 1 built-in, although it does not (as of press time) provide XSLT functionality. Hopefully, future releases will support this very important complementary technology to the DOM.

Additionally, many open-source implementations of the DOM exist. Some of these are beginning to implement Level 2 features, such as events and traversal. A good example of this is the Xerces parser (available as a Java or COM library from http://xml.apache.org).

The HTML DOM As a Special Case of the XML DOM

To understand the differences between HTML and XML, it's important to understand their evolution from a common parent: SGML.

HTML isn't XML

SGML is an acronym for **Standard Generalized Markup Language**. SGML was the first markup language system to become widely used, and it is still heavily used in many businesses today, especially those that handle documents frequently (such as publishing firms). Rather than being a markup language like HTML, SGML is actually a way to *define* markup languages. This is much like XML, but with more freedom in the way tags are nested and information is specified.

HTML is a particular implementation of SGML, that is, it abides by the grammar rules of SGML, but contains a specific definition of elements and attributes that are permissible in an HTML document. In fact, there is a DTD (document type definition) for SGML of HTML, describing the vocabulary and rules. It may be found at http://www.w3.org/TR/html40/sgml/dtd.html.

XML, on the other hand, is a direct descendant of SGML. One of the major goals behind the design of XML was to create a markup definition language that would retain much of the flexibility of SGML, but would be easier to parse. As a result, many of the constructs that were valid in SGML (and hence HTML) are invalid in XML documents.

Problems with the HTML DOM

The HTML DOM is not particularly flexible in the way it allows developers to access the contents of an HTML document. In particular, it is hampered by the need to support what is informally referred to as "DOM Level 0" – functionality implemented in versions 3.0 of Internet Explorer and Netscape (incompatible functionality, we might add) before any effort to standardize an object model for the behavior of HTML pages. This requires the HTML DOM to implement several functions simply for the purposes of backwards compatibility. Additionally, the HTML DOM supports a specific implementation of SGML (relying on the presence of a predefined DTD that governs the possible layout of the document).

The Future of the Web: XHTML

The W3C has produced a recommendation for an implementation of XML known as XHTML 1.0 (and a proposed recommendation for XHTML 1.1). This implementation obeys all of the grammar rules of XML (properly nested elements, quoted attributes, and so on), while conforming to the vocabulary of HTML (the elements and attributes that are available for use and their relationships to one another).

Browsers (such as Amaya) are already available that support XHTML and more mainstream browsers, such as Netscape, Mozilla, Opera, and Internet Explorer are soon to follow. The following points describe the differences between classical HTML and XHTML:

- Documents must be well-formed, all elements must be properly closed, and elements must be properly nested
- Element and attribute names must be in lower case
- Empty elements must either have an end tag or their start tag must end with /
- Attribute-value pairs must be explicitly defined, and their values must be quoted
- The contents of script elements and style elements should be enclosed in a CDATA section to avoid improper parsing
- The `id` attribute should be used to store element identifiers

Let's look at each of these rules in more detail.

Documents Must Be Well-Formed, All Elements Must Be Properly Closed, and Elements Must Be Properly Nested

HTML has certain elements that do not need to be explicitly closed, such as the **paragraph** element `<P>`. The parser determines where the element should be closed by examining the elements that follow. For example, the following HTML fragment is invalid in XHTML:

```
<p>This is the first paragraph.
<p>This is the second paragraph.
```

Instead, the following code (which is functionally equivalent in HTML) should be used:

```
<p>This is the first paragraph.</p>
<p>This is the second paragraph.</p>
```

Element and Attribute Names Must Be in Lower Case

XML is case-sensitive, and treats tags with different cases as different tags. In the XHTML DTD, it was decided that lowercase tags should be used for all elements and attributes, and XHTML documents must follow this rule if you intend them to be processed by XML parsers.

So instead of using this code,

```
<INPUT TYPE="button" ID="button1" VALUE="Click me!">
```

use:

```
<input type="button" id="button1" value="Click Me!" />
```

Note that we added a slash at the end of the corrected version. This brings us to our next rule:

Empty Elements Must Either Have an End Tag or their Start Tag Must End with /

In XML, all elements must be closed; if they are defined as `EMPTY` (having no information associated with them except attributes) or do not have any content, they may be closed either by a separate end tag or by including the slash at the end of the start tag.

Attribute-Value Pairs Must Be Explicitly Defined, and their Values Must Be Quoted

If you want to specify a value for an enumerated attribute on an element, it may no longer be specified without the attribute name.

Instead of,

```
<dl compact>
```

use:

```
<dl compact="compact">
```

Additionally, values for attributes must always appear in either single or double quotes – in HTML, attribute values may optionally not be quoted.

Script Elements and Style Elements Should Be Enclosed in a CDATA Section To Avoid Improper Parsing

Because `script` and `style` elements are declared as `#PCDATA` elements in the XHTML DTD, parsers will treat `<` and `&` as the start of markup. To avoid this, `script` and `style` elements should be enclosed in a CDATA element to allow them to contain unescaped text.

Rather than,

```
<script>
  ...
</script>
```

use:

```
<script>
   <![CDATA[
      ...
   ]]>
</script>
```

If you prefer, you can use entities for markup characters that appear in the script (such as < and &); however, for readability purposes enclosing the entire script in a CDATA block is the better choice.

The id Attribute Should Be Used to Store Element Identifiers

In the XHTML DTD, the `id` attribute is given a type of `ID`; therefore, it should be used to identify the element instead of the `name` attribute. For certain controls, such as radio buttons, you will still need to use the `name` attribute to allow proper form processing.

By following these instructions, you will ensure the highest level of compatibility possible with future browsers that make the move to XHTML. Additionally, the XHTML documents you create may be sent to the client with a `mime-type` of HTML or XML, allowing the greatest flexibility at the client. The XML DOM may then be used to manipulate the contents of the XHTML document directly.

Working with the DOM

We've discussed how the DOM is structured, taking XML documents and transforming them into node trees that may be accessed programmatically. We've also talked about how the specification provided by the W3C is only a description of access mechanisms, and not a particular implementation. But how can we take this information and apply it to a particular problem? To do so, we'll need to use the DOM API.

DOM APIs

When writing a piece of software that accesses XML files using the DOM, a particular implementation of the DOM must be used. The implementation is a library of some kind, designed to be run on a particular hardware and software platform and to access a particular data store (such as a text file, a relational database, and so on).

The DOM is Not an API

As we've seen before, the W3C DOM specification only provides the interface definition for the DOM libraries, not the specifics of their implementation. It then falls to third parties to provide implementations of the DOM that may be used by programmers. When planning to use the DOM to manipulate XML structures in your application, you will need to obtain platform-specific implementations of the DOM for each platform your application targets. In most cases, these libraries will need to be bundled with your application and deployed along with your application binaries.

Be aware that implementations of the DOM, just like implementations of HTML parsers, need to assert a compliance level to the W3C specifications. Given the state at press time of the W3C specifications (DOM Level 1 and 2 are recommendations, Level 3 is in the initial stages), all implementations of the DOM should provide at least the functionality described in the Level 1 document. Many implementations of the DOM will also provide additional functionality – either behavior described in the Level 2 document, or additional behavior that the developers of the implementation felt would be useful.

For example, the Microsoft DOM supports all of the Level 1 specification, as well as additional navigation methods, methods and properties to support style sheets, and so on. As with any other development effort, you need to take into account your target platform(s) before deciding whether or not to take advantage of additional functionality provided in a particular implementation of the DOM.

Programming for XML Data Structures

When using the DOM to access information in an XML node tree, it is helpful to design your system around the access mechanisms the DOM provides. For example, if you are using an object-oriented database, you might tailor your objects to correspond to XML elements. If you know what elements you are expecting, you can create objects that encapsulate other objects, replicating the XML tree in memory in the most useful way possible.

Also, you should bear in mind that XML files can be extremely large, so memory management becomes very important. A good implementation of the DOM will provide just-in-time extraction for elements, but it's crucial that your program manages memory well to avoid excessive swapping or failure.

Client Side and Server Side

While there are a great variety of applications for the DOM and XML, they can be loosely grouped into two types: those deployed on a server (or in a controlled environment, such as a client-server system), and those deployed on a client. We'll take a look at some potential applications for DOM for each of these types.

DOM On the Server Side

Since Internet developers have much more control over the software deployed to their servers, the first applications of DOM have been on the server. The DOM can be used to greatly simplify data interchange between disparate business systems, as well as providing an ideal mechanism for the archival and retrieval of data.

Document Interchange

One of the first applications of XML in the enterprise will be to facilitate inter-process or inter-business communications. XML has many advantages over other transmission formats such as flat files or database dumps:

- XML files are **platform-independent** – unlike an Access database or a SQL Server dump, an XML file can be read and understood by virtually any system simply by reading the text and parsing it into a node tree using the DOM implementation on that system.
- XML files are **self-describing** – unlike a flat file (which requires a programmer to sit down with a format description and do a translation), a well-designed XML file needs little external documentation to decipher – each element that describes an author is clearly marked `<author>`, and so on.
- XML files show **hierarchical information** – unlike flat files, which may contain repeating groups for child elements (such as the books an author has written), XML files are designed to represent hierarchical information in a natural way – via a node tree. If the XML file contains seven authors and 22 books, for example, it's immediately obvious which books are associated with which authors simply by walking the node tree created by the DOM.

There is a strong trend in the software industry at the moment to standardize XML formats for business-to-business transfers of information. Groups like BizTalk (http://www.biztalk.org) and the Mortgage Industry Standards Maintenance Organization (http://www.mismo.org) are creating DTDs, schemas, and data dictionaries that will help businesses communicate with each other more effectively.

Archival

XML is an ideal storage medium for archived information – especially if it comes from a relational or hierarchical database. XML files compress very well due to their text-based nature and their tendency to repeat text (tags). A typical, fairly large XML file will compress to a tenth or twentieth of its original size. By walking the hierarchical or relational tree in a database and using the DOM to construct the appropriate node tree, entire sets of information may be easily archived to one XML file.

A typical example might be an invoicing system that removes invoices older than a year. An automated process might run once a night, scanning the database for invoices that are ready to be archived. Using the DOM, the process could then navigate through the hierarchical or relational tree of information associated with the invoice. Customer information, shipping information, line item information, and so on would all be packaged together in one file that would represent the invoice as a whole. That file could then be compressed and stored to tape or some other archival medium. If there was a question about a particular invoice, the XML file associated with it could be retrieved and decompressed. Someone could then visually scan the file looking for the information needed, or the information could be loaded back into the database using the DOM for manipulation there.

DOM On the Client Side

As of press time, both Microsoft Internet Explorer and Netscape Navigator come with DOM Level 1 libraries built-in. Now that client-side DOM libraries are becoming widely available, Internet developers can take advantage of the DOM on the client to improve the way information is rendered and decrease round trips to the server.

Flexible Client Rendering

It is becoming more and more important for documents to be viewable by a variety of different clients. These clients may need to render the document in various ways, depending on the type of client and the purpose of the file. For example, various cellular telephone providers are starting to provide a limited form of browsing from the tiny LCD screen on the telephone itself. HTML is not ideal for this purpose, since it doesn't include information about the meaning of the content in the various tags, only how to render it. Thus, a rendering engine on a telephone might not know whether it was important to tell the user what color a snake is, or if it's poisonous. XML solves this problem by including information about the content as part of the markup. A customized browser might use the DOM to walk the node tree of the document received by such a device, and selectively identify information that could be discarded.

Client Data Entry

As the DOM is integrated into the major browsers, it will be possible to use client-side DOM manipulation of XML documents to provide a greater level of interaction with the user. Structured information may be collected from the client and shipped back to the server in one transaction, rather than a series of form calls spanning several HTML pages.

Scenarios for Using the DOM in the Publishing Process

Let's take a look at some ways the DOM can be used to generate and manipulate XML documents in enterprise environments.

The DOM and Databases

XML provides one possible mechanism for transferring information between different databases. By their nature, databases are proprietary – each database has a different naming structure for elements, a different normalization level, and even different methods of describing enumerated information. Using the DOM, we can simplify the way information is passed between various databases.

Normally, when data is transferred between databases, a customized translator must be built for each transfer:

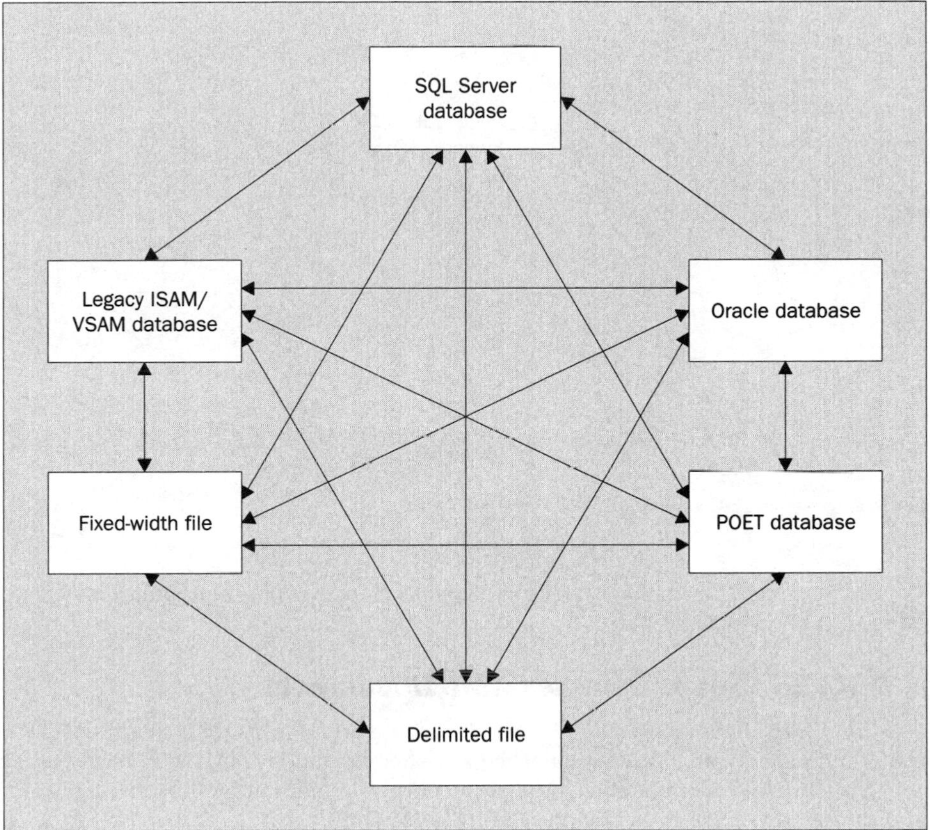

By using XML as the common transfer mechanism, the number of translators that need to be written is greatly simplified – each database needs only to be able to import and export from a common, agreed-upon XML structure:

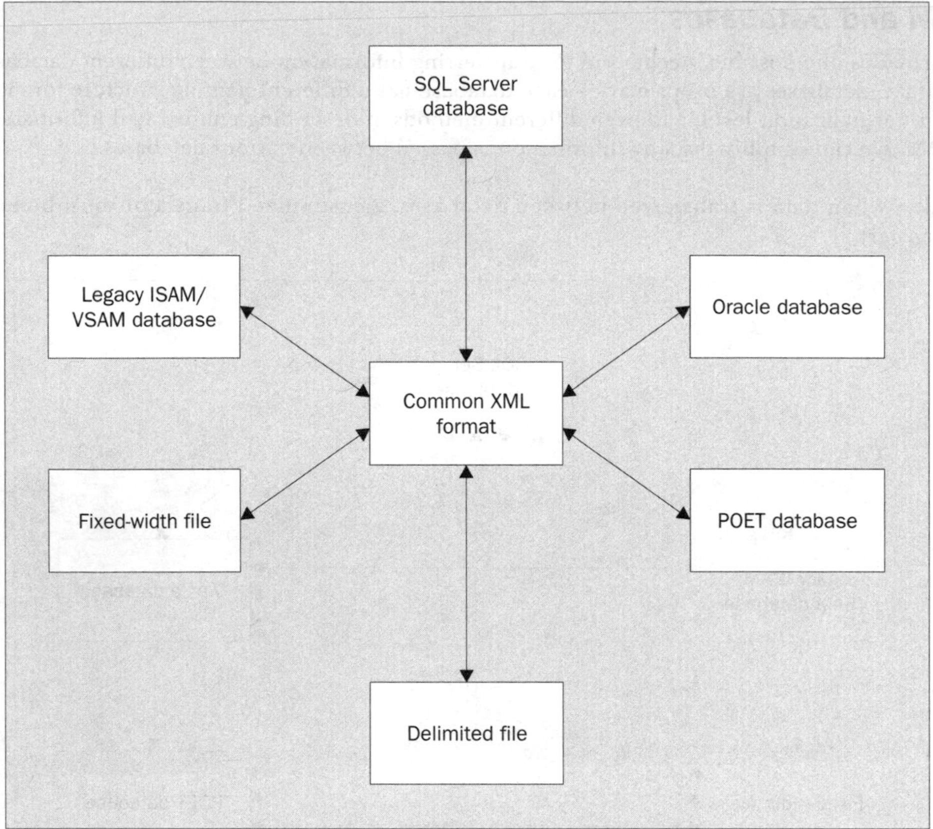

The DOM can be used to create these translation mechanisms. Another method is data binding, which you can see in action in Chapter 15.

Using the DOM To Create Complex XML Documents

One of the nice things about manipulating XML documents with the DOM is that the DOM is **random-access**, that is, a node may be created or attached anywhere within the XML tree at any time. This proves to be quite useful when building XML documents from information in a hierarchical or relational database. An example will help to illustrate this point.

Let's suppose we have the following tables in a database:

```
CREATE TABLE customer(
   customerid int,
   customername varchar(100),
   city varchar(50),
   state char(2),
   zip varchar(10))

CREATE TABLE invoice(
   invoiceid int,
   customerid int,
   invoicedate datetime)
```

```
CREATE TABLE lineitem(
   lineitemid int,
   invoiceid int,
   product varchar(50),
   units int)
```

We'd like to produce an XML file for a particular customer ID from the information stored in these tables, which should look like the following:

```
<customer id="customer1"
         customername="Homer J. Simpson"
         address="142 Evergreen Terrace"
         city="Springfield"
         state="VA"
         zip="00000">
   <invoice id="invoice1"
       invoicedate="11/7/1999">
      <lineitem id="lineitem1"
                product="Plutonium"
                units="17"/>
      <lineitem id="lineitem2"
                product="Donuts"
                units="8726"/>
   </invoice>
   <invoice id="invoice2"
         invoicedate="11/9/1999">
      <lineitem id="lineitem3"
                product="Beer"
                units="37816"/>
      <lineitem id="lineitem4"
                product="Peanuts"
                units="1"/>
   </invoice>
</customer>
```

To write this to an XML document manually, we'd have to perform the following steps:

```
Get the information for the customer from the customer table
Write the information for the customer to the XML file
Get all the invoices for the customer from the invoice table
For each invoice retrieved this way:
     Write the information for the invoice to the XML file
     Get all the line items for this invoice from the lineitem table
     For each line item retrieved this way:
          Write the information for the line item to the XML file
     Write the close tag for the invoice object
Write the close tag for the customer object
```

Whereas, using the DOM, we could generate the node tree this way:

```
Generate the customer root node
Get all the invoices for the customer
Create a node for each invoice and append it to the customer node
Get all the line items for the customer
Create a node for each line item and append it to the appropriate invoice node
```

This is a simple example, but it should be clear that building an XML document using the DOM is much more straightforward than doing so by writing the information to a text file. Rather than jumping back and forth between tables to obtain the information needed, all the information in each table may be written at the same time. As the depth of the node tree increases, the first method becomes more and more cumbersome, while the second method scales easily. Also, generating the document using the DOM guarantees that it will be well-formed. In our first example, say we had forgotten to write the close tag for the invoice object – our XML document would no longer parse.

Sample Application Using DOM and XML

Next, we'll take a look at a couple of ways the DOM can be used in real-world applications.

A Simple Client Side Example

In this section, we'll be using JScript and the DOM objects on the client side to create an XML document representing a set of invoices. Because the DOM objects are being used on the client, this sample must be run using Internet Explorer 5 or higher. The example will let you create an XML document representing an invoice, given form elements to fill in as shown in the following screen shot and we will use the DOM to construct an XML document representing the information:

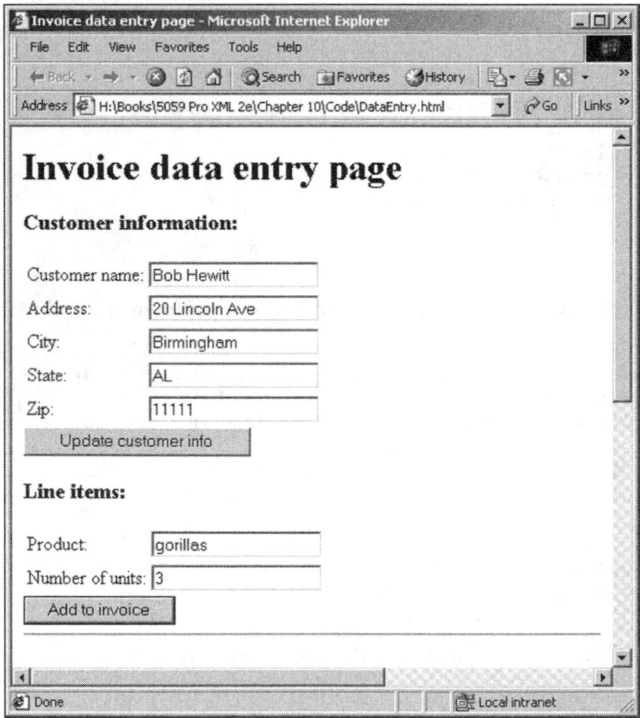

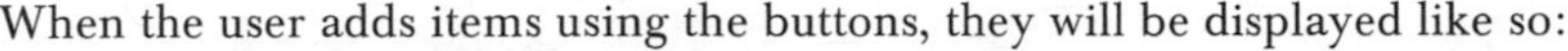

When the user adds items using the buttons, they will be displayed like so:

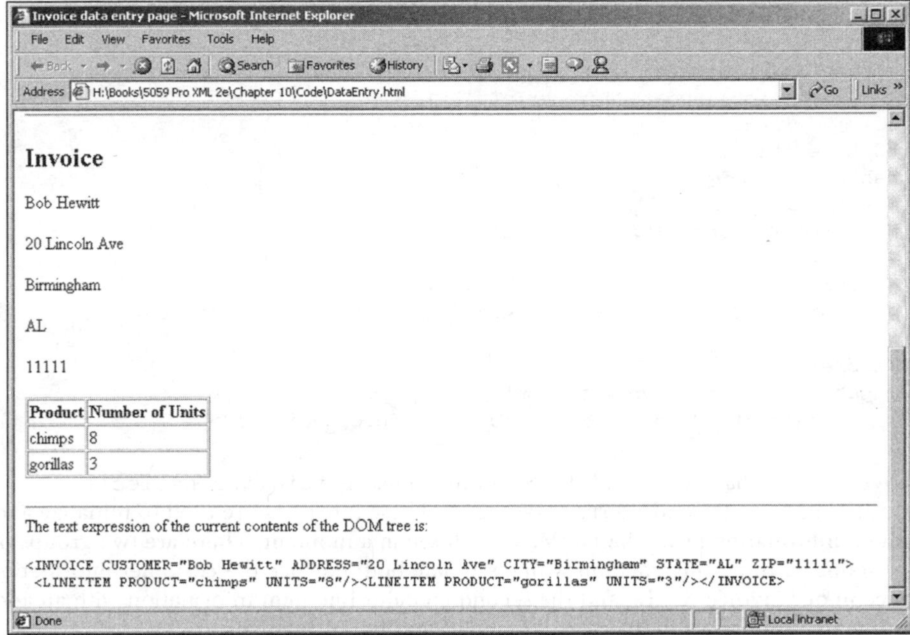

You can see an HTML representation of the invoice below the form, and the created XML at the bottom of the page. This demonstrates using the DOM to create an XML document programmatically.

Using the DOM To Let the User Modify the Page

First, let's create an HTML page that will be our invoice search system. We'll start the page with a form allowing the user to enter customer and line item information for the invoice:

```
<html>
<head>
   <title>Invoice data entry page</title>
</head>
<body onload="initializeInvoice()">
   <h1>Invoice data entry page</h1>
   <h3>Customer information:</h3>
   <table>
      <tr>
         <td>Customer name:</td><td><input id="txtCustomer"></td>
      </tr>
      <tr>
         <td>Address:</td><td><input id="txtAddress"></td>
      </tr>
      <tr>
         <td>City:</td><td><input id="txtCity"></td>
      </tr>
      <tr>
         <td>State:</td><td><input id="txtState"></td>
      </tr>
```

```
    <tr>
       <td>Zip:</td><td><input id="txtZip"></td>
    </tr>
 </table>
 <input id="btnUpdate" type="button" value="Update customer info"
       onclick="updateCustomerInfo()">

 <h3>Line items:</h3>
 <table>
    <tr>
       <td>Product:</td><td><input id="txtProduct"></td>
    </tr>
    <tr>
       <td>Number of units:</td><td><input id="txtUnits"></td>
    </tr>
 </table>
 <input id="btnAdd" type="button"
       value="Add to invoice" onclick="addToInvoice()">
```

In the above code, we have three calls to JScript functions: `initializeInvoice()`, `updateCustomerInfo()`, and `addToInvoice()`. These functions are used to initialize and modify the document information using the DOM, as we'll see in a moment. There are two groups of controls: the first contains customer information with an update button (since the customer information will only appear once in our invoice XML), and the second contains line item information with an add button (since the line item information may appear many times in our invoice).

Next, we'll create the XML **data island** that will contain our finished invoice:

```
 <XML id="docInvoice">
    <INVOICE>
    </INVOICE>
 </XML>
```

In this case, we are using the data island as a signal to Internet Explorer 5 that we want to manipulate an XML document called `docInvoice` from within our code. Note that we have chosen to specify the root object for the XML document, an empty element called `INVOICE`. If we chose, we could have left the data island completely empty, or we could have populated it with some initial information (like an invoice ID) before sending it to the client.

The next section of the code contains the script for manipulating the invoice:

```
 <SCRIPT>

 var docInvoice;
```

We specify `docInvoice` as a global here so that we don't have to keep accessing the XML document by its fully qualified name:

```
 document.all("docInvoice").XMLDocument
```

This syntax, new for IE 5, allows the XML DOM operations to be used from JScript on the client side – it exposes all the functionality of the `XMLDOMDocument` object. We'll initialize its value in the `initializeInvoice()` function, which as you'll recall is called in the `onload` event for the `<BODY>` tag.

```
function initializeInvoice()
{
    docInvoice = document.all("docInvoice").XMLDocument;
    docInvoice.async = false;
    renderElements();
}
```

Here, we're initializing the `docInvoice` variable to point to the `docInvoice` document. We're also setting the `async` property on the document to `false`. This forces all operations on the document to be performed **synchronously** – returning only when they have completed. This allows us to avoid accessing the document when it's still in the process of being updated. Finally, we call a procedure that will show the contents of the DOM – both in a raw format and using XSL style sheets.

Next, we implement the function that allows us to update the customer information in our document:

```
function updateCustomerInfo()
{
    docInvoice.documentElement.setAttribute("CUSTOMER", txtCustomer.value);
    docInvoice.documentElement.setAttribute("ADDRESS", txtAddress.value);
    docInvoice.documentElement.setAttribute("CITY", txtCity.value);
    docInvoice.documentElement.setAttribute("STATE", txtState.value);
    docInvoice.documentElement.setAttribute("ZIP", txtZip.value);

    renderElements();
}
```

This code simply takes the contents of the text fields for the customer information and uses them to attach attributes to the root element in the document. Note that `setAttribute()` will add the attributes if they do not already exist.

The next function adds a line item to the invoice:

```
function addToInvoice()
{
    var elementLineItem;

    elementLineItem = docInvoice.createElement("LINEITEM");

    elementLineItem.setAttribute("PRODUCT", txtProduct.value);
    elementLineItem.setAttribute("UNITS", txtUnits.value);

    docInvoice.documentElement.appendChild(elementLineItem);

    renderElements();
}
```

Here, we're adding an element, so we declare a variable to hold it. Then, we use the `createElement()` method to create a new element that is part of the document. Note that we have not yet chosen to attach the node to any other node – at the moment it's an orphan. Before we attach it, though, we go ahead and set the `PRODUCT` and `UNITS` attributes on the element based on the information entered in the text elements above. We then use the `appendChild()` method to add it as a child of the root node of the document. Finally, we refresh the document again to update our style-sheet formatted invoice and our raw XML section.

Up to this point, the XML document exists only as a tree of nodes in memory in the XML DOM. In order for the user to see the changes, we need to **render** the document. The next function does just that, using both style sheets and in a raw form.

```
function renderElements()
{
   document.all("divRawXML").innerText = docInvoice.xml;
   customerInfo.innerHTML =
      docInvoice.transformNode(customerXSL.documentElement);
   invoiceTable.innerHTML =
      docInvoice.transformNode(lineitemXSL.documentElement);
}

</SCRIPT>
```

Using the `xml` property of the document, we can get the raw text-output XML for the entire document. This is what most people think of when they think about XML 'files'. We set the `divRawXML` element's text (at the bottom of the page) to be the raw text output. Next, we transform the XML document using style sheets for a more human-readable output. More information on XSLT may be found in Chapter 9.

Finally, we have the two in-line style sheets (using the old-style XSLT from Microsoft in IE 5.5) and the rest of the HTML page, containing the `<DIV>` elements that are populated by the `renderElements()` function.

```
<XML id=customerXSL>
   <div xmlns:xsl="http://www.w3.org/TR/WD-xsl">
      <xsl:choose>
         <xsl:when test="/INVOICE/@CUSTOMER[. $ne$ '']">
            <xsl:value-of select="/INVOICE/@CUSTOMER"/><BR></BR>
            <xsl:value-of select="/INVOICE/@ADDRESS"/><BR></BR>
            <xsl:value-of select="/INVOICE/@CITY"/><BR></BR>
            <xsl:value-of select="/INVOICE/@STATE"/><BR></BR>
            <xsl:value-of select="/INVOICE/@ZIP"/>
         </xsl:when>
         <xsl:otherwise>
            Customer information not yet specified.
        </xsl:otherwise>
      </xsl:choose>
   </div>
</XML>

<XML id=lineitemXSL>
   <div xmlns:xsl="http://www.w3.org/TR/WD-xsl">
      <table border="1" cellspacing="1">
         <tr>
            <td><strong>Product</strong></td>
            <td><strong>Number of Units</strong></td>
         </tr>
         <xsl:for-each select="/INVOICE/LINEITEM">
            <tr>
               <td><xsl:value-of select="@PRODUCT"/></td>
               <td><xsl:value-of select="@UNITS"/></td>
            </tr>
         </xsl:for-each>
```

```
        </table>
      </div>
    </XML>

    <hr>
    <h2>Invoice</h2>
    <p><div id=customerInfo></div></p>
    <p><div id=invoiceTable></div></p>
    <hr>
    The text expression of the current contents of the DOM tree is:
    <pre><div id=divRawXML></div></pre>
</body>
</html>
```

Although it's beyond the scope of this example, the XML document created on the client this way can now be passed back to the server for manipulation. The easiest way to do so is to set an input element, typically a hidden one, to the value of the `xml` property of the document, then, when the form is submitted, the information will be part of the submitted elements. Documents on the client that are too large to be transmitted as part of a form submission may be transmitted via FTP, via HTTP using Posting Acceptor or some other HTTP file submitter, or via the SOAP protocol (discussed in Chapter 24).

Another Example (with Java)

As an alternative to the Microsoft parser, I've coded a simple example of DOM use with the Invoice XML and Xerces 1.3.1, which has DOM Level 2 support that we'll see later.

In this example we'll see:

- How to parse a document
- How to get started with navigating it (through the `DocumentElement`)
- How to add nodes and attributes, by creating and then appending them
- How to use recursion to output information
- How the DOM separates information on nodes and attributes
- How to find elements by name
- How to check that features are supported

Getting Started

We import the packages for the DOM, and for the Xerces parser:

```
import org.apache.xerces.parsers.*;
import org.w3c.dom.*;

public class BasicDOMExample {

  public static void main(String[] args) {

    if (args.length > 0) {
```

```
        String filename = args[0];
        BasicDOMExample exampleDOM = new BasicDOMExample(filename);
      }
    }
```

The program takes in the filename of the XML file and passes it to the constructor.

```
    public BasicDOMExample(String filename) {
      try {
        // Parse in XML file, and construct a document
        DOMParser parser = new DOMParser();

        parser.parse(filename);
        Document document = parser.getDocument();
        ...
      } catch (Exception e) {
        e.printStackTrace(System.err);
      }
    }
  }
```

Here we create the DOMParser, parse the XML file and get the Document object for the parsed document. Any errors in the parsing are caught and printed out.

Checking for DOM Level Support

Next we get the DOMImplementation and check it supports Level 1 Core.

```
        DOMImplementation domImpl = document.getImplementation();
        boolean levelCoreSupport = domImpl.hasFeature("CORE", "1.0");
        if (levelCoreSupport)
          System.out.println("DOM implementation supports DOM Level 1.0 Core");
        else
          System.out.println("DOM implementation doesn't support DOM Level 1.0
                                  Core");
```

We have the Document object of the DOM tree, from which we can access all the other nodes.

Accessing the Document Element

Let's start by getting the name of the document element (the root node in the DOM tree), and outputting the tag name:

```
        Element documentElement = document.getDocumentElement();
        System.out.println("Document node name: " + documentElement.getTagName());
```

Iterating Over Attributes

Next we can iterate over the document element's attributes, using a NamedNodeMap and output them:

```
      attributeInformation(documentElement);
      ...
    }

  public void attributeInformation(Element element) {
    NamedNodeMap attributes = element.getAttributes();

    for (int i = 0; i < attributes.getLength(); i++) {
      Attr attribute = (Attr)attributes.item(i);
      System.out.println("Element: " + attribute.getOwnerElement() +
                         " has attribute " + attribute.getName() +
                         " with the value " + attribute.getValue());
    }
  }
```

For the invoice we saw at the start of the chapter, we'll get the following output:

```
Document node name: INVOICE

Element: [INVOICE: null] has attribute ADDRESS with
                         the value 142 Evergreen Terrace
Element: [INVOICE: null] has attribute CITY with the value Springfield
Element: [INVOICE: null] has attribute CUSTOMER with the value Homer J. Simpson
Element: [INVOICE: null] has attribute STATE with the value VA
Element: [INVOICE: null] has attribute ZIP with the value 00000
```

Creating an Attribute

We can create an attribute using the document element object:

```
documentElement.setAttribute("TESTATTRIBUTE", "TESTING");

if (documentElement.hasAttribute("TESTATTRIBUTE"))
  System.out.println("Attribute has been successfully added");
```

We can output the new attribute in one of two ways. Firstly, we can get the attribute as an `Attr` object and use its methods to output details:

```
Attr testAttribute = documentElement.getAttributeNode("TESTATTRIBUTE");
System.out.println("Element: " + testAttribute.getOwnerElement() +
                   " has attribute " + testAttribute.getName() +
                   " with the value " + testAttribute.getValue());
```

Or we can access the attribute by name in the `Element.getAttribute()` method to get the attribute value:

```
System.out.println("New attribute, TESTATTRIBUTE has value: " +
                   documentElement.getAttribute("TESTATTRIBUTE"));
```

Creating a Child Element

To create a child element we use the `Document` object to create the element, adding an attribute for good measure:

```
Element testElement = document.createElement("TESTELEMENT");
testElement.setAttribute("TESTATTRIBUTE", "In TESTELEMENT");
```

Then we can append the new element to its parent node:

```
documentElement.appendChild(testElement);
```

We also add a text node to the new child element:

```
Text testTextNode = document.createTextNode("Test Text");
testElement.appendChild(testTextNode);
```

Retrieving Elements By Tag Name

To get elements by tag name, call:

```
NodeList testTags = document.getElementsByTagName("TESTELEMENT");
System.out.println("TESTELEMENT tags found: " + testTags.getLength());
```

This will return, `TESTELEMENT tags found: 1`, for our document, confirming that the element was added correctly.

Outputting Nodes Recursively

To output the DOM tree to the screen, we need to visit all the nodes recursively, down from the document node.

The `nodeInformation()` method makes this easier. It holds all the DOM node types as a switch statement, and outputs information depending on the node type:

```
    nodeInformation(document);
    ...

  public void nodeInformation(Node node) {
    // Is there anything to do?
    if (node == null) {
      return;
    }

    // Output the NodeType and values
    int type = node.getNodeType();
    switch (type) {
      case Node.ATTRIBUTE_NODE: {
        System.out.println("Attribute node: " + ((Attr)node).getName() +
                           " has value: " + ((Attr)node).getValue());
        break;
      }
      case Node.CDATA_SECTION_NODE: {
        System.out.println("CDATA node: " + node.getNodeName() +
                           " has value: " + node.getNodeValue());
        break;
      }
```

```
        case Node.COMMENT_NODE: {
          System.out.println("Comment node: " + node.getNodeName() +
                             " has value: " + node.getNodeValue());
          break;
        }
        case Node.DOCUMENT_FRAGMENT_NODE: {
          System.out.println("Document fragment node: " + node.getNodeName());
          outputChildNodes(node);
          break;
        }
        case Node.DOCUMENT_NODE: {
          System.out.println("Document node: " + node.getNodeName());
          outputChildNodes(node);
          break;
        }
        case Node.DOCUMENT_TYPE_NODE: {
          System.out.println("Document type node: " + node.getNodeName());
          break;
        }
        case Node.ELEMENT_NODE: {
          System.out.println("");
          System.out.println("Element node: " + ((Element)node).getTagName());
          outputAttributes(node);
          outputChildNodes(node);
          break;
        }
        case Node.ENTITY_NODE: {
          System.out.println("Entity node: " + node.getNodeName());
          break;
        }
        case Node.ENTITY_REFERENCE_NODE: {
          System.out.println("Entity reference node: " + node.getNodeName());
          break;
        }
        case Node.NOTATION_NODE: {
          System.out.println("Notation node: " + node.getNodeName());
          break;
        }
        case Node.PROCESSING_INSTRUCTION_NODE: {
          System.out.println("Processing instruction node: " + node.getNodeName() +
                             " has value: " + node.getNodeValue());
          break;
        }
        case Node.TEXT_NODE: {
          System.out.println("Text node: " + node.getNodeName() +
                             " has value: " + node.getNodeValue());
          break;
        }
      }
    }
```

Code for `DocumentFragment`, `Document`, and `Element` nodes makes a further call to `outputChildNodes()` to recurse any child nodes. The list of children is retrieved into a `NodeList` object:

```
public void outputChildNodes(Node node) {
  // Output all the child nodes from this node recursively, using a NodeList
  NodeList children = node.getChildNodes();

  for (int i = 0; i < children.getLength(); i++) {
    Node child = children.item(i);
    nodeInformation(child);
  }
}
```

The code for the `Element` node also calls `outputAttributes()` to print out attribute information:

```
public void outputAttributes(Node node) {
  // Output all the attributes from this node recursively, using a NamedNodeMap
  NamedNodeMap attributes = node.getAttributes();

  for (int i = 0; i < attributes.getLength(); i++) {
    Attr attribute = (Attr)attributes.item(i);
    nodeInformation(attribute);
  }
}
```

The output from this pass over the DOM tree looks like:

```
Recursive output of node information:
Document node: #document

Element node: INVOICE
Attribute node: ADDRESS has value: 142 Evergreen Terrace
Attribute node: CITY has value: Springfield
Attribute node: CUSTOMER has value: Homer J. Simpson
Attribute node: STATE has value: VA
Attribute node: TESTATTRIBUTE has value: TESTING
Attribute node: ZIP has value: 00000
Text node: #text has value:

Element node: LINEITEM
Attribute node: PRODUCT has value: Plutonium
Attribute node: UNITS has value: 10
Text node: #text has value:

...

Element node: TESTELEMENT
Attribute node: TESTATTRIBUTE has value: In TESTELEMENT
Text node: #text has value: Test Text
```

DOM Level 2

Since the first edition of this book, the W3C DOM Level 2 specification has been promoted to the status of Recommendation. Some implementations of the Level 2 interfaces are beginning to emerge (in processors like Xerces) – we'll see some examples of Level 2 functionality a little later in the chapter. The Level 2 specification contains all of the objects from the DOM Level 1, and adds the following:

- **Modifications to the core specification** – the Level 2 DOM makes some modifications to the core specification for the DOM.
- **Views** – the Level 2 DOM provides a way to distinguish between different views of an XML document.
- **Events** – the Level 2 DOM adds a full-featured event system to the DOM, designed to handle UI-style navigation (such as that found in HTML) and mutation events.
- **Styles** – the Level 2 DOM adds programmatic support for the declaration of stylesheets.
- **Traversal and Ranges** – the Level 2 DOM adds programmatic support for new traversal methods for XML documents (the `NodeIterator` and `TreeWalker` interfaces) and range manipulation (especially good for XML editing software).

Identifying What DOM Level 2 Features Are Present

Unlike the DOM Level 1, the DOM Level 2 can be implemented in a piecemeal fashion. Many of the emergent DOM Level 2 implementations only provide part of the overall Level 2 functionality. To discover what features of the DOM Level 2 are provided in a specific implementation, you can call the `hasFeature()` method of the `DOMImplementation` interface to ask about the presence or absence of the feature you wish to use. We'll see examples of how to do this as we take a look at each of the different sections of the DOM Level 2 specs.

Modifications To the Core Specification

To identify whether a particular implementation of the DOM supports the features in the DOM Level 2 core specification, call the `hasFeature()` method on the `DOMImplementation` interface with the feature parameter set to `Core` and the version parameter set to `2.0`.

In the DOM Level 2, there are some important modifications to the core DOM specification to facilitate the use of namespaces in your XML documents. Also, some additional properties have been added to some of the interfaces to make it easier to navigate around your XML document. Let's see these new functions and how they work.

The modifications include the addition of some new exceptions – `INVALID_STATE_ERR`, `SYNTAX_ERR`, `INVALID_MODIFICATION_ERR`, `NAMESPACE_ERR`, and `INVALID_ACCESS_ERR`.

The Attr Interface

Property	Description
`Element ownerElement`	This property returns the element node with which this property is associated.

The Document Interface

Five methods have been added to the `Document` interface. These methods make it easier to move nodes between documents and to work with namespaces.

Method	Description
`Node importNode ( Node importedNode, boolean deep)`	This method allows a document to import a node from another document. If the node type allows children, setting the `deep` parameter to `true` will also import all of the children of that node. The node must still be associated with a parent node or an owner element node (if it is an attribute). This method returns the added node. May raise the following `DOMException` error: ❑ NOT_SUPPORTED_ERR
`Element createElementNS ( DOMString namespaceURI, DOMString qualifiedName)`	This method allows elements to be created in a particular namespace. By specifying both the qualified name and the namespace URI, the DOM can properly associate the URI with the given prefix. This method returns the created element. May raise the following `DOMException` errors: ❑ INVALID_CHARACTER_ERR ❑ NAMESPACE_ERR
`Attr createAttributeNS ( DOMString namespaceURI, DOMString qualifiedName)`	This method allows attributes to be created in a particular namespace. By specifying both the qualified name and the namespace URI, the DOM can properly associate the URI with the given prefix. This method returns the created attribute. May raise the following `DOMException` errors: ❑ INVALID_CHARACTER_ERR ❑ NAMESPACE_ERR
`NodeList getElementsByTagNameNS ( DOMString namespaceURI, DOMString localName)`	This method allows elements to be selected from a document based on their namespace URI and local name, rather than just on their qualified name. This allows a document to search for elements in a particular namespace regardless of the prefix used for that namespace. It returns a node list containing all the elements that match the search criteria.

Method	Description
`Element getElementById ( DOMString elementID)`	This method provides a standardized way of selecting an element based on the value of its attribute that has type `ID`. Many implementations of the DOM Level 1 had helper functions to find elements by their IDs. This allows `IDREF` and `IDREFS` pointers to be easily navigated when manipulating a document using the DOM. It returns the element with the given ID.

The NamedNodeMap Interface

Three methods have been added to the `NamedNodeMap` interface, all of which make it easier to work with namespaces.

Method	Description
`Node getNamedItemNS ( DOMString namespaceURI, DOMString localName)`	This method allows the named node map to be searched based on a namespace URI and a local name to match nodes in particular namespaces. It returns the matched node.
`Node setNamedItemNS (Node arg)`	This method allows an item to be added to a named node map along with namespace information. Note that if you have a node in a particular namespace you want to add to a `NamedNodeMap`, and you want the namespace information to be retained, you should use this method (rather than `setNamedItem()`). The method returns the added node. May raise the following `DOMException` errors: ❑ `WRONG_DOCUMENT_ERR` ❑ `INUSE_ATTRIBUTE_ERR` ❑ `NO_MODIFICATION_ALLOWED_ERR`
`Node removeNamedItemNS ( DOMString namespaceURI, DOMString localName)`	This method removes an item from the named node map based on its namespace URI and local name. The method returns the node that was removed. May raise the following `DOMException` errors: ❑ `NOT_FOUND_ERR` ❑ `NO_MODIFICATION_ALLOWED_ERR`

The Node Interface

Three methods and three properties have been added to the Node interface.

Property	Description
DOMString namespaceURI	This property returns the URI (if present) of the namespace associated with this node.
DOMString prefix	This property returns the namespace prefix (if present) of the namespace associated with this node.
DOMString localName	This property returns the local name of this node.

Method	Description
boolean isSupported (DOMString feature, DOMString version)	This method determines whether a particular DOM feature is supported by this node. The `feature` and `version` parameters should be set as if this were a call to the `hasFeature()` method on the `DOMImplementation` interface. The method returns a `boolean` indicating whether this node supports this feature or not.
boolean hasAttributes ()	This helper method provides a quick way to determine whether this node has attributes associated with it. It returns a `boolean` indicating whether there are attributes present.
void normalize()	This method has been promoted from the DOM Level 1, where it was found in the `Element` interface. It eliminates empty `Text` nodes and combines adjacent `Text` nodes in the full depth of the subtree beneath this node. It has no return value.

The DocumentType Interface

Three properties have been added to the `DocumentType` interface. These properties extend the document type functionality of the DOM Level 1. Note that since the schema representation language was in flux as the DOM Level 2 specification was being created, the DOM Level 2 still does not provide atomic programmatic control over document type specifications.

Property	Description
DOMString publicID	This property returns the public identifier of the document type.
DOMString systemID	This property returns the system identifier of the document type.
DOMString internalSubset	This property returns the internal subset declarations as a string.

The DOMImplementation Interface

There are two new methods added to the DOMImplementation interface in the DOM Level 2.

Method	Description
`DocumentType createDocumentType ( DOMString qualifiedName, DOMString publicId, DOMString systemId)`	This method allows an empty DocumentType node to be created. While the internal subset of a document type may not be manipulated using the DOM Level 2, this method (along with the createDocument() method, below) allow us to associate an external subset with our documents. May raise the following DOMException errors: ❑ INVALID_CHARACTER_ERR ❑ NAMESPACE_ERR
`Document createDocument ( DOMString namespaceURI, DOMString qualifiedName, DocumentType doctype)`	This method allows a document to be created with a specific namespace and document type association. Creating a document this way (as opposed to simply creating an instance of the Document object) allows you to associate a document type with the new document. May raise the following DOMException errors: ❑ INVALID_CHARACTER_ERR ❑ NAMESPACE_ERR ❑ WRONG_DOCUMENT_ERR

The Element Interface

There are eight new methods for the Element interface. Most of the methods provide extended namespace support for existing Element methods.

Method	Description
`DOMString getAttributeNS ( DOMString namespaceURI, DOMString localName)`	This method returns the string value of the attribute with the given namespace URI and local name.

Table continued on following page

Method	Description

`void setAttributeNS (`
`  DOMString namespaceURI,`
`  DOMString qualifiedName,`
`  DOMString value)`
	This method sets the value of the attribute with the given namespace URI and qualified name to the specified value. If an attribute with a matching local name and namespace URI are already present for this element, it is replaced; otherwise, a new attribute is added.
	
	May raise the following `DOMException` errors:
	
	❑ `INVALID_CHARACTER_ERR`
	❑ `NAMESPACE_ERR`
	❑ `NO_MODIFICATION_ALLOWED_ERR`

`void removeAttributeNS (`
`  DOMString namespaceURI,`
`  DOMString localName)`
	This method removes the attribute for this element with the matching namespace URI and local name.
	
	May raise the following `DOMException` error:
	
	❑ `NO_MODIFICATION_ALLOWED_ERR`

`Attr getAttributeNodeNS (`
`  DOMString namespaceURI,`
`  DOMString localName)`
	This method returns the attribute node for this element with the matching namespace URI and local name.

`Attr setAttributeNS (Attr newAttr)`	This method adds the given attribute node to this element. It returns the added attribute node.

`NodeList getElementsByTagNameNS(`
`  DOMString namespaceURI,`
`  DOMString localName)`
	This method returns a node list containing all of the subelements of this element that match the given namespace URI and local name.

`boolean hasAttribute (DOMString name)`	This helper method returns a `Boolean` indicating whether an attribute with the given name exists for this element.

`boolean hasAttributeNS (`
`  DOMString namespaceURI,`
`  DOMString localName)`
	This helper method returns a `Boolean` indicating whether an attribute with the given namespace URI and local name exists for this element.

The Views Specification

This section of the DOM Level 2 specification provides a way to associate views of an XML document with that XML document. This is used primarily as a placeholder for future DOM interface definitions – you won't have much call to use these in DOM Level 2 compliant parsers.

The Events Specification

This section of the DOM Level 2 specification describes an event model for XML documents.

To determine whether this specification is supported by a particular implementation of the DOM, you may call the `hasFeature()` *method on the* `DOMImplementation` *interface, with a* `feature` *of* `Events` *and a* `version` *of* `2.0`.

The EventTarget Interface

In DOM implementations that support the Events specification, there is an `EventTarget` interface that `Node` objects support. The implementation will vary based on the specific binding of the language – either the `Node` object may be cast to an `EventTarget` object, or the `Node` object may simply support the `EventTarget` methods. In any case, the `EventTarget` interface allows the registration of event listeners for a particular node and messages to be dispatched to that node.

Method	Description

`void addEventListener ( DOMString type, EventListener listener, boolean useCapture)`	This method registers an event listener on this node. The type of event being registered may come from any of the possible event types. Later in the chapter we'll enumerate the event types defined in the DOM Level 2. If the `useCapture` flag is `true`, then this listener will attempt to handle events triggered on subnodes of this node before dispatching the event further down the document tree. For example, say we have the following document:
	`<a>`
	`  <b>`
	`    <c />`
	`  </b>`
	`</a>`
	If we register an event listener on the `b` element, and set `useCapture` to `true`, then the `b` element will attempt to handle any events triggered on the `c` element before dispatching them to the `c` element.
	Note that if there was also an event listener on the `a` element with `useCapture` set to `true`, an event triggered on the `c` element would be first processed by the listener on `a`, then the listener on `b`, before finally being dispatched to the `c` element.

Table continued on following page

Method	Description
`void removeEventListener ( DOMString type, EventListener listener, boolean useCapture)`	This method removes the event listener from the node (if present) with the specified type, listener, and capture settings.
`boolean dispatchEvent (Event evt)`	This allows events to be triggered programmatically. This call triggers the event specified by `evt` on this node.

The EventListener Interface

To use event handling, you must write code that implements the `EventListener` interface (based on the binding that is appropriate to your library). It must implement one method – `handleEvent()` – that takes an `Event` object as a parameter – and that has no return value. Be aware that event listeners that you implement must be able to handle event capturing (if you register your listeners with `useCapture` set to `true`) or event bubbling.

The Event Interface

The `Event` interface describes all of the details about an event. It can be received by an `EventListener` when an event triggers on the node carrying the `EventListener`, or you can create an `Event` object when you dispatch an event manually to a listener.

Property	Description
`DOMString type`	This property contains the type of event that was triggered. We'll take a look at the list of types of events that are defined for the DOM Level 2 later in the chapter.
`EventTarget target`	This property indicates the event target, or node, to which this event was originally targeted (disregarding any bubbling or capturing that may affect the current status of the event).
`EventTarget currentTarget`	This property indicates the current event target, or node, of this event (taking into account any bubbling or capturing that have occurred).
`unsigned short eventPhase`	This flag indicates what type of processing is taking place for the event. There are three possible values: ❑ `CAPTURING_PHASE` – The event is being handled as part of a capture (the event is being pre-emptively processed by an ancestor of the event's original target). ❑ `AT_TARGET` – The event is being handled at its original target. ❑ `BUBBLING_PHASE` – The event is being handled as part of a bubble (the event is moving up through the ancestors of the original target, trying to find a handler that can process it).

Property	Description
`boolean bubbles`	This flag indicates whether the event can bubble or not; if it is `true`, then the event can bubble.
`boolean cancelable`	This flag indicates whether the event may have its default action prevented or not – if it is `true`, then the event's default action may be cancelled.
`DOMTimeStamp timestamp`	This property specified the time, in milliseconds relative to some common base time (system start time, for example, or since the start of January 1, 1970 GMT) when the event was triggered. It's intended to help ensure events are triggered in the proper order. However, not all implementations of the DOM Level 2 event specification are guaranteed to be able to provide this information.

Method	Description
`void stopPropagation()`	This method allows the termination of the event's propagation through the document tree. For example, it would be called to stop further processing of the event when a capturing event handler has processed the event. However, any other listeners on the current target will still have an opportunity to process the event.
`void preventDefault()`	This method is called when a particular behavior of an event specific to the implementation is to be cancelled. For example, canceling an `onClick` event on an XHTML form submit button would prevent the form from being submitted (if the data on the form did not validate correctly, for example).
`void initEvent ( DOMString eventTypeArg, boolean canBubbleArg, boolean cancelableArg)`	This method is used to initialize an event that is created programmatically (for example, to pass to a listener via `dispatchEvent()`). As we've stated before, we'll look at the allowable event types later in the chapter. The other two parameters indicate whether the event bubbles up through the document tree and whether the event may be cancelled.

The DocumentEvent Interface

This interface provides a way to create `Event` objects for a particular implementation. As with `EventTarget` and `Node` objects, the specific way this is done will vary based on the implementation – either the `Document` object may be cast to a `DocumentEvent` object, or it will simply implement the methods and properties in the `DocumentEvent` interface.

Method	Description
`Event createEvent (eventType)`	This method creates an `Event` object of the specified type.

Event Types

Event types declared in the DOM Level 2 events specification are divided into groups. Some of the groups of events are provided for compatibility with legacy "DOM Level 0" implementations; others, like mutation events, are specific to XML. Let's take a look at the various groups and event types that are available.

UI Events

UI events correspond roughly to the events defined in HTML 4.0 and additional events that correspond to the DOM Level 0. To determine whether a particular implementation supports UI events, you may call `hasFeature` with the feature set to `UIEvents` and the version set to `2.0`.

UI events may take the following types:

- `DOMFocusIn` – This event occurs when an `EventTarget` receives focus, as defined by the implementation. For example, this event might fire when a user clicks on a text box to type information. These events bubble, and are not cancelable.
- `DOMFocusOut` – This event occurs when an `EventTarget` loses focus, as defined by the implementation. For example, this event might fire for a text box when the user clicks away from it. These events bubble, and are not cancelable.
- `DOMActivate` – This event occurs when an `EventTarget` is activated, as defined by the implementation. For example, this event might fire when a button on a form is clicked. These events bubble, and are cancelable.

UI events must also implement the `UIEvent` interface, which provides additional contextual information about UI events. This interface includes the following properties and methods:

Property	Description
`views::AbstractView view`	This property returns the view associated with this UI event.
`long detail`	This property returns additional information about this event. For this specification, this is only used for `DOMActivate` – it allows the system to make the distinction between a normal activation (a single click, for example) – with a `detail` value of `1` - and a hyperactivation (a double-click, for example), with a `detail` value of `2`.

Method	Description

`void initUIEvent (`
`  DOMString typeArg,`
`  boolean canBubbleArg,`
`  boolean cancelableArg,`
`  views::AbstractView viewArg,`
`  long detailArg)`
	This method extends the `initEvent()` method, and allows the additional information for a UI event to be specified (the view with which it is associated and any additional contextual information).

Mouse Events

Mouse events represent pointer actions taken by the user on a document. To determine whether a particular implementation supports mouse events, you may call `hasFeature()` with the feature set to `MouseEvents` and the version set to `2.0`.

Mouse events may take the following types:

- `click` – This event occurs when the user clicks and releases the pointing device over a particular `EventTarget`. Note that when this happens, three events are actually triggered – `mousedown`, `mouseup`, and `click`. If more than one click is made on a target (within the specifications of the particular implementation), this will be reflected in the `detail` attribute of the event that is generated. These events bubble and are cancelable.
- `mousedown` – This event occurs when the user presses the pointing device button over a particular `EventTarget`. These events bubble, and are cancelable.
- `mouseup` – This event occurs when the user releases the pointing device button over a particular `EventTarget`. These events bubble, and are cancelable.
- `mouseover` – This event occurs when the user moves the pointer from outside a particular `EventTarget` to inside it. In this case, the `relatedTarget` attribute on the `mouseEvent` interface (see below) indicates the `EventTarget` from which the pointer was moved. These events bubble, and are cancelable.
- `mousemove` – This event occurs when the user moves the pointer within the representation of a particular `EventTarget`. These events bubble, and are not cancelable.
- `mouseout` – This event occurs when the user moves the pointer from inside a particular `EventTarget` to outside it. In this case, the `relatedTarget` attribute on the `mouseEvent` interface (see below) indicates the `EventTarget` to which the pointer was moved. These events bubble, and are cancelable.

Mouse events must also implement the `MouseEvent` interface, which provides additional contextual information about mouse events. Note that this interface inherits from the `UIEvent` interface. This interface includes the following properties and methods:

Property	Description
`long screenX`	This property is the horizontal coordinate (relative to the screen) of the pointer when the event took place.
`long screenY`	This property is the vertical coordinate (relative to the screen) of the pointer when the event took place.
`long clientX`	This property is the horizontal coordinate (relative to the client area of the DOM implementation) of the pointer when the event took place.
`long clientY`	This property is the vertical coordinate (relative to the client area of the DOM implementation) of the pointer when the event took place.
`boolean ctrlKey`	This flag indicates whether the control key was being pressed when the event occurred.

Table continued on following page

Property	Description
`boolean shiftKey`	This flag indicates whether the shift key was being pressed when the event occurred.
`boolean altKey`	This flag indicates whether the alt key was being pressed when the event occurred.
`boolean metaKey`	This flag indicates whether another meta key was being pressed when the event occurred (the precise name of this key will vary based on the platform of the implementation).
`unsigned short button`	This indicates which button was used to take an action (for those event types that involve a mouse button). The leftmost (primary) button on the pointing device corresponds to a value of zero; if there is a middle button, it corresponds to a value of one; and the right button corresponds to a value of two.
`EventTarget relatedTarget`	Indicates what other `EventTarget` was part of the event; for example, in the `mouseover` and `mouseout` events, this indicates what other `EventTarget` previously contained the pointer in the case of `mouseover`, or now contains the pointer in the case of `mouseout`.

Method	Description
`void initMouseEvent (DOMString typeArg, boolean canBubbleArg, boolean cancelableArg, views::abstractView viewArg, long detailArg, long screenXArg, long screenYArg, long clientXArg, long clientYArg, boolean ctrlKeyArg, boolean shiftKeyArg, boolean altKeyArg, boolean metaKeyArg, unsigned short buttonArg, EventTarget relatedTargetArg)`	This method extends the `initEvent()` method, and allows the additional information for a mouse event to be specified (all the additional contextual information).

Mutation Events

Mutation events are triggered when the structure of a document itself changes. To determine whether a particular implementation supports mutation events, you may call `hasFeature()` with the feature set to `MutationEvents` and the version set to `2.0`.

Mutation events may take the following types:

- `DOMSubtreeModified` – This general event fires whenever any change occurs to the document. The implementation may fire this event once for each change, or at its discretion aggregate several rapid document changes into one triggering of this event. When this event triggers, it is targeted to the lowest common ancestor of the changed nodes. These events bubble and are not cancelable.
- `DOMNodeInserted` – This event fires whenever a node has been added as the child of another node. It is dispatched after the document tree has already been modified. It is targeted to the node being inserted. The parent node of the insertion may be found in the `relatedNode` attribute of the `MutationEvent` interface (see below). These events bubble and are not cancelable.
- `DOMNodeRemoved` – This event fires whenever a node is being removed from its parent node. It is dispatched before the document tree is modified. The target of the event is the node being removed. The parent node of the node being removed may be found in the `relatedNode` attribute of the `MutationEvent` interface (see below). These events bubble and are not cancelable.
- `DOMNodeRemovedFromDocument` – This event fires whenever a node is being removed from the document, either through direct removal or removal of a subtree containing the node. Note that while the preceding event will only fire once for a subtree being removed, this event will fire for each node in the subtree. It is dispatched before the document tree is modified. The target of the event is the node being removed. If this node is being removed directly, the `DOMNodeRemoved` event will fire before the `DOMNodeRemovedFromDocument` event. These events bubble and are not cancelable.
- `DOMNodeInsertedIntoDocument` – This event fires whenever a node is being added to the document, either through direct insertion or insertion of a subtree containing the node. Note that while the `DOMNodeInserted` event will only fire once for a subtree being inserted, this event will fire for each node in the subtree. It is dispatched before the document tree is modified. The target of the event is the node being inserted. If this node is being removed directly, the `DOMNodeInserted` event will fire before the `DOMNodeInsertedIntoDocument` event. These events bubble and are not cancelable.
- `DOMAttrModified` – This event fires whenever an attribute is modified. The target of the event is the element whose attribute was changed. The `attrChange` property of the `MutationEvent` interface (see below) indicates whether the attribute was modified, added, or removed. The original and new values of the attribute may be found in the `prevValue` and `newValue` properties of the `MutationEvent`. These events bubble and are not cancelable.
- `DOMCharacterDataModified` – This event fires whenever character data in the document is modified. This event is also fired when processing instructions are changed. The target of the event is the `CharacterData` or `PI` node whose text value was changed. The original and new values of the text may be found in the `prevValue` and `newValue` properties of the `MutationEvent`. These events bubble and are not cancelable.

Mutation events must also implement the `MutationEvent` interface, which provides additional contextual information about mutation events. Note that this interface inherits from the `Event` interface. This interface includes the following properties and methods:

Property	Description
`Node relatedNode`	This property contains information about another node related to the event that was triggered. The exact meaning of this property depends on the type of event being fired.
`DOMString prevValue`	This property contains information about the previous value of attributes or character data before an event was fired.
`DOMString newValue`	This property contains information about the new value of attributes or character data after an event was fired.
`DOMString attrName`	This property contains the name of the attribute that was changed in a `DOMAttrModified` event.
`unsigned short attrChange`	This property indicates the way in which an attribute was changed. If the attribute was modified, this value is one; if it was added, this value is two; and if it was removed, this value is three.

Method	Description
`void initMutationEvent( DOMString typeArg, boolean canBubbleArg, boolean cancelableArg, Node relatedNodeArg, DOMString prevValueArg, DOMString newValueArg, DOMString attrNameArg, unsigned short attrChangeArg)`	This method extends the `initEvent()` method, and allows the additional information for a mutation event to be specified (all the additional contextual information).

HTML Events

These event types correspond to other legacy HTML 4.0 and DOM Level 0 event types; as such, they do not have any direct bearing on XML documents and are thus outside the scope of this book.

The Styles Specification

The DOM Level 2 Styles specification allows the platform-neutral, language-neutral specification of style sheets. The intent of this specification is to grow into a way to easily make flexible documents that behave predictably across different media. However, for Level 2, the specification is fairly feature-poor, and few programmers will find it necessary to implement the interfaces found in this specification.

To identify whether a particular implementation of the DOM supports the features in the DOM Level 2 styles specification, you can do so by calling the `hasFeature()` method on the `DOMImplementation` interface with the feature parameter set to `Styles` and the version parameter set to `2.0`.

The Traversal and Ranges Specification

As its title suggests, this specification actually has two parts. The traversal section of the specification describes some additional mechanisms for the traversal of XML documents, while the range specification describes some interfaces and behaviors for the selection, insertion, and deletion of ranges of content within an XML document.

To determine whether a particular implementation of the DOM supports the traversal features found in this specification, you can do so by calling the `hasFeature()` method on the `DOMImplementation` interface with the feature parameter set to `Traversal` and the version parameter set to `2.0`; to determine if ranges are supported, pass `Range` as the feature parameter instead.

Traversal features: NodeIterators, NodeFilters, and TreeWalkers

Let's face it – parsing XML documents using the DOM 1.0 mechanisms isn't the simplest or fastest process in the world. In the case where only a certain subset of elements in the document have content that is relevant to the code at hand, sifting through all of the extraneous content can lead to poor performance and longer coding time. The features in the traversal portion of the Traversal and Ranges specification introduce some new interfaces intended to make this process easier.

The NodeIterator Interface

The `NodeIterator` interface takes a subset of the XML document tree and flattens it, so that its contents are returned in document order. For example, say we have the following document structure:

```
<a>
  <b>
    <c />
  </b>
  <d>
    <e />
  </d>
</a>
```

A `NodeIterator` created on the subtree of the document starting at the `a` element would return a list of nodes that looks like the following:

```
a b c d e
```

Note that the nodes made available by a `NodeIterator` are `Node` objects, so you can use a combination of traversal objects and DOM Level 1 objects to obtain the results you need in the most direct way possible.

Once a `NodeIterator` object is created, it functions much like a recordset in data manipulation – methods are made available to move forward and backward through the list. A detailed description of how the current position in the list is maintained may be found in the traversal specification, but generally it behaves like a recordset would behave.

Another important point about `NodeIterators` (and `TreeWalkers`, for that matter) is that they are live – that is, they automatically reflect changes to the underlying XML document. You can't change a `NodeIterator` directly – instead you change what it points to. For example, if we added a `f` element after the `c` element, like so:

```
<a>
  <b>
    <c />
    <f />
  </b>
  <d>
    <e />
  </d>
</a>
```

Then the list available to the NodeIterator object would automatically change to reflect this:

```
a b c f d e
```

The types of nodes visible to NodeIterator and TreeWalker objects may be further constrained by filters, as we'll see later.

To create a NodeIterator object, call the createNodeIterator method on the DocumentTraversal interface:

```
NodeIterator createNodeIterator (Node root, unsigned long whatToShow,
                                 NodeFilter filter,
                                 boolean entityReferenceExpansion)
```

This interface will typically be implemented as additional methods on the Document object in the DOM implementation.

The root parameter is the node that will serve as the starting point for the NodeIterator created. The NodeIterator will traverse the entire subtree of that node to determine what nodes to show in the resulting node list.

The whatToShow parameter is a bitmask that sets the allowable node types in the resulting node list. Set the following bits to allow the corresponding node type to appear in the result:

Name	Value
SHOW_ALL	0xFFFFFFFF
SHOW_ELEMENT	0x00000001
SHOW_ATTRIBUTE	0x00000002
SHOW_TEXT	0x00000004
SHOW_CDATA_SECTION	0x00000008
SHOW_ENTITY_REFERENCE	0x00000010
SHOW_ENTITY	0x00000020
SHOW_PROCESSING_INSTRUCTION	0x00000040
SHOW_COMMENT	0x00000080

Name	Value
SHOW_DOCUMENT	0x00000100
SHOW_DOCUMENT_TYPE	0x00000200
SHOW_DOCUMENT_FRAGMENT	0x00000400
SHOW_NOTATION	0x00000800

For example, a whatToShow value of 0x07 would show elements, attributes, and text nodes, but no other types of nodes in the document.

The filter parameter allows you to further constrain the allowable nodes in the resultant NodeIterator. We'll see how NodeFilter objects work later in the chapter.

The entityReferenceExpansion flag is used to determine whether the expanded content of entity reference nodes is available in the result of the NodeIterator object. By combining this with the SHOW_ENTITY_REFERENCE flag in the whatToShow parameter, entities may be rendered in the way that is the most appropriate to the programming task at hand.

Here are the NodeIterator interface properties and methods:

Property	Description
Node root	Returns the root node used to create the NodeIterator object. Note that this property, as well as all the others, is read-only – to change the parameters of a NodeIterator object, discard it and create a new one.
unsigned long whatToShow	Returns the settings of the whatToShow flags for this NodeIterator.
NodeFilter filter	Returns the NodeFilter used when creating this NodeIterator.
boolean expandEntityReferences	Indicates whether the NodeIterator is set to expand entity references.

Method	Description
Node nextNode()	Returns the next node in the NodeIterator's resultant node list, and advances the cursor for the NodeIterator. This method returns null if there are no more nodes beyond the cursor location in the list.
Node previousNode()	Returns the previous node in the NodeIterator's resultant node list, and moves the cursor back. This method returns null if the cursor is at the beginning of the list.

Table continued on following page

Method	Description
void detach()	Releases the NodeIterator, freeing up any resources it was consuming to maintain its list. Note that if you wish to use the NodeIterator after detaching it, you will need to create a new one.

The TreeWalker Interface

The TreeWalker interface works similarly to the NodeIterator interface. It takes a root node, a bitmasked field indicating what node types are to be shown, and an optional filter. It then uses these to create a dynamic view of the contents of that root node.

However, while the NodeIterator interface flattens the subtree it operates on to a simple list, the TreeWalker interface retains an understanding of the overarching document structure. As well as navigating the list in document order with nextNode() and previousNode(), using the TreeWalker allows navigating to parents, siblings, and children. We'll see how this is done later in the chapter.

The benefit to using a TreeWalker, rather than the DOM Level 1 tree navigation methods, is that the TreeWalker may be filtered to return only the nodes of interest.

To create a TreeWalker object, call the createTreeWalker() method on the DocumentTraversal interface:

```
TreeWalker createTreeWalker (Node root, unsigned long whatToShow,
                             NodeFilter filter,
                             boolean entityReferenceExpansion)
```

This interface will again typically be implemented as additional methods on the Document object in the DOM implementation.

The root parameter is the node that will serve as the starting point for the TreeWalker created. The TreeWalker will traverse the entire subtree of that node to determine what nodes to show in the resulting node list.

The whatToShow parameter is a bitmask that sets the allowable node types in the resulting node list. See the discussion of whatToShow earlier in the chapter for a list of these values.

The filter parameter allows you to further constrain the allowable nodes in the resultant TreeWalker. We'll see how NodeFilter objects work later in the chapter.

The entityReferenceExpansion flag is used to determine whether the expanded content of entity reference nodes is available in the result of the TreeWalker object. By combining this with the SHOW_ENTITY_REFERENCE flag in the whatToShow parameter, entities may be rendered in the way that is the most appropriate to the programming task at hand.

Let's take a look at the methods and properties of the TreeWalker interface:

Property	Description
`Node root`	Returns the root node used to create the `TreeWalker` object. Note that this property, as well as all the others, is read-only – to change the parameters of a `TreeWalker` object, discard it and create a new one.
`unsigned long whatToShow`	Returns the settings of the `whatToShow` flags for this `TreeWalker`.
`NodeFilter filter`	Returns the `NodeFilter` used when creating this `TreeWalker`.
`boolean expandEntityReferences`	Indicates whether the `TreeWalker` is set to expand entity references.
`Node currentNode`	This node contains the node that is the current position of the `TreeWalker`. This node may also be set; if so, then the cursor is moved to the nearest node (in document order) to the node specified, even if the node specified is not part of the `TreeWalker` view.

Method	Description
`Node parentNode()`	This method returns the parent of the current node for the `TreeWalker`, and moves the cursor to that node. If the parent is not visible in the `TreeWalker`, it will attempt to return the latest possible ancestor that is visible, or `null` if no ancestor is visible.
`Node firstChild()`	This method returns the first visible child (in document order) of the current node and moves the cursor to that node. If there are no visible children of the current node in the `TreeWalker`, this method returns `null`.
`Node lastChild()`	This method returns the last visible child (in document order) of the current node and moves the cursor to that node. If there are no visible children of the current node in the `TreeWalker`, this method returns `null`.
`Node previousSibling()`	This method returns the closest possible visible previous sibling (in document order) of the current node and moves the cursor to that node. If there are no visible previous siblings of the current node in the `TreeWalker`, this method returns `null`.
`Node nextSibling()`	This method returns the closest possible visible following sibling (in document order) of the current node and moves the cursor to that node. If there are no visible following siblings of the current node in the `TreeWalker`, this method returns `null`.

Table continued on following page

Method	Description
`Node previousNode()`	This method returns the closest visible node (in document order) before the current node, and moves the cursor to that node. If there is no visible node that comes before the current node, this method returns `null`.
`Node nextNode()`	This method returns the next visible node (in document order) after the current node, and moves the cursor to that node. If there is no visible node that comes after the current node, this method returns `null`.

The NodeFilter Interface

The real power of the DOM Level 2 traversal engines is found in the `NodeFilter` interface. This interface is implemented by you, the programmer – so you can show or hide nodes in `NodeIterator` and `TreeWalker` interfaces based on any arbitrarily complex rule you choose. To implement the `NodeFilter` interface, the programmer needs only to implement one method:

```
short acceptNode(Node n)
```

When `NodeIterator` and `TreeWalker` objects attempt to determine whether a node is visible or not and you have assigned an object to be the `NodeFilter` for that object, the `acceptNode()` method will be called for each node. Your code must return a `short` indicating whether the node may appear in the result or not:

- `FILTER_ACCEPT (1)`: The node appears in the results of the `NodeIterator` or `TreeWalker`.
- `FILTER_REJECT (2)`: The node does not appear in the results of the `NodeIterator` or `TreeWalker`. Additionally, children of the node do not appear for a `TreeWalker` object.
- `FILTER_SKIP (3)`: The node does not appear in the results of the `NodeIterator` or `TreeWalker`. However, children of the node may still be processed and appear.

As you can see, the new traversal interfaces for the DOM Level 2 make it much easier to navigate through DOM documents and obtain the information you need in a timely manner.

Range Features

The features in the range portion of the Traversal and Range specification pertain specifically to the manipulation of sections of XML documents. This is particularly germane to those who are writing XML editors, as it allows for operations that cross element boundaries. The range specification may be found at http://www.w3.org/TR/DOM-Level-2-Traversal-Range/ranges.html.

In this specification, thorough details are provided for the behavior of XML documents when range manipulations are performed on them (although a full discussion of this behavior is outside the scope of this book).

A Quick Example

Xerces 1.3.1 has DOM Level 2 support for Core, Events, and Traversal and Range. We'll now extend our earlier Java example to see how to use `TreeWalker` and `NodeIterator` objects.

```
import org.apache.xerces.parsers.*;
import org.w3c.dom.*;
import org.w3c.dom.traversal.*;
```

First add the `org.w3c.dom.traversal.*` package to the package declarations.

We should check that the parser supports DOM Level 2 Traversals. We can use the `DOMImplementation.hasFeature()`, as we did before. Or, in Xerces, you can use the `Node.isSupported()` method to get the same information:

```
      if(document.isSupported("Traversal", "2.0")) {
```

Using the TreeWalker

Next we walk the DOM tree for this document using the `TreeWalker` interface:

```
      TreeWalker walker = ((DocumentTraversal)document).createTreeWalker(
                     documentElement,
                     NodeFilter.SHOW_ELEMENT,
                     null,
                     true);

      walker.firstChild();

      do {
        Node currentNode = walker.getCurrentNode();
        System.out.println("Node name: " + currentNode.getNodeName());

        if (currentNode.getNodeType() == Node.ELEMENT_NODE &&
            currentNode.hasAttributes()) {
          // Extract attribute information
          attributeInformation((Element)currentNode);
        }
      } while (walker.nextSibling() != null);
```

We cast the `document` object to the `DocumentTraversal` interface, and use the factory method to get the `TreeWalker` instance. We use the document element as the root node, and set the filter to show just elements. The `NodeFilter` interface contains a whole host of static constants representing node types.

We call the `firstChild()` method to position our cursor on the first child of the document element, and then, while the `nextSibling()` doesn't return `null`, we get and output that sibling node. If the current node is an element node and has attributes we output them too.

For the invoice example at the start of the chapter we get the following result:

```
Walk tree to output LINEITEM node information:
Node name: LINEITEM
Element: [LINEITEM: null] has attribute PRODUCT with the value Plutonium
Element: [LINEITEM: null] has attribute UNITS with the value 10
```

```
Node name: LINEITEM
Element: [LINEITEM: null] has attribute PRODUCT with the value Donuts
Element: [LINEITEM: null] has attribute UNITS with the value 937
Node name: LINEITEM
Element: [LINEITEM: null] has attribute PRODUCT with the value Beer
Element: [LINEITEM: null] has attribute UNITS with the value 1028
Node name: LINEITEM
Element: [LINEITEM: null] has attribute PRODUCT with the value Peanuts
Element: [LINEITEM: null] has attribute UNITS with the value 1
Node name: TESTELEMENT
Element: [TESTELEMENT: null] has attribute TESTATTRIBUTE with
                              the value In TESTELEMENT
```

Using the NodeIterator

We can iterate over the same DOM tree using the `NodeIterator` interface:

```
      NodeIterator iterator = ((DocumentTraversal)document).createNodeIterator(
                    documentElement,
                    NodeFilter.SHOW_ALL,
                    null,
                    true);

      Node iteratedNode = iterator.nextNode();

      while (iteratedNode != null) {
        System.out.println("Node name: " + iteratedNode.getNodeName());

        if (iteratedNode.getNodeType() == Node.ELEMENT_NODE &&
            iteratedNode.hasAttributes()) {
          // Extract attribute information
          attributeInformation((Element)iteratedNode);
        }

        iteratedNode = iterator.nextNode();
      }
    }
```

This is fairly similar to the `TreeWalker` example we just saw, except:

- We set the filter to `NodeFilter.SHOW_ALL` to show all elements
- The `NodeIterator` uses the `nextNode()` method to advance through the flattened node list

Here's the output for the same old invoice example:

```
Iterate over nodes to output element information:
Node name: INVOICE
Element: [INVOICE: null] has attribute ADDRESS with
                         the value 142 Evergreen Terrace
Element: [INVOICE: null] has attribute CITY with the value Springfield
Element: [INVOICE: null] has attribute CUSTOMER with the value Homer J. Simpson
Element: [INVOICE: null] has attribute STATE with the value VA
Element: [INVOICE: null] has attribute TESTATTRIBUTE with the value TESTING
Element: [INVOICE: null] has attribute ZIP with the value 00000
```

```
Node name: #text
Node name: LINEITEM
Element: [LINEITEM: null] has attribute PRODUCT with the value Plutonium
Element: [LINEITEM: null] has attribute UNITS with the value 10
Node name: #text
Node name: LINEITEM
Element: [LINEITEM: null] has attribute PRODUCT with the value Donuts
Element: [LINEITEM: null] has attribute UNITS with the value 937
Node name: #text
Node name: LINEITEM
Element: [LINEITEM: null] has attribute PRODUCT with the value Beer
Element: [LINEITEM: null] has attribute UNITS with the value 1028
Node name: #text
Node name: LINEITEM
Element: [LINEITEM: null] has attribute PRODUCT with the value Peanuts
Element: [LINEITEM: null] has attribute UNITS with the value 1
Node name: #text
Node name: TESTELEMENT
Element: [TESTELEMENT: null] has attribute TESTATTRIBUTE with
                             the value In TESTELEMENT
Node name: #text
```

What's Next? DOM Level 3

Before we stop talking about W3C specifications, we should take a quick look at what some of the specifications have in store for the DOM Level 3.

Core

There are several enhancements planned for the DOM Level 3 core specification. Helper functions are added to uniquely identify nodes within a document, compare the relative position in a document of two nodes, and move nodes from one document to another.

The latest version of this specification may be found at http://www.w3.org/TR/DOM-Level-3-Core/.

Load and Save and Content Models

This specification, currently in working draft status, attempts to standardize two of the most diversely-implemented parts of DOM libraries – the way documents are loaded and saved, and the way content models are manipulated and validated against. With the advent of XML Schemas, it's going to become even more important to be able to manage content model definitions and associate them with the appropriate XML documents they describe.

The latest version of this specification may be found at http://www.w3.org/TR/DOM-Level-3-CMLS/.

Views and Formatting

This specification, the next logical extension of the DOM Level 2.0 Views specification, describes a generic way to define views and formatting for a particular view of an XML document. It describes both a general way and a flattened mechanism specific to a visual medium. As with many W3C specifications, it remains to be seen how this evolves and how programmers take advantage of its functionality.

The latest version of this specification may be found at http://www.w3.org/TR/DOM-Level-3-Views/, but, at the time of writing, the DOM summary page (http://www.w3.org/DOM/DOMTR) states that it's no longer part of DOM Level 3.

Events

The Level 3 version of the DOM Events specification continues to build on the Level 2 specification by adding new event types and interfaces. Events to trap key presses are added, as well as a way to group event listeners and event targets to facilitate multiple views of a document. As more implementations implement XML event handling, this specification will become central to writing flexible, successful XML code.

The latest version of this specification may be found at http://www.w3.org/TR/DOM-Level-3-Events/.

Future of the DOM and XML

The suite of XML tools is still in the early stages of development. If you were doing HTML work when the HTML 1.0 specification was released, you know that the tools have changed dramatically since then – and you can expect the XML toolsets to follow the same pattern. In this section, we'll take a look at the ways the DOM and XML are expected to change, and some of the implications those changes will have for our industry.

Work By the W3C

The W3C is still in the process of defining XML and the DOM. As of press time, the Level 2 specification of the DOM is a recommendation. DOM Level 3 is in working draft status, and will certainly become a recommendation before too much longer.

Applications

There are myriad third-party developers that are building tools to access and modify XML files. These developers will likely be taking advantage of the DOM functionality to do so. In many instances, these tools will form a layer wrapping the DOM that allows developers to access information at a higher level (rather than having to traverse the node tree manually). One such application would be XML Query, which provides querying facilities and a querying language to control the traversal of the node tree and retrieval of data (see Chapter 16). As the DOM changes over the next year or two, you can expect the tools that facilitate access to XML documents to change as well.

Databases, Schema, and the DOM

The line between databases and XML documents is becoming narrower and narrower. As query languages develop to access XML documents, and XML schema are used to strongly type the content of those documents, the transfer of information between databases and the DOM will become more and more error-free.

Microsoft and Oracle, for example, are already building native XML support into their applications (see Chapter 17). There are also generic data-binding mechanisms, one of which is detailed in Chapter 15, that map XML documents to object models transparently.

Summary

We have seen that the DOM provides a natural, object-oriented mechanism for traversing the node tree that makes up an XML document and retrieving the information stored there. In particular, we have seen that:

- The DOM provides a programmatic means of processing XML documents.
- The DOM allows us to manipulate XML data structures on both the client and the server.
- The DOM provides an ideal mechanism for transferring information between databases using the DOM.
- The DOM may be implemented differently on different platforms.

In short, when reading and manipulating XML documents, using the DOM will ensure the greatest level of interoperability between various platforms.

In the next chapter, we'll see some another method for programmatic control of XML – using SAX (the Simple API for XML).

12

SAX 2

This chapter will focus on the Simple API for XML (SAX), version 2. SAX is an industry-standard API intended for high-performance XML document processing.

We will start this chapter with a short introduction to SAX, its origin and evolution, and give an overview of the most common SAX parsers. Then we will cover: why we need SAX, the difference between SAX and DOM, and how to choose between those two. SAX event-driven processing will be explained, and a step-by-step example given to introduce the SAX handlers. Finally we take a look at some real-life examples.

After reading this chapter, the reader should have good knowledge of the Simple API for XML, and feel confident in parsing XML documents using a SAX-compliant parser.

Introduction

SAX (unlike DOM) is not a W3C Recommendation. It is public domain software, created by members of the XML-DEV mailing list, led by David Megginson. The original SAX implementation was released in May 1998, and was superseded by SAX 2.0 in May 2000. SAX was developed with Java in mind, but today's implementations support many other languages. More information about SAX can be found at http://www.megginson.com/SAX.

It is important to realize that SAX is an API, providing interfaces for parsers to implement. Therefore, SAX by itself cannot be used to parse documents. To do that we need SAX parsers, which are parsers conforming to the SAX specification; in other words, they implement the interfaces defined by SAX.

The current SAX version 2 API can be downloaded from http://www.megginson.com/SAX/Java/sax2.zip.

SAX Parsers

The following table provides a list of common SAX parsers, and where to get them.

Name	Creator	SAX version supported	Download from	Language
Xerces	Apache XML Project	2.0	http://xml.apache.org	Java, C++
MSXML3	Microsoft	2.0	http://msdn.microsoft.com/downloads/default.asp	C++, VB
Saxon	Michael Kay	2.0	http://users.iclway.co.uk/mhkay/saxon/	Java
JAXP	Sun	2.0	http://java.sun.com/xml/download.html	Java
Oracle's XML Parser	Oracle	2.0	http://technet.oracle.com/tech/xml/parser_java2/	Java, C++, PL/SQL

The Need for SAX

As the Document Object Model (DOM) allows complete manipulation of XML documents, the reader might be wondering why we need SAX at all. The answer is simple: performance. SAX parsing proves to be up to twice as fast as DOM parsing. We'll now explain the reasons for this, detailing the difference between these two APIs. Also we'll discuss the advantages and disadvantages of each standard, and how to select the correct one for your task.

SAX Versus DOM – The Tradeoffs

The performance difference between SAX and DOM is caused by the different approaches that these specifications take in the parsing process. SAX parsers process the XML document *sequentially* while DOM parsers typically load the entire document into memory and store it in a tree structure. A SAX parser reads through the input XML document, and notifies us of any interesting events. After processing input data, the SAX parser throws it away, and therefore only stores in memory the data currently being processed.

Unfortunately, there is a catch. This fast, memory friendly, sequential processing has its shortcomings:

- **No random access**. The sequential model that SAX provides does not allow for random access to an XML document. The element being parsed has no knowledge of past or future elements. Therefore, searching through an XML document is a hard task with SAX. **No lateral movement**. The access provided with SAX is not only sequential, but also very hierarchical. This makes tasks like moving laterally between elements difficult. Each element is parsed down to its leaf nodes before moving on to the next sibling of that element. Therefore at no point is there any clear relation of what level of the tree we are at. Because of this, the DOM approach is used for input into any processor needing random access to the XML instance (such as XSLT processors).

SAX development is also more complex than DOM, because you have to write a SAX handler to interpret the SAX events.

However, the SAX handlers have been made easy to write, and if you master SAX, you will find that it is much more flexible for custom solutions than DOM. In many cases, if you need random access to a document, you can still use SAX to create the subset of the document you need as a tree. There are still significant performance increases to be gained from making your own less heavyweight DOM. The lack of a document representation leaves you with the challenge of manipulating, serializing, and traversing the XML document.

So, there's the tradeoff: performance versus easy programming.

Which One To Choose

Some applications do not require the functionality provided by DOM. Parsing with DOM can become very memory hungry, and can dramatically decrease the performance of your application when dealing with large documents. For example, if you're parsing a 10-15 MB XML document with cross-references, the last thing you want to do is load the whole thing into memory, since the memory used for the DOM tree can be 10 times the file size!

Generally, for quick, less-intensive parsing and processing, SAX is the better choice. Also, when no tree manipulation is needed, SAX is better. In other cases, DOM provides an easy-to-use, clean interface to data in a desirable format.

Each API has strengths and weaknesses that you can use depending on the task in hand.

When To Choose SAX

Let's have a look at a few instances that SAX would be better suited to handle:

- **Large document handling.** The strength of the SAX specification is that it can scan and parse gigabytes worth of XML documents without hitting resource limits, because it does not try to create the DOM representation in memory. If you have limited resources on your server, you should definitely use SAX.
- **Retrieving a specific value from a document.** We can abort the SAX processing during any event handling. Therefore, when we have what we want from the document, we can simply abort the processing.
- **Creating a subset document.** When dealing with a large document, SAX can be used to create a subset of it containing the required data, and DOM can then be used to process that data.

When To Choose DOM

Now, for a few issues that DOM handles better:

- **Modifying the document.** As SAX is read-only, it cannot modify an XML document. Of course, SAX can create a new document with modifications, but DOM provides a much easier way to handle this since it allows you to modify the document directly. Thus, DOM is more adept in modifying documents and changing their structure (but again, tends to be heavyweight!).
- **Random access.** As I said earlier, DOM is better suited for randomly accessing the XML document, since it keeps the whole tree in memory.

Understanding SAX

SAX gives you access to the information in your XML document, not as a tree of nodes, but as a sequence of events. It does not create an object model on top of the document (as DOM does), and therefore it can process the document much faster. All that the SAX parser does is to read through the XML documents and fire some events depending on the tags encountered. For example, the `startElement` event marks the beginning of reading a specific element. The developer is then responsible for creating a handler class, which makes sense of the events and perhaps creates an object model.

To enable our application to take actions on specific events, we must implement the *handler* interfaces which the parser calls, and register the handlers with the parser. A handler is just an interface that defines methods for specific events. SAX 2.0 defines four core handler interfaces:

- `org.xml.sax.ContentHandler`
- `org.xml.sax.ErrorHandler`
- `org.xml.sax.DTDHandler`
- `org.xml.sax.EntityResolver`

The use of these handlers is best demonstrated by examples. So, let's just dive right into the code!

Setting Up the Environment

Before we can start the parsing, we need to make sure that we have the software required and that it is set up correctly. I'll use the Apache Xerces parser, which is a robust and highly compliant implementation of SAX. It can be freely downloaded from http://xml.apache.org. Here I used the Xerces Java parser 1.2.3 release. All examples in this chapter will be coded in Java.

Follow these instructions to set up your environment correctly:

1. Download the Java 1.3 development kit from Sun: http://java.sun.com/j2se/1.3 and install it on your system (if it is not already installed). Make sure that the necessary files are reachable in your path and class path.

2. Download the Apache Xerces parser (Java version), and unzip it.

3. Make sure that your Java environment has the XML parser classes in its classpath. The parser classes are contained in a jar file named `xerces.jar`, which can be found in the root directory of the unzipped Xerces. This file therefore needs to be in the classpath.

4. Finally, the path to the classes we will create in this chapter needs to be in the classpath.

No parsing can be done unless we have an XML document ready. In the examples I'll use the following XML document (`example.xml`):

```
<?xml version="1.0"?>
<ProXML:Company xmlns:ProXML="http://www.wrox.com/ProXML">
   <ProXML:Name>Useless Products Corp.</ProXML:Name>
   <ProXML:Address>
      <ProXML:Street>Broadway</ProXML:Street>
      <ProXML:City>New York</ProXML:City>
```

```
        <ProXML:Zip>10005</ProXML:Zip>
        <ProXML:Country>USA</ProXML:Country>
    </ProXML:Address>
    <ProXML:Description>
        This company manufactures useless products.
    </ProXML:Description>
    <ProXML:Employees>
        <ProXML:Employee>
            <ProXML:Name>Johnny Purtvein</ProXML:Name>
            <ProXML:Position>CEO</ProXML:Position>
        </ProXML:Employee>
        <ProXML:Employee>
            <ProXML:Name>Mathilde Hammerstein</ProXML:Name>
            <ProXML:Position>Secretary</ProXML:Position>
        </ProXML:Employee>
    </ProXML:Employees>
</ProXML:Company>
```

Compiling Java Classes

Since all the code in this chapter will be in Java, we'll just give a quick overview of what you need to know to compile and run the Java classes. The classes in this chapter are in a package called `wrox.proxml`. This means that the Java files must be created and compiled in a `/wrox/proxml/` directory.

When the Java file (which is the source code in a file with the `.java` extension) has been created, we use the java compiler to compile it into a `.class` file (which is bytecode). For this purpose we use the `javac` command:

```
D:\xerces\MyCode\wrox\proxml> javac SAXDemo.java
```

This creates a file called `SAXDemo.class` in the same directory. To run the created class we use the `java` command:

```
D:\xerces\MyCode> java wrox.proxml.SAXDemo example.xml
```

Note that the extension should not be used with the `java` command. Also note that the `<JAVA_HOME>/bin` directory must be in the system path, and the `<JAVA_HOME>/lib` directory must be in the class path. In the above example, the current directory must also be in the class path. Finally, it's important to note that the name of the `.java` file must have exactly the same name as the class declared in that file.

OK, with this out of the way we're ready for the fun!

Loading a Reader

The first thing we need to do is to build a program that instantiates a SAX parser. Each SAX parser needs to supply a class that implements the `org.xml.sax.XMLReader` interface. For example, Xerces supplies the `org.apache.xerces.parsers.SAXParser`, which is an implementation of the reader interface. So, we instantiate the reader as an instance of the implementation class:

```
XMLReader reader = new org.apache.xerces.parsers.SAXParser();
```

Let's have a look at our class (`SAXDemo.java`):

```
package wrox.proxml;

// import the SAX reader interface:
import org.xml.sax.XMLReader;

// import exception classes:
import org.xml.sax.SAXException;
import java.io.IOException;

/**
 * A simple SAX demo. Takes an XML document, parses it and
 * outputs all callbacks.
 *
 * @author Oli Gauti Gudmundsson.
 */
public class SAXDemo {

   public static void main( String[] args ) {

      if ( args.length != 1 ) {
         System.out.println(
            "Usage: java SAXDemo <path to XML document>");
         System.exit(0);
      }

      // Instantiate the reader:
      XMLReader reader = new org.apache.xerces.parsers.SAXParser();

      System.out.println("Starting to parse " + args[0]);
      try {
         // Parse:
         reader.parse(args[0]);
      } catch ( IOException e ) {
         System.out.println("Error reading file: " + e.getMessage());
      } catch ( SAXException e ) {
         System.out.println("Error parsing file: " + e.getMessage());
      }
   }
}
```

This class does not do anything useful yet. It is a command line program that parses the XML document given as an argument by calling the parse method:

```
reader.parse(args[0]);
```

but as of yet, we have not registered any handlers to handle the events of the parsing process. Let's go to the directory of our `example.xml` document and try running this example (remember to compile the class first!):

```
D:\xerces\MyCode> java wrox.proxml.SAXDemo example.xml
Starting to parse example.xml
```

One thing is worth noticing. If we wanted to use another SAX implementation than Xerces, we would have to change the source code of our class and recompile it. This is not good practice, as our application is not portable. So, to be able to load the parser with as loose a coupling as possible, we use a method provided by the `org.xml.sax.helpers.XMLReaderFactory` class:

```
package wrox.proxml;

// import the SAX reader interface:
import org.xml.sax.XMLReader;

// import the helper class:
import org.xml.sax.helpers.XMLReaderFactory;

// import exception classes:
import org.xml.sax.SAXException;
import java.io.IOException;

/**
 * A simple SAX demo. Takes an XML document, parses it and
 * outputs all callbacks.
 *
 * @author Oli Gauti Gudmundsson.
 */
public class SAXDemo {

   public static void main( String[] args ) {

      if ( args.length != 1 ) {
         System.out.println("Usage: java SAXDemo <path to XML document>");
         System.exit(0);
      }

      System.out.println("Starting to parse " + args[0]);
      try {
         // Instantiate the reader:
         XMLReader reader = XMLReaderFactory.createXMLReader(
            "org.apache.xerces.parsers.SAXParser");
         // Parse:
         reader.parse(args[0]);
      } catch ( IOException e ) {
         System.out.println("Error reading file: " + e.getMessage());
      } catch ( SAXException e ) {
         System.out.println("Error parsing file: " + e.getMessage());
      }
   }
}
```

Here, the name of the reader implementation class has simply been hard-coded, but ideally we would just read the implementation to use from a configuration file. Now we've made our code portable.

The next step is to implement some handlers and register them.

Content Handlers

The first handler interface we'll implement is the `org.xml.sax.ContentHandler` interface. The `ContentHandler` interface defines methods to handle the following events:

Event	Description
setDocumentLocator()	This is actually not an event! This method is called before any other to provide us with a Locator object, which can be used to obtain the location within the document of subsequent events.
startDocument()	Notifies about the beginning of a document.
endDocument()	Notifies about the end of a document.
processingInstruction()	Notifies about a processing instruction (other than the XML declaration).
startPrefixMapping()	Indicates the beginning of an XML namespace prefix mapping.
endPrefixMapping()	Indicates the end of a scope of a prefix mapping; when the namespace reported through startPrefixMapping() is no longer available.
startElement()	Notifies about the beginning of an element.
endElement()	Notifies about the end of an element.
characters()	Reports character data within an element.
ignorableWhitespace()	Reports ignorable whitespace in element content.
skippedEntity()	Reports an entity that is skipped by the parser.

First, let's look at how we implement each event handling method. At the end of this section we'll then look at them all together. Our implementation class simply prints messages indicating what is currently happening in the parsing process.

setDocumentLocator()

The first method we define sets an `org.xml.sax.Locator` for a SAX event. This method is called before any events. The `Locator` class contains methods to retrieve the location of the event within the document, such as `getLineNumber()` and `getColumnNumber()`. Here we'll simply store the `Locator` in case we need it later.

```
public void setDocumentLocator( Locator locator ) {

    System.out.println("setDocumentLocator called");

    // store the locator:
    this.locator = locator;
}
```

startDocument()

This method is called only once for the parsing of a document, before any other event callbacks (including methods within other handlers, which we'll discuss later). It defines the beginning of the parsing.

```
public void startDocument() throws SAXException {
   System.out.println("*** The beginning of parsing!");
}
```

endDocument()

The SAX parser will invoke this method only once, and it will be the last method invoked during the parse. The parser will not invoke this method until it has either abandoned parsing (because of an unrecoverable error) or reached the end of input.

```
public void endDocument() throws SAXException {
   System.out.println("*** The end of parsing!");
}
```

processingInstruction()

This method is called when the parser encounters a processing instruction. A processing instruction is of the form `<?target instruction?>`. Because a processing instruction is not an element, a special method is needed for its processing. This method receives two parameters: the target and the instruction.

```
public void processingInstruction( String target, String instruction )
   throws SAXException {

   System.out.println("PI - Target:" + target + " Instruction:" + instruction);
}
```

startPrefixMapping()

This method is called when the parser reaches the start of a prefix mapping. A prefix mapping is simply an element that uses the `xmlns` attribute to declare a namespace (for more information about XML namespaces, see Chapter 3). This method receives two parameters: the prefix itself and the URI to which the prefix is mapped. For example:

```
<rootElement>
   <someNamespace:parentElement
      xmlns:someNamespace=" http://mappingUrl.com">
      <someNamespace:childElement>Text</someNamespace:childElement>
   </someNamespace:parentElement>
</rootElement>
```

Here, the attribute `xmlns:someNamspace:=` "`http://mappingUrl.com`" maps the `someNamespace` prefix to the `http://mappingUrl.com` URI.

```
public void startPrefixMapping( String prefix, String uri ) {
   System.out.println("Start mapping - Prefix:" + prefix + " URI:" + uri);
}
```

endPrefixMapping()

As you might have guessed, this method is called when the parser reaches the close tag of the element in which the prefix mapping was declared. The mapping is therefore out of scope. It receives the prefix as parameter.

```
public void endPrefixMapping( String prefix ) {
   System.out.println("End mapping - Prefix:" + prefix);
}
```

startElement()

This method is called when the parser reaches an opening tag of an actual element. The parameters to this method are the name of the element, its attributes, and the namespace URI (if one is present). The attributes are given in an instance of the class `org.xml.sax.Attributes` class, which is a helper class that allows easy iteration (The complete JavaDoc for the SAX API can be found at http://www.megginson.com/SAX/Java/javadoc/index.html). The name of an element is given in two forms: `localName` (without a prefix) and `fullName` (the full name, including the prefix).
Here we'll just print the element name, its full name if it is associated with a namespace, and then iterate through its attributes.

```
public void startElement( String namespaceURI, String localName,
                     String fullName, Attributes attributes )
   throws SAXException {

   System.out.println("Start element - Name: " + localName);
   if ( !namespaceURI.equals("") ) {
      System.out.println("\tIs in namespace, full name: " + fullName);
   }

   // Print the attributes:
   for ( int i = 0; i < attributes.getLength(); i++ ) {
      System.out.println("\tAttribute - Name:" + attributes.getLocalName(i)
         + " Value:" + attributes.getValue(i));
   }
}
```

endElement()

This method is called when the parser reaches the closing tag of an element. It receives the name of the element as a parameter (the same variations as in the `startElement()` method).

```
public void endElement( String namespaceURI, String localName,
               String fullName )throws SAXException {

   System.out.println("End element - Name: " + localName);
   if ( !namespaceURI.equals("") ) {
      System.out.println("\tIs in namespace, full name: " + fullName);
   }
}
```

characters()

This method is called when textual data within an element is encountered. It receives three parameters: a character array containing the characters, the start index in the array, and the end index in the array.

```
public void characters( char[] chars, int start, int end )
      throws SAXException {

      String str = new String( chars,start,end );
      System.out.println("\tCharacters: [" + str + "]");
}
```

It should be noted that SAX does not define how a parser should use this method. That is, the parser may return all the textual data in one callback, but it may also return it in multiple callbacks. Also, non-validating parsers can return whitespace either through the `ignorableWhitespace()` method or the `characters()` method. Thus, the `characters()` method might return only whitespace.

ignorableWhitespace()

This method handles whitespace that the parser sees as ignorable. Validating parsers must use this method to report each chunk of whitespace in element content. As is the case with `characters()`, white space can be returned in one callback, or many. The parameters to this method are of the same form as the parameters for the `characters()` method.

```
public void ignorableWhitespace( char[] chars, int start, int end )
   throws SAXException {

   String whitespace = new String( chars,start,end );
   System.out.println("Ignorable whitespace: \"" + whitespace + "\"");
}
```

skippedEntity()

Non-validating parsers are not required to resolve entity references (except the 5 built-in entity references), so they may simply skip them. This method is called whenever the parser skips an entity. The parameter to this method is the name of the entity.

```
public void skippedEntity( String name ) throws SAXException {
   System.out.println("Skipped entity: " + name);
}
```

The Result

Now that we've implemented all the methods (all methods of the interface need to be implemented in the class implementing the interface), the only thing we have left is to register our content handler with the reader. First let's have a look at our content handler implementation class, which contains all the methods we've been defining (`DemoContentHandler.java`):

```
package wrox.proxml;

import org.xml.sax.Attributes;
import org.xml.sax.ContentHandler;
```

```
import org.xml.sax.Locator;
import org.xml.sax.SAXException;

/**
 * A demo implementation of the org.xml.sax.ContentHandler class.
 */
public class DemoContentHandler implements ContentHandler {

   // The locator provides the location of a callback within a document
   private Locator locator;

   public void setDocumentLocator( Locator locator ) {

         System.out.println("setDocumentLocator called");

      // store the locator:
      this.locator = locator;
   }

   public void startDocument() throws SAXException {
      System.out.println("*** The beginning of parsing!");
   }

   public void endDocument() throws SAXException {
      System.out.println("*** The end of parsing!");
   }

   public void processingInstruction( String target, String instruction )
      throws SAXException {

      System.out.println("PI - Target:" + target + " Instruction:" + instruction);
   }

   public void startPrefixMapping( String prefix, String uri ) {
      System.out.println("Start mapping - Prefix:" + prefix + " URI:" + uri);
   }

   public void endPrefixMapping( String prefix ) {
      System.out.println("End mapping - Prefix:" + prefix);
   }

   public void startElement( String namespaceURI, String localName,
                      String fullName, Attributes attributes )
      throws SAXException {

      System.out.println("\nStart element - Name: " + localName);
      if ( !namespaceURI.equals("") ) {
         System.out.println("\tIs in namespace, full name: " + fullName);
      }

      // Print the attributes:
      for ( int i = 0; i < attributes.getLength(); i++ ) {
```

```
         System.out.println("\tAttribute - Name:" + attributes.getLocalName(i)
         + " Value:" + attributes.getValue(i));
      }
   }

   public void endElement( String namespaceURI, String localName,
                           String fullName )
      throws SAXException {

      System.out.println("End element - Name: " + localName);
      if ( !namespaceURI.equals("") ) {
         System.out.println("\tIs in namespace, full name: " + fullName);
      }
   }

   public void characters( char[] chars, int start, int end )
      throws SAXException {

      String str = new String( chars,start,end );
      System.out.println("\tCharacters: " + str);
   }

   public void ignorableWhitespace( char[] chars, int start, int end )
      throws SAXException {

     String whitespace = new String( chars,start,end );
      System.out.println("Ignorable whitespace: \"" + whitespace + "\"");
   }

   public void skippedEntity( String name ) throws SAXException {
      System.out.println("Skipped entity: " + name);
   }
}
```

Finally we have to register this class in our SAXDemo class, which we created in the last section:

```
package wrox.proxml;

// import the SAX reader interface:
import org.xml.sax.XMLReader;

// import the helper class:
import org.xml.sax.helpers.XMLReaderFactory;

// import handler interfaces:
import org.xml.sax.ContentHandler;

// import exception classes:
import org.xml.sax.SAXException;
import java.io.IOException;


/**
 * A simple SAX demo. Takes an XML document, parses it and

   outputs all callbacks.
```

```
 *
 * @author Oli Gauti Gudmundsson.
 */
public class SAXDemo {

   public static void main( String[] args ) {

      if ( args.length != 1 ) {
         System.out.println("Usage: java SAXDemo <path to XML document>");
         System.exit(0);
      }

      System.out.println("Starting to parse " + args[0]);
      try {
      // Instantiate the reader:
      XMLReader reader = XMLReaderFactory.createXMLReader(
            "org.apache.xerces.parsers.SAXParser");

         // Create an instance of the handlers:
         ContentHandler contentHandler = new DemoContentHandler();

         // Register the handlers:
         reader.setContentHandler( contentHandler );

        // Parse:
         reader.parse(args[0]);
      } catch ( IOException e ) {
         System.out.println("Error reading file: " + e.getMessage());
      } catch ( SAXException e ) {
         System.out.println("Error parsing file: " + e.getMessage());
      }
   }
}
```

First we need to compile the class. Then, if we run the `SAXDemo` class, we will get output that looks like this:

```
D:\xerces\MyCode>java wrox.proxml.SAXDemo example.xml
Starting to parse .\example.xml
setDocumentLocator called
*** The beginning of parsing!
Start mapping – Prefix:ProXML URI:http://www.wrox.com/ProXML

Start element – Name: Company
      Is in namespace, full name: ProXML:Company
      Characters:


Start element – Name: Name
      Is in namespace, full name: ProXML:Name
      Characters: Useless Products Corp.
End element – Name: Name
      Is in namespace, full name: ProXML:Name
      Characters:

...
```

```
End element – Name: Company
      Is in namespace, full name: ProXML:Company
End mapping – Prefix:ProXML
*** The end of parsing!
```

That's interesting, but what if we encounter errors in the parsing process? This is the subject of the next section.

Error Handlers

Just as SAX provides the `ContentHandler` interface to handle content parsing events, it also provides the `ErrorHandler` interface to deal with various errors that may occur during the parsing process. Errors are categorized into three categories: *warnings*, *errors*, and *fatal-errors.*

Each error method receives a parameter of the type `SAXParseException`. Information about the error can be retrieved from this parameter through various methods provided in the `SAXParseException` class. Let's have a look at each of the error types.

warning()

SAX parsers will use this method to report conditions that are not errors or fatal errors as defined by the XML 1.0 recommendation. The default behavior is to take no action.
The SAX parser must continue to provide normal parsing events after invoking this method: it should still be possible for the application to process the document through to the end.

```
public void warning( SAXParseException exception ) {
   System.out.println("--- WARNING ---");
   System.out.println("\tLine number:\t" + exception.getLineNumber());
   System.out.println("\tColumn number:\t" +
      exception.getColumnNumber());
   System.out.println("\tMessage:\t" + exception.getMessage());
   System.out.println("---------------\n");
}
```

error()

This corresponds to the definition of "error" in section 1.2 of the W3C XML 1.0 Recommendation. For example, a validating parser would use this callback to report the violation of a validity constraint. The default behavior is to take no action.

The SAX parser must continue to provide normal parsing events after invoking this method: it should still be possible for the application to process the document through to the end. If the application cannot do so, then the parser should report a fatal error even if the XML 1.0 recommendation does not require it to do so.

```
public void error( SAXParseException exception ) {
   System.out.println("--- ERROR ---");
   System.out.println("\tLine number:\t" + exception.getLineNumber());
   System.out.println("\tColumn number:\t" +
```

```
        exception.getColumnNumber());
    System.out.println("\tMessage:\t" + exception.getMessage());
    System.out.println("-------------\n");
}
```

fatalError()

This corresponds to the definition of "fatal error" in section 1.2 of the W3C XML 1.0 Recommendation. For example, a parser would use this callback to report the violation of a well-formedness constraint.

The application must assume that the document is unusable after the parser has invoked this method, and should continue (if at all) only for the sake of collecting additional error messages; in fact, SAX parsers are free to stop reporting any other events once this method has been invoked.

```
public void fatalError( SAXParseException exception ) throws SAXException {
   System.out.println("--- FATAL ERROR ---");
   System.out.println("\tLine number:\t" + exception.getLineNumber());
   System.out.println("\tColumn number:\t" + exception.getColumnNumber());
   System.out.println("\tMessage:\t" + exception.getMessage());
   System.out.println("-------------------\n");
   throw new SAXException("Fatal Error encountered - parsing terminated.");
}
```

The Result

Our `DemoErrorHandler` class, containing the implemented error handling methods, looks like this (`DemoErrorHandler.java`):

```
package wrox.proxml;

import org.xml.sax.ErrorHandler;
import org.xml.sax.SAXParseException;
import org.xml.sax.SAXException;

/**
 * A demo implementation of the org.xml.sax.ErrorHandler class.
 */
public class DemoErrorHandler implements ErrorHandler {

   public void warning( SAXParseException exception ) {
      System.out.println("--- WARNING ---");
      System.out.println("\tLine number:\t" + exception.getLineNumber());
      System.out.println("\tColumn number:\t" + exception.getColumnNumber());
      System.out.println("\tMessage:\t" + exception.getMessage());
      System.out.println("---------------\n");
   }

   public void error( SAXParseException exception ) {
      System.out.println("--- ERROR ---");
      System.out.println("\tLine number:\t" + exception.getLineNumber());
      System.out.println("\tColumn number:\t" + exception.getColumnNumber());
      System.out.println("\tMessage:\t" + exception.getMessage());
```

```
        System.out.println("-------------\n");
    }

    public void fatalError( SAXParseException exception ) throws SAXException {
        System.out.println("--- FATAL ERROR ---");
        System.out.println("\tLine number:\t" + exception.getLineNumber());
        System.out.println("\tColumn number:\t" + exception.getColumnNumber());
        System.out.println("\tMessage:\t" + exception.getMessage());
        System.out.println("------------------\n");
        throw new SAXException("Fatal Error encountered - parsing terminated.");
    }
}
```

Finally, we register our error handler in the `SAXDemo` class:

```
package wrox.proxml;

// import the SAX reader interface:
import org.xml.sax.XMLReader;

// import the helper class:
import org.xml.sax.helpers.XMLReaderFactory;

// import handler interfaces:
import org.xml.sax.ContentHandler;
import org.xml.sax.ErrorHandler;

// import exception classes:
import org.xml.sax.SAXException;
import java.io.IOException;

...

// Create an instance of the handlers:
ContentHandler contentHandler = new DemoContentHandler();
ErrorHandler errorHandler = new DemoErrorHandler();

// Register the handlers:
reader.setContentHandler( contentHandler );
reader.setErrorHandler( errorHandler );

...
```

If we try running our example once again, we will see no messages from the error handler, because the example document contains no errors. But we want to see our error handler in action, so let's create some errors. First let's try removing the namespace declaration for the `ProXML` prefix. This would generate the following error:

```
D:\xerces\MyCode>java wrox.proxml.SAXDemo example.xml
Starting to parse example.xml
setDocumentLocator called
*** The beginning of parsing!
--- ERROR ---
    Line number:    2
```

```
    Column number:  17
    Message:        The namespace prefix "ProXML" was not declared.
-------------

...
```

The parsing is not terminated, because this is not a fatal error. Now, let's correct the error we created, and generate a fatal error. For example, this can be done by removing the closing tag for the `<ProXML:Name>` element. This results in the following fatal error:

```
D:\xerces\MyCode>java wrox.proxml.SAXDemo .\example.xml
Starting to parse example.xml
setDocumentLocator called
*** The beginning of parsing!
...
--- FATAL ERROR ---
    Line number:    23
    Column number:  17
    Message:        The element type "ProXML:Name" must be terminated
              by the matching end-tag "</ProXML:Name>".
-------------------

Error parsing file: Fatal Error encountered – parsing terminated.
```

Now, let's move on to the `DTDHandler` interface.

DTD Handlers

The `DTDHandler` interface provides methods that handle events that occur while reading and parsing an XML document's DTD. Note that: *it does not define events associated with the validation itself*, just events associated with the parsing of the DTD. We won't spend too long discussing this handler; we will just introduce it so that the reader is familiar with it. The reason for this is that DTDs are getting superseded by XML Schemas, and although many say that DTDs will always have a part to play in XML, they should be used instead. Two event methods are defined:

Event	Description
`notationDecl()`	Reports a notation declaration.
`unparsedEntityDecl()`	Reports an entity declaration that should not be parsed.

A `DTDHandler` implementation can be registered in the same way as other handlers:

```
DTDHandler dtdHandler = new DemoDTDHandler();
reader.setDTDHandler( dtdHandler );
```

Here the `DemoDTDHandler` class would be an implementation of the `DTDHandler` interface (just as `DemoContentHandler` was an implementation of the `ContentHandler` class). Note that we have not created this class (although the reader could easily create it), so the above code is for illustration only.

Note also that using this interface does not turn on validation – it simply makes sure that the DTD is parsed.

Validation

Now, let's have a look at how we can use SAX classes and interfaces to enforce validity constraints in our XML documents. To validate a document, we have to turn on the validation feature of the parser. This can be done with the `setFeature` method of the `org.xml.sax.XMLReader` interface:

```
try {
   // Instantiate the reader:
   XMLReader reader = XMLReaderFactory.createXMLReader(
      "org.apache.xerces.parsers.SAXParser");

   // Create an instance of the handlers:
   ContentHandler contentHandler = new DemoContentHandler();
   ErrorHandler errorHandler = new DemoErrorHandler();

   // Register the handlers:
   reader.setContentHandler( contentHandler );
   reader.setErrorHandler( errorHandler );

   // Turn on validation:
   reader.setFeature("http://xml.org/sax/features/validation",true);

   // Parse:
   reader.parse(args[0]);
} catch ( IOException e ) {
   System.out.println("Error reading file: " + e.getMessage());
} catch ( SAXException e ) {
   System.out.println("Error parsing file: " + e.getMessage());
}
```

Now the parser performs validation, and uses our `DemoErrorHandler` class to output any error messages concerning the validation process.

DTD Validation and Namespaces

Validating parsers have trouble processing documents that use DTD and namespaces, simply because namespaces are not supported by DTDs. Therefore, we need to turn off one or the other. We can turn off namespace awareness with the `setFeature` method:

```
reader.setFeature("http://xml.org/sax/features/namespaces",false);
```

When namespace awareness has been turned off, all element names are treated as containing both the namespace prefix and the local name.

The DefaultHandler

If we are only interested in specific events, and not all of them, it is bothersome to have to implement all of the event methods. SAX provides the helper class `org.xml.sax.helpers.DefaultHandler` to aid developers with these concerns. The `DefaultHandler` provides a default implementation for all of the callbacks in the four core SAX2 handler interfaces.

We can therefore just let our handler class extend the `DefaultHandler`, and override the methods we are interested in. This is very useful when we only need to implement part of a handler interface. The `DefaultHandler` is used in the examples section below.

Common Pitfalls

Before we get to the examples, I'd like to point out some of those annoying pitfalls commonly encountered in the parsing process.

The Order of Attributes

The `Attributes` implementation parameter given to the `startElement` method does not necessarily contain the attributes in the order in which they were parsed. The SAX documentation establishes this: "The order of attributes in the list is unspecified, and will vary from implementation to implementation". It is therefore important to never write code that presumes that they will be in the same order.

Textual Data

Two important points need to be made about textual data within an element, returned by the `characters()` method. First, we should never count on having all the textual data for an element within one callback method. A parser may return all the data in one method call, or split it up into multiple callbacks (the code in the examples section shows one way to deal with this). Secondly, it is very important to read only from the start index to the end index in the character array. The following code can therefore cause problems:

```
for ( int i = 0; i < chars.length; i++ ) {
   // wrong!
}
```

Here the `chars` variable is the character array given as a parameter to the `characters()` method. It is better to read from the start index to the end index (both given as parameters to the `characters()` method):

```
for ( int i = start; i <= end; i++ ) {
   // correct!
   chars[i];
}
```

No Reading Ahead

It is important to realize that SAX does not do any reading ahead. For example, let's have a look at the following structure:

```
<paragraph>Click <link>here</link> to see the results</paragraph>
```

One might assume that this structure would invoke the following events when parsed:

```
Start element - Name: paragraph
```

```
      Characters: Click to see the results
Start element – Name: link
      Characters: here
End element – Name: link
End element – Name: paragraph
```

But as SAX does not read ahead, the above output is wrong. The structure would produce the following events when parsed:

```
Start element – Name: paragraph
      Characters: Click
Start element – Name: link
      Characters: here
End element – Name: link
      Characters: to see the results
End element – Name: paragraph
```

Examples

Now that we've gained an insight into the structure of the event-based processing, and the handlers that deal with the events, it is time to put together some real-life examples, where our new knowledge can be exploited.

Retrieving Data

In this example we'll create a handler class that retrieves specific data from an XML document. For this example we'll use the `hamlet.xml` file, which contains the play: Hamlet, by Shakespeare, in XML format (Jon Bosak has transformed a collection of Shakespeare's plays into XML format, which can be downloaded from http://metalab.unc.edu/bosak/xml/eg/shaks200.zip).

Here is an excerpt from `hamlet.xml`:

```
<?xml version="1.0"?>
<!DOCTYPE PLAY SYSTEM "play.dtd">

<PLAY>
<TITLE>The Tragedy of Hamlet, Prince of Denmark</TITLE>

<PERSONAE>
<TITLE>Dramatis Personae</TITLE>

<PERSONA>CLAUDIUS, king of Denmark. </PERSONA>
<PERSONA>HAMLET, son to the late, and nephew to the present king.</PERSONA>
<PERSONA>POLONIUS, lord chamberlain. </PERSONA>
<PERSONA>HORATIO, friend to Hamlet.</PERSONA>
<PERSONA>LAERTES, son to Polonius.</PERSONA>
<PERSONA>LUCIANUS, nephew to the king.</PERSONA>

<PGROUP>
<PERSONA>VOLTIMAND</PERSONA>
<PERSONA>CORNELIUS</PERSONA>
```

```
<PERSONA>ROSENCRANTZ</PERSONA>
<PERSONA>GUILDENSTERN</PERSONA>
<PERSONA>OSRIC</PERSONA>
<GRPDESCR>courtiers.</GRPDESCR>
</PGROUP>

<PERSONA>A Gentleman</PERSONA>
<PERSONA>A Priest. </PERSONA>

<PGROUP>
<PERSONA>MARCELLUS</PERSONA>
<PERSONA>BERNARDO</PERSONA>
<GRPDESCR>officers.</GRPDESCR>
</PGROUP>

<PERSONA>FRANCISCO, a soldier.</PERSONA>
<PERSONA>REYNALDO, servant to Polonius.</PERSONA>
<PERSONA>Players.</PERSONA>
<PERSONA>Two Clowns, grave-diggers.</PERSONA>
<PERSONA>FORTINBRAS, prince of Norway. </PERSONA>
<PERSONA>A Captain.</PERSONA>
<PERSONA>English Ambassadors. </PERSONA>
<PERSONA>GERTRUDE, queen of Denmark, and mother to Hamlet. </PERSONA>
<PERSONA>OPHELIA, daughter to Polonius.</PERSONA>
<PERSONA>Lords, Ladies, Officers, Soldiers, Sailors, Messengers, and other
Attendants.</PERSONA>
<PERSONA>Ghost of Hamlet's Father. </PERSONA>
</PERSONAE>

<SCNDESCR>SCENE  Denmark.</SCNDESCR>

<PLAYSUBT>HAMLET</PLAYSUBT>

   <ACT><TITLE>ACT I</TITLE>

   <SCENE>
   <TITLE>SCENE I.  Elsinore. A platform before the castle.</TITLE>
   <STAGEDIR>FRANCISCO at his post. Enter to him BERNARDO</STAGEDIR>

      <SPEECH>
      <SPEAKER>BERNARDO</SPEAKER>
         <LINE>Who's there?</LINE>
      </SPEECH>
      ...
    ...
   </SCENE>
   ...
   </ACT>
 ...
</PLAY>
```

This file is quite long (its size is 281K). Let's say that we want to build an application that creates an overview of all the characters in Shakespeare's plays. This involves reading each play and extracting the personae information. This task would prove very memory absorbent if done with DOM.

With SAX we can build a class that accomplishes this task very efficiently. The personae information is only a small part of the document, so we are just going to abort the processing of a play when we have this info (instead of reading the whole document into memory with DOM). Let's take a look at our Java class (`PlayReader.java`) that accomplishes this task:

```
package wrox.proxml;

import org.xml.sax.*;              // The main SAX package
import org.xml.sax.helpers.*;      // SAX helper classes
import java.io.*;                  // For reading the input file
import java.util.Vector;

/**
 * Parse a play file using the SAX2 API and the Xerces parser.
 *
 */
public class PlayReader extends DefaultHandler {

   /* We use the Xerces SAX implementation */
   private static final String READER = "org.apache.xerces.parsers.SAXParser";

   private XMLReader reader;
   private StringBuffer accumulator;
   private String playTitle;
   private Vector personae;

   /** Constructor **/
   public PlayReader() throws SAXException {

      Instantiate the reader:
      reader = XMLReaderFactory.createXMLReader(READER);

      // This class does all handling:
      reader.setContentHandler( this );
      reader.setErrorHandler( this );
   }

   public void readPlay( String playPath ) throws SAXException,IOException
   {
   reader.parse( playPath );
   }

    /** Called at the beginning of parsing **/
    public void startDocument() {
        we initialize our string buffer, and reset the play title
        and the personae at the beginning of parsing **/
        accumulator = new StringBuffer();
        playTitle = null;
        personae = new Vector();
    }

    /**
     * This method is called when the parser encounters textual data.
     * Since the parser may call this method multiple times (without
     * intervening elements), we accumulate the characters in a string buffer.
```

```
     */
    public void characters(char[] buffer, int start, int length) {
        accumulator.append(buffer, start, length);
    }

    /**
     * When beginning to parse a new element, we erase all data from
     * the string buffer.
     */
    public void startElement(String namespaceURI, String localName,
                             String fullName, Attributes attributes) {
        accumulator.setLength(0);
    }

    /**
     * We take special action when we reach the end of selected elements.
     */
    public void endElement(String namespaceURI, String localName, String fullName)
{

        if ( localName.equals("TITLE") && playTitle == null ) {
         // Store the name of the play being parsed
            playTitle = accumulator.toString().trim();
        } else if ( localName.equals("PERSONA") ) {
         // Store the persona
            personae.add( accumulator.toString().trim() );
        } else if (localName.equals("PERSONAE")) {
         // We've reached the end of the PERSONAE element,
         // so we abort the parsing of this play
         try {
            reader = XMLReaderFactory.createXMLReader(READER);
         } catch ( SAXException e ) {}
         }
    }

   /**
   * Returns the personae of the play last parsed.
   */
   public String[] getPersonae() {
      String[] temp = (String[])personae.toArray(new String[0]);
      return temp;
   }

   /**
   * Returns the title of the play last parsed.
    */
   public String getPlayTitle() {
      return playTitle;
   }

   /**
   * The main method can be used for command line testing.
   */
   public static void main( String[] args ) throws IOException, SAXException {

      if ( args.length == 0 ) {
```

```
      System.out.println("Usage: java PlayReader <playFile> [<playFile>
                         ...]");
      System.exit(0);
   }
   PlayReader pr = new PlayReader();

   // extract the personae:
   String[] playPersonae;
   try {
      for ( int i = 0; i < args.length; i++ ) {
         pr.readPlay( args[i] );
         System.out.println("*************************");
         System.out.println("Personae from \"" + pr.getPlayTitle() +
                            "\":\n");
         playPersonae = pr.getPersonae();
         for ( int j = 0; j < playPersonae.length; j++ ) {
            System.out.println( playPersonae[j] );
         }
         System.out.println("*************************");
      }
   } catch ( IOException e ) {
      System.out.println("Error reading file: " + e.getMessage());
   } catch ( SAXException e ) {
      System.out.println("Error parsing file: " + e.getMessage());
   }
}

/** Report a warning **/
public void warning(SAXParseException exception) {
   System.err.println("WARNING: line " + exception.getLineNumber() + ": "+
                      exception.getMessage());
}

/** Report a parsing error **/
public void error(SAXParseException exception) {
   System.err.println("ERROR: line " + exception.getLineNumber() + ": " +
                      exception.getMessage());
}

/** Report a fatal error and exit **/
public void fatalError(SAXParseException exception) throws SAXException {
   System.err.println("FATAL: line " + exception.getLineNumber() + ": " +
                      exception.getMessage());
   throw(exception);
}
}
```

Notice that this class extends `DefaultHandler`, so we simply override the event callback methods that we're interested in. We gather all the personae into a Vector, which we return as a String array with the `getPersonae()` method. In the `endElement()` method, we check if we've reached the end of the `<PERSONAE>` element, and if that proves true we abort the parsing.

To run this example, just type (assuming that the `hamlet.xml` file is in the `MyCode` folder):

```
D:\xerces\MyCode>java wrox.proxml.PlayReader hamlet.xml
```

And remember that the `PlayReader` class must be on the classpath. This would produce the following output:

```
***************************
Personae from "The Tragedy of Hamlet, Prince of Denmark":

CLAUDIUS, king of Denmark.
HAMLET, son to the late, and nephew to the present king.
POLONIUS, lord chamberlain.
HORATIO, friend to Hamlet.
LAERTES, son to Polonius.
LUCIANUS, nephew to the king.
VOLTIMAND
CORNELIUS
ROSENCRANTZ
GUILDENSTERN
OSRIC
A Gentleman
A Priest.
MARCELLUS
BERNARDO
FRANCISCO, a soldier.
REYNALDO, servant to Polonius.
Players.
Two Clowns, grave-diggers.
FORTINBRAS, prince of Norway.
A Captain.
English Ambassadors.
GERTRUDE, queen of Denmark, and mother to Hamlet.
OPHELIA, daughter to Polonius.
Lords, Ladies, Officers, Soldiers, Sailors, Messengers, and other Attendants.
Ghost of Hamlet's Father.
***************************
```

This task is accomplished very quickly with SAX, since the parser does not have to read through the whole document, or store it in memory like DOM would. And even if we had to parse the whole document, SAX would be much faster than DOM (and use less memory).

Word Counter

Now we're going to create a simple word counter with SAX. This word counter, when supplied an XML document, counts all words within elements. It also has an advanced feature: we can specify the element types we want to count words within. Let's have a look at the class (`WordCounter.java`):

```
package wrox.proxml;

import org.xml.sax.*;              // The main SAX package
import org.xml.sax.helpers.*;      // SAX helper classes
import java.io.*;                  // For reading the input file
import java.util.*;                // Vector, StringTokenizer, ...

/**
 * Parse a file using the SAX2 API and the Xerces parser, and count the
 * words contained within specific elements.
 */
```

```
public class WordCounter extends DefaultHandler {

   /* We use the Xerces SAX implementation */
   private static final String READER = "org.apache.xerces.parsers.SAXParser";

   private XMLReader reader;
   private StringBuffer accumulator;
   private int wordCount;
   private Vector elements;
   private boolean countThisElement;

   /** Constructor **/
   public WordCounter() throws SAXException {

      // Instantiate the reader:
      reader = XMLReaderFactory.createXMLReader(READER);

      // This class does all handling:
      reader.setContentHandler( this );
      reader.setErrorHandler( this );
   }

   /**
   * Counts words from the file specified, contained within
   * all elements.
   */
   public void countWords( String filePath ) throws SAXException,IOException {
      countWords( filePath,null );
   }

   /**
   * Counts words from the file specified, contained within
   * the elements specified in the Vector.
   */
   public void countWords( String filePath, Vector elements ) throws
SAXException,IOException {
      this.elements = elements;
      reader.parse( filePath );
   }

   /** Returns the number of words counted in the last file parsed **/
   public int getWordCount() {
      return wordCount;
   }

   /**
   * Counts the words in the string buffer, and
   * adds to the total.
   */
   private void addToCount() {
      if ( accumulator.toString() != null ) {
         StringTokenizer strTok = new StringTokenizer(
                                          accumulator.toString().trim() );
         wordCount += strTok.countTokens();
      }
```

```
    }

    /** Called at the beginning of parsing **/
    public void startDocument() {
        // we initialize our string buffer, and
        // reset the word count at the beginning of parsing
        accumulator = new StringBuffer();
        wordCount = 0;
    }

    /**
     * This method is called when the parser encounters textual data.
     * Since the parser may call this method multiple times (without
     * intervening elements), we accumulate the characters in a string
     * buffer.
     */
    public void characters(char[] buffer, int start, int length) {
        accumulator.append(buffer, start, length);
    }

    /**
    * When beginning to parse a new element, we erase all data from
    * the string buffer. We also determine if we should count the
    * words contained within this element.
    */
    public void startElement(String namespaceURI, String localName,
                         String fullName, Attributes attributes) {
        accumulator.setLength(0);
        countThisElement = ( elements == null || elements.contains(localName) );
    }

   /**
   * After having parsed an element we count the words in the
   * string buffer.
   */
    public void endElement(String namespaceURI, String localName, String fullName)
 {
        if ( countThisElement ) {
            addToCount();
        }
    }

    /**
     * The main method can be used for command line testing.
     */
   public static void main( String[] args ) throws IOException, SAXException {

      if ( args.length == 0 ) {
         System.out.println("Usage: java WordCounter <XMLFile>
                              [<elementName> ...]");
         System.exit(0);
      }
      WordCounter wc = new WordCounter();

      // get the file path:
      String filePath = args[0];
```

```
        // get elements from which words are to be counted:
        // (if no elements are supplied, all words will be counted)
        Vector countElements = null;
        if ( args.length > 1 ) {
            countElements = new Vector();
            for ( int i = 1; i < args.length; i++ ) {
                countElements.add(args[i]);
            }
        }

        // count:
        try {
            wc.countWords( filePath, countElements );
            System.out.println("Total number of words: " + wc.getWordCount());
        } catch ( IOException e ) {
            System.out.println("Error reading file: " + e.getMessage());
        } catch ( SAXException e ) {
            System.out.println("Error parsing file: " + e.getMessage());
        }
    }

    /** Report a warning **/
    public void warning(SAXParseException exception) {
        System.err.println("WARNING: line " + exception.getLineNumber() + ": "+
                           exception.getMessage());
    }

    /** Report a parsing error **/
    public void error(SAXParseException exception) {
        System.err.println("ERROR: line " + exception.getLineNumber() + ": " +
                           exception.getMessage());
    }

    /** Report a fatal error and exit **/
    public void fatalError(SAXParseException exception) throws SAXException {
        System.err.println("FATAL: line " + exception.getLineNumber() + ": " +
                           exception.getMessage());
        throw(exception);
    }
}
```

There are two `countWords()` methods. The first one receives only one parameter, namely the path to the XML file to count from. The latter also receives a Vector containing the names of the elements of which the words are to be counted. Each time the counter reaches the end of an element, it checks whether it should count the words within the element.

To run this example (after the class has been compiled), just type (assuming that the `hamlet.xml` file is in the `MyCode` folder):

```
D:\xerces\MyCode>java wrox.proxml.WordCounter hamlet.xml
```

And remember that the `WordCounter` class must be in the CLASSPATH. This would produce the following output:

```
Total number of words: 38778
```

We can also specify the names of the elements of which the words are to be counted:

```
D:\xerces\Code>java wrox.proxml.WordCounter hamlet.xml LINE
Total number of words: 35677

D:\xerces\Code>java wrox.proxml.WordCounter hamlet.xml PERSONA
Total number of words: 90

D:\xerces\Code>java wrox.proxml.WordCounter hamlet.xml PERSONA STAGEDIR
Total number of words: 1376
```

Using Filters

In this example we'll use a design pattern called *filtering* (or pipelining). In such design, the processing consists of a number of stages. The data flows through a pipe, and in that pipe there are a number of filters filtering the data flowing through. This is described in the diagram below.

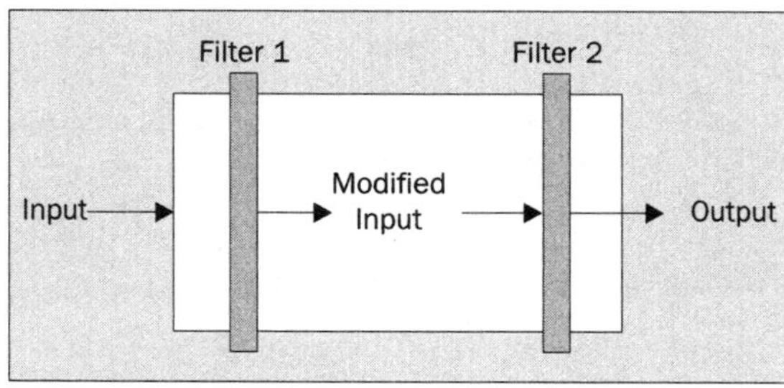

Each filter can make changes to the stream of events as it passes through, but the whole chain of filters still appears to be a single SAX driver to the application. Filtering can be useful on a number of occasions. For example, filters can be used to:

- Remove unwanted elements
- Modify elements or attributes
- Perform validation
- Normalize data values

Also, complex applications are often easier to build if you split the structure to specialized SAX filters, so that each filter performs a specific task. SAX2 formalizes this design technique by adding a new interface, `org.xml.sax.XMLFilter`, and a new helper class, `org.xml.sax.XMLFilterImpl`, which is a default implementation of the interface.

In this example we'll create two simple filters. The first one removes a certain element from the input document, and the other one validates element data. Take a look at this very simple XML document (`filter-input.xml`):

```
<?xml version="1.0"?>
<Users>
```

```
    <User id="144-2334">
       <Username>JP</Username>
       <Password>MyPassword</Password>
       <FullName>Johnny Purtvein</FullName>
       <E-mail>Johnny@anonymous.org</E-mail>
    </User>
    ...
</Users>
```

First we are going to build a filter that filters out the `<Password>` element, because we don't want the application requesting the user data to have access to that element. Our filter class (`PasswordFilter.java`) looks like this:

```
package wrox.proxml;

import org.xml.sax.*;              // The main SAX package
import org.xml.sax.helpers.*;      // SAX helper classes
import java.io.*;                  // For reading the input file

/**
 * Filters out the <Password> element.
 */
public class PasswordFilter extends XMLFilterImpl {

   private String currentElement;

   /** Constructor **/
   public PasswordFilter( XMLReader parent ) {
      super(parent);
   }

   /** Passes all elements on, except the <Password> element. **/
    public void startElement( String namespaceURI, String localName,
                              String fullName, Attributes attributes )
      throws SAXException {

         currentElement = localName;
         if ( !localName.equals("Password") ) {
         super.startElement(namespaceURI, localName, fullName, attributes);
         }
      }

   /** Passes the event on, except when dealing with the <Password> element.
   **/
   public void endElement(String namespaceURI, String localName, String
                          fullName)
      throws SAXException {

         if ( !localName.equals("Password") ) {
            super.endElement(namespaceURI, localName, fullName);
         }
    }

    /** Do not process the contents of the <Password> element. **/
```

```
    public void characters(char[] buffer, int start, int length) throws
SAXException {
        if ( !currentElement.equals("Password") ) {
               super.characters( buffer,start,length );
               }
            }
}
```

The class extends the `org.xml.sax.XMLFilterImpl`, which provides default implementation of `XMLFilter` and the core handlers. Note the use of `super.startElement`, `super.endElement` and `super.characters` to send the event on to the client. When these events are fired, the `PasswordFilter` filters out those contained within the `<Password>` element, but passes all other events on.

Our second filter (`Validator.java`) validates the character data contained within an element specified, and uses a regular expression to check the data. Let's have a look:

```
package wrox.proxml;

import org.xml.sax.*;               // The main SAX package
import org.xml.sax.helpers.*;       // SAX helper classes
import java.io.*;                   // For reading the input file
import org.apache.regexp.*;         // Regular Expressions

/**
 * Validates selected elements.
 */
public class Validator extends XMLFilterImpl {

    private String currentElement;
    private String elementName;
    private StringBuffer accumulator;
    private RE regExp;
    private int lineNumber;

    // The locator provides the location of a callback within a document
    private Locator locator;

    /** Constructor **/
    public Validator( XMLReader parent, String elementName, String pattern )
throws SAXException {
        super(parent);
        this.elementName = elementName;
        accumulator = new StringBuffer();

        // initialize the Regular Expression:
        try {
            regExp = new RE(pattern);
        } catch( RESyntaxException e ) {
            throw new SAXException( e.getMessage() );
        }

    }
```

```
    /** Store the document locator, so that we can report the line number of the
invalid data **/
    public void setDocumentLocator( Locator locator ) {
        this.locator = locator;
        super.setDocumentLocator(locator);
    }

    /** Set some variables, and then pass the event on **/
    public void startElement( String namespaceURI, String localName,
                              String fullName, Attributes attributes )
        throws SAXException {

        currentElement = localName;
        lineNumber = locator.getLineNumber();
        // reset the string buffer
        accumulator.setLength(0);
        super.startElement(namespaceURI, localName, fullName, attributes);
    }

    /**
     * Here we have accumulated all the character data within the element. We can
     * therefore check whether this element should be validated, and if so, then
     * we do (and report any errors).
     */
    public void endElement(String namespaceURI, String localName, String fullName)
        throws SAXException {

        if ( localName.equals(elementName) ) {
            if ( !regExp.match( accumulator.toString() ) ) {
                String errorMessage = "Invalid data [" + accumulator.toString() +
"] ";
                errorMessage += "in element <" + elementName + ">";
                super.error( new SAXParseException(errorMessage,locator) );
            } else {
                super.endElement(namespaceURI, localName, fullName);
            }
        } else {
            super.endElement(namespaceURI, localName, fullName);
        }
    }

    /**
     * Accumulate the characters, and pass the event on.
     */
    public void characters(char[] buffer, int start, int length) throws
    SAXException {
      accumulator.append(buffer, start, length);
      super.characters(buffer,start,length);
    }
}
```

The purpose of this filter is to check whether the character data of a specified element matches a regular expression. If the data does not match the expression, the error method of the parent reader is called. The constructor takes three arguments: the parent `XMLReader`, the name of the element that should be validated, and the regular expression pattern to use.

In this filter we implement four callback methods. We implement the `setDocumentLocator` so that we can report the line number of invalid data. We implement the `startElement` to initialize variables. In the characters method we accumulate the character data for the element currently being parsed in a `StringBuffer`. Most of our work is done in the `endElement` method. There we first check whether the element that has ended should be validated. If so, we check whether the accumulated string data matches the regular expression. If it does not, we fire an error event.

In order to be able to compile and use the `Validator` class, you need to download the `org.apache.regexp` package from Jakarta (it can be downloaded at http://jakarta.apache.org/builds/jakarta-regexp/release/v1.2/). The `jakarta-regexp-1.2.jar` file (which is in the downloadable zip file) must be in your classpath.

Now we have to create a class that uses the filters. The following class (`UserHandler.java`) does that. It prints out the names and values of all elements it encounters during the parsing.

```
package wrox.proxml;

import org.xml.sax.*;              // The main SAX package
import org.xml.sax.helpers.*;      // SAX helper classes
import java.io.*;                  // For reading the input file
import java.util.Vector;

/**
 * Parses an XML document, using the PasswordFilter class.
 */
public class UserHandler extends DefaultHandler {

   /* We use the Xerces SAX implementation */
   private static final String READER = "org.apache.xerces.parsers.SAXParser";

   private XMLReader reader;
   private PasswordFilter pf;
   private Validator validator;
   private StringBuffer accumulator;
   private int level;

   /** Constructor **/
   public UserHandler() throws SAXException {

      // Instantiate the reader:
      reader = XMLReaderFactory.createXMLReader(READER);

      // create the filters:
      validator = new Validator(reader,"E-mail",
           "^(((\\w|\\d)+\\.)*)((\\w|\\d)+)@(((\\w|\\d)+\\.)+)((\\w|\\d)+)$");
      pf = new PasswordFilter(validator);

      // this class handles the events
      validator.setContentHandler(this);
      validator.setErrorHandler(this);
      pf.setContentHandler(this);
      pf.setErrorHandler(this);
   }
```

```
/** Parses the document **/
public void parse( String inputFile ) throws SAXException,IOException {
  level = 0;
   // all parsing is filtered by the password filter
   pf.parse( inputFile );
}

/** Handles indent **/
private void indent() {
     for ( int i = 0; i < level; i++ ) {
      System.out.print("  ");
    }
}

 /** Called at the beginning of parsing **/
 public void startDocument() {
     accumulator = new StringBuffer();
     System.out.println("Starting parsing process...");
 }

 /** Called at the end of parsing **/
 public void endDocument() {
     System.out.println("Parsing finished...");
 }

 /**
  * This method is called when the parser encounters textual data.
  * Since the parser may call this method multiple times (without
  * intervening elements), we accumulate the characters in a string buffer.
  */
 public void characters(char[] buffer, int start, int length) {
     accumulator.append(buffer, start, length);
 }

 /**
  * When beginning to parse a new element, we erase all data from
  * the string buffer.
  */
 public void startElement(String namespaceURI, String localName,
                          String fullName, Attributes attributes)
      throws SAXException {
   indent();
     level++;
     System.out.print("Element encountered: " + localName + "\n");
 }

 /**
  * We take special action when we reach the end of selected elements.
  */
 public void endElement(String namespaceURI, String localName, String fullName)
  throws SAXException {

     indent();
     level--;
```

```
        if ( !accumulator.toString().trim().equals("") ) {
            System.out.print("Element value: [" +
            accumulator.toString().trim() + "]\n");
      } else {
          System.out.print("\n");
      }
        accumulator.setLength(0);
    }

    /**
     * The main method can be used for command line testing.
     */
   public static void main( String[] args ) {

      if ( args.length != 1 ) {
         System.out.println("Usage: java UserHandler <inputFile>");
         System.exit(0);
      }

      try {
         // parse the document specified as an argument
         UserHandler uh = new UserHandler();
         uh.parse(args[0]);
      } catch ( IOException e ) {
         System.out.println("Error reading file: " + e.getMessage());
      } catch ( SAXException e ) {
         System.out.println("Error parsing file: " + e.getMessage());
      }
    }

    /** Report a warning **/
    public void warning(SAXParseException exception) {
        System.err.println("WARNING: line " + exception.getLineNumber() + ": "+
                           exception.getMessage());
    }

    /** Report a parsing error **/
    public void error(SAXParseException exception) {
        System.err.println("ERROR: line " + exception.getLineNumber() + ": " +
                           exception.getMessage());
    }

    /** Report a fatal error and exit **/
    public void fatalError(SAXParseException exception) throws SAXException {
        System.err.println("FATAL: line " + exception.getLineNumber() + ": " +
                           exception.getMessage());
        throw(exception);
    }
}
```

First we create the `reader`, then we create the `validator` using the `reader` as its parent. And finally we create the password filter, using the `validator` as its parent:

```
// Instantiate the reader:
reader = XMLReaderFactory.createXMLReader(READER);

// create the filters:
validator = new Validator(reader,"E-mail",
      "^(((\\w|\\d)+\\.)*)((\\w|\\d)+)@(((\\w|\\d)+\\.)+)((\\w|\\d)+)$");
pf = new PasswordFilter(validator);
```

The `Validator` constructor takes three parameters: the parent reader, the name of the element to validate (in this case we're validating the `<E-mail>` element), and finally the pattern by which to validate (in this case a regular expression to validate an e-mail address).

Notice that we set the `UserHandler` class as the content and error handler for the filters:

```
// this class handles the events
validator.setContentHandler(this);
validator.setErrorHandler(this);
pf.setContentHandler(this);
pf.setErrorHandler(this);
```

And we parse the input document with the first filter (which is not a parent of other filters), the password filter:

```
pf.parse( inputFile );
```

The `password` filter filters out the `<Password>` element and passes the others on to the `validator` filter. The `validator` filter checks the validity of the e-mail address. If the e-mail is invalid an exception is thrown and the parsing is aborted, otherwise the events are passed on to the next reader.

Now that we have the classes ready, let's try them out. To run them, type:

```
D:\xercoo\MyCode>java wrox.proxml.UserHandler filter-input.xml
```

This produces the following output:

```
Starting parsing process...
Element encountered: Users
  Element encountered: User
    Element encountered: Username
      Element value: [JV]
    Element encountered: FullName
      Element value: [Johnny Purtvein]
    Element encountered: E-mail
      Element value: [Johnny@anonymous.org]

Parsing finished...
```

Notice that the `<Password>` element is never mentioned. That's because all events associated with it have been filtered out!

The e-mail address is valid, and therefore no error message is printed. If we change the e-mail address to "`Johnnyanonymous.org`" and run again, we get the following output:

```
Starting parsing process...
Element encountered: Users
  Element encountered: User
    Element encountered: Username
      Element value: [JV]
    Element encountered: FullName
      Element value: [Johnny Purtvein]
```

```
   Element encountered: E-mail
ERROR: line 7: Invalid data [Johnnyanonymous.org] in element <E-mail>
    Element value: [Johnnyanonymous.org]

Parsing finished...
```

In this example we've just used two filters, but we can of course use as many filters as we like, creating different stages in a pipe-like processing sequence.

Summary

In this chapter we've learned how to use the core SAX API. We've learned the differences between SAX and DOM, and how to choose between those two. We've seen how to implement the core handler interfaces, and the reader should feel confident in parsing XML documents using a SAX compliant parser. We discussed some common pitfalls, and had a look at some real-life examples.

Because of its design, the SAX implementation is generally faster and requires fewer resources. On the other hand, SAX code is frequently complex, and the lack of a document representation leaves you with the challenge of manipulating, serializing, and traversing the XML document.

SAX does not solve all XML issues – but it is reliable, memory friendly and extremely fast. SAX is definitely a very important tool in the arsenal of every developer.

13

Schema Based Programming

If you've been reading each chapter so far, you've read about the mainstream of XML. You've also read about a few technologies that are on the cutting edge of XML practice; technologies that are, perhaps, still gestating. This chapter is something different. We're inviting you to read about an idea whose time is yet to come. This is a research project pursued by two Wrox authors. It has been presented in various venues, but even the principal researchers do not know where their ideas will lead. We invite you to join a journey. We do not know where the path will lead, but we can promise you interesting sights along the way. We invite you to investigate schema based programming.

The term schema based programming (SBP) comes from Michael Corning, the proponent of schema based programming in the form described in this chapter. He is known to audiences for promoting the phrase "the schema is the API". This phrase, which appears to have been floating around the XML community for some time, neatly sums up the idea. An XML document describes some entity we wish to use in computation. Unlike a conventional program, an SBP application is implemented almost entirely as a series of XSLT transformations on XML models. XSLT is critically dependent on the form of the class of documents on which it operates. You cannot transform what is not there. Thus, the form of the document determines what you can do. The schema *is* the API.

That may not seem very important to you. As we will show in the rest of this chapter, however, that simple idea has some very important yet not so obvious implications. Before we are done, a strange cast of characters from the world of computing will be brought across the SBP stage. In this chapter, we'll mention declarative programming languages, Petri Nets, and the pi calculus. Fear not; they'll be introduced, take their bow, and exit the stage. As I said, we do not know ourselves where this will lead. We simply followed the path of SBP from its humble origins to the next idea that suggested itself, and from there to the next, and so on. We can only see a few steps down the road, but what we see is sufficiently interesting to encourage us. We hope you will feel the same way and join us. Perhaps you will add your contribution to SBP. Unlike so many projects in our field today, you can actively participate in SBP with only a computer, an XML parser, an XSLT processor, and an active mind. You do not yet need a network and powerful server.

Of course, no chapter in a Wrox book would be complete without some serious code examples. We will not disappoint you. Michael's first foray into SBP has been documented elsewhere (see The Polymorphic Spreadsheet on ASPToday, http://www.asptoday.com/, as well as http://www.aspalliance.com/mcorning/ for an example of the SBPNews application). When the other researcher, Stephen Mohr, joined the project, he realized that he needed to write an SBP application of his own, to begin to come to grips with the programming metaphor inherent in SBP, a "Hello, world" example if you will. This code documents the Living XML Tree. With this tree, you can keep abreast of the latest state of W3C standards related to XML, all neatly categorized according to function. Things happen in the user interface: colors change when you click, boxes appear and disappear, links are forged dynamically. All this is done with a very few lines of procedural script code and an awful lot of XSLT.

By itself, the application doesn't break new ground. You can easily achieve the same effects with standard procedural code and DHTML. It may, however, suggest to you a new approach to writing applications. This approach, **declarative programming**, is not new to computing. In declarative programming, the code tells the processor what to do, but neither how or in what order to do it. The purported advantage is in making the intentions of the programmer clear to future programmers as well as making it easier to modify the code without side effects. Although declarative programming languages have been in existence for some time – Prolog, ML, and Lisp are but a few examples that are declarative in whole or in part – they have never entirely caught on in the mainstream of programming practice. SBP may provide an additional benefit in that it makes the data equally visible and constrains the programmer with the data – hence, "the schema is the API". Whether SBP will prove to be a valuable way to write applications is anyone's guess. The purpose of this chapter is to explore something different. At the very least, you will have some fun and gain new insight into the strengths and weaknesses of procedural code by trying a simple application in a declarative language.

This is a very different chapter. It is firmly in the realm of XML, so even if you don't have your imagination fired by SBP, you will have a rigorous workout in XML and XSLT. The ideas in this chapter are just over the line that separates the coming thing in XML practice from theory and research. SBP, like XML itself, is a very simple idea that takes you to many important places if you give it a little thought. To understand this, we need to take you back to our humble beginnings.

A Short History of Our Short History

Two years ago, Michael Corning decided to see what he could do with the then-new XSL support in Microsoft's XML parser component. XSL was still in the earliest stages of the W3C process, and XML itself was still in the future for most programmers. Microsoft implemented support for the then-current draft of XSL on a technology preview basis. For the first time, a Windows programmer could easily explore XML transformations. In the fall of 1999 Michael débuted his polymorphic spreadsheet for an audience of developers at the Wrox Web Developer's Conferences in Washington D.C. and London; the application was of a rudimentary spreadsheet in a Web page. It summed a column of numbers and it permitted user data entry. If you clicked on a column header, the data was sorted according to that column. The interface was suggestive of Excel, yet it existed inside Internet Explorer. This was no ActiveX control, and Java was nowhere to be found. The document consisted of an XML document associated with an XSL stylesheet and a very small amount of JavaScript. XSL, it seemed, could take you further than pretty styling of data on the page. The conference sessions devoted to what would become SBP were a hit. In fact, they fell somewhere between a religious revival and a rock concert. Michael has that effect on people.

Michael also isn't one to drop a good idea until it produces another good idea. He went back to his job and pondered what he had wrought. Could other applications be built as a series of transforms on data? Could he use this new thing in his work? We cannot speak for the nature of his work, but by the following year, the term SBP was used to describe the idea and the SBPNews application was its demonstration. The application was again implemented as a series of transforms and an XML document. Even more developers flocked to his sessions, even when his highly theoretical final session was scheduled at the end of the last day of the conference. Clearly, something exciting was going on.

Origins of This Incarnation

During this time, another author, Stephen Mohr, was content to critique the topic of SBP from the sidelines. He had a nagging feeling, however, that SBP was like his first encounter with object oriented programming. Until you write some code using either of these metaphors, you won't fully understand it. While Stephen is famously lazy and resists writing "Hello, world" type applications, it quickly became clear to him that he would be unable to contribute anything of worth to SBP until he wrote a simple SBP program and got the process firmly fixed in his mind. What to do for that first project?

If you've been around XML for any length of time, you may have encountered the problem of explaining all the branches of XML to newcomers. There is one single XML Recommendation from the W3C, but it is only one tiny part of what we commonly mean when we refer to the field of XML. The W3C cover page for its technical reports (http://www.w3.org/TR/) announces new publications and lists all publications, but it contains much that is unrelated to XML. Also, if you don't browse it every few days, you'll miss the latest start of the XML world. This is more effort than a novice is likely to put in, particularly if that novice is a project manager who remains to be sold on the value of XML. It would be very nice to have a single page, easily updated, that would graphically display the entire scope of XML and bring order to it. The result is the Living XML Tree we will see later in this chapter. That application, shown below, consists of a user interface that is DHTML source dynamically generated from an XML document by an XSLT transformation. If you change the XML source document, the user interface will reflect the changes on the next request. Events generated by clicking on the boxes result in more transformations that further update the interface. The XML document, moreover, contains everything it needs to stand alone – a combined data store and application. An ASP-based version exists for those clients who lack the MSXML3 parser.

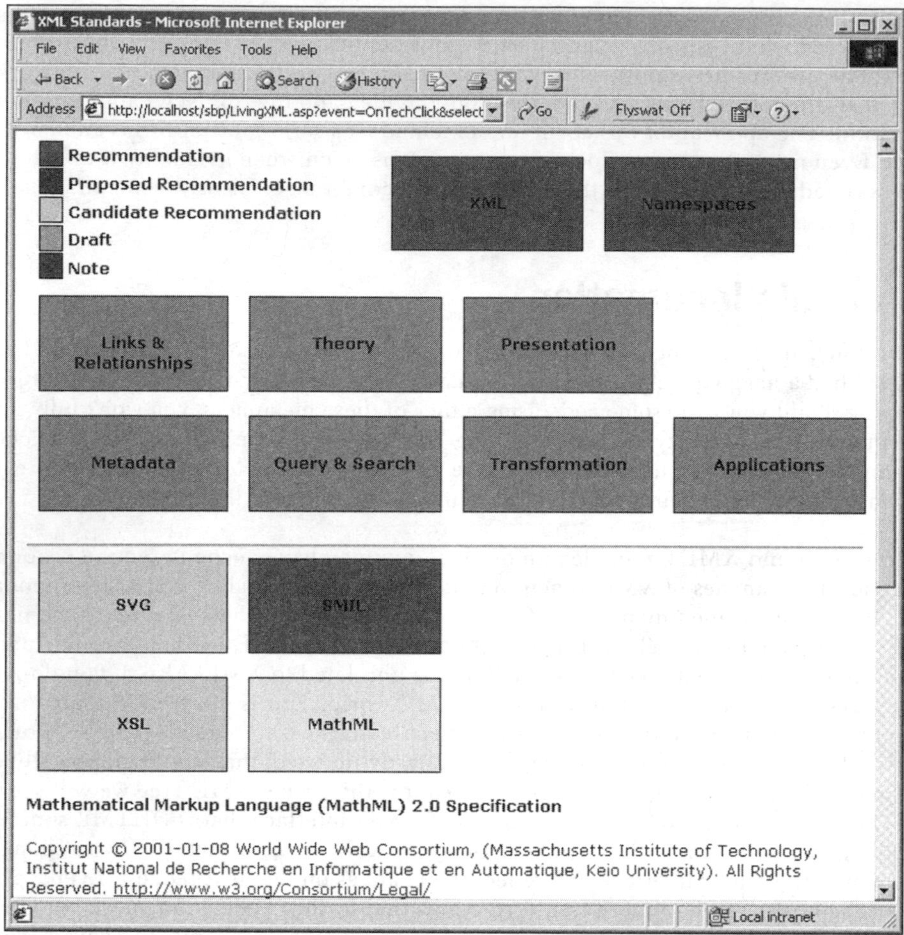

Now that we have, hopefully, intrigued you with what can be done with SBP, we need to clear up what SBP means before we get to the code for the Living XML application. Without some idea of our objectives for SBP, some of the code and markup will seem needlessly verbose. SBP isn't just about a novel way to write flashy applications, it's about a better way to program. Of course, many features that are taken for granted in procedural languages have yet to be explored in SBP, so it is far from being a language for everyday use. Even if SBP isn't the way programs get written five years from now, we hope that our foray into SBP moves the practice of programming forward. If SBP has any merit, it will leave behind lessons and techniques that survive it, should it pass from the scene. Right now we don't know whether we have the "next big thing" or just a better way of designing applications.

Schema Based Programming Objectives

The objectives of SBP are a moving target, sliding forward as we try new things and learn from the results. Michael, in his eloquent coda to Professional XSL (Wrox Press, 2001, ISBN 1-861003-57-9), likens the use of XML in programming to the primitive machines of the ancients. When you were in elementary school, you undoubtedly were introduced to these machines: the inclined plane, the pulley, the screw, etc. The plane allowed primitive man to move heavy objects up a slope into position.

Turning the idea on its head, two inclined planes make a wedge. A wedge, unlike its father the inclined plane, is not a static surface on which things move. Instead, it moves, cleaving a monolithic block into two pieces. Our forebears were terribly excited by this breakthrough. Some unknown genius turned the world on its head when he or she combined the wedge with the wheel to create the screw. The screw is the basis not only for fasteners, but also for the propeller (both nautical and aeronautical), various sorts of material conveyors, and other machines.

XML is like the inclined plane. Getting everyone onto a common and simple way to represent data is making it far easier to move data around and work with it. Schemas, whether the proprietary XDR format offered early on by Microsoft or the 'candidate-recommendation-status' (March 16, 2001) XSD format of the W3C, are the wedge of data representation. Like the wedge before it, schemas turn an existing device to new use. DTDs explained the structure of XML documents, but were not themselves XML and therefore derived no benefit from the very tools they enabled. Schemas are themselves XML. You may do to them anything you can do to – or with – any other sort of XML document. You can traverse the parts of an XML schema to discover the structure of an entire class of documents. You can manipulate a schema with the DOM to create a new class of XML documents. You can create cross-references to documents. The simple notion of marking up meta-data as XML opens up new possibilities in the field of XML.

XPath and XSLT are the screw of XML technology. XSLT is an application of XML, so, like schemas, you can manipulate and read XSLT stylesheets as you would an XML document. Both XPath and XSLT, like applying the wedge to an axle, take a different direction. They are declarative in nature. That is, they express what to do, not how. Submerging the algorithmic "how" beneath the declarative "what" makes the job of understanding the high-level purpose of the programming task easier.

SBP is an effort to move the practice of programming from the grit of procedural, algorithmic code to the rarefied level of declarative programming. SBP programs should be easier to build and maintain because they are clearly understood, intellectually complete, and provably correct. As defined earlier, declarative programming makes the intentions of the programmer clear to anyone viewing the code, without being obscured by code that tells the processor how to implement the intentions. Since SBP relies on a series of transformations, it should be possible, in theory, to logically prove the correctness of a given SBP application. We see the following concise objectives for SBP:

- Provide code clarity
- Form the basis of a universal, largely declarative programming model
- Facilitate the application of formal methods to the task of proving designs correct

Code Clarity

Procedural code – the stuff we write today – is hard to understand, and, consequently, hard to maintain. Designs are divorced from code. Source comments are compiled out of the running executable, and may not be current in the source code itself. Code may be versioned, but not in the source itself. Reconstructing the evolution of a program requires obtaining multiple source models from a version control system and hoping they were well commented. The source instructions of the current version of the software are the only thing guaranteed to be in a source file, and their clarity depends on the programming style of the individual programmer. Procedural code by its very nature makes it too easy for the programmer to stray from the data on which he wishes to operate.

If you are new to XSLT, you may feel that transformations are harder to read than procedural code. We would argue otherwise. A procedural program tells you what to do and when to do it; the data that flows through it is invisible until run-time. You can write entire applications without having live data. Perhaps this is one reason why the current practice of programming favors debugging over design. Eventually the client or employer has to furnish live data, if only to run the program. If there is a critical fault, we reach for the debugger. XSLT, however, reacts to the data it is given. You can look at a template and know exactly when it will execute, or at least what it will respond to. Too often, the impact of procedural code is obscured because a programmer reading the code cannot easily know the state of the application when the code is executed. Consider how often you have gotten sudden insight into a program you have written while debugging it. You assumed one set of behavior and conditions, but discovered an entirely different set of conditions – the state of the application at run-time – that caused the code to behave in a manner different from what you expected or intended. In SBP, you have an event – the occurrence of a certain pattern – and some lines of code that are executed in response. If you want to write a non-trivial XSLT application, you need realistic data. An SBP application takes things a step further. The data is resident with the code. Both are XML markup. You can see the code and the data on which it acts. The only thing that is hidden is data arising at run-time.

In addition to the formal mechanism of a declarative language, the implementation we will see (suggested by the earlier SBPNews application) embodies two constructs that promote code clarity. There are elements for inserting comments, and elements for maintaining source revisions. That is, you may remove a transform from an application by wrapping it in a particular element that will be ignored by the application at run time. The deprecated code is visible in the raw source file, and it is not hard to imagine an XSLT-based development environment that would let you selectively view different generations of the code. You can do the same thing using a version control tool and some custom code, but the versions do not live inside the current source code files. With SBP's approach, everything is in one place and you ignore what you don't need. In the classic version control scheme, everything is hidden and you go in search of what you do need.

A Better Programming Model

This is where the catch phrase "the schema is the API" comes into play. The data structures in a well-designed procedural program are faithful to the real-world objects they are intended to represent. The language, however, lets you create your own structures that may or may not track well with reality. Perhaps the program is attempting to do something unrealistic. Perhaps the programmer isn't talented enough to get the job done with the structures he's given. Whatever the cause, the ability to create structures disconnected from the data submitted to the application, whenever the programmer needs a way around a problem, is seductive. Once you start down that path, there is no guarantee that the results that come out of your program mean anything with respect to the real world.

Declarative languages have no assignment operator. You cannot set the value of a variable after creation, so there are no side effects from running code. If it was correct when created, it will always be correct. This clarity is bought at the price of some difficulty, however. You have to write your code in terms of different views of the data. What you are given is all that you have to work with, and you may not modify it. You may build up new views, but the underlying data is the same as that which you were given. As we shall see, this requires some effort and adjustment for procedural programmers.

SBP uses XSLT, which is a declarative language. That makes SBP pure in the sense of keeping you close to the data. Procedural languages start with algorithms as their fundamental metaphor. Data is strictly a second-class construct. Declarative languages, by contrast, are based on data. A template in an XSLT stylesheet will only fire when triggered by a pattern in the data, so you cannot inject anything into the data without cause. Since there is no assignment operator in XSLT, you have to work with the data to get anything done. Put another way, what you are allowed to do is constrained by the data. The application is always data-driven – the schema is the API.

Formal Methods

There are a lot of formal methods in computer science. These are mathematically rigorous disciplines that allow you to model some algorithm, application, or system and make provable predictions about its performance. For example, Carl Petri gave us Petri Nets in the early 1960s, which are graphs of nodes and edges that describe the behavior of systems. Each such Petri Net has **places** and **transitions**. Each is a kind of node, though transitions are indicated by the edges between these nodes. A transition reflects some activity in the system. A system's state is represented by **tokens**. A token is a mark in a place indicating that a place has A state. A system is in a particular state if tokens are found in the places that describe the state. Tokens follow transitions to new places to describe a transition from one state to another. That would have but narrow interest to programmers except that there exists a rich body of mathematical tools for predicting the behavior of systems modeled as Petri Nets. For example, Ruediger Asche, writing for MSDN in 1994, described how to use Petri Nets to predict deadlocks in Win32 multithreaded applications. Such bugs are notoriously difficult to diagnose after the fact because it is hard to precisely replicate the timing conditions leading to them. A product will often be in use for some time before a customer reports the first example of a deadlock, and then the product team will have difficulties tracking the problem down. Asche demonstrated a utility for modeling a multithreaded algorithm as a Petri Net, then predicting deadlocks.

For the first part of the three-part series on Petri Nets and deadlocks, go to *http://msdn.microsoft.com/library/techart/msdn_deadlock.htm.*

Petri Nets are not the only formal method useful to computer scientists and engineers. There are multiple variations on Petri Nets, as well as additional formalisms such as labeled transition systems and the Pi calculus. A shipping server product, the XLANG Scheduler in Microsoft BizTalk Server 2000 is explicitly built on a model from the Pi calculus.

Formal methods suggest themselves as complements to SBP because of the mathematical clarity of using XSLT transforms to implement state transitions. There are many problems in engineering and physics that are modeled using transformations. It would seem, intuitively, that we should be able to bring formal methods to bear on describing the behavior of a system that can be represented as a series of XSLT transformations. In particular, Petri Nets are described as a series of transformations. If we can use Petri Net formalisms to power SBP applications, we should be able to write applications that can be proven to have the desired behavior before we deploy them. Prediction is always cheaper than exhaustive debugging, and a lot more fun if you know how to do both. How far we can go with formal methods and SBP is a critical research issue, and we'll have more to say about it later in this chapter.

Best Uses for Declarative Programming

We can see some eyes rolling and heads shaking in the back of the audience right now. Using formal methods to build applications? Declarative applications powered by XSLT? Is this stuff a toy for the terminally academic or something a programmer can actually use to solve real-world problems? Unfortunately, the definitive answer is not yet in. Theory suggests that it is so, and a number of efforts are quietly being pursued that should give us more insight. In fact, we hope that with a wider pool of programmers attempting SBP applications we'll have a better grasp of this question. You can make a difference by attempting some experiments yourself. One thing seems certain at this point, however. SBP will not replace procedural programming for all tasks. It is another tool in the programmer's arsenal, to be selected when appropriate.

There are two reasons to make this assertion, both admittedly less than scientific in their rigor. For one thing, XSLT and SBP are definitely not the first declarative languages. In addition to a number of obscure academic languages, Lisp has been around for a number of years. While Lisp makes procedural concessions to programming practice, is substantially declarative in nature. Large programs have been written in it, and it is a popular language in the artificial intelligence community. Lisp, though, has not taken the world by storm. There's probably a good reason for this, and the conceptual shift required by declarative programming is one reason.

Another is the intuitive observation of the SBP researchers that some things that are very easy in procedural languages are very hard in declarative programming: harder, in fact, than they need to be. This is particularly true of numerical methods and things that are easily described as step-by-step algorithms. It seems to us, that small utility components such as COM components, and Java classes, are an ideal complement to SBP. That is, we feel that declarative languages in general, and SBP in particular, are best suited to describing the high-level behavior of a system or application. Somewhere between that level and the bottom-most reaches of the implementation is a line. Below that line, procedural approaches will be most productive. Above the line, declarative approaches that use procedural building blocks will have greater clarity and offer more productivity because they can be formally proven correct. The existence of this dividing line seems obvious. Like so many things in life, though, the idea of the line is of little use without knowing where to draw it, and that location is still a mystery.

Schema Based Programming in Practice

By now we've scared away the dilettantes with our talk of formal methods and uncertainty. We shall now treat the remaining survivors to some running code. We'll examine the Living XML application in due course, but first we'll describe our tools and techniques. Remember, this leads to running code. All the tools are freely available and require nothing special in the way of hardware to run them. You'll need XML and XSLT, of course, in your toolkit of programming technologies. We'll be using version 3.0 of Microsoft's XML parser component, MSXML, although any XSLT-compliant processor will work. The Living XML example requires Internet Explorer 5.x, but that is a function of its use of DHTML and does not reflect anything inherent in SBP per se. We also need to introduce you to a programming theory called Model-View-Controller (MVC) programming. This is easy to understand. In fact, you've probably used it before without knowing.

XML and XSLT

Make no mistake about it: SBP requires XML and XSLT. These are the primitive machines from which the slightly less primitive SBP machine is built. XML describes the world under discussion, while XSLT tells us how to change it.

The XML document that makes up our application contains the state of our application in addition to the transforms that will be applied to that state to create the next state. The portion of the document that addresses the state of the application, then, is dynamic. There is no prescribed vocabulary for implementing SBP applications. We anticipate programmers will devise descriptive vocabularies that suit the task at hand. Indeed, they have to do this. The schema is the API. You may only do easily what is described in the XML model, so the form of that model is critically important. At present, we do not use schemas formally. As research progresses, we expect this will become important. The applications built so far only, as we shall shortly see, modify their state in minor ways, and then using the DOM. A hot topic for future development is the use of XSLT to modify the model document in more substantial ways, such as occurs in serious, real world applications. When that is successfully demonstrated, it will be desirable to safety check state transitions by validating the document.

XSLT is the tool that takes the application from one state to another. Now, you may wonder at this assertion. I just finished saying that we haven't used XSLT to modify the model document. For now, know that the outward appearance of the application *is* modified by XSLT. That is, we expose a view of the model document to the user through XSLT. We'll explain this distinction in the next major section.

We are using the current W3C Recommendation on XSLT for several reasons. First, it is the standard and tool support is available for it. Using XSLT rather than the XSL Technology Preview implementation offered in earlier versions of Microsoft's parser opens the field to practitioners with other parsers and XSLT processors. More importantly, XSLT is fully declarative, thereby forcing the schema to be the API. This is so to the extent that the document's schema – whether a schema document actually exists or is implicit – controls what appears in conformant XML documents, and these documents control the operation of the XSLT transformation. Templates in a stylesheet will have no effect on the transformation if the pattern they match does not appear in the XML document. This is not merely an exercise in academic purity. We believe correct, provable code to be an important feature of SBP. Declarative code offers the hope of formal proof. The use of an assignment operator in procedural languages introduces side effects on variable values as a result of running the code. You cannot determine the value of a variable at an arbitrary time by any means other than executing the code to that point. This is another reason why debugging rules the current state of programming practice. We want to change that.

MSXML 3.0

If you want to test our code for yourself, you will need version 3.0 of Microsoft's XML parser, MSXML (`msxml3.dll`). This is the first version to be fully compliant with XSLT. Prior, beta versions had increasing support for the XSLT Recommendation, but we have not tested this particular application with them. Version 3.0, incidentally, is a separate download from Internet Explorer 5.5. While a number of new products are introducing MSXML 3.0 as part of their installation, you do not get it with the latest browser. You may install MSXML 3.0 side-by-side with an earlier parser, or you may install it so that it replaces your current parser. To operate the sample application correctly in its client-side only implementation, however, the new version must be installed so as to replace older versions. MSXML is backwards compatible with earlier interfaces and the XSL preview, so you should not have any problem upgrading.

The download for MSXML 3.0 is found at http://msdn.microsoft.com/xml/ along with a discussion of installation issues and backward compatibility.

SBP is not restricted to Microsoft technology. If you have an XML parser compliant with DOM Level I and an XSLT processor compliant with XSLT 1.0, you should be able to create SBP applications. Both researchers are fans of MSXML, so our code tends toward its use. Feel free to use whatever works for you. SBP doesn't mind.

Model – View – Controller Programming

We use one final programming technique that, strictly speaking, is not a consequence of using SBP. We have, however, found it a useful and natural way to implement SBP applications. If you want to try a different approach, we'd be interested in hearing from you. This technique, a programming metaphor really, is the Model-View-Controller (MVC) approach. The Microsoft Foundation Classes (MFC) in C++ are an MVC implementation. The use of forms and code modules in Visual Basic is MVC to a lesser extent. The distinction there can get blurred. Java's AWT and Swing classes are MVC. It is a popular, tested approach to programming applications. To some extent, MVC does for applications what XML does for data. Both separate data from its visual presentation.

As the name implies, an MVC application consists of three classes of entities: a **model** consisting of the application data, one or more **views** of that data, and a **controller** that pumps events between the views and the model. The model holds the application state and its behavior. Everything the application is meant to describe is held in the model, and all its behavior is implemented in code belonging to the model.

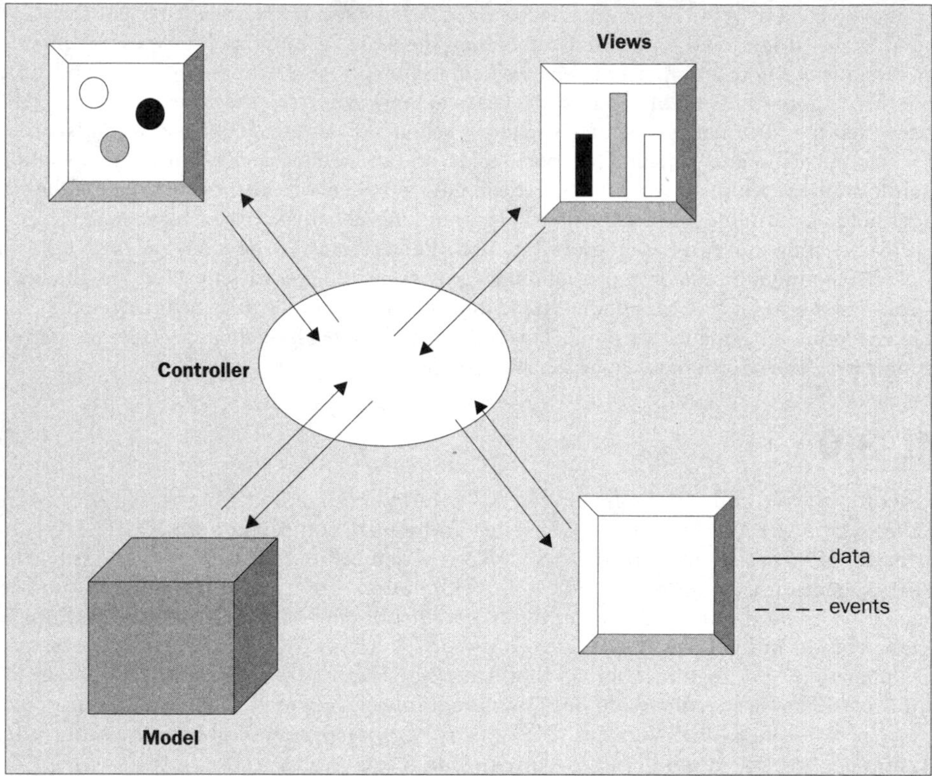

The views are the visual representation of some part of the model. They act as the user interface. Changes in the data are communicated to views, which respond by updating themselves with the latest version of the model's data. Conversely, changes in the views, such as user-initiated events, must be communicated back to the model where they may trigger changes in the model.

The controller is a small piece of code that receives events from the views and communicates them to the relevant entities in the model. The controller keeps track of which view needs which piece of information. When the model signals a change in state, the controller notifies the affected views. When a view conveys an event to the controller, the controller notifies the model, then responds to any events coming out of the model in response to the notification.

There are a number of advantages to the MVC approach. For one thing, the state and behavior of the application is implemented in one place, and implemented only one time. This ensures that the application is consistent in its behavior, and bug fixes related to the underlying behavior of the application get fixed in all places. Views have little or no knowledge of the model. They are confined to visual representation. A change to one view does not affect the others, and it is easy to add a new view to an existing application.

Implementations

Let's tie everything together to give you a rough idea how SBP applications as we are studying them are currently written. They are Web hosted for simplicity. Each consists of an XML document and a Web page that is associated with it. This is where things start to diverge. If you have Internet Explorer and MSXML 3.0, you can load the XML page directly. The XML document has an embedded link to a XSLT stylesheet that generates the initial HTML page. Named sections – typically `<DIV>` elements – comprise the views. The XML document contains four crucial elements:

- Model document – a subtree of the XML containing the state of the model
- Intentions – script code that performs a controller action for an event
- Events – elements that link intensions to views in the Web page
- Views – elements that contain XSLT transform elements (stylesheets) that implement the behavior needed to update a particular view

Nomenclature varies somewhat between the various published SBP applications. Here is the shell of the XML document:

```
<?xml version="1.0" ?>
<?xml-stylesheet type="text/xsl" href="LivingXML.xsl"?>
<Application>
   <Model>
      . . .
   </Model>
   <Intentions>
      . . .
      <codeBlock id="permanentBlock" mode="XML">
         <code id="OnTechClick" boundTo="specsView" event="OnTechClick">
            . . . // procedural script code here
         </code>
      </codeBlock>
   </Intentions>
   <event id="start" notify="showCore highlightCategory showSelSpecs"/>
      . . .
   <view id="showCore" boundTo="coreView">
      <xsl:transform version="1.0"
       xmlns:xsl="http://www.w3.org/1999/XSL/Transform">
         . . .
      </xsl:transform>
   </view>
      . . .
</Application>
```

Now, all this is a little more complicated than we would like. MVC consists of three parts, but it currently takes four in our XML document to have the same effect. We'll return to this issue when we critique the sample application, but largely it turns out to be a result of the fact that the model is updated using DOM code. We have hopes that when the model is updated solely through XSLT transforms, we can tighten the XML schema for closer correspondence with MVC.

I mentioned that things diverge depending on what parser you have available. If you have an XSLT-capable processor resident locally, we can implement all three parts of the MVC metaphor on the client. Otherwise, we must rely on server-side processing. We're going to walk through the code in some depth in a moment, but we want to lay out the outlines of the application now, without a specific implementation, to help you identify what you are seeing in the detailed implementation.

Client-Side: Nothing But XML

As noted previously, the client-side version starts with a request for an XML document that contains the four pieces noted. The XML document contains a link to an XSLT stylesheet. Since Internet Explorer is inherently XML-aware, it requests the stylesheet and performs the transformation, placing the results in the browser window.

Our stylesheet is only used once, to provide startup processing. It generates the HTML document that contains the views. In the course of creating the document, it copies the intentions, events, and view elements into the HTML document. The intentions contain script that implements the controller. After rendering the model into the physical views, we are finished with the stylesheet. User events thereafter go to the controller.

The controller, in turn, uses a naming convention to find the event element associated with the user event. Each event element contains a list of the view elements associated with the event. The controller retrieves these views – which contain XSLT transforms – from the XML document and applies them to the model. Since each view element also contains the name of the physical view to which it applies, the controller is able to programmatically insert the HTML which results from the transformation, completing the application's response to the user event. Here's the sequence of processing:

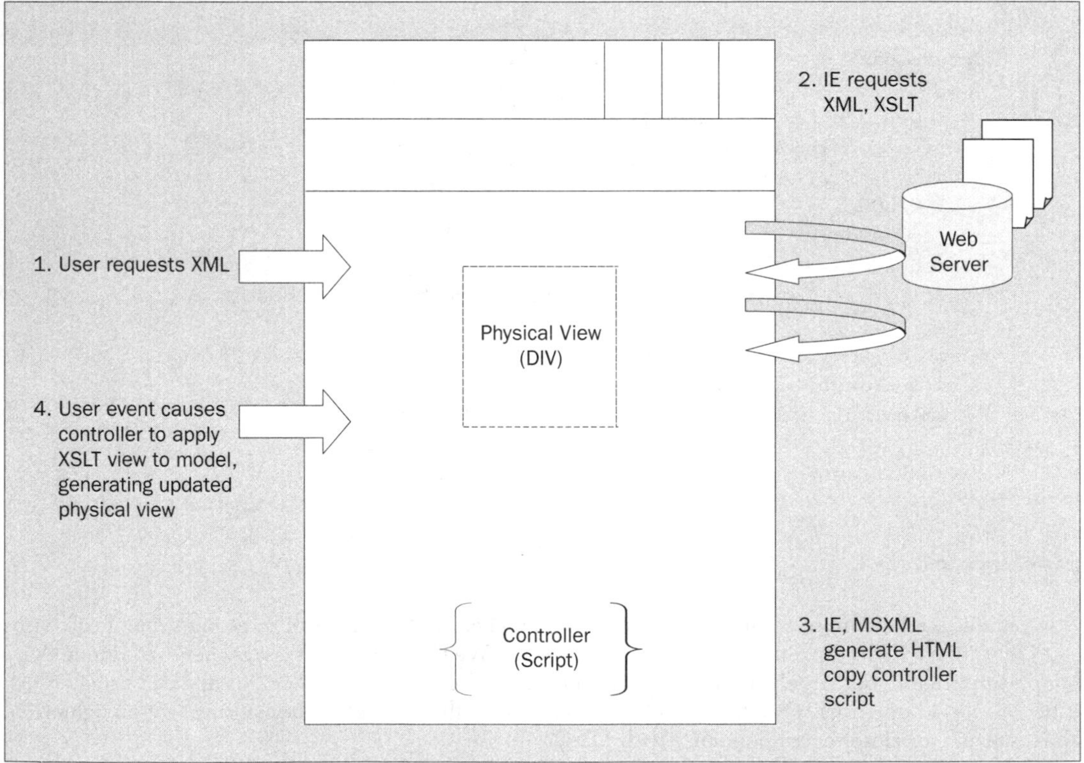

This sequence has several advantages. For one thing, it only requires two round-trips to the server, one to get the XML document and the other to retrieve the stylesheet referenced therein. Once the initial HTML page is created, everything happens in script and XSLT on the client. The generated HTML page is self-contained.

The implementation sticks close to the MVC metaphor. Each user event goes to the controller, which selects an intention in the model. The intention identifies the physical view, and the naming convention associates that with a view element. The controller retrieves the transform inside the view element, applies it to the model, and stuffs the resultant HTML into the physical view. Model (XML document) -View (physical `<DIV>` element + XML view element/XSLT)- Controller (script)

Server-Side: Some Compromises

As selfish as we are in requiring Internet Explorer, we still can't assume that everyone will have MSXML 3.0. Therefore, a second take on the application is to implement it as a client-server application. The application is now implemented as an Active Server Page (ASP). Each request results in the application of the XSLT stylesheet to the XML document. The stylesheet, though, is more complicated in this case. Since the entire user interface will be rendered on every request, and since we have one stylesheet containing all the transformation code that was formerly distributed throughout the view elements, we pass the name of the event to the ASP. The ASP takes advantage of MSXML's support for global XSLT parameters by setting the name of the event as a parameter before applying the transformation. The results of the transformation, an HTML page reflecting the visual state of the application after the event, are returned to the browser.

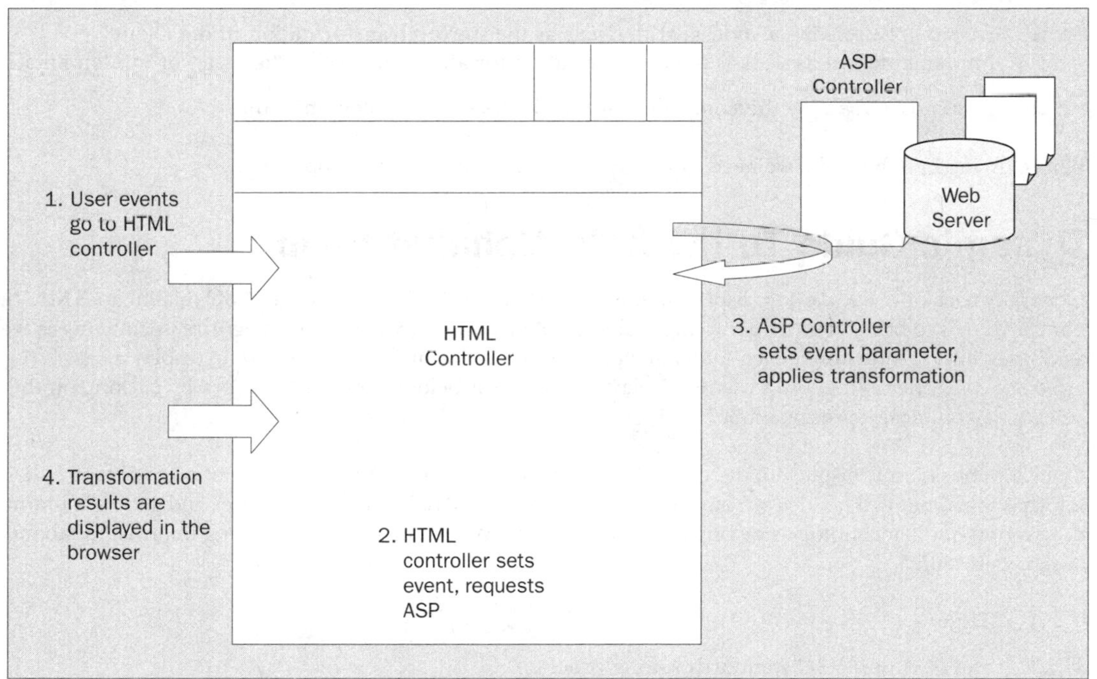

This implementation has the advantage of working with more types of clients. It also requires less processing on startup. Where the client-side implementation has to copy the view elements and intentions into the HTML page, things in the client-server implementation stay in one place. The bulk of the controller code lives in the ASP, with a small portion copied out to the client. The XSLT stylesheet contains a single transformation that is always applied. The controller code no longer needs to identify view elements and physical views. One transformation works for every event, with processing controlled by the parameter that is set by the event.

Unfortunately, this implementation requires a lot more processing. The entire stylesheet is applied in response to every event. A round trip is required to the server for each event. Every event, therefore, regardless of complexity, requires a round trip and a big transformation.

The purity of the MVC metaphor begins to break down as well. The controller, while simplified, is split between the browser and the ASP. All the views are mixed together in one XSLT stylesheet. The client-side implementation explicitly linked events to views. If you want to understand how the event is processed by the view, you inspect the associated transform and see what it does to the model. If you want to have the same understanding of the client-server implementation, you have to trace through one large stylesheet and see what the effects are. The entire user interface – every view regardless of its binding to the active event – is updated in response to every event.

Living XML Tree Example

With that rough outline in mind, let's develop the sample application. Recall from our earlier discussion that we want a visual guide to the many W3C documents specifying XML-related technologies. We'll execute both implementations. We'll have three files when we are finished (all of which are available in the code download for this book):

- `LivingXML.xml` – a document containing the model and the full client-side implementation
- `LivingXML.xsl` – a stylesheet that acts as the startup transformation in the client implementation as well as the transformation for all events in the client-server implementation
- `LivingXML.asp` – the controller for the client-server implementation

Before diving into the code, we need to specify the requirements for our application.

A Dynamic Guide To the XML Alphabet Soup

Generally speaking, we want to display all the major standards published by the W3C relating to XML. Since our purpose is to bring some order to the multitude of documents, we want to categorize documents as well as display information about each individual publication. We would, therefore, like to display a set of arbitrary categories and allow a user to display the standards belonging to the category by clicking on the category's graphical representation.

Once a publication is displayed, the user should be able to interact with its representation to obtain information about it. The idea we have is of a user, new to XML, browsing categories and getting a thumbnail description of the technologies belonging to the category. We would like the following information about each publication:

- Title
- Status in the W3C standards-setting process
- Brief description of the technology
- Link to the full text of the document on the W3C Web site

If we can implement this as an SBP application, the display may be kept up to date by editing the XML model. The next request for information would cause the view to be generated with the latest data. Now take a look at the finished user interface for a moment and then we'll refine the requirements.

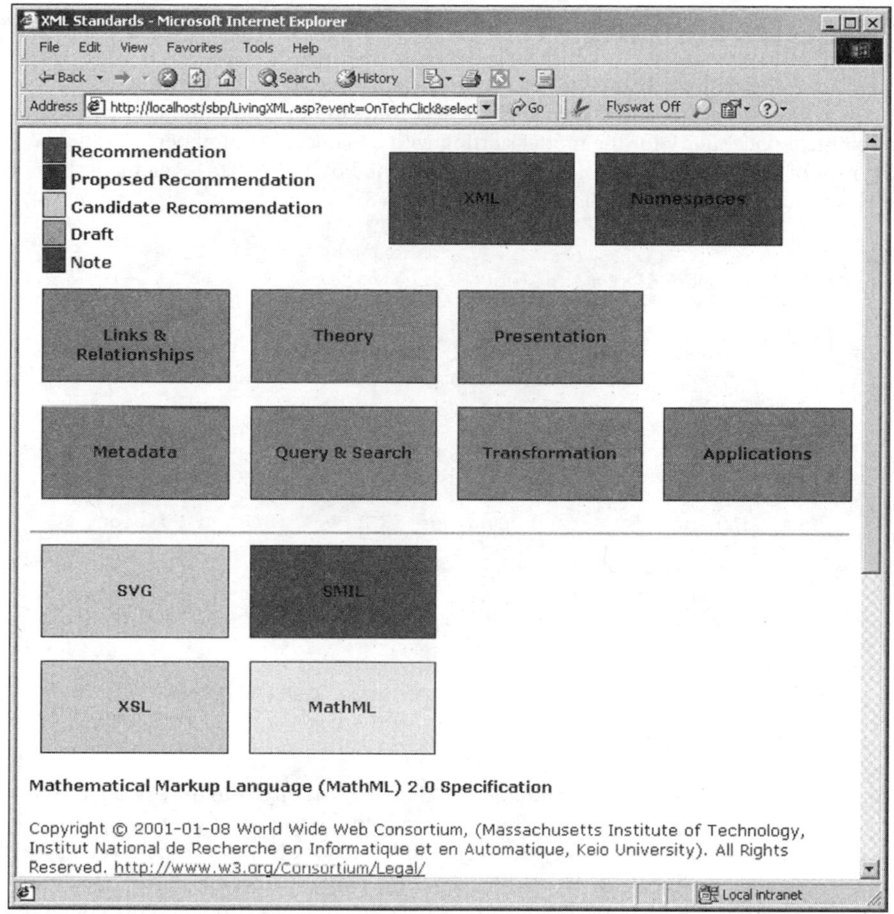

The color-coded legend, core documents (XML and Namespaces), and functional categories (Theory, Presentation, et al) should always be displayed. Hovering the cursor over any title should display a one-line synopsis of the document in a tool-tip. Clicking on the title should open the W3C document in a new window. Clicking on one of the category boxes outside the title should display boxes for each technology belonging to the category. In the client-side implementation, the category is highlighted in yellow when selected.

The behavior for the technology boxes is similar to the category boxes, except that clicking on the box outside the title displays the full title of the publication and the full text of the publication's abstract. Since the W3C has strict guidelines on copyright, we need to display a notice that complies with their guidelines. Briefly stated, the W3C requires that you display the document's copyright notice, or, if none appears, a default notice. The default copyright notice requires the date of the document. It is convenient, therefore, to capture the publication date of the document somewhere in the model.

> *Curiously, almost all the publications have the same copyright text. It is not the same as the default copyright notice.*

Each technology is color-coded according to its progress through the W3C process. When selected, the box is drawn with a yellow background to indicate its selection.

Model: XML Document

Since the schema is the API, we had better be sure the schema captures the information we wish to display and does so in a way that is amenable to processing according to our requirements. Happily, we have the luxury of creating a vocabulary for the model starting with a blank sheet of paper. Recall that our SBP shell contains the root of the model as the sole and immediate child of the <Model> element. Here is an excerpt of the model we settled on for the application:

```
<Model>
   <XMLTree selectedCat="" selectedSpec="">
      <Category id="meta-data">
         <Name>Meta-data</Name>
         <ShortTitle>Meta-data</ShortTitle>
         <Abstract>Structure and content declarations</Abstract>
      </Category>
         . . .
      <Technology status="REC" statusDate="2000-10-06" category="core"
                  id="xml" source="http://www.w3.org/TR/REC-xml">
         <Title>
            Extensible Markup Language (XML)1.0 (Second Edition)
         </Title>
         <ShortTitle>XML</ShortTitle>
         <Abstract>Extensible Markup Language core syntax</Abstract>
         <FullAbstract>The Extensible Markup Language (XML) is . . .
         </FullAbstract>
      </Technology>
         . . .
   </XMLTree>
</Model>
```

The root of the subtree that describes our model, <XMLTree>, captures the only two pieces of state information in the system: the currently selected category and the currently selected specification document. These data are found in the attributes selectedCat and selectedSpec, respectively. The values of these attributes are IDREFs that point to the ID attributes of each individual technology. <XMLTree> has a series of Category elements followed a list of Technology elements. Category captures the information regarding a single category, while Technology describes a specific W3C technology publication.

The question of selection of what publications to include and how to categorize them is somewhat arbitrary. We have restricted ourselves to the most important documents, and to those that directly bear on or are directed at the use and theory of XML. Thus, for example, XHTML is not included. Moreover, when a Recommendation exists for a given technology and a draft of the next version also exists, we have chosen to document the Recommendation. Publications that state requirements for future specifications are also omitted on the belief that they are primarily of interest to those in the standards process and not practitioners. The XML included in the download is current as of the close of the editorial process (Spring 2001).

Category elements have an ID attribute, id, with which we can refer to them in the application. Like all XML ID values, these are unique within the scope of the document. In this case, that only means they are unique within the sub tree rooted by the <XMLTree> element, as we will use XPath to resolve IDREF values into the associated ID value. The XPath expression will be explicitly confined to the model, as we know that is where the information we desire will be found. Each category must display a title that will fit into one of our boxes. For simplicity, we elected to have a fixed-size box without automatic word-wrap capabilities or text sizing, so we need a title that is generally shorter than we might wish. In addition, we need a one-line synopsis of the category. The <Name> element captures a lengthy title for the category, while <ShortTitle> exists to capture a length-constrained variation of that title. <Abstract> contains the synopsis we will display.

Technology elements require a bit more information. They too, need ID-typed attributes, also named id. The value of the status attribute is a value belonging to the enumeration REC, PR, CR, DRAFT, and NOTE. The statusDate attribute is the ISO-format publication date of the document. Technologies are related to categories through the category attribute. As you would expect, these are IDREF-typed values that refer to the value of the associated <Category> element's id attribute. The source attribute is the HTTP URL of the document on the W3C Web site. Note that these items are generally not displayed directly. Instead, they are bookkeeping items that enable various bits of the processing specified in our requirements.

The exception to this is the value of statusDate. This value will be displayed as the copyright date of the document when the default copyright notice is used.

The child elements of <Technology> contain the information that is explicitly displayed in the user interface. The <Title>, <ShortTitle>, and <Abstract> elements function as they did for <Category>. Since technologies can quote text from the W3C document they model, we have added the <FullAbstract> element. An optional element, named <Copyright> and not shown in the fragment above, serves to capture the text of the explicit copyright notice, if any, as it appears on the W3C document.

We are not using a formal schema for this vocabulary. If we were, FullAbstract and Copyright would be open model content to allow us to include HTML from the W3C documents for formatting the text. In practice, a schema will be essential to document the API contract for programmers. It is convenient, however, during research, to be able to make ad hoc changes to the schema without requiring a formal change to a schema document.

Client-Side

We've mentioned that the client-side implementation differs from the server-side implementation in terms of how the controller is implemented and how views are updated. The client-side implementation is wholly self-contained (after the initial page requests), but must copy all the transforms and script it requires into the HTML page when it is initially generated. Besides avoiding round-trips, the client-side implementation has an additional advantage: views are updated individually. Only those views affected by a given event require a refresh. Because the transformations are focused, they are shorter than the server-side implementation's stylesheet. There is a drawback lurking in here, but that is best understood after we've written some XSLT instructions, so we'll save that for later.

Controller: Client-Side Javascript

The freestanding stylesheet that the XML document references sets up the shell of the user interface. It has one very important task beyond this, which is copying the controller script code down to the shell. Without this, the client-side implementation will not function.

Stylesheet Processing for the Controller

Here is the root-matching template in the XSLT stylesheet, LivingXML.xsl:

```
<xsl:template match="/">
   <HTML>
   <HEAD>
   <TITLE>XML Standards</TITLE>

   <script language="Javascript">
```

```
    <xsl:for-each select="Application/Intentions">
       <xsl:apply-templates />
    </xsl:for-each>

    </script>
    </HEAD>
    <BODY>
       . . . <!-- user interface DIV elements go here -->
    </BODY>
    </HTML>
 </xsl:template>
```

For our present purposes, constructing the controller, the template creates a `script` element in the `<HEAD>` element in the HTML page, then processes any elements in the XML document found under the `<Intentions>` element of the `<Application>` element. If you inspect `LivingXML.xml`, you will find the following child elements:

- `<comment>` – single line source comments
- `<commentBlock>` – multiline source comments
- `<codeBlock>` – script code

Since the comments are to appear within a `<script>` element, we need to wrap them in the language-appropriate construct and copy the comment.

> *For our present purposes, we need only copy the comments. A programming tool for SBP such as we envisioned earlier, might do something else with these elements to provide various sorts of support to the programmer.*

We've taken the shortcut of assuming JavaScript for our script language, so the templates look like this:

```
    <xsl:template match="commentBlock">
       /*<xsl:value-of select="." />*/
    </xsl:template>

    <xsl:template match="comment">
       //<xsl:value-of select="." />
    </xsl:template>
```

The template for `<codeBlock>` elements should be simple. We want to copy the value of the element into our output document. Since the XML document is shared between the client-side-only, and server-side implementations, we have an additional complication. Here is the template:

```
    <xsl:template match="codeBlock">
       <xsl:if test="@mode=$mode">
           <xsl:apply-templates />
       </xsl:if>
    </xsl:template>
```

The server-side implementation must distinguish between the initial request, when the client-side portion of the controller must be copied, and subsequent requests. We introduce the `$mode` variable to make this distinction. For the client-side only implementation, though, the stylesheet will only be executed once and there is no need to make this distinction. Fortunately, since the stylesheet is invoked through an `<?xml-stylesheet?>` processing instruction, there is no need to set that parameter. In the body of the stylesheet, we set a default value of `XML` for the `mode variable`, and set the value of the `mode` attribute to `XML,` for those code blocks that are unique to the client-side only implementation. The two match, so template processing continues. There are no further relevant templates in our stylesheet, so the default template for copying text takes over and moves the code we desire into the output HTML document.

Other SBP applications have made use of three additional elements. When we refine the concept sufficiently to warrant writing a formal schema for SBP applications, these elements will likely be there as children of `<Intentions>`:

- `<spec>` – note on the application's requirements
- `<rev>` – version controlled content
- `<limitation>` – comments indicating some known limitation of the application

The `<spec>` and `<limitation>` elements can and should be suppressed in the client-side source. The `<rev>` element has a `deprecated` attribute, which is a date value that indicates when the material was dropped from the current source. In this way, outdated material may be kept with the source so that some hypothetical development environment could reconstruct the text of the source as of any specified date. If the `deprecated` attribute appears, however, the material is outdated and must be omitted. All three elements are suppressed with the following template:

```
<xsl:template match="spec | rev[@deprecated] | limitation" />
```

Controller Script Code

The code that is copied into the HTML document consists of an initialization script, which executes in response to the `onload` event, some utility functions that make the controller work, and DHTML expansion functions that are attached to the physical view `<DIV>` elements that make up the user interface as event handlers for the `onclick` events. Here is the code that executes when the page is parsed:

```
var model=document.XMLDocument;
var catSelected=
   model.selectSingleNode("/Application/Model/XMLTree/@selectedCat");
var specSelected=
   model.selectSingleNode("/Application/Model/XMLTree/@selectedSpec");
var view=null;

var nlstCode=model.getElementsByTagName("code")
var nlstEvent=model.getElementsByTagName("event")
var nlstView=model.getElementsByTagName("view")
window.onload=initialize;
```

The first few lines set up some global variables so that they contain commonly referenced material. The variable `model` points to the entire XML document. The `catSelected` and `specSelected` variables are initialized by using an XPath expression to retrieve our state information; the attributes of the model's root element that track the IDs of the currently selected category and technology publication. Next, `view` is declared. We'll use it later when we bind views to events. The last three variable declarations declare and initialize lists of useful elements from the XML. All the code elements are stored in `nlstCode`, all events in `nlstEvent`, and all views – the logical views in the XML, not the physical views in the HTML – in `nlstView`. These collections will be needed when we bind events, views, and transformations. The last line sets the `initialize` function as the event handler for the main window's onload event.

When the `onload` event occurs, the HTML page is fully loaded, so the functions are resident within the page. At this time, the function `initialize` is called:

```
function initialize()
{
   catView.onclick=OnClickCat;
   catView.transform = transform;
   specsView.onclick=OnTechClick;
   specsView.transform = transform;
   coreView.onclick = OnCoreClick;
   coreView.transform = transform;
   abstractView.transform = transform;
   notify("start");
}
```

When that event happens, `initialize` is called to set event handlers for the `onclick` events of the various views. The name `catView`, as we shall see, is a `<DIV>` element that contains the category boxes. The `<DIV>` named `specsView` contains the boxes for the specifications belonging to the chosen category, and so forth. Each gets a specialized function as an event handler. Each `<DIV>`'s functionality is expanded with the addition of the `transform` function as a method of the `<DIV>`. Let's look at that function.

```
function transform(xslView)
{
   try
   {
      this.innerHTML= model.transformNode(xslView)
   }
   catch(e)
   {
      alert("Error during transform:\n\n"+e.description)
   }
}
```

This single function allows us to write some critical controller code in one place, and then call it from wherever it needs to be used without writing a lot of code to determine what view is being updated. The `this` object refers to the object bearing the method being called. This is why the `transform` function is assigned as an expansion of each `<DIV>`. All this function does is accept an XSLT transformation as a parameter, apply it to the XML model using MSXML's `transformNode` method, and push the resulting HTML into the `<DIV>`. The `transform` function is a key part of the controller, as it is the trigger for performing the XSLT transformations that updates views. To fully understand the controller, though, we have to find out how transform is called.

Let's inspect one of the `onclick` event handlers, specifically `OnCatClick`. From initialize, we can see this will be called when Internet Explorer detects a user click within the `<DIV>` named `catView`. We know that this `<DIV>` contains nothing but the gray boxes representing XML technology categories. This means the user is selecting a new category. Here is the source for that event handler:

```
function OnClickCat()
{
   catSelected.nodeValue=event.srcElement.id;
   specSelected.nodeValue="";
   notify("OnCatClick");
}
```

From an inspection of the code, you could plausibly argue that these event handlers should be classified as part of the model, since they update state information. Whatever the pedantic classification, though, they are essential. `OnClickCat` responds to a user click on a category box by setting the value of the `selectedCat` attribute, referenced by the `catSelected` variable to the `id` of the element originating the event. When we look at the XSLT that generates the physical views, we will see that we have contrived to give the dynamically generated IDs, which match the value of the `id` attribute of the `Category` element in the XML document that models the category. Thus, the box labeled **Applications** has the `id`, `apps`, which matches the value of the `id` attribute on the `Category` element that represents the **Applications** category. In short, we're updating the state information to reflect the currently selected category. A change of category will necessarily invalidate the current specification selection as a new category has a different set of specifications assigned to it. To reflect this, `OnCatClick` sets the value of the `selectedSpec` attribute to an empty string. Finally, it calls a function called `notify`, passing it the name of the event. Here is the source for the `notify` function:

```
function notify(event)
{
   var aNotify=getEvent(event).getAttribute("notify").split(" ");
   for (each in aNotify)
   {
      view=model.selectSingleNode("/Application//view
                                  [@id='"+aNotify[each]+"']");
      document.all(view.getAttribute("boundTo")).transform(view.firstChild);
   }
}
```

This is where things get as tricky as they ever get in the controller. First we have to identify the views requiring notification of the event, that is, we have to bind views to the current event. We start by calling the utility function `getEvent` to retrieve the event element in the XML document whose name matches the name passed as a parameter to this function. For our example, we need an `event` element whose `id` attribute has the value `OnCatClick`. Here is that function and its helper `getNodeFromID`:

```
function getEvent(strID)
{
   return getNodeFromID(strID, nlstEvent)
}

function getNodeFromID(strID, nlst)
{
   var node=null;
   nlst.reset();
   while(node=nlst.nextNode())
      if(strID==node.getAttribute("id")) break;
   return node;
}
```

This is where those list variables we set up when the page was initially loaded come into play. Since we are looking for an event, `getEvent` passes in the requested event name, `strID`, and the list of event elements, `nlstEvent`, as parameters to `getNodeFromID`. We have a similar utility routine for getting view elements. The function `getNodeFromID` walks the list until it finds a node whose `id` attribute's value matches the value of `strID`, then returns the node.

Returning to notify, we are still in the first line, but we have gotten the event node:

```
var aNotify=getEvent(event).getAttribute("notify").split(" ");
```

As you can see from the <event> element for this event, this attribute is a whitespace-delimited list of view element names:

```
<event id="OnCatClick"
       notify="showCore highlightCategory showSelSpecs showAbstract"/>
```

In essence, we need to notify the logical view for the core specifications, highlighted categories, selected specifications, and the displayed abstract. We call the DOM method `getAttribute` to retrieve the value of the `event` element's `notify` attribute. Calling the JavaScript `split` method on this string object completes the line by returning an array of the logical view names. Now we iterate through the list performing notifications:

```
for (each in aNotify)
{
   view=model.selectSingleNode("/Application//view
                              [@id='"+aNotify[each]+"']");
   document.all(view.getAttribute("boundTo")).transform(view.firstChild);
}
```

In each iteration, we call `selectSingleNode` on the XML model, passing it an XPath expression that locates the `view` element whose `id` attribute has a value matching the name of the logical view. What we really want is the physical view associated with it. When we have that object, we can call `transform` on it to physically update the user interface; the view. Here is the <view> element for the logical view `showCore`:

```
<view id="showCore" boundTo="coreView">
   <xsl:transform version="1.0"
                  xmlns:xsl="http://www.w3.org/1999/XSL/Transform">
      . . . <!-- lots of XSLT here -->
   </xsl:transform>
</view>
```

Using this, we see the name of the physical view associated with this logical view; in other words, the <DIV> we want to stuff with new HTML markup is given in the value of `boundTo`. So, returning to the last line of the `for-each` loop in `notify`, we see that we get the value of `boundTo`, and use the DHTML object model to call its `transform` method (which we assigned in `initialize`). The `transform` function requires an XSLT stylesheet, which happens to be the first child element of the `view` element. In short, the `for-each` loop traces the binding from events to logical views to physical views, then effects the view update by triggering the appropriate XSLT transformation and stuffing the output into the content of the physical view <DIV> element.

The MVC programming metaphor provides for dynamically associating views with events. This implementation does not extend that far. The linkage is established at design-time with the creation of the event elements. There is no conceptual reason why this cannot be accomplished dynamically using DOM calls to add, edit, and delete event elements to reflect changes in event registration; although this would likely introduce side effects such as we saw in procedural programming. Each event-handler transformation would remain invariant and provably correct.

Views: Different Transforms

Now we understand the model and the controller, but we've done an awful lot of hand waving with respect to the views. We assume that the HTML page is generated somehow on the initial request for the XML document, and we assume that physical views, <DIV>'s set up in that notional HTML page, are updated when the controller calls `transform`. Everything occurs as an XSLT transformation. Let's start with the transformation that initially creates the HTML page, and then look at a transformation that updates one of the views.

Page Creation XSLT

Several pages ago, we listed the template in `LivingXML.xsl` that matches the root element of the document `LivingXML.xml`, but omitted the contents of the HTML <BODY> element. Let's look at that now:

```
<xsl:template match="/">
   <HTML>
      <HEAD>
         <TITLE>XML Standards</TITLE>
         <script language="Javascript">
            <xsl:for-each select="Application/Intentions">
               <xsl:apply-templates />
            </xsl:for-each>
         </script>
      </HEAD>
      <BODY>

        <DIV id="coreView" event="OnCoreClick">
        <DIV title="Recommendation - W3C consensus is that the ideas are
                    appropriate for widespread adoption"
             style="position:absolute;top:0.2cm;left:0.5cm;width:0.5cm;
                    background:red;border:1px solid black;">
        </DIV>

        <DIV style="position:absolute;top:0.3cm;left:1.1cm;
                    font-family:verdana;font-size:10pt;font-weight:bold;"
                    class="status">
           Recommendation
        </DIV>

        <DIV title="Proposed Recommendation - the ideas are forwarded to the
                    W3C Advisory Committee following implementation
                    experience"
             style="position:absolute;top:.8cm;left:0.5cm;width:0.5cm;
                    height:0.2cm;background:#990000;border:1px solid
                    black;">
        </DIV>

        <DIV style="position:absolute;top:.9cm;left:1.1cm;
             font-family:verdana;font-size:10pt;font-weight:bold;"
             class="status">
           Proposed Recommendation
        </DIV>
      . . .
```

We begin by creating the `coreView` <DIV> element. This is the physical view containing the legend and the two core XML technology specifications, XML 1.0 and XML Namespaces. Note that it has an attribute named `OnCoreClick`. Creating the legend is a matter of writing hard-coded DHTML to the output document. Each colored box in the legend is created as a <DIV> with absolute positioning. Each <DIV> has a title, thereby utilizing Internet Explorer's tool-tip feature to display a brief bit of descriptive text explaining each step in the W3C process.

```
      <xsl:call-template name="list">
         <xsl:with-param name="x" select="8.0"/>
         <xsl:with-param name="y" select="0.5"/>
```

```
        <xsl:with-param name="nodelist" select=
            "/Application/Model/XMLTree/Technology[@category='core']"/>
      </xsl:call-template>
   </DIV>
```

The core technologies might have been hard-coded in the model. Instead, to enable the application to accommodate possible future additions to core XML technology, we label the `<Technology>` elements in the model that represent these publications with a `category` attribute value of `core`. We have a named template, `list`, which will do most of the hard work throughout our application. It takes a starting position and a list of nodes and renders them as a horizontal row of fixed size boxes at regular intervals. In this case, we start 8 centimeters into the document in the horizontal direction and 0.5 centimeters down from the top (the units are assumed and will be added in the template). For our node list, we use XPath to select all those `<Technology>` elements whose `category` attribute has the value `core`.

Next, we create another physical view, `catView`, for the categories:

```
      <DIV id="catView" event="OnCatClick">
       <xsl:call-template name="list">
         <xsl:with-param name="x" select="0.5"/>
         <xsl:with-param name="y" select="3.5"/>
         <xsl:with-param name="nodelist" select=
           "/Application/Model/XMLTree/Category[(position() div 2) =
            floor(position() div 2)]"/>
       </xsl:call-template>

       <xsl:call-template name="list">
         <xsl:with-param name="x" select="0.5"/>
         <xsl:with-param name="y" select="6.0"/>
         <xsl:with-param name="nodelist" select=
           "/Application/Model/XMLTree/Category[(position() div 2) >
            floor(position() div 2)]"/>
       </xsl:call-template>
      </DIV>
```

As before, we are using `list` to render the boxes that are the visual representation of `<Category>` elements. There are too many elements to fit in a single row that would be visible without scrolling, but we do not anticipate so many that we need to do complex calculations to determine the number of rows needed. We assume that two rows will be good enough. The filter:

```
   position() div 2 = floor(position() div 2)
```

gives us all the elements whose ordinal position in the node list is an even integer. Hence, our first call to the `list` template renders the even numbered `<Category>` elements, while the second call renders the odd-numbered categories (since the `floor` function will truncate the results of the integer division).

The next view on the page is the view for technology specifications. We name this `specsView` and assign it an event name of `OnTechClick`:

```
     <DIV id="specsView" event="OnTechClick">
        <xsl:if test="$selNode and $event != 'OnCoreClick'">
           <xsl:variable name="catID">
```

```
            <xsl:choose>
               <xsl:when test="name($selNode)='Technology'">
                  <xsl:value-of select="$selNode/@category"/>
               </xsl:when>
               <xsl:when test="name($selNode)='Category'">
                  <xsl:value-of select="$selNode/@id"/>
               </xsl:when>
            </xsl:choose>
         </xsl:variable>
```

The task here is to obtain all the <Technology> elements belonging to the currently selected category. In general, there should be no selected category since this code is only executed on the initial request, but this will not be true when we implement the server-side solution. In order to share the same XSLT stylesheet between implementations, we have to have code that determines the selected category, whenever there is a selected technology that does not belong to the core category. The variables selNode and event will be set up for the server-side solution. In the current case, these will always evaluate to false. When it is executed (in the server-side implementation), we determine the selected category by looking at the value of the category attribute if the selected node is a <Technology> element and by looking at the id attribute if the selected node is a <Category> element.

```
      <xsl:call-template name="list">
         <xsl:with-param name="x" select="0.5"/>
         <xsl:with-param name="y" select="9.0"/>
         <xsl:with-param name="nodelist" select=
              "/Application/Model/XMLTree/Technology[@category=
              $catID and (position() div 2) > floor(position() div 2)]"/>
      </xsl:call-template>

      <xsl:call-template name="list">
         <xsl:with-param name="x" select="0.5"/>
         <xsl:with-param name="y" select="11.5"/>
         <xsl:with-param name="nodelist" select=
              "/Application/Model/XMLTree/Technology[@category=
              $catID and (position() div 2) = floor(position() div 2)]"/>
      </xsl:call-template>
   </xsl:if>
   </DIV>
```

Similarly to the catView view, we use two calls to the list template to render our technologies in the view. In the initial pass of the client-side implementation, there is no selected category so no specifications are displayed. Finally, we throw in a horizontal rule to set off the publication's abstract, and then create the physical view, abstractView, for it. Since there is no selected category, there are no specifications. Without specifications, there can be no selected specification, and therefore there is nothing to display in this view initially. We shall study this part of the template in more detail when we look at the server-side solution. A similar body of XSLT will appear in the transformation associated with this view.

```
      <HR style="position:absolute;top:8.7cm"/>
      <DIV id="abstractView" style="position:absolute;top:14.0cm;font-
           family:verdana;font-size:10pt;">
         <xsl:choose>
            <xsl:when test = "$selNode and name($selNode)='Technology'">
               <xsl:call-template name="Abstract_TM_Statement">
```

```
                <xsl:with-param name="node" select="$selNode"/>
            </xsl:call-template>
         </xsl:when>
      </xsl:choose>
   </DIV>
</BODY>
</HTML>
</xsl:template>
```

An Event Handler Transformation

When LivingXML.xsl completes its processing, a finished HTML with the initial representation of the views and the controller script code is returned to the requesting browser. At that point and for this implementation, LivingXML.xsl is finished. All further transformations come in response to user events and originate in the logical views embedded in the page. The transformation that handles the rendering of the specifications view is representative. It is found in the <view> element whose id attribute is showSelSpecs. Each logical view contains exactly one child element, an XSLT <xsl:transform> element. This is synonymous with the <xsl:stylesheet> element and is a complete XSLT stylesheet:

```
<view id="showSelSpecs" boundTo="specsView">
```

The task in this view is to render boxes for all the <Technology> elements belonging to the selected category. This view may be asked to render in response to a number of events other than a change in category, so we have to provide for the case in which a specification is selected.

```
<xsl:template match="/">
   <xsl:variable name="selected"
                 select="/Application/Model/XMLTree/@selectedCat"/>
   <xsl:call-template name="list">
      <xsl:with-param name="x" select="0.5"/>
      <xsl:with-param name="y" select="9.0"/>
      <xsl:with-param name="nodelist" select=
               "/Application/Model/XMLTree/*[@category=$selected and
               (position() div 2) = floor(position() div 2)]"/>
   </xsl:call-template>

   <xsl:call-template name="list">
      <xsl:with-param name="x" select="0.5"/>
      <xsl:with-param name="y" select="11.5"/>
      <xsl:with-param name="nodelist" select=
               "/Application/Model/XMLTree/*[@category=$selected and
               (position() div 2) > floor(position() div 2)]"/>
   </xsl:call-template>
</xsl:template>
```

As with categories, we assume that two rows will fit everything in well enough. We begin with a root-matching template that we call list. This is where we run into our first problem. Since list is written in LivingXML.xsl and this <xsl:transform> element is in the body of the HTML page, we have to repeat list here. This is a problem with the client-side only implementation. We have no mechanism for reuse. We could use an <xsl:include> element or an <xsl:import> element, but that would violate the spirit of a self-contained entity. This area requires further study. For now, copying the list template and its dependencies is sufficient for our purposes. We check the selectedCat attribute of <XMLTree> to determine which category is selected. This helps us with the XPath expression that selects the nodelist we pass to list.

We never studied the `list` template when we discussed `LivingXML.xsl`. Since the only thing left in this event handler transform is `list` and its dependencies, this is a good time to look into it. Here is the `list` template:

```
<xsl:template name="list">
    <xsl:param name="x"/>
    <xsl:param name="y"/>
    <xsl:param name="nodelist"/>
    <xsl:variable name="firstnode" select="$nodelist[1]"/>
    <xsl:variable name="rest-of-list" select="$nodelist[position()!=1]"/>
    <xsl:variable name="selID"
                  select="/Application/Model/XMLTree/@selectedSpec"/>
    <xsl:if test="$nodelist">
        <xsl:call-template name="output-box" >
            <xsl:with-param name="selected"
                     select="boolean($selID = $firstnode/@id)"/>
            <xsl:with-param name="node" select="$firstnode"/>
            <xsl:with-param name="x" select="$x"/>
            <xsl:with-param name="y" select="$y"/>
        </xsl:call-template>

        <xsl:if test="$rest-of-list">
            <xsl:call-template name="list">
                <xsl:with param name="x" select="number($x) + 4.5"/>
                <xsl:with-param name="y" select="$y"/>
                <xsl:with-param name="nodelist" select="$rest-of-list"/>
            </xsl:call-template>
        </xsl:if>

    </xsl:if>
</xsl:template>
```

This template is an excellent example of some of the changes in technique that result from the shift to declarative programming. In a procedural language, you would normally iterate through the nodelist outputting boxes on the view. You would have some sort of explicit (as in a for-next loop) or implicit (as in a for-every loop) iteration variable. The value of this variable would change with each iteration. XSLT, however, lacks an assignment operator. Once created, a variable holds its value. We have need of two changing values in `list`: the current node (`$firstnode`) and the current x coordinate (`$x`). Recursion gets around this lack. When we enter `list`, we test to see if a `null` list has been passed. This is because a selected category might be empty. In addition, the first call to update this view will occur when the page is loaded and no category is selected.

> *The other views have no such problem and can guarantee that their nodelists will never be empty. If you examine the other copies of list in `LivingXML.xml`, you will find they do not perform this test.*

If a non-empty list was passed, we immediately split the nodelist into two parts: the first node and the rest of the list. We call the named template `output-box` to render the first node. That template takes `x` and `y` coordinates, the node itself, and a Boolean value indicating whether the specification is currently selected. We determine the value of the Boolean to pass, by comparing the first node's `id` attribute against the value of the attribute, `selectedSpec`, which tells us the name of the currently selected specification.

Now we have one box on the view and we need to know what to do next. First we see if there is anything left to process. If the remainder of the nodelist, `rest-of-list`, is not null, there are nodes left to render. At this point, `list` recursively calls itself. Now the passed nodelist is `rest-of-list`, and we can pass in the current `x` coordinate plus a known offset of 4.5 centimeters as the new value of `$x`. The value of the `$x` variable has not changed: on the call stack for this call, `$x` has the value that was passed in. The next call to `list` will have the incremented value for its `$x` value, and it will never change this. Eventually we will make a call to `list` with a nodelist consisting of a single node. We will output that box, discover `rest-of-list` is null, and terminate processing.

The `output-box` template is fairly simple. We will make fairly extensive use of DHTML and the `style` attribute in particular to create boxes with the interactive behavior we specified at the outset:

```
<xsl:template name="output-box">
   <xsl:param name="selected"/>
   <xsl:param name="node"/>
   <xsl:param name="x"/>
   <xsl:param name="y"/>
      <xsl:element name="DIV">
         <xsl:attribute name="title">
            <xsl:value-of select="$node/Abstract"/>
         </xsl:attribute>
         <xsl:attribute name="id">
            <xsl:value-of select="$node/@id"/>
         </xsl:attribute>
```

Each box consists of an HTML `<DIV>` element. We establish a `title` attribute whose value is the `Abstract` element in our model – remember, this is the short, one line abstract we provided – to get the tool-tip feature of Internet Explorer to give us some information about the publication when we hover over it. The `id` of the box, needed to update our selection state when the user generates a click event, is set equal to the value of the `id` attribute for the `Technology` element. This allows us to tie events in the view to the corresponding element in the model.

```
         <xsl:attribute name="style">
            cursor:help;border:1px solid black;position:absolute;
            top:<xsl:value-of select="$y"/>cm;
            left:<xsl:value-of select="$x"/>cm;
```

The `style` attribute of the `<DIV>` controls the appearance and placement of the box. In this case, we set the absolute position of the `<DIV>` on the page to match the `x` and `y` coordinates we passed into the template.

```
            z-index:1;width:4cm;height:2cm;
            background:
               <xsl:choose>
                  <xsl:when test="$selected">yellow</xsl:when>
                  <xsl:otherwise>
                     <xsl:call-template name="color-code">
                        <xsl:with-param name="status" select="$node/@status"/>
                     </xsl:call-template>
                  </xsl:otherwise>
               </xsl:choose>;
         </xsl:attribute>
```

The background of the box should be yellow if the specification is selected, or the proper color representing the publication's status in the W3C process otherwise. If the Boolean parameter `$selected` is `true`, we can generate the string `yellow` to control the background. Otherwise, we pass the value of the `<Technology>` element's `status` attribute to the `color-code` template to get the proper color:

```
<xsl:template name="color-code">
   <xsl:param name="status"/>
   <xsl:choose>
      <xsl:when test="$status='REC'">red</xsl:when>
      <xsl:when test="$status='CR'">blue</xsl:when>
      <xsl:when test="$status='PR'">#990000</xsl:when>
      <xsl:when test="$status='WD'">#cc9966</xsl:when>
      <xsl:when test="$status='NOTE'">#663300</xsl:when>
      <xsl:otherwise>white</xsl:otherwise>
   </xsl:choose>
</xsl:template>
```

That template outputs a named color or hexadecimal color code based on the value of the `status` attribute. The label placed in the box is going to be a hyperlink to the text of the publication on the W3C site. To accomplish this, we generate an anchor element:

```
<xsl:element name="A">
   <xsl:attribute name="style">
      color:black;text-decoration:none;font-family:verdana;
      font-weight:bold;font-size:10pt;position:relative;
      top:0.75cm;width:4cm;text-align:center;
   </xsl:attribute>
   <xsl:attribute name="target">new</xsl:attribute>
   <xsl:attribute name="href">
      <xsl:value-of select="$node/@source"/>
   </xsl:attribute>
   <xsl:value-of select="$node/ShortTitle"/>
</xsl:element>
```

Since we don't want to lose the application if the user follows the hyperlink, we set the `target` attribute of the anchor element to the value `new` so that the browser will open the publication in a new window. The text of the hyperlink is the `<ShortTitle>` element's value. You'll recall that we created this element precisely for this purpose because of concerns that the full title of the publication would not fit in our boxes. After that, we simply close all our open XSLT elements to complete the template.

As you can see, there is quite a lot of source to the templates `list`, `output-box`, and `color-code`. In the client-side implementation, these are repeated three times, once for each view. Obviously, we need to devise some mechanism that will permit us to reference templates that are not physically contained within a given logical view. The server-side implementation also suffers from this problem because it uses the same XML document. Although it will not call the client-side views, the text must be passed to the requesting browser, and that will include all this dead code.

Server-Side

If you've mastered the client-side implementation, you will find the server-side implementation much easier. Even though the controller is split between the client and the server, it is simpler than its client-side counterpart. This is because there is no need to link events and views. All views are updated on each server round-trip. The full body of `LivingXML.xsl` is executed for each request.

In addition, much of the XSLT is similar to what you have seen in the client-side implementation. Where this is the case, we'll mention it in passing and pass quickly over the common source with little comment.

Controller: HTML

We recall from our discussion of the client-side implementation, that the templates that copy code into the HTML page control use`<codeBlock>` elements, which are copied based on the `mode` parameter:

```
<xsl:template match="codeBlock">
   <xsl:if test="@mode=$mode">
      <xsl:apply-templates />
   </xsl:if>
</xsl:template>
```

We looked at what is copied when the mode is XML. If you request the server-side version instead, that is, by calling for the ASP rather than the XML document, the ASP code which we shall see in a bit sets the mode parameter to ASP before performing the transformation. Here is the script code that is copied when the mode is ASP:

```
window.onload = initialize;
function initialize()
{
   catView.onclick = notify;
   specsView.onclick = notify;
   coreView.onclick = notify;
}

function notify()
{
   if (event.srcElement.id != "")
      location.href = "LivingXML.asp?event="+
      this.event+"&amp;selected="+event.srcElement.id;
}
```

This makes up the entire client-side controller for our server-side implementation. As with the client-side implementation, we invoke `initialize`, but this version is a good deal simpler. There is no longer a need for `transform`, and there are no functions to perform the linkage between events and views. We simply pass the name of the event off to the server-side controller as a parameter in the request URL. In this version of the notify function, note that we are setting the current page's `href` property to be a URL to `LivingXML.asp` that includes the current selection and the name of the event. This triggers an HTTP request for the ASP causing the server portion of the controller takes over.

Controller: ASP

The server-side portion of the controller consists of an ASP page whose only function is to set some parameters and perform an XSLT transformation using `LivingXML.xml` and `LivingXML.xsl`. The most efficient way to do this using MSXML 3.0 on the server is with two free-threaded instances of the parser, one for each document, and an XSLT template object. The latter object is Microsoft's optimization for server-side XSLT processing. It allows a stylesheet to be compiled and cached for use in subsequent requests. We create the three objects with `<OBJECT>` tags. Note the `RUNAT` attributes. The `SERVER` value tells the ASP processor that these objects are to be instantiated on the server and that the `<OBJECT>` tags are not to be passed to the client:

```
<OBJECT ID="Model" PROGID="MSXML2.FreeThreadedDOMDocument" RUNAT="SERVER"/>
<OBJECT ID="xslt" PROGID="MSXML2.FreeThreadedDOMDocument" RUNAT="SERVER"/>
<OBJECT ID="xslTemplate" PROGID="MSXML2.XSLTemplate" RUNAT="SERVER"/>
```

Now we need to run some script on the server to perform the transformation and pass it back to the client. The first thing we need to do is get two parameters passed in the URL:

```
<%@ Language=JScript %>
<SCRIPT LANGUAGE="JScript" RUNAT="Server">
   var event=Request.QueryString("event").Item;
   if ("undefined"==typeof event)
      event="startUp";
   var selected=Request.QueryString("selected").Item;
   var bSelected=("undefined"!=typeof selected)
```

The initial request will have no parameters, so if `event` is undefined we set it to `startUp`. That way, our stylesheet can assume that it will always be passed an event parameter. The `ID` of the selected specification is found in `selected`. If it is not passed, as on the initial request, we want to set a flag so that we do not set a `selection` parameter for the stylesheet.

If we go to the trouble of creating a template object and pre-compiling the stylesheet, we want to get a performance benefit by caching the XML documents in the ASP `Application` object. That way, we bypass file I/O and parsing on subsequent requests. On each request to the server, therefore, we must check and see if such objects exist. If they do not, we load the documents from disk and cache them.

```
   if ('undefined'==typeof Application("Model"))
   {
      Model.async=false;
      Model.load(Server.MapPath("LivingXML.xml"));
      xslt.async=false;
      xslt.load(Server.MapPath("LivingXML.xsl"));
      Session("Model")=Model;
      Session("xslt")=xslt;
   }
   else
   {
      Model.load(Session("Model"));
      xslt.load(Session("xslt"));
   }
```

Now we need to use the Microsoft XSLT template object to create a processor for us. It is this object that is used in the transformation. This is done setting the cached stylesheet as the value of the template's `stylesheet` property and calling the `createProcessor` method:

```
   xslTemplate.stylesheet=xslt;
   xslProc=xslTemplate.createProcessor();
```

Now the processor needs an XML document on which to operate. We set the `input` property of the processor to be the object containing the parsed XML document. The processor's `output` property is set to the ASP `Response` object. That way, the processor will perform the transformation and put it into the `Response` object to return it directly to the browser.

```
    xslProc.input=Model;
    xslProc.output=Response;
```

We still have not executed the transformation and with good reason. Unlike our client-side implementation, which used the DOM to indicate state changes in the model, this implementation passes the current state to the stylesheet as global XSLT parameters. The XSLT Recommendation does not specify how processor implementations are to do this. In MSXML 3.0, we can accomplish this using the `addParameter` method on the XSLT processor object:

```
    xslProc.addParameter("event",event);
    xslProc.addParameter("mode","ASP");
    if (bSelected)
       xslProc.addParameter("selected", selected);

    xslProc.transform;
 </SCRIPT>
```

Once the parameters have been set, the processor is commanded to perform the transformation. When the script finishes, ASP streams the `Response` object, which now contains the HTML page with updated views, back to the client.

Although the server-side controller is a good deal simpler than its client-side equivalent, this simplicity comes at the cost of the purity of the MVC implementation. The client-side implementation enforced the strict linkage between events and the views created by them. The server-side implementation blindly updates all views in response to each event.

View: Transforms

All the views are created physically by the stylesheet with each request to the server. Since the controller is simplified, there is no need for logical views. The remainder of the server-side implementation's behavior, therefore, is found in the XSLT stylesheet. Although much of the XSLT is similar to what you have seen before, we will be investigating some processing that we glossed over in our previous discussion. In the client-case, the parameters did not exist, so certain paths through the XSLT were never executed. The server-side controller sets those parameters, so we need to look at what those elements do in our application.

To refresh your memory of the stylesheet, here are the parameters declarations:

```
<xsl:transform version="1.0"
               xmlns:xsl="http://www.w3.org/1999/XSL/Transform" >
   <xsl:output method="html" indent="yes" omit-xml-declaration="yes" />
   <xsl:param name="event">OnCatClick</xsl:param>
   <xsl:param name="mode">XML</xsl:param>
   <xsl:param name="selected"> </xsl:param>
   <xsl:variable name="selNode"
                 select="/Application/Model/XMLTree/*[@id=$selected]"/>
```

Note that this time, `event`, `mode`, and possibly `selected` will be overridden with values passed into the stylesheet by the processor. In particular, `mode` will have the value `ASP`.

Core Material

Processing begins with the creation of the shell of an HTML document:

```
<xsl:template match="/">
   <HTML>
      <HEAD>
         <TITLE>XML Standards</TITLE>
         <script language="Javascript">
            <xsl:for-each select="Application/Intentions">
               <xsl:apply-templates />
            </xsl:for-each>
         </script>
      </HEAD>
```

This is unchanged from the previous implementation, but since the `mode` parameter is now `ASP`, different `<codeBlock>` elements are copied into the client page. This is the controller code you saw in the section on the client-side controller.

Next, we enter the body of the page and create the `<DIV>` that contains the legend and the core XML technology boxes. This is unchanged from the preceding version, and processing is exactly the same:

```
   <BODY>
      <DIV id="coreView" event="OnCoreClick">
      <DIV title="Recommendation - W3C consensus is that the ideas are
                  appropriate for widespread adoption"
           style="position:absolute;top:0.2cm;left:0.5cm;
                  width:0.5cm;background:red;border:1px solid black;">
      </DIV>
      <DIV style="position:absolute;top:0.3cm;left:1.1cm;
                  font-family:verdana;font-size:10pt;font-weight:bold;"
           class="status">
         Recommendation
      </DIV>
      . . .
      <xsl:call-template name="list">
         <xsl:with-param name="x" select="8.0"/>
         <xsl:with-param name="y" select="0.5"/>
         <xsl:with-param name="nodelist" select=
              "/Application/Model/XMLTree/Technology[@category='core']"/>
         </xsl:call-template>
      </DIV>
```

As before, we rely on `list` to generate a row of boxes corresponding to the `<Technology>` elements selected by matching their `category` attribute value against the string `core`. `List` is the same, but `output-box` is a bit different this time. Since it is called from a variety of places, we need to test what sort of node is being processing by looking at the element's name:

```
<xsl:template name="output-box">
   <xsl:param name="selected"/>
   <xsl:param name="node"/>
   <xsl:param name="x"/>
   <xsl:param name="y"/>
```

```
<xsl:choose>
   <xsl:when test="name($node)='Technology'">
      <xsl:element name="DIV">
         <xsl:attribute name="title">
            <xsl:value-of select="$node/Abstract"/>
         </xsl:attribute>
         <xsl:attribute name="id">
            <xsl:value-of select="$node/@id"/>
         </xsl:attribute>
         <xsl:attribute name="style">
            cursor:help;border:1px solid black;position:absolute;
            top:<xsl:value-of select="$y"/>cm;
            left:<xsl:value-of select="$x"/>cm;
            z-index:1;width:4cm;height:2cm;
            background:
            <xsl:choose>
               <xsl:when test="$selected">yellow</xsl:when>
               <xsl:otherwise>
                  <xsl:call-template name="color-code">
                     <xsl:with-param name="status"
                          select="$node/@status"/>
                  </xsl:call-template>
               </xsl:otherwise>
            </xsl:choose>;
         </xsl:attribute>
         <xsl:element name="A">
         <xsl:attribute name="style">
            color:black;text-decoration:none;font-family:verdana;
            font-weight:bold;font-size:10pt;position:relative;
            top:0.75cm;width:4cm;text-align:center;
         </xsl:attribute>
         <xsl:attribute name="target">new</xsl:attribute>
         <xsl:attribute name="href">
            <xsl:value-of select="$node/@source"/>
         </xsl:attribute>
         <xsl:value-of select="$node/ShortTitle"/>
      </xsl:element>
   </xsl:element>
   </xsl:when>
   <xsl:when test="name($node)='Category'">
      <xsl:element name="DIV">
         <xsl:attribute name="title">Category:
            <xsl:value-of select="$node/Abstract"/>
         </xsl:attribute>
         <xsl:attribute name="id">
            <xsl:value-of select="$node/@id"/>
         </xsl:attribute>
         <xsl:attribute name="style">
            cursor:help;border:1px solid black;position:absolute;
            top:<xsl:value-of select="$y"/>cm;
            left:<xsl:value-of select="$x"/>cm;
            z-index:1;width:4cm;height:2cm;
            background:
               <xsl:choose>
                  <xsl:when test="$selected">yellow</xsl:when>
```

```
                        <xsl:otherwise>gray;</xsl:otherwise>
                     </xsl:choose>;
                </xsl:attribute>
                <xsl:element name="DIV">
                   <xsl:attribute name="style">
                      color:black;text-decoration:none;font-family:verdana;
                      font-weight:bold;font-size:10pt;position:relative;
                      top:0.75cm;width:4cm;text-align:center;
                   </xsl:attribute>
                   <xsl:value-of select="$node/ShortTitle"/>
                </xsl:element>
             </xsl:element>
          </xsl:when>
       </xsl:choose>
    </xsl:template>
```

We use the XPath function `name` to give us the element name of the node being processed, then output the DHTML for a box with slight adjustments to what is contained therein based on whether we are processing a `Category` or `Technology` element.

Categories

Next, the view containing the category boxes is generated. This is fixed data and the server-side code merely calls the `list` template with fixed XPath expressions:

```
<DIV id="catView" event="OnCatClick">
   <xsl:call-template name="list">
      <xsl:with-param name="x" select="0.5"/>+
      <xsl:with-param name="y" select="3.5"/>
      <xsl:with-param name="nodelist"
           select="/Application/Model/XMLTree/Category[(position() div 2)
           = floor(position() div 2)]"/>
   </xsl:call-template>

   <xsl:call-template name="list">
      <xsl:with-param name="x" select="0.5"/>
      <xsl:with-param name="y" select="6.0"/>
      <xsl:with-param name="nodelist"
           select="/Application/Model/XMLTree/Category[(position() div 2)
           > floor(position() div 2)]"/>
   </xsl:call-template>
</DIV>
```

Although this is unchanged from what got executed in the client-side implementation's initial pass through the data, there is one slight difference in behavior. This gets executed every time a request is made. Unlike the initial pass, there may be a category selected. Since the controller does not modify the model document using DOM calls (and cannot, as the document is cached and may be shared by multiple clients), the `selectedCat` attribute will not have a non-empty value set for it. The server-side implementation, consequently, does not keep track of the selected category when a specification is selected. The only time a category box will be drawn with a yellow background is when the category is initially selected and no specification selection has been made. Since the specifications themselves indicate which category is selected, this is a minor loss.

Selected Specifications

We are still inside the template that matches the document element. We now create the view for the specifications. The client-side implementation bypassed a lot of the processing since no category was selected. This is where processing begins to differ between the implementations. This template will be processed many times, so we need to see if a category has been selected and if a specification is selected:

```
<DIV id="specsView" event="OnTechClick">
   <xsl:if test="$selNode and $event != 'OnCoreClick'">
```

If the user is clicking on one of the core specification boxes, the selection category is cleared and no specification boxes should be displayed. Otherwise, we proceed.

```
      <xsl:variable name="catID">
         <xsl:choose>
            <xsl:when test="name($selNode)='Technology'">
               <xsl:value-of select="$selNode/@category"/>
            </xsl:when>
            <xsl:when test="name($selNode)='Category'">
               <xsl:value-of select="$selNode/@id"/>
            </xsl:when>
         </xsl:choose>
      </xsl:variable>
      <xsl:call-template name="list">
         <xsl:with-param name="x" select="0.5"/>
         <xsl:with-param name="y" select="9.0"/>
         <xsl:with-param name="nodelist" select=
                  "/Application/Model/XMLTree/Technology[@category=$catID and
                  (position() div 2) > floor(position() div 2)]"/>
      </xsl:call-template>

      <xsl:call-template name="list">
         <xsl:with-param name="x" select="0.5"/>
         <xsl:with-param name="y" select="11.5"/>
         <xsl:with-param name="nodelist" select=
                  "/Application/Model/XMLTree/Technology[@category=$catID and
                  (position() div 2) = floor(position() div 2)]"/>
      </xsl:call-template>
   </xsl:if>
</DIV>
```

If we are processing a `<Technology>` element, the `category` attribute gives us the category ID. If it is a `<Category>` element, then the `id` attribute does the same thing. We process specifications in two rows, first selecting all elements whose position in the node list is an odd number, then all elements whose position is an even number.

Abstract

Finally, we have to decide whether we need to display the full text of an abstract, which we have to do if a specification is selected. The client-side implementation did not deal with this in the stylesheet because nothing could possibly be selected on the initial pass. Since the stylesheet is always involved in the server-side implementation, this part of the template will get executed whenever a specification is selected.

Besides outputting the horizontal rule, we generate a <DIV> element with the id abstractView. This is the view for the abstracts in our application:

```
<HR style="position:absolute;top:8.7cm"/>
<DIV id="abstractView"
     style="position:absolute;top:14.0cm;font-family:verdana;font-size:10pt;">
   <xsl:choose>
      <xsl:when test = "$selNode and name($selNode)='Technology'">
```

The only case where we want to display an abstract is if a specification is selected. The first half of the XPath test expression tells us whether the selNode variable is empty. Since we may have selected a <Category> element, we have to use name to see if the selected node is a <Technology> element.

```
         <xsl:call-template name="Abstract_TM_Statement">
            <xsl:with-param name="node" select="$selNode"/>
         </xsl:call-template>
      </xsl:when>
   </xsl:choose>
</DIV>
</BODY>
</HTML>
</xsl:template>
```

If a <Technology> element corresponds to the selected box in the user interface, we proceed to call the named template Abstract_TM_Statement. This template is responsible for displaying the correct copyright notice. Although the full abstract is stored in our model, it is excerpted from a W3C document and we must comply with their legal requirements.

It is not possible to link to the copyright notice in the original document. Most W3C publications are published as HTML and therefore the copyright information is not consistently tagged. Also, some documents do not have a copyright notice, in which case we must display the default notice specified by the W3C.

Since we did not discuss the template that generates the abstract, we shall do so here.

```
<xsl:template name="Abstract_TM_Statement">
   <xsl:param name="node"/>
   <B><xsl:value-of select="$node/Title"/></B><P/>
```

This template starts by copying the full title of the publication from the node's <Title> element. This is within an HTML boldface element, and is followed by a paragraph element to ensure the title goes on a line by itself. Now we face a choice: if the Technology element has a child <Copyright> element, it means the publication has its own copyright notice that needs to be displayed; otherwise, we copy the default notice from the stylesheet to the output. Notice that the default has embedded HTML links. Also note that in the default case, we use the publication date, taken from the <Technology> element's statusDate attribute, for the copyright date:

```
   <xsl:choose>
      <xsl:when test="$node/Copyright">
         <xsl:copy-of select="$node/Copyright"/>
      </xsl:when>
      <xsl:otherwise>
         Copyright &#169; <xsl:value-of select="$node/@statusDate"/> World
```

```
            Wide Web Consortium, (Massachusetts Institute of Technology,
            Institut National de Recherche en Informatique et en Automatique,
            Keio University).All Rights Reserved.
            <xsl:element name="A">
               <xsl:attribute name="href">
                  http://www.w3.org/Consortium/Legal/
               </xsl:attribute>
               <xsl:attribute name="target">new</xsl:attribute>
                  http://www.w3.org/Consortium/Legal/
            </xsl:element>
         </xsl:otherwise>
      </xsl:choose>
```

Finally, we write a horizontal rule to separate the title and copyright from the abstract, copy the text of the `FullAbstract` element to the output. If you examine the model, you will find that some of the publications have embedded HTML in their abstracts.

```
      <HR/>
      <xsl:copy-of select="$selNode/FullAbstract"/><P/>
   </xsl:template>
```

Lessons Learned

This application was intended to be the "Hello, world" SBP application for one of the researchers. It served its purpose, but it also raised some interesting questions for the future as well as illuminating the current state of SBP practice. A fresh look by a newcomer often has that effect.

The client-side implementation, while very close to the pure MVC metaphor, is somewhat complicated in terms of the linkage between views and events. The controller code needed to effect this linkage is not complex, but understanding the XML markup and implementing it properly in the absence of a dedicated development tool is hard. There is no such linkage in the server-side implementation, but this loses some of the benefits of the MVC approach. Clearly, additional thought could be given to the schema for SBP documents.

Reuse of named templates is a problem for the client-side implementation. This is particularly true now that we are using XSLT rather than the earlier XSL preview. XSLT 1.0 introduced named templates and parameters, making it possible and desirable to accomplish with declarative XSLT what had previously been accomplished in script. As noted before, the standard `<xsl:import>` and `<xsl:include>` elements would serve, but this would diminish the benefit of having a single, self-sufficient XML document. Using DOM methods to insert reusable templates into logical views that use them would accomplish this. This would require the addition of SBP elements to indicate which views required which reusable templates, and it would require an additional procedural function to perform the reconstitution at load time. The relative merits of this remain to be explored in the laboratory.

Despite the complexity of the linking mechanism, it is impressive how much can be accomplished with transforms alone. Both controller versions are short sections of straightforward code. All the features of the application were accomplished through declarative means. Whether this will hold true for SBP in general is another issue. All the SBP applications so far – the polymorphic spreadsheet, SBPNews, and the Living XML Tree – are primarily information retrieval and display applications. An effort now underway promises to explore applications that require complex state and behavior.

Interfacing Procedural and Declarative Code

An interesting question is how to effectively interface procedural and declarative code. It is the nature of new paradigms to sweep the old methods before them and demand ideological purity, but we are practicing programmers and therefore skeptical of any method that prescribes a certain approach solely on the basis of theory. It might be an interesting intellectual exercise to build complex machines solely from wheels on axles – "The wheel is the future! Renounce that old, inefficient, inclined plane!" – but scarcely practical. Theories come in and out of fashion; what remains is a residue of the theory that has actual merit. The practice of programming is advanced, but the theorists are unhappy. Visual Basic owes much to object oriented programming – think of the "object.method" notation – but fails many of the critical litmus tests of that theory. No objective observer, however, would argue that Visual Basic is not the better for the additions.

Are our SBP applications easier than procedural implementations because these particular programs benefit so much from the procedural HTML processing implemented in Internet Explorer? We would argue not. Some useful and necessary things will be hard to accomplish in a strictly SBP approach. We remain convinced that real-world SBP applications will make liberal use of procedural components. What we do not know, though, is where that line should be drawn. Certainly procedural methods are suited for small-scale, focused tasks, but what is the right scale? What is the degree of focus past which we drop the declarative in favor of the procedural?

The answer seems to lie in deciding what declarative programs do best. This will imply what SBP does best, and therein will lie the answer to our question. The SBP applications produced so far, unfortunately, serve merely to introduce the practitioner to the implementation aspects of SBP. They merely hint at what SBP does best.

State Machines

SBP is declarative: it tells the computer what to do, not how to do it. This implies a distinction between high-level application logic and low-level implementations. Coupling declarative logic with declarative programming – the deliberate lack of an assignment operator being a prime example of the latter – makes possible the specification of applications that can make use of formal methods to prove program correctness. Theories such as automata and Petri Nets have been used to explore the theoretical underpinnings of computer science. The benefit of such theories is that they have a mathematical basis that allows formal proof of theorems. We can work forward from a declaration – the theorem – to a result. Procedural approaches and languages, with their messy side effects of executing algorithms, resist such proof. Debugging reigns supreme.

Of course, formal methods have kept academics busy for decades with only minimal benefits for practicing programmers. The audience for Wrox books tends toward people who need to write running code and away from those who admire an elegant theorem. Theorems are nice, but running code pays better and keeps the team leader at bay. If SBP cannot offer the practical programmer something, it is on a short, fast trip to the ash heap of computing history.

State machines are practical. Lift the cover of an Internet-related protocol implementation and you will likely find a state machine inside. State machines are declarative in that they specify what can happen in a given state. State machines are also close cousins of Petri Nets. One criticism we leveled at the Living XML application is that it did little in the way of modifying its own state, limiting itself to bits of dynamic state information: the selected category and specification. Even then, it used procedural DOM calls to modify its state rather than declarative calls. If we scaled this practice to applications with complex state, we would be unable to leverage the advantages of formal methods in SBP because we failed to use declarative methods to update the state.

Our model is an XML document, and we know XSLT is a good tool for turning one XML document into another. Generally, XML-to-XML transformations are used to convert from one vocabulary to another but there is no reason why we cannot use XSLT to move from one state in an XML document to another. That is, we can use XSLT to effect the transition from one state to another, provided we replace the initial XML model document with the document resulting from the transformation. We can implement a state machine using XML for recording states and XSLT for implementing transitions.

Petri Nets

Rather than reinvent the wheel, we can use Petri Nets for modeling a state machine. This has the happy side effect of bringing in the formal methods that other, smarter people have devised since 1964. A Petri Net is a graphical depiction of a state machine. If you want to impress your friends and confuse your managers, you can refer to it as a directed graph, or digraph for short. The rest of us will refer to it as a diagram with circles, rectangles, and arcs between the two of them. Faint attempts at humor aside, consider the diagram below. It is a Petri Net depicting an insanely simplified state machine for a word processor. The circles are **places**, the rectangles **transitions**, and the directed lines between places and transitions are **arcs**.

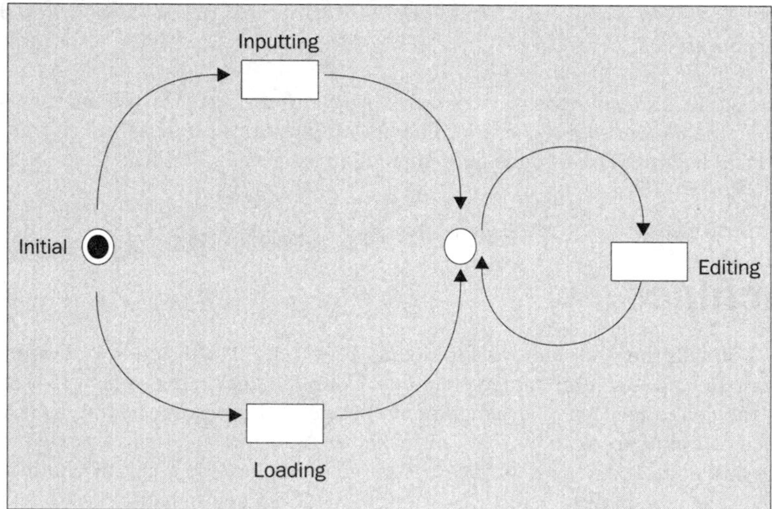

When the word processor has started but has no document in it, it is in the place named initial. Because it has a filled circle within it, we say the place is marked with a token. A marked place indicates the application is in that state. There can be multiple marks in a Petri Net. Moving through a transition removes the mark from the source place and transfers it to the destination place. For example, opening a file takes our notional word processor through the state transition loading, while entering text results in the inputting transition. Both transitions arrive at the ready to edit state. Further work moves the token repeatedly through the editing transition and back to the ready to edit state. Our net has a cycle in it and remains in the ready to edit state for the rest of eternity; clearly, our model is incomplete.

Once you have a Petri Net that accurately models your application, you can apply various algorithms to determine some properties of your system. For example, the utility we mentioned earlier in this chapter takes a Petri Net modeling a multithreaded application and predicts deadlocks.

The Shape of SBP Applications that Use Petri Nets

To use Petri Nets as the basis for our models, we need to replace the <Model> element in our sample application with a document written in an XML vocabulary that has enough information to represent a Petri Net. Happily, just such a vocabulary exists, the Petri Net Markup Language (PNML). PNML resulted from a desire to have a vocabulary for exchanging Petri Nets between modeling tools and is the work of researchers from Humboldt University in Berlin.

> *A summary of PNML is found at* http://www.informatik.hu-berlin.de/top/pnml/download/JKW_PNML.ps. *An XML schema for PNML, conforming to the W3C XML Schemas Working Draft of 7 April 2000, is available from* http://www.informatik.hu-berlin.de/top/pnml/download/stNet.xsd.

PNML documents include information about the topology of the nets they represent. They also include graphical information regarding the placement of symbols on a page.

> *There is a discrepancy between the document cited above and the PNML schema. The document states that the graphics element is optional, while the schema clearly marks it as mandatory. Our sample below conforms to the schema.*

PNML is still in its formative phases, and the use of PNML for SBP remains in the laboratory, so we will not go into the syntax of PNML. It is fairly simple, and fully described in the source above. To give you a taste of it, however, here is a minimal PNML representation of the Petri Net depicted in the previous section:

```
<pnml xmlns:xsi="http://www.w3.org/1999/XMLSchema-instance"
      xsi:noNamespaceSchemaLocation="stNet.xsd">
   <net id="wp1" type="stNet">
      <place id="p1">
         <graphics>
            <position x="10" y="20"/>
         </graphics>
         <name>
            <value>initial</value>
            <graphics>
               <offset x="-10" y="0"/>
            </graphics>
         </name>
         <initialMarking>
            <value>1</value>
            <graphics>
               <offset x="0" y="0"/>
            </graphics>
         </initialMarking>
      </place>
```

Because this place has an <initialMarking> element, it has a token in the initial state of the Petri Net. Note how the value of the <name> is a string that is displayed at an offset to the graphical position of the place itself. Transitions follow a similar structure:

```
   <transition id="t1">
      <graphics>
         <position x="20" y="10"/>
      </graphics>
```

```
      <name>
         <value>inputting</value>
         <graphics>
            <offset x="0" y="-5"/>
         </graphics>
      </name>
   </transition>
   <transition id="t2">
      <graphics>
         <position x="20" y="30"/>
      </graphics>
      <name>
         <value>loading</value>
         <graphics>
            <offset x="0" y="5"/>
         </graphics>
      </name>
   </transition>
   <place id="p2">
      <graphics>
         <position x="30" y="20"/>
      </graphics>
      <name>
         <value>ready to edit</value>
         <graphics>
            <offset x="-10" y="0"/>
         </graphics>
      </name>
   </place>
   <transition id="t3">
      <graphics>
         <position x="40" y="20"/>
      </graphics>
      <name>
         <value>editing</value>
         <graphics>
            <offset x="10" y="0"/>
         </graphics>
      </name>
   </transition>
```

Now that we've established all the places and transitions, we have to connect them with arcs. The graphics elements within `arc` elements are intended to represent positions on the arcs. Note how the connections are denoted by the `source` and `target` attributes. Since we don't have a graphical editing tool for these, we've taken the liberty of providing only a single point to demonstrate the structure:

```
   <arc id="a1" source="p1" target="t1">
      <graphics>
         <position x="12" y="19"/>
      </graphics>
      <inscription>
         <value>1</value>
         <graphics>
            <offset x="0" y="0"/>
```

```
            </graphics>
         </inscription>
      </arc>
      <arc id="a2" source="p1" target="t2">
         <graphics>
            <position x="12" y="22"/>
         </graphics>
         <inscription>
            <value>1</value>
            <graphics>
               <offset x="0" y="0"/>
            </graphics>
         </inscription>
      </arc>
      <arc id="a3" source="t1" target="p2">
         <graphics>
            <position x="24" y="11"/>
         </graphics>
         <inscription>
            <value>1</value>
            <graphics>
               <offset x="0" y="0"/>
            </graphics>
         </inscription>
      </arc>
      <arc id="a4" source="t2" target="p2">
         <graphics>
            <position x="32" y="22"/>
         </graphics>
         <inscription>
            <value>1</value>
            <graphics>
               <offset x="0" y="0"/>
            </graphics>
         </inscription>
      </arc>
      <arc id="a5" source="p2" target="t3">
         <graphics>
            <position x="32" y="19"/>
         </graphics>
         <inscription>
            <value>1</value>
            <graphics>
               <offset x="0" y="0"/>
            </graphics>
         </inscription>
      </arc>
      <arc id="a6" source="t3" target="p2">
         <graphics>
            <position x="42" y="22"/>
         </graphics>
         <inscription>
            <value>1</value>
            <graphics>
               <offset x="0" y="0"/>
```

```
            </graphics>
        </inscription>
    </arc>
    </net>
</pnml>
```

Now, PNML might not be enough by itself. It is restricted to modeling Petri Nets. Places and transitions are black boxes to PNML. However, we can certainly use XML namespaces to mix PNML constructs with our own, application-specific vocabulary. We might, for example, add `IDREF` attributes to places and transitions to locate model and view elements. As an alternative, we could open the content model for our model vocabulary and include PNML fragments as child elements.

Since we don't have a Petri Net utility in hand for modeling, we will need to do more. In fact, if we want to use PNML and SBP for applications, not just modeling and prediction, we will need to do much more. We need to build an engine to move tokens through the Petri Net. Put another way, PNML is the static representation of our state machine. We need an engine that brings it to life. As you might expect, we think a declarative Petri Net engine is in order; in fact, we can write a stylesheet that will take a given PNML document from one state to the next. Repetitively applying the stylesheet to the PNML document yields a new PNML document. Applying it again yields a new PNML document for the next state, and so forth. In fact, just such a stylesheet is in the preliminary stages of development and is described in "Professional XSL", Chapter 15 (ISBN: 1-861003-57-9).

We contend that bringing declarative methods to the model takes XML to a new level. We started with XML for data representation, then we added messaging (think SOAP and BizTalk) to facilitate e-commerce and application integration. With SBP and some formal mechanism to power the model, not just the views, we are actually using XML as a programming tool. We've gone from a dusty inclined plane for moving stones around the desert to the simple screw, and we all know where that led. Because it is built from an open medium, XML, and is declarative in nature, SBP is an open vessel suited to incorporating many different influences. After you have absorbed the basic SBP concepts of controllers and views in XML, the Living XML application is little more than an interesting parlor trick for programmers. Adding non-visual computing techniques such as Petri Nets to the model will extend SBP, we think, to the point of utility in production. Will such additions make SBP useful for producing real-world applications, or will SBP be most useful as a design tool? We will not know without further exploration. We have seen enough, however, to think that there is something substantial hiding in SBP and believe the most exciting discoveries in SBP lie ahead.

Distributed Systems

Petri Nets are closed systems. They model a single application or environment with an unchanging set of places, transitions, and arcs. They are more than adequate to model the behavior of monolithic applications. Increasingly, though, practicing programmers are getting involved with distributed systems. If the resources and interactions remain fixed, such as in a simple client-server system, Petri Nets in one of their variations remain adequate to model the behavior of the system. Dynamic distributed systems, with resources coming and going and actors dropping in and out of the system, go beyond the capabilities of Petri Nets. In fact, they go beyond the descriptive capabilities of automata theory, the really theoretical stuff that explains computing, as we have known it for fifty years. Such systems are not uncommon. B2B e-commerce systems fit this description, as do cellular telephone systems. You may be working on a system right now that classical computer science cannot explain. This is somewhat more serious than having a manager who cannot explain what you are doing. SBP, which is lashed to the masthead of Web development with ropes of XML, wants to go out and play with such systems. It's no fun developing the next new thing if that thing remains stuck in the twentieth century.

Happily, Professor Robin Milner of Cambridge University had thoughts such as these more than twenty years ago. The fruits of his labors (and many others in academia) are known as the Pi calculus. The Pi calculus is a mathematical tool for describing systems in which resources are transferred from one system to another, and interactions between systems are highly dynamic and transient. The Pi calculus is the foundation of at least one e-commerce tool shipping today.

If you want to see what the Pi calculus can lead to, turn to Chapter 25, and read the sections relating to the XLANG Scheduler and orchestration. If you are inclined toward the theoretical and have a firm mathematical background, you can begin your study of the Pi calculus with Communicating and Mobile Systems: the Pi-Calculus (Cambridge University Press, 1999 , ISBN 0-521658-69-1).

If the application of Petri Nets to SBP applications remains in the laboratory, the use of the Pi calculus in SBP is standing outside the laboratory door looking in. Whether it makes it into the model of an application, or webs of SBP applications will be controlled by another SBP application running a Pi calculus engine is unknown. It would seem, however, that distributed systems amenable to description with the pi calculus would be good candidates for implementation with SBP. BizTalk's XLANG Scheduler, after all, does something very much like this, though it certainly isn't implemented in XML.

Descriptions of systems for implementation with XLANG Scheduler are, however, written in an XML vocabulary named XLANG. This is an example of the second stage of XML applications: XML for communications. Applying Pi calculus to SBP would place us firmly in the third stage.

Is MVC the Last Word?

Is MVC an integral part of SBP applications? It has been so to date, and likely will remain the dominant way to write SBP applications with a visual component. Note though, our emphasis on the visual component. The V in MVC dominates. We must consider applications that are inherently non-visual, such as numerical applications or batch processing of data.

Even here, MVC cannot be ruled out. At some point you will need to extract some data for presentation to the user. Even if that data is stored and displayed by another application, for example a text file read in Notepad, you can think of this extraction as an MVC view. Consequently, MVC might still be useful in computing-intensive applications.

One place where MVC may not have a home is in coordinating, or meta-applications such as we suggested in our mention of the Pi calculus. An SBP application that exists to coordinate a dynamic and distributed system would not have an interface unless you wanted to provide a monitor for the system. A small, compact SBP implementation of such an application might forego views and concentrate on the model.

In general, MVC, Petri Nets, and other formalisms are useful tools that we intend to apply to the practice of SBP. SBP by itself requires nothing more than XML and declarative processing in which "the schema is the API". Join the research effort and you are free to explore your own programming metaphors.

Summary

We introduced you to a small yet interesting corner of the XML world, one that is still under construction. Schema Based Programming is an attempt to take the practice of XML-related programming from the first and second levels – data representation and messaging applications – to a third level in which XML-related technologies are used to implement the application. Since processing in such an application cannot do anything not provided for in the schema describing the model, we say, "the schema is the API". SBP, though still experimental, has the following working set of objectives:

- Introduce clarity of intent to application code
- Form the basis of a universal, declarative programming model
- Apply formal methods to the task of proving designs correct

We explored an SBP application that used the MVC programming metaphor to implement a guide to the W3C XML publications. We demonstrated this in two forms: one which downloads to the browser and executes thereafter entirely on the client-side, and one which is available to clients lacking XSLT support but which requires a server-side implementation. Both implementations demonstrated the following points:

- An XML document for the Model
- A series of XML elements and their associated transforms to implement Views
- A limited amount of script to implement the controller

Since SBP is an experimental work in progress, there is much exciting work to be done. One area in which prior SBP applications have been weak is in the area of the model. These applications have implemented simple behaviors in their models. We anticipate the future use of formal methods in SBP as engines that power the model. We devoted some time to an introduction to Petri Nets and the PNML vocabulary. Such formal implementations will bring the benefits of formal mathematical methods for prediction and analysis to the practice of programming. We hope for a world in which design, not debugging dominates the practice of software development. If we can attain this state, programming may stop being an art and become an engineering discipline.

We close this chapter by noting that SBP is as yet a small seed nurtured by too few researchers. It requires few tools and resources and is accessible to almost any programmer. A laptop or home system is a perfectly adequate development environment. SBP requires imagination and intellectual ability, not expensive hardware. If you worked through this chapter, you are more than qualified to join us in exploring SBP. SBP is a new frontier in programming, and there is enough unclaimed territory for everyone.

14

Data Modeling

Because we can write our own markup languages in XML, it is easy to jump straight into an XML project and define document structures without putting sufficient thought into it. The topic of data modeling in the relational database world is mature, and material on designing relational databases is common. However, there is comparatively little material available for those who are working with XML data models.

The design of the XML for our applications will affect how well our application works, and how long it will last. Our data model has to carry all the necessary information that the application and users require, but also has to be flexible enough to accommodate any changes that are required in the future. Many early adopters of XML jumped straight into creating their DTDs and models for their data, only to find that with hindsight they were not robust enough to withstand time. As their business needs changed, many had to go back to the drawing board and start again. So, in this chapter we will be looking at some key concepts that we need to be aware of when designing XML document structures to help create more robust, longer lasting models for our data.

Large portions of the data modeling process can seem quite theoretical. The whole idea of data modeling will be foreign to a significant number of programmers, as it was largely the realm of the relational database designer. But with the increasing use of XML, both programmers and database designers have to learn and understand what it means to create a data model. In this chapter we will introduce data modeling in three sections:

- Information modeling – understanding the information that will be carried in documents: its structure and meaning
- Document design – how we translate the information model into XML documents
- Creating Schemas – which allow us to record document design so that processing applications and other users can work with the schema

We will talk about the processes involved in each of these stages and then look at some more specific issues regarding how we use the XML syntax to model some specific types of information along the way. We will also look at some of the new features that XML Schemas will allow document authors to utilize.

When I use the term schema, I mean it in its generic sense of a DTD, XML Schema or any other schema technology. I will specifically use the term ***XML Schema*** *when I am referring to the W3Cs Proposed Recommendation.*

Introducing Data Modeling

There are three key processes to creating a data model – information modeling, document design, and writing the schemas. The level of detail that we will be able to go into depends on the time we have available to work on the project. In the real world, it is unlikely that we will be able to spend as long as we would like to on the information modeling stage of a project. However, by understanding the key concepts to modeling data we will be able to select those that we feel are most important to the task in hand.

One key thing to remember is that it always pays to look at what is already available to us when we start working on a project. Later in this chapter we will look at schema repositories where we can look for schemas that are already used in our problem domain. Whether it is a case of borrowing structures from these schemas, or just clarifying what tag and attribute names others are using, looking around at other projects is time well spent before starting our own. In particular it is worth remembering that, if there is already a schema for some aspect of our industry, a lot of work may well have gone into this already and studying any available resources will only help us in our task.

Information Modeling

We start the three part modeling process with the **information modeling** stage. In this stage we look at the problem domain, and decide on the concepts that we need to model to get the job done. By the end of this stage we will have a list of objects and properties that are involved in the process we are trying to model, descriptions for each of them, and an idea of where the information goes from and to in each stage of the task at hand.

Information modeling is totally independent from any technology that we might use to implement the project.

The independence of an information model from the technology that is used to implement it means that it would be just as valid to perform the information modeling stage for, say, creating paper forms, as it would for a system using XML. It is still important to look at, because this stage is the foundation for creating our markup; despite the removal from technology we will see that the objects and properties we define in this stage often end up becoming element and attribute names later in the modeling process.

Whether we share the information model with others or keep it in our head, there will be one for every project. Of course, there is a strong advantage to sharing the information model with those who are working on the project. Ideally we would be sharing it with others who may use the schema afterwards as well, because the terms we come out with at the end are core to the business and it would help if everyone could share them. There are two types of information model that we must think about:

- **The Static Information Model**. Representing the objects that are involved in the problem domain – we have to give them names and a description, for example: **customer**, **invoice**, and **transaction**. We also have to describe:

    - The different states that a system can be in, for example – "a customer can have one or more accounts"
    - Properties, such as "a dress can be small, medium, large or extra large"
    - Relationships, for example "a refund is a type of transaction"

    At the end of the static information model we should end up with a document that acts as a dictionary of terms to describe concepts used in our business domain, with diagrams of how these objects relate to each other.

- **The Dynamic Information Model**. Representing how the information gets created and then moved from one place to another to get the job done, for example "the sales department generates an invoice and passes it on to the accounts department". It could involve a workflow or process diagram, and an object life history or data flow model.

    Dynamic models are generally used to represent transient information, such as messages.

There are specific methodologies that we can apply for information modeling, such as **UML** (**Unified Modeling Language**), but we will be focusing on general principles here. We will avoid a specific methodology because there are two objectives involved in information modeling that can seem to work against each other:

- Achieving a precise definitions for the concepts we are modeling
- Communicating the model effectively to all users

The problem lies in the way that, while formal methodologies can offer greater precision in defining the concepts we are modeling, we have to be familiar with the notations they use and how they represent the information. Those who are not familiar with the notation used by a specific methodology will not be able to makes sense of the model, so the use of such a notation can restrict the effectiveness of the model in getting the concepts across. So, in this chapter we will be using a general form of diagrams that is easily understandable to all with minimal explanation.

> *If you want to find out more about UML, visit the rational web site –* *http://www.rational.com/media/uml/resources/media/ad970803_UML11_Summary.pdf* *is a good place to start, or check out a book such as* ***Instant UML*** *(ISBN 1861000871) by Pierre-Alain Muller, published by Wrox Press.*

We should note that some information modeling processes use the terms *entity* and *attribute* in quite a different way to what we are used to in XML, so to help prevent confusion we will use the following alternative terms:

- **objects** rather than entities
- **properties** to represent characteristics of objects rather than attributes.

Whether you start with the static or dynamic modeling stage is up to you, but one important thing to remember is not to consider one stage finished before moving onto the next one. Whether you start by defining the static or dynamic models, you should always be prepared to come back and change the other.

Indeed the boundaries between the two can often appear to be blurred, as objects may appear to be events (a sale of a product can be seen as an event, and an order can start life as a document); how we model these ambiguous items is up to the developer and the situation they are in.

It is usually helpful to start with the static model, as these items find their way into the dynamic model. Or at least start with the first step of the static model, which as we shall see shortly involves identifying, naming and defining objects.

Whether you start with the static or dynamic model, the first step is to find out where you are now and what is already defined:

- What is the scope and purpose of the system?
- How much influence do we have over the project, and the decisions that are going to be made?
- Is there already a set of well-defined business processes (has a business analyst defined what happens at each of the stages involved in a problem domain)?
- Do we need to develop new processes (are we integrating an e-commerce system with our existing applications)?
- Is there an existing schema that applies either to our industry or to a part of the problem domain that we can draw ideas from?

If we are just going to reproduce an existing system, we can use the documents that are already in place as a good starting point and guidance for structure and names for electronic counterparts, then we can talk to users about how the information gets recorded and where it comes from, and goes to. More often, however, it will be necessary to go into more depth. For example, if we are creating an e-commerce system for a bricks and mortar company, we will not be completely mirroring the existing process – there may be all sorts of new factors to consider, such as how we get the goods to the customer, how we can track the goods if the customer claims that they have not received them, and how we can maintain the catalog of products on the web site.

Anyway, let's get on and look at the information models, starting with the static information model.

The Static Information Model

We will be creating our static information model in four steps:

- Step 1: Identify objects, name them, and define them
- Step 2: Organize them into a class hierarchy
- Step 3: Define relationships, cardinality and constraints
- Step 4: Add properties to objects

Step 1: Identify Objects, Name Them, and Define Them

The first step is easy to get started on – simply write down all of the things in the system: **customer**, **purchase order**, **product**, **service**, **supplier, employee**, and **department**. We shouldn't take too long over this stage; we can always come back and add things as the need is found later on in the modeling process. We will refer to these *things* as **Object Types**.

Always try to come up with names that people in the relevant field will be able to understand quickly and easily. This may mean that you come up with longer names, or use standard abbreviations, either of which is acceptable because people will not always be checking your definitions and clarity is the key here.

Once we have done this, we should produce a definition for each of these. The definition is important because it has to remove ambiguities – for example, if an order becomes an object in our model, we need to know whether an amended order is the same order, or a different one. As we will see, there are a lot of questions we can use, and statements we can make to help us tie down the definition, such as:

- If a customer wants two of the same product delivered, one to themselves and one to a friend, is it one order or two?
- Is a service the same object as a physical product?
- Is a returned product counted as the same type of object as a product that is for sale?

There are two very useful questions for most business domains here:

- Is X an order?
- Are X and Y the same thing?

The first question helps draw boundaries, while the second helps us distinguish things. If we asked different people, we would probably get different answers to the same questions, which only serves to highlight the importance of the information modeling process. We need to make sure that all those involved in creating and using the system understand what it is they are working with.

It is also worth thinking about how we are going to identify individual instances of these objects. For example, books already have ISBN numbers to identify them uniquely (we can see the ISBN for this book on the back cover by the bar code – it is the number 1-86100-5059). There may already be an industry term to define some objects, whereas others we will have to come up with ourself, such as customer identification numbers.

At the end of this step we should have a list of objects and their definitions, but remember there is always time to change and add to it later – do not worry if it is not completely exhaustive, we will find other things that we may need as we continue through the process.

Step 2: Organize Objects Into a Class Hierarchy

Once we have our objects, we need to organise them into types or classes (and by this, I don't necessarily mean "classes" in the OOP sense). We will see that this is very useful when we come to take the information model across to a schema, but for now we just want to create a hierarchy of related definitions:

- There are two types of Customer: they are Individual and Company
- Any Service is a different object than a Product

This information is represented in the diagram below:

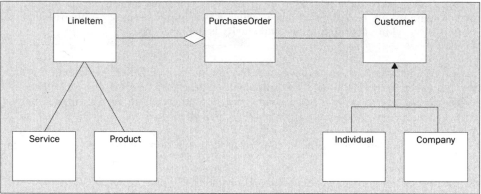

LineItem
PurchaseOrder
Customer
Service
Product
Individual
Company

Here we can see that there are naturally two types of customer, and that we classify a service differently than a product. This is the process of deciding whether something is an instance or type: a Company is a type of Customer. The **is-a** relationship is very useful to represent a relationship, and allows us to define subtypes in our hierarchy (x is a type of y). It is important that as we travel down the tree, we don't have instances of an item existing without the class above it.

While experience in object oriented design may help, be careful not to think in terms of classes as modules of functionality – they should instead be named after the things they represent in the real world. If we use verbs rather than nouns, we may well be falling into this trap.

Step 3: Finding Relationships

Once we have defined our object types, we need to find the relationships between them and add them to the information model. A good way to approach this stage is to use sentences:

- A PurchaseOrder is made up of one or more LineItems
- A LineItem can be made up of a Service or a Product

These relationships or associations can be shown in a diagrammatic form – we have added them to our diagram below.

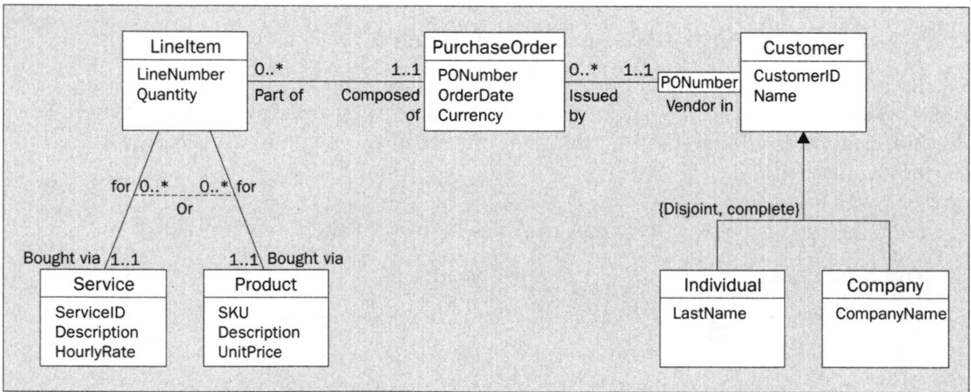

There are many different forms of notation to define the relationships. Here we will look at the two most important aspects of relationships: cardinality and containment. The numbers at the end of each line are the same notation as UML to indicate how many occurrences of an object can occur at each end of the relationships:

- 1..1 – a minimum and maximum of one (for example a customer should only have one billing address).
- 0..*n* – from zero to n objects (the order may involve zero to many copies of an Album in CD format).
- 1..*n* – there will be a minimum of one, and no limit on the maximum number of items (for example we will have at least one shipping address, but different items may need to be delivered to different addresses).

Along with the lines, these numbers represent the **cardinality** of a relationship, how many of each object type can take part in a relationship:

- **One-to-many** – this is the most common: an order can request several albums and singles. At this point we also have to say how many of the objects can be at the end, for example, at each end we may always have a direct mapping of one child for every object (such as a customer having a name) or we may have anything from zero to many objects at the destination of the relationship (an order may include several CDs or none).
- **Many-to-many** – for example an artist may record several albums, or an album may have several artists if it is a compilation.
- **One-to-one** - which is less common, but may relate to a person and their available credit.

One particularly important kind of relationship is that of containment, which is always one to many or one to one. Again we are best off deciding **containment** using sentences, such as an order requires a delivery address. There are two types of containment:

- **aggregation –** where objects form a group of things that are treated for a period of time as a whole (such as an order with several products and customer details). This makes their relationships many-to-many, so we should be careful not to stretch this type of containment to relationships that are one-to-may.
- **composition –** where the parts have no existence of their own, for example if a CD is a double CD we would not want to model the two CDs independently of each other. This is represented using a diamond at the end of the relationship, in a UML diagram. If we see a diamond at the end of a line we should be able to represent the relationship in XML as a containing element and a child element. For example:

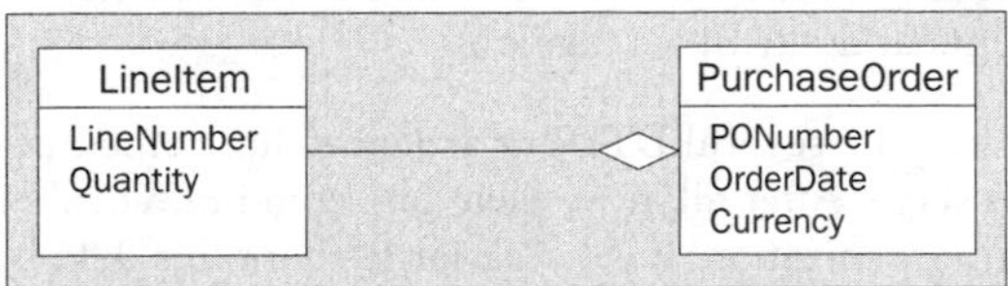

The level of information you choose to add to the diagrams is up to you, but personally I find it better to keep the diagrams relatively simple – only indicating key points, then adding finer grained detail in a text document to accompany the diagram, which also makes them easy to maintain (although it is important to get the key concepts in the diagram as you cannot be sure that people will read the accompanying documentation and update it when changes are made).

By the end of Step 3 we should have added relationships to the object types in the model.

Step 4: Defining Properties

Properties are what really flesh out the objects – they have values that are associated with the objects. Typically they represent concepts that would not exist without the object. For example, a CD may have a unique identifying number, a price, and a category they should be shelved under. Properties do not need to include relationships, as they are implicitly modeled in the relationship stage. We do, however, need to know their data type; whether there is a fixed range of allowable values, whether it is numeric, what are the units we measure the property in, whether it is optional and what the default is if any.

Those who are familiar with relational databases will probably be used to creating tables in which an object's properties have only single facets (for example, a price would just have an amount, not a currency as well); otherwise we normalize the data by adding another table. With XML this discipline no longer has to apply, as it is possible for a property of an object to have different facets, for example we could make a price element, which carries attributes for or has child elements representing amount and a currency. Remember that we are still operating at a level removed from the technology – we are just adding properties to the abstract model; we are not saying that all properties must be modeled as attributes when we come to creating a schema.

In UML we can model the properties of an object in a box, which describes the object. Some people choose to show the properties separately from the diagram as it can get rather complicated, for example we may wish to add them to a spreadsheet, but if we choose to do this it is still helpful to include some of the key properties as it helps remove ambiguity.

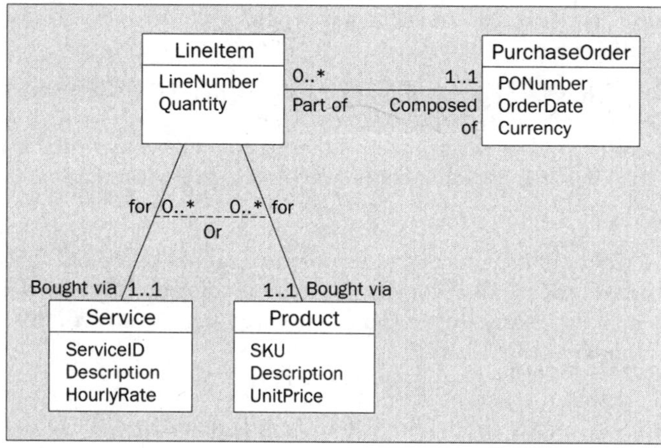

By the end of Step 4 we have a complete static model, with a definition of types of objects available to the system, the relationships between them, and their properties. The definition of object types will undoubtedly become the focus of element and attribute names, while the relationships will affect the structures that these elements and attributes take on.

When you think that there may be several DTDs or schemas that come out of this model, you can appreciate the worth of this stage. After all, if we have one common vocabulary and set of definitions, which is used throughout an organization, it is far easier to share this data between parties that need it. You can easily imagine that if two departments were left to create their own schemas for information that would be passed between them, they may come up with very different schemas using different terms and different structures. If you start by defining the terms that can be used and the relationships between these objects, then it is possible to generate many schemas that form this base point. They will be a lot more interoperable because they are sharing common terms that have a set meaning, and uniform coding.

So, now lets turn our attention to how the data flows through a system.

Dynamic Modeling

Dynamic modeling determines what happens to the data that we have already defined in the static information model. However, it is wrong to think that it is now too late to change the static model – it is not unusual to go back and forth between the two, changing both as is necessary. We have to look into how the data will be flowing through the system – we often look at dynamic models in terms of **messages** flowing through a system.

Note we use the term message here in a generic sense in that the message can be a document, object data, or data from a database.

There are many ways in which we can approach dynamic modeling, and indeed whole books are written on these topics, so we will be taking a brief look at several of the possible approaches, so that you can choose which ones you want to learn about. The approaches we will outline here are:

- Process and workflow models
- Data flow models
- Object interaction diagrams
- Object models and Object life histories
- Use cases

Essentially, when we are looking at dynamic modeling we are looking at the different stages the information goes through in its journey from being created, through processing, to where it is stored.

- Where does the data come from? Which part of the process passes it to the current stage? You should also look at *how* the data is created (whether this becomes part of the dynamic model depends on the approach you use).
- When each stage receives some data you then have to look at what has to be done to it. What tasks need to be performed (and sometimes how are these tasks achieved)?
- What happens to the data after this stage has been completed?

For example, imagine we were designing an e-commerce application. Who creates the purchase order? In this case it is likely to be the customer interacting with the application we have provided. The purchase order may be dynamically created server side (perhaps using Active Server Pages or Java Server Pages), but we are not yet worried about the implementation, we just need to know what information is required to make up a purchase order, and who creates it. What then happens when we have their order? We may need to calculate totals for the items that they have ordered. Finally, where does the information go? If we provide items on account the next stage may be to check their credit-worthiness before allowing the order to be processed. All these things are the types of data we need to be aware of and how they achieve the task in hand.

At each stage of the dynamic model you are looking at what data needs to be passed from one party to the next, and what operations can take place at each stage during the flow of the data.

Once we have this information it will be easy to see what each message in a system needs to relay to the next part of the application, and we can get on with designing our document structure, knowing what information they need to carry.

We will not have time to use all of the dynamic approaches, but by looking at how the different approaches let us model the flow of data through an application, we will get an idea of the tools available to help us understand how data is created, where it goes from and to, and then where (although not how) it will be persisted.

Process and Workflow Models

Process and workflow models are possibly the most common form of dynamic model. They take the form of a flowchart, which represents the roles of individuals or departments in creating, processing, and storing the data throughout an organization. For example, who deals with collecting orders first, how do we ensure payment of accounts, how do we get the product to the person, who ordered it, etc. It is essentially the different stages of any process the system is intended to deal with. The information stores take second place in this kind of model; we just say when the data gets persisted, not how. Here is an example of a workflow diagram:

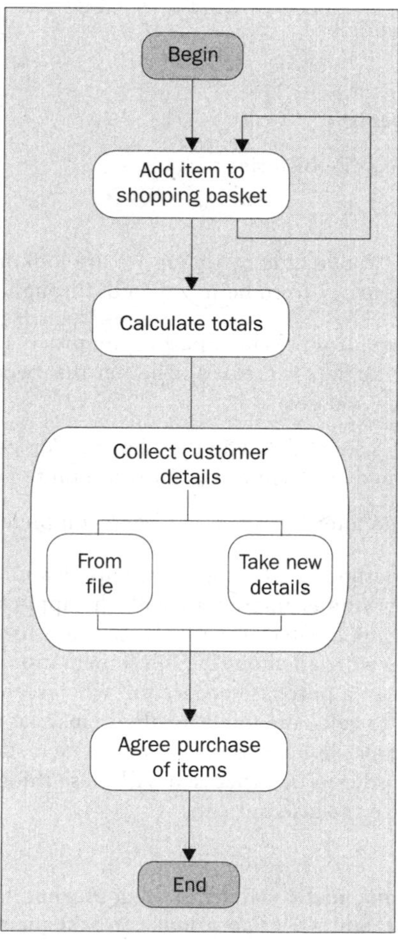

There are a number of tools that are available to us to help in this process. Some people use a tool such as **Visio** to create flow charts, while others use specific enterprise modeling tools such as **Rational** (http://www.rational.com), or Popkin Software's **System Architect 2001** (http://www.popkin.com).

The granularity with which you create a process or workflow model is up to you, but it is often worth dividing up processes so that you do not end up with extremely complicated diagrams which barely fit on a piece of paper. Once you have done this, you should trace the flows between separate stages to ensure that you have not missed any stage and that the information flows are coherent.

Data Flow Models

Data flow models are very similar to process and workflow diagrams, but have more focus on the information systems than the business. A data flow model describes data stores where information is held persistently (whether in a database or a filing cabinet), processors that manipulate the data, and data flows that transfer the data between processors and data stores. It relies heavily on the concepts described in the static model, as it might say that x type of information is held in y type of database, and that information in the y database represents orders that have been shipped. This database will only hold the summary of the sale, while the accounts database will hold details of the financial transaction.

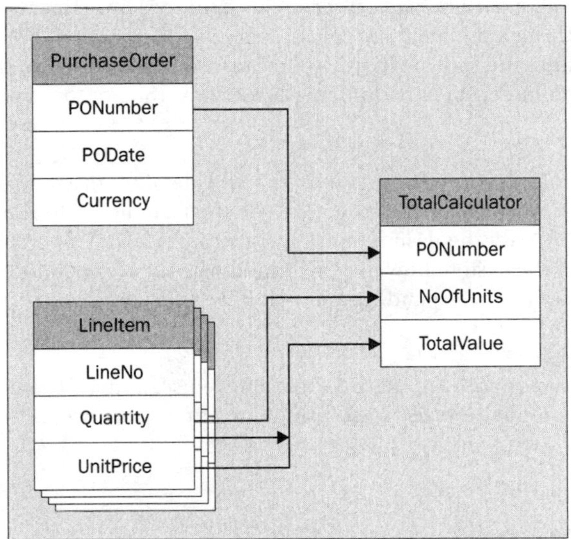

Object Models and Object Life Histories

Object models describe the methods and calls that can be made on data held in an object (essentially what can be done to each object), while object life histories (also known as object lifelines) also include how the component is created and destroyed on top of the capabilities of each.

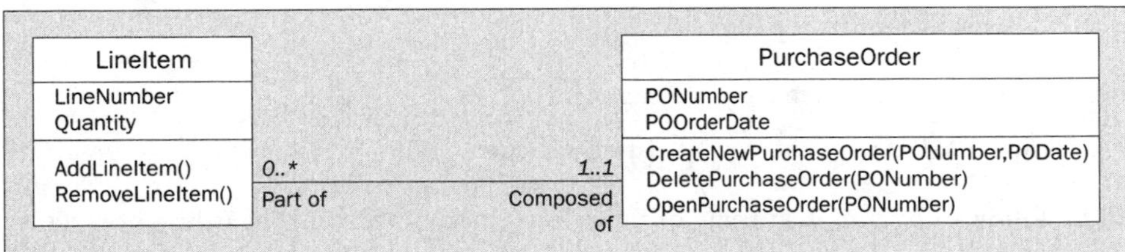

These two dynamic modeling processes can be useful, but tread on interesting ground. Remember that we are still supposed to be abstracted from the implementation of the project. Personally, I find them more useful when the data modeling is completed and you get into system design. In any case, they can both be used at this stage.

Use Cases

Use cases analyse how a user accomplishes a task, such as how someone buys a CD or returns it. A use case is rather like a process model, but generally focuses on the activity of one particular user. It is difficult with this approach to separate the user from the behavior of the system, as the two are often intertwined (especially at the user-interface level – but remember to focus on the information being passed between the two, not how it is presented to the user). They can be particularly useful for checking the integrity of the other dynamic modeling approaches, especially process, workflow and data models.

Choosing a Dynamic Model

As we can see, there are several ways that we can model the flow of information around a system. Indeed, many of them are complementary, and it would be great if we could follow through each before designing the documents that will be passed throughout the system. However, time is rarely on our side, and if we really are to create a dynamic model, we may only be able to choose one approach. As we can see there are several different options when it comes to creating a dynamic model, unfortunately there is not space to go into them in depth, but some might sound as though they suit our situation more than others.

Remember that we do not have to be meticulous in every detail of the models, monitor version control, etc. They could just be a sketch on a piece of paper on the train home to share with others, or written on a whiteboard in a meeting with the design team. Just getting a feeling for how the information should flow through the parts of the system however, will help when it comes to designing the system itself. The models are particularly worth spending time on if we are working on a project that integrates different existing systems together.

So, having generated a static model of the information we use, and a dynamic model of how it flows through the system, we should be ready to start looking at the structure of the XML documents that will be passing through the system.

Designing XML Documents

By this stage, we already have both static and dynamic models for our information, so now it is time to design our XML documents. This will involve creating XML documents to pass information between the various stages of the dynamic model that we have identified, relying heavily on the dictionary of objects and properties, along with their relationships that we have defined in the static model.

In this section, we will start with a look at:

- Creating XML documents for messages
- Creating XML documents for persistent storage

This will be followed by a look at some of the related modeling issues regarding how we structure these documents:

- The size of our documents, and the effects size can have on processing and retrieval
- Naming Conventions

- The old element versus attribute debate
- Handling binary data
- Encoding of property values
- Representing relationships
- Modeling the object type hierarchy

When we are working in this document design stage, we have to consider the different types of document that may apply.

If you are familiar with designing schemas, you may choose to get straight on with the design of the schema, but if you prepare some sample documents first it will help you to create the correct type of schema. If you are to start on the schema straight away it is easy to miss some of the different types of document that a schema may address.

> **Remember that there may be different structures in document instances that are constrained by the same schema.**

When we looked at defining objects that have properties, we specifically said that they did not directly correspond to elements and attributes. Whether we want to go for element content or attribute values for the information represented by any part of the model is still open. For example, we may have defined an `Employee` object like so:

Employee	
EmployeeID	ID
ContractType	(perm|shortTerm|temp|intern)
ContractedFrom	Date
ContractedTo	Date
EmployeeName	String
Department	(sales|marketing|manufacturing|distribution|systems)
Manager	String
Rank	String

It does not mean that the properties: `EmployeeID`, `ContractType`, `ContractedFrom`, `ContractedTo`, `EmployeeName`, `Department`, `Manager`, and `Rank` should all be attributes on an `Employee` element.

There is an important distinction to make when we are looking at the XML messages we are defining:

- the transient messages that get passed between parts of the system
- the persistent storage of the data that is held in the messages

Both of these are forms of XML documents, although they have different purposes.

The static model provides a list of concepts that we must model into our documents, most of which will have to be represented in a persistent form. The dynamic model, meanwhile, tells us which of these makes up the transient messages that are passed between different sections of the application. The static model can also act as a set of building blocks from which we can build our XML documents and schemas.

The hierarchies and relationships that we have defined will help us with structuring these object types. Overall this will also help us to determine what information we will need to store as we should have an idea of the key concepts to our business.

> *Some people call the object types and properties of the static information model the **vocabulary** from which we build documents and schemas, because they tend to reflect the element and attribute names that we will be using in our documents. If you end up using the same names for elements and attributes this is more accurate as the term vocabulary is often also associated with the names of the markup used in a schema. In any case, you might find that you change some of these names when it comes to creating the documents.*

One thing to beware of at this stage is that, if we have a loose structure for our documents, that is, if they can convey a number of scenarios, it is good practice to work through different possibilities rather than just focus on one. Whereas if we have a tight document structure there will be fewer possible states that the document is able to describe. For example, if we are dealing with a transaction, are we as prepared for documents that are dealing with returns as those that are sales? Both documents are just as important as each other.

We will then come back to look at specific schema related issues in the final stage of the data modeling process, but for now let's look at designing the documents that we will be using in the system.

With the dynamic model we will know what information needs to flow from one place to another, so we can start to design the documents that will carry this information. This is what we will look at in the next section.

XML For Messages

It can be easier to design XML for messages than for persistent data, because all of the information that we will need to transport is in the message (with persistent data we have to decide which information blocks to store together and answer questions relating to normalization and how much information to store). Having developed a dynamic model we will have a good idea of what information our message needs to contain; of course there will be some information that we will deem unnecessary to be kept in the message, but this is just a question of removing unnecessary data. One good example of this is any information that can be calculated such as totals – it is often best to leave this to the application rather than including them in the message, to save on message size. Here are some other points that we should remember in our message design:

- **Messages should reflect the information they contain - not their use**. This is because *how* the information is used may well change over time, while the core information content is likely to remain the same. For example, if we had to send a catalog to a purchaser before they bought something, it should act as a catalog, not the first step of a purchase process – so that we could then use it as a catalog for those who just wanted to browse products as well. Note that the message should not be designed around how we are going to present the message to an end user (although if it is for display with CSS you should remember that you cannot directly use CSS to display attributes in a browser without a transformation).

- **The design should anticipate change and allow for it**. Sometimes it is difficult to know whether to include unnecessary information that may be required in the future, but there is no easy answer to this question – we have to evaluate it on a project-by-project basis (a good indicator can be if we intend to implement further parts of the project in future iterations). Sometimes it is easier to include all properties of an object and let the recipient decide whether they want to use the properties, although this has the drawback of costing more in bandwidth, and there may be security concerns associated with sending all the data. We can also explicitly state versions, either through the use of message wrappers, version attributes on our root element, or namespaces. We will look at implementing these techniques later in the chapter.

- **If there is already a standard message type, use that one rather than creating our own**. Look in the repositories (covered later in this chapter) to see if there is something already suitable for us to use in our work – even if we cannot use the messages in the form they are provided in, do use them for ideas or extend them with our own message formats. Initially, these should help we with the division and structure of the messages that we impose on our system. There are also some generic message types that handle general issues of message massing, such as SOAP and XML-RPC, although we can end up getting tied into such a system and it is difficult to move away from such an implementation if we start relying on tools designed to work with such message types.

- **The data encoding should be as close to the original encoding as we can achieve**. Use identifiers that are already used in the business, for example if we are working with books, they have individual ISBN numbers, which are better to use than creating our own numbering system. We should also avoid identifiers that create a dependency between messages and some existing database or application (such as a primary key in the database, in case we change data stores in the future). Keeping the identifiers free from technological dependencies helps prolong the lifetime of our data model beyond that of a specific implementation.

When dealing with messages we should also try to include some generic information (even if it duplicates that of a messaging system we are using) as a wrapper.

For example, looking back at the purchase order that we defined:

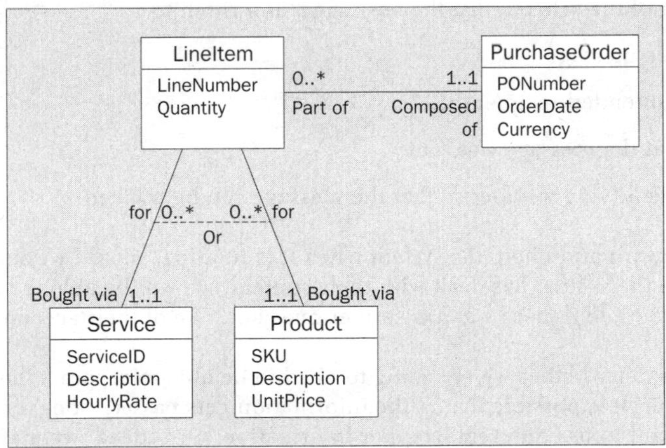

We might end up with a document along these lines:

```
<?xml version = "1.0" ?>

<PurchaseOrder  PONumber = "124442" OrderDate = "2001-03-14"
                Currency = "US$">

   <LineItem LineNumber = "1" Quantity = "3" >
      <Product SKU = "14414" Description = "Widgets"
               UnitPrice = "2.50" />
   </LineItem>

   <LineItem LineNumber = "2" Quantity = "5" >
      <Product SKU = "14236" Description = "Grommets"
               UnitPrice"2.50" />
   </LineItem>

</PurchaseOrder>
```

As we can see, this document contains information about a purchase order that we have just defined. We have also added an element of future proofing in adding the `currency` attribute to the `PurchaseOrder` element. While we only sell to the United States at the moment, if business goes well, we hope that we will be able to enter other markets. As mentioned earlier, we might want to create more than one sample document, as this example only shows we can sell both products and services, but we have only created a document for selling products.

Message Wrappers

Each message should contain some important wrapping information, which should be enforced through the schema when we come to write it. This has to be additional information beyond that we already defined in the dynamic model (unless we already included these anyway), and it should really exist even if it means repeating information supplied by an application (after all the application may change, while we hope our data model will continue to be used in its existing form). Typically, information that should be included in the wrapper would be:

- The version of the schema that the message was written to
- Who sent the message
- Who is the intended recipient
- The date that the message was sent
- A unique identifying number so that the message can be tracked

Not only does this information help the system when it is running, should we store the messages in a persistent store once the system has dealt with their content, we will be able to track details down better at a later date (for example if there was a customer query on one of their accounts.)

We should also consider whether we are going to need to be able to separate the payload from the wrapping information. It is possible that as the information gets passed along, or when the system is upgraded, we will want to use different wrapper information. Or indeed, we may have different wrappers for different parts of the system. So, it is worth considering whether the main contents can still be validated against the original schema if the wrapper changes.

XML for Persistent Data

When it comes to storing XML there are a number of options available to us. We can store it in:

- plain flatfiles (such as plain text files held on the operating system's native file system)
- a relational database (such as Oracle, SQL Server or DB2)
- an object database (which stores DOM representations of the document)
- a directory service (such as Novell NDS or Microsoft Active Directory)

The first two options are by far the most common. If we use flatfiles they tend to be accessed from the file system of the operating system we are running. It is just like holding a collection of text documents or word processing documents on our file server. The important thing to do if we take this approach is to make sure that we have a good naming convention for our files so that they are easily accessed.

Relational databases, however, are still by far the most common data storage format. Increasingly, relational database vendors are adding more sophisticated XML support to their RDBMS so that users can store data in relational tables, but simply send the database XML for it to insert, update or delete the information it holds; they can also request that contents of the database be retrieved and output in XML format. It is no longer necessary with many databases to convert the XML into another form before the database can accept it – if we are able to just send the database an XML file this will save us doing the conversion ourself. For example, SQL Server 2000 has a number of capabilities that allow us – with minimum programming effort – to relate the XML structures we want to send to it, and for it to generate, to the internal model it uses (and is very fast at performing the conversions).

How we store the XML in a database is another question – there is information on this topic in Chapter 17. This chapter will give you a good guide on how to create persistent stores for XML data and how you can model the information, using techniques such as using `ID`s and `IDREF`s to create relationships between data rather than duplicating it (rather like some normalization concepts in relational databases). For example, if we are going to store details of each order, we can relate the order details to the customer information using a customer ID rather than repeating the customer information in every order they make. This is one key example of where message information will differ from our persistent storage data, because the message form of the order will probably contain certain customer details (though probably not all). We should also be careful how the representations will work in the future, for example if a customer moves from New York to California, we do not want the system to indicate that all packages have always been sent to their new address if they may be queried later. The one thing that we do not have to do with normalization, which we may be tempted to do if we are from a relational database background, is to start a new document for each property that has more than one facet, for example XML can easily cope with the concept of a price that has more than one property (say currency and amount).

General Design Issues

Having looked at the two types of document we will be dealing with when designing document structure, let's look at some general concerns that we should think about when devising our message design and persistent store.

- The size of our documents, and the effects size can have on processing and retrieval
- Naming conventions, as it is good to have a standard convention used across the organization
- The old element versus attribute debate

- Modeling the object type hierarchy
- Representing relationships
- How we handle binary data
- Encoding of property values

Let's start with looking at how the size of the document can affect the design.

Size of Document

Whether we are creating our messages and data stores, for every document we will have to answer the question "how large should my documents be?" Or more specifically:

- How much information should be in each message?
- How should we split up persistent stores?

These are helpful questions to bear in mind while we are designing our documents, even if we do not come up with an explicit answer before we start.

How Much Information Should Each Message Contain?

The first question is fairly easy to answer. Our dynamic model should give us a good idea of the information we need to pass between parts of the application. From this model we will know what we have at any one stage in the application and what the next stage needs to use. The only other things to decide at this point in time are:

- Do we include more information in the model to help future proof our design? This can be a good idea but depends on the sensitivity of information that should only be accessed by certain people, as we do not want to be sending all of the data all of the time. It also affects the amount of bandwidth we use; the more data we send, the more bandwidth we take up. Of course, this would be more of an issue, for, say, an application on a wireless device, than an application on a desktop machine in a corporate LAN.
- Do we let the application gather some of the information from a persistent store rather than sending it with every message if possible? For example, we could just send the details of customer orders and enquiries with a customer ID and let the application pull information about the customer that it needs from its data store. Whether we do this will probably depend on factors such as:
    - where this data is stored and whether bandwidth is a premium – will we save anything by not sending all the information?
    - the processing application we are using – and whether it is capable of performing this kind of operation, if indeed we have control over this aspect of the project.

When we consider that XML is not suited to having specific parts of documents directly accessed, especially in the case of very large XML documents, this might help us in our split. Parsing the whole thing could take a long time, and significant processor resources. While we can use SAX to read out values far quicker than loading the document into the DOM, the SAX approach could require several passes of the data if we had to go back and forth through the records.

If we are using components that are quite complex, there might be a natural mapping of a business object to an XML document, so we might have an XML document for each employee or customer.

It is also worth remembering that, if we have a number of smaller documents that relate to a department or task, it will be easier for those who are going to use them to understand what they need to, and they will not be forced to learn a lot of unrelated information just to use the section they are interested in.

How Should We Split Up Persistent Stores?

There are a lot more choices to make regarding how we store persistent details in XML. One of the main issues relates to finding the information once we have stored it in some form or other – after all, if we have trouble accessing information we have stored it detracts from the effort of keeping it in the first place. When using XML to hold persistent data, finding the information will always be a two-part process: finding the file/database that holds the information we are interested in, and then extracting the particular data we are interested in from that file or database.

In order to find the document that we are interested in, we have a number of strategies at our disposal:

- Use the directory structure of the operating systems' filestore to locate documents by name – here, the naming convention we use for the files is very important – we need to create a system that makes it easy to locate the correct file. For example, if we are storing information about people, the file name could make use of their employee or customer ID. For performance reasons, we should not let these folders get too full, keeping the maximum number of files in a particular directory to 256 (as a rule of thumb) and then using hashing to organize the tree structure if we need more.
- Index documents separately, but with a "link document", that is, a document that contains links to access the others. For example, we could have a collection of quarterly reports, each containing one XML document, and we could create a separate link document that will act as an index to the individual reports. This way we end up with the summary information in one file that is used to access others. If we do choose to create link documents, it is worth creating one for each type of information or document rather than one master link document, as it keeps the size down, and helps narrow down the search to the correct document type.
- Create an index for documents within a relational database, whether we may also hold the documents in the database or not, or even if we generate them from the database. We can query the database using SQL queries to find the document that we are interested in.
- Index documents using a free text search engine. This approach is more useful for human consumers rather than other programs that want to consume the XML.

Once we have decided how to store our documents, the second part of the information retrieval process is finding the relevant information from that file. The ability to find the relevant information largely depends upon the size of the document. So, how do we decide how much information to put in each document?

Realistically, XML is not ideally suited to working with large documents. While SAX is far better than the DOM at reading information from large documents, it is only really suitable if we know what information we want from the document. If we have to navigate between nodes, SAX requires multiple passes of the document through the processor. Furthermore it is not ideally suited to creating documents. If we have to create documents programmatically, or recursively navigate nodes, the DOM is a far better approach. However, the DOM does incur a large processing overhead. Furthermore, if our documents are narrowly focussed, it will be easier to process and generate queries on the data within them.

So, one of the key factors in making information easily retrievable from a document is limiting its size. As more applications use relational databases to generate XML, the file size worry will be of less concern than if we had to use a flat file format. In any case, some of the things we should consider when dividing the information are:

- Storing unrelated objects in different files or tables – we do not really want to store the customer information in the same flat file or table as our product catalog. By careful use of relationships we can create sensible splits in chunks of related information. For example, if we store orders separately from customers we can just use a customer ID to relate the two together rather than repeating customer information for each invoice (resulting in smaller documents).

- If there are different departments that are going to use the same information, although each department may require some slightly different information, if we can store it in one place it saves on replication of data. This idea of centralizing the data makes it easier to maintain integrity, because if a customer brings something in for repair, and lets the repair department know that they have changed address, the change of address will then be available to all departments (and yes that also means that the marketing department will be able to send those new catalogs and offers to our new address). There may be a small price of increased bandwidth to pay, and processing power if we are having to create documents from more than one source, but XML is ideally suited to this kind of task (and if we are worried about peak loads we can incorporate a message queuing service to deal with non-critical tasks at quieter times, after all it is easy to put XML messages into message queuing software as plain text). Unfortunately, however, managers are often wary of allowing us to do this, as each department wants control over their own data.

Of course, it can be all too easy to go too far the other way and create too many individual documents, which doesn't make sense either, as we would not be able to make use of the rich capabilities for representing relationships that XML allows internally in documents, and we would have a lot more files or records to sort through to get the appropriate entry. So, it is important to strike a balance between the size of files and the number of them. As is the case with data warehousing techniques, we may choose to replicate individual data stores for different departments that include different subsets of data from any main store, or we may choose to centralise storage of certain types of information within a single department.

If we have to work with large files there are ways to work around file size limits. For example, we can use SAX to read out a subset of data from a large document, which can then be navigated using the DOM, although it adds another layer to the processing.

So, how granular should we aim to make our document stores? This really depends on the main uses for the documents; if we are more likely to require individual customer details than all of them, then it is a good idea to store each customer's details in a separate file. Of course, there will be occasions when we might want a subset of all customer information (such as for marketing purposes), but this can be generated as a batch process rather than trawling through all customer records every time we want to access one customer's details. However, if we are much more likely to want to look at all customer details at once (rather than individual ones) we will end up with a larger file. Realistically speaking, however, the first is more common, where we will want all the customer details in one place even if different departments only require a subset of the information.

If the document contains a lot more detail than we are going to require from the average query on it, we should think about splitting it up further into logical sub units. But again, remember not to go too granular, as we will end up opening lots of documents or making lots of queries to gain the information we need.

We should also avoid storing information that can otherwise be calculated by an application. For example, in an order we might not want to store the totals, as this can be calculated programmatically and saves on the amount of data we actually have to store.

> *When you are working on a web project using Active Server Pages or Java Server Pages, you also have the option of working with the files in application scope, as long as the document is not too large – it can be read into memory when the web server starts and remains there until it is closed down. This, however, is less common than requiring a persistent format that is written to disk, and should not be used for critical data that is subject to change (in case it gets lost should the server crash).*

Having looked at these questions, before we start deciding on the actually defining documents and their structure, we should decide on a naming convention.

Naming Conventions

When it comes to choosing the names for elements and attributes we have some more choices to make. The first thing to say is choose a way of naming elements and attributes and stick to it throughout our documents.

While the names of these often come from the static model, we may want to slightly alter them for the purposes of making it clear whether they are elements or attributes, and whether they are part of a class of elements or attributes.

Firstly we have to ask how much information should be going in the name, for example if we are representing an address, should we use an element called `Address` or should we be more specific, such as `BillingAddress`. While the longer forms may take up more storage space and bandwidth, making sure that the markup is understood is also very important. By giving more descriptive names we reduce the chance of the data being incorrectly marked up or misinterpreted.

Some people like to create abbreviated tag names, as they think that it makes it easier to read the content of the document. Indeed, one way in which this could be said to be true is that smaller tag names allow us to fit more of the document on the screen, making it easier to browse, and as an additional advantage we have less to type. However, the amount of time we spend actually reading the XML document with markup in it these days is quite limited. Others say abbreviated tags are good when we are intending the documents be used by a processing application, in which case descriptive tags do not matter so much. Realistically though, a good data model will outlast an application, and those that come to work with other applications of the data would certainly appreciate clarity in the markup. If we must use short forms for tags and attributes, where possible we should always stick to industry-recognized abbreviations rather than just making up our own.

Because our names should be descriptive, they will often contain more than one word. This may be because they belong to a class of elements or attributes, or it may be because it is just required to distinguish one name from another similar one when the two actually represent very different things.

If the name is made up of more than one word there are a number of options we can use to make the names clearer:

We can use different types of capitalization, such as lowerCamelCase where the first letter of the second word (and each word after) is capitalized, or we could use UpperCamelCase and capitalize the first letter of every word. For example:

```
BillingAddress
billingAddress
```

We can also use a separating character, for example a dot notation. Character separation is clean, and we can use the notation in software that we have written. While the dot is a legal character in an XML name, it has no more significance in XML than any other character, for example:

```
Billing.Address
```

We may also choose a character such as an underscore or a hyphen:

```
Billing_Address
Billing-Address
```

Indeed some people use different capitalization or separating characters for elements and attributes, which can be a good idea to help distinguish them clearly. For example, we could use UpperCamelCase for elements, and lowerCamelCase for attributes.

Whether or not we are using specific names in elements, such as `BillingAddress`, we might still want to add a `type` attribute to the element to indicate a class of element: `<BillingAddress type=billing">`. We could make this a fixed attribute in the DTD, but it does not ensure that every element that has a type attribute whose value is `address` has the same content model (if we are using XML Schema we might like to use a different attribute than `type`, for example `form`, as `type` is a commonly used attribute in XML Schema). We'll look at this more when we come to look at classes of elements.

> **While you can use the same name for an element, a notation, and an entity without causing an error, it can lead to confusion, and you are best to be clear about which is which.**

Another question is whether to overload names and properties that appear in more than one object type; for example, do we use `Name` for customers and for suppliers? Generally speaking we should only try to use the same name if it means the same thing regardless of where it appears. Of course we can overload property names for different elements, but if they mean completely different things it is a good idea to be more specific and avoid confusion. For example, while we might be tempted to use `Name` to represent a customer name and the name of a store, we would be better off clarifying the one that is less obvious, in this case `StoreName`. While the parent element may help to remove confusion and put the item in question into context, it is still a good idea to be as clear as possible (and if we are using SAX we would not have to program so that we remember the context of the current element).

Where possible our naming should try to encourage a one-to-one relationship between child information items (whether attributes or child elements) and their parents. For example, rather than using a `title` attribute for a CD and a `title` attribute for each of the tracks on that CD, we should try to make the distinction clear – use an attribute such as `SongTitle` instead (of course, remember that we would need to have some sort of system involving a separate element for each track in this case – we couldn't have multiple `SongTitle` attributes on one `Album` element, say.)

> **Whichever naming convention you use, you should stick to it throughout all our documents.**

Elements Versus Attributes

Having decided upon the size of documents and a naming convention, we will be ready to start creating our documents. At which point, we will be faced by yet more questions... One of the first we are likely to run into is the argument over whether it is best to use elements or attributes to store values, which has been raging since the XML 1.0 specification was released. It is still one of the hottest contested arguments in the XML world and, despite the amount of bandwidth that has been spent discussing the topic, there is still no definitive answer as to which is best to use. Some of the leading names in the XML community are still divided over this issue. In the real world, we are best off assessing each project on an individual basis, and there are a number of questions we will look at to help us decide which is more appropriate for our particular situation.

If we were using element content, we might mark minimal details about a CD up like so:

```
<CD>
   <Artist>Sade</Artist>
   <Title>Lovers Rock</Title>
</CD>
```

This is sometimes known as a **Hierarchical Model**, because the nested element structures create a hierarchy of data, whereas if we were using attribute content, it would look more like this:

```
<CD artist="Sade" title="Lovers Rock"> … </CD>
```

This form is sometimes known as a **Canonical Model** (or form) for the data (don't get this confused with **Canonical XML**, a subset of XML used to test XML processors).

With most projects, we are going to end up using a mixture of hierarchical and canonical representations in any document, although it may lean more towards one approach than the other.

People have come up with all sorts of suggestions of how we should decide whether to use elements or attributes to contain which data. Let's look at a couple of these before looking at some questions we can ask to assess individual projects.

Because XML had its roots in SGML for document markup one of the most common distinctions that has been suggested has been to:

> *Use elements to hold data that should be visible when displayed on a screen or in ink on a page, then to use attributes to hold meta data about the information printed on the page or screen that processing applications require, such as canvas size.*

This distinction can fit well for human readable matter – especially for those who are designing XML for documents that will be displayed in browsers using CSS, as CSS does not render attribute values on screen – but unfortunately it does not necessarily apply when we are marking up other forms of data than those intended for display to humans. (Note, however, that this does not mean that attributes cannot produce something that is visible, as we could still use attributes for cross-references.

If we consider the case of HTML, this distinction was followed in early versions of the markup. However, the introduction of tags such as `<Script>`, which were not intended to be seen and therefore resulted in the misuse of the comment element, led to the rules being broken.

With data that is not intended to generate human readable matter, we need to think along different lines. So, if we think about the information model we generated, we can translate this theory to something that is more fitting.

> *Use an element to represent objects in the information model that can exist on their own independent of any container element that they may be a child of, and attributes to represent its properties, which cannot exist without the object.*

An alternative way to put this would be to say – "use an element when the info we are recording is a constituent part of the parent element", which will always work as we need a root element. Then use an attribute when the information is inherent to the parent but not a constituent part. Your head and height are both required for you to be a human – what would you be like without a head? However, head is a constituent part, while height is not – you can remove a height attribute and still be a human. This fits with the theory that meta data describes the container – such as height – while the content is the info the container conveys, so an ID attribute is clearly meta data describing the content. We can distinguish metadata by asking, if we removed the data, would my understanding or ability to understand the document change?

Generally we can work with this kind of distinction, however we have to be careful when we come up against some exceptions to the rule. For example, we could consider age to be an attribute, but place of birth to be an element.

Having said that, there are some major proponents of greater attribute use, for example the BizTalk Framework promotes the use of attributes a lot more, and there are plenty of reasons for suggesting such an approach. Whichever you choose, you will be in good company.

Rather than trying to prescribe a general rule of thumb, here are some key things we should consider when dealing with this question:

- What does the designer expect from the `CD` element declaration?
- What is the processing application required to do with the data?
- How will the processing application use the data?

Let's have a look at some of these questions in more depth.

> **Whatever the choice, the application should not have to struggle against what the designer decided when retrieving or creating character data or attribute values.**

Is the Data Flat or Hierarchical?

Attributes can only hold a single level of data – they cannot have any child elements or attributes of their own, so the information they contain is flat unless we link them to `IDREF`s or `ENTITY`s.

Elements, on the other hand, can have much more complex content models of their own. Child elements can be used to represent relationships between containing elements and their children, and we can prescribe the order of multiple child elements.

Do We Need to Order Child Information Items?

If we want to constrain the order in which child information items are provided, then we will have to use elements to store that information. Attributes are unordered; we cannot control the order in which they appear on an element.

Does the Data Represent Information About Content or is it the Content Itself?

This is the distinction we met first, which suggests that content should appear in elements, while metadata about the content should appear in attributes.

Do We Expect the Model To Change Much?

Because attributes cannot have child information items, unlike elements, we may be wise to choose element content where we might need to expand the data model in the future. For example, if we were recording information about the names of plants in a flower bed, we might want to start recording them in single elements, using an attribute called `name` for their name. However, if we then wanted `name` to have two child information items, one for the plant's common name and one for its Latin name, then the children would have to appear in an element called `name` (either as child elements or as attributes), because the attributes cannot hold child information items themselves.

Are the Values Going To Be Consumed By a Program or Human?

Element content is generally easier for humans to read than attribute content, but it takes up more bandwidth (and this does make a difference when we are dealing with very large, or great numbers of documents). Applications, on the other hand, will find it easier to deal with attribute values, which also take up less bandwidth.

Does the Value Have One of an Enumeration of Values?

If there is an enumerated list of values that can be made into name token groups then enumerated attribute values are a good way to enforce the attribute value, for example if we wanted to enumerate a list of states in a country, or if we wanted to offer a fixed set of clothing sizes. This is because there is no equivalent restriction on element content. This can be done using an XML DTD or schema.

Do We Need To Offer Multiple Values?

We are only allowed one instance of an attribute per element; we cannot have several attributes of the same name on an individual element. Nor can attributes contain multiple values, unless we use tokens such as `NMTOKENS` or references to other elements such as `IDREF`s (in which case we need to use a DTD or schema to let the schema know how to interpret the tokens or build in some logic into the application so that it can deal with them). Strictly speaking `NMTOKENS` should only be used to hold formal atomic data that conforms to a grammar, not free-form data.

As we can see, by addressing these questions, we will often find that our decision over whether to use element or attribute content is made for us. Here is a summary of some of the advantages and disadvantages of each.

	Advantages	Disadvantages
XML Attributes	DTD can constrain the values: useful when there is a small set of allowed values, such as "yes" and "no".	Simple string values only.
	DTD can define a default value.	No support for metadata (or "attributes of attributes").
	ID and IDREF validation.	Unordered
	Lower space overhead (makes a difference if we ever need to send gigabytes of data over the network). In the future, this will be more and more likely as XML becomes more widely used.	More escaping required in attributes than in elements, for example quote marks.
	Whitespace normalization is available for certain data types (such as NMTOKENS), which saves the application some parsing effort.	
	Easier to process using DOM and SAX interfaces.	
	Access to unparsed external entities, such as binary data.	
Child Elements	Support arbitrarily complex values and repeating values.	Slightly higher space usage.
	Ordered.	More complex programming.
	Support "attributes of attributes".	
	Extensible when the data model changes, and simply adding more attributes is unfeasible.	

Modeling the Object Type Hierarchy

Having looked at the questions over whether to use elements or attributes, it is time to look at the object type hierarchy and how we can preserve this in our documents. We should have created a Class Hierarchy in Step 2 of the static information modeling process, which reflects the class hierarchy that we will be modeling. When we have classes of objects, we should try to preserve the content model of each as much as possible.

There is no explicit concept of type hierarchy in XML, although we can simulate it. This not only has the advantage of making the schema easier to learn (both when first learning the syntax and when reading document instances, because there is less to learn overall and the structure becomes familiar quicker), but also enables reuse of content models.

> *Remember that if something has an* ***is-a-type-of*** *relationship, we cannot have one without the other, so in the hierarchy we cannot have the child information item without the parent.*

Transitioning Types and Type Hierarchies

Where the object type is part of a type hierarchy we have to decide at what level do we make the transition from elements to attributes (if we need to) – for example we could have:

```
<Transaction type="sale" />
<Transaction type="return" />
<Transaction type="order" />
```

Alternatively, we could have:

```
<Transaction>
   <Order>
      ...
   </Order>
   <Return>
      ...
   </Return>
   ...
</Transaction>
```

The more specific we are, the more specific the schema can be about what attributes and child elements are associated with the element. For example, we may want a completely different set of child elements for a `<Return>` than we do for a sale; by having this as a child element, we can control the content model of that element easier. Alternatively we could have a separate namespace for returns as opposed to sales.

Clear Use of Types

In order to make it clear to the user that we are using a class of information, we can either make the element name clear using a long form, such as `BillingAddress`:

```
<BillingAddress street="10 Loxley Street"
                city="Harsworth"
                state="New Jersey"
                zipCode="120012" />
```

or we can just use the element name `Address` and add a `type` attribute to it:

```
<Address type="billing"
         street="10 Loxley Street"
         city="Harsworth"
         state="New Jersey"
         zipCode="120012" />
```

The disadvantage of the shorter element name with the `type` attribute is that there is no way of enforcing the content model just from the attribute as shown, whereas we can define the content model in the schema to make sure that the `BillingAddress` element contains the correct attributes, for example. If there is more than one address as a child element, we should really include the longer form of a name, for more clarity.

If we can group element types into classes implicitly and explicitly using similar names, attributes and content models for all elements of a class, it will make it easier for authors to use the documents and schema. This is known as **internal consistency**. It is also helpful if we can make sure that it is consistent with the authors' expectations, which can be affected by nationality, industry or even departments in the same company. For example, if we are dealing with cars, the service department may use an element called `Warranty` to indicate how long a warranty has left to run, while the sales department might use it to indicate how long the warranty on a car they are selling will last.

When we are dealing with CDs, records, and tapes, it helps to keep similar content models such as:

```
<CD>
   <Artists>
      <Artist>Sade</Artist>
   </Artists>
   <Title>Lovers Rock</Title>
   <ISSN>7567-91659-2</ISSN>
   <TrackListing>
      <Track>By Your Side</Track>
      <Track>Flow</Track>
      <Track>King of Sorrow</Track>
      <Track>Somebody Already Broke My Heart</Track>
      <Track>All About Our Love</Track>
   </TrackListing>
</CD>
```

```
<Cassette>
   <Artists>
      <Artist>Sade</Artist>
   </Artists>
   <Title>Lovers Rock</Title>
   <ISSN>7567-91659-2</ISSN>
   <TrackListing>
      <Track>By Your Side</Track>
      <Track>Flow</Track>
      <Track>King of Sorrow</Track>
      <Track>Somebody Already Broke My Heart</Track>
      <Track>All About Our Love</Track>
   </TrackListing>
</Cassette>
```

Here, because the CD and cassette elements have similar content models they become a lot easier to learn because the elements have the same class of content. It is much easier to learn similar elements, having learnt the first one. Similar element types should be similar in content models and attribute definitions, and if they differ they should be clearly stated. It helps if they can be used in the same or similar contexts as well.

Encoding Property Values

When it comes to passing the property values from an object to a processing application, we either have to let the application know what data type the value is in, or let the application know the order in which the values will appear, so that it can do the conversion to the appropriate data type. We noted the data type of the values in the static model when defining them.

If we want to tell the processing application what data type the values represent, and are using DTDs, we will have to either use element content with an attribute as a data type, or standardize the data type, for example measurements, and leave the processing application to deal with them. However, if we are using XML Schemas, as described in Chapter 6, we will be able to indicate the data type in the schema as it has introduced a strong data typing mechanism.

The following table indicates ways of dealing with some common data types that properties are likely to display:

Measurement	Examples	How to deal with in DTDs	How to deal with in schemas

Quantities	weight, height, width	Standardise data type (for example, measurements – always use meters) or use an attribute to indicate measurement, and make this the default.
		
		`<height measure="meters">`
		`1.67</height>`
			Specify the datatype in the schema.

Table continued on following page

Measurement	Examples	How to deal with in DTDs	How to deal with in schemas

Boolean	true/false; yes/no	Enumerated attributes.
		
		We cannot use the same name to indicate different values, so we have to create different names.
		
		If we are using attributes, no two attributes can have the same name, so again we can use different names.
		
		`border = "yes"`
		`valid = "true"`
			Use the Boolean data type where possible or create our own with the allowable values we want to limit it to.

Dates and Times	YYYY-MM-DD	Always try to stick to a standard, such as ISO-8601 shown to the left.	Use the built-in data types specified in the data types specification.

It always helps if we stick to an agreed standard for data types. Of course, there is no obligation to use any of these standards, but there are two great advantages if we do:

- Someone else has given more thought to the difficulties than we probably have time for
- Telling people we're going to conform to a standard is a good way of cutting short unproductive debate

The following table shows some of the standards we should be aware of, and are likely to want to use:

Standard	Scope	Description
ISO 2955	Metric measurements (Système Internationale)	Method for representing SI and other units in information systems with limited character sets (without using Greek letters).
ISO 3166	Country codes	Specification of codes for the representation of names of countries; a set of two-letter and three-letter codes. The two-letter codes are most familiar as internet domain names, such as `de` for Germany.
ISO 4217	Currency codes	Codes for national currencies.
ISO 5218	Human sexes	Codes to represent male and female.

Standard	Scope	Description
ISO 6093	Numeric values	Three presentations of numerical values, represented in character strings in machine readable form, and recognizable by humans
ISO 6709	Location of points	A format and representation for unique identification of points on, above, or below the earth's surface by longitude, latitude, and altitude.
ISO 8601	Dates and Times	Expression of dates, including calendar dates, ordinal dates, week numbers and times in numeric form, with punctuation to avoid ambiguity.

Representing Relationships

During the creation of the static model, we defined relationships between the objects. Relationships can also be used to minimize the amount of data in a message or store, or to indicate relationships between data.

The first and most common way of showing relationships is that of **containment**. One-to-one and one-to-many relationships are best modeled in XML using containment. For example, line items on an invoice could be represented like so:

```
<Invoice>
   <LineItem productDescription="Widgets (0.5 inch)"
             quantity="17" unitPrice="0.10" />
   <LineItem productDescription="Grommets (2 inch)"
             quantity="22" unitPrice="0.05" />
</Invoice>
```

We can clearly see here that the `LineItems` are part of the `Invoice`. However, there will often be times when we need to model more complex relationships.

An element can only be contained by one element, however, so we must use other types of relationship in more complicated structures:

- `ID/IDREF` - the `ID` attribute contains a value that identifies the element uniquely with the document, while the `IDREF` contains a value that is the same as one of the `ID` attribute's values. So the `ID` acts like a primary key while the `IDREF` acts as a foreign key. We can also use `IDREFS` to create a space-separated list of `IDREF` values to create a one-to-many relationship (can enforce uniqueness using unique identity constrain in XML schemas).
- `Key/KeyRef` in schema. These are similar to `ID` and `IDREF` types, but we can have more than one `Key` in a document, and we can use XPath syntax to limit the extent to which it applies within a document.
- XPointer references in attributes.
- Use application-defined primary and foreign keys and let our application process the relationships.

We will be covering this further in Chapter 17, "XML and databases"

If we extend this idea of an invoice, we could add a relationship between an LineItem and a Product, so that many products can appear on one invoice and one product may appear on many invoices, as shown below:

```
<OrderData>
   <Invoice>
      <LineItem productIDREF="prod1"
                quantity="17" unitPrice="0.10" />
      <LineItem productIDREF="prod2"
                quantity="22" unitPrice="0.05" />
   </Invoice>
   <Invoice>
      <LineItem productIDREF="prod2"
                quantity="30" unitPrice="0.05" />
      <LineItem productIDREF="prod3"
                quantity="19" unitPrice="0.15" />
   </Invoice>
   <Product productID="prod1"
            productShortName="Widgets (0.5 inch)"
            productDescription="Rubberized Brown Widgets (half-inch)" />
   <Product productID="prod2"
            productShortName="Grommets (2 inch)"
            productDescription="Vulcanized Orange Grommets (two inch)" />
   <Product productID="prod3"
            productShortName="Sprockets (1 inch)"
            productDescription="Anodized Silver Sprockets (one inch)" />
</OrderData>
```

Here we are creating a relationship between the line items and the products. Note how the first invoice contains orders for Widgets and Grommets, while the second contains orders for Grommets and Sprockets. But we have only had to include the information for the Grommets once, because we are pointing to it by the line items that use it.

This is an effective mechanism for describing relationships, however it can have some drawbacks:

- ID and IDREFs are only unidirectional, there is no easy way to navigate from an ID to its associated IDREF, unless we are using XSLT; there is no standard DOM interface to allow us to find an element given its ID (although many parsers offer some way of doing this, such as the Microsoft addition to MSXML which provides the nodeFrom ID() method).
- If we are using ID IDREFs relationships the problem is exaggerated because each token needs to be compared against the ID being examined.
- Neither the DOM nor SAX provide a way to easily navigate ID/IDREF relationships, so it can slow processing down. If the ID appears before an IDREF, we will have to go back to that element with the DOM or pass the whole document through SAX again.
- We can only have one ID attribute per element.

The XML Schema solution is a lot more powerful as it allows us to:

- use any element or attribute as a key
- specify ranges in which the ID value must be unique (it can just be for a set of elements)
- have as many constraints as we want as child elements in the schema

- use the new key and keyref features which allow us to specify keys and their references within a limited scope, so that their values do not have to be unique to a whole document.

However, there is still the likelihood that this will require significant processing overhead. Of course, we could use more complicated containment solutions:

```
<OrderData>
   <Invoice>
      <LineItem quantity="17" unitPrice="0.10">
         <Product productShortName="Widgets (0.5 inch)"
                  productDescription="Rubberized Brown Widgets (half-inch)"
          />
      </LineItem>
      <LineItem quantity="22" unitPrice="0.05">
         <Product productShortName="Grommets (2 inch)"
                  productDescription="Vulcanized Orange Grommets (two inch)"
         />
      </LineItem>
   </Invoice>
   <Invoice>
      <LineItem quantity="30" unitPrice="0.05">
         <Product productShortName="Grommets (2 inch)"
                  productDescription="Vulcanized Orange Grommets (two inch)"
         />
      </LineItem>
      <LineItem quantity="19" unitPrice="0.15">
         <Product productShortName="Sprockets (1 inch)"
                  productDescription="Anodized Silver Sprockets (one inch)"
         />
      </LineItem>
   </Invoice>
</OrderData>
```

This document repeats the information, but is a better solution for many applications, because there are not the same issues regarding processing using DOM and SAX when dealing with containment. If the processing application needed to know that the grommets in the first invoice are the same as the ones in the second invoice. We could just add a productNumber attribute to the Product element carrying a product identification number as a value.

The containment approach is often better when consuming applications will need to work with the data. While there is an expense in slightly larger document size, we save the processing application from having to navigate the relationships (and we should be especially careful of our use of ID and IDREF attributes when we are going to be using SAX to process the documents).

Handling Binary Data

Another issue we are likely to come across is the need to handle binary data. For example, we might need to handle multimedia data (images, audio, or video), which is binary in nature. Binary data is important for information that cannot easily be represented in character strings, and can either be internal, in which case it is part of the XML data stream, or external where it is kept in an external file.

The most common form for internal inclusion in an XML document is Base64 encoding, whereby each sequence of binary information is encoded as an ASCII character, which is good for working with XML as they do not include the characters that are reserved for markup such as "<" and "]]". So, there is no risk of a delimiter appearing in the data for an image. We do, however, need to create or use an application that will transform from the format it is in into binary data so that it can be included in the XML document, and the reverse to use it again.

If we do use the external approach, we would use external unparsed entities and notations. So, to include a GIF image in an XML file, we might choose something like this to our DTD:

```
<!NOTATION gif SYSTEM "gifeditor.exe">
<!ENTITY picture1 SYSTEM "picture1.gif" NDATA gif>
```

where `gifeditor.exe` is the program that handles this kind of format. To include the picture in the XML document, all we need to do is add this:

```
<picture name="picture1"/>
```

Now we can build it into the application logic, so that the application has to decide that, whenever it comes up against a picture element, it has to retrieve the picture from the URL that is in the `name` attribute. If we are going to be using the image in a browser, this may be the best option in any case.

By now we should have an idea of some of the key considerations we should bear in mind when creating the documents that will be used in messages to pass information around an application, and the documents that store the XML. Once we have created these documents it is time to define the constraints of these documents in a schema. This is the final stage of the data modeling process.

Writing Schemas

Having determined the set of XML documents that will be used in our application, they should be represented in a schema that will constrain the allowable content of each type of document.

Schemas describe a set or class of documents, and contain constructs that constrain document meanings, usages of, and relationships between:

- Elements
- Their content and content models
- Attribute use and attribute values
- Entities
- Notations
- Data types

They can also add default values.

If we are familiar with writing schemas, we may have started with the schema already. Whether we have started writing the schema or are about to embark upon it having decided what information is required in each document, we have to be careful because there may be different options of document instances within each schema. If not, we need to take all the possible variations of document instance into account. Here we will look at both DTDs and W3C XML Schema.

Schemas should define the difference between a valid document and an invalid one, so that the software which validates the document instance can decide whether the incoming data is what is expected, although there will be some which only human beings can interpret (such as the Latin name being given for an entry for a flower).

These constraints serve two purposes:

- processing reasons: so that an application can be sure that it has the correct type of information for a particular stage of a business process.
- stylistic reasons: branding, in-house style and consistency in electronic forms of documents.

While it is usually best to try to constrain our documents as much as possible, we have to be very careful to think of the potential uses of the model, in particular international concerns, where we may have problems with address structures or allowable characters, and different interpretation of element names, where different departments or countries may use the same name for different meanings.

We should try to validate as much incoming data as we can before putting it on our server (or when we change it). This way we do not have to validate it on the way out unless we have generated it dynamically – we already know it is valid. Having said this, it can lead to a lot of processing overhead, and we will have to use our judgement as to when we can skip this.

There are some useful schema authoring tools available if we want to get straight on with this (covered in Chapter 6, "Introducing XML Schema").

In the next section we will look at:

- Constraints we can express in DTDs and Schemas
- Content models
- Representing the Object Type Hierarchy that we have defined
- Creating Reusable Content
- Namespaces
- Versioning
- Local and Global Declarations of Content

But before we do, we should take a quick look at where we can find some example schemas that may help us on our way.

Schema Repositories

When it comes to designing our schemas, it is well worth looking to see if one already exists which, even if not exactly what we want, we can borrow from.

There are a number of schema repositories where we can check whether schemas have already been written; these include:

- **BizTalk.org** (http://www.BizTalk.org) – A repository set up by Microsoft, for those working with the BizTalk framework.
- **ebXML** (http://www.ebXML.org) – An organization set up with over 800 participating companies and support of the United Nations.
- **XML.org** (http://www.XML.org) – set up by **OASIS** (the **O**rganization for the **A**dvancement of **S**tructured **I**nformation **S**tandards).

Constraints We Can Express in DTDs and Schemas

DTDs are really quite limited as a language for constraining documents in XML. They are a legacy of XML, born from SGML and using the same syntax that SGML DTDs use – **Extended Backus Naur Form**. While there are tools that allow us to create DTDs, we will have to learn the syntax if we are going to read someone else's. They provide a level of control as to the content model of an element, and which child elements an element can take, but say nothing about the text contained within the elements. There is slightly more control available over attribute values, but it is still limited because we cannot specify a data type for attribute values.

Therefore, much of the real validation becomes the responsibility of the application code or a separate program. Many application authors decided to avoid using DTDs for validation because of their limits, instead writing completely custom validation code as this was necessary in any case before passing information to an application (particularly where it was for a system that is not just maintaining visual documents and where processing of the content was required).

Another drawback with DTDs is that they do not support XML Namespaces, which allow us to mix elements from different DTDs or information models, and clarify their meaning of different elements that share the same name (see later on in the chapter for more information about Namespaces in XML Schemas).

As we saw in Chapter 6, XML Schemas offer a lot more flexibility (and allow us to constrain documents more tightly) than DTDs. However, at the time of writing they are still a Proposed Recommendation – one step away from an official W3C Recommendation, and there are not many parsers that support them, so their use might not be an option for us.

Of course, it is up to the document writer whether a document instance references the schema in any case, and document instances can override the schema by having internal references of their own. Indeed the recipient also needs a copy of the correct version of the schema if it is to be validated (and `ID/IDREF` pairs are to be correctly interpreted), so we need to make sure that we send a copy with the document, if they don't already have it. So, key points to consider are:

- Is the parser at the receiving end a validating parser?
- Does the parser handle XML Schemas or DTDs?
- Does the recipient have a copy of the schema?
- Is the recipient's copy of the schema the correct version?
- Does the document instance contain the correct `<!DOCTYPE>` declaration pointing to the correct schema? (Most APIs will not offer a method to check this.)
- Does the document instance contain an internal DTD subset that overrides all of the key validation rules in the external DTD (as internal DTDs override external rules if there is a collision).

So, how would we go about creating a schema from the Information Model we have created and the sample documents? We have already seen some of the concerns related to creating a translation into XML (such as when to use elements and when to use attributes), but some will become clear only when we start to write the schema.

There are two main kinds of declarations: element and attribute, which make up the majority of markup in XML documents.

Defining Element Content:

When we define an element we have to define its content, which can consist of a **content model**. There are five types of content model (or a type in XML Schemas):

- `EMPTY`
- `ANY`
- `element`
- `MixedCDATA`

Let's take a look at each of these five models available.

EMPTY

`Empty` elements are idea for placeholders, and do not have any child elements or element content, although they may carry attributes, and can therefore represent objects whose properties are solely expressed through attributes. For example:

```
<Address street="" city="" state="" zipCode="" />
```

ANY

An element whose content type is `any` can have any child elements or attributes as long as they have been defined in the DTD (we cannot just start inserting random elements and attributes that have not been declared). It is unlikely to come from the information model, and more likely to be used when the information model of a section of the document is unknown, or when there is likely to be a need for future documents to change as an extension mechanism. It can be especially helpful at the start of a schemas development, but we should try to restrict its use as soon as possible and tighten down the schema as soon as possible, as it allows for errors to creep in.

Element

`Element` content is used when character data cannot appear in the element content, rather it defines which elements can appear as children of the element being defined. The children are known as **Content Particles**, and we can specify their order, whether they are required to appear or are optional, and if they do appear, whether they can appear more than once (using the basic cardinality operators in DTDs and the `use` attribute in XML Schema. This is the option that gives the designer most control over validation.

The drawback of using `element` content is that it constrains the order of the elements in the case of DTDs, so for example, there is no way of listing 10 optional non-repeatable child elements without specifying their order (although we can use `Sequence` in XML Schemas). This can pose difficulty for marking up textual documents, but is a good thing for applications so that they know what order the information is likely to appear in.

If we do allow authors of documents to choose whether an element appears or not, we should try to limit the choices available to the author. This can be done by introducing subsets of elements, so rather than offering a huge list of allowable content, create context-specific choices.

When the content is predictable, for example:

```
<!ELEMENT subtree (a, b, c)>
```

This is good because it means that we have to have elements a, b and c in that order. So the author has no choices and the processing application knows what to expect. Sometimes, however, we need to offer the author a choice:

```
<!ELEMENT subtree (a, b?, c+)>
```

The processing software no longer requires that the b element will appear, and the c element could appear any number of times. However, if we are using XML Schemas we could use annotation elements to indicate to the processing application the intention of the document. Indeed if we are generating forms directly from the schema we could indicate the fields that are optional or repeatable content in the form.

Sometimes it is also helpful to create groups of elements to indicate a class of element content, for example if we were creating an element content model to represent address information, this could be reused in different types of address for customers, suppliers and employees. If we were using DTDs this would involve the use of parameter entities, whereas with XML Schemas we could either create a model group or a type (we will look at these options shortly).

When we create content models like this, we should try to section off the hierarchy so that, if an author is not going to need to use an element, they will not need any of its children in this context or any other. Also, where possible, keep them as consistent as possible to make learning and using the schema a lot easier. For example, if every time we come across an address element we know that it will always contain the same child elements the DTD will be easier to use, while if we are not going to need the address element, then we will not need to know any of its children either. This is particularly helpful to create an address subtype in contact details, because some people may only deal with names and telephone numbers and e-mails, and will never need to know about the address information. Limiting the amount that people need to learn makes the schema easier to adopt and understand.

Mixed

Mixed content contains a mix of elements and text. It often arises with documents whose intention is to be read, and where tags are used to mark other sections of text within that section, for example, a paragraph. In other contexts we should try to avoid it because they cannot be validated with DTDs and cannot be validated as tightly as other models with XML Schemas (although they are an improvement over DTDs).

Mixed content tends to be used for capturing subtleties or ambiguities, such as emphasis or intention in text, and their use is often subjective. For example we might find mixed content suitable for something like the following:

```
<Paragraph>
Bob Wilson said that he thought my plan was <sarcasm> a great idea</sarcasm>
</Paragraph>
```

Character Data – CDATA

CDATA is used for the elements that only contain text; these are the atoms from which a document is constructed to build up more complicated structures and content models. For example:

```
<Paragraph>This paragraph will contain nothing but text.</Paragraph>
```

Permissive and Restrictive Content Models

When we are defining our content model we can either be very strict, nailing down every element, or we can allow a lot more flexibility. In situations where documents are going to be processed by applications, it often helps to be more rigid about the structure so that the document maps directly to an internal structure of the application. Here most elements should only be allowed to appear once and in a strict position.

In document-oriented applications, however, there is often a need for more flexibility. However, there are still some useful structures that we can impose, such as each paper, article or book must contain a title, and that title can then have a paragraph followed by a repeatable level one heading, which in turn can contain paragraphs or a level two heading. This way we do not get lower level headings directly adjacent to one another, and the paragraphs can contain markup that reflects content of paragraphs as opposed to section headings.

Representing the Object Type Hierarchy

We saw in the previous stage some of the issues in modeling object type hierarchies. So, how do we represent these in our schema? In the case of DTDs we would use parameter entities, or with XML Schemas, groups or types.

These reusable content models can be shared between different definitions or as definitions in their own right.

Several Properties with the Same Data Type

Let's come back to the `BillingAddress` and `DeliveryAddress`, which we looked at earlier – we could end up with several element types with the same data type (or same validation rules). In DTDs we can represent this with parameter entities.

```
<!ENTITY % Address "Street, City, State, ZipCode" >
<!ELEMENT BillingAddress ( %Address; ) >
<!ELEMENT DeliveryAddress ( %Address; ) >
```

If we cannot do this directly, we should try to keep the content model similar. For example, a refund is a specialization of payment that has additional properties such as `Reason` and `AuthorizedBy`.

```
<!ENTITY % Payment "Amount, Date, Account, Notes?" >
<!ELEMENT Payment ( %Payment; ) >
<!ENTITY % Refund "%Payment;, Reason?, AuthorizedBy" >
<!ELEMENT Refund ( %Refund; )
```

If we need to make changes between the content models we can use the `Redefine` element or `Specialize` a type to create a new data type.

Defining Attributes

There are fewer choices to make when it comes to modeling attributes, and they tend to follow the information model. Let's look again at the ideas we discussed earlier in the book:

- Should they be optional or mandatory?
- Should there be a default value if one is not given?

- Should the value be fixed so it is always the same (this can be helpful when defining data types for a processing application, to identify a super-type such as `<BillingAddress type="Address">`)?
- What type should the attribute be? It is common just to use `CDATA` as the default type, although we might like to use a `NMTOKEN` or `NMTOKENS` type. A `NMTOKEN` is a sequence of one or more letters, digits, or certain punctuation characters such as ".", "-" and "," while an `NMTOKENS` type is a whitespace separated list of values. We might also like to use an `ID` or `IDREF` type. If we use XML Schemas, this is not a problem as we can define simple types.

We can also tighten down our attributes using default values. There are two types of default value:

- Literal values
- Keywords `#IMPLIED` and `#REQUIRED`

The literal values allow us to provide a list of allowable values (which is good practice when we can limit values) for the attribute, and also provide a default in case one is not specified:

```
<!ATTLIST Account
   status (active|hold|revoked) "active">
```

Here the `Account` element has a status attribute whose default is `active`, although it can be specified as `hold` or `revoked`. It also helps the author of a document, whether they are creating it manually or we are using it to offer them options in a UI. If we added the keyword `#FIXED` before it, authors would not be able to override this. Here is another example of where enumerating attribute content is useful:

```
<Review rating="5">This book was very interesting and informative</Review>.
```

As it is, the `Review` element contains a `rating` attribute for reviewers to give it marks out of 5, while the content is the comment they add to the review. As it is, there is no way of telling what the rating is out of, is it 5 out of 5, 5 out of 10, 5 out of 100? It could even indicate that it is suitable reading for children of about 5 years old. By constraining allowable values of the `rating` attribute we can offer a list of allowable values for the `rating` attribute.

If the same attributes may appear on different elements, it is also good practice to use a parameter entity for the attribute list in DTDs or global attribute groups in Schemas, and use them as properties of a class of elements. If this introduces conflicting attribute definitions, the first will take precedence.

Splitting Up DTDs and Schemas

When we think about document types, it is not as simple as one per schema. This is because we can have a set of top-level elements, which act as a choice of what document types we can work with.

For example, we could create a common schema for employee details, customer details, and supplier details, with each of the elements being a top-level element (rather than creating a schema for each), in other words we are grouping them in the same schema for convenience, although we could have three different document types.

- We could have had a separate schema for each one, or we can define external parameter entities, or include type definitions
- Or we could have the same schema using a different top level element for each – as it is possible in DTDs and XML Schemas to define several top level elements

Both approaches have their merits. If we have a collection of top-level elements representing different messages, while it ends up in a more complicated schema, we can reuse classes with greater ease.

We should always try to standardize details such as addresses, naming conventions, message stamps (time, date sender, recipient).

Of course, we may have decided that the DTD was not able to perform strong enough validation on the document and placed it in the application logic instead, so we might not have created one for any message. With XML Schemas, however, in particular their ability to offer strong data typing, there is a much better argument for using the schema to validate the document content, in which case it is advisable to have a schema for each message. Still we might also like to keep an overall schema for all of the information in a department, or a data store.

If we have a schema for every type of message and data store, this helps describe the split of the data model to those working with the application.

If we think about data stores, this can be especially useful when dealing with a class of information such as contact details, which may hold a sub-class of an address type. By including all of this information in one section, we can create a more manageable set of parameter entities when using DTDs or a set of smaller schemas that can be included or imported when working with XML Schemas.

When we have these sections of information, those who are using the schema only need to learn the bits specific to their domain, and if different departments want to use different sections of DTDs they can create their own. It also means that the data that has been marked up becomes a lot more useful to different people and saves on replication of data, for example the sales, marketing, accounts, customer support, and repair departments can all make use of the same customer contact information if it is stored in a common format.

Creating Reusable Content

If we want to create reusable content for common content models (or data types if we are using XML Schemas), the mechanism we use will depend on the schema technology we are using.

- If we are using DTDs we will be using Entities to create reusable content
- If we are using XML Schemas we will be defining Types that we can import or include in our schema

In this section, we will take a look at each approach.

Creating Reusable Content with DTDs

If we need to create reusable content when writing DTDs we can either define our elements and attributes in global scope so that they can be reused through the DTD (we look at this shortly), or for more flexibility or power, a common technique is to use entities. Entities may be declared in a DTD for reuse within that DTD or in a stored file that is referenced from the DTD if we want to make it available to other DTDs. There are different types of entity that we can use:

Parameter entities can only be used within a schema, so we can build modular schemas and combine them to form larger structures. Parameter entities may either include modularized groups of complete declarations within a larger schema, or define fragments of declarations that can be reused within other declarations. Parameter entities can be internal or external:

- Internal parameter entities only have a name and value with the replacement content
- External parameter entities may have system IDs and public identifiers, and are generally used to import declarations from external files

General entities are used for content that may be reused within documents (such as boilerplate text and foreign characters). They may be internal or external, and external entities may be parsed or unparsed

- Internal general entities only have a name and value, the value associated with the name is expanded on parsing. The value can be plain text or well formed markup.
- External general entities need a name and a system identifier. The system identifier is the file name or URL for the content of the entity. It can have a public identifier using formal public identifier syntax of SGML, but there is no standard way to resolve the public identifier to the location so use is completely optional. We should only use these when the project requires it.

Unparsed entities can reference external content that is not in XML and tell the processing application what the content type is.

Creating Reusable Content with XML Schemas

When working with XML Schemas we do not work with entities, rather there are alternative ways of creating reusable content. As we shall see shortly, we have the options of:

- Declaring elements and attributes in global scope.
- Defining elements and types that can be reused internally or across schemas.
- Using the import and include mechanisms to incorporate other schemas (or parts of them). We use the import mechanism when we want to use declarations and definitions from the namespaces of other schemas and for them to remain in the same schema, or we can include declarations and definitions from a different namespace when they are to be treated as part of the schema we are writing.
- Referencing elements, attributes and data types from other schemas using namespaces.

We need to be aware that if we use components from multiple other separate schemas that require validation, it can slow processing down.

Versioning Our Schemas

Even with the best designed schemas, it is likely that there will be need for change at some point in the future, whether this is because users require new feature as they see the benefits of using XML, because of business needs changing, or because we have found mistakes. Because of this, we should always include a way of indicating changes between versions of schemas.

This is important for different reasons:

- The receiving application may not understand the latest DTD, so it will need to be able to take action, for example, skipping the information it does not understand, or raising an exception.
- The application needs to know that potentially different elements of an object pertain to the same object. So, if the structure of an element changes between versions, we should ignore the earlier version's content in favor of the newer so that the structure change does not confuse the application.

In fact, it is likely that we will see less static schemas in the future, as markets change and advance, and in doing so push schemas to support new capabilities, whether these be new clients or new standards. If we think about the number of new clients that we currently see appearing it is likely that markets will drive standards.

If we think about any schema that represents a modern, advancing technology, then as new features are added, companies will want to be able to exploit them, but if there is a standard schema for that technology, the companies will want to make that available. If we imagine a catalog, a company might want to express that it has the capability to support future features for which the markup is not yet written. As a result, schemas will often include an open, readily extensible element to cover this. Applications that do not understand the new part of the schema will either be able to skip it or put it in some standard form, which also means that new applications can be rolled out when possible rather than having to update them with each change in the specification.

There are two main ways of adding versioning to our schemas:

- Using different namespaces for different versions
- Using a `Version` attribute on the root element

Let's take a quick look at each of these approaches.

Using Namespaces for Version Control

One option for handling versions of schemas is to give them a different namespace, for example:

```
http://www.myorganisation.com/schemas/2001-02-08/orders.xsd
```

Here we have put the most current versions of the schema in a folder with its date. This is a similar method to that used by the W3C for their specifications.

Using a Version Attribute on the Root Element

This second technique for versioning can, if we know an element is likely to change, also work at the element level just as well as it can at the document level. It simply involves adding an attribute called `Version` to either the root element (for versioning the whole document) or to the element in question if we are just trying to version-control a specific component of the data model. The value of this `Version` attribute should be a version number of the latest DTD in use. There are a number of conventions that we can use for the value of this attribute, although we should make sure that we are consistent within our organization once we have chosen one. Popular values are a date string `vYYYY-MM-DD` or a major/minor string, for example `v1.02`. This way it is clear to a user or application when one version is later than another.

If we have several versions of a document structure, or components of a document structure, we may also find that it is helpful to add an `EarliestVersion` attribute, which can indicate the earliest version of the structure this document can work with, which is handy if the applications are forced to change at some point because of a radical change in the structure.

As an attribute alone, `Version` does not indicate groups of elements that are from different versions (perhaps when we are creating a document from schemas that are of different versions themselves). At this point we would need to be able to indicate that groups of elements are from a particular version. To do this, we can resort to adding structure to our documents, with a sub-element. Here we push the version controlled sub-elements into an element whose tag is the version they pertain to.

```
<Person Version="v2001-02-08" EarliestVersion="v1998-04-16">
   <v1998-04-16>
      <Name>Bob Winnings</Name>
      <Address>3 Billingsworth Gardens, Hope Street, Arkansas, AS 19012</Address>
   </v1998-04-16>
   <v1999-08-27>
      <Name>
         <FirstName>Bob</FirstName>
         <LastName>Winnings</LastName>
      </Name>
   </v1999-08-27>
   <v2001-02-08>
      <EmployeeType>Full-time</EmployeeType>
   </v2001-02-08>
</Person>
```

Here we can see that the latest version is 8th February 2001. The earliest version was 16th April 1998, when a person was just written as a string. Then, on the 27th August a new version split `Name` up to contain child elements of `FirstName` and `LastName`. Finally, the latest version added an `EmployeeType` element to indicate whether they are full-time, part-time, or contract workers.

Depending on how an application is written, it will be able to deal with the changes in different ways. A recent application would be able to skip the name until it found the version with the latest date offered. Alternatively it could use brute force and just replace any information for which it found a later version. Obviously it would be preferable to just read the latest version available.

In our schema, we can always provide default values for the latest applications to fill in if the data is from an earlier version.

We could transform our data to make sure that information was broken in to latest versions and provide defaults where not given.

Namespaces

Namespace support in XML Schemas is flexible yet straightforward, and allows we to specify whether the elements and attributes in a schema are considered to be a part of that schema. It uses prefixes within the value of some attributes to identify the namespace of elements, attributes, data types, etc. This mechanism can be extended to import definitions from any other namespace and so reuse them in our own schemas. This is an advantage over DTDs as it allows us to open schemas to elements and attributes from other known or unknown schemas.

Each Schema document is bound to a specific namespace through the `targetNamespace` attribute or to the absence of namespace through the lack of such an attribute. So far we have been working without namespaces in the XML Schemas we have been looking at, because we have omitted the `targetNamespace` attribute.

To use namespaces, let's imagine that our example XML belongs to a single namespace:

```
<CD xmlns="http://www.mymusicshop.org/ns/CD/">
```

The least intrusive way to adapt our schema is to add more attributes to the `xsd:schema` element of our schema, as shown below:

```
<xsd:schema
      xmlns:xsd="http://www.w3.org/2000/10/XMLSchema"
      xmlns="http://www.mymusicshop.org/ns/CD/"
      targetNamespace="http://www.mymusicshop.org/ns/CD/"
      elementFormDefault="qualified"
      attributeFormDefault="unqualified" >
```

The namespace declarations play an important role. The first:

```
xmlns:xsd=http://www.w3.org/2000/10/XMLSchema
```

says that we've chosen to use the prefix `xsd` to identify the elements that are defined in the XML Schema specification, and that we will prefix the predefined data types provided by XML Schema with `xsd`; although we could have chosen any prefix, `xsd` is commonly accepted as the one to use. We could even make this our default namespace so that we do not have to prefix the W3C XML Schema elements.

Since we are working with the `http://www.mymusicshop.org/ns/CD/` namespace, we make this our default namespace. This means that we won't prefix the references to our own elements, attributes, data types, etc. we are creating for this schema as belonging to this namespace. Again we could have chosen any prefix to identify this namespace.

```
      xmlns="http://www.mymusicshop.org/ns/CD/"
```

The `targetNamespace` attribute lets us define the namespace of the schema we are creating, independently of the other namespace declarations used.

```
      targetNamespace="http://www.mymusicshop.org/ns/CD/"
```

The `elementFormDefault` and `attributeFormDefault` attributes are a defaulting mechanism used to specify whether attributes and elements are qualified (in a namespace). When declared like this in the `schema` element they work across the whole schema. If we need more control, we can specify it for individual elements and attributes using the `form` attribute on the element or attribute declaration, which takes a value of `qualified` or `unqualified`.

```
      elementFormDefault="qualified"
      attributeFormDefault="unqualified" >
```

All globally defined elements and attributes must always be qualified. Only local elements and attributes can be specified as unqualified.

Elements and attributes without namespaces can be defined in any schema, but we need at least one schema document per namespace we want to define.

If you need to reference objects belonging to this namespace (which is usually the case except when using a pure Russian Doll design – see below for a definition!) you need to provide a namespace declaration in addition to the target Namespace.

Importing Definitions from External Namespaces

Reusing definitions from other namespaces is done through a three-step process. This process needs to be done even for the XML 1.0 namespace in order to declare attributes such as `xml:lang`.

First, the namespace must be defined as usual.

```
<xsd:schema
   xmlns:xsd="http://www.w3.org/2000/10/XMLSchema"
   targetNamespace="http://www.mymusicshop.org/ns/CD/"
   xmlns:xml="http://www.w3.org/XML/1998/namespace"
   elementFormDefault="qualified" >
```

Secondly, the `schema` needs to be informed of the location at which it can find the schema corresponding to the namespace. This is done using an `xsd:import` element.

```
<xsd:import namespace="http://www.w3.org/XML/1998/namespace"
  schemaLocation="myxml.xsd"/>
```

The schema now knows that it should attempt to find any reference belonging to the XML namespace in a schema located at `myxml.xsd`. So, the third and final step is to use the external definition.

```
<xsd:element name="Title">
   <xsd:complexType>
      <xsd:simpleContent>
         <xsd:extension base="xsd:string">
            <xsd:attribute ref="xml:lang"/>
         </xsd:extension>
      </xsd:simpleContent>
   </xsd:complexType>
</xsd:element>
```

We may wonder why we've chosen to reference the `xml:lang` attribute from the XML namespace rather than creating an attribute with a type `xml:lang`. We've done so because there is an important difference between referencing an attribute (or an element) and referencing a data type when namespaces are concerned.

- Referencing an element or an attribute imports the whole thing with its name and namespace.
- Referencing a data type imports only its definition, leaving us with the task of giving a name to the element or attribute we're defining, and places our definition in the target namespace (or no namespace if our attribute or element is unqualified).

Elements Versus Types

During the development of XML Schemas, there have been questions asked about when to use elements and when to declare types. As a result of this, three common design patterns have emerged.

Often it is not obvious whether we should declare something as an element and then reuse that element or to define it as a type and reuse the type we have declared. Here we declare an element that restricts order numbers from a minimum of 1 to a maximum of 10:

```
<element name="LimitedOrderQuantity">
   <simpleType>
      <restriction base="integer">
         <minInclusive value="1"/>
         <maxInclusive value="10"/>
      </restriction>
   </simpleType>
</element>
```

Having declared the element, we can then reuse it in specific products:

```
<element name="Widgets">
   <complexType>
      <sequence>
         <element ref="LimitedOrderQuantity"/>
      </sequence>
   </complexType>
</element>
```

Whereas we can also declare a type to do the same job:

```
<simpleType name="LimitedOrderQuantity"
   <restriction base="integer">
      <minInclusive value="1"/>
      <maxInclusive value="10"/>
   </restriction>
</simpleType>
```

Having declared the type, we can reuse it in an element declaration:

```
<element name="Products">
   <complexType>
      <sequence>
         <element name="Widget" type="LimitedOrderQuantity"/>
      </sequence>
   </complexType>
</element>
```

Should we declare `LimitedOrderQuantity` as an element and reuse the element or should we declare it as a type and reuse that type?

- Declaring it as an element allows `substitionGroups` to be created – this enables the `LimitedOrderQuantity` element to be substituted by members of the `substitutionGroup`.
- Declaring it as a type will allow derived types to be created, thus enabling the `LimitedOrderQuantity` type to be substituted by derived types.

In programming languages types are the items that get reused, and it has been suggested that XML Schemas are a "type-based system", therefore the idea behind schemas is to reuse types. But is this really the case? Here are some general rules that can help us decide:

We should create a type if:

- we are in doubt, because we can always create an element from the type. And with a type, other elements can reuse the type.
- the item is not intended to be an element in instance documents.
- the element or attribute content is to be reused by other items.
- the item is intended to be used as an element in instance documents, it's required that sometimes it be nullable and other times not.

Whereas we should declare an element when:

- the item is intended to be used as an element in instance documents and synonyms/aliases are to be allowed to substitute for the element.

Elements and types can have the same name, because they are in different symbol spaces, but it is wise to given them separate names to avoid confusion. We can always add the word Type to the names of our types to clarify.

Local Versus Global Declarations and Definitions

Having decided whether to declare an element or define a type, we then have to decide whether to declare or define them globally, or whether to nest them locally.

XML Schema users note:

All globally defined elements and attributes must always be qualified by a namespace. Only local elements and attributes can be specified as unqualified.

If an element, `complexType`, or `simpleType` is global, it is an immediate child of `<schema>`:

```
<element name="Album" type="Listing" />
   <complexType name= "Listing">
      <sequence>
         <element ref="Title"/>
         <element ref="Artist"/>
      </sequence>
   </complexType>
<element name="Title" type="string"/>
<element name="Artist" type="string"/>
```

Whereas it is local if it is not an immediate child of `<schema>`, that is, it is nested within another component:

```
<element name="Album">
   <complexType>
      <sequence>
```

```
            <element name="Title" type="string"/>
            <element name="Artist" type="string"/>
        </sequence>
    </complexType>
</element>
```

So, when should we make a type or element global? It is easy to see the benefit of declaring elements or types globally, as they can be reused (not only within a schema, but also across schemas). But there are some benefits to hiding elements/types.

There are three different design models, which were discussed and developed by members of the XML-Dev mailing list, that deal with the question of whether schema components should be declared locally or globally:

- Russian Doll Design
- Salami Slice Design
- Venetian Blind Model

We will study the three models with the same simple XML:

```
<Album>
    <Title>Illusions</Title>
    <Artist>Richard Dach</Artist>
</Album>
```

Let's start with the Russian Doll Design:

Russian Doll Design

In this approach, the structure mirrors the instance document structure, declares an `Album`, and within it a `title`, followed by an `Artist`.

```
<element name="Album">
    <complexType>
        <sequence>
            <element name="Title" type="string"
                     minOccurs="1" maxOccurs="1"/>
            <element name="Artist" type="string"
                     minOccurs="1" maxOccurs="1"/>
        </sequence>
    </complexType>
</element>
```

The instance document has all of its components bundled together, and the schema is designed to bundle together all element declarations.

Salami Slice Design

This is at the other end of the spectrum from the Russian Doll design; we disassemble the instance document into its individual components. In the schema we define each component (as a separate element declaration), and then assemble them together using references to the declaration in a content model or `complexType`.

```
<element name="Title" type="string"/>

<element name="Artist" type="string"/>

<element name="Album">
   <complexType>
      <sequence>
         <element ref="cat:Title"
                  minOccurs="1" maxOccurs="1"/>
         <element ref="cat:Artist"
                  minOccurs="1" maxOccurs="1"/>
      </sequence>
   </complexType>
</element>
```

Note how the schema declared each component individually (`Title`, and `Artist`) and then assembled them together by referencing them in the creation of the `Album` component.

If we think about boxes, where a box represents an element or type:

- The Russian Doll design corresponds to having a single box, and it has nested within it boxes, which in turn have boxes nested within them, and so on, like Russian Dolls.
- The Salami Slice design corresponds to having many separate boxes that are assembled together - some boxes are combined just like salami slices are in sandwiches.

Let's examine the characteristics of each design.

Russian Doll Characteristics

This design is compact and clean, with everything bundled together into a tidy single unit. Because the related data is grouped together into self-contained components, the components are considered **cohesive**. This has some interesting effects that we should note:

- Because the components are **decoupled** – each component is self-contained (they don't interact with other components) – any changes to that component will have limited impact. If the `Title` or `Artist` elements change, the changes will have no effect outside of the `Album` element.
- The `Title` and `Artist` elements have been declared inside the `Album` element, which means they have **localized scope**; they only apply inside the `Album` element, and are not re-usable by themselves. This is known as an **opaque** declaration of content. If the schema has `elementFormDefault="unqualified"` then the `Title` and `Artist` namespaces are hidden within the schema.

Salami Slice Design Characteristics

This design is quite verbose, but everything is laid out clearly and is visible. The effects of this design are quite different to those of the Russian Doll design:

With Salami Slice design, the elements are **coupled**: `Album` depends on `Title` and `Artist`, so if these elements were to change it would impact the `Album` element. So, this design produces a set of interconnected (coupled) components.

Because the components of the `Album` element are declared outside the `Album` element, they have **global scope,** which means they are available to other schemas, which means they are reusable. This is known as **transparent** (rather than opaque) content. This is irrespective of the value of `elementFormDefault`; the namespaces of `Title` and `Artist` will be exposed in the instance documents.

The two approaches differ in a couple of important ways:

- The Russian Doll design facilitates hiding (localizing) namespace complexities. The salami slice design does not.
- The Salami Slice design facilitates component reuse, the Russian Doll design does not.

There is an alternative, which hides the namespace complexities, and still facilitates component reuse.

Venetian Blind Design

Venetian Blind design uses a global type definition with `Title` and `Artist` nested within it to hide the namespace complexities while still facilitating component reuse.

```
<complexType name="PersonType">
   <sequence>
      <element name="Title" type="string"
               minOccurs="1" maxOccurs="1"/>
      <element name="Name" type="string"
               minOccurs="1" maxOccurs="1"/>
   </sequence>
</complexType>

<element name="Person" type="cat:Person"/>
```

Namespaces are hidden, but the `Person` type component is reusable.

With this design, we disassemble the problem into individual components, as Salami Slice does, but instead of creating element declarations, we create type definitions. Here is what our example looks like with this approach:

```
<simpleType name="Title">
   <restriction base="string">
      <enumeration value="Mr."/>
      <enumeration value="Mrs."/>
      <enumeration value="Dr."/>
   </restriction>
</simpleType>

<simpleType name="Name">
   <restriction base="string">
      <minLength value="1"/>
   </restriction>
</simpleType>

<complexType name="Person">
   <sequence>
      <element name="Title" type="cat:Title"
               minOccurs="1" maxOccurs="1"/>
```

```
            <element name="Name" type="cat:Name"
                     minOccurs="1" maxOccurs="1"/>
        </sequence>
    </complexType>

    <element name="Customer" type="cat:Person"/>
```

It maximises reuse by allowing us to reuse the `Title` and `Name` types, the `Person` type and the `Customer` element.

Whether the namespaces of `Title` and `Artist` are hidden or exposed is still determined by the `elementFormDefault` value, they will be shown if the value is `qualified`, and hidden if the value is `unqualified`.

The Salami Slice design allows us to expose namespaces in our instance documents. However, if this should annoy authors, we will have to re-design the schema, whereas if we use the Venetian Blind design, we can control the namespace appearance just by re-setting the value of the `elementFormDefault` attribute, without having to re-design the schema.

Explaining Our Schemas

We should always consider those who have to use the schema by looking for classes of elements, and defining structures that are intuitive, thus helping to promote adoption and use of our schemas. Remember that documentation of our schema is important if others are to take up its use, from commenting to additional documents – any information will help. If we do not we may end up with **semantic drift**, where users change meanings, and alter meaning of fields of data without processing applications knowing.

As with any programming task, sensible use of comments will make the DTD much easier to use. If we are using DTDs, these take the form of normal XML comments, whereas we can use the `Annotation` element in XML Schemas. In addition, if we can make any of the other models we created available to others (especially the static model with the core concepts) it will be much easier for them to see what we were intending with the schema, and it will help prevent semantic drift.

Summary

In this chapter we have looked at various aspects of data modeling. We have gone through the lifespan of a project, from looking at a problem domain and defining the key objects involved, their relationships, and how data flows around an application, through the design of the document, to the design of schemas, with some specific references to both DTD and XML Schema authoring.

We have seen how to create:

- Static and Dynamic information models to represent the parts of a business that we need to represent electronically, and how the data flows around the system.
- How to structure the documents that are messages and that need to be stored persistently.
- How to model specific concepts in schemas, such as:
    - when to use types and elements
    - how to define classes of information and represent them

- how to version control our schemas
- when we should show namespaces

Unfortunately, there is no substitute for experience when creating schemas. If we remember to look for other related schemas before we start on our project we will be able to take advantage of others' experience. Hopefully with some of the concepts you will have learned from this chapter, you will be better armed with the knowledge to start on a project and create a data model that should outlast any application that uses it.

15

XML Data Binding

Introduction

Application data, whether stored as a plain text file, in a RDBMS, or in a custom binary format typically needs to be converted to native data formats before being manipulated by the application. Storing or representing data in XML is no exception.

With the growing use of XML in many applications today, application developers often have the need to access and manipulate the content of XML documents. There are standard ways for a programmer to access this content, such as the W3C DOM API and the de facto standard SAX API from David Megginson (http://www.megginson.com) , but these APIs are used for lower level XML manipulation. They deal with the structure of the XML document. For most applications which need to manipulate XML data, these APIs will be cumbersome, forcing us to deal with the structural components of the XML document to access the data, and they offer no way to depict the meaning of the data. We can write custom APIs or utilities to access the data, but this would be a laborious task. What is needed is a way to access the data without knowing how it is represented, and in a form more natural for our programming language, in a format that depicts its intended meaning.

One solution is data binding. In the next few sections we will explain what data binding is and how it can be used to simplify programming applications that need to interact with XML data.

Note: The Professional XML 2nd Edition code download available from http://www.wrox.com *comes with not only the full code for all the examples, but also Castor, Jakarta Regex library, Xerces, and xslp, to save you some time with your setup for this chapter.*

What is Data Binding?

Data binding is the process of mapping the components of a given data format, such as SQL tables or an XML schema, into a specific representation for a given programming language that depicts the intended meaning of the data format (such as objects, for example). Data binding allows programmers to work naturally in the native code of the programming language, while at the same time preserving the meaning of the original data. It allows us to model the logical structure of the data without imposing the actual specific structure imposed by the format in which the data is stored.

Let's look at an XML example. In most cases the content of an XML document, though stored in XML as simply character data, represents a number of different data types such as strings, integers, real numbers, dates, and encoded binary data to name a few. These different data types are usually grouped together in some logical hierarchy to represent some special meaning for the domain in which the XML data is intended. Ideally, interacting with the XML content as a data model represented as objects, data structures, and primitive types native to the programming language we are using, and in a manner which closely reflects the meaning of that data, would make programming with XML more natural, much less tedious, and improve code readability and maintainability.

What does all this mean? It simply means that instead of dealing with such things as parse trees, event models, or record sets, we interact with objects, integers, floats, arrays, and other programming data types and structures. To summarize, data binding gives us a way to:

- Represent data and structure in the natural format of the programming language we decide to program in.
- Represent data in a way that depicts the intended meaning.
- Allows us to be agnostic about how the data is actually stored.

XML Data Binding

Now that we have an understanding of what data binding is, let's continue with our look at how it works with XML. XML data binding simply refers to the mapping of structural XML components, such as elements and attributes, into a programmatic data model that preserves the logical hierarchy of the components, exposes the actual meaning of the data, and represents the components in the native format of the programming language. This chapter will focus on XML data binding specifically for the Java programming language. In Java, our data model would be represented as an **Object Model**.

An object model in Java is simply a set of classes and primitive types that are typically grouped into a logical hierarchy to model or represent real-world or conceptual objects. An object model could be as simple as consisting of only one class, or very complex consisting of hundreds of classes.

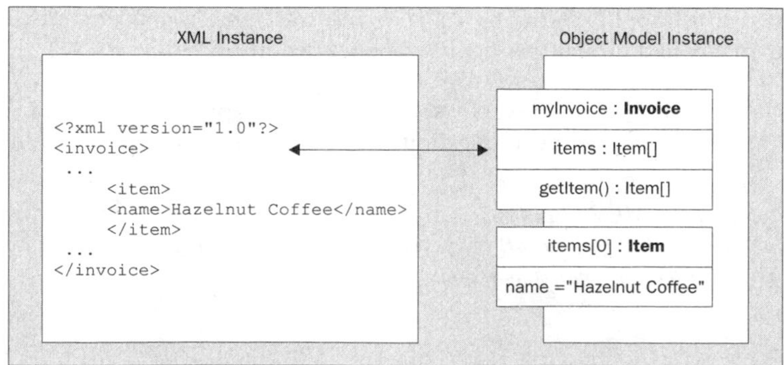

Most XML based applications written today do some form of data binding, perhaps without the programmer even being aware of it. Unless our application was designed specifically to handle generic XML instances it's hard to imagine interacting with XML data without first needing to convert it to a more manageable format. Each time that we convert the value of an attribute to an integer, or create an object to represent an element structure we are performing data binding.

Simple Data Binding Concepts

At this point we already have a good understanding of what data binding is, and hopefully you're convinced that data binding is more practical and more natural to use than generic structure based APIs for typical application development. Structure based APIs are very useful for what they were designed for, interacting with data in the generic format in which it is stored, but if our intent is to interact with the data in a form that closely models the meaning of the data, then data binding is clearly the better choice. This is true for XML data binding, RDBMS data binding, and almost any kind of data binding you can think of. It's always more natural to manipulate data in the native formats of the programming language.

> *While data binding may be the clear choice for interacting with data for many XML applications it may not always be the best choice. If there is no need to interact with the data in a form that models the meaning of the data, or if we only want to grab small bits and pieces of the data, then data binding will probably be more trouble than it's worth.*

How do we bind our XML instances to a Java object model? We have two options; we can write our own data binding utilities, or we can use a data-binding framework (the best solution in most cases). A data-binding framework is an application (or set of applications) that allows data binding solutions to be developed more easily – these frameworks typically come with a number of features, such as source code generation and automatic data binding. We'll see examples of using such features later in the chapter.

XML data binding consists of three primary concepts – **the specification of XML to object model bindings**, **marshaling**, and **unmarshaling**. Different binding frameworks will specify bindings differently and typically a data binding framework will have more than one way to specify such bindings.

When we convert an object model instance into an XML instance we call it marshaling, and when we go in the other direction, from an XML instance to an object model we call it unmarshaling. Many people often get these two terms mixed up. The best way to remember it is that we always look at it from the point of view of writing the program. Our desired format to interact with the data is when it's in the programming language's own natural format. So we start with our Java object model. When we want to store the data we need to marshal it into the proper format. When we want to access the data again we need to unmarshal it back into the object model.

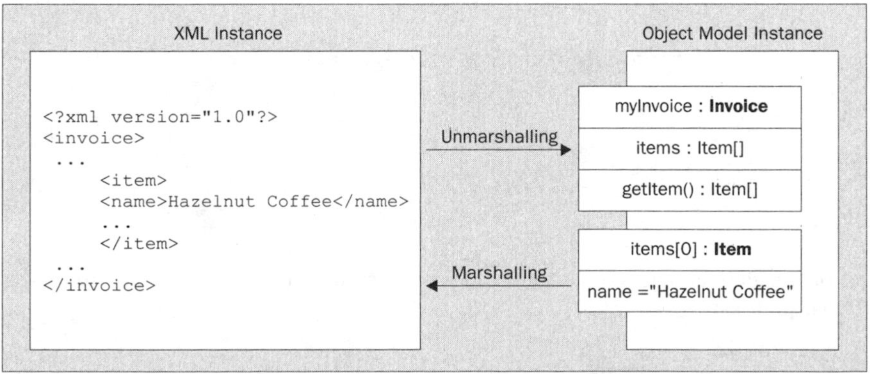

Data Objects

In order to interact with our XML instances and manipulate the data, we'd like to convert the XML instances into a more manageable model that is native to the programming language that we are using. This allows for a more natural way of working with the data and makes our code more readable and maintainable. In our case we'd like to convert the XML model into a Java object model for manipulation and then back into the XML representation when we are finished. In most cases, however, the objects in our model simply do nothing more than hold the data that was once stored as XML, and preserve the logical structure of the XML document. Since these objects have no complex programming or business logic, and just contain typed data, we call them **Data Objects**.

Typically our data objects will also be **Java Beans** (or COM objects if we were working in an MS environment). A Java Bean is a Java class that adheres to the Java Bean design pattern. This means that we follow some basic guidelines when writing our classes so that information can be obtained about our data objects. In most cases, following the method naming conventions of the design pattern for Java Beans is sufficient for tools to obtain information about the fields (also called properties) of our classes by examining the method signatures of a given class. This examination process is called **Introspection** (as defined by the Java Beans Specification). The main guideline for the design pattern is that all publicly accessible fields have proper **getter** and **setter** access methods. For a given field, a getter method is quite simply a method that returns the value of that field, while a setter method is one that allows us to set the value of the field.

The Java Beans design pattern indicates that getter methods should begin with "`get`", followed by the field name, with the first letter of the field name capitalized. The setter methods follow the same pattern, but begin with "`set`". For example, if we had a field called `Name`, the getter method should be called `getName` and the setter method `setName`.

Let's look at a simple Java Bean. If we had an `Invoice` class that contained a shipping address, a billing address and a collection of items, our Java Bean would look something like the following:

```
public class Invoice {

   public Invoice() { ... }


   public BillingAddress getBillingAddress();

   public void setBillingAddress(BillingAddress address);

   public ShippingAddress getShippingAddress();

   public void setShippingAddress(ShippingAddress address);

   public Vector getItem();

   public void setItem(Vector items);

}
```

For indexed properties such as our `Vector` of items it is often useful to provide indexed setter and getter methods, such as:

```
    public Item getItem(int index);

    public void setItem(int index, Item item);
```

The indexed setter and getter methods would apply to arrays, vectors, and ordered lists, but doesn't make sense for other types of collections such as sets, or hash tables, which do not preserve the order of the collection.

It's not required that our data objects be Java Bean compliant, but it is good practice. The main reason is that a data-binding framework will most likely need to determine certain information about a given object such as the field names and Java types by examining the class type of the object, using introspection. This will be discussed in more detail later in the chapter.

For more information on Java Beans see the Java Beans specification version 1.01 (http://java.sun.com/products/javabeans/docs/spec.html)

What's Wrong with APIs Such As DOM and SAX?

Most readers should be familiar by now with the DOM and SAX APIs discussed in earlier chapters (11 and 12, respectively). The W3C DOM is tree-based while SAX is event-based, but both APIs are structure-centric in that they deal purely with the structural representation of an XML document. The basic format of an XML document is a hierarchical structure comprised mainly of elements, attributes and character data. There is nothing actually wrong with these APIs if they are used for their intended purpose, manipulating XML documents in a way that represents the generic structure of the XML document.

Most applications that need to access the contents of an XML document, however, will not need to know whether data was represented as an attribute or an element, but simply that the data is structured and has a certain meaning. APIs such as the DOM and SAX, while providing meaningful representations of the data, can only provide extremely generic representations that make accessing our data long winded, which for high-level XML manipulation adds complexity to our applications that is unnecessary. Programmers must essentially walk the structure of the XML in order to access the data. This data also often needs to be converted into its proper format before it can be manipulated, which can be a very tedious process. This is necessary because the data returned using these APIs is simply a set of characters, or a string. If the contents of an element should represent some sort of date or time instance, then the programmer must take the character data and convert it to a date representation in the programming language. In Java this would most likely be an instance of `java.util.Date` (the Java date function). If the element itself represents a set of other elements, we would need to create the appropriate object representation and continue converting sub-elements.

There are specifications, such as the W3C XPath Recommendation, which improve our ability to easily access the data within an XML document without the need for walking the complete structure. XPath is great for extracting small pieces of information from an XML document. Unfortunately the data still needs to be converted to the proper format if it is to be manipulated. It also tends to add complexity and extra overhead to our applications if our goal is to access data throughout the entire document.

Let's look at an example to demonstrate how one would use SAX to handle data binding (`Invoice.java`, below). Recall our `Invoice` class from the previous section. For simplicity let's assume for that the invoice only contains a set of items, where each item in our set has a unique product identifier called an SKU number, a product name, a quantity, unit price, and a description. We will also assume the price is in US dollars.

For brevity we've removed most of the code and comments and we show only the method signatures. The complete code for can be found in the code download at http://www.wrox.com.

```
public class Invoice {

    public Invoice() { ... }

    public void addItem(Item item);

    public Vector getItem();

    public void setItem(Vector items);
}
```

For convenience I've taken the liberty to include an `addItem()` method that will add the items incrementally to the internal `Vector` of items for us. We could also have added a `removeItem()` method, but we won't use it in our example. Often classes like to abstract how a collection of objects is implemented, and "add" and "remove" methods are a good way to do this. The add/remove methods actually stray slightly from the standard Java Beans design pattern. In Java Beans add/remove methods are usually used for Event Listeners. Nonetheless, the approach of using add/remove methods is a good one if you want to abstract implementation details from your class definitions.

Let's take a look at our `Item` class (`item.java`) :

```
public class Item {


    private int _quantity = 0;

    ...

    public Item() { ... };

    public String getDescription() { ... };

    public void setDescription(String desc) { ... };

    public String getName() { ... };

    public void setName(String name) { ... };

    public double getPrice() { ... };

    public void setPrice(double price) { ... };

    public String getProductSku() { ... };

    public void setProductSku(String sku) { ... };

    /**
     * Returns the desired quantity for this Item.
     *
     * @returns the desired quantity for this Item.
    **/
```

```
    public int getQuantity() { return _quantity };

    /**
     * Sets the desired quantity of this Item.
     *
     * @param quantity the desired quantity for this Item.
    **/
    public void setQuantity(int quantity) {
       _quantity = quantity;
    }

} //-- Item
```

You'll notice our representation of an item also conforms to the Java Beans design pattern we discussed in the previous section, as we have proper getter and setter methods for each field in our class.

Now that we have our object model, let's look at a sample XML instance for our invoice:

```
<?xml version="1.0"?>
<invoice>
   <item>
      <name>ACME Rocket Powered Roller Blades</name>
      <description>ACME's model R2 Roller Blades</description>
      <price>999.98</price>
      <product-sku>9153556177842</product-sku>
      <quantity>1</quantity>
   </item>
   <item>
      <name>ACME Bird Feed</name>
      <description>25 pound bag of Bird feed.</description>
      <price>17.49</price>
      <product-sku>9128973676533</product-sku>
      <quantity>2</quantity>
   </item>
</invoice>
```

We can see that our object model and XML instance look very similar. Both XML and Object Oriented programming are ideal for modeling real-world objects.

How do we unmarshal our XML instance of our invoice into an instance of `Invoice`? To do this in SAX 2.0 we need to create an implementation of the SAX `ContentHandler` interface.

The `ContentHandler` interface specifies many methods that allow us to receive events for elements with their associated attributes, character data, and other XML components. In our implementation of this interface we have to create methods that handle the events for all the different types of XML components that a `ContentHandler` declares methods for. In most cases, we only truly need to implement three methods: `startElement`, `endElement`, and `characters`. In order to be a valid implementation, however, we must create empty methods for all of the declared methods of the interface. Hopefully you're already getting the feeling we're not going to be doing too much!

> *For readability I will not show the empty methods, but the full source can be found in the code download at* http://www.wrox.com.

Let's look at the code for InvoiceContentHandler.java:

To start we need to import the SAX package and declare that our class implements the ContentHandler interface.

```
/* import sax related class */

import org.xml.sax.*;

...

public class InvoiceContentHandler
   implements org.xml.sax.ContentHandler
{
```

In order to build our Invoice object model our ContentHandler must keep track of some state while we are handling the XML events. We need the Invoice instance that we are creating, the current item that is being created and a buffer to hold character data.

```
   private Invoice _invoice = null;

   private Item _current = null;

   private StringBuffer _buffer = null;
```

The constructor for our ContentHandler will initialize the StringBuffer, but our Invoice instance and Item instances will get initialized as our handler receives events.

```
   public InvoiceContentHandler() {
      super();
      _buffer = new StringBuffer();
    } //-- InvoiceContentHandler
```

We also create a method that is used to obtain the Invoice instance when we are finished handling the events:

```
   public Invoice getInvoice() {
      return _invoice;
   } //-- getItems
```

Now let's look at the startElement() method. When we receive the start element events for Invoice and Item we simply create new instances of these classes. We also add some error handling code to make sure we receive a correct XML instance:

```
   public void startElement
      (String namespaceURI, String localName, String qName, Attributes atts)
   throws SAXException
{
   if (localName.equals("invoice")) {
```

```
        _invoice = new Invoice();
        _buffer.setLength(0);
    }
    else {
        if (_invoice == null) {
            throw new SAXException("Invalid XML Instance, missing <invoice>
element.");
        }
        else if (localName.equals("item")) {
            _current = new Item();
            _invoice.addItem( _current );
        }
        else {
            _buffer.setLength(0);
        }
    }
} //-- startElement
```

You'll notice that for all elements other than `invoice` and `item` we simply clear the `StringBuffer`. The reason is that all the other possible elements in our XML instance simply hold character data that represents either String values or primitive types. Therefore we don't have any classes that need to get created for them.

> *For validation purposes we could also use a Validating XML parser in conjunction with some sort of XML schema. A DTD wouldn't suffice here because DTDs contain no type information, but could be used to simply validate the structure. This might be overkill for our simple example, but for large XML instances it would greatly reduce the amount of hard-coded checking that we need to perform.*

The `characters()` method will simply save the characters to the `StringBuffer` so that they are available when we receive the end element event.

```
    public void characters (char[] chars, int start, int length)
    throws SAXException
{
    //-- save characters for later use
    _buffer.append(chars, start, length);

} //-- characters
```

The `endElement()` method looks for each of the elements in our XML instance and converts the saved `StringBuffer` into the appropriate type.

```
    public void endElement
        (String namespaceURI, String localName, String qName)
    throws SAXException
{
    if (localName.equals("item")) {
        _current = null;
    }
    else if (localName.equals("name")) {
        _current.setName( _buffer.toString() );
```

```
    }
    else if (localName.equals("description")) {
       _current.setDescription( _buffer.toString() );
    }
    else if (localName.equals("product-sku")) {
       _current.setProductSku( _buffer.toString() );
    }
    else if (localName.equals("price")) {
       //-- we need to convert string buffer to a double
       try {
          Double price = Double.valueOf ( _buffer.toString() );
          _current.setPrice( price.doubleValue() );
       }
       catch (NumberFormatException nfe) {
          //-- handle error
          throw new SAXException( nfe );
       }
    }
    else if (localName.equals("quantity")) {
       //-- we need to convert string buffer to an int
       try {
          _current.setQuantity( Integer.parseInt( _buffer.toString() ) );
       }
       catch (NumberFormatException nfe) {
          //-- handle error
          throw new SAXException( nfe );
       }
    }

 } //-- endElement
```

Notice that we need to convert the `StringBuffer` to a `double` for the price field, and to an `int` for the quantity field.

We've finished the necessary binding and unmarshaling code for our example. I don't know about you, but for me that was too much work to simply create the object model for our XML instance! In addition, maintaining this piece of code would be rather tedious and the larger the document structure, the greater the possibility of errors. Any time the structure of the document changes you will most assuredly need to modify the `startElement`/`endElement` methods, which are the most complicated methods in the `ContentHandler` to implement.

We now need to call the SAX `XMLReader` to read our XML instance using our implementation of `ContentHandler`. This code is sufficient (`SAXInvoiceExample.java`):

```
 //-- Create an instance of our ContentHandler
 InvoiceContentHandler invoiceHandler = new InvoiceContentHandler();

 //-- Create and configure SAX XMLReader
 XMLReader parser = new SAXParser();
 parser.setContentHandler( invoiceHandler );

 //-- Parse our example XML instance
 parser.parse( new InputSource("invoice.xml") );
```

```
//-- Get Invoice instance
Invoice invoice = invoiceHandler.getInvoice();
```

The full example code in the download will also display the newly created `Invoice` instance on the screen.

Our example was actually quite small, but imagine having to manually write data binding code for hundreds of elements and attributes in order to manipulate it. It's just too tedious, time consuming, and potentially very error-prone. In our example we only covered unmarshaling. Marshaling would be a bit simpler as we might not need to include any validation code, but it's basically just as tedious.

Using the W3C DOM API is quite similar to SAX, but instead of dealing with events we deal with a tree structure. In our SAX `ContentHandler` the events were passed to us, and we simply built our Invoice object model. Using the DOM we would simply start with the `Document` node, obtain the document element, which in our case is the `<invoice>` element, and recursively process all of its associated attributes and child nodes.

Both of these APIs are great if our application needs to deal with XML at this lower level. In most cases however our applications will not need such low-level interaction and these APIs simply add more work than is necessary to solve our problems.

The Need for a Data Binding Framework

I hope that by now I have convinced you that using APIs like DOM and SAX are just too tedious for most large-scale XML-based programming projects. I asked you at the end of the last section to imagine having to write data binding code for hundreds of elements and attributes. Now imagine having to do it for all your XML-enabled applications. This would be very tedious and extremely boring, as well as error-prone, and tricky to test and debug. You'd probably end up needing counseling, your spouse would divorce you because your nightmares about elements, attributes, and `NumberFormatExceptions` would be just too strange for him or her to deal with, and ultimately you would end up quitting your job for something more exciting!

If that wasn't enough, imagine having to maintain all that code. Each time your boss decides he or she wants to change the XML schema you'd have to go back through all that binding code and find the right code to change. Code maintenance would be pretty difficult for large XML schemas.

The good news is that we don't need to use these types of API at all!

> **What we need is a simple framework that allows us to specify how an XML schema should map into an object model and automatically handle the data binding for us.**

As we have discussed above, such a framework is called a data-binding framework. Using such a framework allows us to easily perform XML data binding, as well as to easily maintain our code when we need to change the representation of our XML data – the framework will handle the marshaling and unmarshaling automatically.

The even better news, as we'll see in the next section, is that such a data-binding framework exists, and it's free!

XML Data Binding with Castor

So far we've introduced XML data binding, discovered that APIs such as SAX and DOM are not always the best choice when it comes to writing XML based applications, witnessed the tediousness of hand-coded data binding using SAX, and have discussed the need for a data-binding framework. Now I'd like to introduce you to a project called **Castor**, an open source data-binding framework for Java that supports binding XML, relational databases, and LDAP. For this chapter we will only concern ourselves with the XML data binding capabilities. Castor is freely downloadable at http://www.castor.org.

Before we jump into the code, I want to give you a brief background on the project. Castor was started when Assaf Arkin, the CTO of Intalio, Inc., decided that he wanted to use XML files to store configuration data for another open source project that he was writing. To read the configuration files he wanted to use XML data binding and not one of the XML APIs, for all the reasons we have specified in the previous sections. However, there was a big problem. There wasn't an XML data binding framework freely available for him to use. So he asked me to write a simple framework for him.

Castor XML was initially based on the Java specification request for XML data binding (JSR 31) from Sun Microsystems, Inc. The first draft of JSR 31 was very small and vague, but outlined enough concepts for me to try to follow during my initial implementation. Depending on what happens with the JSR 31 specification in the future Castor may or may not adhere to it.

Today, Castor has benefited from a large user community as its current design has been influenced by feedback and numerous contributions from the users. The core development of Castor is funded by Exolab.org (http://www.exolab.org), which hosts and sponsors a number of open source projects, but Castor wouldn't be the product it is today without the valuable contributions, such as bug reports, suggestions, and code that it receives from its user base.

Castor is written in Java and performs data binding specific to the Java language; in other words, you cannot use Castor to perform XML data binding in C++. Internally Castor XML uses the SAX API as it's underlying XML API. Castor actually interacts with the SAX API during marshaling/unmarshaling so that you don't have to! We'll discuss this more in the following sections.

Castor is designed to not only to work with existing Java object models, but it can generate complete object models based on a given XML Schema! Castor has three core data binding methodologies: automatic data binding using built-in introspection, user specified data binding, and XML Schema based data binding with complete source code generation. These methodologies can be used independently or together, which makes Castor a very powerful and easy to use data binding framework. We will discuss these approaches in the following sections.

You will notice throughout the next few sections that I often refer to different ways to configure Castor. Most of the configuration takes place in a file called `castor.properties`. This file is located in the Castor `.jar` file (`org/exolab/castor/castor.properties`). If you need to configure Castor, simply place a copy of this file in your current working directory and make any necessary modifications. The actual configuration changes are explained further in the following sections.

Now that we know a little history of the project and some basics, let's get to the code!

Using Castor's Built-in Introspection

The easiest way to get started with Castor is to simply rely on its default capabilities to automatically handle simple data binding. Using the default capabilities of Castor is so easy you might wonder why you were ever using an XML API to begin with! The best way to learn anything is to simply try it, so we'll start with a simple example and then explain what Castor is doing behind the scenes.

We'll continue with our invoice theme. Recall our data object representation of an invoice item from the previous section – I've repeated `Item.java` here so that I can make a few additional points about the class.

```
public class Item {

   public Item() { ... };

   public String getDescription() { ... };

   public void setDescription(String name) { ... };

   public String getName() { ... };

   public void setName(String name) { ... };

   public double getPrice() { ... };

   public void setPrice(double price) { ... };

   public String getProductSku() { ... };

   public void setProductSku(String sku) { ... };

   public int getQuantity() { ... };

   public void setQuantity(int quantity) { ... };

} //-- Item
```

This is the same class definition that we used in the first example. No modifications are necessary. As mentioned previously, we have followed the Java Beans design pattern when creating this class definition, which will be important for Castor to be able to automatically determine information about our data object. Castor will need to introspect this class and examine the method signatures during the marshaling and unmarshaling processes. We also have a default constructor. A default constructor is simply a constructor that takes no arguments. This is important since Castor needs to be able to instantiate our objects during unmarshaling. If our objects only had constructors that required arguments, Castor wouldn't know how to create them.

In the following two sections we will demonstrate both marshaling and unmarshaling instances of our `Item` class. We will start with the unmarshaling process first because it's usually more complicated than marshaling and then we'll move into the marshaling process.

Default Unmarshaling

Let's take a look at an XML instance of an item that we would like to unmarshal into an instance of our `Item` class (`item.xml`):

```
<?xml version="1.0"?>
<item>
   <name>ACME Hazelnut Coffee</name>
   <product-sku>9123456123456</product-sku>
   <description>A pound of ACME Hazelnut Coffee - Whole Bean</description>
   <price>9.99</price>
   <quantity>2</quantity>
</item>
```

Since most programmers, at least the ones that I know, including myself, spend more time drinking coffee than actually writing code, our invoice item appropriately represents an order for 2 pounds of coffee from the company that produces everything from rocket-powered roller skates to quick dry cement.

We now have our object model representation and our XML instance document, so let's take a look at the code necessary to unmarshal our XML instance into our object model (`ItemTest.java`):

```
//-- import Castor XML classes
import org.exolab.castor.xml.*;
```

At the top of the class we need to import Castor related packages.

```
...
...
   public static void main() {

      //-- unmarshal instance of item
      Item item = (Item) Unmarshaller.unmarshal(Item.class,
                     new FileReader("item.xml"));
```

That's all that's needed. Let's add a few lines of code to print some of the values of our item:

```
//-- Display unmarshalled address to the screen
System.out.println("Invoice Item");
System.out.println("------------");
System.out.println("Product Name: " + item.getName());
System.out.println("Sku Number : " + item.getProductSku());
System.out.println("Price      : " + item.getPrice());
System.out.println("Quantity   : " + item.getQuantity());
```

Sample output:

> java ItemTest

```
Invoice Item
------------

Product Name: ACME Hazelnut Coffee
Sku Number : 9123456123456
Price     : 9.99
Quantity  : 2
```

Now that was pretty easy, right? What happens, however, if we change our XML file slightly by renaming our element name of the SKU number, currently `product-sku`, to simply `sku`? Let's give it a try and find out (`modified_item.xml`):

```
<?xml version="1.0" standalone="yes"?>
<item>
   <name>ACME Hazelnut Coffee</name>
   <sku>9123456123456</sku>
   <description>A pound of ACME Hazelnut Coffee - Whole Bean</description>
   <price>9.99</price>
   <quantity>2</quantity>
</item>
```

Now we re-run our test case and we get the following result:

```
> java ItemTest

Invoice Item
------------

Product Name: ACME Hazelnut Coffee
Sku Number : null
Price     : 9.99
Quantity   : 2
```

What happened? Why is the SKU number listed as `null`? The simple answer is that we are relying on the default capabilities of Castor. When we changed the element name, Castor was unable to match this name to the proper field in our `Item` class because it was expecting a method, that did not exist. Element naming is important if we are relying on Castor to automatically figure out our data binding. We will see in the section "Using Castor Mapping Files" how we can properly unmarshal the modified version of our XML instance, but first let's take a look at default marshaling.

Default Marshaling

We have seen how simple it is to unmarshal an XML instance into an object model. How about going in the other direction? Let's expand on our example a bit by modifying the quantity field. We all know that 2 pounds of coffee won't last too long for most IT professionals. We will change the example so that after we unmarshal our XML instance into an `Item` object, we will double the quantity to 4 pounds, and then we will marshal this `Item` into a new XML instance.

Let's look at the code necessary to update and marshal our XML instance (`ItemUpdate.java`):

```
...
/* unmarshaling code removed for brevity */
...
//-- update quantity to 4 pounds instead of 2
item.setQuantity( 4 );

//-- marshal item
FileWriter writer = new FileWriter("item_updated.xml");
Marshaller.marshal(item, writer);
writer.close();
```

That's it! `ItemUpdate.java` will save our new XML instance into a file called `item_updated.xml`:

```
<?xml version="1.0"?>
<item>
   <name>ACME Hazelnut Coffee</name>
   <quantity>4</quantity>
   <description>A pound of ACME Hazelnut Coffee - Whole Bean</description>
   <price>9.99</price>
   <product-sku>9123456123456</product-sku>
</item>
```

You might have noticed that our elements are not in the same order. Using Castor's default capabilities ordering of elements is not preserved. In most cases the ordering is not important (although element ordering is important from a valid XML point of view). We'll see how ordering can be preserved in the sections on *Mapping* and *The Complete Data Binding Solution.*

For the advanced reader, who might be a bit curious, the ordering for the default behavior will actually depend on the order in which the method names for the class are examined. This is actually dependent on the class loader. Castor uses the Java Reflection API to obtain the information about the methods of a given class. The order in which the methods are obtained using the Java Reflection API is the order in which Castor will marshal fields. For more information on the Java Reflection API please see http://java.sun.com/products/jdk/1.1/docs/guide/reflection/

A Closer Look At the Default Behavior of Castor XML

Using the default behavior of Castor XML is pretty simple, but let's take a closer look at what is actually happening during the unmarshaling and marshaling of our XML instances. The key to the default behavior in Castor is introspection – recall that this is the process in which the design of a class is examined in order to deduce certain information about it.

Unmarshaling

During unmarshaling, Castor starts with the **document element** of the XML instance. The document element is automatically mapped to an instance of the class passed to the `unmarshal` method. Recall how we invoked the unmarshaller on our `Item` class:

```
//-- unmarshal instance of item
Item item = (Item) Unmarshaller.unmarshal(Item.class,
        new FileReader("item.xml"));
```

We gave the unmarshaller the starting point for our object model. It isn't always necessary to do this, however, when using the default data binding capabilities, it's necessary to give Castor the starting class of our object model when:

- Our starting class does not have a name that can be inferred from the document element name; for example, if we have an element named `<foo>`, but our class name is `FooImpl`.
- Our starting class belongs to a **package** (a Java facility that allows classes to be logically grouped together as well as way to differentiate from classes provided by others), which will be the majority of the time, because it is always good practice to use packages.

There are some special features in Castor that allow us to circumvent this requirement, but discussion of these features is beyond the scope of this chapter.

After Castor has mapped the document element, introspection is used to examine the method signatures of the class. For each sub-element and attribute that exists in the document element, Castor attempts to map to a specific `setter` method by comparing the name of the element or attribute to the name of the method. Castor uses the design patterns specified in the Java Beans specification to find the proper method. For example, Castor will map our `<quantity>` element to a method called `setQuantity`. If the XML name contains a hyphen, Castor will remove the hyphen and capitalize the following character. For example, `<product-sku>` will be mapped to a method called `setProductSku()`.

Once a method is found, the method signature is examined to determine the proper Java type for the argument. Castor will then attempt to convert the data to the proper format. For example, our `setQuantity()` method in our `Item` class has a Java primitive `int` type as the argument, so Castor converts the character data from our `<quantity>` element to an `int` and invokes the `setQuantity()` method using this value.

For all complex elements, which are elements that contain sub-elements and attributes, the same process that is used on the document element is followed. The only difference is that the class type that the element is mapped to is obtained by the examination of the method signatures as discussed above. If Castor cannot find an appropriate setter method, the data for that element or attribute will simply be ignored. Castor takes a "do the best you can" approach to automatic data binding.

This entire process is continued recursively until the entire document is processed.

Marshaling

The marshaling process is much like the unmarshaling process except that we start with our object model and produce an XML instance. The document element for the XML instance is the object instance that we pass into the `marshal()` method:

```
...
Marshaller.marshal(item, writer);
...
```

In our example, the `item` object will be marshalled as the document element. The name for the document element is derived from the class name of the object. By default, when Castor converts Java names to XML names the first character is converted to lower case. All subsequent upper case characters, which typically identify new words, are converted to lower case and preceded by a hyphen. The following chart shows some examples of Java names and their corresponding default XML name. If two or more characters in a row are in upper case they will be not be converted to lower case.

Java class or field name	Castor's default conversion for XML
`Invoice`	`<invoice>`
`ShippingAddress`	`<shipping-address>`
`Item`	`<item>`
`NAME`	`<NAME>`

Castor can be configured to allow mixed case in XML names modifying the `org.exolab.castor.xml.naming` property in the `castor.properties` file as follows:

```
...
# change naming algorithm to allow mixed-case
org.exolab.castor.xml.naming=mixed
...
```

In this configuration only the first character is converted to lower case, so no hyphen is needed to separate words (known as camelCasing). The above names would all be converted the same except for `ShippingAddress`, which would be converted to `shippingAddress`.

Castor also allows custom naming algorithms by simply implementing the `org.exolab.castor.xml.XMLNaming` *interface. This is actually beyond the scope of this chapter, but for more information on configuring Castor, please see the Castor documentation available from* www.castor.org.

Based on the above naming conversions the instance of our `Item` class will have an XML instance name of `<item>`. Once the document element is created, Castor uses introspection to examine all public `getter` methods of the class. For each `getter` method, Castor will create an appropriate XML node, either an attribute or an element, based on the return type of the method. Castor can be configured to handle primitive types (such as `int`, `float`, etc.) as either attributes or elements. In our example we have configured Castor to treat all primitive types as elements. If however the return type is an object, Castor will always create an element. The names of the `getter` methods will be used to create XML names, using the above naming conversions, for their respective fields. For example, our `getQuantity` method will be used to create an element called `<quantity>`.

```
...
  <quantity>4</quantity>
...
```

This entire process is repeated recursively for all objects in the object model.

Conclusion

We've been introduced to the default binding capabilities of Castor, and seen that it's very easy to automatically have Castor handling our binding for us. Even though it's very easy to use the default capabilities it might be difficult to understand what's actually happening if something doesn't marshal or unmarshal properly; for example, when we wanted to use `<sku>` instead of `<product-sku>` we received a `null` value. We also have to make sure that we follow the Java Beans design pattern by using proper getter and setter methods and making sure we have a default constructor, otherwise the default introspection won't work properly. There is also some overhead to having Castor examine all fields of a class, and use the Java Reflection API to interact with class instances, especially if there are many classes in the object model. In the next section we will see how to overcome some of these limitations and have more control over the binding process by using a **mapping file**.

Using Castor Mapping Files

Now that we've seen how easy it is using Castor's default introspection capabilities to automatically handle data binding for us, let's look at how we can have greater control over our XML bindings. It is often the case that the default introspection capabilities are not sufficient to perform the desired data binding. Recall in the previous section we changed our `<product-sku>` element to simply `<sku>`, like so:

```
<?xml version="1.0"?>
<item>
   <name>ACME Hazelnut Coffee</name>
   <sku>9123456123456</sku>
   <description>A pound of ACME Hazelnut Coffee - Whole Bean</description>
   <price>9.99</price>
   <quantity>2</quantity>
</item>
```

The default capabilities were no longer able to perform the automatic binding for us. To solve problems like this, Castor has a binding mechanism called a mapping file. The mapping file is actually an XML document that is written from the point of view of the object model. It describes our object model and allows us specify some XML binding information when needed.

The mapping file allows us to specify how a given Java class and its fields "map" to and from XML; we call this the **XML binding** for the class. The following XML bindings can be specified:

- The node type that a given field should be "bound" to (element, attribute, or text).
- The XML name for a class or a field.
- Namespace declarations for a class

A node is the core component of the XML structure. Elements, attributes, character data, processing instructions, and comments are all examples of nodes.

The mapping file also lets us specify the name of the getter and setter methods for each field in the class. This allows us to perform XML data binding on class definitions that do follow the Java Beans design pattern. We'll examine this in more detail in the next section.

The Mapping File

The mapping file contains two types of information, a description of the object model, and information on how the object model relates to the XML document (or database).

The easiest way to explain the mapping file is to simply show an example. We will show how to write the mapping for our `Item` class so that we can properly marshal and unmarshal instances of the modified version of our XML schema for our invoice item.

We will look at the features necessary for expressing XML bindings only, but the mapping file is also used for relational database bindings. As mentioned in the introduction, Castor supports RDB data binding for Java. Both the XML and RDB bindings can be specified in the same file for classes that will be used in both forms of data binding.

Let's take a look at how to specify the mapping file.

The mapping file conforms to an XML schema, which can be found in the Castor `.jar` file: org/exolab/castor/mapping/mapping.xsd.

The <mapping> Element

A mapping file starts with the `<mapping>` element. This is the document element and simply contains zero or more class mappings.

```
<?xml version="1.0"?>
<mapping>

   <description>Mapping example for our Item class</description>

   <!-- class mappings -->
   ...
</mapping>
```

The `<mapping>` element also allows an optional `<description>` element as we can see in our example above. It also supports the inclusion of other mapping files, but we won't be discussing includes in this chapter.

The <class> Element

The class mapping consists of the `<class>` element. This element specifies the name of the class, and contains zero or more field mappings. It may also contain an optional `map-to` element, which is used to specify an XML name mapping and namespace declaration for the described class. We don't need the `<map-to>` element in our example, but it's often needed for classes that may appear as a document element. This is explained in more detail in the Castor documentation. Our example will deal only with field mappings:

```
<?xml version="1.0"?>
<mapping>

   <description>Mapping example for the Item class</description>

   <class name="Item">
      <!—field mappings -->
   </class>
</mapping>
```

The `name` attribute of the `<class>` element simply specifies the class name. This must be the full package name of the class. Since our `Item` class does not use a package we don't specify one. If we were using the package `org.acme.invoice`, our class mapping would look like:

```
<class name="org.acme.invoice.Item">
   <!-- field mappings -->
</class>
```

The `<class>` element also supports an optional `extends` attribute, which can be used to specify a super class (also called a base class) for the described class. This is really only needed if the described class extends another class which also has a class mapping. This allows us to reuse field mappings (see the next section) from the super class without having to re-specify the mappings. All that needs to be specified is the new fields from the subclass.

We don't need to use the `extends` attribute in our class mapping for the `Item` class, but an example of what this would look like is as follows:

```
<class name="org.acme.invoice.InvoiceObject">
   <!-- local field mappings -->
</class>
...
<class name="org.acme.invoice.Item"
       extends="org.acme.invoice.InvoiceObject">
   <!-- inherits field mappings from InvoiceObject -->
   <!-- local field mappings -->
</class>
```

The <field> Element

The `<field>` element allows us to specify field mappings. A field mapping is where we actually express some data binding information. The field mapping describes the field name, its class type, and optionally the setter and getter methods. The field mapping may also optionally contain the `<bind-xml>` element which allows use to specify specific XML bindings for the given field.

Let's look at the field mapping for our product SKU number:

```
...
   <field name="productSku"
      type="string"/>
...
```

Here we have specified the field name as `productSku` and its type as "`string`".

The `name` attribute is simply the name of the field. The value of the `name` attribute is not always important if we provide full specification of the field mapping, but is important if we do not specify `getter` and `setter` methods (we'll see how to specify these later in this section), as introspection will be used to determine these methods. Therefore in the above field mapping, introspection will be used and Castor will deduce that `getProductSku` and `setProductSku` are the appropriate access methods.

Since the mapping file is written from the point of view of the object model, the `type` attribute specifies the Java class type of the field. You'll notice that our field mapping simply used "`string`" as the type, which doesn't look like the Java string type, `java.lang.String`. Since writing "`java.lang.String`" is rather tedious Castor has aliases, or short cuts, for many of the native Java types.

The following is a list of some of the common type aliases. A complete list may be found in the mapping documentation for Castor.

Alias	Java Class Type	Java Primtive Type
`string`	`java.lang.String`	N/A
`integer`	`java.lang.Integer.TYPE`	int
`double`	`java.lang.Double.TYPE`	double
`boolean`	`java.lang.Boolean.TYPE`	boolean
`long`	`java.lang.Long.TYPE`	long
`float`	`java.lang.Float.TYPE`	float
`date`	`java.util.Date`	N/A

You'll notice in the table that for a primitive type the actual Java class instances of those types are actually used. For example, the `int` type is actually represented by the class `java.lang.Integer.TYPE`.

If a type is a collection, such as a `java.util.Vector`, the optional `collection` attribute is used to specify the type of the collection, and the `type` attribute is used to specify the type of the elements of in the collection. If, for example, we expanded our mapping example to include the `Invoice` class, which contains a collection of `Item` objects, such as:

```
public class Invoice {
    ...
    public void addItem(Item item);
    ...
    public Vector getItems();
    ...
}
```

We could use the following field mapping for the items:

```
...
    <field name="items"
       type="Item" collection="vector"/>
...
```

We'll see an example of using collections later in this section.

The following is a partial list of the collection type aliases:

Alias	Java Class Type
array	type[ ].class
vector	java.util.Vector
arraylist	java.util.ArrayList
set	java.util.Set
hashtable (not yet fully supported)	java.util.Hashtable

Though we didn't need to specify getter and setter methods for our example it's quite easy to do so. We simply add `get-method()` and `set-method()` attributes respectively. An example of this is as follows:

```
...
    <field name="productSku" type="string"
          get-method="getProductSku" set-method="setProductSku"/>
...
```

Again, the specification of setter and getter methods is redundant for our specific case, but if our method names do not follow the Java Beans design pattern then we need to specify this information. For example, if our `setProductSku()` method is changed to `updateProductSku()` we would need to have the following mapping:

```
...
    <field name="productSku" type="string"
          get-method="getProductSku" set-method="updateProductSku"/>
...
```

Note that if we specify either a `set-method()` or `get-method()`, but not both, then the non-specified accessor method will be ignored. This means that if the `get-method()` is specified, but the `set-method()` is not, then during marshaling the value will appear in the XML instance, but during unmarshaling the value will be ignored. The opposite is true if the `set-method()` is specified but no `get-method()`. We will see an example of this later in the chapter.

The <bind-xml> Element

Recall that in the previous section on using Castor's default capabilities we wanted to change the XML element name of `<product-sku>` to simply `<sku>`, but Castor was unable to handle this properly. For this to work we need to tell Castor what the new element name is. We do that with the `<bind-xml>` element.

The <bind-xml> element allows us to specify the XML name and node type (element, attribute, or text) of a field:

```
<field name="productSku" type="string">
   <bind-xml name="sku"/>
</field>
```

The name attribute specifies the XML name binding. You can see that we have now specified that the XML name for our productSku field should be "sku".

Notice that we didn't specify a node type. Recall in the previous section, about Castor's default capabilities, that we discussed how primitive types and objects are mapped to a specific node type. Since the type of the productSku field is a string, or object, it maps to an element. We could have used the following:

```
<field name="productSku" type="string">
   <bind-xml name="sku" node="element"/>
</field>
```

The node attribute is used to specify the node type. In our example specifying the node type is not necessary.

The Mapping File for the Item Class

We now know enough to write the complete mapping for our Item class, so here goes (mapping.xml):

```
<?xml version="1.0"?>
<mapping>

<description>Mapping example for the Item class</description>

<class name="Item">
   <field name="productSku" type="string">
      <bind-xml name="sku"/>
   </field>
   <field name="description" type="string"/>
   <field name="name"        type="string"/>
   <field name="price"       type="double"/>
   <field name="quantity"    type="integer"/>
</class>
</mapping>
```

Notice that for the description, name, price, and quantity fields we didn't specify a <bind-xml> element. This is because Castor can automatically handle the XML bindings for us.

Unmarshaling with a Mapping File

Now that we have our mapping file, let's look at the code necessary to unmarshal our XML instance. We will simply change our ItemTest class to load our mapping file:

We first must import the mapping package as follows:

```
//-- we need to import the mapping package
import org.exolab.castor.mapping.*;
```

```
...
import org.exolab.castor.xml.*;
...
...
```

We then load the mapping just before we call the unmarshaller:

```
    //-- Load Mapping
    Mapping mapping = new Mapping();
    mapping.loadMapping("mapping.xml");
```

After we've loaded the mapping we simply give this mapping to the unmarshaller:

```
    Unmarshaller unmarshaller = new Unmarshaller(Item.class);
    unmarshaller.setMapping( mapping );

    Item item = (Item) unmarshaller.unmarshal(new FileReader("item.xml"));

    /* print item - code removed for brevity */
```

Now we can re-run our test case on the modified version of our XML instance (shown in the beginning of this section) and we get the following:

```
> java ItemTest

Invoice Item
------------

Product Name: ACME Hazelnut Coffee
Sku Number  : 9123456123456
Price       : 9.99
Quantity    : 2
```

As you can see, Castor can now properly handle our XML instance.

Something a Little More Advanced

Now that we have seen how to use a mapping file, let's make a few changes to demonstrate more complicated mappings. First let's change our XML instance so that sku is an attribute instead of an element as follows (modified_item.xml):

```
<?xml version="1.0" standalone="yes"?>
<item sku="9123456123456">
   <name>ACME Hazelnut Coffee</name>
   <description>A pound of ACME Hazelnut Coffee - Whole Bean</description>
   <price>9.99</price>
   <quantity>2</quantity>
</item>
```

If you re-run the test case using the new XML instance, you'll notice that the SKU number is null again:

```
...
Sku Number : null
...
```

To fix this, we make a simple change to our mapping file, which gives us the following (`modified_mapping.xml`):

```
...
   <field name="productSku" type="string">
      <bind-xml name="sku" node="attribute"/>
   </field>
...
```

Notice we've specified the new node type as "`attribute`".

Now we can re-run our test case and we notice that our example is working again.

```
> java ItemTest2

Invoice Item
------------

Product Name: ACME Hazelnut Coffee
Sku Number  : 9123456123456
Price       : 9.99
Quantity    : 2
```

So you can see it's quite easy to specify the node type and XML name for the fields of our classes.

Let's expand our example by introducing the `Invoice` class. In this example our `Invoice` class will simply contain a collection of `Items`, and a total price field. The total price field will have some logic to calculate the total price of the invoice. This field will not have a `set` method, but will have a `get` method. Below you can see `Invoice.java`:

```
public class Invoice {


    /**
       * The collection of items
    **/
    Vector _items = null;

    /**
       * Creates a new Invoice.
    **/
    public Invoice() {
        super();
        _items = new Vector();
    } //-- Item()

    /**
       * Adds an Item to this Invoice
       *
```

```
    * @param item the Item to add
  **/
  public void addItem(Item item) {
     _items.addElement(item);
  } //-- addItem

  /**
     * Returns the Vector of Items for this Invoice
     *
     * @return the Vector of Items for this Invoice
  **/
  public Vector getItems() {
     return _items;
  } //-- getItems

  /**
     * Returns the total for all the Items for this Invoice
     *
     * @returns the total for all the Items for this Invoice
  **/
  public double getTotal() {

     double total = 0.0;

     for (int i = 0; i < _items.size(); i++) {
        Item item = (Item) _items.elementAt(i);
        total += item.getPrice() * item.getQuantity();
     }
     return total;
  } //-- getTotal


} //-- Invoice
```

We can see that the `getTotal()` method does not return a stored value, but calculates the total price of all the items in our invoice. The total price is something that we'd like to have marshalled in the XML instance so we have the `getter` method, but we have no `setter` method because the value is recalculated when it's needed.

A sample XML instance of our invoice will look as follows (`invoice.xml`):

```
<?xml version="1.0"?>
<invoice>
   <item sku="9123456123456">
      <name>ACME Hazelnut Coffee</name>
      <description>A pound of ACME Hazelnut Coffee -
         Whole Bean
      </description>
      <price>9.99</price>
      <quantity>2</quantity>
   </item>
   <item sku="9123456654321">
      <name>ACME Ultra II Coffee Maker</name>
      <description>ACME's best coffee maker,
```

```
            includes intravenous attachment.
        </description>
        <price>149.99</price>
        <quantity>1</quantity>
    </item>
    <total-price>169.97</total-price>
</invoice>
```

The mapping file is quite similar to the previous example, we just need to add the class mapping for our `Invoice` class (see below, `invoice_mapping.xml`):

```
...
<class name="Invoice">
    <field name="items" type="Item" collection="vector"/>
    <field name="total" type="double" get-method="getTotal">
        <bind-xml name="total-price"/>
    </field>
</class>
...
```

Notice that we needed a `bind-xml` element for the `total` field since the XML name that we used in our `invoice.xml` file was `total-price`.

The code to unmarshal is similar to that in our previous example. We've added some additional code to loop over all the items in the invoice, and print out the total price, giving us `InvoiceDisplay.java`:

```
//-- Load Mapping
Mapping mapping = new Mapping();
mapping.loadMapping("invoice_mapping.xml");

//-- Unmarshal Invoice
Unmarshaller unmarshaller = new Unmarshaller(Invoice.class);
unmarshaller.setMapping( mapping );

FileReader reader = new FileReader("invoice.xml");
Invoice invoice = (Invoice) unmarshaller.unmarshal(reader);
reader.close();

//-- Display Invoice
System.out.println("Invoice");
System.out.println("-------");

Vector items = invoice.getItems();

for (int i = 0; i < items.size(); i++) {

    Item item = (Item) items.elementAt(i);

    System.out.println();
    System.out.print(i+1);
    System.out.println(". Product Name: " + item.getName());
    System.out.println("   Sku Number : " + item.getProductSku());
    System.out.println("   Price      : " + item.getPrice());
    System.out.println("   Quantity   : " + item.getQuantity());
}
System.out.println();
System.out.println("Total: " + invoice.getTotal());
```

When we run our `InvoiceDisplay` class we get the following result:

```
> java InvoiceDisplay

Invoice
-------

1. Product Name: ACME Hazelnut Coffee
   Sku Number : 9123456123456
   Price     : 9.99
   Quantity  : 2

2. Product Name: ACME Ultra II Coffee Maker
   Sku Number : 9123456654321
   Price     : 149.99
   Quantity  : 1

Total: 169.97
```

Now that we've seen how to unmarshal with a mapping file we'll take a quick look at marshaling.

Marshaling with a Mapping File

Marshaling using a mapping file is just as easy as unmarshaling. The marshaller also has a `setMapping` method, which is used to specify the mapping file. Since we can use the same mapping file for both unmarshaling and marshaling, we can just take a look at the source code necessary to call the marshaller. We'll modify our `ItemUpdate` class, from the section on marshaling using the default capabilities, to use the mapping file. This gives us `ItemUpdate.java`:

```
...

//-- Load Mapping
Mapping mapping = new Mapping();
mapping.loadMapping("modified_mapping.xml");

/* unmarshaling code removed for brevity */
...
//-- update quantity to 4 pounds instead of 2
item.setQuantity( 4 );

//-- marshal item
FileWriter writer = new FileWriter("item_updated.xml");
Marshaller marshaller = new Marshaller(writer);
marshaller.setMapping(mapping);
marshaller.marshal(item);
writer.close();
```

That's all that's needed! The contents of `item_updated.xml` are:

```
<?xml version="1.0"?>
<item sku="9123456123456">
   <description>A pound of ACME Hazlenut Coffee - Whole Bean</description>
   <name>ACME Hazlenut Coffee</name>
```

```
      <price>9.99</price>
      <quantity>4</quantity>
   </item>
```

Notice that the order in which the elements appear is the same order in which they were specified in our mapping file.

Conclusion

We have seen how easy it is to use a mapping file to specify our XML bindings when the default capabilities are not sufficient to handle the job. We've shown how to specify node types for specific Java fields, how to specify the XML names for a given field, as well as how to specify getter and setter methods. In the next section will discuss using XML Schema to specify our bindings and we will have Castor automatically generate our object model.

> *For more information on the how to use XML mapping files, please see http://castor.exolab.org/xml-mapping.html.*

Using Castor's Source Code Generator

We have seen how to use automatic XML data binding with Castor, and how to use mapping files, but what if we don't have an existing object model to represent our XML instances? It can often be a tedious and time consuming task writing an object model. Luckily, Castor has a solution – a source code generator, which can automatically generate a Java object model to represent a given XML schema. The source code generator will not only create the Java object model, but also all necessary XML binding information needed by the marshaling framework to properly marshal, unmarshal, and validate instances of the given schema. A source code generator is a valuable time-saving tool when it comes to writing XML enabled applications.

This section is meant to give a general introduction to using and understanding Castor's source code generator.

Using XML Schema To Express Bindings

The source code generator takes as input a schema written in the W3C XML Schema language, and produces the Java object model for that schema. Since XML Schema is not yet a W3C Recommendation, we are using the latest version as of this writing, which is the March 30, 2001 Proposed Recommendation. Castor uses XML Schema because of its rich typing and similarities to an object oriented paradigm.

> *This section is intended to introduce how Castor uses XML Schema – you may need to read Chapter 6 on XML Schema, or the W3C XML Schema page (http://www.w3.org/XML/Schema), before continuing.*

Why not use DTDs? Using a DTD (Document Type Definition) we can specify XML structure such as elements and attributes, but we can't specify that an attribute's value should represent an integer or a date. Some of you might be thinking about using the DTD Notation mechanism. Notations are a weak form of typing since they are nothing more than some meta-data, which, in order to work properly, must be respected by people and applications that read and write instances of the given DTD. There is actually a W3C Note (basically a submission), called DT4DTD, or simply Datatypes for DTD, on providing some form of data types for DTD (see http://www.w3.org/TR/dt4dtd). The submission actually seems to try and provide some standard notations that can be used to represent the data types. There also may be some other external types specifications for DTDs, but there is nothing within the language itself.

Unlike DTDs XML Schemas are very expressive and contain a large set of built-in data types. These data types allow us to precisely specify what the value of attributes and elements should be. XML Schema uses the core concepts of **Simple Types** and **Complex Types**. Simple types are basically the set of built-in schema data types and restrictions there of. A complex type is similar to the content model used in DTDs in that it allows us to express an ordering of elements essentially defining the structural representation. Complex types can also define attributes, extend other complex types or simple types, or even restrict other complex types.

> *Castor actually has the ability to convert a DTD into an XML Schema. All the types will basically be strings, but these can be changed by hand to take advantage of the XML Schema types. We currently don't provide a GUI for this, but it's still quite useful. There are also a number of other tools available for doing DTD to XML Schema conversion, such as XML Spy (http://www.xmlspy.com) and TIBCO's Turbo XML (http://www.extensibility.com/tibco/solutions/turbo_xml/index.htm).*

Mapping Schema Components To Java

Mapping XML Schema components to Java is typically a straightforward task. In an ideal world all the data types for XML Schema would have a 1 to 1 mapping with a data type of the programming language we are binding to, in our case the Java language. This is not always the case however. XML Schema has quite a rich set of built-in data types and these types don't always match perfectly with Java. For instance, the XML Schema `date` type doesn't actually map cleanly into a `java.util.Date`, but the XML Schema `timeInstant` type does. So data binding isn't always perfect, but allows us to access and represent the data in way that resembles, as close as possible, the data model of the XML schema. Castor has a defined set of classes that are used to handle the cases when a schema type doesn't map properly into a Java type.

Simple Types

As mentioned above simple types are set of built-in XML Schema types, as well as restrictions there of. Castor will map most simple schema types to Java primitives, such as `int`, `double`, `float`, etc. Other simple types that are more complex such as dates are mapped into either native Java types, such as `java.util.Date`, or, as mentioned above, if no native Java type exists, a Castor defined type. Simple types often support a number of *facets* that allow them to be customizable. For example the `integer` type allows the minimum and maximum values to be specified. Below is a brief list of the commonly used schema simple types and their corresponding Java type. For a complete list, as well as a list of supported facets for each type, see the Castor documentation at http://www.castor.org.

Schema type	Java type
`string`	`java.lang.String`
`boolean`	`Boolean`
`Int`	`Int`
`Long`	`Long`
`Float`	`Float`
`double`	`Double`
`Date`	`org.exolab.castor.types.Date`
`Time`	`org.exolab.castor.types.Time`

Schema type	Java type
`timeInstant`	`java.util.Date`
`binary`	`byte array (byte[])`
`NCName`	`java.lang.String`
`positiveInteger`	`Int`

For simple types that are restrictions of other simple types, such as the built-in types `positiveInteger` and `NCName`, as well as simple types that have been restricted by using facets, Castor will map to the closest Java type and then generate necessary validation code to perform validation when marshaling and unmarshaling. For example, when using the `positiveInteger` type,the source code generator will generate validation code to make sure the values of the integer are greater than zero.

Unlike a validating XML parser, the validation code generated validates the object model and not the XML instance. This code will automatically be called by Castor during the marshaling and unmarshaling process, but may be called by the application at any point to force validation. Validation can be disabled by modifying the `castor.properties` file as follows:

```
...
# disable validation during marshaling and unmarshaling
org.exolab.castor.marshaling.validation=false
...
```

By default Castor also disables the underlying XML parser from performing validation of the XML instance. This is to prevent unnecessary overhead of validating both the object model and the XML instance. If object model validation is disabled, the user may want to enable XML parser validation by modifying the `castor.properties` file as follows:

```
...
# enable XML instance validation during unmarshaling
org.exolab.castor.parser.validation=true
...
```

Note that XML instance validation occurs only during the unmarshaling process, but object model validation occurs during both unmarshaling and marshaling.

> *Some of you might be wondering why the validation code is not simply generated in the class definition itself. Early versions of Castor actually did this. The main reason that it's generated externally is to take advantage of the validation framework that exists in Castor for allowing validation of class definitions that were not generated by Castor. It was a design decision to simply keep all validation consistent throughout the framework. Another reason is for a future plan to expose validation information for third party tools, such as GUI editors that might desire access to such information.*
>
> *There are plans to allow control over whether the validation code is generated externally or internally to the class definition, but this feature was not available at the time of this writing.*

Given the following simple type definition:

```
<simpleType name="priceType">
   <restriction base="double">
      <minInclusive value="0"/>
   </restriction>
</simpleType>
```

the source generator will create a field using the Java primitive type `double` for any class definition that is generated that uses the `priceType`. Additional validation code will be generated, external to the generated class, to guarantee values for this field are greater than or equal to zero. The marshaling framework will use the validation code in order to validate instances of the field during the marshaling and unmarshaling process.

For example, for the following element definition:

```
<complexType ... >
   ...
   <element name="price" type="priceType"/>
   ...
</complexType>
```

The source code generator will create the following field definition and accessor methods (getters and setters):

```
public class ... {
   ...
   private double _price;
   ...
   public double getPrice() {
      return _price;
   }
   ...
   public void setPrice(double price) {
      _price = price;
   }
   ...
}
```

Complex Types

Now let's look at complex types and element definitions. Castor has two ways to map complex types and elements into Java. The first, and default, approach is called the **element-method**. When using this approach, the source code generator maps all element definitions that have types specified using a complex type definition into Java class definitions that represent the structure of the complex type.

All top-level complex types are mapped into abstract Java class definitions. Top-level complex types are complex types that are globally defined for the given schema. They may be extended by other complex type definitions or simply used directly by element definitions.

The following is an example of a top-level complex type definition:

```
<schema xmlns="http://www.w3.org/2000/10/XMLSchema" ... >
   ...
   <!-- top-level complex type definition -->
   <complexType name="address">
```

```
        <sequence>
          ...
          <element name="name" type="string"/>
          <element name="city" type="string"/>
          ...
        </sequence>
      </complexType>
      ...
   </schema>
```

The above complex type definition simply defines an address (we'll assume a US postal address) which contains a sequence of elements (name, city, street, etc.) For simplicity we only defined the name and city elements, which are both defined as strings. The source generator will create an abstract class definition called `Address` as follows:

```
public abstract class Address {

   private String _name = null;
   private String _city = null;
   ...

   public String getCity() { ... };

   public void setCity(String city) { ... };

   public String getName() { ... };

   public void setName(String name) { ... };
   ...

}
```

Any class definitions created for elements that use a top-level complex type definition will extend the class definition for the given complex type.

For example, for the following element definition,

```
<element name="shipping-address" type="address"/>
```

the source generator will create a class definition that extends the `Address` class as follows:

```
public class ShippingAddress extends Address {
   ...
}
```

The element-method approach models closely the XML instance document where each element in the XML instances maps to the class definition generated for the given element.

For all element definitions that have anonymous complex type definitions, which are complex type definitions that appear inside the element definition, the source code generator will simply create a class definition that represents the structure of the complex type. For example, given the following element definition:

```
<element name="item">
   <complexType>
      <sequence>
         ...
         <element name="price" type="priceType"/>
         ...
      </sequence>
   </complexType>
</element>
```

the source code generator will create a class definition as follows:

```
public class Item {

   private double _price = 0.0;

   ...

   public double getPrice() {
      return _price;
   }

   public void setPrice(double price) {
      _price = price;
   }

   ...

   public void validate()
      throws ValidationException;
   ...
}
```

You'll notice the `Item` class looks just like a typical Java Bean. The `validate()` method can be called to make sure that instances of `Item` are valid. This method will actually call Castor's validator, which is part of the marshaling framework, to perform the validation using the validation code that was generated separately from the class definition.

The second approach, called the type-method, is similar to the element-method, but differs on a couple of aspects. Like the element-method, when using top-level element definitions, or element definitions that contain an anonymous complex type definition, the source code generator will create a class definition, which models the structure of the complex type.

With the type-method, however, top-level complex types are not treated as abstract classes as they are with the element-method. For example, our address type definition above will get mapped into the following class definition:

```
public class Address {

   private String _name = null;

   ...

   public String getName() { ... };
```

```
    public void setName(String name) { ... };

    ...

}
```

Also unlike the element-method, with the type-method any element definition that is not top-level, but uses a top-level complex type as its defined type will simply be treated as a field in the class definition for the surrounding complex type definition (the complex type definition in which the element is defined). For example, if we have the following element definition:

```
<element name="invoice">
   <complexType>
      <sequence>
         ...
         <element name="shippingAddress" type="address"/>
         ...
      </sequence>
   </complexType>
</element>
```

in the case of the type-method, the source generator will create a class definition as follows:

```
public class Invoice {

   ...
   private Address _shippingAddress = null;
   ...
}
```

whereas using the element-method the source code generator will create a class definition as follows:

```
public class Invoice {

   ...
   private ShippingAddress _shippingAddress = null;
   ...
}
```

We will be using the element-method for our examples. I encourage the reader to try both methods to determine which one is more appropriate for their needs. Configuring the method to use is quite simple. The source code generator has a file called `castorbuilder.properties`, which is located in `org/exolab/castor/builder` path within the Castor `.jar` file. Simply copy this file to your local working directory and modify the `org.exolab.castor.builder.javaclassmapping` property to read as follows:

```
...
# change class generation method to the type-method
org.exolab.castor.builder.javaclassmapping=type
...
```

The basic rule of thumb when choosing which approach to use is to think about how you want your data modeled. If you want each element definition to map to their own separate class definitions, then choose the `element-method`. With this approach the object model looks very much like the XML instance. For example, if we have an element called `<shipping-address>`, it will map to a class called `ShippingAddress`.

If, on the other hand, you want each element definition to map to the class definition of its corresponding complex type definition, then choose the `type-method`. With this approach the object model looks very much like the types defined within your schema. For example if we have an element called `<shipping-address>` it will map to whatever class definition was generated for its corresponding complex type definition. This may be `ShippingAddress` or `Address` or whatever was defined in the XML schema. We can't guess by simply looking at the XML name of the element, we need to look at the XML schema itself.

The developers of Castor couldn't decide which approach was best, so we simply allow you to choose the one that makes most sense to you.

Now that we have a basic understanding of how Castor's Source Code Generator maps XML Schema types into Java we'll look at a simple example.

> *For more information on how Castor maps XML Schema into Java please read the Source Code Generator documentation at* http://www.castor.org/sourcegen.html.

Generating the Class Definitions for an XML Schema

Recall our invoice example from the previous sections. Let's define the XML schema that represents our invoice. For simplicity our invoice will only contain a shipping address and a collection of items. A sample XML instance would read as follows (`invoice.xml`):

```
<?xml version="1.0"?>
<invoice>

   <shipping-address country="US">
      <name>Joe Smith</name>
      <street>10 Huntington Ave</street>
      <city>Boston</city>
      <state>MA</state>
      <zip>02116</zip>
   </shipping-address>
   ...
   <item sku="9123456123456">
      <name>ACME Hazelnut Coffee</name>
      <description>
         A pound of ACME Hazelnut Coffee - Whole Bean
      </description>
      <price>9.99</price>
      <quantity>2</quantity>
   </item>
   ...
</invoice>
```

Our schema to represent the above XML looks like this (`invoice.xsd`):

```
<?xml version="1.0"?>
<schema xmlns="http://www.w3.org/2000/10/XMLSchema"
   targetNamespace="acme.org/Invoice">

   <!-- invoice definition -->
   <element name="invoice">
      <complexType>
         <sequence>
            <element ref="shipping-address"/>
            <element ref="item" maxOccurs="unbounded" minOccurs="1"/>
         </sequence>
      </complexType>
   </element>

   <!-- item definition-->
   <element name="item">
      <complexType>
         <sequence>
            <element name="name"     type="string"/>
            <element name="quantity"  type="integer"/>
            <element name="price"     type="priceType"/>
            <element name="description" type="string"/>
        </sequence>
        <attribute name="sku" type="ID" use="required"/>
      </complexType>
   </element>

   <!-- Shipping address definition, A simple US based address structure -->
   <element name="shipping-address">
      <complexType>
         <sequence>
            <element name="name"  type="string"/>
            <element name="street" type="string"/>
            <element name="city"  type="string"/>
            <element name="state" type="stateCode"/>
            <element name="zip"  type="zipCode"/>
         </sequence>
      </complexType>
   </element>

   <!-- A US Zip Code -->
   <simpleType name="zipCode">
      <restriction base="string">
         <pattern value="[0-9]{5}(-[0-9]{4})?"/>
      </restriction>
   </simpleType>

   <!-- State Code, simply restrict string to two letters.
        Obviously a non valid state code can be used....but this is just
        an example.
   -->
   <simpleType name="stateCode">
      <restriction base="string">
         <pattern value="[A-Z]{2}"/>
      </restriction>
   </simpleType>
```

```
    <!-- priceType definition -->
    <simpleType name="priceType">
       <restriction base="double">
          <minInclusive value="0"/>
       </restriction>
    </simpleType>

</schema>
```

Notice that we use the pattern facet for `zipCode` and `stateCode` simple type definitions. The pattern facet is a regular expression that allows us to define the production of the string value.

Now that we have our XML Schema all we need to do is run the source code generator so that it can create our object model for us. We do this using the command line interface:

>java org.exolab.castor.builder.SourceGenerator –i invoice.xsd –package org.acme.invoice

This invokes the source code generator on our invoice schema and creates our source code using the package "`org.acme.invoice`". The source code generator will create the source files, which will then need to be compiled. If the directory for the package (in our example this would be `org/acme/invoice`) does not exist it will automatically create and all generated source will be placed in this directory.

The source code generator allows a number of different command line options to be specified. For more information on these options please refer to the Castor documentation.

Let's take a look at one of the source files generated (`invoice.java`). The method bodies, comments, and some helper methods have been removed so that the file doesn't take up too much page space:

```
package org.acme.invoice;

/* imports and javadoc removed for brevity */

public class Invoice implements java.io.Serializable {

   private ShippingAddress _shippingAddress;

   private java.util.Vector _itemList;

   public Invoice() { ... };

   public void addItem(Item vItem)
      throws java.lang.IndexOutOfBoundsException { ... };

   public Item getItem(int index)
      throws java.lang.IndexOutOfBoundsException { ... };

   public Item[] getItem() { ... };

   public ShippingAddress getShippingAddress() { ... };

   public void marshal(java.io.Writer out)
```

```
        throws org.exolab.castor.xml.MarshalException,
org.exolab.castor.xml.ValidationException
    {

        Marshaller.marshal(this, out);
    } //-- void marshal(java.io.Writer)

    public void setItem(Item vItem, int index)
      throws java.lang.IndexOutOfBoundsException { ... };

    public void setItem(Item[] itemArray) { ... };

    public void setShippingAddress(ShippingAddress shippingAddress) { ... };

     public static org.acme.invoice.Invoice unmarshal(java.io.Reader reader)
        throws org.exolab.castor.xml.MarshalException,
            org.exolab.castor.xml.ValidationException
    {
        return (org.acme.invoice.Invoice)
Unmarshaller.unmarshal(org.acme.invoice.Invoice.class, reader);
    } //-- org.acme.invoice.Invoice unmarshal(java.io.Reader)

     public void validate()
        throws org.exolab.castor.xml.ValidationException { ... };

}
```

As you can see, the generated class definition is a typical Java Bean, which represents the invoice that we have described in our schema. Also notice that `marshal()` and `unmarshal()` methods have been created for convenience (the generation of these methods can be disabled using the special option on the command line when invoking the source code generator, currently called `-nomarshall`). These methods simply call Castor's marshaller and unmarshaller as we have done in earlier sections.

If you look at the generated files you will notice that for each class definition created, such as `Invoice.java`, there is an associated class definition, called a **Class Descriptor**, which is also generated, such as `InvoiceDescriptor.java`. The class descriptors are classes that hold the binding and validation information for their associated class and are used by the marshaling framework. Essentially they are equivalent to the mapping files we discussed earlier.

Discussion of the Class Descriptor API goes beyond the scope of this chapter, but more information can be found in the Castor documentation.

Marshaling and Unmarshaling

Now that we've generated our object model from our schema, let's look at the code necessary to unmarshal and marshal instances of our schema.

As can be seen from the following code (`InvoiceDisplay.java`), when we want to unmarshal an instance of an invoice we simply call the `unmarshal()` method:

```
//-- import our generated classes
import org.acme.invoice.*;
```

```
...
try {
    //-- Unmarshal Invoice
    FileReader reader = new FileReader ("invoice.xml" );
    Invoice invoice = Invoice.unmarshal(reader);

    //-- Display Invoice
    System.out.println("Invoice");
    System.out.println("-------");

    System.out.println("Shipping:");
    System.out.println();

    ShippingAddress address = invoice.getShippingAddress();

    System.out.println("    " + address.getName());
    System.out.println("    " + address.getStreet());
    System.out.print("    " + address.getCity() + ", ");
    System.out.println(address.getState() + "  " + address.getZip());

    System.out.println();
    System.out.println("Items: ");

    Item[] items = invoice.getItem();

    for (int i = 0; i < items.length; i++) {
         Item item = items[i];
         System.out.println();
         System.out.print(i+1);
         System.out.println(". Product Name: " + item.getName());
         System.out.println("   Sku Number   : " + item.getSku());
         System.out.println("   Price        : " + item.getPrice());
         System.out.println("   Quantity     : " + item.getQuantity());
    }
 }
 catch(MarshalException mx) {...}
 catch(ValidationException vx) {...}
 catch(IOException iox) {...}
```

The full source code for `InvoiceDisplay.java` is available in the code download for the book from the Wrox web site at http://www.wrox.com.

After running `InvoiceDisplay` we get the following result:

```
>java InvoiceDisplay

Invoice
-------
Shipping:

   Joe Smith
   10 Huntington Ave
   Boston, MA  02116
```

```
Items:

1. Product Name: ACME Hazelnut Coffee
   Sku Number  : 9123456123456
   Price       : 9.99
   Quantity    : 2

2. Product Name: ACME Ultra II Coffee Maker
   Sku Number  : 9123456654321
   Price       : 149.99
   Quantity    : 1
```

When we want to marshal an instance of our `Invoice` class we simply call the `marshal()` method, again in our example we will update the quantity of coffee from 2 pounds to 4 (`InvoiceUpdate.java`):

```
    //-- Unmarshal Invoice
    Invoice invoice = Invoice.unmarshal( new FileReader ("invoice.xml" ));

    //-- find item for our Hazelnut coffee
    String sku = "9123456123456";

     Item[] items = invoice.getItem();

     for (int i = 0; i < items.length; i++) {
         //-- compare sku numbers
         if (items[i].getSku().equals(sku)) {
             //-- update quantity
             items[i].setQuantity(4);
             break;
         }
     }

     //-- marshal our updated invoice
     FileWriter writer = new FileWriter("invoice_updated.xml");
     invoice.marshal( writer );
```

That's all there is to it!

Simply run `InvoiceUpdate` as follows:

```
>java InvoiceUpdate
```

If we run our `InvoiceDisplay` program using the `invoice_updated.xml` document created by our `InvoiceUpdate` program we will get the following:

```
>java InvoiceDisplay invoice_updated.xml

Invoice
-------
Shipping:

   Joe Smith
```

```
    10 Huntington Ave
    Boston, MA  02116

Items:

1. Product Name: ACME Hazelnut Coffee
   Sku Number  : 9123456123456
   Price       : 9.99
   Quantity    : 4

2. Product Name: ACME Ultra II Coffee Maker
   Sku Number  : 9123456654321
   Price       : 149.99
   Quantity    : 1
```

Conclusion

We've discussed briefly how to specify structure and types for our XML documents using a W3C XML Schema, and we've seen how to use the source code generator to automatically create an object model for our schema. The main benefit of using the source code generator is that we have very little work to do as developers in order to access our XML instances in Java. The entire object model to represent the schema is created automatically, including all data binding and validation code, which can save us valuable time when writing our XML applications. If our XML schema changes, it's very easy to regenerate the object model and maintain our applications.

Using XSLT with XML Data Binding

XSLT, the W3C's language for performing XML transformations, seems to have relevance in almost any topic on XML so it should be no surprise that XSLT can be used in conjunction with XML data binding.

One interesting use of XSLT with XML data binding is to create presentable views of our object model for use in web applications. Two other important issues in data binding where XSLT plays an important role is with the handling of complex schema and sharing data with other systems. Both of these issues typically deal with schema conversion – when faced with the need to convert between one XML structure and another we turn to XSLT.

This section is meant to give you some ideas about how you can use XSLT with XML data binding to solve real-world problems. We'll begin with a brief discussion about using XSLT to create presentable views of our object model, and then we will discuss schema conversion.

It might be necessary to read Chapter 9, "Transforming XML", which covers XSLT, before continuing.

Creating Presentable Views of Object Models

When writing applications we often have the need to present application data to the user. Consider our Invoice object model. An invoice is something that should clearly be displayed to the user of our application after an order has been placed.

Imagine that we needed to provide an HTML view of our invoice. We could write a lot of Java code to output our `Invoice` object as HTML. This would be pretty ugly, because our code would have lots of `print` statements with embedded HTML markup. Not only would writing the initial display code be tedious and time consuming, but also maintaining this code would pose some serious headaches.

A better solution would be to separate the presentation information from our application. Since XML data binding allows us to marshal our object models in an XML format, adding presentation information to our data can be quite easy.

Castor supports marshaling object models to both SAX and DOM APIs. This makes connecting the XML output of Castor to an XSLT processor that supports either of these standard APIs straightforward.

Schema Conversion

Converting Complex Schemas To Simpler Ones

It may be the case that a schema is too complex to be handled properly by a data-binding framework (or it might be that our object model and the schema are too far removed from each other to be directly connected by mapping). This often happens with automatically generated schemas, such as schemas generated from DTDs. XML Schema is very expressive and there is more than one way to write a schema that describes the same structure.

In a complex schema, information contained in attributes, child elements or potentially elsewhere in the XML document may be needed to determine the proper binding type for a given element. For example we could have the following element declaration:

```
...
<xsd:element name="address" type="address"/>
...
<xsd:complexType name="address">
  <xsd:all>
      <xsd:element name="name"  type="xsd:string"/>
      <xsd:element name="street" type="xsd:string"/>
      <xsd:element name="city"  type="xsd:string"/>
      <xsd:element name="state" type="stateAbbrev"/>
      <xsd:element name="zip"  type="zip-code"/>
  </xsd:all>
  <xsd:attribute name="type">
      <xsd:simpleType>
         <xsd:restriction>
            <xsd:enumeration value="shipping"/>
            <xsd:enumeration value="billing"/>
         </xsd:restriction>
      </xsd:simpleType>
   </xsd:attribute>
</xsd:complexType>
...
```

Though we didn't show it, assume we have declared `stateAbbrev` type to be an enumeration of the available US state codes, and that we have declared the `zip-code` type to be a pattern consisting of 5 digits, followed by an optional hyphen and 4 digits.

A sample instance of the address element would look like:

```
<address type="shipping">
   <name>Pita Thomas</name>
   <street>2000 Endless Loop</street>
```

```
        <city>Redmond</city>
        <state>WA</state>
        <zip>98052</zip>
    </address>
```

Now assume in our object model that we have two separate objects for the address; we have a `BillingAddress`, and a `ShippingAddress` object, both of which extend an abstract base class called `Address`.

During unmarshaling we need know that an address element with a `type` attribute value of "`shipping`" should be mapped to the `ShippingAddress` class. This poses a problem since this involves more than simply mapping the address element to a particular class. It also involves the value of the `type` attribute. This situation is a one-to-many mapping between element and class definition. Our example isn't very complex, but sometimes one-to-many mappings can be very difficult to handle with a data binding framework.

To make things simple we can use an XSLT stylesheet to convert our above XML instance into an XML instance that adheres to the following schema representation:

```
    ...
    <xsd:element name="shipping-address" type="address"/>
    <xsd:element name="billing-address" type="address"/>
    ...
    <xsd:complexType name="address">
        <xsd:all>
            <xsd:element name="name"  type="xsd:string"/>
            <xsd:element name="street" type="xsd:string"/>
            <xsd:element name="city"  type="xsd:string"/>
            <xsd:element name="state" type="stateAbbrev"/>
            <xsd:element name="zip"  type="zip-code"/>
        <xsd:all>
    </xsd:complexType>
    ...
```

So instead of having an attribute that specifies the type of address, we simply have two separate elements. We've basically reduced our one-to-many mapping situation into a one-to-one mapping situation, which is very easy to handle.

The new XML instance would look like the following:

```
    <shipping-address>
        <name>Pita Thomas</name>
        <street>2000 Endless Loop</street>
        <city>Redmond</city>
        <state>WA</state>
        <zip>98052</zip>
    </shipping-address>
```

Now that there is a one-to-one mapping between the shipping-address element and the `ShippingAddress` class, we can easily perform unmarshaling and marshaling of the XML instances.

The following XSLT stylesheet can be used to convert the first format into the second so that we can perform unmarshaling:

```
<?xml version="1.0"?>
<xsl:stylesheet xmlns:xsl="http://www.w3.org/1999/XSL/Transform"
        version="1.0">
   <xsl:template match="address">
      <xsl:choose>
         <xsl:when test="@type='shipping'">
            <shipping-address>
               <xsl:copy-of select="*"/>
            </shipping-address>
         </xsl:when>
         <xsl:otherwise>
           <billing-address>
              <xsl:copy-of select="*"/>
           </billing-address>
         </xsl:otherwise>
      </xsl:choose>
   </xsl:template>
</xsl:stylesheet>
```

This stylesheet needs just one template for our `address` element. Based on the value of the `type` attribute we simply create either a `<shipping-address>` or `<billing-address>` element, and then copy the remaining data.

This stylesheet only performs the transformation in one direction; when we marshal we would need another stylesheet, or at least another template, that would then convert the marshalled XML instance back into the first format. I won't show it here, but it would be quite similar to the above.

So we see how XSLT can play an important role in allowing us to perform data binding on schemas that might be too complex for our data-binding framework. Of course, using XSLT before unmarshaling and after marshaling will impose additional overhead and degrade performance.

Converting Schemas in Order To Share Data

When writing non-trivial applications we often find that we must share data with other applications and systems within our own organization and, as with B2B applications, potentially with other organizations. It is more common than not for two systems or organizations to have different schemas for representing the same data. With this in mind, it may be necessary to transform the XML data before data binding takes place. XSLT can be used to convert our schemas into other schemas so that we can share our data.

To illustrate this suppose that we work in a particular division of a company that has shipping information that needs to shared with another division of our company, or another company for that matter. Suppose that our division within the company has decided to represent shipping addresses as follows:

```
<shipping-address country="US">
   <name>Gignoux Coffee House</name>
   <street>24 Kernel Street</street>
   <city>Redmond</city>
   <state>WA</state>
   <zip>98052</zip>
</shipping-address>
```

All of our data binding code will unmarshal and marshal XML instances as long as they are in the above format.

Now let's assume that the other division or company uses the following XML format to represent the same data:

```
<shipTo>
   <name>Gignoux Coffee House</name>
   <address country="US">
      <street>24 Kernel Street</street>
      <city>Redmond</city>
      <state>WA</state>
      <zip-code>98052</zip-code>
   </address>
</shipTo>
```

All of their data binding code relies on the shipping addresses to be in the above format in order to be properly unmarshalled.

When we need to share the data we can use an XSLT stylesheet to convert to and from both formats. If our division needs to give the other division or company the data in their respective format, we can simply use an XSLT stylesheet just after we marshal our object model to convert the resulting XML instance into the proper format. If the other division or company is responsible for the data conversion, they can simply use an XSLT stylesheet just before unmarshaling to convert the data into the proper format.

We can use the following XSLT stylesheet to convert from the first format into the second:

```
<?xml version="1.0"?>
<xsl:stylesheet xmlns:xsl="http://www.w3.org/1999/XSL/Transform"
        version="1.0">

   <xsl:template match="shipping-address">
      <shipTo>
         <xsl:copy-of select="name"/>
         <address country="{@country}">
            <xsl:apply-templates select="street | city | state | zip"/>
         </address>
      </shipTo>
   </xsl:template>

   <xsl:template match="*">
      <xsl:copy-of select="."/>
   </xsl:template>

   <xsl:template match="zip">
      <zip-code><xsl:value-of select="text()"/></zip-code>
   </xsl:template>

</xsl:stylesheet>
```

Again this stylesheet only transforms the first format into the second, so we would need another stylesheet that we could use after marshaling.

We can see how XSLT can play an import role in enabling us to share XML data and aid us with integration of data that is not in the proper format.

XML Data Binding Instead of Object Serialization

Serialization refers to Java's built-in persistence mechanism for saving object instance information. The value of each field in the object instance is saved along with type information so that the object instance can be recreated when needed. It is quite analogous to the XML marshaling we have been discussing in previous sections, except that instead of an XML instance, the data is stored in a binary format. Of course, I'm simplifying the analogy a bit as there are other differences than simply how the data is stored and we'll see some of that throughout this section.

If both XML data binding and Java Serialization can save and recreate object instances, how do we determine which method to use? It really depends on the situation at hand, such as what we need to do with the persisted state information or how fast our application needs to be. In most cases XML data binding has clear advantages over serialization. There are some key areas to look at when making a decision on which one to use; these are sharing data, data accessibility, performance, and object model constraints. There are some other differences as well, which will be noted at the end of the section.

Sharing Data Across Systems

Java Serialization is class specific. This means that in order to de-serialize (or restore) an object, we must use the exact same class definition that was used during serialization. If we want to share serialized object instances with other systems, then those systems or applications must also have the same set of classes. This is because the job of serialization is to save an object's instance...not simply the data of the object. There are some workarounds to this issue, such as having the class definition maintain the `serialVersionUID` to trick the JVM into thinking we have the same class definition, or implementing the `Externalizable` interface, which would be a lot of work.

XML data binding does not have this limitation because we're not actually saving object instances, but instead we are simply saving the data of the object. As we have seen, an XML instance can be mapped into different object models.

One goal of data binding is to be agnostic about how the data is stored. Using data binding we can control the stored representation of the object. The format for Java serialization is a binary format that we have no control over.

Java Serialization only works with Java! Serialized objects cannot be de-serialized in a different programming language. XML data binding can be done in almost any language. For example we can marshal a Java object model and unmarshal into a C++ object model. This of course requires that either a data-binding framework exists in the language or we create the data binding code. Being language agnostic is important if we need to share data with other applications, especially if we need to share our data with other companies.

XML data binding can also be used to take advantage of the growing number of XML based messaging formats and protocols by simply marshaling our objects directly to the desired XML format.

Data Accessibility

Java Serialization saves the persisted data in a binary format. This means it's not human readable. If we have the need to read the persisted data then a binary format is not very desirable. It is also means we couldn't easily open this data in a text editor and update values. XML on the other hand is character data, simply formatted using a special syntax. This means that humans can easily read it. Some XML instances may be very long, and not very nice to read, but we can still read it if we need to. We can also update values using a simple text editor.

Performance

Performance is where serialization has a distinct advantage over data binding. Since Castor generated classes implementing the `Serializable` interface, it's actually quite easy to compare the two approaches.

Here's a simple performance test (`PerformanceTest.java`) using our `Invoice` object model that we created earlier with Castor's source code generator. The test case performs a number of iterations

of serializing, deserializing, marshaling and unmarshaling and simply averages the result for each separate test.

```
int    attempts   = 1000;
...
// perform serialization
start = System.currentTimeMillis();
for (int i = 0; i < attempts; i++) {
    FileOutputStream fstream = new FileOutputStream("invoice.ser");
    ObjectOutputStream ostream = new ObjectOutputStream(fstream);
    ostream.writeObject( invoice );
    ostream.close();
}
stop = System.currentTimeMillis();
total = stop - start;
average = (double)total/(double)attempts;
...
// print average
System.out.println("avg time to serialize: " + average + " milliseconds");
...
// perform marshaling
start = System.currentTimeMillis();
for (int i = 0; i < attempts; i++) {
   FileWriter writer = new FileWriter("invoice2.xml");
   invoice.marshal( writer );
   writer.close();
}
stop = System.currentTimeMillis();
total = stop - start;
average = (double)total/(double)attempts;
```

Note: Running this test with virus software running in the background may seriously affect the performance of the marshaling as some virus programs scan reading and writing of files with ".xml" extensions. This is particularly true when running Windows.

I chose to perform 1000 iterations, but feel free to modify this number.

On average, serializing an instance of our Invoice is about 3 times faster than marshaling the same instance using Castor. Deserializing is also about 3 times faster than unmarshaling. It is also interesting to note that the file size for the serialized Invoice instance (839 bytes) is larger than the file size for the XML instance (594 bytes). This will reverse as we add more Items to our invoice and eventually the file size for the serialization will become smaller than the XML instance. I encourage the reader to play around with the test, as results will vary.

For larger object models there are some things we could actually do to speed up the performance of marshaling and unmarshaling such as disabling validation, or caching the descriptors. For example, even with our small `Invoice` instance, if we disable validation and we cache the descriptors by modifying our example as follows (`PerformanceTestOptimized.java`):

```
// import class ClassDescriptorResolverImpl in order to cache
// our class descriptors
import org.exolab.castor.xml.util.ClassDescriptorResolverImpl;
...
    // use our own instance of a ClassDescriptorResolver to
    // cache class descriptors across instances of marshaller
    // and unmarshaller.
    ClassDescriptorResolver cdr = new ClassDescriptorResolverImpl();
    //-- marshaling
    System.out.println();
    System.out.println("Marshaling Invoice object " + attempts + " times");
    start = System.currentTimeMillis();

    for (int i = 0; i < attempts; i++) {
        FileWriter writer = new FileWriter("invoice2.xml");
        Marshaller marshaller = new Marshaller(writer);
        marshaller.setResolver(cdr);
        marshaller.setValidation(false);
        marshaller.marshal(invoice);
        writer.close();
    }
...
```

Notice that we construct our own marshaller, pass in our instance of `ClassDescriptorResolver`, and disable validation. The `ClassDescriptorResolver` is used by the marshaller to load all class descriptors; by passing in our own instance we prevent the marshaller from creating a new one. This allows us to save any class descriptors loaded during the marshaling process. We do the same thing for the unmarshaling process.

So we can see that we've improved our marshaling significantly. Serialization only becomes 2 times faster than marshaling, instead of the previous 3 with the unoptimized version. This improvement should be even better for larger files. Again results will vary, so I encourage the reader to experiment on their own system.

Some Additional Differences

New Class Instances

Since the goal of Serialization is to save an object instance, the JVM will not call any constructors of the object. A new instance is actually created, but no constructors are called and therefore no instructions within the constructors will be executed. To work around this the class definition can supply its own `readObject()` method to perform any initialization that may be necessary.

A data binding framework, like Castor, will actually create new instances of the objects. As we have already seen, Castor typically requires that all class definitions have a default constructor, because Castor will create new instances and therefore must invoke the constructor. Actually, Castor really has no choice in the matter as only the JVM can create an object without calling a constructor.

Public vs. Private

When performing Serialization the JVM has access to all fields: public, protected or private. So it simply deals with the fields directly and not the accessor methods (getters and setters) to save and restore values. A data binding framework can access public fields directly, but has no access to the protected or private fields. Therefore it typically needs to use the public accessor methods to save and restore values of the fields.

There are pros and cons to both approaches. With Serialization we are not required to expose public methods to access private data that needs to be persisted. A drawback to the direct field manipulation of serialization is that if there is any business logic in the accessor methods for a given field it will not be executed. This can be overcome by implementing the `writeObject` and `readObject` methods used by the Serialization API to handle the business logic, however this is more difficult to maintain.

Conclusion

Java Serialization and XML data binding both allow us to save and recreate object instances. Choosing the right approach depends on the situation, but XML data binding has many clear advantages.

Using XML data binding instead of Serialization enables us to:

- Share persisted data across systems
- Obtain object model independence
- Become programming language agnostic
- Read and manually update the persisted information using any text editor

The benefits to Java Object Serialization over XML Data Binding:

- No need to expose access to private fields in order to be persisted
- Faster than XML data binding

Summary

It is typically easier to interact with data in the native format of our programming language, in a manner that depicts the intended meaning of the data, without concern for how the data is stored. Data binding provides the concepts for allowing us to interact with data formats in such a fashion. We learned that, for many XML applications, using XML APIs such as SAX and DOM are often very tedious, lack specific meaning, and force us to work in a format that depicts how the data is stored. Using these APIs is desirable if our applications need to interact with generic XML instances.

Using a data-binding framework allows us to easily write and maintain XML-enabled applications. We have shown examples of using a data binding framework and in doing so we have seen that a data-binding framework allows us to:

- Perform simple XML data binding using an existing object without specifying any binding information
- Express bindings for an existing object model for more complex XML data binding
- Generate a complete object model, including all binding and validation code for a given XML schema

Sometimes an XML schema may be too complex for a specific data-binding framework. We have discussed how we could use XSLT to simplify our XML schema instances to aid data binding. Sharing data with other companies or applications is very common and we have seen how XSLT can help us perform data binding on schemas that are different from what our system expects.

It is often necessary for an application to persist object instances. We have discussed using XML data binding instead of Java Serialization for this purpose, especially when we need to access the data in another system, or if we need to make the persisted data human readable or updateable.

There are many uses for XML data binding and hopefully by reading this chapter you have discovered a way to make programming your XML-enabled applications, easier, more natural, and more enjoyable.

Resources:

Castor

http://castor.exolab.org

Java Beans Specification, version 1.01

http://java.sun.com/products/javabeans/docs/spec.html

Java Serialization

http://www.javasoft.com/products/jdk/1.2/docs/guide/serialization/index.html

JSR 31

http://java.sun.com/aboutJava/communityprocess/jsr/jsr_031_xmld.html

W3C XML Schema

http://www.w3.org/XML/Schema

There are other data binding frameworks apart from Castor. We didn't have time to discuss them in this chapter, but more information about some of them can be found here:

Zeus

http://zeus.enhydra.org

Quick

http://jxquick.sourceforge.net/

Breeze XML Studio

http://www.breezefactor.com/overview.html

16

Querying XML

Consider the following statement:

> **An XML query language accesses an XML document or collection of XML documents like a database.**

Why do we need an **XML Query Language**? Isn't XML just an interchange format that can be used to communicate between existing databases? After all, aren't RDBMSs already showing support for XML? For example, Microsoft's XML views in SQL Server 2000 and Oracle's XSQL enable us to access relational data as XML, as we saw in Chapter 15. By defining custom mappings between tables and standard XML document types, we can facilitate communication between systems that otherwise have incompatible ways of storing data. XML, as a serializable, mediating view of the data, can help us bridge this gap.

But if XML is just another serialization format, like comma-separated values, why should there be a query language for it? No one ever suggested supplementing SQL with a language for querying CSV files (If they did, I don't want to hear about it!).

The answer is that XML provides more than just a serialization format for relational data. Its flexible, hierarchical structure enables it to model not only relational data, but data that doesn't fit so well within the confines of the relational data model. Structured documents are probably the premier example of this. Anyone who has tried to map the components of an HTML page to fields in a relational database knows what I'm talking about. A data model for XML could provide a unified way of viewing both document-centric and data-centric information. Also, an XML query language would provide a unified way to search, extract, manipulate, and otherwise process this information.

That's why the W3C **XML Query Working Group** was chartered – "to provide flexible query facilities to extract data from real and virtual XML documents on the Web".

- The W3C XML Activity Statement: http://www.w3.org/XML/Activity.html#query-wg
- The W3C XML Query home page: http://www.w3.org/XML/Query

The mention of "virtual documents" indicates that we're not just talking about querying XML *files*. From the perspective of a query language, it is immaterial whether the data is stored in flat files, a relational database, or an index. All an XML query language requires is that the data is *viewed* as an XML document or collection of XML documents.

While it may be immaterial to the query language, how the data is stored could make a big difference to the user. Relational databases require you to spend time mapping between two different data models and updating that mapping every time the structure of your data changes. In contrast, "native" XML databases promise to eliminate this expensive overhead by dispensing with the relational model altogether, at least from the user's point of view.

Enter **XQuery**. Though currently only an early working draft, XQuery promises to become a very important W3C recommendation. In this chapter, we will learn the basics of XQuery, its data model, how it relates to other W3C specifications (including XML Schemas, XPath, and XSLT), and what the future might hold for it. Be forewarned that the information in this chapter may soon become out of date, as there are a number of unresolved issues in XQuery. That said, many of the things we will learn here will be valuable, regardless of the particular changes that are made to the language.

The W3C XML Query Language

The W3C XML Query working group has published five documents. The URLs for the most recent versions of these documents can be found below. At the time of this writing, the latest documents were working drafts published on 15 February, 2001.

- XML Query Requirements: http://www.w3.org/TR/xmlquery-req
- XML Query Use Cases: http://www.w3.org/TR/xmlquery-use-cases
- XML Query Data Model: http://www.w3.org/TR/query-datamodel
- The XML Query Algebra: http://www.w3.org/TR/query-algebra
- XQuery: A Query Language for XML: http://www.w3.org/TR/xquery

We'll briefly discuss each of the first four documents, and then we'll delve more deeply into XQuery, which defines the actual syntax (or at least one possible syntax), of the XML Query language.

Requirements

The XML Query language must be **declarative**, that is, it must not enforce a particular evaluation strategy. This means that, unlike imperative programming languages such as Java and C++, XML Query language programs declare the *what* of the relationship between input and output, not the *how*. In this way, it is like SQL and XSLT, where the query optimizer or stylesheet processor – not the user – decides what sequence of steps to take to evaluate expressions and return results.

See Chapter 9 for more information on XSLT and the functional programming paradigm.

Queries must be **closed** with respect to the **XML Query Data Model**. This means that the output from one query could always function as input to another query. This is because they are both instances of the same data model. This is also the case with SQL and XSLT, where the input and output data models are the same (tables and trees, respectively).

The XML Query language may have more than one syntax. There must be an XML syntax, and there must be a syntax that is "convenient for humans to read and write." The requirements are worded in such a way that either one syntax could fulfill both requirements, or two syntaxes could be specified. As it turns out, XQuery is designed to fulfill only the "human-readable" requirement, because it provides a non-XML syntax for the XML Query Language. The XML syntax has not yet been defined. As we'll see later, XQuery uses a succinct SQL-like syntax that might look somewhat familiar to traditional database users.

Queries must be able to select parts of trees, perform arbitrary transformations, construct new instances, and perform operations that preserve the hierarchy and sequence of the original XML documents. Examples of these kinds of queries will be given in the "XQuery" section later in this chapter.

The XML Query language must be able to perform operations on collections of XML documents, references between and within documents, and XML Schema datatypes. See the "Data Model" section below for more information.

The first version of the XML Query language will not support updates. However, it must not preclude the ability to add update-capabilities in a future version of the language.

In this section, we've just touched on some of the most noteworthy requirements for the XML Query language. For the complete list of requirements, see http://www.w3.org/TR/xmlquery-req.

Use-Cases

The XML Query use-cases document includes over 70 example use-cases, grouped into nine categories. Each use-case consists of an XML input document or documents, a prose description of what the query should do, and the XML output it should produce. In addition, possible solutions to each problem are presented in XQuery syntax.

This document can serve as a great learning aid. Try solving some of the use-cases on your own. Write or type the whole query before you check the answer. If you learn well by example, you may find that treating the use-cases document like a tutorial will enable you to more quickly get up to speed with XQuery. You can get started at http://www.w3.org/TR/xmlquery-use-cases.

Data Model

A data model for XML is an abstract way of looking at XML documents; it defines what aspects of XML documents are significant. What is XML's data model? If we look to the XML 1.0 recommendation for the answer to this question, we'll be disappointed. It actually defines a text format, not a data model (although there are hints otherwise, such as the statement that "the order of attributes is not significant").

We've already seen that a data model is necessary for certain kinds of XML applications, including XPath navigation and XSLT transformations. Also, the DOM, though it doesn't define an explicit data model, certainly uses an implicit one. Conflicting (or complementary, depending on your perspective) data models have arisen due to the diverse needs of XML applications. For example, in XPath, whether a character occurs in a CDATA section or not is insignificant and unknown to the XPath user. Compare that to the DOM, where CDATA sections are reported to applications as instances of a particular type of node.

The W3C is working to unify the data models used by various W3C specifications to whatever extent it is possible and reasonable to do so. The **XML Information Set**, or Infoset (also currently in working draft stage) is an attempt to "provide a consistent set of definitions for use in other specifications that need to refer to the information in a well-formed XML document". Rather than providing an exhaustive list of all the possible items that an application might consider significant, the Infoset defines a common subset that is used by multiple specifications. In this sense, it covers the intersection, rather than the union, of information items used by W3C specs. For example, the Infoset defines the "document information item", which is an abstraction of XPath's "root node" and the DOM's "document node". More about the XML Infoset can be found in Chapter 4 and at the URLs below:

- The XML Information Set: http://www.w3.org/TR/xml-infoset
- The XML Schema home page: http://www.w3.org/XML/Schema

The XML Query data model is based on the "post-schema-validation Infoset", or PSV Infoset. This term describes the XML Infoset, augmented by any simple or complex schema type information provided by an XML Schema.

See Chapter 6 for more information on XML Schema structures and datatypes.

In addition to the PSV Infoset, the XML Query data model includes the concepts of collections and references. Collections, such as "ordered forests" and "unordered forests", are used to model collections of multiple XML documents, or document fragments. They also model collections of nodes, similar to XPath node-sets.

References are used to model both intra- and inter-document references, over which query language operators can traverse. An example of an intra-document reference is the use of attributes of type `ID` and `IDREF`. An example of an inter-document reference is the use of XLink for linking between documents and parts of documents. References are important because they enable XML to model not only trees, but any graph as well.

See Chapter 10 for more information on linking XML documents with XLink.

An instance of the query data model serves as input to, and output from queries. For more information on the XML Query data model, see http://www.w3.org/TR/query-datamodel.

Algebra

The **XML Query Algebra** defines the core operators of the XML Query language. Based on the XML Query data model, it includes a complete type system and abstract and concrete syntaxes for that system. It defines a **strongly typed** query language, which means that the datatypes returned by all expressions will be known at compile-time. This enables more sophisticated static query analysis and compile-time error checking.

The algebra also defines equivalence laws for queries, which implementers can use for various query optimization strategies. Since the XML Query language is a declarative language like SQL, implementations should have many opportunities for query optimization. The algebra is intended to highlight and allude to some of these opportunities.

The XML Query algebra grants first-order importance to *expressions*, enabling queries to be composed. **Composability** describes the ability to use the output of one expression as input to another expression. This characteristic further aids the formulation of equivalence laws and, consequently, optimization strategies.

XQuery, which currently describes the "human-readable syntax" of the query language, will be conceptually based on this algebra. Learning the algebra could certainly help you better understand the underlying semantics of XQuery. However, as a user, you can probably get away with not reading the algebra, the precise definition of the semantics of the language will be most important for implementers. For this reason, in this chapter we will focus more on the higher-level XQuery language, examining concrete examples as we go.

Since all of these documents are still working drafts, you can expect that there will be a good deal of give-and-take between XQuery and the algebra, as the working group continues to resolve inconsistencies between the relevant specifications. The latest XML Query algebra document can be found at http://www.w3.org/TR/query-algebra.

XQuery

Now that we've had a brief overview of the requirements, use-cases, data model, and algebra, we'll take a more in-depth look at the actual syntax of the XML Query language, which is what you'll spend most of your time directly using.

> **XQuery is the non-XML syntax for the XML Query language. An XML syntax is still under development.**

In accordance with the XML Query algebra, expressions play a prominent role in XQuery. Queries are made up of expressions, which can be composed into larger expressions. Two notable types of expressions that we'll explore here are **path expressions** and **FLWR** (**F**or **L**et **W**here **R**eturn) **expressions** (pronounced "flower").

In this section, we won't attempt to describe the precise semantics of XQuery, because there are too many unresolved issues and ambiguities in the current working draft. For example, we will not discuss the exact semantics of what is returned by each expression, such as: whether it constitutes a node *copy* (where the returned node has a different identity than the selected node) or a node *reference* (where the node's identity is maintained). Such a discussion would certainly be helpful, but not at this stage in the game. Instead, we will adopt a style similar to that of the XQuery spec, which consists of a tutorial-like introduction, making use of examples to demonstrate XQuery's functionality.

The latest XQuery specification can be found at http://www.w3.org/TR/xquery.

Sample Data

Most of the example queries in this chapter will use one or both of the following XML documents as their input. These examples were designed to exploit XQuery's ability to perform queries across individual documents as well as across multiple documents.

The first example file is called `artists.xml`, and looks like this:

```
<artists>
   <artist>
      <name>Chicago Symphony Orchestra &amp; Chorus</name>
      <album>
         <name>The 9th Symphony</name>
         <composer>Ludwig van Beethoven</composer>
         <conductor>Sir Georg Solti</conductor>
         <year>1995</year>
      </album>
      <album>
         <name>Symphony no 1, Romeo &amp; Juliet, etc.</name>
         <composer>Sergei Prokofiev</composer>
         <conductor>Claudio Abbado, Mstislav Rostropovich, et
                    al.</conductor>
         <year>2000</year>
      </album>
   </artist>
   <artist>
      <name>Johnny Cash</name>
      <album live="no">
         <name>Live and on the Air</name>
         <year>1997</year>
      </album>
      <single>
         <name>Ring of Fire</name>
         <year>1963</year>
      </single>
   </artist>
</artists>
```

The second is called `moreArtists.xml`:

```
<artists>
   <artist>
      <name>John Denver</name>
      <album live="no">
         <name>John Denver</name>
         <year>1979</year>
      </album>
      <album live="yes">
         <name>The Best of John Denver Live</name>
         <year>1997</year>
      </album>
   </artist>
   <artist>
      <name>Elton John</name>
      <album live="yes">
```

```
            <name>
                Elton John Live in Australia with the Melbourne Symphony
                Orchestra
            </name>
            <year>1976</year>
        </album>
        <single>
            <name>Candle in the Wind</name>
            <year>1997</year>
        </single>
    </artist>
</artists>
```

Path Expressions

Path expressions in XQuery are very similar to XPath expressions, but there are some notable differences. XQuery path expressions use the abbreviated syntax of XPath. This effectively reduces the number of axes available for use within location paths.

See Chapter 8 for more information on XPath and the XPath axes.

Also, XQuery path expressions currently are not sufficiently defined in terms of XPath 1.0's semantics. For this reason, we won't push the comparison too far. In the XPath 2.0 Requirements document, however, we are told that both XSLT and the XML Query language will share XPath 2.0. At that time, these semantic differences should be resolved.

- XPath Requirements Version 2.0: http://www.w3.org/TR/xpath20req
- XSLT Requirements Version 2.0: http://www.w3.org/TR/xslt20req

XQuery path expressions can stand alone as queries. This helps fulfill the requirement that queries are easy for humans to read and write, but also that queries be usable in different syntactic environments. For example: by using the path expression syntax, a query could easily be embedded in a URL.

Example Queries

1. From the sample document artists.xml, get all albums released in 1997:

```
document("artists.xml")/artists/artist/album[year = "1997"]
```

The result of this query is:

```
<album live="no">
    <name>Live and on the Air</name>
    <year>1997</year>
</album>
```

The document() function is borrowed from XSLT. It returns the root node of the document identified by its string argument. Otherwise, the above query looks exactly the same as an XPath expression. A notable difference here is that, with XQuery, there is an implied serialization, which is to return a deep copy of each node selected by the path expression. XPath, on the other hand, relies on an external specification, such as XSLT or XPointer, to define what to do with the selected node-set. That said, the above result is fairly intuitive. And the query is certainly convenient in its succinctness.

2. From the implicit root node (containing both XML documents), get all albums released in 1997.

```
/artists/artist/album[year = "1997"]
```

The result of this query is:

```
<album live="no">
   <name>Live and on the Air</name>
   <year>1997</year>
</album>
<album live="yes">
   <name>The Best of John Denver Live</name>
   <year>1997</year>
</album>
```

Note that this query is exactly the same as the first one, except that it does not begin with the `document()` function. Instead, the slash (/) on its own signifies "an implicit root node, determined by the environment in which the query is executed". We are defining the environment to consist of two documents, `artists.xml`, and `moreArtists.xml`, in that order. In the XQuery spec, this is called an "ordered forest" of trees.

3. Get all albums and singles released before 1970.

```
/artists/artist/*[year < 1970]
```

The result of this query is:

```
<single>
   <name>Ring of Fire</name>
   <year>1963</year>
</single>
```

This query shows that, as with XPath, the asterisk (*) can be used as a wildcard. In this case, it matches both `album` and `single` elements, as well as `name` elements. The predicate filters out everything but the one single released before 1970.

FLWR Expressions

FLWR expressions supplement path expressions by providing the ability to iterate through collections of nodes, perform transformations, construct arbitrary results, and do conditional processing, among other things. The SQL-like syntax is designed to be easily readable and familiar to SQL programmers.

```
F - FOR
L - LET
W - WHERE
R - RETURN
```

Example Queries

4. Produce a new, well-formed XML document that contains, for each artist, a `musician` element that contains the text corresponding to the name of that artist.

```
<musicians>
   FOR $a IN /artists/artist
   RETURN
      <musician> $a/name/text() </musician>
</musicians>
```

The result of this query is:

```
<musicians>
   <musician>Chicago Symphony Orchestra &amp; Chorus</musician>
   <musician>Johnny Cash</musician>
   <musician>John Denver</musician>
   <musician>Elton John</musician>
</musicians>
```

The `FOR` clause iterates through the "ordered forest" of nodes returned by the path expression. For each node in that collection, a variable is bound, which is then referenced in the `RETURN` statement. Note the XML-like syntax used for constructing the result. These are called **element constructors**, which constitute another type of XQuery expression.

5. Produce a new well-formed XML document that contains a list of the distinct years in which albums or singles were released, constrained to those within the 10 years prior to the year the last album or single was released:

```
<withinLast10Years>
   FOR $y IN distinct (/artists/artist/*/year)
   LET $d := max(/artists/artist/*/year) - $y
   WHERE $d < 10
   RETURN
      <releaseYear> $y/text() </releaseYear>
</withinLast10Years>
```

The result of this query is:

```
<withinLast10Years>
   <releaseYear>1995</releaseYear>
   <releaseYear>2000</releaseYear>
   <releaseYear>1997</releaseYear>
</withinLast10Years>
```

This query demonstrates the convenience of the `LET` clause, which produces a variable binding, which can be referenced in the `RETURN` statement. It also introduces the `distinct()` function, which returns an unordered collection of nodes – one for each unique value found among the nodes returned by the path expression argument. In this case, the duplicate `year` elements (containing `1997`) are removed. The `WHERE` clause further filters the collection, removing all years apart from ones whose difference with the latest year is less than 10. The `max()` function is used to determine the highest (latest) year. The `distinct()` and `max()` functions (as well as some other aggregation functions including `avg()` and `min()`) are unique to XQuery; they are not currently part of XPath, although they will likely become a part of XPath 2.0.

Conditional Expressions

XQuery also supports conditional processing. This is necessary, for example, when you want the result to be constructed differently based on certain conditions holding.

Example Query

6. For each album, return an element whose name depends on whether the album has a conductor listed for it or not.

```
FOR $a IN /artists/artist/album
IF $a/conductor
THEN
   <classical> $a/name/text() </classical>
ELSE
   <notClassical> $a/name/text() </notClassical>
```

The result of this query is:

```
<classical>The 9th Symphony</classical>
<classical>Symphony no 1, Romeo &amp; Juliet, etc.</classical>
<notClassical>Live and on the Air</notClassical>
<notClassical>John Denver</notClassical>
<notClassical>The Best of John Denver Live</notClassical>
<notClassical>Elton John Live in Australia with the Melbourne Symphony
              Orchestra</notClassical>
```

Quantifiers

XQuery supports **existential** and **universal** quantifiers. An existential quantifier tests to see whether at least one node within a collection that satisfies a given condition exists. A universal quantifier tests to see whether *all* the nodes in a collection satisfy a given condition.

Example Queries

7. Get the name of all the artists; that have at least one album or single with the name containing "John".

```
FOR $a IN /artists/artist
WHERE SOME $n IN $a/*/name SATISFIES
   contains($n, "John")
RETURN
   <floristsFavorite> $a/name/text() </floristsFavorite>
```

The result of this query is:

```
<floristsFavorite>John Denver</floristsFavorite>
<floristsFavorite>Elton John</floristsFavorite>
```

The `SOME/SATISFIES` clause corresponds to the existential quantifier. Note that this could also easily be expressed in the path language. Existential quantifiers are XPath's normal mode of operation as well. Moving the existential quantifier into the path expression would look like this:

```
FOR $a IN /artists/artist[contains(*/name, "John")]
RETURN
   <floristsFavorite> $a/name/text() </floristsFavorite>
```

The predicate will filter out everything but those artists that have at least one album or single name containing "John".

8. Get the name of all the artists, whose album and single names *all* contain "John."

```
FOR $a IN /artists/artist
WHERE EVERY $n IN $a/*/name SATISFIES
   contains($n, "John")
RETURN
   <butchersBest> $a/name/text() </butchersBest>
```

The result of this query is:

```
<butchersBest>John Denver</butchersBest>
```

The EVERY/SATISFIES clause corresponds to the universal quantifier. There is currently not an equivalent mechanism to this in XPath, but such a mechanism is listed among the XPath 2.0 requirements.

Filtering

In addition to the `distinct()` function introduced in "Example 5", XQuery provides a `filter()` function that takes two node collections as arguments. It then filters out all descendant nodes of those in the first list, that aren't in the second, resulting in a tree that consists of a shallow copy of each remaining node preserved in its original hierarchy with respect to the other remaining nodes. It's probably impossible to understand that mouthful without a concrete example.

9. Create a table of contents for `sample.xml`.

First, here's `sample.xml`:

```
<section>
   <title>Learning XQuery</title>
   <abstract>Lots of interesting stuff about XQuery.</abstract>
   <section>
      <title>XML Query Languages</title>
      <para>Some interesting things</para>
      <section>
         <title>XPath</title>
         <para>XPath is...</para>
      </section>
      <section>
         <title>XSLT</title>
         <para>XSLT is...</para>
      </section>
   </section>
   <section>
      <title>XQuery</title>
      <para>XQuery is...</para>
   </section>
</section>
```

Here's the query to produce the table of contents for `sample.xml`:

```
LET $s := document("sample.xml")
RETURN
   filter($s, $s//section | $s//section/title | $s//section/title/text() )
```

The result of this query is:

```
<section>
   <title>Learning XQuery</title>
   <section>
      <title>XML Query Languages</title>
      <section>
         <title>XPath</title>
      </section>
      <section>
         <title>XSLT</title>
      </section>
   </section>
   <section>
      <title>XQuery</title>
   </section>
</section>
```

As you can see, the effect of this query is to prune parts of the original document that we don't want to explicitly retain. In this case, the query effectively prunes all `para` and `abstract` elements from the resulting tree.

Functions, Operators, and Datatypes

The XQuery path expression language includes all the functions in the XPath core function library, as well as the common SQL aggregation functions (`avg()`, `count()`, `min()`, `max()`, `sum()`).

In addition to the built-in functions, XQuery provides a mechanism for user-defined functions. These functions may be recursive, that is, they may invoke themselves. The nature of XQuery as a declarative, functional programming language means that certain tasks will require defining a recursive function, because side-effect-producing assignment statements are not allowed. Some examples of this are included in the XQuery spec.

XQuery's path language also introduces some new constructs to XPath, some of which consist of a syntax change meant to make the path language more readable. Changes in syntax include the `RANGE` predicate, the `UNION` operator, and the dereference operator (`->`). The `BEFORE` and `AFTER` operators allow for comparisons based on document order, providing similar functionality to XPath 1.0's `preceding` and `following` axes. For complete details, see the XQuery specification.

The relationship between XML Schema datatypes and XQuery is still largely unspecified. There are some example queries in the XQuery specification that use simple datatypes, but there are many unresolved issues. These relationships will become more clear as the XML Query data model, XML Schema, and XQuery specifications move closer to finalization.

Querying Relational Data

There is a significant emphasis in the XQuery draft on querying relational data. In fact, the XQuery syntax is arguably optimized for queries that involve joins across multiple documents. One way in which XQuery could be used to query existing relational data is to define a general-purpose, default mapping of relational tables to individual XML documents, which contain the records in those tables. How that mapping might be done is detailed in the XQuery specification.

Here's an example query that could be specified across such data:

10. Return a list of counselor names and their students' grades, in alphabetic order.

```
FOR $cs IN document("counselor-students.xml")//cs_tuple,
    $s IN document("students.xml")//s_tuple[id = $cs/sid],
    $c IN document("counselors.xml")//c_tuple[id = $cs/cid]
RETURN
   <cs_pair>
      $c/name ,
      $s/grade
   </cs_pair> SORTBY (name, grade)
```

The `FOR` clause iterates through the cross product of the collections returned by the three path expressions. This is similar to the behavior of nested `xsl:for-each` instructions in XSLT.

This general way of viewing relational data as XML will be most useful for querying existing relational data for which a custom XML mapping has not been defined. In our opinion, while this can be useful, it seems to bring XML back down to the status of a serialization format rather than a desirable data model, and consequently, it should not be viewed as the most important use-case of an XML query language. After all, XML generally requires fewer joins than the relational data model. This is because the data is usually brought closer together (within the same document or element), rather than being spread out across multiple tables, as necessitated by the relational model.

XQuery vs. XSLT

By now, you may have noticed that many of XQuery's features are similar to those provided by XSLT. In fact, XSLT could easily solve most of the example queries in this chapter, and there has been some controversy over XQuery's overlapping functionality with XSLT. The XSL and XML Query Working Groups are addressing this problem to some extent, with the commitment to make XPath 2.0 compatible with both XSLT and the XML Query language. This will require a good deal of give-and-take on both sides and may result in two languages that are even more similar than they look now.

Currently, one of the most significant things lacking in XSLT, in comparison to the XML Query language, is support for XML Schema datatypes. The XSLT 2.0 and XPath 2.0 Requirements documents (referenced earlier in this chapter under "Path Expressions") both include the requirement to support XML Schema simple and complex types, so this gap will be narrowing.

Another significant difference is that the XML Query language does not provide any mechanism akin to XSLT's template rules. The reasoning behind this is that template rules are not as easy to optimize for large data sets. In addition, the XML Query language does not support all of the XPath axes. This pared-down functionality is designed to make XML Query more optimizable.

XSLT 1.0 is not as easily composed as XQuery. XSLT 1.1 will be changing this, at least to some extent, by introducing the ability to treat arbitrarily constructed trees as node-sets, without requiring the need for an extension function. These node-sets can then be used to compose further expressions.

XSLT models single documents, whereas XQuery can model collections of documents. While this is true, there is nothing fundamentally different between the two data models that would keep XSLT from being able to model multiple documents in one tree as well. In any case, XPath 2.0 will be providing both languages with the same data model, so this may turn out to be a moot point.

Needless to say, it will be quite interesting to see how the story unfolds. Who knows, maybe the XML Query language's XML-based syntax will come in the form of XSLT 2.0 or an XSLT 2.0 subset.

Summary

In this chapter we have seen why we need an XML Query language, and compared it to XSLT. We have seen several examples showing how to find search terms using: Path expressions, FLWR expressions, Conditional expressions and Quantifiers. We have also talked about Filtering, Functions, Operators, and Datatypes, as well as querying relational data.

- The XML Query data model defines a data model for XML, including node types, datatypes, collections, and references.
- The XML Query algebra defines a set of operators on that data model.
- The XML Query language is declarative, closed, and composable.
- XQuery defines a human-readable syntax for that language.

There is also a requirement for an XML-based syntax, which is currently under development. The XPath 2.0 data model and expression language will be a part of both XSLT and the XML Query language.

There are few XQuery implementations currently available, because the XQuery specification is so new and unstable. However, a partial implementation of XQuery's predecessor, Quilt, is available at the following URL:

- Kweelt: Querying XML in the New Millennium: http://db.cis.upenn.edu/Kweelt/

17

Case Study: Databases and XML

In this chapter, we are going to look at a practical application of XML for a real-world problem – the management and retrieval of résumé information for a consulting company. We will take the problem from business case all the way through code, and see how all the pieces fit together to form a flexible, extensible whole. We'll see examples of the following techniques:

- Using a relational database as an index into an XML document repository
- Optimizing the XML structure and the relational database schema for the information being handled
- Using XSLT stylesheets to generate HTML pages
- Using XSLT stylesheets to generate HTML input forms

Technologies Used

In this case study, we have chosen to use ASP pages with VBScript and SQL Server to develop the solution for the Microsoft platform. However, all of the examples use techniques that are perfectly portable to platforms such as Java and Apache, if that is desired. To run the sample code, we will need SQL Server 6.5 or higher, IIS 4.0 or higher, and MSXML 3.0 loaded on our system. Note that we aren't taking advantages of the XML features in SQL Server 2000 – in order to demonstrate the way document meta-data indexing is performed, our structures are designed in such a way that these features wouldn't be a great deal of help to us. Finally, we've chosen to demonstrate client-side creation of XML documents using JavaScript, and we'll need to use IE 5 or higher to view the document on the client.

The Business Problem

We have been given the task of designing a system to hold résumé and skills information for our consulting company. The information gathered for each consultant looks something like this:

Albert Q. Example

Architect

Employee ID:	12345
Qualifications:	Albert has several years of consulting experience working in the financial and pharmaceutical industries. He has focused primarily on database and XML work.
Experience:	Database architect – Designed a relational database for a large financial services application.
	Project management – Managed a small group of developers working on a pharmaceutical supply application
Skills:	Financial systems
	Pharmaceuticals

Competency:	**None**	**Novice**	**Intermediate**	**Expert**
XML		X		
XSLT		X		
C++	X			
COM	X			
CORBA	X			
SOAP	X			
Visual Basic	X			
Windows NT/2000	X			
UNIX	X			
Perl	X			
Python	X			
ASP	X			
Java	X			
JavaScript	X			

The following features need to be implemented:

- A way to add or update résumés over the Internet.
- A way to search the résumés database over the Internet.
- A way to display résumés as the result of searches.
- A competency matrix showing how all returned résumés stack up against each other.
- We also know that we're only interested in searching on skill, title, and competencies – name, employee ID, qualifications, and experience are used for display purposes only. We will take advantage of these assumptions when we design our relational index later in the chapter.

Proposed Architecture

When designing the typical data-oriented application, there are (loosely speaking) four major functions it must perform:

- Gathering the data
- Displaying the data
- Searching the data
- Summarizing the data

Understanding the role each part of our data set plays in each of these functions, will help us understand what our architecture needs to be. As we examine the proposed feature set for our application, we can see that it segments neatly into the categories above:

- Inserting or updating résumés in the repository (gathering the data)
- Displaying résumés as a result of searches (displaying the data)
- Searching for particular résumés in our system (searching the data)

Note that we do not have any summarization needs for this implementation.

Information that is used for display (at the detail level) is best suited to XML (using XSLT to style it for presentation); information that needs to be searched or summarized makes more sense in a relational database. Since our search information comprises only a small part of the entire XML document content, we will use an indexing approach, where SQL Server holds a copy of the information that may be searched against, linked to a pointer into an XML document repository stored as individual files on the filesystem. This saves pages in the relational database (at the expense of greater overall disk usage) and makes our information easily portable – to move a résumé to another system, simply move the associated XML file. By using the employee ID of the particular résumé as the name of the XML file representing the résumé, it makes it very easy to locate the document corresponding to a particular employee.

We will use IIS as the web server for the application. ASP and XSLT stylesheets will be used to move information between the relational database, the XML document store, and HTML. The XML file document repository will reside in a directory on the server; in the examples, this directory is "`d:\resumes`".

Analyzing the Data

Next, we need to take a look at the information found in our résumé and figure out what belongs in our XML documents and what belongs in our SQL Server index. Since we have chosen to make the XML document the "document of record" – that is, the "original" copy of the résumé as it was submitted – that document will need to contain all the information found in the résumé. Our structure should reflect the internal structure of the résumé itself. On the other hand, the SQL Server portion of our database will be smaller, as it needs only to contain the information required for searching (the title, skills, and competencies) – the qualifications and experience fields are not necessary, as we will only be showing those when we show the résumé details.

Designing the XML structure

As we examine our résumé, we see that we have the following information:

- Name
- Title
- Employee ID
- Qualifications
- Experience (may occur more than once)
- Skills (may occur more than once)
- Competencies (may occur more than once):
- Competency Type
- Competency Level

We also know that we have a master list of competency types and a master list of titles that we will use as the only allowable possible values for these attributes. Here are some ways that the lists could be implemented:

- As attributes with enumerated lists in the XML DTD or schema
- As numerical values with related tables in the relational database that provide a text description
- As numerical values with related information in a separate XML document that provide a text description

The first method provides the greatest level of portability for our résumés – a résumé that spells out the text description of these attributes does not need any supporting documentation to explain what the values mean – but it makes it more difficult to implement global changes. For example, if we wanted to change the title of "Architect" to "Designer", we would have to open every single XML document and make the change. The other problem with this technique is that it does not allow for flexible descriptions (since we're using a DTD to describe our document) – each of the allowable tokens must abide by the XML naming convention, making descriptions with spaces (such as "Senior Architect") impossible.

The second method provides the lowest level of portability – in order to make sense of an XML document, the associated table in SQL Server must be accessed. In addition, we cannot simply use a stylesheet to return the text value for the column – other code must be used to access the relational database (and the description).

The third method is a good compromise for our purposes. Titles and competencies are maintained in atomic documents, easily added to or updated, while XSLT stylesheets may access the descriptions of the titles and competencies (using the `document()` function, as we'll see) without requiring a database call.

Given this analysis, we arrive at the following document structure for the XML documents (`resume.dtd`):

```
<!ELEMENT resume (name, title, employeeID, qualifications, experience*,
   skill*, competency*)>
<!ELEMENT name #PCDATA>
<!ELEMENT title #PCDATA>
<!ELEMENT employeeID #PCDATA>
<!ELEMENT qualifications #PCDATA>
<!ELEMENT experience #PCDATA>
<!ELEMENT skill #PCDATA>
<!ELEMENT competency EMPTY>
<!ATTLIST competency
   type CDATA REQUIRED
   value CDATA REQUIRED>
```

Here is an example document for the résumé we have already seen, named after the employee ID (`12345.xml`):

```
<resume>
   <name>Albert Q. Example</name>
   <title>2</title>
   <employeeID>12345</employeeID>
   <qualifications>Albert has several years of consulting experience working in
the financial and pharmaceutical industries. He has focused primarily on database
and XML work.</qualifications>
   <experience> Database designer - Designed a relational database for a large
financial services application.</experience>
   <experience> Project management - Managed a small group of developers working
on a pharmaceutical supply application.</experience>
   <skill>Financial systems</skill>
   <skill>Pharmaceuticals</skill>
   <competency type="1" value="1" />
   <competency type="2" value="1" />
</resume>
```

Remember that we have chosen to store titles and competency types in lookup documents – the integer values seen in our XML document correspond to rows in those documents. Also, note that we've chosen to represent the competencies in a terse way – if the résumé states that the consultant has no skills in a particular competency, that row is omitted from the XML document.

Here is the title lookup document (`titles.xml`):

```
<titles>
   <title name="" value="0" />
   <title name="Senior Architect" value="1" />
   <title name="Architect" value="2" />
   <title name="Senior Programmer" value="3" />
```

```
    <title name="Programmer" value="4" />
    <title name="Staff Programmer" value="5" />
    <title name="Business Analyst" value="6" />
    <title name="Network Architect" value="7" />
    <title name="Project Manager" value="8" />
</titles>
```

Here is the competency-type lookup document (competencies.xml):

```
<competencies>
    <competency name="XML" value="1" />
    <competency name="XSLT" value="2" />
    <competency name="C++" value="3" />
    <competency name="COM" value="4" />
    <competency name="CORBA" value="5" />
    <competency name="SOAP" value="6" />
    <competency name="Visual Basic" value="7" />
    <competency name="Windows NT/2000" value="8" />
    <competency name="*nix" value="9" />
    <competency name="Perl" value="10" />
    <competency name="Python" value="11" />
    <competency name="ASP" value="12" />
    <competency name="Java" value="13" />
    <competency name="JavaScript" value="14" />
</competencies>
```

Note that in our sample résumé, we have omitted the DTD declaration. This is intentional, and illustrates an important point about XML document design. If the document is being created by a trusted source (in our case, JavaScript code in our page) and is known to abide by a certain structure, introducing a parsing step by including a DTD only serves to slow processing of the documents down. They can be helpful during development, but once a system is working, they are not as necessary. DTD references are more useful when documents are coming from a non-trusted source (such as a user editing an XML document by hand) or when a document needs to clearly include information about its internal structure (such as a mixed repository of documents). For our purposes, we will leave it out.

Designing the Relational Database Structure

Next, we need to design the relational structures that will hold our indexing information. Loosely speaking, these should follow the same structure as the XML documents; after all, informational structure is independent of the platform on which the information is being represented. Information should be omitted that does not belong in the index (for example, the information we're not going to be searching on – the qualifications and experience). Additionally, we'll create identity columns in each table, a good practice when designing relational databases in any circumstance, and use these columns as foreign keys to relate our tables together. We will call our database, resume, in this case.

Since we're discarding experience information, we need to have three tables in our structure – one for the résumé, one for each skill, and one for each competency. We end up with the following table structure (tables.sql):

```
CREATE TABLE resume (
    resumeID INT PRIMARY KEY IDENTITY,
    employeeID VARCHAR(20) NOT NULL UNIQUE,
    name VARCHAR(60) NOT NULL,
```

```
      titleType TINYINT)

   CREATE TABLE skill (
      skillID INT IDENTITY,
      resumeID INT NOT NULL
         FOREIGN KEY REFERENCES resume (resumeID),
      description VARCHAR(30))

   CREATE TABLE competency (
      competencyID INT NOT NULL IDENTITY,
      resumeID INT
         FOREIGN KEY REFERENCES resume (resumeID),
      competencyType TINYINT,
      competencyLevel TINYINT)
```

We'll also be creating some support stored procedures in our database for use by our document indexing and searching code, but we'll see the scripts for those later in the chapter.

Showing a Résumé: The Display Code

Of the three functions that our system will need to perform, perhaps the most straightforward is displaying a résumé in HTML form. Since we have chosen to keep our entire résumé in an XML document, one document per résumé, we can easily use an XSLT stylesheet to manipulate that document into the HTML form we desire. Let's take a look at how this is done (`resumeDisplay.xsl`):

```
   <xsl:stylesheet xmlns:xsl="http://www.w3.org/1999/XSL/Transform"
      version="1.0">
      <xsl:output method="html" />
```

Whenever styling XML to HTML, you should always include the `<xsl:output>` element shown above. This ensures that HTML standards, such as dropping the close element marker for certain empty elements, will be followed in the output – most browsers that are written to use HTML 4.01 cannot correctly interpret HTML documents formatted as XHTML.

```
      <xsl:template match="/">
```

When styling data, it's often easier to simply use one template to do so – as opposed to styling documents, where we may want text in an `<importantWord>` element to always appear in a <b> element in the output regardless of where it appears. In this example, we're using just one template that matches on the root of the document.

```
         <html>
         <head>
            <title>Resume</title>
         </head>
         <body>
```

Of course, XSLT allows us to include our elements in this form (rather than using the `<xsl:element>` element), if we so desire. Here it makes the stylesheet shorter and easier to understand. We use attribute templates to include attributes on these elements where necessary, as we'll see later in the example.

```
        <h2>
           <xsl:value-of select="resume/name/text()" />
        </h2>
```

The name of the person whose résumé this is, formatted as a heading level 2.

```
        <h3>
           <xsl:variable name="selectedTitle">
              <xsl:value-of select="resume/title/text()" />
           </xsl:variable>
           <xsl:for-each select="document('titles.xml')/titles/title">
              <xsl:if test="$selectedTitle=@value">
                 <xsl:value-of select="@name" />
              </xsl:if>
           </xsl:for-each>
        </h3>
```

Here we see the first bit of trickery – looking up the text value of the title for this résumé. This is one way of doing it, by iterating through the title elements until the one that matches the value specified in our résumé document is matched. We chose to do this because we could then reuse code that iterates the elements in the `titles.xml` document in our other stylesheets. We could also match directly on the specific name we wanted in the `<xsl:value-of>` element, thereby avoiding the `<xsl:for-each>` process entirely.

```
        <p>
           Employee ID: <xsl:value-of select="resume/employeeID/text()" />
        </p>
        <p>
           Qualifications:
           <xsl:value-of select="resume/qualifications/text()" />
        </p>
```

Again, these values are taken directly from the source XML document.

```
           Experience:
           <ul>
              <xsl:for-each select="/resume/experience">
                 <li>
                    <xsl:value-of select="text()" />
                 </li>
              </xsl:for-each>
           </ul>
```

Here, we create an unordered list. We then iterate through each experience element in our source document and create a list item element for that element.

```
           Skills:
           <ul>
              <xsl:for-each select="/resume/skill">
                 <li>
                    <xsl:value-of select="text()" />
                 </li>
              </xsl:for-each>
           </ul>
```

Here we're using the same technique, only for the skills.

```
          <p />
          <table>
             <tr>
                <td>Competency</td>
                <td>None</td>
                <td>Novice</td>
                <td>Intermediate</td>
                <td>Expert</td>
             </tr>
```

Now we're building the table that will contain the information about the competency level of this person in each of the competencies we have defined.

```
             <xsl:variable name="currentRoot" select="/" />
```

This next part is a little tricky. When we have an <xsl:for-each> element, the context for the processing of stylesheet instructions inside that element becomes the context of the element selected in the <xsl:for-each> element. If this is in another document altogether (as it is here), there's no way to reference the main document being processed. We sidestep the issue by sticking the root node of the current document into a variable called `currentRoot` and using it later, as we will see.

```
             <xsl:for-each select =
                "document('competencies.xml')/competencies/competency">
                <tr>
```

Each row of our table corresponds to one of the competencies in our competency lookup XML document. We iterate through those elements and create a row for each one, using an <xsl:for-each> element.

```
                   <xsl:variable name="compValue">
                      <xsl:value-of select="@value" />
                   </xsl:variable>
```

Again, we need to create a variable to allow our information to be referenced from a different context – in this case, the <xsl:when> test we are performing will be in the context of the main document, so we need to retain the information from the competency lookup document we want to compare against.

```
                   <td><xsl:value-of select="@name" /></td>
```

Each row is going to consist of five columns – the name of the competency type, and four columns for each of the four possible levels of competency for that competency type. Here we populate the first column.

```
                   <td align="center">
                   <xsl:choose>
                      <xsl:when test =
                         "$currentRoot/resume/competency[@type=$compValue
                         and @value='0']">
                        <xsl:text>X</xsl:text>
                      </xsl:when>
```

We have three possibilities for the setting of zero (no skills in a particular competency type):

- An element for the competency is present and the value is stated as zero
- An element for the competency is present and the value is stated as something other than zero
- An element for the competency is not present

Remember that we chose to discard elements that corresponded to no experience with a given competency type. To handle this properly when rendering the XML document to HTML, we need to use an <xsl:when> statement with all three possibilities handled properly.

In the first case above, presented with a stated value of zero, we put an X in this column.

```
                    <xsl:when test =
                       "$currentRoot/resume/competency[@type=$compValue
                       and @value!='0']">
                    </xsl:when>
```

In the second case – presented with a value other than zero – we leave this column blank.

```
                    <xsl:otherwise>
                       <xsl:text>X</xsl:text>
                    </xsl:otherwise>
```

Otherwise (if the competency element is not present), we assume that the value is zero and put an X in this column.

```
                 </xsl:choose>
              </td>
              <td align="center">
                 <xsl:if test =
                    "$currentRoot/resume/competency[@type=$compValue and
                     @value='1']">
                     <xsl:text>X</xsl:text>
                 </xsl:if>
              </td>
```

Here, we check to see if a competency is specified with a value of 1; if so, we put an X in this column, otherwise we leave it blank.

```
              <td align="center">
                 <xsl:if test =
                    "$currentRoot/resume/competency[@type=$compValue and
                    @value='2']">
                    <xsl:text>X</xsl:text>
                 </xsl:if>
              </td>
              <td align="center">
                  <xsl:if test =
                     "$currentRoot/resume/competency[@type=$compValue
                     and @value='3']">
                     <xsl:text>X</xsl:text>
                  </xsl:if>
              </td>
```

We perform the same checks for the values 2 and 3, respectively. We could go one step further and create a document, perhaps called `competencyLevels.xml`, that specifies the allowable values for the competency level and descriptions for each – that document could then be used to drive both the column headers and the specific column generation code.

```
            </tr>
         </xsl:for-each>
      </table>
```

And now that we've iterated through all the columns, we close our table.

```
      <p />
      <input
         id="cmdEdit"
         value="Edit resume"
         type="button"
         onClick="document.URL=
            'editResume.asp?employeeID={resume/employeeID}';" />
```

Finally, we want to provide a way for the client to edit the résumé if he or she so desires. Looking forward a little bit, we will be writing an ASP file called `editResume.asp` that takes an `employeeID` as a parameter; it will then open the appropriate résumé XML document (if it exists) and style it for editing. This code creates a button that takes just that action, taking the `employeeID` from the original XML document.

```
      </body>
      </html>

   </xsl:template>
</xsl:stylesheet>
```

The above stylesheet could have been made more compact, but parts of it are going to be reused, and it illustrates this example better. Since we're going to style our XML documents differently based on the circumstances, we can't embed a reference to the stylesheet directly into the XML; instead, we'll need to dynamically style the XML document on demand and return it to the user. The following ASP code does just that (`displayResume.asp`):

```
<%

Dim doc, docStyle
Dim oXMLError
Dim styleFile

styleFile = Server.MapPath("resumeDisplay.xsl")

Set docStyle = Server.CreateObject("MSXML2.DOMDocument")
docStyle.async = False
docStyle.load styleFile

Set doc = Server.CreateObject("MSXML.DOMDocument")
doc.async = False
doc.load "d:\resumes\" & Request("employeeID") & ".xml"
```

```
Response.Write doc.transformNode(docStyle)

%>
```

This takes an employee ID as a parameter and returns the appropriate résumé, styled for display. It's worth pointing out that for MSXML, XML documents that reside on the server should be resolved to their local paths (rather than URLs) – there's a quirk with the way documents are loaded by MSXML. That's why the call to `Server.MapPath` is present.

This ASP code, as well as some of the others we'll be looking at, could easily be replaced by one ASP document that performs all our styling and transformation, using a parameter to indicate what the destination format should be.

Inserting or Updating a Résumé: The Edit Code

Next, we need to design the code that will allow us to insert a résumé into the repository or update an existing résumé in the repository. This will consist of two steps: producing the input form (pre-populated, if we're editing an existing résumé) and processing the input form when it is submitted. Let's see how this is done.

Building the Form and Sending It To the User

We need to decide how we're going to create the form that gets sent to the user when the user chooses to input or update a résumé. We could create the form using a simple ASP script, and populate it by parsing the existing XML résumé document using the DOM when an update is requested; however, it turns out to be simpler to style an existing résumé, using XSLT, into the input format.

The other decision we have to make is where the XML document gets generated – on the server or on the client. Generating the document on the client is preferable, assuming that the client already has the proper software installed – it moves some of the burden from the server to the client, and allows the server to focus on the document warehousing process. The downside is that unless our client has MSXML installed, they won't be able to view the pages. We've chosen to create the documents on the client side to demonstrate how this is done.

Here's the stylesheet that styles a résumé into the edit form (`resumeInput.xsl`). Let's look at how it works and how the transformation from XML to an HTML form occurs:

```
<xsl:stylesheet xmlns:xsl="http://www.w3.org/1999/XSL/Transform"
   version="1.0">
   <xsl:output method="html" />
   <xsl:template match="/">
```

Again, set the output mode to `html` whenever an HTML browser is the consumer. We have one template that performs all the processing.

```
      <xsl:variable
         name="competencyDoc"
         select="document('competencies.xml')" />
```

Here, we're opening the `competencies.xml` document for later use and assigning it to the `competencyDoc` variable.

```
<html>
<head>
   <title>Resume data entry</title>
</head>
<body>
   <form id="frmDataEntry" action="resumeInput.asp" method="post">
```

The form will be processed by the `resumeInput.asp` script, which we'll look at a little later.

```
      <input name="xmlResume" type="hidden" />
```

We use a hidden input field to hold the XML results created by the JavaScript code in the document – this field will be referenced directly by the ASP script.

```
      <table>
         <tr>
            <td valign="top">Employee Name:</td>
            <td>
               <input
                  id="txtName"
                  type="text"
                  size="60"
                  maxlength="60"
                  value="{resume/name}" />
            </td>
         </tr>
```

First, we have an input field for the name. Note that we use an attribute template to assign the initial value of the input field. We take the text value of the name element in the original document (if provided) and set the value appropriately.

```
         <tr>
            <td valign="top">Title:</td>
            <td>
               <select id="cboTitle">
                  <xsl:variable name="selectedTitle">
                     <xsl:value-of select="resume/title/text()" />
                  </xsl:variable>
```

We set the current title for this résumé aside (if it's present), so that we can set the appropriate option as selected in the drop-down for the title.

```
                  <xsl:for-each select =
                     "document('titles.xml')/titles/title">
                     <option
                        value="{@value}">
                        <xsl:if test="$selectedTitle=@value">
                           <xsl:attribute name="selected">
                              selected
```

```
                    </xsl:attribute>
                 </xsl:if>
                 <xsl:value-of select="@name" />
              </option>
           </xsl:for-each>
```

Here, we loop through all the titles in the `titles.xml` document and add an option element for each one. If the title code for the title happens to match the setting in the `$selectedTitle` variable (the value currently set for this consultant), we add the selected attribute to that particular option element.

```
           </select>
        </td>
     </tr>
     <tr>
        <td valign="top">Employee ID:</td>
        <td>
           <input
              id="txtID"
              type="text"
              size="20"
              maxlength="20"
              value="{resume/employeeID}" />
        </td>
     </tr>
```

Another input field, this one for the employee ID, created from the original value provided (if there is one).

```
     <tr>
        <td valign="top">Qualifications:</td>
        <td>
           <textarea id="txtQualifications" cols="30" rows="5">
              <xsl:value-of select="resume/qualifications/text()"
                 />
           </textarea>
        </td>
     </tr>
```

Here we use a `<textarea>` element, rather than a text input element, but the concept is the same – except that here we embed the value of the `<textarea>` element as content of that element rather than as an attribute of the element.

```
     <tr>
        <td valign="top">Experience:</td>
        <td>
           <select id="lstExperience" size="5">
```

Here, we're creating the list of the experience items the consultant has listed on his or her résumé. We're showing this as a multiple-line select, usually rendered as a listbox – this allows us to add or delete experience items as necessary.

```
              <xsl:for-each select="/resume/experience">
                 <option value="{position()}">
```

In order for us to be able to determine which one of the options is currently selected in our list, we assign a numeric value to each one by setting its value attribute to the position of the experience item in the original résumé. This way, if the user chooses to delete one of the options, we'll be able to do so programmatically.

```
                        <xsl:value-of select="text()" />
```

As always, the text content of the <option> element is the text that appears in the listbox.

```
                     </option>
                  </xsl:for-each>
               </select>
            </td>
         </tr>
         <tr>
            <td />
            <td>
               <input id="cmdAddExperience" value="Add" type="button"
                  onclick="addExperience();" />
               <input id="cmdDelExperience" value="Delete"
                  type="button" onclick="delExperience()" />
            </td>
         </tr>
```

Here, we're putting two buttons in our table that will allow the user to add or delete experience items. These call JavaScript functions, which we'll see later in the source listing.

```
         <tr>
            <td valign="top">Skills:</td>
            <td>
               <select id="lstSkills" size="5">
                  <xsl:for-each select="/resume/skill">
                     <option value="{position()}">
                        <xsl:value-of select="text()" />
                     </option>
                  </xsl:for-each>
               </select>
            </td>
         </tr>
```

Here, we're creating another listbox to hold the list of skills for this consultant. The process is the same as before – add an option element for each skill element that appears in the original résumé.

```
         <tr>
            <td />
            <td>
               <input id="cmdAddSkill" value="Add" type="button"
                  onclick="addSkill();" />
               <input id="cmdDelSkill" value="Delete" type="button"
                  onclick="delSkill()" />
            </td>
         </tr>
```

Again, we have buttons to allow the user to add or delete skills, which call JavaScript functions.

```
</table>
<p />
<input
   id="competencyCount"
   type="hidden"
   value="{count($competencyDoc/competencies/competency)}" />
```

Here, we create a hidden element that will contain the number of competencies that are possible (based on the number that exist in competencies.xml). This gives us an easy way to iterate through all the possible competency values in the JavaScript when we build the XML document, as we'll see later.

```
<table border="1">
   <tr>
      <th>Competency</th>
      <th>None</th>
      <th>Novice</th>
      <th>Intermediate</th>
      <th>Expert</th>
   </tr>
   <xsl:variable name="currentRoot" select="/" />
```

As we saw in the display code, we need to hang on to the current root node so that we can reference it once the original document has become out of context.

```
   <xsl:for-each select =
      "document('competencies.xml')/competencies/competency">
      <tr>
         <td><xsl:value-of select="@name" /></td>
```

The name of the competency is the first column in the table. Note that since we're performing an <xsl:for-each> on the competencies.xml file, all competencies will be listed regardless of whether they appear in the original résumé (if present).

```
         <xsl:variable name="value">
            <xsl:value-of select="@value" />
         </xsl:variable>
```

We hang on to the numeric value here so that we can check against the original document and see if a level is specified for this competency.

```
         <td>
            <input
               name="competency{@value}"
```

Here, we dynamically create the name of the input field by concatenating the prefix competency and the value of the value attribute for that competency in competencies.xml. For example, the first skill (XML) will generate the input field called competency1.

```
               value="0"
               id="competency{@value}_0"
```

For a unique ID for the element, we concatenate the name we cooked up before with _0 – so this input will be called competency1_0 for the first competency in the lookup document.

```
                    type="radio">
                    <xsl:choose>
                       <xsl:when test =
                         "$currentRoot/resume/competency[@type=$value
                         and @value='0']">
                          <xsl:attribute name="checked">
                             true
                          </xsl:attribute>
                       </xsl:when>
```

Again, this is similar to the display code. In the case where the competency level is zero, it may either appear with a value of zero or not appear at all. This <xsl:choose> block tests the various possibilities – not present, present with a value of zero, or present with a non-zero value. Here, if it is present with a value of zero, the radio button is set.

```
                       <xsl:when test =
                         "$currentRoot/resume/competency[@type=$value
                         and @value!='0']">
                       </xsl:when>
```

If the competency level is present but has a non-zero value, the radio button is left unselected.

```
                       <xsl:otherwise>
                          <xsl:attribute name="checked">
                             true
                          </xsl:attribute>
                       </xsl:otherwise>
```

Otherwise, it's not present and assumed to be zero, so the radio button is checked.

```
                    </xsl:choose>
                 </input>
              </td>
              <td>
                 <input
                    name="competency{@value}"
                    value="1"
                    id="competency{@value}_1"
                    type="radio">
                    <xsl:if test =
                       "$currentRoot/resume/competency[@type=$value
                       and @value='1']">
                       <xsl:attribute name="checked">
                          true
                       </xsl:attribute>
                    </xsl:if>
                 </input>
              </td>
```

Here, we construct the column for the competency level of "Novice". In this case, there are only two possibilities. If the competency appears in the original document with a value of 1, the radio button should be selected; otherwise, it should be left unselected.

```
                  <td>
                     <input
                        name="competency{@value}"
                        value="2"
                        id="competency{@value}_2"
                        type="radio">
                        <xsl:if test =
                           "$currentRoot/resume/competency[@type=$value
                           and @value='2']">
                           <xsl:attribute name="checked">
                              true
                           </xsl:attribute>
                        </xsl:if>
                     </input>
                  </td>
                  <td>
                     <input
                        name="competency{@value}"
                        value="3"
                        id="competency{@value}_3"
                        type="radio">
                        <xsl:if test =
                           "$currentRoot/resume/competency[@type=$value
                           and @value='3']">
                           <xsl:attribute name="checked">
                              true
                           </xsl:attribute>
                        </xsl:if>
                     </input>
                  </td>
               </tr>
```

Here, similar code creates the columns for intermediate and expert levels of experience.

```
            </xsl:for-each>
         </table>
         <p />
         <input id="cmdSave" value="Save resume" type="button"
            onclick="composeXML();" />
```

Finally, when the user chooses to save the résumé, a JavaScript function is called that will compose the XML and submit the form.

```
      </form>
   </body>

   <SCRIPT LANGUAGE="JavaScript">
      <![CDATA[
      <!--
```

This header is very important. If we want to include script blocks in our HTML code, typically we need to comment it out using the <!-- and --> delimiters. However, an XSLT processor will interpret (correctly) these delimiters as comment delimiters, and at its discretion discard this comment entirely! This is not an optimal outcome. To get around it, we enclose the contents of the <SCRIPT> element in the CDATA delimiters. This tells the XSLT processor to ignore the markup inside the block (and hence ignore the comment delimiters), and the JavaScript code will show up in the styled HTML properly.

```
function addExperience() {
   var oOption = document.createElement("OPTION");
   var oList = document.forms("frmDataEntry").lstExperience;
   oOption.text=
      prompt("Enter the description of the new experience:", "");
   oOption.value=oOption.text;
   document.forms("frmDataEntry").lstExperience.add(oOption);
}
```

This function is called when the user chooses to add a new experience entry. It simply pops up a JavaScript prompt, the user keys in the new experience description, and the code adds it to the list using DHTML.

```
function delExperience() {
   var oList = document.forms("frmDataEntry").lstExperience;
   var oColl = oList.options;
   if (oColl != null)
      for (i=0; i<oColl.length; i++)
         if (oColl.item(i).selected > 0)
            oColl.remove(i);
}
```

This is called when the user chooses to delete an experience entry. DHTML is used to identify which row in the list is selected (if any), and then removes that <option> element from the <select> element.

```
function addSkill() {
   var oOption = document.createElement("OPTION");
   var oList = document.forms("frmDataEntry").lstSkills;
   oOption.text=
      prompt("Enter the description of the new skill:", "");
   oOption.value=oOption.text;
   document.forms("frmDataEntry").lstSkills.add(oOption);
}

function delSkill() {
   var oList = document.forms("frmDataEntry").lstSkills;
   var oColl = oList.options;
   if (oColl != null)
      for (i=0; i<oColl.length; i++)
         if (oColl.item(i).selected > 0)
            oColl.remove(i);
}
```

These two functions are identical to the addExperience() and deleteExperience() functions, except that they operate on the skills list in the lstSkills <select> element.

```
function helperAppendElement(parentDoc, parentNode,
   childElementName, childElementValue) {

   var elChild = parentDoc.createElement(childElementName);
   var txtChild = parentDoc.createTextNode(childElementValue);
   elChild.appendChild(txtChild);
   parentNode.appendChild(elChild);
}
```

This is a quick helper function to add a text-content element to an XML document. If the document structure you're using has text-only elements (as ours does), it can be a little annoying to add these elements to the XML document – we have to create the element and the text node separately, and then associate each with its proper parents (assuming we're writing to the core DOM functionality). This helper function creates an element with a particular name and a particular text value for a particular parent in a particular document.

```
function composeXML() {
   var docXML = new ActiveXObject("MSXML2.DOMDocument");

   var elResume = docXML.createElement("resume");
   docXML.appendChild(elResume);

   helperAppendElement(docXML, elResume, "name",
      document.forms("frmDataEntry").txtName.value);
   helperAppendElement(docXML, elResume, "title",
      document.forms("frmDataEntry").cboTitle.value);
   helperAppendElement(docXML, elResume, "employeeID",
      document.forms("frmDataEntry").txtID.value);
   helperAppendElement(docXML, elResume, "qualifications",
      document.forms("frmDataEntry").txtQualifications.value);
```

This is straightforward – we've instantiated a `DOMDocument` object, created our root element (`<resume>`), and then started adding text elements to it based on the values in the entered form (retrieved using DHTML).

```
   var oList = document.forms("frmDataEntry").lstExperience;
   var oColl = oList.options;
   if (oColl != null)
      for (i=0; i<oColl.length; i++)
         helperAppendElement(docXML, elResume, "experience",
            oColl.item(i).innerText);
```

Here, we're walking through all the `<option>` elements in the `lstExperience` `<select>` element (in other words, all the various experience entries submitted on the form). For each one, we create an experience element containing the string value of the `<option>`.

```
   var oList = document.forms("frmDataEntry").lstSkills;
   var oColl = oList.options;
   if (oColl != null)
      for (i=0; i<oColl.length; i++)
         helperAppendElement(docXML, elResume, "skill",
            oColl.item(i).innerText);
```

The same process is used here to create all the <skill> elements:

```
            for (i=1;
               i<=document.forms("frmDataEntry").competencyCount.value; i++)
               for (j=1; j<4; j++)
                  if (document.forms("frmDataEntry").all("competency" + i +
                     "_" + j).checked) {
```

Here, we're walking through all the competencies on the form – we know how many because of the competencyCount hidden data field we populate at style time (thinking ahead is good). We also iterate through each radio button for each competency – since we're doing this on the client side, DHTML gives us access to the radio buttons directly.

```
                     var elCompetency = docXML.createElement("competency");
                     elCompetency.setAttribute("type", i);
                     elCompetency.setAttribute("value", j);
                     elResume.appendChild(elCompetency);
                  }
```

If the value of this particular radio button is set, a <competency> element is added to our document stating what competency type and value the consultant claims. Note that we don't check the "None" column – if this radio button is checked, we simply omit the competency element from the document we are creating altogether.

```
            document.forms("frmDataEntry").xmlResume.value =
               docXML.xml;
            document.forms("frmDataEntry").submit();
         }
```

Finally, we set the value of the hidden input, xmlResume, to the XML for our document (we're exposing it here through the MSXML xml property – other platforms may require more effort, such as serializing the document manually).

```
         //-->
         ]]>
      </SCRIPT>
      </html>

   </xsl:template>
</xsl:stylesheet>
```

Again, since we're dynamically styling the XML, we need some code that will transform our résumé document according to the stylesheet for the edit page. The following code, like the display code, accepts an employee ID as a parameter and returns the form styled up from the XML document for that employee. Because we designed our stylesheet correctly, it happens to work properly if no employeeID is provided –calling editResume.asp with no parameters brings up a blank entry form. Here's the code (editResume.asp):

```
<%

   Dim doc, docStyle
```

```
    Dim oXMLError
    Dim styleFile

    styleFile = Server.MapPath("resumeInput.xsl")

    Set docStyle = Server.CreateObject("Msxml2.DOMDocument")
    docStyle.async = False
    docStyle.load styleFile

    Set doc = Server.CreateObject("Msxml2.DOMDocument")
    doc.async = False
    doc.load "d:\resumes\" & Request("employeeID") & ".xml"

    Response.Write doc.transformNode(docStyle)

    Set doc = Nothing
    Set docStyle = Nothing
%>
```

The reader is encouraged to try to combine this simple styling active server page with the others presented in the chapter to produce a generic styling engine that will accept a stylesheet type as well as an employee ID.

Receiving and Processing the Response from the User

Next, we're going to need to write the ASP code that accepts the submitted form. This code needs to do three things: it needs to write the XML document to the document repository, it needs to write the indexing information to the SQL Server database, and it needs to let the user know that the résumé was saved. Here's the code (`resumeInput.asp`):

```
<%

    Dim doc
    Dim db
    Dim el, skills, competencies
    Dim employeeID, name, titleType, description
    Dim compType, compValue

    Set doc = Server.CreateObject("Msxml2.DOMdocument")
    doc.loadXML (Request("xmlResume"))
```

Here, we instantiate a `DOMDocument` object and load the string passed to us in the `xmlResume` hidden data field.

```
    Set db = Server.CreateObject("ADODB.Connection")
    db.Open "UID=sa;PWD=;DATABASE=resume;SERVER=MYSERVER;" & _
       "DRIVER={SQL SERVER};DSN='';"
```

We'll also open an ADO connection to our SQL Server database (the server may not be called `MYSERVER` – change as necessary).

```
Set el = doc.getElementsByTagName("employeeID")
employeeID = el(0).childNodes(0).nodeValue

Set el = doc.getElementsByTagName("name")
name = el(0).childNodes(0).nodeValue

Set el = doc.getElementsByTagName("title")
titleType = el(0).childNodes(0).nodeValue
```

Here, we're pulling out the employee ID, name, and title submitted as part of the XML. Note that we could also have taken the information directly from submitted fields, but doing it this way makes it clear how information in an XML document is referenced.

```
db.Execute "AddResume('" & employeeID & "', '" & name & "', " & _
   titleType & ")"
```

This stored procedure commits the résumé data to the database. We'll see the source code for this stored procedure later in the chapter.

```
Set skills = doc.getElementsByTagName("skill")
For i = 0 to skills.length - 1
   db.Execute "AddSkill('" & employeeID & "', '" & _
      skills(i).childNodes(0).nodeValue & "')"
Next
```

Similarly, here we are extracting each skill in the XML document and calling a stored procedure to associate that skill with this résumé.

```
Set competencies = doc.getElementsByTagName("competency")
For i = 0 to competencies.length - 1
   compType = competencies(i).getAttribute("type")
   compValue = competencies(i).getAttribute("value")
   db.Execute "AddCompetency('" & employeeID & "', '" & compType & _
      "', '" & compValue & "')"
Next
```

Finally, we extract the competency information from the database and call a stored procedure to associate it with our résumé as well.

```
Dim fso, tf

Set fso = CreateObject("Scripting.FileSystemObject")
If fso.FileExists("d:\resumes\" & employeeID & ".xml") Then
   fso.DeleteFile("d:\resumes\" & employeeID & ".xml")
End If
Set tf = fso.CreateTextFile("d:\resumes\" & employeeID & ".xml", True)
tf.Write doc.xml
tf.Close
```

Here, we're saving the XML content of our document to our flat file repository. Note that we are using the employee ID as the filename, so we should really add some data scrubbing checks to ensure that the employee ID doesn't contain anything nasty like backslashes – but for the purposes of this example, we'll leave it the way it is.

```
    Response.Redirect "resumeSaved.htm"

  db.close
  Set tf = Nothing
  Set fso = Nothing
  Set doc = Nothing
  Set db = Nothing

  %>
```

Finally, we alert the user that the résumé was saved to the database. (We won't bother to discuss `resumeSaved.htm`, as it's just a static web page – it can be downloaded from the Wrox web site).

Recall that we called three stored procedures to update the data in our SQL Server database. Here are the scripts that create those stored procedures: (`addResume.sql`, `addCompetency.sql`, and `addSkill.sql`)

```
CREATE PROC AddResume (@employeeID varchar(20),
   @name varchar(60), @titleType tinyint)
AS
BEGIN

   IF (SELECT COUNT(*) FROM resume WHERE employeeID = @employeeID) > 0
   BEGIN
      DELETE skill FROM skill s, resume r
         WHERE s.resumeID = r.resumeID AND r.employeeID = @employeeID
      DELETE competency FROM competency c, resume r
         WHERE c.resumeID = r.resumeID AND r.employeeID = @employeeID
      DELETE resume WHERE employeeID = @employeeID
   END

   INSERT resume (employeeID, name, titleType)
      VALUES (@employeeID, @name, @titleType)

END
GO
```

Note that in this stored procedure, we delete all the information that matches the submitted employee ID – the assumption is that the employee ID is an alternative key that uniquely identifies our consultant.

```
CREATE PROC AddCompetency (@employeeID varchar(20),
   @competencyType tinyint, @competencyLevel tinyint)
AS
BEGIN
   INSERT competency (resumeID, competencyType, competencyLevel)
      SELECT r.resumeID, @competencyType, @competencyLevel FROM resume r
      WHERE r.employeeID = @employeeID
END
GO
```

This procedure adds a competency to our database index.

```
CREATE PROC AddSkill (@employeeID varchar(20), @description varchar(30))
AS
BEGIN
   INSERT skill (resumeID, description)
   SELECT r.resumeID, @description
      FROM resume r
      WHERE r.employeeID = @employeeID
END
GO
```

This procedure adds a skill to our database index.

Searching the Repository: The Search Code

Now that we've managed to add some résumés to our repository, we come to the final step in our design – building a way to search through the résumé database to match on particular titles, skills, and/or competency levels. Let's see how this is done.

Dynamic Generation of the Search Form

First, we need to create a form that the user may fill out and submit to search the résumé database. This form has to allow the user to enter a title, skill, and/or a set of competency levels that describe the type of consultant they are searching for. Since the title and competency information is being driven by XML documents, the most flexible way to create the search form is by styling these documents. Here's the stylesheet that does this (`resumeSearch.xsl`):

```
<xsl:stylesheet xmlns:xsl="http://www.w3.org/1999/XSL/Transform"
   version="1.0">
   <xsl:output method="html" />
   <xsl:template match="/">

   <xsl:variable
      name="competencyDoc"
      select="document('competencies.xml')" />
   <xsl:variable
      name="titleDoc"
      select="document('titles.xml')" />
      <html>
      <head>
         <title>R&eacute;sum&eacute; search</title>
         <!-- &eacute; makes an e with an acute accent, needed for resume-->
      </head>
      <body>
         <form id="frmDataEntry" action="resumeSearch.asp" method="get">
            <table>
               <tr>
                  <td valign="top">Title:</td>
                  <td>
                     <select id="cboTitle" name="cboTitle">
                        <xsl:for-each select =
                           "$titleDoc/titles/title">
```

```
                    <option value="{@value}">
                        <xsl:value-of select="@name" />
                    </option>
                </xsl:for-each>
            </select>
        </td>
    </tr>
```

Most of this code should look familiar. Here, we're creating an `<option>` element for each title found in `titles.xml` and building our `cboTitle` `<select>` element.

```
    <tr>
        <td valign="top">Skill:</td>
        <td>
            <input id="txtSkill" name="txtSkill" type="text"
                size="20" maxlength="20" />
        </td>
    </tr>
```

We then add a text input so that the user may enter one skill to be matched on.

```
</table>
<p />
<input
    id="competencyCount"
    name="competencyCount"
    type="hidden"
    value="{count($competencyDoc/competencies/competency)}" />
```

Here, we generate our `competencyCount` hidden field; we'll use this when iterating through all the competencies in the ASP code when we create the SQL statement to search the database.

```
<table border="1">
    <tr>
        <th>Competency at least:</th>
        <th>None</th>
        <th>Novice</th>
        <th>Intermediate</th>
        <th>Expert</th>
    </tr>
    <xsl:for-each select=
        "document('competencies.xml')/competencies/competency">
        <tr>
            <td><xsl:value-of select="@name" /></td>
            <td>
                <input
                    name="competency{@value}"
                    value="0"
                    id="competency{@value}_0"
                    type="radio"
                    checked="true" />
            </td>
            <td>
```

```
                    <input
                        name="competency{@value}"
                        value="1"
                        id="competency{@value}_1"
                        type="radio" />
                </td>
                <td>
                    <input
                        name="competency{@value}"
                        value="2"
                        id="competency{@value}_2"
                        type="radio" />
                </td>
                <td>
                    <input
                        name="competency{@value}"
                        value="3"
                        id="competency{@value}_3"
                        type="radio" />
                </td>
            </tr>
        </xsl:for-each>
```

Again, this code should look familiar – we loop through all the competencies and create radio buttons corresponding to each one. We set a competency level of "None" as the default for each competency type.

```
            </table>
            <p />
            <input id="cmdSearch" value="Search" type="submit" />
        </form>
    </body>
    </html>

  </xsl:template>
</xsl:stylesheet>
```

The next thing we'll need is an ASP script to style the `titles.xml` and `competencies.xml` documents into the search input format. Note that we chose to make our stylesheet use only the document command to obtain information – therefore, we can style an empty document to create the output we're looking for (`searchResumes.asp`).

```
<%

   Dim doc, docStyle
   Dim oXMLError
   Dim styleFile

   styleFile = Server.MapPath("resumeSearch.xsl")

   Set docStyle = Server.CreateObject("Msxml2.DOMDocument")
   docStyle.async = False
   docStyle.load styleFile
```

```
    Set doc = Server.CreateObject("Msxml2.DOMDocument")

    Response.Write doc.transformNode(docStyle)

  %>
```

Processing the Search

Once the form is submitted, an active server page is required to accept the form, query the database, and return information about the résumés found that match the specified criteria. Here's the code that handles the search (`resumeSearch.asp`):

```
<html>
<head>
   <title>Resume search results</title>
</head>
<body>

   <%

      Dim db
      Dim rec, recCompetencies
      Dim queryString
      Dim selectedTables
      Dim sql
      Dim i, j
      Dim doc

      queryString = ""

      selectedTables = "resume"
```

We're going to build up our SQL call little by little. The `queryString` variable contains what will effectively become the `WHERE` clause of our call to the server, while the `selectedTables` variable contains a list of all the tables that participate in the query. Clauses will be added to each variable based on the values provided on the search form.

```
      If Request("cboTitle") > 0 Then
         queryString = "titleType = " & Request("cboTitle")
      End If
```

If the user chose to search on a particular title, we add a check on the `titleType` column in the `resume` table to our query string.

```
      If Request("txtSkill") > "" Then
         selectedTables = selectedTables & ", skill"
         If queryString > "" Then
            queryString = queryString & " AND "
         End If
         queryString = queryString & "skill.resumeID = resume.resumeID"
         queryString = queryString & " AND skill.description = '" & _
            Request("txtSkill") & "'"
      End If
```

If a particular skill was entered, we need to add a query to check to see if that skill is present. We can do this by joining to the skill table and searching for a matching description for that resumeID. We add the skill table to the list of tables participating in the join, and add the check for the matching description to the WHERE clause (with an AND in between if necessary).

```
For i = 1 to Request("competencyCount")
   If Request("competency" & i) > 0 Then
      ' We need to add this one to the query
      If queryString > "" Then
         queryString = queryString & " AND "
      End If
      queryString = queryString & "c" & i & _
         ".resumeID = resume.resumeID" & " AND c" & i & _
         ".competencyType = " & i & " AND c" & i & _
         ".competencyLevel >= " & Request("competency" & i)
      selectedTables = selectedTables & ", competency c" & i
   End If
Next
```

Here's where things get a little weird. We can assume that a relatively small number of competencies are going to be specified for a search – typically, the user is going to be looking for a strong XML consultant, or an intermediate XSLT consultant. To save repeated calls to the database, we implement this check using an implicit JOIN to a different instance of the competency table for each competency that was specified. We do this by aliasing the table based on the number of the competency. If, for example, competency 2 were specified as needing to be at least at an intermediate level, the code would add a join to the competency table, aliased as c2, where c2.value is greater than or equal to 2. The aliased instance of the table is then also added to the list of joined tables.

```
sql = "SELECT resume.resumeID, name, employeeID FROM " & _
   selectedTables
If queryString > "" Then
   sql = sql & " WHERE " & queryString
End If
sql = sql & " ORDER BY name"
```

Here we construct the full query string from the fragments we have created.

```
Set db = Server.CreateObject("ADODB.Connection")
db.Open "UID=sa;PWD=;DATABASE=resume;SERVER=SERVERNAME" & _
   "DRIVER={SQL SERVER};DSN='';"
' Replace the SERVERNAME with the name of the database server

Set rec = Server.CreateObject("adodb.Recordset")
rec.Open sql, db

If rec.EOF Then
   Response.Write "<h2>No matches found.</h2>"
Else
   Response.Write "<h2>Resume search results</h2>"
```

If matches were found, we indicate to the user that this was the case and describe the matches found. We have chosen to display a competency array for each consultant that was matched – this allows the user to easily compare the skills of the different consultants before drilling down into their specific résumés. We also choose to make the consultants' names the first column of the table, and have the name string itself be a hyperlink to a displayed version of the résumé (by adding the appropriate link to displayResume.asp).

```
Set recCompetencies = Server.CreateObject("ADODB.Recordset")
Set doc = Server.CreateObject("Msxml2.DOMDocument")
doc.load (Server.MapPath("competencies.xml"))
Set elComps = doc.getElementsByTagName("competency")
Response.Write "<table rules='all'>"
Response.Write "<tr>"
Response.Write "<td></td>"
For i = 0 to elComps.Length - 1
  Response.Write "<td>" & elComps(i).getAttribute("name") & _
    "</td>"
Next
```

We put the names of the competencies (taken from `competencies.xml`) into the top row of the table.

```
Response.Write "</tr>"
While Not rec.EOF
```

This loop is processed for each returned row from the query – in other words, for each consultant that matched the search criteria.

```
  Response.Write "<tr>"
  Response.Write "<td><a href='displayResume.asp?employeeID=" & _
    rec("employeeID") & "'>" & rec("name") & "</a>"
```

Here, we're putting the name of the consultant in the first column, with a hyperlink that leads to a detailed display of the résumé for that consultant.

```
  sql = "SELECT competencyType, competencyLevel FROM competency"
  sql = sql & " WHERE resumeID = " & rec("resumeID") & _
    " ORDER BY competencyType"
```

In order to properly indicate what competencies the consultant claims, we create another recordset that returns all the competencies in the database for this row's consultant. Note that if we were using the XML features of SQL Server 2000, we could have returned this information in one pass – but we're working within the limitations we've set for ourselves. Since this recordset is sparsely populated, we walk through the list of competencies and the list of returned records at the same time to determine what competencies are present.

```
  recCompetencies.Open sql, db
  For i = 0 to elComps.Length - 1
    Response.Write "<td align='center'>"
    If Not recCompetencies.EOF Then
      If recCompetencies("competencyType") = i + 1 Then
        For j = 1 to recCompetencies("competencyLevel")
          Response.Write "X"
        Next
```

If the competency number in the returned record corresponds to the column currently being written, then we write a number of X's to the cell in the table based on the level of expertise claimed by the consultant. We then move to the next record in the recordset containing the returned competencies for the consultant.

```
                recCompetencies.MoveNext
             Else
                Response.Write " "
```

If the competency number in the returned record does not match, then the consultant must not have any expertise in that particular competency; a placeholder is written to the table to ensure that the borders for the cell are drawn.

```
             End If
          Else
             Response.Write " "
```

If the recordset containing the competencies is at end-of-file (in other words, all the competencies have already been shown), then the consultant must not be claiming any level of experience with this competency; again, a placeholder is written to the table.

```
          End If
          Response.Write "</td>"
       Next
       recCompetencies.Close
       Response.Write "</tr>"
       rec.MoveNext
    Wend
    Response.Write "</table>"
 End If

%>

<p />
<a href="resume.htm">Return to main</a>
</body>
</html>
```

Finally, we put a hyperlink that allows us to go back to the main résumé page. This is just a static HTML page, and may be downloaded from the Wrox web site.

Further Enhancements

In this example, we've seen a very simplistic way to use an XML document repository, indexed by a relational database, to maintain résumé information. Here are some suggestions for modifications that could be made to this case study:

- Add wireless support. As our user interfaces are created by styling XML documents, it would be a simple matter to add stylesheets for other platforms such as WML or iMode. The requesting browser could be checked for what markup language it accepted, and the XML could be styled appropriately.
- Add full-text search capabilities. Since the document repository itself is in the form of files, many third-party tools can index those files and create a full text search capability for the résumés.

- Add access control. Right now, anyone who is viewing a résumé is allowed to edit it. By adding access control information, branching can be added to the ASP scripts to ensure that only those who are allowed to edit a particular résumé may do so.
- Add voice support using VoiceXML. As all the presentation is styled with stylesheets, then it can easily be styled to and from VoiceXML and so résumés could be amended and listened to over the telephone.

Summary

In this case study, we've seen how a combination of an XML document repository and a relational database index may be used to maintain a data store. We've seen how XSLT, when properly applied, can free our information of its HTML bonds and make it more flexible and reusable. Although the example that we've just worked our way through is a highly simple one, the concepts introduced are robust enough to scale to much larger applications.

18

Presenting XML Graphically

To coin a phrase, "A picture is worth a thousand start and end tags!"

XML-based information systems can be rich and expressive for programmers who, at least at times, can find deep satisfaction in the elegant solutions which XML offers to some data interchange problems. But, for most ordinary mortals – the users and customers of our XML Web-based systems – it is often much more meaningful to see visual representations of data rather than text-based summaries.

People want striking or informative pictures. Until recently XML-based information systems haven't been able to provide those for users, at least not in a way which is based on XML. With the emergence of technologies such as Scalable Vector Graphics, **SVG**, and **SMIL** Animation (Synchronized Multimedia Integration Language) it becomes possible to provide our customers with XML-based graphics, which can be static or can also incorporate animation and/or interactivity.

In this chapter we will take a brief tour of XML-based graphics and animation technologies currently available, or likely soon to be finalized, and demonstrate their application in producing some simple business graphics.

> *Be aware that all the XML-based graphics and multimedia formats are under active development at the World Wide Web Consortium, W3C. Therefore points of detail regarding how to use them may vary from those that we will see later in this chapter.*

The specifications of the various XML-based graphics and multimedia formats under development at the World Wide Web Consortium, W3C, total about 1,000 pages of highly condensed and sometimes cryptic text. Therefore in this chapter there can be little more than a flavor of what these technologies have to offer. However, we will see the use of SVG and a little SMIL Animation in the creation of a range of graphics from XML-based business related data. We will be focusing most on Scalable Vector Graphics, since the specification and tools for its display are the most advanced.

More specifically, the material in this chapter consists of

- An overview of XML-based graphics and animation technologies
- An account of the differences between SVG and other graphics technologies
- An overview of SVG
- A brief overview of SVG elements with emphasis on those elements we will be using later in the chapter
- A look at available SVG viewers which you will need for the mini-projects which follow
- Creating a horizontal bar chart in SVG
- Adding interactivity declaratively to the horizontal bar chart
- Using SVG with Cascading Style Sheets
- Creating an SVG horizontal bar chart using XSLT
- Creating a vertical bar chart using XSLT
- Incorporating SVG graphics in XSL-FO
- A look at some commercially available tools which generate SVG graphics

XML-based Graphics and Animation Technologies

The W3C has produced or is developing four inter-related graphics and multimedia specifications:

- Scalable Vector Graphics, SVG
- Synchronized Multimedia Integration Language, SMIL, version 1
- SMIL Animation
- SMIL version 2

In this chapter we will focus primarily on SVG and SMIL Animation.

SVG is the primary XML-based graphics solution, which at the time of writing is likely shortly to be released as a full Recommendation by the W3C (World Wide Web Consortium). SVG includes both static and animated graphics.

Animated SVG elements are particularly closely related to the SMIL Animation specification, but SVG has inter-relationships to all three flavors of SMIL – SMIL Animation, and the two versions of the Synchronized Multimedia Integration Language, (often pronounced "smile") – SMIL 1.0, and SMIL 2.0.

Current Status

At the time of writing only SMIL 1.0 is a full W3C Recommendation, released in 1998. The 1998 Recommendation is located at http://www.w3.org/TR/1998/REC-smil-19980615. The focus of SMIL 1.0 is essentially multimedia presentations, which goes beyond the scope of this chapter.

SVG is currently at Candidate Recommendation stage, although it is quite likely that it may be either a Proposed Recommendation or a full Recommendation by the time you read this. The November 2000 SVG Candidate Recommendation on which this chapter is based is located at http://www.w3.org/TR/2000/CR-SVG-20001102/. To find out what progress has been made from Candidate Recommendation please check the most up to date information on the status of SVG which is located at http://www.w3.org/TR/SVG/. If that URL still refers to the November 2000 Candidate Recommendation then nothing has changed since this chapter was written.

Both SMIL Animation and SMIL 2.0 are still at Working Draft stage. The most up to date versions of those specifications are located at http://www.w3.org/TR/smil-animation/ and http://www.w3.org/TR/smil20/ respectively. The SMIL Animation elements are used in SVG animations, and you will see some straightforward examples in the mini-projects later in this chapter.

The SVG Candidate Recommendation alone runs to some 513 pages. It is obvious that this chapter can only begin to give a flavor of what these W3C graphics and animation/multimedia specifications can offer.

The Graphics Facilities Users Demand

Cast your mind back ten years or so to the time before the Mosaic graphical browser arrived on the scene. Think how dull, in comparison to today's Web, a text-only World Wide Web must have been. Before the graphical Mosaic web browser appeared, the WWW was a text-only interface. It still worked, allowing the format and display of textual information, and easy links to other documents, but it was the introduction of multimedia content that brought it to life and got the millions of people hooked on it that there are today.

Users routinely demand, or expect, attractive or striking colored images, animation, interactivity or a combination of all three. There are some exceptions where a text-only presentation of information may be sufficiently informative, but even in that situation users now expect and demand a visually attractive setting for the text. Similarly, for business data, graphical presentation can be much more expressive for most users than a lengthy text-based summary of data.

To provide users with Web graphics we have two broad options. The first option is to embed familiar bitmap graphics, which are essentially arrays of individually characterized pixels, within HTML/XHTML. We can have static JPEGs, PNGs, GIFs, or animated GIFs. The second, is to create and display SVG graphics which themselves are vector-based images or an alternate vector format. So, can SVG and SMIL also provide the desired combination of color, animation and interactivity we are used to from bitmap graphics? Absolutely!

Working together, SVG, SMIL Animation, and SMIL offer exciting combinations of visual appearance and animation, which can be manipulated programmatically, either declaratively or by using a scripting language such as ECMAScript! That's right, you the programmer can, in a text editor (or other SVG/SMIL authoring environment), create the source code for SVG graphics. Similarly, you will be able to generate dynamically SVG-based graphs, for example of stock prices, currency exchange rates, etc. Declarative animation and scripting of elements are described in the SVG specification. Some examples are accessible online at http://www.kevlindev.com.

In one sense, an SVG "image" is also an SVG "document" which conforms to the XML 1.0 well-formedness constraints, etc. From a programming point of view, an SVG image/document is XML 1.0 compliant. Any programmer with visual awareness and understanding of how SVG elements define a graphical layout can create SVG graphics de novo. An alternative, and probably more likely workflow in a production setting, is to have a Web graphic designer create SVG graphics, for example using Jasc WebDraw (http://www.jasc.com/) or Adobe Illustrator, which the user can then adapt to create dynamically generated, "personalized" images to display to customers.

Exciting times lie ahead for Scalable Vector Graphics and the SMIL technologies. But to begin to be able to make use of that potential, we need to understand more of how they work and how they differ from existing technologies.

How Does SVG Differ from Typical Web Graphics?

In this section we will examine how SVG differs from typical GIFs and JPEG images, which are a familiar sight on the Web. Since SVG is an animate-able vector format, we will also briefly look at the currently available non-XML vector technology, Macromedia Flash.

After reading any Web graphics book, the distinction that is often drawn (sorry for the pun) between bitmap graphics and vector graphics will probably be familiar. Bitmap graphics, such as GIFs, JPEGs, and PNGs hold information about an image in a two dimensional array with each element in the array holding color information about one pixel. (Compressed bitmap formats are not exactly like that but the description is sufficiently accurate for the purposes of this comparison). By contrast, the description of a vector graphic image is typically held as a binary description of how to draw the graphic. Flash is a binary vector format, but in SVG the description of the graphic is held in the SVG elements, which are compliant with XML 1.0 syntax.

However, if we step back a little from that classical distinction we can get a new insight into what is going on. Any image you view on your computer screen, whether it be "bitmap" or "vector" is actually seen as a two-dimensional array of colored pixels.In other words, all graphics whether "bitmap" or "vector" are actually displayed on screen as bitmap graphics.

The difference then between "bitmap graphics" and "vector graphics" is not in the final display format – that is always bitmap – but in the storage format (bitmap or vector) and, by implication, in the time or place when the image is rendered to a bitmap format.

To create a simple Web button we may draw a particular shape, and our image editing software (for example: Adobe Photoshop or Jasc PaintShop Pro) **renders** the image as a bitmap GIF, or other format, when we save the file. Once the image has been rendered and exported it is essentially fixed.

A GIF image is limited to 256 colors, or the 216 colors of the "Web safe" palette. With SVG we are not limited in that way. If the monitor and software allows the display of 16.7 million colors, SVG will provide that if we so choose.

SVG graphics are always stored as a set of SVG elements (just like all other XML elements), which describe how to "draw" or "paint" the graphic. An "SVG viewer" is actually a rendering engine that interprets the vector description of an image, and renders it as a bitmap for display on screen. The fact that the rendering of an SVG image can be carried out on a client machine dynamically, also means that it is possible to adjust certain parameters of the rendered image at the client's choice. For example, an SVG image can typically be zoomed in or out on screen and can be scrolled and panned to view particular areas in detail. For example, the following screen shot shows some text in the Batik SVG Viewer zoomed to about x50 magnification. Notice that the outline of the letters remains sharp. Imagine the "jaggies" and loss of quality if a bitmap image were magnified 50 times.

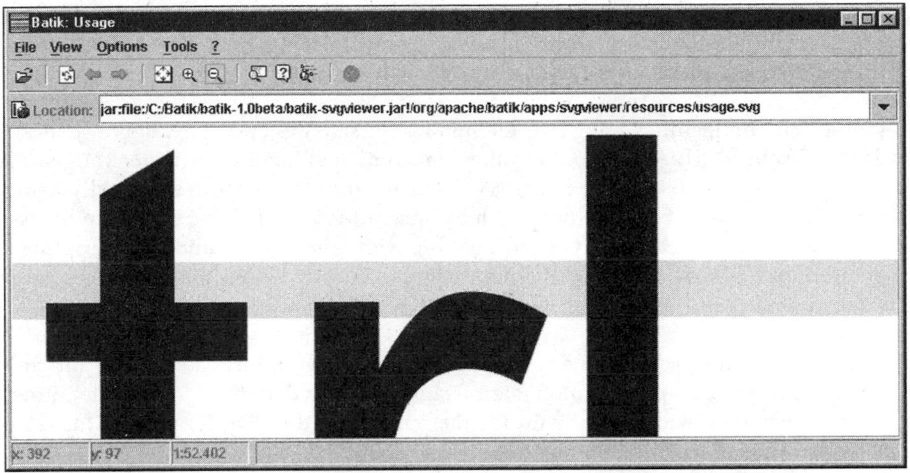

This zooming capability of SVG has huge potential in the production of maps, for example. Imagine starting off with an overview of a city we are visiting, and being able to zoom in on the map, so that we can see more detail to help us locate the street or building we want to get to. Another application where the zooming capability is of immense potential is that of technical drawings. If we are creating a new piece of machinery or circuit board, it is a huge benefit to be able to zoom in and out to look at detail, or take an overview as needed.

SVG also includes XLink and (limited) XPointer capabilities, which means that we can build hypertext links between SVG images or documents, thus opening up a use of SVG for creating XML-based teaching materials. Also, of course, those SVG teaching materials can both include animations and allow other interactions, so providing a totally customized learning experience. Remember that those images can include both SVG text and SVG graphics, so someone with poor sight can zoom in to be able to read the text better too.

Hopefully we have shown a glimpse of the huge potential of SVG. But we need to keep focus, and take a closer look at how SVG actually works.

Overview of Scalable Vector Graphics

Having had a very high level look at what SVG may be able to do let's take a closer look at SVG.

SVG is an application of XML. It is compliant with the Namespaces in XML Recommendation and therefore can be used, in suitable browsers, with other XML application languages. For example, in Chapter 20 we introduce the Extensible Stylesheet Language – Formatting Objects (XSL-FO), and show how an SVG image can be embedded in an XSL-FO document for viewing on screen, either locally or across the Web. In the latter part of this chapter we will embed one of the SVG charts we have created in a simple XSL-FO business report.

SVG is designed to be able to display three things:

- Two dimensional vector graphic shapes
- Text
- Bitmap graphics

The SVG specification offers a rich set of functionality that allows vector graphic objects to be manipulated. Functionality includes: grouping, styling, transforming, compositing into previously rendered objects, clipping paths, alpha masks, and filter effects.

SVG provides animation facilities using two techniques. First, SVG makes available several animation elements, derived from SMIL Animation, to allow declarative animation. A wider range of animation can be achieved by the use of scripting of the SVG Document Object Model, typically using JavaScript (ECMAScript). A rich set of event handlers such as `onmouseover` and `onclick` can be assigned to any SVG graphical object, and because SVG is compatible with other Web standards, scripting can, in principle, be used on XHTML and SVG elements simultaneously within the same Web page. The potential is enormous.

These capabilities allow the creation of a wide range of subtle or sophisticated static and animated graphics. File size for SVG graphics is often significantly smaller than for comparable bitmap graphics, and therefore uses less bandwidth. However, for the purpose of this chapter we will focus on what we need to know to create some straightforward business charts.

An Overview of SVG Elements

Let's move to take a look at the structure of an SVG document/image. Not all SVG elements are relevant to the small projects that we will be undertaking later in the chapter, so we won't attempt to be comprehensive here.

The MIME type for an SVG image/document is "`image/svg+xml`". The typical file extension for an SVG image is "`.svg`". On a Mac it is "`svg `" (`svg` with a trailing space character). There is also a compressed SVG format that some SVG viewers can handle, which uses the file extension "`.svgz`".

All SVG documents/images have an `<svg>` element as the root element. All other elements in an SVG image are nested within that `<svg>` root element. In other words an SVG image is also a well-formed XML document.

The SVG `<title>` element can be displayed in the title bar of a suitable SVG viewer.

The `<desc>` element permits an SVG image/document, or its component parts, to be fully documented internally.

SVG elements may be grouped within `<g>` elements. Such elements can be animated as a group or transformed. The `<g>` element is not the only grouping element. It is permissible for there to be other `<svg>` elements nested within the `<svg>` element that is the element root. Thus, in principle, an **SVG document fragment** may be created and reused within other SVG documents. The SVG `<image>` element will provide that functionality once it is fully supported by SVG viewers.

SVG also promotes reusability of code by another technique, by providing a `<defs>` element where an SVG object can be defined. This could then potentially be used in a number of ways or instances later in the same SVG document, by employing the `<use>` element.

SVG provides a range of **basic shapes** – the `<rect>`, `<circle>`, `<ellipse>`, `<line>`, `<polyline>`, and `<polygon>` elements. More complex shapes are often created using the `<path>` element. The names of these elements are pretty self-explanatory.

SVG provides declarative animation by means of the <animate>, <set>, <animateMotion>, <animateColor>, and <animateTransform> elements. In addition animation may be scripted using JavaScript for example.

Already we can see that SVG documents/images can be potentially very complex, with multiple nested elements, some of which may be grouped, some animated, some scripted and some used as "visual components" by reusing external SVG document fragments.

It will probably be a relief to know that we don't have to master all that potential complexity in the next few pages. We will focus on one aspect of SVG – the creation of some fairly simple business graphics. So, having given a hint of the range of SVG elements, let's move on to take a close look at the SVG elements which we will be using in our charts later in the chapter.

The <rect> Element

We will be using the <rect> element to create the bars of our bar charts later in the chapter so we need to understand how to describe a <rect> element.

Let's create a very simple SVG document to illustrate how to use the <rect> element. When writing SVG code, remember to save it with an .svg file extension ("svg " on the Mac). Without the appropriate file extension the SVG will simply be displayed as tagged text.

```
<?xml version="1.0" standalone="no"?>
<!DOCTYPE svg PUBLIC "-//W3C//DTD SVG 20001102//EN"
          "http://www.w3.org/TR/2000/CR-SVG-20001102/DTD/svg-20001102.dtd">

<svg width="500" height="400">

<rect x="100" y="100" width="300" height="200" style="stroke:black;
      fill:red; stroke-width:3;"/>

</svg>
```

The XML declaration will be familiar. The DOCTYPE definition is that for the November 2000 SVG Candidate Recommendation, the version current at the time of writing.

The <svg> element that is the element root requires its dimensions to be defined using the width and height attributes. This can be expressed in a variety of units, but plain numbers (which default to pixels) will suffice for our present purpose.

To be able to display an SVG <rect> element we need to define its x, y, width and height attributes. The x and y attributes define the coordinates of its top left corner. If any of those are inadvertently omitted, or syntax errors made, the rectangle may not display at all.

In the style attribute of the <rect> element we have defined three CSS properties. The fill of the rectangle is red, the stroke (the edge) is black, and the stroke-width is 3 pixels. We used named colors above but we could equally well have created the same rectangle like this:

```
<rect x="100" y="100" width="300" height="200" style="stroke:#000000;
      fill:#FF0000; stroke-width:3;"/>
```

Or this:

```
<rect x="100" y="100" width="300" height="200" style="stroke:rgb(0,0,0);
      fill:rgb(255,0,0); stroke-width:3;"/>
```

In Internet Explorer 5.5, with the Adobe SVG Viewer, our rectangle is displayed as below. For installation instructions on installing the Adobe SVG Viewer see later. (The code has been changed to make a gray box, to address printing issues.)

```
<rect x="100" y="100" width="300" height="200" style="stroke:rgb(0,0,0);
      fill:rgb(204,204,204); stroke-width:3;"/>
```

The amended file is SimpleRect.svg.

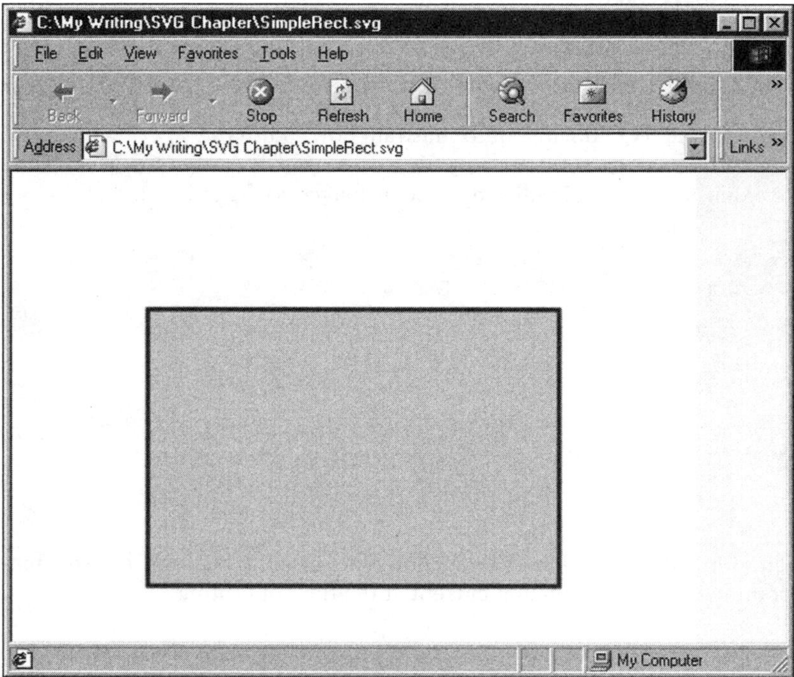

We will use <rect> elements widely in the examples later in the chapter.

The <line> Element

Another SVG element we will be using is the <line> element. To display a line in SVG we need to describe the x and y coordinates of its start and finish points.

The simple SVG document, SimpleLine.svg:

```
<?xml version="1.0" standalone="no"?>
<!DOCTYPE svg PUBLIC "-//W3C//DTD SVG 20001102//EN"
        "http://www.w3.org/TR/2000/CR-SVG-20001102/DTD/svg-20001102.dtd">
```

```
<svg width="500" height="200">
<line x1="10" y1="10" x2="490" y2="190" style="stroke:#000000; stroke-
     width:5;"/>

</svg>
```

displays like this:

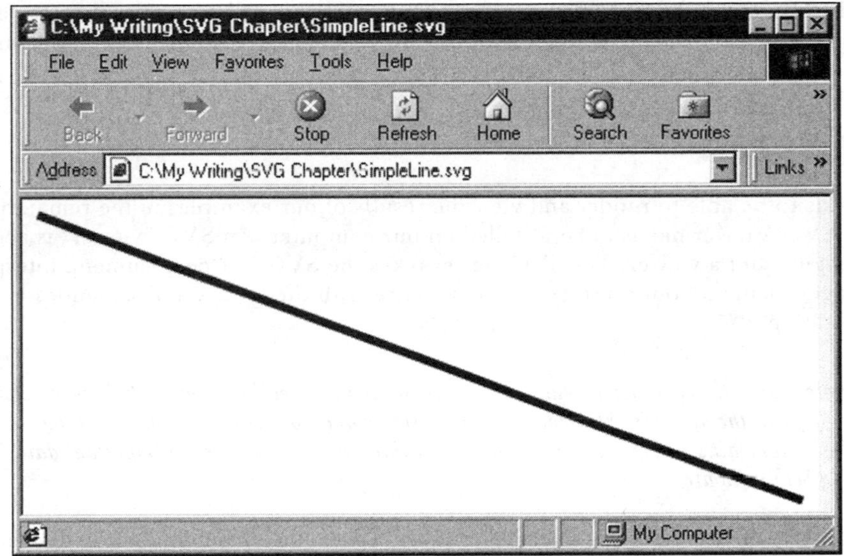

The x1 and y1 attributes describe the starting point of the line, and the x2 and y2 define its other end. The color and thickness of the line are defined by the stroke and stroke-width attributes.

The <text> and <tspan> Elements

The <text> element is the prime means for laying out text in SVG. Text can be laid out solely using <text> elements but a useful option is to nest <tspan> elements within <text> elements.

Here is a simple SVG document, SimpleText.svg, which uses the <text> element.

```
<?xml version="1.0" standalone="no"?>
<!DOCTYPE svg PUBLIC "-//W3C//DTD SVG 20001102//EN"
        "http://www.w3.org/TR/2000/CR-SVG-20001102/DTD/svg-20001102.dtd">

<svg width="500" height="400">

  <text x="100" y="100" style="font-family:Arial, sans-serif; font-size:18;
        stroke:#FF0000; fill:#FF0000;">
      Hello World!
  </text>

</svg>
```

Notice, that in order to display text we must provide values for the x and y attributes. Without those the text will not be displayed, since the SVG viewer/rendering engine does not have sufficient information to allow it to place the text.

It may have been a surprise to notice that for the style attribute of the <text> element there were both stroke and fill properties within the style attribute. We can, if we so choose, create two-color text with the stroke and fill properties defining the colors. Many SVG attributes are derived from CSS2 properties.

Having looked briefly at the SVG elements, which we will be using later in the chapter, let's move on to take a look at the viewers (actually rendering engines) which let us display SVG on screen.

SVG Viewers

In order for us to be able to render and view the results of our examples in the remainder of the chapter, an SVG Viewer needs to be installed on our computer. An SVG "viewer" is actually both a rendering engine and a viewer. The SVG viewer takes the SVG source document, interprets it and lays the image/document out on screen in accordance with the syntax and semantics defined in the SVG specification.

Please note that both SVG viewers suggested in this section are available currently in beta versions. Both, at least in the author's experience, have been stable and have caused no problems, but please remember to take all sensible precautions, such as making suitable backups of important data before installing beta software.

We would suggest the use of the Adobe SVG Viewer to view the examples later in the chapter, since it has the best overall implementation of the SVG Candidate Recommendation, including a far better implementation of SVG animations than any other viewer.

The Adobe SVG Viewer can be downloaded from http://www.adobe.com/svg/. At the time of writing two download options are offered: Adobe SVG Viewer version 1 and SVG Viewer version 2 Release Candidate 1. The code in this chapter has been checked and will run on both. By the time of reading this, it is likely that the final release of Version 2 will have been released (and therefore version 1 may have been withdrawn).

Note that Adobe have quite understandably decided to focus on development for the Internet Explorer and Netscape Navigator browsers for Windows and Mac platforms, since those are the dominant Web browsers used by the graphics community and by general users. The Version 1 Viewer is designed to operate on Internet Explorer 4.0 to 5.0 (but also works well on IE5.5) and Netscape Navigator version 4.0 to 4.73. To get the Adobe SVG Viewer working with Netscape 6.0 or with Opera 5.0, on a Windows platform, you need to have one of the supported Netscape browsers. Install the viewer and then copy three files from that browser's plugins directory to the respective plugins directories. The files that need to be copied are, SVGViewer.zip, SVGView.dll, *and,* NPSVGVw.dll. *Thereafter, with very minor differences in layout, you can view SVG files. The following screen shot shows* www.SVGSpider.com, *the world's "first" all SVG web site viewed using Opera 5 (available free at:* http://www.opera.com) *and the Adobe SVG Viewer.*

When manually copying the Adobe SVG Viewer files to either the Netscape or Opera plugins directory, be sure to remember that upgrades to later versions will again need versions of those same files (unless Adobe changes the necessary files) copied into the relevant plugins directory. As far as the author can establish, it is not possible to, say, run version 2 Release Candidate 1 of the SVG Viewer under Internet Explorer while being able to running SVG Viewer version 1 under Netscape 6. On the Windows platform it is straightforward to use the Add/Remove Programs facility to effectively switch from one to the other, assuming the respective downloads have been suitably labeled.

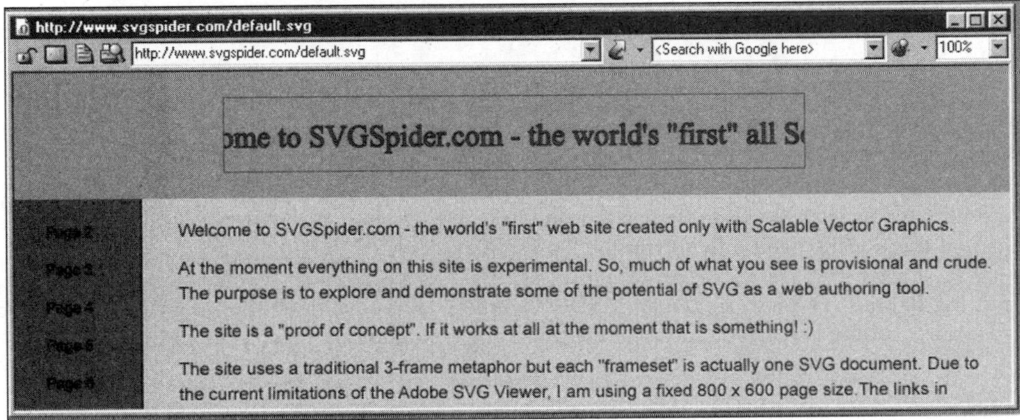

Due to an extraordinary design decision, now being reviewed after vigorous user feedback, Adobe decided that scroll bars could be omitted. SVG provides panning capabilities, which vary depending on SVG viewer and operating system. On a Windows system with the Adobe SVG viewer, we can now pan around by holding the ALT key down together with the left mouse button and moving the mouse.

Platforms other than Windows or Mac are not able to use the Adobe SVG Viewer.

One cross-platform SVG Viewer is the Batik SVG Viewer, currently available as a beta version, from the Apache Foundation. Batik is a Java-based SVG Viewer that can be expected to run on any platform with a suitable Java Virtual Machine. The Apache Batik SVG Toolkit consists of much more than an SVG Viewer – it includes an SVG generator and an SVG rasterizer (converts the vector description of the graphic to a bitmap) – but here we will focus only on Batik as an SVG viewer.

The Batik project is described at http://xml.apache.org/batik/index.html. Batik may be downloaded from http://xml.apache.org/batik/dist/. At the time of writing the latest stable version of Batik is http://xml.apache.org/batik/dist/batik-1.0beta.zip, although other more experimental releases are also available for download. The beta mentioned has, in the authors experience, been very stable, at least on the Windows platform. It seems to be "beta" more in the sense of being a partial implementation, than in being an unstable one.

Running Batik requires Java Virtual Machine 1.2 or later. The Apache web site states that it runs better with Java 1.3, although does not specify what problems you may encounter with earlier versions.

The Batik `batik-1.0beta.zip` file contains a binary executable as well as a range of sample SVG images.

The Java Virtual Machine version 1.3 can be downloaded from the java.sun.com Web site.

On a Windows platform, the directory into which you install the JVM needs adding to the PATH environment variable. For Windows 98SE (used for testing), this involves adding the relevant information to the PATH in the `Autoexec.bat` file.

After downloading the author installed Batik into `C:\Batik`. The JAR executable files are placed by the installation routine in the C:\Batik\batik-1.0beta directory.

The Java Virtual Machine needs to be made aware of where the JAR files are located. The author added the following to his `Autoexec.bat` file:

```
SET CLASSPATH=%CLASSPATH%c:\Batik\batik-1.0beta\batik-
    svgviewer.jar;c:\Batik\batik-1.0beta\batik-rasterizer.jar;
```

An alternative approach is to run Batik from the directory in which the JAR files are installed. This is adequate if there is the need only to run Batik as an SVG Viewer.

To start the Batik SVG Viewer open an MSDOS window and move to the directory in which the batik-`svgviewer.jar` file is located, and type the following command at the command prompt:

```
java -jar batik-svgviewer.jar
```

Assuming that the installation worked properly, the Batik SVG Viewer will open with an appearance very much like the following screen shot.

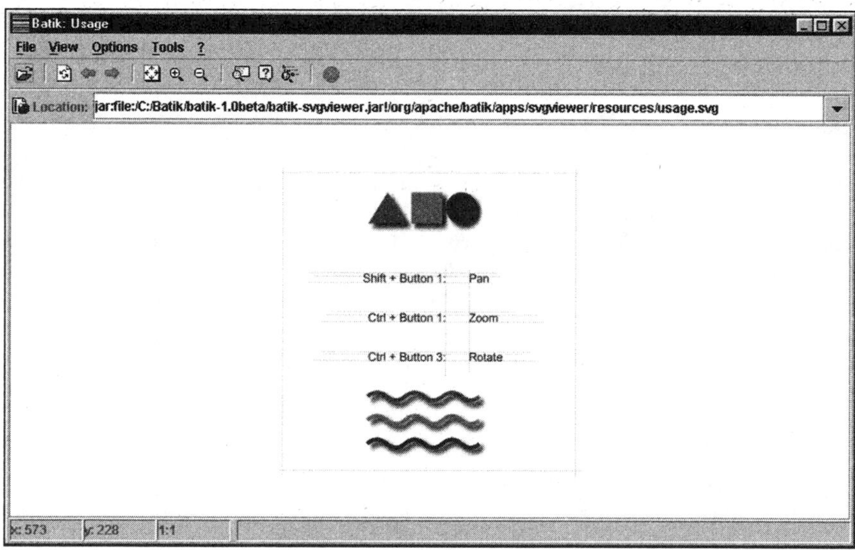

Notice in the screen shot that the default file, which Batik opens, indicates the combined keyboard and mouse commands for navigating an SVG image in Batik. For example, if the Shift key is held down at the same time as the left mouse button (mouse button 1) we can pan around the image.

Assuming that we now have an SVG viewer available, let's move on to create some fairly simple SVG business charts.

A Horizontal Bar Chart

Having already looked fairly briefly at the elements which we are likely to need in creating simple SVG graphs, etc, let's move on to create a simple Bar Chart. Our first example will create a simple horizontal bar chart, which will display quarterly sales figures.

As we can see, our source XML document, `QuarterlySales.xml` perhaps produced as the result of a simple database query, is fairly straightforward. Typically, we might manipulate the XML with XSLT (we will see this later) to produce SVG, but for the next few sections we will statically create the SVG for a clear demonstration of the SVG syntax.

```
<?xml version='1.0'?>
<QuarterlySales>
   <Year>2001</Year>
   <Quarter name="Q1">40</Quarter>
   <Quarter name="Q2">60</Quarter>
   <Quarter name="Q3">80</Quarter>
   <Quarter name="Q4">100</Quarter>
</QuarterlySales>
```

We want our final horizontal bar chart to look like this:

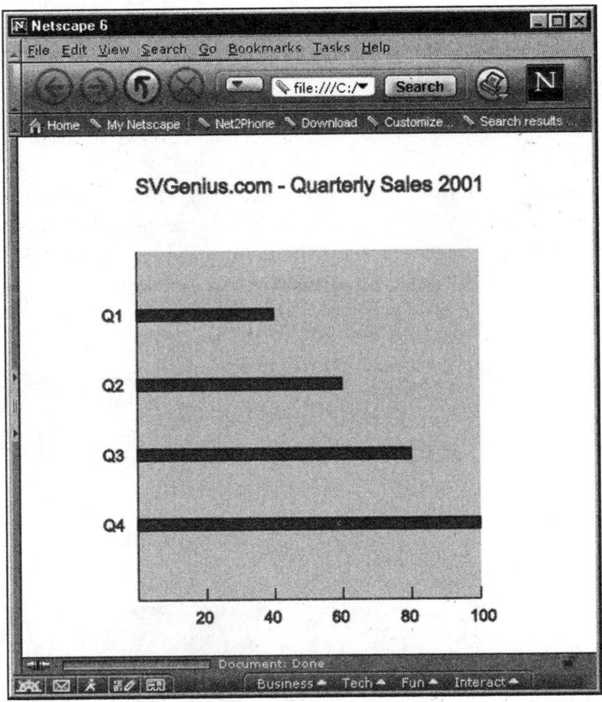

As a first step we will create the gray background and the lines at the left and bottom of the background area.

Our SVG file, `HorizBarv1.svg`, at this stage looks like this:

```
<?xml version="1.0" standalone="no"?>
<!DOCTYPE svg PUBLIC "-//W3C//DTD SVG 20001102//EN"
        "http://www.w3.org/TR/2000/CR-SVG-20001102/DTD/svg-20001102.dtd">

<svg width="500" height="500">
<title>Horizontal Bar Chart</title>
<rect id="Background" x="100" y="100" width="300" height="300"
      style="fill:#cccccc"/>

<g id="LeftLine">
<line x1="100" y1="100" x2="100" y2="400" style="stroke:black;"/>
<line x1="100" y1="160" x2="110" y2="160" style="stroke:black;"/>
<line x1="100" y1="220" x2="110" y2="220" style="stroke:black;"/>
<line x1="100" y1="280" x2="110" y2="280" style="stroke:black;"/>
<line x1="100" y1="340" x2="110" y2="340" style="stroke:black;"/>
</g>

<g id="BottomLine">
<line x1="100" y1="400" x2="400" y2="400" style="stroke:black;"/>
<line x1="160" y1="400" x2="160" y2="390" style="stroke:black;"/>
<line x1="220" y1="400" x2="220" y2="390" style="stroke:black;"/>
<line x1="280" y1="400" x2="280" y2="390" style="stroke:black;"/>
<line x1="340" y1="400" x2="340" y2="390" style="stroke:black;"/>
</g>

</svg>
```

We have included a `<title>` element to describe the nature of our file but, unfortunately, the Adobe Viewer has not, at the time of writing, implemented that feature.

The gray background is produced by using a `<rect>` element with the various attributes as described within the code.

For clarity, the various `<line>` elements that make up the vertical line and its markings to the left of the gray area, are grouped within an SVG `<g>` element, which has an `id` attribute. However, for our immediate purposes we could equally well omit the grouping `<g>` element and add a comment instead to remind you what the purpose of particular elements might be.

So far our code produces a screen display that looks like this:

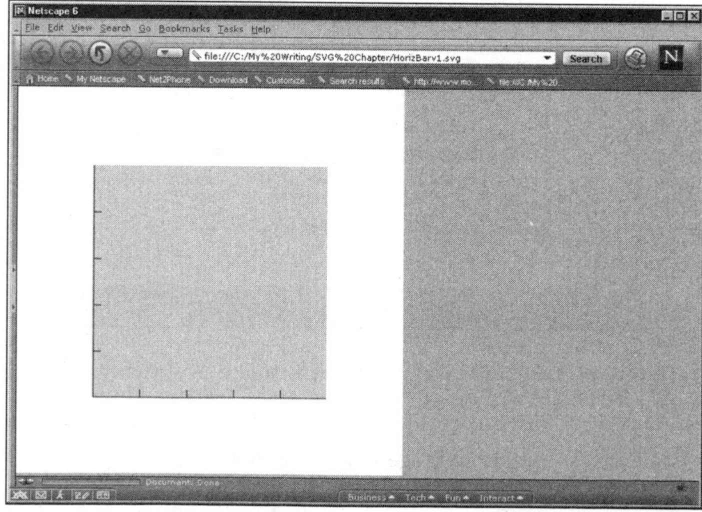

We can see that we have created an appropriately sized gray colored background area, with vertical and horizontal lines to represent the axes of our graph.

So far, so good. Let's go on and add the horizontal bars, which display the growth in sales over the four quarters of 2001 for www.SVGenius.com.

We will display our data as horizontal bars. Since the maximum value of 100 must fit within our 300 pixel gray background area we will scale the actual value of sales by three, for display.

Thus our SVG code, `HorizBarv2.svg` looks like this:

```
<?xml version="1.0" standalone="no"?>
<!-- HorizBarv2.svg -->
<!DOCTYPE svg PUBLIC "-//W3C//DTD SVG 20001102//EN"
          "http://www.w3.org/TR/2000/CR-SVG-20001102/DTD/svg-20001102.dtd">

<svg width="500" height="500">
<title>Horizontal Bar Chart</title>
<rect id="Background" x="100" y="100" width="300" height="300"
      style="fill:#cccccc"/>

<g id="LeftLine">
   . . .
</g>
<g id="BottomLine">
   . . .
</g>

<g id="Quarters1to4">
<rect x="100" y="150" width="120" height="10" style="fill:red;
      stroke:black;"/>
<rect x="100" y="210" width="180" height="10" style="fill:red;
      stroke:black;"/>
<rect x="100" y="270" width="240" height="10" style="fill:red;
      stroke:black;"/>
<rect x="100" y="330" width="300" height="10" style="fill:red;
      stroke:black;"/>
</g>

</svg>
```

Each of the bars in the bar chart is represented in our source code by a `<rect>` element. We have defined the `x`, `y`, `width` and `height` attributes to produce an appearance appropriate to our needs. The style of each `<rect>` element is the same, with a red fill and a black stroke. You may notice that there is repetition in the manner of defining the style attribute, which suggests that, at least in some settings, the use of Cascading Style Sheets to hold the style information may be useful. We will see how to do that in a later section.

If we check our code with another screen shot we see that we are making progress.

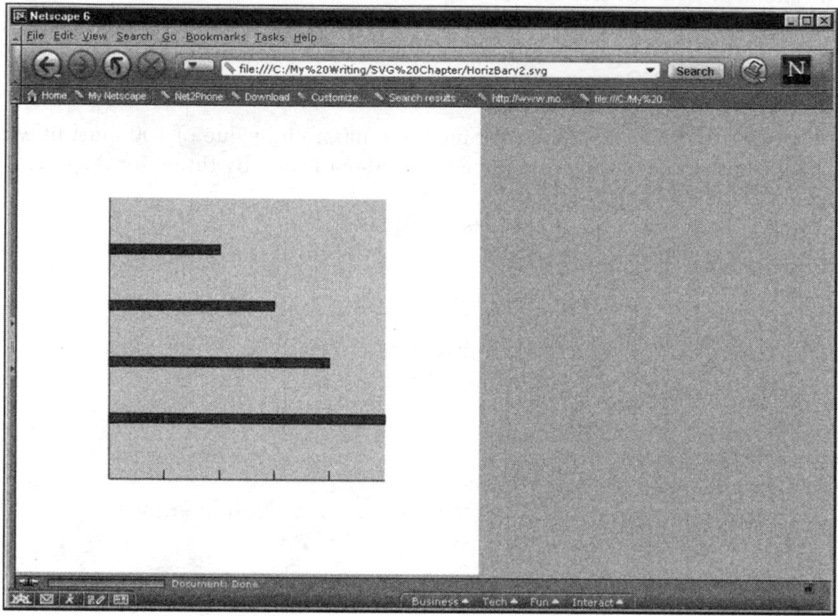

We now have appropriately scaled horizontal bars appropriately placed on our gray background, although as it stands, the graphic is very bare. We need to add some text to explain what the display is referring to. Our final step in creating the horizontal bar graph is to add a heading and other text to indicate what each bar represents and text to indicate the scale which applies to our graphic.

So after we have added our heading and label text the final version, `HorizBarv3.svg`, has code which looks like this:

```
<?xml version="1.0" standalone="no"?>
<!-- HorizBarv3.svg -->
<!DOCTYPE svg PUBLIC "-//W3C//DTD SVG 20001102//EN"
          "http://www.w3.org/TR/2000/CR-SVG-20001102/DTD/svg-20001102.dtd">

<svg width="500" height="500">
<title>Horizontal Bar Chart - SVGenius.com sales by Quarter 2001</title>

<!-- Header text goes here. -->
<text x="100" y="50" style="font-size:18; font-weight:normal; stroke:red;
      fill:red;">SVGenius.com - Quarterly Sales 2001</text>

<!-- Left text goes here. -->
<text x="70" y="160" style="font-size:14; stroke: red; fill:red;">Q1</text>
<text x="70" y="220" style="font-size:14; stroke: red; fill:red;">Q2</text>
<text x="70" y="280" style="font-size:14; stroke: red; fill:red;">Q3</text>
<text x="70" y="340" style="font-size:14; stroke: red; fill:red;">Q4</text>

<!-- Bottom text goes here. -->
<text x="150" y="420" style="font-size:14; stroke: red; fill:red;">20</text>
<text x="210" y="420" style="font-size:14; stroke: red; fill:red;">40</text>
```

```
<text x="270" y="420" style="font-size:14; stroke: red; fill:red;">60</text>
<text x="330" y="420" style="font-size:14; stroke: red; fill:red;">80</text>
<text x="390" y="420" style="font-size:14; stroke: red;
      fill:red;">100</text>

<!-- This rectangle is the gray background. -->
<rect id="Background" x="100" y="100" width="300" height="300"
      style="fill:#cccccc"/>

<!-- These lines are the vertical axis and scale marks. -->
<g id="LeftLine">
<line x1="100" y1="100" x2="100" y2="400" style="stroke:black;"/>
<line x1="100" y1="160" x2="110" y2="160" style="stroke:black;"/>
<line x1="100" y1="220" x2="110" y2="220" style="stroke:black;"/>
<line x1="100" y1="280" x2="110" y2="280" style="stroke:black;"/>
<line x1="100" y1="340" x2="110" y2="340" style="stroke:black;"/>
</g>

<!-- These lines are the horizontal axis and scale marks. -->
<g id="BottomLine">
<line x1="100" y1="400" x2="400" y2="400" style="stroke:black;"/>
<line x1="160" y1="400" x2="160" y2="390" style="stroke:black;"/>
<line x1="220" y1="400" x2="220" y2="390" style="stroke:black;"/>
<line x1="280" y1="400" x2="280" y2="390" style="stroke:black;"/>
<line x1="340" y1="400" x2="340" y2="390" style="stroke:black;"/>
<line x1="400" y1="400" x2="400" y2="390" style="stroke:black;"/>
</g>

<!-- These rectangles are the horizontal bars of the bar chart. -->
<g id="Quarters1to4">
<rect x="100" y="150" width="120" height="10" style="fill:red; stroke:black;"/>
<rect x="100" y="210" width="180" height="10" style="fill:red; stroke:black;"/>
<rect x="100" y="270" width="240" height="10" style="fill:red; stroke:black;"/>
<rect x="100" y="330" width="300" height="10" style="fill:red; stroke:black;"/>
</g>
</svg>
```

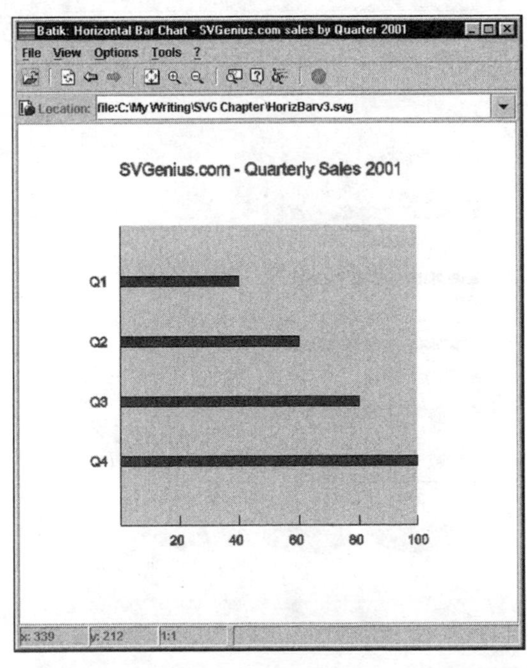

For our final screen shot in this section we've chosen to use Batik, in part to demonstrate that Batik displays the SVG `<title>` element in the title bar. If you compare this with the two previous screen shots, which were in Netscape 6, you will note that the content of the SVG `<title>` element is not shown, since (at the time of writing) the Adobe SVG Viewer does not support display of the `<title>` element.

We have created a straightforward bar chart using only five SVG elements – the `<svg>` root element, which is, of course, a required element, plus the `<rect>`, `<line>`, `<text>`, and `<title>` elements.

In the sections that follow we will see a number of other things that can be done to improve our bar chart. First, let's look at adding some simple interactivity to our bar chart.

An Interactive Bar Chart

You are seeing SVG presented on paper where only a static graphic can be displayed. Imagine that the managers of SVGenius.com might be due to meet, to discuss the quarterly sales figures. For whatever reason the sales manager may wish to focus the attendee's attention on particular parts of our bar chart at any one time. S/he would like the data to be presented to his/her colleagues with only the Q1 results showing, but with the option of revealing the results of each successive quarter at the appropriate point in the discussion.

In other words we need to add some interactivity and animation to our bar chart. So we need to make use of some of the animation elements that SVG "borrows" from SMIL Animation.

First, let's look at the final version of the bar chart with some simple controls which will allow the sales manager to display the results for each successive quarter when s/he chooses to.

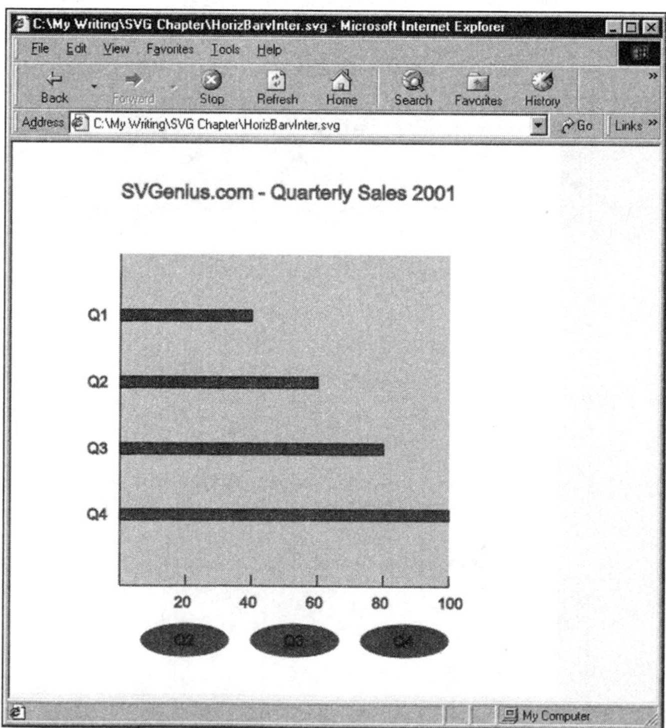

The three simple controls at the bottom of the screen-shot use SVG <ellipse> elements with <text> elements to contain the label text. Some comments have been added within the existing code, just to remind you what is going on, and new or changed code has been highlighted.

```
<?xml version="1.0" standalone="no"?>
<!-- HorizBarvInter.svg -->
<!DOCTYPE svg PUBLIC "-//W3C//DTD SVG 20001102//EN"
          "http://www.w3.org/TR/2000/CR-SVG-20001102/DTD/svg-20001102.dtd">
<svg width="500" height="500">
<title>Horizontal Bar Chart - SVGenius.com sales by Quarter 2001</title>

<!-- Header text goes here. -->
<text x="100" y="50" style="font-size:18; font-weight:normal; stroke:red;
      fill:red;">SVGenius.com - Quarterly Sales 2001</text>
<!-- Left text goes here. -->
<text x="70" y="160" style="font-size:14; stroke: red; fill:red;">Q1</text>
   . . .
<!-- Bottom text goes here. -->
<text x="150" y="420" style="font-size:14; stroke: red; fill:red;">20</text>
   . . .
<!-- This rectangle is the gray background. -->
<rect id="Background" x="100" y="100" width="300" height="300"
      style="fill:#cccccc"/>
<!-- These lines are the vertical axis and scale marks. -->
<g id="LeftLine">
   . . .
</g>
<!-- These lines are the horizontal axis and scale marks. -->
<g id="BottomLine">
   . . .
</g>
<!-- These rectangles are the horizontal bars of the bar chart. -->
<g id="Quarters1to4">
<rect x="100" y="150" width="120" height="10" style="fill:red;
      stroke:black;"/>

<rect id="Q2Sales" x="100" y="210" width="180" height="10" style="fill:red;
stroke:black; display:none;">
<animate begin="Q2Button.click" dur="1s" attributeName="display" from="none"
        to="block" fill="freeze"/>
</rect>

<rect id="Q3Sales" x="100" y="270" width="0" height="10" style="fill:red;
stroke:black;">
<animate begin="Q3Button.click" dur="3s" attributeName="width" from="0"
        to="240" fill="freeze"/>
</rect>

<rect x="100" y="330" width="0" height="10" style="fill:red; stroke:black;">
<animate begin="Q4Button.click" dur="3s" attributeName="width" from="0"
        to="300" fill="freeze"/>
</rect>
</g>

<g id="Controls">
<a id="Q2Button">
```

```
<ellipse cx="160" cy="450" rx="40" ry="15" style="stroke:red; fill:red;"/>
<text x="150" y="455" style="font-size:14; fill:black;
      stroke:black;">Q2</text>
</a>

<a id="Q3Button">
<ellipse cx="260" cy="450" rx="40" ry="15" style="stroke:red; fill:red;"/>
<text x="250" y="455" style="font-size:14; fill:black;
      stroke:black;">Q3</text>
</a>

<a id="Q4Button">
<ellipse cx="360" cy="450" rx="40" ry="15" style="stroke:red; fill:red;"/>
<text x="350" y="455" style="font-size:14; fill:black;
      stroke:black;">Q4</text>
</a>
</g>

</svg>
```

Let's take a look at the new or changed code, step by step. We have added two animation elements with their attributes set differently, which will respond to a single click on the appropriate element that we are using as a control. The first uses an `<animate>` element:

```
<rect id="Q2Sales" x="100" y="210" width="180" height="10" style="fill:red;
      stroke:black; display:none;">
<animate begin="Q2Button.click" dur="1s" attributeName="display" from="none"
         to="block" fill="freeze"/>
</rect>
```

Notice first that we have split our `<rect>` element into separate start and end tags, whereas previously we had used the abbreviated empty element form. Nested within the `<rect>` element is an SVG `<animate>` element, which is "borrowed" from SMIL Animation. To apply an animation to any SVG element, you need to nest the animation element between the start and end tags of the element to be animated.

Let's take a closer look at the animation:

```
<animate begin="Q2Button.click" dur="1s" attributeName="display" from="none"
         to="block" fill="freeze"/>
```

The `begin` attribute tells us that the animation begins when the `Q2Button` is clicked. Not surprisingly, the `Q2Button` refers to the ellipse labeled "`Q2`" which we will look at in more detail shortly. The `dur` (duration) attribute tells us that it will take 1 second for the animation to complete. But what are we going to animate? The value of the `attributeName` attribute tells us. We are going to animate the `display` property. We are going to change the `display` property from a value of `none` (that is; hidden) to a value of `block`, which means in this context that it becomes visible. The `fill` attribute tells us that once the animation completes, the `display` property will be frozen as `block` instead of returning to the previous value of `none`.

To translate all that to the user's perspective: we see that when a user clicks the "`Q2`" elliptical button, the `<rect>` element which displays as a red bar changes in 1 second from hidden to visible. Thus our sales manager can control when the Q2 results are shown to his/her audience.

Our sales manager also has other animation options available, which the animation for Quarter 3 shows. Again, we use an <animate> element but the attribute to be animated is different.

```
<rect id="Q3Sales" x="100" y="270" width="0" height="10" style="fill:red;
      stroke:black;">
<animate begin="Q3Button.click" dur="3s" attributeName="width" from="0"
         to="240" fill="freeze"/>
</rect>
```

The begin attribute of the <animate> element tells us that the animation begins when the object with id attribute Q3Button is clicked. Over a period of 3 seconds the width attribute of the rectangle representing the Quarter 3 sales figures increases in value from 0 to 240. When the width attribute had a value of 0 (before the animation) it was, for all practical purposes, hidden. By animating the width attribute rather than the display property we can get a more visual sense of growth of sales during that Quarter 3 period.

The elements, which relate to the three controls, are nested within a <g> element below:

```
<g id="Controls">
<a id="Q2Button">
<ellipse cx="160" cy="450" rx="40" ry="15" style="stroke:red; fill:red;"/>
<text x="150" y="455" style="font-size:14; fill:black;
      stroke:black;">Q2</text>
</a>

<a id="Q3Button">
<ellipse cx="260" cy="450" rx="40" ry="15" style="stroke:red; fill:red;"/>
<text x="250" y="455" style="font-size:14; fill:black;
      stroke:black;">Q3</text>
</a>

<a id="Q4Button">
<ellipse cx="360" cy="450" rx="40" ry="15" style="stroke:red; fill:red;"/>
<text x="350" y="455" style="font-size:14; fill:black;
      stroke:black;">Q4</text>
</a>
</g>
```

Each control has a similar structure. The control is an <a> element with an id attribute of value Q2Button or similar. You will recognize that it is the value of this id attribute, that makes up the value of the begin attribute of the <animate> elements we looked at a little earlier (such as begin="Button2.click").

The SVG <a> element has a usage similar to the <a> element of HTML and XHTML 1.0. It is used for linking purposes. In our example the <a> element associates the control with the element being animated. It has wider usage such as providing XLinks (see Chapter 10) to other SVG images or web pages. Examples of working XLinks in SVG can be seen on the Web at www.SVGSpider.com/default.svg.

The <ellipse> element is an SVG element that we haven't considered yet. To display an <ellipse> element we need to define the x and y coordinates of its center using the cx and cy attributes, and the x and y radii, using the rx and ry attributes. The style attribute is similar to that which you saw previously for the <rect> element.

Notice that the <ellipse> element precedes the <text> element in the control. SVG has a "painter's model" which determines the order in which elements are rendered. By putting the <ellipse> element first followed by the <text> element, it essentially means that the ellipse is painted and then the text is painted on top, which is what we want. If we had reversed the order of the elements, we would have caused the text to be rendered then painted over by the ellipse (and the text would no longer be visible to us). So, if elements become invisible, consider the possibility that they have been painted over with another SVG element.

Here is our final interactive bar chart (in Internet Explorer 5.5), after the Q2 and Q3 bars have been animated, and while the horizontal bar representing Quarter 4 is in the process of animating:

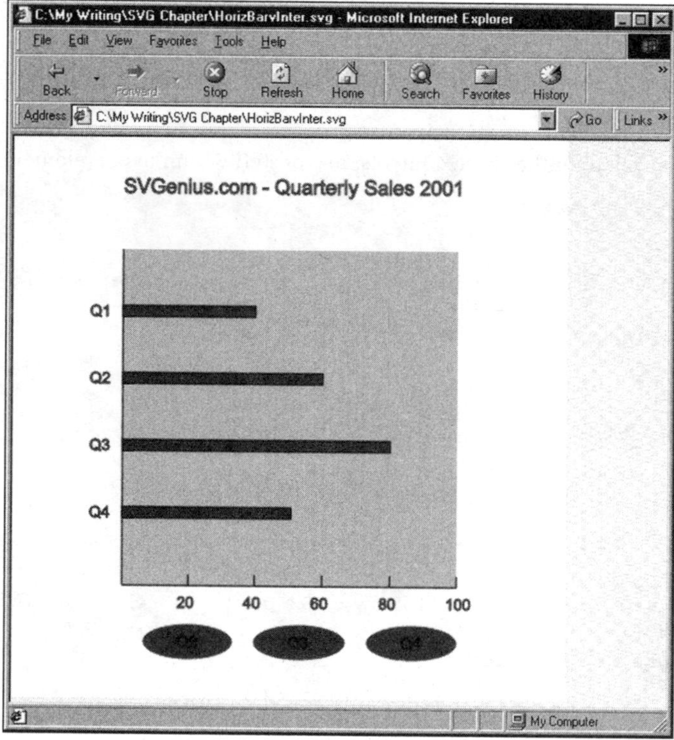

Up until this point Batik has given us a good display; in fact it outdid both IE5.5 and Netscape 6 in that it could make use of the SVG <title> element. When we come to animations though, Batik, at least at the time of writing, is very weak.

Here is the initial display of the interactive bar chart in Batik:

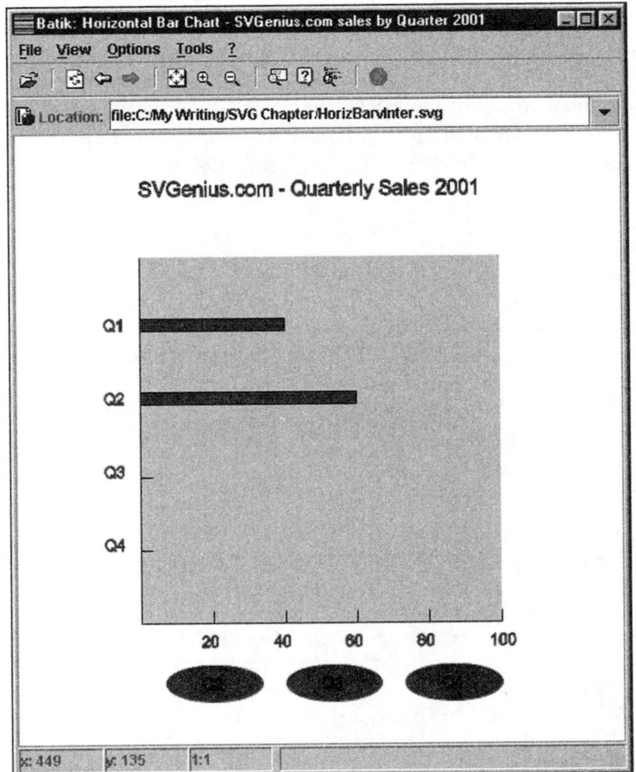

Note that the horizontal bar for Quarter 2 is visible instead of being hidden. So, in Batik, we have lost the ability to animate the Q2 bar by animating the `display` property. Furthermore, clicking on the button for either Q3 or Q4 has no useful effect. The screen simply clears and the same incorrect display as shown above is repeated. Thus, to create and view the interactive bar chart for the time being, we need to use the Adobe SVG Viewer.

The Batik and Adobe SVG viewers are under ongoing development. Features lacking or incomplete at the time of writing may have been implemented by the time of reading this book. Check the URLs given earlier for the most up to date information.

Using SVG with Cascading Style Sheets

In the first version of the horizontal bar chart we created, we hard-coded all our styling information as CSS properties within the `style` attributes of various SVG elements. For very simple documents or for one-off documents that is a reasonable approach. However, if we are to include our SVG bar chart on a corporate web site then we might find that we need to conform to corporate image guidelines regarding colors, acceptable fonts, etc. If we are producing lots of images we certainly don't want to start fiddling around in dozens or hundreds of files changing CSS properties if the company's web site is re-styled.

There are many advantages to keeping our style information separate in a Cascading Style Sheets file. In that file, or files, we can centrally store all the styling information for both the text and graphics in our SVG images. If the company color scheme changes, our SVG images can be adapted in a straightforward way to match the new colors chosen.

So let's look at how we need to adapt our SVG document to allow for separating style into an external CSS style sheet. We will use `class` attributes on the SVG elements to allow us to create suitable CSS rules. The modified code is shown in `HorizBarCSS.svg` below:

```
<?xml version="1.0" standalone="no"?>
<?xml-stylesheet href="HorizBar.css" type="text/css" ?>
<!-- HorizBarvCSS.svg -->
<!DOCTYPE svg PUBLIC "-//W3C//DTD SVG 20001102//EN"
         "http://www.w3.org/TR/2000/CR-SVG-20001102/DTD/svg-20001102.dtd">

<svg width="500" height="500">
<title>Horizontal Bar Chart - SVGenius.com sales by Quarter 2001</title>

<!-- Header text goes here. -->
<text x="100" y="50" class="header">SVGenius.com - Quarterly Sales
      2001</text>

<!-- Left text goes here. -->
<text x="70" y="160" class="label">Q1</text>
<text x="70" y="220" class="label">Q2</text>
<text x="70" y="280" class="label">Q3</text>
<text x="70" y="340" class="label">Q4</text>

<!-- Bottom text goes here. -->
<text x="150" y="420" class="label">20</text>
<text x="210" y="420" class="label">40</text>
<text x="270" y="420" class="label">60</text>
<text x="330" y="420" class="label">80</text>
<text x="390" y="420" class="label">100</text>

<!-- This rectangle is the gray background. -->
<rect id="Background" x="100" y="100" width="300" height="300"
      style="fill:#cccccc"/>

<!-- These lines are the vertical axis and scale marks. -->
<g id="LeftLine">
<line x1="100" y1="100" x2="100" y2="400" style="stroke:black;"/>
<line x1="100" y1="160" x2="110" y2="160" style="stroke:black;"/>
<line x1="100" y1="220" x2="110" y2="220" style="stroke:black;"/>
<line x1="100" y1="280" x2="110" y2="280" style="stroke:black;"/>
<line x1="100" y1="340" x2="110" y2="340" style="stroke:black;"/>
</g>

<!-- These lines are the horizontal axis and scale marks. -->
<g id="BottomLine">
<line x1="100" y1="400" x2="400" y2="400" style="stroke:black;"/>
<line x1="160" y1="400" x2="160" y2="390" style="stroke:black;"/>
<line x1="220" y1="400" x2="220" y2="390" style="stroke:black;"/>
<line x1="280" y1="400" x2="280" y2="390" style="stroke:black;"/>
<line x1="340" y1="400" x2="340" y2="390" style="stroke:black;"/>
<line x1="400" y1="400" x2="400" y2="390" style="stroke:black;"/>
</g>

<!-- These rectangles are the horizontal bars of the bar chart. -->
<g id="Quarters1to4">
<rect x="100" y="150" width="120" height="10" class="bar"/>
```

```
<rect id="Q2Sales" x="100" y="210" width="180" height="10" style="display:none;"
class="bar">
<animate begin="Q2Button.click" dur="1s" attributeName="display" from="none"
        to="block" fill="freeze"/>
</rect>

<rect id="Q3Sales" x="100" y="270" width="0" height="10" class="bar">
<animate begin="Q3Button.click" dur="3s" attributeName="width" from="0"
        to="240" fill="freeze"/>
</rect>

<rect x="100" y="330" width="0" height="10" class="bar">
<animate begin="Q4Button.click" dur="3s" attributeName="width" from="0"
        to="300" fill="freeze"/>
</rect>
</g>

<g id="Controls">
<a id="Q2Button">
<ellipse cx="160" cy="450" rx="40" ry="15" class="button"/>
<text x="150" y="455" style="font-size:14; fill:black;
      stroke:black;">Q2</text>
</a>

<a id="Q3Button">
<ellipse cx="260" cy="450" rx="40" ry="15" class="button"/>
<text x="250" y="455" style="font-size:14; fill:black;
      stroke:black;">Q3</text>
</a>

<a id="Q4Button">
<ellipse cx="360" cy="450" rx="40" ry="15" class="button"/>
<text x="350" y="455" style="font-size:14; fill:black;
      stroke:black;">Q4</text>
</a>
</g>

</svg>
```

The line:

```
<?xml-stylesheet href="HorizBar.css" type="text/css" ?>
```

associates the CSS style sheet named `HorizBar.css` with our SVG image.

Essentially, what we have done is to remove all the `style` attributes from our SVG elements and replaced them with `class` attributes with varying values.

For example: in the `<text>` element, which describes the chart header, we have added a `class` attribute with the value of `header`:

```
<text x="100" y="50" class="header">SVGenius.com - Quarterly Sales 2001</text>
```

If you are familiar with Cascading Style Sheets you will probably recall that there is syntax, widely used with HTML, to allow the application of style using **class selectors**. For example, to apply a particular style to `<text>` elements where the `class` attribute has the value of `header` we have a rule, which takes a form like this:

```
text.header
   {
   font-size:18;
   font-weight:normal;
   stroke:red;
   fill:red;
   }
```

The syntax `text.header` indicates that the CSS rule applies to text elements with a `class` attribute value of `header`. The full stop is the separator between the element name and the class value in the CSS class selector. The content within the curly braces describes the styling of the elements chosen using the class selector. The latter is essentially the same as the styling information within the corresponding `style` attribute.

So, if we want to simply maintain the visual appearance of our bar chart, the CSS that is linked to our SVG (`HorizBar.css`), looks like this:

```
/* This is HorizBar.css */

text.header
   {
   font-size:18;
   font-weight:normal;
   stroke:red;
   fill:red;
   }

text.label
   {
   font-size:14;
   stroke: red;
   fill:red;
   }

rect.bar
   {
   fill:red;
   stroke:black;
   }

ellipse.button
   {
   stroke:red;
   fill:red;
   }
```

If you open `HorizBarvCSS.svg` in an SVG Viewer its visual appearance and its functionality will not have changed. But the manner in which it derives its visual appearance has changed significantly.

Let's suppose that a manager comes up with the idea that a more subdued color scheme is preferable to the bright color scheme of black and red. With much of our style information held in a separate CSS style sheet, it is a straightforward exercise to redefine the colors used for display of our graphic.

We can change the content of the CSS style sheet easily, and see the changes in color scheme ripple throughout the graphic. Here is the code for the amended CSS style sheet, `HorizBar2.css`:

```
/* This is HorizBar2.css */

text.header
   {
   font-size:18;
   font-weight:normal;
   stroke:#990066;
   fill:#990066;
   }

text.label
   {
   font-size:14;
   stroke: navy;
   fill:navy;
   }

rect.bar
  {
   fill:#990066;
   stroke:black;
   }

ellipse.button
   {
   stroke:navy;
   fill:#cccccc;
   stroke-width:1;
   }
```

If we want to associate this more subdued color scheme with our SVG image, we need to alter the following line (in `HorizBarCSS.svg`) as below:

```
<?xml-stylesheet href="HorizBar2.css" type="text/css" ?>
```

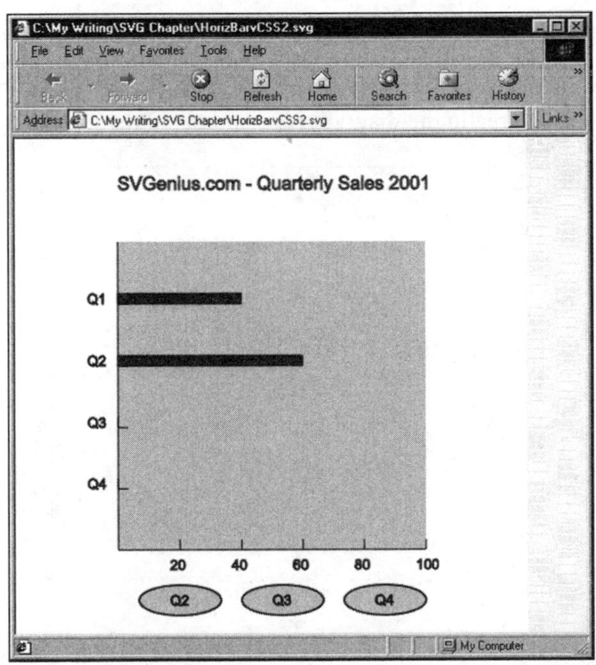

Visually this looks very like the screen shot of Batik shown earlier. The difference is that the horizontal bar visible beside the label "Q2" has been correctly animated. And, if the "Q3" and "Q4" controls at the bottom of the screen shot are activated they will animate correctly.

Creating SVG Using XSLT

Up to this point we have created our SVG statically. In practice you may often need to create SVG dynamically. One tool for such dynamic generation of SVG is XSLT.

In Chapter 9 we introduced the use of Extensible Stylesheet Language Transformations, XSLT. If the reader is not yet up to speed with XPath location paths we recommend the introduction to XPath in Chapter 8. In this section we will use XSLT to dynamically create the SVG image that we have just seen.

Much earlier in the chapter we used a simple XML source document (`QuarterlySales.xml`) as the basis for the various versions of the horizontal bar chart. In order to create our XSLT stylesheet, we need to understand the structure of our source XML document. Note the added second line that associates the file with the XSLT stylesheet, which we will look at in a moment.

```
<?xml version="1.0"?>
<?xml-stylesheet href="HorizBarvXSLT.xsl" type="text/xsl" ?>
<QuarterlySales>
   <Year>2001</Year>
   <Quarter name="Q1">40</Quarter>
   <Quarter name="Q2">60</Quarter>
   <Quarter name="Q3">80</Quarter>
   <Quarter name="Q4">100</Quarter>
</QuarterlySales>
```

If we are going to programmatically create our SVG rather than doing a bit of mental arithmetic as we write the code, we need some sort of model for the layout that will yield some variables for us to use. In the following diagram you can see a possible model for the layout of the SVG horizontal bar graph we have already seen. The gray area in the diagram corresponds to the gray area in our previous bar charts.

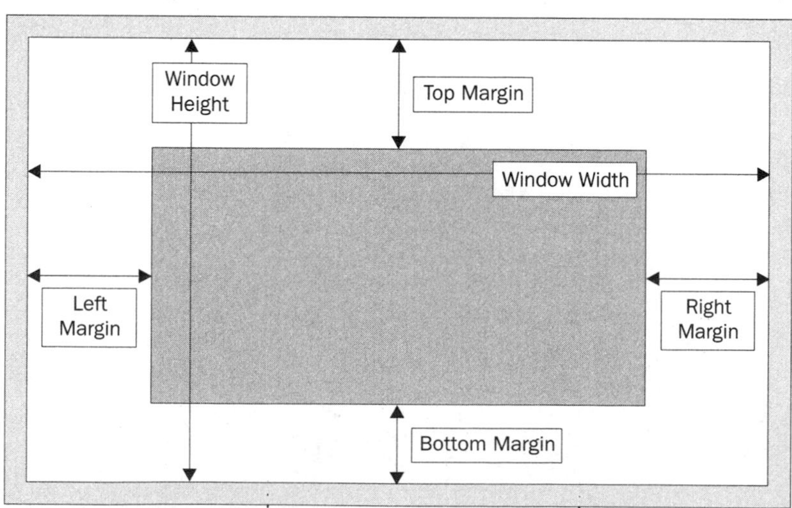

While reading through the XSLT stylesheet, `HorizBarvXSLT.xsl`, it is helpful to refer to the above diagram to help visualize what the calculations refer to.

In the code (`HorizBarvXSLT.xsl`) that follows, we will introduce the use of XSLT global variables, and XSLT named templates, to produce our interactive SVG chart. Most of the chart is created within a single XSLT template. That is done not to show good practice, but to make it easier to understand how XSLT global variables and named templates work.

```
<?xml version='1.0'?>
<xsl:stylesheet version="1.0"
                xmlns:xsl="http://www.w3.org/1999/XSL/Transform">

<xsl:output indent="yes"/>

<!-- Hard code the size of the SVG window to the dimensions as in previous
     examples. -->
<xsl:variable name="WindowWidth">500</xsl:variable>
<xsl:variable name="WindowHeight">500</xsl:variable>

<!-- Hard code the top, bottom, left and right margins. They are equal, as
     in previous examples, but they do not need to be equal. -->
<xsl:variable name="WindowTopMargin">100</xsl:variable>
<xsl:variable name="WindowBottomMargin">100</xsl:variable>
<xsl:variable name="WindowLeftMargin">100</xsl:variable>
<xsl:variable name="WindowRightMargin">100</xsl:variable>

<xsl:template match="/">

<!-- Use the $WindowWidth and $WindowHeight variables in the defining of
     the width and height attributes of the <svg> element root. -->
<svg width="{$WindowWidth}" height="{$WindowHeight}">

   <!-- Use the content of the <Year> element in the source document. -->
   <title>Horizontal Bar Chart - SVGenius.com sales by Quarter
      <xsl:value-of select="/QuarterlySales/Year"/>
   </title>

   <!-- Header text goes here. -->
   <!-- Use the content of the <Year> element in the source document in our
        header. -->
   <text x="100" y="50" style="font-size:18; font-weight:normal; stroke:red;
         fill:red;">SVGenius.com - Quarterly Sales
      <xsl:value-of select="/QuarterlySales/Year"/>
   </text>

   <!-- Left text goes here. -->
   <!-- Use an <xsl:value-of> element and an XPath location path to define
        the label text to be printed beside our vertical line. -->
   <text x="70" y="160" style="font-size:14; stroke: red; fill:red;">
      <xsl:value-of select="/QuarterlySales/Quarter[position()=1]/@name"/>
   </text>
   <text x="70" y="220" style="font-size:14; stroke: red; fill:red;">
      <xsl:value-of select="/QuarterlySales/Quarter[position()=2]/@name"/>
   </text>
   <text x="70" y="280" style="font-size:14; stroke: red; fill:red;">
```

```
        <xsl:value-of select="/QuarterlySales/Quarter[position()=3]/@name"/>
     </text>
     <text x="70" y="340" style="font-size:14; stroke: red; fill:red;">
        <xsl:value-of select="/QuarterlySales/Quarter[position()=4]/@name"/>
     </text>

     <!-- Bottom text goes here. -->
     <!-- For the first text label calculate its y coordinate using the
          $WindowHeight and $WindowBottomMargin variables. -->
     <text x="150" y="{$WindowHeight +20 - $WindowBottomMargin}" style="font-
           size:14; stroke: red; fill:red;">20</text>
     <text x="210" y="420" style="font-size:14; stroke: red;
           fill:red;">40</text>
     <text x="270" y="420" style="font-size:14; stroke: red;
           fill:red;">60</text>
     <text x="330" y="420" style="font-size:14; stroke: red;
           fill:red;">80</text>
     <text x="390" y="420" style="font-size:14; stroke: red;
           fill:red;">100</text>

     <!-- This rectangle is the gray background. -->
     <rect id="Background" x="100" y="100" width="300" height="300"
           style="fill:#cccccc"/>

     <!-- These lines are the vertical axis and scale marks. -->
     <g id="LeftLine">
        <line x1="100" y1="100" x2="100" y2="400" style="stroke:black;"/>
        <line x1="100" y1="160" x2="110" y2="160" style="stroke:black;"/>
        <line x1="100" y1="220" x2="110" y2="220" style="stroke:black;"/>
        <line x1="100" y1="280" x2="110" y2="280" style="stroke:black;"/>
        <line x1="100" y1="340" x2="110" y2="340" style="stroke:black;"/>
     </g>

     <!-- These lines are the horizontal axis and scale marks. -->
     <g id="BottomLine">

        <!-- Use the $WindowLeftMargin variable to define the x1 attribute of
        the base line. -->
        <line x1="{$WindowLeftMargin}" y1="400" x2="400" y2="400"
              style="stroke:black;"/>
        <line x1="160" y1="400" x2="160" y2="390" style="stroke:black;"/>
        <line x1="220" y1="400" x2="220" y2="390" style="stroke:black;"/>
        <line x1="280" y1="400" x2="280" y2="390" style="stroke:black;"/>
        <line x1="340" y1="400" x2="340" y2="390" style="stroke:black;"/>
        <line x1="400" y1="400" x2="400" y2="390" style="stroke:black;"/>
     </g>

     <!-- These rectangles are the horizontal bars of the bar chart. -->
     <g id="Quarters1to4">
        <rect x="100" y="150" width="120" height="10" style="fill:red;
              stroke:black;"/>
        <rect id="Q2Sales" x="100" y="210" width="180" height="10"
              style="fill:red; stroke:black; display:none;">
           <animate begin="Q2Button.click" dur="1s" attributeName="display"
                    from="none" to="block" fill="freeze"/>
```

```
      </rect>
      <rect id="Q3Sales" x="100" y="270" width="0" height="10"
            style="fill:red; stroke:black;">
         <animate begin="Q3Button.click" dur="3s" attributeName="width"
                  from="0" to="240" fill="freeze"/>
      </rect>
      <rect x="100" y="330" width="0" height="10" style="fill:red;
            stroke:black;">
         <animate begin="Q4Button.click" dur="3s" attributeName="width"
                  from="0" to="300" fill="freeze"/>
      </rect>
   </g>

   <!-- The creation of the controls (the ellipses and accompanying text) has
        been broken out into a named XSLT template. -->
   <xsl:call-template name="Controls">
   </xsl:call-template>
</svg>

<!-- End of the template which matches the root element -->
</xsl:template>

<xsl:template name="Controls">

<!-- The controls. Note that an XPath location path is used to select the
     text to be included on individual ellipses below. -->
   <g id="Controls">
      <a id="Q2Button">
         <ellipse cx="160" cy="450" rx="40" ry="15" style="stroke:red;
                  fill:red;"/>
         <text x="150" y="455" style="font-size:14; fill:black;
               stroke:black;">
            <xsl:value-of select="/QuarterlySales/Quarter[position()=2]
                                  /@name"/>
         </text>
      </a>
      <a id="Q3Button">
         <ellipse cx="260" cy="450" rx="40" ry="15" style="stroke:red;
                  fill:red;"/>
         <text x="250" y="455" style="font-size:14; fill:black;
               stroke:black;">
            <xsl:value-of select="/QuarterlySales/Quarter[position()=3]
                                  /@name"/>
         </text>
      </a>
      <a id="Q4Button">
         <ellipse cx="360" cy="450" rx="40" ry="15" style="stroke:red;
                  fill:red;"/>
         <text x="350" y="455" style="font-size:14; fill:black;
               stroke:black;">
            <xsl:value-of select="/QuarterlySales/Quarter[position()=4]
                                  /@name"/>
         </text>
      </a>
   </g>
</xsl:template>
</xsl:stylesheet>
```

To create the SVG, an XSLT processor such as Instant Saxon is needed. To create the SVG image, which is displayed below, enter the following command on the command line:

```
c:\InstantSaxon>saxon QuarterlySales.xml HorizBarvXSLT.xsl HorizBarvXSLT.svg
```

For alternative XSLT tools see Chapter 9 on XSLT.

Happily, the code in `HorizBarvXSLT.xsl` produces the desired end product, `HorizBarvXSLT.svg`:

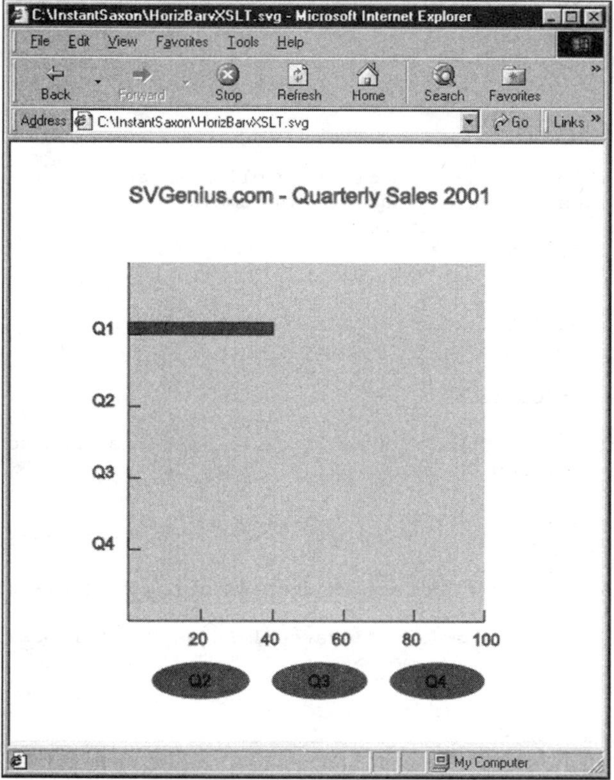

The above screen shot shows the chart generated using XSLT before any of the three animations have been activated.

A Vertical Bar Chart Created Using XSLT

In this section we will build on the use of XSLT shown in the preceding section. We will see a more complex, but more real-world, use of XSLT to create SVG. We will make use of several XSLT `<xsl:variable>` elements as well as several XSLT named templates to enable us to calculate the values of various parts of our bar chart.

Just to make things a little more interesting, this time we will create a vertical bar chart rather than a horizontal one. We will also tidy up a few minor issues from the previous charts. Did you notice that the check mark for a value of 100 went slightly outside the gray area? That was because half of an SVG stroke is painted inside an area and half outside. Because our check marks were fairly thick the overlap on to the white background was visible. So this time we will slightly extend the gray area. We will also extend the check marks right across the gray area, since this time we are going to display monthly sales rather than quarterly sales, and adding lines representing particular values will make it easier to make comparisons between months.

For readers not overly familiar with XSLT, the code has a text narrative interspersed, to help explain what is happening. If this section is a little overwhelming, it may help to go back and study the XSLT transformation in the previous section, then come back and take another look at this one – although more complex, it uses the same instructions.

As will be seen in the final result we can assume that the salesmen for SVGenius.com have worked successfully during all of 2001 but took a long, and well-deserved, break during July and August.

Here is the final display of the vertical bar chart:

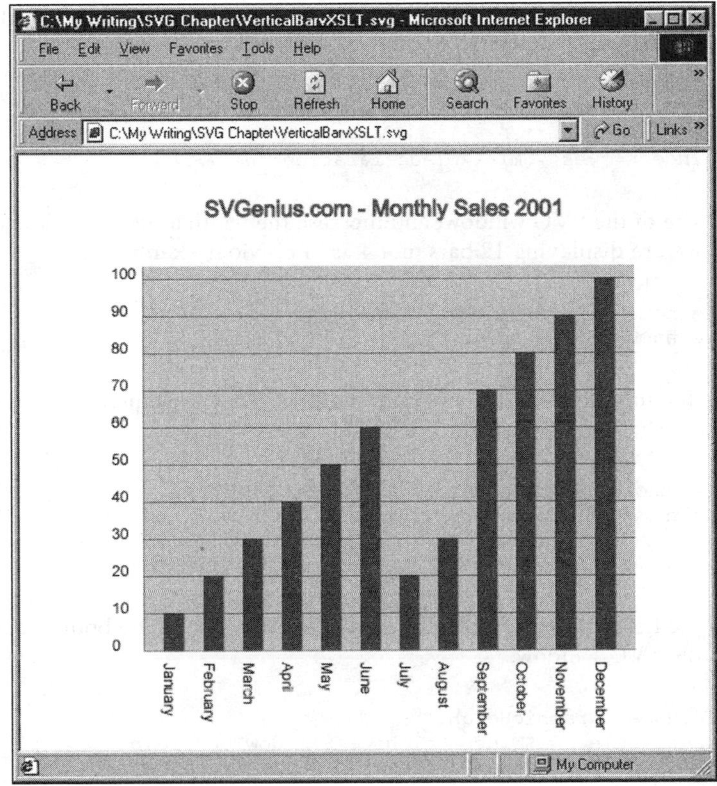

Below, the source XML document, `VerticalBarvXSLT.xml`, contains sales data for each month:

```
<?xml version='1.0'?>
<?xml-stylesheet href="VerticalBarvXSLT.xsl" type="text/xsl" ?>
<MonthlySales >
   <Year>2001</Year>
   <MaxValue>100</MaxValue>
      <Month name="January">10</Month>
      <Month name="February">20</Month>
      <Month name="March">30</Month>
      <Month name="April">40</Month>
      <Month name="May">50</Month>
      <Month name="June">60</Month>
      <Month name="July">20</Month>
      <Month name="August">30</Month>
```

```
        <Month name="September">70</Month>
        <Month name="October">80</Month>
        <Month name="November">90</Month>
        <Month name="December">100</Month>
</MonthlySales>
```

Here is the XSLT stylesheet, `VerticalBarvXSLT.xsl`:

```
<?xml version="1.0" encoding="UTF-8"?>
```

This stylesheet produces a vertical bar chart and makes extensive use of both global and local XSLT variables and named templates.

```
<xsl:stylesheet xmlns:xsl="http://www.w3.org/1999/XSL/Transform"
                version="1.0">
<xsl:output indent="yes" omit-xml-declaration="no"/>
```

We hard code the size of the SVG window, and increase the width a little, to allow for additional vertical bars since we are displaying 12 bars (not 4 as in previous examples).

```
<xsl:variable name="WindowWidth">600</xsl:variable>
<xsl:variable name="WindowHeight">500</xsl:variable>
```

We also hard code the top, bottom, left, and right margins. They are equal, as in previous examples, but they do not need to be.

```
<xsl:variable name="WindowTopMargin">100</xsl:variable>
<xsl:variable name="WindowBottomMargin">100</xsl:variable>
<xsl:variable name="WindowLeftMargin">100</xsl:variable>
<xsl:variable name="WindowRightMargin">100</xsl:variable>
```

Then we calculate the height of our graphic by subtracting the size of the bottom and the top margins from the height of the SVG window.

```
<xsl:variable name="GraphicHeight">
   <xsl:value-of select="$WindowHeight - $WindowTopMargin -
                 $WindowBottomMargin"/>
</xsl:variable>
```

The we calculate the Y coordinate of the bottom of the graphic (the bottom of the gray area).

```
<xsl:variable name="GraphicBottom">
   <xsl:value-of select="$WindowHeight - $WindowBottomMargin"/>
</xsl:variable>
```

Then we calculate the width of our graphic by subtracting the size of the left and right margins from the width of the SVG window.

```
<xsl:variable name="GraphicWidth">
   <xsl:value-of select="$WindowWidth - $WindowLeftMargin -
                 $WindowRightMargin"/>
</xsl:variable>
```

We now determine the number of vertical bars to be displayed by using the count() function to find the number of occurrences of Month in the source XML document. This allows the XSLT to be generalized to any (sensible) number of periods.

```
<xsl:variable name="NumBars">
   <xsl:value-of select="count(//Month)"/>
</xsl:variable>
```

To calculate the width of a bar, we divide the width of the gray area by twice the number returned by the count() function +1. This allows for even spacing.

```
<xsl:variable name="BarWidth">
   <xsl:value-of select="$GraphicWidth div ($NumBars * 2 + 1)"/>
</xsl:variable>
```

Now we determine, using the MaxValue from the XML source document, the maximum value to be displayed. A more generalized approach would be to determine the maximum value in the XML source and calculate a suitable MaxValue.

```
<xsl:variable name="MaxValue">
   <xsl:value-of select="/MonthlySales/MaxValue"/>
</xsl:variable>
```

The interval for labels and horizontal lines is hard coded. Again, this could be calculated to provide a sensible number of bars for the source data.

```
<xsl:variable name="IntervalValue">10</xsl:variable>
```

This is the XSLT template that matches the root of our source XML document. Most of the work of the XSLT is either carried out within, or called from this template. See also the global XSLT variables defined above.

```
<xsl:template match="/">
   <svg width="{$WindowWidth}" height="{$WindowHeight}">
```

This part creates the header information.

```
<text x="150" y="50" style="font-size:18; font-weight:normal; stroke:red;
      fill:red;">SVGenius.com - Monthly Sales
   <xsl:value-of select="/MonthlySales/Year"/>
</text>
```

We make our gray area just a little taller (10 pixels), than the maximum allowed value (MaxValue)

```
   <rect x="{$WindowLeftMargin}"
         y="{$WindowTopMargin - 10}"
         width="{$GraphicWidth}"
         height="{$GraphicHeight + 10}"
         style="fill:#CCCCCC;"/>
```

Then draw the vertical line up the left of the gray area, by calling a named template.

```
    <xsl:call-template name="VerticalLine"/>
```

Now we draw the horizontal line at the base of the gray area, plus the horizontal lines within the gray area, which represent the value of sales.

```
    <xsl:call-template name="HorizontalLines"/>
```

This applies the XSLT template for each <Month> element.

```
    <xsl:apply-templates select="//Month"/>
  </svg>
  </xsl:template>
```

Here, we create a vertical bar for each <Month> element in the XML source document, and add appropriate text.

```
  <xsl:template match="/MonthlySales/Month">
    <xsl:call-template name="VerticalBar">
      <xsl:with-param name="NumberofBar">
        <xsl:number count="*"/>
      </xsl:with-param>
    </xsl:call-template>

    <g style="fill:#000000; font-size:12; font-family:Arial">
      <xsl:call-template name="HorizLabels">
        <xsl:with-param name="NumberofBar">
          <xsl:number count="*"/>
        </xsl:with-param>
      </xsl:call-template>
    </g>
  </xsl:template>
```

This is the end of the template for `match="/MonthlySales/Month"`.

Here is the template to create the vertical bars to be displayed. Notice that stroke-width is reduced so as to produce a more elegant output line.

```
  <xsl:template name="VerticalBar">
    <xsl:param name="NumberofBar"></xsl:param>
    <xsl:variable name="BarValue">
      <xsl:value-of select="."/>
    </xsl:variable>

    <xsl:variable name="BarHeight">
      <xsl:value-of select="$BarValue * $GraphicHeight div $MaxValue"/>
    </xsl:variable>
    <rect x="{$WindowLeftMargin +$BarWidth +($BarWidth * 2 *($NumberofBar -
            3))}"
        y="{$GraphicBottom - $BarHeight}" style="fill:red;
            stroke:black; stroke-width:0.1"
        width="{$BarWidth}"
        height="{$BarHeight}"/>
  </xsl:template>
```

This template draws the line up the left side of the graph. We increase the height of the line by 10 pixels to allow for display of values equal to the `MaxValue` in the source document.

```
<xsl:template name="VerticalLine">
   <line x1="{$WindowLeftMargin}"
         y1="{$WindowTopMargin - 10}"
         x2="{$WindowLeftMargin}"
         y2="{$GraphicBottom}"
         style="stroke:#000099; stroke-width:0.1" />
</xsl:template>
```

This template creates, directly or by calling other named templates, the horizontal lines on the graphic – both the base line and those corresponding to non-zero values.

```
<xsl:template name="HorizontalLines">
   <xsl:variable name="NumHorizLines">
      <xsl:value-of select="$MaxValue div $IntervalValue"/>
   </xsl:variable>
   <xsl:call-template name="BaseLine">
      <xsl:with-param name="NumHorizLines">
         <xsl:value-of select="$NumHorizLines"/>
      </xsl:with-param>
   </xsl:call-template>
</xsl:template>
```

This named template creates a horizontal line at the bottom of the gray area, and calls another named template to create the other horizontal lines.

```
<xsl:template name="BaseLine">
   <xsl:param name="NumHorizLines"></xsl:param>
   <xsl:param name="CurrLineNumber">0</xsl:param>
   <xsl:variable name="LineSpacing">
      <xsl:value-of select="$GraphicHeight div $NumHorizLines"/>
   </xsl:variable>
   <xsl:if test="$NumHorizLines + 1 > $CurrLineNumber">

   <g style="fill:#000000; font-size:12; font-family:Arial">
      <xsl:call-template name="VertLabels">
         <xsl:with-param name="VertLabelText">
            <xsl:value-of select="$CurrLineNumber * $IntervalValue"/>
         </xsl:with-param>
         <xsl:with-param name="LineYCoord">
            <xsl:value-of select="$GraphicBottom - $LineSpacing *
                          $CurrLineNumber"/>
         </xsl:with-param>
      </xsl:call-template>
   </g>
```

Here we create the other horizontal lines within the gray area.

```
   <xsl:call-template name="OtherLines">
      <xsl:with-param name="LineYCoord">
         <xsl:value-of select="$GraphicBottom - $LineSpacing *
```

```
                           $CurrLineNumber"/>
      </xsl:with-param>
   </xsl:call-template>
   <xsl:call-template name="BaseLine">
      <xsl:with-param name="NumHorizLines">
         <xsl:value-of select="$NumHorizLines"/>
      </xsl:with-param>
      <xsl:with-param name="CurrLineNumber">
         <xsl:value-of select="$CurrLineNumber + 1"/>
      </xsl:with-param>
   </xsl:call-template>
   </xsl:if>
</xsl:template>
```

These templates draw the horizontal lines and labels indicating values within the gray area.

```
<xsl:template name="OtherLines">
   <xsl:param name="LineYCoord"></xsl:param>
   <line x1="{$WindowLeftMargin}"
         y1="{$LineYCoord}"
         x2="{$WindowLeftMargin + $GraphicWidth}"
         y2="{$LineYCoord}"
         style="stroke:#000000; stroke-width:0.2" />
</xsl:template>

<xsl:template name="VertLabels">
  <xsl:param name="VertLabelText"></xsl:param>
  <xsl:param name="LineYCoord"></xsl:param>
  <text x="{$WindowLeftMargin - 25}" y="{$LineYCoord}">
      <xsl:value-of select="$VertLabelText"/>
  </text>
</xsl:template>

<xsl:template name="HorizLabels">
   <xsl:param name="NumberofBar"></xsl:param>
   <xsl:variable name="TextxCoord">
      <xsl:value-of select="$WindowLeftMargin + $BarWidth +($BarWidth * 2
                      *($NumberofBar - 3))"/>
   </xsl:variable>
   <xsl:variable name="TextYCoord">
      <xsl:value-of select="$GraphicHeight + ($WindowTopMargin+10)"/>
   </xsl:variable>
```

Here we take the value of the name attribute from the source document, and use it as a label for the base line by transforming its position.

```
   <text x="{$TextxCoord}" y="{$TextYCoord}"
         transform="translate({$TextxCoord},{$TextYCoord}) rotate(90)
         translate(-{$TextxCoord},-{$TextYCoord})">
      <xsl:value-of select="@name"/>
   </text>
</xsl:template>
```

The end of the `HorizLabels` template.

```
</xsl:stylesheet>
```

The SVG code, `VerticalBarvXSLT.svg,` can be generated by Instant Saxon or any other XSLT processor and is also available in the code download from www.wrox.com.

Incorporating SVG in XSL-FO

The use of SVG we have seen so far in the chapter has been intended only for display on screen. Many business reports require presentation both on screen and on paper.

In Chapter 20 of this book there is an introduction to XSL-FO. Unless the reader is pretty much up to speed with XSL-FO, it would be worth reading this chapter before trying to follow the code in this section in detail.

Let's briefly take a look at how we might present the annual sales figures from the previous section as an SVG graphic embedded within an XSL-FO document. We do not deal with creating XSL-FO documents in this chapter, so we shall simply see the XSL-FO document with commented code, and show the result with the vertical bar chart placed within the report.

In the Antenna House XSL Formatter, our XSL-FO and SVG sales report, with a different explanation for the fall in sales in July and August, looks like this:

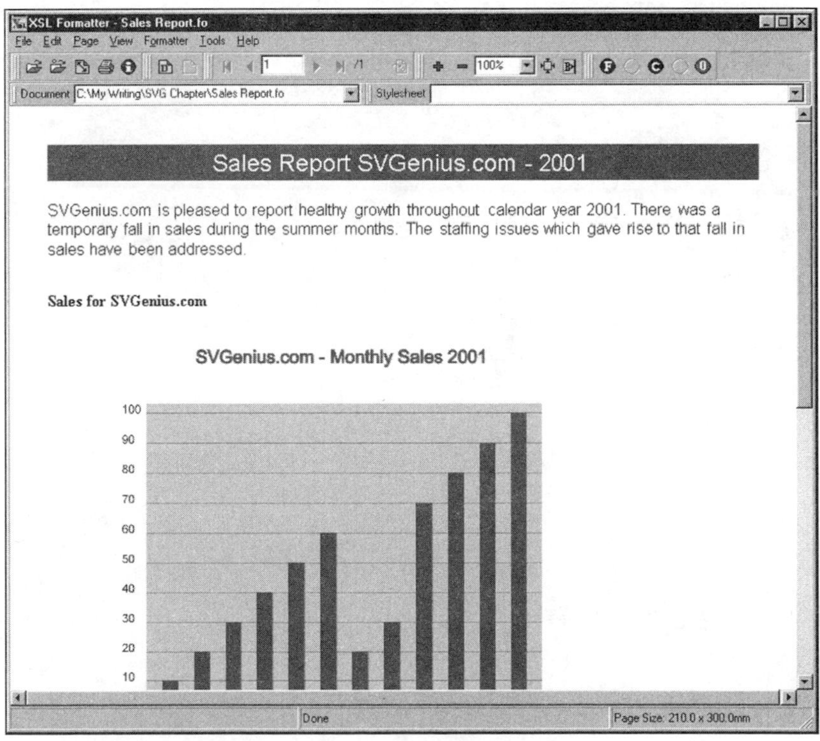

The image displayed was produced statically. It is possible to produce multiple output documents using XSLT but that is beyond the scope of this chapter.

The XSL-FO file, `SalesReport.fo`, used to produce the screen shot is shown here:

```
<?xml version='1.0'?>

<!-- This is SalesReport.fo. It will display an annual sales report for
     www.SVGenius.com for the calender year 2001. -->
<fo:root xmlns:fo="http://www.w3.org/1999/XSL/Format">
<fo:layout-master-set>

<!-- Page layout information for a page to be displayed on screen. -->
<fo:simple-page-master master-name="Report"
                       page-height="30cm"
                       page-width="21cm"
                       margin-top="1cm"
                       margin-bottom="1cm"
                       margin-left="1cm"
                       margin-right="1cm">
   <fo:region-body margin-top="0cm"/>
   <fo:region-before extent="2cm"/>
   <fo:region-after extent="1cm"/>
</fo:simple-page-master>

</fo:layout-master-set>

<fo:page-sequence master-name="Report">
<fo:flow flow-name="xsl-region-body">

<!-- This defines a header in white text on a red colored background -->
   <fo:block
      font-size="18pt"
      font-family="sans-serif"
      line-height="24pt"
      space-after.optimum="15pt"
      background-color="red"
      color="white"
      text-align="center"
      padding-top="3pt">
         Sales Report SVGenius.com - 2001
   </fo:block>

<!-- This defines plain paragraph text for this document. -->
   <fo:block font-size="12pt"
             font-family="sans-serif"
             space-after.optimum="15pt"
             text-align="left">
      SVGenius.com is pleased to report healthy growth throughout
      calendar year 2001. There was a temporary fall in sales during the
      summer months. The staffing issues, which gave rise to that fall,
      have been addressed.
   </fo:block>

   <fo:block space-before="2em" font="bold large serif" keep-with-
```

```
                                    next="always">
        Sales for SVGenius.com
    </fo:block>
    <fo:block>
        <fo:external-graphic content-width="600px" content-height="500px"
                                    src="VerticalBarvXSLT.svg"/>
    </fo:block>

<!-- This defines plain paragraph text for this document. -->
    <fo:block font-size="12pt"
              font-family="sans-serif"
              space-after.optimum="15pt"
              text-align="left">
        The Antenna House XSL Formatter displays the SVG image using the
        &lt;fo:external-graphic&gt; element. At the present time the Antenna
        House XSL Formatter does not support the &lt;fo:instream-foreign-
        object&gt; element but is likely to do so in a future release.
    </fo:block>

</fo:flow>
</fo:page-sequence>
</fo:root>
```

Some Commercial Tools To Produce SVG

In this chapter we have seen some basic techniques which allow us to begin creating charts with SVG graphics. In many circumstances the reader may wish to incorporate a generation of SVG charts and graphics within their own programs. However, there are also commercially available tools that will produce SVG charts "off the shelf".

In the following section there will be a brief description of two such tools, Corda PopChart Image Server Pro, and SVGMaker. Corda PopChart Image Server Pro is a cross-platform tool capable of producing SVG statically or dynamically. SVGMaker is available for the Windows platform and produces static SVG images. It is to be expected that a range of new SVG-capable graphing programs will appear during the lifetime of this book, so further choices are likely to be available to suit many project types.

Corda PopChart Image Server Pro

Corda PopChart Image Server Pro (PCIS) is a Java-based charting server, which is capable of producing graphs in a range of formats including PNG, GIF, Flash, and of relevance for this chapter, SVG. PCIS can be used with JSP, ASP, and ColdFusion. Further information on Corda PopChart Image Server Pro is available at http://www.corda.com including several online examples. An evaluation version is available for download.

The author downloaded the version for Window 98, and installed it without difficulty. To run PCIS you will need a Java Virtual Machine already installed, or use the option to download a JVM with PCIS. Also included in the download are copious help files, which deal with most likely scenarios. The only difficulty encountered was that it recommends installing the "appearance files" in the `apfiles` directory, but this is not the default; include the path in a URL, so the appearance files for SVG images to be found and will display.

To customize the colors, etc. for a particular type of graph, an "appearance file" needs to be created, which consists of various color and other settings for the desired type of graph to be produced. The following screen shot shows the use of PopChart Builder to create a grayscale "appearance file" for a line chart.

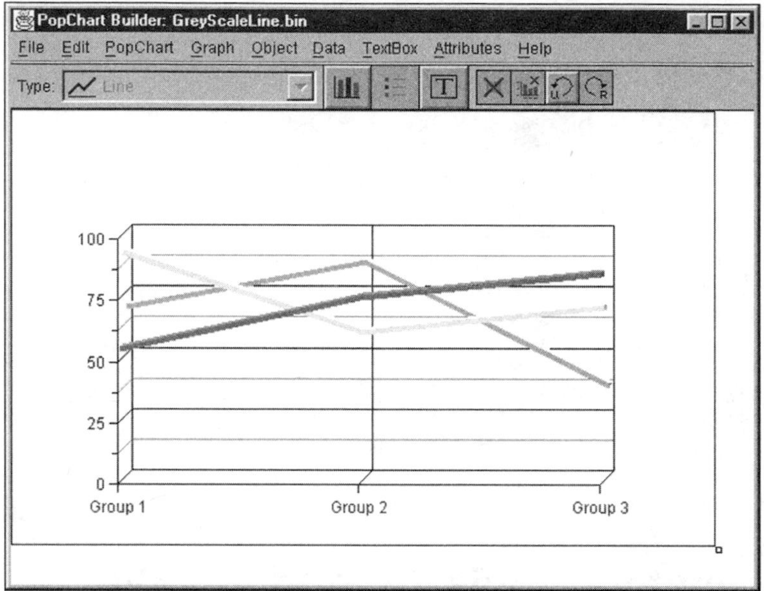

As is visible in the above image, there is an extensive range of menus available within PopChart Builder, allowing choices of the type of graph, and customizations for it. The appearance file can be saved and applied to multiple sets of raw data, if required.

PCIS can produce an extensive range of charts, of which several examples are provided with ready-made "appearance files". The following screen shot shows a 3D bar graph in SVG in Internet Explorer 5.5. The URL in the browser bar will give you some impression of the syntax that PCIS uses to locate desired files in an appropriate format.

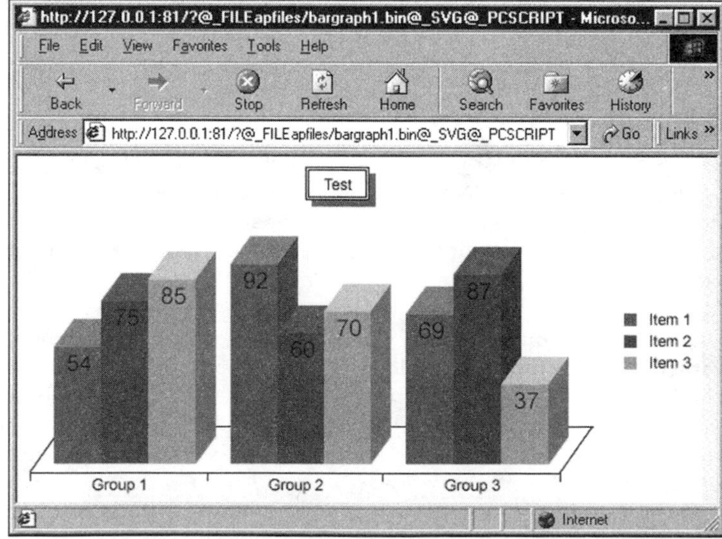

SVGMaker

SVGMaker can produce static SVG graphics of the type that we developed by hand earlier in this chapter, and more sophisticated variants from a range of Windows illustration or CAD programs. SVGMaker functions as a "printer driver" for Windows based illustration, CAD or graphing programs. For example, Excel 97 was used to produce the SVG output files shown later. SVG is output either as standard (`.svg`) or as compressed files (`.svgz`). A beta version of SVGMaker is available for Windows 98, and this was used to produce the screen shots shown below. Versions of SVGMaker are also available for Windows NT and Windows 2000.

Installation of SVGMaker is straightforward. It is as simple as adding a new printer driver to your Windows machine and is fully explained in the documentation provided with the program. To generate an SVG file, either in normal or compressed format, simply "print" your illustration using SVGMaker as the printer driver and be sure to select the "Print to file" option as shown in this screen shot:

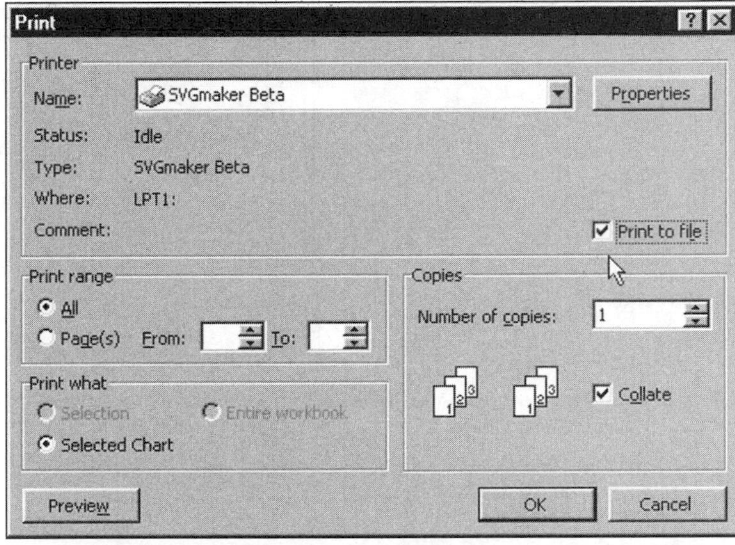

The Windows graphing software, from which you are "printing" determines the range of graphs. For example, this screen shot shows a simple bar graph produced from Excel 97.

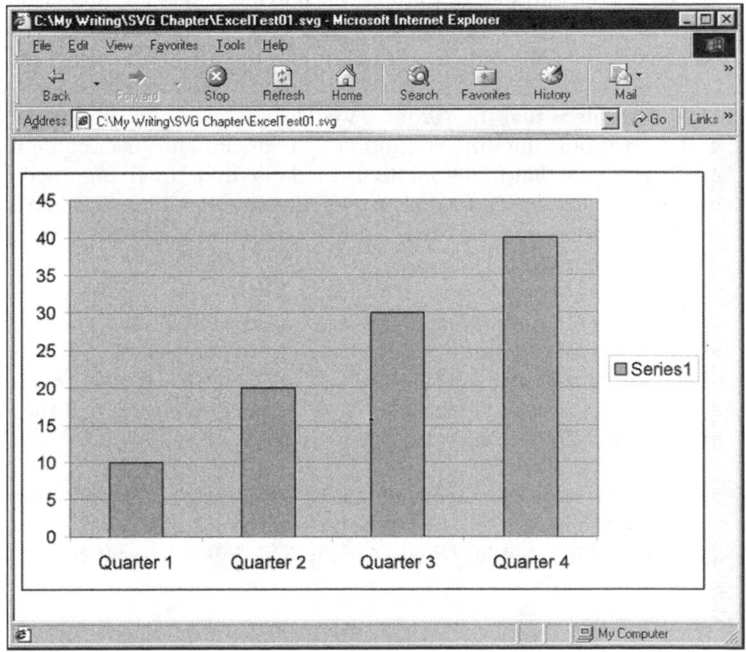

SVGMaker can display the full range of pre-defined or customized graphics produced by the program whose graphical output is "printing". For example, in this screen shot you can see the 3-D line chart output from some simple sales figures in Excel 97.

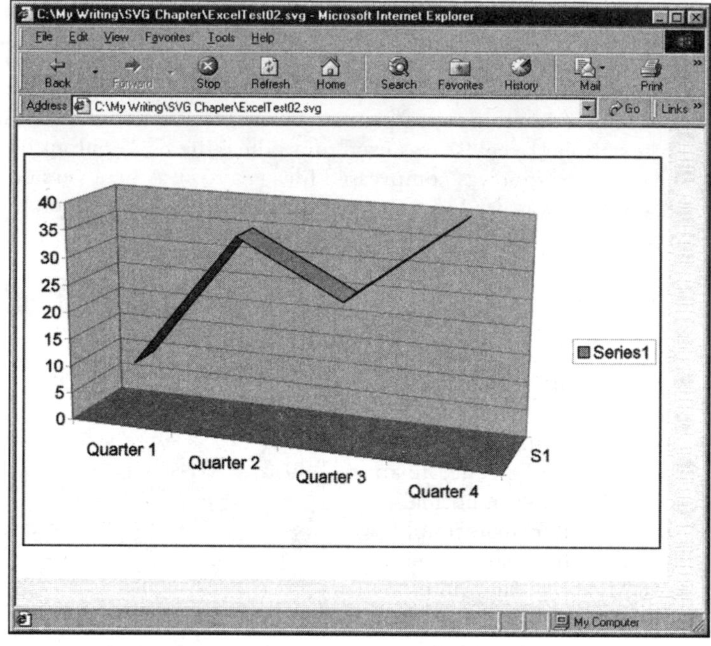

Further information on SVGMaker is available at http://www.svgmaker.com.

Looking Ahead

We have concentrated in this chapter mostly on SVG. One reason for that is that SVG tools, including viewers, are readily available and are pretty stable. Yet not one of the tools shown in the earlier part of this chapter is complete. So there is more potential, still to be unleashed.

One example is that the Adobe SVG Viewer (Version 2 Release Candidate 1) does not, at the time of writing, support the import of other SVG documents or document fragments using the SVG `<image>` element. Once that functionality is available then it will be possible to import standard parts of SVG images. For example, if a company has a standard logo, or copyright statement that they wish to include in all their SVG images, then that SVG fragment could be stored separately and imported using the `<image>` element.

SVG allows the embedding of foreign objects within an SVG image, using the `<foreignObject>` element. Thus it should be possible to embed, say, an XHTML form within an SVG image, to allow collection of data. Since both the XHTML and SVG can use external Cascading Style Sheets for storing style information, such CSS files could be used to ensure that the styling of the SVG and the XHTML embedded within it remain coordinated.

SVG can be used by other XML-based technologies. The X-Smiles browser (http://www.x-smiles.org), currently available as a preview release can combine SVG with XSL-FO, SMIL and XForms. See the section on the X-Smiles browser in the XSL-FO chapter (Chapter 20).

The remit for this chapter was to introduce the display of business data using SVG. SVG though, is a general-purpose XML-based graphics format. SVG can be used to produce navigation bars and other web page elements, to produce interactive graphical reports, and for many other purposes. At present no book length material on SVG is available, but if this chapter has been of interest, we would encourage you to explore SVG's many strengths. SVG can add a new, colorful and animated dimension to your XML skills.

Summary

We have covered a lot of ground in this chapter, but there has been space only to scratch the surface of SVG's capabilities.

We looked briefly at how SVG compares to other available Web graphics technologies. We had a very brief look at SVG generally and looked more specifically at some SVG elements, which we would need for our examples within the chapter.

We created a horizontal bar in SVG then added some interactivity to it, in the process making use of two straightforward types of SVG animation, based on SMIL Animation. We looked at how to separate the styling information from other content in an SVG document, using Cascading Style Sheets.

We looked at how to use XSLT to create a horizontal bar chart and then used more complex XSLT to create a vertical bar chart. We then took that vertical bar chart and created a simple sales report, by embedding our SVG bar chart in an XSL-FO document.

We briefly looked at two commercially available graphics generators, which can provide an alternative approach to generating SVG images. Finally, we looked ahead to the potential that later releases of SVG tools could bring to the XML community.

The future for SVG is bright. Visual display of XML-based information is an excellent fit with SVG's capabilities. When SVG is combined more fully with SMIL 2.0 and SMIL Animation, programmatic control of the multimedia display of XML-based information will have exciting new possibilities.

Online Resources

Tools:

As mentioned earlier in the chapter SVG Viewers may be downloaded from:

- Adobe SVG Viewer – http://www.adobe.com/svg/
- Apache Batik Viewer & toolkit – http://xml.apache.org/

SVG Online Tutorials:

- KevLinDev.com – Kevin Lindsey's SVG tutorial and demos. http://www.kevlindev.com

SVG Web Sites:

- SVGSpider.com The world's "first" all-SVG web site. A proof-of-concept, that SVG can be used to author web pages. http://www.svgspider.com/default.svg

19

VoiceXML

The promise of communicating with computing devices using natural language has long attracted the imagination of the public, the creative energy of technologists and fabulists, and the resources of investors. From the passive, benign example of Star Trek: ("Earl Grey, hot," says Captain Picard to an empty room and, in a heartbeat, a wall panel opens revealing a steaming mug), to Stanley Kubrick's befuddled and maleficent HAL, the futures we envision are all populated with machines that hear, speak, and hopefully obey.

The current state of the art falls short of this vision, but speech recognition and its sister technologies, speech synthesis (also called text-to-speech or TTS) and speaker verification, are sufficiently mature that applications using them can be developed and deployed in mission-critical settings. Speech technology is ready for prime time.

In this chapter, we will:

- Introduce the emerging Voice Web and its historical context
- Discuss voice application architecture and the unique challenges presented by voice application development
- Describe the VoiceXML 1.0 Specification
- Discuss its limitations
- Direct you to online resources for developing voice applications

The Voice Web

The WWW is a medium for the exchange of distributed data. Since our primary means of accessing that data is via a Graphical User Interface, we are accustomed to regarding that data as intrinsically graphical. However, HTML provides only a representation of that data, a particular view. As we know, XML technologies help separate data from presentation, providing for a wide range of user interface modalities.

VoiceXML provides an alternative presentation of that data – platform-independent, amenable to tools and techniques familiar to Web developers, and accessible to anybody with a telephone.

The Voice Web is the network of gateways, servers, and applications that provide telephone access to Web-based information and transactions. It is growing rapidly, and the emergence and adoption of the VoiceXML standard will help the Voice Web reach its full commercial potential.

We can take the comparison between HTML and VoiceXML a step further and examine the means by which information is gathered from the user and sent upstream for each markup language. The following HTML form gathers information from the user and sends it to a Java servlet for processing.

```
<form method="post" action="./servlets/survey">
   Do you have ketchup with scrambled eggs?
   <br>
   <select name="selExample" size="3">
      <option>Always
      <option>Sometimes
      <option>Never
   </select>
   <br>
   <input type="submit"/>
</form>
```

The following VoiceXML snippet prompts the user, gathers the response, and matches the utterance against a grammar. As in the HTML example, the result is sent to a Java servlet for processing. (Program logic for missed recognition, cases in which the software failed to match voice input to grammar rules, is omitted from this example).

```
<form>
   <field name="select">
      <prompt>Do you have ketchup with scrambled eggs?</prompt>
      <grammar>[always sometimes never] </grammar>
   </field>
   <block>
      <submit next="./servlets/survey"/>
   </block>
</form>
```

Details about these tags will be provided later in this chapter. For now, just note the similarities between the two examples. In HTML, we use:

- A `form` to structure the gathering of data
- `select` and `option` tags to provide bullets and entry boxes
- `submit` to send the results off back to the server

In VoiceXML:

- `form` has the identical role of encapsulating the interaction
- `prompt` and `grammar` gather the data
- `submit` moves it upstream

A Pocket Lexicon for Speech Technology

Speech technology is rife with acronyms and domain-specific terminology. The following is a brief glossary to ease the road ahead.

- **Active grammar** – a speech or DTMF grammar referred to by the currently executing element
- **ASR** – Automatic Speech Recognition
- **DTMF** – the tones used in telephones for 'touch-tone' dialing. DTMF actually stands for Dual Tone Multi Frequency, because a DTMF tone is the sum of two sine waves.
- **Earcon** – an auditory cue to provide reference or feedback to the user of a speech application
- **Grammar** – a schema for designating the well-formed phrases or sentences drawn from a vocabulary
- **Implementation platform** – A computer with the software and hardware required to support the interactions defined by VoiceXML, also called a **voice browser** or **VoiceXML Gateway**
- **IVR** – Interactive Voice Response
- **Language model** – a probabilistic description of the distribution of words within a language. For instance, *walk* is more likely to be followed by *the* than *stentorian*
- **Mixed initiative** – a human-machine interaction in which either the human or the computer can initiate an action
- **PSTN** – Public Switched Telephone Network
- **Reference model** – a computer representation of vocabulary for speech recognition or of speakers' voices for speaker verification
- **Speaker identification** – determining the identity of a speaker by computationally processing his or her voice
- **Speaker verification** – determining that a speaker is who they claim to be by computationally processing his or her voice
- **Template** – a computer representation of a vocabulary item
- **Text-to-Speech** – often referred to as **TTS**, machine synthesis of human speech from text
- **Vocabulary** – the specific utterances for which the recognizer contains models or templates
- **Voiceprint** – also called a **spectogram**, a graphical display of an utterance in which frequency is plotted against time, with the signal amplitude indicated by a gray-scale
- **VUI** – Voice User Interface
- **Wizard of Oz scenario** – a VUI design exercise involving two people in which one person plays the role of the machine and the other plays the role of the user

Recent History of Speech Recognition

Speech recognition technology has evolved along two parallel, largely independent tracks. Early research in the eighties focused on telephone-based, limited dictionary, speaker-independent systems capable of recognizing digits and a few commands. The computing power required for effective deployment of these systems was prohibitive by the standards of the day, however, and the UI design limitations imposed by such small vocabularies were steep. The technology languished.

At the same time, work was being done to commercialize speaker-dependent dictation software targeted at personal computer users. IBM, Lernout & Hauspie, and Dragon Systems all delivered shrink-wrapped products that worked fairly well. However, these products all required the user to 'train' the software, and even after such training, the error rate was often unacceptably high.

In the nineties, much progress was made on the telephony side. Speech recognition algorithms based on hidden Markov models (a two-pronged probabilistic approach for predicting states and state transitions) advanced considerably, as did the price and performance of computers. It soon became practical to deploy systems capable of recognizing hundreds, even thousands, of utterances. Current successful speech recognition applications are enabled by a threshold of accuracy and speed achieved about two years ago; a casual metric for that threshold is the ability to enter a 16 digit credit card number or any city and state in the US or a company on the NYSE with 85-90% utterance accuracy and less than 4 seconds latency. Furthermore, recognition errors or ambiguities have less impact in applications where they can be resolved by effective VUI (Voice User Interface) design.

> **Human**: "*(cough)* Uh, get – what's my ... account – *(cough)* – *account* balance."
>
> **Computer**: "Excuse me, could you repeat that?"
>
> **Human**: "What is my account balance?"
>
> **Computer**: "Just a moment ... "

In this example, the ASR system was unable to match the utterance against the active grammar and returned a confidence score below the threshold set by the application architect, triggering the polite request for clarification.

The year 2000 was a banner year for speech recognition:

- Nuance and SpeechWorks, two of the leaders in the provision of core speech technologies, both had successful IPOs
- Locus Dialogue, another leading technology provider, was acquired by Infospace
- The **voice portal**, an aggregation of services accessed by speech recognition through a single phone number, became a familiar fixture in the industry press and several such entities were launched, including TellMe Networks, BeVocal, and HeyAnita
- Several large companies (IBM, Microsoft, Siebel) articulated their positions regarding the emerging **voice web**
- A host of startups, including Webversa, VoiceGenie, and Speechwise Technologies, announced product or service offerings

In May 2000, the VoiceXML Forum (http://www.VoiceXML.org), an industry consortium founded by IBM, Lucent, Motorola, and AT&T, whose membership at time of writing numbers 460 companies, submitted Version 1.0 of the VoiceXML Specification to the W3C. At its May meetings in Paris, the W3C's Voice Browser Working Group agreed to adopt VoiceXML 1.0 as the basis for a W3C dialog markup language.

Voice Application Architecture

Telephone-based speech technology in its current form is really a convergence of three technologies: speech services (recognition, verification, and synthesis), telephony, and the Internet. It is therefore not surprising that the architecture of a typical speech application can be somewhat more complex than its conventional web-based counterpart.

It is convenient to decompose server-side speech applications into layers: hardware, speech, presentation, middleware, and data.

Data	Enterprise Applications	Databases	Other Data Sources	
Middleware	Session Manager Configuration Manager User Profiles Logging and Monitoring	Publishing Engine	Back-end Integration (object-relational mapping, enterprise API's etc)	Business Logic
Presentation	Prompts	Grammars	Call Flow	
Speech	Speech Recognition	Speaker Verification	Speech Synthesis	
Hardware	Telephony Platform	Servers		

Hardware

The hardware layer consists of a telephony platform and various servers: for ASR, Web hosting, and the application. The hardware itself consists typically of industry standard Windows or UNIX servers with standard telephony boards providing an interface to the PSTN or to Voice-Over-IP.

There is much latitude here in configuration. An Application Service Provider deployment model will have different requirements than a single enterprise deployment.

Speech

The speech layer has three primary components: the recognition engine, a TTS (text-to-speech) engine, and speaker verification software. In addition, this layer contains any support for dynamic grammar generation and audio recording software.

Presentation

The presentation layer consists of the various files and components that comprise the Voice User Interface.

- Prompts and **earcons** are typically `.wav` or `.vox` audio files
- Grammars are text files that provide rules for extracting semantic content from recognized utterances
- The call flow provides the connective logic between VUI states. It is here that the boundary between presentation and application logic can blur – the Achilles heel of speech application design.

Middleware

One has to preface any discussion of middleware for speech applications with the observation that there are few middleware products on the market today. Like Gertrude Stein's Oakland, "there's no there there". However, as the demands on speech application run-time environments increase, and as development costs drive the use of Rapid Application Development methodologies to deliver timely, robust software, middleware products will emerge, just as they did for the 'vanilla' Web.

Speech application middleware mediates between speech and telephony services and enterprise APIs. An ideal platform will provide a dynamic binding between VUI states on the one hand and enterprise components on the other. Such a platform will also provide prosaic but essential services such as logging, monitoring, configuration management, and session management, and encapsulate the messy business of conforming to proprietary back ends. Finally, the keystone of any such platform will be a publishing engine that folds result sets from the data layer into a presentation format such as VoiceXML.

Currently, almost all of the above must be built on a custom basis.

Data

The data layer consists of enterprise applications, relational databases, and HTTP servers that deliver XML, HTML, and VoiceXML documents.

It should be noted that speech applications do not require all of these services. A simple speech application may only require a VoiceXML Gateway and a VoiceXML Document Server.

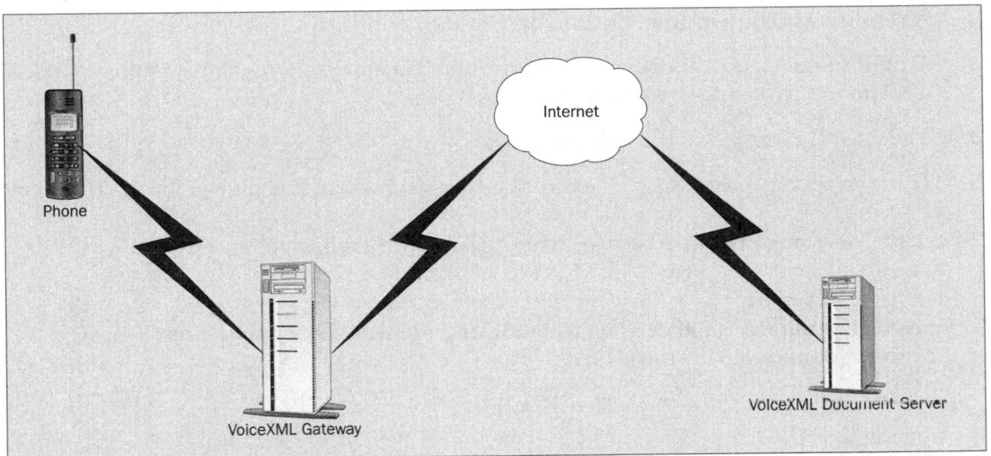

Anatomy of Request-Response in Voice Applications

Let's look at how a GUI and a VUI might use the same enterprise application resources.

In a typical three-tier database-driven application, the request-response lifecycle is structured as follows.

- User requests a page by clicking on a link or typing a URL in the browser window
- The browser creates an HTTP request and sends it to the web server
- The web server resolves the path and forwards the request to the middleware, probably residing on another machine
- Business logic and application logic are invoked (for example, a SQL query is composed and executed)
- A resultset is returned from the database to the middleware (XML-based formats for interchanging and working with the data are possible)
- A publishing engine applies HTML markup to the data to produce a web page
- The page is returned to the web server
- The web server passes the page on to the browser client.

Here is the request-response lifecycle for a VoiceXML application integrated with the above back end:

- User requests data over the telephone, using natural language. "I want to hear a description of Gone With the Wind"
- The ASR engine matches the utterance against the active grammar, then uses the grammar semantic to set the tokens `[description, GoneWithTheWind]`
- The Gateway wraps the resulting name-value pairs in an HTTP request and sends it to the web server
- The web server resolves the path and forwards the request to the middleware, probably residing on another machine
- Business logic and application logic are invoked, probably culminating in the composition of a SQL query which is passed on to the database server

- A resultset is returned from the database to the middleware
- A publishing engine, perhaps in concert with a personalization engine, applies VoiceXML markup to the data to produce a Voice Web page
- The page is returned to the web server
- The web server passes the page on to the Gateway, where it is played for the telephony client

As you can see, the similarities in these two scenarios far outweigh the differences.

VoiceXML facilitates rapid development of Internet-based speech applications by using the existing application infrastructure.

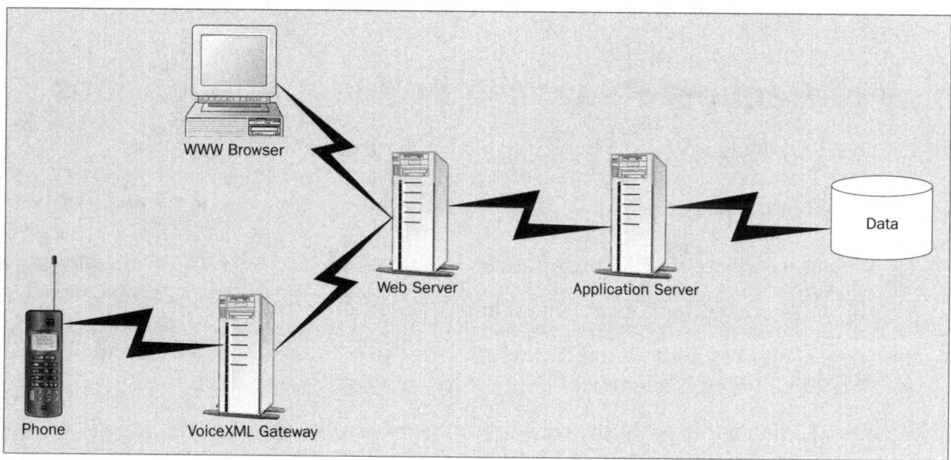

VoiceXML Basics

A VoiceXML application, consisting of one or more VoiceXML documents, is a finite state machine. Each state, or **dialog**, determines the next dialog in the call flow.

Two kinds of dialogs are permitted: **forms** and **menus**:

- Forms gather input and present information to the user
- Menus offer choices to the user and transition to another dialog based on the user input

Forms

Let's examine a simple VoiceXML document.

```
<?xml version="1.0" encoding="utf-8"?>

<vxml version="1.0">
   <form>
```

```
        <block> Would you like to play a game?</block>
      </form>
   </vxml>
```

You can test this script by registering at http://café.bevocal.com, *and uploading the file to your account. Activate the file, and run it in the Vocal Scripter to see the output. This tool really helps in building and debugging VoiceXML documents.*

As in all XML documents, it is recommended that VoiceXML documents begin with the XML version declaration. The document itself should be enclosed by the `<vxml tags>`. The `<block>` tags denote a container for non-interactive code. The above document causes the gateway to play the text enclosed by the `<block>` tags in TTS and hang up.

Consider the call flow for a retail v-commerce application (voice-driven electronic commerce). The user logs on, searches for one or more items and adds then to a shopping cart, and checks out.

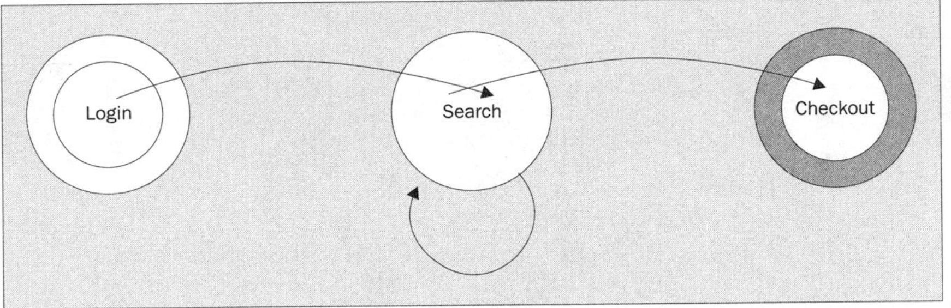

The corresponding VoiceXML application might be structured as follows

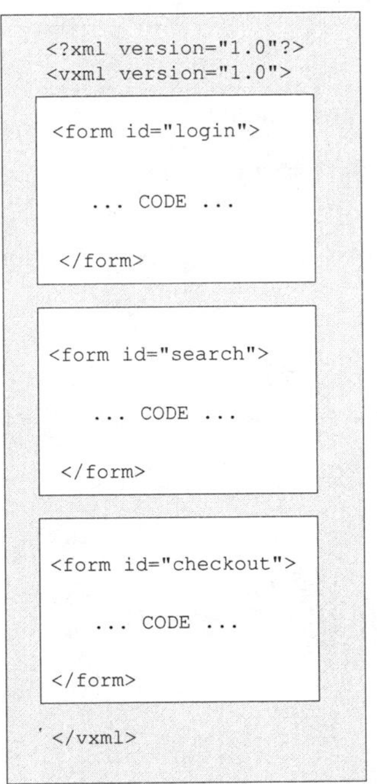

In practice, one would most likely factor an application such as this into separate documents. The point is that forms provide a convenient encapsulation for VUI tasks.

The <goto> element dictates transitions between forms:

```
<form id="login">
   ... CODE ...
   <block>
      <goto next="#search"/>
   </block>
</form>
```

Form Items

Form items are elements visited in the course of form interpretation that perform various tasks. **Field items** gather data; **Control items** are associated with non-recognition-based tasks that assist in gathering data.

Field Item	Description
<field>	Gathers input via speech recognition or DTMF ('touch tone')
<record>	Records an audio clip from the user
<transfer>	Transfers the user to another telephone number. The bridge attribute specifies whether the original caller can resume his or her session with the interpreter (bridging), or whether no resumption is possible (blind transfer)
<object>	Invokes a platform-specific object
<subdialog>	Analogous to a function call; invokes another dialog

Control Item	Description
<block>	A sequence of procedural statements used for prompting and computation
<initial>	Controls initial interaction in a mixed-initiative form

With the above tags, we can begin to construct interactive applications:

```
<form id="loginForm">
   <field name="userName">
      <prompt>What is your name?</prompt>
      <grammar src="./grammars/staff.gram" type="application/x-jsgf" />
      <filled>
         <prompt>Hello, <value expr="userName"/> </prompt>
      </filled>
   </field>
   <field name="userPin">
      <prompt>Please say your four digit pin</prompt>
      <grammar src="./grammars/pins.gram" type="application/x-jsgf" />

      ... etc ...
   </field>
</form>
```

The first field element indicates that we must find a value for the variable `userName`. Within the grammar element, the path to the grammar file and the MIME type are specified. The `<filled>` element encloses actions to be taken when the utterance is successfully matched against the active grammar.

The corresponding dialog fragment goes something like this:

> **Computer**: What is your name
>
> **Human**: Tony Blair
>
> **Computer**: Hello, Tony Blair. Please say your four-digit pin...

Grammars

A grammar specifies the allowable utterances that can be assigned to the field. Simple grammars can be specified inline.

```
      <prompt>What is your favorite primary color?</prompt>
      <grammar>[vanilla chocolate strawberry]</grammar>
```

VoiceXML defines several built-in grammars that can be specified by a `field`'s `type` attribute:

```
   <field name="sale" type="boolean">
      <prompt>Would you like to buy this fine automobile?</prompt>
      <filled>
         <prompt>I heard <value expr="sale" /> </prompt>
      </filled>
   </field>
```

Other built-in grammar types are `date`, `digits`, `currency`, `number`, `phone`, and `time`.

Variables and Execution Flow

VoiceXML variables are equivalent to ECMAScript variables. In addition to field declarations, which we have seen, they can also be declared by `<var>` elements. The snippet below assigns the value `Casablanca` to the `movie` variable:

```
   <var name="movie" expr="Casablanca" />
```

The following variable scopes are available, in ascending order: anonymous, dialog, document, application, and session. Variable declaration is scoped to the parent element. A variable `X` declared within `vxml` tags has document scope and can be referred to as `X` or `document.X`. A variable `Y` declared within `form` tags, has dialog scope and can be referred to as `Y` or `dialog.Y`.

VoiceXML also supports limited control flow constructs. Conditional logic can be implemented in simple `if...elseif` blocks.

```
<if cond="userChoice=='calendar'" />
   <prompt>Your calendar items for today are ... </prompt>
<elseif cond="userChoice=='to-do'" />
   <prompt>Items remaining on your to do list are ... </prompt>
...
```

The <goto> element is used in transitions to:

- Another form item in the current form
- Another dialog in the current document
- Another document

The <submit> element also allows you to change to another document. It also allows you submit name-value pairs to the document server via HTTP GET or POST.

Menus

A VoiceXML menu is a form with a heaped teaspoon of syntactic sugar to simplify choosing from a range of options. An anonymous field collects data from the user and transfers control to different places based on the results.

This menu offers the user a choice between News, Weather, and Stocks.

```
<menu>
   <prompt> Would you like news, weather or sports?</prompt>
   <choice next="./news.vxml">News</choice>
   <choice next="./weather.vxml">Weather</choice>
   <choice next="./sports.vxml">Sports</choice>
</menu>
```

Another method for describing choices is the <enumerate> element, which provides a mechanism for automatically generating the choices available to the user. The code enclosed by a pair of <enumerate> tags is a template that is applied to each choice in the order they appear between the menu tags. When <enumerate> is empty, a default template listing all the choices is applied.

```
<menu>
   <prompt> Please choose one of the following: <enumerate/></prompt>
   <choice next="./news.vxml">News</choice>
   <choice next="./weather.vxml">Weather</choice>
   <choice next="./sports.vxml">Sports</choice>
</menu>
```

The corresponding dialog is as follows:

> **Computer**: Please choose one of the following: news, weather, sports.

Directed Dialog Versus Mixed Initiative

In directed dialogs, forms are filled in the order they appear in the VoiceXML document. All of the examples we have seen so far are directed dialogs. The user experience is modal, a short evolutionary step from ancestral IVR (interactive voice response) applications, in which the user pressed touch-tone phone buttons to navigate menu choices.

> **Computer**: Would you like to access your checking or savings account?
>
> **Human**: Checking

Computer: Would you like to hear your account balance or transfer funds?

Human: Transfer funds

Computer: To which account?

Directed dialogs have field-level grammars. That is, each field to be filled has an associated grammar that dictates the allowable values for that field.

It is more desirable for an application to allow for an interaction that follows a more natural speech pattern.

Computer: Welcome to Bank By Voice. What would you like to do?

Human: Transfer a thousand dollars from savings to checking

Mixed-initiative dialogs like this allow either the computer or the user to initiate conversation. The user can usually fill several fields without waiting to be prompted. Mixed-initiative dialogs have form-level grammars. Their fields can be filled in any order, and more than one field can be filled with a single utterance. These grammars can span several dialogs, allowing a user to accomplish complex tasks very efficiently.

However, the grammars can become very complex, application design is trickier, and the implementation is more prone to error. Something we know about web applications is that users will try interactions with the site that the designers will never imagine. Mixed-initiative design encourages users to try things that you didn't anticipate!

The initial interaction with a mixed-initiative form is specified with the `<initial>` tag. Some, but possibly not all, of the fields will be filled as a result of that prompt. The rest of the required fields are filled via directed dialogs.

Links

Links contain grammars that, when matched, trigger either a transition to a new document or the throwing of an event. This link will activate when `pizza` is uttered, or the user presses `1`.

```
<link next="./pizza.vxml">
   <grammar>[pizza dtmf-1]</grammar>
</link>
```

This link throws a `help` event when a small set of frustrated utterances is matched.

```
<link event="help">
   <grammar>[doh dammit (help me)]</grammar>
</link>
```

Events

The platform can throw events in response to error conditions such as no input, unintelligible input, or accidental disconnect. Application-specific events can also be thrown from within executable content, invoking an associated event handler.

The `<throw>` element throws an event, whether built-in or application defined.

Available catch elements include <catch>, <error>, <help>, <noinput>, and <nomatch>. Form items contain counters that allow us to construct different behaviors, if the same event is thrown multiple times.

```
<form id="pick_a_number">
   <field name="guess">
      <prompt>Pick a number from one to ten</prompt>
      <grammar>three</grammar>
      <help>It is less than four and more than two</help>
      <catch event ="nomatch noinput" count="3">
         <prompt> Try again!</prompt>
      </catch>
   </field>
   <block>
      <goto next="#lucky_winner"/>
   </block>
</form>
```

Object

Through the <object> element, the VoiceXML application can access platform-specific services, for example, speaker verification, VUI components such as Nuance Speech Objects, native components, additional telephony functionality, and so on. The <param> element is used to pass parameters to the object.

Multiple Document Applications

Just as a web GUI can span multiple HTML documents, a VoiceXML application can consist of more than one VoiceXML document. In these cases, we must select one document to be the application root document, and refer to it in the other documents' <vxml> elements.

```
<?xml version="1.0"?>
<!-- rootdoc.vxml -->
<vxml version="1.0">
   <var name ="greeting" expr="howdy" />
   ...
</vxml>
```

```
<?xml version="1.0"?>
<!-- hello.vxml -->
<vxml version="1.0" application="rootdoc.vxml">
   <form id ="login">
      <prompt> <value expr="application.greeting"/> world! </prompt>
      ...
   </form>
</vxml>
```

Every time the interpreter is told to load a document that is part of a multi-document application, it loads the root document as well. Therefore, a variable `foo` declared in the application root document has application scope and can be referred to using the 'dot' notation – *`application.foo`*. Another benefit of multiple document applications is that grammars of the application root document may remain active in other documents, resulting in a richer palette for VUI design.

An Example

The Wrox Café is the hottest greasy spoon this side of Silicon Alley. They do a brisk lunch business, particularly call-in orders. The proprietor, Frankie Four-Fingers, earned his nickname trying to multitask taking orders and chopping onions. To ease his cognitive load, he has implemented an automated telephone ordering system.

This demo can be tested in the US by calling 1-800-4-BEVOCAL; say "BeVocal Café" and enter the Demo I.D. 1000240.

```
<?xml version="1.0"?>
<vxml version="1.0">

   <!-- DEFAULT MESSAGES -->
   <!-- ************************************************** -->
   <help>I'm sorry. There's no help available here. </help>
   <noinput>
      I'm sorry. I didn't hear anything.
      <reprompt />
   </noinput>
   <nomatch>
      I didn't get that.
      <reprompt />
   </nomatch>
   <!-- ************************************************** -->

   <!-- MAIN FORM  -->
   <!-- ************************************************** -->
   <menu id="restaurantMenu">
      <prompt>
         Welcome to the Wrox Cafe Telephone Ordering System.
         Would you like pizza or tofu?
      </prompt>
      <choice next="#pizzaForm">pizza</choice>
      <choice next="#tofuForm">tofu</choice>
   </menu>

   <form id="pizzaForm">
      <field name="topping">
         <prompt>
            What kind of topping would you like?
            Your choices are sausage, clams, or pineapple
         </prompt>
         <grammar>[sausage clams pineapple]</grammar>
         <filled>
            <prompt> Okay,<value expr="topping" />pizza!</prompt>
            <goto next="#exitForm" />
         </filled>
      </field>
   </form>

   <form id="tofuForm">
      <field name="prep">
         <prompt>
            How would you like your tofu? Baked, steamed, or fried.
         </prompt>
         <grammar>[baked steamed fried]</grammar>
         <filled>
            <prompt>Okay, <value expr="prep" />tofu!</prompt>
```

```
            <goto next="#exitForm" />
         </filled>
      </field>
   </form>

   <form id="exitForm">
      <block>
         <prompt>Your order will be ready in ten minutes!</prompt>
      </block>
   </form>
</vxml>
```

It is always a good idea to provide your application with default behaviors for routine exceptional conditions. The user should be able to say, "Help" at any point in your application and receive more information. The application should do something reasonable if it detects no input (`noinput` and `reprompt`), or if it is unable to identify an utterance (`nomatch` and `reprompt`). These default behaviors can be overridden anywhere in the application by providing alternative implementations.

The first form encountered is `restaurantMenu`, which provides the user with a choice of pizza or tofu. After successfully navigating to the next appropriate form, the user is prompted for elaboration. When the order is complete, the user is sent to the exit form.

Limitations of VoiceXML

As we have seen, VoiceXML offers a straightforward paradigm for the construction of simple voice applications. However, a VUI that simulates natural language interaction with complex business processes will pose demands that VoiceXML simply cannot handle.

Architecture

One of the advantages which XML brings to web application development, is that it helps separate presentation logic from application logic. This provides many benefits: defects are more easily isolated, prototyping is accelerated, code reuse is encouraged and development team resources are more efficiently assigned, to name but a few.

Speech application development is notoriously difficult, and any benefit it can derive from this corner is very welcome. Unfortunately, the control flow mechanisms the language provides embed the call flow in the presentation logic, negating to a great extent the advantages described above.

Do such control flow mechanisms belong in a markup language? Whatever your opinion, they are here, probably to stay. However, anything but very sparse and judicious use of these constructs will lengthen and complicate the application development lifecycle.

Lowest Common Denominator

VoiceXML is an easy to use, high-level markup language that allows individuals with only a moderate level of training build relatively simple speech applications. It is aimed at the broadest audience possible. But the very benefits it achieves by abstracting away platform requirements constitute a glass ceiling of sorts for the level of complexity that VoiceXML applications can attain. There is little intrinsic support for reusability beyond the `<subdialog>` element, a crude equivalent to a function call. User interface guidelines and advanced application features, such as state management, are beyond the scope of the specification.

Although the language formally supports mixed-initiative navigation, it does so poorly. Complex navigation and data gathering is difficult to support; the resulting VUIs are still very modal.

Complex Development Environment

There are some great VoiceXML development environments available for free; the reader is directed to the web sites in the section on VoiceXML resources. However, to develop dynamic VoiceXML applications, one must navigate concurrently not one but three development environments and paradigms: VoiceXML itself, ECMAScript, and a server-side publishing mechanism such as JSP.

Alternatives

One way to rearrange the limitations of VoiceXML, is to provide a finer level of control with platform components accessed through the `<object>` tag.

One example of such platform components is Nuance SpeechObjects. SpeechObjects are reusable dialog components written in Java that enable a richer VUI, hide complexity via encapsulation, offer more complex error recovery strategies, and provide access to the underlying platform for tuning, debugging, and testing.

Recent applications have successfully leveraged a hybrid approach, combining platform components for complex dialogs with VoiceXML for transport of recognition results. This is a very promising approach and will most likely become a common way to develop voice applications.

VoiceXML Resources

There are a number of excellent VoiceXML resources available, and more become available online all the time. The following list is not exhaustive, but will give the developer a jump-start with building voice applications. Of particular value are the web-based development environments offered by companies such as TellMe, BeVocal, and VoiceGenie. Most of these services are free, and some provide a very rich toolkit.

Site	URL	Description
VoiceXML version 1.0	http://www.w3.org/TR/voicexml/	The complete specification. This is a submission to the W3C by the VoiceXML Forum. In May 2000, the W3C's Voice Browser Working group agreed to adopt VoiceXML 1.0 as the basis for a W3C dialog markup language.
BeVocal Café	http://cafe.bevocal.com/	VUI development, testing, and deployment tools, documentation, and tutorials.
TellMe Studio	http://studio.tellme.com/	
VoiceGenie Developers' Workshop	http://developer.voicegenie.com/	

Table continued on following page

Site	URL	Description
The VoiceXML Forum	http://www.voicexml.org	The mother of all VoiceXML sites and home of the excellent webzine, The VoiceXML Review.

Summary

It is instructive to compare the current state of speech application development with the relational database industry, circa 1990.

- Small, highly specialized developer community
- Long implementation cycles
- Legacy integration problems
- Core technology providers dominated deployment as well as technology provision
- Few architectural standards

What changed all that, was the emergence of tools, technologies, and standards that empowered the developer community and facilitated the development of large-scale, complex business applications. Currently, developing speech applications is difficult and error-prone. Although the core technology has achieved a reasonable state of maturity, the marriage of speech, telephony, and the Internet is still young. Platform dependence is a given. Configuration management is at best a challenge. Applications are highly customized and integrating with back-end systems is tricky and time-consuming. Presentation logic couples with application logic in novel and unfamiliar ways. A philosophy has not yet emerged to guide the developer community in the design, implementation, and deployment of speech applications.

VoiceXML is a step in the right direction. Its primary goal is to use tools and techniques from web development and content management in the creation of interactive voice applications. It shields application authors from platform dependence, separates service logic from interaction behavior, promotes cross-platform portability, provides a few simple execution flow mechanisms, and is easy to learn.

20

XSL Formatting Objects: XSL-FO

XSL Formatting Objects (**XSL-FO**) is a powerful and complex XML-based technology from the W3C for the presentation of XML on screen and on paper. The XML jigsaw has many pieces and XSL-FO is, we believe, a very important piece in that jigsaw whose power and usefulness have not yet been fully appreciated.

As the individual pieces of that jigsaw become available and developers understand how to use them better, so the power, which is inherent in XSL-FO, can be more fully unleashed. In this chapter, we will look at the power of XML-based technologies in presenting XML using text and graphical means, and describe and demonstrate the use of XSL-FO.

XSL-FO is one part of the two-part Extensible Stylesheet Language, XSL. The other part of XSL, which consists of XSL Transformations (XSLT) is described in Chapter 9. Creation of XSL-FO documents, using XSLT, relies on XPath expressions to select relevant parts of an XML source document for appropriate presentation.

> *In this chapter, we will use the term "XSL-FO" to refer to XSL Formatting Objects, "XSLT" to refer to XSL Transformations and "XSL" to refer to the Extensible Stylesheet Language generally. The official Candidate Recommendation on XSL-FO refers to it often as "XSL", which can serve to confuse rather than clarify.*

Previously, much of the usage of XSLT has been to convert XML to HTML or XHTML, for display or to convert an XML document to another XML-based document format, for example in B2B data interchange. Those applications are important, and will remain so, but essentially the primary purpose for which XSLT was created – as a preliminary step to presenting XML visually using XSL-FO – has not yet been fully explored or realized. Cascading Style Sheets (CSS) can be used to present XML, but CSS employs a non-XML syntax, whereas XSL-FO can present XML using an XML-compliant syntax. Most of this chapter will be about XSL-FO itself, but we will also demonstrate briefly how to use XSLT to create an XSL-FO document. In practice, most XSL-FO will be created using XSLT, but to aid clarity, most examples skip the transformation step and go straight to the XSL-FO. Once you understand the XSL-FO you intend to produce, you are in a better position to create XSLT stylesheets to produce it.

It is not surprising that XSL-FO has received relatively little attention so far. At the time of writing (March 2001), the XSL Formatting Objects specification was not yet final and was a Candidate Recommendation at the W3C. The full text of the November 2000 XSL-FO Candidate Recommendation can be accessed online at http://www.w3.org/TR/2000/CR-xsl-20001121/. Note that although the document essentially describes XSL-FO, it is labeled as "Extensible Stylesheet Language (XSL)". If you want to explore the detail of the XSL-FO specification, we would suggest that either you download the PDF version of the specification, or the large HTML file which contains the entire specification.

During the lifetime of this book, the XSL-FO specification is likely to progress to a Proposed Recommendation and then a Full Recommendation. The most up-to-date version of the XSL-FO specification can be accessed at http://www.w3.org/TR/xsl/.

The XSL-FO Candidate Recommendation is over 400 pages in length, so here we can only give you a broad outline of the capabilities of XSL-FO and demonstrate how to use XSL-FO to create relatively simple documents. This chapter includes the following sections:

- XSL-FO Overview
- Comparison of XSL-FO and CSS
- XSL-FO Tools
- Creating simple XSL-FO documents
- Creating a simple XSL-FO invoice
- Using XSL-FO to produce PDF documents
- Using XSL-FO with SVG
- Using an XSL Formatter as a Web Browser

Remember that all of what follows is based on a draft specification at the W3C. It is unlikely that any major changes will take place in the specification at this stage, but it is possible, so if you find that anything behaves oddly when you try out this chapter's code, visit the errata page for this book on the Wrox web site, and in addition, check the W3C web site at the URL given earlier for any indication that the details of the XSL-FO specification has changed.

However, before we start delving into the detail of XSL-FO, let's look at this screen shot of XSL-FO being displayed using the Antenna House XSL Formatter. The code for this screenshot, the capabilities of the Antenna House XSL Formatter and how to obtain it will be described in more detail later in the chapter.

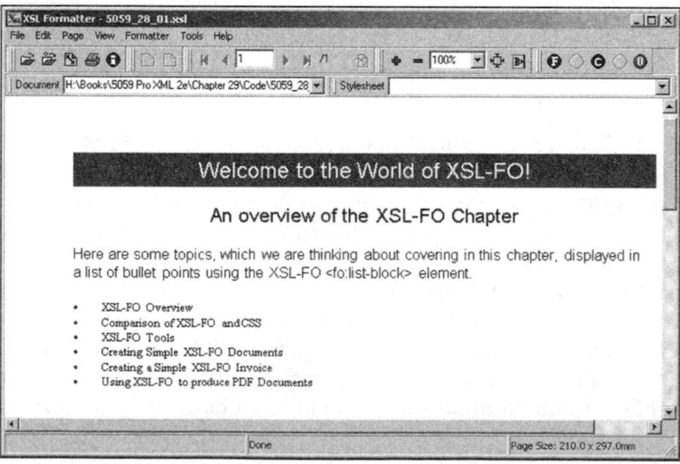

Most people have only had experience of seeing XSL-FO after it has been converted to PDF for printing, so it might have been something of a surprise to see XSL-FO displayed on screen. It is also perhaps a little shocking to see the length of the code required to produce such a simple display.

We know that many readers like to get their hands dirty with code straight away, so here is the code for `Welcome2.fo`, which is the XSL-FO document displayed above. As can be seen, brevity is not one of its features! One reason for its length is that it has been commented to make it more comprehensible to read, but as can be seen, XSL-FO is *not* succinct. We will be explaining more about this later in the chapter.

```
<?xml version="1.0" encoding="utf-8"?>

<!-- Welcome to the World of XSL-FO - an example using list elements -->

<!-- Each XSL-FO document has an <fo:root> element, which refers to the XSL-FO
Namespace.-->

<fo:root xmlns:fo="http://www.w3.org/1999/XSL/Format">

<!--  At the beginning of all XSL-FO documents the page layout is defined. -->

<!--   Each <fo:root> element has a single <fo:layout-master-set> element, which
defines one or more page layouts in the document. -->

<fo:layout-master-set>

<!-- Page layout information for an A4 page. -->
<!-- If we want to use US Letter size change the "page-height" to "11in" and the
"page-width" to "8.5in". We may also want to express the margin sizes in inches. -
->

   <fo:simple-page-master master-name="Simple"
      page-height="29.7cm"
      page-width="21.0cm"
      margin-top="2cm"
      margin-bottom="2cm"
      margin-left="2cm"
      margin-right="2cm">
      <fo:region-body margin-top="0cm" />
      <fo:region-before extent="2cm" />
      <fo:region-after extent="1cm" />
   </fo:simple-page-master>
</fo:layout-master-set>

<!-- The text to be displayed on the page or screen starts here, contained in a
<page-sequence> element which uses the <simple-page-master> named in its "master-
name" attribute. -->

<fo:page-sequence master-name="Simple">
   <fo:flow flow-name="xsl-region-body">

   <!-- Each header or paragraph is encapsulated in an <fo:block> element
   -->

   <!-- This defines a header in white text on a red colored background -->
   <fo:block
```

```
      font-size="18pt"
      font-family="sans-serif"
      line-height="24pt"
      space-after.optimum="15pt"
      background-color="red"
      color="white"
      text-align="center"
      padding-top="3pt">
      Welcome to the World of XSL-FO!
   </fo:block>

   <!-- This defines a smaller title in black text on white. -->
   <fo:block
      font-size="16pt"
      font-family="sans-serif"
      space-after.optimum="15pt"
      text-align="center">
      An overview of the XSL-FO Chapter
   </fo:block>

   <!-- This defines plain paragraph text for this document. -->
   <fo:block
      font-size="12pt"
      font-family="sans-serif"
      space-after.optimum="15pt"
      text-align="left">

      Here are some topics, which we are thinking about covering in this chapter,
 displayed in a list of bullet points using the XSL-FO
 &lt;fo:list-block&gt; element.

   </fo:block>

   <!-- The list of sections planned for the chapter begins here. -->
   <fo:list-block >

      <!-- An individual list item -->
      <fo:list-item>
         <!-- Insert a bullet (a list-item-label) here -->
         <fo:list-item-label>
            <fo:block>
               <fo:inline font-family="Symbol">&#183;</fo:inline>
            </fo:block>
         </fo:list-item-label>
         <!-- The text of the list item, the list-item-body goes here. -->
         <fo:list-item-body>
            <fo:block>
               XSL-FO Overview
            </fo:block>
         </fo:list-item-body>
      </fo:list-item>

      <fo:list-item>
         <fo:list-item-label>
            <fo:block>
               <fo:inline font-family="Symbol">&#183;</fo:inline>
```

```
            </fo:block>
         </fo:list-item-label>
         <fo:list-item-body>
            <fo:block>
               Comparison of XSL-FO and CSS
            </fo:block>
         </fo:list-item-body>
      </fo:list-item>

      <fo:list-item>
         <fo:list-item-label>
            <fo:block>
               <fo:inline font-family="Symbol">&#183;</fo:inline>
            </fo:block>
         </fo:list-item-label>
         <fo:list-item-body>
            <fo:block>
               XSL-FO Tools
            </fo:block>
         </fo:list-item-body>
      </fo:list-item>

      <fo:list-item>
         <fo:list-item-label>
            <fo:block>
               <fo:inline font-family="Symbol">&#183;</fo:inline>
            </fo:block>
         </fo:list-item-label>
         <fo:list-item-body>
            <fo:block>
               Creating Simple XSL-FO Documents
            </fo:block>
         </fo:list-item-body>
      </fo:list-item>

      <fo:list-item>
         <fo:list-item-label>
            <fo:block>
               <fo:inline font-family="Symbol">&#183;</fo:inline>
            </fo:block>
         </fo:list-item-label>
         <fo:list-item-body>
            <fo:block>
               Creating a Simple XSL-FO Invoice
            </fo:block>
         </fo:list-item-body>
      </fo:list-item>

      <fo:list-item>
         <fo:list-item-label>
            <fo:block>
               <fo:inline font-family="Symbol">&#183;</fo:inline>
            </fo:block>
         </fo:list-item-label>
         <fo:list-item-body>
```

```
            <fo:block>
               Using XSL-FO to produce PDF Documents
            </fo:block>
         </fo:list-item-body>
      </fo:list-item>
   </fo:list-block>
   </fo:flow> <!-- The end tag for the flow element-->
</fo:page-sequence> <!-- The end tag for the page-sequence element -->
</fo:root> <!-- The end tag for the XSL-FO document -->
```

Having shown that XSL-FO can be natively displayed on screen and having given a flavor of what XSL-FO code looks like, let's move on to take a bird's eye view of XSL-FO.

XSL-FO Overview

Historically, sophisticated presentation of text on paper has typically involved proprietary or binary formats, which limit interoperability. HTML does not provide the detailed control for precise layout on paper. The introduction of XSL-FO brings to page layout, both on paper and on screen, the potential improvements in interoperability common to members of the XML family together with precision presentation and layout of text and graphics needed for presentation on paper. For many larger companies, the ability to hold information in XML and to present it on screen and on paper using a single XML-based technology will have potentially attractive business benefits.

As we have already mentioned, XSLT and XSL-FO are the two parts of the Extensible Stylesheet Language, XSL. Up until now, XSLT has mostly been used separately from XSL-FO due to the time lag between the finalization of the XSLT Recommendation in November 1999 and the slower progress on the XSL-FO part of XSL. Now that XSL-FO tools are emerging, we can expect to see XSLT used frequently in the production of XSL-FO.

XML was designed with a view to its use on the Web. Initially, the vision (at least of some) for XSL-FO was that it too would be an XML-based Web display format. However, over time, a change in the positioning of XSL-FO took place, to place significantly more emphasis on the capabilities of XSL-FO to provide sophisticated on-paper page layout. The attraction, particularly for large corporations, of that capability is that it would become possible to store information as XML and then display it either on paper (as XSL-FO), or on the Web. Display on the Web could use one or more of a variety of technologies; for example, we could use XSLT to output HTML/XHTML, style XML directly with CSS, display as XSL-FO, or use SVG's capabilities to display both text and graphics in SVG-based web pages.

The potential cost savings of having a "store once, write anywhere" information strategy are enormous, particularly for large corporations. In parallel, assuming XML-based information strategies are well thought out, potentially significant improvements in accuracy are also possible.

As we have just mentioned, XSL-FO has powerful and precise page layout capabilities. However, it would be a mistake to think of XSL-FO primarily as a *page* description language. It is better to think of XSL-FO as a *document* description language. An XSL-FO document, as we shall see later, includes information on how different page layouts are used within the overall structure of a document, as well as including detailed information about how information should be laid out on the page.

The fact that XSL-FO is a document description language has disadvantages for the production of short (1 page or so) XSL-FO documents. The structure of all XSL-FO documents must carry the overhead appropriate to a structure that allows very lengthy documents to be produced. The overhead is expressed not so much in speed but in verbosity.

So, let's move on to examine how these notions are put into practice. We will look at the individual parts of an XSL-FO page, then look at the overall structure of an XSL-FO document. Later in the chapter, we will look at creating some of our own straightforward documents.

As we would expect, all elements within an XSL-FO document correspond to the XML 1.0 syntax. XSL-FO documents use the http://www.w3.org/1999/XSL/Format namespace URI. The typical namespace prefix used at the time of writing is **fo.**. Of course, we can use any namespace prefix that we want to, but throughout this chapter, we will use the `fo` prefix that refers to the above namespace.

Let's look at the terminology that describes the dimensions of a page in XSL-FO. Take careful note of the terminology of this, as it is more complex than that which we may be familiar with for page layout, since it is designed for the display of a broad range of natural languages, whether they are written from left to right, right to left or vertically.

In the diagram that follows, the overall size of the gray area corresponds to the width of the chosen paper. The horizontal double-headed arrow in the gray area indicates the page width size (and is represented by the `page-width` attribute of the `<fo:simple-page-master>` element) and the vertical double-headed arrow in the gray area indicates the page height (represented by the `page-height` attribute of a `<fo:simple-page-master>` element). The areas indicated as Top Margin, Bottom Margin, Left Margin and Right Margin respectively are represented by the `margin-top`, `margin-bottom`, `margin-left`, and `margin-right` attributes of the `<fo:simple-page-master>` element. Text is not displayed in the margins in the gray area.

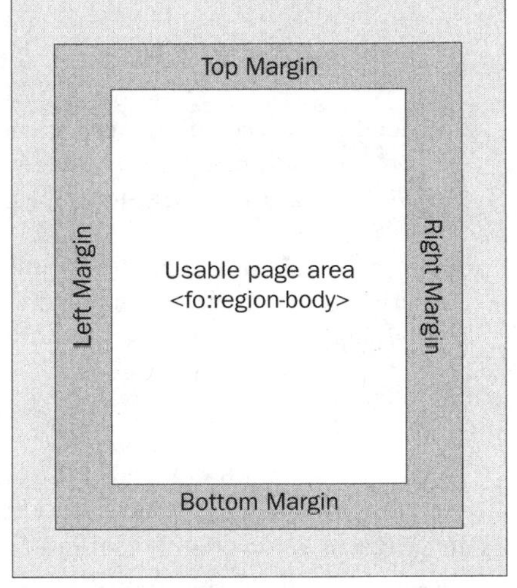

The following diagram represents the white area in the previous diagram, that is, the overall page less each of its margins. The white area is represented by the `<fo:region-body>` element.

It might appear a strange concept at first sight but within the overall dimensions of the `<fo:region-body>` element, four other XSL-FO elements are placed:

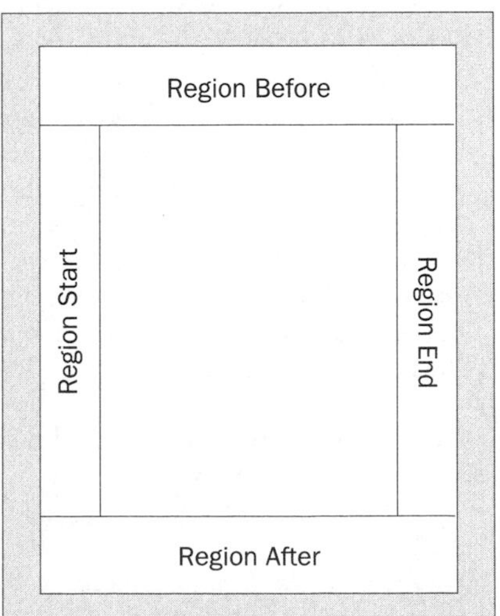

The region before is represented by the `<fo:region-before>` element, whose `extent` attribute defines the extent (unsurprisingly) of the page area available for (in this case) a page header. We need to be careful to avoid placing page content on top of the header content. We can use the `margin-top` attribute of the `<fo:region-body>` element to ensure that the area defined by `<fo:region-before>` is not overwritten.

> *We need to be careful to ensure that we have understood the difference between the area referred to by the `margin-top` attribute of the `<fo:simple-page-master>` element seen in the first diagram into which no page content is placed, and the `margin-top` attribute of the `<fo:region-body>` element, which represents an area that can overlap with the `<fo:region-before>` element and which may contain page content.*

The region after is similarly represented by the `<fo:region-after>` element and similar considerations apply. It is necessary to avoid overwriting any footer, by setting an appropriate value for the `margin-bottom` attribute on the `<fo:region-body>` element. The region start represents the `<fo:region-start>` element and the region end represents the `<fo:region-end>` element.

The need for this seemingly cumbersome construction to describe a page is to allow XSL-FO to fully support internationalization, where script may be written not only left-to-right, as in, for example, English and German, but also right-to-left, as in Arabic or Hebrew, or vertically as in Chinese and Japanese.

Please note that although "start" and "begin" carry very similar meanings in ordinary English, in XSL-FO terminology there are major differences in meaning. Notice from the second diagram that for English text (written left to right), the region before, which is represented by the `<fo:region-before>` element, is effectively the header for the page, whereas the region start, represented in XSL-FO code by the `<fo:region-start>` element, is at the left of the page – effectively a left sidebar.

To complicate matters further, the absolute positions of, for example, the `<fo:region-before>` and `<fo:region-start>` elements, alter if the direction of a line of writing changes. The positions given in the diagram are correct for left-to-right writing such as English. For right-to-left script, such as Hebrew, the positions of `<fo:region-start>` and `<fo:region-end>` elements are reversed. That is, instead of approximating to a left sidebar, the `<fo:region:start>` element approximates to a right sidebar.

In document layout for English language text, the `<fo:region-before>` and the `<fo:region-after>` elements would consist of header and footer material respectively. Typically, the content of the headers and footers is static, in the sense that they are displayed on each page, whereas the page content is displayed once on each particular page. Of course, that does not necessarily mean that every page has identical headers. The pages you are currently reading will, unless the publisher changes the page layout, have a header on left pages which consists of the chapter number, while the header on right hand pages will be a running title for the chapter. Those headers would, in XSL-FO, both be represented by `<fo:static-content>` elements. In other words, in an XSL-FO page the content of a header is displayed within the region before using an `<fo:static-content>` element. The `<fo:static element>` for a header is associated with the region before by setting the value of its `flow-name` attribute to have a value of "`xsl-region-before`". For a footer, the `flow-name` attribute has a value of "`xsl-region-after`".

A very simplified page might be encoded like this:

```
<fo:page-sequence master-name="Simple">

   <fo:static-content flow-name="xsl-region-before">
      <fo:block>
```

```
      Our Page Header
    </fo:block>
  </fo:static-content>

  <fo:static-content flow-name="xsl-region-after">
    <fo:block>
      Our Page Footer
    </fo:block>
  </fo:static-content>

  <fo:flow flow-name="xsl-region-body">
    <!-- The page body region content goes here. -->
  </fo:flow>

</fo:page-sequence>
```

Notice in the above code that the `<fo:static-content>` element has a `flow-name` attribute, which has the value `xsl-region-before`. That means that the static content for a particular page sequence will be placed in the before region – at the top of the page for left-to-right languages such as English. Note also that the `<fo:static-content>` elements for both header and footer precede the `<fo:flow>` element for the main page content.

The actual page content *flows* from page to page and is contained within `<fo:flow>` elements, which are themselves direct children of `<fo:page-sequence>` elements. The page area, within which the page content is flowed, is defined by the `flow-name` attribute of the `<fo:flow>` element. Typically, the flowed content will be placed within the region body, as indicated in the following code snippet:

```
<fo:flow flow-name="xsl-region-body">
  <!-- The page body region content goes here>
</fo:flow>
```

Within the `<fo:flow>` elements we can expect to find a variety of XSL-FO elements, which represent block level elements:

- `fo:block`
- `fo:block-container`
- `fo:table-and-caption`
- `fo:table`
- `fo:list-block`

These block level elements may themselves contain other block level elements. For example, if we looked at the code for the example earlier in the chapter, we may have noticed that nested within the `<fo:list-block>` element there were `<fo:list-item>` elements.

```
<fo:list-block >

    <!-- An individual list item -->
    <fo:list-item>
      <!-- Insert a bullet (a list-item-label) here -->
      <fo:list-item-label>
        <fo:block>
```

```
                <fo:inline font-family="Symbol">&#183;</fo:inline>
            </fo:block>
        </fo:list-item-label>
        <!-- The text of the list item, the list-item-body goes here. -->
        <fo:list-item-body>
            <fo:block>
                XSL-FO Overview
            </fo:block>
        </fo:list-item-body>
    </fo:list-item>
<!-- Other <fo:list-item> elements could go here
</fo:list-block>
```

Some block elements contain nested line level elements and in-line elements. Together those different types of XSL-FO elements make up the space that the content of the page occupies.

In addition to these basic layout facilities, XSL-FO provides many other page layout and document management capabilities within its elements and attributes. For example, we can control how page numbers are to be applied within a long document, whether chapters start on odd or even pages, which headers or footers are used on left or right hand pages, and a myriad other facilities. Since the purpose of this chapter is to give you an introduction to what XSL-FO can do now and what it is likely to be doing in the future, we won't dwell on such details now, although they are of significant importance in production-quality use of XSL-FO.

Before we move on to other issues let's just recap.

Within an XSL-FO document, there are two basic parts:

- The layout for the entire document is contained within a `<fo:layout-master-set>` element, which will contain layout information for one or more page layouts.
- The content to be displayed on the pages of the document is nested within `<fo:page-sequence>` elements, which are linked by their `master-name` attribute to a particular page layout specified in a `<fo:simple-page-master>` element.

The page content is contained within what can be a very deeply nested set of XSL-FO elements, which define how the content is to be displayed on page.

XSL-FO and Web Accessibility

The W3C attaches a significant amount of importance to the accessibility of web-based documents. See, for example, information on the **Web Accessibility Initiative**, **WAI**, at http://www.w3.org/WAI/. If future XSL-FO browsers implement a zooming facility such as that available in the Antenna House XSL Formatter (see later), it might be preferable to those with impaired sight, rather than the capabilities shown by web-browsers (for example, IE and Netscape) of adjusting font size. If you look at the screen shot of the Antenna House XSL Formatter shown earlier you can see + and – symbols in the central upper part of the screen that zoom in and out respectively, and a drop down list which allows a numerical zoom level to be chosen. In addition, XSL-FO provides what it terms **Common Aural Properties** to provide an alternative audio rendition of XSL-FO elements for the visually impaired.

Comparison of XSL-FO and CSS

If you have come to this chapter from an HTML/XHTML background, you may well be familiar with at least some of the capabilities of Cascading Style Sheets (CSS), and you may have realized that CSS has some of the same styling abilities offered by XSL-FO.

You may be asking yourself what advantages XSL-FO brings. If you want to have a fully XML-based syntax, then XSL-FO is in the lead since CSS has a rule-based syntax that is distinctly non-XML. The functionality offered, at least in theory, by XSL-FO gives it an advantage over CSS at present, especially if you have a need for right-to-left text or vertical text or footnotes, margin notes etc. However, the working drafts of the CSS3 specification at the W3C indicate that CSS is likely to soon provide functionality such as multi-column layout that brings it closer to the layout functionality offered by XSL-FO.

Of course, CSS has so far been largely targeted at presentation on the Web and the variation between browsers in how much of CSS2 is implemented causes many practical problems for Web authors. The advent of XSL-FO *might* offer a chance for more consistent presentation standards, but it is too early at present to know. Much depends on how a final XSL-FO specification is implemented.

At one time, it was possible to characterize CSS as simple and XSL-FO as complex, but as was indicated, CSS is becoming less simple. The variability in browser support of CSS2 is another important issue.

If you have data stored as XML, which you want to present both on the Web and on paper, both CSS and XSL-FO have, or are likely to soon have, viable solutions. A careful evaluation in the light of the needs of your particular project will need to be made.

XSL-FO Tools

During the lifetime of this book, we can expect many new tools to process and display XSL-FO to appear. One useful online resource is the list of XSL-FO tools at http://www.xmlsoftware.com/xslfo/. Another place to look for information on tools is the Links page of the XSL-FO mailing list at **YahooGroups.com**: http://www.yahoogroups.com/group/XSL-FO/links.

At the time of writing, there are no final releases of XSL-FO tools available, which is not very surprising given that the XSL-FO specification is not yet finalized. However, there are a small number of tools available, which allow us to explore some of the potential of XSL-FO. While they provide useful functionality, be aware that there may be gaps in implementation of certain XSL-FO elements. Check the feature list of each product to make sure that the layout functionality you may need is actually provided. The preview releases offer adequate functionality for our purposes, in this chapter, of demonstrating the basics of XSL-FO by laying out simple pages.

> *All the tools mentioned here are preview releases, or similar, so be aware that they may not be fully stable. So, ideally you should run those tools on a machine dedicated to the evaluation of beta software where no production data is stored. If that is not possible, be sure to back up every important file before running pre-release software.*

Many XSL-FO developers at the time of writing seem to be routinely processing XSL-FO into PDF format, which is probably understandable given that XSL formatters, which display XSL-FO natively on screen, are a very recent development and PDF is a well-established document format.

In the examples later in this chapter, we are going to concentrate mostly on using two of the available XSL-FO tools: the Antenna House XSL Formatter, and the open source FOP XSL-FO to PDF processor from the Apache Foundation. We will tell you more about those in a moment.

Other XSL-FO tools, which are available for download, include the RenderX XEP processor that creates PDF files and PostScript from XSL-FO. Further information is available at http://www.renderx.com/. Unicorn offers UFO (Unicorn Formatting Objects), which is downloadable from http://www.unicorn-enterprises.com/products.html.

The Antenna House XSL Formatter can be downloaded from http://www.AntennaHouse.com. The version used in this chapter was 0.1.0.1227.The Antenna House XSL Formatter uses the MSXML3 component and is available only for the MS Windows platform at present. There is an option to download sample files to use initially if you are not up to speed with XSL-FO. After download, simply double click on the downloaded file and installation proceeds without problem (at least it did for me). If you do get a problem, then it is most likely that we will need a more recent version of the Windows Installer tool, which can be downloaded using the Windows Update facility (http://windowsupdate.microsoft.com/).

The Antenna House XSL Formatter supports many, but not all, of the elements in the November 2000 XSL-FO Candidate Recommendation. We won't list in detail the elements supported since these may have changed by the time you read this and download the XSL Formatter. The help files contain a list of supported and unsupported elements. The Antenna House Formatter lets us produce single or multi-page documents for display on screen or for printing.

The interface is straightforward. The Antenna House Formatter has small windows for inserting the name of an XML source document and an XSL stylesheet. We can quickly reselect documents or stylesheets used recently using drop down menus as shown in the following screen shot:

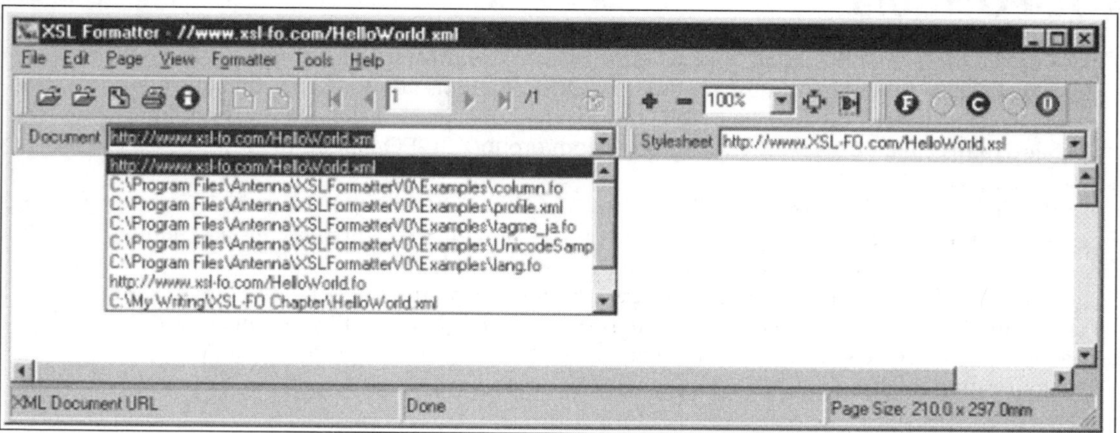

Having chosen a suitable document and stylesheet, we run the XSL Formatter by clicking on the blue circle with the F in it, towards the right hand side of the screen shot – the XSL-FO document is displayed on screen. We may then choose where to save the XSL-FO files you produce.

As we explained earlier in the chapter, XSL-FO describes a number of block level elements. The Antenna House XSL Formatter lets us optionally see the representation of those on screen, which can be very useful when diagnosing layout problems. The next screen shot shows a display with the Show border facility toggled on, which is done using the rectangular yellow button with a B on it. This allows us to see how the layout of each block element on the page relates to one another. Notice on the right of the screen that the size of the right hand column of the table has extended further than desirable, a mistake that might have been missed had this facility not been available.

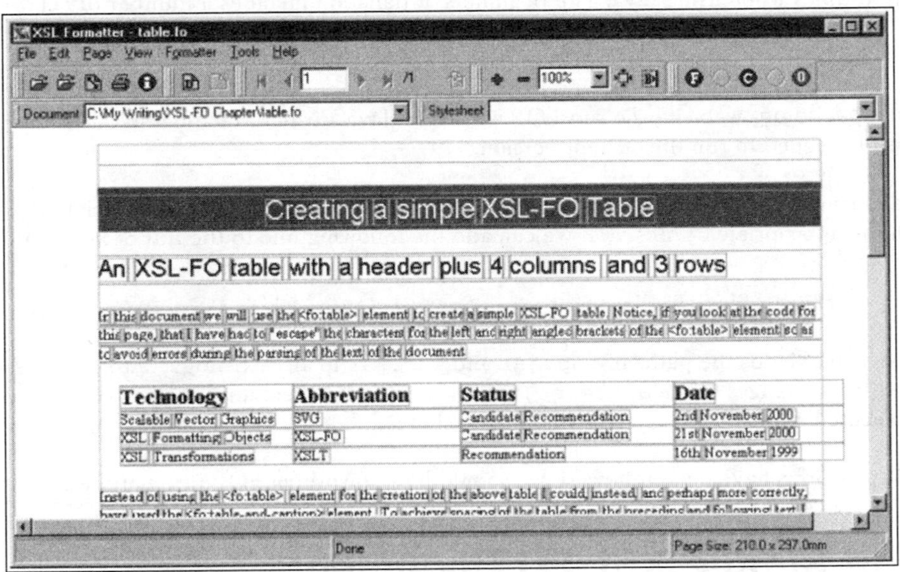

Notice the difference from the earlier screen shot. This time we are displaying an XSL-FO document produced earlier, which requires no stylesheet for its display. The XSL-FO source is rendered by the Antenna House Formatter.

When there is more than one page in a document, it is possible to move from page to page using the arrows just below and to the right of the Help menu (giving a paging metaphor, rather than the scrolling metaphor of HTML web browsers). To the left of that are two icons that allow the XML document and the XSL stylesheet to be edited. The latter is grayed out in the screenshot since it is displaying an XSL-FO document directly, rather than generating it dynamically using an XML source document and an XSL stylesheet. We can select which XML editor we wish to use. In addition, it is possible to zoom in or out of a document using the drop down menu set in the screenshot to 100%. There is also, immediately to the right of that menu, a fit to window option. Of course, there is also an option to print any XSL-FO displayed.

To summarize, the Antenna House XSL Formatter allows us to display XSL-FO documents using a variety of XML source documents and XSL stylesheets.

The FOP processor, which we will use later in the chapter, converts an XSL-FO document, typically having a `.fo` suffix, to a PDF document. For general information about FOP, follow the FOP link on the xml.apache.org home page. To download a suitable version of FOP, visit http://xml.apache.org/dist/fop/ where the available versions for download are indicated. At the time of writing, the latest available version is 0.17.0. Versions with or without documentation or example files are available as zipped or tarball files. There is also a beginner's version, with many example files that are well worth studying. We will be using the most recent beginner's version for the examples in this chapter: http://xml.apache.org/dist/fop/recent/fop-0_15_0-forBeginners.zip. Depending on our needs, our operating system, and the latest available versions when we visit the Apache site, we may want to make an alternative download.

FOP may be run from the command line, or can be embedded in your own Java applications. Instructions on how to embed FOP are to be found at http://xml.apache.org/fop/embedding.html. In this section, we will be describing the use of FOP from the command line.

The following description of installation is for the Windows platform, using the Beginner's version. Once the FOP zip file is downloaded, simply unzip it into an appropriately named directory, such as `C:\fop`. It is better to avoid using directory names which include spaces, as including them can cause problems at times when using Java. The beginners' installation includes a number of HTML files that can be accessed from:`C:\fop\docs\html-docs\index.html`.

The documentation provided is very similar to the information about FOP found on the http://xml.apache.org web site. To run FOP we need a Java Virtual Machine on our computer. JDK 1.1 (or higher) is needed to run the current version.

The Java Virtual Machine needs to know where the FOP files are located. To associate the Java `.jar` files with the appropriate `CLASSPATH` we can add the following line to the `autoexec.bat` file:

```
set CLASSPATH=%CLASSPATH%c:\fop\build\fop.jar;c:\fop\lib\w3c.jar;
```

The above syntax adds the paths of `fop.jar` and `w3c.jar` to any existing `CLASSPATH` settings. Remember that changes to the `autoexec.bat` file don't take effect until the `autoexec.bat` batch file is next executed, typically when restarting the machine.

If these instructions have been followed, we should have a working FOP installation.

Creating Simple XSL-FO Documents

In this section we will show you a little about how to produce simple XSL-FO documents which include some of the more common XSL-FO elements. In the space available, we can't hope to cover everything, but will simply describe and demonstrate some foundational techniques. In these sections you will begin to get an idea of how to create XSL-FO documents.

One of the notions that we have found most helpful in grasping the structure of an XSL-FO document, is to think of XSL-FO as a *document* description language, not a *page* description language. An XSL-FO document therefore contains not only the content of a document but also the complete layout information for the document.

Let's briefly consider what we might need to know if this book were to be produced entirely from XSL-FO. If we look at some of the material at the front of the book, we see that several pages, including the Table of Contents, have their own page layouts. When we move into the body of the book, we notice that the header for the left pages differs from that on the facing right pages. In addition, the first page of each chapter has yet another page layout. The index uses a two-column layout, rather than the single column layout typical within the main text. To produce the entire layout information for a book like this one will require a number of different layouts.

The power that XSL-FO potentially has when used to produce a book has a downside too. When we come to produce a simple, single-page document we still need to include all the sections necessary for producing a lengthy document like a book, although within each section there will be very little information. In practice that will be less of a problem since we will probably have an XSLT/XSL-FO stylesheet to create a basic XSL-FO document. Nevertheless, at this initial stage it can seem a little intimidating. So let's look systematically at building up a bare document skeleton.

Each XSL-FO document has, as root element, an <fo:root> element, assuming that the prefix fo is linked to the namespace http://www.w3.org/1999/XSL/Format. Within that <fo:root> element, an initial section describes the layout(s) to be used in the document, and a subsequent section describes the actual content of the document. Therefore, a skeleton XSL-FO document looks something like this:

```
<fo:root xmlns:fo="http://www.w3.org/1999/XSL/Format">
   <!--Page layout information goes here. There can be one or more
      layouts.-->

   <!-- Page content goes here -->
</fo:root>
```

When we translate this general structure into a skeleton of XSL-FO elements we see the following:

```
<fo:root xmlns:fo="http://www.w3.org/1999/XSL/Format">
   <fo:layout-master-set>
      <!-- The information about the available page layouts goes here in one
         or more fo:simple-page-master elements -->
   </fo:layout-master-set>

   <fo:page-sequence>
      <!-- Some page content goes here -->
   </fo:page-sequence>

   <!-- Other fo:page-sequence elements can go here -->
</fo:root>
```

Let's move on to look more closely at the information structure at the beginning of each XSL-FO document that describes the layout(s) contained within the document. All the layout information is contained within a <fo:layout-master-set> element. Within this element, we find one or more descriptions of the individual types of page that the document may contain. Each description of a page layout is contained in, for example, a <fo:simple-page-master> element. Typically, each <fo:simple-page-master> element would have several attributes defined which contain information for page height, page width etc.

Therefore, if we want to create an A4 size page we would create a <fo:simple-page-master> element within the <fo:layout-master-set> element, similar to that in the following code snippet:

```
   <fo:layout-master-set>

      <!-- Page layout information for an A4 page. -->
      <!-- If you use US Letter size change the "page-height" to "11in" and
         the "page-width" to "8.5in".You may also want to express the margin
         sizes in inches. -->

      <fo:simple-page-master master-name="Simple"
         page-height="29.7cm"
         page-width="21.0cm"
         margin-top="2cm"
         margin-bottom="2cm"
         margin-left="2cm"
         margin-right="2cm">
         <fo:region-body margin-top="0cm"/>
```

```
            <fo:region-before extent="2cm"/>
            <fo:region-after extent="1cm"/>
        </fo:simple-page-master>
    </fo:layout-master-set>
```

A <fo:simple-page-master> element must include master-name, page-height, and page-width attributes. The master-name attribute is essential so that a <fo:page-sequence> element may make use of the named <fo:simple-page-master> element. The page-height and page-width attributes are needed to inform the XSL formatting engine of the page size. Typically, the four attributes that define the page margins, margin-top, margin-bottom, margin-left, and margin-right, will also be present. In addition there will frequently be further XSL-FO elements that define the extent of the regions within the page. In the example above, we have used the <fo:region-body> element (effectively the main part of the page), the <fo:region-before> element (effectively the header), and the <fo:region-after> element (effectively the footer for the page).

Please note that this has been presented for languages written from left to right. If we are using a language such as Hebrew or Arabic, written right to left, then the visual positioning of the <fo:region-start> and <fo:region-end> are reversed. If we are using a language where the direction of a line of text is top-to-bottom, or bottom-to-top, then the positioning of the various regions changes correspondingly.

Therefore, if our XSL-FO document had the above as its <fo:layout-master-set> element, it would tell us that the XSL-FO document has only one page layout defined for it – a layout for an A4 size page, with margins as specified in the attributes of the <fo:simple-page-master> element. As indicated in the comment within the code, the page size can be easily modified to correspond to US Letter size or any other desired layout dimensions. Among the permitted units are centimeters, inches, points, and pixels.

For our single page document, we only need to include one <fo:simple-page-master> element within the <fo:layout-master-set> element. If we were to use XSL-FO to create a book similar to this one, then we would need several <fo:simple-page-master>,<fo:repeatable-page-master> or <fo:conditional-page-master> elements. In our examples, we will use only the <fo:simple-page-master> element.

So, having looked briefly at how to create the layout information for our XSL-FO document, let's move on to look at how we structure the content of our document.

We need to use one or more <fo:page-sequence> elements. For our simple single-page document we need only one <fo:page-sequence> element. How does the XSL formatter know how to lay out the content of our page? In other words, how do we tell the formatter which of the <fo:simple-page-master> elements (if there is more than one) to use? We use the master-name attribute of the <fo:page-sequence> element, and ensure that the value of the master-name attribute matches the master-name attribute of a <fo:simple-page-master> element within our <fo:layout-master-set>. We assigned the value Simple to the master-name attribute of our <fo:simple-page-master>, so we use that same name in the master-name attribute of the <fo:page-sequence> element.

```
    <fo:page-sequence master-name="Simple">
```

So, now we have defined an A4 page (or a US Letter size page, if the earlier code was modified) to contain our content, how do we describe how we want the content to be laid out within that page?

Most content within XSL-FO pages is *flowed* into the available space using algorithms whose complexity goes far beyond the scope of this chapter. However, the important thing for our purpose is to recognize the importance of the <fo:flow> element, which is the one that the content is nested in. In other words, the code for the content of a typical XSL-FO page will look something like this:

```
<fo:page-sequence master-name="Simple">
   <fo:flow>

   <!-- The page content which is to be flowed into the space defined by
      the <fo:page-sequence> element goes in here. It can be brief or
      very extensive. -->

   </fo:flow>
</fo:page-sequence>
```

Actual content is nested within <fo:flow> elements, typically within <fo:block> elements. Therefore, if we wanted to display the text "Hello World!" in our XSL-FO document, we would nest code such as this within <fo:flow>:

```
      <!-- This defines plain paragraph text for this document. -->
      <fo:block
         font-size="12pt"
         font-family="sans-serif"
         space-after.optimum="15pt"
         text align="left">
         Hello World!
      </fo:block>
```

Putting all these ideas together, we arrive at a completed XSL-FO document, HelloWorld.fo. Notice that working code includes the XML declaration and the namespace declaration of the XSL-FO Namespace URI, which were omitted from earlier code fragments:

```
<?xml version="1.0" encoding="utf-8"?>
<fo:root xmlns:fo="http://www.w3.org/1999/XSL/Format">

   <fo:layout-master-set>

      <!-- Page layout information for an A4 page. -->

      <fo:simple-page-master master-name="Simple"
         page-height="29.7cm"
         page-width="21.0cm"
         margin-top="2cm"
         margin-bottom="2cm"
         margin-left="2cm"
         margin-right="2cm">
         <fo:region-body margin-top="0cm"/>
         <fo:region-before extent="2cm"/>
         <fo:region-after extent="1cm"/>
      </fo:simple-page-master>
   </fo:layout-master-set>

   <fo:page-sequence master-name="Simple">
```

```
        <fo:flow>

            <!-- This defines plain paragraph text for this document. -->
            <fo:block
               font-size="12pt"
               font-family="sans-serif"
               space-after.optimum="15pt"
               text-align="left">
               Hello World!
            </fo:block>

        </fo:flow>
    </fo:page-sequence>

</fo:root>
```

As you can see, a lot of code goes into producing such a trivial result:

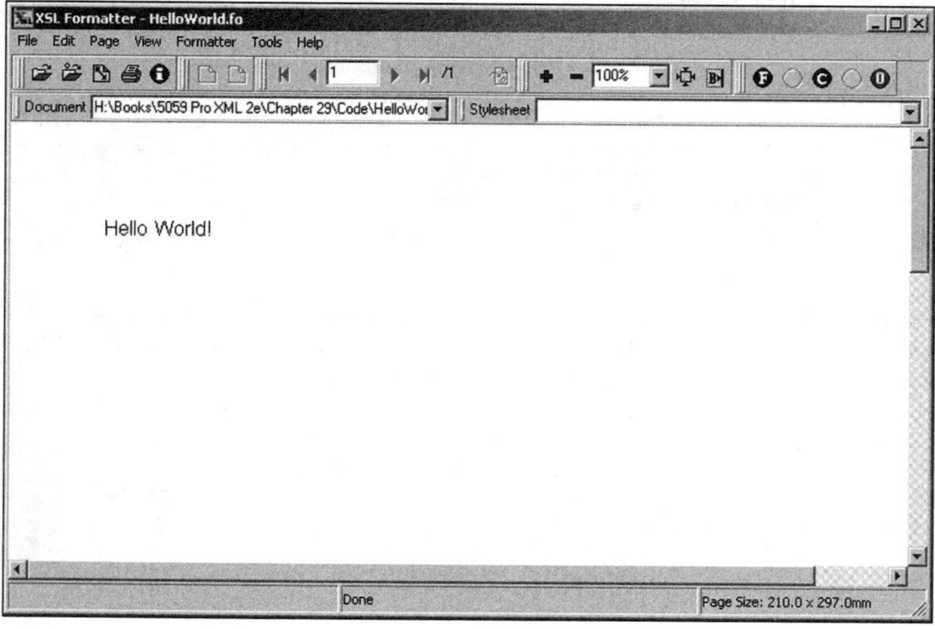

Now we have seen how to put together some of the basic building blocks of XSL-FO to produce a displayed XSL-FO document, let's go on to build on this simple start by adding a bulleted list to our capabilities in XSL-FO.

Creating a Simple XSL-FO Document Including a List

Having created a simple "Hello World!" document, let's take a closer look at how we can produce some slightly more useful XSL-FO, incorporating a list of items, which looks like the one shown in the first screenshot we saw. We also saw the full text of the code earlier in the chapter. In this section, we will provide additional explanation, going through the code step-by-step.

As you step through the code, it will be helpful to review the output in the first screenshot shown in this chapter, to help associate the visual effect with the relevant XSL-FO element(s). Here is the screenshot again to save flipping through pages:

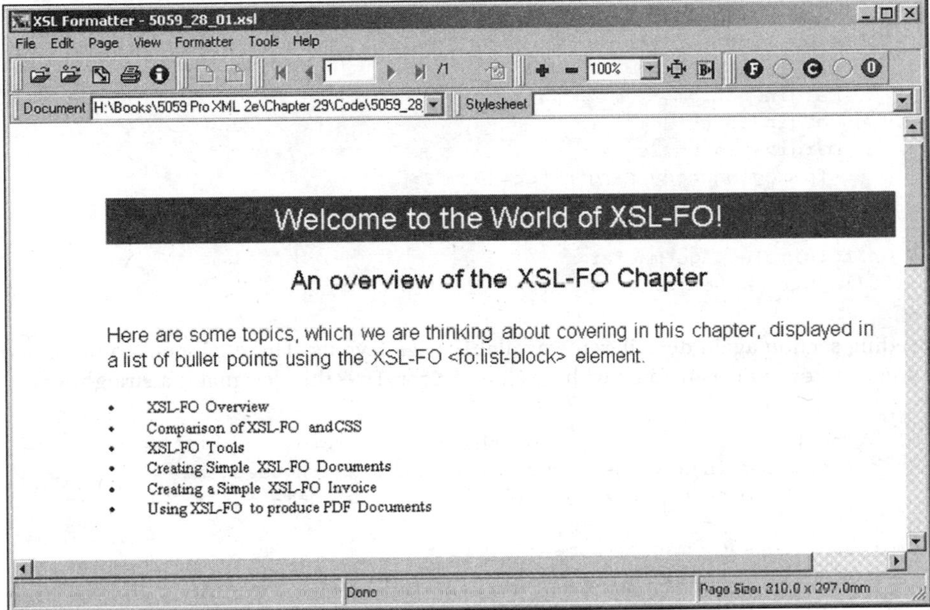

Now it is time to look at the code in detail, section by section:

```
<?xml version="1.0" encoding="utf-8"?>
```

XSL-FO is XML, and therefore the XML declaration, with or without attributes, is typically the first line of all XSL-FO documents.

```
<!-- Welcome to the World of XSL-FO - an example using list elements
     Each XSL-FO document has a <fo:root> element, which refers to the
     XSL-FO Namespace. -->

<fo:root xmlns:fo="http://www.w3.org/1999/XSL/Format">
```

Every XSL-FO document has, assuming the conventional `fo` prefix, an `<fo:root>` element as the root element of the document. You will notice that the relevant namespace is included in the root.

```
   <!-- At the beginning of all XSL-FO documents
        the page layout is defined. -->

   <!-- Each <fo:root> element has a single <fo:layout-master-set> element
        which defines one or more page layouts in the document. -->

   <fo:layout-master-set>

      <!-- Page layout information for an A4 page.
           If we use US Letter size, change the "page-height" to
```

```
            "11in" and the "page-width" to "8.5in". We may also want to
            express the margin sizes in inches. -->

      <fo:simple-page-master master-name="Simple"
         page-height="29.7cm"
         page-width="21.0cm"
         margin-top="2cm"
         margin-bottom="2cm"
         margin-left="2cm"
         margin-right="2cm">
         <fo:region-body margin-top="0cm"/>
         <fo:region-before extent="2cm"/>
         <fo:region-after extent="1cm"/>
      </fo:simple-page-master>
   </fo:layout-master-set>
```

The preceding section again describes the available page layouts. There happens to be only one element that has the `master-name` attribute with a value of `Simple` – this designates a straightforward A4 page.

```
   <!-- The text to be displayed on the page or screen starts here,
        contained in a <page-sequence> element which uses the
        <simple-page-master> named in its "master-name" attribute. -->

   <fo:page-sequence master-name="Simple">
```

Note that the `master-name` attribute of the `<fo:page-sequence>` element must, in our example, match a name of a `<fo:simple-page-master>` element nested within the `<fo:layout-master-set>` element. In our case the two `master-name` attributes match.

```
      <fo:flow flow-name="xsl-region-body">
```

Our content is contained within a `<fo:flow>` element.

```
         <!-- Each header or paragraph is encapsulated in an <fo:block>
              element. This defines a header in white text on a red colored
              background -->
         <fo:block
            font-size="18pt"
            font-family="sans-serif"
            line-height="24pt"
            space-after.optimum="15pt"
            background-color="red"
            color="white"
            text-align="center"
            padding-top="3pt">
            Welcome to the World of XSL-FO!
         </fo:block>
```

The above code describes the font size, background color, etc. of the headline on our page.

```
         <!-- This defines a smaller title in black text on white. -->
         <fo:block
```

```
      font-size="16pt"
      font-family="sans-serif"
      space-after.optimum="15pt"
      text-align="center">
      An overview of the XSL-FO Chapter
   </fo:block>
```

This code produces the display of the text "An overview of the XSL-FO Chapter", in a smaller font and without a colored background.

```
   <!-- This defines plain paragraph text for this document. -->
   <fo:block
      font-size="12pt"
      font family="sans serif"
      space-after.optimum="15pt"
      text-align="left">
      Here are some topics, which I am thinking about covering in this
      chapter, displayed in a list of bullet points using the XSL-FO
      &lt;fo:list-block&gt; element.
   </fo:block>
```

The above section of code lays out our first paragraph of text.

```
   <!-- The list of sections planned for the chapter begins here. -->
   <fo:list-block >
```

Our bulleted list is nested within a <fo:list-block> element.

```
      <!-- A individual list item -->
      <fo:list-item>
         <!-- Insert a bullet here -->
         <fo:list-item-label>
            <fo:block>
               <fo:inline font-family="Symbol">&#183;</fo:inline>
            </fo:block>
         </fo:list-item-label>
```

Each item within the list is represented by a <fo:list-item> element, inside which there is a <fo:list-item-label> element, which may contain a bullet, an image identifier etc.

```
         <!-- The text of the list item goes here. -->
         <fo:list-item-body>
            <fo:block>
               XSL-FO Overview
            </fo:block>
         </fo:list-item-body>
      </fo:list-item>
```

The other part of the <fo:list-item> element is the <fo:list-item-body> element, which contains the actual text of a list item.

```
            <fo:list-item>
               <fo:list-item-label>
                  <fo:block>
                     <fo:inline font-family="Symbol">&#183;</fo:inline>
                  </fo:block>
               </fo:list-item-label>
               <fo:list-item-body>
                  <fo:block>
                     Comparison of XSL-FO and CSS
                  </fo:block>
               </fo:list-item-body>
            </fo:list-item>
```

Here we see a further <fo:list-item> element, with <fo:list-item-label> and <fo:list-item-body> elements nested within it.

```
            <fo:list-item>
               <fo:list-item-label>
                  <fo:block>
                     <fo:inline font-family="Symbol">&#183;</fo:inline>
                  </fo:block>
               </fo:list-item-label>
               <fo:list-item-body>
                  <fo:block>
                     XSL-FO Tools
                  </fo:block>
               </fo:list-item-body>
            </fo:list-item>

            <fo:list-item>
               <fo:list-item-label>
                  <fo:block>
                     <fo:inline font-family="Symbol">&#183;</fo:inline>
                  </fo:block>
               </fo:list-item-label>
               <fo:list-item-body>
                  <fo:block>
                     Creating Simple XSL-FO Documents
                  </fo:block>
               </fo:list-item-body>
            </fo:list-item>

            <fo:list-item>
               <fo:list-item-label>
                  <fo:block>
                     <fo:inline font-family="Symbol">&#183;</fo:inline>
                  </fo:block>
               </fo:list-item-label>
               <fo:list-item-body>
                  <fo:block>
                     Creating a Simple XSL-FO Invoice
                  </fo:block>
               </fo:list-item-body>
            </fo:list-item>
```

```
          <fo:list-item>
             <fo:list-item-label>
                <fo:block>
                   <fo:inline font-family="Symbol">&#183;</fo:inline>
                </fo:block>
             </fo:list-item-label>
             <fo:list-item-body>
                <fo:block>
                   Using XSL-FO to produce PDF Documents
                </fo:block>
             </fo:list-item-body>
          </fo:list-item>

       </fo:list-block>
```

Our list ends here.

```
      </fo:flow> <!-- The end tag for the flow element-->
   </fo:page-sequence> <!-- The end tag for the page-sequence element -->
</fo:root> <!-- The end tag for the XSL-FO document -->
```

In the correct order, we need to provide closing tags for the `<fo:flow>`, `<fo:page-sequence>` and `<fo:root>` elements.

Creating a Simple XSL-FO Table

Having created a simple XSL-FO document incorporating a list, let's move on and create an XSL-FO document that includes a table, by using the `<fo:table>` element.

Our final XSL-FO document will look like this in the Antenna House XSL Formatter:

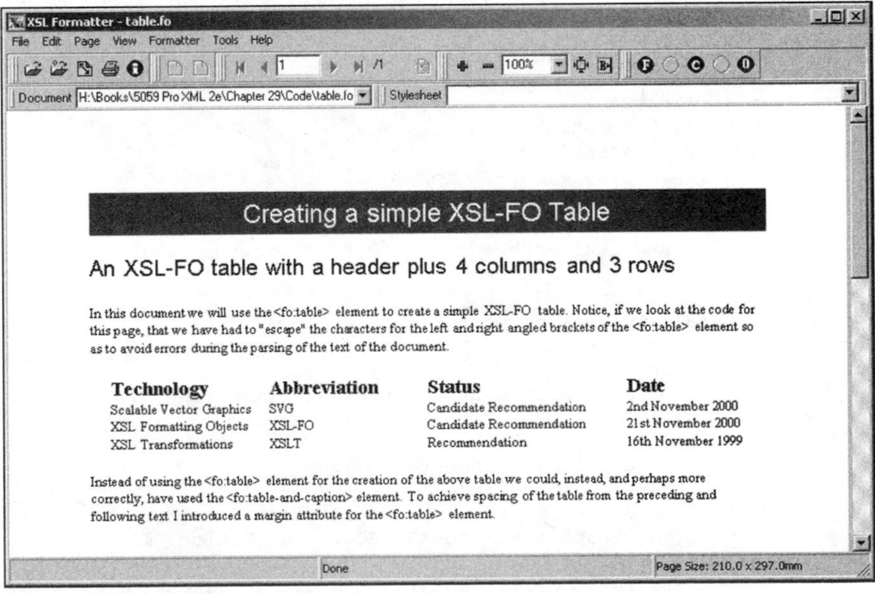

So, let's take a look at the XSL-FO code used to produce the document, which incorporates the table. Some of this is very similar to the code that was used to produce the previous document, and that will potentially form the basis for all the XSL-FO documents produced. Again, as we read the code, compare the visual output with the XSL-FO elements that underpin the visual effect.

```
<?xml version="1.0" encoding="utf-8"?>

<fo:root xmlns:fo="http://www.w3.org/1999/XSL/Format">

   <!-- This part of the XSL-FO document describes the layout master set.
        Page layout information for an A4 page; if we use US Letter size
        change the "page-height" to "11in" and the "page-width" to "8.5in".
        We may also want to express the margin sizes in inches. -->

   <fo:layout-master-set>
      <fo:simple-page-master
         master-name="Simple"
         page-height="29.7cm"
         page-width="21cm"
         margin-top="1cm"
         margin-bottom="2cm"
         margin-left="2cm"
         margin-right="2cm">
         <fo:region-body margin-top="1cm"/>
         <fo:region-before extent="0.5cm"/>
         <fo:region-after extent="1cm"/>
      </fo:simple-page-master>
   </fo:layout-master-set>

   <!-- The actual document layout starts here. -->
   <fo:page-sequence master-name="Simple">
      <fo:flow flow-name="xsl-region-body">

         <!-- This is a main header. -->
         <fo:block
            font-size="18pt"
            font-family="sans-serif"
            line-height="24pt"
            space-after.optimum="15pt"
            background-color="red"
            color="white"
            text-align="center"
            padding-top="5pt">
            Creating a simple XSL-FO Table
         </fo:block>

         <!-- This is a smaller header, with black text on white. -->
         <fo:block
            font-size="16pt"
            font-family="sans-serif"
            space-after.optimum="15pt"
            text-align="left">
            An XSL-FO table with a header plus 4 columns and 3 rows
         </fo:block>

         <!-- This is normal paragraph text -->
         <fo:block text-align="start">
            In this document we will use the &lt;fo:table&gt;
            element to create a simple XSL-FO table. Notice, if we look at
            the code for this page, that we have had to "escape" the
            characters for the left and right angled brackets of the
            &lt;fo:table&gt; element so as to avoid errors during the
```

```
   parsing of the text of the document.
</fo:block>
```

```
<!-- The table starts here. -->
<fo:table margin="0.5cm">
   <fo:table-column column-width="40mm"/>
   <fo:table-column column-width="40mm"/>
   <fo:table-column column-width="50mm"/>
   <fo:table-column column-width="40mm"/>
   <fo:table-body>
      <fo:table-row font-size="14pt" font-weight="bold">
         <fo:table-cell >
            <fo:block>Technology</fo:block>
         </fo:table-cell>
         <fo:table-cell >
            <fo:block>Abbreviation</fo:block>
         </fo:table-cell>
         <fo:table-cell >
            <fo:block>Status</fo:block>
         </fo:table-cell>
         <fo:table-cell >
            <fo:block>Date</fo:block>
         </fo:table-cell>
      </fo:table-row>
      <fo:table-row>
         <fo:table-cell >
            <fo:block>Scalable Vector Graphics</fo:block>
         </fo:table-cell>
         <fo:table-cell >
            <fo:block>SVG</fo:block>
         </fo:table-cell>
         <fo:table-cell >
            <fo:block>Candidate Recommendation</fo:block>
         </fo:table-cell>
         <fo:table-cell >
            <fo:block>2nd November 2000</fo:block>
         </fo:table-cell>
      </fo:table-row>
      <fo:table-row>
         <fo:table-cell >
            <fo:block>XSL Formatting Objects</fo:block>
         </fo:table-cell>
         <fo:table-cell >
            <fo:block>XSL-FO</fo:block>
         </fo:table-cell>
         <fo:table-cell>
            <fo:block>Candidate Recommendation</fo:block>
         </fo:table-cell>
         <fo:table-cell >
            <fo:block>21st November 2000</fo:block>
         </fo:table-cell>
      </fo:table-row>
      <fo:table-row>
         <fo:table-cell >
            <fo:block>XSL Transformations</fo:block>
         </fo:table-cell>
         <fo:table-cell >
            <fo:block>XSLT</fo:block>
         </fo:table-cell>
         <fo:table-cell>
            <fo:block>Recommendation</fo:block>
         </fo:table-cell>
```

```
                <fo:table-cell>
                   <fo:block>16th November 1999</fo:block>
                </fo:table-cell>
             </fo:table-row>
          </fo:table-body>
       </fo:table>
       <!-- The table ends here. -->

       <!-- Back to normal paragraph text -->
       <fo:block text-align="left">
          Instead of using the &lt;fo:table&gt; element for the creation
          of the above table we could instead, and perhaps more
          correctly, have used the &lt;fo:table-and-caption&gt; element.
          To achieve spacing of the table from the preceding and following
          text I introduced a margin attribute for the &lt;fo:table&gt;
          element.
       </fo:block>

    </fo:flow>
  </fo:page-sequence>
</fo:root>
```

Notice that the table is nested within a <fo:table> element. We used different font settings in the first row of the table to create the appearance of a column header. The <fo:column> elements define the number and width of the columns in our table. Within the <fo:table> element are several <fo:table-row> elements, one for each row of the table. Within each <fo:table-row> element there are <fo:table-cell> elements, each of which contains an <fo:block> element in the table shown. The content of each <fo:table-cell> element is nested within a <fo:block> element.

Creating a Simple XSL-FO Invoice

So, let's move on to create a simple invoice using XSL-FO. Since we have created our earlier documents in A4 paper size, we will take this opportunity to demonstrate use of US Letter size paper for our invoices. Similarly, we will use margins measured in inches, rather than in metric measure. Our previous documents did not include content in the <fo:region-before> or <fo:region-after> elements. On this occasion we will create a simple page header and footer, so we will need both a <fo:region-before> and a <fo:region-after> element nested within the <fo:page-sequence> element.

Later in the chapter, we will go on to further process our XSL-FO document as PDF. Since the version of the FOP processor that we will be using to produce PDF does not currently support <fo:region:start> and <fo:region-end>, we will only use <fo:region-before> and <fo:region-after> in this section to ease this further processing.

The invoice that we will create will be from XSL-FO.com to Wrox.com. XSL-FO.com uses data similar but not identical to that used elsewhere in this book.

We will present this as though the source XML was a static file. In practice, it might be created dynamically using a database query. Our XML source file, Invoice.xml, looks like this:

```
<?xml version="1.0"?>
<?xml-stylesheet href="Invoice.xsl" type="text/xsl"?>
```

```
<invoice>

   <ourAddress>
      <ourStreet>123 Formatting Street</ourStreet>
      <ourCity>Format City</ourCity>
      <ourState>Delirious State</ourState>
      <ourZip>012345</ourZip>
   </ourAddress>

   <billingAddress>
      <billingStreet>22222 Supercalifragilistic Street</billingStreet>
      <billingCity>Fiction City</billingCity>
      <billingState>New York</billingState>
      <billingZip>234567</billingZip>
   </billingAddress>

   <invoiceItems>
      <product id="1234" quantity="5" unitPrice="3"
         description="Web widgets" />
      <product id="2345" quantity="2" unitPrice="7"
         description="Wonder wobbles" />
      <product id="3456" quantity="8" unitPrice="2"
         description="Dynamic doodas" />
      <product id="4567" quantity="3" unitPrice="5"
         description="Marvel mysteries" />
   </invoiceItems>

</invoice>
```

The invoice we will produce looks like this:

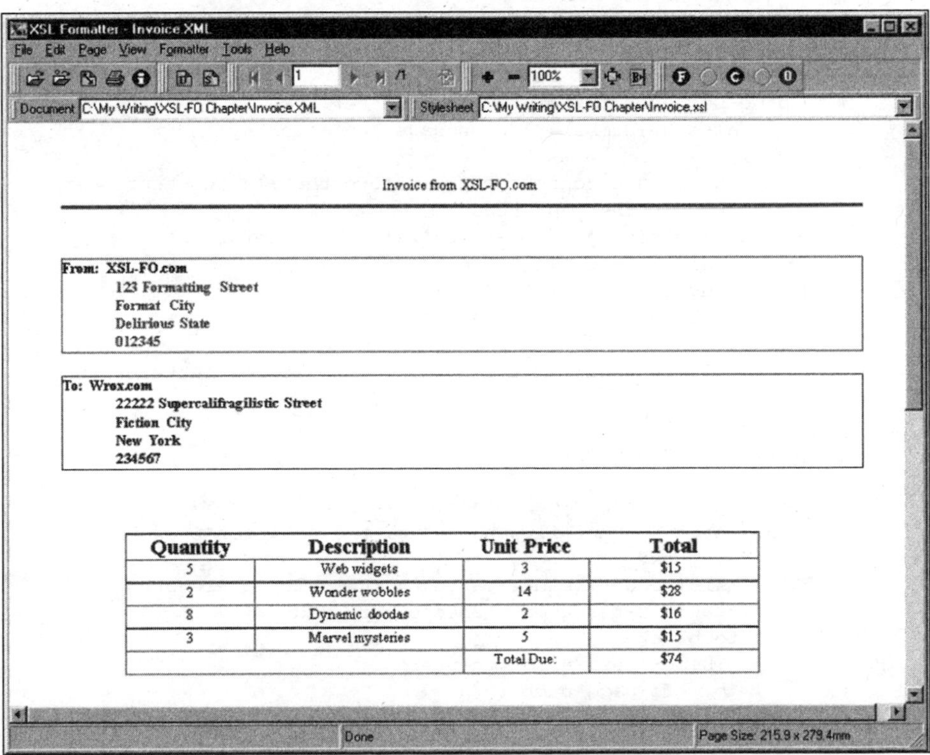

The invoice includes both a header in `xsl-region-before` and a footer (not visible in the screen shot) in `xsl-region-after`. In creating the invoice, we have used several XSL-FO elements and attributes that haven't been met so far in this chapter. As we step through the code, which is commented internally, the usage of these new elements and attributes should be fairly self-explanatory.

Here is the file, `Invoice.xsl`, which produced the invoice shown above:

```
<?xml version="1.0"?>
<xsl:stylesheet version="1.0"
   xmlns:xsl="http://www.w3.org/1999/XSL/Transform"
   xmlns:fo="http://www.w3.org/1999/XSL/Format">

   <!-- This is the template which does much of the work generating the
        Invoice. -->
   <xsl:template match="/">
      <fo:root xmlns:fo="http://www.w3.org/1999/XSL/Format">

         <!-- Set up the page master to have space for a header (using
              "region before") and a footer (using "region-after"). -->
         <fo:layout-master-set>
            <fo:simple-page-master  master-name="US-Letter"
               page-height="11in"  page-width="8.5in"
               margin-top="0.5in"  margin-bottom="0.5in"
               margin-left="0.5in"  margin-right="0.5in">
              <fo:region-body margin-top="0.75in" />
              <fo:region-before extent="0.75in"/>
              <fo:region-after extent="0.75in"/>
            </fo:simple-page-master>
         </fo:layout-master-set>

         <!-- The page content begins here. -->
         <fo:page-sequence master-name="US-Letter"
            initial-page-number="1" language="en" country="us">

            <!-- The static content comes before the flow content. -->
            <!-- This is the page header. -->
            <fo:static-content flow-name="xsl-region-before">
               <fo:block text-align="center">
                  Invoice from XSL-FO.com
               </fo:block>
               <fo:block>
                  <fo:leader leader-length="7.5in" leader-pattern="rule"
                     rule-thickness="2pt" color="red" />
               </fo:block>
            </fo:static-content>

            <!-- This is the page footer. -->
            <fo:static-content flow-name="xsl-region-after">
               <fo:block>
                  <fo:leader leader-pattern="rule" leader-length="7.5in"
                     rule-thickness="2pt" color="red" />
               </fo:block>
               <fo:block text-align="center">
                  p. <fo:page-number />
               </fo:block>
```

```
</fo:static-content>

<!-- This begins the page body content. -->
<fo:flow flow-name="xsl-region-body">
   <fo:block border="1pt double red" space-after.optimum="15pt"
      font-weight="bold">
      From: XSL-FO.com<xsl:apply-templates
      select="//ourStreet | //ourCity | //ourState | //ourZip"/>
   </fo:block>
   <fo:block border="1pt double blue" font-weight="bold">
      To: Wrox.com<xsl:apply-templates
      select="//billingStreet | //billingCity | //billingState |
      //billingZip"/>
   </fo:block>

   <!-- Use a <fo:table> element to hold the itemized data in
        the invoice. -->
   <fo:table margin="1.5cm" border="1pt double green" >
      <fo:table-column column-width="30mm" />
      <fo:table-column column-width="50mm" />
      <fo:table-column column-width="30mm" />
      <fo:table-column column-width="40mm" />
      <fo:table-body>

         <!-- Create a header row for the column labels. -->
         <fo:table-row font-size="14pt" font-weight="bold">
            <fo:table-cell >
               <fo:block text-align="center">
                  Quantity
               </fo:block>
            </fo:table-cell>
            <fo:table-cell >
               <fo:block text-align="center">
                  Description
               </fo:block>
            </fo:table-cell>
            <fo:table-cell >
               <fo:block text-align="center">
                  Unit Price
               </fo:block>
            </fo:table-cell>
            <fo:table-cell >
               <fo:block text-align="center">
                  Total
               </fo:block>
            </fo:table-cell>
         </fo:table-row>

         <!-- Use an XSLT <xsl:for-each> element to step through
              each product in the source file. -->
         <xsl:for-each select="/invoice/invoiceItems/product">
            <xsl:variable name="quantity" select="@quantity" />
            <xsl:variable name="unitPrice" select="@unitPrice"/>
            <fo:table-row>
               <fo:table-cell border="1pt double green"
```

```
                        text-align="center">
                        <fo:block text-align="center">
                           <xsl:value-of select="@quantity" />
                        </fo:block>
                     </fo:table-cell>
                     <fo:table-cell border="1pt double green"
                        text-align="center">
                        <fo:block>
                           <xsl:value-of select="@description"/>
                        </fo:block>
                     </fo:table-cell>
                     <fo:table-cell border="1pt double green"
                        text-align="center">
                        <fo:block text-align="center">
                           <xsl:value-of select="@unitPrice" />
                        </fo:block>
                     </fo:table-cell>
                     <fo:table-cell border="1pt double green"
                        text-align="center">
                        <fo:block>
                           $<xsl:value-of
                              select="$quantity * $unitPrice" />
                        </fo:block>
                     </fo:table-cell>
                  </fo:table-row>
               </xsl:for-each>

               <!-- Carry out the calculation of the grand total due
                    for the items being invoiced. -->
               <xsl:variable name="total">
                  <xsl:call-template name="runningTotal">
                     <xsl:with-param name="list" select="//product"/>
                  </xsl:call-template>
               </xsl:variable>

               <!-- Create the final row of the table including the
                    grand total due. -->
               <fo:table-row>
                  <fo:table-cell >
                     <fo:block></fo:block>
                  </fo:table-cell>
                  <fo:table-cell >
                     <fo:block></fo:block>
                  </fo:table-cell>
                  <fo:table-cell border="1pt double green"
                     text-align="center" >
                     <fo:block>Total Due:</fo:block>
                  </fo:table-cell>
                  <fo:table-cell border="1pt double green"
                     text-align="center">
                     <fo:block>
                        $<xsl:value-of select="$total"/>
                     </fo:block>
                  </fo:table-cell>
               </fo:table-row>
```

```
            </fo:table-body>
         </fo:table> <!--The table containing the items ends here.-->

         <!-- Add a reminder of when payment is due. -->
         <fo:block text-align="center" font-weight="bold">
            Terms: Payment is due within 30 days.
         </fo:block>

      </fo:flow>
   </fo:page-sequence>
  </fo:root> <!-- Root element template stops here. -->
 </xsl:template>

 <xsl:template match="*">
   <fo:block text-align="left" space-after.optimum="15pt">
      <xsl:value-of select="."/></fo:block>
 </xsl:template>

 <xsl:template match="/invoice/ourAddress/*">
   <fo:block text-indent="0.5in" color="red">
      <xsl:value-of select="."/></fo:block>
 </xsl:template>

 <xsl:template match="/invoice/billingAddress/*">
   <fo:block text-indent="0.5in" color="blue">
      <xsl:value-of select="."/></fo:block>
 </xsl:template>

 <!-- This named template calculates the running total due. -->
 <xsl:template name="runningTotal">
   <xsl:param name="list" />
   <xsl:choose>
      <xsl:when test="$list">
         <xsl:variable name="first" select="$list[1]"/>
         <xsl:variable name="othersTotal">
            <xsl:call-template name="runningTotal">
               <xsl:with-param name="list"
                  select="$list[position()!=1]"/>
            </xsl:call-template>
         </xsl:variable>
         <xsl:value-of select="$first/@quantity * $first/@unitPrice +
            $othersTotal" />
      </xsl:when>
      <xsl:otherwise>0</xsl:otherwise>
   </xsl:choose>
 </xsl:template>

</xsl:stylesheet>
```

Remember, you will need an XSL Formatter such as the Antenna House XML Formatter to view the XSL-FO. A standard Web browser, such as Internet Explorer, is not capable of rendering it.

Our XSL-FO output can be printed directly from the Antenna House XSL Formatter. For some users, having the invoice as a PDF file might better suit their current needs, so we will move on to examine how to convert our XSL-FO file, `Invoice.fo`, to PDF.

Using XSL-FO to produce PDF documents

In this section, we will process our XSL-FO invoice one step further. As indicated in the previous sections, this may not be necessary for some purposes, but until XSL Formatters become more mainstream, you may feel more comfortable handling at least some of your documents in the longer established PDF.

For the rest of this section we will use the FOP formatter, which can be downloaded as described in the XSL-FO tools section earlier in the chapter. Of course, if you prefer another XSL-FO to PDF tool, for example the RenderX XEP processor, please feel free to use that instead.

The beginner's installation of FOP, mentioned earlier, in the XSL-FO Tools section, includes a number of `.fo` files that you can use for test purposes. To test that your installation is working, on Windows 98, run the `autoexec.bat` file (to apply the `CLASSPATH` changes), and then at a command prompt change to the directory in which you installed FOP (`c:\fop`). Then to test the installation, making use of the `test.fo` file that should have been installed when you unzipped the FOP file, type the following at the command line:

```
> java org.apache.fop.apps.CommandLine test.fo test.pdf
```

Alternatively, to use the file that we used earlier in the chapter, we should be able to enter this:

```
> java org.apache.fop.apps.CommandLine Welcome2.fo Welcome2.pdf
```

We should then be able to view the file either directly within the Adobe Acrobat Reader (available for download from www.adobe.com) or within a web browser.

If all has gone well, we should see a series of messages; something like this:

```
MS-DOS Prompt
C:\My Writing\XSL-FO Chapter>java org.apache.fop.apps.CommandLine Welcome2.fo We
lcome2.pdf
FOP 0.15
using SAX parser org.apache.xerces.parsers.SAXParser
using renderer org.apache.fop.render.pdf.PDFRenderer
using element mapping org.apache.fop.fo.StandardElementMapping
using element mapping org.apache.fop.svg.SVGElementMapping
using property list mapping org.apache.fop.fo.StandardPropertyListMapping
using property list mapping org.apache.fop.svg.SVGPropertyListMapping
building formatting object tree
WARNING: Unknown value for property 'text-align': left
setting up fonts
formatting FOs into areas
 [1]
rendering areas to PDF
writing out PDF

C:\My Writing\XSL-FO Chapter>_
```

Remember to ensure that the source file, `Welcome2.fo`, is either in the same directory as the one from which you are issuing the command, or is within a directory specified by the PATH environment variable. We specified that our output file be `Welcome2.pdf`. Here it is, displayed in the Adobe Acrobat Reader.

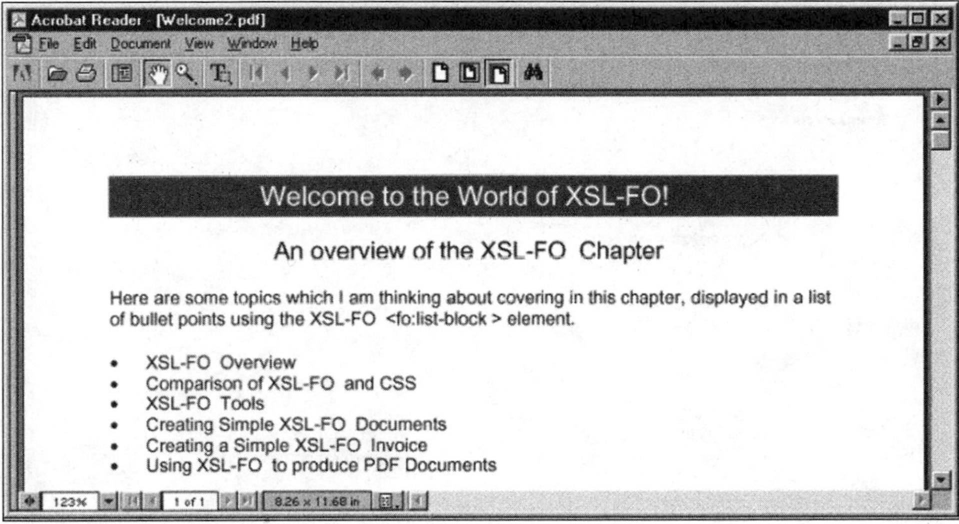

We can see that if the FOP installation is correct, then it is straightforward to convert an XSL-FO file to an equivalent PDF file.

Using XSL-FO with SVG

In Chapter 18, we showed how to use **Scalable Vector Graphics** (**SVG**) to create some graphical output from some business data. XSL-FO and SVG are designed to work together. In fact, XSL-FO can display several graphics formats within a document. Since the main point of interest is how to embed images within XSL-FO documents, we will use very simple XSL-FO documents whose structure should already be familiar to us.

So, let's look at an SVG image embedded in an XSL-FO document. The SVG image correctly displays as a static image, but the animation and interactivity it displays when viewed in a dedicated SVG viewer, such as the Adobe SVG Viewer, is not accessible in the embedded image.

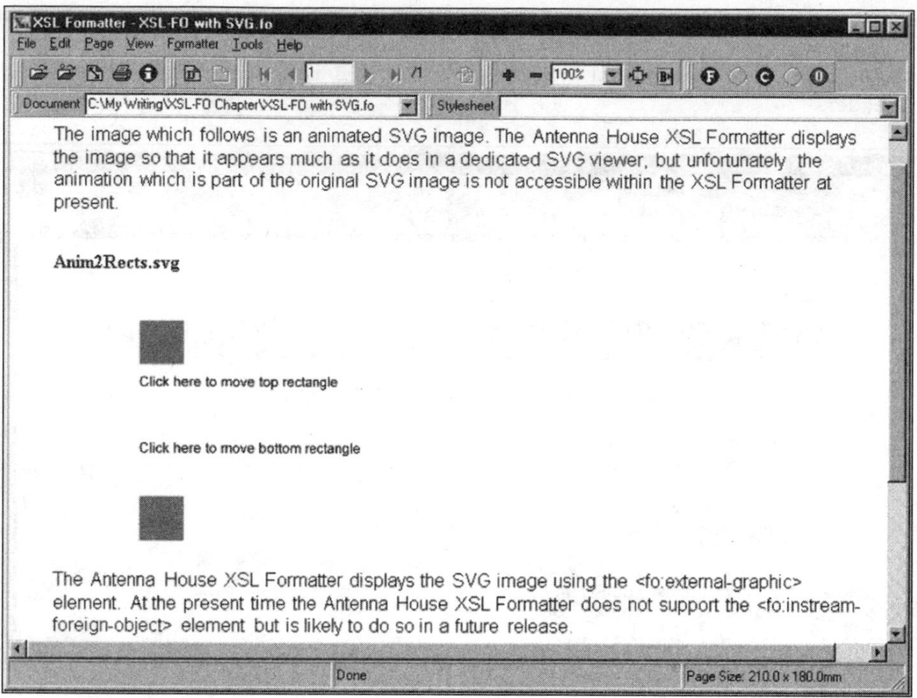

To produce this screen shot, we needed the simple SVG image (`Anim2Rects.svg`) to be contained in the same directory as the `SVG.fo` file, which contains the following code:

```
<?xml version="1.0"?>
<fo:root xmlns:fo="http://www.w3.org/1999/XSL/Format">

   <fo:layout-master-set>

      <!-- Page layout information for a page to be displayed on screen. -->

      <fo:simple-page-master master-name="Screen"
         page-height="18cm"
         page-width="21cm"
         margin-top="1cm"
         margin-bottom="1cm"
         margin-left="1cm"
         margin-right="1cm">
         <fo:region-body margin-top="0cm" />
         <fo:region-before extent="2cm" />
         <fo:region-after extent="1cm" />
      </fo:simple-page-master>

   </fo:layout-master-set>
```

Note that we have altered the dimensions of our `<fo:simple-page-master>` element to correspond a little more closely to a screen shape, since this document was intended only for display on screen. Note too that we altered the value of the `master-name` attribute of the `<fo:simple-page-master>` element to `Screen`, and made a corresponding change in the `master-name` attribute of the `<fo:page-sequence>` element that follows.

```
  <fo:page-sequence master-name="Screen">
     <fo:flow flow-name="xsl-region-body">

        <!-- This defines plain paragraph text for this document. -->
        <fo:block
           font-size="12pt"
           font-family="sans-serif"
           space-after.optimum="15pt"
           text-align="left">
           The image that follows is an animated SVG image. The Antenna
           House XSL Formatter displays the image so that it appears much
           as it does in a dedicated SVG viewer, but unfortunately the
           animation, which is part of the original SVG image, is not
           accessible within the XSL Formatter at present.
        </fo:block>

        <fo:block space-before="2em" font="bold large serif"
           keep-with-next="always">
           Anim2Rects.svg
        </fo:block>
        <fo:block>
           <fo:external-graphic content-width="300px"
              content-height="250px" src="Anim2Rects.svg" />
        </fo:block>
```

The code section above does the work of embedding the SVG image. The `<fo:external graphic>` element is used. The `content-width` and `content-height` attributes define the screen area to be used to display the image. The `src` attribute specifies the name of the SVG image that is to be displayed.

```
        <!-- This defines plain paragraph text for this document. -->
        <fo:block
           font-size="12pt"
           font-family="sans-serif"
           space-after.optimum="15pt"
           text-align="left">
           The Antenna House XSL Formatter displays the SVG image using the
           &lt;fo:external-graphic&gt; element. At the present time the
           Antenna House XSL Formatter does not support the
           &lt;fo:instream-foreign-object&gt; element but is likely to do
           so in a future release.
        </fo:block>

     </fo:flow>
  </fo:page-sequence>

</fo:root>
```

We can use very similar code to display `.gif`, `.jpg` or `.png` images. Simply provide a filename appropriate to the image type that we wish to display, specify appropriate dimensions for the screen area on which the image is to be displayed, and all should be well.

Using an XSL Formatter As an XSL-FO Web Browser

Imagine having web pages in XSL-FO which can show precisely the layout of a document on paper and which can be printed, with confidence, on the assumption that the computer understands XSL-FO, since we are using an XSL formatter. Contrast that with the sometimes-haphazard output if we try to print an HTML/XHTML web page.

The first step in achieving that potentially attractive concept is to be able to access XSL-FO documents directly across the Web, which is now possible. The screen shot that follows is of a very short XSL-FO document stored on the www.XSL-FO.com web site. In the Antenna House XSL Formatter, type in http://www.XSL-FO.com/HelloWorld.fo in the Document window, and then we can simply press the blue F button to run the XSL Formatter, and the XSL-FO document is displayed across the Web.

Of course, the layout of the "Hello World" document is hardly earth shattering in its design but we might want to try printing it to see how the computer copes with that.

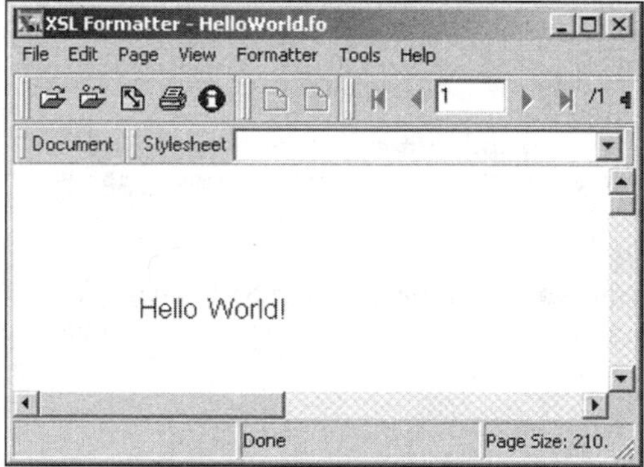

Access to XSL-FO documents across the Web is not only limited to only text. It is also possible to access XSL-FO documents with embedded SVG and other graphic elements. The following screenshot shows the simple XSL-FO document we saw in an earlier section, when accessed across the Web. Note the URL: http:www.xsl-fo.com/XSL-FO%20with%20SVG.fo in the Document window of the Antenna House XSL Formatter.

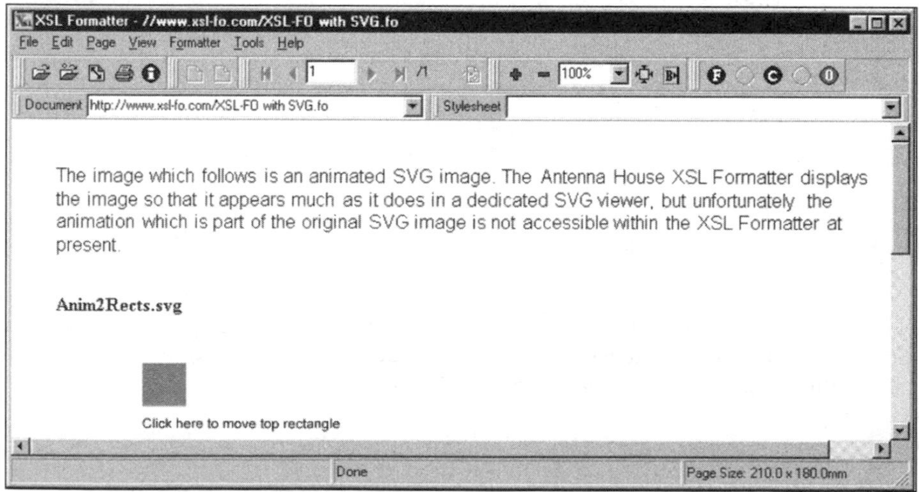

Of course, this process isn't limited to simply displaying static XSL-FO documents. It is also possible to display XSL-FO that is accessed across the Web as separate XML documents, and their associated XSL stylesheets.

Below is a similar "Hello World" screenshot to the one that we saw earlier. Notice that both the XML source document and the XSL stylesheet are each situated on the www.XSL-FO.com web site.

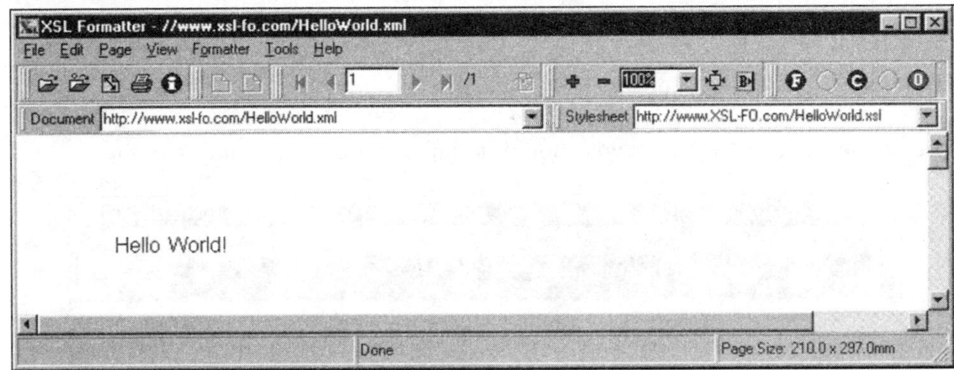

The URL for the XML source document is http://www.xsl-fo.com/HelloWorld.xml. The URL for the stylesheet is http://www.xsl-fo.com/HelloWorld.xsl.

With documents that are more significant, the opportunities open up to apply different stylesheets to one XML source document (or XML generated from a RDBMS). This can be performed locally of course, but as can be seen from the screenshot, it can also be done across the Web.

The opportunity to apply different XSL style sheets to XML source documents across the Web opens up many interesting possibilities. The most straightforward use is to apply the XSL stylesheet designed by the author. However, the author of the XML source document may have provided more than one XSL stylesheet, allowing multiple possible outputs on screen or paper. The further possibility exists to create our own XSL stylesheet to display data on screen – either simply as XSL-FO, but with the option of selecting certain parts of the XML source document for display as SVG. Therefore, with appropriate knowledge of XSLT, XSL-FO, and SVG, we could create our own customized graphical output from any XML source file on the Web. The possibility of opening up web applications using XSL-FO and SVG is an exciting one.

When we bear in mind that XSL-FO includes a `<fo:basic-link>` element, and may potentially also allow the more complex linking functionality of the XML Linking Language, XLink, and the XML Pointer Language, XPointer, it should be clear that powerful and flexible web-based XSL-FO functionality is possible. To what extent it is implemented depends on many factors outside the scope of this chapter. Our purpose was simply to whet your appetite and to recognize exciting, if perhaps unanticipated, possibilities.

Shortly before this chapter was completed, an exciting new preview release of a multi-namespace XML browser called X-Smiles was made available. X-Smiles can display XSL-FO, SVG, **SMIL** (**Synchronized Multimedia Integration Language**) and XForms. Since only version 1.0 of SMIL is a full W3C Recommendation at the time of writing, expect some gaps within the preview release of X-Smiles, but what is already there opens up exciting new possibilities.

The X-Smiles browser, which is Java-based, can be downloaded from the X-Smiles Web site: http://www.xsmiles.org/. The version tested was 0.31.

If you download the binary version it can be unzipped into a suitably named directory. I installed it into `c:\XSmiles`. When unzipping the download be sure to enable use of folders, since X-Smiles expects a particular directory hierarchy to be present. If you unzip into a single directory, X-Smiles won't run. Also be aware that X-Smiles uses the Apache Xalan and Xerces processors, so be careful that you have no other, possibly older, versions of Xalan or Xerces in your Classpath – that could cause problems.

From the command line, if you have observed the above cautions, you can start X-Smiles using the following command:

```
c:\XSmiles> java -jar xsmiles.jar
```

If the installation has gone well then you should see an opening screen similar to this:

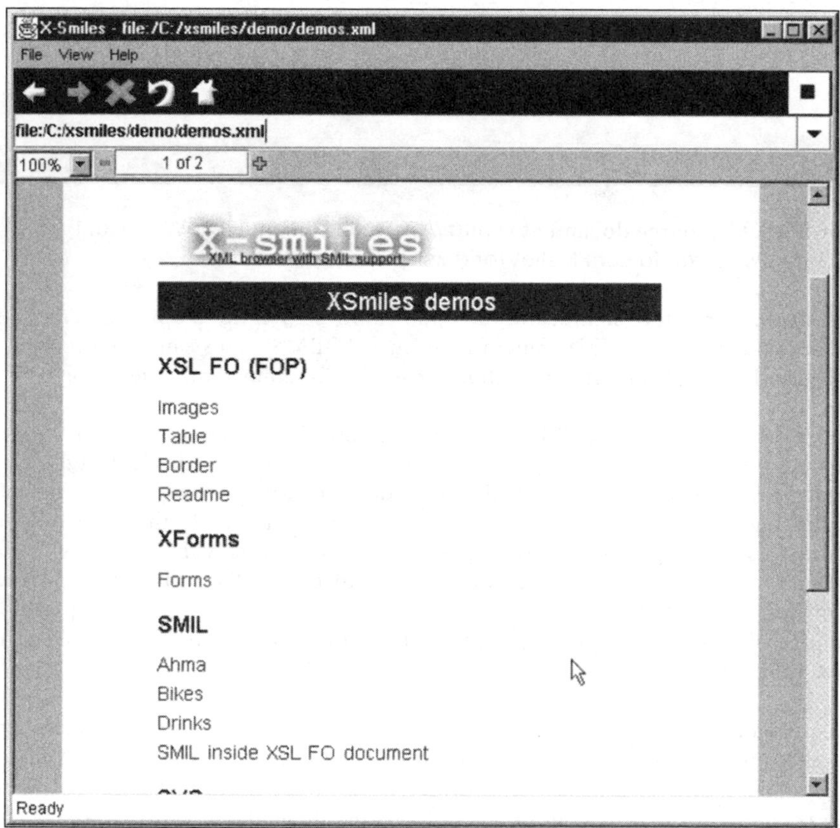

Notice that there are links to online demos for XSL-FO, as well as XForms, SMIL and SVG.

X-Smiles allows the embedding of one XML namespace within another. For example, if we embed the SVG vertical bar chart from Chapter 18 in a simple XSL-FO document, we can view them together within X-Smiles:

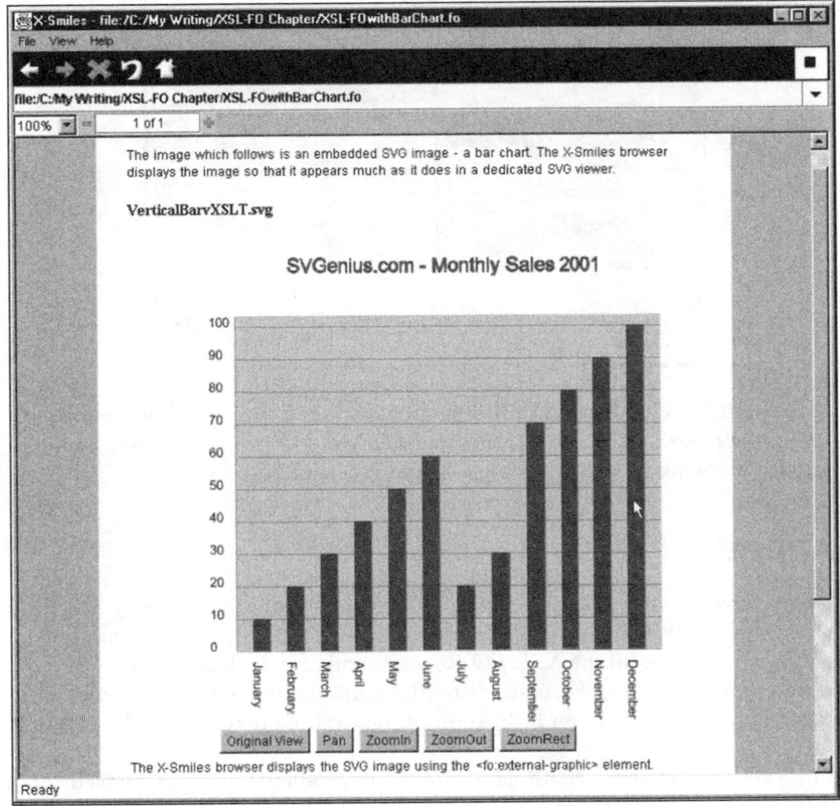

The buttons labelled Pan, ZoomIn, etc provide the zooming and panning capabilities common to SVG Viewers. See Chapter 18 for further information on SVG.

Both X-Smiles and the Antenna House XSL Formatter are very much preview releases and neither is, at the time of writing, a complete implementation of XSL-FO. Therefore expect to have to tweak some code since what works on one browser/formatter may not work unchanged on the other. We can expect that situation to improve as further versions are released.

You can also download, as a separate zipped file, a range of demo files from the X-Smiles site. Among them is a demo of a SMIL presentation embedded within an XSL-FO document. It is a little startling to listen to lively music and a slide show within an XSL-FO document. Company reports may never be the same again!

X-Smiles also allows XSL-FO, SVG, SMIL and XForms to be downloaded across the Web. In that context X-Smiles has a benefit over the Antenna House XSL Formatter in that you can use the URL for an XML source document and X-Smiles will find and load the linked XSLT stylesheet, so preserving the XML source for viewing. The X-Smiles browser allows the XSL-FO source, the XML source or the XSLT source to be viewed:

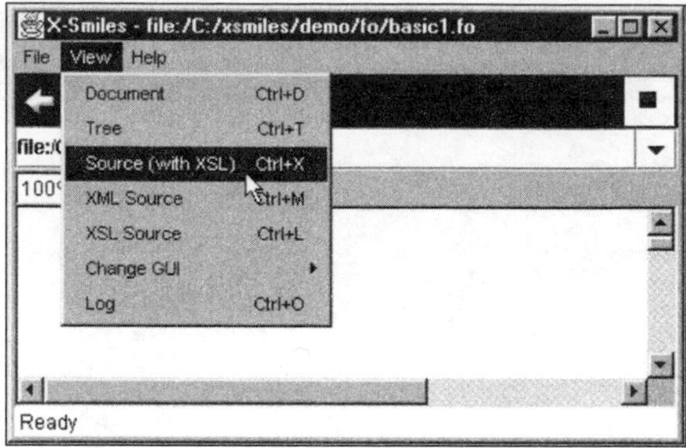

In addition, it is possible to view the output document as a tree. By switching between these various views of the XML source, the XSLT stylesheet and the XSL-FO produced from them, X-Smiles can be a great learning tool, allowing us to explore the various facets of XSL-FO.

Looking Ahead

In this chapter we have given you an indication of some facets of using parts of XSL-FO. There is a great deal of detail which it wasn't possible to cover. At present XSL-FO tools are few in number, and will likely continue to be so until the XSL-FO Recommendation is finalized. However, the emergence of tools like the Antenna House XSL Formatter and the multi-namespace XML browser, X-Smiles (http://www.x-smiles.org/), gives us an indication of the exciting potential of the technology.

XSL-FO can be expected to play a significant role in the production of XML-based reports, quite possibly in combination with SVG. Those same reports may be presented online using not only XSL-FO and SVG but also incorporating XForms to add interactivity and SMIL to provide embedded multimedia, so potentially providing business documents whose functionality goes far beyond the presentation of XML statically on paper. Alternatively XSL-FO with suitable embedded SVG or SMIL could provide powerful XML-based training "documents", although it is debatable whether these exciting interactive multimedia entities are adequately described by such a prosaic term.

XSL-FO may equally carve out a significant role in production of lengthy paper-based documents. Perhaps a future edition of this book will be produced using XSL-FO.

Summary

We have covered quite a bit of ground in this chapter and we have been introduced to some relatively straightforward usage of XSL-FO, as well as some exciting new possibilities of combining XSL-FO with SVG or SMIL.

By far the best way to learn how to use XSL-FO is to practice using real code. Therefore, we would encourage you to download one of the available XSL formatters to start playing with it – each has useful example XSL-FO files. The code in this chapter is straightforward, so feel free to experiment with changing attribute values, adding additional `<fo:simple-page-master>` elements with different page sizes, margin settings etc. If the Beginner's version of the FOP processor that we mentioned earlier was downloaded, there are many sample files to examine and learn from.

Dave Pawson, a member of the W3C, has recently produced an XSL demo on his web site at http://www.dpawson.co.uk/. There is also a dedicated XSL-FO mailing list at http://www.yahoogroups.com/group/XSL-FO with a page of useful links.

XSL-FO (and SVG) will assume increasing importance in the textual and graphical presentation of XML data. We can't pretend that it is a trivial task to master either XSL-FO or SVG, particularly when XSLT may be generating both, but we would encourage the exploration of those technologies since their future importance is in little doubt.

We hope that we have shown you enough to convince you that exciting times lie ahead for XSL-FO development, not least in combination with SVG graphics and SMIL multimedia.

21

Case Study: Generating a Site Index

Have you ever been frustrated doing a web search? That's a quite common experience when using a global search site, but it's true doing searches even within a single large site. A wealth of information on a web site isn't worth much if you can't find a specific piece of information even when you know it's there.

This problem was first experienced in books a long time ago. The evolution of library science helped to reduce the problem of finding information among books. Library card catalogs and book indexes are examples of searchable meta-data. Creating and using searchable meta-data, whether in books or on the web, makes existing information more useful. It still takes people though to do a good job of creating that meta-data.

While human judgment and effort is required, machines can remove the drudgery of creating an index. An **index generator** is a computer program that takes documents and their index marks, along with the **thesaurus** of index terms and relationships between the terms, and then creates an index that reflects the combination document marks and their meanings.

Here's what this might look like when generating an index for a book about cars. The diagram shows a sample of three pages from the book, along with the key words on each page. In general, a thesaurus lists the words, phrases, or concepts to be found in a book and the relationships between them. In this case, the thesaurus is capturing the relationship between car model lines and their origin. The index generator combines the thesaurus with the pages of the books containing the words in the thesaurus, to produce an index. The index displays the category groupings found in the thesaurus, along with a display of each of the words, and the location where each word was found.

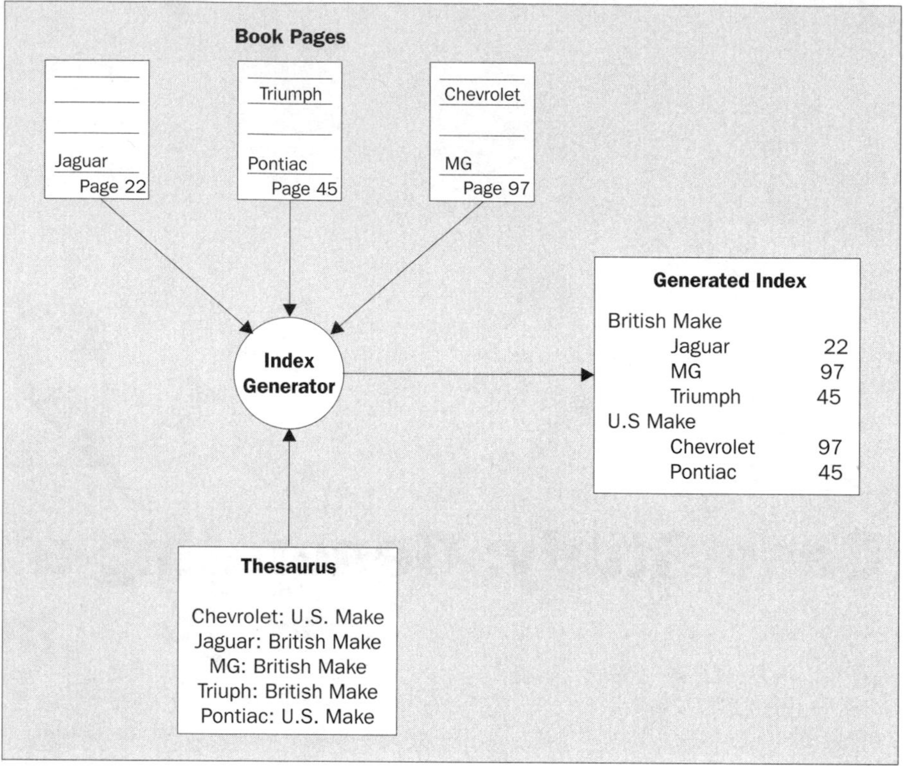

The index generator we'll describe reads XML or HTML source documents to produce XML documents that describe and link to pre-determined terms in the source documents. Since it's easier to see the relationships on a rendered web page, we'll first describe the generation of an HTML web site index. Later, we'll apply the same process in a pure XML environment. Lastly, we'll see the design and code for the generator.

What Is a Site Index?

Much like the index in this book, a web site index presents pointers from words and phrases to locations in a web site. The words and phrases in the index are determined by human judgment, and the pages to which the index entries link, are also determined by choices made while the page is being created. In contrast, a *search* function looks for combinations of words dynamically. A search can attempt to provide some guidance as to the importance of a word on each page in which it is found, but cannot show the relative importance of a word in relation to the entire site.

For instance, on a financial web site, a conventional search of a term as common as "stock" would show many dozens of pages, with good descriptions of the term buried among mere mentions of the term. In contrast, a user who looks up "stock" in the index would only find pages with significant descriptions or uses of the term. The user may also see in the index several choices to narrow down what s/he's trying to find. For instance, looking for "stock", s/he may find a list that includes "stock funds", "stock options", and "stock, international".

The American Society of Indexers (ASI) at www.asindexing.org has a good introduction to the science of indexing, as well as references to examples of site indexes. That site shows there are as many different ways to organize a set of documents, as there are document sets. The rest of this chapter will focus on a simple scheme that's appropriate for the indexing of small-scale web sites, but keep in mind that the generator mechanism could support more sophisticated indexing.

Index Example

The following screen shots show three pages from a simple example site. The lower right page is a source document, to the left is the main index page, and the upper right shows one of several available index term pages. Hidden information in the source document causes an index entry to be made to the source document for the word "saxophone". The "saxophone" link on the main index page points to an index page listing all documents related to "saxophone". One of the entries in the table points to the source document.

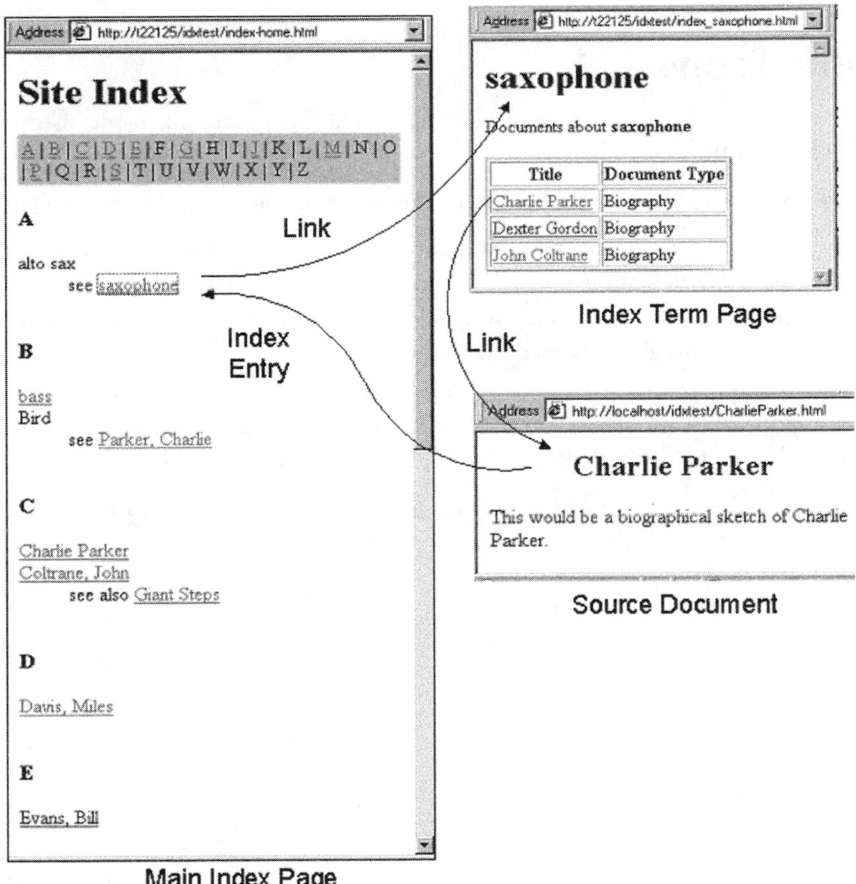

The Index Term Page is the analogue of the list of pages found after an index term in a book. By linking to that list, we can show the list more comfortably and add valuable features, such as the title and type for each link. That helps the user pick a particular entry. There is also almost no loss of context by moving off the main Site Index Page since it is organized alphabetically, and the choice of term has no obvious semantic relationship to the terms next to it on the main list.

Thesaurus and Page Markup Design

Looking again at the earlier car book example or the web site example, the primary design decisions for an index generator are:

- ❑ What are the key words we want to find in the book?
- ❑ What word relationships do we want to capture in the thesaurus?
- ❑ How do we find the key words in the book?
- ❑ What is the format of the generated output?

In this section, we'll talk about the design of this chapter's thesaurus and page markup. It is only one of many possible designs. The ability to create more sophisticated models is limited only by willingness, and the resources available.

Thesaurus Terms

Each word or phrase that names a concept useful for searching is a **term**. The model used by the generator has four classes of terms:

- ❑ A **preferred** term is the spelling for a concept that is used as the key for the concept.
- ❑ A **synonym** is a word or phrase that names the same concept, or very similar concept, as a preferred term.
- ❑ A **rotated** term has the same words as a preferred term, but in a different order. A rotation almost always usually occurs around a comma.
- ❑ A **related** term forms a relationship from one preferred term to another preferred term. It is a peer-to-peer relationship in contrast to the other terms that are subservient to a preferred term. The relationship is less strong than a synonym.

The relationship between these term classes can be illustrated like this, using "Parker, Charlie" as the preferred term from our example site:

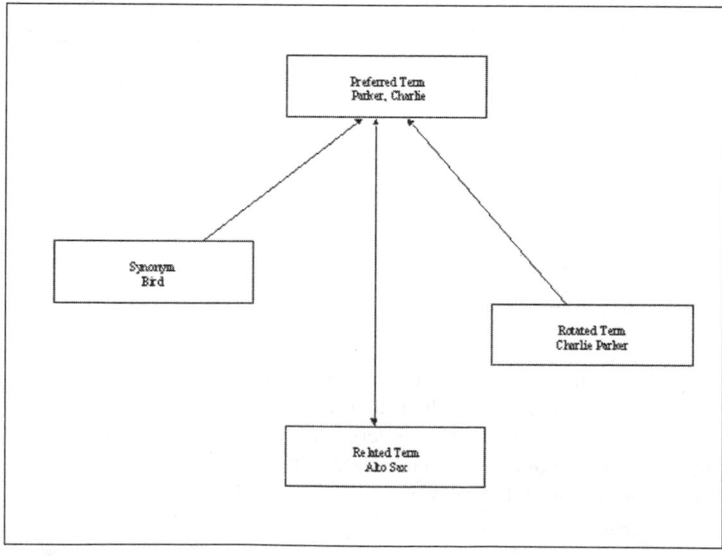

Examples of these term classes can also be seen on the main index page below:

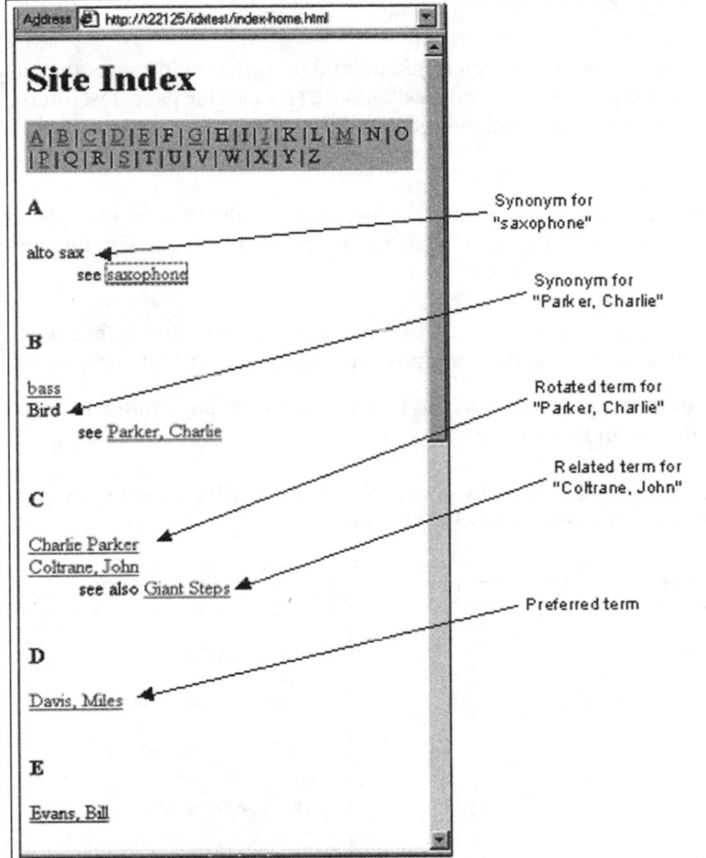

The list of terms, their classifications, and their relationships form a **thesaurus**. A small thesaurus may be kept in a spreadsheet; a large one would be maintained better in a database. An XML representation is used to provide a common format that may be read by our generator.

Page Markup for Indexing

The rest of the work for index generation is attaching indexing information to source documents – in this case HTML pages. Each page to be indexed must have one or more preferred terms attached from the thesaurus. Although the indexing information can be performed in an XML linkbase or other external store, placing the tags within the document has advantages:

- There is no chance that the indexing information will be wrongly associated with a different page (or vice-versa).
- A conventional search engine can be configured to give a strong preference for the preferred terms displayed in the page. Conventional searches and index searches complement each other, so it's preferable for the relatively expensive indexing work to be leveraged by conventional searching.

To place tags in the pages' HTML or XML source requires that the indexer can modify the source, or in more sophisticated production environments, that page indexing is integrated into the automated page generation process of the web site's content management system.

The HTML `<META>` tag elements are well suited to hold this information since they allow a natural name/value pair, and search engines already look in `<META>` tags for page description information. We'll see later how embedded indexing information is gathered from XML documents more flexibly than from `<META>` tags.

Two other pieces of information will improve the look and usability of the index page entries. Each is associated with the HTML or XML source page, so they are stored along with the preferred terms of the source page.

- A title for the page to be displayed as the text of the link (that is, between the `<A>` and `</A>` tags) will allow the link to be descriptive in the context of the index entry.
- A document type name to be displayed along with the page title will help the user find the most useful page in the list.

We can see how the `<META>` tags work by going back to the first illustration of the site index, but this time we'll replace the source document with its HTML code.

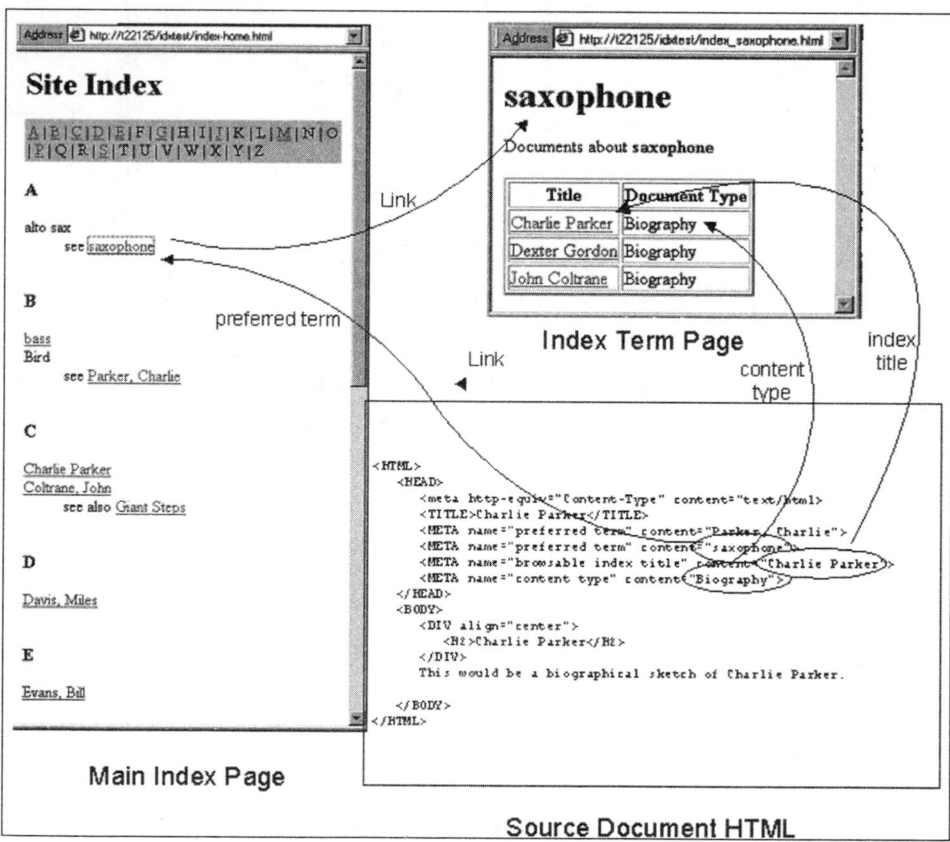

The Indexer and the Generator

An **indexer** is a person skilled in natural language, typically with a background in Library Science, who creates and maintains the index. Much of this work is maintaining the thesaurus for the site, which is the controlled vocabulary for the index. The indexer analyzes the whole web site, creating and later adjusting the thesaurus for the information on the site. Each page to be indexed is categorized with terms from the thesaurus, and in this particular design, the `<META>` tags of the page are updated with indexing information. Whenever needed, the indexer causes the index generator to be run, which reads the page indexing information and the thesaurus to generate web index pages and a report on the index process. The indexer then examines the index generation report, and the whole site, to make additional adjustments.

The following process diagram shows a simple indexing cycle; eight steps of the process are performed from the beginning, and the process continues after the first round. On a controlled and complex web site, the indexers' job is made more difficult by restrictions of web site updates, the introduction of new content pages, and longer-than-desired cycle times to validate changes.

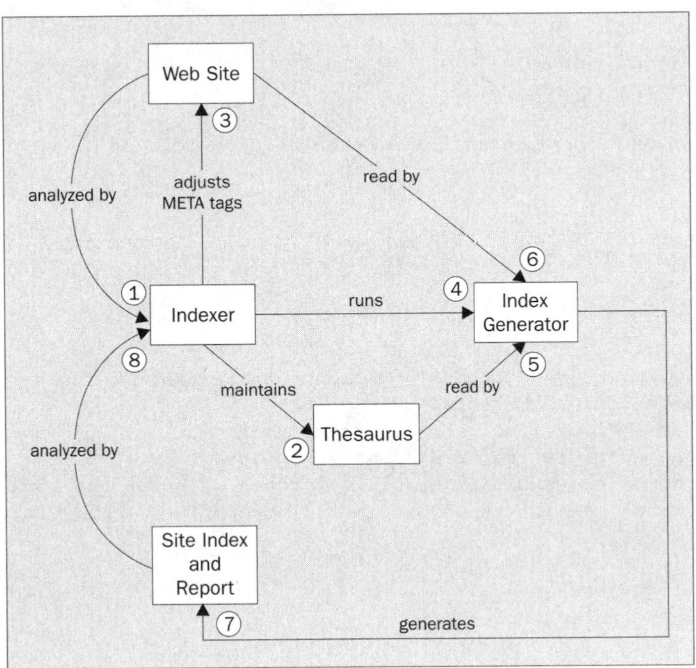

An indexer with a language arts background is probably not going to change `<META>` tags or run a generator personally. Technical personnel will make page changes and run the generator, or provide tools for indexers to do so indirectly. Of course, in working environments where the site production process and roles are less formal, indexers themselves may edit HTML files and directly run the generator.

HTML Example

Let's look at some example files. The entire example can also be downloaded from the Wrox site (http://www.wrox.com). First, we'll see the starting documents and the ending documents to get a feel for the end points of the process. The starting documents are the site HTML pages and the thesaurus XML document; the ending documents are the XML index documents, and then the HTML rendering of the index.

Example Site

The example site has biographies of jazz musicians. Here are two example pages; the others are similar. Notice the <META> tag values.

John Coltrane's page, `JohnColtrane.html`:

```
<HTML>
   <HEAD>
      <META http-equiv="Content-Type" content="text/html; charset=utf-8">
      <TITLE>John Coltrane</TITLE>
      <META name="preferred term" content="Coltrane, John">
      <META name="preferred term" content="saxophone">
      <META name="preferred term" content="Giant Steps">
      <META name="browsable index title" content="John Coltrane">
      <META name="content type" content="Biography">
   </HEAD>
   <BODY>
      <DIV align="center">
         <H2>John Coltrane</H2>
      </DIV>
      This would be a biographical sketch of John Coltrane.
   </BODY>
</HTML>
```

Thelonious Monk's page, `TheloniousMonk.html`:

```
<HTML>
   <HEAD>
      <META http-equiv="Content-Type" content="text/html; charset=utf-8">
      <TITLE>Thelonious Monk</TITLE>
      <META name="preferred term" content="Monk, Thelonious">
      <META name="preferred term" content="piano">
      <META name="browsable index title" content="Thelonious Monk">
      <META name="content type" content="Biography">
   </HEAD>
   <BODY>
      <DIV align="center">
         <H2>Thelonious Monk</H2>
      </DIV>
      This would be a biographical sketch of Thelonious Monk.
   </BODY>
</HTML>
```

The home page (below) of the site, `JazzHome.html`, simply links to the others, and has no indexing <META> tags:

```
<HTML>
   <HEAD>
      <meta http-equiv="Content-Type" content="text/html; charset=utf-8">
      <TITLE>Jazz Home</TITLE>
   </HEAD>
   <BODY>
      <DIV align="center">
```

```
            <H2>Jazz Home</H2>
         </DIV>
         <UL>
            <LI><A href="MilesDavis.html">Miles Davis</A></LI>
            <LI><A href="GrantGreen.html">Grant Green</A></LI>
            <LI><A href="BillEvans.html">Bill Evans</A></LI>
            <LI><A href="WyntonMarsalis.html">Wynton Marsalis</A></LI>
            <LI><A href="CharlesMingus.html">Charles Mingus</A></LI>
            <LI><A href="CharlieParker.html">Charlie Parker</A></LI>
            <LI><A href="DexterGordon.html">Dexter Gordon</A></LI>
            <LI><A href="JohnColtrane.html">John Coltrane</A></LI>
            <LI><A href="TheloniousMonk.html">Thelonious Monk</A></LI>
            <LI><A href="WesMontgomery.html">Wes Montgomery</A></LI>
         </UL>
      </BODY>
   </HTML>
```

Reading the Source Documents

An HTML **spider** reads the HTML source documents. This is an application that uses the HTTP protocol to go to, and record accurate URLs, and then read more documents by following links in HTML `<A>` tags.

> *A "spider" is the traditional name for an automaton that reads a web page (or other hypertext document) and follows the links it finds to read more pages. A spider crawls over the web – get it?*

In our simple example site, we need only seed the spider with the URL to the `JazzHome.html` page. All the links on that page to the 10 biography pages are relative to the current directory, and therefore the spider reads those 10 pages. As the author used a web server on his local machine, with the example HTML pages in the `idxtest` document directory, the home page URI is http://localhost/idxtest/JazzHome.html. The links placed in output files have this URI pattern because that's where the spider picked up the source documents.

We'll have more to say about operating the spider and other generator components later.

Thesaurus

The thesaurus is represented in XML. There is a DTD to allow validation.

Example Site Thesaurus

The example thesaurus (`Thesaurus.xml`) is very simple, but contains at least one of each of the classes of terms. The terms include musician names, musical instruments, and famous albums. The direct mapping of site pages for each musician to their preferred terms is not unusual for a site that is setting out to educate its visitors about the preferred terms. However, the ratio of pages overtly defining preferred terms, to those that only use the terms, is higher than most real sites would be.

```
<?xml version="1.0" ?>
<!DOCTYPE Thesaurus SYSTEM "Thesaurus.dtd" >

<Thesaurus>

<TermClasses>
```

```
    <TermClass code="P" name="Related" text="Preferred term related to
               enclosing preferred term" />
    <TermClass code="R" name="Rotated" text="Term is a comma-rotation of a
               preferred term" />
    <TermClass code="S" name="Synonym" text="Term is a synonym for a
               preferred term" />
    <TermClass code="V" name="Variant" text="Term is a variant of another" />
  </TermClasses>

  <PrefTermTypes>
    <PrefTermType code="I" name="Internal" text="Only used by indexers" />
    <PrefTermType code="P" name="Pointer" text="Points to another
                  description" />
    <PrefTermType code="C" name="Concept" text="A general concept" />
    <PerfTermType code="V" name="Proprietary" text="Proprietary term" />
  </PrefTermTypes>

  <PreferredTerms>

    <PreferredTerm>
      <text>Davis, Miles</text>
      <gloss>Influential trumpet player, 1926-1991</gloss>
      <OtherTerms>
        <Term class="Rotated">Miles Davis</Term>
      </OtherTerms>
    </PreferredTerm>
    <PreferredTerm>
      <text>saxophone</text>
      <OtherTerms>
        <Term class="Synonym">alto sax</Term>
      </OtherTerms>
    </PreferredTerm>
    <PreferredTerm>
      <text>bass</text>
      <OtherTerms>
        <Term class="Related">Mingus, Charles</Term>
      </OtherTerms>
    </PreferredTerm>
    <PreferredTerm>
      <text>Mingus, Charles</text>
      <gloss>Influential bass player</gloss>
    </PreferredTerm>
    <PreferredTerm>
      <text>Parker, Charlie</text>
      <gloss>Influential alto sax player</gloss>
      <OtherTerms>
        <Term class="Rotated">Charlie Parker</Term>
        <Term class="Related">saxophone</Term>
        <Term class="Synonym">Bird</Term>
      </OtherTerms>
    </PreferredTerm>
    <PreferredTerm>
      <text>Coltrane, John</text>
      <gloss>Influential tenor sax player</gloss>
      <OtherTerms>
        <Term class="Rotated">John Coltrane</Term>
```

```
         <Term class="Related">saxophone</Term>
      </OtherTerms>
   </PreferredTerm>
   <PreferredTerm>
      <text>Evans, Bill</text>
   </PreferredTerm>
   <PreferredTerm>
      <text>Giant Steps</text>
      <gloss>A seminal album by John Coltrane</gloss>
      <OtherTerms>
         <Term class="Related">Coltrane, John</Term>
      </OtherTerms>
   </PreferredTerm>
   <PreferredTerm>
      <text>Gordon, Dexter</text>
   </PreferredTerm>
   <PreferredTerm>
      <text>Green, Grant</text>
   </PreferredTerm>
   <PreferredTerm>
      <text>guitar</text>
      <OtherTerms>
         <Term class="Related">Green, Grant</Term>
         <Term class="Related">Montgomery, Wes</Term>
      </OtherTerms>
   </PreferredTerm>
   <PreferredTerm>
      <text>Montgomery, Wes</text>
   </PreferredTerm>
   <PreferredTerm>
      <text>Marsalis, Wynton</text>
   </PreferredTerm>
   <PreferredTerm>
      <text>Monk, Thelonious</text>
   </PreferredTerm>

</PreferredTerms>

</Thesaurus>
```

We can see the three term classes we defined earlier being declared in the `<TermClass>` elements. The codes `P`, `R`, and `S` tell the generator what the semantics for each class are. The purpose of having single-letter class codes that simply map to class names is to allow indexers to change the name of classes without having to change the index generator program. For instance, the senior indexer may someday decide that "approved" would be a better name than "preferred", and "peer" would be a better name than "related". Remember that indexers are experts at word meanings, so they should have the right to change the vocabulary in which they have to work.

> *The **variant** term class is defined, but not used in our example. A variant is a different spelling for a term; for instance, a "401(k) plan" versus a "401k plan". The preferred term types just default to* `Concept`*; we won't be seeing any processing examples of preferred term types (but they can be used by indexers to document preferred terms that are not yet indexed, and to provide special reporting).*

The <PreferredTerm> elements include at least a <text> element to define the name of the term. <OtherTerms> declares the relationship with other terms in a list of <Term> elements. If a <Term> element has a class attribute of value "Related", then the text of the <Term> element *must* match a <PreferredTerm>. The impact to the generator is that it needs to perform two passes through the thesaurus. One other restriction not captured in the syntax is that two <PreferredTerm> elements may not have the same <text>.

Thesaurus Structure

There are two major sections of the Thesaurus XML source:

- The first section is a definition of the classes of terms. We saw the logical definitions of term classes before; we also include types of preferred terms mostly for internal record keeping and reporting. The preferred term types are defaulted to "Concept" because we won't be discussing preferred term types further.
- The second section contains the terms themselves. The section is a list of preferred terms. Within each preferred term are the terms related to it.

Here is the DTD, creatively named Thesaurus.dtd:

```
<!ELEMENT Thesaurus (TermClasses, PrefTermTypes, PreferredTerms) >

<!ELEMENT TermClasses (TermClass+) >

<!ELEMENT PrefTermTypes (PrefTermType+) >

<!ELEMENT TermClass EMPTY>
<!ATTLIST TermClass
   code (P|R|V|S) #REQUIRED
   name ID        #REQUIRED
   text CDATA     #IMPLIED
   >

<!ELEMENT PrefTermType EMPTY>
<!ATTLIST PrefTermType
   code (I|P|C|V) #REQUIRED
   name ID        #REQUIRED
   text CDATA     #IMPLIED
   >

<!ELEMENT PreferredTerms (PreferredTerm*) >

<!ELEMENT PreferredTerm (text, gloss?, OtherTerms?) >
<!ATTLIST PreferredTerm type IDREF "Concept" >

<!ELEMENT text        (#PCDATA) >
<!ELEMENT gloss       (#PCDATA) >
<!ELEMENT OtherTerms  (Term+)   >

<!ELEMENT Term (#PCDATA) >
<!ATTLIST Term class IDREF #REQUIRED >
```

The code attribute in the <TermClass> and <PrefTermType> elements tell the thesaurus reader program the semantics of each class and type.

The name attribute in <TermClass> is used as the class attribute in <Term> elements, and similarly the name attribute in <PrefTermType> is used as the type attribute in <PreferredTerm> elements.

The meat of the thesaurus is within the <PreferredTerms> element. Each <PreferredTerm> contains the preferred term name (in the <text> element), a displayable definition (in the <gloss> element), and an optional list of related terms under <OtherTerms>. Each related <Term> element must include the class attribute of the term, whose name and semantics were defined earlier in <TermClass> elements.

Generated Index Pages

After the index generator runs, a set of XML documents will be produced. There are two document types:

- Many index term documents, one for each preferred term mentioned at least once in a <META> tag. URL links to the HTML site content pages are embedded in <XLink> elements.
- A single main index document with <XLink> elements pointing to the index term documents.

Index Term Documents

One index term document is generated for each preferred term. The preferred term must also have been mentioned at least once in a <META> tag to generate a document.

Example

Here is a generated index term document, index_saxophone.html, with three entries pointing to HTML pages in which "saxophone" is a "preferred term" in a <META> tag. (They are not the same HTML pages shown earlier; please see downloadable files for the complete set of examples.)

```
<?xml version="1.0" ?>
<!DOCTYPE Term SYSTEM "index-page.dtd" >

<Term title="saxophone"
      EntryCount="3"
      xmlns:xlink="http://www.w3.org/1999/xlink" >

   <Entry xlink:type="simple"
          xlink:show="new"
          xlink:actuate="onRequest"
          xlink:title="Charlie Parker"
          xlink:href="http://localhost/idxtest/CharlieParker.html"
          xlink:role="Biography"
          />
   <Entry xlink:type="simple"
          xlink:show="new"
          xlink:actuate="onRequest"
          xlink:title="Dexter Gordon"
          xlink:href="http://localhost/idxtest/DexterGordon.html"
          xlink:role="Biography"
          />
   <Entry xlink:type="simple"
          xlink:show="new"
          xlink:actuate="onRequest"
          xlink:title="John Coltrane"
```

```
            xlink:href="http://localhost/idxtest/JohnColtrane.html"
            xlink:role="Biography"
            />
  </Term>
```

The index term page title is the `<Term>` element's `title` attribute. This is the name of the preferred term "saxophone" in the thesaurus, and in an HTML `<META>` tag found on the indexed page. For example this line, found in `JohnColtrane.html`, is what causes `JohnColtrane.html` to be listed in the third `<Entry>` element above:

```
        <META name="preferred term" content="saxophone">
```

This is just one of the "preferred term" `<META>` tags found in `JohnColtrane.html`, but it is the one that creates the `<Entry>` tag in `index_saxophone.htm`.

While there can be more than one "preferred term" `<META>` tag on a source page, an indexed page contains just one "content type" and one "browsable index title":

```
        <META name="browsable index title" content="John Coltrane">
        <META name="content type" content="Biography">
```

These two specifications from `JohnColtrane.html` are carried to the `<Entry>` element `for that` indexed page, along with the URL of `JohnColtrane.html`. They are set in the `<Entry>` element's `attributes: xlink:role, xlink:title`, and `xlink:href`, respectively.

Syntax

The DTD for the index term documents, `index-page.dtd` is below:

```
<!ELEMENT Term (Gloss?, Entry+) >
<!ATTLIST Term
   title        CDATA    #REQUIRED
   EntryCount   CDATA    #REQUIRED
   xmlns:xlink  CDATA    #FIXED "http://www.w3.org/1999/xlink"
   >

<!ELEMENT Entry EMPTY >
<!ATTLIST Entry
   title     CDATA       #REQUIRED
   href      CDATA       #REQUIRED
   role      CDATA       #REQUIRED
   type      (simple)    #FIXED "simple"
   show      (new)       #FIXED "new"
   actuate   (onRequest) #FIXED "onRequest"
   >

<!ELEMENT Gloss (#PCDATA) >
```

The outer `<Term>` element contains:

- The title for the index term page in the `title` attribute, which is the name of the preferred term in the thesaurus.

- The `EntryCount` attribute, which is a convenience for XML translators; it is the number of `<Entry>` elements that follow.
- The `xmlns:xlink, which` attribute declares the standard namespace for XLink.
- The glossary element `<Gloss>`, when that element is defined for the preferred term in the thesaurus.

There is one `<Entry>` element for each HTML page found by the spider with this index page's preferred term. For each such page, there are three items associated with the `<META>` tag entry: the "browsable index title", the "content type" from the `<META>` tag attributes, and the URL of the page in which the preferred term was found.

Three variable XLink attributes are used to define the three items:

- `title` – from the "browsable index title" `<META>` tag on the source page.
- `role` – from the "content type" `<META>` tag on the source page. We use the `xlink:role` attribute since there are no required semantics for that attribute.
- `href` – which is the URL from which the HTML page was read.

Main Index Page Document

Example

The full version of the generated main index document `index-home.xml`, which contains links to all 14 index term documents, is available in the code download. Below is an abbreviated version:

```
<?xml version="1.0" ?>
<!DOCTYPE Index SYSTEM "index-home.dtd" >

<Index GroupCount="26"
       xmlns:xlink="http://www.w3.org/1999/xlink" >

<GroupName name="A" empty="no" />
<GroupName name="B" empty="no" />
<GroupName name="C" empty="no" />
<GroupName name="D" empty="no" />
   . . .
<GroupName name="P" empty="no" />
<GroupName name="Q" empty="yes" />
<GroupName name="R" empty="yes" />
<GroupName name="S" empty="no" />
<GroupName name="T" empty="yes" />
<GroupName name="U" empty="yes" />
<GroupName name="V" empty="yes" />
<GroupName name="W" empty="yes" />
<GroupName name="X" empty="yes" />
<GroupName name="Y" empty="yes" />
<GroupName name="Z" empty="yes" />

<Group name="A" count="1" >
   <Entry related-count="1" >
   <Term title="alto sax" />
      <Link xlink:type="simple"
```

```
            xlink:title="saxophone"
            xlink:href="index_saxophone.xml"
            xlink:role="synonym"
            xlink:show="none"
            xlink:actuate="onRequest"
            />
    </Entry>
  </Group>
  <Group name="B" count="2" >
    <Link xlink:type="simple"
          xlink:title="bass"
          xlink:href="index_bass.xml"
          xlink:role="preferred"
          xlink:show="none"
          xlink:actuate="onRequest"
          />
    <Entry related-count="1" >
    <Term title="Bird" />
      <Link xlink:type="simple"
            xlink:title="Parker, Charlie"
            xlink:href="index_parker__charlie.xml"
            xlink:role="synonym"
            xlink:show="none"
            xlink:actuate="onRequest"
            />
    </Entry>
  </Group>
  <Group name="C" count="2" >
    <Link xlink:type="simple"
          xlink:title="Charlie Parker"
          xlink:href="index_parker__charlie.xml"
          xlink:role="preferred"
          xlink:show="none"
          xlink:actuate="onRequest"
          />
    <Entry related-count="1" >
    <Link xlink:type="simple"
          xlink:title="Coltrane, John"
          xlink:href="index_coltrane__john.xml"
          xlink:role="preferred"
          xlink:show="none"
          xlink:actuate="onRequest"
          />
      <Link xlink:type="simple"
            xlink:title="Giant Steps"
            xlink:href="index_giant_steps.xml"
            xlink:role="related"
            xlink:show="none"
            xlink:actuate="onRequest"
            />
    </Entry>
  </Group>
  <Group name="D" count="1" >
    . . .
      . . .
```

```
. . .
<Group name="P" count="1" >
   <Link xlink:type="simple"
         xlink:title="Parker, Charlie"
         xlink:href="index_parker__charlie.xml"
         xlink:role="preferred"
         xlink:show="none"
         xlink:actuate="onRequst"
         />
</Group>
<Group name="S" count="1" >
   <Entry related-count="2" >
      <Link xlink:type="simple"
            xlink:title="saxophone"
            xlink:href="index_saxophone.xml"
            xlink:role="preferred"
            xlink:show="none"
            xlink:actuate="onRequest"
            />
      <Link xlink:type="simple"
            xlink:title="Coltrane, John"
            xlink:href="index_coltrane__john.xml"
            xlink:role="related"
            xlink:show="none"
            xlink:actuate="onRequest"
            />
      <Link xlink:type="simple"
            xlink:title="Parker, Charlie"
            xlink:href="index_parker__charlie.xml"
            xlink:role="related"
            xlink:show="none"
            xlink:actuate="onRequest"
            />
   </Entry>
</Group>

</Index>
```

We can see a new concept of "group" here. A `<Group>` element is just a way to abstract the idea of separating the items on the page into alphabetical sets. As far as the generation of index pages is concerned, `<Group>` elements are not important. The explicit `<Group>` elements allow a simpler HTML translator to implement groups in the HTML, but in theory all the information needed by a translator to create groups, already exists in the `Link xlink:title` attributes.

Syntax

The single main index page has the following syntax shown in `index-home.dtd`:

```
<!ELEMENT Index (GroupName+, Group*) >
<!ATTLIST Index
   GroupCount  CDATA    #REQUIRED
   xmlns:xlink CDATA    #FIXED "http://www.w3.org/1999/xlink"
   >

<!ELEMENT GroupName EMPTY >
```

```
<!ATTLIST GroupName
   name ID #REQUIRED
   empty (yes|no) "no"
   >

<!ELEMENT Group ((Entry | Link)*) >
<!ATTLIST Group
   name  IDREF #REQUIRED
   count CDATA #REQUIRED
   >

<!ELEMENT Entry ( (Link | Term), Link* ) >
<!ATTLIST Entry related-count CDATA #REQUIRED>

<!ELEMENT Link EMPTY >
<!ATTLIST Link
   type     (simple)     #FIXED "simple"
   title    CDATA        #REQUIRED
   href     CDATA        #REQUIRED
   show     (none)       #FIXED "none"
   actuate  (onRequest) #FIXED "onRequest"
   role     (preferred|related|synonym)    #REQUIRED
   >

<!ELEMENT Term EMPTY >
<!ATTLIST Term title CDATA #REQUIRED >
```

Entry and Link Elements

Each <Group> contains a list of either <Entry> or <Link> elements. Each <Entry> element can contain an initial <Term> or <Link> element, followed by zero or more <Link> elements. Each <Link> or <Term> element represents some general thesaurus term, not just preferred terms. The <Link> points to the index term XML document. The following list describes how the three classes of terms would be represented in this document.

- Preferred terms always link to an index term document, and may also have links to related preferred term index documents. If the preferred term has no related terms, then it will be a <Link> element. If it has related terms, then it will be represented by an <Entry> element containing one <Link> for the subject preferred term, and one or more for each related preferred term.
- Synonyms do not have a link, so the first element in a synonym <Entry> is a <Term> element, which is just text. There should always be one <Link> element following the <Term> element, representing links to the index term documents of the preferred term, to which the synonym term is related.
- Rotated terms link to the same index term document as their rotated preferred term. Therefore, rotated terms are represented by a single <Link> element.

Group and GroupName Elements

Although a list of <Entry> and <Link> elements ought to be sufficient to represent all linkages needed, as a convenience to the XML translation processing we added the concept of "groups". These are meant to separate the index into entries with the same first letter; see how the Site Index Page image has a bold letter (A, B, C...) before each group. The grouping concept is generalized in the syntax so that other types of groupings are possible.

The <Index> element has the GroupCount attribute containing the count of groups. The first elements inside <Index> are the <GroupName> elements with two attributes: name and empty. A group can be defined but be empty as indicated as a <GroupName> element with the empty attribute having the value "yes". After all the <GroupName> elements are done, <Group> elements contain <Entry> and <Link> elements. The <Group> element's name attribute is an IDREF to a <GroupName> element's name attribute. The count attribute is just another convenience count for XML generators.

Index Translation To HTML

To go full circle back to HTML, we can translate the XML index documents using XSLT. Although the resulting pages are quite basic, we can see one obvious application of the XML index documents, as well as showing the XLink attributes being translated into <A> tags.

In the following example the Saxon XSLT Processor with its embedded parser and XPath evaluator was used in the Java code. The Saxon Processor by Michael Kay can be downloaded from http://users.iclway.co.uk/mhkay/saxon/.

Translation of an Index Term Document

The sample index page translator is index-page.xsl. Notice that we need two namespace declarations (xmlns:xsl and xmlns:xlink). One is expected for use of the XSL namespace, but we also need the XLink namespace because we have XPath expressions with xlink: names.

```
<?xml version="1.0" ?>
<xsl:stylesheet version="1.0"
   xmlns:xsl="http://www.w3.org/1999/XSL/Transform"
   xmlns:xlink="http://www.w3.org/1999/xlink"
   >
<xsl:output method="html" indent="yes" />
<xsl:template match="/Term">

<HTML>
<HEAD>
<TITLE>Index of <xsl:value-of select="@title" /></TITLE>
</HEAD>

<BODY>
<H1><xsl:value-of select="@title" /></H1>
<xsl:if test="Gloss">
   <xsl:value-of select="Gloss"/>
   <P/>
</xsl:if>
Documents about <B><xsl:value-of select="@title" /></B>
<P/>
<TABLE border="2">
   <TR>
      <TH>Title</TH>
      <TH>Document Type</TH>
   </TR>
   <xsl:for-each select="Entry">
      <TR>
         <TD>
            <A HREF="{@xlink:href}"><xsl:value-of select=
               "@xlink:title"/>
```

```
            </A>
         </TD>
         <TD>
            <xsl:value-of select="@xlink:role"/>
         </TD>
      </TR>
   </xsl:for-each>
</TABLE>
</BODY>
</HTML>
</xsl:template>
</xsl:stylesheet>
```

Above, we iterate over the `<Entry>` elements, and select the three XLink attributes that vary, and make up each line in the table.

Applying `index-page.xsl` against our index term document, this is the resulting index term page:

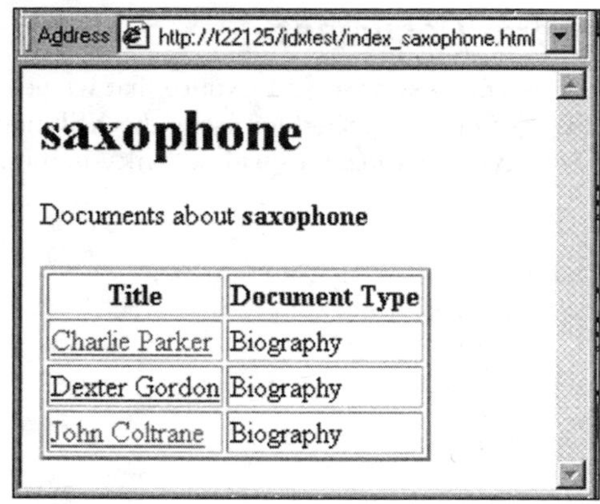

Below is the HTML code for this index term page:

```
<HTML xmlns:xlink="http://www.w3.org/1999/xlink">
   <HEAD>
      <meta http-equiv="Content-Type" content="text/html; charset=utf-8">
      <TITLE>Index of saxophone</TITLE>
   </HEAD>
   <BODY>
      <H1>saxophone</H1>
      Documents about <B>saxophone</B><P></P>
      <TABLE border="2">
         <TR>
            <TH>Title</TH>
            <TH>Document Type</TH>
         </TR>
         <TR>
            <TD>
               <A HREF="http://localhost/idxtest/CharlieParker.html">
                  Charlie Parker
               </A>
            </TD>
```

```
            <TD>Biography</TD>
         </TR>
         <TR>
            <TD>
               <A HREF="http://localhost/idxtest/DexterGordon.html">
                  Dexter Gordon
               </A>
            </TD>
            <TD>Biography</TD>
         </TR>
         <TR>
            <TD>
               <A HREF="http://localhost/idxtest/JohnColtrane.html">
                  John Coltrane
               </A>
            </TD>
            <TD>Biography</TD>
         </TR>
      </TABLE>
   </BODY>
</HTML>
```

Translation of the Main Index Document

The XSLT code for the main index document, `index-home.xsl`, is a little more interesting. It generates a "bar navigator" of letters to link to anchors in the main part of the document. The advantage of using groups and pre-declaring the groups, which might have been hard to justify when we looked at the DTD, is now apparent. Notice also the explicit tests for "`preferred`", "`synonym`", and "`related`"; the rules we were putting into words for these three cases may be easier to understand here in code.

```
<?xml version="1.0" ?>
<xsl:stylesheet version="1.0"
   xmlns:xsl="http://www.w3.org/1999/XSL/Transform"
   xmlns:xlink="http://www.w3.org/1999/xlink"
   >
<xsl:output method="html" indent="yes" />
<xsl:strip-space elements="*" />

<xsl:template match="/Index">
<HTML>
   <HEAD>
      <TITLE>Site Index</TITLE>
   </HEAD>
   <BODY>
      <H1>Site Index</H1><P/>
      <TABLE bgcolor="cccc99">
         <TR>
            <TD>
               <xsl:for-each select="GroupName">
                  <xsl:if test="position() > 1" >
                     |
                  </xsl:if>
                  <xsl:choose>
                     <xsl:when test="@empty != 'yes'">
```

```
                        <A HREF="#{@name}"><xsl:value-of select="@name" /></A>
                     </xsl:when>
                     <xsl:otherwise>
                        <xsl:value-of select="@name" />
                     </xsl:otherwise>
                  </xsl:choose>
               </xsl:for-each>
            </TD>
         </TR>
      </TABLE>
      <xsl:for-each select="Group">
         <BR/>
         <H3 id="{@name}">
            <xsl:value-of select="@name" />
         </H3>
         <DL>
            <xsl:apply-templates />
         </DL>
      </xsl:for-each>
   </BODY>
</HTML>
</xsl:template>

<xsl:template match="Entry">
   <xsl:apply-templates />
</xsl:template>

<xsl:template match="Term">
   <DT>
      <xsl:value-of select="@title" />
   </DT>
</xsl:template>

<xsl:template match="Link">
   <xsl:choose>
      <xsl:when test="@xlink:role = 'preferred'" >
         <DT>
            <xsl:call-template name="CreateLink" />
         </DT>
      </xsl:when>
      <xsl:when test="@xlink:role = 'synonym'" >
         <DD>see <xsl:call-template name="CreateLink" /></DD>
      </xsl:when>
      <xsl:when test="@xlink:role = 'related'" >
         <DD>see also <xsl:call-template name="CreateLink" /></DD>
      </xsl:when>
   </xsl:choose>
</xsl:template>

<xsl:template name="CreateLink">
   <A HREF="{concat(substring-before(@xlink:href,'.xml'),'.html')}">
```

```
      <xsl:value-of select="@xlink:title" />
    </A>
  </xsl:template>

  </xsl:stylesheet>
```

Notice the use of a `<DL>` list; it is well suited to the simple indentation we're looking for. Within a `<DL>` list, `<DT>` creates left-justified list element, and `<DD>` creates an indented list element. We want to show the "`see`" and "`see also`" entries created from "`synonym`" and "`related`" terms visually embedded in the enclosing term.

Sometimes it's hard to see the logic in markup languages like XSLT (or JSP), so below the logic for `index-home.xsl` is shown:

```
Emit page start tags, including title and heading.
Start a one-row, one-column table
For each GroupName element:
   If not the first GroupName, emit '|'
   If the group is not empty,
      Emit the group name in a link to an anchor of the same name
   Else
      Emit just the group name
End the table

For each Group:
   Emit the group name with anchor target of the same name
   Start a "definition list" (<DL>)
   For each element:
      If element is Link,
         Call EmitLink
      Else if element is Entry,
         For each element in Entry:
            If element is Term,
               Emit title attribute within a <DT> pair
            If element is Link,
               Call EmitLink
   End the definition list (</DL>)
Emit page end tags
Done.


Subroutine EmitLink:
   If the XLink role attribute is "preferred",
      Emit .html link within a <DT> pair
   If the XLink role attribute is "synonym",
      Emit "see" and .html link within a <DD> pair
   If the XLink role attribute is "related",
      Emit "see also" and .html link within a <DD> pair
End subroutine EmitLink
```

Main Index in HTML

This is the result of applying `index-home.xsl` against `index-home.xml`, producing `index-home.html`.

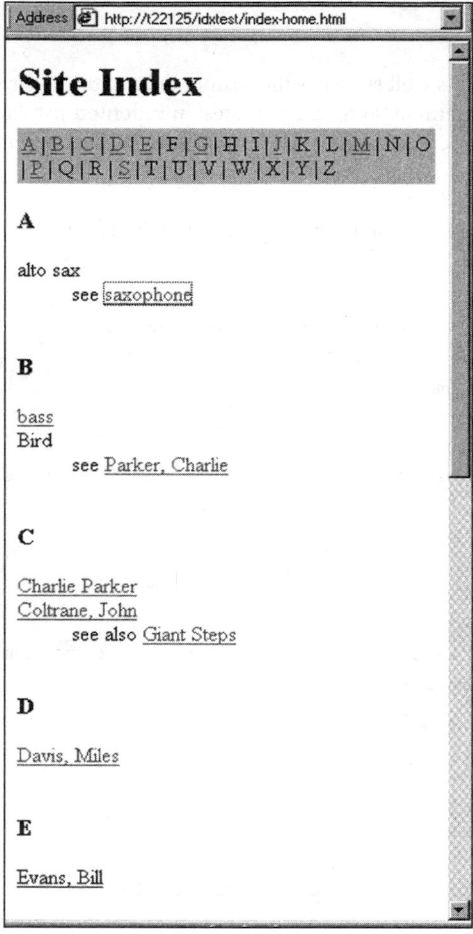

Here is the actual HTML code for `index-home.html`:

```
<HTML xmlns:xlink="http://www.w3.org/1999/xlink">
   <HEAD>
      <meta http-equiv="Content-Type" content="text/html; charset=utf-8">
      <TITLE>Site Index</TITLE>
   </HEAD>
   <BODY>
      <H1>Site Index</H1>
      <P></P>
      <TABLE bgcolor="cccc99">
         <TR>
            <TD><A HREF="#A">A</A>
                |<A HREF="#B">B</A>
                |<A HREF="#C">C</A>
                |<A HREF="#D">D</A>
```

```
            |<A HREF="#E">E</A>
            |F
            |<A HREF="#G">G</A>
            |H|I
            |<A HREF="#J">J</A>
            |K|L
            |<A HREF="#M">M</A>
            |N|O
            |<A HREF="#P">P</A>
            |Q|R
            |<A HREF="#S">S</A>
            |T|U|V|W|X|Y|Z
         </TD>
      </TR>
   </TABLE><BR><H3 id="A">A</H3>
   <DL>
      <DT>alto sax</DT>
      <DD>see <A HREF="index_saxophone.html">saxophone</A></DD>
   </DL><BR><H3 id="B">B</H3>
   <DL>
      <DT><A HREF="index_bass.html">bass</A></DT>
      <DT>Bird</DT>
      <DD>see <A HREF="index_parker__charlie.html">Parker, Charlie</A></DD>
   </DL><BR><H3 id="C">C</H3>
   <DL>
      <DT><A HREF="index_parker__charlie.html">Charlie Parker</A></DT>
      <DT><A HREF="index_coltrane__john.html">Coltrane, John</A></DT>
      <DD>see also <A HREF="index_giant_steps.html">Giant Steps</A></DD>
   </DL><BR><H3 id="D">D</H3>
   <DL>
      <DT><A HREF="index_davis__miles.html">Davis, Miles</A></DT>
   </DL><BR><H3 id="E">E</H3>
   <DL>
      <DT><A HREF="index_evans__bill.html">Evans, Bill</A></DT>
   </DL><BR><H3 id="G">G</H3>
   <DL>
      <DT><A HREF="index_giant_steps.html">Giant Steps</A></DT>
      <DT><A HREF="index_gordon__dexter.html">Gordon, Dexter</A></DT>
      <DT><A HREF="index_green__grant.html">Green, Grant</A></DT>
      <DD>see also <A HREF="index_guitar.html">guitar</A></DD>
      <DT><A HREF="index_guitar.html">guitar</A></DT>
   </DL><BR><H3 id="J">J</H3>
   <DL>
      <DT><A HREF="index_coltrane__john.html">John Coltrane</A></DT>
   </DL><BR><H3 id="M">M</H3>
   <DL>
      <DT><A HREF="index_marsalis__wynton.html">Marsalis, Wynton</A></DT>
      <DT><A HREF="index_davis__miles.html">Miles Davis</A></DT>
      <DT><A HREF="index_mingus__charles.html">Mingus, Charles</A></DT>
      <DD>see also <A HREF="index_bass.html">bass</A></DD>
      <DT><A HREF="index_monk__thelonious.html">Monk, Thelonious</A></DT>
      <DT><A HREF="index_montgomery__wes.html">Montgomery, Wes</A></DT>
      <DD>see also <A HREF="index_guitar.html">guitar</A></DD>
   </DL><BR><H3 id="P">P</H3>
   <DL>
```

```
            <DT><A HREF="index_parker__charlie.html">Parker, Charlie</A></DT>
         </DL><BR><H3 id="S">S</H3>
         <DL>
            <DT><A HREF="index_saxophone.html">saxophone</A></DT>
            <DD>see also <A HREF="index_coltrane__john.html">Coltrane, John</A></DD>
            <DD>see also <A HREF="index_parker__charlie.html">Parker,
                                Charlie</A></DD>
         </DL>
      </BODY>
   </HTML>
```

XML Source Documents

The examples have assumed that we have a web site with HTML documents that need to be indexed. To create accurate URLs to the documents, a "spider", using HTTP, would read the pages and follow the links found.

However, we may want to index XML documents instead. For XML documents, the XLink `href` attribute can be followed just like `<A>` tags are followed in HTML. However, it is not practical to require XLinks on XML documents to gather them all, since XLink is new and there are few XML documents supporting XLink. Therefore, we'll need to have the option to read files (using file system calls or the file: URL protocol) and to specify them with wildcard expressions and directory sweeps. The file system method of reading XML documents supplements the HTTP method of reading HTML. The system doesn't have a bias; HTML documents can be read from files, and XML documents can read using HTTP.

To read XML documents, the other feature that's needed is to be able to specify the indexing values using XPath expressions instead of the fixed `<META>` tags of HTML. This gives more flexibility in using non-conflicting elements, or even existing elements in source documents. There may already be a set of XML documents containing fields that we'd like to use as preferred terms, so by accepting XPath expressions, the spider can leverage the information already in the documents. Of course, we could also take the approach described earlier by defining and using special tags (like the `<META>` tags in HTML). XPath expressions give lots of options for indexing.

Since there is no HTML involved, indexing from XML source documents to XML index documents is actually cleaner and simpler. The only change in the XML index documents from that described earlier, is that since the links back to the source documents will use whatever URL was used to read them, they're much more likely to be file: rather than http: URLs, because indexing XML documents will more likely use a file system protocol than HTTP.

Index Generator Components

Now that we understand the transformation performed by the index generator, let's look at components that make up the generator.

Logical Relationship Analysis

The following diagram shows the logical relationships among the components of the system.

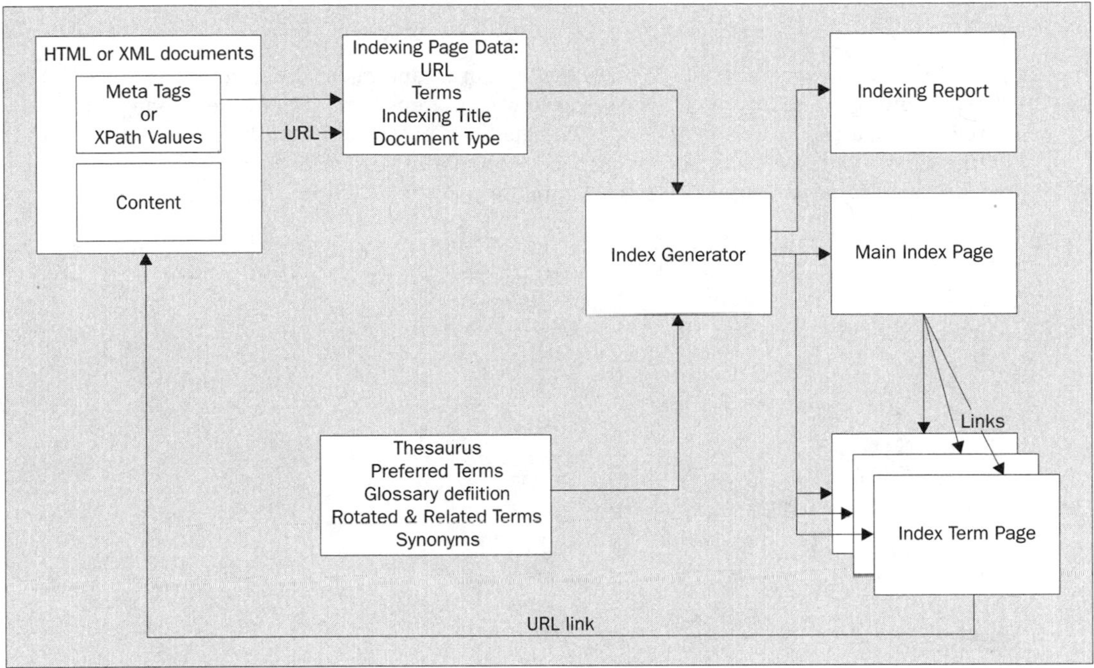

There are two major types of data needed by the generator: the Thesaurus and Indexing Page Data. The Thesaurus is modeled as a single object. Indexing Page Data is an object containing all the indexing information found on a source document:

- The URL of the document.
- The list of preferred terms for the page, found in one or more <META> tags.
- The indexing title and document type, each found in its own <META> tag.

There is one Thesaurus object for the system and the Index Generator creates one Main Index Page object, and many Indexing Page Data objects (one for each source document). These output page objects contain all the information needed to create a generated index page, whether the output file format is HTML or XML. The Index generator also creates a single Indexing Report. There are hyperlinks from the Main Index Page to each Index Term Page, and hyperlinks from each Index Term Page back to the originating documents.

An Indexing Page Data object comes from tags or elements within the source document, as well as the URL for the document itself.

Not shown at this level is the mechanism for creating Indexing Page Data objects, or for creating the closure of source documents to be indexed. (We already described a spider for this purpose.)

The words "object", and "class", are used here with their high-level analysis meanings, although they will inform our design of real Java classes.

Physical Design

The index generator is built with three major components, and an optional translation. Each component is run as a separate program. Files are passed from two components in the first stage to a component in the second stage. These are:

- The Thesaurus program, which reads the thesaurus, and generates a file with a Java object representing the thesaurus. This frees us to use any representation of the thesaurus that can be read by Java code. It also guarantees a single-file representation of the thesaurus in the output file, which could be useful for taking a snapshot of the thesaurus for version control. The Thesaurus program supports an XML input format.

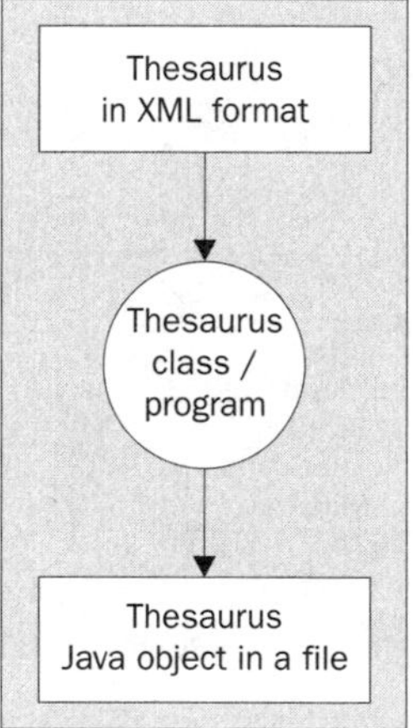

- The IndexingSpider program, which reads the site's content pages and records the `<META>` tags (HTML) or XPath (XML) information in them. The spider can read pages using the FILE and HTTP protocols. Along with file system reading, HTTP requests are also supported, so that accurate URLs are recorded for web site pages, and dynamically generated pages (from cgi-bin or JSPs or ASPs). The output of the program is a file containing a sequence of `IndexedPage` objects, each containing a reference to a page along with the Indexing Page Data found on that page.

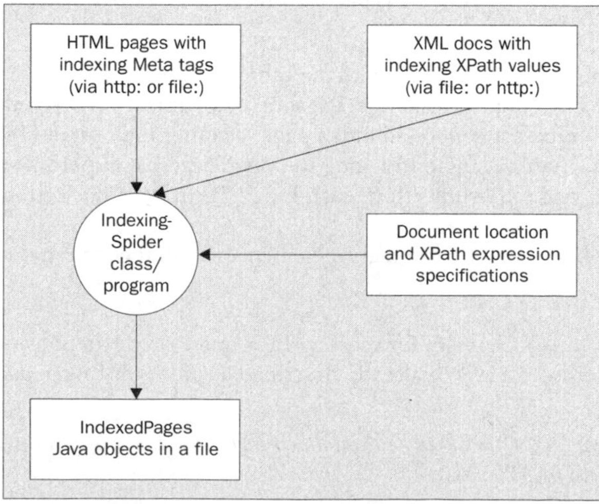

- The BrowsableIndex program, which reads the output files of the previous two components. The programs output is XML documents describing the main index page and the many index term pages. In addition, a text report is produced to give feedback to the indexers.

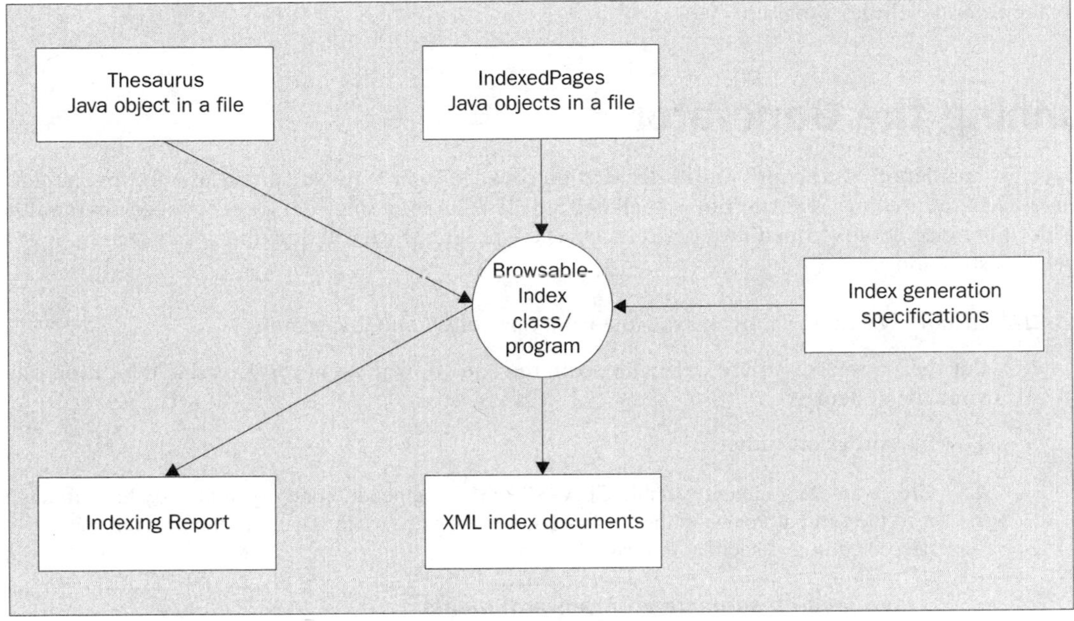

- An optional XSLT translation from XML index documents to HMTL index documents, if your final form needs to be HTML.

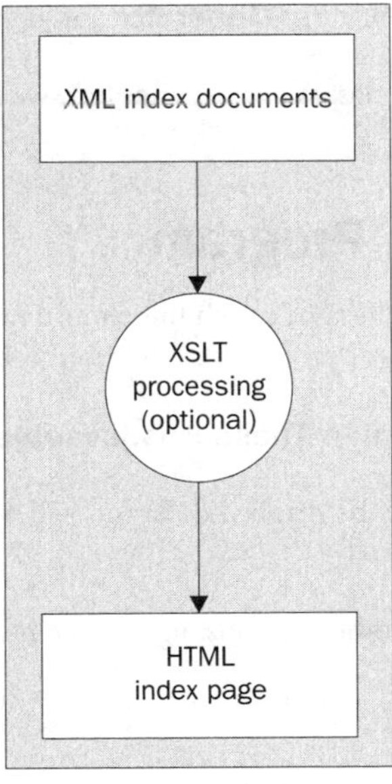

The Java class design for the main programs are similar. Each "program" above is implemented in a Java class of the same name. The `main()` method creates an instance of its enclosing class, which is both an object model of the information, and contains serial operations to take input files and create output files. The Thesaurus and IndexingSpider programs create files that contain Serialized Java objects, which are then read by the BrowsableIndex program.

Running the Generator

Specific installation instructions for the distribution package from Wrox are given later in this chapter. The IndexGenerator comes ready to run with all needed class files in a single jar file. For those not familiar with running programs from a Java jar file, such as the programs we will describe in this section, follow the below instructions:

- Install Java 1.2 (or above), available from Sun (http://sun.java.com).
- Put the `IndexGenerator.jar` file from the code download in some readable location on your file system.
- To run a program, either:

  a. Create an environment variable CLASSPATH, or append to one if you already have it, and set it to the full path name to the `IndexGenerator.jar` file. Then run the programs as described in this section, in form of:

     > java *java-class-name program-arguments*

  b. Put the full or relative path to the `IndexGenerator.jar` file as the argument to the command line option -cp. This is the approach taken by the scripts in the distribution package, but it can be tedious to do by hand. This command line form looks like:

     > java -cp c:/myinstall/IndexGenerator.jar *java-class-name program-arguments*

Given a proper installation of the Java classes of the generator, we'll describe the parameters needed for each of three programs.

Running the Thesaurus Program

Assuming we have prepared an XML thesaurus with the name `Thesaurus.xml`, here is a command that creates an output file `Thesaurus.javaobject` for later use by BrowsableIndex:

> java Thesaurus -x Thesaurus.xml -o Thesaurus.javaobject

If problems occur, a Java exception will be displayed. Saxon will write the location of a syntax error in the XML to `System.err` (the console usually).

Although we probably don't need any other options, here is the help displayed by the program when we run it without parameters:

```
Thesaurus class converter.
Reads Indexing Thesaurus from ODBC database, XML, or Java object file
Usage:
java Thesaurus -nojit
```

```
    [ -x[mlFile] XML-file-name ]
    [ -r[eadDatabase] ODBC-database-name ]
    [ -i[nputFile] Java-object-file ]
    [ -o[utputFile] Java-object-file ]
    [ -d[umpObject] dump-file | '-' ]

where:
XML-file-name is the name of an XML file on the file system
   (can be located by a Java File object). The XML must conform
   to the Thesaurus XML syntax described in Thesaurus.dtd.
ODBC-database-name is an ODBC database configured on the current system
   to connect to the Microsoft Access database containing the Thesaurus.
   When used, the program checks for all needed data integrity.
Java-object-file is a file written by a Java object stream.
   -o Writes the object to the specified file, overwriting existing file.
   -i Reads the object from the specified previously-written file.
-d Dumps the object to a file or '-' for stdout;
   it is not a programming interface.
```

You may be curious about the ODBC support. The original Thesaurus class was written to read an Access database that was directly maintained by indexers. That support is still in the code, but we won't be discussing it in this chapter. The `-d` option creates a text "dump" of the internal object state. This can be useful for debugging, or if you need to be sure that the XML was interpreted correctly.

Running the IndexingSpider Program

The IndexingSpider has the most complex specifications of the three components. For more than a handful of documents, it will also take by far the longest to run. We must prepare a text file containing name/value pairs for the spider specifications, which we'll name `Spider.properties`. The syntax of the input file, described below, is an extension of the `java.util.properties` file format. The command to create an output file `Spider.javaobject` containing a sequence of Java objects looks like this:

> java IndexingSpider Spider.properties Spider.javaobject

The first parameter can be "-" to read the properties from standard input. This is especially useful if the shell scripting language can embed files in the script (such as the Unix Korn shell's *here-document* feature).

The second parameter can have a "+" prefix to append to the output file, instead of overwriting. This feature can be useful if the set of documents we need to read cannot be reached by a single set of specifications – we can run IndexingSpider multiple times with different specifications and produce one concatenated output file for BrowsableIndex.

Here's a list of the parameters supported by IndexingSpider. You can look at the distribution tests to see some real examples. Only one of the first two parameters is required to operate the spider. If http: documents are found, then `SPIDER_INCLUSIVE_HOST_SUFFIX` and `SPIDER_INCLUSIVE_FILE_PREFIX` must both be valued as well. If XML documents are found (`content-type="application/xml"`), then the last four parameters must be valued.

Parameter name	Meaning
SPIDER_SEED_FILES	The set of files to start the spider on its journey. If the path is a directory, all the files in the directory are seeds. If the path is a directory followed by a name with a single '*', all the files in the directory satisfying the wildcard are seeds. All files matching each path are read with the `file:` protocol.
SPIDER_SEED_URLS	The set of initial URLs to start the spider on its journey. Port number is supported. Protocols supported by `java.net.URLConnection` are supported, which include `http:` and `file:`.
SPIDER_INCLUSIVE_HOST_SUFFIX	To be followed, the host part of the URL must end with one of the hosts in this list. Port number is supported. Ignored for `file:` URLs.
SPIDER_INCLUSIVE_FILE_PREFIX	To be followed, the file part of the URL must begin with one of the files in this list. Ignored for `file:` URLs.
SPIDER_EXCLUDE_HOST_PREFIX	If the host part of a URL is found beginning with one of the hosts in this list, it is not followed. Port number is supported. Ignored for `file:` URLs.
SPIDER_EXCLUDE_FILE_PREFIX	If the file part of a URL is found beginning with one of the files in this list, it is not followed. Ignored for `file:` URLs.
SPIDER_HOST_TRANSLATION	A set of host name pairs to allow a host found in an `HREF` to be translated to a different host. The property value must be a list of host names; there must be an even number of hosts, the first name of the pair is the host to translate from, the second of the pair is the host to translate to.
SPIDER_MAX_THREADS	The maximum number of threads to be created for spidering. Limited to between `1` and `100`, if not specified, the default is `10`.
SPIDER_PROGRESS_FILE	Set to "`DEFAULT`" to get a report of the current URL being read every 2 seconds, written to standard error stream.
SPIDER_LOG_FILE	Set to "`DEFAULT`" to get a log of all URLs read, URLs found on each page, and exceptions thrown while reading. The log is written to file `Spider.log`.
SPIDER_XSL_TEMPLATE	For XML, this is the XPath to match to apply the following `XSL_VALUE` expressions.
SPIDER_XSL_VALUE_TERMS	For XML, this is the XPath for the nodeset whose string values are the *preferred terms* for the document. This is the analogue to the `<META>` tag "preferred term" in HTML.
SPIDER_XSL_VALUE_TITLE	For XML, this is the XPath for the string value for the title of the document in an Index Term Page. This is the analogue to the `<META>` tag "browsable index title" in HTML.

Parameter name	Meaning
SPIDER_XSL_VALUE_TYPE	For XML, this is the XPath for the string value for the type of the document in an Index Term Page. This is the analogue to the <META> tag "content type" in HTML.

For the first six items, the parameter value is a list. The syntax of a parameter list requires an initial separator character, followed by a list item, repeated for each parameter in the list. Note that the initial separator character is required even if only one parameter is specified. Comments can be included with a '#' in the first column.

Here is an example `IndexingSpider` file used for `.html` files; and when `SPIDER_SEED_FILES` is uncommented, for `.xml` files:

```
SPIDER_LOG_FILE=DEFAULT
SPIDER_PROGRESS_FILE=DEFAULT
SPIDER_SEED_URLS=;http://localhost/idxtest/JazzHome.html
#SPIDER_SEED_FILES=;*.xml
SPIDER_INCLUSIVE_HOST_SUFFIX=;localhost
SPIDER_INCLUSIVE_FILE_PREFIX=;/
#SPIDER_EXCLUDE_FILE_PREFIX=;/cgi-bin
SPIDER_XSL_TEMPLATE=Term
SPIDER_XSL_VALUE_TERMS=Entry/@xlink:role
SPIDER_XSL_VALUE_TITLE=@title
SPIDER_XSL_VALUE_TYPE=Gloss
```

Running the BrowsableIndex Program

The BrowsableIndex program has a simple command specifying a parameter file with a format similar to the parameter file for IndexingSpider. To run BrowsableIndex, the Java object output files from Thesaurus and IndexingSpider must be already available.

> java BrowsableIndex Index.properties

The help text, displayed if there are no program arguments, shows the parameter file syntax:

```
Creates browsable index pages
Usage: java BrowsableIndex properties-file
   where properties-file is a file in Java Properties class format,
   specifying parameters to the BrowsableIndex program.
   It may be '-' to specify standard input instead of a file name

Properties-file content:
   THESAURUS= Java object file created by the Thesaurus class.
   INDEXING= Java object file created by IndexedPages class.
   [BACKDOOR= Text input file in CSV format with backdoor
      indexed page substitutions.
   [OUTPUT= Output Java object file.
      Can be read later by the IndexTerms object.
   [XML_FILES= Set to TRUE to create .xml index files.
   [VAR_FILES= Set to TRUE to create .var index files.
   [REPORT= Text output file for the indexer report; '-' for stdout.]
```

```
[DUMP= Text output file for an object dump; '-' for stdout.]
[ALLOW_MISSING_TITLETYPE= Set to true to allow an index table entry
   even if the title or content type is missing (default is FALSE).]
[URL_PREFIX_MAP= A series of pairs of URLs, representing a remapping of
   URL prefixes from the first of the pair to the second of the pair.
   Each URL is separated by a semicolon. Used to rehost the generated files.
```

The THESAURUS and INDEXING files are the output of the Thesaurus and IndexingSpider programs. They are always required. To generate XML, you include an entry XML_FILES=true.

The other index generation output format is a .var file, which is a proprietary template-driven text substitution format. We will not discuss that format further, although there is still code to support that format.

Setting the REPORT parameter can generate a text report. Indexers use this file; to find pages with <META> tag errors, measure the coverage of their thesaurus, and keep a record of the generated index.

Distribution

The index generator described in this chapter can be found on the Wrox site in a Zip file. It includes a .jar with all needed classes, including Saxon. Java source files, test files as described in this chapter, and DOS batch files for running tests are also available in the Zip.

Installation

Extract the zip file into an empty directory, letting it create the subdirectories stored in the Zip. There should now have a directory with an IndexGenerator.jar file, and 6 subdirectories. IndexGenerator.jar contains my generator classes, as well as the contents of the Saxon distribution, so that the single .jar has everything needed (besides Java 1.2.x itself).

site/xml contains the XML sources for the example site. The first test will generate the HTML sources into Site\html.

java/source contains Java source files, and java/javadoc contains javadoc .html files for all classes.

data contains Thesaurus.xml, .xsl, and .dtd files as shown in this chapter.

test1 contains a test of basic installation. Go to that directory and run test1.bat. It should do a Saxon XSLT translation of the XML sources in site/xml to HTML sources in site/html.

test2 contains the operations for creating XML index files from HTML.

test3 is similar to test2, but operates on XML source files instead of HTML, and follows XLink elements in the XML just like the HTML version follows <A> tags.

Summary

XLink provides hyperlink capabilities significantly beyond that available in HTML. We only touched on the possibilities for interlinking XML documents here. For instance, an intermediate state of the generator is an object representation of the source document pages and the indexing information found on them. This could be output as a linkbase, which is an XML document containing only (or at least dominated by) extended XLink elements, which serve to relate documents to one another. There are exciting possibilities to extend this index generator to automatically create widely different hypertext views of XML document sets, represented by agnostic XML linkbases, and requiring no modification to the original XML documents.

This may be one of the first spiders to read XLink elements just like HTML `<A>` tags are read by traditional HTML document spiders. In addition, this spider reads both XML and HTML documents in the same run, and applies an entirely different parsing method depending on the MIME type of the source document. While supporting the two different approaches, the spider still generates a consistent index representation of all successfully scanned documents.

The Saxon XSLT tool was relatively easy to integrate into this application, which was previously unaware of XML. Because the Saxon processor became a part of the application, the spider can be configured to process arbitrarily complex XPath expressions, both to find preferred terms, and to transform XML elements from source documents into index documents. This is flexibility well beyond what the author had originally envisioned, and would not have even been attempted were it not for Saxon.

The evolution of the generator is a powerful example of the promise of object-oriented development being fulfilled. The generator was originally an HTML-only tool used to create a proprietary output format. It was later modified to allow it to be run without resorting to proprietary formats. A much more significant modification added XML processing to result in the generator described in this chapter. All these modifications were possible because at its core, the generator is the realization of an object model discovered in analysis of the real-world properties and relationships of the input and output objects. Because the core objects modeled the real world, modifications could be limited to the format used to instantiate the core objects. For instance, the Thesaurus was originally instantiated from an ODBC connection to a Microsoft Access database. The objects created within the Thesaurus class modeled the real world, not the Access database. Therefore, when the Thesaurus was modified to instantiate itself from XML, the object design did not have to change.

Overall, in this chapter we covered:

- What a site index is, we also explored the various *terms* (preferred, synonym, related, and rotated) and the design of page markup, and thesauri, as well as looking at the concept of a spider.
- We took an in-depth look at the indexing of an example HTML site, and the use of `<Group>` and `<GroupName>` elements. We covered generated index pages (specifically Index Term documents and a Main Index document), and used XSLT to transform them to a hyperlinked HTML format.
- For indexing XML documents, we saw how the XLink `href` attribute can be followed, just as `<A>` tags can in HTML.
- After following the transformations performed by the index generator, we looked at its components, namely the Thesaurus, IndexingSpider, and BrowsableIndex programs, as well as the optional transformation of XML index documents to HTML.
- Finally we gave details of how to run the Thesaurus, IndexingSpider, and BrowsableIndex programs from the zip file contained in the code download (at http://www.wrox.com).

22

RDF

The Resource Descriptor Framework (RDF) provides a technique for describing resources on the web. By 'resources' we simply mean anything that has a web address, whether it's a web site, or a single page. By 'describing' we mean that we might say this page is good and that one bad (if we were reviewing sites) or we might say this is for adults and this for children (if we were building a ratings system), or that this one is about football and this one is about gardening (if we were addressing search issues). All of the information that we need for reviewing, rating, searching, and more, is supplementary data *about* our original data. It is data *about* the web page or web site. This is usually referred to as **meta data**.

Meta data is everywhere. It is used in all your favorite search engines (this article is about sport), stored in your word processing documents (the date of the last edit and who made the changes) and used to categorize sites to prevent access to children. Yet if you wanted to swap meta data with some other system, there is no easy way to do it. RDF therefore provides two things:

- The first is an abstract 'model' for meta data, so that we can all talk about the same thing when we discuss meta data
- The second is an XML representation of that model, so that we can transport it

RDF expressed in XML provides a powerful way of sending meta data from one place to another, since it takes advantage of the fact that XML can be sent over the web, can hold information in many different character sets, and can be parsed for accuracy. The subject of the next two chapters is to show you how XML can be used to transport meta data, and to provide a few example applications to help you decide if RDF is for you.

The RDF specification is divided into two parts, the model and syntax side, which we have just mentioned, and the schema side. In this book we focus solely on the model and syntax of RDF.

Before we launch into the Resource Descriptor Framework (RDF) proper, we need to familiarize ourselves with some of the problems that RDF helps to solve. Specifically we need to remind ourselves about meta data.After that we will look in detail at RDF, looking at the abstract model as well as the XML syntax. In the next chapter we will look at some RDF applications, as well as show some sample code.

Introduction to Meta data

Most readers of this book will be familiar with the concept of *meta data*. For those not familiar with the idea, we are referring to data *about* data. We might have some data, like a file – perhaps an image or sound file – and we may also have information *about* the file – when it was created, who by, and how large it is. At the end of the day all meta data is really just data – there's little to choose between the data that makes up the image and the data that is the author's name. But by using the prefix *meta,* we can indicate that one set of data is in reference to some more fundamental data.

One side effect of this is that we can establish common meta data for very different sets of data. For example, the meta data about the file that we mentioned might be the date the file was created, the name of the person who created the file, the date the file was last accessed, and so on. This information can be stored for any file, regardless of the fact that one file is a picture of your cat and another is the novel that you still haven't finished.

Another interesting aspect – that we will go into in more detail later – is that different people could have different meta data about the same data. As a student of English literature, you might have different meta data for *The Merchant of Venice* than I would as a publisher. You may be writing a thesis on the play, and need to refer to particular speeches by the different characters, whilst I might want to arrange the play into pages for printing. We are both referring to the same data, but we each have different meta data.

Of course, since meta data is merely data, we could also establish some *meta-meta data*. Take the example of music on a CD. Let's say you own the single version of Wyclef Jean's song 911. Your data and meta data could be represented like this:

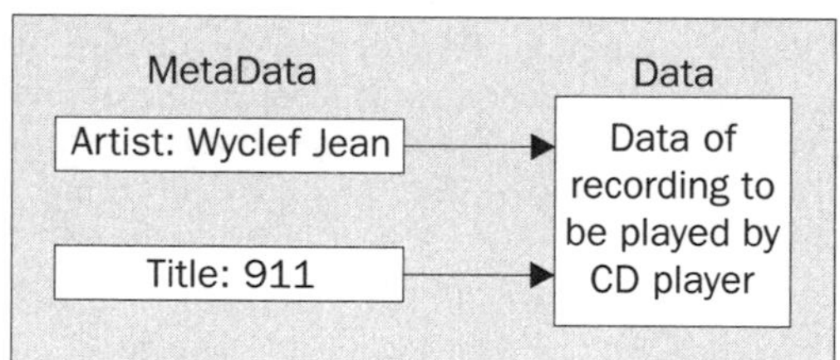

We have the actual data for the track, which in this case is a digital recording, ready for playing on your CD player. We then have data *about* the track – the name of the recording artist and its length. But imagine we put this track on Wyclef Jean's album *The Ecleftic: 2 Sides II a Book*? The track is sixth on the album, so we could represent this like this (with another track shown):

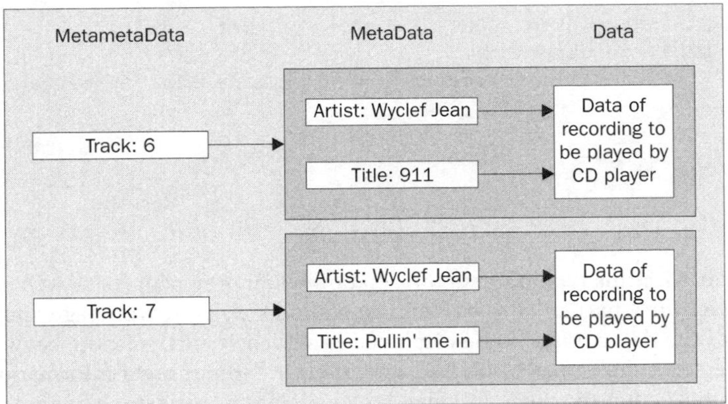

So each song on the album is data, the length of the song and its title is meta data, and the fact that *in this context* one track is 'track six' and another is 'track seven', could be called meta-meta data. However, before you get too worried about this, we don't generally use the 'meta-meta' term. As we said before, data is data is data; what makes a particular piece of data *meta data* is its context. So we could say that from the standpoint of an *album*, the data about a track comprises the digitally recorded music (what we were calling the data) *and* the title of the track and its length (what we were calling the meta data). And now the information about which is the sixth track, and which is the seventh, becomes the meta data.

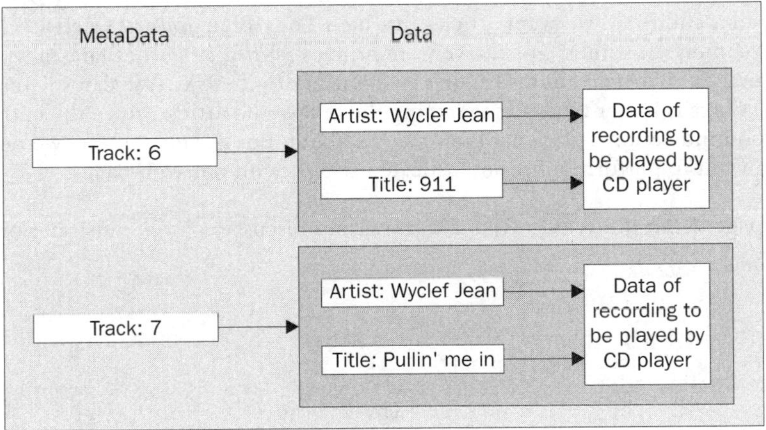

To be clear then, meta data is just good old, common or garden data. We simply use the term *meta data* so that we know in some particular case the data performs a certain role, that of helping describe some other data that we want to deal with. But whether some information is data or meta data is determined only by where you are viewing it from – it is determined solely by the role that it is playing.

Meta data Inside Web Pages

Let's look at a specific couplet of data and meta data – web pages and their meta-information. The following tags are typical of those that you would find in many HTML pages:

```
<HTML>
   <HEAD>
      <TITLE>A Page About Meta data</TITLE>
```

```
        <META NAME="keywords" CONTENT="web page, meta data">
        <META NAME="description"
                   CONTENT="A description of meta data as it pertains to web pages">
    </HEAD>
    <BODY>
        ...
    </BODY>
</HTML>
```

You will be familiar with this type of meta-information when preparing your web sites for search engines. The crawler for a particular search engine will pick up your web page and extract the title of the page, as well as the description (to be displayed in search results) and the keywords (for matching a user's search). The `META` tag is part of HTML, and allows us to put meta-information into web pages. The advantage of this is that the page designer can give clues to the search engine about the subject matter of the page. It may be the case that the theme of the page is not explicitly referred to in the text, and so a search within the words in the text for the page would not help. For example, a page that contains an article about British Prime Minister Tony Blair, might not actually contain the words 'prime minister', but simply say, "Today Tony Blair announced that...". The page designer may choose to put 'prime minister' into the `keywords` `META` tag, so that a search for 'prime minister' in some search engine would yield their page.

Of course, if you are at all familiar with meta data, you will know that this opens up a whole *other* can of worms. When we search for 'Tony Blair' are we searching for articles *about* Tony Blair (such as he and his wife have had a child), do we want articles in which Tony Blair *features* (such as "Today Tony Blair addressed the Women's Institute"), or do we want articles *written by* Tony Blair, in which he may not feature at all (such as an article about Britain's relationship to the US). We can see that searching on the `keywords` `META` tags is better than just searching the text of the article, since the author will hopefully have given a good indication as to what their page is about. But as you can see, we need more precise meta data if we want to perform more sophisticated searches on our web pages.

The following page, from the W3C's RDF interest group discussion area, illustrates one solution:

```
<HTML>
    <HEAD>
        <TITLE>www-rdf-interest@w3.org from March 2000: XSLT for
                    screen-scraping</TITLE>
        <META NAME="Author" CONTENT="Dan Connolly (connolly@w3.org)">
        <META NAME="Subject" CONTENT="XSLT for screen-scraping RDF
                    out of real-world data">
        <LINK REL="Stylesheet" HREF="http://www.w3.org/StyleSheets/
                                             Mail/public-message">
    </HEAD>
    <BODY>
        <H1>XSLT for screen-scraping RDF out of real-world data</H1>
        <!-- received="Tue Mar 21 13:42:25 2000" -->
        <!-- isoreceived="20000321184225" -->
        <!-- sent="Tue, 21 Mar 2000 12:39:40 -0600" -->
        <!-- isosent="20000321183940" -->
        <!-- name="Dan Connolly" -->
        <!-- e-mail="connolly@w3.org" -->
        <!-- subject="XSLT for screen-scraping RDF out of real-world data" -->
        <!-- id="38D7C1EC.2062AB7E@w3.org" -->
        ...
    </BODY>
</HTML>
```

The page contains a posting to the discussion board, and, so that searches on the web site can search for all postings by a particular author, the site has created a `META` tag called `Author`, and made the content of that `META` tag the author's name. The site has also added a `Subject META` tag, which is the subject line that Dan would have entered when he initially typed up his post. That certainly seems to be a positive step, doesn't it?

Well, for data that you have complete control over, yes. If we go to the RDF interest group area (see http://www.w3.org/RDF/Interest for RDFIG, and http://lists.w3.org/Archives/Public/www-rdf-interest for the discussion area) we can group together all posts written by Dan. The software on the web site is fully aware of the meta-information contained in the tag named `Author`, and can use it to group the posts together.

But what if we were searching for everything that Dan Connolly has ever written, from a completely different search engine? The search engine we're using may well have indexed the W3C site, and so indexed all of these pages from the discussion area. But that search engine may have no concept of the RDF Interest Group's tag `Author`. Our search for 'Dan Connolly' will yield all pages that contain 'Dan Connolly' as a string of text, and so the search results that come from the RDF Interest Group discussion area will include those posts that are replies to Dan, or even just mention him by name – but they won't be limited to those *written by* him. To make matters worse we have no control over the order in which they will appear, either, so that if there are lots of posts replying to Dan's comments, we may have to wade through these to find the posts for which Dan is the author. And of course, when we do find them, how will we know that the Dan Connolly we are interested in wrote them, and not some other?

We will discuss these issues in more detail as we go through this chapter. We will look here at one solution to this problem, which is to adopt a standard set of names for the properties in the `META` tags. If all search engines recognized the same name for the property that indicates the page's author, the property used for its creation date, and so on, then it would go some way to solving this problem. One such standardization is called the Dublin Core initiative.

Dublin Core

The Dublin Core (DC) initiative takes its name from a workshop that discussed meta data semantics, which took place at a conference in 1995, in Dublin, Ohio. The aim of the discussion was to establish a set of common semantics that would help when categorizing the web, and make for easier search and retrieval.

The elements that DC believes to be common to most sets of data are:

- Title
- Creator
- Subject and Keywords
- Description
- Publisher
- Contributor
- Date
- Resource Type
- Format

- Resource Identifier
- Source
- Language
- Relation
- Coverage
- Rights Management

The full description of these elements can be found at http://dublincore.org/documents/dces/. We will just look at `Title`, `Creator`, and `Subject and Keywords` to give an idea of how DC can be used.

DC and HTML

DC is primarily intended for use with RDF, but since we haven't yet looked at RDF – we're still discussing meta data, don't forget! – I will postpone showing you how DC fits in. Instead we will look at how we can use DC in our web pages to try to provide standard names for the meta data elements of a web site.

Title

The `Title` element is a name given to the referred resource. In the case of a web page it might contain the title from the `TITLE` HTML tag. The information can be placed in an HTML `META` tag using `DC.Title`.

Creator

The `Creator` element contains information about who, or what, is responsible for creating the resource. This could be a person, but it might also be an organization. The information can be placed in an HTML `META` tag using `DC.Creator`.

Subject and Keywords

The `Subject and Keywords` element should contain the topic of the resource. This will often be keywords or key phrases, or preferably, some values from a controlled vocabulary or a formal classification scheme. A controlled vocabulary is often called a **taxonomy**, and is a very important concept in meta data so we'll return to it later on. The information can be placed in an HTML `META` tag using `DC.Subject`.

Example

There are many more elements in the DC set, but these three give us enough to illustrate how DC can be used in HTML pages. The following is Dan's posting that we saw earlier, but this time we have tried to use 'standard' tags to encode our meta data:

```
<HTML>
   <HEAD>
      <TITLE>www-rdf-interest@w3.org from March 2000: XSLT for
                 screen-scraping</TITLE>
      <META NAME="DC.Title" CONTENT="XSLT for screen-scraping RDF
                 out of real-world data">
      <META NAME="DC.Creator" CONTENT="Dan Connolly">
      <META NAME="DC.Subject" CONTENT="RDF, screen-scraping, XSLT">
      <LINK REL="Stylesheet" HREF="http://www.w3.org/StyleSheets/
```

```
                                              Mail/public-message">
    </HEAD>
    <BODY>
      ...
    </BODY>
  </HTML>
```

Providing that the search engine software has been geared up to recognize the DC meta tags, then a search for anything 'created by' Dan should now yield any page in which the `DC.Creator` `META` tag has been set to 'Dan Connolly'. Importantly, we no longer have ambiguity; the '`DC.`' prefix is being used much like namespaces in XML, to try and ensure that keywords with the same name do not get mixed up. For example, in the original, the `Subject` `META` tag actually held the title of the post. Other systems might have used the name `Subject` for something completely different again. By choosing to use DC we now have a standardized meaning for the tag, that is, it indicates keywords that identify the topic matter of the document. (Of course there is nothing to stop anyone using `DC.Title` for a completely different purpose, for example the title of a person, like Sir or Lord.)

Extensibility

DC is not meant to be all encompassing, but is rather intended to provide a starting-point for other vocabularies. For example, a vocabulary relating to music may have its own elements for the key and tempo of a piece, but could still use DC for the composer, subject matter, and title:

```
<META NAME="DC.Title" CONTENT="Eine Kleine Nacht Muzik">
<META NAME="DC.Creator" CONTENT="Mozart">
<META NAME="DC.Subject" CONTENT="Classical Music">
<META NAME="MUSIC.Key" CONTENT="E Flat">
<META NAME="MUSIC.Tempo" CONTENT="2/4">
```

DC itself can also be extended or *qualified*. For example, to express an alternative title for the resource to the one set in the `Title` tag, you would use the following **qualifier**:

```
<META NAME="DC.Title.Alternative" CONTENT="Another title">
```

The dot notation can be used to extend the element names, but this then introduces the possibility that a particular search engine will not recognize your extension. The intended behavior is that the search engine will 'fall back' to the part of the element name that it understands.

> *The basic fifteen DC elements listed above (`Title`, `Creator`, and so on) are together known as* Simple Dublin Core *and have the advantage that any user agent that intends to understand DC will at least understand these basic elements. The DC initiative also provides a set of* ***standard qualifiers****, such as `Alternative`, used above, which make up* Qualified Dublin Core, *sometimes referred to as qDC. (More information is available at* http://dublincore.org/documents/dcmes-qualifiers/).

Note that in HTML 4.0, the `META` tag has been extended to provide more information to the user agent processing the document. For example, if we were using classification codes from the Dewey Decimal Classification (DDC), for the `Subjects and Keywords` element, we could use the following syntax:

```
<META NAME="DC.Subject" SCHEME="DDC" CONTENT="781.68">
```

This indicates to the user agent, whether a search engine or an intelligent web browser, that the classification code used is from a predefined set. The possible values for the SCHEME attribute are not defined though; instead the user agent in the context of the element name understands them. In the example given here, subject code '761.68' from DDC is "Classical Music".

We can see here that not only is there an advantage to having a standard set of names for the fields, but also a standard set of *values*. Even if two sites use DC.Subject to hold the keywords that describe a page, it still may be difficult to successfully search on 'Classical Music' if one site has,

```
<META NAME="DC.Subject" CONTENT="Classical Music">
```

another site has,

```
<META NAME="DC.Subject" CONTENT="Music, Classical">
```

and yet another has:

```
<META NAME="DC.Subject" CONTENT="The Classics">
```

By using standard sets of values, such as DDC, we can bring data into conformity, and can instead search for the Dewey code '761.68'. We will discuss this in more detail later, since it is one of the key design concepts behind RDF.

Problems

One of the ongoing problems with HTML – or more precisely, one of the problems with how HTML has been used until now– is that it merges many different levels of abstraction together. As someone familiar with XML, you will already know that HTML merges data with the visual representation of that data. Using XSLT with our XML documents allows us to break that link, and use HTML only as a rendering standard. However, HTML pulls a similar stunt by merging meta data with data – using the META tag that we saw above.

Of course, once a document is indexed the meta data is stored separately from the source document itself, but this makes little difference since that meta data will not change unless the META tags change – in other words the document itself controls its own meta data.

Another problem with embedding the source meta data inside an object, in the manner that HTML does, is that it prevents two people from creating different sets of meta data for the same object. This is obvious for example, when classifying web sites. A portal site for children may want to classify other web sites in such a way that sites are ranked depending on their subject. A site for web designers designing children's sites may want to classify web sites by how easy they are to use, or whether designers can learn something from them. This would require the two different classification web sites – one for children and one for web designers – to be able to store completely different meta data about the same web sites.

A further problem is that each search engine creates different sets of indexes for the document, in different formats. This does not allow us to process meta data in the same way that we might process any other data. Remember what we said about meta data being just plain old data, when viewed from another angle? We should be able to manipulate meta data as easily as we can our ordinary data. I should be able to find meta data about a document in the search indexes on a sports portal, and I should be able to merge it with meta data about the same document in the search indexes of a medical portal. We need an easy way to *interchange* meta data.

Resource Descriptor Framework (RDF) is an attempt to address these problems.

RDF: An XML Standard for Meta data

As we mentioned in the introduction, the RDF specification is actually made up of two W3C documents:

- The first, the *RDF Model and Syntax Specification* (http://www.w3.org/TR/REC-rdf-syntax) is currently a W3C recommendation document. If you decided to read around the subject you will often see this document referred to as RDFMS or MS.
- The second document is the *RDF Schema Specification 1.0* (http://www.w3.org/TR/rdf-schema), which sits at Candidate Recommendation stage. This is often abbreviated to RDFS. In this book we will only look at the model and syntax specification.

A Model for Meta data

Although the **syntax** part of the specification gives us a way of expressing meta data in XML, it is important to understand that the specification actually tries to discuss meta data at a more generalized level, XML being only one possible form that the meta data could be represented in. The advantage of taking this approach is that many different physical XML documents could actually represent the same RDF meta data model, allowing for different formats in different situations.

Note that this is not the case in ordinary XML – a fact that causes a lot of confusion for those new to RDF. Whilst XML does have an abstract model, it is a hierarchical set of nodes. The relationships between the nodes are simply things like 'is a child of', 'is a parent of' or 'is an attribute of'. So, whether there is congruence in terms of meaning between the following XML documents, is determined completely by the application that is interpreting the document:

```
<play>
   <author>William Shakespeare</author>
   <title>The Merchant of Venice</title>
</play>
```

```
<play author="William Shakespeare" title="The Merchant of Venice" />
```

```
<play>
   <author name="William Shakespeare" />
   <title>The Merchant of Venice</title>
</play>
```

As far as an XML parser is concerned these three documents have nothing in common, since they represent different data models (that is, different hierarchical node structures). Yet from a meta data point of view the intention of whoever created these documents may well have been that their meanings should be identical.

> **To make it clear about which level we are talking about, we will reserve the term *RDF* for the abstract model of meta data. When we talk of RDF we are talking about the properties of meta data *in general,* with no particular concern for how it is represented. If we want to talk about the XML form of RDF we use the term *RDF/XML.***

Let's look at how RDF models meta data more closely.

Resources and Statements

RDF essentially allows us to make **statements** about **resources**. A resource is some object that we are referring to, such as a web site or a play, and is identified using a **Universal Resource Identifier** (URI). The URLs that you are familiar with for addressing web sites are just one specific form of a URI, but whilst RDF is often used to describe meta data about web sites (and so uses URLs a lot), it has far greater potential than that. Much of this potential stems from the fact that anything can have a URI. This means that RDF can be used to specify meta data about anything we choose. If you haven't already read it, take a look at Chapter 3 where the difference between URIs and URLs is discussed in detail. In the following examples we use URLs of real online articles to make things easier to explain and understand. But bear in mind throughout that a resource is not limited to being a web page, and is simply anything that can have a URI.

We now know what resources are, but what of statements? Well, these are simply the **facts** that we want to state about the resource being described – the meta data. A statement is made up of the resource being referred to, and the meta data or **property** being specified. An example would be:

```
Mick Hume is the author of http://www.spiked-online.com/Articles/0000000054C3.htm
```

The statement can be broken down as follows:

- The resource is http://www.spiked-online.com/Articles/0000000054C3.htm
- The property of that resource that we are specifying is "author"
- The **value** of that property has been set to "Mick Hume"

This simple arrangement of the three parts of a statement – known in RDF terminology as a **triple** – gives us a powerful way of defining meta data outside of the resource that is being referred to. We may not have any control over the web site http://www.spiked-online.com/ but we can still make statements about it. Of course, why on earth anybody else should *believe* our statements is another matter altogether! I may after all, be wrong, that Mick Hume is the author of that article.

Note that this mechanism of using triples to describe meta data is not really that new to you. If we go back to our HTML `META` example, we had what at first sight appears like a series of traditional **property/value pairs**:

```
<HTML>
   <HEAD>
      <TITLE>A Page About Meta data</TITLE>
      <META NAME="keywords" CONTENT="web page, meta data">
      <META NAME="description" CONTENT="A description of meta data as it pertains
to web pages">
   </HEAD>
   <BODY>
      ...
   </BODY>
</HTML>
```

We could represent these pairs in many different ways, such as this:

```
keywords: web page, meta data
description: A description of meta data as it pertains to web pages
```

But don't forget that this information is in relation to a web page, and that the web page has a URL. Let's say that the URL is http://www.wrox.com/RDF/AboutMeta data.htm.

The META tags we have just seen are actually implicitly triples:

```
"web page, meta data" are the keywords for web page
http://www.wrox.com/RDF/AboutMeta data.htm

"A description of meta data as it pertains to web pages" is the description for
web page http://www.wrox.com/RDF/AboutMeta data.htm
```

Just as in our statement earlier about Mick Hume being the author of a particular article, we were able to express this meta data with three parts – the resource, the property name and its value – so too here we have seen that property/value pairs inside web pages are also triples. Let's continue with triples (or **3-tuples**, as they are sometimes called) for a bit, since they are key to understanding RDF.

Triples

Since the RDF specification is concerned as much with establishing a *model* for representing meta data, as it is with its syntactic representation, it uses a number of different ways to represent these triples. It also uses a more formal terminology to name the three component parts of a triple, where the resource being described becomes the **subject**, the property of that resource is the **predicate**, and the value assigned to that property is known as the **object**. When reading the RDF documentation you will need to be familiar with both sets of terminology.

It is particularly important to be comfortable with the more formal one (predicate/subject/object) since it used extensively when creating meta data about your (or anyone else's) meta data. Why would you want to do that? Well, to control meta data you need to be able to make statements about it as easily as you can make statements about any other data. Just as I can make a statement about an article on the web:

```
Mick Hume is the author of http://www.spiked-online.com/Articles/0000000054C3.htm
```

you might want to say something about my statement:

```
Mark Birbeck says that "Mick Hume is the author of http://www.spiked-
online.com/Articles/0000000054C3.htm"
```

In the documentation, creating this type of meta data is known as **making statements about statements**, and we will return to this topic near the end of the chapter.

So, what are the different ways that statements, or triples, are represented? Well, the first of them we have already met; simple sentences such as:

```
Mick Hume is the author of http://www.spiked-online.com/Articles/0000000054C3.htm
```

In this case http://www.spiked-online.com/Articles/0000000054C3.htm is the resource, or subject of the statement. The property, or predicate, that we are defining for the article at that URL is *author,* and the value of that property – the object of the statement – is *Mick Hume.*

Another form for representing the model is through **directed labeled graphs**. You may well be familiar with these constructions from database design – they are often called **nodes and arcs diagrams**. The statement we just made about one of Mick Hume's articles would be represented graphically as follows:

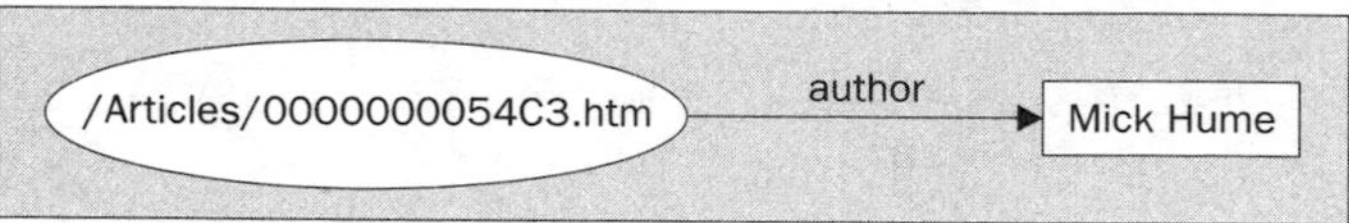

This graph can be 'read' as any of the following sentences:

```
Mick Hume is the value of author for http://www.spiked-
online.com/Articles/0000000054C3.htm
```

```
http://www.spiked-online.com/Articles/0000000054C3.htm has a property author with
a value Mick Hume
```

```
The author of http://www.spiked-online.com/Articles/0000000054C3.htm is Mick Hume
```

Since the basic unit of the RDF model can be expressed as an arc joining two vertexes then it is obvious that RDF only enables you to express **binary relationships**; that is, a statement can only establish a relationship between two resources. This doesn't mean that more complex structures cannot be created – they can. It just means that they will ultimately be made up of many connected binary relationships. For example, we may say that the publisher of the article written by Mick, is spiked Ltd.:

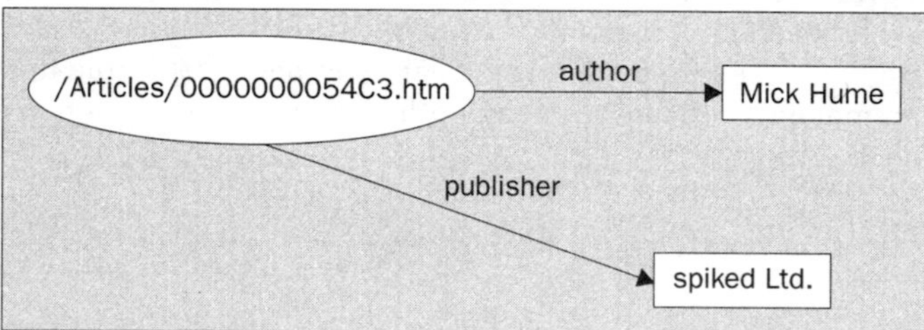

As you can see, this more complex statement is actually made up of two binary statements.

The final way that triples are represented in the RDF documentation is as follows:

```
{ predicate, subject, object }
```

The two statements that we made earlier would therefore be shown as follows:

```
{ author, [http://www.spiked-online.com/Articles/0000000054C3.htm], "Mick Hume" }
{ author, [http://www.spiked-online.com/Articles/0000000054C3.htm], "spiked" }
```

The syntax uses square brackets to indicate that the resource being referred to is actually a URI, whilst the quotation marks indicate that the resource is simply a string literal. The difference is important. Although all of our example statements so far have set the value of the property to a string literal (for example, "`Mick Hume`") part of the real power of RDF comes from our ability to set the value of a property to another resource. It's worth looking at this distinction in a little more detail.

String Literals and URIs

Recall our discussion earlier about the Dewey Decimal Classification, in which we said that it was preferable to use some fixed code like '781.68' rather than the text 'Classical Music'. We suggested that by choosing from a list of predefined values we would create more consistent and accurate meta data.

Where does this leave our example in the previous section, where we said that Mick Hume was the author of an article? Let's begin with the article address, which is completely unambiguous, so that's good. Any search for meta data about the article 'http://www.spiked-online.com/Articles/0000000054C3.htm' will not cause any problems, and were we looking to combine meta data about this article from a number of sources, we could do so safe in the knowledge that everyone was referring to the same article. (Actually this is almost true! There is still discussion about how to test whether URIs are equal. For now assume that the string representation of the URIs is equal.)

But what if we searched for any articles written by Mick Hume? What if someone had entered the data as 'Michael Hume' or what if there were two Mick Humes writing articles on the web? The search would no longer be unambiguous. This becomes worse with the name of the publisher; imagine searching for 'spiked'!

As we've seen, RDF makes great use of URIs to create a unique way of identifying the resource being described, but it also allows URIs to be used when setting the values of the properties. In this case, each author on the spiked web site has their own directory to store their biography, list of articles, pictures and whatever else. Let's use the directory name to uniquely identify *this* Mick Hume, as opposed to any other Mick Hume that might write articles:

```
http://www.spiked-online.com/Authors/Mick%20Hume
```

Of course anything could be used to create a unique URI, and it doesn't have to point to some real web site. In this case this URL is not ideal, because if Mick was to move on to another publication in years to come, his unique identifier would change, creating just the problem we are trying to avoid. Ideally we would have a unique URI for each individual, provided by some authority that can guarantee that uniqueness.

For now though, we'll assume that URI fits the bill; here's how the statement modeling the triple now looks:

```
{
    author,
    [http://www.spiked-online.com/Articles/0000000054C3.htm],
    [http://www.spiked-online.com/Authors/Mick%20Hume]
}
```

The same thing can be done for the publisher:

```
{
    publisher,
    [http://www.spiked-online.com/Articles/0000000054C3.htm],
    [http://www.spiked-online.com/]
}
```

In this case we can probably be more confident that the URI we've used is a good choice, since it is owned by spiked. However, an even better choice would be some identifier from the offices of the authority that registers companies. In the UK this is Companies House.

Let's pretend that Companies House in the UK, through which all companies are registered, provides a URI for all companies, and that spiked Ltd.'s URI is:

```
http://www.companieshouse.gov.uk/companynumber/3935644
```

As we said before, this doesn't necessarily point to anything. The only reason for using the *web site* of Companies House to name the URIs is because it is something that Companies House can guarantee is unique to them. We could use,

```
urn:companieshouse:spiked
```

but then there would be no way of knowing whether someone else has used the same identifier.

We've used a different syntax in our triples to convey the difference between resources and string literals – using square brackets and quotes – but there is also a difference in the way that the diagrams we introduced earlier are displayed:

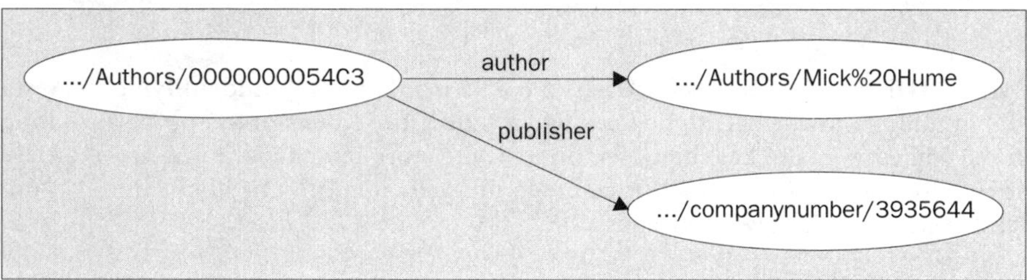

You can see from the diagram that resources are shown as ovals, and the string literals that we saw earlier are represented as rectangles:

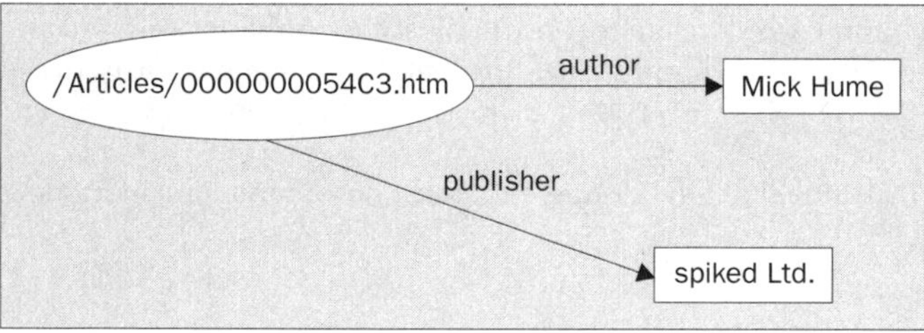

Now that we've seen different ways to model meta data, you're probably itching to see some real RDF. Let's look at how RDF represents meta data syntactically.

RDF Syntax

Introduction

We've looked at how RDF *models* meta data, now we want to see how this information is actually represented in XML. Let's stick with the statement that we just made about an article on the spiked-online website having been created by "Mick Hume". The XML for this statement looks like this:

```
<rdf:Description
 xmlns:rdf="http://www.w3.org/1999/02/22-rdf-syntax-ns#"
 xmlns:dc="http://purl.org/meta data/dublin_core#"
 about="http://www.spiked-online.com/Articles/0000000054C3.htm"
>
  <dc:Creator>Mick Hume</dc:Creator>
</rdf:Description>
```

Look at how a statement is formed:

- The statement begins with a reference to the resource that the statement is about. This is in the `about` attribute of the `rdf:Description` element.
- The statement is located inside the `rdf:Description` element, and says that there is a property of this resource – the `Creator` – that has a value of `"Mick Hume"`.

Note that the property name is `Creator`, or more precisely `dc:Creator`. This is familiar to us from our discussion of Dublin Core earlier, and is an illustration of why namespaces are extremely important in RDF. In this case we are able to distinguish the property from some other property with the same name. We are specifying that the property is the `creator` property from the set of Dublin Core properties, not the `creator` property from some other set of properties.

When there are many namespaces in an RDF document I find it more convenient to group them on an `rdf:RDF` element, so that they stand out:

```
<rdf:RDF
 xmlns:rdf="http://www.w3.org/1999/02/22-rdf-syntax-ns#"
 xmlns:dc="http://purl.org/meta data/dublin_core#"
>
  <rdf:Description about="http://www.spiked-online.com/Articles/0000000054C3.htm">
    <dc:Creator>Mick Hume</dc:Creator>
  </rdf:Description>
</rdf:RDF>
```

This element is optional, and we didn't include it in the first example. If the processor that will deal with your document is expecting an RDF structure, then you are free to omit this enclosing element. However, the `rdf:RDF` element is necessary if you want to make statements about more than one resource in the same document, as illustrated here:

```
<rdf:RDF
 xmlns:rdf="http://www.w3.org/1999/02/22-rdf-syntax-ns#"
 xmlns:dc=http://purl.org/meta data/dublin_core#
>
  <rdf:Description about="http://www.spiked-online.com/Articles/0000000054C3.htm">
    <dc:Creator>Mick Hume</dc:Creator>
  </rdf:Description>

  <rdf:Description about="http://www.spiked-online.com/Articles/0000000054E9.htm">
    <dc:Creator>Mick Hume</dc:Creator>
  </rdf:Description>
</rdf:RDF>
```

We have now listed two articles that were created by Mick Hume. For completeness let's show the different meta data models that are represented by this syntax. First, we'll use sentences:

```
Mick Hume is the creator of http://www.spiked-online.com/Articles/0000000054C3.htm
Mick Hume is the creator of http://www.spiked-online.com/Articles/0000000054E9.htm
```

Secondly, we'll use a labeled graph:

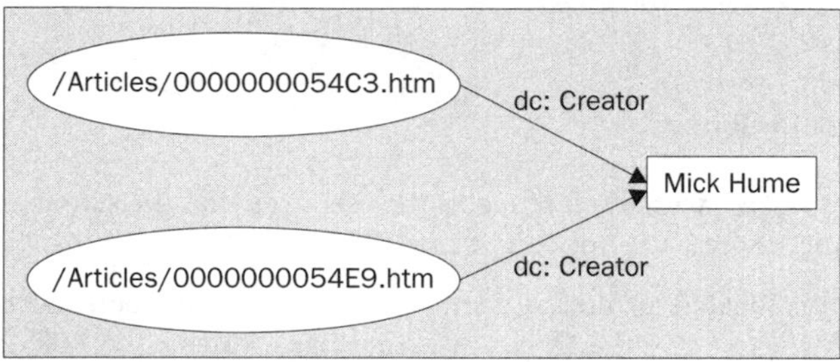

And finally, we'll show the underlying meta data model as a set of triples:

```
{ dc:Creator, [http://www.spiked-online.com/Articles/0000000054C3.htm],
              "Mick Hume" }
{ dc:Creator, [http://www.spiked-online.com/Articles/0000000054E9.htm],
              "Mick Hume" }
```

Note that I've not actually revealed everything yet about this particular way of describing triples, since the predicates – or properties – would not actually be represented as I have shown them here. I'll clear this up for you when we get to the discussion on namespaces.

One of the keys to getting the most from RDF is to be able to move easily backwards and forwards between these abstract models, and the syntactic representation of that model.

Now that we have introduced the basis RDF syntax, let's look in more detail at the elements that make up the syntax. I have grouped them as:

- The `rdf:Description` element
- Property elements
- Containers
- Statements about statements

The rdf:Description Element

We've seen how the `rdf:Description` element contains within it the URI for the resource that is being described, and we've also seen that a child XML element is used to describe the properties that are being defined. In terms of triples, the `rdf:Description` element contains the subject, whilst a child element defines a predicate/object pair.

Just as a quick reminder, here's the example we were dealing with earlier (note that I will tend to omit the namespace declarations from now on, unless they are under discussion. This makes the examples a little easier to read):

```
<rdf:RDF>
  <rdf:Description about="http://www.spiked-online.com/Articles/0000000054C3.htm">
    <dc:Creator>Mick Hume</dc:Creator>
  </rdf:Description>
</rdf:RDF>
```

Now we will look in more detail at the `rdf:Description` element, examining:

- Multiple properties for the same resource
- Nesting statements
- The `about` attribute
- The `ID` attribute
- Anonymous resources
- The `type` attribute

Multiple Properties for the Same Resource

You may well have noticed this already, but the `rdf:Description` element is actually a container for as many predicate/object pairs as you want. Just as graphically we can show a number of statements being made about the same resource like this,

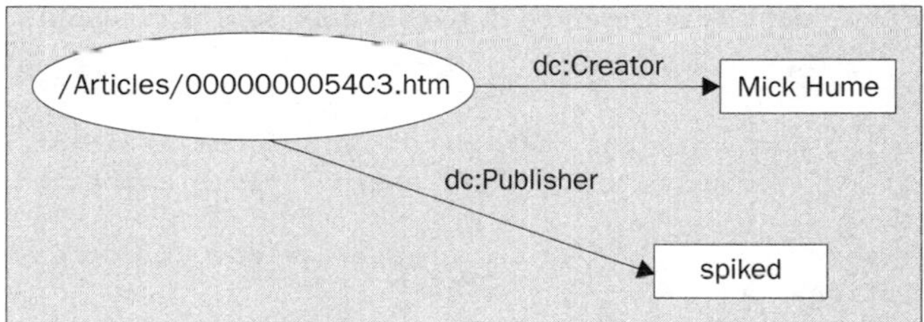

so too we have the flexibility in the syntax to specify a number of properties for the same URI:

```
<rdf:RDF>
  <rdf:Description about="http://www.spiked-online.com/Articles/0000000054C3.htm">
    <dc:Creator>Mick Hume</dc:Creator>
    <dc:Publisher>spiked</dc:Publisher>
  </rdf:Description>
</rdf:RDF>
```

It's also possible to represent the same meta data model using a slightly different syntax, using attributes in place of the child elements. The previous example can be represented as follows:

```
<rdf:RDF>
  <rdf:Description about=http://www.spiked-online.com/Articles/0000000054C3.htm
    dc:Creator="Mick Hume"
    dc:Publisher="spiked"
  />
</rdf:RDF>
```

It is important to keep stressing though, that the underlying meta data model does not change when we are given flexibility with the syntax. The labeled graph, set of triples, or statements represented by this different syntax are exactly the same as before.

String Literals and Resource URIs

We spoke in the section *A Model for Meta data* about the distinction between a string literal and a resource, for the value of a property. We have also briefly seen how this is represented in RDF syntax, using the `resource` attribute. Let's look at this issue in a little more detail.

Recall in the discussion on string literals and resources that we established URIs for the author and publisher of an article, and that the triples produced were as follows:

```
{
    dc:Creator,
    [http://www.spiked-online.com/Articles/0000000054C3.htm],
    [http://www.spiked-online.com/Authors/Mick%20Hume]
}
{
    dc:Publisher,
    [http://www.spiked-online.com/Articles/0000000054C3.htm],
    [http://www.companieshouse.gov.uk/companynumber/3935644]
}
```

We didn't show how this could be represented in RDF syntax, so let's do so now:

```
<rdf:RDF>
  <rdf:Description about="http://www.spiked-online.com/Articles/0000000054C3.htm">
    <dc:Creator rdf:resource="http://www.spiked-online.com/Authors/Mick%20Hume"/>
    <dc:Publisher
          rdf:resource="http://www.companieshouse.gov.uk/companynumber/3935644"/>
  </rdf:Description>
</rdf:RDF>
```

This creates a powerful combination of factors.

- Firstly, we have used a known and shared name for the property that we are defining – for example, `dc:Publisher` or `dc:Creator`
- Secondly, we have given that property a value that is unique

In the case of the publisher property, we have given it a value that will uniquely identify the company amongst all other companies in the world – the UK registered company, spiked Ltd. Provided other search engines use the same means of describing meta data, then this allows us to find any resource that has a property that has been set to the same company.

Nesting Statements

The RDF syntax that we have just shown can be expressed in the following nodes and arcs diagram:

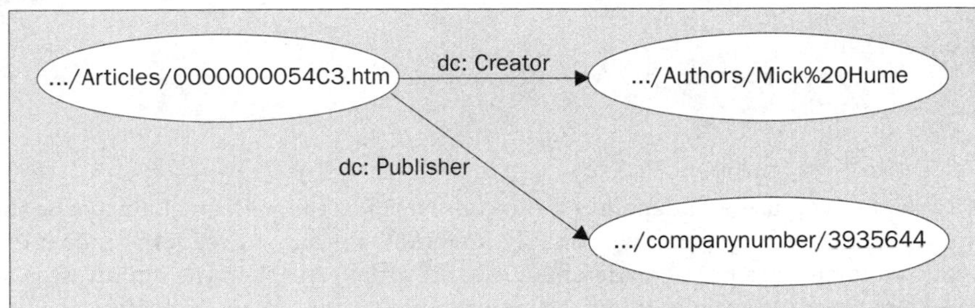

There is nothing to stop us extending this diagram, and making statements about any of these resources, for example:

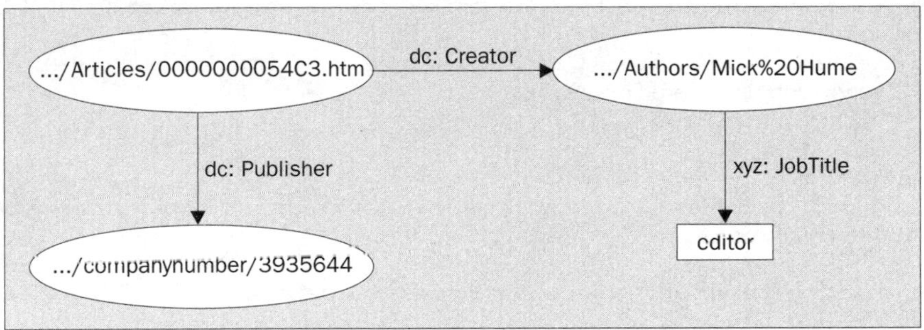

Here, we have added a statement about the author of the article, saying that he is also the editor of the web site. The property 'editor' comes from some schema that we haven't defined, but perhaps the namespace xyz might be a news information format. How should this be represented in RDF? Well, of course we could just add our statement, straight after our other statements, as we saw in the introduction to this section:

```
<rdf:RDF>
  <rdf:Description about="http://www.spiked-online.com/Articles/0000000054C3.htm">
    <dc:Creator rdf:resource="http://www.spiked-online.com/Authors/Mick%20Hume"/>
    <dc:Publisher
          rdf:resource="http://www.companieshouse.gov.uk/companynumber/3935644"/>
  </rdf:Description>

  <rdf:Description about="http://www.spiked-online.com/Authors/Mick%20Hume">
    <xyz:JobTitle>editor</xyz:JobTitle>
  </rdf:Description>
</rdf:RDF>
```

But RDF syntax also allows us to nest rdf:Description elements. We could use this approach to represent the same set of statements like this:

```
<rdf:RDF>
  <rdf:Description about="http://www.spiked-online.com/Articles/0000000054C3.htm">
    <dc:Creator>
```

```
        <rdf:Description about="http://www.spiked-online.com/Authors/Mick%20Hume">
          <xyz:JobTitle>editor</xyz:JobTitle>
        </rdf:Description>
      </dc:Creator>
      <dc:Publisher
            rdf:resource="http://www.companieshouse.gov.uk/companynumber/3935644"/>
    </rdf:Description>
  </rdf:RDF>
```

Exactly which syntax you use will depend on the context, since the *model* will always be the same. In the example just given, the nested syntax is probably preferable for human readers, since it draws attention to the fact that statements are being made about first the article and then the author. It is less efficient though when there are more articles in our list; we wouldn't want to keep repeating the fact that Mick Hume's job title was editor if we had a lot of articles:

```
  <rdf:RDF>
    <rdf:Description about="http://www.spiked-online.com/Articles/0000000054C3.htm">
      <dc:Creator>
        <rdf:Description about=" http://www.spiked-online.com/Authors/Mick%20Hume">
          <xyz:JobTitle>editor</xyz:JobTitle>
        </rdf:Description>
      </dc:Creator>
      <dc:Publisher
            rdf:resource="http://www.companieshouse.gov.uk/companynumber/3935644"/>
    </rdf:Description>

    <rdf:Description about="http://www.spiked-online.com/Articles/0000000054E9.htm">
      <dc:Creator>
        <rdf:Description about="http://www.spiked-online.com/Authors/Mick%20Hume">
          <xyz:JobTitle>editor</xyz:JobTitle>
        </rdf:Description>
      </dc:Creator>
      <dc:Publisher
            rdf:resource="http://www.companieshouse.gov.uk/companynumber/3935644"/>
    </rdf:Description>
  </rdf:RDF>
```

In such a scenario the following would be more efficient:

```
  <rdf:RDF>
    <rdf:Description about="http://www.spiked-online.com/Articles/0000000054C3.htm">
      <dc:Creator rdf:resource="http://www.spiked-online.com/Authors/Mick%20Hume"/>
      <dc:Publisher
            rdf:resource="http://www.companieshouse.gov.uk/companynumber/3935644"/>
    </rdf:Description>

    <rdf:Description about="http://www.spiked-online.com/Articles/0000000054E9.htm">
      <dc:Creator rdf:resource="http://www.spiked-online.com/Authors/Mick%20Hume"/>
      <dc:Publisher
            rdf:resource="http://www.companieshouse.gov.uk/companynumber/3935644"/>
    </rdf:Description>

    <rdf:Description about="http://www.spiked-online.com/Authors/Mick%20Hume">
      <xyz:JobTitle>editor</xyz:JobTitle>
    </rdf:Description>
  </rdf:RDF>
```

This second arrangement is most likely the one you would use if generating an RDF syntax document automatically from some triple storage medium, since you can just throw out information about any resource that you know anything about. But remember that no matter which of these syntaxes we use, the meta data model is unchanged, as follows:

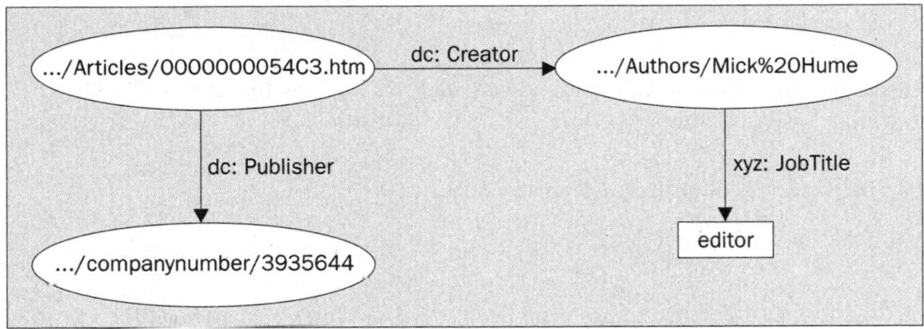

You're probably wondering whether we could refine this syntax even further, and take out the repetition of having the same author and publisher for both articles. RDF syntax does provide us with an easy way to do just this, using **containers**, which we will look at shortly.

The about Attribute

There are a number of different attributes that can be used with the `rdf:Description` element. The one we have seen so far, and probably the one you will see most in the examples you look at, is the `about` attribute. The contents of the `about` attribute are a Uniform Resource Identifier (URI). Full details of URIs are discussed in Chapter 3 and are contained in RFC2396 (see http://www.isi.edu/in-notes/rfc2396.txt). Much of the power of RDF comes from its use of URIs as the key identifier around which to group meta data.

RFC2396 defines a resource as "anything that has identity", before going on to illustrate this point with examples:

> Familiar examples include an electronic document, an image, a service (e.g., "today's weather report for Los Angeles"), and a collection of other resources.

Note the example of "today's weather". This is important, since URIs are conceptual mappings to an entity or set of entities. This means that the exact information represented by a URI can change, even though the resource does not, provided of course that the mapping between the resource and the conceptual mapping does not change.

Note also that URIs are not limited to resources on the Internet:

> Not all resources are network "retrievable"; e.g., human beings, corporations, and bound books in a library can also be considered resources.

A book, for example, may be identified with a URI like this:

```
urn:isbn:1861005059
```

This creates the powerful possibility that if you create meta data about this book, and use this URI to identify your meta data, and I in turn create my own meta data about the same book, and use the same URI *our meta data could be merged.* We can confidently say that we are both talking about the same book.

Uniform Resource Locators (URLs) are a subset of URIs. They refer to resources by specifying a path to find the resource and a protocol by which to access it. The following are all URLs:

```
http://www.spiked-online.com/
mailto:Mick.Hume@spiked-online.com
ftp://ftp.wrox.com/software/
```

A lot of confusion arises because URLs are a very easy way of creating unique URIs. If I want to create a unique identifier for Mick Hume, I could use a URI like this:

```
<rdf:Description about="uri:person:MickHume">
  <xyz:JobTitle>editor</xyz:JobTitle>
</rdf:Description>
```

However, it is difficult to be sure of keeping such a URI unique. A much better approach is to build into the URI something over which the producer of the meta data has control, say a domain name they have registered:

```
<rdf:Description about="http://www.spiked-online.com/Authors/Mick%20Hume">
  <xyz:JobTitle>editor</xyz:JobTitle>
</rdf:Description>
```

From the point of view of being a unique identifier it does not matter whether there is anything actually at the URL, since this URL is playing the role of a URI. That is, we have created the reference to be unique, not to retrieve anything.

However, the ability to create unique identifiers means that statements can be made about resources that do not belong to you – the meta data becomes external to the object being described. I am no longer relying on you to put information *inside* your resource for me to search; I can create my own information and describe *your resource*. And many other people could do the same if they wanted.

Since the content of an `about` attribute is a URI it can take many different forms. We'll go through some of the forms of URIs to show how they are valid in RDF statements. First, here is the fully specified absolute path:

```
<rdf:RDF>
  <rdf:Description about="http://www.spiked-online.com/Articles/0000000054C3.htm">
    <dc:Creator>Mick Hume</dc:Creator>
  </rdf:Description>
</rdf:RDF>
```

This form used an absolute path for a URI, completely specifying the path to the resource. As with web sites, we can also specify a path, which has the same root as the document that is being processed. If the following document was stored at http://www.spiked-online.com/Meta data.rdf, then URIs could be expressed as follows:

```
<rdf:RDF>
  <rdf:Description about="/Articles/0000000054C3.htm">
    <dc:Creator>Mick Hume</dc:Creator>
  </rdf:Description>
</rdf:RDF>
```

The next example uses a fragment identifier. This will again be relative to the URI of the document containing the statements. Note that there is nothing to say that the `ID` referred to by the fragment must exist:

```
<rdf:RDF>
  <rdf:Description about="#MickHume">
    <v:E-mail>Mick.Hume@spiked-online.com</v:E-mail>
  </rdf:Description>
</rdf:RDF>
```

Note however, that RDF stipulates that in all cases the URI is converted to an absolute URI when creating triples. So both the first and second examples would give us this triple,

```
{ dc:Creator, [http://www.spiked-online.com/Articles/0000000054C3.htm], "Mick
Hume" }
```

although for the second example the RDF document would have to be in the root directory for the relative URI to be resolved to this absolute one. The third example would give us this,

```
{
    v:E-mail,
    [http://www.spiked-online.com/Meta data.rdf#MickHume],
    "Mick.Hume@spiked-online.com"
}
```

assuming that the RDF we were looking at was contained in a document called:

```
http://www.spiked-online.com/Meta data.rdf
```

Be aware that in this last example, the resource `#MickHume` doesn't actually exist. As we have repeated over and over, it is not a requirement that the URI points to anything in particular. It may do, but it also may be just a convenient way to group together statements that are being made about the same identifier.

The ID Attribute

Although we just said that the resource identified by the fragment identifier does not need to exist, there is no reason why it can't. RDF provides a way to create a resource inside a document that can be referred to within that document. Let's extend the example we just had:

```
<rdf:RDF>
  <rdf:Description about="#MickHume">
    <v:E-mail>Mick.Hume@spiked-online.com</v:E-mail>
  </rdf:Description>

  <rdf:Description ID="MickHume">
    <v:Name>Mick Hume</v:Name>
  </rdf:Description>
</rdf:RDF>
```

By using the `ID` attribute we have created a local resource about which we can make further statements. Note that the `about` and `ID` attributes are mutually exclusive – the `rdf:Description` element can only have one or other, but not both. (The other permutation is to have neither, as we will see in a moment.)

The fragment identifier isn't only usable in the relative format we have here. Let's say we had a document listing the various authors who contribute to the spiked web site, along with some of their properties:

```
<rdf:RDF>
  <rdf:Description ID="MickHume">
    <v:Name>Mick Hume</v:Name>
    <v:E-mail>Mick.Hume@spiked-online.com</v:E-mail>
  </rdf:Description>

  <rdf:Description ID="JennieBristow">
    <v:Name>Jennie Bristow</v:Name>
    <v:E-mail>Jennie.Bristow@spiked-online.com</v:E-mail>
  </rdf:Description>

  ...

  <rdf:Description ID="BrendanONeill">
    <v:Name>Brendan O'Neill</v:Name>
    <v:E-mail>Brendan.ONeill@spiked-online.com</v:E-mail>
  </rdf:Description>
</rdf:RDF>
```

Let's say this RDF document is located at:

```
http://www.spiked-online.com/Authors.rdf
```

We could now refer to any of the authors from other RDF documents within the spiked web site, as in the following example:

```
<rdf:RDF>
  <rdf:Description about="http://www.spiked-online.com/Articles/0000000054C3.htm">
    <dc:Creator resource="http://www.spiked-online.com/Authors.rdf#MickHume" />
  </rdf:Description>

  <rdf:Description about="http://www.spiked-online.com/Articles/0000000054E5.htm">
    <dc:Creator resource="http://www.spiked-online.com/Authors.rdf#BrendanONeill"
/>
  </rdf:Description>

  <rdf:Description about="http://www.spiked-online.com/Articles/0000000054F3.htm">
    <dc:Creator resource="http://www.spiked-online.com/Authors.rdf#JennieBristow"
/>
  </rdf:Description>
</rdf:RDF>
```

This uses the `resource` attribute that we touched on briefly earlier, but will be explained in more detail in the next section. Just note for now that URIs are very flexible, and any of the normal forms you would use for a URI – absolute or relative, with or without fragment identifiers – can be used within RDF when a URI is called for.

But to labor the point once more, so that there is no chance of any confusion, these URIs could just as easily point into the ether, to nothing, and the meaning of this document would be not one jot different to what it was before:

```
<rdf:RDF>
  <rdf:Description about="http://www.spiked-online.com/Articles/0000000054C3.htm">
    <dc:Creator resource="http://www.spiked-online.com/Authors#MickHume" />
  </rdf:Description>

  <rdf:Description about="http://www.spiked-online.com/Articles/0000000054E5.htm">
    <dc:Creator resource="http://www.spiked-online.com/Authors#BrendanONeill" />
  </rdf:Description>

  <rdf:Description about="http://www.spiked-online.com/Articles/0000000054F3.htm">
    <dc:Creator resource="http://www.spiked-online.com/Authors#JennieBristow" />
  </rdf:Description>
</rdf:RDF>
```

However, we would no longer be able to combine this meta data with the meta data in the `Authors.rdf` document; *not* because we can't retrieve the other data, but because when we query the store that holds the meta data from the two RDF documents, the unique identifiers for each author will not match. One would be `.../Authors.rdf#MickHume` and the other would be `.../Author#MickHume`. As far as the meta data system is concerned they will be completely different resources.

One final point on the RDF document that we just 'created' for the author details (`Authors.rdf`); I'm sure you will have noticed that statements were being made about the resource declared with the `ID` attribute, just as statements were made about a resource when using the `about` attribute. In fact the triples generated by an `rdf:Description` that uses an `about` attribute and those for an `rdf:Description` with an `ID` attribute are exactly the same. All that has changed is that on the one hand you are creating statements *about* another resource, and on the other you are creating the resource that you want to make statements about. Now other systems can add statements to your statements, since the resource identifier is available.

If you always think in terms of *statements* then you should have no problem with this. Read the format that uses the `about` attribute as "The following are statements about resource *xyz*". Read the format that uses the `ID` attribute as "Create a resource with the name *xyz*. The following are statements are about that resource.".

Anonymous Resources

One more option for the `rdf:Description` element is to not specify an `about` or `ID` attribute. It is quite legitimate in the RDF model to have **anonymous resources** – a description element that exists for no other reason than to be given properties. This might be the case if, for example, we wanted to make additional statements about the author of an article, but we had no external resource by which we could refer to the author (using the `about` attribute) and we weren't interested in making the resource available outside our document (using the `ID` attribute). The following is a modified version of the example we gave when looking at nesting `rdf:Description` statements:

```
<rdf:RDF>
  <rdf:Description about="http://www.spiked-online.com/Articles/0000000054C3.htm">
    <dc:Creator>
      <rdf:Description>
        <v:Name>Mick Hume</v:Name>
        <v:E-mail>Mick.Hume@spiked-online.com</v:E-mail>
        <xyz:JobTitle>editor</xyz:JobTitle>
      </rdf:Description>
    </dc:Creator>
```

```
    <dc:Publisher
          rdf:resource="http://www.companieshouse.gov.uk/companynumber/3935644"/>
  </rdf:Description>
</rdf:RDF>
```

It's important to note that how the URI for an anonymous resource is specified when modeling the meta data as triples, is undefined. On the one hand we must give the anonymous resource a value so that we can distinguish it from other anonymous resources; a document may have many more than one. But how we actually do that doesn't matter, since no external system can query for this resource *since it's anonymous!* So we could use the following triples:

```
{
    dc:Creator,
    [http://www.spiked-online.com/Articles/0000000054C3.htm],
    [anon:1]
}
{ v:Name, [anon:1], "Mick Hume" }
{ v:E-mail, [anon:1], "Mick.Hume@spiked-online.com" }
{ xyz:JobTitle, [anon:1], "editor" }
```

The graphical representation of this RDF is very straightforward; the oval representing the anonymous resource is simply left empty:

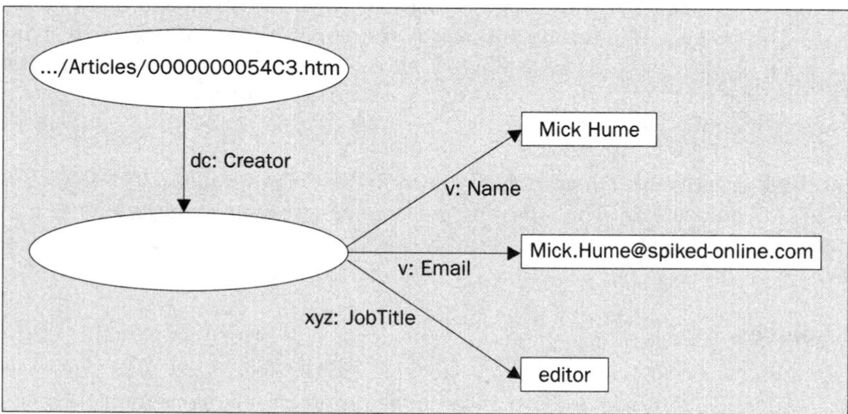

There are many situations where RDF will create anonymous resources automatically. Or to be more precise, there are situations where an RDF parser will create anonymous resources in order to correctly represent the meta data that it is processing. This means that in a given meta data model, there may be triples that refer to anonymous resources that have not been explicitly defined by creating an `rdf:Document` element without an `about` or `ID` attribute. We'll see a number of these later when we look at **containers**. For now we'll discuss a simple example of when the parser creates an anonymous resource automatically.

Let's go back to Mozart, and assume that some authority on classical music has given the piece *Eine Kleine Nachtmusik* the URL:

```
http://www.music.com/233456
```

Recall also that we gave the piece the Dewey Decimal Classification (DDC) code of `781.68`, which means classical music. One statement we could make would be:

```
http://www.music.com/233456 has a dc:Subject of 781.68
```

The RDF for this statement is simply:

```
<rdf:Description about="http://www.music.com/233456">
  <dc:Subject>781.68</dc:Subject>
</rdf:Description>
```

However, what if we wanted to indicate that the code `781.68` comes from DDC? The syntax to do this is very straightforward. We haven't met the `rdf:value` element before, but it shouldn't cause you any trouble here:

```
<rdf:Description about="http://www.music.com/233456">
  <dc:Subject>
    <rdf:Description>
      <rdf:value>781.68</rdf:value>
      <xyz:Classification>DDC</xyz:Classification>
    </rdf:Description>
  </dc:Subject>
</rdf:Description>
```

But how would we represent this using nodes and arcs? We have given properties to a resource that has not been explicitly defined, even though we can see its position in the document. We need an extra node as a placeholder for this resource, and then we can attach both the value, and the classification of that value to this node. An RDF parser will create such a resource in just the same way that we might explicitly create an `rdf:Description` with no attributes:

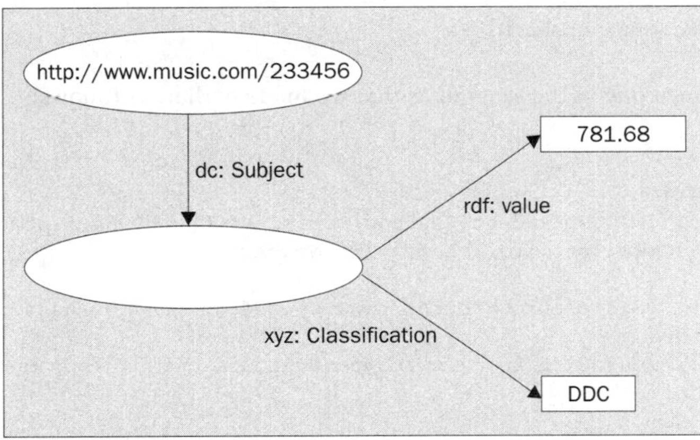

As in our previous example, the node is still a resource just like any other, but since it is anonymous it cannot be referred to by other statements outside of this immediate collection of statements. Another way of saying the same thing is that the only facts you will ever know about this resource are the facts that we have just created.

Finally, let's take a quick look at how the triples might be represented:

```
{ dc:Subject, [http://www.music.com/233456], [anon:2} }
{ rdf:value, [anon:2], "781.68" }
{ xyz:Classification, [anon:2], "DDC" }
```

It is important to be clear that the name of the anonymous resource really does not matter. The only criterion for it is that it can be differentiated from other anonymous resources in the same document. Although I have made up the format `anon:1` to illustrate my points, some parsers use the prefix `genid:` in their output, to indicate that the resource is anonymous, and that the URI has therefore been generated.

The type Attribute

Another property that can be applied to `rdf:Description` elements is `type`. This is a very powerful feature of RDF, linking the worlds of knowledge representation and object orientation.

The `type` attribute allows us to indicate that the resource being referred to is of a particular class. This will allow parsers that are able to process this information to glean more about the meta data. For instance a class-aware parser would be able to check whether the statements being made about a certain resource are actually valid. I'll explain this in more detail, but let's first build up the pieces of the jigsaw that we need.

Let's assume that the organization International Press Tele-Communnication (IPTC) – who are responsible for the XML format used in the spiked articles we have been using – has defined a URI that allows us to indicate that the article being referred to is in their NITF format. NITF stands for the News Interchange Format, and is widely used to transfer news articles between organizations, such as publishers and syndicators. The URL for all object types that belong to the NITF group of objects might be something like this:

```
http://www.iptc.org/schema/NITF#
```

We could then enhance one of the statements that we made earlier, as follows:

```
<rdf:RDF>
  <rdf:Description
   about="http://www.spiked-online.com/Articles/0000000054C3.htm"
   type="http://www.iptc.org/schema/NITF#NewsArticle"
  >
    <dc:Creator rdf:resource="http://www.spiked-online.com/Authors/Mick%20Hume"/>
    <dc:Publisher
          rdf:resource="http://www.companieshouse.gov.uk/companynumber/3935644"/>
  </rdf:Description>
</rdf:RDF>
```

Here we are saying that the resource being referred to is not just any resource, but is actually an NITF news article. We have created the full URI for the object type by adding the specific type, `NewsArticle`, to the broad grouping – NITF object types. This is because the IPTC have other groups of objects for pictures, video, audio, and so on.

This aspect of RDF is incredibly powerful and is very close to principles of object-oriented programming (OOP). By saying that the resource is a news article, we create the possibility for checking whether the meta data provided is in fact valid for that resource. For example, it is probably wrong to indicate that a person has a `dc:Format` property (the Dublin Core `Format` property is used to specify the MIME type of documents) as we have done here:

```
<rdf:Description about="http://www.spiked-online.com/Authors/Mick%20Hume">
  <dc:Format>text/html</dc:Format>
</rdf:Description>
```

But as things stand there is no way of knowing anything more about this resource:

```
http://www.spiked-online.com/Authors/Mick%20Hume
```

By specifying a type in the `type` attribute, we can give a parser more information:

```
<rdf:Description
 about="http://www.spiked-online.com/Authors/Mick%20Hume"
 type="http://www.schemas.org/Schemas#Person"
>
  <dc:Format>text/html</dc:Format>
</rdf:Description>
```

The triples represented by this syntax are:

```
{
    rdf:type,
    [http://www.spiked-online.com/Authors/Mick%20Hume],
    [http://www.schemas.org/Schemas#Person]
}
{ dc:Format, [http://www.spiked-online.com/Authors/Mick%20Hume], "text/html" }
```

Exactly what makes up a `Person` object can be defined using the RDF Schema mechanism, which is beyond the scope of this book. For now we will look at the different ways that type information can be specified in the syntax. This is important to understand for our later discussion on containers.

As we know from previous sections, specifying a value by using an attribute on an `rdf:Description` element is the same as specifying the value as an element that is a child of the `rdf:Description` element. This is almost the same with a `type` attribute, except that the contents are a resource, and not a string literal. Our previous example can therefore be expressed using the following syntax, with no loss of meaning at the meta data level:

```
<rdf:Description about="http://www.spiked-online.com/Authors/Mick%20Hume">
  <rdf:type resource="http://www.schemas.org/Schemas#Person" />
  <dc:Format>text/html</dc:Format>
</rdf:Description>
```

Just to highlight the slight difference, since `dc:Format` is a string literal we can express it as an attribute like this:

```
<rdf:Description
 about="http://www.spiked-online.com/Authors/Mick%20Hume"
 dc:Format="text/html"
>
  <rdf:type resource="http://www.schemas.org/Schemas#Person" />
</rdf:Description>
```

Typed Elements

There is another syntax that can be used to express the same type information we have just seen, which is to create what are known as **typed elements**. These XML elements represent the resource that we've seen referred to in the `type` attribute. Let's go through this a step at a time.

Remember that we assumed that we had a prefix for objects created by the IPTC for their NITF standard, and we said that this prefix was:

```
http://www.iptc.org/schema/NITF#
```

We then said that we could create object types – or references to schemas – by specifying a full URI. In this case we simply appended the class of the object to the prefix:

```
http://www.iptc.org/schema/NITF#NewsArticle
```

The RDF syntax provides us with a further convenient abbreviation to specify type information where we simply assign the prefix we have just defined to a namespace variable, and then use the class name as the name of an element. We then replace the `rdf:Description` element with this whole construction. The previous statements,

```
<rdf:RDF>
  <rdf:Description about="http://www.spiked-online.com/Articles/0000000054C3.htm">
    <rdf:type resource="http://www.iptc.org/schema/NITF#NewsArticle" />
    <dc:Creator rdf:resource="http://www.spiked-online.com/Authors/Mick%20Hume"/>
    <dc:Publisher
          rdf:resource="http://www.companieshouse.gov.uk/companynumber/3935644"/>
  </rdf:Description>
</rdf:RDF>
```

can now be represented like this:

```
<rdf:RDF
 xmlns:nitf="http://www.iptc.org/schema/NITF#"
>
  <nitf:NewsArticle rdf:about="http://www.spiked-online.com/
                          Articles/0000000054C3.htm">
    <dc:Creator rdf:resource="http://www.spiked-online.com/Authors/Mick%20Hume" />
    <dc:Publisher
          rdf:resource="http://www.companieshouse.gov.uk/companynumber/3935644"/>
  </nitf:NewsArticle>
</rdf:RDF>
```

As far as the model is concerned these two lots of RDF are exactly the same. Both of them produce this list of triples:

```
{
    [http://www.w3.org/1999/02/22-rdf-syntax-ns#type],
    [http://www.spiked-online.com/Articles/0000000054C3.htm],
    [http://www.iptc.org/schema/NITF#NewsArticle]
}
{
```

```
    [http://purl.org/meta data/dublin_core#Creator],
    [http://www.spiked-online.com/Articles/0000000054C3.htm],
    [http://www.spiked-online.com/Authors/Mick%20Hume]
}
{
    [http://purl.org/meta data/dublin_core#Publisher],
    [http://www.spiked-online.com/Articles/0000000054C3.htm],
    [http://www.companieshouse.gov.uk/companynumber/3935644]
}
```

As you can see, RDF allows a namespace-qualified element name to be equivalent to a resource type, simply by concatenating the namespace and the element, so that,

```
nitf:NewsArticle
```

is effectively,

```
http://www.iptc.org/schema/NITF#NewsArticle
```

provided of course that the `nitf` namespace was declared as:

```
http://www.iptc.org/schema/NITF#
```

This is quite an important feature of the RDF syntax so we'll go into it in more detail in a moment. Before we do, there's just one final point to emphasize on the typed element syntax, which is that anything that is valid on an `rdf:Description` element is valid when using a typed element. For example, we can use anonymous resources – the `v:vCard` element here contains an invented vCard syntax:

```
<rdf:RDF xmlns:v="http://www.vCard.org/Schemas#">
  <rdf:Description about="http://www.spiked-online.com/Articles/0000000054C3.htm">
    <dc:Creator>
      <v:vCard>
        <v:Name>Mick Hume</v:Name>
        <v:E-mail>Mick.Hume@spiked-online.com</v:E-mail>
        <xyz:JobTitle>editor</xyz:JobTitle>
      </v:vCard>
    </dc:Creator>
    <dc:Publisher
         rdf:resource="http://www.companieshouse.gov.uk/companynumber/3935644"/>
  </rdf:Description>
</rdf:RDF>
```

We can also turn some or all of the elements specifying the predicates, into attributes:

```
<rdf:RDF xmlns:v="http://www.vCard.org/Schemas#">
  <rdf:Description about="http://www.spiked-online.com/Articles/0000000054C3.htm">
    <dc:Creator>
      <v:vCard v:Name="Mick Hume" v:E-mail="Mick.Hume@spiked-online.com">
        <xyz:JobTitle>editor</xyz:JobTitle>
      </v:vCard>
```

```
    </dc:Creator>
    <dc:Publisher
         rdf:resource="http://www.companieshouse.gov.uk/companynumber/3935644"/>
  </rdf:Description>
</rdf:RDF>
```

As I said earlier, this last abbreviation is very useful for extracting meta data from existing XML documents, since it gives us a way of interpreting ordinary XML as a set of triples. Remember from our introduction that if the context allows it you can omit the `rdf:RDF` declaration and go straight into `rdf:Description`. Of course you can only do this if your processor knows that the only document types arriving are RDF, but if it does, you can see that the following document is actually acceptable RDF syntax, even though it makes no mention of any RDF attributes or elements:

```
<v:vCard xmlns:v="http://www.vCard.org/Schemas#">
  <v:Name>Mick Hume</v:Name>
  <v:E-mail>Mick.Hume@spiked-online.com</v:E-mail>
</v:vCard>
```

Assuming the document was called http://www.spiked-online.com/Authors/MickHume.rdf, then if you interpreted this as XML, the triples produced would be:

```
{
    [http://www.w3.org/1999/02/22-rdf-syntax-ns#type],
    [http://www.spiked-online.com/Authors/MickHume.rdf],
    [http://www.vCard.org/Schemas#vCard]
}
{
    [http://www.vCard.org/Schemas#Name],
    [http://www.spiked-online.com/Authors/MickHume.rdf],
    "Mick Hume"
}
{
    [http://www.vCard.org/Schemas#E-mail],
    [http://www.spiked-online.com/Authors/MickHume.rdf],
    "Mick.Hume@spiked-online.com"
}
```

The labeled graph would be:

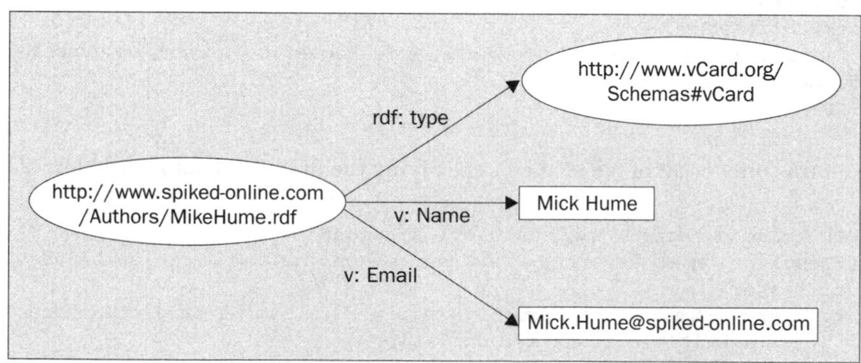

Namespaces in RDF

Let's look a bit more into how namespaces are used in RDF. As things stand with RDF, all we did in the previous examples was to join two strings together – the namespace and the local name of the element. This does raise a problem when trying to re-create the original RDF from a set of triples. Take one of the triples we had earlier:

```
{
    [http://purl.org/meta data/dublin_core#Creator],
    [http://www.spiked-online.com/Articles/0000000054C3.htm],
    [http://www.spiked-online.com/Authors/Mick%20Hume]
}
```

We know that the RDF that generated this was:

```
<rdf:RDF
 xmlns:rdf="http://www.w3.org/1999/02/22-rdf-syntax-ns#"
 xmlns:dc="http://purl.org/meta data/dublin_core#"
>
  <rdf:Description about="http://www.spiked-online.com/Articles/0000000054C3.htm">
    <dc:Creator rdf:resource="http://www.spiked-online.com/Authors/Mick%20Hume"/>
  </rdf:Description>
</rdf:RDF>
```

However, given the previous triple, how do we know that the original RDF did not have a namespace of,

```
http://purl.org/meta data/dublin_core#Cre
```

and an element name:

```
ator
```

The source document could well have looked like this:

```
<rdf:RDF
 xmlns:rdf="http://www.w3.org/1999/02/22-rdf-syntax-ns#"
 xmlns:dc="http://purl.org/meta data/dublin_core#Cre"
>
  <rdf:Description about="http://www.spiked-online.com/Articles/0000000054C3.htm">
    <dc:ator rdf:resource="http://www.spiked-online.com/Authors/Mick%20Hume"/>
  </rdf:Description>
</rdf:RDF>
```

This would have produced exactly the same set of triples as we saw before. This leads to the interesting conclusion that whilst the RDF *syntax* is namespace aware, the *model* is not. This shouldn't surprise you too much, if you have understood the distinction between the model and the syntax, since the syntax is merely an XML mechanism for transporting triples – and triples are the key to RDF. However, it has caused a great deal of discussion in various RDF forums.

Since the XML form of RDF is intended only as a way of conveying the RDF model, then this namespace problem is actually *not* a problem. The RDF model does not provide enough information to round-trip your original XML document anyway, so the best way to deal with this is to treat namespaces as simply a convenient abbreviation, and understand them only at the level of *one possible representation of RDF,* and that is, using XML. What I mean by this is that although it is convenient to write this,

```
<dc:Creator>Mick Hume</dc:Creator>
```

you should always remember that this is merely the XML representation for the predicate/object statement:

```
http://purl.org/meta data/dublin_core#Creator = "Mick Hume"
```

In other words, the model has no knowledge of namespaces, it only knows about absolute URIs.

When converting back to XML we can do pretty much anything we want as long as we faithfully represent the *model;* we are not required to come up with the original XML. We could therefore transport the triples from our example in the typed nodes discussion earlier,

```
<rdf:RDF
 xmlns:rdf="http://www.w3.org/1999/02/22-rdf-syntax-ns#"
 xmlns:nitf="http://www.iptc.org/schema/NITF#"
 xmlns:dc="http://purl.org/meta data/dublin_core#"
>
  <nitf:NewsArticle rdf:about="http://www.spiked-online.com/
                               Articles/0000000054C3.htm">
    <dc:Creator rdf:resource="http://www.spiked-online.com/Authors/Mick%20Hume" />
    <dc:Publisher
          rdf:resource="http://www.companieshouse.gov.uk/companynumber/3935644"/>
  </nitf:NewsArticle>
</rdf:RDF>
```

in the following format, without any loss of meaning at the model level:

```
<ns1:Description
 xmlns:ns1="http://www.w3.org/1999/02/22-rdf-syntax-ns#"
 xmlns:ns2="http://purl.org/meta data/dublin_core#Cre"
 xmlns:ns3="http://purl.org/meta data/dublin_core#Publi"
 about="http://www.spiked-online.com/Articles/0000000054C3.htm"
>
  <ns1:type resource="http://www.iptc.org/schema/NITF#NewsArticle" />
  <ns2:ator rdf:resource="http://www.spiked-online.com/Authors/Mick%20Hume"/>
  <ns2:sher
         rdf:resource="http://www.companieshouse.gov.uk/companynumber/3935644"/>
</ns1:Description>
```

Most parsers, however, will work backwards from the end of the URI until they find a character that is not valid in the local part of an element name, and then treat the rest of the URI as the namespace. This approach would have yielded this:

```
<ns1:Description
 xmlns:ns1="http://www.w3.org/1999/02/22-rdf-syntax-ns#"
 xmlns:ns2="http://purl.org/meta data/dublin_core#"
 about="http://www.spiked-online.com/Articles/0000000054C3.htm"
>
  <ns1:type resource="http://www.iptc.org/schema/NITF#NewsArticle" />
  <ns2:Creator rdf:resource="http://www.spiked-online.com/Authors/Mick%20Hume"/>
  <ns2:Publisher
        rdf:resource="http://www.companieshouse.gov.uk/companynumber/3935644"/>
</ns1:Description>
```

This is quite a neat solution, and it's probably advisable for you to adopt the approach that many are already doing and use a # suffix to help create a suitable break. It would also cover you should some future version of RDF make the model more aware of namespaces.

But there is nothing to force you to do this, and if the Dublin Core had decided not to do so, our example would instead look like this:

```
<ns1:Description
 xmlns:ns1="http://www.w3.org/1999/02/22-rdf-syntax-ns#"
 xmlns:ns2="http://purl.org/meta data/"
 about="http://www.spiked-online.com/Articles/0000000054C3.htm"
>
  <ns1:type resource="http://www.iptc.org/schema/NITF#NewsArticle" />
  <ns2:dublin_coreCreator rdf:resource="http://www.spiked-online.com/
                                            Authors/Mick%20Hume"/>
  <ns2:dublin_corePublisher
        rdf:resource="http://www.companieshouse.gov.uk/companynumber/3935644"/>
</ns1:Description>
```

Here we stick with the approach of finding the first non-valid Qname character to turn a URI into a namespace/local name pair, in this case /.

This would still be perfectly OK from our meta data point of view.

Summary

The rdf:Description property can take a number of attributes, although we have still not yet met all of them. The remainder we will look at later. Those that we have discussed are:

- about
- ID
- type
- attributes with a namespace prefix (other than xmlns and xml), which can be used to specify properties

We saw:

- How not specifying an ID or about attribute meant that the resource was anonymous
- How type information could also be provided using namespace-qualified element names
- As far as the element itself is concerned, the rdf:Description element can be used to make a number of statements about the same resource
- How the contents of this rdf:Description element would be a number of properties, or name/value pairs

Formal Grammar

The RDF documentation defines a formal grammar – using an Extended Backus-Naur Format (EBNF) – for the features that we have just seen. It is not imperative that you understand this, and you are welcome to skip straight to the next section. However, if you think you will be involved in the nitty-gritty of RDF such as:

- Using a number of different parsers
- Even writing a parser
- Designing storage mechanisms
- Experimenting with querying technologies

or you're just plain curious, then you would do well to familiarize yourself with the formal definitions for the syntax that we have been looking at.

The formal statements that follow are usually call **productions**. You will often find that discussions and articles that refer to the formal definitions of RDF will use the production numbers listed below. Since the definition of the grammar occurs in section 6 of the RDF Model and Schema document, all production numbers begin with 6 (6.5, 6.6, and so on). I have retained the prefix and the numbering of the productions so that you can cross-reference with other information on RDF that you might read.

The following lists only those statements in EBNF that we have discussed fully:

<table>
<tr><th>Section</th><th>Production</th><th>Syntax</th></tr>
<tr><td>[6.1]</td><td>RDF</td><td>::= ['<rdf:RDF>'] obj* ['</rdf:RDF>']</td></tr>
<tr><td>[6.2]</td><td>obj</td><td>::= description</td></tr>
<tr><td>[6.3]</td><td>description</td><td>::= '<rdf:Description' idAboutAttr? propAttr* '/>'
| '<rdf:Description' idAboutAttr? propAttr* '>'
propertyElt* '</rdf:Description>'
| typedNode</td></tr>
<tr><td>[6.5]</td><td>idAboutAttr</td><td>::= idAttr | aboutAttr</td></tr>
<tr><td>[6.6]</td><td>idAttr</td><td>::= ' ID="' IDsymbol '"'</td></tr>
<tr><td>[6.7]</td><td>aboutAttr</td><td>::= ' about="' URI-reference '"'</td></tr>
<tr><td>[6.10]</td><td>propAttr</td><td>::= typeAttr | propName '="' string '"'</td></tr>
<tr><td>[6.11]</td><td>typeAttr</td><td>::= ' type="' URI-reference '"'</td></tr>
<tr><td>[6.13]</td><td>typedNode</td><td>::= '<' typeName idAboutAttr? propAttr* '/>'
| '<' typeName idAboutAttr? propAttr* '>'
propertyElt* '</' typeName '>'</td></tr>
<tr><td>[6.14]</td><td>propName</td><td>::= Qname</td></tr>
<tr><td>[6.15]</td><td>typeName</td><td>::= Qname</td></tr>
<tr><td>[6.19]</td><td>Qname</td><td>::= [NSprefix ':'] name</td></tr>
<tr><td>[6.20]</td><td>URI-reference</td><td>::= string, interpreted as a URI</td></tr>
<tr><td>[6.21]</td><td>IDsymbol</td><td>::= (any legal XML name symbol)</td></tr>
<tr><td>[6.22]</td><td>name</td><td>::= (any legal XML name symbol)</td></tr>
<tr><td>[6.23]</td><td>NSprefix</td><td>::= (any legal XML namespace prefix)</td></tr>
<tr><td>[6.24]</td><td>string</td><td>::= (any XML text, with "<", ">" and "&" escaped)</td></tr>
</table>

To help you get acquainted with this form of expressing the syntax, I'll go through each production and spell out the meaning:

- [6.1]: A valid `RDF` document optionally begins with `<rdf:RDF>`, is then following by one or more `obj`s, before finishing – optionally – with `</rdf:RDF>`. The namespace is in italics to indicate that the actual letters used for the namespace prefix are irrelevant, it is the mapping that is important
- [6.2]: A valid `obj` is made up of a valid `description`
- [6.3]: A valid `description` is made up of one of the following:
  - An `<rdf:Description>` element with zero or one idAboutAttrs and zero or more propAttrs
  - An `<rdf:Description>` element with zero or one idAboutAttrs and zero or more propAttrs and zero or more propertyElts
  - A typedNode
- [6.5]: An `idAboutAttr` is either an `idAttr` or an `aboutAttr`
- [6.6]: An `idAttr` is the text `ID="` followed by an `IDsymbol`, followed by the text `"`
- [6.7]: An `aboutAttr` is the text `about="` followed by a `URI-reference`, followed by the text `"`
- [6.10]: A `propAttr` is one of the following:
  - A `typeAttr`
  - A `propName` followed by the text =" followed by a `string`, and then the text "
- [6.11]: A `typeAttr` is the text `type="` followed by a `URI-reference`, followed by the text `"`
- [6.13]: A `typedNode` is one of the following:
  - An element whose name conforms to `typeName` with zero or one `idAboutAttrs` and zero or more `propAttrs`
  - An element whose name conforms to typeName with zero or one `idAboutAttrs` and zero or more `propAttrs` and zero or more `propertyElts`
- [6.14]: A `propName` is a `Qname`
- [6.15]: A `typeName` is a `Qname`
- [6.19]: A `Qname` is an optional `NSprefix` and ':', followed by a `name`
- [6.20]: A `URI-reference` is a `string` that must conform to RFC2396 (http://www.isi.edu/in-notes/rfc2396.txt)
- [6.21]: An `IDsymbol` is any legal XML name symbol, as per http://www.w3.org/TR/REC-xml#NT-Nmtoken
- [6.22]: A `name` is any legal XML name symbol, as per http://www.w3.org/TR/REC-xml#NT-Nmtoken
- [6.23]: An `NSprefix` is any legal XML namespace prefix
- [6.24]: A `string` is any legal XML text, with the usual XML characters escaped

Let's now look in more detail at what can go inside an `rdf:Description` element by looking at the syntax of properties in more detail.

Property Elements

Although in the previous section we discussed the `rdf:Description` element, it was inevitable that we'd actually say quite a lot about the properties that this element could contain. We'll recap on what we have seen so far, before looking at other features that are available.

We have already seen three ways that property information can be expressed.

String Literals

The first creates a string literal that is the value for a predicate that is defined by the name of the element containing the literal:

```
<rdf:Description about="http://www.spiked-online.com/Articles/0000000054C3.htm">
  <dc:Creator>Mick Hume</dc:Creator>
  <dc:Publisher>spiked</dc:Publisher>
</rdf:Description>
```

Resources

The second way to express properties for a resource is to say that the value of the predicate is actually another resource, and to use a URI to specify which resource that is:

```
<rdf:Description about="http://www.spiked-online.com/Articles/0000000054C3.htm">
  <dc:Creator rdf:resource="http://www.spiked-online.com/Authors/Mick%20Hume"/>
  <dc:Publisher
       rdf:resource="http://www.companieshouse.gov.uk/companynumber/3935644"/>
</rdf:Description>
```

Nesting Statements

The third syntax that you have seen involved nesting RDF statements within other statements. Recall that we are able to do the following:

```
<rdf:Description about="http://www.spiked-online.com/Articles/0000000054C3.htm">
  <dc:Creator>
    <rdf:Description about="http://www.spiked-online.com/Authors/Mick%20Hume">
      <xyz:JobTitle>editor</xyz:JobTitle>
    </rdf:Description>
  </dc:Creator>
  <dc:Publisher
       rdf:resource="http://www.companieshouse.gov.uk/companynumber/3935644"/>
</rdf:Description>
```

This is saying that the value of the property `dc:Creator` is itself a resource, and that we have statements to make about that resource.

We are also able to specify type information in the content of a property element:

```
<rdf:Description about="http://www.spiked-online.com/Articles/0000000054C3.htm">
  <dc:Creator>
    <rdf:Description>
      <rdf:type resource="http://www.vcard.org/Schemas#vCard" />
      <v:Name>Mick Hume</v:Name>
```

```
      <v:E-mail>Mick.Hume@spiked-online.com</v:E-mail>
    </rdf:Description>
  </dc:Creator>
</rdf:Description>
```

We saw that this could be abbreviated, by taking the type of the resource and turning it into a namespace qualified element name:

```
<rdf:Description about="http://www.spiked-online.com/Articles/0000000054C3.htm">
  <dc:Creator>
    <v:vCard>
      <v:Name>Mick Hume</v:Name>
      <v:E-mail>Mick.Hume@spiked-online.com</v:E-mail>
    </v:vCard>
  </dc:Creator>
</rdf:Description>
```

The pattern then is that an `rdf:Description` element will contain properties, but those properties can in turn contain `rdf:Description` elements.

parseType="Literal"

But what if that was not our intention? What if the XML inside the `dc:Creator` element was not meant to be interpreted by the RDF parser? Perhaps it was meant to be stored as is. Let's pick a better example to illustrate our point – one of the examples in the RDF Model and Syntax documentation (from Section 7).

Say we have a mathematical paper whose title is *Ramifications of* $(a+b)^2$ *to World Peace.* We would like to use MathML to specify this title, since it can help us format the various symbols properly, but if we place the MathML inside a `dc:Title` element we need some way of telling an RDF parser not to interpret the XML as RDF. This is achieved using an attribute named `parseType`:

```
<rdf:Description
 xmlns:rdf="http://www.w3.org/1999/02/22-rdf-syntax-ns#"
 xmlns:dc="http://purl.org/metadata/dublin_core#"
 xmlns="http://www.w3.org/TR/REC-mathml"
 rdf:about="http://mycorp.com/papers/NobelPaper1"
>
  <dc:Title rdf:parseType="Literal">
    Ramifications of
    <apply>
      <power/>
      <apply>
        <plus/>
        <ci>a</ci>
        <ci>b</ci>
      </apply>
      <cn>2</cn>
    </apply>
    to World Peace
  </dc:Title>
  <dc:Creator>David Hume</dc:Creator>
</rdf:Description>
```

Note that the contents of this element are not simply a string. For a start the text must be well formed XML, otherwise the RDF parser will fail. It is not the same as wrapping a CDATA section around everything; as you can see in the previous example the XML inside the dc:Title element is integral to the structure of the document. In addition to this, the XML requires all its namespace information, since at some point this fragment will need to re-emerge as:

```
Ramifications of
<m:apply>
  <m:power/>
  <m:apply>
    <m:plus/>
    <m:ci>a</m:ci>
    <m:ci>b</m:ci>
  </m:apply>
  <m:cn>2</m:cn>
</m:apply>
to World Peace
```

in order to be displayed correctly.

The parseType="Literal" attribute can be applied to any text, so the following would be valid:

```
<rdf:Description>
  <rdf:type resource="http://www.vcard.org/Schemas#vCard" />
  <v:Name parseType="Literal">Mick Hume</v:Name>
  <v:E-mail parseType="Literal">Mick.Hume@spiked-online.com</v:E-mail>
</rdf:Description>
```

However, the RDF documentation makes clear that anything inside a property element that *does not* contain XML markup will be interpreted as a string literal. We therefore only need to use the Literal parse type when we want to prevent the RDF parser from interpreting any XML that it encounters inside an element.

parseType="Resource"

We've seen how we can prevent an RDF parser from interpreting XML inside a property element as if it was RDF, but there is another related situation that can cause problems, when the parser cannot tell the difference between a property value and a resource.

As you know from the previous section we normally have properties inside an rdf:Description element, such as this:

```
<rdf:Description about="http://www.spiked-online.com/Articles/0000000054C3.htm">
  <dc:Creator>Mick Hume</dc:Creator>
</rdf:Description>
```

or this:

```
<rdf:Description about="http://www.spiked-online.com/Articles/0000000054C3.htm">
  <dc:Creator rdf:resource="http://www.spiked-online.com/Authors/Mick%20Hume"/>
</rdf:Description>
```

The RDF syntax allows us to make more statements about the author though, like this:

```
<rdf:Description about="http://www.spiked-online.com/Articles/0000000054C3.htm">
  <dc:Creator>
    <rdf:Description about="http://www.spiked-online.com/Authors/Mick%20Hume">
      <v:E-mail>Mick.Hume@spiked-online.com</v:E-mail>
    </rdf:Description>
  </dc:Creator>
</rdf:Description>
```

However, what if all we wanted to say was that the author had an e-mail address of `Mick.Hume@spiked-online.com`, but we weren't bothered about identifying the author. Of course we could remove the resource reference, like this:

```
<rdf:Description about="http://www.spiked-online.com/Articles/0000000054C3.htm">
  <dc:Creator>
    <rdf:Description>
      <v:E-mail>Mick.Hume@spiked-online.com</v:E-mail>
    </rdf:Description>
  </dc:Creator>
</rdf:Description>
```

but that seems overly elaborate. Surely we should be able to simply do this:

```
<rdf:Description about="http://www.spiked-online.com/Articles/0000000054C3.htm">
  <dc:Creator>
    <v:E-mail>Mick.Hume@spiked-online.com</v:E-mail>
  </dc:Creator>
</rdf:Description>
```

This unfortunately raises an ambiguity. If you started from the inside out, you would say you have an anonymous `dc:Creator` element, which in turn has a `v:E-mail` property:

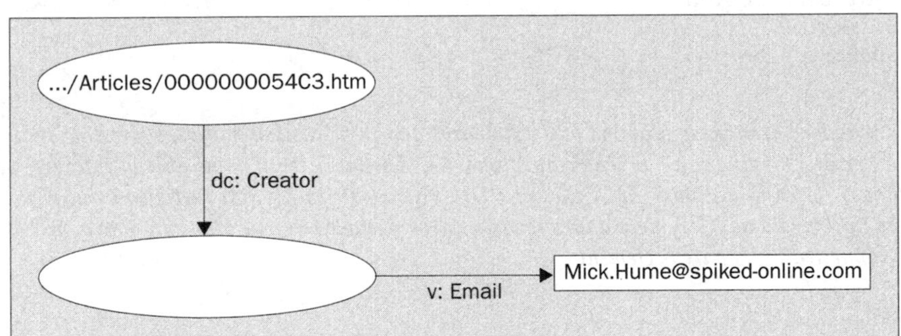

But if you started from the outside in, you would say you had a resource of a web page, that had a `dc:Creator` property, and that this `dc:Creator` property refers to an anonymous resource of type `v:E-mail`:

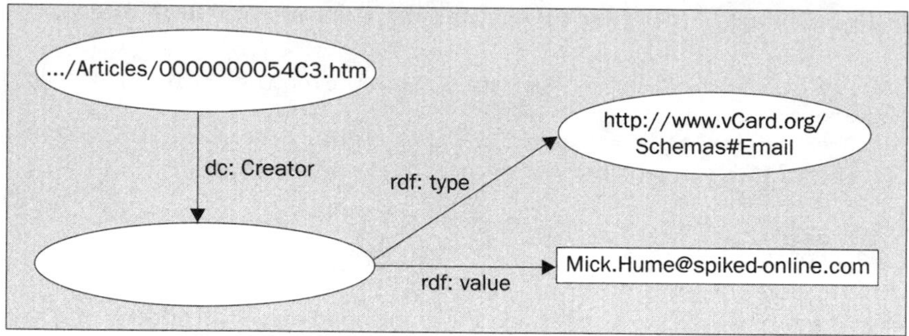

This second diagram is in fact the correct interpretation of the RDF/XML as it stands at the moment. The problem is that we need the `dc:Creator` element to be interpreted as both a property of the web page, but also as an anonymous resource in its own right so that we can attach properties to it.

RDF/XML does allow us to force the `dc:Creator` element to be interpreted as if it was both a predicate *and* an anonymous resource. The `parseType="Resource"` attribute does exactly that, so the following RDF syntax gives us just the model we want:

```
<rdf:Description about="http://www.spiked-online.com/Articles/0000000054C3.htm">
  <dc:Creator rdf:parseType="Resource">
    <v:E-mail>Mick.Hume@spiked-online.com</v:E-mail>
  </dc:Creator>
</rdf:Description>
```

This is exactly the same as specifying the anonymous resource explicitly:

```
<rdf:Description about="http://www.spiked-online.com/Articles/0000000054C3.htm">
  <dc:Creator>
    <rdf:Description>
      <v:E-mail>Mick.Hume@spiked-online.com</v:E-mail>
    </rdf:Description>
  </dc:Creator>
</rdf:Description>
```

Some discussions are taking place on bulletin boards and in discussion papers, suggesting that `parseType="Resource"` *is the default behavior. The intention is to be able to interpret meta data that is stored in ordinary XML files as RDF. This would mean that just about any XML file could be interpreted as RDF meta data, by making every single element into an anonymous resource that is connected to its parent element.*

Summary

We have seen a number of different ways of expressing the value of a statement property:

- As a string literal
- As a URI which refers to a resource
- As well-formed XML
- As an anonymous resource with its own properties
- As a named resource with its own properties

Formal Grammar

As before, we list here the formal grammar that defines the features that we have just seen:

Section	Production	Syntax
[6.12]	propertyElt	::= '<' propName idAttr? '>' value '</' propName '>' | '<' propName idAttr? parseLiteral '>' literal '</' propName '>' | '<' propName idAttr? parseResource '>' propertyElt* '</' propName '>' | '<' propName idRefAttr? propAttr* '/>'
[6.16]	idRefAttr	::= idAttr | resourceAttr
[6.17]	value	::= obj | string
[6.18]	resourceAttr	::= ' resource="' URI-reference '"'
[6.32]	parseLiteral	::= ' parseType="Literal"'
[6.33]	parseResource	::= ' parseType="Resource"'
[6.34]	literal	::= (any well-formed XML)

If you managed to work your way through the last lot of formal grammar then this piece is probably easy for you! If not, then I'll expand a little on the meaning:

- [6.12]: A `propertyElt` is one of the following:
  - An element whose name conforms to `propName` (see [6.14] in the previous section), with zero or one `idAttr` attributes and whose content is a value
  - An element whose name conforms to `propName`, with zero or one `idAttr` attributes, one `parseLiteral` attribute and whose content is a `literal`
  - An element whose name conforms to `propName`, with zero or one `idAttr` attributes, one `parseResource` attribute and whose content is one or more `propertyElts`
  - An element whose name conforms to `propName`, with zero or one `idRefAttr` attributes, and one or more `propertyAttrs`
- [6.16]: An `idRefAttr` is either an `idAttr` (see [6.6]) or a `resourceAttr`
- [6.17]: A `value` is either an `obj` (see [6.2]) or a `string` (see [6.24])
- [6.18]: A `resourceAttr` is an attribute called '`resource`' which has a value of `URI-reference` (see [6.20])
- [6.32]: A `parseLiteral` is an attribute called '`parseType`' which has a value of "`Literal`"
- [6.33]: A `parseResource` is an attribute called '`parseType`' which has a value of "`Resource`"
- [6.34]: A `literal` is any well-formed XML

Containers

A container is simply a list, or collection, of resources. The collection might be a list of articles that make up a web site or a list of authors who have contributed to an article. RDF has three different types of container – a **bag**, a **sequence**, and an **alternative** – and they can be used anywhere that the `rdf:Description` element can be used.

rdf:Bag

The simplest container is a bag, and it is used to contain multiple values for a property when there is no significance to the order in which the values are listed. The following shows the RDF syntax for a bag that enables more than one author to be specified for an article on the spiked website:

```
<rdf:RDF>
  <rdf:Description about="http://www.spiked-online.com/Articles/0000000054C4.htm">
    <dc:Creator>
      <rdf:Bag>
        <rdf:li resource="http://www.spiked-online.com/
                          Authors/Victor%20Rortvedt"/>
        <rdf:li resource="http://www.spiked-online.com/Authors/Sandy%20Starr"/>
        <rdf:li resource="http://www.spiked-online.com/Authors/Josie%20Appleton"/>
      </rdf:Bag>
    </dc:Creator>
  </rdf:Description>
</rdf:RDF>
```

The syntax for a bag is simply the enclosing element, `rdf:Bag`, followed by the list of resources in the bag. The members of the container are identified using `rdf:li` elements (so named because of the HTML 'list item' tag), and although in this example they have resource attributes to indicate their value, they could also be string literals:

```
<rdf:RDF>
  <rdf:Description about="http://www.spiked-online.com/Articles/0000000054C3.htm">
    <dc:Subject>
      <rdf:Bag>
        <rdf:li>democracy</rdf:li>
        <rdf:li>voter apathy</rdf:li>
        <rdf:li>general election</rdf:li>
      </rdf:Bag>
    </dc:Subject>
  </rdf:Description>
</rdf:RDF>
```

Note that as far as the meta data in this example is concerned, the resource being referred to – the article .../Articles/0000000054C3.htm – only has *one* property, but that property (`dc:Subject`) has three values. This is very different to not using a bag, and giving the resource three values:

```
<rdf:RDF>
  <rdf:Description about="http://www.spiked-online.com/Articles/0000000054C3.htm">
    <dc:Subject>democracy</dc:Subject>
    <dc:Subject>voter apathy</dc:Subject>
    <dc:Subject>general election</dc:Subject>
  </rdf:Description>
</rdf:RDF>
```

This repeated properties syntax – in this case we have three occurrences of the same property – is modeled as follows:

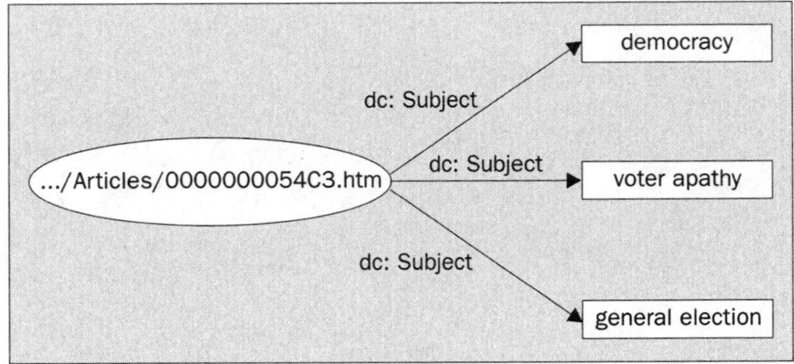

That is straightforward, and we have met it before. But the container syntax requires a resource to represent the bag that holds the values for the subject. This is modeled differently, as follows:

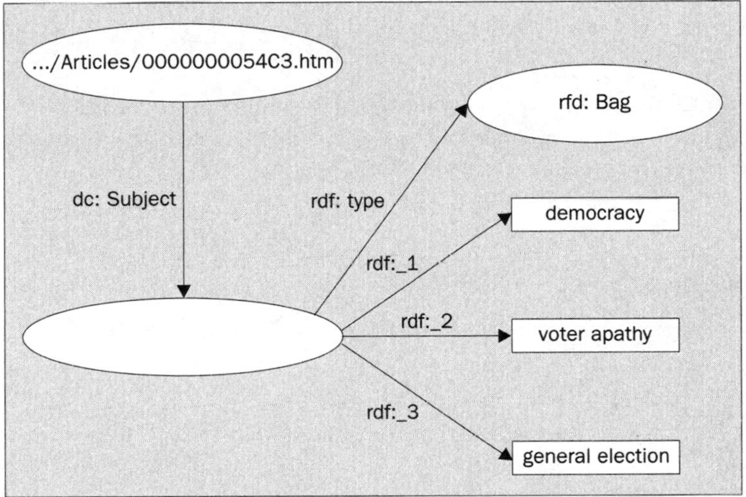

With `rdf:Bag`, we are saying that the resource *article* is connected to another resource *container,* and that this container has three items within it. In the previous diagram we were saying that the resource *article* is connected to three other resources (in this case, string literals), which are each subject values in their own right.

You may recall that I said earlier that there were a number of situations where an RDF parser would automatically create anonymous resources in order to correctly model your meta data. The processing of containers is one such situation. As we can see, an anonymous resource has automatically been created as a placeholder, on to which the resource `type` can be added, as well as the string literals that represent the values.

You will have noticed that an RDF parser will also automatically name the predicates for the `rdf:li` values. If this were not the case then the above model would have looked like this, with each arc from the anonymous resource to the string literals labeled with `rdf:li`:

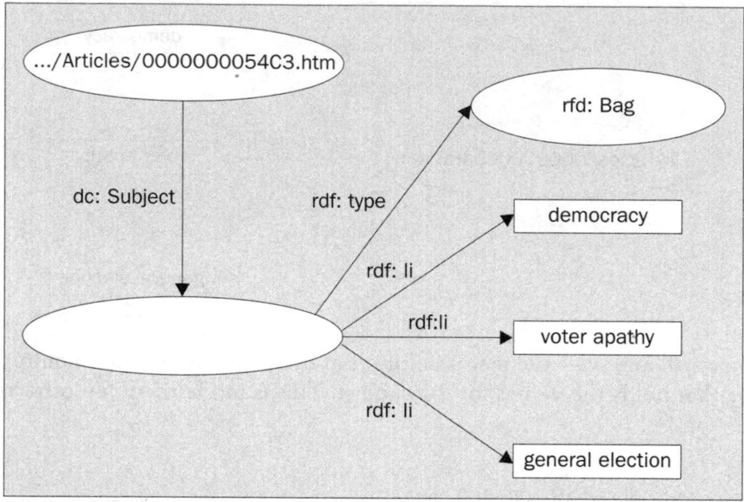

At first sight there seems nothing wrong with this, but recall that properties can be specified with attributes on a resource, just as easily as they can with child elements. This means that the above graph *should* be able to be represented something like this:

```
<rdf:Description about="http://www.spiked-online.com/Articles/0000000054C3.htm">
  <dc:Subject>
    <rdf:Bag
     rdf:li="democracy"
     rdf:li="voter apathy"
     rdf:li="general election"
    />
  </dc:Subject>
</rdf:Description>
```

But of course this is not possible since XML does not allow a repeat of an attribute with the same name. RDF therefore allows us to use this syntax:

```
<rdf:Description about="http://www.spiked-online.com/Articles/0000000054C3.htm">
  <dc:Subject>
    <rdf:Bag
     rdf:_1="democracy"
     rdf:_2="voter apathy"
     rdf:_3="general election"
    />
  </dc:Subject>
</rdf:Description>
```

Whilst we only need to explicitly use these names if we are using the attribute syntax, by making the parser automatically create these names when using the element syntax, we can be sure that whichever format is used the model will be the same. The attribute syntax just used would create the following graph, which is exactly the same as our first example:

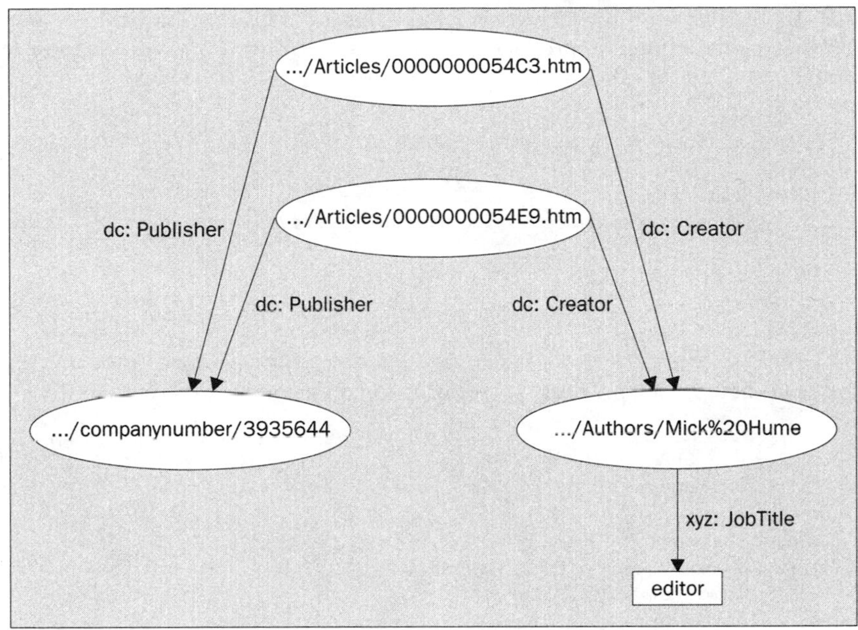

There's yet another way that this model can be expressed syntactically. So far we have used elements as children of an rdf:Bag element, and we have attached attributes to the rdf:Bag element, but we can also specify a type property on an rdf:Description element. I'm sure you spotted this possibility when you saw the graph, but we may as well spell this out. In this syntax we explicitly create an anonymous resource onto which we can attach a resource type and the three string literals:

```
<rdf:Description about="http://www.spiked-online.com/Articles/0000000054C3.htm">
  <dc:Subject>
    <rdf:Description>
      <rdf:type resource="http://www.w3.org/1999/02/22-rdf-syntax-ns#Bag" />
      <rdf:li>democracy</rdf:li>
      <rdf:li>voter apathy</rdf:li>
      <rdf:li>general election</rdf:li>
    </rdf:Description>
  </dc:Subject>
</rdf:Description>
```

As a little diversion, I'll just demonstrate that RDF is completely consistent, no matter where you start. Let's put aside all of the previous discussion on rdf:Bags, and begin with the idea that a container can be an anonymous resource:

```
<rdf:Description about="http://www.spiked-online.com/Articles/0000000054C3.htm">
  <dc:Subject>
    <rdf:Description>
      ...
    </rdf:Description>
  </dc:Subject>
</rdf:Description>
```

Let's treat this as a base class onto which we will build. Just as in OO you might have an abstract notion of a container that is then refined to produce lists, sequences, arrays, and so on, so too we will give this abstract container a type:

```
<rdf:Description about="http://www.spiked-online.com/Articles/0000000054C3.htm">
  <dc:Subject>
    <rdf:Description>
      <rdf:type resource="http://www.w3.org/1999/02/22-rdf-syntax-ns#Bag" />
      ...
    </rdf:Description>
  </dc:Subject>
</rdf:Description>
```

We'll also throw in the `rdf:li` property to allow us to add as many members to the collection as we want:

```
<rdf:Description about="http://www.spiked-online.com/Articles/0000000054C3.htm">
  <dc:Subject>
    <rdf:Description>
      <rdf:type resource="http://www.w3.org/1999/02/22-rdf-syntax-ns#Bag" />
      <rdf:li>democracy</rdf:li>
      <rdf:li>voter apathy</rdf:li>
      <rdf:li>general election</rdf:li>
    </rdf:Description>
  </dc:Subject>
</rdf:Description>
```

Note that this time we have started with the expanded syntax, directly corresponding to the graph that we saw earlier. Now, let's use the abbreviated format where we can create typed nodes by using the type `value` of an `rdf:Description` as the namespace qualified element name:

```
<rdf:Description about="http://www.spiked-online.com/Articles/0000000054C3.htm">
  <dc:Subject>
    <rdf:Bag>
      <rdf:li>democracy</rdf:li>
      <rdf:li>voter apathy</rdf:li>
      <rdf:li>general election</rdf:li>
    </rdf:Bag>
  </dc:Subject>
</rdf:Description>
```

Which is where we came in! This point is not integral to understanding containers, but it does illustrate the consistency within the RDF model and its corresponding syntax. As you can see we can move backwards and forwards from model to syntax, making abbreviations here and adding detail there – with no loss of meaning.

rdf:Seq

Whilst the contents of `rdf:Bags` are unordered – that is there is no implied order to the contents and any software processing, the list can treat them in whatever order it likes – there will always be a need for ordered lists of resources. Such lists can be created using the `rdf:Seq` element. Let's create a list of the articles that appear in the election section of the spiked web site:

```
<rdf:RDF>
  <rdf:Description about="http://www.spiked-online.com/Sections/election">
    <xyz:Contents>
      <rdf:Seq>
        <rdf:li resource="http://www.spiked-online.com/
                                  Articles/0000000054E5.htm"/>
        <rdf:li resource="http://www.spiked-online.com/
                                  Articles/0000000054E8.htm"/>
        <rdf:li resource="http://www.spiked-online.com/
                                  Articles/0000000054C0.htm"/>
        <rdf:li resource="http://www.spiked-online.com/
                                  Articles/0000000054BF.htm"/>
        <rdf:li resource="http://www.spiked-online.com/
                                  Articles/0000000054C1.htm"/>
        <rdf:li resource="http://www.spiked-online.com/
                                  Articles/0000000054AF.htm"/>
        <rdf:li resource="http://www.spiked-online.com/
                                  Articles/00000000546B.htm"/>
      </rdf:Seq>
    </xyz:Contents>
  </rdf:Description>
</rdf:RDF>
```

As before, we are simply saying that the `rdf:type` of the element `xyz:Contents` is `rdf:Seq`. However, this time we are saying to any software that processes this RDF, that the order of the articles in the `Contents` container is important.

rdf:Alt

Whilst `rdf:Bag` and `rdf:Seq` provide us with a way of creating lists of resources, it is also useful to be able to provide a selection from which any one resource can be chosen. The `rdf:Alt` container is a means by which a number of resources can be specified which are deemed to be equivalent. A processor of the RDF can then choose one of these based on whatever criteria seem applicable.

For example, the spiked website might have different language versions of the same article. The absolute URL of the article may stay the same – to assist when moving our meta data around – but a container could be created with other articles that could be deemed to be equivalent. Some software engine might then map all hyperlinks within the spiked site to the correct language version of the article:

```
<rdf:RDF>
  <rdf:Description about="http://www.spiked-online.com/Articles/0000000054E8.htm">
    <xyz:Translations>
      <rdf:Alt>
        <rdf:li resource="http://www.spiked-online.com/
                                  Articles/0000000054E8.htm"/>
        <rdf:li resource="http://www.spiked-online.com/
                                  Articles/Italian/54E8.htm"/>
        <rdf:li resource="http://www.spiked-online.com/Articles/French/54E8.htm"/>
      </rdf:Alt>
    </xyz:Translations>
  </rdf:Description>
</rdf:RDF>
```

Note that I have included the original, English version of the article in the rdf:Alt list. This is because the first item in the list of alternatives is deemed to be the default and preferred selection. If I didn't include it then the default would become the Italian version. As it happens, in this case that is completely application dependent, and we could just as easily have left the English version out and just not processed the alternatives if we were dealing with English users. I mention it because there is a more significant point, which is that the consequence of the first item in the list being the default means that an rdf:Alt *must always contain at least one member.*

rdf:li

So far we have seen two ways that the rdf:li element is used to identify the items in a container. The first was to simply contain a string literal, whilst the second was to refer to some external resource. Since both of these ways of declaring an item in a container are similar to the syntax alternatives available when specifying property elements (see [6.12]), you may well have wondered whether we can use the other syntax alternatives, such as nesting rdf:Descriptions or using parseType="Literal" attributes.

Well, your intuition was right. We can indeed use any of the forms available to us when specifying property elements, the only difference being that if we want to add further properties to the collection member, we have to use the parseType="Resource" attribute that we discussed earlier. Let's look at a few examples.

The first example shows how we might embed some translated XHTML into our RDF document:

```
<rdf:RDF>
  <rdf:Description about="http://www.w3.org/Meta data/">
    <xyz:Translations>
      <rdf:Alt>
        <rdf:li parseType="Literal" xmlns:lang="en">
          <H1>Meta data and Resource Description</H1>
        </rdf:li>
        <rdf:li parseType="Literal" xmlns:lang="fr">
          <H1>Meta data et description de ressources</H1>
        </rdf:li>
      </rdf:Alt>
    </xyz:Translations>
  </rdf:Description>
</rdf:RDF>
```

Note that I have used the xml:lang attribute on the rdf:li element. However, I tend to avoid doing this since this attribute does not create a triple, and so any useful information is lost when the document is parsed. If this information were important then you would need to add it to the main meta data.

The next example shows how we might add information to the illustration we had in the rdf:Bag section – where an article was written by a number of people – by nesting rdf:Description elements:

```
<rdf:Description about="/Articles/0000000054C4.htm">
  <dc:Creator>
    <rdf:Bag>
      <rdf:li>
        <rdf:Description about="/Authors/Victor%20Rortvedt">
          <v:E-mail>Victor.Rortvedt@spiked-online.com</v:E-mail>
        </rdf:Description>
      </rdf:li>
```

```
        <rdf:li>
          <rdf:Description about="/Authors/Sandy%20Starr">
            <v:E-mail>Sandy.Starr@spiked-online.com</v:E-mail>
          </rdf:Description>
        </rdf:li>

        <rdf:li>
          <rdf:Description about="/Authors/Josie%20Appleton">
            <v:E-mail>Josie.Appleton@spiked-online.com</v:E-mail>
          </rdf:Description>
        </rdf:li>
      </rdf:Bag>
    </dc:Creator>
  </rdf:Description>
```

The final format is to simply add a property to the `rdf:li` resource itself. Of course the resource will not be accessible from anywhere else, since it will be anonymous. Adding properties to an `rdf:li` anonymous resource can be achieved by using the `parseType="Resource"`, as follows:

```
  <rdf:Description about="/Articles/0000000054C4.htm">
    <dc:Creator>
      <rdf:Bag>
        <rdf:li parseType="Resource">
          <v:E-mail>Victor.Rortvedt@spiked-online.com</v:E-mail>
        </rdf:li>

        <rdf:li parseType="Resource">
          <v:E-mail>Sandy.Starr@spiked-online.com</v:E-mail>
        </rdf:li>

        <rdf:li parseType="Resource">
          <v:E-mail>Josie.Appleton@spiked-online.com</v:E-mail>
        </rdf:li>
      </rdf:Bag>
    </dc:Creator>
  </rdf:Description>
```

Don't forget that if you don't use the `parseType="Resource"` then the parser will think that it has a typed node, that is, the abbreviated form of an `rdf:Description` that has an `rdf:type` property set to indicate its type.

The ID Attribute on Containers

Although we have tended to create anonymous resources for our collections, there will be situations where we want to make statements about the collection in just the same way that we make statements about any other resource. Let's go back to a shortened version of the contents page that we created for the election section of the spiked website:

```
  <rdf:Description about="http://www.spiked-online.com/Sections/election">
    <xyz:Contents>
      <rdf:Seq>
        <rdf:li resource="http://www.spiked-online.com/Articles/0000000054E5.htm"/>
        <rdf:li resource="http://www.spiked-online.com/Articles/0000000054E8.htm"/>
```

```
        <rdf:li resource="http://www.spiked-online.com/Articles/0000000054C0.htm"/>
      </rdf:Seq>
    </xyz:Contents>
  </rdf:Description>
```

Instead of just specifying one section in this document, let's use it to express all the sections. Note that it is perfectly legitimate to have a container within another container. You just need to use the `rdf:li` element to achieve this nesting:

```
<rdf:Description about="http://www.spiked-online.com/Sections">
  <xyz:Contents>
    <rdf:Bag>
      <rdf:li>
        <rdf:Seq ID="election">
          <rdf:li resource="http://www.spiked-online.com/
                            Articles/0000000054E5.htm"/>
          <rdf:li resource="http://www.spiked-online.com/
                            Articles/0000000054E8.htm"/>
          <rdf:li resource="http://www.spiked-online.com/
                            Articles/0000000054C0.htm"/>
        </rdf:Seq>
      </rdf:li>

      <rdf:li>
        <rdf:Seq ID="science">
          <rdf:li resource="http://www.spiked-online.com/
                            Articles/000000005527.htm"/>
          <rdf:li resource="http://www.spiked-online.com/
                            Articles/000000005513.htm"/>
          <rdf:li resource="http://www.spiked-online.com/
                            Articles/000000005526.htm"/>
        </rdf:Seq>
      </rdf:li>

      <rdf:li>
        <rdf:Seq ID="culture">
          <rdf:li resource="http://www.spiked-online.com/
                            Articles/000000005474.htm"/>
          <rdf:li resource="http://www.spiked-online.com/
                            Articles/00000000552B.htm"/>
          <rdf:li resource="http://www.spiked-online.com/
                            Articles/00000000551F.htm"/>
        </rdf:Seq>
      </rdf:li>
    </rdf:Bag>
  </xyz:Contents>
</rdf:Description>
```

Now that we have added `ID` attributes to each bag we can reference the containers just like any other resource. We might indicate what order the sections should appear in when shown inside a menu, for example:

```
<rdf:Description about="http://www.spiked-online.com/MainMenu">
  <xyz:Menu>
    <rdf:Seq>
      <rdf:li resource="#culture"/>
      <rdf:li resource="#election"/>
      <rdf:li resource="#science"/>
```

```
    </rdf:Seq>
  </xyz:Menu>
</rdf:Description>
```

We might also indicate the e-mail address for readers' enquiries, which could then be displayed on each contents page:

```
<rdf:RDF>
  <rdf:Description about="#election">
    <v:E-mail>election@spiked-online.com</v:E-mail>
  </rdf:Description>

  <rdf:Description about="#science">
    <v:E-mail>science@spiked-online.com</v:E-mail>
  </rdf:Description>

  <rdf:Description about="#culture">
    <v:E-mail>culture@spiked-online.com</v:E-mail>
  </rdf:Description>
</rdf:RDF>
```

The aboutEach Attribute

The `ID` attribute that we have attached to a container has allowed us to make statements about that container. However, there may be situations where we want to make statements not about the container but *the members of the container.*

You may recall that when we were discussing nesting statements in the section on `rdf:Description`, we speculated on whether a certain meta data model could be abbreviated further. Let's go back to that example to see how this might be done. The model is as follows:

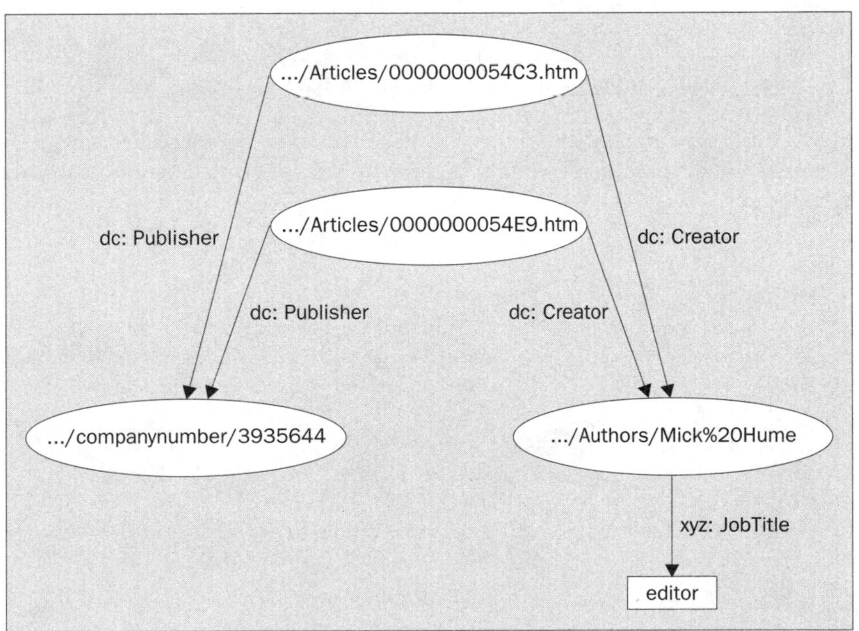

The syntax for this model is this:

```
<rdf:RDF>
  <rdf:Description about="http://www.spiked-online.com/Articles/0000000054C3.htm">
    <dc:Creator rdf:resource="http://www.spiked-online.com/Authors/Mick%20Hume"/>
    <dc:Publisher
          rdf:resource="http://www.companieshouse.gov.uk/companynumber/3935644"/>
  </rdf:Description>

  <rdf:Description about="http://www.spiked-online.com/Articles/0000000054E9.htm">
    <dc:Creator rdf:resource="http://www.spiked-online.com/Authors/Mick%20Hume"/>
    <dc:Publisher
          rdf:resource="http://www.companieshouse.gov.uk/companynumber/3935644"/>
  </rdf:Description>

  <rdf:Description about="http://www.spiked-online.com/Authors/Mick%20Hume">
    <xyz:JobTitle>editor</xyz:JobTitle>
  </rdf:Description>
</rdf:RDF>
```

Intuitively we felt that we must be able to abbreviate this syntax further, since each article has the same publisher and the same author, and indeed we can. The first step is to create a bag that contains the two articles being referred to and give the bag an identifier so that we can make statements about it:

```
<rdf:RDF>
  <rdf:Bag ID="articles">
    <rdf:li resource="http://www.spiked-online.com/Articles/0000000054C3.htm" />
    <rdf:li resource="http://www.spiked-online.com/Articles/0000000054E9.htm" />
  </rdf:Bag>
</rdf:RDF>
```

Note that a container is an acceptable top-level element in RDF.

Now we can use a different attribute on the `rdf:Description` element, called `aboutEach`, which applies whatever statements are made within the `rdf:Description` element to each of the resources in the bag referred to:

```
<rdf:RDF>
  <rdf:Bag ID="articles">
    <rdf:li resource="http://www.spiked-online.com/Articles/0000000054C3.htm" />
    <rdf:li resource="http://www.spiked-online.com/Articles/0000000054E9.htm" />
  </rdf:Bag>

  <rdf:Description aboutEach="#articles">
    <dc:Creator rdf:resource="http://www.spiked-online.com/Authors/Mick%20Hume"/>
    <dc:Publisher
          rdf:resource="http://www.companieshouse.gov.uk/companynumber/3935644"/>
  </rdf:Description>
</rdf:RDF>
```

As you can imagine, the real power of this syntax comes when the bag is filled with hundreds – or even thousands – of articles. But bear in mind that the only abbreviation we are getting here is in the syntax. The model is *exactly the same* as if each of the statements about each of the articles had been made separately. The `aboutEach` attribute does not create anything special in the model. Instead it simply acts as if the statements within the `rdf:Description` element were applied one at a time across each member of the container referred to. (For this reason the `aboutEach` attribute is called a **distributive referent**.)

In other words, when you look at the model produced, whether a graph or triples, there would be no indication that `aboutEach` had been used in the source. In our example here, the only difference between the model produced in the earlier scenario and this one is that the later one has a resource for the bag. But note that the `dc:Creator` and `dc:Publisher` properties are not attached to the bag, they are attached to each member individually, so the existence of the bag is irrelevant as far as the model of the meta data is concerned.

This doesn't mean that some RDF parser might not store the fact that the statements created originated with a distributive referent. How triples and other information are stored is not defined in the specification. What we are saying though, is that if some system comes to query the meta data store, it should be able to query as if the statements were made individually.

> *The question of what the RDF parser stores is important when you consider whether to accumulate statements from different RDF documents. If I add another list of articles that are unknown to this document, should the referent apply across them too? This is undefined, but has led me to think that you need to store the source of statements in a triple store, so that you can decide when querying whether you want just statements that you received in one document, and all statements regardless of where they originated.*
>
> *Also, if the distributed referent were ever removed, you'd need to remove all the individual statements. And then you'd need to know if those individual statements were created by the distributant or independently. All in all, it makes sense to store the notion of* `aboutEach`.

The aboutEachPrefix Attribute

The final attribute that can be applied to an `rdf:Description` element is `aboutEachPrefix`. This attribute is also a distributive referent, but this time the distribution takes place across any resource that begins with the specified characters. For example, to indicate that anything that appears on the spiked website is published by spiked Ltd, we could use this syntax:

```
<rdf:Description aboutEachPrefix="http://www.spiked-online.com/">
  <dc:Publisher
        rdf:resource="http://www.companieshouse.gov.uk/companynumber/3935644"/>
</rdf:Description>
```

The model for this is an anonymous bag that contains all of the resources that begin with the specified prefix. The statements that are in the `rdf:Description` element are being made about each of the resources in this anonymous bag.

Summary

In this section we looked at the containers that RDF provides:

- Bags
- Sequences
- Alternatives

We also looked at how the members of a container can contain any of the formats from the RDF syntax that can appear in other parts of an RDF document. Finally, we looked at ways that we can make statements about all resources in a collection, rather than just the collection itself.

Formal Grammar

The formal grammar for the features that we have seen is specified as follows:

<table>
<tr><th>Section</th><th>Production</th><th>Syntax</th></tr>
<tr><td>[6.2]</td><td>obj</td><td>::= description | container</td></tr>
<tr><td>[6.4]</td><td>container</td><td>::= sequence | bag | alternative</td></tr>
<tr><td>[6.25]</td><td>sequence</td><td>::= '<rdf:Seq' idAttr? '>' member* '</rdf:Seq>'
| '<rdf:Seq' idAttr? memberAttr* '/>'</td></tr>
<tr><td>[6.26]</td><td>bag</td><td>::= '<rdf:Bag' idAttr? '>' member* '</rdf:Bag>'
| '<rdf:Bag' idAttr? memberAttr* '/>'</td></tr>
<tr><td>[6.27]</td><td>alternative</td><td>::= '<rdf:Alt' idAttr? '>' member+ '</rdf:Alt>'
| '<rdf:Alt' idAttr? memberAttr? '/>'</td></tr>
<tr><td>[6.28]</td><td>member</td><td>::= referencedItem | inlineItem</td></tr>
<tr><td>[6.29]</td><td>referencedItem</td><td>::= '<rdf:li' resourceAttr '/>'</td></tr>
<tr><td>[6.30]</td><td>inlineItem</td><td>::= '<rdf:li' '>' value </rdf:li>'
| '<rdf:li' parseLiteral '>' literal </rdf:li>'
| '<rdf:li' parseResource '>' propertyElt* </rdf:li>'</td></tr>
<tr><td>[6.31]</td><td>memberAttr</td><td>::= ' rdf:_n="' string '"' (where n is an integer)</td></tr>
</table>

The meaning of each production is:

- [6.2]: An `obj` is one of the following:
  - A `description` (see [6.3])
  - A `container`
- [6.4]: A `container` is one of the following:
  - A `sequence`
  - A `bag`
  - An `alternative`
- [6.25]: A `sequence` is an element named `rdf:Seq` with zero or one `idAttr` (see [6.6]) attributes and one of the following:
  - Zero or more `member` elements
  - Zero or more `memberAttr` attributes
- [6.26]: A `bag` is an element named `rdf:Bag` with zero or one `idAttr` (see [6.6]) attributes and one of the following:
  - Zero or more `member` elements

- Zero or more memberAttr attributes

- [6.27]: An alternative is an element named rdf:Alt with zero or one idAttr (see [6.6]) attributes and one of the following:
  - One or more member elements
  - One or more memberAttr attributes
- [6.28]: A member is one of the following:
  - A referencedItem
  - An inlineItem
- [6.29]: A referencedItem is an element named rdf:li with one resourceAttr (see [6.18])
- [6.30]: An inlineItem is an element named rdf:li with one of the following:
  - A child element of value (see [6.17])
  - One parseLiteral (see [6.32]) attribute and a child element of literal
  - One parseResource (see [6.33]) attribute and zero or more propertyElts (see [6.12])
- [6.31]: A memberAttr is an attribute named rdf:_n where n is an integer

Statements About Statements

The final area of the RDF Model and Syntax specification that we need to discuss concerns what we called in the introduction *meta-meta data*. Just as RDF provides us with facilities to make statements about resources, so too it provides us with a way of making statements about other statements.

Much of what follows may seem largely esoteric, and often seems irrelevant to most real-world uses of meta data. After all, most of us are used to dealing with search engines and ratings systems but they may well be the limit of our experience of meta data.

But recall that the aim of RDF is to be a model for meta data in all its forms. As much as it provides us with a framework within which we can say that:

```
the rating for the spiked website is 100
```

so too it must be able to cope with a statement such as:

```
the web ranking service says that:
  the rating for the spiked website is 100
```

This is not the same as chaining together a series of statements. At first sight it looks like we are saying nothing much different to what we have done in the rest of this chapter. But just as in mathematics this:

```
(5 + 7) * 6
```

yields a different result to this:

```
5 + (7 * 6)
```

so too we have a world of difference between:

```
the web ranking service says that
  there is a rating
    which refers to the spiked website
    and has a value of 100
```

and,

```
the web ranking service says (X)
```

with X itself being an entire statement.

Why might you want to make the distinction? Chances are you wouldn't. Much of this will seem like chasing clouds if you are not involved in fairly specialized areas. But if you are involved in the worlds of knowledge representation, logic, artificial intelligence, and so on, you will often be dealing with data about meta data, and since this second level of meta data is meta data just like any other, so the same RDF model can be used. In RDF terms, what we are doing is described as making **statements about statements**, and RDF adds some extra features to make this easier.

When we made our 'statement about a statement' earlier, it would seem at first glance that all we need do is give a statement an identifier, and then we have the facility to make second-level statements about it.

The problem with this is that the statement that you are making statements about may not actually exist, as we will illustrate in a moment. This sounds odd, given that we said we would be making 'statements about statements' but if we work through the logic it creates *more* flexibility, not less.

Let's take an example from the world of knowledge representation – I want to record someone's beliefs, independent of the fact that they believe. For example, I can *believe* that the world is flat, even if it isn't. So imagine that I wish to record that Columbus believed that he had reached India. I might think that I could use the following syntax to express this:

```
<rdf:RDF>
  <rdf:Description about="#ChristopherColumbus">
    <xyz:Believes rdf:resource="#fact" />
  </rdf:Description>

  <rdf:Description ID="fact">
    <xyz:Belief>
      <rdf:Description about="#ChristopherColumbus">
        <xyz:Reached rdf:resource="http://www.countries.org/India" />
      </rdf:Description>
    </xyz:Belief>
  </rdf:Description>
</rdf:RDF>
```

Alternatively, I might decide to just group what it is that Columbus believes inside an `rdf:Bag`, rather than inventing an element to contain it:

```
<rdf:RDF>
  <rdf:Description about="#ChristopherColumbus">
    <xyz:Believes rdf:resource="#fact" />
  </rdf:Description>
```

```
    <rdf:Bag ID="fact">
      <rdf:li>
        <rdf:Description about="#ChristopherColumbus">
          <xyz:Reached rdf:resource="http://www.countries.org/India" />
        </rdf:Description>
      </rdf:li>
    </rdf:Bag>
  </rdf:RDF>
```

Whichever approach we take, the problem is we are left at the end with an unfortunate by-product; our meta data model contains the statement that Columbus reached India, which we know is wrong. That's not to say that we would never model data that is incorrect – RDF is dependent on us humans after all – it's just that in our example we never intended to say anything about Columbus' travels or India; we were only trying to store what *Columbus believed*. To make this clear, look at the triples produced by this statement, and note the last triple:

```
{ [#ChristopherColumbus], [xyz:Believes], [#fact] }
{
    [http://www.w3.org/1999/02/22-rdf-syntax-ns#type],
    [#fact],
    [http://www.w3.org/1999/02/22-rdf-syntax-ns#Bag]
}
{
    [http://www.w3.org/1999/02/22-rdf-syntax-ns#_1],
    [#fact],
    [#ChristopherColumbus]
}
{ [#ChristopherColumbus], [xyz:Reached], [http://www.countries.org/India] }
```

If this example doesn't convince you, imagine that you are using RDF in some publishing system to hold information about the processes. I have checked the spelling on my document and the system needs to record this. Just as storing the statement *believed* by Columbus has the consequence of creating the statement that the person believes, if we try to model that I believe that the document is spelled correctly, we end up with a statement that says that the document *is* spelled correctly.

And it's not just this spurious statement that is a problem. If you look at the triples again, you will see that the first is OK, since it simply says that Columbus believes the resource identified by `fact`. However, the bag identified by `fact` is actually connected to the resource `ChristopherColumbus`, not the entire statement. What we need is a way of grouping the parts of a statement together as one unit, and then making our statement about that unit. We also need to avoid creating a 'real' statement, when all we want is the model of the statement.

RDF addresses these problems through a process called **reification**.

Reification

A reified statement is simply a representation of a statement, rather than the statement itself. We can create a model of Columbus's mistaken belief, as follows (assuming that http://xyz.com# is the namespace for `xyz`):

```
<rdf:RDF>
  <rdf:Description>
    <rdf:subject resource="#ChristopherColumbus" />
    <rdf:predicate resource="http://xyz.com#Reached" />
```

```
    <rdf:object resource="http://www.countries.org/India" />
    <rdf:type resource="http://www.w3.org/1999/02/22-rdf-syntax-ns#Statement" />
  </rdf:Description>
</rdf:RDF>
```

As you can see, RDF syntax has given us three more typed elements that we can use to specify the subject, predicate, and object of a statement. There's also a new type added with which we can indicate the type of the resource – `rdf:Statement`. I'm sure I don't need to spell it out, but the type information can also be expressed like this:

```
<rdf:RDF>
  <rdf:Statement>
    <rdf:subject resource="#ChristopherColumbus" />
    <rdf:predicate resource="http://xyz.com#Discovered" />
    <rdf:object resource="http://www.countries.org/India" />
  </rdf:Statement>
</rdf:RDF>
```

As you can see from the triples produced, we no longer have a statement about who reached India; instead we have a *representation of a statement* about who traveled to India:

```
{
    [local#fact],
    [http://www.w3.org/1999/02/22-rdf-syntax-ns#subject],
    [#ChristopherColumbus]
}
{
    [local#fact],
    [http://www.w3.org/1999/02/22-rdf-syntax-ns#predicate],
    [http://xyz.com#Discovered]
}
{
    [local#fact],
    [http://www.w3.org/1999/02/22-rdf-syntax-ns#object],
    [http://www.countries.org/India]
}
{
    [local#fact],
    [http://www.w3.org/1999/02/22-rdf-syntax-ns#type],
    [http://www.w3.org/1999/02/22-rdf-syntax-ns#Statement]
}
```

Now that we have this statement we can do with it whatever we can do with any other resource. In particular we want to say that Columbus believes this statement to be true:

```
<rdf:RDF>
  <rdf:Description about="#ChristopherColumbus">
    <xyz:Believes resource="#fact" />
  </rdf:Description>

  <rdf:Statement ID="fact">
    <rdf:subject resource="#ChristopherColumbus" />
    <rdf:predicate resource="http://xyz.com#Discovered" />
```

```
    <rdf:object resource="http://www.countries.org/India" />
  </rdf:Statement>
</rdf:RDF>
```

One new triple is generated:

```
{ [#ChristopherColumbus], [xyz:Believes], [#fact] }
```

For completeness here is the graph of our syntax:

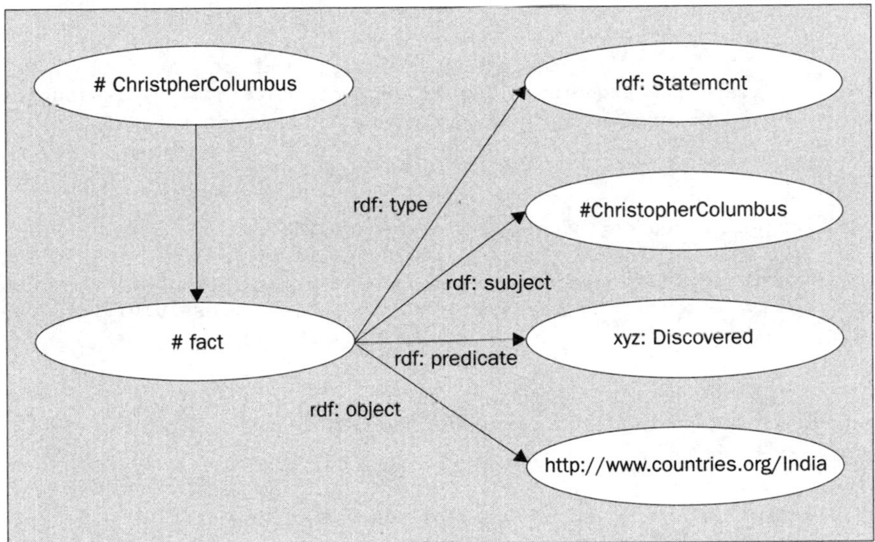

It's all very well dealing with the case of making statements about mistaken beliefs, but what of statements about things we believe are true? In this case we would want to store both the reified statement, *and* the original statement of fact. Let's develop an example.

When articles are entered into the spiked publishing system they are categorized:

```
<rdf:Description about="http://www.spiked-online.com/Articles/0000000054C3.htm">
  <dc:Creator>Mick Hume</dc:Creator>
  <dc:Subject rdf:resource="http://www.iptc.org/SubjectCodes#10101010" />
  <dc:Subject rdf:resource="http://www.iptc.org/SubjectCodes#10101011" />
  <dc:Subject rdf:resource="http://www.iptc.org/SubjectCodes#10101012" />
</rdf:Description>
```

However, more than one person can categorize the article, depending on their particular area of expertise. Let's say that we want to keep track of who added which category to an article. The first thing we would need to do is create reified statements that model the statements we have made about the subject codes. This will give us something to refer to:

```
<rdf:RDF>
  <rdf:Description about="http://www.spiked-online.com/Articles/0000000054C3.htm">
    <dc:Creator>Mick Hume</dc:Creator>
    <dc:Subject rdf:resource="http://www.iptc.org/SubjectCodes#10101010" />
```

```
    <dc:Subject rdf:resource="http://www.iptc.org/SubjectCodes#10101011" />
    <dc:Subject rdf:resource="http://www.iptc.org/SubjectCodes#10101012" />
  </rdf:Description>

  <rdf:Statement ID="subject1">
    <rdf:subject resource="http://www.spiked-online.com/
                           Articles/0000000054C3.htm" />
    <rdf:predicate resource="http://purl.org/meta data/dublin_core#Subject" />
    <rdf:object resource="http://www.iptc.org/SubjectCodes#10101010" />
  </rdf:Statement>

  <rdf:Statement ID="subject2">
    <rdf:subject resource="http://www.spiked-online.com/
                           Articles/0000000054C3.htm" />
    <rdf:predicate resource="http://purl.org/meta data/dublin_core#Subject" />
    <rdf:object resource="http://www.iptc.org/SubjectCodes#10101011" />
  </rdf:Statement>

  <rdf:Statement ID="subject3">
    <rdf:subject resource="http://www.spiked-online.com/
                           Articles/0000000054C3.htm" />
    <rdf:predicate resource="http://purl.org/meta data/dublin_core#Subject" />
    <rdf:object resource="http://www.iptc.org/SubjectCodes#10101012" />
  </rdf:Statement>
</rdf:RDF>
```

Now we can add our statements about these reified statements:

```
<rdf:RDF>
  <rdf:Description about="http://www.spiked-online.com/Articles/0000000054C3.htm">
    <dc:Creator>Mick Hume</dc:Creator>
    <dc:Subject rdf:resource="http://www.iptc.org/SubjectCodes#10101010" />
    <dc:Subject rdf:resource="http://www.iptc.org/SubjectCodes#10101011" />
    <dc:Subject rdf:resource="http://www.iptc.org/SubjectCodes#10101012" />
  </rdf:Description>

  <rdf:Statement ID="subject1">
    <rdf:subject resource="http://www.spiked-online.com/
                           Articles/0000000054C3.htm" />
    <rdf:predicate resource="http://purl.org/meta data/dublin_core#Subject" />
    <rdf:object resource="http://www.iptc.org/SubjectCodes#10101010" />
  </rdf:Statement>

  <rdf:Statement ID="subject2">
    <rdf:subject resource="http://www.spiked-online.com/
                           Articles/0000000054C3.htm" />
    <rdf:predicate resource="http://purl.org/meta data/dublin_core#Subject" />
    <rdf:object resource="http://www.iptc.org/SubjectCodes#10101011" />
  </rdf:Statement>

  <rdf:Statement ID="subject3">
    <rdf:subject resource="http://www.spiked-online.com/
                           Articles/0000000054C3.htm" />
    <rdf:predicate resource="http://purl.org/meta data/dublin_core#Subject" />
```

```
    <rdf:object resource="http://www.iptc.org/SubjectCodes#10101012" />
  </rdf:Statement>

  <rdf:Description about="#subject1">
    <dc:Creator>Mick Hume</dc:Creator>
  </rdf:Description>

  <rdf:Description about="#subject2">
    <dc:Creator>Jennie Bristow</dc:Creator>
  </rdf:Description>

  <rdf:Description about="#subject3">
    <dc:Creator>Jennie Bristow</dc:Creator>
  </rdf:Description>
</rdf:RDF>
```

We've achieved what we set out to do, which is to attribute various statements about the subject matter to the person who actually set that category. And since the category is valid for the article, regardless of who set it, then we also have the actual statement of fact to sit alongside our reified version.

If you are feeling that this may be a little long-winded, then you are right. But there is also another problem besides verbosity. Note that there is a direct correlation between each statement of fact and a reified version. Any changes or additions to the subject codes in the first description element would need to be reflected in our reified statements. It is not like our example earlier where the statement that Columbus believed – that he had reached India – did not exist in our version of truth, but the statement that *he believed that statement* was in our world-view. No. In fact here the situation is almost the opposite in that for every real statement there must be a matching reified statement, and there must be no reified statements for which there is not a real statement. In other words, we do not want a statement,

```
Jennie Bristow was responsible for the fact that article x has subject code y
```

if article x no longer has subject code y. Of course, if you were tracking the history of changes to the meta data about a document, then you may well retain the reified statements, even after the subject codes have been changed. This would take us back to our Columbus scenario – the fact that we have a statement that says,

```
On Monday Jennie Bristow set the subject code of article x to the value y
```

does not imply that the subject code for the article *is* y, since on Tuesday someone might have deleted it. Anyway, let's stick with the example, in which we want there to be a reified statement for every ordinary statement. RDF syntax has a neat way to achieve this using one final attribute on the `rdf:Description` element – `bagID`.

The bagID Attribute

The `bagID` attribute does not replace any of the other attributes that can appear on an `rdf:Description` element, but sits alongside them. The reason for this is that the `rdf:Description` element still needs to do its main job of reflecting statements about a resource – and so still needs the attributes `ID`, `about`, `aboutEach`, and so on. Instead, adding a `bagID` effectively says, create an `rdf:Bag` element, give it the `ID` specified, and then fill it with a reified version of each of the statements in the `rdf:Description` element.

We could therefore create all the statements and reified statements for Jennie in one go, with the more convenient syntax that follows:

```
<rdf:Description
 about="http://www.spiked-online.com/Articles/0000000054C3.htm"
 bagID="reify"
>
  <dc:Subject rdf:resource="http://www.iptc.org/SubjectCodes#10101011" />
  <dc:Subject rdf:resource="http://www.iptc.org/SubjectCodes#10101012" />
</rdf:Description>
```

This is an extremely convenient abbreviation, and you will use it a lot if you enter the world of meta-meta data! So, to make sure that we are completely clear on what is being stated, the shortened form we have just seen is completely equivalent to:

```
<rdf:RDF>
  <rdf:Description
   about="http://www.spiked-online.com/Articles/0000000054C3.htm"
   bagID="reify"
  >
    <dc:Subject rdf:resource="http://www.iptc.org/SubjectCodes#10101011" />
    <dc:Subject rdf:resource="http://www.iptc.org/SubjectCodes#10101012" />
  </rdf:Description>

  <rdf:Bag ID="reify">
    <rdf:li>
      <rdf:Statement>
        <rdf:subject resource="http://www.spiked-online.com/
                                   Articles/0000000054C3.htm" />
        <rdf:predicate resource="http://purl.org/meta data/dublin_core#Subject" />
        <rdf:object resource="http://www.iptc.org/SubjectCodes#10101011" />
      </rdf:Statement>
    </rdf:li>

    <rdf:li>
      <rdf:Statement>
        <rdf:subject resource="http://www.spiked-online.com/
                                   Articles/0000000054C3.htm" />
        <rdf:predicate resource="http://purl.org/meta data/dublin_core#Subject" />
        <rdf:object resource="http://www.iptc.org/SubjectCodes#10101012" />
      </rdf:Statement>
    </rdf:li>
  </rdf:Bag>
</rdf:RDF>
```

And if you spotted the other convenience that is thrown up by the abbreviation, then you are a fully qualified RDF master; we can now use `aboutEach` when making statements about these statements. Recall that Jennie was responsible for the two statements about the subject codes of the article in question. We can state in the following way:

```
<rdf:Description aboutEach="reify">
  <dc:Creator>Jennie Bristow</dc:Creator>
</rdf:Description>
```

Since we were only showing the rdf:Bag element to make clear what was happening behind the scenes when we used the bagID, let's finish off by showing the fully abbreviated syntax for the statements that Jennie has made about the subject codes of the article:

```
<rdf:RDF>
  <rdf:Description
   about="http://www.spiked-online.com/Articles/0000000054C3.htm"
   bagID="reify"
  >
    <dc:Subject rdf:resource="http://www.iptc.org/SubjectCodes#10101011" />
    <dc:Subject rdf:resource="http://www.iptc.org/SubjectCodes#10101012" />
  </rdf:Description>

  <rdf:Description aboutEach="reify">
    <dc:Creator>Jennie Bristow</dc:Creator>
  </rdf:Description>
</rdf:RDF>
```

Although the bag is implied by the use of the bagID attribute but not explicitly declared, we can still use aboutEach to distribute our statements across the bag. And along with the advantages of using this compact syntax we have the ease of maintaining only the original statements, with all reifications being produced 'behind the scenes'.

Summary

In this section we looked at the facilities RDF provides that allow us to make statements about statements. We looked at:

- Reification, which creates a model of a statement
- The bagID attribute which automatically causes statements to be reified

Formal Grammar

The formal grammar for the features that we have seen is specified as follows:

Section	Production	Syntax
[6.3]	description	::= '<rdf:description' idAboutAttr? bagIdAttr? propAttr* '/>' | '<rdf:description' idAboutAttr? bagIdAttr? propAttr* '>' propertyElt* '</rdf:description>' | typedNode
[6.9]	bagIdAttr	::= ' bagID="' IDsymbol '"'
[6.12]	propertyElt	::= '<' propName idAttr? '>' value '</' propName '>' | '<' propName idAttr? parseLiteral '>' literal '</' propName '>' | '<' propName idAttr? parseResource '>' propertyElt* '</' propName '>' | '<' propName idRefAttr? bagIdAttr? propAttr* '/>'

Table continued on following page

<table>
<tr><th>Section</th><th>Production</th><th>Syntax</th></tr>
<tr><td>[6.13]</td><td>typedNode</td><td>::= '<' typeName idAboutAttr? bagIdAttr? propAttr* '/>'
| '<' typeName idAboutAttr? bagIdAttr? propAttr* '>'
propertyElt* '</' typeName '>'</td></tr>
</table>

Summary

In this chapter we have seen how RDF models meta data, using the key concept of triples to represent statements that are made about resources. We also saw how RDF provides syntax for representing this model in an XML format. Much of the promise of the web hinges on being able to communicate meta data between systems as well as indicating who is responsible for a particular set of meta data. Both of these requirements can be met through RDF, and so the wider adoption of this standard points towards a more powerful and flexible Internet.

In the next chapter we will look at some real uses of RDF, as well as discuss some of the implementation issues that arise when trying to parse RDF and store the results.

23

RDF Code Samples and RDDL

In the last chapter we looked in a lot of detail at the theory of RDF. We examined the need for meta data, and in particular, why we would want to be able to use common values for meta data chosen from well-known ranges of values (or taxonomies). We also looked at how this meta data could be represented as sets of triples and directed labeled graphs (the RDF model), before seeing how the RDF/XML syntax allows us to transport the model so that meta data can be exchanged.

We covered much on RDF in the last chapter, but in this chapter we will look at:

- An application in which RDF is the key component – annotating documents over the Internet
- Issues to consider when writing RDF parsers
- The need for an RDF API
- How to store RDF statements
- How to search and retrieve RDF statements

Throughout the chapter we will use as many real examples of RDF as we can, to show how RDF is beginning to be applied.

A Real-World Use for RDF: Annotation

As RDF is only slowly gaining support – although the last year has seen gradually accelerating activity – case studies are not plentiful. However, the W3C has shown how serious it takes the issues that RDF aims to address, by creating an area on their site listing activity relating to "The Semantic Web".

The Semantic Web (**SW**) is the concept – championed by many, but most famously by Tim Berners-Lee (the creator of the WWW) – that it should be possible for a machine to find and use the data published on the Web. Although we didn't use this term in the last chapter, the concepts will be familiar to you from the discussion at the beginning of the previous chapter about standardizing category codes and property names.

Semantic Web activity at the W3C can be found at http://www.w3.org/2001/sw/. It is worth keeping an eye on this if we have a serious interest in meta data and RDF.

One of the interesting projects initiated under the SW banner is Annotea, an attempt to allow annotation of web documents by people as they browse. It is an ideal illustration of both RDF and some of the meta data concepts that we have discussed.

Annotea

The idea behind annotation of web pages is simple; when we are viewing a site, our browser software should be capable of:

- Taking comments from the user about the page s/he is viewing, and adding them to a database.
- Showing other people's comments that have been made about the page we are viewing.

As can be deduced from the above, RDF is ideal for expressing the data about each page. The resource that we want to make statements about is the page being viewed, while the annotation itself, the name of the person making the annotation, and so on, can be represented as statements about that resource. We would encourage you to install Annotea and have a play – it may well give ideas for other applications. Currently, Annotea is a UNIX based system, using an Open Source database and web server, MySQL and Apache. The installation instructions are located at: http://www.w3.org/1999/02/26-modules/User/Annotations-HOWTO.

Installation

The first step to installation is to download the W3C web browser Amaya. The purpose of the W3C software is as a reference browser containing features that the W3C is working on or would like to see adopted in browser technology. Although look-and-feel takes second place to functionality, the browser works adequately if we want to use it as an everyday browser. But the most important feature for our current purposes is its ability to annotate documents and even parts of a document. The program can be downloaded and installed from http://www.w3.org/Amaya/User/BinDist.

Once the software is installed, we need to connect the annotation feature to an annotation server. The W3C provides a test server for this, but we will need to register with the service in order to gain access. To begin the registration process, go to http://annotest.w3.org/access.

Once we have registered (and this requires that a confirmation e-mail is sent, so it may take a few minutes), we can then enter the following annotation server details into Amaya's configuration settings, http://annotest.w3.org/annotations, by going into Annotations | Configuration, and doing as follows:

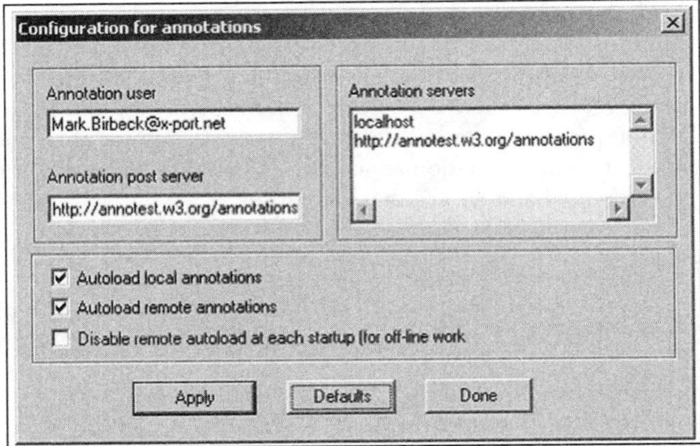

Note that we need to leave the `localhost` entry in the server list since our annotations are initially saved locally, with the option of moving them to a remote server later. Note also that we have set the autoload feature on, so that whenever we move to a new web page, the browser will check with all the listed servers to see if they have any annotations for the new page.

Viewing Annotations

Now that we have Amaya installed, let's see what an annotation looks like. Point the browser to the article we referred to in the previous chapter: http://www.spiked-online.com/Articles/000000005464.htm

We should see the following display:

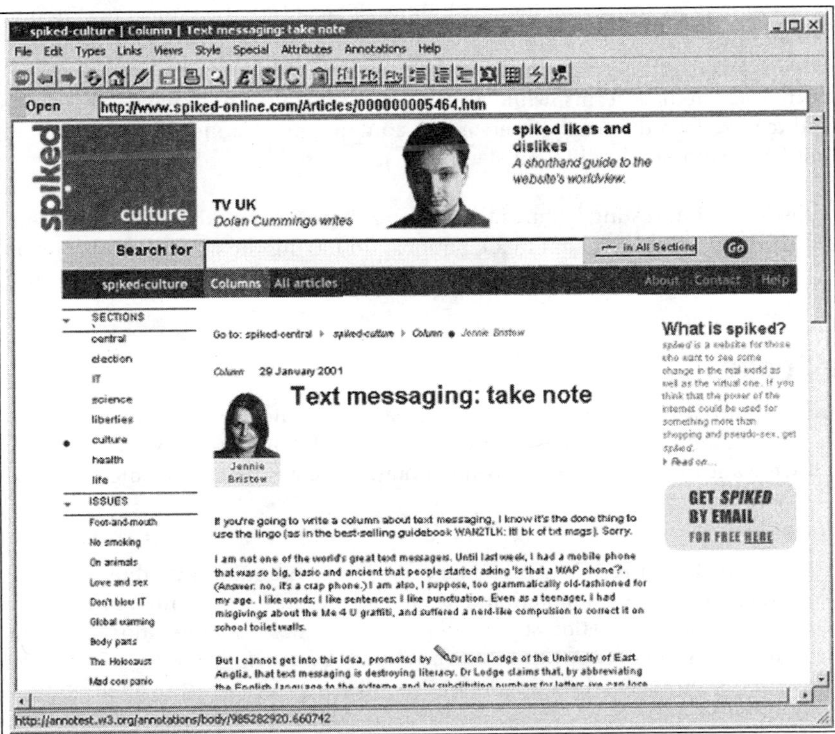

Note the small picture of a pencil followed by text highlighted in yellow. This was not in the original document, but has been inserted by the Amaya browser. As we loaded the page, the browser queried the annotation server – whose address we configured in the previous section – to see if the server had any information about the resource specified by the URL of the document. In this case, the resource was specified as an XPointer (see Chapter 10) so that the annotation could be added to a specific part of the document. Having located an annotation about this document, Amaya inserted it in the correct place. Double-click on the pencil and we see the annotation:

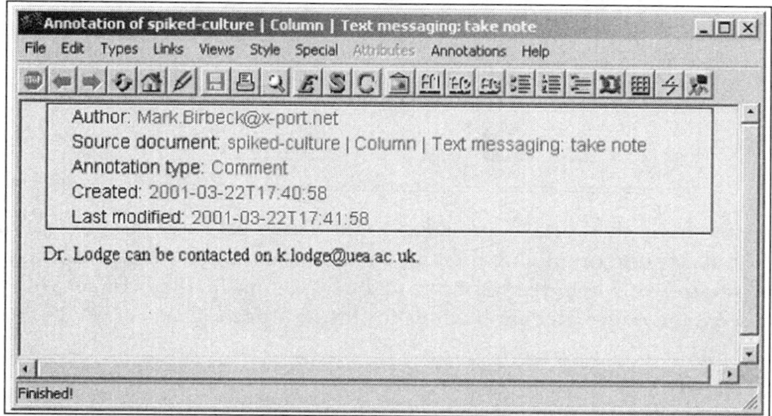

Of course, there might be a lot more pencil icons in the document than the ones in this screenshot – that will depend on whether other people, such as the readers of this book, have added annotations to the same document.

The whole concept creates some exciting possibilities. The ability to connect to different annotation servers means that different interest groups could have different servers with comments on documents pertinent to them. For example, a group of medical users could have annotations added to documents that explain different medical terms, while a group of sports fans might have annotations with comments on players and teams. Two different servers might contain annotations about exactly the same document, but from completely different standpoints.

Amaya provides some interesting features that point to how this could go in the future, such as having our own local annotations that are not made public, and having the ability to filter on annotations by author and server source, so that we might only see the medical annotations, or only see the sports ones, for example.

Behind the Scenes

We won't say any more on the software, since you can experiment with that yourself. What we will do now, though, is look behind the scenes at how Annotea and Amaya achieve what they are doing, which should help if we want to implement our own annotation viewer or storage medium.

Annotation Format

Annotations are expressed in RDF's XML syntax. When an annotation is edited on the user's machine – in software such as Amaya – the annotation that the user creates is formatted into XML, and then `POST`ed using HTTP to an annotation server. We can query the test annotation server using URLs like the following, which will look for any annotations about our article from the spiked web site:
http://annotest.w3.org/annotations?w3c_annotates=http://www.spiked-online.com/Articles/000000005464.htm

Let's look at how the annotation that we saw in the screenshots a moment ago, would be expressed in RDF/XML format.

First Annotea declares the namespaces that it needs:

```
<r:RDF
   xmlns:d="http://purl.org/dc/elements/1.0/"
   xmlns:http="http://www.w3.org/1999/xx/http#"
   xmlns:a="http://www.w3.org/2000/10/annotation-ns#"
   xmlns:r="http://www.w3.org/1999/02/22-rdf-syntax-ns#">
```

Next we need an indication of the resource we are about to make statements about. Note that the `<rdf:Description>` element has the `about` attribute set to the URI for the annotation, and not the URI for the web page being annotated. This creates the possibility of making statements about the annotation itself. Refer to the discussion in the previous chapter on "statements about statements". If someone wanted to, they could say that the author's statement about Dr. Lodge was actually incorrect:

```
<r:Description
   about="http://annotest.w3.org/annotations/annotation/985282920.660742"
>
```

After the creator and modified dates have been specified (`<d:creator>` and `<d:date>`), the type of the resource is indicated. The type is firstly an `Annotation`, but in addition the type of the annotation is set, in this case a `Comment`:

```
<d:creator>Mark.Birbeck@x-port.net</d:creator>
<d:date>2001-03-22T17:41:58</d:date>
<r:type
   resource="http://www.w3.org/2000/10/annotation-ns#Annotation" />
<r:type resource="http://www.w3.org/2000/10/annotationType#Comment" />
```

The next element – `<a:Attribution>` – points to a resource on the annotation server, which if retrieved actually contains exactly the same document as we have retrieved here, but with the whole body of our annotation inserted as a literal. We'll show that in a moment, when we get to the `<a:body>` property. In the meantime, note that after the `<a:Attribution>` element, we have the author's e-mail address and full name. The author didn't post this information –only the e-mail address was needed when the annotation was submitted. However, the rest of the information was retrieved from the server, as it matched up the e-mail address with the initial registration details:

```
<a:Attribution
   r:resource =
   "http://annotest.w3.org/annotations/attribution/985282920.660742"
/>
<a:Email r:resource="mailto:Mark.Birbeck@x-port.net" />
<a:Family>Birbeck</a:Family>
<a:Given>Mark</a:Given>
```

After the details of the person making the annotations, there is a property that indicates the resource that we are annotating (`<a:annotates>`):

```
<a:annotates
   r:resource="http://www.spiked-online.com/Articles/000000005464.htm"
/>
```

The <a:body> property is next, and this contains a reference to the actual annotation:

```
<a:body r:resource =
    "http://annotest.w3.org/annotations/body/985282920.660742" />
```

The actual annotation is stored in HTML format as a separate file, which creates the possibility that we could annotate an annotation, and the client software can go on to retrieve this further resource. As we said a moment ago, the <a:body> element could just as easily contain the entire HTML document inline. This is achieved by using the <http:Body> property, with the parseType="Literal" attribute. Referring to the previous chapter, we recall that the contents of an element with a parseType="Literal" attribute must still be valid XML, but the elements are not to be interpreted as RDF by an RDF parser:

```
<a:body>
    <r:Description
        about="http://annotest.w3.org/annotations/body/985282920.660742"
    >
        <http:Body r:parseType="Literal">
            <html xmlns="http://www.w3.org/1999/xhtml">
                <head>
                    <title>
                        Annotation of spiked-culture | Column | Text
                        messaging: take note
                    </title>
                </head>
                <body>
                    <p>Dr. Lodge can be contacted on k.lodge@uea.ac.uk.</p>
                </body>
            </html>
        </http:Body>
```

The http namespace allows more than just the HTML document to be defined inside <a:body>. Properties are provided to allow the content type and length to be specified, which means that a full HTTP transaction can be created:

```
        <http:ContentLength>246</http:ContentLength>
        <http:ContentType>text/html</http:ContentType>
    </r:Description>
</a:body>
```

The advantage here is that we can reduce the number of transactions between the client software and the server. In the first scenario we were given a URL that pointed to the text of the annotation, which we would then have to retrieve, requiring two requests to the server. In the second scenario we can get everything we need from the server in one go (including the MIME type of the document, since there is no reason why the annotation text need be in HTML).

The http namespace is also used when posting documents to the server for the same reasons, as we shall see shortly. Before we look at this, we'll finish our examination of the annotation data returned by looking at the two properties, <a:context> and <a:created>.

XPointer and Annotation Context

The <a:context> property indicates exactly what part of the resource is being annotated. Annotations can be added to the document as a whole, or to highlighted parts of the document. To annotate a document section requires the use of XPointer.

For detailed information about XPointer, see Chapter 10. All we need to know at this point is that XPointer enables us to make XPath statements in URLs. XPath is covered in Chapter 8. As an example, we could refer to all bold text in an XHTML document like this: http://www.spiked-online.com/Articles/000000005464.htm#xpointer(/html[1]/body[1]//b)

Or this: http://www.spiked-online.com/Articles/000000005464.htm#xpointer(//b)

XPointer also adds to XPath the ability to specify ranges. As can be seen from the `<a:context>` property, which defines the highlighted text for the annotation, Annotea has used the `string-range` function of XPointer to specify first the node that contains the text, then the position at which the highlighting should begin, followed by the length of the highlight:

```
        <a:context>
          http://www.spiked online.com/Articles/000000005464.htm#
            xpointer(string-range(/html[1]/body[1]/table[1]
            /tbody[1]/tr[5]/td[1]/table[1]/tbody[1]/tr[1]/td[4]/table[1]/
            tbody[1]/tr[1]/td[1]/table[2]/tbody[1]/tr[2]/td[1]/
            table[1]/tbody[1]/tr[3]/td[1],&quot;&quot;,46,45))
        </a:context>
```

Note that these long XPointers are very vulnerable to changes in the original document. Ideally when creating documents that might be annotated, we would place `id` values in the HTML elements, which would then allow us to have XPointer values such as:

```
            xpointer(id("Paragraph1"))
```

The final property of an annotation is the time and date that the annotation was created:

```
        <a:created>2001-03-22T17:40:58</a:created>
      </r:Description>
    </r:RDF>
```

More Information

Annotea annotation servers use ordinary HTTP requests to add, delete and modify annotations. Full details on the format for new annotations, or modifications for existing ones, can be found at: http://www.w3.org/2001/Annotea/User/Protocol.html.

Building Our Own Annotation Server

Let's use the structure of the annotation application to see what components are needed when dealing with RDF. Information about running our own annotation store under UNIX can be found at: http://www.w3.org/1999/02/26-modules/User/Annotations-HOWTO.

An annotation store is not that difficult to program, provided that we have the right RDF components. Let's follow through the functionality of the application to see what components are needed, beginning with the user making a comment.

Posting an Annotation

The first requirement is that the browser, or other software, takes the user's comments and creates an HTML document containing these comments. The application also creates an RDF document that contains these comments in an `<http:body>` element, as well as containing the meta data about the annotation. The RDF document is then posted to the annotation server. The transport for the document is simply an HTTP `POST`.

The RDF document could be built using simple string manipulation or an XML DOM. However, it would be much easier if we had some form of RDF DOM – an API that could handle the manipulation of statements rather than simply XML nodes.

Storing an Annotation

The annotation server receives the annotation via `POST` and then parses the RDF/XML document. Once the meta data model has been determined from the syntax, the server can store the statements that have been made, ready for retrieval when someone wants to see annotations on a particular document.

The server will need to parse the RDF/XML with an RDF parser, such as SiRPAC – see the section "*Event-driven RDF Parsers*". Once the statements are established they can be stored in an RDF store.

Retrieving Annotations

When a user views a web page through Amaya, the browser contacts the annotation server to see if there are any annotations for the page being viewed. The RDF/XML representing any relevant annotations is then returned to the browser.

The server is contacted via simple HTTP `GET` commands. Once the server receives the request, it needs to query the RDF store to find which statements are pertinent, and those statements are then built into an RDF document. As before, this could simply use the XML DOM, but it could also be carried out more efficiently with an RDF API.

Components

The components that are specifically RDF-related are:

- RDF DOM or API
- RDF parser
- RDF data store
- RDF data store query mechanism

Although we could do without the RDF DOM for building RDF documents, and we could even store our statements in whatever way we want, the component we *must* have is a means to parse RDF. Most of the rest of this chapter is devoted to looking at issues that should be considered when writing software to carry out the tasks outlined here. Before we look at them, here is a summary of the components needed to build an annotation system:

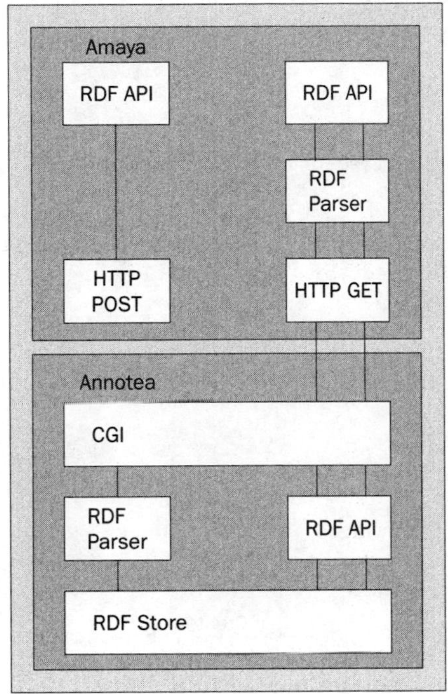

RDF Parsers

One of the many confusing issues for those new to RDF, is why we should even need an RDF parser at all. Why can't we just use an XML parser? The simple answer is that the two parsers produce very different abstract models. An XML parser has the task of producing a hierarchical node set, where each node corresponds to one of the XML elements – or attributes, text, comments and so on – in the original document. The parser can ensure that the XML document conforms to some DTD or schema, but beyond that infers no meaning to the document.

The underlying abstract model for RDF, as we saw in the previous chapter, is very different. Here we are dealing with meta data, or the properties of a particular resource. Recall that the two very different XML documents that follow, with their correspondingly varied node hierarchies, would yield exactly the same RDF model:

```
<rdf:RDF>
   <rdf:Description
      about="http://www.spiked-online.com/Articles/0000000054C3.htm">
      <dc:Creator
         resource="http://www.spiked-online.com/Authors/Mick%20Hume"/>
      <dc:Publisher
         resource="http://www.companieshouse.gov.uk/companynumber/3935644"/>
   </rdf:Description>

   <rdf:Description
      about=" http://www.spiked-online.com/Authors/Mick%20Hume">
      <xyz:JobTitle>editor</xyz:JobTitle>
```

```
    </rdf:Description>
</rdf:RDF>

<rdf:RDF>
    <rdf:Description
        about="http://www.spiked-online.com/Articles/0000000054C3.htm">
        <dc:Creator>
            <rdf:Description
                about=" http://www.spiked-online.com/Authors/Mick%20Hume">
                <xyz:JobTitle>editor</xyz:JobTitle>
            </rdf:Description>
        </dc:Creator>
        <dc:Publisher
            resource="http://www.companieshouse.gov.uk/companynumber/3935644"
        />
    </rdf:Description>
</rdf:RDF>
```

In both cases the model is the following:

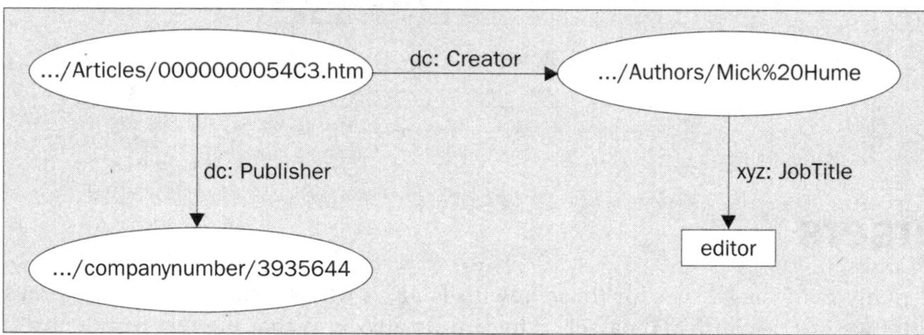

Although dealing with this at the level of the RDF model should be easy, it wouldn't be if we tried it at the level of XML. Although we *could* write plenty of code to walk through the node hierarchy and then process the RDF however we wanted, it would be a lot easier to convert the RDF/XML to the model first, and then manipulate the model.

For this reason we need to have a distinct processor for RDF documents. This processor will obviously be built on top of an XML parser, since RDF/XML documents must be well-formed XML. But the parser must understand these documents as a collection of meta data.

So what is the output of an RDF parser? If an XML parser produces a hierarchical tree of nodes, what does the RDF parser produce?

Parser Output

An RDF parser will produce statements in the form of triples, which are `<statement>` nodes containing `<subject>`, `<predicate>`, and `<object>` nodes. Note that there is nothing in the documentation that says this is all that can be produced. Just as the XML 1.0 specification does not rule out producing a series of 'events' when processing an XML document (as we have seen in the chapter on SAX – Chapter 12) so the RDF Model and Syntax specification is not prescriptive about how the underlying model should be represented.

We could mirror the node structure of XML DOM and represent triples as a series of 'objects', and we could mirror SAX and represent triples as a series of events. We'll look at both approaches.

At the moment there are very few RDF parsers available, which is perhaps responsible in part for the slow adoption of RDF. However, there is enough code out there for us to play with and see what is possible, and as more and more people get interested in RDF, the range of tools will surely grow. The easiest group of tools that we can use to play with RDF makes use of an XSLT stylesheet to convert RDF into a set of triples. This is a useful approach since it uses all the software that we will have already been using in this book.

XSLT Stylesheets

It has probably already occurred to you that one way of creating a collection of triples would be to run an RDF/XML document through a stylesheet that produces a list of subject/predicate/object sets. This is indeed a good way to proceed, and is especially useful to those who are new to RDF since it makes use of all the tools with which you are familiar.

Although the approach is simple and does not involve writing a parser proper, the XSLT stylesheets produced are very complex. A number of people have produced very thorough XSLT stylesheets to transform RDF into a list of the triples that would represent the underlying data model. The stylesheet from Jason Diamond (available at http://injektilo.org/rdf/rdft.xsl) is a good place to start, since it covers most parts of RDF, as well as it being used by others inside stylesheets that have different purposes. An example of the latter is Jonathan Borden's RDF Extractor (http://www.openhealth.org/RDF/rdf_Syntax_and_Names.htm), which takes HTML with embedded RDF, and produces RDF from it.

If we run our earlier annotation through Jason's stylesheet we get:

```
<?xml version="1.0" encoding="UTF-16"?>
<model>
   <statement>
      <subject>
         http://annotest.w3.org/annotations/annotation/985282920.660742
      </subject>
      <predicate>http://purl.org/dc/elements/1.0/creator</predicate>
      <object type="literal">Mark.Birbeck@x-port.net</object>
   </statement>

   <statement>
      <subject>
         http://annotest.w3.org/annotations/annotation/985282920.660742
      </subject>
      <predicate>http://purl.org/dc/elements/1.0/date</predicate>
      <object type="literal">2001-03-22T17:41:58</object>
   </statement>

   <statement>
      <subject>
         http://annotest.w3.org/annotations/annotation/985282920.660742
      </subject>
      <predicate>http://www.w3.org/1999/02/22-rdf-syntax-ns#type</predicate>
      <object type="resource">
         http://www.w3.org/2000/10/annotation-ns#Annotation
```

```
    </object>
  </statement>

  <statement>
    <subject>
      http://annotest.w3.org/annotations/annotation/985282920.660742
    </subject>
    <predicate>http://www.w3.org/1999/02/22-rdf-syntax-ns#type</predicate>
    <object type="resource">
      http://www.w3.org/2000/10/annotationType#Comment
    </object>
  </statement>

  <statement>
    <subject>
      http://annotest.w3.org/annotations/annotation/985282920.660742
    </subject>
    <predicate>
      http://www.w3.org/2000/10/annotation-ns#Attribution
    </predicate>
    <object type="resource">
      http://annotest.w3.org/annotations/attribution/985282920.660742
    </object>
  </statement>

  <statement>
    <subject>
      http://annotest.w3.org/annotations/annotation/985282920.660742
    </subject>
    <predicate>http://www.w3.org/2000/10/annotation-ns#Email</predicate>
    <object type="resource">mailto:Mark.Birbeck@x-port.net</object>
  </statement>

  <statement>
    <subject>
      http://annotest.w3.org/annotations/annotation/985282920.660742
    </subject>
    <predicate>http://www.w3.org/2000/10/annotation-ns#Family</predicate>
    <object type="literal">Birbeck</object>
  </statement>

  <statement>
    <subject>
      http://annotest.w3.org/annotations/annotation/985282920.660742
    </subject>
    <predicate>http://www.w3.org/2000/10/annotation-ns#Given</predicate>
    <object type="literal">Mark</object>
  </statement>

  <statement>
    <subject>
      http://annotest.w3.org/annotations/annotation/985282920.660742
    </subject>
    <predicate>
      http://www.w3.org/2000/10/annotation-ns#annotates
```

```
      </predicate>
      <object type="resource">
         http://www.spiked-online.com/Articles/000000005464.htm
      </object>
   </statement>

   <statement>
      <subject>
         http://annotest.w3.org/annotations/annotation/985282920.660742
      </subject>
      <predicate>http://www.w3.org/2000/10/annotation-ns#body</predicate>
      <object type="resource">
         http://annotest.w3.org/annotations/body/985282920.660742
      </object>
   </statement>

   <statement>
      <subject>
         http://annotest.w3.org/annotations/annotation/985282920.660742
      </subject>
      <predicate>http://www.w3.org/2000/10/annotation-ns#context</predicate>
      <object type="literal">
         http://www.spiked-online.com/Articles/000000005464.htm
         #xpointer(string-range(/html[1]/body[1]/table[1]/tbody[1]/tr[5]/
         td[1]/table[1]/tbody[1]/tr[1]/td[4]/table[1]/tbody[1]/tr[1]/
         td[1]/table[2]/tbody[1]/tr[2]/td[1]/table[1]/tbody[1]/
         tr[3]/td[1],"",46,45))
      </object>
   </statement>

   <statement>
      <subject>
         http://annotest.w3.org/annotations/annotation/985282920.660742
      </subject>
      <predicate>http://www.w3.org/2000/10/annotation-ns#created</predicate>
      <object type="literal">2001-03-22T17:40:58</object>
   </statement>
</model>
```

This is perfect for our needs. Navigating through these nodes with the XML DOM is much easier than before, and we could easily use this output to create database entries, and so on.

For small documents like our annotation, using stylesheets is fine. But we need to bear in mind that the DOM needs to read the entire source document before it can style it. This can be very expensive in processing terms, if the source document is large.

Take WordNet for example. WordNet is a project at Princeton, which intends to provide an interconnected network of words in English and other languages (see http://www.cogsci.princeton.edu/~wn/). The idea is to provide a hierarchy of words (so that a human is a type of mammal, or a shark is a type of fish), along with their meanings and synonyms. The data is constantly being updated, but what is most exciting here is that the data is available in RDF. The following section from the information on nouns, shows some different words for the different types of cat:

```
<rdf:RDF
  xmlns:rdf="http://www.w3.org/1999/02/22-rdf-syntax-ns#"
  xmlns:a="http://www.cogsci.princeton.edu/~wn/concept#"
  xmlns:b="http://www.cogsci.princeton.edu/~wn/schema/">
  ...
  <b:Noun
    rdf:about="http://www.cogsci.princeton.edu/~wn/concept#101630921">
    <b:wordForm>Felis catus</b:wordForm>
    <b:wordForm>Felis domesticus</b:wordForm>
    <b:wordForm>domestic cat</b:wordForm>
    <b:wordForm>house cat</b:wordForm>
  </b:Noun>
  <b:Noun
    rdf:about="http://www.cogsci.princeton.edu/~wn/concept#101631393"
    b:wordForm="pussycat">
    <b:wordForm>kitty</b:wordForm>
    <b:wordForm>kitty-cat</b:wordForm>
    <b:wordForm>puss</b:wordForm>
    <b:wordForm>pussy</b:wordForm>
  </b:Noun>
  <b:Noun
    rdf:about="http://www.cogsci.princeton.edu/~wn/concept#101631497"
    b:wordForm="mouser" />
  <b:Noun
    rdf:about=" http://www.cogsci.princeton.edu/~wn/concept#101631577">
    <b:wordForm>alley cat</b:wordForm>
    <b:wordForm>stray</b:wordForm>
  </b:Noun>
  <b:Noun
    rdf:about="http://www.cogsci.princeton.edu/~wn/concept#101631653">
    <b:wordForm>tom</b:wordForm>
    <b:wordForm>tomcat</b:wordForm>
  </b:Noun>
  ...
</rdf:RDF>
```

The problem here is that the document that this excerpt comes from is 9MB in size. Using Microsoft Internet Explorer 5 as a very rough test, it seems to take over 60Mb of memory at peak, to run this document through an XSLT stylesheet. But worse – the document takes an incredible amount of time to transform with IE's default stylesheet. And before XSLT can get to work on the document, it must be fully loaded. Yet if we look at the structure of the document, it is very **flat**; there is no reason why we couldn't be performing some action on all the meta data for alternative words for domestic cat, for example, once that block is finished.

It is problems like these that SAX was designed to solve, so it makes sense that we can do the same if we build RDF parsers on SAX.

Event-driven RDF Parsers

The most widely used RDF parser is SiRPAC, which stands for the Simple RDF Parser and Compiler. Written in Java, the parser is available at http://www.w3.org/RDF/Implementations/SiRPAC/. The parser can also be accessed remotely at this URL, which means that we can cut and paste some RDF into a form and get the results back as a set of triples. This is very useful when we are experimenting with our own RDF.

As well as the XSLT solution offered earlier, Jason Diamond is also responsible for repat, a C version of the Java-based RDF Filter by David Megginson. repat is available at http://injektilo.org/rdf/repat.html, while RDF Filter is available at http://www.megginson.com/Software/.

There are a few other parsers, and a good place to find resources is at http://www.w3.org/RDF/, but we won't list them all here since they all rely on much the same principles. Instead we will look at some of the issues we would need to address if we were going to write an RDF parser.

SAX

To briefly recap on SAX, recall that we are given events whenever the processor establishes that some fundamental XML unit has been received. For example, examine the following XML fragment:

```
<x>text</x>
```

We would see an event for the beginning of the element when the <x> tag was processed, then we would see another event for the text, and lastly an event when we saw the closing <x> tag. SAX has distinct callback functions for each of these events, so if we provided the right processing code for it, we would get:

```
StartElement();
Characters();
EndElement();
```

To build an RDF parser on top of SAX we would want to trigger a different set of events. We may want to get very detailed and say,

```
StartSubject();
```

followed by:

```
StartPredicate();
```

but at the very least, we will want to fire an event such as:

```
Statement();
```

Walk-through

Let's walk through the following document and parse it as if we were an event-driven RDF parser, firing `Statement()` events as soon as we are sure we have a statement:

```
<rdf:RDF
   xmlns:rdf="http://www.w3.org/1999/02/22-rdf-syntax-ns#"
   xmlns:a="http://www.cogsci.princeton.edu/~wn/concept#"
   xmlns:b="http://www.cogsci.princeton.edu/~wn/schema/">
   <b:Noun
      rdf:about=" http://www.cogsci.princeton.edu/~wn/concept#101631577">
      <b:wordForm>alley cat</b:wordForm>
      <b:wordForm>stray</b:wordForm>
   </b:Noun>
</rdf:RDF>
```

<rdf:RDF>

The first event we will get is for the `<rdf:RDF>` element. All we need to do here is simply note that we have received this element, so that if we receive it again, there is an error; but beyond that, there is no other processing. As we remember from our detailed discussion of RDF syntax in the previous chapter, an RDF/XML document can open with the `<rdf:RDF>` element, or go straight to an `<rdf:Description>`, or a typed node.

Note also that we don't need to process the namespaces since SAX2 is namespace aware. When we receive our events as we step through the document, we will be told the namespace of each element. For example, the C function prototype for Jason's element handler function is as follows:

```
void start_element_handler(
   void* user_data,
   const XML_Char* name,
   const XML_Char** attributes);
```

The `name` parameter will include the namespace and the local name of the element separated by a colon. The Microsoft implementation of SAX2, which has been included in MSXML 3, gives us more information but is much the same:

```
HRESULT STDMETHODCALLTYPE MyContent::startElement(
   /* [in] */ wchar_t __RPC_FAR *pwchNamespaceUri,
   /* [in] */ int cchNamespaceUri,
   /* [in] */ wchar_t __RPC_FAR *pwchLocalName,
   /* [in] */ int cchLocalName,
   /* [in] */ wchar_t __RPC_FAR *pwchRawName,
   /* [in] */ int cchRawName,
   /* [in] */ ISAXAttributes __RPC_FAR *pAttributes);
```

This time we get the namespace and local name as separate parameters, as well as the original element tag. Microsoft has modeled this C++ implementation on the original Java implementation of SAX. The function prototype in Java looks like:

```
public void startElement(java.lang.String namespaceURI,
   java.lang.String localName,
   java.lang.String qName,
   Attributes atts)
```

So we can see that whichever implementation of SAX we build our RDF parser on, namespaces will be quite simple to process.

Namespaces

Namespaces seem to me to be one of the most confused aspects of RDF parser writing. One of the criticisms often leveled at the RDF model is that it is not namespace aware. As can be read in the previous chapter, this is an advantage, not a disadvantage. If we think back to the distinction between the model and syntax discussed in the last chapter, we established that at the level of the model, statements could be made about a resource, and those statements comprised a subject, predicate, and object. All three could be specified using URIs, which is where the power of RDF lies.

We then moved on to see that these statements could be transported and interchanged if they were expressed in a common syntax. The most obvious tool for that was XML, so we looked at RDF expressed as XML. But it is important to note that the fact that XML has a feature that we know as namespaces, is unimportant to the RDF *model*. XML also has features such as entities and comments, but these have no impact on the model.

To make the point more explicitly, examine this XML:

```
<rdf:RDF
   xmlns:rdf="http://www.w3.org/1999/02/22-rdf-syntax-ns#"
   xmlns:a="http://www.cogsci.princeton.edu/~wn/concept#"
   xmlns:b="http://www.cogsci.princeton.edu/~wn/schema/">
   <b:Noun
      rdf:about=" http://www.cogsci.princeton.edu/~wn/concept#101631577">
      <b:wordForm>alley cat</b:wordForm>
      <b:wordForm>stray</b:wordForm>
   </b:Noun>
</rdf:RDF>
```

As far as XML is concerned, it bears no relation to this XML fragment:

```
<rdf:RDF
   xmlns:rdf="http://www.w3.org/1999/02/22-rdf-syntax-ns#"
   xmlns:a="http://www.cogsci.princeton.edu/~wn/concept#"
   xmlns:b="http://www.cogsci.princeton.edu/~wn/schema/No"
   xmlns:c="http://www.cogsci.princeton.edu/~wn/schema/wordF">
   <b:un rdf:about=" http://www.cogsci.princeton.edu/~wn/concept#101631577">
      <c:orm>alley cat</c:orm>
      <c:orm>stray</c:orm>
   </b:un>
</rdf:RDF>
```

Nevertheless, from an RDF standpoint they are identical. Either of the above two documents would result in exactly the same set of triples. The conclusion? If we want to save the original RDF/XML document then go ahead, but store it in some XML store. Once we convert it to the RDF model then we have to understand that going back to RDF/XML is simply a means of transporting that model, and any process that creates RDF/XML from our triples is under no obligation to try to recreate the original RDF/XML exactly as it was provided.

As a final point, the previous comments do *not* apply to the RDF namespace, since this carries important information to bridge the gap between the RDF syntax and the model.

<b:Noun>

After that brief detour, let's get back to the document we were parsing. Our next event indicates that we have another element. We need to save the fact that we received the `<rdf:RDF>` element so that we can spot errors like this:

```
<rdf:RDF
   xmlns:rdf="http://www.w3.org/1999/02/22-rdf-syntax-ns#"
   xmlns:a="http://www.cogsci.princeton.edu/~wn/concept#"
   xmlns:b="http://www.cogsci.princeton.edu/~wn/schema/">
   <b:Noun
```

```
        rdf:about="http://www.cogsci.princeton.edu/~wn/concept#101631577">
        <b:wordForm>alley cat</b:wordForm>
        <b:wordForm>stray</b:wordForm>
     </b:Noun>
     <!-- rdf:RDF is only allowed at the top level of a document -->
     <rdf:RDF
        xmlns:rdf="http://www.w3.org/1999/02/22-rdf-syntax-ns#"
        xmlns:a="http://www.cogsci.princeton.edu/~wn/concept#"
        xmlns:b="http://www.cogsci.princeton.edu/~wn/schema/">
        <b:Noun
           rdf:about=" http://www.cogsci.princeton.edu/~wn/concept#101631577">
           <b:wordForm>alley cat</b:wordForm>
           <b:wordForm>stray</b:wordForm>
        </b:Noun>
     </rdf:RDF>
  </rdf:RDF>
```

This means that we need some form of stack onto which to push the state that the parser is in when we get opening elements, and then pop it off when we get closing elements. If we add a ready state as well, then our stack would look like this after processing the `<b:Noun>` element:

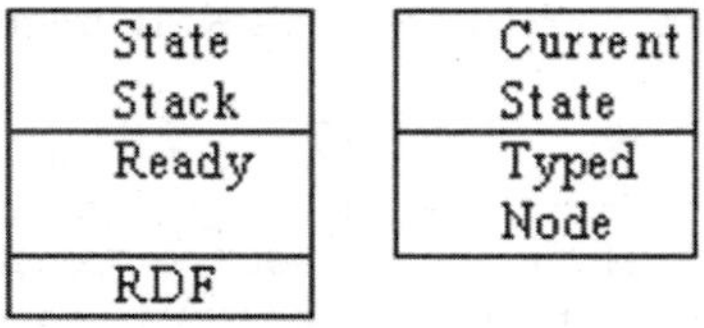

State Stack
Ready
RDF

Current State
Typed Node

Once the previous state has been saved, we need to process the element that we have found. At this point in the document, the only elements that are allowed are an `<rdf:Description>`, a container (`<rdf:Bag>`, `<rdf:Seq>`, or `<rdf:Alt>`), or a typed node. In this case we have a typed node, so we are already in a position to make a statement. Here are the triples our parser should generate for this first statement:

```
  {
     [http://www.w3.org/1999/02/22-rdf-syntax-ns#type],
     [http://www.cogsci.princeton.edu/~wn/concept#101631577],
     [http://www.cogsci.princeton.edu/~wn/schema/Noun]
  }
```

We should remember from the previous chapter that this means that the resource specified has a property `<rdf:type>`, which has a value of `<b:Noun>`.

Any subsequent element inside this typed node is going to be a property of the resource, so we need another stack, which stores the most recently encountered resource URI. As with the state stack we push and pop the URIs as we open and close elements. After we have finished processing the `<b:Noun>` opening element, our stacks look like this:

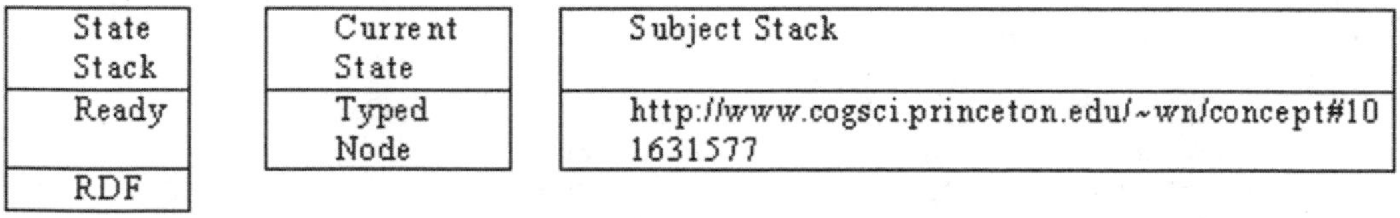

State Stack
Ready
RDF

Current State
Typed Node

Subject Stack
http://www.cogsci.princeton.edu/~wn/concept#101631577

<b:wordForm>

The next open element event indicates that we have a predicate. This too is stored on a stack. Although in the current RDF syntax, the following is not valid:

```
<rdf:Description
   about="http://www.spiked-online.com/Articles/000000054C3.htm">
   <dc:Creator>
      <rdf:Description
         about="http://www.spiked-online.com/Authors/Mick%20Hume">
         <xyz:JobTitle>editor</xyz:JobTitle>
      </rdf:Description>
         <!-- Cannot have another resource here -->
         <rdf:Description
            about="http://www.spiked online.com/Authors/Jennie%20Bristow">
            <xyz:JobTitle>commissioning editor</xyz:JobTitle>
         </rdf:Description>
      </dc:Creator>
   <dc:Publisher
resource="http://www.companieshouse.gov.uk/companynumber/3935644"/>
</rdf:Description>
```

As we saw in the previous chapter, we can express the same information with an element, like this:

```
<rdf:Description about="/Articles/000000054C4.htm">
   <dc:Creator>
      <rdf:Bag>
         <rdf:li>
            <rdf:Description about="/Authors/Victor%20Rortvedt">
               <v:Email>Victor.Rortvedt@spiked-online.com</v:Email>
            </rdf:Description>
         </rdf:li>

         <rdf:li>
            <rdf:Description about="/Authors/Sandy%20Starr">
               <v:Email>Sandy.Starr@spiked-online.com</v:Email>
            </rdf:Description>
         </rdf:li>

         <rdf:li>
            <rdf:Description about="/Authors/Josie%20Appleton">
               <v:Email>Josie.Appleton@spiked-online.com</v:Email>
            </rdf:Description>
         </rdf:li>
      </rdf:Bag>
   </dc:Creator>
</rdf:Description>
```

But as you know, the `<rdf:Bag>` statement creates a new resource level, so the saved predicate will not be used again. However, storing the predicate onto a stack is useful in case the syntax ever changes to allow multiple values for a predicate.

Our stack is now like this:

State Stack
Ready
RDF
Typed Node

Current State
Property

Subject Stack
http://www.cogsci.princeton.edu/~wn/concept#101631577

"alley cat"

The processing of character text in SAX2 may be a bit of a problem if our SAX2 implementation is non-validating. This means that the processor cannot tell whether mixed content is allowed or not and is therefore unsure as to how to interpret whitespace. The consequence is that we get character data events triggered between opening elements, even if the character data itself consists only of carriage returns, tabs, or spaces.

If we are writing an RDF parser using SAX2 that is non-validating, we at least have a slight advantage in that we know that mixed content is not allowed. This means that we can ignore character events where the content is only whitespace, if it occurs between two starting element events:

```
<x>    <y>text</y>     </x>
```

But we should take the content into account if it occurs between a starting event and a closing event:

```
<x>
  <y>     </y>
</x>
```

Of course, if the string is not whitespace and occurs between two open element events then we have an error. For this reason, at this stage in our walk-through we can't assume that we have a complete statement when we have received character data, and instead we should store the string "`alley cat`" and then wait for the closing element event. By doing this we are able to spot errors like the following:

```
<b:Noun rdf:about="http://www.cogsci.princeton.edu/~wn/concept#101631577">
   <b:wordForm>
      alley cat
      <!-- Mixed content not allowed -->
      <b:wordForm>stray</b:wordForm>
   </b:wordForm>
</b:Noun>
```

Our stack is now:

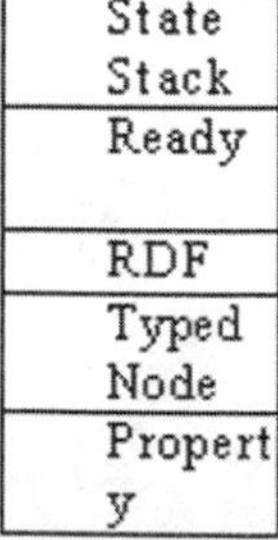

State Stack
Ready
RDF
Typed Node
Propert y

Current State
String

Subject Stack
http://www.cogsci.princeton.edu/~wn/concept#101631577

</b:wordForm>

We now receive our first closing element event. With closing events we need to pop off the stack to go back to the state the parser was in when it received the opening element that we are about to close. First though, you must test the state that you are in for additional processing.

In this particular case the additional processing is to say that we have finished receiving a string value, and so we have enough information to make a statement:

```
{
    [http://www.cogsci.princeton.edu/~wn/schema/wordForm],
    [http://www.cogsci.princeton.edu/~wn/concept#101631577],
    "alley cat"
}
```

Note that the subject of the statement comes from the top of the subject stack, and the predicate comes from the top of the predicate stack. We can then pop the previous parser state off the stack, to give us this:

State Stack
Ready
RDF
Typed Node

Current State
Property

Subject Stack
http://www.cogsci.princeton.edu/~wn/concept#101631577

However, since we are closing the element `<b:wordForm>` we should also close out the fact that we are in a property. You will find that implementing the close state often requires more than one pop off the state stack. In this case popping a property requires us to pop the predicate URI. The subject URI is *not* popped off the subject stack until we see the closing element of the typed node that originally set the resource URI.

After popping the property element state, our stack is now like this:

State Stack
Ready
RDF

Current State
Typed Node

Subject Stack
http://www.cogsci.princeton.edu/~wn/concept#101631577

We are now back in typed node state, ready and waiting for another property element.

Conclusion

To build an event-driven RDF parser is not difficult. The main techniques required are to build a number of stacks that allow statements to be nested. As elements open and close, values are pushed and popped to the stack. Once enough information is available to make a statement, a `Statement()` event can be fired. This event could simply output the statement as text, or store the statement in a database.

RDF DOM or API

Although we know that the parser produces triples, we don't have a standard interface for accessing those triples. As we saw in the chapter on XML DOM, a standard interface to the hierarchical node set produced when parsing an XML document has gained wide support, and is one of the most common interfaces used in the wide range of XML parsers available. But the XML DOM is not just useful for navigating an existing XML document; it is also the most convenient way of building a document under program control.

The same goes for RDF. When building up an RDF document from a set of statements, it would be desirable if we could just do something like:

```
x = new RDFDocument();
x.AddStatement(p, s, o);
x.AddStatement(p, s, o);
x.Output();
```

All we need to worry about are statements – the actual form that the statements take, as RDF/XML, would be handled by the API. (If this is confusing, the XML DOM is discussed in detail in Chapter 11, and although it relates to XML rather than RDF, should help in understanding this concept.)

Some important work has been done in this area, and the most widely used is Stanford's API, maintained by Sergey Melnik. More information is available online at http://www-db.stanford.edu/~melnik/rdf/api.html. Just to briefly illustrate our points though, here is an excerpt that shows some of the methods available for the Model class. As you can see it has the features we need – the ability to add and remove triples, determine how many triples are in the model, and so on.

Methods	Description
`public int size() throws ModelException`	Number of triples in the model Returns: number of triples, `-1` if unknown
`public boolean isEmpty() throws ModelException`	`true` if the model contains no triples
`public java.util.Enumeration elements() throws ModelException`	Enumerate triples
`public boolean contains(Statement t) throws ModelException`	Tests if the model contains the given triple. Returns: `true` if the triple belongs to the model; `false` otherwise
`public void add(Statement t) throws ModelException`	Adds a new triple to the model
`public void remove(Statement t) throws ModelException`	Removes the triple from the model

Methods	Description
`public Model find(Resource subject, Resource predicate, RDFNode object) throws ModelException`	General method to search for triples. `Null` input for any parameter will match anything. Example: `Model result = m.find(null, RDF.type, m.getNodeFactory().createResource("http://...#MyClass"))` finds all instances of the class `MyClass`

If we are building complex documents from a data source, then we would do well to evaluate using an API such as Stanford's.

RDF Data Stores

As more and more people add annotations about different documents, we need an efficient way of retrieving them quickly. This is particularly important given the dynamic nature of the user's interaction with the annotations. Since every time a user views a web page the browser could query an annotation server for any comments that exist about that web page, the whole process needs to be fast. In this section we'll look at how we might store and retrieve RDF information.

In the previous chapter we spent a lot of time discussing the model for RDF being a series of triples. It seems pretty obvious then that we need to look at the efficient storage of triples, and ways to access them quickly. Of the current database technologies around, relational databases seem ideally suited to the task, so we will stick with them.

A Triple Table

There are obviously a number of ways that triples could be stored in a database for retrieval. Given the consistent nature of triples a relational database is ideal for this. A number of suggestions as to how to achieve this are at http://www-db.stanford.edu/~melnik/rdf/db.html.

The common approach is to create tables for each of the types of information that can make up a triple – a resource, a predicate, and an object. A triple table then indexes into these other tables to get the parts of the triple. Most solutions seem also to store namespaces, although, as I said in the discussion on parsing, there is no explicit need to maintain the namespace of the source documents. Obviously, if this were to change in the future, you'll be glad you stored them!

Reification

Another issue that seems to separate the different approaches to storing statements is how to approach reification. As we saw in the previous chapter, statements can be reified by creating four more statements, so in principle these could all be stored in exactly the same statement table as all other statements. Some suggest storing reified statements separately from the other statements, whilst others suggest having a flag on each statement to indicate whether it is reified or not.

This second approach has the advantage that it saves on storage, since a reified statement takes up no more space than an ordinary one. It does have the disadvantage though, that since the individual components of the statement do not exist independently in the database, queries have to be mapped. So for example, I should be able to query for all reified statements in which a certain resource is the *object* and the results should include situations where the resource is a component of a reified statement.

aboutEach and aboutEachPrefix

Similar issues are raised when storing `aboutEach` and `aboutEachPrefix`. Since it is not possible most of the time for the parser and data store to know what values are valid at any given time for these two statements, the store must again do some mapping. For example, if we said that all of spiked-online pages were published by spiked:

```
<rdf:Description aboutEachPrefix="http://www.spiked-online.com/">
   <dc:Publisher
      resource="http://www.companieshouse.gov.uk/companynumber/3935644"/>
</rdf:Description>
```

we would need to ensure that every time a resource beginning `http://www.spiked-online.com/` was returned, we returned the extra triple:

```
{
   dc:Publisher,
   [http://www.spiked-online.com/xyz],
   [http://www.companieshouse.gov.uk/companynumber/3935644]
}
```

Storage

As with most proposed implementations we would want to store the component parts of triple separately. We could probably store everything we needed in only two tables. One table would contain the component parts of our statements, which would be a string plus a type. The type would indicate whether the sting was a literal, a resource URI, an `aboutEach` URI, or an `aboutEachPrefix` URI. summary

The other table would contain the triples, each part of the triple being an index into the table of component parts. For example:

Triple Table

subjectID	predicateID	objectID
1	2	3
4	5	6

Value Table

ID	Type	Value
1	Resource	http://www.cogsci.princeton.edu/~wn/concept#101631577
2	Resource	http://www.cogsci.princeton.edu/~wn/schema/wordForm

ID	Type	Value
3	Literal	`alley cat`
4	AboutEachPrefix	http://www.cogsci.princeton.edu/~wn/concept#
5	Resource	http://www.w3.org/1999/02/22-rdf-syntax-ns#type
6	Resource	http://www.cogsci.princeton.edu/~wn/schema/Noun

Note that we have said that all concepts are of type `Noun`. This may not be true with WordNet, we have just added it to show how we might store `aboutEachPrefix`.

One interesting issue is whether loading a number of different files into a database should be cumulative. For example, what if the two different statements above came from different source files? Should a query return both statements in the same document, if the need arose? Or should all statements only apply to the document from which they came? The advantage of the first approach is that you begin to accumulate knowledge about resources from different sources – which was always the advantage of using URIs to identify the target of your statements. We also avoid multiple copies of the same statement. However, the advantage of the second approach is that you can modify an RDF document and re-import it, and the statements should change.

This second approach is catered for in R V Guha's **rdfDB**, available at http://www.guha.com/rdfdb/. A facility is provided to unload from the database the RDF that originated from a particular place.

One way round to get the best of both worlds, might be to store the origin of statements in the database, but then allow queries against the database to choose whether they want to match against a particular source document or all document sources in the database.

Querying Metadata Stores

In this section we look at two sides to the querying of meta data stores.

- One is the querying of a store which has been created specifically to house RDF statements, as we saw in the previous section.
- The other shows how you might query meta data in some non-RDF system – in our case Microsoft Index Server – but returns it as RDF/XML ready for interchange.

Query an RDF Data Store

If we were to store our RDF statements in a relational database as discussed in the previous section, then obviously our queries on the database would be expressed in SQL. However, what we are more concerned with here is expressing queries in a way that is independent of how the triples are stored. One person may have stored their statements in an object database, another in a relational database using ten tables, and another in a relational database using three.

An interesting project from IntelliDimension provides a layer on non-RDF stores that allows them to be queried as if they contain RDF statements. Have a look at their RDF Gateway at http://www.intellidimension.com/. The approach they take is quite important for the further growth of RDF, since it allows legacy data to be treated as if it were RDF – the great advantage of creating an interchange format.

RDF Query Language

One proposal for querying RDF came from IBM (see http://www.w3.org/TandS/QL/QL98/pp/rdfquery.html), which involves specifying the data to return in an XML document:

```
<rdfq:rdfquery>
   <rdfq:From eachResource="http://www.research.ibm.com/people/neel"/>
      <rdfq:Select>
         <rdfq:Condition>
            <rdfq:equals>
               <rdfq:Property name="Project" />
               <rdf:String>Web Technologies</rdf:String>
            </rdfq:equals>
         </rdfq:Condition>
      </rdfq:Select>
   </rdfq:From>
</rdfq:rdfquery>
```

This query would return all items in the collection referred to by `eachResource` that has the property, `Project`, set to "`Web Technologies`".

This is an interesting way to proceed, and would make for a very flexible querying facility. One problem is that the syntax as it stands queries across a collection, but this could be easily modified if the general structure suited our needs.

Algernon

The Annotea pages provide a facility for querying their store using the query part of the language *Algernon*. This language aims to represent knowledge electronically in the form of Access-Limited Logic (see http://www.cs.utexas.edu/users/qr/algernon.html for more information). While knowledge of such subjects is not important for the use of RDF, we mention it here because it offers an interesting way of querying the meta data that has been modeled by RDF.

Let's look at an example, which would bring up the annotation data that we were dealing with at the beginning of the chapter:

```
(ask
   '(
      (
         http://www.w3.org/1999/02/22-rdf-syntax-ns#type
         ?annotation
         http://www.w3.org/2000/10/annotation-ns#Annotation
      )
      (
         http://www.w3.org/2000/10/annotation-ns#annotates
         ?annotation
         http://www.spiked-online.com/Articles/000000005464.htm
      )
      (http://www.w3.org/2000/10/annotation-ns#context ?annotation ?context)
      (http://purl.org/dc/elements/1.0/creator ?annotation ?creator)
      (http://purl.org/dc/elements/1.0/date ?annotation ?date)
      (http://www.w3.org/2000/10/annotation-ns#body ?annotation ?body)
   )
   :collect '(?annotation ?context ?creator ?date ?body)
)
```

The opening line, ask, indicates that we have an Algernon query. The next two bracketed sections are querying the database to return any statements that have the web page we are looking at as the object:

```
(
   http://www.w3.org/2000/10/annotation-ns#annotates
   ?annotation
   http://www.spiked-online.com/Articles/000000005464.htm
)
```

as well as being of type a:Annotation:

```
(
   http://www.w3.org/1999/02/22-rdf-syntax-ns#type
   ?annotation
   http://www.w3.org/2000/10/annotation-ns#Annotation
)
```

This is effectively a join on the field ?annotation, since only statements where the subject is the same will be returned. The next four statements take this same URI and locate statements where the predicate is:

```
a:Context
dc:Creator
dc:Date
a:Body
```

as follows:

```
(http://www.w3.org/2000/10/annotation-ns#context ?annotation ?context)
(http://purl.org/dc/elements/1.0/creator ?annotation ?creator)
(http://purl.org/dc/elements/1.0/date ?annotation ?date)
(http://www.w3.org/2000/10/annotation-ns#body ?annotation ?body)
```

All told, we now have the following variables that will have been filled from the various joined query parts:

```
annotation
context
creator
date
body
```

The final part of the query simply indicates that the returned values should be a collection of these variables:

```
:collect '(?annotation ?context ?creator ?date ?body)
```

Although this is quite a complex querying syntax, when compared to something simple like SQL, we will need something like it, if RDF is to gain in popularity. RDF requires queries to be made up of a number of components as we have seen here, and the Algernon ask interface is a useful starting-point.

Making Microsoft Index Server Return RDF Syntax

Usually when we see discussions on XML and databases, our first example will be a simple script to return data from the database as XML. The example we're presenting here is analogous to that; a sort of "Hello, World" for meta data. We will take Microsoft Index Server, which is effectively a meta data store, and write a simple script to make it return RDF. The code is available for download, but we'll discuss some of the key points here.

Search-RDF.asp

The main file we use is `Search-RDF.asp`. This short ASP script calls a search function that returns an XML DOM object containing our RDF. The parameters for the script are the standard Index Server parameters, such as,

```
/Search-RDF.asp?qu=paris
```

to retrieve meta data for all articles that mention Paris or,

```
/Search-RDF.asp?q1=election&c1=EPX.Section
```

to retrieve all articles that are in the election section of the site. For more information on formatting searches through a URL, see the Index Server documentation. Before we step through the code in this script, we'll show some typical output here, so that we can have a picture of what the code is building towards:

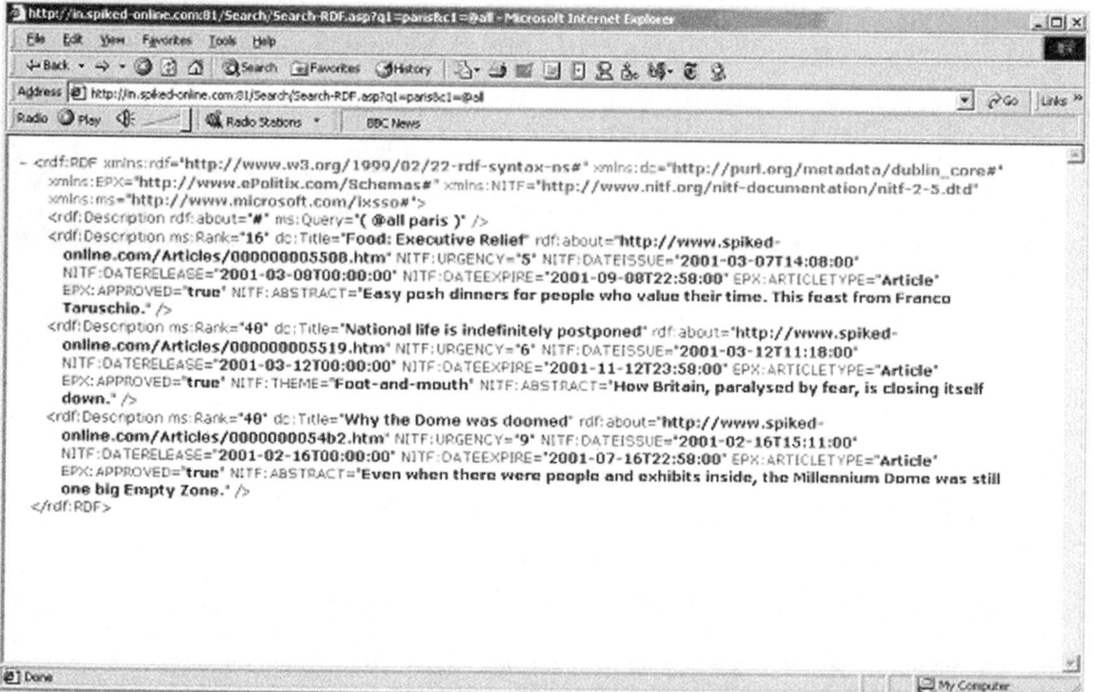

Now let's look at the code. First set up our include files. These are discussed in more detail in a moment:

```
<%@ Language=JScript %>
<!-- #include file="xml.inc" -->
<!-- #include file="ixSearch.inc" -->
```

Next we establish our script block and error handling:

```
<SCRIPT LANGUAGE="JScript" RUNAT="Server">
   try
   {
```

We call the search function, which is defined in `ixSearch.inc`. The function returns a `CXMLParser` object, which is defined in `xml.inc`:

```
      var oSrc = ixSearch(
         500,
         Request.QueryString,
         "Spiked-Online",
         "rank, DocTitle, Path, NITF.Urgency, NITF.DateIssue, ↵
         NITF.DateRelease, NITF.DateExpire, EPX.ArticleType, ↵
         EPX.Approved, EPX.Theme, NITF.Abstract",
         "NITF.Urgency"
      );
```

The parameters are as follows:

- The page size, which indicates to index server how many results should be returned in one go
- The entire query that was entered as part of the URL
- The name of the Index Server catalog to query
- The names of the columns that we want returning
- The columns that will determine the sort order of the results

Note that when we first set up Index Server we chose to use a dot in the name of the META tags to indicate a namespace. You could use whatever convention you wanted to, though, but since this is the convention used by Dublin Core when putting data into META tags, we have decided to adopt it. In the `ixSearch.inc` code, we use the dot to help us add namespaces to our RDF syntax.

Once we have the results of the search as a `CXMLParser` object, we can write it out. If there are processing or transformation stylesheets then we apply them first. (This is a feature we use a lot in sites like spiked and ePolitix, whereby we first run a *processing* stylesheet, and then a *presentation* one before finally showing the output. This feature is not important here.)

```
      var sXSLProcess = "" + Request.QueryString("xslProcess");
      var sXSLPresent = "";

      oSrc.write(Response, "text/xml", sXSLProcess, sXSLPresent);

      delete oSrc;
      delete oBrowser;
   }
```

If there are any errors then we return an error description as HTML. If this were a fully automated system you would want to return XML, so that a remote server could then act upon the error:

```
    catch(exception)
    {
        var sError;

        if (typeof(exception) == "string")
            sError = exception;
        else
            sError = exception.description;
        Response.ContentType = "text/html";
        Response.Write("Error: " + sError);
    }
</SCRIPT>
```

ixSearch.inc

The include file `ixSearch.inc` runs a search with the parameters passed and then returns the results in a `CXMLParser` object, as XML that complies with the RDF syntax. Since Index Server returns its results as an ADO recordset, then the functions here could be generalized to work with any data source. Let's step through the code.

At the top we have a couple of routines for breaking apart multi-valued properties from Index Server. These functions deal with VB arrays so we have to put them in a VB code block. Of course we could have put all the code into VB, but we prefer JavaScript with objects, since it makes the transition to COM easier should we decide we need better performance. We therefore need this short VBScript section:

```
<script language="VBScript" runat="Server">
    Dim oUtil : Set oUtil = Server.CreateObject("ixsso.util")

    Function GetSearchArrayElement(v, i)
        GetSearchArrayElement = oUtil.GetArrayElement(v, i)
    End Function

    Function VBArrayToString(o, sSep)
        if IsArray(o.Value) then
            Dim arr : arr = o.Value
            VBArrayToString = ""
            dim i, sElem
            for i = LBound(arr) to UBound(arr) - 1
                VBArrayToString = VBArrayToString &
                    GetSearchArrayElement(arr, i) & sSep
            next
            VBArrayToString = VBArrayToString & GetSearchArrayElement(arr, i)
        else
            VBArrayToString = o.Value
        end if
    End Function
</script>
```

Next we can declare our JavaScript block, and declare a global variable that will hold our XML DOM object for use throughout the scripts:

```
<script language="JScript" runat="Server">
   var oParser;
```

We also establish a global array to hold the namespaces that we will need when mapping the META tag names to URIs for RDF. We could make this array a parameter to the function. Note that we have completely made up a Microsoft namespace for any properties that we want to set that come from Index Server. However, we will see with new products coming from Microsoft, such as Exchange 2000, that namespaces are increasingly being defined for different data sets:

```
   var ns = new Array();
   ns["RDF"] = "http://www.w3.org/1999/02/22-rdf-syntax-ns#";
   ns["DC"] = "http://purl.org/metadata/dublin_core#";
   ns["EPX"] = "http://www.ePolitix.com/Schemas#";
   ns["NITF"] = "http://www.nitf.org/nitf-documentation/nitf-2-5.dtd#";
   ns["MS"] = "http://www.microsoft.com/ixsso#";
```

Now declare the function that will do the searching. The five parameters that we need were described earlier, when we made the call to this function:

```
   function ixSearch(iPageSize, sURL, sCatalog, sColumns, sSortBy)
   {
```

Create a `CXMLParser` object in which we will build our RDF/XML results, and set a pointer to the XML DOM object for faster access:

```
      oCParser = new CXMLParser();
      oParser = oCParser.m_oDOM;
      var oNode;
      var sCreateError = "";
```

Now create the `<rdf:RDF>` element to hold the meta data. Add to this element any namespaces that might be needed by our Index Server data:

```
      var oResults = oParser.createNode(1, "rdf:RDF", ns["RDF"]);
      oResults.setAttribute("xmlns:rdf", ns["RDF"]);
      oResults.setAttribute("xmlns:dc", ns["DC"]);
      oResults.setAttribute("xmlns:EPX", ns["EPX"]);
      oResults.setAttribute("xmlns:NITF", ns["NITF"]);
      oResults.setAttribute("xmlns:ms", ns["MS"]);
```

We now create the query object, and set any column names that we will need, with their data types. See the Index Server documentation if you need more information on why this is necessary. Note that we are using the Index Server that comes with Windows 2000. We may need to change the `Server.CreateObject()` call to suit our own data sources. The `Query` object has a feature that allows us to set the query parameters from the URL that was passed to the script, so we'll use that:

```
      var Q;
      var RS;
      try
      {
         Q = Server.CreateObject("ixsso.Query");
```

```
Q.DefineColumn('"NITF.DateIssue"(VT_FILETIME) = ↵
      d1b5d3f0-c0b3-11cf-9a92-00a0c908dbf1 nitf.dateissue');
Q.DefineColumn('"EPX.Approved"(DBTYPE_WSTR) = ↵
      d1b5d3f0-c0b3-11cf-9a92-00a0c908dbf1 epx.approved');
Q.DefineColumn('"NITF.Urgency"(DBTYPE_WSTR) = ↵
      d1b5d3f0-c0b3-11cf-9a92-00a0c908dbf1 nitf.urgency');
Q.DefineColumn('"EPX.ArticleType"(DBTYPE_WSTR) = ↵
      d1b5d3f0-c0b3-11cf-9a92-00a0c908dbf1 epx.articletype');
Q.DefineColumn('"NITF.DateRelease"(DBTYPE_WSTR) = ↵
      d1b5d3f0-c0b3-11cf-9a92-00a0c908dbf1 nitf.daterelease');
Q.DefineColumn('"NITF.DateExpire"(DBTYPE_WSTR) = ↵
      d1b5d3f0-c0b3-11cf-9a92-00a0c908dbf1 nitf.dateexpire');
Q.DefineColumn('"NITF.Theme"(DBTYPE_WSTR) = ↵
      d1b5d3f0-c0b3-11cf-9a92-00a0c908dbf1 nitf.theme');
Q.DefineColumn('"NITF.Abstract"(DBTYPE_WSTR) = ↵
      d1b5d3f0-c0b3-11cf-9a92-00a0c908dbf1 nitf.abstract');

Q.SetQueryFromURL(sURL);
Q.SortBy = sSortBy;
Q.MaxRecords = iPageSize;
Q.Catalog = sCatalog;
Q.Columns = sColumns;
```

Inside the <rdf:RDF> block, we create an <rdf:Description> element, which refers to the resulting document as its resource. Onto this element we attach any information that we want about the query itself. This could be anything we like, but here we have just put in the actual query that was executed:

```
var oSearchNode =
   oParser.createNode(1, "rdf:Description", ns["RDF"]);
oSearchNode.setAttribute("rdf:about", "#");
oSearchNode.setAttribute("ms:Query", Q.Query);
oResults.appendChild(oSearchNode);
```

Now we are ready to execute the query and step through the recordset returned. For each record we create an <rdf:Description> element and then add all of the attributes in the record to this element. We'll see the code to add attributes in a moment:

```
RS = Q.CreateRecordSet("nonsequential");

while (!RS.EOF)
{
   var oRSNode = oParser.createNode(1, "rdf:Description",
      ns["RDF"]);
   addPropertyListAsAttributes(oRSNode, RS.Fields);
   oResults.appendChild(oRSNode);
   RS.MoveNext();
}
```

Finally we can place the completed RDF document inside our XML DOM object, before returning the CXMLParser object. If there are errors we will still return an XML DOM object, but the object will contain nodes indicating the error:

```
        oParser.documentElement = oResults;
    }
    catch(exception)
    {
        var sError;

        if (typeof(exception) == "string")
            sError = exception;
        else
            sError = exception.description;
        oNode = oParser.createElement("error");
        oNode.setAttribute("description", "ixSearch - general: " + sError);
        oResults.appendChild(oNode);
        oParser.documentElement = oResults;
        sCreateError = sError;
    }

    return oCParser;
}
```

The `addPropertyListAsAttributes()` function takes a node and a collection as parameters, and simply loops through the collection adding each name/value pair to the node as an attribute. It would be straightforward to produce another version of this routine that makes each property/value pair into a child element of the node:

```
function addPropertyListAsAttributes(oNode, oList)
{
    var i;
    for (i = 0; i < oList.Count; i++)
    {
        var p = oList(i);
        if (typeof(p.value) != "undefined")
        {
            try
            {
```

Note that we convert multi-valued properties to a single string, with each value separated by a comma. In some situations this is convenient. However, we could easily extend this part to make each of the values into a member of a bag, which is itself a child of the property:

```
                setAttr(oNode, p.Name, VBArrayToString(p, ", "));
            }
            catch(e)
            {
```

If there is an error we place the value of the error into the returned XML. This is not ideal, but it does mean that the script can continue running, and we just get an error message as the value of the particular attribute that caused a problem. This is useful for debugging since we can see lots of errors at the same time, but a live system should make the error message into an `<error />` element so that a processor can check for it:

```
                var sError;
                if (typeof(e) == "string")
                    sError = e;
                else
                    sError = e.description;
```

```
                setAttr(oNode, p.Name, sError);
            }
        }
    }
}
```

The `setAttr()` function simply creates an attribute on an element and sets its value. We use the first full-stop in the property name to find the namespace:

```
function setAttr(oNode, sName, vValue)
{
    var oAttr;
    var sNS = "";

    var i = sName.indexOf(".");
    if (i != -1)
    {
        sNS = sName.slice(0, i);
        sName = sName.slice(i + 1);
    }
```

If there is no namespace then we assume we have some of the built-in Index Server properties and map them to standard property names. Obviously the URL maps to `rdf:about` and the document title maps to `dc:Title`, but the rank mapping I have just made up as a property within the fictitious Microsoft namespace, so as to give us a hook to hang it on:

```
    if (sNS == "")
    {
        if (sName == "PATH")
        {
            sName = "rdf:about";
            sNS = ns["RDF"];
        }
        else if (sName == "DOCTITLE")
        {
            sName = "dc:Title";
            sNS = ns["DC"];
        }
        else if (sName == "RANK")
        {
            sName = "ms:Rank";
            sNS = ns["MS"];
        }
    }
```

If there *was* a specified namespace then we restore it to the front of the element name that we have, and do a lookup for the full URI of the namespace:

```
    else
    {
        sName = sNS + ":" + sName;
        sNS = ns[sNS];
    }
```

Now we can create an attribute with the correct name and namespace, set its value and then add it to the element node:

```
      oAttr = oParser.createNode(2, sName, sNS);
      oAttr.nodeValue = new String(vValue);
      oNode.setAttributeNode(oAttr);
   }
</script>
```

xml.inc

The final module that we need is `xml.inc`. This file contains everything that we need for handling XML. The approach we have taken is to wrap the XML DOM that we are using inside a JavaScript object, so that the specific DOM being used is hidden and localized. This allows us to add features to our object that we would like to see in the parser itself, such as XInclude and XPointer.

We won't go into the entire source here since it isn't really important to understand the generation of the RDF syntax. We'll just show the declaration of the `CXMLParser` object, since that is what is returned from `ixSearch()`:

```
function CXMLParser()
{
   try
   {
      var oDOM = Server.CreateObject("MSXML2.DOMDocument");

      oDOM.async = false;
      oDOM.resolveExternals = false;
      oDOM.validateOnParse = false;
      this.m_oDOM = oDOM;

      this.load = xmlparser_load;
      this.loadXML = xmlparser_loadXML;
      this.ProcessIncludes = xmlparser_ProcessIncludes;
      this.ProcessOutputs = xmlparser_ProcessOutputs;
      this.transform = xmlparser_transform;
      this.write = xmlparser_write;
      this.save = xmlparser_save;
   }
   catch(exception)
   {
      if (typeof(exception) == "string")
         throw(exception);
      else
         throw(exception.description);
   }
}
```

Conclusion

For RDF to really take off will require a number of factors. Most obviously, the RDF toolbox will need to continue growing. A lot of good code is out there, and the number of parsers and data stores is growing. These will increasingly need to become industrial-strength components that people can drop into their applications.

But probably most obviously, *people need to start using it.* Sounds obvious, but there are a lot of great meta data applications out there, which use proprietary formats for their data, rather than building on a standard such as RDF. Take QuickClick (http://www.quickclick.com/) from NBCi, for example. This application is based on FlySwat, a rather clever piece of technology that creates links on the web pages that we are viewing. The links are picked up from documents containing links on a wide range of topics – you can choose your topics by adding 'booster packs'. As with our annotation example earlier, I might choose to use the medical booster pack, while you might choose the golfing booster pack. Both you and I could read the same page, but we would both see different links.

But the application does not use RDF. The XML format for these meta data links is non-standard, so I could not easily connect my QuickClick software to an RDF document returned by some thirdparty. Someone would have to convert it to the QuickClick format. Having said that, it's still worth a look since the concept is sound.

In conclusion, in this chapter we have seen some of the software that would be needed to build real systems that use RDF. We looked at issues that we would need to address when

- Coding a parser
- Storing the RDF statements that the parser would extract from RDF/XML
- Searching stores of meta data

Namespaces in RDF and XML

What does a namespace URI resolve to? The answer to this riddle depends entirely on whom you ask. In this section, we will cover a technology that allows namespaces to become more than just pointers that each application needs an implementation of.

The Namespaces in XML Recommendation states, "The namespace name, to serve its intended purpose, should have the characteristics of uniqueness and persistence." These are, in fact, the *only* properties necessary to unambiguously identify an element or attribute – the resource identified by the namespace name need not physically exist. The Recommendation reinforces this when it states, "It is not a goal that it be directly usable for retrieval of a schema (if any exists)."

However, the fact that namespace names are represented using URIs certainly adds to the confusion. Virtually all URIs that we deal with are actually URLs – addresses that we can enter into our browser and visit. We have an almost irresistible urge to do just that with anything that starts with http://. Moreover, when we see the dreaded 404 Resource Not Found message, we are left shocked and grief-stricken.

Therefore, despite the W3C's explicit warning that a namespace URI need not resolve to anything, many of their namespaces actually do. Try pointing a browser to:

- http://www.w3.org/XML/1998/namespace
- http://www.w3.org/1999/XSL/Transform
- http://www.w3.org/1999/xhtml
- http://www.w3.org/1999/02/22-rdf-syntax-ns#

Some of these namespace URIs should be familiar by now – however, how many people have actually navigated to them, and what did they find? Below is what can be found at the above URLs:

- An HTML file explaining why we should use the "`xml:`" prefix
- A plain text file containing the sentence, "This is the XSLT namespace"
- An outdated XML Schema with an annotation claiming that "Someday a schema for XHTML will live here"
- An RDF Schema describing the intrinsic classes and properties found in RDF

Since the Namespaces in XML Recommendation (http://www.w3.org/TR/REC-xml-names/) does not mandate what, if anything, a namespace URI resolves to, these resources are all perfectly acceptable and in compliance with the specification – as they would have been if no resources at all were found at those URLs. But are they useful?

Interestingly, they contain either human or machine-readable information but not both. Humans attempting to de-reference the XML or XSLT namespace URIs using a browser – perhaps out of nothing more than pure curiosity – might be pleasantly surprised when they encounter a description of the vocabulary identified by that namespace. What will they think, though, when de-referencing the RDF namespace URI? Wouldn't it be helpful for those intrepid surfers if they could find a human-readable description of RDF at that location – perhaps even the RDF Recommendation itself? Or do RDF processors expect and rely on the specific RDF Schema that's currently located there in order to function correctly?

If a specification like RDF decides that it's vitally important that RDF Schemas be located at the other end of a namespace URI, then there's nothing we can do to prevent this. This is still compliant with the Namespaces Recommendation. While it states, "it is not a goal that [a namespace name] be directly usable for retrieval of a schema" it does not explicitly forbid it. The authors of the specifications documenting namespace names are free to place whatever entity they desire, or even nothing at all, at the end of their namespace URIs.

There are those that fear, however, that the W3C will start requiring namespace URIs to resolve to W3C XML Schema documents. The controversy lies in the fact that the W3C's XML Schema specification is not the only XML schema specification. Microsoft's XDR, Murata Makoto's RELAX, Rick Jelliffe's Schematron, and James Clark's TREX are just a few of the more widely known alternatives (see Chapters 6 and 7 for more details). Proponents of these schemas don't wish to be locked into using the W3C's XML Schema simply because it's only possible to include a single resource at the end of any particular URI.

Resource Directory Description Language

The Resource Directory Description Language (**RDDL**) provides a layer of indirection that allows any arbitrary namespace URI to reference multiple resources. Started as an experimental project by a group of subscribers to the XML-DEV mailing list, RDDL documents are quickly becoming the answer to the question: What does a namespace URI resolve to? The RDDL specification (which is, itself, a RDDL document) can be found at http://www.rddl.org/.

A RDDL document can be both automatically queried for resources of a specific type or usage and also perused and understood by us mere mortals. It does this by extending the human-readable XHTML Basic specification (http://www.w3.org/TR/xhtml-basic/) with a hidden, embedded element meant for consumption by machines. Since our typical (X)HTML browsers have no understanding of this new element, they ignore them. And since RDDL-aware processors only need scan for the RDDL-specific elements, they can ignore all of the ambiguous human verbiage we're so fond of using when trying to communicate to each other.

Let's see an example. Afterwards, we'll look at the part of the RDDL DTD that describes the attributes that are allowed on the new element. The following is an exceedingly simple, but valid, RDDL document that 'describes' a namespace with two related resources:

```
<?xml version="1.0"?>
<!DOCTYPE html
   PUBLIC "-//XML-DEV//DTD XHTML RDDL 1.0//EN"
   "http://www.rddl.org/rddl-xhtml.dtd">
<html
   xmlns="http://www.w3.org/1999/xhtml"
   xmlns:xlink="http://www.w3.org/1999/xlink"
   xmlns:rddl="http://www.rddl.org/"
>
   <head>
      <title>My Favorite Namespace</title>
   </head>

   <body>
      <h1>Resources Associated With My Favorite Namespace</h1>

      <rddl:resource
         id="DTD"
         xlink:title="My Favorite DTD"
         xlink:role="http://www.isi.edu/in-notes/iana/
            assignments/media-types/application/xml-dtd"
         xlink:arcrole="http://www.rddl.org/purposes#validation"
         xlink:href="my.dtd">
         <h2>My Favorite DTD</h2>

         <p>This <a href="my.dtd">DTD</a> validates XML documents
         conforming to My Favorite Namespace.</p>

      </rddl:resource>

      <rddl:resource
         id="XMLSchema"
         xlink:title="My Favorite Schema"
         xlink:role="http://www.w3.org/2001/XMLSchema"
         xlink:arcrole="http://www.rddl.org/purposes#schema-validation"
         xlink:href="my.xsd">
         <h2>My Favorite XML Schema</h2>

         <p>This <a href="my.xsd">XML Schema</a> augments the infoset
         of XML documents conforming to My Favorite Namespace.</p>

      </rddl:resource>

   </body>
</html>
```

With the exception of the <rddl:resource> elements and XLink attributes, it looks like XHTML, doesn't it? It is.

RDDL's One Tag

RDDL actually extends XHTML Basic 1.0 with just a single element, `<rddl:resource>`. Using the techniques defined in the XHTML Modularization Recommendation (http://www.w3.org/TR/xhtml-modularization/), the `<rddl:resource>` element is allowed anywhere a `<div>` or `<p>` element can appear. The content model for `<rddl:resource>` allows anything allowed by the `<div>` element, including more `<rddl:resource>` elements.

The `ATTLIST` declaration for `<rddl:resource>` elements looks like this:

```
<!ATTLIST rddl:resource
   id             ID         #IMPLIED
   xml:lang       NMTOKEN    #IMPLIED
   xml:base       CDATA      #IMPLIED
   xmlns:rddl     CDATA      #FIXED    "http://www.rddl.org/"
   xlink:type     (simple)   #FIXED    "simple"
   xlink:arcrole  CDATA      #IMPLIED
   xlink:role     CDATA                "http://www.rddl.org/#resource"
   xlink:href     CDATA      #IMPLIED
   xlink:title    CDATA      #IMPLIED
   xlink:embed    CDATA      #FIXED    "none"
   xlink:actuate  CDATA      #FIXED    "none"
>
```

The XLink attributes that will consistently have the same value, have been declared as `#FIXED`. The standard `id`, `xml:lang`, and `xml:base` attributes are optional. It's usually a good idea to give your resources unique `ID`s so that they can be referenced directly. The `xlink:title` attribute is optional and can be used to provide a human-readable label for the resource. The remaining attributes, `xlink:href`, `xlink:role`, and `xlink:arcrole` will be described shortly.

With the exception of this new element, RDDL is the same well-formed XHTML we've come to know and love. We can enter text, links, tables, images, and even forms.

What a RDDL Resource Represents

So what does a `<rddl:resource>` element represent? It represents a resource, of course – hopefully, one that's somehow related to the namespace URI at which the document resides. The actual URI of the resource and its relationship to the namespace are identified by attributes from the XLink namespace:

- The resource's URI is indicated using an `xlink:href` attribute
- The `xlink:role` and `xlink:arcrole` attributes specify the nature and purpose of the related resource

Natures and purposes in the general sense aren't specific to RDDL but the terminology is. Basically, a resource's **nature** (specified using an `xlink:role` attribute) describes the resource's *type*. The word "type" is far too overloaded in developer circles, and so the synonym "nature" was adopted by RDDL in an attempt to be less ambiguous in our discourse.

When describing a resource, we could ask, for example, if it's a DTD, an XSLT stylesheet, or an HTML document. These natures are identified by a URI. If the resource nature is already known by some commonly accepted URI (like a namespace URI), then it's preferred that that URI be used to identify the resource's nature. XML Schema documents, for example, should specify http://www.w3.org/2001/XMLSchema as their nature. RDF Schema documents would most likely use http://www.w3.org/2000/01/rdf-schema#.

It is not a requirement that resources be XML documents, however. DTDs, legacy HTML documents, CSS stylesheets, plain text files, ZIP archives, and more, can all be described using RDDL. Since these types of resources don't have well-known namespace URIs, their MIME type can be used to create a suitable URI in its place. Practically everything has a MIME type. To create the URI, append the MIME type to http://www.isi.edu/in-notes/iana/assignments/media-types/. Try appending application/xml to that URI and resolving it and see why we do this.

A list of common natures can be found at http://www.rddl.org/natures. Some of them are listed below:

Nature	URI
Legacy HTML	http://www.isi.edu/in-notes/iana/assignments/media-types/text/html
CSS Stylesheet	http://www.isi.edu/in-notes/iana/assignments/media-types/text/css
XHTML Document	http://www.w3.org/1999/xhtml
RELAX Grammar	http://www.xml.gr.jp/xmlns/relaxCore
Schematron Schema	http://www.ascc.net/xml/schematron
TREX Pattern	http://www.thaiopensource.com/trex

Like natures, **purposes** (specified using an `xlink:arcrole` attribute) also use URIs. But a resource's purpose identifies how it's meant to be used. The purpose of an XML Schema is most likely to validate an instance document. The URI we would use would probably be http://www.rddl.org/purposes#schema-validation. RELAX grammars can be used for the same purpose, though. And so can Schematron schemas or TREX patterns. It's the combination of nature and purpose that allows RDDL-aware processors (of which none currently exist) to select and use the validation technology that they prefer.

A list of common purposes is found at http://www.rddl.org/purposes. We highlight some of them below:

Purpose	URI
Parse-time validation (DTDs)	http://www.rddl.org/purposes#validation
Post-parse validation (Schemas)	http://www.rddl.org/purposes#schema-validation
Software Implementation	http://www.rddl.org/purposes#software-package
Documentation	http://www.rddl.org/purposes#reference
Specification	http://www.rddl.org/purposes#normative-reference
Representative image	http://www.rddl.org/purposes#icon

Arbitrary Transforms

One particularly interesting combination of natures and purposes occurs when relating an XSLT resource (using the http://www.w3.org/1999/XSL/Transform as its nature URI) capable of transforming an instance document from this namespace into an instance of some other namespace. The purpose URI should be set to the nature URI of the result of the transform. This isn't easy to explain, so perhaps an example can help make it clearer:

```
...

<rddl:resource
   id="xhtml-transform"
   xlink:role="http://www.w3.org/1999/XSL/Transform"
   xlink:arcrole="http://www.w3.org/1999/xhtml"
   xlink:href="xhtml.xsl">
   <h2>My Favorite Namespace to XHTML Transform</h2>

   ...

</rddl:resource>

<rddl:resource
   id="rss-transform"
   xlink:role="http://www.w3.org/1999/XSL/Transform"
   xlink:arcrole="http://purl.org/rss/1.0/"
   xlink:href="rss.xsl">
   <h2>My Favorite Namespace to RSS Transform</h2>

   ...

</rddl:resource>

...
```

In a world where every namespace URI resolves to a RDDL document, it's conceivable that a RDDL-aware tool could attempt to transform a document conforming to some arbitrary namespace, to a document conforming to some other arbitrary namespace without any special knowledge of either. Resolving the namespace URI of the source document and searching for a `<rddl:resource>` element with a nature equal to the XSLT namespace URI, and a purpose equal to the namespace URI of the desired result document could yield a transform capable of performing this task (as indicated by that `<rddl:resource>` element's `xlink:href` attribute). This tool need not have *any* hard-coded knowledge of the namespaces it's working with. And that's the beauty of the whole concept behind RDDL. If a stylesheet exists with the appropriate nature and purpose values then it can be discovered and applied automatically. Of course, RDDL isn't restricted to stylesheets – any type of resource usable for just about any reason can be located via a RDDL document at the end of a namespace URI.

RDDL Examples

Since XHTML and, therefore, RDDL are well-formed XML, we can use our favorite XML tools to process and discover resources within it.

Getting the RDDL DTD

When creating our own RDDL directories, it'd probably be a good idea to copy the RDDL DTD files to our local machine (and modify DOCTYPE accordingly) to improve performance and reduce the load on the www.rddl.org. Since RDDL only adds a single element to XHTML, the chances of it changing frequently are slim.

The files that make up the RDDL DTD are bundled into a convenient ZIP archive and available for download. To discover the current URI for this archive, try searching the RDDL document at http://www.rddl.org/ for a resource with an ID of "ZIP" (either by viewing the source, using some sort of RDDL-aware processor or a custom tool – we'll be making our own using XSLT later on).

At the time of writing, the RDDL doc has the following RDDL resource to hold the link to the ZIP file containing the DTD.

```
<rddl:resource id="ZIP"
   xlink:role="http://www.isi.edu/in-notes/iana/
      assignments/media-types/application/zip"
   xlink:arcrole="http://www.rddl.org/purposes#software-package"
   xlink:href="rddl-20010122.zip" >
```

The RDDL Report Transform

A simple XSLT transform like the following could generate a report containing all of the resources in a directory.

```
<xsl:transform
   version="1.0"
   xmlns:xsl="http://www.w3.org/1999/XSL/Transform"
   xmlns:xlink="http://www.w3.org/1999/xlink"
   xmlns:rddl="http://www.rddl.org/">
   <xsl:output method="text" encoding="UTF-8"/>

   <xsl:template match="rddl:resource">
      <xsl:text>&#10;Resource: </xsl:text>
      <xsl:value-of select="@id"/>
      <xsl:text>&#10;Nature: </xsl:text>
      <xsl:value-of select="@xlink:role"/>
      <xsl:text>&#10;Purpose: </xsl:text>
      <xsl:value-of select="@xlink:arcrole"/>
      <xsl:text>&#10;URI: </xsl:text>
      <xsl:value-of select="@xlink:href"/>
      <xsl:text>&#10;</xsl:text>
   </xsl:template>

   <!-- don't output text nodes -->
   <xsl:template match="text()"/>

</xsl:transform>
```

As it is, if an RDDL document contains a `<rddl:resource>` element with an `xlink:href` attribute containing a relative URI (like our example, below), then the report will output just the relative URI instead of resolving it to an absolute URI as specified in RFC 2396. Of course, this report could be much more useful if XSLT included standard functions to retrieve the base URI of the RDDL document and resolve the URI references found within against that base URI. (Michael Kay's excellent XSLT engine, SAXON, can actually retrieve the base URI using an extension function, but the resolving is left up to the developer. An Open Source, pure XSLT implementation of the URI resolving, described in RFC 2396, can be found in the XSLT Standard Library at http://xsltsl.sourceforge.net/.)

Running the above transform against the W3C's only known RDDL document at the time of writing (which is located at http://www.w3.org/2001/XMLSchema) results in the following report:

Resource:
Nature: http://www.isi.edu/in-notes/iana/assignments/media-types/text/xml-dtd
Purpose: http://www.rddl.org/purposes#validation
URI: XMLSchema.dtd

Resource: xmlschema
Nature: http://www.w3.org/2001/XMLSchema
Purpose: http://www.rddl.org/purposes#schema-validation
URI: XMLSchema.xsd

Resource: xmlschemap1
Nature: http://www.w3.org/TR/html4
Purpose: http://www.rddl.org/purposes#normative-reference
URI: http://www.w3.org/XML/Group/xmlschema-current/structures/structures.html

It looks like someone forgot to give that first resource an ID.

User-specified Transforms with .NET

We could parameterize the above report to retrieve just the URI of a transform capable of producing results of a specific nature for our hypothetical RDDL-aware tool. Or, we could use any of the currently available APIs implemented for more traditional programming languages.

The following sample uses the only (currently) known .NET API to retrieve the URI for a user-specified transform:

```
using System;
using Injektilo.RDDL;

public class GetTransformURI
{
   private const string XSLT_NAMESPACE =
      "http://www.w3.org/1999/XSL/Transform";

   public static void Main(string[] args)
   {
      if (args.Length < 2)
      {
         Console.WriteLine(
           "usage: GetTransformURI sourceNamespaceURI resultNamespaceURI");
      }
      else
      {
         string sourceNamespaceURI = args[0];
         string resultNamespaceURI = args[1];

         string transformURI = null;

         RddlReader rddlReader = new RddlReader(sourceNamespaceURI);

         while (transformURI == null && rddlReader.Read())
         {
```

```
            if (rddlReader.Role == XSLT_NAMESPACE &&
               rddlReader.Arcrole == resultNamespaceURI)
            {
               transformURI = rddlReader.Href;
            }
         }

         if (transformURI == null)
         {
            Console.WriteLine(
               "There is no resource to perform that transformation.");
         }
         else
         {
            Console.WriteLine(transformURI);
         }
      }
   }
}
```

Let's say that we want to transform a RDDL document into an RSS document. If we run the above code with http://www.rddl.org/ and http://purl.org/rss/1.0/ as parameters, it will print out the URI of an XSLT transform capable of performing that task for us (which is currently http://www.rddl.org/rddl2rss.xsl).

The details of the .NET API aren't that important for this illustration. For more information, we can read the documentation bundled with the code. This tool could have been written in any language (try searching the RDDL document at http://www.rddl.org/ for resources with a purpose of http://www.rddl.org/purposes#implementation to see what's currently available) and could have retrieved the URIs of any other type of resource. It's that extra layer of indirection between a namespace URI and RDDL that makes this possible.

Summary

In this chapter, we have covered a number of topics relating to RDF and RDDL. Following on from the previous chapter, we have shown examples of RDF in practice. We covered:

- Annotations using Amaya and Annotea
- RDF Parsers – XSLT and event driven
- The RDF API
- Storing RDF
- Querying RDF
- Using Microsoft Index Server for an example RDF application

We have also seen that the Resource Directory Description Language (RDDL) provides one answer to the question of what a namespace URI represents and one solution to packaging resources that pertain to the elements of a namespace, whether for validation purposes, programmatic support, or standard transformations of the namespace elements to other formats.

24

SOAP

In this chapter, we will introduce you to **SOAP** (**Simple Object Access Protocol**), a new language and platform-neutral communication protocol:

- We will cover the core concepts of SOAP (Simple Object Access Protocol), the XML describing its messages, and provide examples of how it can be used for synchronous and asynchronous communication between servers with different programming environments.
- We will see how SOAP came into being, cover its message syntax, and briefly cover WSDL (Web Services Description Language) as it relates to SOAP. This will provide you with the knowledge to create basic SOAP documents.
- We will review some important characteristics of two of the most popular protocols on the Internet: HTTP (Hypertext Transfer Protocol) and SMTP (Simple Mail Transfer Protocol).
- We will look at some of the programming languages and the way that they handle SOAP documents, and we will review some of the most popular implementations of SOAP provided by leading vendors or communities of developers.
- At this point we will be ready to focus on using SOAP to implement computer-to-computer communication in a synchronous and then in an asynchronous way. The examples provided in this chapter will show how to do this, using the tools available today.

By the end of this chapter you will be able to choose the appropriate tools and make decisions about the type of communication you would like to set up between your servers. We will wrap up our discussion with a look into the future of SOAP as the core of the XML Protocol (XP), support for SOAP in various languages, and a few of the upcoming releases of the most popular SOAP implementations.

You can find the SOAP 1.1 specification submitted to W3C (World Wide Web Consortium) at: http://www.w3.org/TR/SOAP *or go to* http://www.w3.org/TR *and look for the most current SOAP document. This specification is at the state of a "note", which means that it is not a standard endorsed by W3C as of yet, but it is considered by it and by vendors to be a potential future standard.*

Introduction To SOAP

As we have already seen, SOAP is a communication protocol for exchanging information between computers regardless of their operating system or programming environment. In the specification, SOAP is defined as a lightweight protocol for exchange of structured and typed information between peers (that being computers) in a decentralized and distributed environment. A "decentralized and distributed environment" usually refers to networks such as the Internet, but it does not say anywhere within the SOAP specification that it would have to be limited to these networks. For example, SOAP can easily be used for communication between computers on a LAN (Local Area Network). SOAP is an XML based protocol, designed to enable computers to talk to each other, regardless of their operating system, object model, or language environment. SOAP does not define a programming model or implementation specific semantics (such as **API** or **Application Programming Interface**). It defines a simple mechanism for exchanging messages, by providing a modular packaging model and a way of encoding data within messages.

One of the easiest ways to think about SOAP is to think of it as a protocol that specifies the message format of the communication that occurs between computers. In essence, just like postal mail has to follow certain specifications for most letters that are mailed, SOAP addresses similar needs for computer-to-computer communications. For example, the postal mail system specifies an envelope for standard letters, and SOAP specifies an envelope for the data payload. Furthermore, SOAP defines some of the payload as well, particularly in describing how to implement remote procedure calls and responses to those calls.

More details about the main components of a SOAP message will be given later in the chapter.

An important thing to remember about SOAP is that it does not define the transport protocol that will be used for sending the message. In the same postal mail system analogy, an envelope itself typically does not specify whether a letter is sent via plane or via ground transportation (but the stamps or other stickers on it, typically do). The SOAP specification (version 1.1) does describe how HTTP can be used to carry SOAP messages, but it clearly says that SOAP is not limited to HTTP in any way and that it can be used with a variety of other protocols.

SOAP provides a simple and lightweight mechanism for exchanging structured and typed information between peers in a decentralized and distributed environment using XML.

By supporting SOAP, web sites and applications in general, can offer **web services** that are accessible programmatically to other computers, without the need for human interaction or intermediation. In this way, one application can assemble solutions from any combination of software components, applications, processes, or devices. For example, an ASP (Application Service Provider) can use SOAP to build a generic solution for customer authentication, payment, tax calculation, delivery, and more, and then sell or give away this service.

Web services and **Enterprise Application Integration** (**EAI**) are sometimes understood to be one and the same. However, EAI tends to be more specific to a particular business process, such as connecting a specific human resources application to a specific financial application. In addition, EAI is typically designed as a much tighter bound implementation of connecting systems. Web services are a loose bound collection of services and they are much easier to plug in and out, discover, and bind to dynamically. EAI is less flexible and more expensive to implement than web services using SOAP and XML. The area of web services is bound to bring in an entire range of new opportunities in aggregation, federation, and integration of services anywhere on the Internet.

SOAP and XML are core technologies of web services architectures.

Before going deeper in our discussion of SOAP, let's quickly look at the state of the computer industry before the introduction of XML and more specifically, before the introduction of SOAP.

Life Before SOAP

You may think that living in the time before having SOAP around would have been unbearable, and in a way it was. Often, it is difficult enough connecting computers and having them talk to each other within the same operating system environment. Just how many of you can set up an enterprise DCOM architecture (or CORBA/ IIOP implementation for that matter) on a Saturday afternoon, without having to spend the rest of the weekend and likely much more time adjusting the various settings on multiple machines?

Now, imagine having the same need to connect various computers, but some of your machines are running UNIX with IBM WebSphere and Java on them, some are running Linux with Apache and Perl, and some are running Windows 2000 with COM+ and ASP!

SOAP does not promise to clear away all of these headaches, but it does promise to solve some important aspects of computer-to-computer communication across various platforms in truly distributed and decentralized environments, which are, arguably, the web architectures of the future.

What was really going on before the time of XML, and more recently SOAP? Let's take a look at the state of communication protocols not too long ago.

My Protocol Is Better Than Your Protocol

Back in the 1980s developers did not care much about communications protocols. Making applications talk to each other on the same machine was a challenge enough. But that was quite some time ago in computer terms, and even longer in Internet time. Once networks became much more commonplace in the 1990s, the importance of how you connect from one machine to another became very important. Vendors and organizations that already had their own object models, such as **COM** (**Component Object Model**) and **CORBA** (**Common Object Request Broker Architecture**), extended them to support the ability to communicate across the network. Microsoft came up with **DCOM** (**Distributed COM**) as its **RPC** (**Remote Procedure Call**) protocol that can cross machine boundaries, and the Java community established **IIOP** (**Internet Inter-ORB Protocol**) as the CORBA standard wire protocol. Another very strong contender in the Java community is Sun Microsystems' **RMI** (**Remote Method Invocation**) protocol. Furthermore, RMI provides a bridge over to IIOP as a way for Java applications using RMI to connect to CORBA as well.

In order to implement a rich application-to-application communication across machines, we would typically use DCOM, CORBA/ IIOP, or RMI. However, as rich environments, implementing application-to-application communication with these protocols tends to be quite complex. Configuration, installation, and administration are prone to errors and very difficult to set up to work properly "right out of the box". Once you add security and transaction management, the installation and configuration becomes even more difficult.

Another major obstacle is communication over the Internet – you cannot guarantee that both ends of the communication link will have implemented the same distributed object model. Furthermore, the aforementioned protocols rely on single-vendor solutions in order to gain the maximum advantage of the protocol. There has been some implementation of these protocols on operating systems and language platforms other than their usual ones, but this has been limited and not very successful. For example, the primary language platform for the CORBA/IIOP protocols has been the Java programming language and its use on other language platforms has not been significant. An even more limiting issue is the difficulty of getting these protocols to work over firewalls or proxy servers; in other words, they are quite firewall unfriendly. Of course, there are some workarounds, such as **RDS** (**Remote Data Services**) for DCOM, but these types of workarounds tend to be slower, more challenging to configure properly, and are typically not implemented in various operating systems or language platforms. Firewall administrators are very reluctant to open many ports, except for some widely used ones, such as ports for HTTP and SMTP.

Even though CORBA/IIOP, DCOM, and RMI are respectable protocols, the industry has not yet shifted entirely to one in particular. This lack of full industry **acceptance** was marked by all sides pointing out the other's shortcomings. Each side finally realized that the strategy of attempting to persuade the other side that "my protocol is better than yours, therefore everybody should use it" didn't work. Therefore, the solution seems to be in embracing the use of existing Internet standards.

Do We Really Need Another Protocol?

You may think that we already have too many protocols to worry about, so do we really need yet another one? SOAP came to light as a protocol that tries not to invent anything new, but to use existing technologies such as XML, HTTP, SMTP, and other common Internet protocols. XML defines the format of the message, envelope, and RPC mechanism, and HTTP, SMTP, or other Internet protocols define the transport mechanisms for the message. So, yes, we do need a new protocol to allow for "componentization" of the Web and making these "components" universally accessible. None of today's established standard communication protocols are completely platform and language independent (aside from HTTP, SMTP and other Internet transport protocols that are different from SOAP as described above). If this is the case, then let's see how SOAP compares with some of the currently well-established protocols.

As its name suggests, SOAP is a **simple** protocol, so with only a few lines of code, an XML parser, and an HTTP server, you can quickly have a SOAP object request broker (commercial Object Request Brokers or ORBs are system services that assist in object invocation, and often manage the object lifetime, perform object pooling for enhanced performance, and more). That seems to address the complexity issue with the other protocols. SOAP goes even a step further, by being **extensible** via the use of XML. No single protocol can guarantee that it will be applicable to all situations and all times, and SOAP addresses this via a standard way of extensibility.

SOAP works with the existing Internet infrastructure. No special configurations have to be applied to routers, firewalls, or proxy servers to get SOAP to work. By using HTTP or other common Internet transport protocols, SOAP becomes very easy to deploy with no firewall modifications. One step further, SOAP establishes a framework of sending messages or conducting RPC type communications, but it does not limit to the use of single transportation protocol. In essence, this makes SOAP extensible in the selection of various transportation protocols.

The unusual mix of vendors that have supported the implementation of SOAP – from IBM and Microsoft, to the open-source community – could all address the second issue of vendor acceptability. Finally, being recognized by W3C as a note at this time and likely as a **RFC** (**Request for Comment**) sometime later this year, would ensure that no single vendor has full control over SOAP, and that it becomes as common as some of the other Internet standards, such as HTML, XML, or HTTP and SMTP.

Finally, SOAP does not fully replace the existing protocols such as DCOM, CORBA/ IIOP, or RMI. SOAP purposefully leaves several features from traditional messaging and distributed object systems out of its specification. For example, object type functionality such as activation, object–by–reference, distributed garbage collection, and batching of messages is purposely left to the infrastructure where the SOAP client and server are implemented. SOAP has no object model, but it binds applications implemented in various object models and languages.

A Brief History of SOAP

So, how did web applications achieve interoperability before this move toward Internet web services and SOAP? Web pages started off as islands of information, with links that allowed users to move from one place to another. When using links, however, one had to leave everything that was on the first page in order to move to the second. Probably the most common interoperability between web sites and web applications has been via the use of frames. This brought the impression that users can work with different web applications at the same time. The limitation of the frames approach is that at the end it is quite difficult to get many web applications to look like a single one, in terms of their graphical appearance, layout, form style, and user experience elements.

For example, you may have tried to frame other web sites under your site, so that your users don't completely leave your site (maybe for maps or weather information). It is very likely that users will be able to easily tell that the framed web site is not part of your web site. Now, imagine that the web site you are framing under your web site provides a web service for the information that you need (again, maybe this is for the purpose of dynamically obtaining map or weather information). In this case, you would be able to fully integrate their service under your web site and follow your own graphical, layout, and style choices. This should make your marketing department much happier.

Another approach was to have the web server act as a client to another web application, and then "**screen scrape**" the page for relevant content. This process would recognize key parts of the information, fields, or other items on the web page and then present its version of the content. This was often difficult to do appropriately and it was susceptible to errors due to visual changes in the web application serving the information.

A variation of the screen scraping method is to simply **post information** to a web site (via HTTP `POST` or `GET` methods that will be described in further detail later in this chapter). Sometimes, this is known as the early generation of web services, before the time of XML. However, this method lacked structure (such as the XML structure that is used by SOAP for its message format) and it was difficult to conduct a RPC type of communication between the servers.

A number of first generation portal applications and "digital dashboard" type applications used the methods of links, frames, "screen scraping", and posting information to assemble different applications under one place and single interface. If you have worked with these types of applications, you know that the interoperability was not where users liked it to be.

Web services with SOAP address the need for interoperability between web applications. With this paradigm shift, one needs to think of web sites as functions (in other words, web services). One web application calls another, as a regular application would call another, by invoking a function and getting a result back. Or if communicating in an asynchronous mode, a web application would send information or a message to another web application, without the need to receive an immediate response. Having this type of services programmatic interface, a company can focus on its core competencies within its web application and add the other needed capabilities from others. In this way the end-user can experience a full-fledged application. SOAP enables web applications to do just that.

It's important to mention that SOAP was not the first XML based RPC protocol. One of its XML-based predecessors is **XML-RPC** (**eXtensible Markup Language Remote Procedure Call**). XML-RPC is a very simple protocol, but it has two important shortcomings: it is quite verbose in the way it represents data, and it lacks good data typing. XML-RPC has challenges when encoding structures of data and other more complex data types such as arrays. At the time when XML-RPC was created, the work on XML data types via XML schemas was far from ready. When SOAP was first submitted to W3C, the work on XML schemas had advanced significantly and SOAP was able to utilize it as its solid foundation.

For more information on XML-RPC visit http://www.xmlrpc.com.

SOAP is being portrayed as the standardized protocol for XML messaging and RPC communication between applications on any platform, and between any object models, or languages. The W3C acknowledged the submission of the protocol in May of 2000. Ariba Inc., CommerceOne Inc., Compaq Computer Corp, DevelopMentor Inc., Hewlett-Packard Co., IBM Corp., IONA Technologies PLC, Lotus Development Corp., Microsoft Corp., SAP AG, and Userland Software Inc. jointly submitted the specification to the W3C. Having such a group of diverse companies supporting the submission of SOAP was a good sign towards industry acceptance and implementation of an open standards-based interoperability protocol.

SOAP is a simple and extensible computer-to-computer communication protocol that leverages existing Internet standards: XML for message formatting, HTTP and other Internet protocols for message transport. It requires no special firewall configuration. Up to this date, SOAP has had a surprising mixture of vendors joining the effort.

Other Competing Protocols To SOAP

Besides XML-RPC, most other implementations that would compete with SOAP are technology- or vendor-specific. Some protocols, like CORBA/ IIOP, DCOM, and RMI that we covered earlier, have a strong following of developers and users. They all have the challenges that we described, therefore not making them very suitable for a universal protocol for machine-to-machine communication.

It is worth mentioning that there are other XML-based SOAP contenders, which include:

- **XMOP** (**XML Metadata Object Persistence**), which started to use the SOAP protocol recently, in fact. For more information, go to http://www.openhealth.org/xmop/XMOP.htm.
- **WDDX** (**Web Distributed Data Exchange**) by Allaire Corp, found at http://wddx.org, which specifies a DTD for communication.

For a more complete list of competitors and possible competitors to SOAP, you can visit http://www.w3.org/2000/xp/Group/ *and look for the XML Protocol Matrix link.*

Another contender in this space of computer-to-computer communication is **Electronic Business XML** (**ebXML**). This protocol is managed by **UN/CEFACT** (a United Nations body that has done lots of work on **EDI** (**Electronic Data Interchange**) standards such as the UN/EDIFACT) and **OASIS** (a consortium that operates the XML.org registry for industry XML schemas and vocabularies). ebXML has a different scope than SOAP, however. SOAP is fairly simple and deals with the message format, whereas ebXML has much larger scope and is much more complex. ebXML defines items such as message routing, security, audit trails, quality of service, restart and recovery, etc. Supporting this level of capability is a very complex and difficult task and would likely take some time for it to be more widely implemented. SOAP does not specifically address many of the issues that ebXML does, but it is possible to address many of them by using the extensibility that is provided by the SOAP framework.

> *For more on ebXML go to Chapter 26, or visit* http://www.ebxml.org/

As we go to print, the ebXML group had announced that it plans to incorporate SOAP 1.1 and SOAP Messaging with Attachment specifications into its future releases of ebXML. Building the messaging infrastructure of ebXML on top of SOAP, would give SOAP one more sign of industry-wide acceptance. It would also put to rest any worries of SOAP and ebXML interoperability.

SOAP Message

SOAP messages are fundamentally one-way transmissions from a sender to a receiver. Often messages are combined to implement request/response communication. All SOAP messages are XML documents with their own schema; they include proper namespaces on all elements and attributes. SOAP defines two namespaces, **SOAP envelope** and **SOAP serialization** or **encoding**. Some of the rules that SOAP specifies are stricter than XML itself, for example SOAP messages cannot contain DTDs or Processing Instructions. This should be no surprise, as one of goals of SOAP was to remain a simple protocol.

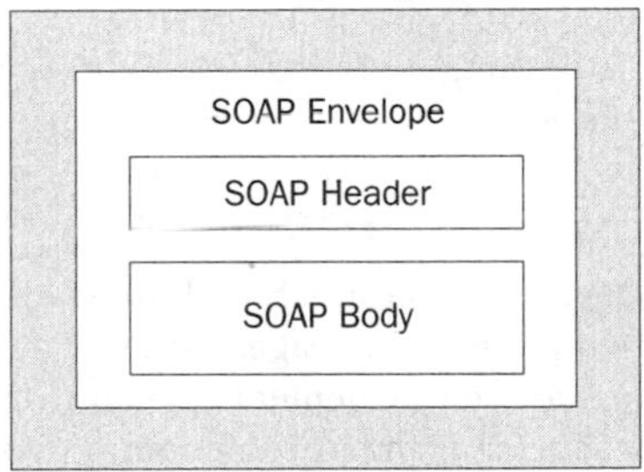

As an XML document, SOAP messages consist of three sections: SOAP envelope, SOAP header, and the SOAP body. The envelope wraps the payload, the header provides identifying information about the payload, and the body contains the payload of the message – more details to follow. The SOAP specification talks about the encoding styles accepted and the handling of RPC type communications. We will look at these aspects as well, before continuing our discussion – looking at implementing SOAP solutions in both synchronous and asynchronous ways.

Simple SOAP Example

The following snippet of code comes from the SOAP specification and illustrates a simple example of a SOAP message used to call a procedure that requires a single parameter. Notice some of the main sections of the SOAP document: the envelope that acts as the document root element (`<SOAP-ENV:Envelope>`), and its element `<SOAP-ENV:Body>`.

```
<SOAP-ENV:Envelope
  xmlns:SOAP-ENV="http://schemas.xmlsoap.org/soap/envelope/"
  SOAP-ENV:encodingStyle="http://schemas.xmlsoap.org/soap/encoding/">
   <SOAP-ENV:Body>
       <m:GetLastTradePrice xmlns:m="Some-URI">
           <symbol>DIS</symbol>
       </m:GetLastTradePrice>
   </SOAP-ENV:Body>
</SOAP-ENV:Envelope>
```

You can also see within the body of this SOAP message that a procedure is being called by the name of `GetLastTradePrice`, and a parameter (`<symbol>`) is being passed to it with a value of `DIS`. Note that the envelope and body have the namespace of `http://schemas.xmlsoap.org/soap/envelope/` and encoding has a namespace of `http://schemas.xmlsoap.org/soap/encoding/`. The method itself references a user–defined schema.

SOAP Message, and Now the Details

In this section, we will cover important points about the individual parts of a SOAP message.

- An **envelope** that defines what is in the message, what should work with it, and whether it is optional or mandatory.
- The **header** as an optional and generic mechanism for adding features to SOAP messages.
- The **body** is the container for the mandatory information, that is, the data payload that is being transferred. Within the body, only the `Fault` element is defined by SOAP.
- **Encoding rules** based on a simple system – generalization of the common features found in type systems in most programming languages, databases, and semi–structured data.
- **RPC** representation, that is nothing more than a convention used to represent remote procedure calls and responses.

SOAP Envelope

The envelope is a mandatory top-level element in a SOAP message. Conceptually, you can think of the envelope as the envelope used to wrap e-mail messages, or even as envelopes used in regular postal mail. Attributes within the envelope, as well as elements, when present, have to be identified by a namespace. The `<SOAP-ENV:Envelope>` element can contain two elements as its immediate children: the optional `<SOAP-ENV:Header>` element, and the `<SOAP-ENV:Body>` element. Any other immediate children elements have to come after the `<SOAP-ENV:Body>` element. These additional immediate children elements have no prescribed use by the SOAP specification at this time and it may be up to vendors or future specifications to utilize their potential.

```
<SOAP-ENV:Envelope
  xmlns:SOAP-ENV="http://schemas.xmlsoap.org/soap/envelope/"
  SOAP-ENV:encodingStyle="http://schemas.xmlsoap.org/soap/encoding/">
   <SOAP-ENV:Body>
       <m:GetLastTradePrice xmlns:m="Some-URI">
           <symbol>DIS</symbol>
       </m:GetLastTradePrice>
   </SOAP-ENV:Body>
</SOAP-ENV:Envelope>
```

The <SOAP-ENV:Envelope> element should be associated with the http://schemas.xmlsoap.org/soap/encoding/ namespace. The attribute SOAP-ENV:encodingStyle can be used to specify the serialization rules used in the SOAP message by referencing the appropriate URI. Its scope is applied in a similar fashion as namespace scopes are applied – to the particular element's content, as well as all child elements that do not specify this attribute. This attribute is an ordered list of one or more URIs indicating the order of most specific to least specific.

SOAP Header

The <SOAP-ENV:Header> element is an optional element, but when present, it has to be the first immediate child of the <SOAP-ENV:Envelope> element and it has to come before the <SOAP-ENV:Body> element. This element may contain attributes and elements within, and they have to be namespace identified.

```
<SOAP-ENV:Header>
   <t:Transaction xmlns:t="some-URI" SOAP-ENV:mustUnderstand="1">
          5
   </t:Transaction>
</SOAP-ENV:Header>
```

The SOAP Header element provides a mechanism for extending a message in a decentralized fashion without prior knowledge between the communicating parties. Some examples of extensions would be header entries for authentication, transaction management, and payment.

The SOAP specification defines two attributes for the <SOAP-ENV:Header> element. One is the SOAP-ENV:mustUnderstand attribute shown in the above example. This attribute can have a value of "1" or "0" (default). A value of "1" indicates that the recipient of the message must understand all of the attributes provided in the header and if not, it is required to return an error message and not process the message. In our example above, unless the recipient understands the transaction specified by the particular namespace, they are not allowed to proceed to the message.

There is another optional attribute for the Header element, and that is the SOAP-ENV:actor attribute. This attribute specifies a SOAP intermediary in situations where the SOAP message may travel from the original sender to the ultimate destination via a set of SOAP intermediaries. A SOAP intermediary is an application that could process SOAP messages and then be able to route them further, analogous but not the same as routers on the Internet that forward TCP/IP packets. When this attribute is omitted, the SOAP message's ultimate recipient is the first recipient.

SOAP Body

The <SOAP-ENV:Body> element contains the payload of the SOAP message. Depending on the type of communication that is occurring, the Body element can contain the RPC call or response, error message, or other one-way SOAP messages. The example below shows a SOAP message that carries a payload of a RPC call to a web service.

```
<SOAP-ENV:Envelope
  xmlns:SOAP-ENV="http://schemas.xmlsoap.org/soap/envelope/"
  SOAP-ENV:encodingStyle="http://schemas.xmlsoap.org/soap/encoding/">
   <SOAP-ENV:Body>
       <m:GetLastTradePrice xmlns:m="Some-URI">
           <symbol>DIS</symbol>
       </m:GetLastTradePrice>
   </SOAP-ENV:Body>
</SOAP-ENV:Envelope>
```

The immediate child elements of the <SOAP-ENV:Body> element are called **body entries**. These elements can be namespace qualified. Only one of these body entries is an element that is defined by the SOAP specification and that is the <SOAP-ENV:Fault> element, which we'll look at next.

SOAP Faults

The Purpose of the <SOAP-ENV:Fault> element is to carry error or status information within a SOAP message. This element, when present, must appear only once and must be within the Body element. The <SOAP-ENV:Fault> element has four sub-elements defined by the SOAP specification; more can be added by qualifying them with a user-defined namespace, if needed.

```
<SOAP-ENV:Envelope
  xmlns:SOAP-ENV="http://schemas.xmlsoap.org/soap/envelope/">
   <SOAP-ENV:Body>
       <SOAP-ENV:Fault>
           <faultcode>SOAP-ENV:Server</faultcode>
           <faultstring>Server Error</faultstring>
           <detail>
               <e:myfaultdetails xmlns:e="Some-URI">
                 <message>My application didn't work</message>
                 <errorcode> 1001 </errorcode>
               </e:myfaultdetails>
           </detail>
       </SOAP-ENV:Fault>
   </SOAP-ENV:Body>
</SOAP-ENV:Envelope>
```

- The <faultcode> element is intended to provide information to the software about the error type. This element must be present in a <SOAP-ENV:Fault> element. SOAP defines only four fault code values:
  - SOAP-ENV:VersionMismatch (invalid namespace likely)
  - SOAP-ENV:MustUnderstand (the SOAP-ENV:mustUnderstand element within the SOAP header could not be satisfied)
  - Client (error in the message sent by the client, should be resubmitted only once corrected)
  - SOAP-ENV:Server (error at the server in the processing of a message)

  This list is extensible with a "." notation, for example: Client.Authentication.
- The <faultstring> element provides human readable information about the error. This element must be present when a <SOAP-ENV:Fault> element is being sent.
- The <faultactor> element is an optional element that provides information about the system that caused the error. It is particularly useful when SOAP intermediary systems are present.
- The <detail> element is for carrying application-specific error information related to the <SOAP-ENV:Body> element. It must be present if the content of the message in the body cannot be processed successfully (in other words, <faultcode> is of the type SOAP-ENV:Server). Header detail information, however, must be carried within the header entries. The absence of the detail element indicates that the fault is not related to processing of the <SOAP-ENV:Body> element – useful for troubleshooting. All immediate elements to the detail element are called detail entries.

SOAP Encoding and Types Supported

The SOAP specification describes an encoding style "that is based on a simple type system that is a generalization of the common features found in type systems of common programming languages, databases, and other semi–structured systems of data". SOAP's **type** is described as "a simple scalar type or a compound type constructed as a composite of several parts, each with a type". The encoding style described by the specification is encouraged but not required; other data models and encoding can be used in conjunction with SOAP.

In comparison with XML, SOAP defines a narrower set of rules for encoding. At a high level, SOAP recognizes values such as **primitive types** (strings, integers, and others), as well as **composite types** (a compound of other types, such as `name` being a compound of the `FirstName` as string and `LastName` as string). **Simple values** are ones that do not have named parts within them. Examples would be strings, integers and enumerated values. SOAP adopts all the built–in datatypes supported by XML Schemas. The XML Schemas specification includes type definitions, but does not include corresponding element declaration, thus the SOAP–ENC schema and namespace (`http://schemas.xmlsoap.org/soap/encoding/`) declares an element for every simple datatype, instead of the "`xsd:primitive`" type of declaration. This allows `id` and `href` attributes to be used. So, in the following example, the first element has an `id` that is referenced within the second element with the `href` attribute.

```
<SOAP-ENC:int id="int1">45</SOAP-ENC:int>
<SOAP-ENC:int href="#int1"/>
```

Another high–level type would be a **compound value** that is an aggregate of relations to other values. Examples would be invoice type, address type and arrays. Compound values can be accessed with an **ordinal accessor** (like arrays, for example `MyArray[4]`) or via a **name accessor** (like collections, for example `MyCollection("TestElement")`). The following example shows a type with both simple and complex members. The simple types are `title`, `name`, `e-mail`, and `web`. The complex types are `author`, `address`, as well as `e:Book`, `e:Person`, and `e:Address`. The prefix "e" that is found in front of these attribute names, simply qualifies the attributes to a custom namespace defined by a unique URI. The exact URI is not important; it is only important to remember that it is unique and it is a namespace.

```
<e:Book>
   <title>My Life and Work</title>
   <author href="#Person-1"/>
</e:Book>
<e:Person id="Person-1">
   <name>Henry Ford</name>
   <address href="#Address-2"/>
</e:Person>
<e:Address id="Address-2">
   <e-mail>mailto:henryford@hotmail.com</e-mail>
   <web>http://www.henryford.com</web>
</e:Address>
```

An important aspect to values as defined by the SOAP specification is the differentiation between "**single–reference**" values and "**multi–reference**" values. In the previous example, `e:Address` and `e:Person` are multi–reference values, because there is more than one reference to them (one reference is implicit and it is from the parent element), and the other reference(s) are in elements with the `href` attribute pointing to the particular multi-reference element. All other elements are single–reference values. Single–reference values are referenced by only one accessor; multi–reference values can be referenced by multiple accessors.

Furthermore, the SOAP encoding terminology differentiates between "**independent**" elements, ones that appear at the top level of the serialization, and "**embedded**" elements – all others. In the previous example, `Address` would be an independent element, and `e-mail` would be an embedded element. Also, there are **locally scoped** types, whose names are unique within the type but not outside, and **Universally scoped** types, that have names based at least in part on an URI. In our example, `e:Address` would be universally scoped because it has a namespace prefix.

For more details on SOAP encoding, refer to the SOAP encoding section at http://www.w3.org/TR/SOAP, and XML Schemas Part 2: Datatypes, at http://www.w3.org/TR/.

RPC and SOAP, Request and Response Examples

SOAP messages can carry communication as one–way or two–way transmissions. The two–way communication is, in essence, RPC calls and replies. They are carried in the Body element of a SOAP message. **Method invocation** is modeled as a single compound datatype with name and type identical to the method name. The parameters are represented as single accessors with name and type matching the actual parameters that they represent. They appear in the order of the method signature. Here's a code snippet, taken from the SOAP specification, showing a simple SOAP request:

```
<SOAP-ENV:Envelope
  xmlns:SOAP-ENV="http://schemas.xmlsoap.org/soap/envelope/"
  SOAP-ENV:encodingStyle="http://schemas.xmlsoap.org/soap/encoding/">
   <SOAP-ENV:Body>
       <m:GetLastTradePrice xmlns:m="Some-URI">
           <symbol>DIS</symbol>
       </m:GetLastTradePrice>
   </SOAP-ENV:Body>
</SOAP-ENV:Envelope>
```

Once the server receives the above message, it will process the message using its SOAP implementation libraries, and optionally forward an answer to another machine or return a response to the machine that sent the request. Assuming that the computer needs to reply to the machine that had originally sent the request, the reply could look something like this:

```
<SOAP-ENV:Envelope
  xmlns:SOAP-ENV="http://schemas.xmlsoap.org/soap/envelope/"
  SOAP-ENV:encodingStyle="http://schemas.xmlsoap.org/soap/encoding/">
   <SOAP-ENV:Body>
       <m:GetLastTradePriceResponse xmlns:m="Some-URI">
           <Price>34.5</Price>
       </m:GetLastTradePriceResponse>
   </SOAP-ENV:Body>
</SOAP-ENV:Envelope>
```

As you can see, the **method response** is modeled as a single element within the SOAP Body containing one accessor for each return value and each out or in/ out parameters. The first accessor is the return value and its name is not significant, although according to convention it is named with the method name with the string "`Response`" after it. The parameters that follow are ordered as the method signature. Finally, it is important to keep in mind that a response cannot return values as well as a `<SOAP-ENV:Fault>` element at the same time. Since we have become familiar with the structure of SOAP messages, let's move on to take a quick look at WSDL.

Brief Overview of WSDL

WSDL (**Web Services Description Language**) is an XML format for describing network services. It does this by considering network services as a set of endpoints operating on messages containing either document–oriented or procedure–oriented information. The operations and procedures are described abstractly first, and then bound to specific network or transportation protocols and message formats. WSDL is extensible to allow describing network services regardless of their network and messaging protocols. The current specification only describes bindings to SOAP 1.1, HTTP `GET`/`POST`, and MIME. The current version of WSDL does not include a complete framework for describing the composition and orchestration of network services.

WSDL was brought together to represent the current thinking of defining web services by Ariba, IBM, and Microsoft. On March of 2001, WSDL received the status of a note with the W3C, meaning that is not a full specification as of yet, but it is being considered by the W3C and vendors. When it comes to defining the services provided with SOAP, the most current implementations use WSDL. In the past, the above vendors used **NASSL** (**Network Accessible Services Specification Language**), **SCL** (**SOAP Contract Language**), or **SDL** (**Services Description Language**). You may recognize some of these from earlier implementations of SOAP toolkits and web services by the aforementioned vendors.

For more coverage of WSDL and UDDI, refer to Chapter 26, or the WSDL specification at *http://www.w3.org/TR/wsdl.*

WSDL Example

Since we would like to look at WSDL in the context of SOAP, let's look at an example of a WSDL document representing the definition of a network service. Then, we'll walk through the code and get familiar with each section. The following code is the network definition of a stock quote service and comes from the WSDL specification.

```
<?xml version="1.0"?>
<definitions name="StockQuote"

targetNamespace="http://example.com/stockquote.wsdl"
          xmlns:tns="http://example.com/stockquote.wsdl"
          xmlns:xsd1="http://example.com/stockquote.xsd"
          xmlns:soap="http://schemas.xmlsoap.org/wsdl/soap/"
          xmlns="http://schemas.xmlsoap.org/wsdl/">

    <message name="SubscribeToQuotes">
        <part name="body" element="xsd1:SubscribeToQuotes"/>
    </message>

    <portType name="StockQuotePortType">
        <operation name="SubscribeToQuotes">
           <input message="tns:SubscribeToQuotes"/>
        </operation>
    </portType>

    <binding name="StockQuoteSoap" type="tns:StockQuotePortType">
        <soap:binding style="document" transport="http://example.com/smtp"/>
        <operation name="SubscribeToQuotes">
           <input message="tns:SubscribeToQuotes">
               <soap:header element="xsd1:SubscriptionHeader"/>
```

```
            </input>
        </operation>
    </binding>

    <service name="StockQuoteService">
      <documentation> This is a stock quote one way service</documentation>
        <port name="StockQuotePort" binding="tns:StockQuoteSoap">
            <soap:address location="mailto://subscribe@example.com"/>
        </port>
    </service>

    <types>
        <schema targetNamespace="http://example.com/stockquote.xsd"
               xmlns="http://www.w3.org/1999/XMLSchema">
            <element name="SubscribeToQuotes">
               <complexType>
                   <all>
                       <element name="tickerSymbol" type="string"/>
                   </all>
               </complexType>
            </element>
            <element name="SubscriptionHeader" type="uriReference"/>
        </schema>
    </types>
</definitions>
```

WSDL Document Structure

WSDL introduces certain terminology that, once grasped, makes reading the content of documents such as the one above quite easy. The document contains multiple levels due to its approach to decouple network services and their abstract definitions from the actual network transport protocols and message format bindings. We will start reading the above document from the bottom up.

A WSDL document defines **services** as collection of network endpoints called ports.

```
    <service name="StockQuoteService">
       <documentation>This is a stock quote one way service</documentation>
        <port name="StockQuotePort" binding="tns:StockQuoteSoap">
           <soap:address location="mailto://subscribe@example.com"/>
        </port>
    </service>
```

A **port** is a single endpoint defined as a combination of a binding and a single network address. In the example above it is an endpoint with a specific SMTP address – `subscribe@example.com`.

Going further, a **binding** brings together a concrete protocol and data format for a particular port type.

```
    <portType name="StockQuotePortType">
        <operation name="SubscribeToQuotes">
           <input message="tns:SubscribeToQuotes"/>
        </operation>
    </portType>
```

```
<binding name="StockQuoteSoap" type="tns:StockQuotePortType">
    <soap:binding style="document" transport="http://example.com/smtp"/>
    <operation name="SubscribeToQuotes">
        <input message="tns:SubscribeToQuotes">
            <soap:header element="xsd1:SubscriptionHeader"/>
        </input>
    </operation>
</binding>
```

The above binding specifies the SOAP protocol as the message format, and SMTP as the one–way asynchronous transportation protocol. The binding is for the particular port type that is specified just above it. A **port type** is an abstract set of operations supported by one or more endpoints. In our example the operation described by the port type is a one–way message – a quote subscription. WSDL defines four transmission operations:

- **one–way** (endpoint receives a message).
- **request–response** (endpoint receives a message and then sends one as a reply to the received message).
- **solicit–response** (the endpoint sends a message, and receives a correlated message).
- **notification** (one–way, the endpoint sends a message).

The **operation** itself refers to messages or actions that are supported by the service. **Messages** in return are type definitions described in the types section. The types definitions can be described using any type system, for example XSD (XML Schema Definition – for more details see Chapter 6.

```
<types>
    <schema targetNamespace="http://example.com/stockquote.xsd"
            xmlns="http://www.w3.org/1999/XMLSchema">
        <element name="SubscribeToQuotes">
            <complexType>
                <all>
                    <element name="tickerSymbol" type="string"/>
                </all>
            </complexType>
        </element>
        <element name="SubscriptionHeader" type="uriReference"/>
    </schema>
</types>

<message name="SubscribeToQuotes">
    <part name="body" element="xsd1:SubscribeToQuotes"/>
</message>
```

Finally, notice that the WSDL document is just an XML document wrapped in a `<definitions>` root element. `<documentation>` elements can optionally be added to make the document more human readable, as we have added within the `<service>` element.

SOAP Bindings To Transport Protocols

We had mentioned at the beginning of this chapter that SOAP does not tie itself to any particular transport protocol; in fact, SOAP documents can be carried by almost any transport protocol. The SOAP specification describes how SOAP can be used in combination with HTTP and the **HTTP Extension Framework**, but it provides this as an example only. SOAP can bind to other protocols such as SMTP, just like the example we provided in the previous section on WSDL.

The HTTP Extension Framework can be used optionally, over just regular HTTP. In order to use the HTTP Extension Framework the client has to support it as well as the server. Currently, the support for the HTTP Extension Framework is not as widespread as the support for standard HTTP and SMTP. See the SOAP specification for more information on this topic.

HTTP As the Standard Synchronous Protocol

HTTP as an Internet transport protocol is ubiquitous with the Web – most web content today is served via HTTP. Firewalls are very friendly to HTTP, naturally, and it typically travels over port 80, which is open on virtually all firewalls. HTTP can be used together with **SSL** (**Secured Sockets Layers**) and certificates to become **HTTPS** (**HTTP Secured**). In this fashion, all of the traffic can be encrypted between the two network endpoints. When SOAP uses HTTP as its transport protocol, it can use all of the strengths of HTTP, such as its ubiquitous nature.

Other than the fact that HTTPS typically travels over port 443 rather than 80, everything else mentioned here about HTTP typically applies to HTTPS as well.

SOAP binds to the HTTP request/response message model very intuitively, particularly when implementing RPC-type communication. In regard to HTTP, there are two highly important HTTP request types: `GET` and `POST`. The `GET` request method encodes all HTTP data behind the URL, and the `POST` request method incorporates all HTTP data within the header of the request. The SOAP specification provides details for binding SOAP to HTTP `POST`. So, let's look at an example of a SOAP HTTP request, particularly its header:

```
POST /StockQuote HTTP/1.1
Content-Type: text/xml; charset="utf-8"
Content-Length: nnnn
SOAPAction: "http://wrox.com/abc#MyMessage"

<SOAP-ENV:Envelope...
```

The first line of the request specifies that this is a HTTP `POST` request for the `/StockQuote` resource following the HTTP/1.1 protocol syntax. This is pretty standard HTTP request information. The second line is more interesting to us; we can see that the `Content-Type` variable is set to "`text/xml`". It is a requirement that all SOAP requests are sent using this encoding, but that should come as no surprise because the payload of the message is in XML. The third line is also a standard HTTP line, which specifies the length of the HTTP message; the fourth line being an additional HTTP header field added by SOAP, specifying a URI of the service (that does not have to be resolvable). The `SOAPAction` HTTP header field is required for SOAP clients making HTTP SOAP requests; it is there in order for firewalls to be able to use it to filter traffic, if that need exists. Finally, the value of this field can be blank, as well, in which case it would simply mean that there are no indications as to the intent of the message.

Now, let's look at the SOAP response, its header in particular, returned via HTTP:

```
HTTP/1.1 200 OK
Content-Type: text/xml; charset="utf-8"
Content-Length: nnnn

<SOAP-ENV:Envelope...
```

The first line of this HTTP message is status information, with the number 2xx indicating that the request was serviced properly. In a case of SOAP error returning a SOAP `Fault` element, HTTP 500 "Internal Server Error" must be returned as the HTTP status code.

For full details about the various HTTP status codes, as well as other information about HTTP 1.1, look at http://www.rfc-editor.org/rfc/rfc2616.txt *(scroll to page 40 and 41 for HTTP status codes).*

Asynchronous Communication Via SMTP and MIME

As we have seen in our discussion of SOAP, this protocol is not limited in using HTTP as its transport mechanism. HTTP is the first and most obvious choice, of course, due to its ubiquitous nature on the Web. Also, HTTP lends itself very nicely for performing RPC type communication across the network. However, when it comes to performing asynchronous communications or message forwarding, HTTP proves to be a bit challenging. One of the most widely spread Internet standard protocols for asynchronous or one–way message transfer protocol is SMTP.

From a business case scenario perspective, you cannot always use synchronous communication as provided by HTTP. For example, you may have a slow system, a system that has to do lots of processing before submitting the reply back, or a system that simply has to wait for human intervention such as an approval before acting on the request. In this case, it would not make sense to wait for the reply, but it would be helpful to perform this communication asynchronously.

The WSDL specification provides an example of how a SOAP one–way message can be sent via a SMTP binding. You can refer to the full example code presented in our earlier discussion on WSDL in this chapter. For now, let's take a look at some of the more interesting points of this example.

```
<binding name="StockQuoteSoap" type="tns:StockQuotePortType">
    <soap:binding style="document" transport="http://example.com/smtp"/>
    <operation name="SubscribeToQuotes">
        <input message="tns:SubscribeToQuotes">
            <soap:header element="xsd1:SubscriptionHeader"/>
        </input>
    </operation>
</binding>
```

The highlighted sections are the ones that differ from what you would find for a WSDL file defining a SOAP message bound to HTTP. The `<soap:binding>` element provides an attribute called `transport` with the value of `http://example.com/smtp`. Furthermore, the `operation` section describes only one input message, but no output message, specifying that this is one–way communication. The final difference in the WSDL is the `location` attribute within the `<soap:address>` section of the port definition section. This attribute contains the value for an endpoint (a destination e-mail address):

```
<service name="StockQuoteService">
  <documentation> This is a stock quote one way service</documentation>
    <port name="StockQuotePort" binding="tns:StockQuoteSoap">
       <soap:address location="mailto://subscribe@example.com"/>
    </port>
</service>
```

When utilizing SMTP to transfer information, particularly information that has richer content than plain text, the content is often encoded with an encoding mechanism called **MIME** (**Multipurpose Internet Mail Extensions**). MIME is a multipart mechanism for encapsulation of compound documents that can be used to bundle not only SOAP messages, but also other documents related to those SOAP messages, such as binary document attachments. If you think about the possibility of being able to submit SOAP messages with attached fax documents or images, various legal documents, medical images, engineering drawings, or any other type of images, you can see the great potential of this use of MIME.

The specification that describes how to bind SOAP 1.1 to MIME in greater detail is "SOAP Messages with Attachments", which can be found at http://www.w3.org/TR/SOAP-attachments.

The following is an example of a SOAP message wrapped in an additional MIME envelope. Note that the root part of this wrapper has to be the primary SOAP message with its XML content, and the content type of the MIME envelope has to be set to "`text/xml`". The SOAP message itself has no specific knowledge that it is being encapsulated in a MIME wrapper; however, the SOAP message does contain URI references to the attached entities, when those attachments are present. The MIME wrapper, from a SOAP perspective, is considered to be part of the transfer protocol binding. This is done in this way to show the capability of transferring attachments with SOAP messages without the need of re–inventing new entities for such interactions. Now, let's take a quick look at an example that was taken out of the SOAP Messages with Attachment specification.

```
MIME-Version: 1.0
Content-Type: Multipart/Related; boundary=MIME_boundary; type=text/xml;
        start="<claim061400a.xml@claiming-it.com>"
Content-Description: This is the optional message description.

--MIME_boundary
Content-Type: text/xml; charset=UTF-8
Content-Transfer-Encoding: 8bit
Content-ID: <claim061400a.xml@claiming-it.com>

<?xml version='1.0' ?>
<SOAP-ENV:Envelope
xmlns:SOAP-ENV="http://schemas.xmlsoap.org/soap/envelope/">
<SOAP-ENV:Body>
..
<theSignedForm href="cid:claim061400a.tiff@claiming-it.com"/>
..
</SOAP-ENV:Body>
</SOAP-ENV:Envelope>

--MIME_boundary
Content-Type: image/tiff
Content-Transfer-Encoding: binary
Content-ID: <claim061400a.tiff@claiming-it.com>

...binary TIFF image...
--MIME_boundary--
```

The MIME version is specified first, with the content type following next. The content type is `multipart/related`, specifically stating the content type of the root part of `text/xml` (the content type for the actual SOAP message itself). Just a bit further down, the SOAP message follows in its typical XML format – the only difference being the `href` references provided to the attachments, when attachments are present. In our example above, we have a TIFF image for an attachment that follows right after the SOAP message. This is a binary format attachment with a content type of `image/tiff`.

SOAP compound messages that are bound to MIME for encoding of other attached content can be carried over any transport mechanism, both SMTP and HTTP. The SOAP Messages with Attachment specification does provide an example of binding SOAP messages with attachments to HTTP 1.1 in the form of HTTP messages with a `Multipart/Related` content type. At this point there is no published specification known that provides an example of how to bind SOAP messages to SMTP, with or without the use of MIME encoding. This simply means that developers and implementers are left to develop their own implementation by simply following the basic SMTP rules of sending e-mail messages and the SOAP specification. We will discuss this a bit further when going over the examples of using SOAP in asynchronous communication via SMTP.

Other Transport Mechanisms

We have limited our discussion of binding SOAP messages to HTTP for synchronous request/response interactions, and SMTP for asynchronous messaging. However, from the perspective of the SOAP specification there is no limitation to binding SOAP to any other transportation mechanisms. SOAP messages defined in XML can be exchanges using enterprise–messaging technologies such as **MSMQ** or **Queued Components** by Microsoft, **MQSeries** by IBM, or **JMS** (**Java Message Service**) for the Java community. These messaging technologies can provide all of their features, such as built–in security and transaction support, to the SOAP messages being submitted in their payloads. While the benefits of using some of the enterprise–messaging technologies are widely known, the drawbacks lie in communication difficulties across platforms and across the Internet, particularly in communicating across firewalls.

Some of benefits of the proprietary messaging protocols mentioned might be outweighed slowly, as new security and transaction addendums to the SOAP specifications come to light. For example, in February of 2001, the W3C recognized a specification for extending SOAP to support digital signatures as a "note". Recall that a "note" in W3C terminology means that it is not a standard endorsed by the W3C as of yet, but it is being considered as a potential future standard. This SOAP extension specifies syntax and rules for processing SOAP header entries to carry digital signatures.

*You can take a look at the latest **SOAP Security Extensions: Digital Signatures** specification at http://www.w3.org/TR/SOAP–dsig/, or go to http://www.w3.org/TR and then look for the latest SOAP and Digital Signatures document.*

Popular Implementations of SOAP

Even though SOAP has been around for a relatively short time, there are already a number of implementations on the market. Most key vendors have their own implementations of SOAP within their preferred programming language. In this chapter, we use three of those implementations to show how you can invoke services from one language platform to another, synchronously or asynchronously. We will now take a brief look at some of the features of:

- **Apache SOAP 2.1** by Apache.org (originally donated by IBM and its alphaWorks division to the care of the Apache organization)
- **SOAP Toolkit 2** by Microsoft
- **SOAP::Lite** for PERL

Apache SOAP and IBM Web Services Toolkit

The Apache Software Foundation handles a number of open-source development initiatives. One of these initiatives was added to its XML Project, when IBM and its alphaWorks division handed over the IBM4J (Java) implementation of SOAP to Apache. Since that time, Apache has released an update to the SOAP implementation – version 2.1.

IBM provides a **Web Services Toolkit** that bundles the SOAP implementation within itself. The earlier releases of the Web Services Toolkit implemented NASSL, whose features were incorporated in WSDL. The early editions of the Web Services Toolkit also supported the **WDS** (**Well Defined Services**) schema for describing various services information. Now these features are handled by the support for UDDI and the UDDI registry.

More recent releases of the web services toolkit by IBM incorporate WSDL, UDDI, and SOAP. However, the current version of the IBM Web Services Toolkit includes Apache SOAP 2.0, rather than the latest release. The examples in this chapter were developed and tested with the Apache SOAP 2.1 release.

This release supports a number of the features listed in the SOAP 1.1 specification, and it has some support for the SOAP Messaging with Attachment specification. WSDL is not supported directly within the Apache SOAP 2.1, but the IBM Web Services Toolkit is to be used for WSDL and UDDI support.

> *More information on the Apache SOAP implementation can be found at http://xml.apache.org/soap/index.html. IBM's Web Services Toolkit can be found at http://www.alphaworks.ibm.com/tech/webservicestoolkit.*

Microsoft's SOAP Toolkit, BizTalk Server, and Web Services in .NET

Microsoft originally released its first implementation of SOAP in the SOAP Toolkit 1.0. This was an unsupported release that did not support WSDL, but rather supported a Microsoft-specific specification called **SDL** (**Services Definition Language**). Also, in terms of XML schemas it supported the older **XML–Data Reduced** (**XDR**) specification. December 2000 was the last release of this toolkit.

Subsequently, Microsoft released its SOAP Toolkit 2.0, which fully supports WSDL 1.0, SOAP 1.1, XSD, and UDDI. The final release which is planned to be ready sometime in the fall of 2001, and should implement just about all of the features of those specifications. At the time of writing, Microsoft has not given any definite indications whether or not it will provide support for asynchronous SOAP messaging.

The SOAP toolkit can be used from any of the Visual Studio languages that can invoke COM objects, such as Visual Basic or Visual C++ (most features are also available to VBScript/JScript). The examples in this chapter were created and tested with the SOAP Toolkit 2, RC0 (Release Candidate 0) of the package. The languages used were Visual Basic and VBScript.

For more information on Microsoft's implementation of SOAP visit: http://msdn.microsoft.com/soap/default.asp.

Microsoft BizTalk Server 2000 implements EAI and B2B integration. It processes BizTalk documents that are simply an extension of a SOAP document, incorporating extra BizTalk-specific XML tags called **BizTags**. The BizTalk Framework, which is a set of guidelines that enable message exchange between organizations and applications, builds upon SOAP. BizTalk Server is one of the first servers from Microsoft that incorporates SOAP. Other products are likely to follow this lead by incorporating SOAP themselves. We will not cover the details of SOAP as it is implemented in BizTalk, in Chapter 25, "B2B with Biztalk".

For more information on BizTalk Server 2000, see Professional BizTalk (ISBN 1-861003-29-3), published by Wrox Press. You can also visit Microsoft's BizTalk site at: http://www.microsoft.com/biztalk/ *and the BizTalk.org community site at* http://www.biztalk.org/.

One of the most widely publicized new technologies from Microsoft has been .NET. The current beta release of .NET (beta 1) supports SDL and XSR, just like SOAP Toolkit 1. However, the next beta release will also support WSDL and XSD, and more complete features of the SOAP specification and UDDI. According to Microsoft, .NET is its long-term strategy for providing web services, so it will not be surprising to see .NET offering a more comprehensive SOAP implementation, as well as including a fuller support for other web services technologies related to SOAP.

To learn more about .NET, go to http://msdn.microsoft.com/net/.

Perl and SOAP::Lite

SOAP::Lite is a collection of Perl modules that implement a subset of the SOAP 1.1 specification. In addition, it has support for aspects of SOAP Messaging with Attachments, and UDDI and WSDL support. The SOAP::Lite module is quite advanced in its support for various SOAP features and functionality, such as arrays.

The version used in this chapter is 0.47. It is interesting to mention that SOAP::Lite for Perl has gone a bit further in implementing some extensions to the base protocol such as object–by–reference with simple garbage collection and activation, as well as FTP client support.

For more information on the SOAP::Lite module for PERL see http://www.soaplite.com.

Synchronous SOAP Example Via HTTP

In this section we will look at an example of implementing web services with SOAP via HTTP. We will use a very simple Invoice Application that implements communication between various language platforms by making SOAP RPC calls.

All of the code in this example is downloadable from the Wrox web site, along with more detailed installation requirements and configuration steps.

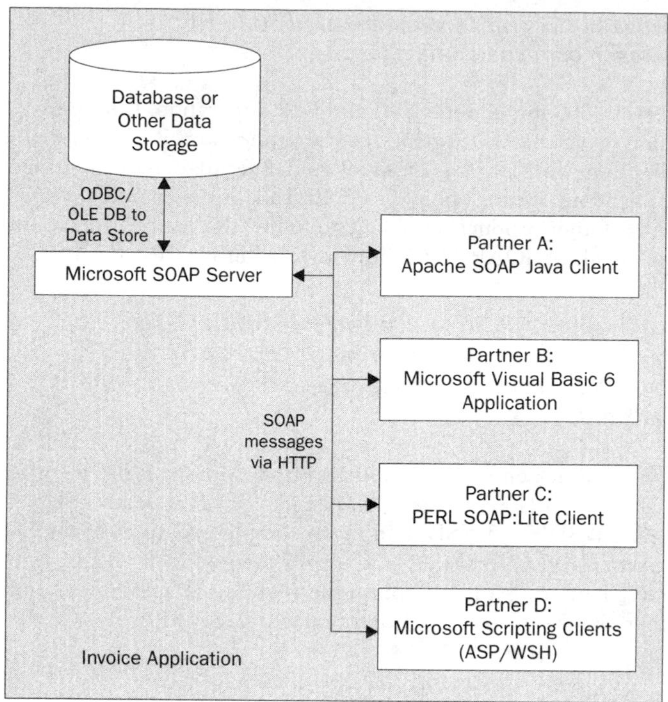

As you can see from the diagram, our simple Invoicing Application has four types of clients talking to one SOAP server. All communication occurs over HTTP, and the message exchange is two-way RPC type message exchange. The client submits a new invoice to the server with every call to its web service exposed via SOAP. Then, the server replies with a status message containing return values, confirming successful submittal or returning an error.

The SOAP messages being submitted in our example are simple, and are meant to illustrate the point of how you can easily interconnect different language platforms by using SOAP and WSDL. You can easily expand these examples with more attributes and more complex messages in order to meet your current technical challenges.

Server Application Implementation

We start our sample application with the generation of a very simple Visual Basic 6 COM object that has one operation (or method) that adds an invoice. When invoked, this component will in practice connect to any backend systems, sending the appropriate invoice information and invoke any other related components. In our example, it does not connect to a database or any other data source, and returns a reply, stating what information it has received and stamping it with the current date and time. Here's the component code, consisting of one class and one method. We chose to implement the server side of our example using Visual Basic, although we could have done it in any other language that has support for SOAP, such as Java or C++. In a real-life scenario, you would select the language that best suits the needs of your particular project.

```
'Visual Basic code
Public Function InvoiceAdd (ByVal InvoiceID As Integer, _
    ByVal CustomerID As Integer, ByVal InvoiceDate As Date, _
    ByVal Notes As String, ByVal DeliveryAddress As String, _
```

```
    ByVal PaymentTerms As String, ByVal Paid As String) As String

    InvoiceAdd = "Invoice with ID=" & CStr(InvoiceID) & _
        " was added for customer with ID=" & CStr(CustomerID) & _
        " at delivery address of " & DeliveryAddress & _
        " on date  " & CStr(InvoiceDate) & _
        ". Payment terms of " & PaymentTerms & " was recorded " &_
        "with a payment status of " & Paid & _
        ". Notes: " & Notes & _
        ". The data was processed at " & CStr(Now())

End Function
```

The **system requirements** at the server end are one of the following operating systems: Windows 2000 Server or Professional, NT 4 Server or Workstation, or Windows 9x/ME. In addition, you will need a Microsoft web server, such as IIS 4 or above, or Personal Web Server, depending on whether you are using a desktop or server OS. Furthermore, you will need the SOAP Toolkit Version 2 and MSXML 3.0 (Microsoft's Implementation of XML and typically included with the SOAP toolkit). You will also need Visual Basic 6 run-time (if you do not have Visual Basic on your machine), Windows Installer 1.1 or above, and Internet Explorer 5 or above.

We tested the code with Windows 2000 Server and IIS 5, MSXML 3, SOAP Toolkit 2 RC0 (Release Candidate 0). For more information on the system requirements for the SOAP Toolkit 2, please check the documentation included with it.

> *You can download the SOAP Toolkit 2 from* http://msdn.microsoft.com/xml/general/soap1and2.asp *– follow the links for SOAP Toolkit version 2. If you do not have the MSXML 3 (typically included with the SOAP Toolkit), you can download it from* http://msdn.microsoft.com/code/sample.asp?url=/msdn-files/027/000/541/msdncompositedoc.xml.
>
> *General information about XML and SOAP related tools and technologies could be obtained by going to the XML section of MSDN at* http://msdn.microsoft.com/xml/default.asp. *You can download the Visual Basic run-time from most download sites, such as* http://www.cnet.com, *just follow their download links and search for the Visual Basic run-time. You can obtain the links to the other required downloads at the SOAP Toolkit download page.*

Our component is created using Visual Basic 6, and compiled as an ActiveX DLL, having been tagged for unattended execution (an important setting for components that will not have visual elements, such as components running on the server). For ease of maintenance, we will add our component to COM+, however we won't make it run into transactions. In a production environment, you may need to do this. With our Web Service ready, the next step is to generate its WSDL file.

The **WSDL file** is generated by the Microsoft WSDL Generator utility provided with the SOAP Toolkit 2. This utility consists of a simple wizard interface that walks you through the steps of generating a WSDL file for any DLL or type library file provided. It also provides a **WSML** (**Web Services Meta Language**) file that is specific to the way Microsoft implements SOAP, designed to assist developers in mapping web services to COM objects easily. Actually, in this way, web services can be connected to COM objects with very few lines of code, as we will show. Finally, the WSDL Generator will automatically generate a web service listener, but more on this item later in this section.

Our sample application has a simple WSDL that requires clients to submit a few items when submitting an invoice: invoice ID, customer ID, invoice date, notes, delivery address, payment terms and paid status. You can see this under the message description of the following WSDL file (`InvoiceSubmit.wsdl`):

```
<?xml version="1.0" encoding="UTF-8"?>
<!-- Generated 04/04/01 by Microsoft SOAP Toolkit WSDL File Generator, Version
1.00.530.0 -->

<definitions name="InvoiceSubmit" targetNamespace="http://localhost/soap/wsdl/"
xmlns:wsdlns="http://localhost/soap/wsdl/"
xmlns:typens="http://localhost/soap/InvoiceSubmit.xsd"
xmlns:soap="http://schemas.xmlsoap.org/wsdl/soap/"
xmlns:xsd="http://www.w3.org/2001/XMLSchema"
xmlns:stk="http://schemas.microsoft.com/soap-toolkit/wsdl-extension"
xmlns="http://schemas.xmlsoap.org/wsdl/">

<types>
    <schema targetNamespace="http://localhost/soap/InvoiceSubmit.xsd"
xmlns="http://www.w3.org/2001/XMLSchema" xmlns:SOAP-
ENC="http://schemas.xmlsoap.org/soap/encoding/"
xmlns:wsdl="http://schemas.xmlsoap.org/wsdl/" elementFormDefault="qualified"/>
</types>

<message name="InvoiceSubmit.InvoiceAdd">
    <part name="InvoiceID" type="xsd:short"/>
    <part name="CustomerID" type="xsd:short"/>
    <part name="InvoiceDate" type="xsd:dateTime"/>
    <part name="Notes" type="xsd:string"/>
    <part name="DeliveryAddress" type="xsd:string"/>
    <part name="PaymentTerms" type="xsd:string"/>
    <part name="Paid" type="xsd:string"/>
</message>
<message name="InvoiceSubmit.InvoiceAddResponse">
    <part name="Result" type="xsd:string"/>
</message>
```

When you look at the description of the operation (`message` tag section in the previous code), you can see that our web service has one input, the `InvoiceAdd` operation that is being invoked, and an output message – the `InvoiceAddResponse`. The input operation defines seven input parameters and the output of the service has one output parameter, that being `Result`. The data types of those parameters are specified in the previous XML code, as well. The order of the parameters is provided next, within the `operation` tag section in the following code. It is interesting to note that within the `binding` section, you can see the `binding style` specified as being `rpc` and the transport being specified as `HTTP`. Next, the `operation` line points to the entry point in this service, that being the `http://localhost/soap/InvoiceSubmit.asp`.

```
<portType name="InvoiceSubmitSoapPort">
    <operation name="InvoiceAdd" parameterOrder="InvoiceID CustomerID InvoiceDate
Notes DeliveryAddress PaymentTerms Paid">
        <input message="wsdlns:InvoiceSubmit.InvoiceAdd"/>
        <output message="wsdlns:InvoiceSubmit.InvoiceAddResponse"/>
    </operation>
</portType>
```

```
<binding name="InvoiceSubmitSoapBinding" type="wsdlns:InvoiceSubmitSoapPort">
    <stk:binding preferredEncoding="UTF-8"/>
    <soap:binding style="rpc" transport="http://schemas.xmlsoap.org/soap/http"/>

<operation name="InvoiceAdd">
    <soap:operation soapAction="http://localhost/soap/InvoiceSubmit.asp"/>
    <input>
        <soap:body use="encoded"
namespace="http://localhost/soap/InvoiceSubmit.xsd"
encodingStyle="http://schemas.xmlsoap.org/soap/encoding/"/>
    </input>
    <output>
        <soap:body use="encoded"
namespace="http://localhost/soap/InvoiceSubmit.xsd"
encodingStyle="http://schemas.xmlsoap.org/soap/encoding/"/>
    </output>
</operation>

</binding>
```

In this last section of the WSDL, you can see that the service name is `InvoiceSubmit`. Finally, within the `service` section of the WSDL, we have the `location` attribute specifying the location of the service being an HTTP address to an ASP page. This is the actual endpoint or listener of our service.

```
<service name="InvoiceSubmit">
    <port name="InvoiceSubmitSoapPort" binding="wsdlns:InvoiceSubmitSoapBinding">
    <soap:address location="http://localhost/soap/InvoiceSubmit.ASP"/>
    </port>
</service>
</definitions>
```

At this point we were ready to look at the ASP that acts as the SOAP listener. The SOAP listener simply connects our COM object with the web server. This file is created automatically by the WSDL Generator utility used to create the WSDL file described earlier. When running the wizard, you can choose to create an **ASP SOAP listener** or an ISAPI (**Internet Server API or Application Programming Interface**) DLL file as the SOAP listener. The ASP version is slower, but it provides more flexibility, such as easy editing. The entire code for the ASP listener file is included in the code download from the Wrox web site, but the core section of this file is the following ASP/ VBScript code:

```
<!--ASP/ VBSript of the ASP listener -->
<%
Option Explicit
On Error Resume Next
Response.ContentType = "text/xml"

If IsEmpty(Application("InvoiceSubmitServer")) Then
    Application.Lock
    If IsEmpty(Application("InvoiceSubmitServer")) Then
        Dim SoapServer
        Dim WSDLFilePath
        Dim WSMLFilePath
        WSDLFilePath = Server.MapPath("InvoiceSubmit.wsdl")
```

```
        WSMLFilePath = Server.MapPath("InvoiceSubmit.wsml")
        Set SoapServer = Server.CreateObject("MSSOAP.SoapServer")
        'Activate tracing of SOAP messages
        soapserver.tracedirectory = "e:\temp\"
        If Err Then
            SendFault "Cannot create SoapServer object." & Err.Description
        End If
        SoapServer.Init WSDLFilePath, WSMLFilePath
        If Err Then
            SendFault "SoapServer.Init failed. " & Err.Description
        End If
        Set Application("InvoiceSubmitServer") = SoapServer
    End If
    Application.UnLock
End If

Set SoapServer = Application("InvoiceSubmitServer")
SoapServer.SoapInvoke Request, Response, ""
%>
```

As the request comes across the Web and HTTP, it comes as an HTTP request. This ASP file receives the request within the `Request` object. The SOAP server object is initialized with the location of the WSDL and WSML file, providing the SOAP server object with the information about this service. The SOAP server object is then cached within application scope. Next, the SOAP server is called by providing it with the `Request` object, which contains the incoming SOAP XML payload. The SOAP object takes care of contacting our COM object and retrieving the results back from the COM object. The SOAP object knows how to do this by using the WSDL, particularly the WSML file. The results from our COM object are returned back to us within the `Response` object that is being returned to the original client that called this service – the reply is a HTTP response with a content type of `text/xml`.

This implementation of the SOAP server was done using the high level API. This API requires much less code to expose our COM objects and it is very simple to do, as you saw from this example. For more flexibility in implementing the server (or the client) of your SOAP implementation you can use the low-level API. The low-level API extensively uses the `SoapSerializer` object and few others, allowing you that finer level of control in creating your SOAP messages. When using the low-level API you would not be able to use the WSDL and WSML files, which increases the amount of code that you would have to write.

Since the server-side coding for our Web Service is done, we just need to add some **configuration** settings, in order to be able to start receiving requests for our web service. First, create a virtual directory for your web service under your default web site in IIS or PWS. Then, allow anonymous access to its files, and allow script or execute access to the virtual folder without giving write access.

The final configuration step to do is to provide a `global.asa` file and place it within your virtual directory. This file is provided within the download from the Wrox site or you can create one yourself, by customizing the one provided with the SOAP Toolkit. Along with the `global.asa` file, you would need to place your ASP listener file, and your WSDL and WSML files within the same directory (all provided in the Wrox download). If you have not registered the SOAP server DLL file, you would want to do that by running `regsvr32 InvoiceSOAPServer.dll` at your command prompt.

Client Application Implementation

The client applications that were designed to communicate with our SOAP server were created in various programming environments: Java application, Visual Basic Application, PERL client, and ASP & WSH (Windows Scripting Host) clients. Although we did not do an example with JSP (Java Server Pages), you could easily modify our Java application code sample and create a JSP version yourself. Let's look at the various client implementations.

Client Application with Java At Partner A

The Java application client submits their invoices without the use of WSDL. The Apache SOAP implementation, as we have stated before, does not include support for WSDL. The IBM Web Services Toolkit does, but we decided not to use the IBM toolkit and see if we can get the Java client to work without the WSDL support. The result was good, and we created the following code:

```
//Java code
import java.util.*;
import java.net.*;
import org.w3c.dom.*;
import org.apache.soap.util.xml.*;
import org.apache.soap.*;
import org.apache.soap.encoding.*;
import org.apache.soap.encoding.soapenc.*;
import org.apache.soap.rpc.*;
import org.apache.soap.transport.http.SOAPHTTPConnection;

//This SOAP Client Using Java calls
//Microsoft SOAP server with Microsoft SOAP Toolkit 2
```

The **system requirements** for the Java implementation of Apache SOAP 2.1 are as follows:

- **Java SDK** 1.2 or above (we used the Java SDK 1.3)
- **Apache Xerces** 1.1.2 or higher, for XML capabilities (we used Xerces 1.3.0)
- **JavaBean Activation Framework** (**JAF**) – we used JAF 1.0.1
- **JavaMail**, but only if SMTP is used (we used JavaMail 1.2)

You can download the required components for Java at the Sun Microsystems web site http://java.sun.com/products/?frontpage-main. *The Apache components can be found at Apache.org and its XML project* http://xml.apache.org/. *You can download Xerces and Apache SOAP at that site. If you decide to use the IBM Web Services Toolkit, you can download that at* http://www.alphaworks.ibm.com/tech/webservicestoolkit.

```
//Java code (cont.)
public class InvoiceSubmitClientJava {
    public static void main(String[] args) throws Exception {

        //Define some variables
        Response oResp;

        //Set the parameters
```

```
Integer idInvoiceID = new Integer (1);
Integer idCustomerID = new Integer (1);
String strInvoiceDate = new String ("2001-01-25T00:00:00");
String strNotes =
    new String ("This is an invoice submitted via the Java client");
String strDeliveryAddress =
    new String ("1234 Java Street, Some City, AZ 00000");
String strPaymentTerms = new String ("Net 120 days");
String strPaymentReceived = new String ("N");
```

In the previous section of the code we set some variables and parameters. We hard-coded the values of the parameters, but in a real-life application you would probably dynamically generate them. Serializing `Date` objects in the current implementation version of the Apache SOAP is a bit of a challenge. The release FAQs mention that a more correct `DateSerializer` is planned for some of the future releases. For our purpose, we opted to send the date as a string in the format that our SOAP server expects. Please look in the latest Apache SOAP implementation for better alternatives. Creating our integer and string types is pretty straightforward.

The different SOAP implementations treat the `type` attribute a bit differently. Understanding this can help you avoid some of the most common errors when using SOAP to connect different systems. For example, it is interesting to note that the Apache SOAP implementation adds the `xsi:type` attribute to each one of the parameters as shown in the following XML code example:

```
<InvoiceID xsi:type="xsd:int">1</InvoiceID>
```

The Apache SOAP implementation requires this attribute in order to know what serializer to use and Microsoft's implementation does not provide this attribute within the SOAP message. Microsoft's implementation does however include this attribute within the WSDL file, but in our Java implementation we are not using the WSDL file as we had mentioned earlier. The SOAP specification states this attribute ought to be optional. We have a similar issue at the point of reading the reply message that was sent to us by the Microsoft SOAP server, as you will see in the following code section.

Next, we start building the call and implement the `SOAPMappingRegistry` to get around the `xsi:type` attribute issue:

```
//Java code (cont.)
// Build the call.
Call oCall = new Call();

//Once again, we have the xsi:type issue
//Need to define the deserializer for the return value sent back by
//MS SOAP Tookit 2, Beta 1 without xsi:type
SOAPMappingRegistry oSOAPMap = new SOAPMappingRegistry ();
StringDeserializer oStrDeserial = new StringDeserializer ();
oSOAPMap.mapTypes (Constants.NS_URI_SOAP_ENC,
    new QName ("", "Result"), null, null, oStrDeserial);
oCall.setSOAPMappingRegistry (oSOAPMap);
oCall.setEncodingStyleURI
    ("http://schemas.xmlsoap.org/soap/encoding/");
oCall.setTargetObjectURI("http://localhost/soap/InvoiceSubmit.xsd");

//Set the method name to call
oCall.setMethodName("InvoiceAdd");
```

You can see that the target object URI to the XSD is the same as the one provided in our WSDL file. The XML schema file that this URI points to does not have to exist, as is the case with many URIs. However, its location seems to have to point to the services directory in this particular release, just as its stated in the WSDL file. After this, we specify the method that we would like to invoke.

Next, we set the parameters by using the `Vector` class. We add an element for each parameter that is a parameter class in itself. The parameter class takes the following as arguments:

- *Parameter name* as a string – this has to match the name of the parameter being submitted. Remember that we are not using a WSDL file for the structure of our service, thus our client has no other way to submit the proper SOAP call but to submit the correct parameter names.
- *Type class* of the parameter. This is related to the encoding that is being used with each type, so see the point on encoding style below.
- *Value* for the parameter being submitted to the SOAP server. When the `type` class and encoding style are correct, Java knows how to map the value correctly. For some complex classes this may be a challenge, particularly in the beta implementations. As the vendors release their SOAP implementations to the market and start doing interoperability testing, this should be less of an issue.
- *Encoding style* URI. Apache SOAP, at its current version, supports SOAP v.1.1, Literal XML, and XML encoding.
    - *XML encoding* is only available when using Java 1.2.2 or above. It allows automatic marshaling and unmarshaling of arbitrary objects.
    - *SOAP encoding* provides support for encoding and decoding primitive types, strings, JavaBeans using reflection, and one-dimensional arrays of these types. For other types, such as `Date` classes, you would have to hand-write encoder and decoder and register it with the SOAP run-time.
    - *Literal XML encoding* provides the capability to send XML elements. The Apache SOAP comes with some examples of doing this.

```
    //Set the parameters
    Vector oParIn = new Vector();
    oParIn.addElement(new Parameter("InvoiceID", Integer.class,
     idInvoiceID, Constants.NS_URI_SOAP_ENC));
    oParIn.addElement(new Parameter("CustomerID", Integer.class,
     idCustomerID, Constants.NS_URI_SOAP_ENC));
    oParIn.addElement(new Parameter("InvoiceDate", String.class,
     strInvoiceDate, Constants.NS_URI_SOAP_ENC));
    oParIn.addElement(new Parameter("Notes", String.class,
     strNotes, Constants.NS_URI_SOAP_ENC));
    oParIn.addElement(new Parameter("DeliveryAddress", String.class,
     strDeliveryAddress, Constants.NS_URI_SOAP_ENC));
    oParIn.addElement(new Parameter("PaymentTerms", String.class,
     strPaymentTerms, Constants.NS_URI_SOAP_ENC));
    oParIn.addElement(new Parameter("Paid", String.class,
     strPaymentReceived, Constants.NS_URI_SOAP_ENC));
    oCall.setParams(oParIn);

  //Set the end point, service URL
    String strServiceURL = new String
       ("http://localhost/soap/InvoiceSubmit.asp");
```

```
        URL oURL = new URL(strServiceURL);

        //Invoke the service
        System.out.println("\n\nSOAP Client Using Java \n");
        System.out.println("Invoice Submitted to " +
            "Microsoft SOAP Server at ");
        System.out.println("\t" + strServiceURL + "\n");
        System.out.println("Reply from Microsoft SOAP Server:\n");
```

After setting up the various parameters, we set the URL for the endpoint that we are calling at the SOAP server and then we try to invoke the service. If we encounter an error we print the contents of the `<SOAP-ENV:Fault>` element; if not, we simply write out the reply that we received by the server:

```
        try {
            oResp = oCall.invoke(oURL, strServiceURL);
        }
        catch (SOAPException e) {
          //Show the Fault information, if there is an error
          System.out.println("The SOAPException is: (" +
                             e.getFaultCode () + "): " +
                             e.getMessage ());
          return;
        }
      //Retrieve the response value
      if (!oResp.generatedFault()) {
        Parameter oParResult = oResp.getReturnValue();
        Object value = oParResult.getValue();
        System.out.println (value);
      }
      else {
        //Or show the Fault information
        Fault oFault = oResp.getFault ();
        System.out.println ("The system fault is: ");
        System.out.println ("  Fault Code   = " + oFault.getFaultCode());
        System.out.println ("  Fault String = " + oFault.getFaultString());
      }
    }
}
```

If everything went well, we should receive the following output, when calling our Java client application.

```
E:\WINNT\System32\cmd.exe

E:\SOAPWebSvc\Web>javac InvoiceSubmitClientJava.java

E:\SOAPWebSvc\Web>java InvoiceSubmitClientJava


SOAP Client Using Java

Invoice Submitted to Microsoft SOAP Server at
        http://localhost/soap/InvoiceSubmit.asp

Reply from Microsoft SOAP Server:

Invoice with ID=1 was added for customer with ID=1 at delivery address of 1234 J
ava Street, Some City, AZ 00000 on date  2/15/2001. Payment terms of Net 120 day
s was recorded with a payment status of N. Notes: This is an invoice submitted v
ia the Java client. The data was processed at 2/26/2001 1:06:18 AM

E:\SOAPWebSvc\Web>
```

SOAP Client in Visual Basic At Partner B

In this example, we have a Visual Basic Application that was compiled to a single executable file. In terms of the **system configuration**, you may need to install the Visual Basic runtime in order to run this executable file if you don't have Visual Basic installed. Furthermore, you will need the SOAP Toolkit 2. The requirements for the SOAP Toolkit are the Visual Basic 6 run-time, Internet Explorer 5 or above, MS XML 3, and Windows Installer 1.1 or above.

You can find MS SOAP Toolkit from http://msdn.microsoft.com/soap/default.asp *– follow the SOAP Toolkit 2 links. You can obtain the links to the other required downloads at the SOAP Toolkit download page. You can download the Visual Basic run-time from most download sites, such as* http://www.cnet.com, *just follow their download links and search for the Visual Basic 6 run-time.*

Within this application, we have a simple entry form where we submit the invoice being entered to a SOAP server. The code that submits the service is quite simple, as we are using the high level API of the Microsoft SOAP Toolkit 2 that takes advantage of the WSDL. We have a single function that gets called when the user clicks the "Submit Invoice to Microsoft SOAP Server" button. The following is from our Visual Basic code:

```
'Visual Basic code
Private Sub btnSubmit_Click()

    'In a case of an error go to the error handler
    On Error GoTo ErrorHandler

    'Create the SoapClient object
    Dim SoapClient As SoapClient
    Set SoapClient = New SoapClient
```

We create a `SoapClient` object and we initiate it by pointing it to the location of the WSDL file and the service name being called. Next, we initiate the `InvoiceAdd` method by passing it the needed parameters.

```
    'Visual Basic code (cont.)

    'Initiate the SoapClient with the correct WSDL file
    'and tell it the service name
    SoapClient.mssoapinit txtWSDLFile.Text, "InvoiceSubmit"

    'Initiate the particular method by passing it the needed parameters
    'Submit text box values and place the result in the text box
    txtResult.Text = CStr(SoapClient.InvoiceAdd(txtInvoiceID, _
        txtCustomerID, CDate(txtInvoiceDate), txtNotes, _
        txtDeliveryAddress, txtPaymentTerms, txtPaymentReceived))

    'Cleanup
    Set SoapClient = Nothing

    Exit Sub
```

At the end we place the result into the textbox for the display of the confirmation that tells the user that their application had submitted the invoice successfully. In the case where we receive an error, we execute the error capturing code and display the information from the `Fault` element in the SOAP reply message.

```
'Visual Basic code (cont.)
ErrorHandler:
    'Show the details of the fault in a case of an error via a pop up box
    MsgBox "The faultstring is: " & SoapClient.faultstring & _
      Chr(13) & " and the faultcode is: " & SoapClient.faultcode & _
      Chr(13) & ", the details of the Fault is: " & _
      SoapClient.detail, vbExclamation

End Sub
```

This client was very easy to implement due to the use of the high level API and the WSDL file. If our invoice submittal was successful, we should get the following screen.

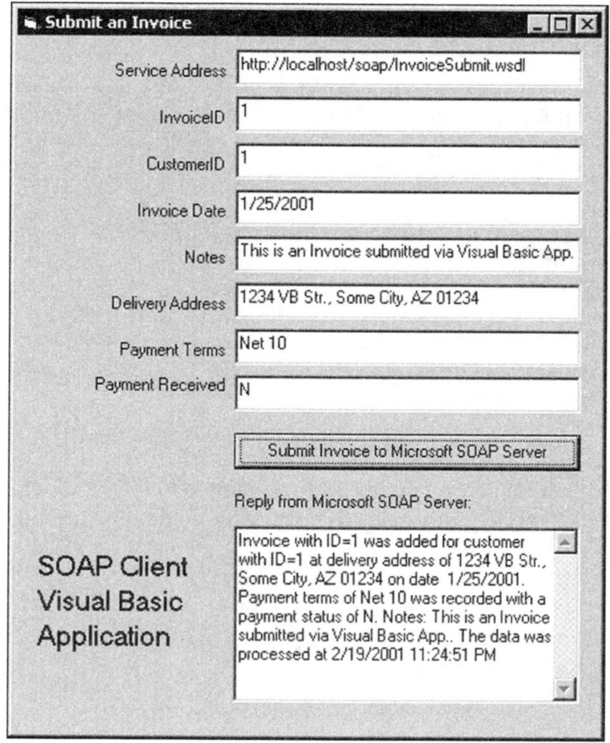

Perl Client At Partner C

In our Perl implementation, we used the SOAP::Lite module for PERL version 0.47. Our **system configuration** used ActivePERL 5.6 by ActiveState. Other PERL modules that we had installed were MIME::Lite 2.106, XML–Parser 2.30, URI 1.10, and MIME–Base64 2.11. Before running any PERL scripts in your virtual directory under IIS, you must mark that directory to allow running executables. You can install SOAP::Lite by running the command perl Makefile.PL within the directory where you have SOAP::Lite (for more information on installation and the requirements of the SOAP::Lite package, please view the readme file and other support information included with the SOAP::Lite download).

> *You can download ActivePERL from ActiveState's web site at* http://www.activestate.com. *For SOAP::Lite you can go to* http://www.soaplite.com, *where you can follow the links for the other necessary components that SOAP::Lite requires.*

Since PERL supports WSDL, the client code for PERL is fairly short. We specify that we would like to use the SOAP::Lite module. Then, if using this script within a web page, we print a basic HTTP header for our HTTP response that will carry back the processed SOAP response. What follows is the beginning of our PERL code.

```
# PERL code
use SOAP::Lite;

# HTTP headers may be needed depending on environment
print "HTTP/1.0 201 Ok \n";
print "Content-type:text/html\n\n";

# Set parametar variables
$idInvoiceID = "1";
$idCustomerID = "3";
. . .
$dtInvoiceDate = "2001-02-08T00:00:00";
$strNotes = "This is an invoice submitted via the PERL client";
$strDeliveryAddress = "1234 PERL Street, Some City, AZ 00000";
$strPaymentTerms = "Net 15 days";
$strPaymentReceived = "N";
```

Next, we set a few variables with values that will be submitted to our SOAP server. PERL seems to be able to read the WSDL file properly and define `xsi:type` attributes properly without us having to specify the type of each parameter manually. You can see this in the following snippet of the call sent by PERL. Notice the highlighted section that shows the various attributes and their types. This is the XML code of the SOAP message sent by our PERL client.

```
<?xml version="1.0" encoding="UTF-8"?>
<SOAP-ENV:Envelope xmlns:SOAP-ENC="http://schemas.xmlsoap.org/soap/encoding/"
SOAP-ENV:encodingStyle="http://schemas.xmlsoap.org/soap/encoding/"
xmlns:xsi="http://www.w3.org/1999/XMLSchema-instance" xmlns:SOAP-
ENV="http://schemas.xmlsoap.org/soap/envelope/"
xmlns:xsd="http://www.w3.org/1999/XMLSchema">
   <SOAP-ENV:Body>
      <namesp1:InvoiceAdd
            xmlns:namesp1="http://localhost/soap/InvoiceSubmit.xsd">
         <InvoiceID xsi:type="xsd:short">1</InvoiceID>
         <CustomerID xsi:type="xsd:short">3</CustomerID>
         <InvoiceDate xsi:type="xsd:dateTime">
            2001-02-08T00:00:00
         </InvoiceDate>
         <Notes xsi:type="xsd:string">
            This is an invoice submitted via the PERL client
         </Notes>
         <DeliveryAddress xsi:type="xsd:string">
            1234 PERL Street, Some City, AZ 00000
         </DeliveryAddress>
         <PaymentTerms xsi:type="xsd:string">Net 15 days</PaymentTerms>
         <Paid xsi:type="xsd:string">N</Paid>
      </namesp1:InvoiceAdd>
   </SOAP-ENV:Body>
</SOAP-ENV:Envelope>
```

Now, going back to our PERL code. We set the WSDL location and the actual service or endpoint location. After printing some introductory notes to the screen, we call the service. Here's the second part of our PERL code:

```
# PERL code (cont.)
$strWSDL = "http://localhost/SOAP/InvoiceSubmit.wsdl";
$strEndPoint = "http://localhost/SOAP/InvoiceSubmit.asp";

# Print the introductory text
print "<HTML>";
print "<HEAD><TITLE>SOAP Client Using PERL";
print "</TITLE></HEAD><BODY><H3>SOAP Client Using PERL</H3>";
print "<H4>Invoice Submitted to Microsoft SOAP Server.<BR><BR>";
print "Reply from Microsoft SOAP Server:</H4>";

# Call the Microsoft SOAP server and print the result
print SOAP::Lite
   -> service($strWSDL)
   -> proxy($strEndPoint)
   -> InvoiceAdd($idInvoiceID, $idCustomerID, $dtInvoiceDate, $strNotes,
       $strDeliveryAddress, $strPaymentTerms, $strPaymentReceived);

print "</BODY></HTML>  ";
```

We call the Microsoft SOAP services by invoking the SOAP::Lite module and providing it with the services information in the form of the WSDL file – within the proxy we provide the location of the service endpoint itself. Next, we call the method that we like to invoke along with the parameters that we like to pass to it. If everything worked well, you should get the following in your browser.

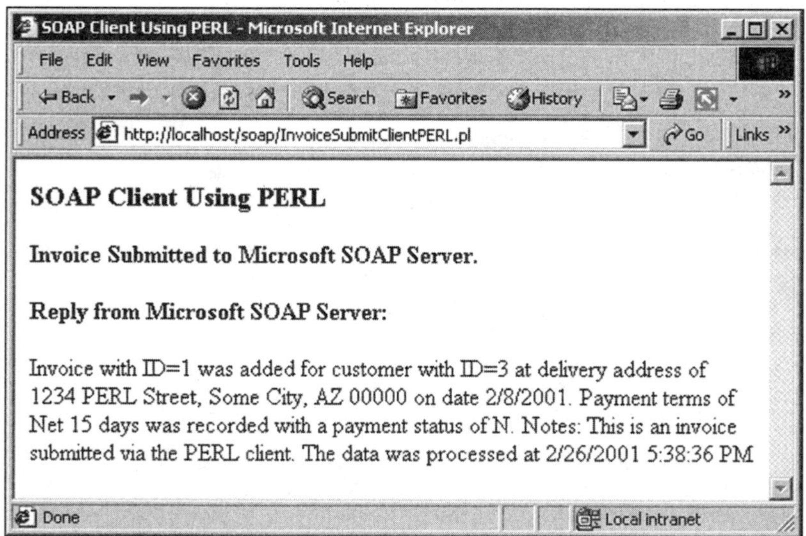

ASP/ WSH Scripting Clients At Partner D

The ASP and **WSH** (**Windows Scripting Host**) clients are very similar in the way they're implemented. They both use VBScript as their language. However, the **system configuration** differs a little bit, particularly in the need for a web server. ASP requires that you have a web server; WSH does not.

WSH is a tool that allows you to run VBScript or JScript automation scripts. WSH can be downloaded for Microsoft Windows 95 and Windows NT, and it comes as part of Windows 2000/ME/98. WSH is primarily used for automating common tasks such as logon scripts.

In our implementation, we used ASP 3.0 and WSH 2.0 included with Windows 2000. Older versions of ASP are included with all web servers and these examples should work fine with them, as long as you upgrade to the latest Windows Scripting version (links provided below). In terms of the web servers, you would need to use IIS for Windows NT 4 and 2000 Server or Personal Web Server for the desktop version of the operating system.

We will cover only the core section of the ASP implementation here. However, within the code that you can download from the Wrox web site, you are able to download the Windows Scripting Host version of the SOAP client.

> *You can download versions for the Windows Scripting Host from Microsoft at* http://msdn.microsoft.com/scripting/windowshost/download/default.htm.
>
> *If you are running older versions of Windows (other than Windows 2000) you can get the latest scripting engine at* http://www.microsoft.com/msdownload/vbscript/scripting.asp. *You should be able to run the examples provided here with Microsoft PWS if you have Windows 9x, NT Workstation, or Windows 2000 Professional.*

```
'ASP/VBScript code
'Declare variables
Dim SoapClient, strWSDL, strInvoiceID, strCustomerID, strInvoiceDate
Dim strNotes, strDeliveryAddress, strPaymentTerms, strPaymentReceived

'Set the parameters
strInvoiceID = "1"
strCustomerID = "3"
strInvoiceDate = "1/20/2001"
strNotes = _
    "This is an invoice submitted via the Active Server Pages (ASP) client"
strDeliveryAddress = "1234 Active Server Pages, Some City, AZ 00000"
strPaymentTerms = "Net 90 days"
strPaymentReceived = "N"
```

In the code above, we declare our variables and set their values. Next, in the code that follows, we set the location of the WSDL file. As a temporary fix for the current release of the software, we set it to its physical location. In newer releases, you can try to use the HTTP path instead (commented line below the physical path). Also, don't forget to modify these lines to reflect the paths found on the actual machine that you are using.

Next, we instantiate the `SoapClient` object and initiate it with the WSDL location, the name of the service and port. This is very much like our Visual Basic implementation. Finally, we invoke our method to submit the new invoice. Notice that the variables in VBScript are all variants (meaning undefined type in general) and they have a specific sub-type of integer or string, etc. In the conversion we simply do this variant to a variant with sub-type conversion.

```
'ASP/VBScript code (cont.)
'Temporary fix for the current versions of the SOAP Toolkit by Microsoft
'For later releases, change this path to match the location of your files
strWSDL = "E:\SOAPWebSvc\Web\InvoiceSubmit.wsdl"
```

```
'strWSDL = "http://localhost/SOAP/InvoiceSubmit.wsdl"

'Initiate the SoapClient object with the correct WSDL file and service name
Set SoapClient = Server.CreateObject("MSSOAP.SoapClient")
SoapClient.mssoapinit strWSDL, "InvoiceSubmit"

'Initiate the particular method by passing it the needed parameters
Response.Write CStr(SoapClient.InvoiceAdd(CInt(strInvoiceID), _
    CInt(strCustomerID), CDate(strInvoiceDate), strNotes, _
    strDeliveryAddress, strPaymentTerms, strPaymentReceived))

'Cleanup
Set SoapClient = Nothing
```

If everything goes well you will get the following message in your browser:

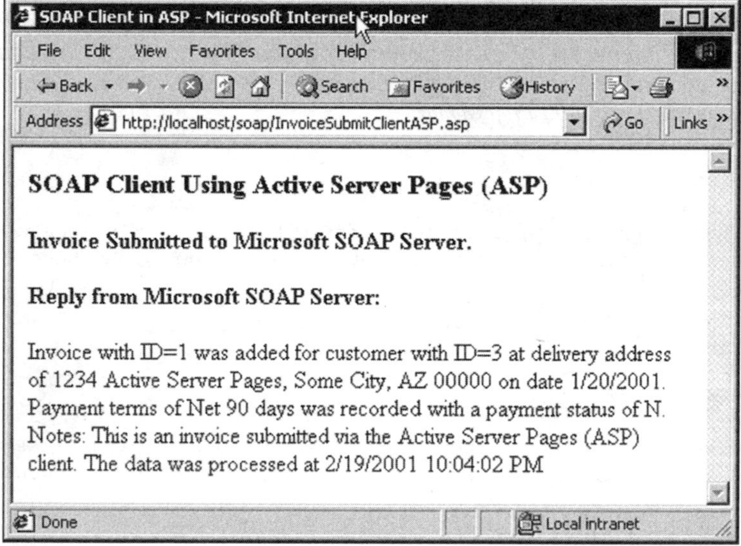

Using this service, ASP, just like our Visual Basic application and the WSH client, creates the following SOAP message (in XML) as the request.

```
<?xml version="1.0" encoding="UTF-8" standalone="no"?>
<SOAP-ENV:Envelope SOAP-
ENV:encodingStyle="http://schemas.xmlsoap.org/soap/encoding/" xmlns:SOAP-
ENV="http://schemas.xmlsoap.org/soap/envelope/">
   <SOAP-ENV:Body>
      <m:InvoiceAdd xmlns:m="http://localhost/soap/InvoiceSubmit.xsd">
         <InvoiceID>1</InvoiceID>
         <CustomerID>3</CustomerID>
         <InvoiceDate>2001-01-20T00:00:00</InvoiceDate>
         <Notes>
           This is an invoice submitted via the Active Server Pages (ASP)
           client
```

```
        </Notes>
         <DeliveryAddress>
            1234 Active Server Pages, Some City, AZ 00000
         </DeliveryAddress>
         <PaymentTerms>Net 90 days</PaymentTerms>
         <Paid>N</Paid>
      </m:InvoiceAdd>
   </SOAP-ENV:Body>
</SOAP-ENV:Envelope>
```

As you can see, the higher-level API of the current version of the Microsoft SOAP toolkit does not generate the `xsi:type` attribute for each of its parameter elements. You could generate these attributes in a more manual process if you were to use the lower-level API provided with the SOAP Toolkit.

Asynchronous SOAP Example Via SMTP

Earlier in this chapter we covered the use of asynchronous SOAP in communications between machines. We saw that the WSDL specification provides examples of defining these types of services. Furthermore, we looked briefly over the SOAP extension specification, SOAP Messages with Attachments.

At the time of writing, the vendors are only starting their efforts of supporting SMTP. Even where they have, they are relying on supporting technologies to make this happen and then simply adding SOAP to this equation. There is little automated implementation, such as the high level API of the Microsoft SOAP Toolkit 2 for HTTP and SOAP, or the equivalent SOAP::Lite for PERL or Apache/IBM SOAP classes. In our examples, we will do just that: use the current SOAP functionality and utilize the current SMTP support that the particular vendors have. For a Microsoft implementation, that means utilizing the current functionality of **CDO** (**Collaboration Date Objects**) or **CDONTS** (**Collaboration Data Objects for NT Services**, which is a component for handling basic e-mail operations and is part of IIS both under Windows NT 4 and Windows 2000). In terms of our Java implementation, it would mean using the JavaMail 1.2 class library, which contains providers for SMTP, **POP3** (**Post Office Protocol 3**), and **IMAP** (**Internet Message Access Protocol**).

The e-mail server that we used in this example was Microsoft Exchange Server 2000. It acted as both the SMTP server to which we submitted our SOAP e-mail messages, as well as the POP3 server from which we had retrieved the SOAP e-mail messages. However, there is no reason why you could not use any other e-mail server that supports SMTP and POP3.

If you follow the "What's Next – XML Protocol?" section further in this chapter you will discover some more information as to where the industry is heading in terms of better SMTP support, built in a similar fashion as HTTP is today.

So, let's look at our updated SOAP implementation, shown on the diagram below. We have an added need to be able to connect our SOAP server that is receiving invoices from our partners, to our Fulfillment Server. Our Invoice Server will act as a client in this interaction and it has Microsoft SOAP Toolkit v2 on it. Our Fulfillment Server has Apache/IBM Java SOAP Toolkit 2.1 and it will act as the server in this case. The code for these upcoming samples is available from the Wrox web site.

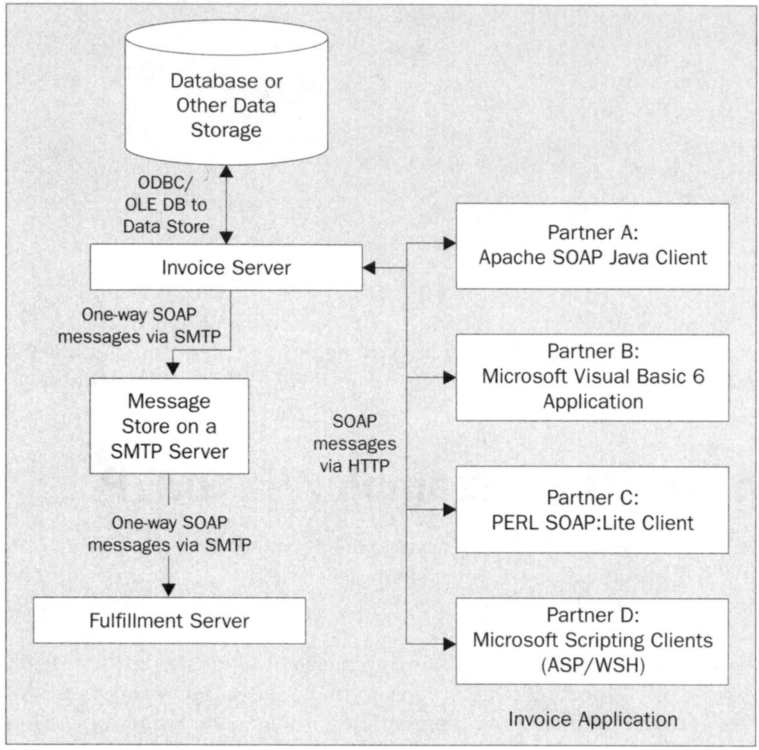

Invoice Server – Microsoft SOAP Client Via SMTP

After an invoice is submitted to our Invoice Server, the client is redirected to a fulfillment web page (`InvoiceFulfillSMTPCli.asp`). From this web page, a request would be sent to our Fulfillment Department to follow through with the fulfillment of the order. The example here is to work with the partners that have web-based invoicing systems. In order to make this functionality work for any clients, we would simply have to transfer our code into a COM object that is running on our server and have our SOAP server COM object that is handling the receipt of invoices, call this fulfillment message forwarding component.

Our Fulfillment Server can either retrieve this data from a database or other date store, or it can use the existing SOAP message and forward the needed data to the Fulfillment Server. In our situation we opted to read the SOAP message from our file system, but in a real-life scenario you may like to dynamically generate the SOAP message by using data provided from a database for example. Most SOAP implementations provide objects that would allow you to create SOAP messages dynamically. In the Microsoft tools, you would use the `SoapSerializer` object to do this.

Keep in mind that, in absence of better SMTP transport support within the existing tools, we are utilizing our current technologies to accomplish most of what is needed for transferring SOAP messages over SMTP as described in the SOAP 1.1, WSDL 1.0, and SOAP Messages with Attachment specifications. There are some differences, for example, in the header specifications of the mail messages that we did not follow, but as long as the server-side does not expect any of that information, this approach would work fine. As the tools and specifications get updated, you can choose to modify this code appropriately.

For the **system configuration** in this example, you need to have the CDONTS library that is provided with IIS 4 or above. We used IIS 5 under Windows 2000 Server. In order to get CDONTS to actually send a message out to a SMTP server (instead of keeping it on your file system), you would have to configure your IIS SMTP service. Setting up the smart-host setting to the name of your destination SMTP server (in our case that was the Exchange 2000 server) is the key configuration item. You may have to set up some of the IIS SMTP service permission settings, depending on the permission settings set on the destination SMTP server. For more tips on properly configuring the IIS SMTP service that works with IIS, you can follow the help provided with the SMTP service in Windows 2000 Server or within the option pack for Windows NT 4 Server.

In our SOAP client code, we start by retrieving the SOAP message. In our case this is a XML file found in the file system.

```
<!-- ASP/VBScript code -->
<%
'Initiate objects
Option Explicit
Dim oReader, oMail, strSOAPXMLurl, strMsgSubject, strSOAPBINurl, intChoice
Set oReader = Server.CreateObject ("MSSOAP.SoapReader")
Set oMail = Server.CreateObject ("CDONTS.NewMail")
'Set these file paths to your own locations
strSOAPXMLurl =  "E:\SOAPWebSvc\Web\InvoiceFulfillSample.xml"
    'SOAP XML Message
strSOAPBINurl = "E:\SOAPWebSvc\Web\InvoiceFulfillBinarySample.gif"
    'Binary attachment
```

As you can see in the code above, we have created a `NewMail` object using the CDONTS library. Sending an e-mail message with CDONTS is very simple, as you will see in our code that follows soon. We utilize the `SoapReader` object to dynamically create a SOAP message by reading its content from a XML file found in our file system.

```
'ASP/VBScript code (cont.)
oReader.load strSOAPXMLurl
```

Next, we specify the typical message attributes, such as the `From`, `To`, and `Subject`. Make sure you adjust the various parameters, such as the `To` attribute to match what is needed in your particular environment. We set the format of the body of the e-mail message to be text instead of html, and we also set the mail format to be MIME instead of plain text, in order to be able to add attachments to our e-mail.

```
'ASP/VBScript code (cont.)
'Set the From and To properties
oMail.From = "InvoiceSrv@ToyCo.com"
'Select a To property that is appropriate for your system configuration
oMail.To = "wrox@saturn2000.com"

oMail.BodyFormat = 1 '0-HTML, 1-Text
'When SOAP Message in Body use 1, When SOAP as Attachment use 1
'oMail.MailFormat = 1 '0-MIME format, 1-Uninterrupted plain text
oMail.MailFormat = 0 '0-MIME format, 1-Uninterrupted plain text
```

We now face a choice of how we would like to package the SOAP message inside a SMTP mail message. One way would be to simply include it as text within the body of the mail message; the other would be to include it as an XML attachment. Both approaches work well; the approach that you use will depend on your needs and preferences. The server can read both successfully. For example, if you would like to filter SOAP messages at your mail server by the type of attachment they include, then you may like to send the SOAP message as an attachment and have your mail server forward only messages with XML attachments and not allow any other attachments. Of course, you will want to filter all of those "I Love You" message attachments!

You can simply select one of these approaches of sending the SOAP message by modifying the `intChoice` variable. The reason that we have four choices instead of two is that we also have an option of including an additional binary attachment. In our code samples that you can download from the Wrox web site we use an image as a binary attachment. Your attachments could be fax images, signed contracts, or any other type of documentation that could be required with your SOAP message.

> *When submitting the SOAP messages with binary attachments, our headers and `href` attributes do not link the parts properly. This is because we are not using tools that have full support for the SOAP Messages with Attachments specifications. You can create your own tools in some of the lower-level languages or wait a little to get these tools from your favorite vendor.*

```
'ASP/VBScript code (cont.)
'***** A FEW DIFFERENT WAYS OF ATTACHING THE SOAP XML MESSAGE *****
'simply change the following variable (1 to 4 valid only) to try other
'ways of sending the SOAP XML payload
intChoice = 3

Select Case intChoice
Case 1
   '1st Version with XML as text in body
   strMsgSubject = "New Invoice Submitted on " & Now() & _
      " (XML as Text in Body)"
   oMail.Subject = strMsgSubject
   oMail.Body = oReader.DOM.xml 'SOAP Message in body as text
Case 2
   '2nd Version with XML as single attachment
   strMsgSubject = "New Invoice Submitted on " & Now() & _
      " (XML as Single Attachment)"
   oMail.Subject = strMsgSubject
   oMail.attachFile strSOAPXMLurl 'SOAP Message as first attachment
Case 3
   '3rd Version with XML as text in body with additional binary attachment
   strMsgSubject = "New Invoice Submitted on " & Now() & _
      " (XML as Text in Body w/ Binary Attachment)"
   oMail.Subject = strMsgSubject
   oMail.Body = oReader.DOM.xml 'SOAP Message in body as text
   oMail.attachFile strSOAPBINurl
      'Additional binary attachment (MIME Encoded)
Case 4
   '4th Version with XML as first attachment with additional binary attachment
   strMsgSubject = "New Invoice Submitted on " & Now() & _
      " (XML as First Attachment w/ Binary Attachment)"
   oMail.Subject = strMsgSubject
   oMail.attachFile strSOAPXMLurl 'SOAP Message as first attachment
   oMail.attachFile strSOAPBINurl
      'Additional binary attachment (MIME Encoded)
End Select
```

Finally, we are ready to send our message and write out a confirmation on the screen.

```
'ASP/VBScript code (cont.)
'Send SOAP message and print confirmation
oMail.Send
Response.Write "<H3>Your order was forwarded to our " & _
    "Fulfillment Department for " & _
    "further processing. <BR>Thank you.<BR></H3><SMALL>" & _
    "For system use ONLY: <BR>" & _
    "<B>" & strMsgSubject & "</B><BR><BR>" & _
    Server.HTMLEncode (oReader.DOM.xml) & "</SMALL>"

Set oMail = Nothing
Set oReader = Nothing
```

This code has submitted an e-mail message from our Invoice Server to the Fulfillment Server, where we have a Java application processing the incoming messages. If everything works well, you should get the following screen (when selecting to send the SOAP XML payload in the body of the message, along with the binary attachment).

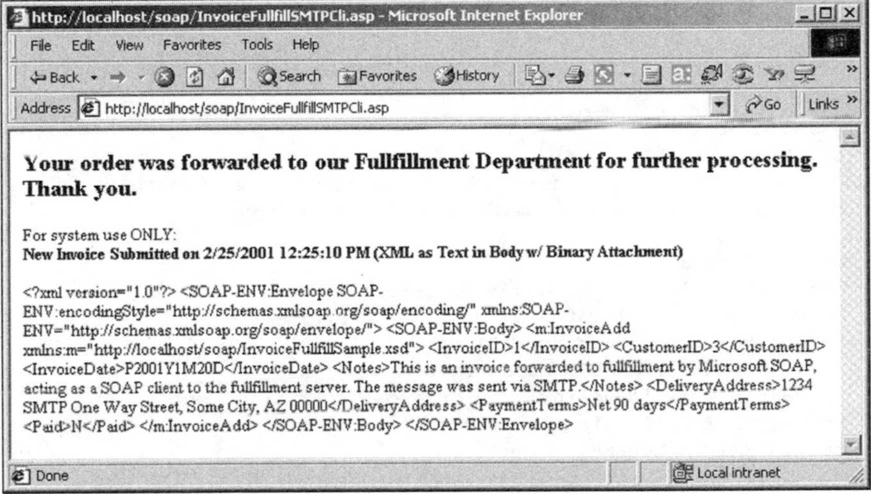

If you were wondering to see what our e-mail transmission looked like, here's part of the actual e-mail text where you can see how the different parts fit together. This e-mail sample is from the situation where we are sending the SOAP message in the body of the e-mail message and we are attaching a binary file to the message, as well. You can see copies of any of the various types of e-mail transmissions from the code download from Wrox.

```
Received: from ToyCo.com ([192.168.1.250]) by saturn2000.saturn2000.com with
Microsoft SMTPSVC(5.0.2195.1600);
    Sun, 25 Feb 2001 12:23:56 -0500
Received: from mail pickup service by ToyCo.com with Microsoft SMTPSVC;
    Sun, 25 Feb 2001 12:25:10 -0500
From: <InvoiceSrv@ToyCo.com>
To: <wrox@saturn2000.com>
Subject: New Invoice Submitted on 2/25/2001 12:25:10 PM (XML as Text in Body w/
Binary Attachment)
```

```
Date: Sun, 25 Feb 2001 12:25:10 -0500
MIME-Version: 1.0
Content-Type: multipart/mixed;   boundary="----
=_NextPart_000_000F_01C09F25.FEF9E450"
X-MimeOLE: Produced By Microsoft MimeOLE V5.50.4133.2400
Message-ID: <InvoiceSrvretKACwc3KeGAK00000017@ToyCo.com>
X-OriginalArrivalTime: 25 Feb 2001 17:25:10.0877 (UTC)
FILETIME=[E7EE70D0:01C09F4F]
Return-Path: InvoiceSrv@ToyCo.com
```

The above part contains the various e-mail message headers. Note that this message is MIME encoded and it has the content type of multipart/mixed. You can also see that these same content type headers are not exactly the same as the SOAP Messages with Attachment specification, as we have explained earlier. Next, you will see the first MIME part, that of the XML being attached to this message. This part is not Base64 encoded (a common way of encoding e-mail content when using MIME). However, quotation marks are being escaped, because of the content transfer encoding of `quoted-printable`:

```
This is a multi-part message in MIME format.

------=_NextPart_000_000F_01C09F25.FEF9E450
Content-Type: text/plain;
   charset="iso-8859-1"
Content-Transfer-Encoding: quoted-printable

<?xml version=3D"1.0"?>
<SOAP-ENV:Envelope =
SOAP-ENV:encodingStyle=3D"http://schemas.xmlsoap.org/soap/encoding/" =
xmlns:SOAP-ENV=3D"http://schemas.xmlsoap.org/soap/envelope/">
   <SOAP-ENV:Body>
      <m:InvoiceAdd =
xmlns:m=3D"http://localhost/soap/InvoiceFullfillSample.xsd">
         <InvoiceID>1</InvoiceID>
         <CustomerID>3</CustomerID>
         <InvoiceDate>P2001Y1M20D</InvoiceDate>
         <Notes>This is an invoice forwarded to fulfillment by Microsoft =
SOAP, acting as a SOAP client to the fulfillment server. The message =
was sent via SMTP.</Notes>
         <DeliveryAddress>1234 SMTP One Way Street, Some City, AZ =
00000</DeliveryAddress>
         <PaymentTerms>Net 90 days</PaymentTerms>
         <Paid>N</Paid>
      </m:InvoiceAdd>
   </SOAP-ENV:Body>
</SOAP-ENV:Envelope>
```

The next attachment is the binary attachment that we are including with this message. This section is Base64 encoded and has a content type of `image/gif`.

```
------=_NextPart_000_000F_01C09F25.FEF9E450
Content-Type: image/gif;
   name="InvoiceFullfillBinarySample.gif"
Content-Transfer-Encoding: base64
Content-Disposition: attachment;
```

```
    filename="InvoiceFullfillBinarySample.gif"
```



```
R0lGODlhnAIPAfcAAAAAAAAAMwAAZgAAmQAAzAAA/wAzAAAzMwAzZgAzmQAzzAAz/wBmAABmMwBm
ZgBmmQBmzABm/wCZAACZMwCZZgCZmQCZzACZ/wDMAADMMwDMZgDMmQDMzADM/wD/AAD/MwD/ZgD/
mQD/zAD//zMAADMAMzMAZjMAmTMAzDMA/zMzADMzMzMzZjMzmTMzzDMz/zNmADNmMzNmZjNmmTNm
zDNm/zOZADOZMzOZZjOZmTOZzDOZ/zPMADPMMzPMZjPMmTPMzDPM/zP/ADP/MzP/ZjP/mTP/zDP/
. . .
```


With this you should have a pretty good idea of how our client-side of the SOAP message exchange is working. Next, we'll look at our server-side implementation of SOAP with SMTP.

For more information on programming with CDONTS or CDO, please see the Wrox Press book Professional CDO Programming (ISBN 1-861002-06-8).

Fulfillment Server – Apache/IBM Java Server Via SMTP

Our Fulfillment Server is running a Java application that connects to our e-mail server and retrieves the e-mail messages that contain SOAP messages. We are using Java 2 SDK, Standard Edition v.1.3.0 with JavaMail 1.2. The current version of JavaMail includes Sun Microsystems' implementation of POP3 already integrated, unlike some of the previous editions, where the library had to be downloaded separately. You would also need the JAF. For ways to download these components please see the previous section on synchronous communication with SOAP over HTTP and the Apache/IBM Java client implementation.

```
//Java code
import java.util.*;
import java.io.*;
import javax.mail.*;
import javax.mail.internet.*;
import javax.activation.*;

//This is an illustration of Java SOAP application
//that uses JavaMail 1.2 to retrieve SOAP messages
//from a POP3 mail server via SMTP
```

In our simple implementation, we have one class with a few methods within. Our main method starts by setting some connection parameters to the SMTP server that supports POP3 for message retrieval. Make sure that you modify those to the appropriate ones within your environment.

```
//Java code (cont.)
public class InvoiceFulfillSMTPSrv {

    public static void main(String argv[]) {

        //Set the connection information for your environment
        String strProtocol = "pop3";
        String strSMTPHost = "saturn2000.saturn2000.com";
        String strUserName = "wrox";
        String strUserPwd = "1234";
        String strMailBoxDefault = "INBOX";
```

```
try {
   //Set an unshared session instance
   //and retrieve the store for this transport protocol
   //In our case the transport protocol is SMTP and
   //the store protocol is POP3
   Properties oProps = System.getProperties();
   Session oSession = Session.getInstance(oProps, null);
   Store oStore = oSession.getStore(strProtocol);
   oStore.connect(strSMTPHost, -1, strUserName, strUserPwd);
```

The typical way of accessing mail with JavaMail starts by opening a mail session and then opening the store for our user. This places us at the root of the mail folder hierarchy. Next, we retrieve a reference to the default folder, which is the one that contains all of the typical folders such as Inbox and Outbox.

```
   //Java code (cont.)
   //First open the user folder and then
   //open the default folder within (typically "Inbox")
   Folder oFolder = oStore.getDefaultFolder();
   if (oFolder == null) {
      System.out.println("No default folder");
      System.exit(1);
   }
   oFolder = oFolder.getFolder(strMailBoxDefault);
   if (oFolder == null) {
      System.out.println("Invalid " + strMailBoxDefault +
         " folder");
      System.exit(1);
   }
   //Attempt read/write open first and then try read only
   try {
      oFolder.open(Folder.READ_WRITE);
   }
   catch (MessagingException oMsgExcept) {
      oFolder.open(Folder.READ_ONLY);
      }
   //What's the total number of messages vs. read messages
   int totalMessages = oFolder.getMessageCount();
   if (totalMessages == 0) {
      System.out.println("No SOAP Messages in Mailbox. " +
         "Try Later.");
      oFolder.close(false);
      oStore.close();
      System.exit(1);
   }
   int newMessages = oFolder.getNewMessageCount();
   System.out.print("Total SOAP Messages = " +
      totalMessages + ", ");
   System.out.println("New SOAP Messages = " + newMessages);
```

Once we open the `Inbox` folder in our mailbox, we can display information about this folder, such as how many new messages we have and how many total messages there are in our mailbox. In deciding whether to attempt to process any further messages, we can base our decision on this information, for example:

```
//Java code (cont.)
  //Get the messages collection and print their content
   Message[] arMsg = oFolder.getMessages();
   for (int iCount = 0; iCount < arMsg.length; iCount++) {
        System.out.print("\n" +
           "***** Message Number: " + (iCount + 1));
        mShowPart(arMsg[iCount]);
      }
   oFolder.close(false);
   oStore.close();
 } catch (Exception oExcept) {
   System.out.println("Error..." + oExcept.getMessage());
   oExcept.printStackTrace();
   System.exit(1);
 }
 System.exit(0);
 }
```

Finally, we can retrieve the messages that are in the `Inbox` folder and loop through them to process them. In our current code example, we simply print the contents of the e-mail message to the console window. In a real–world application of this code, we would probably create a SOAP object model representation of the data, with the help of the particular SOAP implementation toolkit, and/or further process the XML in the SOAP message using some of the XML libraries provided by the SOAP Toolkit for the particular platform.

The following code is the method that shows a part of an e-mail message to the screen. A "part" of an e-mail message can be the entire content or parts of it. MIME messages can often be multi–part, as our example shows. In that case, we would process one part at a time. In our example, the first part that we retrieve is the SOAP message main payload (the XML). The second part is the binary attachment of our graphical file. Depending on the MIME type of the content that we have, we use slightly different ways of displaying it. We deal with binary parts by utilizing the `InputStream` class.

```
//Java code (cont.)
//Display part of message
public static void mShowPart(Part oMsgPart) throws Exception {
  if (oMsgPart instanceof Message)
     mShowHeader((Message)oMsgPart);

  System.out.println("Content-Type: " +
        oMsgPart.getContentType());
  String filename = oMsgPart.getFileName();
  if (filename != null)
     System.out.println("Filename: " + filename);

  //Determine the content type and then output the text to console
  if (oMsgPart.isMimeType("text/plain")) {
     System.out.println("\n" +
        "***** SOAP Message With XML in Body as Text *****");
     System.out.println((String)oMsgPart.getContent());
  } else if (oMsgPart.isMimeType("multipart/*")) {
     System.out.println("***** SOAP Message is Multipart "+
           "*****");
     Multipart oMsgMultiPart =
        (Multipart)oMsgPart.getContent();
```

```
        int iTotalParts = oMsgMultiPart.getCount();
        for (int iCount = 0; iCount < iTotalParts; iCount++)
        mShowPart(oMsgMultiPart.getBodyPart(iCount));
    } else if (oMsgPart.isMimeType("message/rfc822")) {
        System.out.println("***** SOAP Message is Nested *****");
        mShowPart((Part)oMsgPart.getContent());
    } else {

   //Output attachments that are not text or XML
          //(likely binary)
        Object oMsgBin = oMsgPart.getContent();
        if (oMsgBin instanceof String) {
        System.out.println("This is a string");
        System.out.println("________________________");
        System.out.println((String)oMsgBin);
        } else if (oMsgBin instanceof InputStream) {
        System.out.println("This is just an input stream");
        System.out.println("________________________");
        InputStream oInStream = (InputStream)oMsgBin;
        int strInStream;
        while ((strInStream = oInStream.read()) != -1)
           System.out.write(strInStream);
        } else {
        System.out.println("This is an unknown type");
        System.out.println("________________________");
        System.out.println(oMsgBin.toString());
        }
    }
  }
```

The final method that we have in our class is the one that we call at the beginning of each message to display some of the header information for each message. Header information would be items such as the From, To, and Subject fields. In a production type scenario, this information could be used to make decisions before processing each one of the e-mail messages.

```
  //Java code (cont.)
  //Display message header information
  public static void mShowHeader(Message oMsg) throws Exception {
     System.out.println(" " + "Message Header Information Next " +
                          "*****");
     Address[] arrAddress;
     //Display the From, To, Subject, and Date for the message
     if ((arrAddress = oMsg.getFrom()) != null) {
        for (int iCount = 0; iCount < arrAddress.length; iCount++)
        System.out.println("From: " +
           arrAddress[iCount].toString());
     }
     if ((arrAddress =
        oMsg.getRecipients(Message.RecipientType.TO)) != null) {
        for (int iCount = 0; iCount < arrAddress.length; iCount++)
        System.out.println("To: " + arrAddress[iCount].toString());
     }
     System.out.println("Subject: " + oMsg.getSubject());
     Date dtDate = oMsg.getSentDate();
```

```
        System.out.println("Date Message Sent: " +
            (dtDate != null ? dtDate.toString() :
                              "Date Cannot Be Shown"));
    }
}
```

When you run this code you should get something like the following in your console window. The first picture shows the message header information, as well as the beginning of the first part of the SOAP message (the XML part). The second part of the message (the beginning of the binary attachment) is shown in the second image.

```
E:\WINNT\System32\cmd.exe

E:\SOAPWebSvc\Web>java InvoiceFullfillSMTPSrv
Total SOAP Messages = 1, New SOAP Messages = 0

***** Message Number: 1 Message Header Information Next *****
From: InvoiceSrv@ToyCo.com
To: wrox@saturn2000.com
Subject: New Invoice Submitted on 2/25/2001 12:25:10 PM (XML as Text in Body w/
Binary Attachment)
Date Message Sent: Sun Feb 25 12:25:10 EST 2001
Content-Type: multipart/mixed;  boundary="----=_NextPart_000_000F_01C09F25.FEF9E
450"
***** SOAP Message is Multipart *****
Content-Type: text/plain;
        charset="iso-8859-1"

***** SOAP Message With XML in Body as Text *****
<?xml version="1.0"?>
<SOAP-ENV:Envelope SOAP-ENV:encodingStyle="http://schemas.xmlsoap.org/soap/encod
ing/" xmlns:SOAP-ENV="http://schemas.xmlsoap.org/soap/envelope/">
        <SOAP-ENV:Body>
                <m:InvoiceAdd xmlns:m="http://localhost/soap/InvoiceFullfillSamp
le.xsd">
                        <InvoiceID>1</InvoiceID>
                        <CustomerID>3</CustomerID>
```

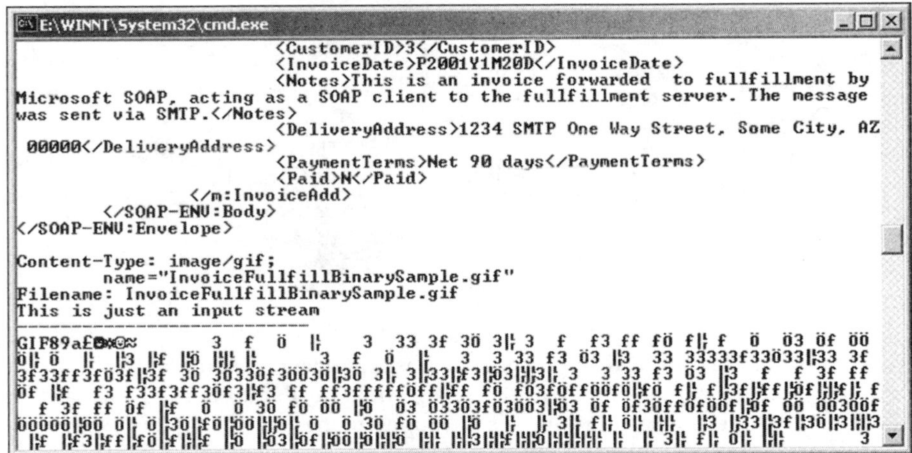

E:\WINNT\System32\cmd.exe
<CustomerID>3</CustomerID>
<InvoiceDate>P2001Y1M20D</InvoiceDate>
<Notes>This is an invoice forwarded to fullfillment by
Microsoft SOAP, acting as a SOAP client to the fullfillment server. The message
was sent via SMTP.</Notes>
<DeliveryAddress>1234 SMTP One Way Street, Some City, AZ
00000</DeliveryAddress>
<PaymentTerms>Net 90 days</PaymentTerms>
<Paid>N</Paid>
</m:InvoiceAdd>
</SOAP-ENV:Body>
</SOAP-ENV:Envelope>
Content-Type: image/gif;
name="InvoiceFullfillBinarySample.gif"
Filename: InvoiceFullfillBinarySample.gif
This is just an input stream

With this we have concluded our discussion of sending SOAP messages with or without attachments via SMTP. We were able to connect a Microsoft SOAP system to an Apache/IBM SOAP server working in Java. Our example was a one-way SOAP messaging implementation that did not expect to have return information provided back.

For more information on utilizing JavaMail, XML with Java, and other Java server programming advice, please see the Wrox Press title Java Server Programming – J2EE Edition (ISBN 1-861004-65-6).

What's Next – an XML Protocol (XP)?

Actually, yes, it appears that an XML Protocol would be the end result of the development of SOAP. The W3C has a list of about 25 editorial and technical issues with SOAP at the current time. Individuals from various organizations and companies are working on these issues, along with looking at details in comparing the various XML protocols that are out today before determining the final draft for an XML Protocol. The XML Protocol working group that was formed under the umbrella of the W3C has a charter, and a quite specific agenda. It plans to have a Candidate Recommendation for the XML Protocol sometime in the summer of 2001, and plans to have a Recommendation for the XML protocol in the fall or winter of 2001 (first final release). The XML Protocol working group is scheduled to last until April 2002. Also, it is interesting to know that the XML Protocol group is planning to coordinate with other groups such as the ebXML standards bodies, in an attempt to coordinate the development of the final XML Protocol.

So, how is this XML Protocol going to relate to SOAP? It appears, by looking at the current stage of affairs of the XML Protocol working group, that SOAP will cover the majority of the needs of the upcoming XML Protocol. In all likelihood, the XML Protocol would be in essence the next version release of SOAP 1.1, where the SOAP functionality would cover the core of the XML Protocol and more would be available in terms of expandability and layered modularity of the entire framework. Some of the current ideas of the overall framework of the upcoming XML Protocol would be as described in the following chart.

XML Protocol Layering

XP Module
XP Module
XML Protocol
XP Binding
XP Binding
XP Binding
XP Binding
HTTP
SMTP
TCP
...

The core section would be the XML Protocol, which is an updated version of SOAP. Below it, very similar to what SOAP does today, the XML Protocol would be able to bind to various transports, HTTP, SMTP or other. The current SOAP specification emphasizes HTTP, but it does not really provide much in terms of examples for any other protocols, aside from HTTP. It appears that the XML protocol would work a bit more in this area. Then, the transport protocols such as HTTP and SMTP would layer on top of TCP or other networking protocols. For those of you who think this will bring the idea of the **OSI** (**Open Systems Interconnection**) model of layering the networking protocols from physical to application layer, you are absolutely right. It almost looks like the XML protocol would expand the OSI model further and in more detail, particularly within the application layer of the OSI model.

The modules that "sit" on top of the XML Protocol are optional modules that will not be specified by the XML Protocol, but it would allow them to "plug-in". These modules would include ones for security, routing, and other similar needs that computer-to-computer communication requires and that some have criticized SOAP for not providing. At the end, only one question remains: are we going to keep the name "SOAP" or are we going to use the less entertaining name of "XML Protocol" or "XP"?

You can follow some of the workings of the XML Protocol group at http://www.w3.org/2000/xp/.

Future Releases of SOAP Implementations

We expect to see frequent new releases of the currently available SOAP implementation by the various vendors. A number of them have already made announcements to expect updates to their code in monthly intervals. This is good news because it means the outstanding bugs will be fixed promptly and that features which are missing in the current releases, are bound to appear very soon in the near future.

IBM's Toolkit and Apache SOAP

The Apache organization as the keeper of the Java SOAP source code is working actively in providing new upgrades to the existing SOAP implementation. IBM on the other hand, as the implementer of the core SOAP implementation that was donated to the care of the Apache organization, has been busy adding a number of features to its Web Services Toolkit. The Web Services Toolkit contains, besides SOAP, the implementations of WSDL, UDDI, as well as sample code and documentation.

For more information visit IBM's alphaWorks Web Services Toolkit site at http://www.alphaworks.ibm.com/tech/webservicestoolkit *and the Apache organization's SOAP project at* http://xml.apache.org/soap/index.html.

Microsoft and .NET

Microsoft is planning to release a production version of the SOAP Toolkit 2 by the fall of 2001. This version is going to be fully supported by Microsoft (unlike version 1) and it will be tested for cross-platform compatibility. At time of writing this book, the Release Candidate 0 (RC0) was released.

Microsoft's longer-term vision is .NET. The .NET implementation of the web services will bring full support for SOAP (or the upcoming XML Protocol) with support for WSDL, UDDI, and more.

For more information visit Microsoft's MSDN site and its SOAP section at http://msdn.microsoft.com/soap/default.asp *and the web services section at* http://msdn.microsoft.com/webservices/default.asp.

Other Java SOAP Implementations

The Apache/IBM SOAP implementation is probably the most well known Java implementation of SOAP. However, there are other Java implementations of SOAP. Here are few: IdooXoap for Java by ZVON.org at http://www.zvon.org/?nav_id=34, SOAP RMI by Indiana University at http://www.extreme.indiana.edu/soap/index.html, DevelopMentor at http://www.develop.com/soap/.

Implementations in Other Languages

There are other SOAP implementations in other languages, too. For example there is another PERL implementation from DevelopMentor at http://www.develop.com/soap/.

C++ Implementations

There are few vendors that provide C++ implementations that are at various stages of their development. You can try:

- White Mesa Software at http://www.whitemesa.com/wmsoapsvc_about.htm
- ZVON.org at http://www.zvon.org/?nav_id=33
- EasySOAP++ at http://sourceforge.net/projects/easysoap/

Python Implementations

You can find a Python implementation of SOAP at PythonWare with SOAP for Python located at http://www.pythonware.com/products/soap/.

PHP Implementation

You can find a PHP implementation of SOAP at http://www.gigaideas.com.cn/phpsoap/.

Some Other Language Implementations

We were somewhat surprised that there were even more SOAP implementations in various other languages, such as SOAP for ADA 95 at http://home.snafu.de/boavista/soap.html, and SOAP for SmallTalk at http://wiki.cs.uiuc.edu/CampSmalltalk/SOAP+Smalltalk+Reference+Implementation. You should not be surprised if you see a SOAP implementation for just about any language out there as interoperability between languages is beneficial to all language communities.

Summary

In this chapter we became familiar with SOAP as the lightweight protocol for exchanging information in decentralized and distributed environment. SOAP enables systems to exchange information not only regardless of their operating environment, but also regardless of their language environment and object implementations. We looked at the history of the distributed protocols, their current state, and their strengths and weaknesses, especially as they relate to SOAP. Furthermore, we looked at the main parts of a SOAP message and how they all fit together. We became familiar with WSDL as a way of describing network services, because most SOAP implementations use WSDL.

Next, we briefly looked at some of the more popular implementations of SOAP. Then, we were able to go into the main topic of this chapter, that being how we can connect different programming environments, firstly via synchronous communication over HTTP, and then in an asynchronous environment using SMTP. We looked at the source code of these implementations in Java, Visual Basic/ASP, and PERL. We examined the messages that these services generated and their structures.

Finally, we looked at the state of the industry today. We saw that the W3C is busy working on the next release of SOAP under the potential name of XML Protocol (XP). Then, we briefly scanned some of the additional implementations of SOAP in other languages.

HTML and HTTP enabled people to connect to machines and browse for information. Then the Web exploded. XML and SOAP (the XML Protocol) will enable machines to talk to other machines, whatever their location and setup. This will give us the opportunity to create new types of applications, services, and opportunities that are difficult to imagine at the moment.

25

B2B with Microsoft BizTalk Server

Business-to-business e-commerce systems increasingly rely on what we will call business servers. Unlike application servers, which provide scalable component services, business servers act as intermediaries between applications and trading partners, providing messaging and format translation services. In addition, some business servers also provide mechanisms for coordinating messaging, and individual applications to accomplish a formally specified business process such as a business might have for purchasing activities. Such servers are sometimes promoted under the heading of **Enterprise Application Integration** (**EAI**). Business servers perform the same functions in this role, but the emphasis is on connecting applications within an organization instead of across organizational boundaries.

One such server is the newly released **Microsoft BizTalk Server 2000**. BizTalk Server builds on the services and technologies of the Windows platform to enable EAI and B2B e-commerce. In this chapter, we'll present a quick overview of BizTalk Server coupled with a worked example demonstrating the major features of the product. When we have finished this chapter, we will understand:

- The needs and driving principles of B2B e-commerce
- The technology issues surrounding B2B e-commerce
- The two major functional areas of BizTalk Server
- The tools provided by BizTalk Server
- How B2B systems are implemented in BizTalk Server

Our code sample is a contrived e-commerce situation, designed to lead you through the different features of the product. In addition, robust, real-world message formats can be quite complex. To facilitate an introduction to B2B e-commerce, we've taken some liberties and streamlined our messages and processes. Therefore, while the sample is far from ready for use in a production e-commerce setting, it realistically presents the issues we might encounter when building B2B systems.

While we cannot cover the entire product in detail in a single chapter, we will be exposed to the major capabilities and services of BizTalk Server. By understanding the technology needs of B2B e-commerce, we will have a better appreciation of BizTalk Server, particularly as it compares to competing products.

For more information on BizTalk, see Professional BizTalk (Wrox Press, ISBN 1-861003-29-3).

Needs of B2B Commerce

B2B e-commerce has three major requirements that must be addressed if a given system is to be scalable, reliable, and effective. These needs are:

- Data representation
- Messaging
- Business process modeling

All commercial B2B business servers cover the first two, however the third is somewhat controversial. Some products make no provision for it. The issue is far from settled. Indeed, standardized B2B frameworks are split on the issue. Some, like BizTalk Framework, make no recommendations regarding process, while others, notably **RosettaNet**, mandate formal processes.

The BizTalk Framework is distinct from BizTalk Server. Although BizTalk Server offers a fully compliant BizTalk Framework implementation, it is completely possible and permissible to use BizTalk Server without using the BizTalk Framework and vice versa. RosettaNet is the product of an industry consortium and provides message formats as well as prescribing specific sequences of events for business transactions. The BizTalk Framework 2.0 specification is published at http://www.biztalk.org, *while RosettaNet is found at* http://www.rosettanet.org.

We will briefly discuss these requirements in order to frame the discussion of BizTalk Server. Following our summary of the requirements, we'll also give some idea of the general solutions emerging from industry practice before launching into the specific solutions found in BizTalk Server.

Data Representation

At the lowest level, every B2B system must represent commercial information in some set of easily exchanged data structures, conventionally termed **messages**. Data about prices, products, billing, and so forth, must be captured in such a way as to be unambiguous to all parties. These structures should also be well suited to transmission over networks.

In a freestanding application, we would probably use proprietary binary data structures. The format of these structures would be described in the source code. It might also be found in off-line, human-readable documentation, but there is always the concern about currency of documentation. In addition to these challenges, binary formats introduce platform dependencies. Certain data types are organized differently on various platforms, so a binary-format file written under one operating system may not be read the same way on a different operating system.

For these reasons, large systems have long exported their data in text form. Whether dumping the contents of a database, or engaging in an earlier B2B scheme like EDI, critical data intended for use by an entity other than the creator of the data has long been written in textual form. Traditionally, this has taken the form of a delimited file (comma separated values being especially popular) or a positional, fixed field format. This solves the portability problem, but the issue of documentation remains. Any B2B system then needs to represent its data in a portable form, most likely text, and do whatever it can to minimize the documentation problem.

Messaging

The "2" in "B2B" implies two-way communication. We are no longer talking only to ourselves. An application on our side must communicate with an application owned and operated by our trading partner. Here again, the issues of platform portability encountered in data representation arise. A number of interprocess communications technologies exist that take this into account. **CORBA**, for example, is supported on many platforms and offers an object-based view of distributed communications. Sockets, the technology upon which the Internet is built, are a lower level view of distributed communications.

The sticking point isn't platform differences, but rather scalability. By its very nature, B2B e-commerce deals with important data. We are dealing with money and the delivery of goods and services. Information must be correct, and it must be guaranteed to arrive. A lost message may leave a partner waiting for supplies that never come, while a system that is unavailable means that an organization is unable to do business.

These problems translate into the related problems of scalability and availability. A large part of availability is handled through the normal mechanisms of redundancy and hardware measures. RAID systems, failover clusters, and backup power systems are important parts of an e-commerce solution, but these measures fall outside the scope of this book. We are concerned with software technologies that translate into an effective architecture. In this light, scalability *is* availability. If the communications scheme doesn't scale well, the server receiving data will be overwhelmed and will be unavailable to other partners. Even though the hardware is up and operating and the data is readable, the server might as well be off line for all the good it does to partners who wish to do business with the server's owning organization.

Traditionally, scaling systems that involve distributed communications has meant the use of **asynchronous messaging**. A discrete chunk of data describes some event or action in the system and is conveyed to the recipient as a message. Processing in the system is oriented around the transmission of such messages. Communication is asynchronous, in that senders do not expect a reply (except, perhaps, a low-level system message indicating that the message was successfully conveyed to the recipient) at the same time that the message is sent. If an acknowledgement is required, a separate message is sent which references the first. While this introduces some complexity to a distributed system, it greatly enhances scalability. If demand exceeds the ability to fully process messages, incoming messages may be placed in a queue to await processing. Since the sender does not expect an immediate reply, the recipient is free to hold those messages until demand drops and resources are available to handle the message. Many platform-proprietary systems, like Microsoft's Message Queue (MSMQ) or IBM's MQSeries, exist to offer queued, asynchronous messaging.

Before we leave this topic, we should note that of the commonly used Internet protocols, only SMTP is asynchronous. HTTP demands an immediate reply. If we are going to implement B2B e-commerce on the public Internet, we will need to add some layer of application logic on top of HTTP to mask this. That is, we will have to have an agreement between partners that a receiving application using HTTP will acknowledge receipt of the raw message, thus satisfying the protocol, but queue the message somehow and defer processing until later, satisfying scalability demands with queuing and asynchronous processing.

Business Process Modeling

The last section hinted at the final requirement of B2B e-commerce. Since we are dealing with serious issues, some idea of the business process must be incorporated into our automated systems. Offline organizations typically have established processes and protocols for specific business tasks. There is, for example, a formal process in most organizations for making a purchase that includes a request, approval of the request, and notifications to the finance office. When dealing with an external partner through manual means, for example making telephone calls and receiving printed letters, human users can enforce the process. Taking this to the Web, we must find some way of describing processes to an automated system so that the system can follow the procedure.

Writing the process into application code is not going to be effective. We cannot generally afford to write and debug code for dozens of procedures. Even when we do so, we cannot afford to pay for reprogramming whenever a process must change. Any commercial system will need flexibility. Business conditions will change, necessitating a change in process. Exceptions will need to be made for partners with special conditions. Since the individual transactions of the process are data driven (through the arrival of messages consisting of structured data), it is highly desirable to be able to drive a business process through descriptive means as well.

Some Solutions

Obviously, a chapter presenting a specific e-commerce solution is going to have specific solutions to these problems in mind. The solutions that the BizTalk Server team arrived at are fairly common to other, similar products, such as WebMethods. Let's briefly outline these solutions, then, before diving into the specifics of Microsoft's product. These solutions are:

- XML for data representation
- The use of open Internet protocols for communication
- Frameworks for business process semantics

XML for Data Representation

We must at least be leaning toward the use of XML to represent data. The requirements presented in the last section strongly pushed us toward the use of text to represent data. XML surpasses the traditional flatfile formats though, by offering everyone a common system of delimiters as well as a commonly understood mechanism for extending and communicating data formats. DTDs and schemas are a recognized way to document and specify some arbitrary format. At the very least, the fact that items of information are tagged in XML allows us as programmers to write applications that degrade gracefully. If an application is expecting a particular item of information at a specific location in a binary format, it has no choice but to read whatever bytes are at that location and try to treat them as the expected item. If a similar application is looking for a `Cost` field at a particular point in an XML document, and instead gets something called `Dimensions`, it can stop processing before it causes a fatal error within the code.

XML, moreover, was designed with the Internet in mind. Some of the early proponents of XML referred to it as "SGML for the Web". Simplicity and the ability to be transported via the protocols commonly in use on the Internet were guiding requirements in the development of XML. The current situation, in which XML has taken the software industry by storm, makes XML an even better choice for B2B data representation. The fact that the technology is widely adopted and tools are widely available means that our partners are likely to be using XML. If they are not, tools exist to transform XML into other formats. If you want to translate legacy flatfile formats like EDI to other legacy flatfile formats, we might have to write our own converters and parsers. At the very least, our choice of software would be limited. With XML, the tools have usually been written and we have a broad selection from which to choose.

Internet Protocols for Communication

EDI traditionally uses **Value Added Networks** (**VANs**) – proprietary communications networks that were expensive to set up and operate. In their favor, we must say that VANs offer reliability and security features that surpass what is found by default on the public Internet. Nevertheless, proprietary networks using proprietary protocols limit our choices, both in terms of available software and hardware, and in terms of business partners capable of communicating with us using these tools.

Contrast that with the public Internet and open communications protocols. By now, almost all businesses in the technically developed world are connected to the Internet. This is not to say that they have adequate bandwidth or sufficient reliability connectivity for large-scale B2B efforts, but the basic infrastructure is there. Small businesses can start limited B2B efforts with ISDN or DSL, while larger operations will require dedicated and reliable lines with quality of service guarantees (at least with respect to connectivity).

Since these businesses are connected to the public Internet, they are also equipped to deal with the basic protocols of the Web, such as HTTP and SMTP. Virtually everyone in business makes use of an SMTP server, and most have their own HTTP servers, whether on site or hosted by a third party. This is enough to make an open standards-based approach attractive. Like the network, the mere fact of having a server isn't sufficient for robust, large-scale B2B e-commerce, but, again, the foundation exists. Software is available and programmers are gaining expertise. The reliability and availability demanded by serious B2B work can be added as a layer of logic above this common core. HTTP, as we have seen, can be used in such a way as to implement asynchronous messaging, even though the protocol itself isn't asynchronous. As we will see in the next section, there are many approaches to adding this functionality to the Web.

B2B Frameworks

Implementing a business process on top of messaging is a difficult problem to solve. On the one hand, we want to have complete flexibility so that businesses can implement whatever business protocol they wish. On the other, we'd like to promote common standards so that organizations can communicate with a minimum of prior coordination. Currently, B2B practice is split on this issue. Some products do not prescribe a business process, leaving that up to the customer to define and implement. Others embrace the work of consortia and standards bodies that are writing fixed frameworks that mandate specific processes for common business problems.

Every standards body in the B2B field is trying to develop a framework of protocols and messages to address the issues we identified in the use of open protocols on the public Internet. The frameworks mandate application semantics such that organizations that adhere to them will gain the reliability they need while using inexpensive software and hardware. The key differentiator is the extent to which the business process is prescribed by the standards body. Some restrict themselves to relatively low-level messaging issues to solve problems of addressing, reliable delivery, and message acknowledgement, while leaving the semantics of e-commerce up to individual customers. Others specify these semantics and require an organization to adjust their processes to conform to the standard. Although there is some disruption for an organization when following the latter course, an established standard with specific business processes will eventually be supported by a selection of third party software. Therefore, if we select one of these frameworks and it takes hold, we can look forward to a day when turnkey implementations exist for our framework. Here is a brief list of some of these standards organizations and their frameworks:

- **cXML** – developed by Ariba, a B2B software vendor; cXML is now a consortium that uses XML messaging for B2B e-commerce (http://www.cxml.org).
- **BizTalk Framework** – founded and operated by Microsoft, BizTalk.org prescribes a reliable messaging framework based on XML as well as a publicly accessible repository of message formats (http://www.biztalk.org).
- **RosettaNet** – a consortium of e-commerce vendors, RosettaNet prescribes specific message formats and business processes. (http://www.rosettanet.org).
- **ebXML** – a joint venture of **OASIS** (the **Organization for the Advancement of Structured Information Standards**) and **UN/CEFACT** (a body of the United Nations devoted to the advancement of electronic commerce), ebXML is a technical framework for message formats and processes for B2B e-commerce (http://www.ebxml.org).
- **UDDI** – although not strictly a B2B e-commerce framework, UDDI (the **Universal Description, Discovery, and Integration standard**) is being promoted by a consortium of vendors, so that potential e-commerce partners can describe the services they offer as well as the technical measures they use to communicate. This means that an organization may search for what they need and find vendors using a compatible framework (http://www.uddi.org).

For more on Biztalk Framework, RosettaNet, and ebXML, read on.

An initiative somewhat similar to UDDI, the Web Services Description Language (WSDL), is under consideration by the W3C at present (Spring 2001). Like UDDI, WSDL is an XML vocabulary, not a framework. The full text of the W3C Note on WSDL is available at http://www.w3.org/TR/wsdl.

BizTalk Server takes a measured approach. First, as we shall see, the product includes a data-driven service that allows customers to develop and implement their own business processes. Consequently, users of BizTalk Server can interoperate without embracing any B2B framework at all, so long as they have an agreement on semantics with their partners. Secondly, BizTalk Server is fully compliant with BizTalk Framework, so customers can use the BizTalk Framework messaging format to introduce a measure of reliability to the exchange of their own messages over the public Internet. Finally, the BizTalk Server team is widely believed to be at work on some sort of extension to the BizTalk SDK that will allow it to interoperate with RosettaNet servers. Although not formally announced as of this date (Spring 2001), the extension, if completed, is expected to become part of a future release of the SDK.

Microsoft BizTalk Server

We now turn our attention away from the theory of B2B e-commerce to the specific feature set of BizTalk Server 2000. Microsoft BizTalk Server 2000 is a first release product and an entirely new offering in the Microsoft server line, so it requires a bit of description before we launch into the sample.

Microsoft BizTalk Server 2000 configuration, administration, and programming is covered in detail in Professional BizTalk (Wrox Press, ISBN 1-861003-29-3).

Data Representation

BizTalk is strongly oriented toward the use of XML for data representation. It ships with pre-defined XML message formats for many common business functions, and the administrative tools for the product support all the features of well-formed XML as well as some extensions available through **XDR Schemas** (see below). In fact, BizTalk Server makes extensive use of XML for its own implementation, and every message that passes through the server and requires translation, regardless of format, goes through an intermediate XML form. Because of the strong influence of legacy formats such as EDI, however, BizTalk Server is built to process any text format.

The key to handling messages in BizTalk Server is the **message specification**, BizTalk's formal document for describing the structure of a class of messages. Specifications are held in a repository common to the BizTalk server group where messaging configurations can reference them. When an interchange of messages requires translation from one format to another, such as when an XML message must be translated to a flatfile format before transmission to a partner, the messaging configuration will also reference a **map**. A map consists of two message specifications and an XSLT stylesheet for converting from one to the other.

Specifications

BizTalk Server reads and writes Microsoft's own **XML – Data Reduced** (**XML – DR** or **XDR**) schema format. When the W3C publishes XML Schema (and this is looking to be imminent), the product will migrate to use that standard. Given Microsoft's commitment to XML, it is imperative that BizTalk Server be able to describe message formats in an open, standard way.

Merely reading schemas, however, is insufficient for the product. Schemas do not describe flatfiles, so BizTalk Server has it's own proprietary specification for messages. If we look at a specification file, we will find an XDR schema adorned with additional attributes and elements from a BizTalk-related namespace. These additional items give the product a place to record information specific to flatfiles, such as delimiters and escape characters. The bulk of the information in a specification, then, can go in a schema. What will not fit into a schema goes in one of the adorning items. In this way, BizTalk is able to leverage Microsoft's standard XML tools, adding only enough additional functionality to process non-XML formats.

Specifications are written using **BizTalk Editor**, an administrative tool that comes with the product. This tool, depicted below, uses a record and field metaphor for document structure in preference to an elements-and-attributes metaphor to be accessible to a wide range of business programmers. The structure of the message is graphically depicted in the tree-view on the left, while the specifics of each item are specified in tabbed property pages on the right.

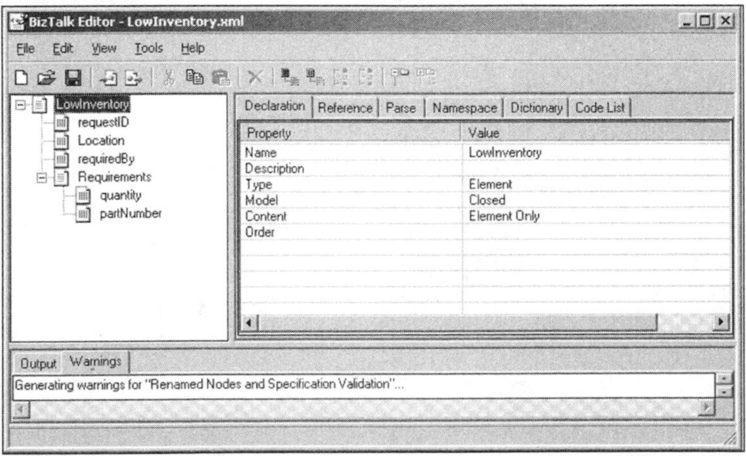

Editor's property pages are organized into six tabs as follows:

- Declaration – basic properties of the record or field
- Reference – cardinality of the item
- Parse – details of delimited or positional flatfile formats
- Namespace – declarations for all XML namespaces used in the specification
- Dictionary – used to specify fields when using dynamic routing or special processing
- Code List – used with EDI format messages to list codes available for use with a particular field

When creating a new message specification, we begin by indicating whether we are starting from scratch, or basing our specification on some existing standard. In addition to its own XML formats, BizTalk Server includes X12 and EDIFACT EDI specifications. If our messages are modified versions of one of those standards, we may begin with one of the templates and edit it, rather than starting from a blank page. In addition to the templates provided, BizTalk Editor is capable of importing an XDR schema, or reading an instance of an XML-based message and generating a specification based on what it sees in the imported document.

Every message that is handled by BizTalk Server must have a message specification written for it. The messaging system uses these specifications to initialize its parser and serializer components. When encountering a new message, it loads a COM+ component built for the appropriate type (XML, flatfile, EDI). Since these are general-purpose components, they must load the proper message specification in order to know how to read and write documents of this type.

Document Repository

As noted, BizTalk must reference the message specification when instances of message pass to the server. Additionally, message editors will need to read and write message specifications in the normal course of their maintenance duties. These people will not want to work on the BizTalk Server, nor should they be working on a production machine. Since so many entities need remote access to message specifications, BizTalk Server incorporates a document repository.

This repository uses **WebDAV** (Distributed Authoring and Versioning), a W3C standard for document management using HTTP (for more information on WebDAV, go to http://www.webdav.org). The message specification files physically reside in a known location on the BizTalk Server machine. Anyone requiring access, a human editor maintaining a specification, or the messaging system itself, uses HTTP to gain access. When we install BizTalk Server, a single folder exists within the repository with the name Microsoft. This is where the pre-built XML specifications are found.

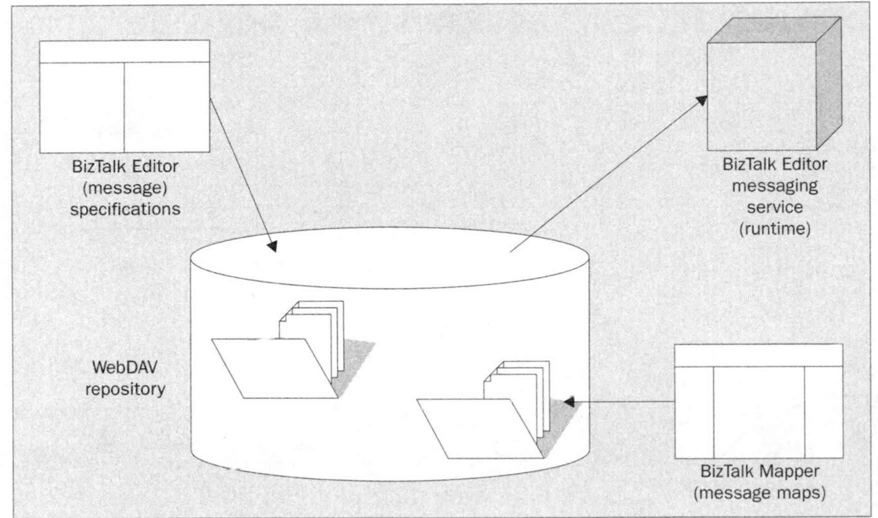

As we shall see in a moment, message specifications are not the only document type required by BizTalk Server. As we have already learned, there is something called a map as well. A separate set of folders is maintained in the repository for maps. The tools used for specifications and maps incorporate knowledge of this folder structure, so that when you are using Editor, you see the folders for specifications, while the tool for maps defaults to the folders dedicated to that document type.

Format Translation

Message format translation is a critical feature for a B2B server. However hard we try to get all interested parties to standardize on a specific set of message formats, universal consensus on the structure of business documents will never be achieved. Even when two partners agree on a common business framework standard, it is possible that one of the partners will use a modification of the standard formats to suit their special requirements. The B2B server should handle this as part of its messaging implementation, rather than in application code.

BizTalk Server terms this feature **mapping**. When a message arrives for transmission, BizTalk Server identifies a configuration that describes what must happen to the message. If the outbound format differs from the format in which the message was presented, a map will be specified. As noted earlier, a map is an XML document that physically includes source and destination specifications and a transformation from the source to the destination. This transformation is, at heart, an XSLT stylesheet. In order to handle flatfiles and accommodate special processing rules, a map may also include **Functoids**. Functoids are graphical components that may be configured in the course of specifying the map. They implement their processing with VBScript run in the course of performing the XSLT transformation.

The tool used to design a map is called **BizTalk Mapper**. This consists of two tree views, one for each message specification. The source document is on the left, while the destination is on the right. A business developer drags and drops links from fields and records in the source message specification to fields and records in the destination message specification. When special processing is required, the analyst drops a functoid onto the central grid and establishes links from the source to the functoid, and from the functoid to the destination. A dialog is used to configure the functoid. Incoming links from the source document are treated as parameters. The Mapper includes a selection of pre-built functoids in a variety of areas such as database retrieval, numeric formatting and conversion, and string manipulation. There is also a script functoid, which permits the analyst to enter his own script for execution. Functoids are COM+ components, and programmers may create new, custom functoids, which are added to the palette of available functoids in the Mapper.

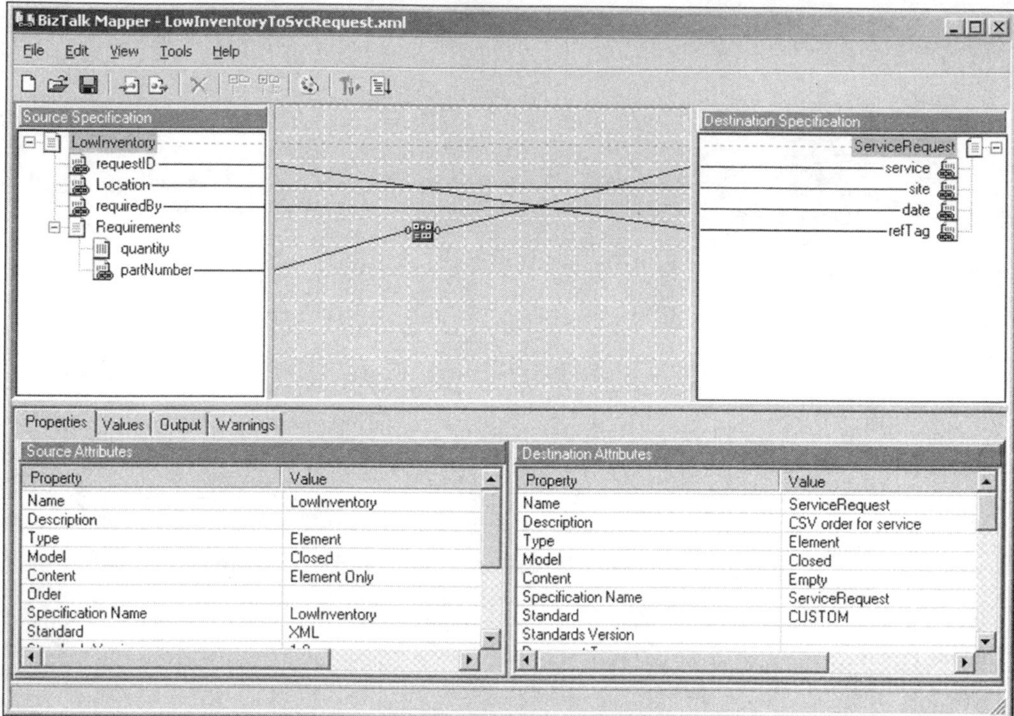

Messaging Service

Specifications and maps are useless unless we are able to actually send messages. This is the function of the BizTalk messaging service. To do this, an administrator configures various aspects of the desired messaging. These separate configurations are tied together through a **channel**, which is simply a collection of pointers to lower-level configurations. The nature of channels will become clearer when we work through the sample application. The messaging service accepts incoming messages and associates them with a previously configured channel based on the document format, source, and destination. Based on the configuration, the format of the message may be changed using a map. The message is sent to a port, which is the abstraction of a protocol endpoint, for example, HTTP or SMTP URL, MSMQ queue, etc. BizTalk works with a variety of open and proprietary protocols, facilitating application integration within the Windows platform as well as B2B integration across platforms.

The messaging service is scalable through server groups. Each group consists of one or more stateless servers that share a common messaging configuration database known as the **messaging management database**. This database is a SQL Server database managed by BizTalk that describes the location and configuration of each server in the group, as well as all the messaging configurations specified for message interchanges. Thus, all the message specifications and message maps are described in this database, as well as the ports to which messages are sent and the channels that use those ports. This gives each server in the group a consistent view of the messaging configurations. Using these configurations and the document repository, any server in the group is able to process any message submitted.

Messaging configurations are established through an application called the **BizTalk Messaging Manager**. It uses an Explorer-style user interface, shown below, to identify configurations in the messaging management database. When creating or maintaining a configuration, a wizard is used to lead an administrator through the tasks needed to fully specify the configuration.

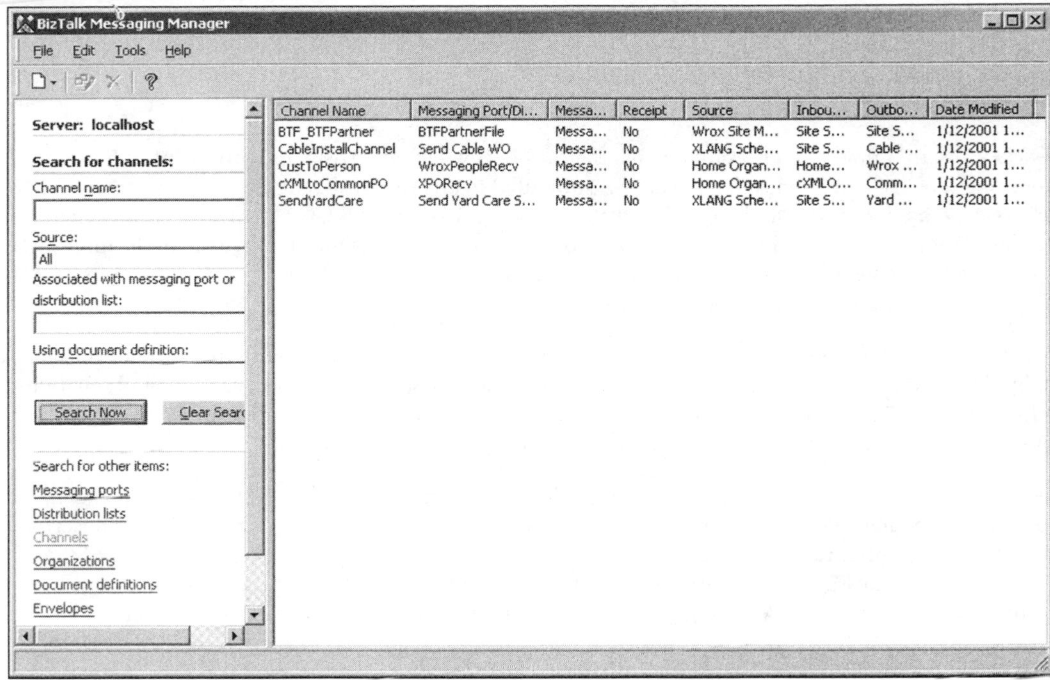

The group shares messages equally through the shared queues. Each server in the group retrieves the next available message in the queue and processes it.

Shared Queues

The shared queues are not queues as we may know them from MSMQ or MQSeries, but rather are logical queues implemented on top of a database. Implementing them in SQL Server not only gives each server in the group an equal view of the message load, but also provides transactional recovery of the shared queues. There are four queues in the shared queues database:

- **Work** – the queue to which all new messages are submitted
- **Scheduled** – the queue to which all messages are assigned after a channel(s) is selected for their processing
- **Retry** – the queue to which messages are sent when transmission fails and multiple attempts are requested in the configuration
- **Suspended** – the queue to which messages are sent when all transmission attempts have failed

We will never interact with the queues directly. BizTalk Server's COM+ API is used to submit messages (except when receive functions are used, as noted below). Internally, access is granted using stored procedures.

Protocols and Protocol Translation

BizTalk supports the following communications protocols:

- COM+
- MSMQ

- File system
- HTTP and HTTPS
- SMTP

COM+ calls are implemented using two interfaces collectively known as **Application Interchange Components** (**AIC**). When used, a message is submitted to an AIC by calling a method of one of the COM+ interfaces defined for AICs and passing in the body of the message. All COM+ messaging sacrifices scalability by forcing synchronous communication, AICs offer a mechanism by which applications with proprietary APIs, such as SAP IDOC, may be called. The proprietary API is simply wrapped in a COM+ component that offers one of the AIC interfaces.

MSMQ is highly favored as a messaging protocol by BizTalk and you should use them whenever integrating applications within an organization that uses MSMQ. The protocol offers robust security and reliability in addition to asynchronous messaging behavior. As we shall see shortly, BizTalk has made a number of optimizations that allow it to scale very well when using MSMQ as a protocol.

Messages may be "sent" using the file system. When receiving from the file system, the messaging service monitors a specified file system folder for the arrival of a file bearing certain characteristics described in the messaging configuration. The arrival is treated as the arrival of a message. The contents of the file are submitted to the messaging service for processing and the file is deleted from the file system. When sending a message via the file system, the outbound message is written to disk in the specified location.

The remaining two protocols are used to support B2B messaging over the public Internet. Both embrace the use of S/MIME for encryption and digital signing of messages. BizTalk includes components for transmitting messages via HTTP, although reception (and SMTP transmission) requires the use of an independent HTTP or SMTP server such as IIS or Exchange.

Protocol Listeners

It is easy enough to envision what happens when a message is sent out via the messaging service. A component within BizTalk that implements the selected protocol is called, and the message is sent. In the case of SMTP, the component invokes the use of an SMTP server. Receiving a message, however, requires a bit more imagination to understand. How does a protocol like HTTP receive a message and submit it to BizTalk's messaging service? The answer is in protocol-specific **receive functions**. In the case of MSMQ and the file system, these are components implemented by BizTalk. HTTP and SMTP require some code component resident on the respective server and calls to the BizTalk messaging API to get the messaging service involved. COM+ may only be used to send a message.

COM+ may be used to receive messages in something called an XLANG Schedule, which we discuss later. The messaging service, though, cannot receive messages using COM+.

Special Components: MSMQ and File System

The BizTalk Server messaging service uses two special components to receive messages from MSMQ queues or the local file system. These are configured through the BizTalk Server Administration console, which is a snap-in for the familiar Windows MMC utility. Both monitor the specified resource, a queue or file folder respectively, for the arrival of a message. Upon arrival, the message is removed from the resource and submitted to the messaging service. The illustration below shows an MSMQ receive function being configured through the Administration snapin.

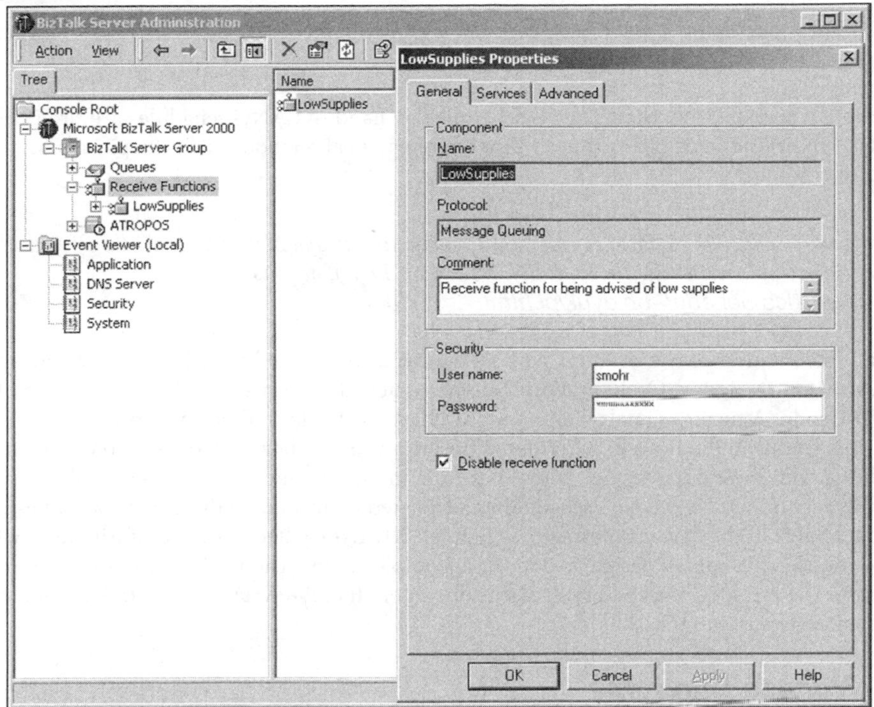

Unlike most other configurations in BizTalk messaging, receive functions are tied to a particular server in the BizTalk server group. In practice, one or more servers in a given group are dedicated to hosting receive functions, leaving the remaining servers free to process the bulk of the message traffic. While the dedicated servers still participate in messaging activities, the load from receiving messages usually precludes them from handling an equal share of the traffic.

Some Code Required: HTTP and SMTP

That leaves HTTP (and its secure variant HTTPS) and SMTP. Here, the receive function is not an actual component implemented by BizTalk but rather consists of some code, usually in script, running on a dedicated server. In the case of HTTP and IIS, this would typically be an ASP, while for SMTP it would be a script running under Exchange. In both cases, a message is sent to an endpoint (ASP or e-mail machine) where the script takes the message from the protocol and submits it to the messaging service using the service's `IInterchange` COM+ interface. As far as the messaging service is concerned, the message arrived via `IInterchange`. As far as the sender is concerned, the message was sent to an HTTP or SMTP address. The script needed to implement the receive function may be as complicated or as simple as the message type requires.

We will see an example of a basic HTTP receive function executed in ASP later in this chapter.

Orchestration and XLANG Scheduler

The messaging service is entirely concerned with single point-to-point message exchanges. This does not answer our requirement for a run-time implementation of business processes. Coordination of business workflows is called orchestration in BizTalk, and the run-time engine for orchestration is called the **XLANG Scheduler**. The scheduler (a COM+ application) is initialized by reading an XML document called an XLANG schedule. It implements a schedule through actions. Each action is a message. Orchestration schedules may use BizTalk messaging, native MSMQ, or COM+ as the implementation of actions.

Orchestration was chosen in preference to the word workflow as that term had previously been used in Exchange CDO.

Happily, there is no need to write XLANG schedules by hand (XLANG schedules are pretty complicated documents). Orchestration is built using a formal mathematical method called the pi calculus, so orchestration is robust.

For a good introduction to the pi calculus, see Communicating and Mobile Systems: the PI-Calculus (Cambridge University Press, 1999 , ISBN 0-521658-69-1), or go to http://www.ics.uci.edu/~bbidyuk/pi.html

Rather than making users write complex XML documents in a text editor, Microsoft provides a tool called the **Orchestration Designer**. Orchestration Designer is actually Visio 2000 with the addition of some highly specific VBA code. A business analyst draws a flowchart for the desired business process. When that is complete, the actions in the flowchart (termed a business process diagram) are tied to orchestration ports. Not to be confused with messaging service ports, these are, in turn, bound to messaging implementations using the protocols mentioned above. The schedule is completed by turning to the data flow and establishing links between data fields in the various messages, which tell XLANG Scheduler how information will flow from message to message. When all design activities are complete, the Visio file is exported as an XML document conforming to the XLANG vocabulary. It is this document that the XLANG Scheduler loads when it is time to execute an orchestration schedule.

Business Process Diagrams

Business process diagrams are very similar to flowcharts. They share many of the same symbols. In orchestration, each symbol, termed shapes, represents an action, decision, or flow of control construct. Orchestration Designer supports the following shapes:

- **Begin** – provided automatically by Orchestration Designer, this shape signifies the start of processing
- **Action** – the fundamental shape in schedules, action shapes represent sending and receiving messages and are the primary means by which things happen
- **Decision** – analogous to both `if` and `switch` (or `case`) statements, decision shapes support one or more rules; the first rule to evaluate `true` causes processing to follow the associated path
- **While** – the schedule follows one path so long as the rule in the while shape evaluates to true, then follows another path out of the loop when the rule is false
- **Fork** – control branches into two or more concurrent paths; as many as 44 concurrent paths are supported
- **Join** – merges multiple paths following a fork or decision shape
- **Transaction** – indicates the boundaries of a transaction; these shapes enclose other shapes in the schedule
- **End** – denotes the end of processing and the termination of the schedule
- **Abort** – terminates a branch of processing or a transaction; if a transaction reaches an abort shape, error recovery mechanisms are invoked

Analysts and programmers drag and drop shapes onto the business process diagram, then connect them together to specify the flow of processing through the schedule. Under normal conditions, processing will flow from one action shape to another, sending and receiving messages. If an action shape is bound to a receive messaging implementation, the schedule will block until the message is received or the implementation times out. The rules in `decision` and `while` shapes may use data fields in messages sent or received by the schedule to control the flow of processing.

Data Flow in Schedules

Each message sent or received by the schedule is represented in the data view. This view is a separate tabbed page in Orchestration Designer. By default, each message has several system-generated fields. When actions are bound to implementations (a process we shall illustrate in the sample), we may also designate specific fields within the message that we wish to work with in the data view. If we do that, the value in that field is retained by the running schedule and may be used in other messages or rules on the business process diagram.

Programmers drag links between message fields in the data view to establish the flow of information within a schedule. For example, we might wish to copy a tracking number from an incoming message into an outgoing message for reference purposes. Rather than write code to read the incoming message and copy the desired data, you would designate the tracking number field in the incoming message and the corresponding field in the outgoing message and establish a link between the two. When the schedule runs, the tracking number would be read from the incoming message. When the outgoing message is generated, the value would be automatically copied to the designated field for us. We will see an example of a data flow later in this chapter.

Advanced Capabilities

The serious nature of B2B messaging requires robust features for error recovery and scalability. Not surprisingly, transactions are supported. This might not seem like a big deal until you consider the nature of what we are doing with orchestration. It is easy enough to imagine how transactions involving transactional resources like MSMQ might be rolled back. The system-level **Distributed Transaction Coordinator** (**DTC**) is able to invoke certain COM+ interfaces and either commit or rollback activities involving these resources. In fact, this is what XLANG Scheduler does in certain classes of transactions. There are other transaction types, though, which are not amenable to DTC-style transactions yet require the commit/rollback semantics we associate with transactions. These are called **long transactions**. They may span intervals of time longer than those involved with a DTC-style transaction, or they may involve non-transactional resources. XLANG Scheduler and Orchestration Designer offer features we can use to cope with this problem.

Because BizTalk Server is intended as an enterprise-class server, scalability and resource use is a major issue. We might expect to see hundreds of concurrently executing schedules in a production environment. While server groups offer a means of bringing additional resources to bear on the messaging traffic, we certainly do not wish to waste expensive server resources. XLANG Scheduler offers a mechanism called **hydration**, which moves idle schedules out of memory and brings them back into memory when they become active.

Transactions: The Long and Short of It

BizTalk orchestration supports three types of transactions: short, long, and timed. Short transactions are based on the DTC and transactional resources. They typically span short intervals of time, hence the name, and are easily rolled back thanks to the DTC. If you have used transactions in SQL, you will be familiar with short transactions.

Long transactions span longer periods. An example might be an activity requiring an HTTP transmission to an external partner that required some sort of reply. The HTTP transmissions themselves might only take a few seconds, but the processing to generate the reply could take minutes or hours. Hopefully, our partner is queuing messages on his side to ensure high availability. Our message might not be processed for some time. This is good for scalability and availability, but the interval of the transaction is longer than we would wish to hold resources. Even if we could use the DTC, the resource consumption might be prohibitive. Timed transactions are a variation on long transactions. In a timed transaction, you establish a timeout period. If the transaction has not completed within that interval, the transaction is rolled back. This is useful when you are in a situation in which you might get no reply from or never establish connectivity with a partner. Rather than hanging, the transaction fails.

Besides the time interval, the three types of transactions are distinguished by how XLANG Scheduler responds to a failed transaction. A short transaction will enlist the DTC to rollback a failed transaction. Transactional resources support certain COM+ interfaces by definition. When these resources indicate a failure, the DTC is able to use these interfaces to rollback the transaction. If no failure is detected, the interfaces are used to commit the transaction. It is incumbent on the schedule designer to ensure all actions within a short transaction are transactional.

Long transactions, however, can't rely on the DTC. Even if they could, we've seen that the time interval is such that holding references to transactional interfaces and consuming various resources, for example, database connections, might be prohibitively expensive. To cope with this, Orchestration Designer offers the On failure page. This is a business process diagram that is invoked whenever the transaction fails. On failure pages have all the capabilities of regular business process diagrams, including transactions and On failure pages of their own. The idea is to allow a programmer or analyst to specify the actions that will compensate for the actions taken by the failed transaction. For example, you might check to see if an HTTP message had been sent. If it had, you could send the recipient another message referencing the first and indicating a desire to rollback the directed activity. You are relying on their good faith, but at least you have a mechanism to signal problems in your process to your partners so that they may take action in their system.

We may also specify an On failure *page for a short transaction. In all cases, after an* On failure *page has completed its processing, control returns to the main business process diagram at the first shape outside the transaction boundaries.*

Hydration

The XLANG Scheduler may have many instances of the same schedule running at the same time, each with different, instance-specific data. The scheduler conserves system resources through a process known as hydration. In this process, schedules which are known to be idle, are serialized to a SQL Server database managed by the scheduler while a stub remains in memory. When a message arrives for a dehydrated schedule, the stub takes note of the event and rehydrates the schedule from the state information stored in the database. B2B scenarios, in particular, are likely to span long periods. Hydration supports scalability by limiting active resource consumption to schedules that are actively exchanging messages.

Hydration is controlled entirely by XLANG Scheduler. When we configure a messaging implementation that involves waiting to receive a message from outside the schedule, we are asked to provide an estimate of how long it will take to receive the message. This is one factor used by the scheduler to determine when to dehydrate a schedule. Other factors may influence this, however, so you should not expect to control hydration. In fact, schedules are always dehydrated on transaction boundaries so that the pre-transaction state may be recovered in the event of a short transaction failure.

Hydration has one important ramification for COM+ components used in schedules. If our component is stateless, and holds no property information of importance between method calls, then we have nothing to worry about. If we have a stateful component though, we should implement the `IPersist` interface. If you do so, you may indicate this support to Orchestration Designer when implementing a COM+ messaging binding. In that case, when XLANG Scheduler dehydrates a schedule it will call on your component's persistence interface, offering it a stream in which to serialize its state information. When rehydrating the schedule, this stream will be passed to the component so that it may restore its state information.

Tracking

Given the nature of the messages passing through BizTalk Server – enterprise level business events – it is essential to be able to track messaging actions. In addition to the messaging management, shared queue, and hydration databases, BizTalk Server creates and manages a final database devoted to document tracking. Every message that passes through the messaging service is, by default, stored in the database. The messaging configuration permits you several options regarding this tracking activity. You may store messages in either their native format or as XML. BizTalk document tracking captures certain fields by default: the message body, source, destination, time of the event, document type, a tracking number, and any error information. You may also specify selected fields within a message for capture. You might, for example, select a tracking ID originating in the message itself. One example of this would be a purchase order number. Although the document-tracking database will have this information in the body of the message, capturing it as a separate column in the database allows you to search on this information without opening the message itself.

Since this information is maintained in SQL Server, we can, of course, create our own reports and search tools. BizTalk Server, however, comes with a web-based application that provides a default search capability. The main page, shown below, allows a user to enter specific search criteria. Note that the application has knowledge of the different organizations and document types configured in the messaging system.

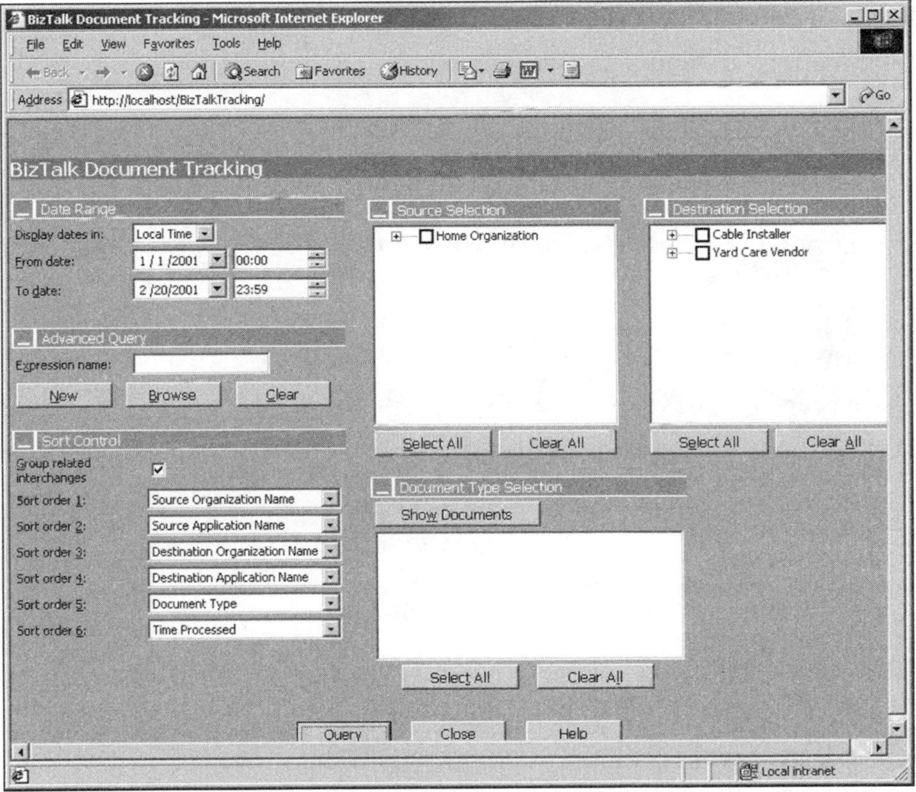

Clicking on the Query button executes a search of the document-tracking database. The results are displayed in a secondary page, which is shown overleaf:

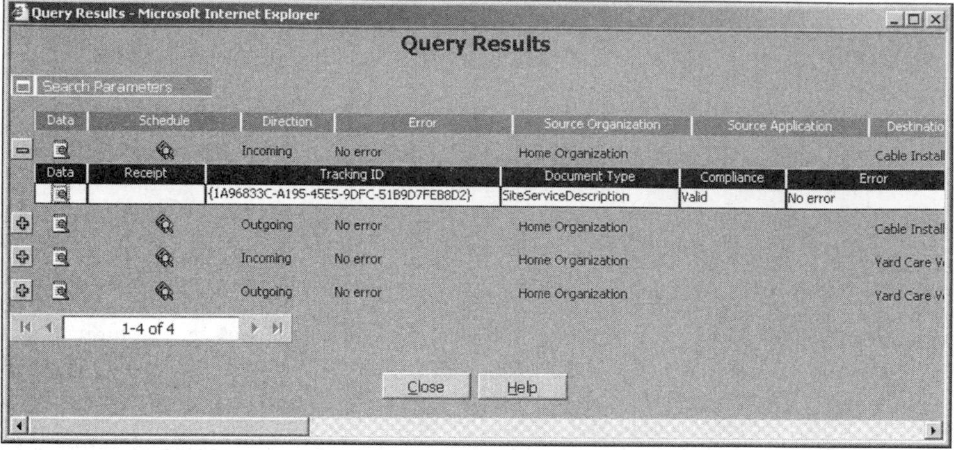

Note that the first column has an icon that indicates expandable information (the first row above is expanded). Clicking the Data icon will bring up another window (not shown), which displays the stored message body.

BizTalk Server Extensibility

BizTalk Server is built from COM+ components. In addition to facilitating the development of this product for Microsoft, this means that programmers have a wide variety of interfaces to use in extending and programming BizTalk Server. Anything that you can do through the Messaging Manager application can be done through the programmatic interfaces. Messages may be submitted using the `IInterchange` interface; indeed, that is how HTTP and SMTP `receive` functions are implemented. Using a variety of interfaces, we may perform the following tasks:

- Read and modify the messaging configuration, to include the dynamic creation of ports and channels
- Submit messages to the messaging service
- Query the document tracking database and retrieve error information for failed message interchanges
- Launch orchestration schedules and access arbitrary ports on running schedules

In addition, BizTalk Server specifies a number of interfaces that we can use to hook into the processing of the services and tools, thereby extending the product. Here are some of the things we can do:

- Perform pre-processing of messages
- Devise custom parsers and serializers for custom message types
- Develop our own mapping functoids that will be integrated into Mapper
- Correlate acknowledgements with the messages to which they respond
- Import specialized message instances into Editor and create new message specifications from them
- Write AICs that may be used in BizTalk messaging and Commerce Server pipelines

Clearing Up Some Confusion

BizTalk Server certainly isn't the only XML-based messaging technology on the market today. In fact, it isn't even the only effort from Microsoft named BizTalk. Considerable confusion has arisen around the relationship of BizTalk Server and the Simple Object Access Protocol (SOAP) as well as over the distinction between BizTalk Server and the BizTalk Framework.

SOAP is also known as XML Protocol (XP) at the W3C, where the independently developed SOAP standard is working its way through the W3C standardization process. The XP activity is found at http://www.w3.org/2000/xp/.

BizTalk Server and SOAP

SOAP is a scheme for exchanging XML documents in such a way as to implement an RPC-like mechanism. SOAP is one basis for building Web-hosted services that may be called by Web applications. Request documents are sent to a server specifying what service is desired and transmitting a parameter list. The result of the service is sent back as a response document in which the results are marked up as XML.

BizTalk Server implements XML-based messaging, but it operates at a higher level of abstraction and offers more complicated semantics. Where SOAP is inherently synchronous, BizTalk is designed to prefer asynchronous communications. Where BizTalk permits rich process information to be conveyed in a single message of arbitrary complexity, SOAP is oriented to the transmission of small chunks of data focused on a particular method or service.

SOAP, then, does not replace BizTalk, nor does it compete with it. There is considerable interest in adding SOAP to BizTalk's list of supported communications protocols in some future release of the product. If this happens, it will be used as yet another transport mechanism for moving a message from one server to another.

BizTalk Server and BizTalk Framework

The ties between BizTalk Server and BizTalk Framework are somewhat closer, although many will be surprised to discover that the two are the fruits of entirely distinct development teams at Microsoft. BizTalk Server, as we have seen, is a server product that is closely tied to the Windows operating system. It may exchange messages with applications on other platforms, but it is a software product developed and sold by Microsoft that requires Windows to run.

BizTalk Framework, on the other hand, is a messaging framework that is distinct from any particular platform or product. It is designed to specify a messaging scheme such that compliant servers gain certain advantages in terms of reliable communications. Although initiated and supported by Microsoft, anyone may use the BizTalk Framework. There is a Web site, http://www.biztalk.org, which publishes the framework specification and hosts a repository of document schemas. Membership on the site is free although registration is required in order to use the repository.

BizTalk Server is fully compliant with version 2.0 of the BizTalk Framework specification. If we examine the wizards in the Messaging Manager tool we see references to reliable messaging. This is the BizTalk Framework implementation. When we select this for a messaging configuration, BizTalk's messaging service will generate a BizTalk Framework envelope for our message.

The BizTalk Framework draws heavily on the SOAP envelope design.

When reliable messaging is used, the BizTalk messaging service will implement the scheme specified in the Framework specification. Basically, we are able to specify the number of times the messaging service will attempt to send a particular message, and how long to wait between attempts. The receiving server is obligated to respond with an acknowledgement within the window specified in the BizTalk message envelope. If the originating server does not receive an acknowledgement within this period, it will assume the message was not received and will follow our instructions regarding repeat attempts. If we use reliable messaging in BizTalk Server, we can watch your message move from the Scheduled queue to the Retry queue and eventually move to the Suspended queue as our attempts are used up.

XYZ: A B2B BizTalk Example

This has been a lot of information in a short amount of time, and even so we've really only scratched the surface of BizTalk Server. The best way to understand what we've covered and uncover areas for further investigation is to work through a sample problem. We're going to tie together all the pieces we've covered so far – orchestration, the messaging service, and message mapping – so our example will necessarily be a bit simplified. Our messages will be brief but indicative of the type of information needed. Production-ready B2B message formats can be quite complex. Take a look at the EDI message templates or the XML templates in the Microsoft folder of the repository and you will see what we mean. We are also going to replace the applications coordinated by orchestration with stubs. Nevertheless, what we are going to show is representative of a B2B workflow. We will take in messages, notify external partners, handle transactions, and send messages. Once we understand the process and the BizTalk tools, we will be ready to expand on what we show and grow into production-scale applications.

The Business Problem

Imagine that we are running a manufacturing organization. Somewhere in one of our lines we have a very specialized piece of equipment that slowly consumes some commodity that must be replaced on an infrequent basis. An example of this might be a catalyst in an oil refinery. The catalytic agent, a very expensive commodity, is replaced every six months or so. Further assume that replacing the material is such a specialized process that it requires the services of outsiders. These may be specially trained employees from a different operating group in our organization or contract technicians from an external vendor. These specialists provide some service, replenishment, calibration, or whatever, necessary to the safe and successful completion of the replacement task.

The replacement is critical to our operation. We do not want to shut down operations for an extended period, but we also do not want to replace the commodity unnecessarily. Over time, we have developed an application that is able to inform us shortly before the commodity must be replaced. Now we want to replace the manual coordination that formerly took place to effect the replacement with an automated process. Once notified by the warning application, we want to automatically order a quantity of the commodity from the supplier and simultaneously schedule a visit from the specialists. For the sake of simplicity, we will assume we have prior arrangements in place authorizing these orders and performing payment. We will also assume that we have a sole-source supplier for each task. Once the orders have been placed, an acknowledgement is sent back to the warning application so that no further notifications are made.

This scheme is going to motivate our use of several BizTalk features. These are:

- Orchestration – we will implement the tasks described above as a schedule
- BizTalk messaging – the vendors are outside organizations that require HTTP communication

- MSMQ messaging – the warning application is inside our organization, so we want to take advantage of proprietary technology; we will also be receiving an acknowledgement from the service vendor via MSMQ
- Message mapping – to make things interesting, we will design a number of XML messages and one CSV-format flatfile message requiring mapping
- Transactions – either order is useless without the other; if either message fails, we must back out of both orders

Messages

There are six distinct messages needed for our schedule:

- **LowInventory** – an XML-format message sent by the warning application indicating what is needed
- **SupplyRequest** – an XML-format message ordering the commodity from an outside vendor
- **ServiceRequest** – a CSV-format message scheduling a service visit from an outside vendor
- **SchedConfirm** – an acknowledgement message in XML format from the service vendor
- **OrderUpdate** – an XML-format message used to advise outside suppliers of a need to modify or cancel an order
- **OrderAck** – an XML-format message sent to the warning application, acting as an acknowledgement of whether resupply has been scheduled

Let's look at the structure of each message now. If we are recreating this sample manually, be sure to create a document definition for each message in Messaging Manager pointing to the document specification. Until we do so, the messaging service has no knowledge of the message and cannot make use of it.

LowInventory

The message that will start the business process is a low inventory advisory from the warning application. This message sends a request for some quantity of a commodity on behalf of a particular operating location. We model this with the `LowInventory` XML vocabulary, a sample of which is shown below:

```
<LowInventory requestID="A-8917-01" requiredBy="2001-02-20">
   <Location>Refinery Unit 7</Location>
   <Requirements quantity="100" partNumber="A8769-B9"/>
</LowInventory>
```

All the attributes and elements seen above are required. The `requestID` attribute is generated by the warning application and must be carried through the entire process so that we can reconcile all orders and advisories with the initiating `LowInventory` request. The `requiredBy` attribute is the date by which the commodity is required. It is typed as a `date` and must be in the standard format of `yyyy-mm-dd`. The `partNumber` attribute is our organization's serial number identifying the commodity needed.

Putting this into the language of BizTalk Editor, we create an XML specification whose root record is `LowInventory`. `Requirements` is also a record as it must bear the `quantity` and `partNumber` fields. Everything else is a field. This includes `Location`. Editor defaults to `Attribute` for the `Type` property of a field, so we must explicitly change this value to `Element`.

The `LowInventory` specification file is in the code download in the `DocSpecs` folder under the name `LowInventory.xml`. If we want to use it directly, without creating it manually, we copy the file to the DocSpecs folder of the `BizTalkServerRepository` folder under our BizTalk Server installation, and create a document definition for it through Messaging Manager. We name the definition Low Inventory Warning. *We must create the definition whether we create the specification through Editor or merely copy the downloaded file.*

If we examine the EDI or XML templates that ship with BizTalk Server, we realize this is a highly simplified request specification. There is no notion of payment, for example. `Location` would probably be more complicated, including contact information for someone at the requesting location. There would probably be delivery instructions as well. Nevertheless, this short message gives us some interesting and instructive tasks. A number of items need to be carried forward to other messages in the workflow. This motivates mapping as well as the data flow on the data view tab in Orchestration Designer.

SupplyRequest

`SupplyRequest` is an XML-format message used to order the desired commodity from the commodity vendor. All the information we need is found in the `LowInventory` message, but we cannot simply send the vendor that message as they use `SupplyRequest`. We will take care of this with message mapping. The schedule will send a `LowInventory` message to the messaging service. The service will invoke the mapping process and forward the resulting `SupplyRequest` message to the vendor. This is one of the great advantages of BizTalk; we work with the document formats we understand, and BizTalk makes sure our partners get messages in the formats they understand. Here is a sample `SupplyRequest` message:

```
<SupplyRequest refID="A-8917-01">
   <Delivery Site="Refinery Unit 7">
      <DeliveryDate>2001-02-20</DeliveryDate>
   </Delivery>
   <ItemOrder>
      <SerialNumber>WD40</SerialNumber>
      <Qty>100</Qty>
   </ItemOrder>
</SupplyRequest>
```

It should be fairly obvious how fields map from `LowInventory` to `SupplyRequest`. There is one wrinkle, however. The value in `SerialNumber` is different from the value in `partNumber` from the `LowInventory` message. This is not uncommon in B2B situations. Organizations frequently generate their own serial numbers for inventory items. Indeed, since `LowInventory` is requesting a combination of a commodity and a service, `partNumber` might easily pertain to the combination, not the commodity alone. In practice, we would have to perform some sort of database lookup to find the appropriate value for `SerialNumber`. In our sample, since we always know what the commodity is in this application, we will take a shortcut.

The message specification for this document is found in the DocSpecs folder of the download in the file `SupplyRequest.xml`. A sample of the message is found in the main folder as `test_supply.xml`.

Create a document definition in Messaging Manager that points to this specification and name it "Resupply Order".

ServiceRequest

The ServiceRequest message orders the service call associated with the commodity order. Just to make things interesting when we get to mapping, we've made this a delimited flatfile message. You might suppose that the service technicians are using a legacy system that pre-dates XML. Here is a sample:

```
AXY1020(A8769-B9),Refinery Unit 7,2001-02-20,A-8917-01
```

The message consists of a single record bearing four fields. The first field is an identifier for the service. This consists of the literal AXY1020 – the service technician's reference for the particular service desired – followed by the originator's identifier in parentheses. The next field is the location where service is desired, followed by the service date, and ending with the requestor's reference ID.

The specification file for this message is found in ServiceRequest.xml.

Create a new specification in BizTalk Editor. Name the root record ServiceRequest, and specify CUSTOM for the Type property on the Reference tab. While on that page, select CR (0xD) for the Default Record Delimiter, (0x2c) for the Default Field Delimiter, and ~ (0x7e) for the Default Escape Character. This establishes a carriage return between records and a comma between fields by default. The default escape character is used when a comma needs to be used inside a field.

On the Parse tab, select Infix for the Field Order property. This puts the delimiter between fields without a delimiter after the final field in a record. Specify the Delimiter Type property as Character, and select (0x2c) for the Delimiter Value property.

Next, return to the tree view and add four fields to the record: service, site, date, and refTag. Select the service field and go to the Reference tab. Select Yes for the Required property, and then go to the site field in the tree view. Once that field is selected, repeat the Required property selection. Do this for the remaining two fields. When done, we may save the specification to the repository, and create a document definition, named Service Request, in Messaging Manager, which points to this specification. We will also need to create an envelope to use this message.

The messaging service implicitly knows the syntax of XML. The delimiters for XML attributes and elements are well known. In a flatfile format, however, we have to give the service some help. It cannot know whether the format is delimited or positional, or some combination of the two. To pass along the information, flatfile messages are sent with an envelope that points to the message specification. When the service encounters this, it loads the specification and uses the information it finds there to initialize the flatfile parser.

To create an envelope, go to Messaging Manager and click on the Envelopes link. Click the Search Now button to see what envelopes are in your system, then right click in the listing and select the New Envelope item from the context menu. In the New Envelope dialog, enter Service Order CSV Envelope for the name, select FLATFILE for the envelope format, check Envelope specification, and browse to the message specification file we just created (or copied from the download).

The ServiceRequest message is also somewhat simplistic, but it is an example of the sort of message format older systems may require. This introduces you to the task of specifying flatfile formats in Editor, and will give us a chance to try out the Mapper later.

SchedConfirmation

We will want to receive confirmation from the service technicians that they can support the service request on the date indicated. Without their service, there is no point in ordering the commodity. Assume that in the past, the scheduling system for their organization was fed manually through some front-end application that generated the CSV files we described for `ServiceRequest`. A technician took requests verbally or in writing, entered the information manually, and replied by voice. Now that they've opened the application up to automated scheduling, they added an automated confirmation capability. Since it is newly created, they chose XML as the message format. This is the `SchedConfirmation` message. Here is a sample:

```
<SchedConfirmation reqID="A-8917-01" status="1"/>
```

This message is going to be passed back to us via MSMQ. Our schedule can check the status attribute, an integer value, to see whether the technicians have accepted the request. If it has a non-zero value, the request was approved.

The message specification file for this message is found in the download file named `SchedConfirm.xml`.

In BizTalk Editor, create a new XML message specification and name the root record `SchedConfirmation`. Select Empty for the value of the Content property on the Declaration tab. On the Reference tab, ensure XML is the value of the Standard property. Add two fields, `reqID` and `status`, and ensure they are typed as attributes on the Declaration tab. Go to the Reference tab for each and indicate that they are required fields. On the Declaration tab for status, select Integer (i4) for Data Type. Save the specification to the repository and create a document definition in Messaging Manager. Name the definition SchedulingConfirmation.

OrderUpdate

If the service technicians cannot accommodate our request, we will want to cancel the commodity order. This is the task of the `OrderUpdate` message. Although our messages are highly simplified, we will give this message the ability to either cancel an order, or modify some of its parameters. The idea is that the commodity vendor receives an `OrderUpdate` message with a request identifier. It checks its database for a `SupplyRequest` message with the same ID. If it finds one, it either deletes it or updates its parameters as indicated in the `OrderUpdate` message. If it does not find one, it ignores the `OrderUpdate` message. Here is a sample:

```
<OrderUpdate requestID="A-8917-01" action="cancel">
   <OrderInfo part="A8769-B9" quantity="100">
      <Location>Refinery Unit 7</Location>
   </OrderInfo>
</OrderUpdate>
```

This message is specified in the file `OrderUpdate.xml`.

All records and fields are required. The action field is an enumerated type with the values `cancel` and `modify`. `OrderUpdate` and `OrderInfo` are records in the specification. The remaining items are fields. As with the other message specifications, you must save it to the document repository and create a document definition that refers to this specification through the Messaging Manager. Give the definition the name Order Update.

OrderAck

When the process is complete, we will want to send an acknowledgement back to the warning application telling it whether or not we are dealing with the low inventory situation. If we've successfully placed our orders, we will want to tell the application to stop worrying about the situation. If we encountered a problem – a messaging failure or a failure to schedule the service technicians – the application should be properly advised so that it can take alternative action or keep notifying us. This will be an XML-format message named `OrderAck`, of which a sample is shown here:

```
<OrderAck requestID="A-8719-01" ackType="ok">
   <Order>
      <Location>Refinery Unit 7</Location>
      <Part>A8769-B9</Part>
   </Order>
</OrderAck>
```

As can be seen, this message references the request identifier originally provided in the `LowInventory` message and repeats the location and part number information. If the value of the `ackType` attribute is the string "`ok`", the process succeeded. If the value is error, the warning application must take alternative action.

The message specification file for this message is named `OrderAck.xml`.

`OrderAck` and `Order` are records; the remaining items are fields. The `Location` and `Part` fields are typed as Element on the Declaration tab. We can accept the default, Attribute, for the others. All fields are required. On the Reference tab for `Order`, specify 1 as the value for both the Minimum Occurrences and Maximum Occurrences properties. When done, create a document definition in Messaging Manager and name it Order Ack (warning ack).

Mapping

Before we get into the schedule for this process, we need to deal with the format translations implied by our messages. `LowInventory` can be mapped directly into `SupplyRequest` and `ServiceRequest`, thereby relieving the schedule of the task of generating these messages. Instead, it just passes the `LowInventory` message it receives to the messaging service twice, once for each order, and the service will translate it into the designated outbound format. We therefore need to create two maps in BizTalk Mapper.

The map files are found in the download in the files `LowInventoryToSupplyRequest.xml` *and* `LowInventoryToSvcRequest.xml` *in the* `Maps` *folder of the download. You may copy these files to your document repository or create them as indicated in the following sections.*

LowInventory to SupplyRequest

This map is a good introduction to Mapper as it uses only a few of Mapper's features. Also, as an XML-to-XML translation, we can use Mapper to test the map and observe output in the `SupplyRequest` vocabulary. When dealing with translations involving flatfiles, as we shall see, the output is an intermediate XML form, not the final flatfile format we might expect. This map will be used as part of a messaging channel invoked by the schedule when ordering commodity supplies.

Open Mapper and use File New... or click on the new document icon to create a new map. When prompted for the source specification, go to the document repository and select `LowInventory.xml`. Immediately after this, we will be prompted for the destination message specification. Select `SupplyRequest.xml` from the repository. The two specifications will open in the tree views of the main window.

The map is composed almost entirely of direct links between a single field in the source document and a single field in the destination document. To create such a link, we select the source field node of the tree view, and then drag the mouse over to the desired destination field. A line will be drawn between the two fields, and the nodes involved will display a chain-link icon. To create the map, establish the following links:

- `requestID` to `refID`
- `Location` to `Site`
- `requiredBy` to `DeliveryDate`
- `quantity` to `Qty`

Conspicuously absent is any link going into the `SerialNumber` field. In a production environment, we'd probably reuse `SupplyRequest` across multiple applications and vendors, so we would have to extract the appropriate value from a database using the database functoids. Our sample is limited to a known commodity, so we can enter a constant value. Select the `SerialNumber` field in the `SupplyRequest` view, and then select the **Values** tab in the window at the bottom of the application. On the right side of this property page is an edit field labeled **Destination constant value**. Enter any value here. This value will be copied into the output `SerialNumber` field whenever the translation is performed.

Readers who have downloaded the message map will notice that I'm not exactly ordering sophisticated, expensive chemicals at this point.

At this point, the map is complete. We should click Tools | Compile Map and check the Output tab for warnings. Unlike a programming language compiler, a warning in BizTalk Mapper is an error. It has to be fixed before using it with channels in the messaging service. Once we have saved the map to the repository, click on Tools | Test Map. A sample `SupplyRequest` document will be generated and displayed in the Output tab using default values. We can verify that selected source fields are actually performing the mapping and entering values for them in the Source test value edit control of the Values tab. When we do so and when we test the map, the values that we input will be used in the mapping and will appear in the output.

LowInventory to ServiceRequest

The last map was a little too easy. This time around, we'll throw in a functoid and show what happens when we test an XML-to-flatfile map. To begin, create a new map specifying `LowInventory.xml` as the source specification and `ServiceRequest.xml` as the destination specification. As before, the specifications arrange themselves in the two tree views. Now establish the following direct links:

- `requestID` to `refTag`
- `Location` to `site`
- `requiredBy` to `date`

There are no constant values used in the map. We are free to enter any source test values we wish. This leaves us with just one more link, the one needed to map `partNumber` into `service`. Recall that the part number we use probably won't be the number the service technicians use. Like the commodity mapping, we would probably have to do some kind of database lookup in a production application. From our discussion of the `ServiceRequest` specification, though, we recall that we said this service uses a fixed value followed by the requestor's part number in parentheses. This would be used by a technician to refer to the originally requested part number when talking to a member of our organization. We can do this translation using a functoid.

Click on the toolbar icon that looks like a painter's palette or click View Functoid Palette... on the main menu. When the functoid palette appears, select the String tab. Drag the Concatenate functoid to the grid between the two tree views.

The names of the functoids are displayed in tooltips if you hover over the functoid icons. In the illustration below, the functoid you are looking for is in the first row, third from the right.

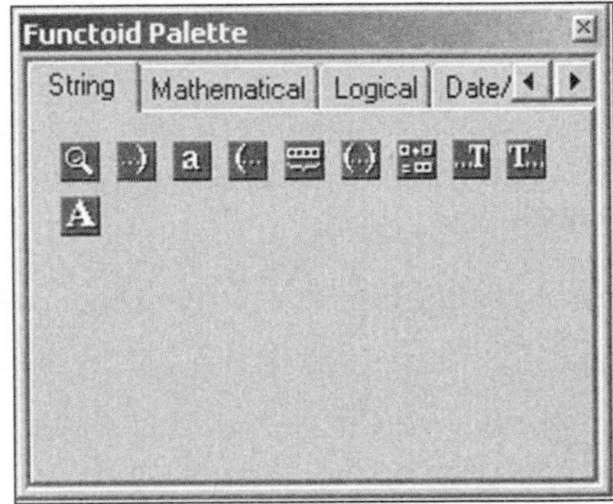

When the functoid is positioned on the grid, drag a link from `partNumber` to the functoid, and then drag a link from the functoid to `service`. Double-click on the functoid. We will see a dialog with two pages. The second, Script, is a read-only copy of the script code that will be embedded in the map and executed at run-time. We are interested in the first page, General. When first seen, the only parameter displayed is the inbound link, represented by the XPath expression `/LowInventory/Requirements/@partNumber`. Click on the Insert New Parameter icon, the left-most one in the dialog's toolbar, to add two new parameters. Enter "`AXY1020(`" into the first one, and "`)`" into the other one. These are constant values that will be used in the map. Click on the up and down arrow buttons to position the first parameter before the linked parameter and the second new parameter after the linked parameter. This will be reflected in the script. Now, when the script is executed, the three parameters will be concatenated in the order in which they appear in our list and the result will be copied to the output service field. The result of our work should look like the map shown in the screenshot found in the "Format Translation" section earlier in this chapter.

After checking then compiling the map, we will want to test it. If we do so, we find that the output window displays an XML document with the names from `ServiceRequest.xml`. This is a function of how mapping takes place in the messaging service when flatfiles are involved. If the source is a flatfile, the flatfile parser component uses the message specification to translate the inbound document into an intermediate XML form. If the source is XML, no translation is necessary. At that point, the XSLT transformation embedded in the map file is applied to generate another XML form. If the output is XML, this is what is output. In this case, where the destination is a flatfile, the flatfile serializer component uses the destination message specification to convert the transformed intermediate XML into the final flatfile format.

BizTalk Mapper does not have access to the parser and serializer components however, so all you will see in the output following a test is the transformed intermediate XML. This should verify that the correct data is being picked up and placed in the proper fields within the proper records. If a channel involving this map fails in practice but the map test succeeds, the problem would be either in the parser or the serializer. The most likely cause will be a problem with one of the message specifications.

At this point, we have all the low-level documents needed to implement the messaging portion of our process. Before building up the ports and channels required, let's build the orchestration schedule so we can gain some idea of the big picture.

The Schedule

We've finally reached the exciting part of the whole process. We are about to specify the high-level coordination that turns a series of discrete messaging actions into a business process. This specification is a declarative way to implement an algorithm involving things like decisions and transactions. In a production application, we would work with a business analyst to ensure the validity of the process. Since there's no one here except programmers, let's get started.

Business Process Diagram

We begin the business process diagram in Orchestration Designer by drawing a flowchart without worrying unduly about the messaging implementations of the various actions. The flowchart, shown below, should reflect the following basic flow of tasks:

- Receive a `LowInventory` message from the warning application
- Begin a timed transaction
- Send the `LowInventory` message to the commodity vendor, relying on the messaging service to perform the translation to `SupplyRequest`
- Send the `LowInventory` message to the service technicians, similarly relying on the messaging service
- Wait for a `SchedConfirmation` message from the service technicians
- Leave the boundaries of the transaction
- If the confirmation arrived with a non-zero status value, send an `OrderAck` message with an `ackType` value of `ok`
- If the confirmation message was never received or was received with a status value of zero, send an `OrderAck` message with `ackType` set to `error`

The Visio file for this schedule is found in the main folder of the download under the name `InventoryOrderProcess.skv`. *Its XLANG export, an XML document, is* `InventoryOrderProcess.skx`.

Drag the shapes from the stencil to the left side of the business process diagram so that it resembles the diagram below. Do not worry about placing the transaction, connecting the shapes, or binding to messaging implementations yet. Double click on each shape and enter the label shown below for each. These are unimportant to schedule execution, but they will help us follow the discussion that follows. When we are done, we will have the start of a flowchart, but no shapes on the right side of the document or on the double-line boundary between the two sides.

To place the transaction shape, drag it from the stencil so that it covers the three action shapes. Depending on your placement, we may need to resize the shape. When we have it in place, double click on it to reach the Transaction Properties dialog. Give the transaction the name Orders Tx. Check the Timed transaction radio button and enter 100 for the Timeout value in the Transaction options group. In the On failure group, click the Add Code button. The Enabled checkbox becomes enabled and the button changes to Delete Code. Check the check box to enable transaction failure processing. We will provide this processing later. When we click OK, the transaction shape is renamed and colored blue, and we will notice a tab labeled On Failure of Orders Tx has been added to the diagram. Ignore this tab for a moment.

We connect two shapes by selecting one shape, then dragging from one of its connection points (indicated by an X on the shape) to a connection point on the next shape. To connect the transaction properly, drag a connection from **Recv Low Inventory** to the top connection point on the transaction, and then connect it to the **Order Commodity** shape. Continue as shown until **Recv Sched Confirm** is connected to the bottom connection point on the transaction, and then connect that to the first decision shape. Connect the remaining shapes. We still will not have any shapes on the boundary or any connections between the action shapes and anything to their right.

The result of the transaction is to establish a group of actions that must complete within 100 seconds. If a system-generated failure occurs with a transactional resource, such as MSMQ, or we remain blocked waiting for a reply until the transaction times out, the transaction will fail. Note that a failure in the HTTP transmission will not trigger an abort, as HTTP is not transactional. That is why we are dependent on getting an acknowledgement from the service technicians. Besides transactional COM+ failures, aborts may be manually caused by placing an abort shape in the flow of processing.

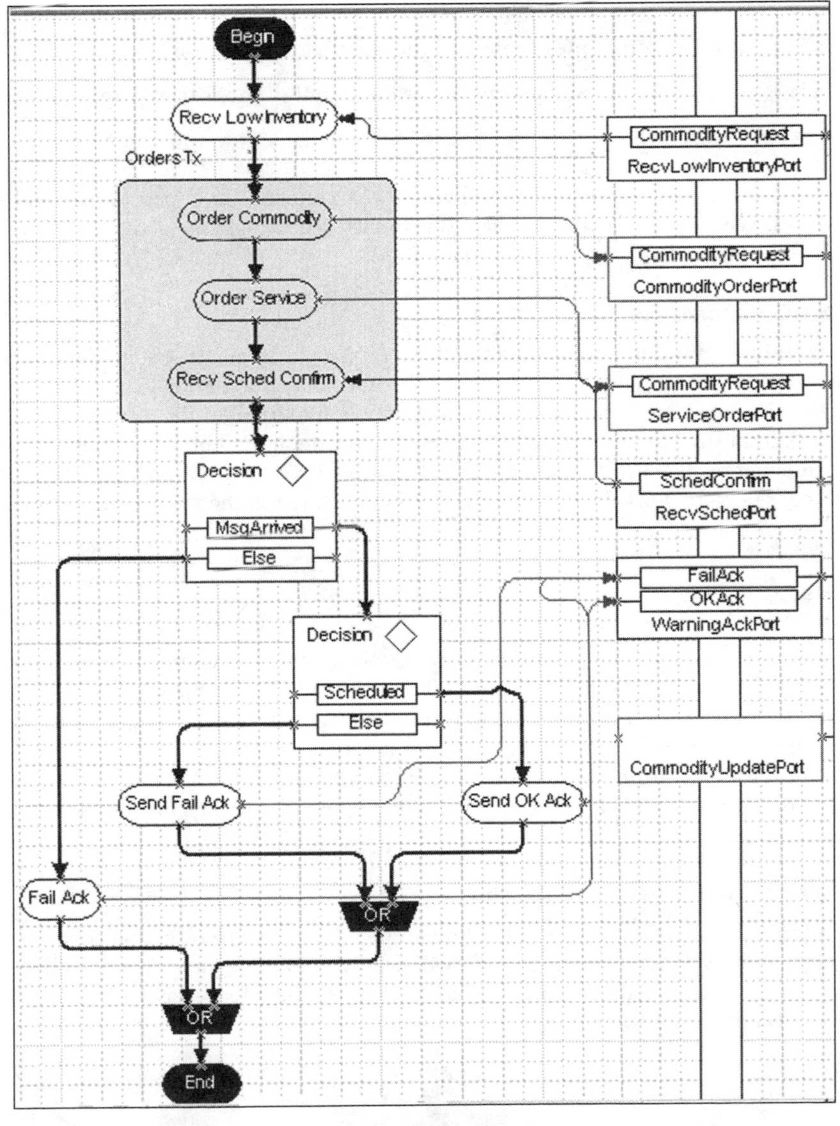

Before we can fill in the rules for the decision shapes, we need some messages. This is accomplished by binding the action shapes to messaging implementations.

Message Queuing Implementations

We're going to use MSMQ to get the `LowInventory` message into our schedule, receive the `SchedConfirmation` message from the service technicians, and send `OrderAck` messages to the warning application. Let's create the queues we'll need, then create the Message Queuing implementations we need in the schedule.

Creating the Queues

We will need to create the following transactional private queues. This may be done through the Computer Management utility usually found through the Administrative Tools menu on most installations. Locate the Message Queuing service, navigate to Private Queues, and right click to create a new private queue. The queues are:

- `Warning_adv` – receives messages from the warning application
- `Warning_ack` – takes `OrderAck` messages on behalf of the warning application
- `Svc_sched` – receives `SchedConfirmation` messages from the service technicians

Ensure each queue is transactional and that the Everyone account has full rights to read and write messages from these queues. We may restrict these rights later. In fact, removing write-access to the `svc_sched` queue is the easiest way to trigger failure of the transaction.

Creating an MSMQ Receive Function

We will have a stub program to send messages to the `warning_adv` queue, but how does the message get into a running instance of the schedule? We'll take advantage of an interesting feature of the messaging service to do this. First, we need an MSMQ `receive` function to monitor the `warning_adv` queue. Go into BizTalk Server Administration and navigate to the Receive Functions node. Right-click on it and create a new message queuing receive function. Give it the name Low Inventory. On the Services tab of the properties dialog, select the BizTalk Server computer on which to run the `receive` function. In the Polling location field, enter the string:

```
DIRECT=OS:your_machine_name\private$\warning_adv
```

Here, *`your_machine_name`* should be replaced by the actual machine name of the server hosting the queue. On the Advanced tab, ensure Openness is Not open, then enter the name ReceiveLowInventoryChannel in the Channel name field. When we get to BizTalk messaging, we will create this channel. Click OK. This creates a `receive` function, which will monitor our queue and pass messages to the BizTalk messaging service using the ReceiveLowInventoryChannel channel. This channel, in turn, will be configured to launch a new instance of the schedule and pass the message to the first port, thereby starting our processing.

Creating MSMQ Implementations and Binding To Them

Now return to Orchestration Designer. The binding to the initial message reception is performed through BizTalk messaging, not MSMQ messaging, so we will defer this for a moment. We need BizTalk messaging, remember, to be able to launch the schedule. Let's create the binding for receiving confirmation messages from the service technicians first.

Drag a Message Queuing shape onto the right side of the schedule diagram, to the right of the double-line boundary. The BizTalk Message Binding Wizard starts. Name the port RecvSchedPort. Click Static Queue on the Static or Dynamic Queue Information page.

Click Use a known queue for all instances on the Queue Information page and enter the string: `.\private$\svc_sched` to tell Orchestration which queue to monitor. Note that private queues are local to the machine using them. We've chosen this for convenience, using a single machine for both BizTalk Server and MSMQ. Since we are not using BizTalk to launch the schedule (it's already running at this step), we can use MSMQ directly.

In a production environment, we would want to use a new queue for each instance to associate a queue with a particular schedule. In that case, we would have to pass the name of the queue to the service technicians in the `ServiceRequest` message. Since we know we will never have concurrent instances of the schedule running, we can use the static queue we created a moment ago.

Click Transactions are required with this queue on the Advanced Port Properties page and click Finish. The wizard terminates and we see a Message Queuing shape on the page connected to a port on the double-line boundary between the business process diagram and the messaging implementations. Now we need to bind the Recv Sched Confirm action to the port. Drag a connection from the action shape to the port you just created to start the XML Communication Wizard.

On the Welcome page, click Receive and enter 60 as the number of seconds we expect the XLANG Scheduler to wait. This is just an estimate used by BizTalk to optimize its hydration decisions (see the "Hydration" section earlier in the chapter). On the Message Information page, create a new message named SchedConfirm. This name is what will appear on the Data view and does not reflect the root element name of the messages we will receive.

On the XML Translation Information page, select Receive XML messages from the queue. On the Message Type Information page, enter SchedConfirmation. Now XLANG Scheduler knows it is receiving XML and understands what element name to look for in incoming messages. On the Message Specification Information page, browse for the message specification you created for this message in the repository. Check Validate messages against the specification. While you are on this page, you need to add a message field to the list in the Message fields group. The ones listed are the ones that will appear for the message in the Data view. Unless we add the status field, we will be unable to see it in the schedule. We want to write rules that check for this value to decide what sort of acknowledgement to send to the warning application. Click on Add... and navigate to the `status` node on the tree view that appears. Orchestration Designer is using the message specification to understand the structure of the incoming messages and generates an XPath expression with which it will retrieve `status` values at run time. These values will be made available to us for use in the schedule.

Now we need to set up an implementation and binding for the `OrderAck` confirmation back to the warning application. Once again drag a Message Queuing shape onto the implementations side of the schedule's business process diagram. In the Wizard, name the port WarningAckPort, select a static queue with a known instance (`.\private$\warning_ack`) for all instances, and indicate that transactions are required.

Next, establish a connection between the Send OK Ack action shape and the newly created port. Select Send as the direction and create a new message named OKAck. For reasons that will become clear when we address the Data view, we need distinct message references in the schedule for OrderAck messages with `ackType` set to `ok` and the same document type with `ackType` set to `error`. Select Send XML messages to the queue, specify `OrderAck` as the message type, and point to the message specification. Add all the fields of the message to the Message fields list on the Message Specification Information page. We're going to set up the message entirely within the schedule using data flows, so we need to be able to see all the fields in the message from the Data view page.

Now drag a connection from the Send Fail Ack shape to the same port and create a message named FailAck. Give it all the same information you provided in OKAck. When finished, the port will have two labeled rectangles inside the port shape to reflect the two messages. Send OK Ack will be connected to one, while Send Fail Ack will be connected to the other. Finally, drag a connection from the Fail Ack action shape to the port. This time, instead of creating a new message, we add a reference to the existing FailAck message. When finished, the connection we just made will be connected to the FailAck shape within the WarningAckPort. This completes the MSMQ messaging implementations for the schedule.

Creating BizTalk Messaging Configurations

Now we need to set up BizTalk messaging services for the schedule. Before we connect anything in the schedule, we'll go to Messaging Manager and create some configurations that build on the document definitions and the envelope that we created earlier.

Application

We'll presume we are the Home Organization that is created by BizTalk during installation. It is possible to rename this organization, but it is the only one that can have applications designated for it. BizTalk Server assumes that external organizations are black boxes as far as you are concerned. Find the Home Organization and double click on it. On the Applications tab of the Organization Properties dialog box, click Add and enter the name warning. This name stands for our warning application in the messaging service. It is merely a name used by the messaging service to keep things straight.

Organizations

The first step is to establish organizations for our external partners. In the Organizations list, right click and select New Organization. Enter the name Commodity Vendor and click the OK button to create the organization that supplies our commodities. Repeat the task for the service technicians, giving their organization the name Service Technicians.

Ports

That's pretty boring stuff. Life starts to get more exciting when we create ports. These are messaging endpoints that refer to some URL, queue name, or COM+ component. We need the following ports:

- `RecvLowInventoryPort` – for receiving `LowInventory` messages from the MSMQ receive function and bringing them into the messaging service
- `CommodityOrderPort` – for sending commodity orders and `OrderUpdate` messages to the commodity vendor
- `ServiceRequestPort` – for sending `ServiceRequest` messages to the service technicians inside the flatfile envelope we created earlier

Even though requests and updates will all use the same protocol – HTTP – we need two ports for the service technicians and only one for the commodity vendor because the commodity vendor uses XML exclusively, while the service technicians use flatfiles for requests (which require an envelope) and XML for updates (which do not).

In the ports listing, right-click and create a new port to an application, and name it RecvLowInventoryPort. From BizTalk's point of view, we will be receiving this message from a receive function and sending it to a new schedule instance. Therefore, on the Destination Application page, select New XLANG schedule. In the Schedule moniker field, enter the file path to the InventoryOrderProcess.skx file. This is the XLANG document we will create from Orchestration Designer that initializes XLANG Scheduler. We can put it anywhere on the server. Enter RecvLowInventoryPort in the port name field. This is an orchestration port we shall create when we bind the initial action shape to the BizTalk messaging implementation. The messaging service will use the information you are entering on this property page to find the schedule, launch it, and pass the message into the schedule. Click Finish to save the port in the messaging management database.

> *The Wizard gives us the option of creating a channel that uses the port. For the purposes of organization, we are going to continue with the port configurations. We may skip ahead to the next section, or bypass the channel creation process for now.*

Now create a new port to an organization and name it CommodityOrderPort. We'll use this to send `SupplyOrder` messages to the commodity vendor via HTTP. Select Organization on the Destination Organization page and browse to the Commodity Vendor. Click the Browse button and select HTTP as the transport type. Enter a URL ending in `CommodityOrders.asp` – the details of the URL will depend on where you choose to locate the ASP on your server. You're going to need to create a virtual directory in IIS to host this page. We will be developing that page as the `receive` function for the commodity vendor. Click OK to close the browse dialog, and then click Finish to save the port.

We'll repeat the process for the ServiceRequestPort. Provide the name, select the Service Technicians organization, and enter an HTTP URL ending in `ServiceOrders.asp`. Inside of clicking Finish, however, proceed to the Envelope Information page and browse to the Service Order CSV Envelope. Click Finish to save the port to the messaging management database. Now we have an HTTP port pointing to an ASP receive function, but the messaging service will wrap the CSV flatfile in an appropriate envelope.

Channels

Channels are the configuration that ties processing instructions for a particular message with the location specified by a port. The action shapes in the schedule refer to channels, so these configurations are the final piece we need to configure in Messaging Manager. We need the following channels:

- `RecvLowInventoryChannel` – delivering `LowInventory` messages to the Recv Low Inventory action
- `SupplyOrdersChannel` – taking `LowInventory` messages from the Order Commodity action and sending it to the commodity vendor after translation to `SupplyRequest`
- `ServiceOrdersChannel` – taking `LowInventory` messages from the Order Service action and sending it to the service technicians after translation to `ServiceRequest`
- `CommodityOrderUpdateChannel` – taking `OrderUpdate` messages in the On Failure of Orders Tx page in response to a transaction abort and sending them to the commodity vendor

We'll start with the channel used to deliver the `LowInventory` message to the schedule. We've referred to this by the name RecvLowInventoryChannel in the MSMQ `receive` function, so we'd better be sure we configure it and give it this name.

In the ports list, right-click on the RecvLowInventoryPort and select New Channel from an Application. In the Channel Wizard, enter the name of the channel and proceed to the Source Application page. Click Application, and then select warning from the list. On the Inbound Document page, browse to the Low Inventory Warning message. Remember, the names in the list are the names we created in the document definitions. Those definitions point to the message specification files, but there is no need for the document definitions to have the exact same name as the document element or the filename. These are just configurations in the database.

On the Outbound Document page, browse to the same message. The messaging service is getting a `LowInventory` message from the MSMQ receive function and passing it along unchanged to the schedule it launches. Click Finish to save this channel.

Commodity orders require the SupplyOrdersChannel channel. In the list of ports, right-click on the CommodityOrderPort and create a channel to an organization. In the Wizard, provide the name SupplyOrdersChannel. On the next page, select XLANG Schedule as the source. This message will be originating in an action in our schedule. For the Inbound Document page, browse to the Low Inventory Warning document definition. Remember that as far as the schedule is concerned, that is what it is sending. On the next page we will specify the map we created to convert the message to the SupplyRequest format.

For the Outbound Document page, browse to the Resupply Order document definition you created for the SupplyRequest document definition. The Wizard will automatically check the Map inbound document to outbound document check box when it detects that the inbound and outbound formats are different. You must browse to the message map we created for this transformation before leaving this page. That map is called `LowInventoryToSupplyRequest.xml`. Click Finish to accept the remaining defaults and save the channel configuration.

The ServiceOrderChannel configuration is similar. In the Wizard, enter the name and proceed to the Source Application page to select XLANG Schedule as the source. The inbound document definition is Low Inventory Warning, the outbound definition is Service Request, and the map specification is `LowInventoryToSvcRequest.xml`. Click Finish to save the channel.

Finally, click on the CommodityOrderPort once again and create a channel to an organization. The name is CommodityOrderUpdateChannel, the source is XLANG Schedule, and the inbound and outbound document definitions are Order Update. We will be creating these messages entirely within the schedule using the Data view and no translation is needed.

At this point we are finished with Messaging Manager. All that remains is to bind the action shapes in our schedule's business process diagram to BizTalk Messaging implementations.

> *We are going to proceed without testing these channels individually. As a practical matter, we highly recommend that you obtain the channel tester utility from the download for Professional BizTalk (Wrox Press, ISBN 1-861003-29-3) or devise your own. That way, you may test the individual channels that implement each action in a schedule before tackling the schedule as a whole. This greatly simplifies troubleshooting as it eliminates the messaging service as a possible cause when a schedule does not work as expected. It is probably worth downloading said download anyway, as it contains some other very useful resources that will help with this chapter.*

Binding To BizTalk Messaging

Returning to the business process diagram in Orchestration Designer, we'll create three BizTalk Messaging implementations on the business process diagram. In the following section, we'll create a very simple process for recovering from transaction failures. That will include a single action that uses a final BizTalk Messaging implementation. Each of these implementations uses one of the channels we created in the last section. Here is the list of implementations and bindings needed on the business process diagram:

- RecvLowInventoryChannel to Recv Low Inventory action
- Order Commodity action to SupplyOrdersChannel
- Order Service action to ServiceOrdersChannel

Drag a BizTalk Messaging shape onto the implementations side of the business process diagram – the BizTalk Messaging Binding Wizard appears. Name the schedule's port RecvLowInventoryPort. Remember, this is the schedule's port and has nothing to do with any of the messaging service's ports we created a few sections ago. On the next page, select receive as the direction of communication. Click Next to proceed to the XLANG Schedule Activation Information page.

We want this channel binding to launch the schedule, so click Yes to confirm this. Click Finish to complete the implementation. The shape appears on the right, and a new port appears on the double-line boundary. Drag a connection from the Recv Low Inventory action shape to the port. The XML Communications Wizard appears.

The direction of communications was set in the implementation, so although the Receive radio button is selected on the Welcome page, both radio buttons are disabled. On the Message Information page, create a new message and name it CommodityRequest. Select Receive XML message from the queue on the XML Translation Information page and enter LowInventory for the message type on the Message Type Information page. This name must match the document element of the XML messages we are going to receive. Proceed to the Message Specification Information page.

Browse to the `LowInventory.xml` message specification file, then add the `requestID`, `Location`, `requiredBy`, `quantity`, and `partNumber` fields. Click Finish to complete the binding in the schedule. The part of the business process diagram dealing with the first action should look something like this:

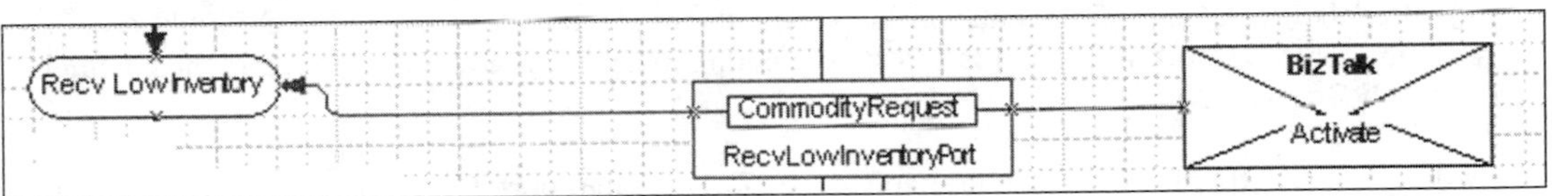

Now we need to create an implementation for the Order Commodity action. Once again, drag a BizTalk Messaging implementation shape from the stencil to the implementation side of the business process diagram. Enter CommodityOrderPort for the port name. The communication direction is Send, and the static channel is SupplyOrdersChannel. Click Finish.

Now drag a connection from the Order Commodity action to the new port. Verify that Send is selected. Add a reference to the CommodityRequest message. Again, as with the first binding, we wish to send XML messages to the queue. The message type is LowInventory as we are going to send a copy of the message we received out of the schedule to the messaging service. The message specification should be provided for us along with the field selections. Click Finish. This part of the diagram will now look like this:

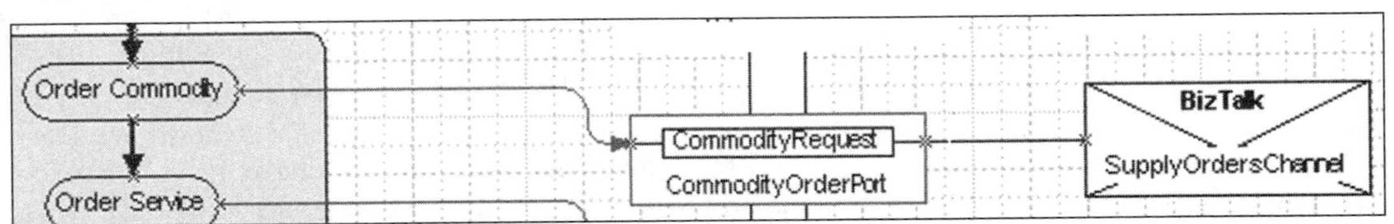

The process for the implementation for sending messages to the service technicians should be familiar by now. Drag the BizTalk Messaging implementation shape onto the diagram. Name the port ServiceOrderPort. The communication direction is Send, and the channel to use is ServiceOrdersChannel, referring to the channel configuration we created in Messaging Manager. Click Finish.

Drag a connection to the port from the Order Service action shape. Add a reference to the Commodity Request message we created for the first implementation. We want to send XML messages to the queue. The message type is LowInventory, and the specification and field selections should be established. It should look something like this:

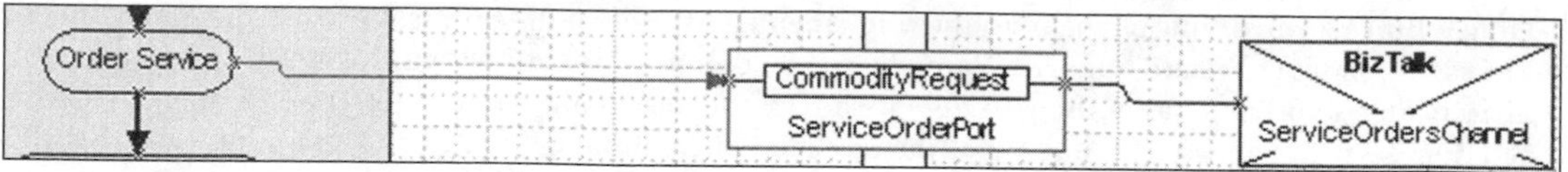

This completes the message implementations that we need if everything works as planned in the business process diagram. Since we have a transaction, however, we have to plan recovery actions in the event the transaction fails. This is the "code" we have to supply for the On Failure of Orders Tx tab that was created when we configured the transaction.

Recovering from Transaction Failures

If the transaction fails, we want to send an `OrderUpdate` message to the commodity vendor to cancel the order. On the On Failure page, add an action shape and name it Update Commodity. Add an End shape, then connect the Begin shape to the action shape and the action shape to the End shape. That's all that is required for the logical flow.

To implement this flow physically, we need a BizTalk Messaging implementation that uses the CommodityOrderUpdateChannel from the messaging service. This sends the `OrderUpdate` message to the commodity vendor's HTTP `receive` function without change.

Drag a BizTalk Messaging implementation shape onto the implementation side of the On Failure page. The port name should be CommodityUpdatePort. The communication direction is Send, and the channel is CommodityOrderUpdateChannel. Click Finish.

Now drag a connection from the action shape to the newly created port. Create a new message (from the schedule's point of view) and name it OrderUpdate. Send XML messages to the queue. The message type is OrderUpdate and the specification file is `OrderUpdate.xml`. Add the `requestID`, `part`, `quantity`, and `Location` fields to the schedule. As with the `OrderAck` message, we will be creating the `OrderUpdate` message within the schedule using the data flow, so we need to have these fields visible to the schedule so we can set their values.

Putting Rules Into the Decision Shapes

Now we can return to the business process diagram and finish it by adding rules to the decision shapes. We'll first turn our attention to the shape that is connected to, and immediately follows, the transaction. Whether the transaction commits or aborts, processing will reach this shape. We need to decide if the transaction completed successfully.

We can do this by checking to see if the `SchedConfirmation` message arrived from the service technicians. The only thing that can abort the transaction is a problem with the MSMQ messaging. Double-click on the shape, or right-click and select the Properties... menu item on the context menu. When the Decision Properties dialog appears, click the Add button. Create a new rule is selected by default in the Add Rule dialog that appears. As we create rules, they are displayed in this dialog so that they may be reused in other decision shapes. Right now, though, we need to create our first rule. Click OK, and the Rule Properties dialog will appear.

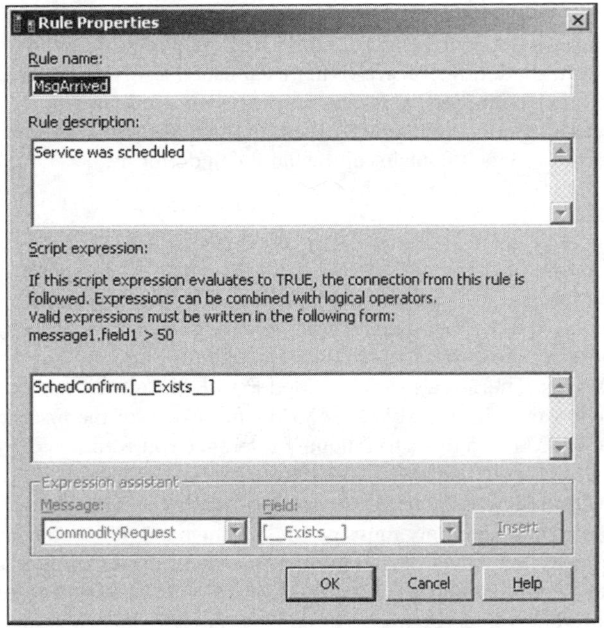

As we can see in the screenshot above, we've named our rule `MsgArrived` and provided a comment. In the **Expression assistant** group (which is unfortunately disabled in the screenshot), we can see a drop-down list box containing a list of the messages we've defined in the schedule. Select **SchedConfirm**, then go to the **Field** list box. The fields we've selected during binding are there, but there are also some fields delimited by brackets and double underscore characters. These are system-provided fields. The field `[__Exists__]` has the value **true** if the message appears in the system at run-time. It will be true for **SchedConfirm** only if we receive that message. Select this field, then click **Insert**. The VBScript fragment `SchedConfim.[__Exists__]` now appears in the **Script expression** box. In general, we may use any VBScript expression that evaluates to a Boolean value as the text of a decision shape rule. Click **OK** to add the rule to the decision shape, then **OK** in the **Decision Properties** dialog to dismiss it and accept the rule. A rectangle labeled with the name of the rule now appears inside the decision shape above the rectangle labeled **Else**. We may add multiple rules to a decision shape, although we don't need that feature in our schedule. Each rule will be evaluated in the order in which it appears. The first one to evaluate `true` controls the flow of execution in the schedule.

Now drag a connection from the rule's connection point to the top of the next decision shape. Drag a connection from the **Else** rectangle to the top of the **Fail Ack** action shape.

Now proceed to the next decision shape and add a rule named **Scheduled**. This rule is a bit more complicated. We want to check and see that the status field in the `SchedConfirmation` message is greater than zero and that no `OrderUpdate` message was sent. This confirms that there were no problems and the service technicians have accepted the schedule. When we are done with the Expression Assistant, the rule should look like this: `SchedConfirm.status > 0 and not OrderUpdate.[__Exists__]`. Connect this rule to the **Send OK Ack** action shape and the **Else** to the **Send Fail Ack** action shape. Ensure that the join shapes read **OR**, if it hasn't been done previously. We can do this by double clicking on the shape and selecting the appropriate radio button in the **Properties** dialog.

At this point, our business process diagram should look like it did in our original screenshot (see the "Business Process Diagram" section). All the action shapes should be bound to message implementations. We might think that the schedule is finished, however we've not established a way to create the `OrderUpdate` or `OrderAck` messages. While a complicated, production-ready schedule might use a call to a COM+ component to do this, we can get by with creating them in the **Data** view. This will give us a chance to inspect that view and see what data it contains and what it can do for us.

Data Flow

Click on the tab at the bottom of the screen labeled **Data**. The page that appears is quite a bit different from the business process diagram. We will see a series of labeled tabular shapes. Each message we created in the message binding process has a table listing the system fields available for it as well as any fields we selected. These tables are what permit us to gain access to the field values passed in the messages at run-time and copy them to subsequent messages. There is also a table titled **Port References** with a list of the messaging implementation ports. The values in this table are COM+ monikers for the instantiated ports. Such monikers are strings that allow the COM+ run times to uniquely reference some entity.

We are going to use the **Data** view, as noted, to create the `OrderAck` and `OrderUpdate` messages. The basic procedure for this is to add an empty message shell to the data view as a constant, then fill in the values of the fields using the appropriate values passed in other messages, for example the request reference ID. To do this, go to the **Constants** table and right mouse click, then select the **Properties...** menu item from the context menu. In the **Constants** message properties dialog that appears, click the **Add...** button. In the **Constant Properties** dialog, enter the name **OrderAckShell**, ensure **string** is the data type, and type the following string into the **value** field:

```
<OrderAck requestType="" ackType="">
   <Order><Location/><Part/></Order>
</OrderAck>
```

This is the empty shell of an `OrderAck` message. We can obtain all the data we need for the fields except for the value for the `ackType` attribute. To provide this, we'll add two more string constants, `OK`, with the value "`ok`", and `Error`, with the value "`error`". Once we have added these, arrange the message tables so that they look something like the diagram overleaf. Ignore the connections for a moment.

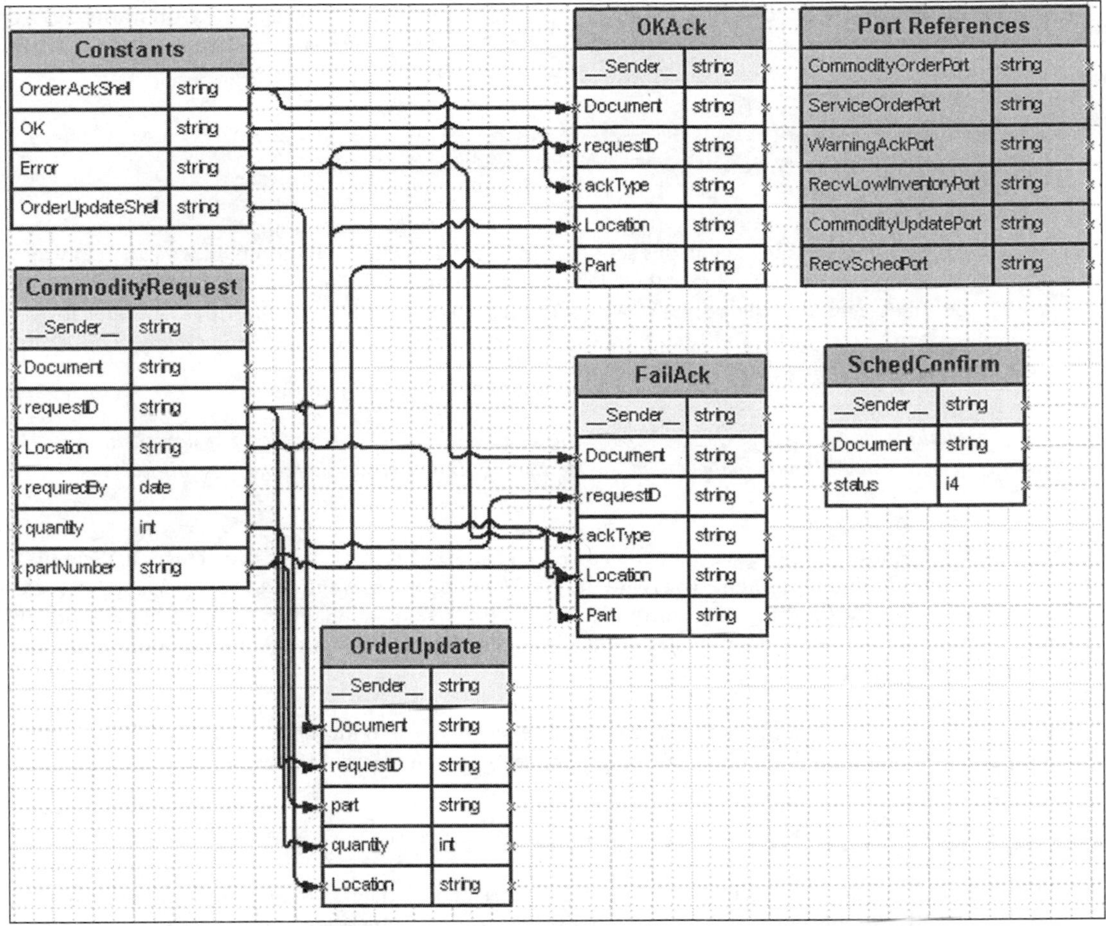

Now that we have things arranged, we are ready to link fields together to create a data flow. From the business process diagram, we know that we have two variations of the `OrderAck` message: `OKAck` and `FailAck`. Let's start with `OKAck`. The first step is to drag a connection from the right side (the output) of the `OrderAckShell` string constant to the `Document` field of the `OKAck` message. This provides the message with a shell. Next, since we want the `ackType` field to have the value "`ok`", drag a connection between the `OK` constant and the `ackType` field. At run-time, XLANG Scheduler will insert the shell, then fill in the `ackType` field with the constant we've provided. The `Location`, `requestID`, and `Part` fields must have values that reflect the actual `LowInventory` message received by the schedule. These values are available in the `CommodityRequest` message table as the `Location`, `requestID`, and `partNumber` fields, so drag connections from them to the `OKAck` message fields. Now that we've done this, XLANG Scheduler can generate a complete `OKAck` message. When the schedule reaches the **Send OK Ack** action, XLANG Scheduler will assemble a complete `OrderAck` message with the `ackType` field set to `ok` based on our data flow and pass this message to the messaging service for transmission.

Now make similar connections between the string constants, the `CommodityRequest` message fields and the `FailAck` message fields. Remember to link the `Error` string constant to the `ackType` field in `FailAck` to properly set the `ackType` field and indicate a failed order request.

Finally, we need to create the data flow for the `OrderUpdate` message. Return to the **Constants** table and add a string constant named `OrderUpDateShell` with this value (whitespace has been added for clarity on the page):

```
<OrderUpdate requestID="" action="cancel">
   <OrderInfo part="" quantity=""><Location/></OrderInfo>
</OrderUpdate>
```

Since we are only using this message in this schedule to cancel an order, not modify it, we can get away with hardcoding the action attribute's value in the shell. Link this constant to the `Document` field in the `OrderUpdate` message. Link the `requestID`, `partNumber`, `quantity`, and `Location` fields to `requestID`, `part`, `quantity` and `Location` in the `OrderUpdate` message, respectively. This completes the data flow for the sample schedule.

We could also have created the `CommodityRequest` message this way, but it would be unrealistic to expect to do this in a production application. In addition, the Data view would become very difficult to read.

With the schedule now complete, save the file as `InventoryOrderProcess.skv`. This is a Visio file, however, not an XLANG document. To create the XLANG document we need to run the schedule, select the main menu's File Make XLANG InventoryOrderProcess.skv... menu item to compile the schedule. Move the file to the location provided in BizTalk Messaging Manager when we configured the port named RecvLowInventoryPort.

All that stands between us and watching this schedule execute is a stub for the warning application and HTTP `receive` functions to accept the messages on behalf of the external vendors.

Putting the Schedule Into Production

The focus of this sample is on BizTalk, not the applications it coordinates. We are only interested in the outside applications to the extent that we can get a `LowInventory` message into the system and watch other messages come out of it. We'll create a simplistic HTML page with some client-side Javascript to put a pre-written and saved `LowInventory` message into the `warning_adv` queue, then create two ASP pages to act as HTTP `receive` functions. Both `receive` functions should write the messages they receive to a log file so that we can verify that messaging is, in fact, taking place. In real life, these pages would access the applications used by the vendors through whatever messaging or API the applications support. In addition to logging the messages it receives, the service technician's `receive` function ASP must also submit a `SchedConfirmation` message to the `svc_sched` queue to keep things going.

Simulating the Warning Application

The stub for the warning application is called `stuff.html`. This page consists of a single button whose `onclick` event is handled by the `Stuff` function:

```
function Stuff()
{
   var mqInfo, mqQueue, mqMessage, ofsFSO, mqTxDisp, mqTx;

   mqInfo = new ActiveXObject("MSMQ.MSMQQueueInfo");
   ofsFSO = new ActiveXObject("Scripting.FileSystemObject");
   mqTxDisp = new ActiveXObject("MSMQ.MSMQTransactionDispenser");
   if (mqInfo != null)
```

```
        {
            mqInfo.FormatName = "DIRECT=OS:.\\private$\\warning_adv";
            mqQueue = mqInfo.Open(2, 0);
            mqQueue.Refresh;

            if (mqQueue != null && mqQueue.IsOpen == true)
            {
                mqMessage = new ActiveXObject("MSMQ.MSMQMessage");
                if (mqMessage != null)
            {
                mqMessage.Body =
                    ofsFSO.OpenTextFile(
                     "c:\\temp\\lowinv_sample.xml",1).ReadAll();
                mqMessage.Label = "LowInventory";
                mqTx = mqTxDisp.BeginTransaction();
                mqMessage.Send(mqQueue, mqTx);
                mqTx.Commit();
                mqMessage = null;
                ofsFSO = null;
            }
                mqQueue = null;
            }
            mqInfo = null;
        }
    }
```

This is relatively straightforward MSMQ and FileSystemObject programming. Note the `FormatName` *string refers to a queue on the same machine as is running this code. You may wish to refer to Designing Distributed Applications (Wrox Press, 1999, ISBN 1-861002-27-0) for an introduction to MSMQ programming in Javascript. The* `FileSystemObject` *programming model is documented for Javascript on the Microsoft Scripting Technologies site at* *http://msdn.microsoft.com/scripting/jscript/doc/jsFSOTutor.htm.*

In this script, we create `MSMQQueueInfo` and `MSMQTransactionDispenser` objects to handle the queue transactionally, and a `FileSystemObject` object to open a text file on disk that contains a sample `LowInventory` message. We've provided `lowinv_sample.xml` in the code download for this purpose. We access the queue by providing the format `DIRECT=OS:.\\private$\\warning_adv` and opening a queue for write-access. If this works, we open the text file and read it in its entirety. The call to `ReadAll` returns the contents of the file as a string, so the following line assigns then opens the file, reads it, and assigns the contents to the body of the message:

```
mqMessage.Body = ofsFSO.OpenTextFile(
    "c:\\temp\\lowinv_sample.xml",1).ReadAll();
```

If you use another sample file or move it on your system, be sure to change the file path appropriately.

The event handler function ends by committing the queue transaction and cleaning up its objects. Opening this page in a browser and clicking the button drops a `LowInventory` message into the `warning_adv` queue. Don't bother looking at the queue for the message, though. If our MSMQ `receive` function is working properly, it plucks the message from the queue and tries to submit it to the messaging service.

Commodity Vendor's HTTP Receive Function

The commodity vendor's `receive` function is an active server page we've adapted from a sample in the BizTalk SDK samples. All it does is grab the text posted to it and, if all goes well, writes it to the end of a textfile named `CommodityLog.txt` on disk, returning an HTTP 200 response. The sample, which is found in the download as `CommodityOrders.asp` (or in the unmodified form as `Sample3.asp` in the `Sample3` folder under the SDK's `Messaging Samples` folder in our BizTalk Server installation), checks the content headers and grabs the posted contents with the following line:

```
EntityBody = Request.BinaryRead (Request.TotalBytes )
```

After converting to Unicode, it writes the contents to the disk file with the following lines:

```
Set objFS = CreateObject("Scripting.FileSystemObject")
Set objStream = objFS.OpenTextFile("c:\temp\CommodityLog.txt", 8, True)

objStream.WriteLine "-------- Received at " & Now() & " ------------"
objStream.WriteLine PostedDocument
objStream.WriteLine "-------- End Received at " & Now() & " --------" & _
   VbCrlf
objStream.Close
Set objStream = Nothing
Set objFS = Nothing
```

Note that this sample is a minimal HTTP `recieve` function, although it performs everything needed to process most simple messages. It is conspicuously lacking support for processing multipart MIME messages (although it does recognize them), so if our messaging applications use binary attachments to go with our text messages, we will need to extend the code found in this sample.

Here is a sample for one such log using our sample message:

```
-------- Received at 2/23/2001 10:06:34 ------------
<SupplyRequest refID="A-8917-01"><Delivery Site="Refinery Unit
7"><DeliveryDate>2001-02-
20</DeliveryDate></Delivery><ItemOrder><SerialNumber>WD40</SerialNumber><Qty>100</
Qty></ItemOrder></SupplyRequest>

-------- End Received at 2/23/2001 10:06:34 --------
```

Make a new virtual directory on your web server that matches the URL entered for the messaging port named CommodityOrderPort and you are ready to receive messages on behalf of the commodity vendor.

Service Technician's HTTP Receive Function

The service technician's `receive()` function must perform the same functions as we just saw, so save the ASP as `ServiceOrders.asp`. Change the following file writing line as follows to reflect a different log file:

```
Set objStream = objFS.OpenTextFile("c:\temp\ServiceLog.txt", 8, True)
```

This `receive()` function must also send a `SchedConfirmation` message to a message queue to keep things going. After the lines that write the message body to the log file, insert the following lines. They constitute a VBScript translation of the MSMQ code we saw in `stuff.html`:

```
Dim mqInfo, mqQueue, mqMessage, ofsFSO, mqTxDisp, mqTx

Set mqInfo = CreateObject("MSMQ.MSMQQueueInfo")

Set mqTxDisp = CreateObject("MSMQ.MSMQTransactionDispenser")
If IsObject(mqInfo) Then
   mqInfo.FormatName = "DIRECT=OS:.\private$\svc_sched"
   Set mqQueue = mqInfo.Open(2, 0)

   If (mqQueue.IsOpen) Then
      Set mqMessage = CreateObject("MSMQ.MSMQMessage")
      If IsObject(mqMessage) Then
         mqMessage.Body = "<SchedConfirmation reqID='unk' status='1'/>"
         mqMessage.Label = "SchedConfirmation"
         Set mqTx = mqTxDisp.BeginTransaction()
         mqMessage.Send mqQueue, mqTx
         mqTx.Commit()
         Set mqMessage = nothing
      End if
      Set mqQueue = Nothing
   End if
   Set mqInfo = nothing
End if
```

There are a few details to note. First, the `FormatName` property value reflects the name of the `svc_sched` queue. Next, the message label matches the document element name of our message. Finally, we've hardcoded the `SchedConfirmation` message body into the script. The `reqID` won't be set properly, of course, but we know that our sample will always be dealing with a single message at a time, so it isn't worth parsing the incoming message to retrieve a value that will never be used by the system. After saving this page, place it in the folder that we configured as a virtual web directory in the preceding section. If we used a different URL when configuring the ServiceRequestPort messaging port in BizTalk, place the page in that folder instead. A sample log entry for this receive function is:

```
-------- Received at 2/23/2001 10:06:34 ------------
AXY1020(A8769-B9),Refinery Unit 7,2001-02-20,A-8917-01
-------- End Received at 2/23/2001 10:06:34 --------
```

We may test the proper operation of the BizTalk application by changing the value of the status field to zero. Since IIS may be configured to cache ASPs, we may have to stop and restart the web server to reflect the changed page.

Testing the Application

When all our `receive` functions and BizTalk configurations are ready, we may test the operation of your completed application by opening `stuff.html` and clicking the button. After a brief interval (longer the first time as the messaging service has not run any messages), we should see the `receive()` function message logs appear (if we did not create them ourselves) in the directory specified in the script. We can open them and verify that the vendors received their messages.

If we go into the Computer Management utility and inspect the queues, we will not see any messages in `warning_adv` because the MSMQ `receive()` function removed them when it submitted the incoming message to the messaging service. The schedule, in turn, removed the `SchedConfirmation` message from the `svc_sched` queue when it arrived, so that queue should be empty as well. If we browse the `warning_ack` queue, however, we should see the `OrderAck` message the schedule sent to the warning application with the `ok` value set in the `ackType` field. Since we didn't bother to implement this portion of the warning application, there is nothing to consume this message. We must manually purge the queue to delete it.

To test the error handling in the queue, deny write-access to the `svc_sched` queue to the **Everyone** account. Click on the button in `stuff.html` again, then look at the commodity log. We should see an `OrderUpdate` message canceling the order. Restore the queue privileges, then modify `ServiceOrders.asp` to send a value of zero in the status field. When the `OrderAck` message arrives in the `warning_ack` queue, view the message body. The `ackType` field should be `error`.

Summary

We've covered a lot of ground in this chapter. You were provided with a necessarily brief overview of the needs, requirements, and technology issues surrounding business-to-business applications. You were introduced to some messaging frameworks and the web sites that discuss them. We reviewed the functional areas of BizTalk Server 2000, a newly released product from Microsoft implementing enterprise application integration and B2B messaging services. These include a messaging service for transmitting XML and flatfile messages over a variety of protocols and a process orchestration engine called the XLANG Scheduler. The messaging service offers the ability to dynamically translate message formats and change protocols. We set up a B2B messaging situation using configuration rather than extensive programming. XLANG Scheduler is a powerful way to implement complex business processes in a declarative fashion. We ended our review of the product with a quick tour of the design and administrative tools that are included in the package.

The second half of the chapter was given over to a sample B2B application implemented with BizTalk Server. We illustrated the main features of the product, including the following:

- Orchestration
- HTTP and MSMQ messaging using the messaging service
- Message format mapping
- HTTP `receive` functions
- MSMQ `receive` functions
- Launching a schedule in response to message arrival

This was a simplified example whose messages are not nearly as complicated as we encounter in a real-world B2B environment, and we did not even begin to cover the tasks involved with programmatically accessing and extending BizTalk Server using the various COM+ interfaces provided. We hope, though, that this sample gave some indication of how XML is being used to implement B2B messaging over Internet protocols.

26

E-Business Integration

Introduction To E-Business

The purpose of this chapter is to illustrate the methods used to link diverse e-business standards and provide a degree of interoperability between standards. Some of the frameworks define not only the format of the standards, but also the implementation and routing details. We will not consider these latter aspects, such as exchange protocols, messaging, registry and repository in any depth, as they are extensive and out of this chapter's scope. However, we will look at how we can use the vocabularies of each to allow operation between the standards.

We will look first at the RosettaNet and xCBL standards, which have been around slightly longer than BizTalk, and ebXML, which is currently still being defined as a standard.

Next we will look at the issues that need to be addressed when looking at e-business integration, and look at the solutions to problems faced.

Finally, we shall look at an actual implementation of these solutions – an application, which generated a RosettaNet Purchase Order, and submits it to a remote marketplace, where it is converted for use by a Biztalk compliant system.

> **You will find the sample code for this chapter in the book's code download, available from Wrox.com, arranged into 5 subfolders inside the chapter folder.**
>
> **Also, bear in mind that this case study (particularly the XSLT section) was developed with the Microsoft XML version 3.0 parser freely downloadable from http://msdn.microsoft.com/xml. To view XML output with Internet Explorer (which you will do at the end of the chapter), you must also download the XMLInst.exe (from the same location) file that replaces the default IE parser.**

RosettaNet

The **RosettaNet** specification can be found at `http://www.rosettanet.org`, and was designed to allow e-business system implementers and solution providers to create or implement interoperable software application components. Business processes such as catalogs, invoices, purchase orders etc. can be defined and exchanged in XML according to RosettaNet XML standard DTD or XDR schema, and routed to software programs running on business partners servers.

RosettaNet defines itself as shown below:

> **"A self-funded, non-profit organization, RosettaNet is a consortium of major Information Technology, Electronic Component and Semiconductor-manufacturing companies, working to create and implement industry-wide, open e-business process standards. These standards form a common e-business language, aligning processes between supply chain partners on a global basis."**

The key to this is the RosettaNet standard set, which defines a set of business and technical specifications such as **Partner Interface Processes** (**PIPs**) for defining processes between trading partners and data dictionaries that define a common set of properties to be used by PIPs. There is also the **RosettaNet Implementation Framework** (**RNIF**) that defines exchange protocols allowing for quick and efficient implementation of PIP's. Finally, there is a series of codes for products and partners to align business processes and definitions.

PIPs are schema definitions for various business processes (such as a purchase order) and are the key components to the RosettaNet standards– based on XML vocabularies as defined in DTDs and schemas – and there are eight clusters (groups of business processes):

- **RosettaNet Support**
- Administrative functionality.
- **Partner, Product and Service Review**
- Allows information collection, maintenance and distribution for the development of trading-partner profiles and product-information subscriptions.
- **Product Information**
- Enables distribution and periodic update of product and detailed design information, including product change notices and product technical specifications.

- **Order Management**
- Allow partners to order catalog products, create custom solutions, manage distribution and deliveries, and support product returns and financial transactions.
- **Inventory Management**
- Enables inventory management, including collaboration, replenishment, price protection, reporting and allocation of constrained product.
- **Marketing Information Management**
- Enables communication of marketing information, including campaign plans, lead information and design registration.
- **Service and Support**
- Provides post-sales technical support, service warranty and asset management capabilities.
- **Manufacturing**
- Enables the exchange of design, configuration, process, quality and other manufacturing floor information to support the "Virtual Manufacturing" environment.

The RNIF can be very technical, and defines how to exchange this information between businesses and facilitate the execution of the business components. It is very extensive and out of scope for the case study. I suggest you have a look at it – the URL is given at the end of the chapter.

xCBL (CommerceOne)

The **Common Business Library** (**xCBL**) is defined by CommerceOne as:

> **A set of XML building blocks and a document framework that allows the creation of robust, reusable, XML documents for e-commerce. These elemental building blocks were defined based on extensive research and collaboration by CommerceOne and the leading XML industry initiatives. xCBL can help accelerate any trading partner's XML efforts by providing these building blocks and a document framework. Consistent with this purpose, xCBL is available free of charge in prominent XML repositories.**

xCBL (the "x" states that there are multiple versions of the CBL, the most up-to-date being 3.0) is a single vocabulary and allows for data typing and validation between documents being exchanged in an e-commerce transaction. It allows you to integrate and create business processes such as the following:

- `Invoice`
- `OrderRequest`
- `PaymentRequest`
- `ProductCatalog`
- `ShippingSchedule`
- `TimeSeries`
- `TradingPartnerUserInformation`

There are many more document types that can be created from the extensive vocabulary. Furthermore, xCBL defines a very detailed list of common data types that can be used industry wide when defining a business document – some examples are shown below (you should look at the CBL Reference Library for more information on these data types):

- **CurrencyCode**

  for example, "CLP" – Chilean Peso. So, a business could use CLP within its XML instance to state that a particular currency was Chilean Pesos (or one of the many other currencies defined in this data type).

- **CountryCode**

  for example, "CL" - Chile

- **DateQualifierCode**

  for example, "36030" – calculation is based on year of 360 days and 30 day months

- **LanguageCode**

  for example, "en" - English

- **RegionCode**

  for example, "CANMB" – Canada, Manitoba

- **ServiceCode**

  for example, "AdvanceChargesHandling" – Advance Charges Handling

- **UOMCode**

  for example, "BX" – Box (for a box of something)

Again, the best way to understand the extensive e-business framework offered by xCBL is to work through an implementation (such as this case study) and extend that understanding to your own particular business needs.

BizTalk (Microsoft)

http://www.BizTalk.org defines its site purpose as follows:

> **"... the goal of providing the software and business communities with resources for learning about and using XML for Enterprise Application Integration (EAI), and business-to-business (B2B) document exchange, both within the enterprise and over the Internet."**

The BizTalk library is not a standards body, but rather a resource of XDR Schemas and vocabulary definitions created and entered by diverse organizations. It is different to xCBL and RosettaNet in that it lets the businesses define the vocabularies and allows users to understand those vocabularies and implement them. For example, there are a few Purchase Order definitions entered by companies that want solution providers to be able to interact directly with their e-commerce systems. When a party uses a schema it is registered, and the business owner can send them update information. To be initially registered, it must pass an XDR schema verification test and is kept on the BizTalk site which controls its versioning of the schema, which can be updated with a new version at any point.

BizTalk has identified the following benefits for working with BizTalk:

- Road map for consistent XML implementations.

  Core set of elements and attributes defined for creating effective business processes.

- Easier mapping across schemas.

  Allows software developers and ISV (Independent Software Vendors) to map business processes between each other.

- Design target for software vendors.

  Allow software vendors to target consistently formatted schemas.

- Framework for standards bodies.

  Allows the migration of existing standards such as EDI to XML and schemas.

- Repository for BizTalk schemas.

  Allows industry groups and developers to publish their schemas with versioning, searching and specialization for support of the BizTalk Framework.

- Showcases for best practices in developing XML interchanges.

  Allows the same groups and developers to discover best practices for implementing their schemas.

The BizTalk Framework architecture defines rules for formatting, transmitting, receiving and processing a standard XML message. Each BizTalk message (such as a Purchase Order) is wrapped in an XML document, which defines routing and location information.

It is a good idea to familiarize yourself with the BizTalk Framework, although a detailed explanation is outside the scope of this study. You can find resources at the end of the chapter.

ebXML (Oasis/UN)

The ebXML initiative (http://www.ebxml.org) is currently still under development and there is a lot of activity surrounding a myriad areas that will eventually form the ebXML framework. It is similar to the other frameworks and is defined as the following:

> **A set of specifications that together enables a modular electronic business framework. The vision of ebXML is to enable a global electronic marketplace where enterprises of any size and in any geographical location can meet and conduct business with each other through the exchange of XML-based messages. ebXML is a joint initiative of the United Nations (UN/CEFACT) and OASIS, developed with global participation for global usage.**

There is some strong support behind ebXML – it is derived from the work processed by the following workgroups:

- ebXML requirements

  Focuses on defining the requirements of an ebXML compliant application.

- Business Process Methodology

  To accomplish cross-industry XML-based business process integration and to allow organizations to build business processes according to a specification while ensuring that they are understandable by other organizations by cross-process integration.

- Technical Architecture

  The focus of this area is to define a technical architecture for the standard, allowing for high-level business views and improvement of business process integration with common standard intra-business standards.

- Core Components

  Contains the context and Metamodel (linking ebXML metamodel with context classification schemes), Methodology (for capturing core components) and Analysis (semantic definitions and cross-industry analysis).

- Transport/Routing and Packaging

  Focusing on defining the specification for a universal business-level messaging service for secure, reliable ebXML business document exchange.

- Registry and Repository

  To define ebXML registry services, and an ebXML registry information model and repository.

- Quality Review

  To review the ebXML deliverables for quality and consistency.

- Proof of concept

  Reinforces the viability of the ebXML specifications by understanding how the initiative will be employed in a global market place.

- Trading Partners

  To provide a **Unified Modeling Language** (**UML**) model for trading partner information as well as its markup and specification.

- Marketing Awareness

  To stimulate, inform and communicate to the business community the opportunities, benefits and outcomes of ebXML.

This case study will not make much use of ebXML as it is currently still being defined, however, it is worth checking out the ebXML site, as it is making fast progress, and it will become a major player in global business e-commerce in the future.

Now that we have had an overview of each of the major technology initiatives, let's look at some of the current problems we run into when integrating these systems.

Integration Issues & Solutions

With the Business-to-Business solutions in place, one would imagine that communication between diverse business systems would be simple. Unfortunately, there are still integration and communication issues because of the differences in the schemas of these frameworks.

Each standard makes a unique contribution to e-business, and to fully exploit the ability to integrate your business processes with other companies, you must be able to use the distributed power of these efforts. RosettaNet is over two years old and is supported by over 200 of the industry leading vendors (such as IBM and Oracle), xCBL also has industry support and works with large software vendors (such a Microsoft and SAP), BizTalk is gaining rapid ground and its growth will continue, while ebXML is expected to be hugely successful with the backing of many major corporations in the industry.

Businesses may not want to support every e-business standard in the market, so they must be able to choose what they want to support and have methods to implement this support. For example, the different purchase order schemas for RosettaNet, xCBL, BizTalk and ebXML are completely different. So, where the RosettaNet schemas may expect the name of the city, the delivery is to be made, the BizTalk schemas may use the street address; and where the xCBL purchase order schema expects a `<PostalCode>` element, in the RosettaNet PO schemas, this element is defined as `<NationalPostCode>`, as illustrated below:

A RosettaNet Purchase Order section instance:

```
<PhysicalAddress>
   <cityName>
      <FreeFormText>Walnut Creek</FreeFormText>
   </cityName>
   <addressLine1>
      <FreeFormText>1600 Riviera Ave</FreeFormText>
   </addressLine1>
   <addressLine2>
      <FreeFormText>Suite# 200</FreeFormText>
   </addressLine2>
   <NationalPostalCode>94596</NationalPostalCode>
   <regionName>
      <FreeFormText>CA</FreeFormText>
   </regionName>
   <GlobalCountryCode>US</GlobalCountryCode>
</PhysicalAddress>
```

A similar CBL Purchase Order section instance:

```
<NameAddress>
   <Name1>Mr. Muljadi Sulistio</Name1>
   <Name2>Attention: Business Service Division</Name2>
   <Address1>1600 Riviera Ave</Address1>
   <Address2>Suite# 200</Address2>
   <City>Walnut Creek</City>
   <StateOrProvince>CA</StateOrProvince>
   <PostalCode>94596</PostalCode>
   <Country>US</Country>
</NameAddress>
```

So, for this reason we would have to effectively "black-box" all of the transactional applications working to similar frameworks. The following diagram illustrates a potential e-business scenario in this case:

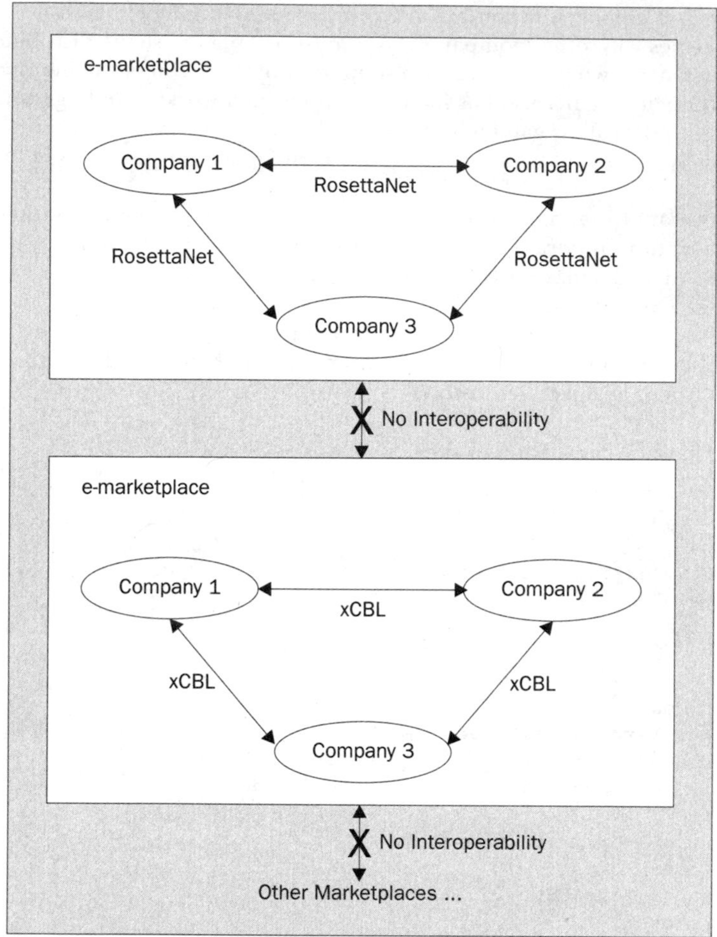

Although this allows tremendous opportunity for businesses to share with and purchase from others in their immediate marketplaces, we can clearly see defined borders and lost opportunity. An even worse scenario is that a business operating in one environment would not be able to work with an existing supplier because they had adopted diverse e-business frameworks. This scenario defeats the goals of all the e-business frameworks, which is to allow universal communication between distributed transactional applications.

However, it is obvious that we are never going to have absolutely everyone talking the same language using the same e-business framework, so some solution much be reached. The following diagram represents a high level (but simple) architecture that would allow interoperability among current and future e-business standard frameworks:

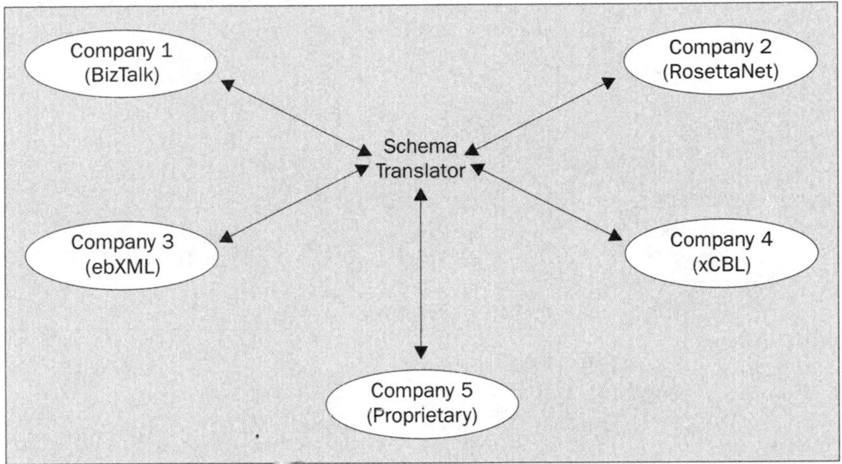

This allows the best of all worlds. It is similar to current market trading throughout the world. There are many varying languages, yet trading across borders is common practice today. The e-business translation world is a lot simpler as there are well-defined structures to each standard (the schema) and so we can understand meaning and context of the instances a system may be presented with. Technically speaking, we can define the above architecture as follows:

> *A global market place based on diverse e-business XML standard vocabularies communicating with XSLT for schema-to-schema translation.*

The location of the XSLT's brings up many issues that are outside the chapter scope, such as their versioning and maintenance, so we will assume that each XSLT is stored with each company and can be applied to any XML file that is sent to that business and has to be transformed. To prove this solution, we are now going to work through an extensive example based on e-business purchase order exchanges.

Integrated Purchase Order

As we stated above, we are going to use a fictitious example (but one very common in the real world) of business purchase orders to illustrate diverse e-business framework interoperation. The following diagram shows a typical process model for an e-commerce solution.

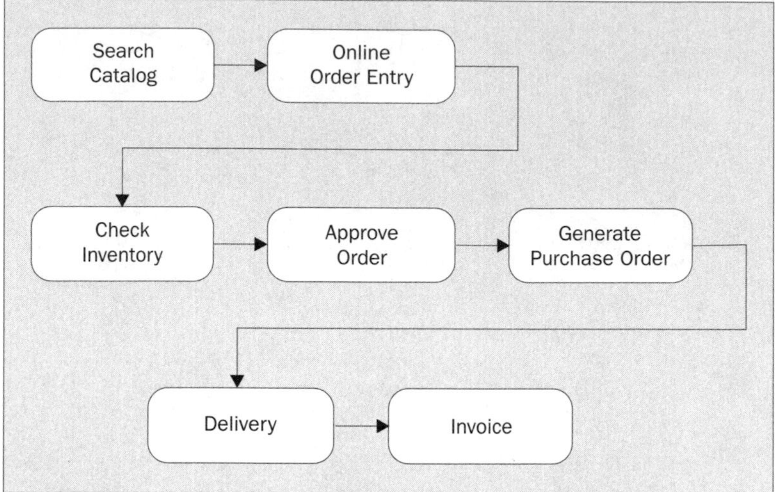

This is a scenario that will become common throughout online business.

Scenario Overview

A high-level diagram of the scenario we will be working with is given below:

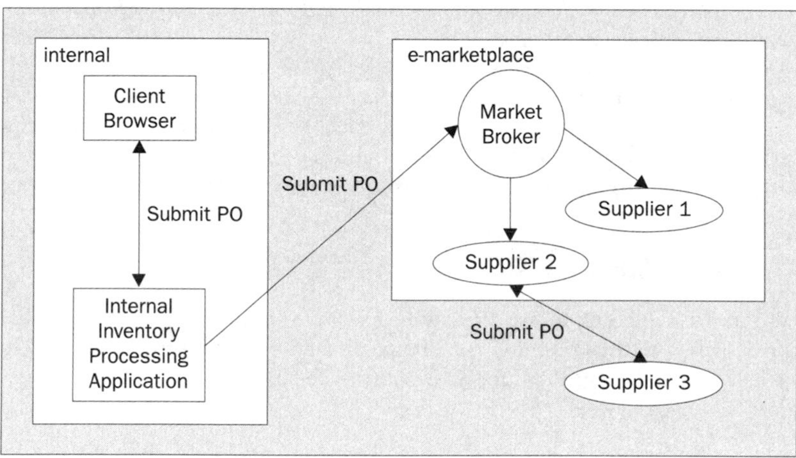

When an employee requires some office items (such as pens, paper etc.), the purchase order is initially submitted internally and processed by the **Internal Inventory Processing Application**. To avoid getting into the details of supply chain management and inventory control, we are going to assume a simplified situation. The internal application will only process orders for simple items, such as pens, pencils etc. When it receives an order for something more extensive such as bulk orders for printing paper it forwards the order to an e-market, which contains two supplier sites, supplier 1 and supplier 2. In turn, orders for heavy goods, such as tables and chairs are forwarded initially to supplier site 2, who uses supplier site 3 to process the orders. In the real world, there would probably be a rather more detailed ordering process, but we are just exploring the important concepts of e-business communication rather than supply-chain and inventory-management issues.

Purchase Order Schemas and Instances

An essential component to any e-business communication is a well-defined structure to the data. This is when we can make use of the various XML vocabularies defining purchase orders. Let's look in turn at each of these vocabularies we are working with and define our sample instances that will be communicated in the sample.

RosettaNet

The full RosettaNet XML standard is rather large so instead let's look at some of the key elements in the XDR Schema that will be important to our sample. XDR is the type of schema that comes with the RosettaNet downloads. You can find the full XDR file in the code download.

The root of the RosettaNet Purchase Order is an element called `Pip3A4PurchaseOrderRequest`, which contains an `xmlns` attribute that references the XDR Schema for validation. It has five child elements, of which the first three, `PurchaseOrder`, `toRole` and `fromRole` play the major roles:

```
<ElementType name="Pip3A4PurchaseOrderRequest" model="closed" content="eltOnly"
order="seq">
   <AttributeType name="xmlns" dt:type="string"/>
   <attribute type="xmlns"/>
   <element type="PurchaseOrder" minOccurs="1" maxOccurs="1"/>
   <element type="fromRole" minOccurs="1" maxOccurs="1"/>
   <element type="toRole" minOccurs="1" maxOccurs="1"/>
   <element type="thisDocumentGenerationDateTime" minOccurs="1" maxOccurs="1"/>
   <element type="thisDocumentIdentifier" minOccurs="1" maxOccurs="1"/>
   <element type="GlobalDocumentFunctionCode" minOccurs="1" maxOccurs="1"/>
</ElementType>
```

The `PurchaseOrder` element contains the delivery information, such as the name and address where the items ordered should be sent to.

```
<ElementType name="PurchaseOrder" model="closed" content="eltOnly" order="seq">


</ElementType>
```

The `toRole` element serves as an important part of the order, containing the `PartnerRoleDescription` element described below:

```
<ElementType name="toRole" model="closed" content="eltOnly" order="seq">
   <element type="PartnerRoleDescription" minOccurs="1" maxOccurs="1"/>
</ElementType>
```

The `PartnerRoleDescription` is a collection of business properties that describes a business partners' role in a partner interface process. It provides a partner classification code and contact details (in `ContactInformation`) for the person from the company that is purchasing the goods, such as the name, telephone number and email address. The `PartnerRoleDescription` identifies business partners' and their function in a supply chain.

```
<ElementType name="PartnerRoleDescription" model="closed" content="eltOnly"
    order="seq">
   <element type="GlobalPartnerRoleClassificationCode" minOccurs="1"
      maxOccurs="1"/>
   <element type="ContactInformation" minOccurs="0" maxOccurs="1"/>
   <element type="PartnerDescription" minOccurs="0" maxOccurs="1"/>
</ElementType>
```

Finally, the `fromRole` element can contain much of the same information as the `toRole`, but is based on the business selling the item(s):

```
<ElementType name="fromRole" model="closed" content="eltOnly" order="seq">
   <element type="PartnerRoleDescription" minOccurs="1" maxOccurs="1"/>
</ElementType>
```

The following instance is based on the RosettaNet standard that we are going to use in our sample because this is what the businesses' existing systems have been using for some years. You should look through it and understand its relationship to the RosettaNet standard, as well as areas you may consider expanding on or removing details based on your own business experiences. A section of the full file is here and you can find the file in the RosettaNet directory in the samples as the file `RosettaNet_PO.xml`.

```
<?xml version="1.0" encoding="UTF-8"?>
<Pip3A4PurchaseOrderRequest xmlns="x-
schema:3A4PurchaseOrderRequestMessageGuideline_V1_4.xdr">
   <PurchaseOrder>
      <deliverTo>
         <PhysicalAddress>
            <cityName>
               <FreeFormText>Winnipeg</FreeFormText>
            </cityName>
            <addressLine1>
               <FreeFormText>223746 Red Oak Drive</FreeFormText>
            </addressLine1>
            <addressLine2>
               <FreeFormText>3rd Floor</FreeFormText>
            </addressLine2>
            <NationalPostalCode>R2J 29A</NationalPostalCode>
            <regionName>
               <FreeFormText>MB</FreeFormText>
            </regionName>
            <GlobalCountryCode>CA</GlobalCountryCode>
         </PhysicalAddress>
      </deliverTo>
      <ProductLineItem>
         <shipFrom>
            <GlobalLocationIdentifier>
               1234123411234
            </GlobalLocationIdentifier>
         </shipFrom>
         <ProductQuantity>10</ProductQuantity>
         <LineNumber>1</LineNumber>

      ...
```

```
        <countryOfOrigin>
           <GlobalCountryCode>US</GlobalCountryCode>
        </countryOfOrigin>
        <requestedShipDate>
           <DateStamp>19990809T14:30:00</DateStamp>
        </requestedShipDate>
     <GlobalProductUnitOfMeasureCode>
        EACH
     </GlobalProductUnitOfMeasureCode>

     ...

  </PurchaseOrder>
  <fromRole>
     <PartnerRoleDescription>
        <GlobalPartnerRoleClassificationCode>
           Seller
        </GlobalPartnerRoleClassificationCode>
     </PartnerRoleDescription>
  </fromRole>
  <toRole>
     <PartnerRoleDescription>
        <GlobalPartnerRoleClassificationCode/>
        <ContactInformation>
           <EmailAddress>stv_ca@hotmail.com</EmailAddress>
           <contactName>
              <FreeFormText>Steven Livingstone</FreeFormText>
           </contactName>
           <telephoneNumber>
              <CommunicationsNumber>
                 (0928) 839 7820
              </CommunicationsNumber>
           </telephoneNumber>
        </ContactInformation>
     </PartnerRoleDescription>
  </toRole>

     ...

</Pip3A4PurchaseOrderRequest>
```

xCBL

Let's now look at the CBL XDR schema elements that will be important to our sample instance. The `BillToParty` element contains information on the person to whom the delivery will be made, such as the name and address information and the contact information:

```
<ElementType name="BillToParty" content="eltOnly">
   <element type="Party" minOccurs="1" maxOccurs="1"/>
</ElementType>
```

It contains the `Party` element, which has various types of contact information and some other related information:

```
<ElementType name="Party" content="eltOnly">
<group order="seq">
<element type="PartyID"/>
<element type="ListOfIdentifier" minOccurs="0" maxOccurs="1"/>
<element type="MDFBusiness" minOccurs="0" maxOccurs="1"/>
<element type="NameAddress" minOccurs="0" maxOccurs="1"/>
<element type="OrderContact" minOccurs="0" maxOccurs="1"/>
<element type="ReceivingContact" minOccurs="0" maxOccurs="1"/>
<element type="ShippingContact" minOccurs="0" maxOccurs="1"/>
<element type="OtherContacts" minOccurs="0" maxOccurs="1"/>
<element type="CorrespondenceLanguage" minOccurs="0" maxOccurs="1"/>
</group>
</ElementType>
```

The `OtherContacts` element contains all the information to contact the person, whether they are the seller of the goods, or the buyer. The `NameAddress` collects postal information about this person.

Details on how the product(s) are moved to the customer are contained in the `Transport` element (shown below), which contains an ID and shipment method (Air, for example):

```
<ElementType name="Transport" content="eltOnly">
   <group order="seq">
      <element type="TransportID"/>
      <element type="TransportMode" minOccurs="0" maxOccurs="1"/>

...

   </group>
</ElementType>
```

The `OrderDetail` element details the item(s) in the PO, as well as the quantity and unit item cost.

```
<ElementType name="OrderDetail" content="eltOnly">
<group order="seq">
<element type="ListOfItemDetail"/>
<element type="ListOfPackageDetail" minOccurs="0" maxOccurs="1"/>
</group>
</ElementType>
```

So now we have discussed some of the sections of the Purchase Order xCBL instance, let's look at the instance we are going to work with in our case study. You should examine this sample – look up the meanings in the xCBL reference in the reference library downloadable from the CBL documentation site at http://www.xcbl.org/xcbl30/xcbl30xdrdoc.html.

```
<?xml version="1.0"?>
<OrderRequest xmlns="x-schema:XCBL30.xdr">
   <OrderRequestHeader>
      <OrderRequestNumber>
         <BuyerOrderRequestNumber>
            REF-002-99-0-3000
         </BuyerOrderRequestNumber>
         <SellerOrderRequestNumber>
            REF002-44556677
```

```
      </SellerOrderRequestNumber>
   </OrderRequestNumber>
   <OrderRequestIssueDate>20010104T09:00:00</OrderRequestIssueDate>
   <OrderRequestReferences>

   ...

   </OrderRequestReferences>
   <Purpose>
      <PurposeCoded>InformationOnly</PurposeCoded>
   </Purpose>
   <RequestedResponse>
      <RequestedResponseCoded>ResponseExpected</RequestedResponseCoded>
   </RequestedResponse>
   <OrderRequestCurrency>
      <Currency>
         <CurrencyCoded>CAD</CurrencyCoded>
      </Currency>
   </OrderRequestCurrency>
   <OrderRequestLanguage>
      <Language>
         <LanguageCoded>en</LanguageCoded>
      </Language>
   </OrderRequestLanguage>
   <OrderRequestParty>
      <SellerParty>
         <Party>

         ...

            <NameAddress>
               <Name1>MyOffice International Inc.</Name1>
               <Department>Supplies</Department>
               <PostalCode>H67 76W</PostalCode>
               <City>Winnipeg</City>
               <Region>
                  <RegionCoded>MB</RegionCoded>
               </Region>
            </NameAddress>
            <OtherContacts>
               <ListOfContact>
                  <Contact>
                     <ContactName>
                        Steven Livingstone
                     </ContactName>
                     <ContactFunction>
                        <ContactFunctionCoded>
                           DeliveryContact
                        </ContactFunctionCoded>
                     </ContactFunction>
                     <ListOfContactNumber>
                        <ContactNumber>
                           <ContactNumberValue>
                              stv_ca@hotmail.com
                           </ContactNumberValue>
```

```
                                        <ContactNumberTypeCoded>
                                           EmailAddress
                                        </ContactNumberTypeCoded>
                                     </ContactNumber>
                                  </ListOfContactNumber>
                               </Contact>
                            </ListOfContact>
                         </OtherContacts>
                      </Party>
                   </SellerParty>
                   <BillToParty>
                      <Party>

                      ...

                      </Party>
                   </BillToParty>
                </OrderRequestParty>
                <ListOfTransport>
                   <Transport>
                      <TransportID>1000</TransportID>
                      <TransportMode>
                         <TransportModeCoded>Air</TransportModeCoded>
                      </TransportMode>
                   </Transport>
                </ListOfTransport>
                <OrderTermsOfDelivery>
                   <TermsOfDelivery>
                      <TermsOfDeliveryFunctionCoded>
                         TransportCondition
                      </TermsOfDeliveryFunctionCoded>
                      <ShipmentMethodOfPaymentCoded>
                         AdvancePrepaid
                      </ShipmentMethodOfPaymentCoded>
                   </TermsOfDelivery>
                </OrderTermsOfDelivery>
             </OrderRequestHeader>
             <OrderRequestDetail>
                <OrderDetail>
                   <ListOfItemDetail>

                   ...

                      </ItemDetail>
                   </ListOfItemDetail>
                </OrderDetail>
             </OrderRequestDetail>
             <OrderRequestSummary>

             ...

             </OrderRequestSummary>
          </OrderRequest>
```

BizTalk

The BizTalk schema is divided into the **header section**, **contact information**, **shipping information**, **billing information** and finally **details on the goods ordered**. However, unlike the previous schemas, this schema is based mainly on attributes and it also uses the XML Data datatypes (see Chapter 6 for more information on these) to define valid types for these attributes. So, for example, consider the following statement.

```
<AttributeType name = "qty" dt:type = "decimal" required = "yes"/>
```

This defines an attribute called `qty`, defining the quantity of goods ordered, and it can accept any number as defined below:

> **Decimal, with no limit on digits; can potentially have a leading sign, fractional digits, and, optionally, an exponent. Punctuation as in U.S. English. (Values have the same range as the most significant number, 1.7976931348623157E+308 to 2.2250738585072014E-308.)**

Let's look at the BizTalk schema below:

```
<?xml version ="1.0"?>
<Schema name = "poSample.biz"
    xmlns = "urn:schemas-microsoft-com:xml-data"
    xmlns:dt = "urn:schemas-microsoft-com:datatypes">
   <ElementType name = "PO" content = "eltOnly" order = "seq">
      <element type = "POHeader"/>
      <element type = "Contact"/>
      <element type = "POShipTo"/>
      <element type = "POBillTo"/>
      <element type = "POLines"/>
   </ElementType>
   <ElementType name = "POHeader" content = "empty">
      <AttributeType name = "refPromise" dt:type = "string" required =
      "yes"/>
      <AttributeType name = "description" dt:type = "string" required =
      "yes"/>
      <AttributeType name = "paymentType" dt:type = "string" required =
      "yes"/>
      <AttributeType name = "shipType" dt:type = "string" required = "yes"/>
      <AttributeType name = "fromCust" dt:type = "string" required = "yes"/>
      <AttributeType name = "poNumber" dt:type = "string" required = "yes"/>
      <attribute type = "refPromise"/>
      <attribute type = "description"/>
      <attribute type = "paymentType"/>
      <attribute type = "shipType"/>
      <attribute type = "fromCust"/>
      <attribute type = "poNumber"/>
   </ElementType>
   <ElementType name = "Contact" content = "empty">
      <AttributeType name = "contactName" dt:type = "string" required =
      "yes"/>
      <AttributeType name = "contactEmail" dt:type = "string" required =
      "yes"/>
```

```
        <AttributeType name = "contactPhone" dt:type = "string" required =
        "yes"/>
        <attribute type = "contactName"/>
        <attribute type = "contactEmail"/>
        <attribute type = "contactPhone"/>
    </ElementType>
    <AttributeType name = "city" dt:type = "string" required = "yes"/>
    <AttributeType name = "attn" dt:type = "string" required = "yes"/>
    <AttributeType name = "country" dt:type = "string" required = "yes"/>
    <AttributeType name = "stateProvince" dt:type = "string" required =
    "yes"/>
    <AttributeType name = "street4" dt:type = "string" required = "yes"/>
    <AttributeType name = "street3" dt:type = "string" required = "yes"/>
    <AttributeType name = "street2" dt:type = "string" required = "yes"/>
    <AttributeType name = "street1" dt:type = "string" required = "yes"/>
    <AttributeType name = "postalCode" dt:type = "string" required = "yes"/>
    <ElementType name = "POShipTo" content = "empty">
        <attribute type = "city"/>
        <attribute type = "attn"/>
        <attribute type = "country"/>
        <attribute type = "stateProvince"/>
        <attribute type = "street4"/>
        <attribute type = "street3"/>
        <attribute type = "street2"/>
        <attribute type = "street1"/>
        <attribute type = "postalCode"/>
    </ElementType>
    <ElementType name = "POBillTo" content = "empty">
        <attribute type = "city"/>
        <attribute type = "attn"/>
        <attribute type = "country"/>
        <attribute type = "stateProvince"/>
        <attribute type = "street4"/>
        <attribute type = "street3"/>
        <attribute type = "street2"/>
        <attribute type = "street1"/>
        <attribute type = "postalCode"/>
    </ElementType>
    <ElementType name = "POLines" content = "eltOnly" order = "seq">
        <AttributeType name = "startAt" dt:type = "int" required = "yes"/>
        <AttributeType name = "count" dt:type = "int" required = "yes"/>
        <attribute type = "startAt"/>
        <attribute type = "count"/>
        <element type = "Item" minOccurs = "1" maxOccurs = "*"/>
    </ElementType>
    <ElementType name = "Item" content = "empty">
        <AttributeType name = "uom" dt:type = "enumeration" dt:values = "PC
        UNIT" required = "yes"/>
        <AttributeType name = "unitPrice" dt:type = "float" required = "yes"/>
        <AttributeType name = "qty" dt:type = "decimal" required = "yes"/>
        <AttributeType name = "partno" dt:type = "string" required = "yes"/>
        <AttributeType name = "needAfter" dt:type = "date" required = "yes"/>
        <AttributeType name = "discount" dt:type = "float" required = "yes"/>
        <AttributeType name = "line" dt:type = "int" required = "yes"/>
        <AttributeType name = "needBefore" dt:type = "date" required = "yes"/>
```

```
        <attribute type = "uom"/>
        <attribute type = "unitPrice"/>
        <attribute type = "qty"/>
        <attribute type = "partno"/>
        <attribute type = "needAfter"/>
        <attribute type = "discount"/>
        <attribute type = "line"/>
        <attribute type = "needBefore"/>
    </ElementType>
</Schema>
```

Now we have seen the schema used for a BizTalk document, here is an example of an instance that will be used in our sample application.

```
<?xml version="1.0" encoding="UTF-8"?>
<PO xmlns="x-schema:cfwau8qx.xml">
   <POHeader refPromise="0" description="" paymentType="CREDIT CARD"
   shipType="AIR" fromCust="22" poNumber="876628"/>
   <Contact contactName="Steven Livingstone"
            contactEmail="stv_ca@hotmail.com"
            contactPhone="(0928) 839 7820"/>
   <POShipTo city="Glasgow" attn="Steven Livingstone" country="Scotland"
      stateProvince="Strathclyde" street4="" street3="" street2="Yoker"
      street1="879A Red Oak Avenue" postalCode="GL1K A6T"/>
   <POBillTo city="" attn="" country="" stateProvince="" street4=""
             street3="" street2="" street1="" postalCode=""/>
   <POLines startAt="1" count="1">
      <Item uom="PC" unitPrice="" qty="50" partno="0018MixClrPens"
         needAfter="2001-03-25" discount="0" line="1"
         needBefore="2001-04-18"/>
   </POLines>
</PO>
```

Schema Translation

As we discussed above, we must use some mechanism to allow purchase order instances derived from separate schemas to talk to each other. In other words, we must be able to send the BizTalk instance above to a business that works with RosettaNet formatted instances and seamless processing occurs and the order works as expected.

Now, to do this, we have to have some way of mapping information within the BizTalk schema to information containers within the RosettaNet schema. So, for example, if we specify the contact information for the delivery of the items in the BizTalk schema, we must be able to specify that same information correctly within the RosettaNet schema. In other words, we must have some way of transforming the contents of the BizTalk `POShipTo` element to the equivalent within the `ContactInformation` element of the RosettaNet schema. This must occur for as much information as possible to satisfy the necessary requirements for each schema. Therefore, we must define some mapping between the elements and attributes of each schema – the diagram below illustrates this:

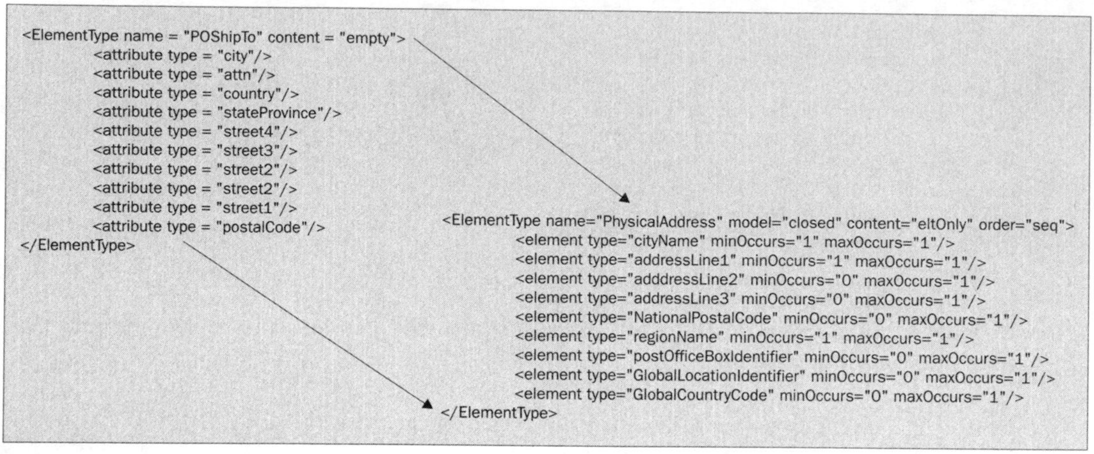

```
<ElementType name = "POShipTo" content = "empty">
        <attribute type = "city"/>
        <attribute type = "attn"/>
        <attribute type = "country"/>
        <attribute type = "stateProvince"/>
        <attribute type = "street4"/>
        <attribute type = "street3"/>
        <attribute type = "street2"/>
        <attribute type = "street2"/>
        <attribute type = "street1"/>
        <attribute type = "postalCode"/>
</ElementType>

<ElementType name="PhysicalAddress" model="closed" content="eltOnly" order="seq">
        <element type="cityName" minOccurs="1" maxOccurs="1"/>
        <element type="addressLine1" minOccurs="1" maxOccurs="1"/>
        <element type="adddressLine2" minOccurs="0" maxOccurs="1"/>
        <element type="addressLine3" minOccurs="0" maxOccurs="1"/>
        <element type="NationalPostalCode" minOccurs="0" maxOccurs="1"/>
        <element type="regionName" minOccurs="1" maxOccurs="1"/>
        <element type="postOfficeBoxIdentifier" minOccurs="0" maxOccurs="1"/>
        <element type="GlobalLocationIdentifier" minOccurs="0" maxOccurs="1"/>
        <element type="GlobalCountryCode" minOccurs="0" maxOccurs="1"/>
</ElementType>
```

Now, let's look at mapping the elements of each schema so we can interoperate between schemas.

Mapping Schema Elements

Now we are going to look at how to map the elements and attributes of the Purchase Order schemas we are going to look at in our sample to each other. First we will look at RosettaNet to BizTalk, followed by BizTalk to ebXML and finally RosettaNet to xCBL.

XSLT Modules

To perform the translation from a given vocabulary (such as BizTalk) to another standard (such as xCBL) we are going to use XSLT. For each translation, a separate XSLT "module" will be created, which will contain the code needed to transform the schema. We can therefore build up a set of XSLT modules that can be applied to one XML instance based on a standard to get another instance based on another standard (for example, to get a BizTalk XML instance from a xCBL defined instance).

Mapping the schema elements can be a difficult and time-consuming job. Understanding the relationships can also be difficult. The method I use for determining the mapping between elements involves creating a table using the instance we want to get to. This is accomplished by creating a structural hierarchy that helps us define the XPath queries we will need in the XSLT transform, by mapping the values of elements back to the source instance.

First you should create a table with two columns. The title of the left column should contain the name of the originating schema (that is, the schema that you are wanting to transform) and the title of the right column should be the title of the result schema (the schema you are transforming TO).

Now, take an instance of the schema you are mapping to (the result). Start from the root of the instance and work down each branch of the tree and, in the right column, write down the XML to get to each node that is either an attribute or element and should have a value (very much similar to how you would define an XPath query). So, you should start at the root – everything below it should be **RELATIVE** to the root **UNTIL** you reach the end of a particular branch, in which case you start at the root again (in my case, I mark each root with a grey cell background color). For those elements or attributes that should have a value, put an equals sign before them. The following diagram illustrates this concept.

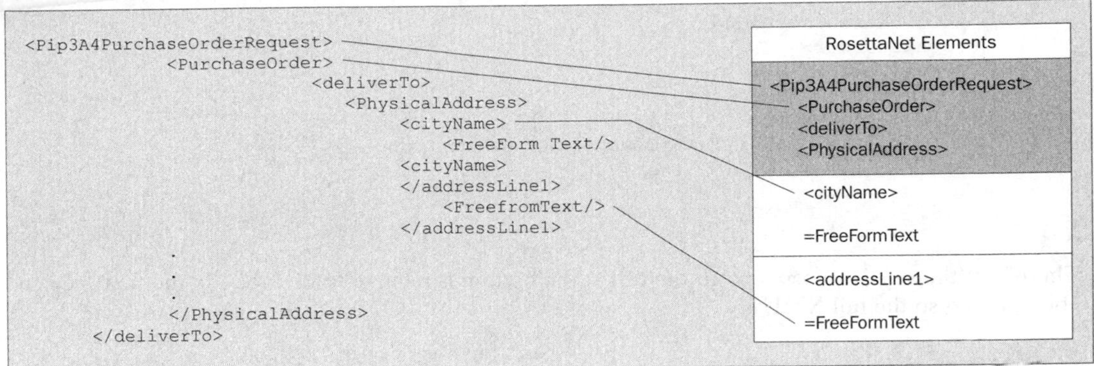

Let's look at an example of what we have just done for the case of wanting to translate from an xCBL PO schema to a RosettaNet PO schema:

xCBL Elements	RosettaNet Elements
	<Pip3A4PurchaseOrderRequest> **<PurchaseOrder>** **<deliverTo>** **<PhysicalAddress>**
	<cityName>
	=FreeFormText
	<addressLine1>
	=FreeFormText
	<Pip3A4PurchaseOrderRequest> **<PurchaseOrder>** **<ProductLineItem>**
	<shipFrom>
	=GlobalLocationIdentifier

So, in the first case, we have the XML from the root node,

```
<Pip3A4PurchaseOrderRequest>
   <PurchaseOrder>
      <deliverTo>
         <PhysicalAddress>
```

and in the following cell, we have,

```
<cityName>
=FreeFormText
```

which is relative to the element in the first grey cell above and actually refers to the `FreeFormText` element in the `Pip3A4PurchaseOrderRequest` schema as below:

```
<Pip3A4PurchaseOrderRequest>
   <PurchaseOrder>
      <deliverTo>
         <PhysicalAddress>
            <cityName>
               <FreeFormText>Glasgow</FreeFormText>

            ...
```

Therefore, the <shipFrom> text in the cell at the bottom is relative to the node in the first grey cell above it and so the full XML is:

```
<Pip3A4PurchaseOrderRequest>
   <PurchaseOrder>
      <ProductLineItem>
         <ShipFrom>
            <GlobalLocationIdentifier>82823</GlobalLocationIdentifier>

         ...
```

This works the same for the entire column and if you write out each column at the end, it should match your XDR schema.

Once the right-hand column has been completed, it is necessary to enter some information in the left-hand column (the source schema) to describe what element(s) map to the element in the result schema. This works in the exact same way as described above, except the source schema does NOT have grey cells highlighted. So, the above schema mapping would look like this:

xCBL Elements	RosettaNet Elements
<OrderRequestHeader> <OrderRequestParty> <BillToParty> <Party> <NameAddress>	**<Pip3A4PurchaseOrderRequest>** **<PurchaseOrder>** **<deliverTo>** **<PhysicalAddress>**
=City	<cityName>
	=FreeFormText
=StreetSuppliment1	<addressLine1> =FreeFormText
<OrderRequest> <OrderRequestHeader> <OrderRequestParty> <SellerParty> <Party> <PartyID> <Identifier>	**<Pip3A4PurchaseOrderRequest>** **<PurchaseOrder>** **<ProductLineItem>**
=Ident	<shipFrom>
	=GlobalLocationIdentifier

Finally, there are some cases where there is no mapping and a default value is provided for the field. To do this, enclose the value in square brackets, such as [Scotland].

You may have another method for doing this work and there are some tools coming out that help you with the process, such as the Microsoft BizTalk Mapper tool, which is a graphical editor that loads the two XML specifications and allows the programmer to specify how the records and fields map to one another. The following tables show how this technique is used to map several schemas that will be used in our sample. Don't rush through them, but work through them and see how they map to the actual schemas we have defined above. You should pick up the technique fairly quickly, and get great benefit from it.

xCBL To RosettaNet

xCBL Elements	RosettaNet Elements
<OrderRequestHeader> <OrderRequestParty> <BillToParty> <Party> <NameAddress>	<Pip3A4PurchaseOrderRequest> <PurchaseOrder> <deliverTo> <PhysicalAddress>
=City	<cityName>
	=FreeFormText
=StreetSuppliment1	<addressLine1>
	=FreeFormText
=StreetSuppliment2	<addressLine2>
	=FreeFormText
=PostalCode	=NationalPostalCode
<Region>	<regionName>
=RegionCoded	=FreeFormText
=Country	=GlobalCountryCode
<OrderRequest> <OrderRequestHeader> <OrderRequestParty> <SellerParty> <Party> <PartyID> <Identifier>	<Pip3A4PurchaseOrderRequest> <PurchaseOrder> <ProductLineItem>
=Ident	<shipFrom>
	=GlobalLocationIdentifier

Table continued on following page

xCBL Elements	RosettaNet Elements
<OrderRequest> <OrderRequestDetail> <OrderDetail> <ListOfItemDetail> <ItemDetail> <BaseItemDetail> <TotalQuantity> <Quantity> =QuantityValue	=ProductQuantity
<OrderRequest> <OrderRequestDetail> <OrderDetail> <ListOfItemDetail> <ItemDetail> <BaseItemDetail> <LineItemNum> =BuyerLineItemNum	=LineNumber
<OrderRequest> <OrderRequestDetail> <OrderDetail> <ListOfItemDetail> <ItemDetail> <BaseItemDetail> <ItemIdentifiers> <PartNumbers> <SellerPartNumber> <PartNum>	<ProductUnit> <ProductPackageDescription> <PartnerProductIdentification>
=PartID	=ProprietaryProductIdentifier
[shopper]	=GlobalPartnerClassificationCode
<OrderRequest> <OrderRequestDetail> <OrderDetail> <ListOfItemDetail> <ItemDetail> <BaseItemDetail> <CountryOfOrigin> <Country> =CountryCoded	<CountryOfOrigin> =GlobalCountryCode

xCBL Elements	RosettaNet Elements
<OrderRequest> <OrderRequestHeader> <OrderRequestReferences> <OrderReferences> <ContractReferences> <ListOfContract> <Contract> <ValidityDates> =StartDate	<RequestedShipDate> =DateStamp
<OrderRequest> <OrderRequestDetail> <OrderDetail> <ListOfItemDetail> <ItemDetail> <BaseItemDetail> <TotalQuantity> <Quantity> <UnitOfMeasurement> = UOMCoded	=GlobalProductUnitOfMeasureCod e
<OrderRequest> <OrderRequestHeader> <ListOfTransport> <Transport> <TransportMode> =TransportModeCoded	<SpecialHandlingInstruction> <specialHandlingText> =FreeFormText
<OrderRequest> <OrderRequestDetail> <OrderDetail> <ListOfItemDetail> <ItemDetail> <PricingDetail> <ListOfPrice> <Price> <UnitPrice> = UnitPriceValue	<RequestedPrice> < FinancialAmount> =MonetaryAmount
<OrderRequest> <OrderRequestHeader> <OrderRequestCurrency> <Currency> =CurrencyCoded	<RequestedPrice> < FinancialAmount> =GlobalCurrencyCode
	<Pip3A4PurchaseOrderRequest> <PurchaseOrder>

Table continued on following page

xCBL Elements	RosettaNet Elements
<OrderRequest> <OrderRequestHeader> <OrderTermsOfDelivery> <TermsOfDelivery> =ShippingMethodOfPaymentCoded	=GlobalShipmentTermsCode
[1]	=RevisionNumber
<OrderRequest> <OrderRequestHeader> <OrderRequestReferences> <OrderReferences> <ContractReferences> <ListOfContract> <Contract> <ContractType> =ContractTypeEncoded	= GlobalFinanceTermsCode
[ ]	=PartnerDescription
[Dropship]	=GlobalPurchaseOrderTypeCode
	<Pip3A4PurchaseOrderRequest> <fromRole> <PartnerRoleDescription>
[Seller] (is defined as this in document)	=GlobalPartnerRoleClassificationCode
	<Pip3A4PurchaseOrderRequest> <toRole> <PartnerRoleDescription>
[Buyer]	=GlobalPartnerRoleClassificationCode
<OrderRequest> <OrderRequestHeader> <OrderRequestParty> <BillToParty> <Party> <OtherContacts> <ListOfContact> <Contact>	<ContactInformation>
<ListOfContactNumber> <ContactNumber> =ContactNumberValue	=EmailAddress

xCBL Elements	RosettaNet Elements
=ContactName	<contactName> =FreeFormText
<ListOfContactNumber> <ContactNumber> = ContactNumberValue	<telephoneNumber> =CommunicationsNumber
<OrderRequest> <OrderRequestHeader> =OrderRequestIssueDate	<Pip3A4PurchaseOrderRequest> <thisDocumentGenerationDateTime > =DateTimeStamp
<OrderRequest> <OrderRequestHeader> <OrderRequestNumber> =SellerOrderRequestNumber	<Pip3A4PurchaseOrderRequest> <thisDocumentIdentifier> =ProprietaryDocumentIdentifier
[Request]	<Pip3A4PurchaseOrderRequest> =GlobalDocumentFunctionCode

RosettaNet to BizTalk

RosettaNet Elements	BizTalk Elements
	<PO> <POHeader>
[0]	=refPromise
[ ]	=description
<Pip3A4PurchaseOrderRequest> <PurchaseOrder> = GlobalFinanceTermsCode	=paymentType
<SpecialHandlingInstruction> <specialHandlingText> =FreeFormText	=shipType
<Pip3A4PurchaseOrderRequest> <PurchaseOrder> <ProductLineItem> <shipFrom> =GlobalLocationIdentifier	=fromCust
<Pip3A4PurchaseOrderRequest> <thisDocumentIdentifier> =ProprietaryDocumentIdentifier	=PoNumber

Table continued on following page

RosettaNet Elements	BizTalk Elements
<Pip3A4PurchaseOrderRequest> <thisDocumentIdentifier> <toRole>	<PO> <Contact>
<PartnerRoleDescription> <ContactInformation>	
=contactName	=contactName
=EmailAddress	=contactEmail
=telephoneNumber	=contactPhone
<Pip3A4PurchaseOrderRequest> <PurchaseOrder> <deliverTo> <PhysicalAddress>	<PO> <POShipTo>
<cityName>	=city
=FreeFormText	
<Pip3A4PurchaseOrderRequest> <thisDocumentIdentifier> <toRole>	=attn
<PartnerRoleDescription> <ContactInformation> =contactName	
=GlobalCountryCode	=country
<regionName>	=startProvince
=FreeFormText	
<addressLine2>	=street2
=FreeFormText	
<addressLine1>	=street1
=FreeFormText	
=NationalPostalCode	=postalCode
<Pip3A4PurchaseOrderRequest> <PurchaseOrder> <ProductLineItem>	<PO> <POLines>
[1]	=startAt
[1]	=count
	<Item>

RosettaNet Elements	BizTalk Elements
=GlobalProductUnitOfMeasureCode	=uom
<RequestedPrice> <FinancialAmount> =MonetaryAmount	=unitPrice
<Pip3A4PurchaseOrderRequest> <PurchaseOrder> <ProductLineItem> =ProductQuantity	=qty
<Pip3A4PurchaseOrderRequest> <PurchaseOrder> <ProductLineItem> <ProductUnit> <ProductPackageDescription> <PartnerProductIdentifier> =ProprietaryProductIdentifier	=partno
<Pip3A4PurchaseOrderRequest> <PurchaseOrder> <ProductLineItem> <RequestedShipDate> =DateStamp	=needAfter
[0]	=discount
<Pip3A4PurchaseOrderRequest> <PurchaseOrder> <ProductLineItem> =LineNumber	=line
<Pip3A4PurchaseOrderRequest> <PurchaseOrder> <ProductLineItem> <requestedShipDate> =DateStamp	=needBefore

Business Rules in Translation

When looking at the schema Translation methodology above, you probably noted that the format of some values in the xCBL schema is slightly or completely different from the values in the RosettaNet schema. The same would apply for conversions to all of the other schema types as well. Let's look at how we can approach and solve these challenges.

The Need for Business Rules Between Schemas

As we previously mentioned, there are many cases when mapping between schemas in which data types between mapped elements differ. This is best illustrated with an example. Let's consider the `<DateStamp>` element of the RosettaNet schema and the `<needBefore>` element of the BizTalk schema.

The RosettaNet schema species that the format of the date within the `<DateStamp>` element is:

> **Based on the ISO 8601 specification. The "Z" following the day identifier (DD) is used to indicate Coordinated Universal Time. Informal format: CCYYMMDDThh:mm:ssZ**

So, in other words, we can specify

```
Wednesday 10 March at 2:30 PM at US Eastern Standard Time
```

as

```
20010310T14:30:00Z-05:00
```

So CC is the century (20), YY is the year (01), MM is the month (03) and DD is the day (10). The `T` represents the Time in hours, minutes and seconds and the `Z` is used to specify the time zone, which is –5 hours in our example.

However, the format of the **BizTalk** date is

CCYY-MM-DD

Or, as in our example,

```
2001-03-10
```

This illustrates a key point that sometimes information can be discarded between translations (as we see the time is lost in this conversion). What it does show, however, is that sometimes some manipulation is required to reformat a particular datatype for a given schema.

We are going to look at how to work with the date type and unit of measurement codes for the different schemas we have be using. We are NOT going to look at others, as converters for every type are out of scope for this chapter – however, with this understanding and some simple scripting, you should be able to write rules for all of your XML business schema needs.

In the case study, we use JavaScript (because it's simple and most scriptors are familiar with it) although you could use any other script of your choice, and depending on your choice of XSL Parser (we work with the Microsoft XML Parser) you could use COM objects or Java objects. Furthermore, using this technique, you can create business objects containing all the rules and reuse the objects within the relevant schemas (for example a BizTalk object may convert other formats to the BizTalk format). Many of the examples you will come across could also be done in XSLT, but these are simple examples.

Often you may have very complex rules when translating. For example, it would be better to call out to a business object to determine more complex statements. For instance, some of the standards use very large enumerations and rather than having 1000 `xsl:if` comparisons, you can call out to a business object that may use an external source (such as a database) to get the result. Remember this as you look through the examples.

The following table summaries the uses and relationships of these types within our schemas.

xCBL	RosettaNet	BizTalk
Element <OrderRequestIssueDate>	Element <DateTimeStamp>	Element <needBefore>
Format CCYYMMDDZ	Format CCYYMMDDZ	Format CCYY-MM-DD
Example 20010310	Example 20010310	Example 2001-03-10
Element <UOMCode>	Element <GlobalProductUnitOfMeasurementCode>	Element <UOM>
Format BX (box), DZ (Dozen) etc...	Format Each, Dozen etc...	Format PC or UNIT
Example BX	Example EACH	Example PC

The JavaScript code below shows how to modify the datatype for the xCBL to RosettaNet transformation. Note that it illustrates the concepts as outlined in this case study and does not cover all the types. This method is used to convert between the definition of a Unit Of Measurement between the xCBL schema and the RosettaNet schema. If you look at these definitions in the relevant specifications, you will see they differ greatly and the list is very extensive. For the purposes of this application, we map only the "BOX" (BX) unit or define it as "Dozen". If you look at the code, you can see that when the measurement unit is "BX", the return value is "EACH", which is the equivalent in the RosettaNet world.

```
function xCBL2RosettaNet_UOM(str_UOM)
{
   //you should increase this to cover every type
   var str_BizUom="";

   if (str_UOM=="BX")
      str_BizUom="EACH";
   else
      str_BizUom="Dozen";

   return(str_BizUom);
}
```

You should enhance this code for your own particular business application to cover the many other measurement types they have.

Similar code is used for the RosettaNet to BizTalk conversion, with the addition of the date format function:

```
function RosettaNet2BizTalk_Date(d_RNet)
{
   // Returns date in CCYYMMYY format
   // for example 2001-03-10

   var d_Rnet = new Date(d_RNet);
   var d_year=d_RNet.substr(0,4);
   var d_month=d_RNet.substr(4,2);
   var d_day=d_RNet.substr(6,2);

   return(d_year+"-"+d_month+"-"+d_day);
}

function RosettaNet2BizTalk_UOM(str_UOM)
{
   //BizTalk says PC or UNIT
   var str_BizUom="";

   //you should increase this to cover every type
   if (str_UOM=="EACH")
      str_BizUom="PC";
   else
      str_BizUom="UNIT";

   return(str_BizUom);
}
```

The date format function simply takes in the date in the RosettaNet format and splits it up and formats it as a BizTalk expected date format.

Solution Architecture

> **In addition to the downloads cited at the start of the chapter, you should download the useful IE XML Validation Tool from http://msdn.microsoft.com/xml, which allows you to view the XSL Output from an XSLT transform.**

Now that we understand the business processes behind integrating diverse e-business systems, we are going to look at how we actually implement this and the architecture of the solution we employ. We will see how we can effectively employ XSL transforms and combine this with the mapping procedure and business logic we worked on in the two sections above.

The following diagram demonstrates the complex marketplace we have in our scenario.

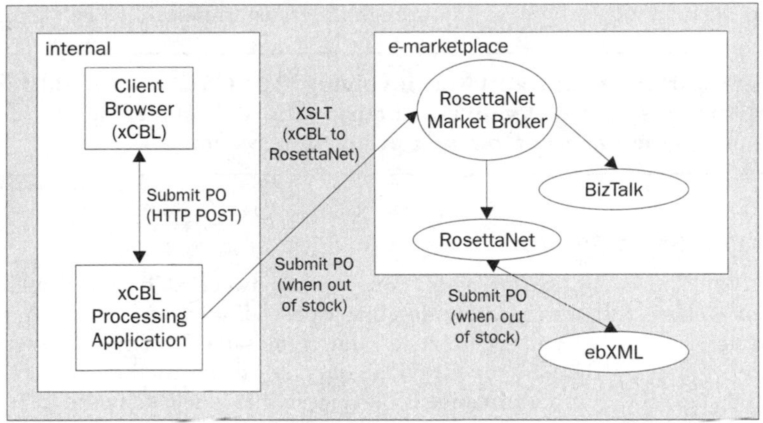

The internal businesses involved have a set of internal processes, which work based on the xCBL standard. However, when they are out of stock of a particular item, they work directly with their online marketplace, which happens to work to the RosettaNet standard. Hence, any purchase orders sent to this marketplace must be converted using one of the XSLTs we will define later. This marketplace works mainly with RosettaNet based businesses, but in order to support as wide a range of businesses as possible, it also supports the BizTalk standard. PO's are also converted to the BizTalk standard when necessary, and posted to the relevant recipients. Finally, there is one business in the marketplace that has a backup supplier, which operates outside the market place using the ebXML standards. PO's to this business must be converted accordingly during processing.

Now we must look at these XML transformation scripts and how we define them.

Integration Practice

You will recall that we have defined all the mappings between the elements in the different schemas above. As a result we can now easily create our own XSLTs that will perform the actual transforms. This is because in the right hand column of the mapping tables we defined earlier, we followed the branching of the XML instance for the result schema (RosettaNet in the first case and BizTalk in the second case). As we move through the schema (and hence down the right hand side of the table), we can quickly look at the corresponding mapping entry in the left of the table and get the information needed to perform successful transformations. This is illustrated below.

xCBL Elements	RosettaNet Elements
<OrderRequestHeader> **<OrderRequestParty>** **<BillToParty>** **<Party>** **<NameAddress>**	**<Pip3A4PurchaseOrderRequest>** **<PurchaseOrder>** **<deliverTo>** **<PhysicalAddress>**
=City	**<cityName>** //OrderRequestHeader/OrderRequestParty/BillToParty/Party/NameAddress/City =FreeFormText
=StreetSuppliment1	**<addressLine1>** =FreeFormText

The best way to illustrate this is by working through the transformations, so let's look at these now.

> **Note: When working with transforms involving the xCBL, you should remove the xmlns attribute as it will validate and can take a considerable amount of time, which may be unacceptable in a production system.**

xCBL To a RosettaNet Based Supplier

The following listing shows the XSLT used for conversion between xCBL and RosettaNet. After we have browsed the code in full, we can examine some aspects of it in more detail. In particular, look at each node with `xsl:value-of` and see how the value is the same as defined in our mapping tables above. Note that we use "//" in many of our XPath queries – this is used to simplify the reading of the code, but I would suggest that if performance is of concern that you specify the full XPath to an element or use templates, as "//" causes the processor to search the entire document for the specified node.

```
<xsl:stylesheet version="1.0" xmlns:xsl="http://www.w3.org/1999/XSL/Transform"
    xmlns:msxsl="urn:schemas-microsoft-com:xslt"
   xmlns:user="http://wrox.com/somenamespace">
   <xsl:output method="xml" version="1.0" encoding="UTF-8" indent="yes"/>
   <xsl:template match="/">
      <Pip3A4PurchaseOrderRequest
       xmlns="x-schema:3A4PurchaseOrderRequestMessageGuideline_V1_4.xdr">
         <PurchaseOrder>
            <deliverTo>
               <PhysicalAddress>
                  <cityName>
                     <FreeFormText>
                        <xsl:value-of
                              select="//BillToParty/Party/NameAddress/City"/>
                     </FreeFormText>
                  </cityName>
                  <addressLine1>
                     <FreeFormText>
                        <xsl:value-of select="//BillToParty/
                                                  Party/NameAddress/
                                                  StreetSupplement1"/>
                     </FreeFormText>
                  </addressLine1>
                  <addressLine2>
                     <FreeFormText>
                        <xsl:value-of select="//BillToParty/
                                                  Party/NameAddress/
                                                  StreetSupplement2"/>
                     </FreeFormText>
                  </addressLine2>
                  <NationalPostalCode>
                     <xsl:value-of select="//BillToParty/Party/
                                            NameAddress/PostalCode"/>
                  </NationalPostalCode>
                  <regionName>
                     <FreeFormText>
                        <xsl:value-of select="//BillToParty/
                                                  Party/NameAddress/Region/
```

```
                                               RegionCoded"/>
                  </FreeFormText>
               </regionName>
               <GlobalCountryCode>
                  <xsl:value-of select="//BillToParty
                                        /Party/NameAddress/Country
                                        /CountryCoded"/>
               </GlobalCountryCode>
            </PhysicalAddress>
         </deliverTo>
         <ProductLineItem>
            <shipFrom>
               <GlobalLocationIdentifier>
                  <xsl:value-of select="//ListOfItemDetail
                                        /ItemDetail/BaseItemDetail
                                        /TotalQuantity/Quantity
                                        /QuantityValue"/>
               </GlobalLocationIdentifier>
            </shipFrom>
            <ProductQuantity>
               <xsl:value-of select="//ListOfItemDetail
                                     /ItemDetail/BaseItemDetail/
                                     TotalQuantity/Quantity/
                                     QuantityValue"/>
            </ProductQuantity>
            <LineNumber>
               <xsl:value-of select="//ListOfItemDetail/ItemDetail
                                     /BaseItemDetail/LineItemNum/
                                     BuyerLineItemNum"/>
            </LineNumber>
            <productUnit>
               <ProductPackageDescription>
                  <ProductIdentification>
                     <PartnerProductIdentification>
                        <GlobalPartnerClassificationCode>
                           <xsl:value-of select="//
                              ListOfItemDetail/ItemDetail/
                              BaseItemDetail/ItemIdentifiers/
                              PartNumbers/SellerPartNumber
                              /PartNum/PartID"/>
                        </GlobalPartnerClassificationCode>
                        <ProprietaryProductIdentifier>
                           Shopper
                        </ProprietaryProductIdentifier>
                     </PartnerProductIdentification>
                  </ProductIdentification>
               </ProductPackageDescription>
            </productUnit>
            <countryOfOrigin>
               <GlobalCountryCode>
                  <xsl:value-of select="//ListOfItemDetail/ItemDetail/
                                        BaseItemDetail/CountryOfOrigin/
                                        Country/CountryCoded"/>
               </GlobalCountryCode>
            </countryOfOrigin>
            <requestedShipDate>
```

```
            <DateStamp>
               <xsl:value-of select="//OrderReferences/
                                     ContractReferences/
                                     ListOfContract/Contract
                                     /ValidityDates/StartDate"/>
            </DateStamp>
         </requestedShipDate>
         <GlobalProductUnitOfMeasureCode>
            <xsl:value-of select="user:xCBL2RosettaNet_UOM(string(//
                                  ListOfItemDetail/ItemDetail
                                  /BaseItemDetail/TotalQuantity
                                  /Quantity/UnitOfMeasurement/
                                  UOMCoded))"/>
         </GlobalProductUnitOfMeasureCode>
         <SpecialHandlingInstruction>
            <specialHandlingText>
               <FreeFormText>
                  <xsl:value-of select="//ListOfTransport/
                                        Transport/TransportMode
                                        /TransportModeCoded"/>
               </FreeFormText>
            </specialHandlingText>
         </SpecialHandlingInstruction>
         <requestedPrice>
            <FinancialAmount>
               <GlobalCurrencyCode>
                  <xsl:value-of select="//OrderRequestCurrency/
                                        Currency/CurrencyCoded"/>
               </GlobalCurrencyCode>
               <MonetaryAmount>
                  <xsl:value-of select="//ListOfItemDetail/ItemDetail/
                                        PricingDetail/ListOfPrice/
                                        Price/UnitPrice/
                                        UnitPriceValue"/>
               </MonetaryAmount>
            </FinancialAmount>
         </requestedPrice>
      </ProductLineItem>
      <GlobalShipmentTermsCode>
         <xsl:value-of select="//OrderTermsOfDelivery/TermsOfDelivery
                               /ShippingMethodOfPaymentCoded"/>
      </GlobalShipmentTermsCode>
      <RevisionNumber>1</RevisionNumber>
      <GlobalFinanceTermsCode>
         <xsl:value-of select="//OrderReferences/ContractReferences
                               /ListOfContract/Contract/ContractType
                               /ContractTypeEncoded"/>
      </GlobalFinanceTermsCode>
      <PartnerDescription/>
      <GlobalPurchaseOrderTypeCode>
         dropship
      </GlobalPurchaseOrderTypeCode>
   </PurchaseOrder>
   <fromRole>
      <PartnerRoleDescription>
         <GlobalPartnerRoleClassificationCode>
```

```
            seller
         </GlobalPartnerRoleClassificationCode>
      </PartnerRoleDescription>
   </fromRole>
   <toRole>
      <PartnerRoleDescription>
         <GlobalPartnerRoleClassificationCode>
            Buyer
         </GlobalPartnerRoleClassificationCode>
         <ContactInformation>
            <EmailAddress>
               <xsl:value-of select="//BillToParty/Party/OtherContacts
                                     /ListOfContact/Contact/
                                     ListOfContactNumber/
                                     ContactNumber[2]/
                                     ContactNumberValue"/>
            </EmailAddress>
            <contactName>
               <FreeFormText>
                  <xsl:value-of select="//BillToParty/
                                        Party/OtherContacts/
                                        ListOfContact/Contact/
                                        ContactName"/>
               </FreeFormText>
            </contactName>
            <telephoneNumber>
               <CommunicationsNumber>
                  <xsl:value-of select="//BillToParty/
                                        Party/OtherContacts/
                                        ListOfContact/Contact/
                                        ListOfContactNumber/
                                        ContactNumber/
                                        ContactNumberValue"/>
               </CommunicationsNumber>
            </telephoneNumber>
         </ContactInformation>
      </PartnerRoleDescription>
   </toRole>
   <thisDocumentGenerationDateTime>
      <DateTimeStamp>
         <xsl:value-of select="//OrderRequestIssueDate"/>
      </DateTimeStamp>
   </thisDocumentGenerationDateTime>
   <thisDocumentIdentifier>
      <ProprietaryDocumentIdentifier>
         <xsl:value-of select="//SellerOrderRequestNumber"/>
      </ProprietaryDocumentIdentifier>
   </thisDocumentIdentifier>
      <GlobalDocumentFunctionCode>Request</GlobalDocumentFunctionCode>
  </Pip3A4PurchaseOrderRequest>
</xsl:template>
<msxsl:script language="JScript" implements-prefix="user">
   function xCBL2RosettaNet_UOM(str_UOM)
   {
      //you should increase this to cover every type
      var str_BizUom="";
```

```
            if (str_UOM=="BX")
               str_BizUom="EACH";
            else
               str_BizUom="Dozen";

            return(str_BizUom);
         }
      </msxsl:script>
   </xsl:stylesheet>
```

Notice that there are two namespace definitions beyond the standard `xmlns:xsl` namespace declaration, which indicates the prefix `xsl` is going to be used for elements defined in the W3C XSLT specification, found at http://www.w3.org/1999/XSL/Transform.There are also namespaces represented by the "`msxsl`" prefix and "`user`" prefix.

```
<xsl:stylesheet version="1.0" xmlns:xsl="http://www.w3.org/1999/XSL/Transform"
   xmlns:msxsl="urn:schemas-microsoft-com:xslt"
   xmlns:user="http://wrox.com/somenamespace">
```

The first namespace is used here to define extension functions that use the Microsoft parser, which we will see below. The second is for user defined functions – namely the business logic routines we discussed above.

Notice that we also have an `xsl:output` tag that defines the output format of the document as **XML, with UTF-8 encoding**. This is the default value (if none is specified), but it is good practice to put it in anyway.

```
<xsl:output method="xml" version="1.0" encoding="UTF-8" indent="yes"/>
```

The business rules we scripted on above are actually defined in script at the bottom of the page in the `msxsl:script` section:

```
<msxsl:script language="JScript" implements-prefix="user">
   ...business logic as defined previously
</msxsl:script>
```

We can then call the routines in this script from anywhere within our XSL code. The following illustrates how to call the `xCBL2RosettaNet_UOM` function to convert a given code from xCBL format to RosettaNet format.

```
<xsl:value-of
select="user:xCBL2RosettaNet_UOM(string(/OrderRequest/OrderDetail/ListOfItemDetail
/ItemDetail/BaseItemDetail/TotalQuantity/Quantity/UnitOfMeasurement/UOMCoded))"/>
```

The `string()` method is used within the method call to convert the return from the XPath query from a node type to a string value.

If you are using Internet Explorer, you can see the following result.

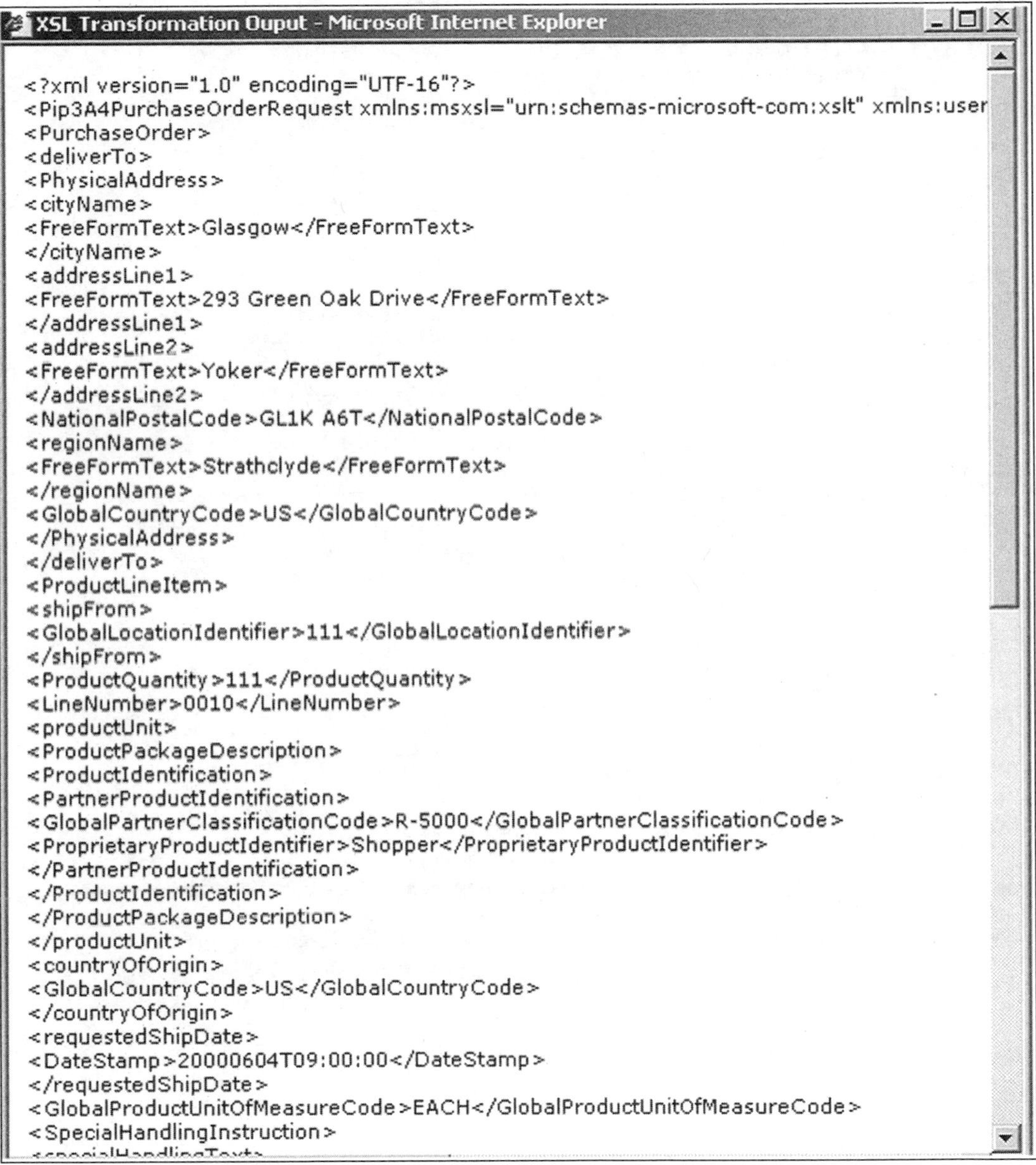


```
<?xml version="1.0" encoding="UTF-16"?>
<Pip3A4PurchaseOrderRequest xmlns:msxsl="urn:schemas-microsoft-com:xslt" xmlns:user
<PurchaseOrder>
<deliverTo>
<PhysicalAddress>
<cityName>
<FreeFormText>Glasgow</FreeFormText>
</cityName>
<addressLine1>
<FreeFormText>293 Green Oak Drive</FreeFormText>
</addressLine1>
<addressLine2>
<FreeFormText>Yoker</FreeFormText>
</addressLine2>
<NationalPostalCode>GL1K A6T</NationalPostalCode>
<regionName>
<FreeFormText>Strathclyde</FreeFormText>
</regionName>
<GlobalCountryCode>US</GlobalCountryCode>
</PhysicalAddress>
</deliverTo>
<ProductLineItem>
<shipFrom>
<GlobalLocationIdentifier>111</GlobalLocationIdentifier>
</shipFrom>
<ProductQuantity>111</ProductQuantity>
<LineNumber>0010</LineNumber>
<productUnit>
<ProductPackageDescription>
<ProductIdentification>
<PartnerProductIdentification>
<GlobalPartnerClassificationCode>R-5000</GlobalPartnerClassificationCode>
<ProprietaryProductIdentifier>Shopper</ProprietaryProductIdentifier>
</PartnerProductIdentification>
</ProductIdentification>
</ProductPackageDescription>
</productUnit>
<countryOfOrigin>
<GlobalCountryCode>US</GlobalCountryCode>
</countryOfOrigin>
<requestedShipDate>
<DateStamp>20000604T09:00:00</DateStamp>
</requestedShipDate>
<GlobalProductUnitOfMeasureCode>EACH</GlobalProductUnitOfMeasureCode>
<SpecialHandlingInstruction>
```

This code takes care of allowing businesses operating to RosettaNet standards to view our PO; however, the marketplace also wants to make the same information available to BizTalk standardized services and this is what we are going to look at now.

RosettaNet To a BizTalk Schema-based Supplier

The following schema shows the XSLT needed to transform a RosettaNet document into a compatible BizTalk schema. Browse the document and see how the mapping table above helps to define the mapping methods we use.

```
<xsl:stylesheet version="1.0" xmlns:xsl="http://www.w3.org/1999/XSL/Transform"
    xmlns:msxsl="urn:schemas-microsoft-com:xslt"
    xmlns:user="http://wrox.com/somenamespace">
    <xsl:output method="xml" version="1.0" encoding="UTF-8" indent="yes"/>
    <xsl:template match="/">
   <PO xmlns="x-schema:cfwau8qx.xml">

      <POHeader refPromise="0" description=""
                paymentType="{//GlobalFinanceTermsCode}"
shipType="{//SpecialHandlingInstruction/specialHandlingText/FreeFormText}"
fromCust="{//ProductLineItem/shipFrom/GlobalLocationIdentifier}"
                poNumber="{//ProprietaryDocumentIdentifier}"/>

      <Contact contactName="{//toRole/PartnerRoleDescription
                             /ContactInformation/contactName}"
              contactEmail="{//toRole/PartnerRoleDescription/
                             ContactInformation/EmailAddress}"
              contactPhone="{//toRole/PartnerRoleDescription/
                             ContactInformation/telephoneNumber}"/>

   <POShipTo city="{//deliverTo/PhysicalAddress/cityName/FreeFormText}"
attn="{//toRole/PartnerRoleDescription/ContactInformation/contactName}"
country="{//deliverTo/PhysicalAddress/GlobalCountryCode}"
stateProvince="{//deliverTo/PhysicalAddress/regionName/FreeFormText}"
street4="" street3=""
street2="{//deliverTo/PhysicalAddress/addressLine2/FreeFormText}"
street1="{//deliverTo/PhysicalAddress/addressLine1/FreeFormText}"
postalCode="{//deliverTo/PhysicalAddress/NationalPostalCode}"/>

   <POBillTo city="" attn="" country="" stateProvince="" street4=""
             street3="" street2="" street1="" postalCode=""/>
   <POLines startAt="1" count="1">
      <Item
       uom="{user:RosettaNet2BizTalk_UOM(string(//
             GlobalProductUnitOfMeasureCode))}"
             unitPrice="{//RequestedPrice/FinancialAmount/MonetaryAmount}"
             qty="{//ProductLineItem/ProductQuantity}"
partno="{//ProductLineItem/ProductUnit/ProductPackageDescription/
             PartnerProductIdentifier/ProprietaryProductIdentifier}"
             needAfter="{user:RosettaNet2BizTalk_Date(string(//
             requestedShipDate/DateStamp))}"
             discount="0" line="{//ProductLineItem/LineNumber}"
             needBefore="{user:RosettaNet2BizTalk_Date(string(//
             requestedShipDate/DateStamp))}"/>
   </POLines>
</PO>
</xsl:template>
   <msxsl:script language="JScript" implements-prefix="user">
      function RosettaNet2BizTalk_Date(d_RNet)
      {
         // Returns date in CCYYMMYY format
         // e.g. 2001-03-10

         var d_Rnet = new Date(d_RNet);
         var d_year=d_RNet.substr(0,4);
         var d_month=d_RNet.substr(4,2);
```

```
            var d_day=d_RNet.substr(6,2);

            return(d_year+"-"+d_month+"-"+d_day);
        }

        function RosettaNet2BizTalk_UOM(str_UOM)
        {
            //BizTalk says PC or UNIT
            var str_BizUom="";

            if (str_UOM=="EACH")
                str_BizUom="PC";
            else
                str_BizUom="UNIT";

            return(str_BizUom);
        }
    </msxsl:script>
</xsl:stylesheet>
```

You will notice that many of the concepts are very similar to the previous XSLT, although there is a slight difference, because the BizTalk XDR schema is designed to make heavy use of attributes. So rather that use the value-of XSL routine, we make use of curly brackets "{}" and enter an Attribute Value Template (XPath query) to return the appropriate node.

An extra function call is also made to convert the date format from RosettaNet format to BizTalk format as we discussed earlier in the chapter. The output is shown below:

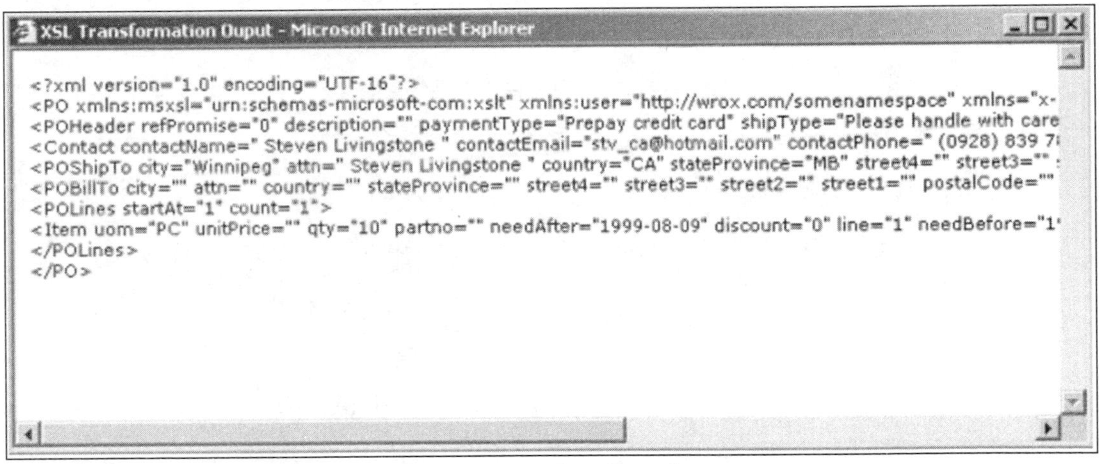

XSL Transformation Ouput - Microsoft Internet Explorer

```
<?xml version="1.0" encoding="UTF-16"?>
<PO xmlns:msxsl="urn:schemas-microsoft-com:xslt" xmlns:user="http://wrox.com/somenamespace" xmlns="x-
<POHeader refPromise="0" description="" paymentType="Prepay credit card" shipType="Please handle with care
<Contact contactName=" Steven Livingstone " contactEmail="stv_ca@hotmail.com" contactPhone=" (0928) 839 7
<POShipTo city="Winnipeg" attn=" Steven Livingstone " country="CA" stateProvince="MB" street4="" street3=""
<POBillTo city="" attn="" country="" stateProvince="" street4="" street3="" street2="" street1="" postalCode=""
<POLines startAt="1" count="1">
<Item uom="PC" unitPrice="" qty="10" partno="" needAfter="1999-08-09" discount="0" line="1" needBefore="1
</POLines>
</PO>
```

EXAMPLE: Submitting a PO (MS XML Parser)

Now we are going to look at how to use all of the above components to represent an actual implementation. Until this point, everything except the MSXSL namespace and script in the XSL files has been platform and language neutral. We are going to implement this example in JScript using the Microsoft XML 3.0 parser, although the concepts are similar for any platform implementation.

> **This sample requires the MSXML 3.0 parser and IIS. You should put the files in the PO folder in the download into a directory called PO on the root of your web server. You also have to ensure that you have write permissions to the Orders sub-directory within the PO directory.**

In this example, `PurchaseOrder.htm` is used to create a purchase order based on the RosettaNet standard, and submit the instance to a server (`po.asp`) at a remote marketplace. When the result is received, it is parsed, transformed to a valid BizTalk instance, and saved to the server. A person at the marketplace or third party business can then view the details of the purchase order using `ShowPurchaseOrder.asp`. Let's examine this process in more detail.

`PurchaseOrder.htm` is the name of the web page that starts off the whole process. A user enters the information about the purchase order and sends it to the remote marketplace. When a user has entered the purchase order details, the submit button is clicked and this invokes the client JavaScript function `submitPO()`.

```
<HTML>
<HEAD>
<TITLE>Internal Inventory Purchase Order Form</TITLE>
<SCRIPT LANGUAGE="JavaScript">
function submitPO()
{
```

The XML RosettaNet instance is built up client-side from the local template file `RosettaNet_POTemp.xml`, which is an empty purchase order instance. This is loaded as an XML document; now we can simply work through the values using the HTML DOM, tying them in with the elements in the loaded XML document, and having the document populated.

```
   var objXML = new ActiveXObject("Microsoft.XMLDOM")
   objXML.async=false
   objXML.load("http://localhost/PO/Rosetta_POTemp.xml")

objXML.selectSingleNode("//addressLine1").childNodes(0).text=
   document.all("addressLine1").value
objXML.selectSingleNode("//addressLine2").childNodes(0).text=
   document.all("addressLine2").value
objXML.selectSingleNode("//NationalPostalCode").text=
   document.all("NationalPostalCode").value
objXML.selectSingleNode("//regionName").childNodes(0).text=
   document.all("regionName").value
objXML.selectSingleNode("//cityName").childNodes(0).text=
   document.all("cityName").value
objXML.selectSingleNode("//PhysicalAddress/GlobalCountryCode").text=
   document.all("PhysicalAddress/GlobalCountryCode").value
```

Once the XML instance as been populated, we have to send it to the remote server; to do this we use the Microsoft XMLHTTP object. This uses the `open()` method to send information to a remote web page. The first parameter specifies that you are going to use the POST method to send data to the web page, the second is the URL of the page the information is to be posted to, and the final parameter is `false`; this tells the server not to return the result until the entire page has been completed.

```
var xmlhttp = new ActiveXObject("Msxml2.XMLHTTP");
xmlhttp.Open("POST", "http://localhost/po/remote/po.asp", false);
```

Finally, the XML document is sent to the remote server, and a message is displayed based on whether the remote page returns a successful or unsuccessful result.

```
xmlhttp.Send(objXML);
if (xmlhttp.responseXML.text=="ok")
   alert("Purchase Order successfully placed.")
else
   alert("There was a problem placing your order.")

}
</SCRIPT>
</HEAD>

<BODY>
<H2>Delivery Information</H2>
<TABLE>
   <TR>
   <TD>Street Address 1</TD>
   <TD>
      <INPUT TYPE="TEXT" NAME="addressLine1" VALUE="223746 Red Oak Drive"/>
   </TD>
   </TR>
   <TR>
   <TD>Street Address 2</TD>
   <TD>
      <INPUT TYPE="TEXT" NAME="addressLine2" VALUE="3rd Floor"/>
   </TD>
   </TR>
   <TR>
   <TD>City</TD>
   <TD>
      <INPUT TYPE="TEXT" NAME="cityName" VALUE="Winnipeg"/>
   </TD>
   </TR>
   <TR>
   <TD>PostalCode</TD>
   <TD>
      <INPUT TYPE="TEXT" NAME="NationalPostalCode" VALUE="R2J 29A"/>
   </TD>
   </TR>
   <TR>
   <TD>Region</TD>
   <TD>
      <INPUT TYPE="TEXT" NAME="regionName" VALUE="MB"/>
   </TD>
   </TR>
   <TR>
   <TD>Country</TD>
   <TD>
      <INPUT TYPE="TEXT" NAME="PhysicalAddress/GlobalCountryCode" VALUE="CA"/>
   </TD>
   </TR>
</TABLE>

<H2>Contact Information</H2>
...
```

```
<H2>Product Line Item</H2>
...

<P>
   <INPUT TYPE="BUTTON" VALUE="Submit PO" onclick="submitPO()"/>
</P>

</BODY>
</HTML>
```

The screen looks like this:

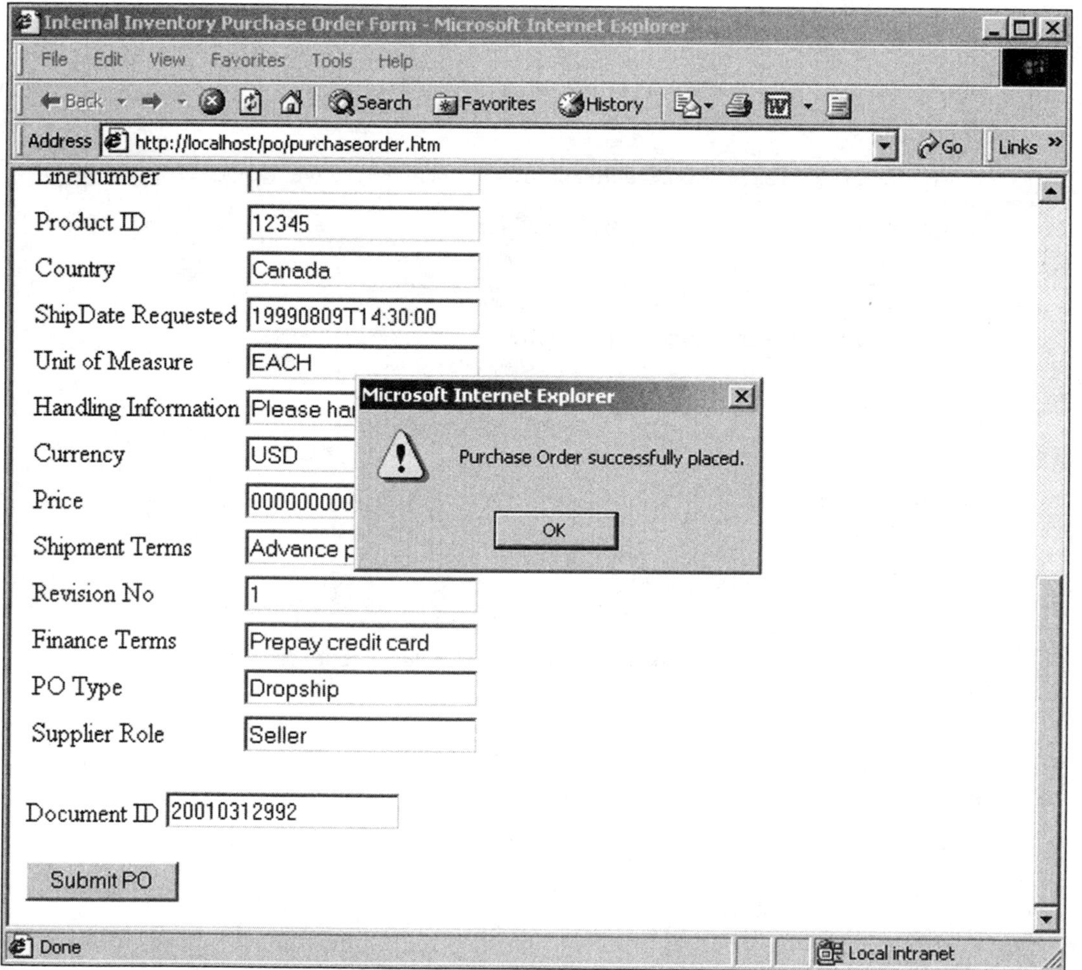

The XML created from the form is posted to a remote site (that is, a marketplace). We are using the local server, but this could be replaced by ANY web-server. The file it is posted to is called `po.asp` and part of its code is shown below – we used JScript to illustrate the example, although you could use a scripting language of your choice.

The `Request` object containing the XML document we posted is loaded as an XML document.

```
<% @Language = "JSCRIPT" %>
<%
var objXML = Server.CreateObject("Microsoft.XMLDOM")
objXML.async=false
objXML.load(Request)
```

Once we have the XML document, we need to perform a transform on it to get it from a RosettaNet PO to a BizTalk PO. This is where we load our `RosettaNet2BizTalk.xsl` transform file.

```
var objXSL = Server.CreateObject("Microsoft.XMLDOM")
objXSL.async=false
objXSL.load(Server.MapPath("RosettaNet2BizTalk.xsl"))

var objNewXML = Server.CreateObject("Microsoft.XMLDOM")
objNewXML.async=false
```

In most cases, when this stylesheet is used in a `transformNode()` call, the encoding will switch to UTF-16. The best way around this is to `transformNodeToObject()`. The difference, of course, is that `transformNode()` returns a bstr (which is, by definition, utf-16), and the `transformNodeToObject()` returns, well, an object. Before we work with the object however, we must specify that the content to be output is XML. This is where we set the `Response.ContentType`, so hence, we store the newly transformed file in a XML Document object called `objNewXML`.

```
Response.ContentType=("text/xml")
str = objXML.transformNodeToObject(objXSL,objNewXML)
```

The order information is then recorded by persisting the file in an Orders subdirectory using the Order Number as the unique file name. Finally, we write back a valid XML "ok" response to indicate that the order was successfully recorded.

```
objNewXML.save(Server.MapPath("Orders")+"/"+
   Request.Form("ProprietaryDocumentIdentifier")+".xml")

Response.Write("<result>ok</result>")
%>
```

At the supplier location, they will want to view the information and see what the request entails. To do this, `ShowPurchaseOrder.asp` is used – the code is shown below.

Initially the order information stored in the XML in our Orders directory is loaded – here we know the order ID we have been working with, but it is likely that either a production version would iterate through the Orders directory to show all orders that have been sent and allow the user to choose one, or an advanced queuing system (using something like MSMQ or IBM MQSeries) could be used to allow the user to view each order on the queue.

```
<% @Language = "JSCRIPT" %>
<%
var objXML = Server.CreateObject("Microsoft.XMLDOM")
objXML.async=false
objXML.load(Server.MapPath("Orders/20010312992.xml"))
```

Next, variables are populated with the equivalent attribute values from the BizTalk PO. This is done for each field we are going to display to the user.

```
poNumber=objXML.selectSingleNode("//@poNumber").text

contactName=objXML.selectSingleNode("//@contactName").text
contactEmail=objXML.selectSingleNode("//@contactEmail").text
contactPhone=objXML.selectSingleNode("//@contactPhone").text
attn=objXML.selectSingleNode("//@attn").text
street1=objXML.selectSingleNode("//@street1").text
street2=objXML.selectSingleNode("//@street2").text
postalCode=objXML.selectSingleNode("//@postalCode").text
city=objXML.selectSingleNode("//@city").text
stateProvince=objXML.selectSingleNode("//@stateProvince").text
country=objXML.selectSingleNode("//@country").text
shipType=objXML.selectSingleNode("//@shipType").text
paymentType=objXML.selectSingleNode("//@paymentType").text
partno=objXML.selectSingleNode("//@partno").text
qty=objXML.selectSingleNode("//@qty").text
uom=objXML.selectSingleNode("//@uom").text
unitPrice=objXML.selectSingleNode("//@unitPrice").text
needBefore=objXML.selectSingleNode("//@needBefore").text
%>
```

Finally, an order page is displayed to the user using the variable values we defined above.

```
<HTML>
<HEAD>
   <TITLE>Internal Inventory Purchase Order Request</TITLE>
</HEAD>

<BODY>
<H2><I>Order #<%=poNumber%></I></H2>
<H2>Contact</H2>
Name : <%=contactName%><BR/>
Email : <%=contactEmail%><BR/>
Tel : <%=contactPhone%><BR/>

<H2>Shipping/Billing Information</H2>
Attn : <%=attn%><BR/>
Street 1 : <%=street1%><BR/>
street 2 : <%=street2%><BR/>
Postal Code : <%=postalCode%><BR/>
City : <%=city%><BR/>
State/Province: <%=stateProvince%><BR/>
Country : <%=country%><BR/>

Shipped by <%=shipType%><BR/>
Payment Method : <%=paymentType%>

<H2>Order Details</H2>
Part : <%=partno%><BR/>
Quantity : <%=qty%><BR/>
<%=uom%> Price : <%=unitPrice%>
Delivery Date : <%=needBefore%><BR/>

</BODY>
</HTML>
```

The final purchase order screen looks like this:

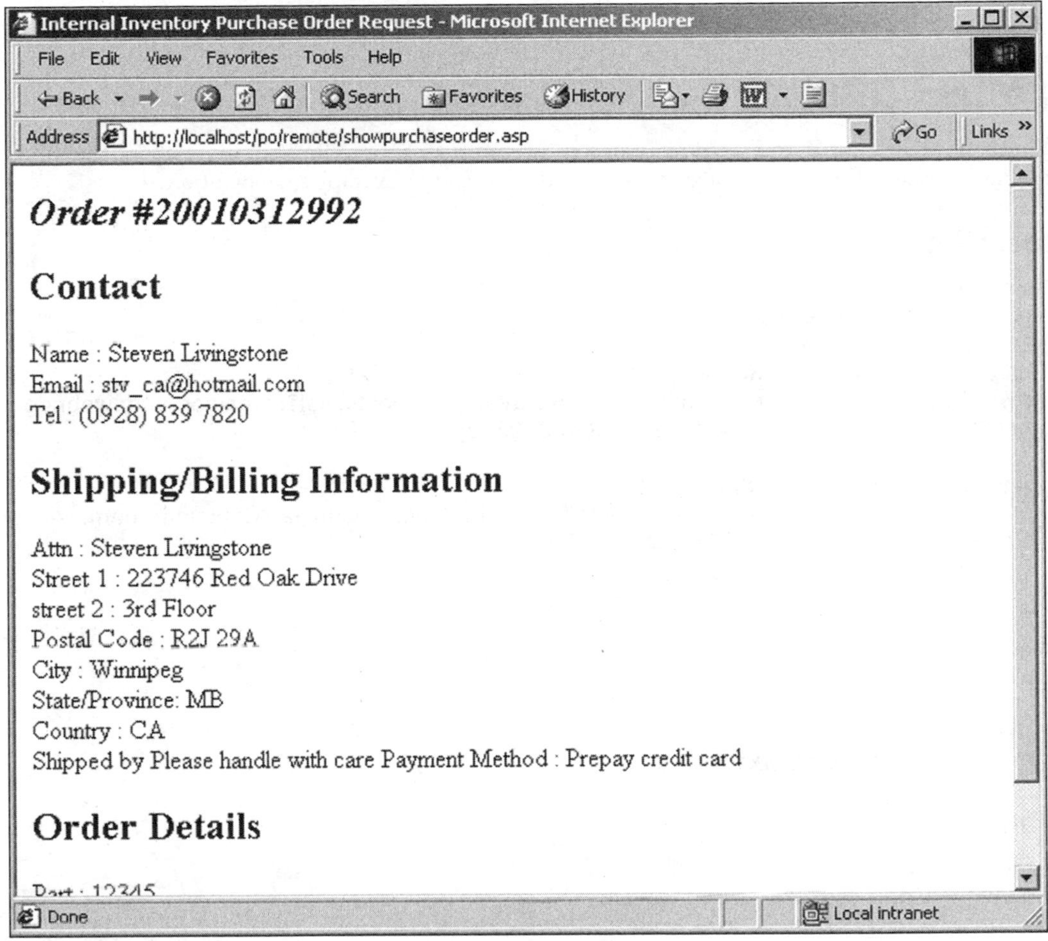

This sample illustrates only one small part of the potentially huge set of sub-processes involved in the process flow of a business transaction. This sample can be built upon to provide advanced functionality such as business-to-business invoice and shipping processes.

Summary

This chapter introduced you to some of the e-business standards that are either being used now, or created on the Internet. It was not intended to give you detailed information on the framework implementations themselves, as there are many resources you can use to understand this (see "Important URLs"). Rather, it was to illustrate how these diverse and changing frameworks can be brought together to enable businesses to integrate their e-business processes.

Using the methods explored in this chapter, you should be able to develop an understanding of how to integrate your e-business systems with partners systems and access the full potential of electronic marketplaces.

Important URLs

What follows is a list of useful online resources for those wishing to find out more about the different standards discussed in this chapter, or download some of the examples we mentioned.

RosettaNet

Homepage
http://www.rosettanet.org

Manage Purchase Order Downloads
http://www.rosettanet.org/rosettanet/rooms/displaypages/layoutinitial?container=com.webridge.entity.Entity[OID[6AB37A9DA92DD411842300C04F689339]]

RosettaNet Implementation Framework
http://www.rosettanet.org/rosettanet/Rooms/DisplayPages/LayoutInitial?Container=com.webridge.entity.Entity[OID[AE9C86B8022CD411841F00C04F689339]]

xCBL

Homepage
http://www.xcbl.org

xCBL 3.0 Download
http://www.xcbl.org/xcbl30/xcbl30.html

BizTalk

Homepage
http://www.biztalk.org

BizTalk PO download
http://www.biztalk.org/Library/library.asp

BizTalk Framework Resources
http://www.biztalk.org/Resources/resources.asp

ebXML

Homepage
http://www.ebxml.org

ebXML Message Specification
http://www.ebxml.org/

ebXML Technical Specification
http://www.ebxml.org/

27

B2B Futures: WSDL and UDDI

Let's Work Together

It's become a commonplace to say that the Internet has changed everything. HTML and the World Wide Web have completely revolutionized the way in which many of us live, work and organize our lives. The way in which the Web has been used so far has been mainly for interactions between users on the one side and computers on the other. The next step, however, is to get those computers to talk to each other in a sensible, structured way, so that program can talk to program, application to application, and, finally, business to business, so that we really do ultimately achieve "Business at the Speed of Thought".

This chapter is about two emerging technologies that are looking to make all this possible. The first of these is the Web Services Description Language, or WSDL. This is a way of formalizing the description of services provided by a system so that another remote system can use those services. The second of these is Universal Description, Discovery and Integration, or UDDI. This provides a framework for the registration and discovery of these services.

Both of these initiatives have the full backing of IBM, Microsoft, and e-commerce specialists Ariba, among others, and in this chapter we're going to see completely independent sets of software from both IBM and Microsoft inter-operating with each other. We can't stress how significant all of this is for the future of systems development. If all goes according to plan, this may well constitute the second phase of development of the Web – the semantic web, as Tim Berners-Lee likes to call it.

This chapter inevitably involves a certain amount of programming; in particular, we're going to be using Microsoft Visual Basic version 6, and Java (JDK version 1.3). Familiarity with one or other of these is therefore an essential requisite for this chapter.

WSDL

We're going to start by looking at how WSDL works. For the purposes of this section, we're going to need access to Microsoft's SOAP Toolkit Version 2.0 and IBM's Web Services Toolkit. The former is available as a free download from http://msdn.microsoft.com/downloads/default.asp?URL=/code/sample.asp?url=/MSDN-FILES/027/001/580/msdncompositedoc.xml, while the latter can be downloaded from http://www.alphaworks.ibm.com/tech/webservicestoolkit (incidentally, it's better to download this in preference to the WSDL toolkit, as this package contains the WSDL toolkit plus a whole lot else; however, you should be aware that there are 15 MBytes of it). The Microsoft toolkit can only be run on Windows systems, while the IBM system is Java-based, and so can, in theory, be executed anywhere. Also, it must be noted that the Visual Basic run-time is required if Visual Basic 6 is not installed.

There is one final word of warning before we get started. At the time of writing, this is all seriously cutting edge stuff. The examples we see here were put together using Beta 2 of the Microsoft SOAP Toolkit and version 2.2 of the IBM Web Services Toolkit. By the time this book is printed, it is quite possible that what we see when we run the various tools will be different from the illustrations in this chapter. Some of the workarounds described in the text may no longer be necessary. It is also even possible that some new ones will be required instead. However, the basic principles will remain unchanged.

WSDL: The Theory

There are two ways of going about introducing WSDL. There is the theoretical approach, where we discuss the entire language in abstract, before launching into an example, or there is the pragmatic approach, where we cover as little of the theory as we can get away with before launching headlong into the practical stuff. The author's preference is for the latter, and it's especially appropriate in this case, because the real meaning of WSDL doesn't really become apparent until we begin to play with it in earnest.

However, much as we'd like not to, we need to go over at least some of the theory. This short section covers as much as we need to get started.

WSDL has an XML format for describing web services. Version 1.0 of the protocol was published on September 25, 2000. WSDL describes which operations can be carried out, and what the messages used should look like. Operations and messages are described in abstract terms, and are then implemented by binding to a suitable network protocol and message format. As at version 1.0, bindings for SOAP 1.1, HTTP `GET`/`POST`, and MIME have been defined. In this chapter, we will be concentrating on SOAP, as this binding is available in both IBM and Microsoft implementations. This is very much an evolving technology, and future versions are expected to define frameworks for composing services and describing the behavior of services.

> *If you're familiar with the Interface Description Language (IDL) used by the likes of COM and CORBA, then you can think of WSDL as a highly generic IDL, rewritten in XML.*

Each WSDL file describes one or more **services**. Each service consists of a group of **ports**, where each port defines an endpoint that can be accessed by a remote system. Readers who are familiar with TCP/IP sockets will recognize the use of the term "port" for a network endpoint, although here we are referring to more than a simple numeric identifier. A port belongs to a particular **port type**, and has a particular **binding** (SOAP or another type), which specifies the address that the remote system must use to access the port. Each port type defines a number of **operations** that may be carried out, each of which may have either an **input message** and an **output message**, or both, depending on the type of the operation. Each message is defined in terms of a number of **parts**. Each part is defined in terms of a name and a **type**. All types are defined, either by reference to a particular schema, or by local definition.

So we can summarize the function of the WSDL file by saying that it defines:

- Where the service is implemented
- What operations the service supports
- What messages need to be passed between the client and server for those operations
- How the parameters for that message are to be encoded

This is how it looks in practice:

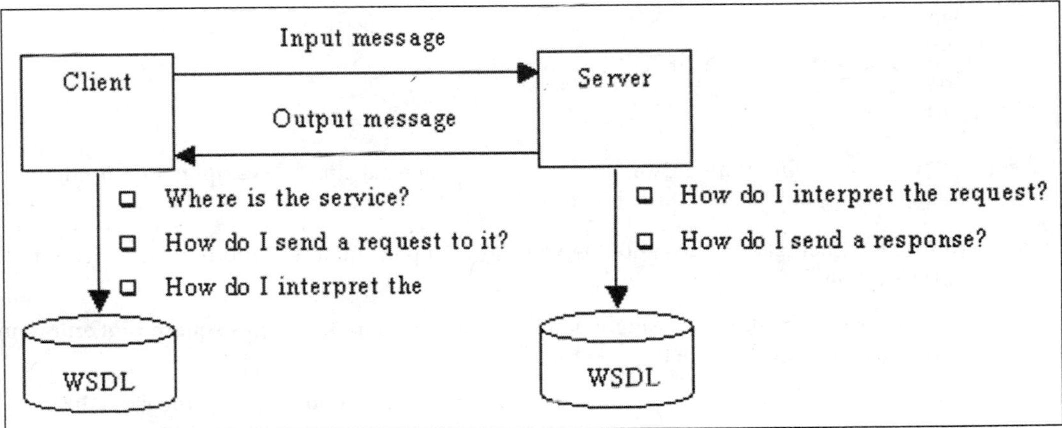

Each of the WSDL elements is defined in a section of the WSDL file, and we'll be looking at an example shortly. However, now it's time for a practical demonstration.

Generating WSDL

In practice, very few people will want to hand craft WSDL. The most likely approach to developing a web service is that a developer will put together a web service component using one of the standard techniques (COM, Java, and of course, .NET), and then use a tool to generate the associated WSDL; and that's exactly what we're going to do. In fact, we're going to do it twice: once the Microsoft way (COM), and once the IBM way (Java).

There are actually plenty of good reasons why we might want to start with the WSDL, but we'll look at that a little later on in the chapter, in the section titled *"Chickens and Eggs"*.

WSDL from COM

Before we get started, we're going to need a COM component, written in Microsoft Visual Basic 6. If Visual Basic isn't available, don't worry, because the COM DLL that we're going to develop is part of the code download from the Wrox site. However, we will need to register it, as so:

```
> regsvr32 ArithServer.dll
```

(Incidentally, on Windows 98, `regsvr32.exe` is located in `c:\windows\system`, in case the path doesn't include this.) Having done that, we can skip the next section, where we discuss how the COM object is developed.

Developing COM objects under Visual Basic is relatively straightforward. We'll start by creating a new Visual Basic project, as type "ActiveX DLL". Save this project as `ArithServer.vbp`. Now create a new class module in the project, called `Arithmetic.cls`. Add the following code to this class module:

```
Option Explicit

Function Square(ByVal InValue As Double) As Double
   Square = InValue * InValue
End Function

Function SquareRoot(ByVal InValue As Double) As Double
   SquareRoot = Sqr(InValue)
End Function

Function Capitalize(ByVal InString As String) As String
   Capitalize = UCase(InString)
End Function
```

In the grand tradition of these things, we have chosen a somewhat simple example: an arithmetic server, which offers the calling application three functions:

- `Square` – which takes a single double value as its input, squares it and returns the result as its double output
- `SquareRoot` – which takes a single double value as its input, takes its square root and returns the result as its double output
- `Capitalize` – which takes a string as its input, capitalizes it and returns the capitalized string as its output.

There is a reason for keeping the server simple, by the way. It will be tricky enough as it is to see the wood for the trees once the WSDL starts to emerge, and the simpler our basic application is, the better.

Once we have set up our code, all we need to do is compile it, and we have our `ArithServer` COM object ready for web delivery.

wsdlgen

The Microsoft WSDL generation tool provided with Version 2 of the SOAP Toolkit is called `wsdlgen`. Let's try it out on `ArithServer.dll`. This is what we see when we execute it:

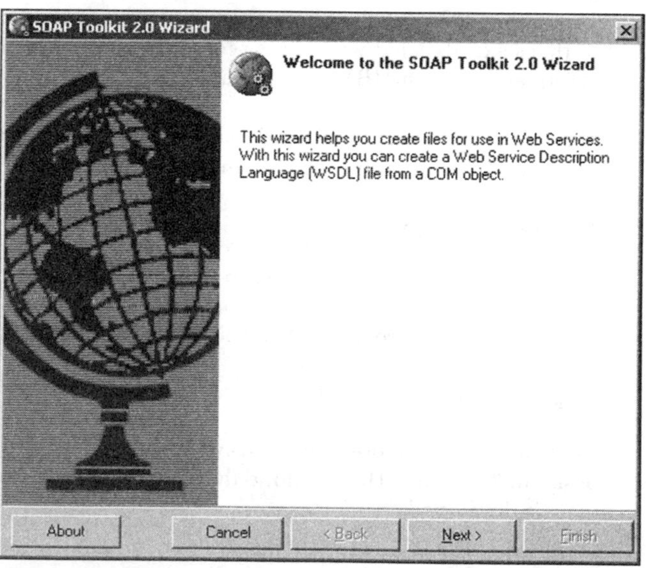

If you don't have Visual Basic installed, this command won't work. The `wsdlstb.exe` *command line utility will have to be invoked instead.*

Moving on, in the next dialog, we need to choose a name for our web service (we've chosen "Arithmetic"), and then browse to locate our COM object:

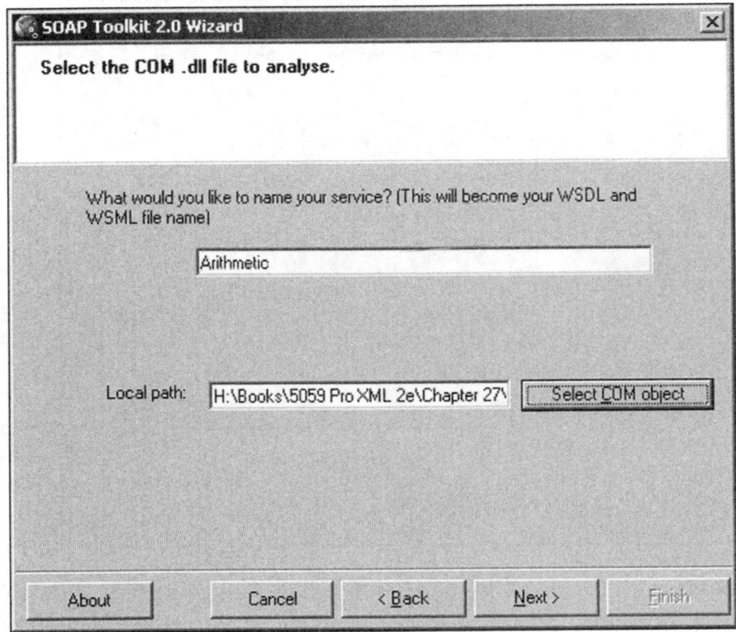

Next, we choose which of the services we wish to expose. We expose all of them:

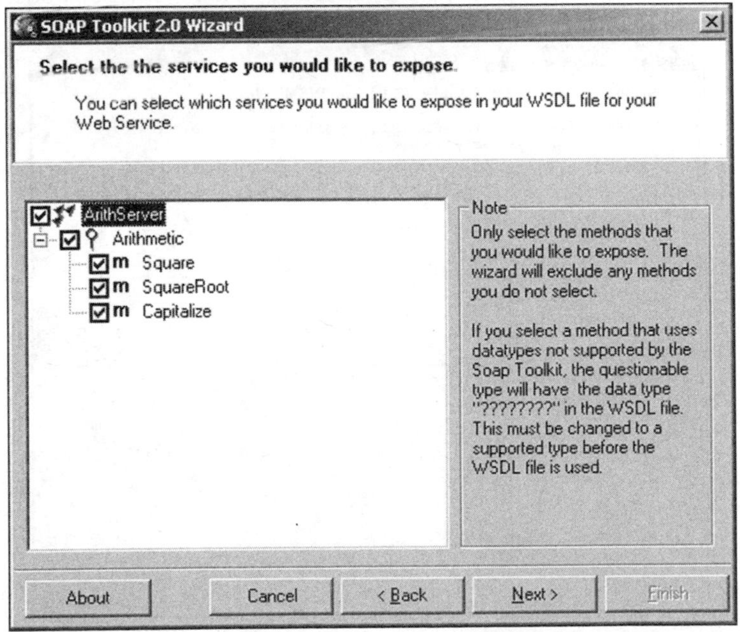

Next, we select where the SOAP listener is going to be located (see Chapter 24). Incidentally, the Microsoft documentation tends to refer to Internet IIS throughout; however, be assured that Personal Web Server works quite satisfactorily as well, provided that we stick to using ASP rather than ISAPI for the listener type:

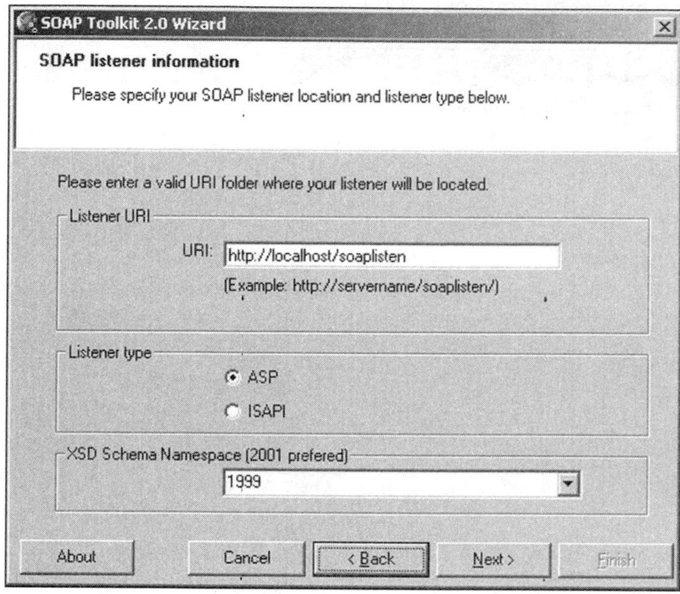

Finally, all we need to do is decide where our generated files are going to be located. For the time being, we'll co-locate them with the server DLL. However, we may subsequently move them around.

Notice that it says "generated file*s*" in the above paragraph. This is because Microsoft have introduced a little extra something themselves, called WSML. We'll take a look at what that does in a little while.

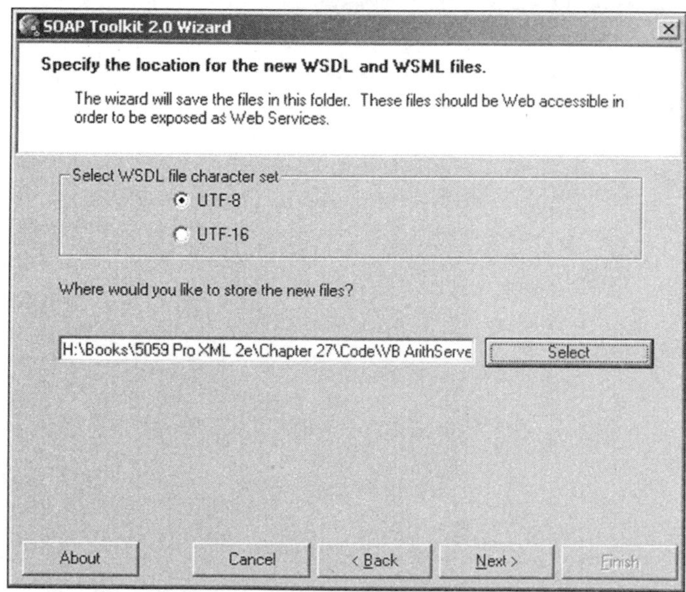

And we're done:

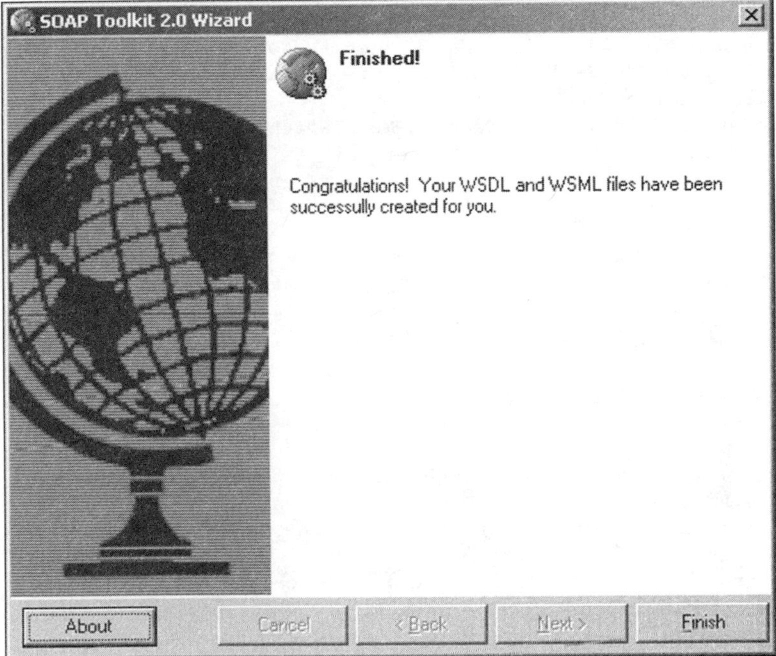

So What Did wsdlgen Do for Us?

Let's look at what we've got. There are basically three things that have been generated:

- An Active Server Page file, `Arithmetic.asp`
- A WSDL file, `Arithmetic.wsdl`
- A WSML file, `Arithmetic.wsml`

We'll deal with each one in turn.

The ASP File

`Arithmetic.asp` is the Active Server Page that will drive our SOAP server. All SOAP requests for `Arithmetic` will be directed towards this. Most of the code is to do with setting up and trapping errors, so we've highlighted the lines that do the real work:

```
<%@ LANGUAGE=VBScript %>
<%
Option Explicit
On Error Resume Next
Response.ContentType = "text/xml"
If IsEmpty(Application("SoapServer")) Then
   Application.Lock
   If IsEmpty(Application("SoapServer")) Then
      Dim SoapServer
      Dim WSDLFilePath
```

```
        Dim WSMLFilePath
        WSDLFilePath = Server.MapPath("Arithmetic.wsdl")
        WSMLFilePath = Server.MapPath("Arithmetic.wsml")
        Set SoapServer = Server.CreateObject("MSSOAP.SoapServer")
        If Err Then SendFault "Cannot create SoapServer object. " & _
           Err.Description
        SoapServer.Init WSDLFilePath, WSMLFilePath
        If Err Then SendFault "SoapServer.Init failed. " & Err.Description
        Set Application("SoapServer") = SoapServer
     End If
     Application.UnLock
  End If
  Set SoapServer = Application("SoapServer")
  SoapServer.SoapInvoke Request, Response, ""
  If Err Then SendFault "SoapServer.SoapInvoke failed. " & Err.Description

  Sub SendFault(ByVal LogMessage)
     Dim Serializer
     On Error Resume Next
     ' "URI Query" logging must be enabled for AppendToLog to work
     Response.AppendToLog " SOAP ERROR: " & LogMessage
     Set Serializer = Server.CreateObject("MSSOAP.SoapSerializer")
     If Err Then
        Response.AppendToLog "Could not create SoapSerializer object. " & _
           Err.Description
         Response.Status = "500 Internal Server Error"
     Else
        Serializer.Init Response
        If Err Then
           Response.AppendToLog "SoapSerializer.Init failed. " & _
              Err.Description
           Response.Status = "500 Internal Server Error"
        Else
           Serializer.startEnvelope
           Serializer.startBody
           Serializer.startFault "Server", _
              "The request could not be processed due to a problem in " & _
              "the server. Please contact the system admistrator. " & _
              LogMessage
           Serializer.endFault
           Serializer.endBody
           Serializer.endEnvelope
           If Err Then
              Response.AppendToLog "SoapSerializer failed. " & Err.Description
              Response.Status = "500 Internal Server Error"
           End If
        End If
     End If
     Response.End
  End Sub
  %>
```

As can be seen, the SOAP ASP creates a `SoapServer` object and tells it where to find an appropriate set of WSDL and WSML files. Those two files contain sufficient information for the `SoapServer` object to interpret the incoming request, locate the required COM object, and encode the required response. So all we need to do is call the `SoapServer` object's `SoapInvoke` method and we're done.

The WSML File

Before we look at the WSDL, we'd better quickly cover WSML. WSML stands for **Web Services Meta Language**. This is an entirely Microsoft-specific concept, and we'll see why it's there and what it does in a minute. This file was generated from our arithmetic server DLL:

```
<?xml version="1.0" encoding="UTF-8" ?>
<!-- Generated 03/13/01 by Microsoft SOAP Toolkit WSDL File Generator,
     Version 1.00.501.1 -->
<servicemapping name="Arithmetic">
   <service name="Arithmetic">
      <using PROGID="ArithServer.Arithmetic" cachable="0"
         ID="ArithmeticObject" />
      <port name="ArithmeticSoapPort">
         <operation name="Capitalize">
            <execute uses="ArithmeticObject" method="Capitalize"
               dispID="1610809346">
               <parameter callIndex="1" name="InString"
                  elementName="InString" />
               <parameter callIndex="-1" name="retval"
                  elementName="Result" />
            </execute>
         </operation>
         <operation name="SquareRoot">
            <execute uses="ArithmeticObject" method="SquareRoot"
               dispID="1610809345">
               <parameter callIndex="1" name="InValue"
                  elementName="InValue" />
               <parameter callIndex="-1" name="retval"
                  elementName="Result" />
            </execute>
         </operation>
         <operation name="Square">
            <execute uses="ArithmeticObject"
               method="Square" dispID="1610809344">
               <parameter callIndex="1" name="InValue"
                  elementName="InValue" />
               <parameter callIndex="-1" name="retval"
                  elementName="Result" />
            </execute>
         </operation>
      </port>
   </service>
</servicemapping>
```

We shan't dwell on this too much, except to highlight one or two points of interest. The `PROGID="ArithServer.Arithmetic"` should ring a few bells if the reader is familiar with COM; this is telling the SOAP server how to create the required object. The COM run-time will then convert this into a class identifier and hence locate the actual registered COM DLL. The `dispID`'s are the dispatch identifiers for the individual methods.

So this file is telling the SOAP server how to use the required COM object to handle an incoming request on the service `Arithmetic`. This is entirely specific to Microsoft, so that is why it is not part of any standard.

The WSDL File

It is time to look at the real meat of the application. This is what the WSDL file that the generator produced looks like:

```
<?xml version="1.0" encoding="UTF-8" ?>
<!-- Generated 03/13/01 by Microsoft SOAP Toolkit WSDL File Generator,
     Version 1.00.501.1 -->
<definitions name="Arithmetic" targetNamespace="http://tempuri.org/wsdl/"
   xmlns:wsdlns="http://tempuri.org/wsdl/"
   xmlns:typens="http://tempuri.org/type"
   xmlns:soap="http://schemas.xmlsoap.org/wsdl/soap/"
   xmlns:xsd="http://www.w3.org/2000/10/XMLSchema"
   xmlns:stk="http://schemas.microsoft.com/soap-toolkit/wsdl-extension"
   xmlns="http://schemas.xmlsoap.org/wsdl/">
   <types>
      <schema targetNamespace="http://tempuri.org/type"
         xmlns="http://www.w3.org/2000/10/XMLSchema"
         xmlns:SOAP-ENC="http://schemas.xmlsoap.org/soap/encoding/"
         xmlns:wsdl="http://schemas.xmlsoap.org/wsdl/"
         elementFormDefault="qualified">
      </schema>
   </types>
   <message name="Arithmetic.Capitalize">
      <part name="InString" type="xsd:string" />
   </message>
   <message name="Arithmetic.CapitalizeResponse">
      <part name="Result" type="xsd:string"/>
   </message>
   <message name="Arithmetic.SquareRoot">
      <part name="InValue" type="xsd:double"/>
   </message>
   <message name="Arithmetic.SquareRootResponse">
      <part name="Result" type="xsd:double"/>
   </message>
   <message name="Arithmetic.Square">
      <part name="InValue" type="xsd:double"/>
   </message>
   <message name="Arithmetic.SquareResponse">
      <part name="Result" type="xsd:double"/>
   </message>
   <portType name="ArithmeticSoapPort">
      <operation name="Capitalize" parameterOrder="InString">
         <input message="wsdlns:Arithmetic.Capitalize" />
         <output message="wsdlns:Arithmetic.CapitalizeResponse" />
      </operation>
      <operation name="SquareRoot" parameterOrder="InValue">
         <input message="wsdlns:Arithmetic.SquareRoot" />
         <output message="wsdlns:Arithmetic.SquareRootResponse" />
      </operation>
      <operation name="Square" parameterOrder="InValue">
         <input message="wsdlns:Arithmetic.Square" />
         <output message="wsdlns:Arithmetic.SquareResponse" />
      </operation>
   </portType>
   <binding name="ArithmeticSoapBinding" type="wsdlns:ArithmeticSoapPort" >
      <stk:binding preferredEncoding="UTF-8" />
      <soap:binding style="rpc"
         transport="http://schemas.xmlsoap.org/soap/http" />
      <operation name="Capitalize" >
         <soap:operation
            soapAction="http://tempuri.org/action/Arithmetic.Capitalize" />
```

```
            <input>
               <soap:body use="encoded" namespace="http://tempuri.org/message/"
                  encodingStyle="http://schemas.xmlsoap.org/soap/encoding/" />
            </input>
            <output>
               <soap:body use="encoded" namespace="http://tempuri.org/message/"
                  encodingStyle="http://schemas.xmlsoap.org/soap/encoding/" />
            </output>
         </operation>
         <operation name="SquareRoot" >
            <soap:operation
               soapAction="http://tempuri.org/action/Arithmetic.SquareRoot" />
            <input>
               <soap:body use="encoded" namespace="http://tempuri.org/message/"
                  encodingStyle="http://schemas.xmlsoap.org/soap/encoding/" />
            </input>
            <output>
               <soap:body use="encoded" namespace="http://tempuri.org/message/"
                  encodingStyle="http://schemas.xmlsoap.org/soap/encoding/" />
            </output>
         </operation>
         <operation name="Square" >
            <soap:operation
               soapAction="http://tempuri.org/action/Arithmetic.Square" />
            <input>
               <soap:body use="encoded" namespace="http://tempuri.org/message/"
                  encodingStyle="http://schemas.xmlsoap.org/soap/encoding/" />
            </input>
            <output>
               <soap:body use="encoded" namespace="http://tempuri.org/message/"
                  encodingStyle="http://schemas.xmlsoap.org/soap/encoding/" />
            </output>
         </operation>
      </binding>
      <service name="Arithmetic">
         <port name="ArithmeticSoapPort"
            binding="wsdlns:ArithmeticSoapBinding" >
            <soap:address
               location="http://laa-laa/soaplisten/Arithmetic.ASP" />
         </port>
      </service>
   </definitions>
```

At this point, it may be obvious why we kept our service as simple as possible! However, it is not quite as complex as it seems. Let's take each section in turn, and see what we can learn from it about WSDL.

Definitions

As we saw earlier, a WSDL file is a set of definitions. Therefore, the root element of our XML is sensibly called `<definitions>`. It has a couple of optional attributes, a name to refer to the service by and a target namespace. The toolkit also declares many other namespaces for later use. Note that the default namespace is `wsdl`. Throughout this document, we will see references to a mythical URI called http://tempuri.org. This is simply a placeholder that we can use if we need to introduce more complex data types and so on. For the purposes of this example, we can leave it as it is. Here's the definitions section again:

```
<definitions  name="Arithmetic" targetNamespace="http://tempuri.org/wsdl/"
   xmlns:wsdlns="http://tempuri.org/wsdl/"
   xmlns:typens="http://tempuri.org/type"
```

```
xmlns:soap="http://schemas.xmlsoap.org/wsdl/soap/"
xmlns:xsd="http://www.w3.org/2000/10/XMLSchema"
xmlns:stk="http://schemas.microsoft.com/soap-toolkit/wsdl-extension"
xmlns="http://schemas.xmlsoap.org/wsdl/" >
```

Types

The <types> element contains data type definitions that are relevant for the messages in this service. For the purposes of this service, we are going to use a standard schema. We're not going to be defining any complex types (see Chapters 6 & 7), so we don't need to extend this at all. Here's the types section of the WSDL file again:

```
<types>
   <schema targetNamespace="http://tempuri.org/type"
      xmlns="http://www.w3.org/2000/10/XMLSchema"
      xmlns:SOAP-ENC="http://schemas.xmlsoap.org/soap/encoding/"
      xmlns:wsdl="http://schemas.xmlsoap.org/wsdl/"
      elementFormDefault="qualified">
   </schema>
</types>
```

Messages

In this section, we define the structure of each message used by the service. As can be seen, our generator has created a pair of messages for each of our three methods. A message can consist of a number of parts, each with its own name and type attributes. In this case, however, our methods have a single input and a single output; so all our messages have just one part. Here's the messages section again:

```
<message name="Arithmetic.Capitalize">
   <part name="InString" type="xsd:string"/>
</message>
<message name="Arithmetic.CapitalizeResponse">
   <part name="Result" type="xsd:string"/>
</message>
<message name="Arithmetic.SquareRoot">
   <part name="InValue" type="xsd:double"/>
</message>
<message name="Arithmetic.SquareRootResponse">
   <part name="Result" type="xsd:double"/>
</message>
<message name="Arithmetic.Square">
   <part name="InValue" type="xsd:double"/>
</message>
<message name="Arithmetic.SquareResponse">
   <part name="Result" type="xsd:double"/>
</message>
```

Port Types

A port type is a set of operations, along with the messages involved. In our case, it amounts to a definition of our original COM object. Each of the three operations is listed, along with its input and output messages. Four operation types can be specified in WSDL:

- **One-way**: this has an input, but no output
- **Request-response**: this has an input, then an output; all of the operations in our example are of this type

- **Solicit-response**: this has an output followed by an input
- **Notification**: this has an output, but no input

The parameter order attribute is optional (and redundant if there is only one parameter), but our generator has provided it anyway. The `parameterOrder` attributes refer to the `<part>` `name` attributes in the previous section. Here's the `<portTypes>` section of the WSDL file again:

```
<portType name="ArithmeticSoapPort">
   <operation name="Capitalize" parameterOrder="InString">
      <input message="wsdlns:Arithmetic.Capitalize" />
      <output message="wsdlns:Arithmetic.CapitalizeResponse" />
   </operation>
   <operation name="SquareRoot" parameterOrder="InValue">
      <input message="wsdlns:Arithmetic.SquareRoot" />
      <output message="wsdlns:Arithmetic.SquareRootResponse" />
   </operation>
   <operation name="Square" parameterOrder="InValue">
      <input message="wsdlns:Arithmetic.Square" />
      <output message="wsdlns:Arithmetic.SquareResponse" />
   </operation>
</portType>
```

Bindings

This section defines how the operations and their messages are actually to be implemented using the underlying protocol. In our case, we are using SOAP, so we use the specific WSDL grammar for the SOAP binding. These elements are as follows.

The `<soap:binding>` element signifies that we are using SOAP binding, along with the default style and transport. The transport here is HTTP, the standard SOAP transport.

Each `<soap:operation>` element describes how the associated WSDL operation is to be encoded within SOAP. Within this, each `<soap:body>` element describes how the messages for the operation are to be encoded within the SOAP body. Here's the bindings section again:

```
<binding name="ArithmeticSoapBinding" type="wsdlns:ArithmeticSoapPort" >
   <stk:binding preferredEncoding="UTF-8" />
   <soap:binding style="rpc"
      transport="http://schemas.xmlsoap.org/soap/http" />
   <operation name="Capitalize">
      <soap:operation
         soapAction="http://tempuri.org/action/Arithmetic.Capitalize" />
      <input>
         <soap:body use="encoded" namespace="http://tempuri.org/message/"
            encodingStyle="http://schemas.xmlsoap.org/soap/encoding/" />
      </input>
      <output>
         <soap:body use="encoded" namespace="http://tempuri.org/message/"
            encodingStyle="http://schemas.xmlsoap.org/soap/encoding/" />
      </output>
   </operation>
   <operation name="SquareRoot" >
      <soap:operation
```

```
            soapAction="http://tempuri.org/action/Arithmetic.SquareRoot" />
         <input>
            <soap:body use="encoded" namespace="http://tempuri.org/message/"
               encodingStyle="http://schemas.xmlsoap.org/soap/encoding/" />
         </input>
         <output>
            <soap:body use="encoded" namespace="http://tempuri.org/message/"
               encodingStyle="http://schemas.xmlsoap.org/soap/encoding/" />
         </output>
      </operation>
      <operation name="Square" >
         <soap:operation
            soapAction="http://tempuri.org/action/Arithmetic.Square" />
         <input>
            <soap:body use="encoded" namespace="http://tempuri.org/message/"
               encodingStyle="http://schemas.xmlsoap.org/soap/encoding/" />
         </input>
         <output>
            <soap:body use="encoded" namespace="http://tempuri.org/message/"
               encodingStyle="http://schemas.xmlsoap.org/soap/encoding/" />
         </output>
      </operation>
   </binding>
```

Services

Finally, we define the services available within this WSDL file. Each service groups together a number of ports, each of which defines an individual endpoint. This set of definitions pulls together all the preceding definitions in the file. For each port, we define its type (as defined in the `<portType>` elements), its binding (as defined in the `<binding>` elements), and its address. Its address is specific to the binding being used, so here we are using a SOAP address. Here's the services section of the WSDL file again:

```
   <service name="Arithmetic" >
      <port name="ArithmeticSoapPort"
         binding="wsdlns:ArithmeticSoapBinding" >
         <soap:address
            location="http://laa-laa/soaplisten/Arithmetic.ASP" />
      </port>
   </service>
```

WSDL Generation the IBM Java Way

Before we move on, we should perhaps look at what happens when we are starting with a Java class rather than a COM object. Here is a suitable Java class with the same methods as our COM object, `ArithServer.java`:

```
import java.lang.Math;

class Arithmetic extends Object
{
   public double Square (double inValue)
   {
```

```
        return inValue * inValue;
     }

     public double SquareRoot (double inValue)
     {
        return Math.sqrt(inValue);
     }

     public String Capitalize (String inString)
     {
        return inString.toUpperCase();
     }
  }
```

We need to compile this:

> **javac ArithServer.java**

Now we can run the IBM web service creation tool. We do this by running the file `serviceWizard.bat` under MS Windows, or `serviceWizard.sh` under UNIX. This is what we see (on Windows):

Having selected a Java class as our input, we move on to the next screen, where we select the class that we want to generate our WSDL from:

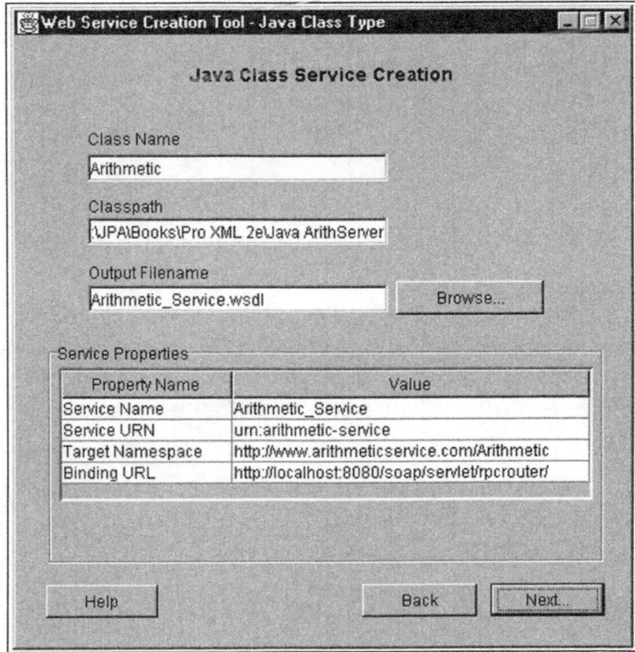

We have to fill in the top three fields, while the tool fills in the rest for us. Next we need to select which methods are to be exposed. These are the same ones as we exposed before: `Square`, `SquareRoot`, and `Capitalize`.

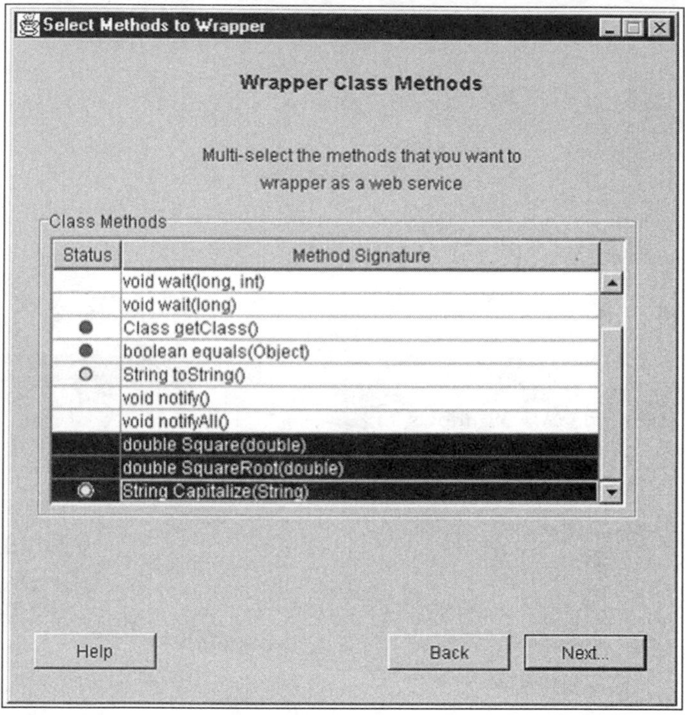

The list contains all the public non-static members of our class and its ancestors, including the ones that we have added ourselves. The status column has the following meanings:

- Blank – the method contains only non-String base types which can be described in XML without any schema definitions.
- Yellow – the method contains base types (including String) which can be described in XML without any schema definitions unless any String represents an XML document type which must be more fully defined in the service description. If we select one of these, the WSDL will be generated on the assumption that these are simple strings; if not, we'll have to modify the generated WSDL manually.
- Red – the method contains complex user-defined or base Java objects and/or arrays of objects which cannot be described in XML without also writing a schema definition in a WSDL document. If we select one of these, we'll be presented with a list of complex types to choose from which will cause a schema definition to be generated for us.

One more step and we're finished:

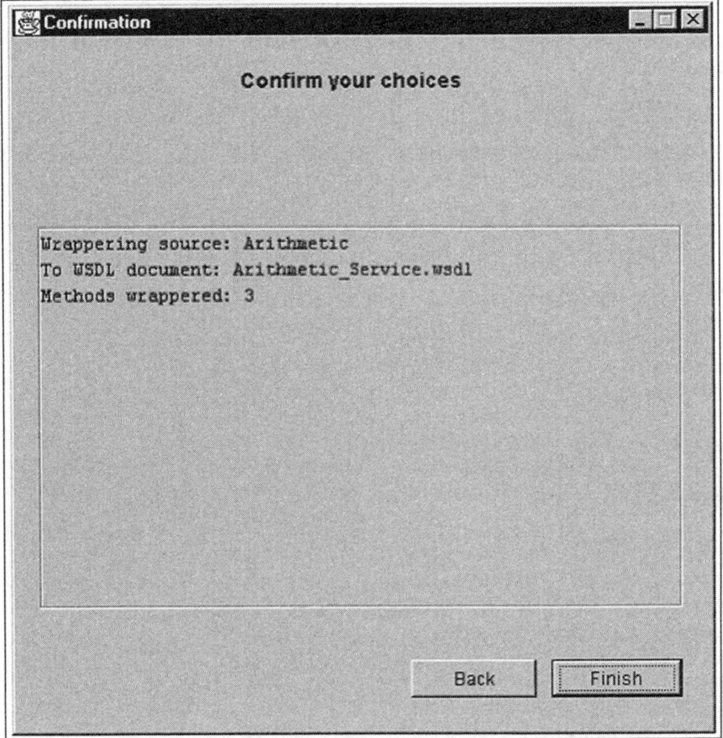

And we're done.

This time we've actually got two WSDL files generated; one a generic service blueprint that can be reused for different service implementations, which can be thought of as client-side (`Arithmetic_Service-interface.wsdl`), and one that is implementation specific that can be thought of as server-side (`Arithmetic_Service-impl.wsdl`). This is what the *client*-side WSDL file looks like this time:

```
<?xml version="1.0" encoding="UTF-8"?>
<definitions name="Arithmetic_Service-interface"
   targetNamespace="http://www.arithmeticservice.com/Arithmetic-interface"
   xmlns="http://schemas.xmlsoap.org/wsdl/"
   xmlns:soap="http://schemas.xmlsoap.org/wsdl/soap/"
   xmlns:tns="http://www.arithmeticservice.com/Arithmetic"
   xmlns:xsd="http://www.w3.org/1999/XMLSchema">
   <message name="InSquareRequest">
      <part name="meth1_inType1" type="xsd:double" />
```

```
   </message>

   <message name="OutSquareResponse">
      <part name="meth1_outType" type="xsd:double" />
   </message>

   <message name="InSquareRootRequest">
      <part name="meth2_inType1" type="xsd:double"/>
   </message>

   <message name="OutSquareRootResponse">
      <part name="meth2_outType" type="xsd:double" />
   </message>

   <message name="InCapitalizeRequest">
      <part name="meth3_inType1" type="xsd:string" />
   </message>

   <message name="OutCapitalizeResponse">
      <part name="meth3_outType" type="xsd:string" />
   </message>

   <portType name="Arithmetic_Service">
      <operation name="Square">
         <input message="InSquareRequest" />
         <output message="OutSquareResponse" />
      </operation>

      <operation name="SquareRoot">
         <input message="InSquareRootRequest" />
         <output message="OutSquareRootResponse"/>
      </operation>

      <operation name="Capitalize">
         <input message="InCapitalizeRequest" />
         <output message="OutCapitalizeResponse" />
      </operation>
   </portType>

   <binding name="Arithmetic_ServiceBinding" type="Arithmetic_Service">
      <soap:binding style="rpc"
         transport="http://schemas.xmlsoap.org/soap/http" />
      <operation name="Square">
         <soap:operation soapAction="urn:arithmetic-service" />
         <input>
            <soap:body
               encodingStyle="http://schemas.xmlsoap.org/soap/encoding/"
               namespace="urn:arithmetic-service" use="encoded" />
         </input>
         <output>
            <soap:body
               encodingStyle="http://schemas.xmlsoap.org/soap/encoding/"
               namespace="urn:arithmetic-service" use="encoded" />
         </output>
      </operation>
```

```
      <operation name="SquareRoot">
         <soap:operation soapAction="urn:arithmetic-service" />
         <input>
            <soap:body
               encodingStyle="http://schemas.xmlsoap.org/soap/encoding/"
               namespace="urn:arithmetic-service" use="encoded" />
         </input>
         <output>
            <soap:body
               encodingStyle="http://schemas.xmlsoap.org/soap/encoding/"
               namespace="urn:arithmetic-service" use="encoded" />
         </output>
      </operation>
      <operation name="Capitalize">
         <soap:operation soapAction="urn:arithmetic-service" />
         <input>
            <soap:body
               encodingStyle="http://schemas.xmlsoap.org/soap/encoding/"
               namespace="urn:arithmetic-service" use="encoded" />
         </input>
         <output>
            <soap:body
               encodingStyle="http://schemas.xmlsoap.org/soap/encoding/"
               namespace="urn:arithmetic-service" use="encoded"/>
         </output>
      </operation>
   </binding>
</definitions>
```

There are not, thankfully, that many differences from the one that `wsdlgen` produced (although that reference to the 1999 schema is slightly startling). The first one that strikes us, is the absence of any type definitions; however, all the types used are namespaced to the standard XML Schema, so the types section *is* redundant. The second, minor, point is that the (again redundant) parameter order has been left out of the message definitions. Finally, the most significant point is that the service definition has been left out altogether. This is slightly startling at first, but, on further reflection, it is only of use to the server-side. Speaking of which, here is the server-side WSDL file, `Arithmetic_Service-impl.wsdl`:

```
<?xml version="1.0" encoding="UTF-8"?>
<definitions name="Arithmetic_Service"
   targetNamespace="http://www.arithmeticservice.com/Arithmetic"
   xmlns="http://schemas.xmlsoap.org/wsdl/"
   xmlns:soap="http://schemas.xmlsoap.org/wsdl/soap/"
   xmlns:tns="http://www.arithmeticservice.com/Arithmetic"
   xmlns:xsd="http://www.w3.org/1999/XMLSchema">

   <service name="Arithmetic_Service">
      <documentation>
         IBM WSTK 2.0 generated service definition file
      </documentation>
      <port
         binding="Arithmetic_ServiceBinding"
         name="Arithmetic_ServicePort">
         <soap:address
            location="http://localhost:8080/soap/servlet/rpcrouter/"/>
```

```
        </port>
    </service>
    <import
        location=
          "http://localhost:8080/wsdl/Arithmetic_Service-interface.wsdl"
        namespace="http://www.arithmeticservice.com/Arithmetic-interface">
    </import>
</definitions>
```

Here's our service definition, along with everything else, *imported* from the main WSDL file. We haven't encountered `import` before – indeed, as of version Beta 2, the Microsoft toolkit doesn't support it yet. This element does what it says: it includes everything in the imported file in the current one.

If we so wished, we could take this file and use it to set up a Java-based arithmetic server, using standard Java servlet technology; however, that is outside the scope of this discussion.

WSDL in Practice

I think it is probably about time that we tried some of this out with a real client. We will start with something nice and easy, by using a Microsoft client with a Microsoft server, then we will move on to the more interesting problem of interoperation between Microsoft and IBM. If all goes well, we'll end up with two entirely disparate systems connected only by their use of a common WSDL definition working together as a single system.

Using a VBScript Client

First, let's take a look at what our client would look like if there were no SOAP in the way. In this next example we use the Windows Scripting Host. Try this simple VBScript program, `ArithTest.vbs`:

```
Set arith = CreateObject("ArithServer.Arithmetic")
WScript.Echo arith.Square(8)
WScript.Echo arith.SquareRoot(4)
WScript.Echo arith.Capitalize("Hello world")
```

If Windows Script Host isn't installed on your machine, pay a visit to the Microsoft Scripting Technologies page at http://msdn.microsoft.com/scripting/.

If we run it, on the same machine that `ArithServer.dll` is registered, we should see three message boxes, containing "64", "2" and "HELLO WORLD" respectively. Our aim is to provide exactly the same functionality when our server is on a different machine altogether.

Let's first ensure that our SOAP server is set up correctly. Remember that we specified the folder `soaplisten` underneath the web root on our server? We need to move all three files that were generated by `wsdlgen` there: `Arithmetic.asp`, `Arithmetic.wsdl` and `Arithmetic.wsml`.

Now, on our client machine, we create a new VBScript program, `ArithClient.vbs`:

```
Set soapclient = CreateObject("MSSOAP.SoapClient")
Call soapclient.mssoapinit("http://laa-laa/soaplisten/Arithmetic.wsdl",
   "Arithmetic", "ArithmeticSoapPort")
WScript.Echo soapclient.Square(8)
WScript.Echo soapclient.SquareRoot(4)
WScript.Echo soapclient.Capitalize("Hello world")
```

Note that all we're doing now is creating a SOAP client object, telling it which WSDL file to use, and which service and port to use from that definition. There really could not be less to specify. Moreover, if we run it, we should see precisely the same result as before.

Using a Java Client

This, unsurprisingly, is where the fun starts. As we have seen above, there is sufficient flexibility in the WSDL and SOAP specifications to ensure that two different implementations of the same simple set of functions can turn out quite dramatically different. Ultimately, of course, the demands of interoperability *should* ensure that the final versions of the various vendors' WSDL toolkits should be able to cope with whatever any other vendor's WSDL toolkit sends them. However, this is not necessarily the case during the beta phase of the development cycle, and, sadly, this is the point at which we presently find ourselves. During the following discussion, please bear in mind the comment that I made at the start of the chapter regarding the various workarounds. By the time this book is printed, there may be a completely different set of issues to deal with.

The first thing we have to do is generate a Java proxy for our WSDL service. This is a class that will handle all the WSDL interactions on our behalf. There is a tool provided with the IBM toolkit to do just this:

> **java com.ibm.wsdl.Main -in Arithmetic.WSDL**

This is the point at which we encounter our first problem:

```
>> Transforming WSDL to NASSL ..
>> Generating Schema to Java bindings ..
>> Generating serializers / deserializers ..
Interface 'wsdlns:ArithmeticSoapPort' not found.
```

The IBM generator does not like the wsdlns namespace in front of the port name in our WSDL file. However, it's not necessary in this particular case, so we can safely remove it:

```
<binding name="ArithmeticSoapBinding" type="ArithmeticSoapPort" >
```

Our next attempt gets a little further:

```
>> Transforming WSDL to NASSL ..
>> Generating Schema to Java bindings ..
>> Generating serializers / deserializers ..
>> Generating proxy ..
Created file E:\JPA\Books\Pro XML 2e\Java ArithClient\ArithmeticSoapPortProxy.ja
va
Call to extension function failed: method call/new failed: java.lang.reflect.Inv
ocationTargetException target exception: java.lang.IllegalArgumentException: The name attribute of all type elements must be namespace-qualified.
I was unable to convert an object from java.lang.Object to null.
```

And so on. Confusingly, what we now have to do is remove that `wsdlns` namespace from the messages as well, therefore:

```
<operation name="Capitalize" parameterOrder="InString">
   <input message="Arithmetic.Capitalize" />
```

```
            <output message="Arithmetic.CapitalizeResponse" />
        </operation>
        <operation name="SquareRoot" parameterOrder="InValue">
            <input message="Arithmetic.SquareRoot" />
            <output message="Arithmetic.SquareRootResponse" />
        </operation>
        <operation name="Square" parameterOrder="InValue">
            <input message="Arithmetic.Square" />
            <output message="Arithmetic.SquareResponse" />
        </operation>
```

Now we get this:

```
>> Transforming WSDL to NASSL ..
>> Generating Schema to Java bindings ..
>> Generating serializers / deserializers ..
>> Generating proxy ..
Created file E:\JPA\Books\Pro XML 2e\Java ArithClient\ArithmeticSoapPortProxy.java
No mapping was found for 'http://www.w3.org/2000/10/XMLSchema:string'.
No mapping was found for 'http://www.w3.org/2000/10/XMLSchema:string'.
No mapping was found for 'http://www.w3.org/2000/10/XMLSchema:string'.
I was unable to convert an object from null to java.lang.Object.
I was unable to convert an object from java.lang.Object to null.
```

And so on. The problem now is that the IBM generator doesn't recognize the 2000 schema, so we need to revert to the 1999 model:

```
        xmlns:xsd='"http://www.w3.org/1999/XMLSchema"
```

This time, it works, and we have a Java proxy class, `ArithmeticSoapPortProxy.java`. Not only that, but the IBM generator will have compiled it for us, too.

Now we need a client. As with our VBScript client, we are going to make it very simple. Here is our Java client, `ArithClient.java`:

```
import ArithmeticSoapPortProxy;

public class ArithClient
{
   public static void main (String[] args) throws Exception
   {
      ArithmeticSoapPortProxy arith = new ArithmeticSoapPortProxy ();
      System.out.println (arith.Capitalize ("Hello world"));

      System.out.println (arith.Square (8));
      System.out.println (arith.SquareRoot (4));
   }
}
```

They come much simpler than that, really. This is how we compile it:

> javac ArithClient.java

So let's see what happens when we run it:

```
Exception in thread "main" [SOAPException: faultCode=SOAP-ENV:Client; msg=No
Deserializer found to deserialize a ':Result' using encoding style 'http://schemas.
xmlsoap.org/soap/encoding/'.; targetException=java.lang.IllegalArgumentException
: No Deserializer found to deserialize a ':Result' using encoding style 'http://
schemas.xmlsoap.org/soap/encoding/'.]
        at org.apache.soap.rpc.Call.invoke(Call.java:244)
        at ArithmeticSoapPortProxy.Capitalize(ArithmeticSoapPortProxy.java:50)
        at ArithClient.main(ArithClient.java:8)
```

We encountered this before in Chapter 24, when we first looked at SOAP, so we will not go into it in any detail here. Suffice to say that we need to make the following couple of small changes to the generated Java class:

```
import java.net.*;
import java.util.*;
import org.apache.soap.*;
import org.apache.soap.encoding.*;
import org.apache.soap.rpc.*;
import org.apache.soap.util.xml.*;
import org.apache.soap.encoding.soapenc.StringDeserializer;
```

and:

```
public ArithmeticSoapPortProxy() throws MalformedURLException
{
   call.setTargetObjectURI("http://tempuri.org/message/");
   call.setEncodingStyleURI("http://schemas.xmlsoap.org/soap/encoding/");
   this.url = new URL("http://laa-laa/soaplisten/Arithmetic.ASP");
   this.SOAPActionURI = "http://tempuri.org/action/Arithmetic.Capitalize";

   StringDeserializer oStrDeserializer = new StringDeserializer ();
   SOAPMappingRegistry smr = new SOAPMappingRegistry ();
   smr.mapTypes ("http://schemas.xmlsoap.org/soap/encoding/",
      new QName ("", "Result"), null, null, oStrDeserializer);
   call.setSOAPMappingRegistry (smr);
}
```

We compile this as follows:

> javac ArithmeticSoapPortProxy.java

This is what we see when we run our client:

```
HELLO WORLD
Exception in thread "main" [SOAPException: faultCode=SOAP-ENV:Server; msg=WSDLRe
ader: The operation requested in the Soap message isn't defined in the WSDL file.
This may be because it is in the wrong namespace or has incorrect case]
        at ArithmeticSoapPortProxy.Square(ArithmeticSoapPortProxy.java:126)
        at ArithClient.main(ArithClient.java:10)
```

Well, the first line is looking good. However, this is the point at which we realize that our interoperability is currently limited to services containing a single method, unless we want to do some severe hacking of our WSDL file. Look at this unusual line in the generated Java class:

```
this.SOAPActionURI = "http://tempuri.org/action/Arithmetic.Capitalize";
```

This effectively pins us down to `Capitalize` for the time being. Moreover, if we want to change to `Square`, for instance, we also need to change our deserializer, like this:

```
//import org.apache.soap.encoding.soapenc.StringDeserializer;
import org.apache.soap.encoding.soapenc.DoubleDeserializer;
```

and:

```
public ArithmeticSoapPortProxy() throws MalformedURLException
{
   call.setTargetObjectURI("http://tempuri.org/message/");
   call.setEncodingStyleURI("http://schemas.xmlsoap.org/soap/encoding/");
   this.url = new URL("http://laa-laa/soaplisten/Arithmetic.ASP");
   // this.SOAPActionURI="http://tempuri.org/action/Arithmetic.Capitalize";
   this.SOAPActionURI = "http://tempuri.org/action/Arithmetic.Square";

// StringDeserializer oStrDeserializer = new StringDeserializer ();
   DoubleDeserializer oDblDeserializer = new DoubleDeserializer ();
   SOAPMappingRegistry smr = new SOAPMappingRegistry ();
// smr.mapTypes ("http://schemas.xmlsoap.org/soap/encoding/",
// new QName ("", "Result"), null, null, oStrDeserializer);
   smr.mapTypes ("http://schemas.xmlsoap.org/soap/encoding/",
      new QName ("", "Result"), null, null, oDblDeserializer);
   call.setSOAPMappingRegistry (smr);
}
```

We had also better change our client:

```
import ArithmeticSoapPortProxy;

public class ArithClient
{
   public static void main (String[] args) throws Exception
   {
      ArithmeticSoapPortProxy arith = new ArithmeticSoapPortProxy ();
      // System.out.println (arith.Capitalize ("Hello world"));

      System.out.println (arith.Square (8));
      // System.out.println (arith.SquareRoot (4));
   }
}
```

When we run it, we get this result:

```
64.0
```

Therefore, we have at least established that we can handle doubles with WSDL.

Let's just pause here for a moment and consider what we've achieved here. We have managed to get two completely disparate systems, without a single line of common code, to talk to each other as if they were instead working as a single program, simply by formalizing the interactions between them in a standard, common, WSDL file. I think that is impressive, by anyone's standards. Also, it must be noted that once we are past the beta stage in these technologies, all of these little glitches should be ironed out and it will work seamlessly. As the chapter title suggests, this gives you a glimpse of the future.

Chickens and Eggs

Here is an interesting question. Which came first the WSDL or the code? Up until this point, we have taken a highly pragmatic approach to WSDL. We took an operational server, derived a WSDL file from it, and used that file to generate a suitable client. This isn't the only way to do it, however. There is another school of thought (the one that prefers not to believe in the concept of the executable specification) that says, actually, WSDL is a neat design tool. It is highly rigorous, platform-independent, concise, and defined using XML – so there are plenty of tools available for manipulating it, as well.

The feeling is that for the present, this is not a viable option, because there are a couple of factors against it. Firstly, there currently aren't any commercially available graphical tools for building definitions, and handcrafting WSDL is just too tedious and time-consuming. Secondly, there is currently no Microsoft tool to generate code from WSDL. However, it is unlikely that either of these will remain true for very long, and perhaps future developments will be WSDL-driven, rather than code-driven.

UDDI

OK, so we know how to talk to each other. However, that's not an enormous amount of help if we don't actually know of each other's existence. Now we *could* try a web search to find out the kind of service that we're looking for, and then hunt around on their web site for a suitable WSDL file.

What we really need is a kind of dating agency, where we can enter the details of our required business partner, run a structured search, and come up with the details of what they do and who to contact there. If we're *really* lucky, we might even get hold of their WSDL file without having to search for it. It so happens that such an agency is being built, although it goes under the more sober title of **the Universal Description, Discovery and Integration Registry**. The parties involved are Ariba Inc., IBM, and Microsoft. All three have their own trial registry implementations, available on the World Wide Web, while the latter two provide toolkits to access the registries. In this half of the chapter, we are going to try out both APIs on all three registries. We're going to start by making inquiries on registries and then we're going to publish to the registries ourselves.

The UDDI protocol is SOAP 1.1 based. However, we have no need to understand or even care about the underlying details, as the APIs nicely wrap all of this up for us. Before we get programming, though, we'd better get to grips with some of the concepts involved.

UDDI Concepts

The UDDI business registry is described as being a cloud, wherein a business can be registered once, but published everywhere. What kind of information is held in this registry? The core element of information is the `businessEntity`. This contains general information about the business (contact names and addresses and so on), as well as `businessService` elements. Each business service contains descriptive data as well as a number of technical web service descriptions, or `bindingTemplate` elements. The binding templates contain the information needed to actually invoke a web service. The key part of this is called a `tModel`; this is meta data about a specification, containing its name, details of who published it and URL pointers to the actual specification. This specification could, of course, be in the form we have been discussing in the first part of this chapter: a WSDL file.

This diagram shows how these elements are related:

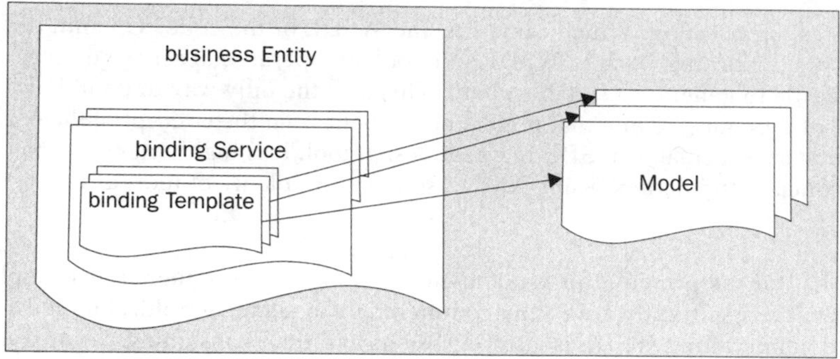

The rest of this chapter is going to look at how we can use the UDDI APIs to make simple inquiries of and publish to the various publicly available registries. We're not actually going to touch on much of the elements involved in a registry entry; once we've established how to access and update a simple part of the business entity (its description), we can extend that process to any other part of the structure.

UDDI Inquiries

Before we can make any inquiries on any of the registries, we need to set up some test data. Since we need to be registered as publishers for the next section (because we're going to be publishing business information as well as making inquiries), we might as well do that now. This is quite a straightforward process, and all we need to do is go to each web site in turn and follow all the steps to register ourselves. The steps involved are different in each case, but they are quite self-explanatory, so we won't waste space by discussing them further here. The sites in question are:

- Ariba: http://uddi.ariba.com
- IBM: http://www.ibm.com/services/uddi
- Microsoft: http://uddi.microsoft.com

Once we've registered ourselves, then we can go on and add a business. In the case of IBM, use the test registry, rather than the live one; in the other two cases, we don't get a choice. For the time being, just create a business with a name and a simple description. For the purposes of this chapter, we created a business called "WroxDemo".

We will also need the APIs. The IBM UDDI API is called `uddi4j` (UDDI for Java), and this is included as part of the Web Services Toolkit that we loaded in the first part of this chapter. You should make sure that the `uddi4j.jar` archive is in the Java CLASSPATH. The Microsoft API can be found at http://msdn.microsoft.com/downloads/default.asp?URL=/code/sample.asp?url=/msdn-files/027/001/527/msdncompositedoc.xml.

Both APIs are essentially the same, although implemented using different technologies (Java for IBM, COM for Microsoft). The Microsoft version, as we shall see, exposes a little more of the underlying SOAP technology than IBM; however, most of the calls are functionally identical.

Inquiries the IBM Way

We will start with a very simple application to get a feel for what we're doing. We'll code it up as a single Java class using command line I/O, called `UDDIClient.java`. Here is how the code starts, importing the necessary UDDI Java classes:

```
import com.ibm.uddi.client.UDDIProxy;
import com.ibm.uddi.response.BusinessList;
import com.ibm.uddi.response.BusinessInfos;
import com.ibm.uddi.response.BusinessInfo;
import java.util.Vector;
```

Here's the `main()` method:

```
public class UDDIClient
{
   public static void main (String[] args) throws Exception
   {
      byte input[] = new byte[128];

      System.out.print ("Search for? ");
      int nRead = System.in.read (input, 0, 128);

      String strSearch = new String (input, 0, nRead - 2);

      System.out.print ("Registry? ");
      nRead = System.in.read (input, 0, 128);
```

All we're doing here is getting a company name to search for, plus an identifier for the registry that we're going to search in (A for Ariba, I for IBM, and M for Microsoft). Let us look a bit further:

```
      String strRegistry;
      String strURL;

      switch (input[0])
      {
      case 'A':
         strRegistry = "Ariba";
         strURL = new
            String("http://uddi.ariba.com/UDDIProcessor.aw/ad/process");
         break;

      case 'I':
         strRegistry = "IBM";
         strURL = new String(
            "http://www-3.ibm.com/services/uddi/testregistry/inquiryapi");
         break;

      case 'M':
         strRegistry = "Microsoft";
         strURL = new String("http://test.uddi.microsoft.com/inquire");
         break;

      default:
         System.out.println ("Invalid registry specified - exiting");
         return;
      }

      System.out.println ("Searching for <" + strSearch +
         "> at " + strRegistry + " ...");
```

Here, we're setting up the URL of the registry that we're going for. Notice that in the case of IBM, we have specified the test registry (http://www-3.ibm.com/services/uddi/testregistry/inquiryapi) rather than the live registry (http://www-3.ibm.com/services/uddi/inquiryapi).

Now comes our first glimpse into the API:

```
UDDIProxy proxy = new UDDIProxy();
proxy.setInquiryURL (strURL);
```

The `UDDIProxy` object is our way of talking to the registry. Every interaction with the registry is done via this object. It needs one URL for inquiries, and another one for publishing; however, we won't need the second one yet. It's time to carry out our search:

```
BusinessList list = proxy.find_business (strSearch, null, 10);
```

At this stage, I've chosen a very simple partial string match search, and I've limited the number of hits to 10, as experience has shown that specifying an unlimited number of hits (-1) can result in an indefinite wait.

Once we have a response, we can extract the information that we need:

```
            BusinessInfos infos = list.getBusinessInfos ();
            Vector vInfo = infos.getBusinessInfoVector ();
            int nInfo = vInfo.size();
            System.out.println (nInfo + " items found:");
            for (int iInfo = 0; iInfo < nInfo; iInfo++)
            {
               BusinessInfo info = (BusinessInfo) vInfo.elementAt (iInfo);
               System.out.println (info.getNameString ());
               Vector vDesc = info.getDescriptionStrings ();
               int nDesc = vDesc.size ();
               for (int iDesc = 0; iDesc < nDesc; iDesc++)
                  System.out.println ((String) vDesc.elementAt (iDesc));
            }
         }
      }
```

A `BusinessInfo` object contains all the information for a single business, so all we're doing here is extracting the name and description for each of the businesses found by our search. In practice, it is only possible to enter a single description via any of the UDDI web sites, so we will only manage to extract one.

Let us see what happens when we try out an extraction from Ariba:

```
Search for? Wrox
Registry? A
Searching for <Wrox> at Ariba ...
1 items found:
WroxDemo
Wrox Demonstration Business (Ariba version)
```

How about IBM:

```
Search for? Wrox
Registry? I
Searching for <Wrox> at IBM ...
1 items found:
WroxDemo
Wrox Demonstration Business (IBM version)
```

Finally, we will try Microsoft:

```
Search for? Wrox
Registry? M
Searching for <Wrox> at Microsoft ...
Exception in thread "main" [SOAPException: faultCode=SOAP-ENV:Protocol; msg=Miss
ing content type.]
        at org.apache.soap.transport.TransportMessage.read(TransportMessage.java
:214)
        at org.apache.soap.util.net.HTTPUtils.post(HTTPUtils.java:296)
        at org.apache.soap.transport.http.SOAPHTTPConnection.send(SOAPHTTPConn
ection.java:208)
        at org.apache.soap.messaging.Message.send(Message.java:120)
        at com.ibm.uddi.client.UDDIProxy.send(UDDIProxy.java:1215)
        at com.ibm.uddi.client.UDDIProxy.send(UDDIProxy.java:1187)
        at com.ibm.uddi.client.UDDIProxy.find_business(UDDIProxy.java:192)
        at UDDIClient.main(UDDIClient.java:52)
```

Now that doesn't look quite right. This problem arose during the period when we were working on this book, and is apparently due to the Microsoft registry returning a content type of `"text/xml;"`, which causes Apache SOAP to enter a loop. With any luck, this will all have been resolved between the various parties by the time this book goes on sale.

Inquiries the Microsoft Way

Let's see how Microsoft does it. There is a moderately sophisticated example provided with the UDDI API, but for clarity's sake, we're going to build something somewhat less ambitious, along very similar lines to the Java one. We'll use Microsoft Visual Basic version 6. Once we've created a new project, we'll need to add references to the two UDDI COM DLL's via Project | References:

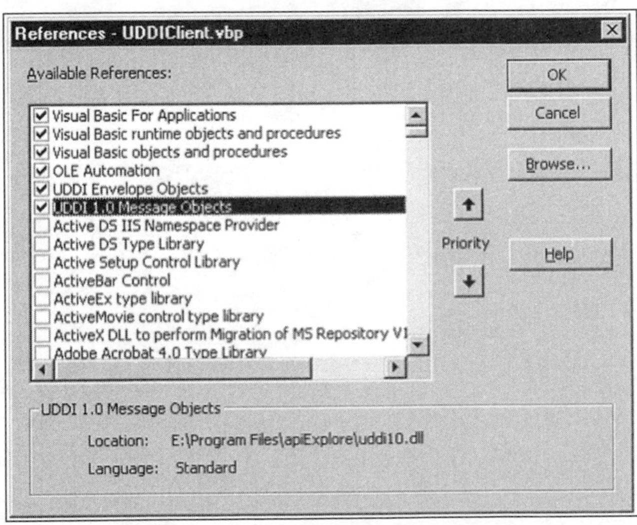

Next, we'll create our form:

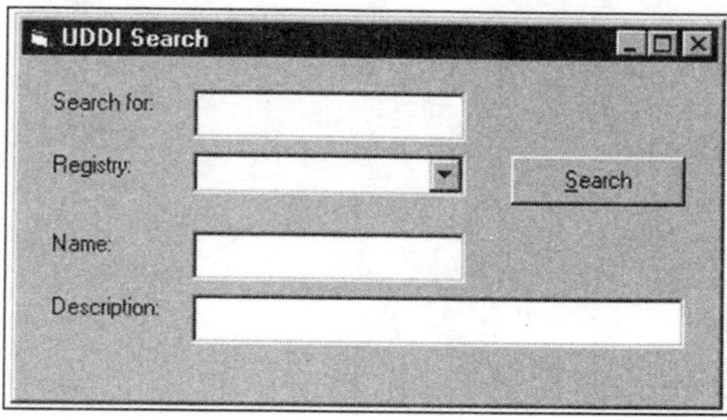

The three text boxes are as follows: `txtSearch`, `txtName` and `txtDescription`. The combo box is `cmbRegistry`, and the command button is `cmdSearch`. We only need to attach any code to two events. In `Form_Load()`, all we need to do is set up the registry selection combo box:

```
Private Sub Form_Load()
   cmbRegistry.AddItem ("Ariba")
   cmbRegistry.AddItem ("IBM")
   cmbRegistry.AddItem ("Microsoft")

   cmbRegistry.ListIndex = 0
End Sub
```

In `cmdSearch_Click()`, we start off by declaring a number of UDDI-related variables, which we'll discuss as we go on. Then we set up the first of these, the UDDI request manager. This is equivalent to the Java `UDDIProxy` object, in that it's the object that every UDDI interaction passes through:

```
Private Sub cmdSearch_Click()
   Dim strSearch As String
   Dim strRegistry As String
   Dim req As UDDIEnv.RequestManager
   Dim envOut As UDDIEnv.Envelope
   Dim findBiz As UDDI10.find_business
   Dim envIn As UDDIEnv.Envelope
   Dim bizList As UDDI10.businessList
   Dim bizInfo As UDDI10.businessInfo

   strSearch = txtSearch.Text
   strRegistry = cmbRegistry.Text

   Set req = New RequestManager

   If (strRegistry = "Ariba") Then
      req.UDDI_Address = "http://uddi.ariba.com/UDDIProcessor.aw/ad/process"
   ElseIf (strRegistry = "IBM") Then
      req.UDDI_Address = _
         "http://www-3.ibm.com/services/uddi/testregistry/inquiryapi"
   Else
      req.UDDI_Address = "http://uddi.microsoft.com/inquire"
   End If
```

Next, we need to set up our `find_business` object. This object defines the parameters for our search:

```
Set findBiz = New find_business
```

Then we have to create a UDDI SOAP envelope, and insert our `find_business` object into it. Once we've done that, we can safely populate it:

```
Set outEnv = New Envelope
Set outEnv.Plugin = findBiz

findBiz.Name = strSearch
findBiz.maxRows = 10
```

This exposes a little more of the underlying architecture than the IBM Java implementation (remember all we did last time was invoke the `find_business` method on the `UDDIProxy` object?).

Now we can send off our request and get a response. The request goes off in one envelope and comes back in another. Strictly speaking, we could reuse the same envelope; however, for the sake of clarity, I've used a separate one:

```
Set inEnv = req.UDDIRequest(outEnv)
```

If all goes well, we can extract a list of businesses from the incoming envelope:

```
Set bizList = New businessList
Set inEnv.Plugin = bizList
```

Having done that, we can simply iterate through the list, displaying the name and description (although we're actually only set up to display one at a time):

```
    For Each bizInfo In bizList.businessInfos
        txtName.Text = bizInfo.Name
        txtDescription.Text = bizInfo.Description(1)
    Next bizInfo
End Sub
```

Let's try it out on Ariba:

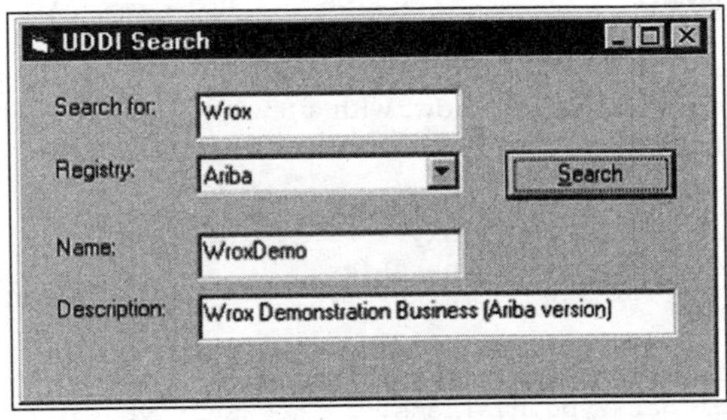

IBM:

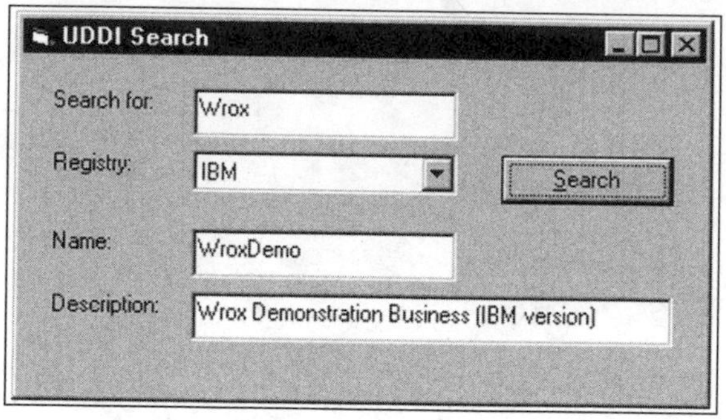

UDDI Search
Search for: Wrox
Registry: IBM
Search
Name: WroxDemo
Description: Wrox Demonstration Business (IBM version)

and, finally, Microsoft:

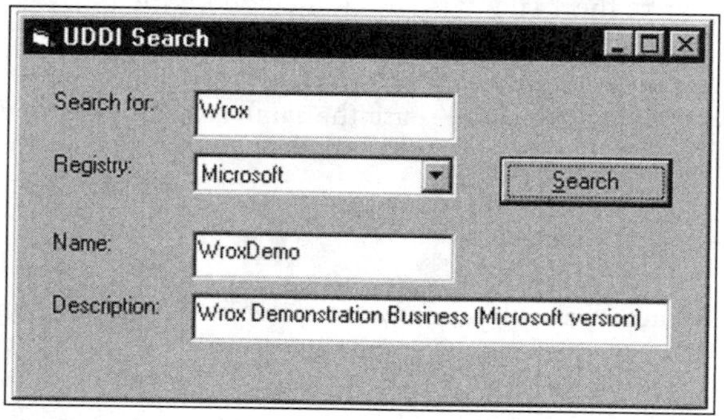

UDDI Search
Search for: Wrox
Registry: Microsoft
Search
Name: WroxDemo
Description: Wrox Demonstration Business (Microsoft version)

Publishing To UDDI

The majority of interactions with UDDI are likely to be inquiries. However, it's also unlikely that corporations in the future will want to be saddled with the hassle of using a web-style user interface every time they want to update their details. In this section, we look at how we can extend the way in which we interact with UDDI to include amendments as well as simple retrievals.

Amending UDDI information involves several additional steps, and we are going to amend both of our implementations accordingly. All we are actually going to do is change the description field. However, once we can do that successfully, we can effectively amend anything.

Publishing the IBM Way

As before, we will start off with the IBM Java implementation. We start by copying our previous class to `UDDIClient2.java`. Here's how it starts now, with a few additional imports (we'll see what these are doing as we go through the rest of the code):

```
import com.ibm.uddi.client.UDDIProxy;
import com.ibm.uddi.response.BusinessList;
import com.ibm.uddi.response.BusinessInfos;
import com.ibm.uddi.response.BusinessInfo;
import com.ibm.uddi.response.BusinessDetail;
import com.ibm.uddi.datatype.business.BusinessEntity;
import com.ibm.uddi.response.AuthToken;
```

```
import java.util.Vector;
import java.security.Security;
import java.util.Properties;
```

In the new version, we are going to have to access the publishing URL for each of the registries, using a secure connection. Therefore, we are going to have to enable secure sockets:

```
public class UDDIClient2
{
   public static void main (String[] args) throws Exception
   {
      Properties props = System.getProperties ();
      props.put ("java.protocol.handler.pkgs",
                 "com.ibm.net.ssl.internal.www.protocol");
      System.setProperties (props);
      Security.addProvider(new com.ibm.jsse.JSSEProvider());
```

The next section remains unchanged:

```
      byte input[] = new byte[128];

      System.out.print ("Search for? ");
      int nRead = System.in.read (input, 0, 128);

      String strSearch = new String (input, 0, nRead - 2);

      System.out.print ("Registry? ");
      nRead = System.in.read (input, 0, 128);
```

We now have to set up a URL for publishing as well as inquiries:

```
      String strRegistry;
      String strInquiryURL;
      String strPublishURL;

      switch (input[0])
      {
      case 'A':
         strRegistry = "Ariba";
         strInquiryURL = new String(
            "http://uddi.ariba.com/UDDIProcessor.aw/ad/process");
         strPublishURL = new String(
            "https://uddi.ariba.com/UDDIProcessor.aw/ad/process");
         break;

      case 'I':
         strRegistry = "IBM";
         strInquiryURL = new String(
            "http://www-3.ibm.com/services/uddi/testregistry/inquiryapi");
         strPublishURL = new String(
            "https://www-3.ibm.com/services/uddi/
                     testregistry/protect/publishapi");
         break;
```

```
case 'M':
   strRegistry = "Microsoft";
   strInquiryURL = new String("http://uddi.microsoft.com/inquire");
   strPublishURL = new String("https://uddi.microsoft.com/publish");
   break;

default:
   System.out.println ("Invalid registry specified - exiting");
   return;
}

System.out.println ("Searching for <" + strSearch + "> at " +
   strRegistry + " ...");

UDDIProxy proxy = new UDDIProxy();
proxy.setInquiryURL (strInquiryURL);
proxy.setPublishURL (strPublishURL);
```

The next section, where we are setting up the initial inquiry, remains unchanged:

```
BusinessList list = proxy.find_business (strSearch, null, 10);
BusinessInfos infos = list.getBusinessInfos ();
Vector vInfo = infos.getBusinessInfoVector ();
```

However, from this point on, we are in new territory. The first difference is that this time around, we're just going to focus on the first item found (if any). The second difference is that we're going to have to get access to the business entity, because that's what we're going to be changing. The first step to doing this is to get hold of the unique key for the record; the registry allocated this when we first registered the business:

```
int nInfo = vInfo.size();

if (nInfo == 0)
{
   System.out.println ("None found");
   return;
}

BusinessInfo info = (BusinessInfo) vInfo.elementAt (0);
String strKey = info.getBusinessKey ();
```

Now we have that, we make a request via the proxy for the business details relating to this key, and from that we can extract the business entity:

```
System.out.println ("Getting business entity for key " + strKey +
   " ...");

BusinessDetail detail = proxy.get_businessDetail (strKey);

Vector vEntity = detail.getBusinessEntityVector ();

int nEntity = vEntity.size ();
```

```
if (nEntity == 0)
{
   System.out.println ("Failed to retrieve business entity");
   return;
}

BusinessEntity entity = (BusinessEntity) vEntity.elementAt (0);
```

As a check that we have the right entity, we output the name and description from this object, rather than the business info object:

```
String strName = entity.getNameString ();
System.out.println ("Name = " + strName);

Vector vDesc = entity.getDescriptionStrings ();

int nDesc = vDesc.size ();

if (nDesc > 0)
   System.out.println ("Description = " +
      (String) vDesc.elementAt (0));
```

Now we ask the user for a new description, and put it into the entity, as the first description. Then we load the entity back into the entity vector:

```
System.out.print ("New description? ");
nRead = System.in.read (input, 0, 128);

String strDescription = new String (input, 0, nRead - 2);

if (nDesc > 0)
   vDesc.setElementAt (strDescription, 0);
else
   vDesc.addElement (strDescription);

entity.setDescriptionStrings (vDesc);
vEntity.setElementAt (entity, 0);
```

In order to publish, we need to give the registry the user name and password that we established when we registered ourselves with UDDI in the first place. We use these to get an authentication token, which we can use for subsequent publishing operations:

```
System.out.print ("User name? ");
nRead = System.in.read (input, 0, 128);

String strUser = new String (input, 0, nRead - 2);

System.out.print ("Password? ");
nRead = System.in.read (input, 0, 128);

String strPassword = new String (input, 0, nRead - 2);

AuthToken auth = proxy.get_authToken (strUser, strPassword);
```

Having got that, we can now save the business entity with its new description:

```
            proxy.save_business (auth.getAuthInfoString (), vEntity);
        }
    }
```

This is what happens when we run it; the username and password is the business name entered when we first registered a company at the start of this section:

```
Search for? Wrox
Registry? A
Searching for <Wrox> at Ariba ...
Getting business entity for key 3d528bf1-00e5-ec77-f22c-cefb19a7aa77 ...
Name = WroxDemo
Description = Wrox Demonstration Business (Ariba version)
New description? Ariba Wrox Demo
User name? ...
Password? ...
```

If we run it again, we can see that the description has indeed been changed. The IBM registry behaves similarly, but once again, the Microsoft registry is currently inaccessible from IBM.

Publishing the Microsoft Way

Let's complete the set now, and extend our VB application to publish a new description. Copy the project and form to `UDDIClient2.vbp` and `UDDIClient2.frm`, respectively, and amend the form as follows:

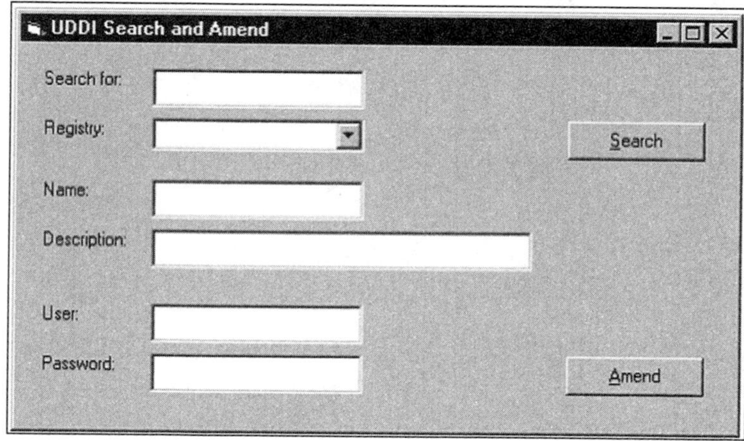

The new text boxes are called `txtUser` and `txtPassword`, respectively. The new command button is called `cmdAmend`. Seeing as we're now going to be holding information between the `Search` and `Amend` commands, we'll need to add a couple of global variables:

```
    Dim mReq As UDDIEnv.RequestManager
    Dim mEntity As UDDI10.businessEntity
```

`Form_Load()` remains unchanged, but we've also got to add one or two new variables to `cmdSearch_Click()`:

```
Private Sub cmdSearch_Click()
   Dim strSearch As String
   Dim strRegistry As String
   Dim outEnv As UDDIEnv.Envelope
   Dim findBiz As UDDI10.find_business
   Dim getBiz As UDDI10.get_businessDetail
   Dim inEnv As UDDIEnv.Envelope
   Dim bizList As UDDI10.businessList
   Dim bizInfo As UDDI10.businessInfo
   Dim bizDetail As UDDI10.businessDetail
   Dim strKey As String
```

As with the Java implementation, we need to set up both the inquiry address and the publishing (or secure, in Microsoft terms) address. We also need to use the global request variable now:

```
   strSearch = txtSearch.Text
   strRegistry = cmbRegistry.Text

   Set mReq = New RequestManager

   If (strRegistry = "Ariba") Then
      mReq.UDDI_Address =
         "http://uddi.ariba.com/UDDIProcessor.aw/ad/process"
      mReq.UDDI_SecureAddress =
         "http://uddi.ariba.com/UDDIProcessor.aw/ad/process"
   ElseIf (strRegistry = "IBM") Then
      mReq.UDDI_Address =
         "http://www-3.ibm.com/services/uddi/testregistry/inquiryapi"
      mReq.UDDI_SecureAddress = "https://www-3.ibm.com/services/uddi" & _
         "/testregistry/protect/publishapi"
   Else
      mReq.UDDI_Address = "http://uddi.microsoft.com/inquire"
      mReq.UDDI_SecureAddress = "https://uddi.microsoft.com/publish"
   End If
```

The next section, which retrieves the business information from UDDI, remains unchanged:

```
   Set findBiz = New find_business
   Set outEnv = New Envelope
   Set outEnv.Plugin = findBiz

   findBiz.Name = strSearch
   findBiz.maxRows = 10

   Set inEnv = mReq.UDDIRequest(outEnv)

   Set bizList = New businessList
   Set inEnv.Plugin = bizList
```

However, as before, from here on we're in uncharted waters. The first thing we need to do is extract the business key:

```
   If (bizList.businessInfos.Count = 0) Then
      MsgBox ("None found")
      Exit Sub
```

```
    End If

    Set bizInfo = bizList.businessInfos(1)
    strKey = bizInfo.businessKey
```

Now we get the business details, and extract the entity from it:

```
    Set getBiz = New get_businessDetail
    Set outEnv = New Envelope
    Set outEnv.Plugin = getBiz

    getBiz.AddbusinessKey = strKey

    Set inEnv = mReq.UDDIRequest(outEnv)

    Set bizDetail = New businessDetail
    Set inEnv.Plugin = bizDetail

    If (bizDetail.Count = 0) Then
       MsgBox ("Failed to retrieve business entity")
       Exit Sub
    End If

    Set mEntity = bizDetail.businessEntity(1)
```

Again, we use this to populate the name and description fields:

```
    txtName.Text = mEntity.Name
    txtDescription.Text = mEntity.Description(1)
End Sub
```

Now let's look at what happens when we click on the **Amend** button:

```
Private Sub cmdAmend_Click()
   Dim save As UDDI10.save_business
   Dim outEnv As UDDIEnv.Envelope
   Dim inEnv As UDDIEnv.Envelope
```

The first thing that we have to do is get our authentication token. The slight difference here is that the actual token is stored within the request object, so we don't actually need to deal with it explicitly:

```
   mReq.Authenticate txtUser.Text, txtPassword.Text
```

Now we can amend our entity, and we're nearly home and dry:

```
   mEntity.Description(1) = txtDescription.Text
```

At this point, we encounter a problem. Because the Microsoft implementation is wrapped in COM objects, there is no easy way to copy across an entire entity into an envelope without copying each element in turn. So that's what we're going to have to do:

```
    Set save = New save_business
    Set outEnv = New Envelope
    Set outEnv.Plugin = save

    With save.AddbusinessEntity
        .Adddescription = mEntity.Description(1)
        .businessKey = mEntity.businessKey
        .Name = mEntity.Name
    End With
```

In fact, in real life, there would be a whole lot more! However, we are nearly finished, and we can send off our save to the registry:

```
    Set inEnv = mReq.UDDIRequest(outEnv)
    MsgBox ("Done")
End Sub
```

Let's try the application out and see if it works. Here is the result of our search on Ariba:

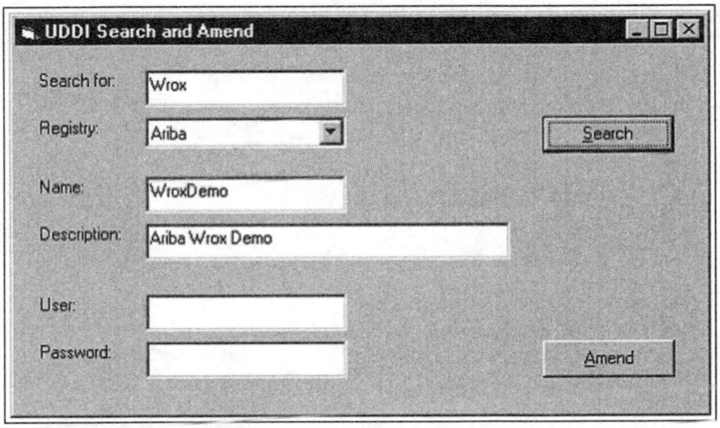

Let's change that description back to what it was before:

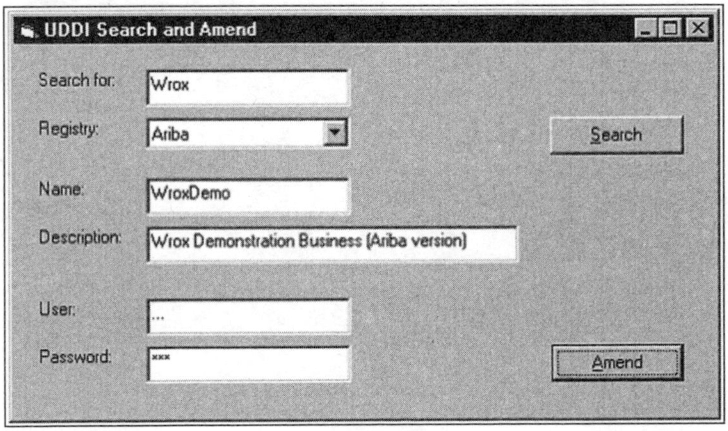

If we now clear that description and issue the search again, the new value will reappear. And the really good news is that this works with the IBM and Microsoft registries as well.

Summary

In this chapter, we have looked a little into the future. In particular, we have:

- Looked at how our systems are going to be talking to each other, using WSDL
- Succeeded in getting two completely unrelated systems to work together in a reasonably satisfactory manner
- Discussed what impact this might have on future software development processes

We have also looked at how:

- Our systems are going to find compatible partners, via the UDDI registry
- We can search this registry to find the information we need
- We can publish data to it

Again, we have done this with two entirely different technologies.

Index

A Guide to the Index

The index is arranged hierarchically, in alphabetical order, with symbols preceding the letter A. Most second-level entries and many third-level entries also occur as first-level entries. This is to ensure that users will find the information they require however they choose to search for it.

Symbols

A

B

C

D

E

F

G

H

I

J

K

L

M

O

P

Q

R

S

T

V

W

X

Z

p2p.wrox.com
The programmer's resource centre

A unique free service from Wrox Press
with the aim of helping programmers to help each other

Wrox Press aims to provide timely and practical information to today's programmer. P2P is a list server offering a host of targeted mailing lists where you can share knowledge with your fellow programmers and find solutions to your problems. Whatever the level of your programming knowledge, and whatever technology you use, P2P can provide you with the information you need.

ASP Support for beginners and professionals, including a resource page with hundreds of links, and a popular ASP+ mailing list.

DATABASES For database programmers, offering support on SQL Server, mySQL, and Oracle.

MOBILE Software development for the mobile market is growing rapidly. We provide lists for the several current standards, including WAP, WindowsCE, and Symbian.

JAVA A complete set of Java lists, covering beginners, professionals,and server-side programmers (including JSP, servlets and EJBs)

.NET Microsoft's new OS platform, covering topics such as ASP+, C#, and general .Net discussion.

VISUAL BASIC Covers all aspects of VB programming, from programming Office macros to creating components for the .Net platform.

WEB DESIGN As web page requirements become more complex, programmer sare taking a more important role in creating web sites. For these programmers, we offer lists covering technologies such as Flash, Coldfusion, and JavaScript.

XML Covering all aspects of XML, including XSLT and schemas.

OPEN SOURCE Many Open Source topics covered including PHP, Apache, Perl, Linux, Python and more.

FOREIGN LANGUAGE Several lists dedicated to Spanish and German speaking programmers, categories include .Net, Java, XML, PHP and XML.

How To Subscribe

Simply visit the P2P site, at **http://p2p.wrox.com/**

Select the 'FAQ' option on the side menu bar for more information about the subscription process and our service.

p2p.wrox.com

Programmer to Programmer™

Wrox writes books for you. Any suggestions, or ideas about how you want information given in your ideal book will be studied by our team. Your comments are always valued at Wrox.

Free phone in USA 800-USE-WROX
Fax (312) 893 8001

UK Tel. (0121) 687 4100 Fax (0121) 687 4101

Professional XML 2nd Edition - Registration Card

Name ______
Address ______
______
______
______
City ______ State/Region ______
Country ______ Postcode/Zip ______
E-mail ______
Occupation ______
How did you hear about this book? ______
- ☐ Book review (name) ______
- ☐ Advertisement (name) ______
- ☐ Recommendation ______
- ☐ Catalog ______
- ☐ Other ______

Where did you buy this book? ______
- ☐ Bookstore (name) ______ City ______
- ☐ Computer Store (name) ______
- ☐ Mail Order ______
- ☐ Other ______

What influenced you in the purchase of this book?
- ☐ Cover Design
- ☐ Contents
- ☐ Other (please specify) ______

How did you rate the overall contents of this book?
- ☐ Excellent ☐ Good
- ☐ Average ☐ Poor

What did you find most useful about this book? ______

What did you find least useful about this book? ______

Please add any additional comments. ______

What other subjects will you buy a computer book on soon? ______

What is the best computer book you have used this year? ______

Note: This information will only be used to keep you updated about new Wrox Press titles and will not be used for any other purpose or passed to any other third party.

5059 Check here if you DO NOT want to receive support for this book ☐ 5059

NB. If you post the bounce back card below in the UK, please send it to:

Wrox Press Ltd., Arden House, 1102 Warwick Road,
Acocks Green, Birmingham B27 6BH. UK.

Computer Book Publishers

NO POSTAGE
NECESSARY
IF MAILED
IN THE
UNITED STATES

BUSINESS REPLY MAIL

FIRST CLASS MAIL PERMIT#64 CHICAGO, IL

POSTAGE WILL BE PAID BY ADDRESSEE

WROX PRESS INC.,
29 S. LA SALLE ST.,
SUITE 520
CHICAGO IL 60603-USA